Also by Walter Isaacson

PRO & CON

THE WISE MEN
(coauthor with Evan Thomas)

KISSI

A Biography

NGER

Walter Isaacson

SIMON & SCHUSTER

NEW YORK • LONDON • TOKYO • SYDNEY • TORONTO • SINGAPORE

SIMON & SCHUSTER
Simon & Schuster Building
Rockefeller Center
1230 Avenue of the Americas
New York, New York 10020

Copyright © 1992 by Walter Isaacson
All rights reserved
including the right of reproduction
in whole or in part in any form.
SIMON & SCHUSTER and colophon are
registered trademarks of Simon & Schuster Inc.
Designed by Edith Fowler
Manufactured in the United States of America

10   9   8   7   6   5   4   3   2   1

Library of Congress Cataloging in Publication Data
Isaacson, Walter.
  Kissinger: a biography/Walter Isaacson.
      p.   cm.
  Includes bibliographical references and index.
    1. Kissinger, Henry, 1923–   .   2. Statesmen—United States
—Biography.   3. Historians—United States—Biography.
I. Title.
E840.8.K58I78   1992
973.924'092—dc20
[B]   *92-16009*
ISBN: 0-671-66323-2   *CIP*

To
BETSY, WHO IS WORTHY OF HER NAME

Contents

Introduction

"As a professor, I tended to think of history as run by impersonal forces. But when you see it in practice, you see the difference personalities make." —KISSINGER, *in a background talk with reporters on his plane after his first Middle East shuttle, January 1974*

As his parents finished packing the few personal belongings that they were permitted to take out of Germany, the bespectacled fifteen-year-old boy stood in the corner of the apartment and memorized the details of the scene. He was a bookish and reflective child, with that odd mixture of ego and insecurity that can come from growing up smart yet persecuted. "I'll be back someday," he said to the customs inspector who was surveying the boxes. Years later, he would recall how the official looked at him "with the disdain of age" and said nothing.[1]

Henry Kissinger was right: he did come back to his Bavarian birthplace, first as a soldier with the U.S. Army counterintelligence corps, then as a renowned scholar of international relations, and eventually as the dominant statesman of his era. But he would return as an American, not as a German. Ever since his discovery, upon his arrival in New York City, that he did not have to cross the street to avoid being beaten by non-Jewish boys coming his way, he was eager to be regarded as, and accepted as, an American.

And so he was. By the time he was made secretary of state in 1973, he had become, according to a Gallup poll, the most admired person in America. In addition, as he conducted foreign policy with the air of a guest of honor at a cocktail party, he became one of the most unlikely celebrities ever to capture the world's imagination. When he visited Bolivia, protocol prevented the president of that country from being part of the welcoming party; but he went to the airport that night anyway, incognito, and stood in the crowd anonymously so that he could witness Kissinger's arrival.[2]

Yet Kissinger was also reviled by large segments of the American public, ranging from liberal intellectuals to conservative activists, who in varying ways considered him a Strangelovian power manipulator dangerously devoid of moral principles. Among the mandarins of the mainstream foreign policy establishment, it became fashionable to deride him even while calling him Henry. When George Ball, the veteran American diplomat, sent the manuscript of a new book to an editor, he was told: "We've got one big problem here. In almost every chapter you stop what you're saying and beat up again on Henry Kissinger." Ball replied: "Tell me what chapters I've missed and I'll add the appropriate calumnies."[3]

Because people hold such divergent opinions of Kissinger, and hold them so strongly, the first question that a person writing a book about him must answer is, Will it be favorable or unfavorable? It's an odd query, not the sort one would make of a biographer of Henry Stimson or George Marshall or even Dean Acheson. Years after he left office, Kissinger still aroused controversy of a distinctly personal sort—hatred and veneration, animosity and awe, all battling it out with little neutral territory in between.

Kissinger's furtive style and chameleon instincts, which make capturing his true colors on any issue difficult, compound the problem of producing an objective assessment. Different people who dealt with him directly on major events—the invasion of Cambodia, the mining of Haiphong harbor, the Christmas bombing of Hanoi, the resupply of Israel during the 1973 war—have conflicting impressions of what he really felt.

That may be why most books about his policies seem to set sail on either a distinctly favorable or unfavorable tack, and also why there has never been a full biography of him. Though I leave it to the reader to decide whether I have succeeded, my goal was to produce an unbiased biography that portrayed Kissinger in all of his complexity. It seemed to me that enough time had passed to permit an objective look: the main players were in the twilight of their careers, still in possession of their memories and personal papers but freed from old strictures of secrecy and ambition.

•

This is not an authorized biography. Kissinger did not get to approve—or even see—its contents before it was published, nor did he have any authority over what I put in. It contains disclosures and judgments that he would surely dispute, especially since his ego and sensitivity are such that he would probably feel that even his own memoirs do not quite do justice to his achievements.

Yet it is not, on the other hand, an unauthorized biography. When I first decided to write it, my only contact with Kissinger had been an interview for a book involving some other modern American statesmen, *The Wise Men.* As a courtesy, I sent him a letter when I decided to undertake a biography of him.

His reply betrayed minimal enthusiasm. He could do nothing to stop me, he said, but he had no desire to see me pursue the project. But as I proceeded to interview his former associates and gather documents, I began to sense a growing interest on his part.

The subject of the book was, after all, one that fascinated him deeply. He had never written any memoirs about his life before the Nixon administration, nor about his personal life, nor about the Ford administration and afterward. Part of his personality is that he cares obsessively about trying to make people understand him: like a moth to flame, he is attracted to his critics and displays a compulsion to convert them, or at least explain himself to them.

So when the time came for me to talk to him, he ended up cooperating fully. He gave me more than two dozen formal interviews plus access to many of his public and private papers. In addition, he asked family members, former aides, business associates, and past presidents to work with me. He even helped me track down some old adversaries.

Although I tried to embark on this project without any biases, certain themes emerged during the reporting that I hope will become evident to the reader, and perhaps even convincing. The most fundamental, I believe, is that Kissinger had an instinctive feel—*Fingerspitzengefühl,* to use the German word—for power and for creating a new global balance that could help America cope with its withdrawal syndrome after Vietnam. But it was not matched by a similar feel for the strength to be derived from the openness of America's democratic system or for the moral values that are the true source of its global influence.

In addition, I have sought to explore how Kissinger's personality —brilliant, conspiratorial, furtive, sensitive to linkages and nuances, prone to rivalries and power struggles, charming yet at times deceitful

—related to the power-oriented realpolitik and secretive diplomatic maneuvering that were the basis of his policies. Policy is rooted in personality, as Kissinger knew from studying Metternich.

Kissinger came to power amid a swirl of great historical forces, including Moscow's achievement of strategic parity with Washington, the American humiliation in Vietnam, and China's need to end its generation of isolation. But it was also a period when complex, larger-than-life personalities played upon the world stage, including Nixon, Mao, Sadat, and Kissinger himself.

As a young academic, Kissinger once wrote of Bismarck and his era: "The new order was tailored to a genius who proposed to constrain the contending forces, both domestic and foreign, by manipulating their antagonisms." Much the same could be said of Kissinger and his era. And Germany in the 1930s was a good place for a sensitive and brilliant child to learn about contending forces and the manipulation of antagonisms.

ONE

FÜRTH

Coming of Age
in Nazi Germany, 1923–1938

*"The point of departure is order, which alone can produce freedom."—*METTERNICH

THE KISSINGERS OF BAVARIA

Among the Jews of Rodelsee, a small Bavarian village near Würzburg, Abraham Kissinger was known for his piety and profound religious knowledge. Because he was successful as a merchant, he was able to honor the Sabbath by closing before sunset on Fridays. But he feared that his four sons might not have that luxury if they, too, went into trade. So he decreed that they should all become teachers, as his own father had been, and thus always be able to keep the Sabbath.

And so it was that Joseph, Maier, Simon, and David Kissinger each went forth from Rodelsee and founded distinguished Jewish schools in the nearby German villages. Of their children, at least five, including David's eldest son, Louis, would also become teachers. And years later, at a famous college in a faraway country, so would Louis's elder son, a studious and introverted young man who, until his family fled to America, was known as Heinz.[1]

The Jews of Bavaria had suffered recurring onslaughts of repression since they first settled in the region in the tenth century. As merchants and moneylenders, they were protected in many Bavarian towns because of the contribution they made to the economy, only to find themselves brutally banished when the mood of princes and populace changed. They were expelled from upper Bavaria in 1276, beginning a wave of oppression that culminated with the persecutions following the Black Death in 1349. By the sixteenth century, few significant Jewish communities remained in the region.

Jews began returning to Bavaria, mainly from Austria, at the beginning of the eighteenth century. Some were bankers brought in to help finance the War of Spanish Succession; others came as traders and cattle dealers. Despite occasional outbreaks of anti-Semitism, they gradually regained a secure place in Bavarian society, or so it seemed. A series of laws between 1804 and 1813, during Napoleon's reign, allowed Jews to attend state schools, join the militia, and enjoy full citizenship. In addition, they were accorded the right to be known by family surnames.

The first member of the family to take the name Kissinger was Abraham's father, Meyer, who was born in Kleinebstadt in 1767. As a young man, Meyer went to live in the resort town of Bad Kissingen, a popular spa north of Würzburg. At the time, Kissingen was home to approximately 180 Jews out of a population of just over 1,000. Later he moved to Rodelsee, where Meyer of Kissingen legally adopted the name Meyer Kissinger in 1817. Abraham was born the following year.[2]

Abraham was the only one of Meyer's ten offspring to survive childhood. He lived until he was eighty-one and became the patriarch of a family that included the four sons who followed his wishes and became teachers, four daughters, and thirty-two grandchildren. Although they were all Orthodox Jews, they were a solidly middle-class German family, one that felt deep loyalty to a nation that treated them well.

David Kissinger, the youngest of Abraham's sons, was born in Rodelsee in 1860 and moved to Ermershausen where he founded a small school and served as the cantor in the local synagogue. Later, he taught in the Jewish seminary in Würzburg. Always somberly dressed, he was referred to by friends as the "Sunday Kissinger," to distinguish him from his brother Simon, a more casual dresser, who was known as the "weekday Kissinger."[3]

David and his wife, Linchen, known as Lina, were sophisticated and well read, the type of Germans who would give their first son, born in 1887, a French name, Louis. Louis was the only one of their seven children to take up teaching, but unlike his father, he decided to do so in secular rather than religious schools. After studying at

Heidelberg University, he enrolled in the teachers' academy in Fürth, a town on the outskirts of Nuremberg.

Because Germany needed teachers, Louis was exempted from service during World War I. He took a job at the Heckmannschule, a bourgeois private school. Directed by gentiles, but with half of its students Jews, it typified the extent of Jewish assimilation in Fürth, a city with a history of religious tolerance.[4]

Fürth had flourished in the fourteenth century, when Jews were denied entry into Nuremberg and settled instead in the riverbank village just outside the walls of the fortified city. Traders, craftsmen, and metalworkers, they turned Fürth into a vibrant commercial center and one of Bavaria's few undisrupted seats of Jewish culture. By 1860, Fürth had a population of 14,000, about half Jewish.

During the industrial revolution, many of the Jewish businessmen built textile and toy factories. The most prosperous formed a Jewish aristocracy, led by such families as the Nathans and the Frankels. Their large sandstone villas overlooked the town, and they endowed a wide array of philanthropies, including an orphanage, hospital, school, and orchestra. The town's seven synagogues were crowded around a large square, which was dominated by that of the most liberal congregation, patronized—at least on the High Holy days —by the more socially prominent Jews.

Louis Kissinger, who joined the most Orthodox of the town's synagogues, the Neuschul, was not part of the world of the Frankels and Nathans. But teaching was a proud and honorable calling in Germany, and Herr Kissinger was a proud and honorable member of the German middle class. In his politics, he was a conservative who liked the kaiser and yearned for him after his abdication. Despite his religious faith, Zionism held no appeal for him; he was a German, patriotic and loyal.

When the kaiser's government shut down most private schools, the Heckmannshule was dissolved. But Louis was able to find a new job as a *"Studienrat"*—a combination of schoolmaster, teacher, and counselor—in the state-run system. First, he worked at a girl's junior high school. Then, he taught geography and accounting at a secondary school, the Mädchenlyzeum, which soon merged with a trade school, the Handelsschule.[5]

Louis Kissinger took great pride in his status as a *Studienrat,* an eminent position in German society. Years later, after he had lost his job at the hands of another German government and fled his homeland, he would write to old acquaintances, signing himself, in his neat handwriting, *"studienrat ausser dienst,"* retired schoolmaster. He was strict but popular. "Goldilocks," the girls called him, sometimes to his face, and also "Kissus," which amused him even more. He had a slight paunch, a faint mustache, a prominent jaw, and a deferential manner. "He was a typical German schoolteacher," according to Jerry Bechhofer, a family friend from Fürth and later New York City. "He was professorial and stern, but wouldn't hurt a fly."[6]

When Louis first came to the Mädchenlyzeum, the school's headmaster told him about a girl named Paula Stern who had graduated the previous year. The headmaster knew how to entice the sober new teacher: he showed him Paula's grades. There were enough A's to kindle Louis's interest. But those marks were a bit misleading. Instead of having the same scholarly demeanor as Louis, Paula was sharp, witty, earthy, and practical. It was a fine pairing: Louis was the wise and somewhat aloof teacher, Paula the energetic and sensible decision-maker.

The Sterns lived in Leutershausen, a village thirty miles east of Nuremberg. Paula's great-grandfather had gone into the cattle trade in the early nineteenth century. Her grandfather, named Bernhardt, and her father, named Falk, built the business into a healthy enterprise.

Falk Stern, a prominent figure among both the Jewish and gentile communities in the area, was far more assimilated than the Kissingers were. His imposing stone house, with its large courtyard and carefully tended garden, was in the center of the village. Yet he remained a simple man: he went to bed every evening shortly after nine P.M. and took little interest in politics or scholarly subjects. His first wife, Beppi Behr, also from a cattle-dealing family, died young. They had one child, Paula, born in 1901. Though her father remarried, Paula remained his only child.

When Paula was sent to Fürth for school, she stayed with her aunt, Berta Fleischmann, wife of one of the town's kosher butchers. Berta helped encourage the match with Louis Kissinger, even though he was thirty-five and Paula only twenty-one. The Sterns also approved. When the couple married in 1922, the Sterns bestowed upon them a dowry large enough to buy a five-room, second-floor corner apartment in a gabled sandstone building on Mathildenstrasse, a cobbled street in a Jewish neighborhood of Fürth. Nine months later, on May 27, 1923, their first child was born there.[7]

Heinz Alfred Kissinger. His first name was chosen because it appealed to Paula. His middle name was, like that of his father's brother Arno, a Germanicized updating of Abraham. From his father, Heinz inherited the nickname Kissus. When he moved to America fifteen years later, he would become known as Henry.[8]

YOUNG HEINZ

By the time Heinz Kissinger was born, the Jewish population of Fürth had shrunk to three thousand. A new period of repression was under way: in reaction to the emasculation Germany suffered in World War I, a nationalism arose that celebrated the purity of the Teutonic, Aryan roots of German culture. Jews were increasingly treated as aliens. Among other things, they were barred from attending public gatherings—including league soccer matches.

Nonetheless, Heinz became an ardent fan of the Kleeblatt Eleven, the Fürth team that had last won the German championships in 1914. He refused to stay away from their games, even though his parents ordered him to obey the law. He would sneak off to the stadium, sometimes with his younger brother, Walter, or a friend, and pretend not to be Jewish. "All we risked was a beating," he later recalled.

That was not an uncommon occurrence. On one occasion, he and Walter were caught at a match and roughed up by a gang of kids. Unwilling to tell their parents, they confided in their family maid, who cleaned them up without revealing their secret.[9]

Kissinger's love of soccer surpassed his ability to play it, though not his enthusiasm for trying. In an unsettled world, it was his favorite outlet. "He was one of the smallest and skinniest in our group," said Paul Stiefel, a friend from Fürth who later immigrated to Chicago. What Kissinger lacked in strength he made up in finesse. One year he was even captain of his class team, selected more for his leadership ability than his agility.

The Jews in Fürth had their own sports club. "My father once played for the city team," said Henry Gitterman, a classmate of Kissinger's. "When the Jews were thrown off, they formed their own teams at a Jewish sports club." The field was merely a plot of dirt with goalposts, and the gym was an old warehouse with a corrugated roof. But it served as a haven from roving Nazi youth gangs and an increasingly threatening world.[10]

Young Kissinger could be very competitive. In the cobblestone yard behind their house, he would play games of one-on-one soccer with John Heiman, a cousin who boarded with his family for five years. "When it was time to go in," Heiman recalled, "if he was ahead, we could go. But if he was losing, I'd have to keep playing until he had a chance to catch up."

Kissinger was better at *Völkerball,* a simple pickup game, usually played with five on a side, in which the object was to hit members of the opposite team with a ball. Kissinger liked being the player who stood behind the enemy lines to catch the balls that his teammates threw. "It was one of the few games I was very good at," he would later say.[11]

It was as a student rather than as an athlete that Kissinger excelled. Like his father, he was scholarly in demeanor. "A bookworm, introverted," recalled his brother, Walter. Tzipora Jochsberger, a childhood friend, said she "always remembered Heinz with a book under his arm, always."

His mother even worried that books had become an escape from an inhospitable world. "He withdrew," she recalled. "Sometimes he wasn't outgoing enough, because he was lost in his books."[12]

Heinz and his brother, Walter, who was a year younger, looked a lot alike. Both were skinny with wiry hair, had high foreheads and their father's large ears. But their personalities contrasted. Heinz was shy, observant, detached, somewhat insecure, earnest, and reflective like his father. Walter was impish, sociable, lively, practical, a better athlete, and down-to-earth like his mother. Though something of a loner, Heinz became a leader because his friends respected his intelligence. Walter, however, was more socially adroit, a wheeler-dealer and an instigator rather than a leader. "Henry was always the thinker," his father once said. "He was more inhibited. Wally was more the doer, more the extrovert."[13]

Louis badly wanted his two children to go to the *Gymnasium,* the state-run high school. After years at a Jewish school, Heinz was likewise eager to make the change. But by the time he applied to the state-run school, the tide of anti-Semitism had risen. Because he was Jewish, he was rejected.[14]

The Israelitische Realschule, where he went instead, was every bit as good academically: the emphasis was on history—both German and Jewish—foreign languages (Kissinger studied English), and literature. It was small, with about thirty children in each grade, half boys and half girls. But it eventually grew to about fifty per class as the state school system barred Jews and as many Orthodox children began commuting there by trolley from Nuremberg. Religion was taken seriously. Each day, Kissinger and his friends spent two hours studying the Bible and the Talmud.

Kissinger regarded his father fondly, but with a touch of detachment. "He was the gentlest person imaginable, extraordinarily gentle," Kissinger later said. "Good and evil didn't arise for him because he couldn't imagine evil. He couldn't imagine what the Nazis represented. His gentleness was genuine, not the sort of obsequiousness that is really a demand on you."

Louis was a cultured man, with a great love of literature and classical music. He had an extensive record collection and an upright piano, both of which he played with great verve. ("Unfortunately, his favorite composer was Mahler," Paula recalled.) Wise and compassionate, he was the sort of person neighbors often called upon for counsel. "He did not hold himself out as a moralist," his son said, "but his own conduct was so extraordinary it served as a lesson."

His children, however, were more reticent about bringing their problems to him. "He couldn't understand children having problems and didn't think they should have real problems," Kissinger recalled. "Nor could he understand the type of problems a ten-year-old would have."

Paula Kissinger, on the other hand, had a knack for handling family crises. "My father was lucky he had an earthy wife who made all the decisions," Kissinger said. She was a survivor, very practical. "She didn't occupy her mind with grand ideas or with ultimate meanings. She looked after necessities."[15]

Paula had sharp eyes and keen instincts. Hidden behind her smile and unaffected grace was a toughness when it came to protecting her family. Though less reflective than her husband (or her son), and less intellectual, she had a better sense of herself and of what people around her were thinking.

As a child, Kissinger was more comfortable having one close friend than being part of a group. In Fürth, his inseparable companion was Heinz Lion (pronounced like *Leon*), who later became a biochemist in Israel and changed his name to Menachem Lion. They spent almost every afternoon and weekend together. On Saturdays, Lion's father would teach the boys the Torah, then take them on hikes.

Kissinger used to discuss with Lion and his father those problems he could not broach with his own father. "They lived near us and he would ride over on his bike," Lion recalled. "It seems to me he had a problem with his father. He was afraid of him because he was a very pedantic man. His father was always checking his homework. He told me more than once that he couldn't discuss anything with his father, especially not girls."

Kissinger and Lion used to take walks on Friday evenings through the park with girlfriends, sometimes stopping to skate on the frozen lake. One Sabbath evening, the two boys were enjoying themselves so much that they came home late. "In Germany, in those days, it was one of the most sacred rules of behavior to return home on time and never to stay out after dark," Lion's mother later said. "And so my husband took off his belt and gave them a thrashing." Rather unfairly, Herr Lion blamed Kissinger for being a bad influence, and he forbade his son to see him for a week. Later, Lion's parents sent him to a summer camp in Czechoslovakia for six weeks to get him away from Kissinger.[16]

When Kissinger was seven, his cousin John Heiman moved in because his native village had no Jewish school. He slept in the same room as Heinz and Walter, becoming a part of the family. "I was very homesick those first few days," recalled Heiman, who later became a hobby-kit manufacturer in Chicago. "I carried on pretty badly." One evening Paula found him in tears. He wanted a school cap, he cried, a blue one like the other boys at the Realschule wore. "The next day I woke up and there was the school cap. That's the type of person she was."[17]

For the young Kissinger, one place was particularly magical: his mother's family home in Leutershausen, where the Kissingers spent the summer. The Stern home was stately and secure, built around a cozy courtyard where Heinz would chase the family's brood of chickens and, as he grew older, play *Völkerball* with his friends.

Falk Stern, with his weathered face, would watch from the window as the boys played, and his wife, Paula's stepmother, would bustle about in her apron. A fastidious woman, she cleaned house every Wednesday, and the children were barred from the living room until the Sabbath ended on Saturday evening. Leutershausen had only a tiny Jewish community, about twenty families. Consequently, the Sterns had many non-Jewish friends, unlike the Kissingers in Fürth.

One of young Kissinger's best friends in Leutershausen was Tzipora Jochsberger. Her family had a big garden where the children would organize their version of a circus. They borrowed ladders and mats in order to produce acrobatic acts. "Even Henry got interested for a while," she recalled. "Usually he was too serious for that sort of thing."

When Tzipora was fourteen, she was expelled with the other Jewish children from her public school. Even though they were Reform Jews, her parents sent her to an Orthodox school. When she came back that summer, she had become an Orthodox Jew, much to her family's chagrin. "My parents were not very religious, and they didn't understand my conversion," she said. "They were very upset." Since she had determined to keep kosher, Tzipora could not even eat with her family. Kissinger, himself Orthodox, was the only person she felt could understand her change. They went on long walks to discuss it. Faith was important, he told her, and she should remain Orthodox if that is what she felt was right for her. "Henry seemed to understand the change. I always liked to listen to him explain matters because he was so smart." [18]

Along with John Heiman and Heinz Lion, Kissinger went to synagogue every morning before school. On Saturdays, Lion's father read and discussed the Torah with them. Young Kissinger "would be totally engulfed in the atmosphere of piety," according to Lion's mother. "He would pray with devotion."

Kissinger, who had mastered the Torah and had a sonorous voice even as a child, chanted the passages at his bar mitzvah with such beauty that those who were there would remark on it years later. Presiding over the service was Rabbi Leo Breslauer, who would later move to New York and officiate at Kissinger's first wedding. At the party after the bar mitzvah, Paula read a poem she had written for the occasion. [19]

When Kissinger graduated from school in Fürth, he went to study at the Jewish seminary in Würzburg. His time there was pleasant enough: life in a dormitory, endless books to distract the mind from the threats of the outside world, and daily visits to his wise grandfather David. But Kissinger had not gone to Würzburg to become a Jewish teacher, for it had become clear that there was no future for Jewish teachers, or even Jews, in Germany. Instead, he went to Würzburg for lack of anything better to do for the moment. By then, the Kissinger family, led by Paula, was coming to an anguishing decision. [20]

A WORLD DESTROYED

In 1923, the year that Kissinger was born, Julius Streicher had founded the rabid anti-Semitic weekly *Der Stuermer* in Nuremberg, where he headed the local branch of Hitler's Nazi party. His incitement of hatred against the Jews was not only fanatic, but sadistic. He demanded the total extermination of Jews, whom he called "germs" and "defilers."

Streicher's newspaper, which achieved a circulation of five hundred thousand, stoked the fire of anti-Semitism in Fürth and Leutershausen. The atmosphere of their summers in Leutershausen changed, Paula Kissinger recalled. "Some gentiles had been our friends, but after Streicher began publishing we were isolated. A few people stuck by us, but only a few. There was hardly anyone for the boys to play with." [21]

Streicher paved the way for the Nuremberg Laws of 1935. These statutes negated the German citizenship of Jews, forbade marriages between Jews and German Christians, and prevented Jews from being teachers in state schools or holding many other professional positions.

As a result, Louis Kissinger was suddenly deemed unfit to teach true Germans and lost the job of which he was so proud. For a while, he worked to establish a Jewish vocational school in Fürth, where he taught accounting. But he was a broken man, humbled and humiliated by forces of hatred that his kindly soul could not comprehend.

In later years, Henry Kissinger would minimize his Jewish heritage. When he discussed his childhood (which he did only rarely and reluctantly), he would describe it as "typical middle-class German," adding only as an afterthought that of course it was German Jewish. His family, he would say, was assimilated, and the Jews of Fürth were not all that segregated or tribal.

He also minimized the traumas he faced as a child, the persecution and the beatings and the daily confrontations with a virulent anti-Semitism that made him feel like an outcast. As he told a reporter from *Die Nachrichten,* a Fürth newspaper, who was writing a profile of him in 1958: "My life in Fürth seems to have passed without leaving any lasting impressions." He said much the same to many other questioners over the years. "That part of my childhood is not a key to anything," Kissinger insisted in a 1971 interview. "I was not consciously unhappy. I was not acutely aware of what was going on. For children, these things are not that serious."[22]

Kissinger's childhood friends regard such talk as an act of denial and self-delusion. Some of them see his escape from memory as a key to his legendary insecurities. The child who had to pretend to be someone else so that he could get into soccer games, they say, became an adult who was prone to deceit and self-deception in the pursuit of acceptance by political and social patrons.

Paula Kissinger was more forthcoming about the traumas of the Nazi period. "Our children weren't allowed to play with the others," she said. "They stayed shut up in the garden. They loved football, Henry most of all, but the games in Nuremberg were banned to them." She especially remembered her children's pitiful fright and puzzlement when the Nazi youths would march by taunting the Jews. "The Hitler Youth, which included almost all the children in Fürth, sang in ranks in the streets and paraded in uniform, and Henry and his brother would watch them, unable to understand why they didn't have the right to do what others did."[23]

"Anti-Semitism was a feature of Bavaria and did not start with Hitler," said Menachem Lion. "We didn't have much if any contact with non-Jewish children. We were afraid when we saw any non-Jewish kids coming down the street. We would experience things that people couldn't imagine today, but we took it for granted. It was like the air we breathed."[24]

Other childhood friends of Kissinger's recalled similar traumas. Werner Gundelfinger: "We couldn't go to the swimming pool, the dances, or the tea room. We couldn't go anywhere without seeing the sign: *Juden Verboten*. These are things that remain in your subconscious." Frank Harris: "We all grew up with a certain amount of inferiority." Otto Pretsfelder: "You can't grow up like we did and be untouched. Every day there were slurs on the street, anti-Semitic remarks, calling you filthy names."[25]

The rise of the Nazis was hardest on Paula Kissinger. Her husband Louis was baffled, almost shell-shocked, struck mute; but Paula was acutely sensitive to what was happening and deeply pained by it. She was the sociable one, the sprightly woman with gentile friends who loved to go swimming every day during the summer in the Leutershausen municipal pool. When her gentile friends began to avoid her, and when Jews were barred from using the pool, she began to realize there was no future for her family in Germany.

"It was my decision," she later said, "and I did it because of the children. I knew there was not a life to be made for them if we stayed."

She had a first cousin who had immigrated years before to Washington Heights on Manhattan's far Upper West Side. Although they had never met, Paula wrote to her late in 1935, just after passage of the Nuremberg Laws, to ask if Heinz and Walter could come live with her. No, replied her cousin, the whole Kissinger family should emigrate, but not the children alone.

Paula was very devoted to her father, who was then dying of cancer. She did not want to leave him. But by the spring of 1938, she realized there was no choice. Her cousin had filed the necessary affidavits to allow them into the U.S., and the papers had come through allowing them to leave Germany.

For the final time, the Kissinger family went to Leutershausen to visit Paula's father and stepmother. "I had never seen my father cry until he said good-bye to my mother's father," said Kissinger. "That shook me more than anything. I suddenly realized we were involved in some big and irrevocable event. It was the first time I had encountered anything my father couldn't cope with."[26]

By that time, Kissinger was ready to leave. The Lion family had immigrated to Palestine in March. They sold their apartment a week before they left, and Heinz Lion moved in with the Kissingers for those final days. The two boys talked about being apart, about leaving

Germany, about whether they would ever return. Lion's father offered some parting words for the young Kissinger: "You'll come back to your birthplace someday and you won't find a stone unturned." With Heinz and Herr Lion gone, Kissinger had little reason to want to stay. "That was when his first real loneliness came," his mother recalled.

On August 20, 1938, less than three months before the mobs of Kristallnacht would destroy their synagogue and most other Jewish institutions in Germany, the Kissingers set sail for London, to spend two weeks with relatives, and then on to America. Henry was fifteen, his brother, Walter, fourteen, his father fifty, and his mother thirty-seven.

Packing was a simple task: even though they had paid a fee to move their belongings out of Germany, they were permitted to take only some furniture and whatever personal possessions could fit into one trunk. Louis had to leave his books behind, and they were allowed to take only a small sum of pocket money.[27]

Kissinger would return, both as a soldier and as a statesman. In December of 1975, when he was secretary of state, he was invited back —along with his parents—for a ceremony awarding him Fürth's Gold Medal for Distinguished Native Citizens. German Foreign Minister Hans-Dietrich Genscher and Mayor Kurt Scherzer were on hand, along with a thousand onlookers and a choir from the school that once would not accept the Kissinger boys. Kissinger's remarks were brief and avoided any mention of the horrors that caused his family to flee. When invited to tour the neighborhood where he used to play soccer and study the Torah and face beatings by Hitler Youth members, Kissinger politely declined.

"My memories are not all that glorious," he later told reporters. "I did it mostly for my parents. They never lost their attachment for this city." His father seemed to agree. At a lunch with the few friends of his still in Fürth, he quoted Euripides and said, "We forget all the bad memories on this day." His mother, however, forgot nothing. "I was offended in my heart that day, but said nothing," she recalled. "In my heart, I knew they would have burned us with the others if we had stayed."[28]

At the restored synagogue where the Kissingers once worshiped there is a plaque. "On the 22d of March 1942," it says, "the last occupants of this building, 33 orphan children, were sent to their deaths in Izbica with their teacher, Dr. Isaak Hallemann."

While on their 1975 visit, the Kissingers visited Falk Stern's grave. He was lucky; he died in his home before the holocaust began. At least thirteen close relatives of Kissinger were sent to the gas chambers or died in concentration camps, including Stern's wife.

One reason so many of them perished is that, as Kissinger has said, they considered themselves loyal German citizens. His grandfather David and granduncle Simon both felt that the family should ride out the Nazi era, that it would pass. David did not flee until after Kristallnacht, when he joined his son Arno (Louis Kissinger's brother) in Sweden. But Simon, even after Kristallnacht, forbade his family to leave. Germany, he said, had been good to the Jews. They should stick with the country and be loyal to it as it went through this phase.

Simon was killed in a German concentration camp. So, too, were his sons Ferdinand and Julius, who like their father and uncles were teachers. All three of Kissinger's aunts—his father's sisters—also perished in the holocaust: Ida and her husband, Siegbert Friedmann, who was a teacher in Mainstocken, and one child; Sara and her husband, Max Blattner, and their daughter, Selma; Fanny and her husband, Jacob Rau, and their son, Norbert. Fanny's daughter, Lina Rau, who had boarded with the Kissingers, managed to escape to New York. "My parents did not expect Hitler to last," she said. "Nobody did. We thought it would blow over."[29]

LEGACIES OF A LOST CHILDHOOD

Kissinger rarely spoke of the holocaust other than to protest now and then that it did not leave a permanent scar on his personality. "It was not a lifelong trauma," he said. "But it had an impact: having lived under totalitarianism, I know what it's like." Only once did he ever show any signs of anger about what happened. During an early visit to Germany as national security adviser, Bonn announced that Kissinger might visit with some of his relatives. "What the hell are they putting out?" he grumbled to aides. "My relatives are soap."[30]

Despite Kissinger's demurrals, the Nazi atrocities left a lasting imprint on him. "Kissinger is a strong man, but the Nazis were able to damage his soul," said Fritz Kraemer, a non-Jewish German who left to fight Hitler and became Kissinger's mentor in the U.S. Army. "For the formative years of his youth, he faced the horror of his world coming apart, of the father he loved being turned into a helpless mouse." Kissinger's most salient personality traits, Kraemer said, can be traced to this experience. "It made him seek order, and it led him to hunger for acceptance, even if it meant trying to please those he considered his intellectual inferiors."[31]

A desire to be accepted, a tendency to be distrustful and insecure:

these were understandable reactions to a childhood upended by one of the most gruesome chapters in human history. Kissinger's desire for social and political acceptance—and his yearning to be liked—was unusually ardent, so much so that it led him to compromise his beliefs at times.[32]

One of Kissinger's insecurities as an adult was his feeling, sometimes half-confessed through mordant humor, that he would not fit in if he was too closely identified with his religion. Only partly in jest, he grumbled that too much reporting about his family background could "bring every anti-Semite out of the woodwork" to attack him.

For Kissinger, the holocaust destroyed the connection between God's will and the progress of history—a tenet that is at the heart of the Jewish faith and is one of the religion's most important contributions to Western philosophy. For faithful Jews, the meaning of history is understood by its link to God's will and divine justice. After witnessing the Nazi horror, Kissinger would abandon the practice of Judaism, and as a young student at Harvard he would embark on an intellectual search for an alternative way to find the meaning of history.[33]

Kissinger's childhood experiences, not surprisingly, also instilled in him a deep distrust of other people. In his self-deprecating way, he would joke about his famous paranoia and his perception that people were always plotting against him. Another noted American statesman, Henry Stimson, lived by the maxim he learned at Yale's Skull and Bones that the only way to earn a man's trust is to trust him. Kissinger, on the other hand, was more like Nixon: he harbored an instinctive distrust of colleagues and outsiders alike. Stimson rejected the notion of a spy service by saying that "gentlemen do not read other people's mail"; Nixon and Kissinger established a series of secret wiretaps on the phones of even their closest aides.

Another legacy of Kissinger's holocaust upbringing was that later in life he would avoid revealing any signs of weakness—a maxim he applied to himself personally and, as the basic premise of his realpolitik, to foreign policy. Kissinger's father, whom he loved deeply, was graced by gentleness and a heart of unquestioning kindness. But such virtues served only to make him seem weak in the face of Nazi humiliations. As Kissinger grew older, he repeatedly attached himself to forceful, often overbearing patrons with powerful personalities: the boisterous and self-assured Prussian Fritz Kraemer in the army, the grandiose Professor William "Wild Bill" Elliott at Harvard, Nelson Rockefeller, Richard Nixon.

In addition, Kissinger, who spent his childhood as an outcast in his own country, became driven by a desire for acceptance. What struck many people as deceitfulness was often the result of Kissinger's attempts to win approval from opposing groups; during Vietnam, for example, he would attempt to convince dovish Harvard intellectuals that he was still one of them while simultaneously trying to impress Nixon with gutsy hardline advice. Kissinger would go out of his way to curry favor with the American Right after they attacked him over détente—while at the same time making disparaging comments about Reagan and prominent Reaganites to his intellectual friends. Historian Arthur Schlesinger, Jr., a longtime friend of Kissinger's, referred to this trait as "his refugee's desire for approval."[34]

Still another legacy of his childhood was his philosophical pessimism. His worldview was dark, suffused with a sense of tragedy. He once wrote that Americans, who have "never suffered disaster, find it difficult to comprehend a policy conducted with a premonition of catastrophe." Although he rejected Spengler's notion of the inevitability of historic decay, he came to believe that statesmen must continually fight against the natural tendency toward international instability.

The Nazi experience could have instilled in Kissinger either of two approaches to foreign policy: an idealistic, moralistic approach dedicated to protecting human rights; or a realist, realpolitik approach that sought to preserve order through balances of power and a willingness to use force as a tool of diplomacy. Kissinger would follow the latter route. Given a choice of order or justice, he often said, paraphrasing Goethe, he would choose order. He had seen too clearly the consequences of disorder.

As a result, Kissinger would become—philosophically, intellectually, politically—a conservative in the truest sense. He developed an instinctive aversion to revolutionary change, an attitude that he explored in his doctoral dissertation on Metternich and Castlereagh and that affected his policies when he came to power.

He also became uncomfortable with the passions of democracy and populism. Like George Kennan, his philosophical predecessor as a conservative and realist, Kissinger would never learn to appreciate the messy glory of the American political system, especially when it affected foreign policy.

Intellectually, his mind would retain its European cast just as his voice would retain its rumbling Bavarian accent. He felt comfortable plunging into Hegel and Kant and Metternich and Dostoyevski. But he never showed any appreciation for such archetypal American imaginations as Mark Twain and Thomas Jefferson and Ben Franklin.

Nonetheless, perhaps the most important effect of the horrors of his youth was the one that Kissinger himself always cited: it instilled a love of his adopted country that far surpassed his occasional disdain for the disorderliness of its democracy. When young Heinz reached Manhattan and became Henry, America's combination of tolerance and order would provide an exhilarating sense of personal freedom to a boy who had never walked the streets without fear. "I therefore," he would later say, "have always had a special feeling for what America means, which native-born citizens perhaps take for granted."[35]

TWO

WASHINGTON HEIGHTS

The Americanization of
an Aspiring Accountant, 1938–1943

*When I came here in 1938, I was asked to write an essay at George
Washington High School about what it meant to be an American. I
wrote that . . . I thought that this was a country where one could
walk across the street with one's head erect.—from a Kissinger farewell speech as secretary of state, January 1977*

A WORLD RESTORED

His first thought was to cross the street—a natural
reaction, one that had been reinforced by years of beatings and taunts.
He was walking alone on Manhattan's West 185th Street, from Am-
sterdam Avenue toward the ice cream parlor he had discovered on
Broadway, when he spotted the group of boys—strangers, not Jewish
—approaching. In Fürth, such an encounter was sure to produce, at
the very least, some small humiliation. He started to step off the
sidewalk. Then he remembered where he was.[1]

Henry Kissinger had been in America only a few months when
this small epiphany occurred. His family had moved into a comfortable but modest three-bedroom apartment in a squat six-story brick
building at Fort Washington Avenue and 187th Street. Across the hall
lived Paula Kissinger's cousin. Other friends from Fürth and Nuremberg were among the hundreds of new Jewish immigrants who filled
similar bulky buildings up and down the bustling avenue.

Washington Heights, from which George Washington's forces
sought (unsuccessfully) to defend Manhattan from the British in Oc-

tober 1776, rises along a rock bluff overlooking the Hudson River. Early in the century, its rows of apartment buildings were populated by Polish and Russian Jews. As they became successful, many moved to the suburbs, leaving a neighborhood filled with synagogues and delicatessens ready to host a new wave of Jewish immigrants. When the refugees from Hitler arrived, the area acquired the nickname the Fourth Reich.

At age fifty, Louis Kissinger had trouble adjusting to life in a new language. Even though he was well schooled in English, or perhaps because of that, he was afraid of making a grammatical error and embarrassed by his thick accent. So he said little, certainly far less than his friends with poorer educations and fewer inhibitions.

There was no demand for his skills as a teacher, and the Depression made it difficult to get any job. On top of that, he arrived in the U.S. with a chronic gall-bladder ailment that, for a while, doctors thought was cancer. From Falk Stern, Paula's father, who died soon after they arrived, the Kissingers received a modest inheritance. But the money soon ran thin. Finally, after two years of only sporadic work, Louis got a low-paying job as a bookkeeper at a factory owned by friends from Germany.

It fell to Paula Kissinger, thirteen years younger and far more adaptable, to support the family. Her sociable nature, nimble mind, and quick tongue stood her in good stead: she soon mastered the language, or at least enough to chat without trepidation. For a while she worked with a local caterer, preparing and serving food at bar mitzvahs and weddings; then she went into business for herself. Mostly she acted as an "accommodator," which is what caterers were often called, handling small parties in private homes.*[2]

Freed from the fear that pervaded Fürth, Henry Kissinger plunged into his new life in Washington Heights with the gusto of a paroled prisoner. Within days he had found his way to Yankee Stadium, mastering the intricacies of a subtle sport he had never before seen. "He was the first to find out how to get there and how much it cost, and to understand baseball," recalled John Sachs, who arrived from Fürth that summer. "A couple of weeks after he went to the stadium the first time, he got my uncle and me to go. Baseball was a sport unknown to us, but he explained the whole game."[3]

When he and Sachs went to take a driving test, Kissinger flunked,

---

* She became so popular that years later, even after her son had become national security adviser, she would still get requests from old clients to work their parties. She generally agreed, though she asked that they call her Paula rather than use her last name so that guests would not know who she was.

then proceeded to flunk it twice more. ("For the life of me, I don't understand why I kept failing it," he later said, though some people who have driven with him can suggest a variety of possible reasons.) Sachs passed easily enough, and with a borrowed car he and Kissinger explored such places as the Catskills.

In September of 1938, a month after he arrived, Kissinger enrolled in George Washington High School. A large Georgian structure built in 1925 on a two-acre campus at 192nd Street, it was then the pride of the city's public school system, serving a neighborhood of educationally ambitious Jews and other refugees. The teachers were among the best in the city, and so was the education they provided.

In Kissinger's records at George Washington High, he is among the many designated as having a "foreign language handicap." In fact, he was handicapped hardly at all. He got a grade of 70 (out of 100) in his first semester of English, but the second semester he raised it to a 90. From then on he got a 90 or better in every course he took—French, American history, European history, economics, algebra, and bookkeeping—except for an 85 in an "Industries and Trade" class. "He was the most serious and mature of the German refugee students," his math teacher, Anne Sindeband, later said, "and I think those students were more serious than our own." One German refugee who was in Kissinger's class recalled: "Of course we were serious. What else was there for us to do but be serious about our studies? We had no other way of making it in America except to do well at school and then make it at City College. Nowadays, kids make fun of the grinds. But back then, we were all grinds." With a little smile, he added: "Especially Henry."[4]

The Kissingers belonged to the Congregation K'hal Adath Jeshurun, a fledgling Orthodox synagogue that was founded the year they arrived. Its first rabbi was the former head of the yeshiva in Frankfurt, Rabbi Joseph Breuer, a noted defender of uncompromising Orthodoxy; in the neighborhood, it was referred to simply as "Breuer's synagogue." Kissinger, wearing his prayer shawl, was a faithful congregant. His mother began to sense, however, that he was going to synagogue more out of fealty to his father than out of fidelity to his faith.[5]

Socially, Kissinger began edging away from his Orthodox heritage and joined a youth group—Beth Hillel—that was mainly the province of Reform Jews, most of them refugees from Bavaria. They met at the Paramount Hall on 183rd Street and St. Nicholas Avenue.

Henry Gitterman, who had been with Kissinger at the Realschule in Fürth, was a president of Beth Hillel. "We would meet most weekends, both boys and girls. It was a way to meet girls from the same background." Even though they were all from Germany, English was the language spoken at Beth Hillel. Leaders from the community, including politicians such as Jacob Javits, would come and give talks. It offered the chance to band together while also assimilating. "There would be about eighteen or twenty of us at each meeting," recalled Kurt Silbermann. "We had discussion sessions, book groups, or sometimes just evenings when we'd go to a movie or listen to the radio."[6]

In addition to John Sachs, Kissinger's other close friend was Walter Oppenheim, also his sometime rival. He had been Kissinger's benchmate at the Realschule in Fürth, their families had both fled in the summer of 1938, and they ended up as neighbors in Washington Heights. Personable and handsome, though not as intellectual as Kissinger, Oppenheim was a natural leader.

On most Saturday evenings, eight or ten friends, Kissinger included, gathered at the Oppenheim home. Sometimes they went to the movies or for ice cream. For a big treat, they would head down to Fifty-ninth Street with their dates to Child's Restaurant, where there was a band. The minimum charge was three dollars, not an inconsiderable amount to the young refugees. They each carefully calculated their orders, spending the minimum and not more.

Sometimes when he came over to Oppenheim's house, Kissinger ended up spending the evening talking to Oppenheim's father, who was interested in politics and a strong partisan of Franklin Roosevelt. "Henry had convinced himself he was a Wendell Willkie Republican, even though all of us refugees were Democrats," recalled Walter Oppenheim. "He would stay up late arguing with my father. He was always reading about politics and history, and he was very thrilled by Willkie's ideas, though I cannot imagine why."[7]

Going through adolescence in a strange land, Kissinger remained almost as withdrawn as he had been in Fürth. He was respected by his crowd of fellow young immigrants for his mind and maturity, but he remained detached and socially insecure. "It was difficult for Henry to find his bearings, to feel in place when we first came, especially when our father had no career," said his brother, Walter.

He was particularly awkward at Edith Peritz's ballroom dance classes, a rite of passage for most Beth Hillel members. A 1941 picture of one of her dances—at Audubon Hall in Washington Heights— shows a diminutive and bespectacled Kissinger in the very last row on the far edge. As in any dance class, large numbers of prizes were given out, almost as many as there were students; Kissinger never won any.

Among the girls in the dance class was Anneliese Fleischer, a refugee from Nuremberg whose father had been successful in the shoe trade before being forced to flee. They lived on Ellwood Street on the northern edge of Washington Heights. She had dark hair, an easy smile, and a Lana Turner figure that to this day her old friends remark upon. She was considered "deep" and "aloof," also "nice but not very ebullient," all of which could have been said about Kissinger.

Literature and music were Ann's special interests; she wrote poems and played the cello. In addition, she had all the talents that would make for a good hausfrau: she and her sister made their own clothes, and Ann liked to baby-sit for the neighborhood children. She also helped take care of her father, who had been partially paralyzed by a stroke and psychologically broken by the Nazi horrors.

Ann and Henry soon started dating. Together they went on the Beth Hillel hikes, often keeping to themselves. Although her family was more casual in its Judaism—they belonged to a Conservative rather than an Orthodox synagogue and certainly did not keep kosher —the Kissingers were happy with the pairing, especially since it made their son seem less withdrawn.

Ann also dated Walter Oppenheim, who was somewhat more polished and certainly a better dresser. Finally, Ann made her choice, one that surprised her friends. She wrote Oppenheim a long letter explaining that she had decided to date Kissinger exclusively. Oppenheim remembers being hurt at first, though the letter was gentle. But they all remained part of the same group of friends and still spent most Saturday evenings together with the rest of their crowd.[8]

The Way Out

Despite his stubborn retention of his Bavarian accent, one trait distinguished Henry Kissinger from his friends: he was more directed, more ambitious, more serious about assimilating and succeeding in America. The others were quite comfortable within their tight-knit German Jewish world. Many of them, even as they became successful in business, continued to identify with their ethnic heritage rather than break from their immigrant style. Not Kissinger. He was more eager to blend into society, more adept at picking up the cultural cues that marked one as an American.

"If I assimilated quicker," Kissinger later explained, "perhaps it was because I had to go to work when I was sixteen. That probably made me more independent." After his first year at George Washington High, he began going to school at night and working by day on West Fifteenth Street at the Leopold Ascher Brush Company, a shaving-brush manufacturer owned by cousins of his mother. As part of the bleaching process, the bristles were dipped in acid, then in water. Kissinger, wearing heavy rubber gloves, had to squeeze the acid and water out of the bristles. He started at $11 a week, rising to about $30 when he became a delivery boy and shipping clerk. "His mind tended to be elsewhere while he was working," said Alan Ascher, who later ran the company. "Whenever he got the chance, he would pull out a book and do some reading or some studying for his night school."[9]

When Kissinger graduated from George Washington, he had no problem getting into the City College of New York. Founded in 1847 as the Free Academy, the school's purpose has always been to provide free higher education to gifted students of New York. By 1940, the college, located on 140th Street in Washington Heights, had more than thirty thousand students—about three-fourths of them Jewish. For immigrant children, it was a first step into the American meritocracy. Among its students were Felix Frankfurter, Bernard Baruch, and Jonas Salk.

Kissinger was able to breeze through his classes at City College, even though he was still working days at the brush company. He got A's in every course he took, except for one B in history. Without great enthusiasm, he was heading toward becoming an accountant, which had become his father's field. "My horizons were not that great when I was in City College," he said. "I never really thought of accounting as a calling, but I thought it might be a nice job."[10]

He was, however, looking around for something more he could do, a way up and out. For young men seeking to escape constricted lives, the army offered a perfect opportunity, all the more so because there was little choice involved. Kissinger's draft notice arrived shortly after his nineteenth birthday, and his farewell party was held at the Iceland Restaurant near Times Square in February of 1943. The next day he left by train for Camp Croft in Spartanburg, South Carolina—where for the first time in his life he would not be part of a German Jewish community.[11]

THREE

THE ARMY

"Mr. Henry" Comes
Marching Home Again, 1943–1947

> *Whenever peace—conceived as the avoidance of war—has been
> the primary objective of a power or a group of powers, the interna-
> tional system has been at the mercy of the most ruthless member.*
> —KISSINGER, A WORLD RESTORED, *1957*

THE MELTING POT

At a dusty training camp in a place more foreign to
him than anywhere he had ever been, Henry Kissinger was made a
citizen of the United States. There was little ceremony: it was March
of 1943, and at Camp Croft in South Carolina, the army routinely
naturalized the new recruits who happened to be immigrants. It was
just part of the daily process of being, as Kissinger described it in a
letter to his brother, "pushed around and inoculated, counted, and
stood at attention."[1]

For perhaps the last time in American history, the experience of
military service was shared by an entire cross section of backgrounds
and classes. As a result, World War II had the side effect of being a
vast democratizing force, one that transformed the way Americans
lived. The United States had always been a mobile society with a fluid
class system; now it was even more so. Soldiers from small towns in
South Carolina and Louisiana for the first time saw places like Paris
and Berlin, turning all-American boys with hardscrabble heritages
into cosmopolitan conquerers. And on a smaller scale, the army took

young refugees from Nuremberg and Fürth, put them in places such as Camp Croft and Camp Claiborne, then marched them off to war in melting-pot platoons, thus turning cosmopolitan aliens into acculturated American citizens.

For immigrant boys such as Kissinger, serving in the war made citizenship more than merely a gift bestowed. It was an honor they had earned. Having defended the U.S., they now had as much claim as any Winthrop or Lowell to feel that it was their nation, their country, their home. They were outsiders no more.

In addition, the army plucked out people such as Kissinger, who had been headed toward a night-school degree in accounting, and offered them new opportunities. "My infantry division was mainly Wisconsin and Illinois and Indiana boys, real middle Americans," Kissinger recalled. "I found that I liked these people very much. The significant thing about the army is that it made me feel like an American." As Helmut Sonnenfeldt, a fellow refugee who served with Kissinger in the army and then government, put it: "The army made the melting pot melt faster."[2]

Kissinger was still a solitary figure, quiet and reticent as he went through basic training. But as always, he was observant. Consequently, he survived boot camp well, displaying the normal hatred of his lieutenant ("we hated him beyond description and probably for no real reason"), but allowing the exhilaration of a new life to resonate in his letters home. As he was finishing basic training, Kissinger provided some brotherly advice to Walter. Go into the service, he wrote, "with your eyes and your ears open and your mouth closed." The two-page typewritten letter says as much about Kissinger as it does about the army:

> Always stand in the middle because details are always picked from the end. Always remain inconspicuous because as long as they don't know you, they can't pick on you. So please repress your natural tendencies and don't push to the forefront. . . .
> Don't become too friendly with the scum you invariably meet there. Don't gamble! There are always a few professional crooks in the crowd and they skin you alive. Don't lend out money. It will be no good to you. You will have a hard time getting your money back and you will lose your friends to the bargain. Don't go to a whore-house. I like a woman as you do. But I wouldn't think of touching those filthy, syphilis-infected camp followers.

Kissinger ended on a personal note, one that has been written by countless older brothers over the years: "You and I sometimes didn't get along so well, but I guess you knew, as I did, that in the 'clutch' we could count on each other. We are in the clutch now."[3]

The army's clutches, however, worked in strange ways. During a battery of aptitude tests administered at nearby Clemson, Kissinger scored well enough (in fact, the highest of his entire unit) to be assigned to the Army Specialized Training Program. Those who qualified—more than one hundred thousand nationwide—were yanked out of combat training and sent to college at government expense. Kissinger was assigned to study engineering at Lafayette College in Easton, Pennsylvania, an idyllic campus less than a hundred miles from Washington Heights.

Kissinger had always been scholarly. Now his own rather strong suspicion that he was a cut above everyone else was reinforced. Even among the brains plucked out of the army, he was considered brainy. He was called upon to tutor the other students in a variety of subjects, especially calculus and physics. The process of learning began to enthrall him, even obsess him. He would skip meals to devour his books, staying in his messy room eating crackers, drinking Coke, and muttering to himself as he read.

Often Kissinger would argue with the books, according to his roommate Charles Coyle. "He didn't read books, he ate them with his eyes, his fingers, his squirming in the chair, and with his mumbling criticism. He'd be slouching over a book and suddenly explode with an indignant, German-accented 'Bullshit!' blasting the author's reasoning."

Kissinger took twelve courses during his academic year at Lafayette. He got an A in every one of them, including a perfect 100 in chemistry. "The guy was so damn bright and so damn intellectual it was strange to most of us—and we were the ones who had been selected for our intelligence," said Coyle. "He'd come into the living room of our suite. Three or four of us would be talking, probably about sex. He'd flop on the couch and start reading a book like Stendhal's *The Red and the Black*—for fun!" There was, as always, a seriousness, a Germanic heaviness, to Kissinger's demeanor. He had seen more than these guys. He was more mature.

At times, a few of the redneck students would toss out anti-Semitic remarks. Kissinger sloughed it off. "He was too smart to get into a fight," said Coyle. "Henry would just be patient with the kids from the hills, and they ended up liking him." Though his sense of humor was not yet developed, Kissinger began to discover how a mixture of sarcasm, wry observations, and self-deprecation could deflect tension. "Sometimes he would ridicule the army, sometimes he would ridicule himself, and there were times when he would ridicule some of us," recalled Coyle. "But he did it with a smile. It was typical New York humor."[4]

On the weekend, when Kissinger would hitchhike home for a visit, he would sometimes go to synagogue with his father. Friends at K'hal Adath Jeshurun remember a few times in 1943 when Kissinger, wearing a private's uniform and yarmulke, would come for the Sabbath service. But he was drifting away from his religion, and he went to synagogue mainly to please his father. "Henry respected him so much," his mother recalled, "that he would never have done anything that would hurt him."

The invasion of Europe made the Specialized Training Program a luxury that the army could not justify. Warm bodies, even overeducated ones, were needed for the front. Nor was the elitist notion of sparing smart boys from combat and sending them to college a particularly popular one. In April 1944, the army canceled the program.

One way to avoid combat was to be selected for training as an army doctor. Kissinger applied, not because he had much interest in medicine, but because he had even less interest in being a combat infantryman. By then, Kissinger knew how to blitz the standardized tests so valued by the army. He easily did well enough to be chosen as one of the twenty-five finalists at Lafayette for medical school.

Among the other finalists was Leonard Weiss, known as Larry. He and Kissinger used to hitchhike to New York on weekends and double-date. Once, Weiss and his girlfriend went with Kissinger and Ann Fleischer to see *The Marriage of Figaro* at the Metropolitan Opera. The two soldiers were at the top of the program at Lafayette, but Weiss considered Kissinger to be the smarter. In the end, however, it was Weiss who made the cut for medical school.

Kissinger claimed that it was his lapse on the standardized test that held him back. "I could usually eat up those standardized tests," he recalled. "But on the day of the one to get into med school, I slept late, missed breakfast, came in after the test began, and spent too much time filling in each section."

Weiss had a different impression. Of the five chosen, he was the only Jew. The rest, who were far below Kissinger in their test results, were two Southern Baptists and two Philadelphia Catholics. "My appearances were less Jewish than Kissinger's," said Weiss, "and I didn't have an accent. When an interviewer asked my religion and I said Jewish, he said they try to 'balance' the religious makeup of the group." In any event, Kissinger was not all that upset. In 1988, when Weiss's brother introduced himself at an American Express board meeting, Kissinger said: "Ah, yes, your brother saved me from being a doctor."[5]

•

Paula Kissinger would later refer to Camp Claiborne, Louisiana, as "that swamp," even though it was amid the dusty dirt farms near upstate Alexandria, far from bayou country. Swamp or not, Kissinger was not happy to find himself plucked from academe and, along with 2,800 other intellectuals, shipped down on a single train to Louisiana to join the 17,000 soldiers of the 84th Infantry Division.

During that searing summer of 1944, as he was subjected to an arduous series of training exercises, Kissinger used to call home collect to complain. For the first time, he was homesick. "Mother, I want to walk out on my hands and crawl home," he told her.

One of his few stimulations was serving as a company education officer. Once a week, instead of target practice, a hundred or so of his fellow infantrymen would gather for an informal briefing on the war and other world events. The duty of giving the talk usually fell to Kissinger. "He always carried *Time* and a couple of newspapers in his knapsack on hikes," recalled Charles Coyle, his roommate from Lafayette College, who had also been sent to Camp Claiborne. "Henry was always the best lecturer. He never talked about his childhood in Germany, but it was clear he knew all about the Nazis."[6]

FRITZ KRAEMER

The dramatic encounter that plucked Kissinger from the pack began with a scene that would have strained the credibility of a grade-B war movie. The soldiers of Kissinger's company had just finished a ten-mile hike and were scattered prostrate on the sun-baked grass of a rifle range. Suddenly, a jeep roared up amid a cloud of dust and out stepped a short thirty-five-year-old Prussian-bred U.S. Army private with a cocksure face and crisply pressed uniform. Wearing a monocle and brandishing a walking stick, he brushed past the startled infantrymen.

"Who is in command here?" the private yelled. A lieutenant colonel, slightly shaken, stepped forward. The private barked out in cannon-fire Prussian tones: "Sir, I am sent by the general and I am going to speak to your company about why we are in this war."

Kissinger, who had been half-asleep, was mesmerized. The jaunty private stood on the jeep and began to lecture, with bombastic volume and clipped cadences, about the philosophy of the Nazi state and why it was necessary—as well as inevitable—that Hitler be crushed. He had flashing eyes, a hypnotic flamboyance, and a bristling electricity.

His arrogance was towering and his mannerisms eccentric, but the effect was to make him seem charismatic rather than absurd. When the lecture was over, Kissinger did something he had never done before: he wrote a fan note. "Dear Pvt. Kraemer. I heard you speak yesterday. This is how it should be done. Can I help you in any way? Pvt. Kissinger."[7]

Fritz Gustav Anton Kraemer, born in 1908, was the son of a Prussian state prosecutor. His mother, from a wealthy chemical-making family, owned a thirty-five-room manor near Wiesbaden. Both parents were foes of Hitler, whom they called that "miserable Bohemian corporal," and his mother established an orphanage on her estate that took in Christian and Jewish children even after the Nazis seized power.

Fritz spent most of his time abroad. He went to school in England, earned a degree from the London School of Economics, then gathered doctorates from Goethe University in Frankfurt and the University of Rome. In 1939, as war loomed, he was working in Rome for the League of Nations. Deciding to remain in exile, he sent his wife and infant son, Sven, back to Wiesbaden to bid farewell to his mother. There they were trapped for six years, during which time Fritz, penniless but exuding bravado, moved to the U.S. and enlisted in the army.

The army had a hard time knowing what to make of Kraemer, or what to do with him. During one training exercise at Camp Claiborne, he was assigned to add realism by shouting rapid-fire military commands in German from a platform. The commander of the 84th Infantry Division, General Alexander Bolling, happened by. "What are you doing, soldier?" he asked. "Making German battle noises, sir," Kraemer responded. They fell into conversation. Bolling, impressed, had Kraemer assigned to his headquarters.

When the trainload of defrocked Special Training Program students arrived, Kraemer went to his commander with a request. "We've got twenty-eight hundred new intellectuals in this division. Permit me to address them; otherwise, they will not understand why they are here." And thus Kissinger and Kraemer, two exiled Germans—one a reluctant religious refugee, the other a proud political expatriate—found themselves face-to-face on a rifle range in Louisiana in May of 1944.[8]

The fan note that arrived from Private Kissinger the next day appealed to Kraemer. He liked its blunt manner, its unadorned brevity. Later he would also claim to admire its lack of flattery, but in fact Kissinger had struck just the right note of flattery. " 'This is how it should be done,' " Kraemer recalled almost fifty years later, repeating and savoring Kissinger's phrase as he paced in his Washington garden. Kraemer, letter in hand, returned the next day to Kissinger's battalion, again roaring up in a jeep and barking at the startled lieutenant colonel. "Who is this Kissinger?" demanded Kraemer, not the last time the question would be asked.

Kissinger and Kraemer talked for twenty minutes. "You have an unusual political mind," Kraemer said. Later, Kissinger would recall that "this really was startling news to me. It hadn't occurred to me."[9]

Kraemer went back to headquarters and told his captain about "this little Jewish refugee" he had met. "He as yet knows nothing, but already he understands everything." In Kraemer's lexicon, this was a compliment; Kissinger, he explained, seemed to have an inner ear for the music of history.

Kraemer's patronage was to prove momentous. During the next three years, he would pluck Kissinger out of the infantry, secure him an assignment as a translator for General Bolling, get him chosen to administer the occupation of captured towns, ease his way into the Counter-Intelligence Corps, have him hired as a teacher at a military intelligence school in Germany, and then convince him to go to Harvard. Kraemer is often described as "the man who discovered Kissinger." He thunders: "My role was not discovering Kissinger! My role was getting Kissinger to discover himself!"

Kraemer saw in Kissinger—and helped nurture in Kissinger—a reflection of his own conservatism. "Henry's knowledge of history, and his respect for it, led to his reverence for order," Kraemer said. "The lay of his soul was conservative. He had an understanding that it was the state's duty to preserve order."

Both men liked conversation, but they were partial to discussions that were intellectual rather than intimate. Neither was immune to flattery. "Henry, you are absolutely unique, you are unbelievably gifted," the older man would say, and Kissinger was not pained by such suggestions. Kissinger, for his part, would question Kraemer about the forces of history, probe him about abstract ideas. "He would squeeze me for my ideas the way one would squeeze a sponge," Kraemer recalled.

Yet it was an explosive combination of egos: many years later, when his former mentor was an adviser at the Pentagon, Kissinger (quite understandably) found Kraemer's long harangues to be overbearing. Kraemer (perhaps just as understandably) began to regard Kissinger as too ambitious and too self-absorbed. "I slowly observed," Kraemer lamented, "that this man who was hungry for knowledge was also concerned about a personal career."

Kissinger would, probably, have found his way out of obscurity even had Kraemer not come along. But the flamboyant Prussian certainly hastened the process and instilled in the insecure refugee a sense of his intellectual distinction. He exposed Kissinger's impressionable twenty-year-old mind to a pantheon of thinkers and philosophers—Spengler, Kant, Dostoyevski, and others—and inspired him to explore the depths of his own mind. No longer did Kissinger aspire to be an accountant. History rather than math became his new fascination.

Kraemer also shored up Kissinger's sense of identity as a German; he insisted that they converse in German and that Kissinger learn German history and philosophy. In the process, some of Kraemer's deep-seated anticommunism rubbed off: Kraemer considered both the Nazis and the communists to be barbarians. A breakdown in social order, he felt, provided a dangerous opening for totalitarian regimes of either the left or the right.

For Kissinger, attaching himself to Kraemer was like adopting a new father figure. He seemed fascinated by Kraemer's aristocratic hauteur and larger-than-life swagger, qualities he would later find in his Harvard mentor, William Elliott. With his Lutheran sense of divine duty, Kraemer was a man of action willing to confront the forces of history. Kraemer's personality offered an antidote to Kissinger's insecurity: he learned to mask it with a Kraemer-like bravado that at times bordered on a Kraemer-like arrogance.

There was, however, one Kraemer attribute that did not rub off on Kissinger. Kraemer had a disdain for money, power, position, recognition, and conventional measures of success. Ambition was alien to him. Not that he was self-effacing—far from it. But he felt that directing his actions toward publicity or personal success was somehow "utilitarian." Once, years later, when he visited Kissinger at Harvard, he was horrified to see photographs on the shelf with inscriptions from famous people. "Why do you do this?" Kraemer roared. "This is not done."

Kraemer now feels he may have been "mistaken" in his early impressions of Kissinger. But even as the resentments of his later years pour out, so do the affection and awe he once felt:

> His motivations may have been more crass than I originally thought. When he was in counterintelligence, there were people who told me that he was a difficult person with a strong ego. Kissinger had a difficult youth. I did not. I knew who I was. He did not. Kissinger may have had all along a desire for power. He obviously hankers for approval. But back then what I remember is how he hankered for knowl-

edge, for truth. He wanted to know everything, not just what might be of use to him. He was—he is—one of the most gifted people you could imagine. The Lord God when picking from his basket of gifts usually distributes carefully. But with Kissinger, he showered the whole basket. [10]

RETURN OF THE NATIVE

The 84th Infantry Division got its orders to move in September 1944, embarking for Europe to be part of the pursuit phase of the war in the wake of D day. Private Kissinger, serial number 32816775, was assigned to G Company of the 335th Infantry Regiment. Their ship—the USS *Stirling Castle*—sailed from Pier 58 in Manhattan, giving Kissinger the chance to pay a quick visit home. On the night of November 1, they crossed the English Channel. While aboard, they were given absentee ballots for the election between Franklin Roosevelt and Thomas Dewey. Kissinger, though now twenty-one and a citizen, did not vote.

With G Company leading the attack, the 84th Division made it to Germany within a week. They poured across the Belgian-German border under heavy fire near Aachen on November 9, the sixth anniversary of Kristallnacht. During those six years, Kissinger had gained a new homeland; as he crossed the border, he thought of himself as an American liberator, not a returning German.

Nor had he come for vengeance. "I felt," he once told the *New York Post,* "to the dismay of my family, that if racial discrimination was bad vis-à-vis the Jews, it was bad vis-à-vis the Germans. I mean, you couldn't blame a whole people." But though his homecoming was not as he might have imagined, it was a dramatic fulfillment of the prophecy he had made to the customs man who had sneered at him in Fürth.

Kissinger crossed the border alone, driving a jeep. Thanks to Fritz Kraemer, he had been yanked out of G Company the day before and ordered to report to division headquarters. General Bolling needed a German-speaking translator-driver, and Kraemer had Kissinger tapped for the assignment. From then on, Kissinger would be assigned to Division Intelligence and later to the Counter-Intelligence Corps, which handled military occupation. In such capacities, he was never called upon to fire his rifle in combat.

The Battle of the Bulge, Germany's last-gasp offensive, began that December. The 84th Division and the rest of the Ninth Army were among those pushed back into Belgium by the onslaught. For the Jewish refugees among the American troops, there was a special danger: many of them who were captured were summarily shot rather than taken prisoner. Nevertheless, when his division was forced to evacuate hastily from the Belgian town of Marche, Kissinger volunteered to be part of the small detachment that stayed behind to fight a delaying action.

The situation in Marche was chaotic. American forces had entered the town only to find German police already ensconced there, and General Bolling ordered a hasty withdrawal. Because Kissinger spoke German, it made sense for him to remain behind to try to discover what the enemy was planning. "He did it with the full knowledge that he would never get out if the Germans took the town," recalled Kraemer. "It was very brave and Kissinger did it without hesitation." Said Kissinger: "In combat, you don't think of yourself as brave."

By March 1945, the 84th Division had pushed back into Germany. The first major town they captured was Krefeld, a Rhine river port with a population of two hundred thousand near the Dutch border. It was in shambles: there was no garbage collection, no water, no gas. The Counter-Intelligence Corps had the task of restoring order.

But typical of army efficiency, no one in the CIC detachment spoke German. They all spoke French. Kraemer, by then a sergeant in division intelligence, was asked to handle the civilian occupation. He demurred. He was engaged, as was his wont, in his own version of psychological warfare: driving along the front with a loudspeaker trying to convince the Germans to surrender. "I have this extraordinarily brilliant young man," he told them. "Why don't you take him?"

And so Kissinger, still a private and with no security clearance, became the administrator of Krefeld. "I relied on the German sense of order," he recalled. He decreed that the people in charge of each municipal function—gas, water, power, transportation, garbage—report to him, then he weeded out the obvious Nazis. They were usually easy to spot, because they were the only ones well fed. If necessary, he tracked down the people who had run certain functions before the Nazis came to power. Within eight days he built a civilian government. "It was an astounding phenomenon," said Kraemer. "And he did it without showing any resentment, any hatred. He showed only that he was a practical man."

As a result, Kissinger was transferred to the Counter-Intelligence Corps, at first as a driver, because there was no other slot for him, then as a Counter-Intelligence agent with the rank of sergeant. The main mission of the CIC was to ferret out the dangerous Nazis and Gestapo members in the territories under Allied control.[11]

While stationed in Hanover, Kissinger again relied on the German character to help him carry out his work. He put up posters asking people with "police experience" to report to him. A beefy man showed up and proudly announced he had been with the state police. Kissinger assumed that he had been with the regular police force, not the dreaded secret police, but he asked anyway, almost as a joke. "Geheime Staatspolizei?" The man proudly said yes, he was indeed with the Gestapo. Kissinger locked him up.

Kissinger then was able to play on the man's German sense of obedience. "He asked me how he could show his goodwill, and I ordered him to find his colleagues," Kissinger recalled. "We rode around in a jeep picking them up. It surprised me because I had the impression that the Gestapo were all monsters. In fact, they were mainly miserable little bureaucrats who were eager to work with us."

Kissinger also played on German pride, perfecting a trick commonly used by the Counter-Intelligence Corps. He would tell each suspected Nazi, "We know you're not important, you're just a small fry," until the suspect's pride would cause him to erupt that he was in fact a high-ranking local Nazi.

Kissinger did not savor the revenge. Despite what the Nazis had inflicted on his family and his fellow Jews, he soon lost his stomach for arresting Gestapo members. "After a while, it got too messy picking up so many Gestapo—wives were crying, children clinging. So I sent an MP around with my Nazi all over lower Saxony. I think I brought in more Gestapo this way than all the rest of the army."[12]

For this, Sergeant Kissinger won his Bronze Star. It was due, he is the first to admit, more to serendipity than bravery, and involved less danger than some of his unheralded actions. But the army's citation piled on the glory: "Sgt. Kissinger, performing duty in charge of a Counter-Intelligence team operating under difficult and extremely hazardous conditions, successfully established chains of informants reaching into every phase of civilian life, resulting in the detection and arrest of numerous persons identified as enemy agents engaged in espionage and sabotage."

"I SAID FAREWELL TO MY YOUTH"

The Allied victory over Hitler in May 1945 gave Kissinger the chance to round out his journey. A few days shy of his twenty-second birthday, the American man went back to see where the German boy had lived. Fürth, Leutershausen, Nuremberg, the surrounding countryside: he retraced the steps where he and his friends used to walk together—Heinz Kissinger, Heinz Lion, Herr Lion—and surveyed the damage, both physical and psychic.

Kissinger was never considered, except by his mother, to be a particularly sentimental person. But upon his return to Fürth, his sentiments poured forth in a most revealing letter home, a ten-page description of his return handwritten as a short story, in English, evoking the ghosts he saw and the emotions he felt.

His first stop was Leutershausen, the small Bavarian village where his mother's family had prospered as cattle dealers. Looking down into the valley at the roofs gleaming in the sun, he marveled at how sleepy and peaceful the town looked:

> I stood on the hill and looked down into the valley, into the valley wherein lay buried part of my youth. The trees were still shady, the dairy was still there. We stopped the jeep where the bus had always stopped.
>
> For a fleeting moment I thought I saw a little fat woman with her apron on and a weather-beaten mustached old man [his grandfather Falk Stern, who had died of cancer shortly after the Kissingers fled Germany, and his wife, who was killed by the Nazis in a concentration camp]. But there was only the street and the tower.
>
> We drove very slowly, past the ghosts of all the men who lived and died in the hatred of the years. I thought of the little boy who had played football in the yard and the old man who used to stand in the window to watch him. All the years came back and for a minute time stood still. It was like when our friends were still alive and we were young.
>
> If we could go back 13 years over the hatred and the intolerance, I would find that it had been a long hard road. It had been covered with humiliation, with disappointment. Thirteen years is a long time to go back to. I thought of the fine old people that had been so kind, of the long walks in the woods, of what was and what might have been. For a minute the valley was alive with the people I used to know. They were all there. Then the illusion faded. . . . I said goodby to my grandparents.

From Leutershausen, Kissinger went to Fürth, driving his jeep along the scarred roads around Nuremberg and through the woods where he used to hike. From the second-floor apartment where the Kissingers had lived—"Houses have a way of shrinking with the years," he wrote—he stared out the window at the cobbled street and park below and thought of the walks he had taken there with Heinz Lion and his father. " 'What are you looking at?' the new tenant asked. Nothing, you'll never understand, I thought. Nothing but my friend and his father. Only the cruelty of the years and the nihilism of a decade."

In front of the school where his father had taught, Kissinger posed for a picture. Inside, a German official was handling administrative work. Kissinger described the scene in his letter: "We walked through the corridors, and wherever we went, men stood at attention, and wherever we walked the past followed. 'Why do you inspect the school?' Dr. Hahn asked. 'I am paying a debt, a debt to my father.' "

Finally, he visited Nuremberg. In his letter, he called it the "Epilogue." He wrote:

> The Opera House, the culture house, the railroad station, the post office were all pounded into ruin. We stood on a hill and looked into the valley. The shell of Nuremberg lay before us. I thought of Herr Lion's words: You'll come back to your birthplace someday and you won't find a stone unturned. A shattered sign lay in the road. Nuremberg 7 km, Fürth 6 km, it said.
>
> Those who live by the sword shall perish by the sword. There on the hill overlooking Nuremberg I said farewell to my youth.[13]

While visiting Fürth, Kissinger searched for old childhood friends. Most had emigrated, others had been killed in the concentration camps. The townspeople told of but one survivor: Helmut Reissner, a classmate at the Realschule and fellow soccer player at the sports club. Kissinger sought him out, finding him in the home of a non-Jewish family in Fürth.

In 1941, the Reissner family, among the town's wealthiest Jews, had been sent by train to concentration camps, eventually ending up at Buchenwald, about one hundred miles to the north. Along with fifty thousand other inmates at the complex, Helmut's parents and other relatives had died from starvation, medical experimentation, or other cruelties. Helmut was among the twenty thousand inmates who were still alive when General George Patton's Third Army liberated the camp in April. He drifted back down to Fürth, searching for someone he knew.

When Kissinger came to the home where he was staying, Reissner recognized him at once. "He was very natural, warm, and had a lot of compassion," Reissner recalled. But both boys refrained from getting emotional in discussing what had happened. "What he told me later,"

Reissner said, "was that if I had wept while telling him this, he could not have listened to me."[14]

Kissinger kept an eye on Reissner for months as he physically recovered, making sure that he had sufficient food and funds. Within a year, Reissner was ready to immigrate to Long Island, where he had an aunt. Kissinger wrote her a long letter telling her what to expect. In the process, he revealed some of the lessons he drew from those who had survived the holocaust:

> I feel it necessary to write to you, because I think a completely erroneous picture exists in the States of the former inmates of the concentration camps. . . .
>
> Concentration camps were not only mills of death. They were also testing grounds. Here men persisted, and in a sense fought for survival, with the stake always nothing less than one's life, with the slightest slip a fatal error. Such was the filth, the compulsion, the debasement, that a person had to be possessed of extraordinary powers, both psychic and of will, to even want to survive. The intellectuals, the idealists, the men of high morals had no chance. . . . Having once made up one's mind to survive, it was a necessity to follow through with a singleness of purpose, inconceivable to you sheltered people in the States. Such singleness of purpose broached no stopping in front of accepted sets of values, it had to disregard ordinary standards of morality. One could only survive through lies, tricks and by somehow acquiring food to fill one's belly. The weak, the old had no chance.
>
> And so liberation came. The survivors were not within the ordinary pale of human events anymore. They had learned that looking back meant sorrow, that sorrow was weakness, and weakness synonymous with death. They knew that having survived the camp, surviving the liberation was no problem. So they applied themselves to the peace with the same singleness of purpose and sometimes the same disregard of accepted standards as they had learned in the camp. Above all they wanted no pity. Pity made them uncomfortable, jumpy. . . .
>
> You would make a terrible mistake, were you to expect a broken boy. Helmut is a man. He has seen more than most people in a lifetime. . . . Helmut will want to be much alone, he will not want to be pampered. He will want to live an ordinary life, but a life of his own making.

Reissner ended up with a life of his own making. He started the Reissner Chemical Co. on Long Island and lived comfortably in New Hyde Park.

Kissinger's letter played on a theme that would recur throughout his career: the tension that often exists, at least in his view, between morality and realism. Survival, he noted, sometimes required a disregard for moral standards that was "inconceivable" to those who had led "sheltered" lives. Kissinger contrasted the cold realist, who survives, with "the men of high morals," who, in brutal situations, have no chance. In later years, Kissinger would sometimes equate an emphasis on morality with weakness. He could also have been describing himself when he wrote of concentration camp victims: "They have seen man from the most evil side, who can blame them for being suspicious?" [15]

THE OCCUPIER

Residents of Bensheim remember him roaring into town in a white 1938 Mercedes he had confiscated from the Nazi owner of a baby-powder company. Past the medieval town houses he drove, through the center of the hillside village, coming to a stop in the alley in front of the tax office. He took the stairs two at a time and, arriving at the top, announced: "I'm Mr. Henry from the Counter-Intelligence Corps, and I'm taking over this floor." [16]

In June of 1945, Sergeant Kissinger, at age twenty-two, was named commandant of a new Counter-Intelligence detachment assigned to provide order and weed out dangerous Nazis in the Bergstrasse district of Hesse. Their headquarters was in Bensheim, population 17,000, a sleepy paper-making town about thirty miles south of Frankfurt and a hundred and ten miles west of Fürth and Nuremberg. Thus did Kissinger become a monarch in a land that had despised his people. "I had absolute authority to arrest people," he noted. "In the CIC, we had more power than even the military government." As Kraemer put it: "He was the absolute ruler of Bensheim."

Nevertheless, Kissinger avoided any expression of hatred toward the Germans, any signs of vengeance. In fact, he reserved his anger for those Counter-Intelligence agents—particularly Jews—who gave vent to anti-German feelings. "I remember one occasion when some of these refugee interpreters were being a little abusive to a civilian couple," one army colleague, Ralph Farris, said. "Henry began yelling at the questioners thusly: 'You lived under the Nazis! You know how abusive they were! How can you turn around and abuse these people the same way?'"

Kissinger went even further: he kept quiet, insofar as it was possible, about the fact that he was Jewish. He no longer practiced his religion and never brought it up. And though his army colleagues of course knew him as Kissinger, he called himself Mr. Henry among the Germans in his jurisdiction because it sounded more American than Jewish. "I used the name Mr. Henry," he later explained, "because I didn't want the Germans to think the Jews were coming back to take revenge." [17]

Kissinger, consciously or subconsciously, became about as German as he could be. Despite the rules against fraternizing with the local citizenry, he took up with a blond and beautiful mistress who was the wife of a German nobleman. He toured the countryside in his Mercedes, becoming a fixture at local soccer matches. And he set up house in a modern palatial villa he confiscated in Zwingenberg, a classy suburb three miles north of Bensheim.

"What a setup!" said Jerry Bechhofer, his friend from Fürth and Washington Heights who was stationed in Heidelberg. Bechhofer used to come for visits and was a guest at the parties Kissinger used to throw. "He had a very elegant villa, modern in the style of the 1930s. His girlfriend was intelligent and beautiful, and they used to give fabulous feasts. You could tell how much he liked the trappings of power, though he never threw his weight around."

Reissner also used to come for visits, staying at the villa and regaining his health after his years in Buchenwald. One weekend they went to the racetrack in Munich, another time to a soccer game.

As the regent of more than twenty towns, Kissinger honed his diplomacy. The mayor of Bensheim was a frequent dinner guest. So, too, was the pre-Hitler police chief, who helped Kissinger identify and arrest the local Nazi leaders until the old chief started taking bribes and had to be arrested himself. "Henry was an excellent diplomat," said Bechhofer. "He was able to get along with German officials and make them do his bidding. In short order, the towns were working and the region had been de-Nazified." [18]

Karl Hezner and his relatives in Leutershausen had been, before the war, friends of Paula and her family. A wealthy, patrician clan of deep German roots, the Hezners were among the few non-Jews to remain friendly with the Sterns and Kissingers throughout the Nazi era. So Kissinger was surprised to find that they had been falsely accused of Nazi sympathies and that the American commandant in the area had confiscated their business. Kissinger intervened, got them back their home, and helped them raise money to restart their business. He also took care of Fritz Kraemer's wife, who was still living at her family villa with their son, Sven. Because she was not a German citizen and had no ration card, Kissinger would send her food packages from Bensheim each week.[19]

Kissinger stayed for almost a year in Bensheim until Kraemer again played patron. Kraemer was one of the founders of the European Command Intelligence School in Oberammergau, a postcard-perfect resort in the Bavarian Alps forty miles south of Munich. The school taught Allied military officers how to uncover Nazis and restore German civil authority. The commandant was taken aback when Kraemer insisted on recruiting for the faculty a sergeant with only a high school diploma. But Kraemer insisted that he would reassign Kissinger to gather firewood if he failed to make the grade as a teacher.

For the next ten months—first as a staff sergeant and then as a civilian employee making the tidy sum of $10,000 a year—Kissinger taught at Oberammergau. Among the others there were Helmut Sonnenfeldt, who would later work as Kissinger's counselor at the State Department, and Henry Rosovsky, later a noted economist and dean at Harvard. "Though he was not long out of high school, Henry had a very authoritative—and authoritarian—manner," said Rosovsky, who attended Kissinger's class on German paramilitary organizations. "He would lecture with great self-confidence and intellectual sophistication." But the director of education, Colonel Donald Strong, regarded Kissinger as arrogant: he refused to submit a lesson plan for approval, and he bucked regulations by keeping a pet dog in the barracks. "He was a problem person," Strong later recalled.[20]

Before he could leave Europe, Kissinger had one last visit to make. His grandfather, the scholarly and wise David Kissinger, was living near his son Arno in a fashionable neighborhood of Stockholm. Kissinger and his best friend from the Bergstrasse Counter-Intelligence Corps, a square-jawed sergeant named Frank Levitch, made the journey by train in December of 1946.

Uncle Arno, Louis Kissinger's brother, was in fine shape. "His business is very good right now," Kissinger wrote home. "Needless to say, he is not the quietest and most even-tempered boss imaginable." David Kissinger, at eighty-six, was also thriving. "He plays cards every evening with a girl of ninety-two who he insists always imposes on his relative youth by cheating."

What most impressed Kissinger was his grandfather's lack of bitterness at what had happened under the Nazis, even though three of his daughters were among those killed in the concentration camps. In his letter home, Kissinger praised his grandfather's ability to eschew hatred, and he implied it should be a model to his father, whose mind was tortured at the time by news of his sisters' deaths:

I spent hours each day talking to him and not just because of a sense of obligation. Grandfather has preserved
such a wonderful agility of mind, so much balanced judgment, such deep humility, such a lack of hatred and bias,
that it is a pleasure to speak with him. He still has the same
wonderful sense of humor. I wish you, dear father, could see
him. Although he suffers as much as any father with the loss
of his daughters, his attitude about it is so deeply decent, so
religiously resigned, that it could be a model to anybody. . . .
I'm sure he wouldn't want you, dear father, to torture yourself just as he doesn't torture himself. [21]

"I MAY HAVE SET UP A DEFENSIVE MECHANISM"

"Living as a Jew under the Nazis, then as a refugee in
America, and then as a private in the army, isn't exactly an experience
that builds confidence," Kissinger once said. He was wrong. Not only
did the army help Americanize him, it toughened him. His insecurity
was still present, but now there was a hard shell and the aura of
confidence that comes from having survived in war and thrived in
command.

Confidence coexisting with insecurities, vanity with vulnerability,
arrogance with a craving for approval: the complexities that were lay-
ered into Kissinger's personality as a young man would persist
throughout his life.

"It was an Americanization process," said Kissinger. "It was the
first time I was not with German Jewish people. I gained confidence
in the army." He felt less self-conscious, so much so that he thought
he had lost his accent, until he returned home and was reminded
otherwise.* Says his brother, Walter: "Both of us found our way, got
ourselves going, became who we are, because of our time in the service." [22]

In giving him a new self-identity, the army also stripped Kissinger
of some of his old one. No longer did he practice his religion. No
longer was he part of the refugee community. And though he loved
and respected his parents all the more with his new maturity, his
distance from them grew. "The army opened a new world for us,"

---

* Kissinger's German accent remained with him throughout his life, even
though his brother, Walter, only a year younger, pretty much shed his. When
asked why he had lost his accent while his brother had not, Walter Kissinger
answered: "Because I am the Kissinger who listens."

Walter Kissinger explained, "one that our parents couldn't share or understand."[23]

Yet what passed for confidence was partly a wall, the wall that arises when innocence and wonder crumble. Shortly after his return, Kissinger explained it in a letter to his parents, who had gone on a week's vacation at Kahn's Hotel in Quebec to celebrate their twenty-fifth anniversary. "If I seem sometimes distant, please remember that for me, the war ended only in July 1947," he wrote, "that for three years I have been deceived, I have had to fight, and argue and lose. I may have set up a defensive mechanism."[24]

That defensive mechanism would be with Kissinger for the rest of his life. So, too, would the detachment and distance he would feel even toward those who knew him well. The war matured Kissinger, broadened his horizons, piqued his ambitions. But it also snuffed out the scholarly innocence that dwelled in the young boy from Fürth who always had a book tucked under his arm. Innocence, naïveté, and being too concerned with moral niceties became identified in his mind with weakness and even death. As he'd stood on the hill overlooking Nuremberg, he had indeed bid farewell to his youth.

By July of 1947, Kissinger was ready to sail from Germany to the U.S. for the second time in nine years. Now twenty-four, he had been away from home for four years, had lived as an occupier in Germany for three.

To his parents, he heralded his imminent return with a telegram: SMOKY ARRIVING BY PLANE TONIGHT. Smoky was a cocker spaniel he had spotted in the window of a Paris pet shop and carted around Europe in a knapsack. Now they were inseparable. "So this telegram comes with instructions to go pick up his dog," Paula Kissinger recalled. "Louis was sick. The floor man had just come in to polish all the floors. I don't have a car. On the subway I have to go to the airport to get this dog. Inside the box is Henry's coat, so the dog would be comforted by the smell. And there's a letter. It says the dog eats hamburgers and string beans. So I feed the dog hamburger and string beans."[25]

Upon Kissinger's departure from Germany, Kraemer had given him a last piece of advice. "You need an education," said the Prussian with two doctorates. "Go to a fine college. A gentleman does not go to the College of the City of New York." The advice reflected Kraemer's elitism and was hardly accurate. But it fit in with Kissinger's new ambitions.[26]

Most colleges were by now filled for the fall term. But Harvard made a special effort to accommodate returning veterans; its president, James Bryant Conant, had been a driving force behind the G.I. Bill, and he had appointed an outreach counselor to make sure that veterans had access to his university.

"In order to adequately prepare myself for a literary carreer [*sic*], with political history as the main field of interest, I consider it essential to acquire a Liberal Arts education," Kissinger wrote in his application to Harvard. He noted in his autobiographical sketch that "racial persecution forced my family to emigrate to the U.S.," but he was otherwise unrevealing in discussing his past. He listed his interests as "writing, classical music, and contemporary literature" and his favorite sports as "tennis, baseball." In the blank for religion, he had typed in "Hebrew." As for a roommate, he said that he would like to be assigned a "Midwesterner," preferably one who was twenty-three or older.[27]

Kissinger also applied to Columbia and Princeton. The reason he finally chose Harvard was simple: it was the only college willing, that late, to have him for the next academic year. As it turned out, it would end up having him for the next twenty.

FOUR

HARVARD

The Ambitious Student, 1947–1955

> *In the life of every person there comes a point when he realizes that out of all the seemingly limitless possibilities of youth he has in fact become one actuality.—opening sentence, Kissinger's undergraduate thesis, 1949*

SMOKY AND THE SCHOLAR

The class of 1950, which Henry Kissinger joined in the fall of 1947 as a twenty-four-year-old sophomore, was the largest in Harvard's history. Most of its 1,588 members were veterans, as were three-quarters of all the students in the university. Fresh-faced high school graduates mixed with mature former soldiers eager to get on with their lives. Although the traditions of the nation's oldest university remained intact—maids still came each morning to make the beds —Harvard had become more democratic. For the first time in its history, more than half of its students came from public schools.

With America donning an unfamiliar mantle of world leadership, Harvard was crackling with the excitement of a new role of its own. At the 1947 commencement, Secretary of State George Marshall had unfurled his plan for reviving war-ravaged Europe. That fall, when Kissinger arrived, a forum featuring I. F. Stone and Joseph Alsop debated the topic "Must We Stop Russia?" The Carnegie Foundation announced it was funding a Russian Research Center at the university; it would be the first of the university's many "area studies" programs designed to accompany America's emergence from its isolationist past. "Harvard was an uncommonly lively place in the early postwar period," recalled McGeorge Bundy, then a government professor. "International affairs was expanding as a discipline. Harvard believed it had a new role because the country had a new role."[1]

Kissinger moved into room 39 of Claverly Hall, a dusty brick dormitory on busy Mt. Auburn Street near the heart of the university. His roommates were Arthur Gilman and Edward Hendel, both veterans, both Jewish.

Jews entering Harvard in 1947 were usually assigned roommates based on religion. Nevertheless, the anti-Semitism that had pervaded the Ivy League before the war had subsided. Jewish enrollment at Harvard was about 17 percent—lower than in the early 1920s when President A. Lawrence Lowell felt compelled to impose de facto quotas, but higher than in the years just before the war. While Kissinger was an undergraduate, the college quit advising the masters of the residential houses not to take more Jews "than the traffic will bear" and discontinued the practice of putting an asterisk next to the names of Jews applying to the houses.

President James Bryant Conant, in his efforts to broaden Harvard after the war, was particularly vigorous in his opposition to anti-Semitism. "Harvard welcomed us refugees with open arms," said Henry Rosovsky, Kissinger's colleague at the U.S. Army intelligence school in Oberammergau, and later an economics professor, dean of the faculty, and the first Jewish member of the Harvard Corporation. Though discrimination continued in some departments, it was least evident in the Government Department, where Louis Hartz, a Jew, was a professor of political theory and onetime chairman.[2]

Kissinger did not talk religion with his roommates. "We never, ever discussed our Jewishness," said Gilman. But in late-night bull sessions, Kissinger strongly opposed the creation of Israel. "He said it would alienate the Arabs and jeopardize U.S. interests. I thought it was a strange view for someone who had been a refugee from Nazi Germany." Herbert Engelhardt, who lived downstairs, said, "I got the impression that Kissinger suffered less anti-Semitism in his youth than I did as a kid in New Jersey."

Kissinger struck his roommates as intensely driven and excessively mature. By seven each morning, he was up and gone to his studies. Back in the room by late afternoon, he would sit in his easy chair reading and biting his fingernails, occasionally letting loose an outburst at some flaw in the author's logic. He read the *New York Times* and the *Boston Globe* each day, but made a point of not looking at the editorials. "He said he had to form his own opinions," recalled Gilman, "not learn those of the editors."

Also sharing the three-room suite was Smoky, Kissinger's misnamed tan cocker spaniel. Harvard had become quite liberal in its student regulations: women were allowed to visit in Claverly, alcohol was permitted, and virtually nothing was forbidden. Except weapons and dogs. "Keeping Smoky was a small way of defying the Harvard system," Kissinger later said. When the maid reported Smoky and Kissinger was ordered to get rid of him, he instead got up each morning, borrowed a car from Engelhardt, and brought Smoky to a kennel across the river, then back at night. When he went to New York for weekends, Gilman's mother would sometimes keep Smoky. "Her claim to fame," her son would later joke.

Despite his professed interest in sports, Kissinger did not go to any of the Harvard games. Nor did he go drinking or to parties with his housemates. He was a member of no club or society, a contributor to no publication, a player of no sport, a participant in no student activity. "Henry could be charming if he decided he wanted to be," said Gilman, "but he was really a loner."

Engelhardt, while professing a grudging affection, is even harsher. "He was deadly serious all the time. He never liked to chase after women. His famous wit and nuance were not in evidence when he was an undergraduate. He had no judgment, no feel for what was happening around him, no empathy for people he was with. He was clumsy, socially awkward, I guess a little shy. Basically he was a very limited person."[3]

In his first term, Kissinger took introductory courses in government, history, math, and French, earning an A in each. He also received permission to take chemistry as a fifth course for no credit. The following year he took another chemistry course for credit, got an A, and toyed with the idea of majoring in the subject. He asked Professor George Kistiakowsky, a chemist and later a presidential science adviser, whether he should. "If you have to ask," Kistiakowsky replied, "you shouldn't." Kissinger later regarded it as one of his lucky breaks in life. "I joked to Kistiakowsky that he could have kept me out of years of trouble by allowing me to become a mediocre chemist."

Instead, Kissinger chose government and philosophy as his fields of concentration, influenced in part by his fascination with William Elliott, the professor of his first-semester course on "The Development of Constitutional Government." On the basis of his first-year grades (all A's), Kissinger was entitled to have a senior faculty member as his tutor. Thus he latched onto the second dynamic patron in his life, the Government Department's *grand seigneur,* a man who was to Southerners what Fritz Kraemer was to Prussians: something between an epitome and a parody.[4]

WILLIAM YANDELL ELLIOTT

Kissinger was endearingly nervous, Engelhardt recalled, as he set out for his first meeting with Elliott. When he arrived at the professor's office, Elliott was busy writing. "Oh, my God," Elliott said upon looking up, "another tutee." He quickly dispatched Kissinger by giving him a list of twenty-five books to read and telling him not to return until he had written a paper comparing Immanuel Kant's *Critique of Pure Reason* with his *Critique of Practical Reason.*

Engelhardt and Gilman got a good laugh when they heard of Elliott's imperious put-down. But Kissinger went to the library, checked out the books, stacked them up next to the overstuffed easy chair in the suite, and began to read. He stayed up until two A.M. night after night. "I'll be damned if he didn't read them all," said Engelhardt. It took him three months to finish the paper, which Kissinger dropped off in Elliott's office one morning.

That afternoon the phone rang in Kissinger's suite. It was Elliott summoning him back. Never before, the professor boomed, had any student read all the books and written such a coherent paper.[5]

"I had a similar relationship with Elliott as I did with Kraemer," Kissinger later said. "Both had large, epic personalities."

Unlike Kraemer, William Yandell Elliott was also epic in size. A towering former all-American tackle at Vanderbilt, he had an orator's drawling boom, bushy eyebrows, a shock of black hair, and outsized features. Known as Wild Bill, he liked to stage cockfights in his basement at Harvard. "He was big, very big—in personality, in ego, and in size," according to Professor Stanley Hoffmann.

As a small-town Tennessee boy at Vanderbilt, Elliott became attached to the poets and writers of the Southern literary movement known as The Fugitives, such as John Crowe Ransom and Allen Tate. He won a Rhodes Scholarship, gloried in Oxford's tutorial system, and donned the mantle of athlete-poet-scholar with great majesty. At Harvard, he swung for the fences at departmental softball games, wrote and published florid poetry, and propounded philosophical notions with more fervor than reflection.

Elliott's best scholarship, on European political relations, was completed in the 1920s. After that, he subsisted on reputation and no small amount of bluster. "He was a glorious ruin," according to Professor Arthur Schlesinger, Jr. John Finley, a classics professor at Harvard, once likened Elliott to "a Pierce-Arrow running on seven cylinders."

Elliott's one professed regret was that his obsession with public service had not been fully consummated. He carried himself like the Southern senator or secretary of state that he never became. "There was a sense of duty that underlay his self-indulgent, vainglorious obsession with government service," wrote David Landau, a Harvard student who did a thesis on Kissinger in 1972. "It was that peculiar combination of lust and purpose that Elliott transmitted to Kissinger."[6]

"On many Sundays we took long walks in Concord," Kissinger recalled in a tribute to Elliott on his retirement in 1963. "He said that the only truly unforgivable sin is to use people as if they were objects." Given Kissinger's later propensity to manipulate people, the lesson may have been regarded as more of an academic analysis than a personal creed. The idea is a basic tenet of Elliott's favorite thinker, Immanuel Kant, the eighteenth-century German philosopher. As part of the formulation of his "categorical imperative," or fundamental moral principle, Kant declares: "Treat humanity whether in your own person or in that of others as an end only and never as a means."[7]

Elliott's patronage provided Kissinger with an enormous boost, both as an undergraduate and later in his quest to become a tenured professor. "He had a feeling for political philosophy," Elliott said. "He was not blind to the epic nature of history." Elliott was struck by the profundity of Kissinger's mind more than he was by its elegance. In recommending him for Phi Beta Kappa, Elliott wrote:

> I would say that I have not had any students in the past five years, even among the summa cum laude group, who have had the depth and philosophical insight shown by Mr. Kissinger. On the other hand, his mind lacks grace and is Teutonic in its systematic thoroughness. He has a certain emotional bent, perhaps from a refugee origin, that occasionally comes out. But I would regard him as on the whole a very balanced and just mind.[8]

When Kissinger attached himself to Elliott as his tutor, he paid a courtesy call on Professor Carl Friedrich to explain his choice. Friedrich and Elliott, the twin pillars of the Government Department, were personal and professional rivals. They shared an interest in Kant, particularly his obscure political tract "Perpetual Peace." Otherwise they were opposites: Friedrich, a German-born Protestant, was a meticulous scholar in the continental tradition, more dogged than creative, who felt contempt for Elliott's intuitive imagination, careless scholarship, charismatic presence, and flamboyant style.

Kissinger would later become famous for his agility at playing both sides of a rivalry. His handling of Friedrich and Elliott showed his early mastery of the maneuver. "He had managed to be on excellent terms with both these supreme rivals of the Harvard Government Department," wrote John Stoessinger, who had been a fellow student. " 'I wonder how he managed that,' one of us wondered wistfully, not without envy."[9]

Indeed, his success at currying favor with both Friedrich and Elliott—a feat no other student of the period matched—was regarded by many at Harvard with the mixture of admiration and resentment that Kissinger was destined to engender wherever he went. In 1971, just as he was becoming a global celebrity, Kissinger surprised Friedrich by flying up to Cambridge for his retirement party. "We went out on the porch together and he made some extravagant remarks," Friedrich recalled. "He said he learned more from me than anyone. He's a very skillful flatterer, which is part of his success as a negotiator."[10]

Under Elliott's guidance, Kissinger concentrated in both government and philosophy—until he collided with a philosophy course called "Relational Logic." Philosophy at Harvard had not yet been rescued by W. V. O. Quine from the excesses of logical positivism, and Kissinger's grasp of the subject was shaky, as he revealed in an essay appended to his undergraduate thesis. He ended up with a B in the course, the first time that he had sunk to such depths. Kissinger altered his major to Government, never took another philosophy class, and never got another B.

But it was not merely for his grades that Kissinger became an academic legend as a Harvard undergraduate.[11]

THE MEANING OF HISTORY

In Harvard's 350-year history, it has learned to take in stride the peculiar combination of intellectual brilliance and quirkiness that occasionally blossoms among its undergraduates. Even so, Henry Kissinger's senior thesis is still described in awed tones.

First of all there was its sheer bulk: 383 pages, longer than any previous undergraduate thesis—or, for that matter, any subsequent one, since it prompted the "Kissinger rule" limiting any future tomes to about one-third that length. There was also its scope, nothing less than "the meaning of history."

Having bitten off more than he could chew, Kissinger then proceeded to chew more than he had bitten off. He packed his pages with turgid, closely argued, and often impenetrable prose. Topping it off was his decision to focus on an incongruous trio of thinkers: he put the towering philosophical giant Immanuel Kant alongside two twentieth-century historical analysts, Oswald Spengler and Arnold Toynbee. Along the way, he roped in Descartes and Dostoyevski, Hegel and Hume, Socrates and Spinoza, the radical empiricists and their cousins the logical positivists. At the very end, having not quite satisfied himself, he tossed in a section called "A Clue from Poetry," featuring Dante, Homer, Milton, and Virgil. Those who found it all quite daunting (including his examiners) had a small consolation: in a feeble stab at making the opus more manageable, he omitted chapters he had written on yet another unlikely pairing: Georg Hegel and Albert Schweitzer.

This unpublished thesis is interesting as philosophy and is fascinating as personal testament. It introduced themes about morality, freedom, revolution, bureaucracy, and creativity that recur throughout Kissinger's life. It gave a taste of the intellectual arrogance for which he would become famous; at one point, for example, he declared, "Descartes' *cogito ergo sum* was not really necessary." And it offered a glimpse of how the future statesman perceived the pursuit of peace to be a constant balancing act that lacked larger meaning.[12]

In order to fathom Kissinger's mind, it is necessary to understand the four Europeans who fascinated him: Spengler, whose gloomy historic determinism infected Kissinger emotionally but repelled him intellectually; Kant, whose concept of moral freedom Kissinger embraced as a basis for political philosophy; Metternich, the Austrian minister who cobbled together a stable European balance through adroit diplomatic maneuvering; and Bismarck, the German unifier whose creativity allowed him to be both a conservative and a revolutionary. The first two of these men were at the core of his undergraduate thesis; the latter two were explored in Kissinger's work as a doctoral student and junior faculty member.[13]

"The Meaning of History" raised one of the most fundamental philosophical issues: the problem of determinism versus free will. Offering a glimpse into his young soul, Kissinger cast it in personal terms. "In the life of every person there comes a point when he realizes that out of all the seemingly limitless possibilities of his youth he has in fact become one actuality," he began. "No longer is life a broad plain with forests and mountains beckoning all-around, but it becomes apparent that one's journey across the meadows has indeed followed a regular path, that one can no longer go this way or that." Kissinger's goal was to show that free will is possible. "The desire to reconcile an experience of freedom with a determined environment is the lament of poetry and the dilemma of philosophy."

In his chapter on Spengler, titled "History as Intuition," Kissinger described the insights of the nationalistic German scholar, whose *Decline of the West* was published in 1918. Great cultures go through stages of youth and maturity until, in Kissinger's paraphrase of Spengler, "amidst a repetition of cataclysmic wars the civilization petrifies and dies." Thus, Spengler portrays history as a doomed power struggle, "a vast succession of catastrophic upheavals of which power is not only the manifestation but the exclusive aim."[14]

It would be wrong to identify Spengler's gloomy views with those of Kissinger, who seeks in his thesis to find a more palatable meaning to history. But it would also be wrong to ignore the perverse fascination that the brooding German refugee had for Spengler. Kissinger's historic pessimism, inbred as a boy, set him apart from the traditional American mavens of manifest destiny. As Professor Stanley Hoffmann noted, "Henry, in his melancholy, seems to walk with the spirit of Spengler at his side."[15]

In his chapter on Toynbee, Kissinger argued that the British theorist, whose twelve-volume *A Study of History* began appearing in 1934, "attempted to transcend Spengler's metaphysical limitations by an assertion of purposiveness." In other words, history is not predetermined; instead, man is engaged in a spiritual struggle that has a purpose. When a civilization does decay, a new one with higher values tends to be erected on the ruins of the old.

Toynbee ultimately failed, according to Kissinger, because he claimed to view human progress in a Christian framework but he relied on empirical methods that left no room for the role of free will. It was an approach "whose exhibition of deep learning tends to obscure its methodological shallowness," Kissinger wrote.[16]

Man's knowledge of freedom, Kissinger argued, must come from an inner intuition. This led him to Immanuel Kant, the German philosopher whose main treatises were written in the 1780s. Kissinger got off to a troublesome start by asserting that the connections between causes and effects exist only in the human mind: "Causality expresses the pattern which the mind imposes on a sequence of events in order to make their appearance comprehensible." He attributed this notion to Kant, who indeed accepted it, although the true credit (or blame) properly rested with the British trio of radical empiricists, Locke, Berkeley, and Hume. Fortunately, Kissinger quickly sidled away from Kant's theories about empirical facts; understanding the nature of freedom, Kissinger decided, requires moving to a "profounder level of meaning . . . revealed to man in his esthetic, theological and, above all, moral experiences."

Kant, a German Protestant raised in the Pietist tradition, had an understanding of morality that was mystical and religious in nature. But he did not provide Kissinger with fulfilling answers. "The transcendental experience of the moral law," wrote Kissinger, "leaves the question of purposes in history undecided."

Kissinger then painted a stark description of historic determinism: "Life is suffering, birth involves death. Transitoriness is the fate of existence." How can it be overcome? Only through the personal awareness and "inward conviction" that we each have of our own freedom, Kissinger concluded. After noting that "the generation of Buchenwald and the Siberian labor camps cannot talk with the same optimism as its fathers," Kissinger proclaimed his new historical creed: "The experience of freedom allows us to rise above the suffering of the past and the frustrations of history."

Although Kissinger ended up liking Kant, it is not clear that Kant would have liked Kissinger. Kissinger never embraced the European-style liberalism, republicanism, and idealism that is associated with Kant, who in "Perpetual Peace" called for a League of Republics that would cooperate based on international law. Instead, Kissinger was more attracted to European conservatism, with its emphasis on national interests and balances of power. "Youthful fascination with Kant's political writings could have moved Kissinger toward a Wilsonian view of America's interests and mission," noted Peter Dickson in a study of Kissinger's philosophy of history. "Instead, the émigré turned to Metternich and Bismarck—the prime practitioners of power politics."[17]

Among the graduate students who haunted the halls of the Government Department, the length and pretense of Kissinger's thesis made him an object of both awe and derision. Friedrich passed the word that he read only 150 pages and refused to go further, and his tale quickly spread. But it was probably not true. Kissinger was awarded a summa cum laude, both on his thesis and on his grades, an honor earned by about 1 percent of his class.

ANNELIESE FLEISCHER KISSINGER

While Kissinger was in the army, his girlfriend Ann Fleischer had been sputtering academically at Hunter College in New York, tending to her ailing father, and slipping away from the rigidity of her upbringing. Feeling restless when Kissinger decided to delay his return to the U.S., she fled the confines of Washington Heights to spend a year in Colorado Springs, where she worked at a hotel, audited some courses, and enjoyed the skiing. But by the time Kissinger returned and enrolled at Harvard, she had moved back to her family home and gone to work as a bookkeeper in Manhattan.

During Kissinger's second year, they decided to get married. He had pretty much abandoned the practice of Judaism, and she was becoming involved in the Ethical Culture Society, a nondenominational movement that attracted many lapsed Jews. Nevertheless, to please Kissinger's parents, they got married in an Orthodox Jewish service on February 6, 1949. Henry was twenty-five, Ann twenty-three.

The ceremony was held in the Kissinger apartment in Washington Heights, partly because Ann's home was not kosher, partly because of her father's illness. Afterward the group went to a dinner at a neighborhood restaurant. There were only twelve guests, all family members. No friends—from Fürth or the neighborhood or Harvard —were invited. Rabbi Leo Breslauer, who had bar mitzvahed Henry at the ultra-Orthodox synagogue in Fürth, insisted that Ann take the ritual prenuptial bath, or mikvah, much to the couple's private annoyance.[18]

The couple moved to a small apartment in Arlington Heights, and Kissinger bought a secondhand 1947 Dodge to commute to campus. "Ann helped him focus on academics," said Henry's brother, Walter. "He had difficulty adapting to the frivolity of college life. Both of us had a hell of a time adjusting to living in a dorm with a bunch of kids just out of prep school. Marrying Ann allowed him to be serious."[19]

Money was tight. For his second year, Kissinger's tuition increased from $400 to $525. Fortunately, he was awarded $600 in scholarship aid for living and tuition, plus he landed work as a teaching assistant to Professor Elliott. Ann worked as a bookkeeper at a suburban furniture store and did other chores to help put her husband through college (among them, typing the 383-page thesis from his longhand scrawl).

In early 1950, Kissinger prepared a financial proposal for his third year at Harvard to justify his request for aid.[20] It included:

RESOURCES		EXPENSES	
Wife's savings	$700	Tuition	$600
Wife's earnings	$1100	Medical fee	$30
Govt. benefits	$1340	Books, fees	$100
		Room	$750
TOTAL:	$3140	Board	$780
		Clothing	$150
		Auto expense	$250
		Insurance	$100
		Recreation	$120
		Miscellany	$170
		TOTAL:	$3040 *

Kissinger considered applying for a fellowship to study in Europe after graduation, but his ponderous personality, married status, and Jewish-refugee background did not help his case. His adviser wrote on his senior-year transcript, "Re Knox fellowship: able, but not quite the obvious personal qualities for Knox. Also is married. Told him he could apply & be considered, but not much chance." Kissinger also discussed applying for a Fulbright or a Rotary fellowship. But in the end, he decided to stay at Harvard and applied to become a doctoral candidate in the Government Department.

"My constant endeavor has been to keep my field of study as broad as possible on the assumption that political life does not consti-tute an end in itself but is merely one manifestation of a general cultural pattern," he wrote in the essay accompanying his application. He explained that he wished to study the relationship between culture and politics during a historic period. He concluded with a prescient statement about his future plans: "I hope upon receiving my graduate degree to become affiliated with a university in a teaching or research capacity, though I have not excluded the possibility of entering gov-ernment service."[21]

THE INTERNATIONAL SEMINAR

Professor Elliott was more of a personal patron than an intellectual mentor to Kissinger. He knew that his tutee was already

* The total is actually $3050. Kissinger added incorrectly.

surpassing him as a thinker, and to his credit, the flamboyant Southern professor was about the only one of Kissinger's Harvard colleagues to display no jealousy about such matters. Instead, he set out to help his fledgling graduate student where he needed it—finding work, making some money, and establishing a social and political base in an academic community that was not enthusiastically embracing him. As the director of the university's summer school, Elliott in 1951 helped Kissinger hatch a project that would be his bailiwick for the next seventeen years: the Harvard International Seminar.

The program invited promising young leaders from around the world to spend the summer at Harvard. Most were not academics but practitioners—young men and women in elective office, civil service jobs, or journalism. Kissinger personally chose the participants and usually sprinkled in a poet or writer. It was a fine notion: the generation of Europeans who had come of age since the late 1930s had not enjoyed the chance to explore the world the way other generations had. As America assumed leadership of the Western alliance, young leaders from abroad were hungering for the opportunity to visit for the summer.[22]

As he built up his new program, Kissinger solicited ideas from various powerful people at Harvard, thus assuring their support. At twenty-eight, he was developing a power base within the academic bureaucracy. There was even patronage to dispense: since the seminar was well funded, it could offer a fat fee to the professors Kissinger invited to lecture.

Kissinger was not shy about calling famous professors, both at Harvard and around the country, pouring on doses of flattery, and asking if they would be kind enough to lecture his students. Those who spoke at Kissinger's behest ranged from Eleanor Roosevelt to the Southern poet John Crowe Ransom, from sociologist David Riesman to the labor leader Walter Reuther.

Money came from the university, the Ford Foundation, the Rockefeller Foundation, and elsewhere. Kissinger spent much of his time hustling funds. Beginning in 1953, a group named Friends of the Middle East began giving grants that eventually totaled just under $250,000. Later it was revealed that the group was a CIA front. Kissinger was panicky at first, fearing that this might ruin his reputation. He stormed into his office the day the story broke and flew into a rage. But the controversy soon blew over.

One morning in July 1953, a batch of similar envelopes arrived in the mail addressed to the forty foreign participants. Curious, Kissinger opened one. It contained flyers filled with ban-the-bomb propaganda and criticism of American military policy. He called the FBI field office in Boston, and an agent was dispatched to take the information and file a confidential report. Nothing came of the incident, but the final part of the agent's report was interesting: "KISSINGER identified himself as an individual who is strongly sympathetic to the FBI. . . . Steps will be taken . . . to make KISSINGER a Confidential Source of this Division." Though he never did any specific work for the FBI, he did become a contact at Harvard occasionally consulted by the local FBI office.[23]

At the core of the International Seminar program were classes in politics and the humanities. But part of the experience was social. Kissinger arranged outings to baseball games, factories, the beach, Marx Brothers and Charlie Chaplin movies, and other cultural events.

Kissinger, who was just honing his sense of humor, gave an amusing talk at the beginning of each summer as the group prepared for its first cocktail party. "One of our American customs is the cocktail party," a participant of the mid-1950s recalled Kissinger lecturing in a droll deadpan. "Now you must understand the custom and not be offended. If you talk to Americans more than ten minutes at a cocktail party, they will get a glassy, hysterical expression and start to look just past your left ear. They may turn away in the middle of a sentence. That is because they feel compelled to make sure that they impress themselves on everyone in the room, and you are holding them up."

Kissinger hosted some of the cocktail parties himself, including a big one that he and Ann threw at the end of each summer. In addition, he gave informal dinners twice a week for seminar students—far more socializing than he did during the academic year. "We combine small groups from the seminar with American guests," Ann Kissinger once said of the dinners, adding that she usually cooked chicken but always kept "an extra supply of eggs on hand in cases the guests are not permitted by their religion to eat meat."

Kissinger's pleasure in dealing with his foreign stars was genuine; he found them interesting, pleasant, and unthreatening. But the program also provided him with a network of contacts around the world. "Henry collected a repertoire of people," said Professor Thomas Schelling. "I don't think it was altruism. He had an instinct for inviting someone who could turn out to be his host later."

Of the six hundred foreign students who participated before the program came to an end in 1969, many went on to become important to Kissinger in power. Among them: Yasuhiro Nakasone of Japan in 1953, Valery Giscard d'Estaing of France in 1954, Yigal Allon of Israel in 1957, Bulent Ecevit of Turkey in 1958, Leo Tindemans of Belgium in 1962, and Mahathir Bin Mohammad of Malaysia in 1968. Others became foreign ministers, newspaper editors, and bank presidents.

Even in the 1990s, Kissinger was still calling on some of them in his work as a private consultant.[24]

CONFLUENCE

Though still a graduate student just starting his dissertation, Kissinger was building quite a reputation among foreign statesmen and journalists because of his duties as director of the International Seminar. While his fellow graduate students gossiped about academic politics and plotted the right moves within their departments, Kissinger was disdainful of such intramural intrigue. Of academia, he was fond of saying: "The disputes are so bitter because the stakes are so small."

Kissinger's sights were set higher. Instead of winning renown as an academic, he sought to make his name among players and policymakers on the world stage. The International Seminar was an ideal vehicle because it helped him build a network of influential contacts. In 1952, the year after the summer program began, Kissinger created another vehicle that helped transform him into an ascending star in the galaxy of international affairs: a gray, sober-looking journal called *Confluence*.

A quarterly magazine filled with foreign affairs disquisitions, *Confluence* had few subscribers, no advertising base, and lasted only six years. But during that time it featured a dazzling array of famous contributors whom Kissinger, as editor, was able to court. Like the International Seminar, *Confluence* became a personal power base that gave him the chance to deal with influential statesmen, professors, and journalists.

"I dreamed it up," Kissinger later said of *Confluence*. "I got a book listing the addresses of foundations and began to write them seeking money." Most of the funds—$26,000—came from the Rockefeller Foundation, a relationship he forged by sending a fulsome letter about the importance of the project. That allowed him to print five thousand or so copies of each issue and send them free to anyone he wanted to impress. Although he paid only $100 per article, he discovered that prominent people were flattered to be asked to write for a Harvard-based academic journal, even one that largely went unread.[25]

The journal provides little insight into Kissinger's thinking. In an editor's note in the second issue, he declared that there would be no editorial comments. "This is not to say we are without opinions, that we are 'neutralists' in the present crisis," he wrote, displaying apparent pleasure at lashing out against neutralism with a royal "we." But his own voice was absent; he never contributed a piece or wrote any comments.

The contributors he enlisted formed an impressive convocation, though one without a discernible philosophic connection. Among them: McGeorge Bundy, Reinhold Niebuhr, John Crowe Ransom, Raymond Aron (three times), Walt Rostow, John Kenneth Galbraith, Oscar Handlin, Hannah Arendt, Enoch Powell, Arthur Schlesinger, Jr., I. A. Richards, Sidney Hook, Russell Kirk, Seymour Martin Lipset, Czeslaw Milosz, Hans Morgenthau, Paul Nitze, and Denis Healey. Kissinger dealt with each personally. "When I met some of the contributors," he later noted with pride, "they were stunned to see how young I was."

One of the few articles Kissinger rejected was from William F. Buckley, Jr., who had been invited to contribute a piece about Joseph McCarthy's communist-hunting tactics and had produced a ringing defense of the senator. Kissinger admitted that it was out of "cowardice" that he spiked Buckley's piece. "He was surely offensive to my colleagues, but that was no reason not to publish him." To make up for it, Kissinger began to invite Buckley each year to his International Seminar, and eventually they became friends.[26]

Though the product was generally quite impressive, the publication of *Confluence* had an odd aspect to it, since it was more a method of mutual self-aggrandizement by Kissinger and his contributors than a true addition to the literature of foreign affairs. It was weighty, it seemed distinguished, but it had few subscribers other than those on Kissinger's list who got it free.

"I always suspected it was a fake," said Professor Schelling. "Kissinger used to keep piles of issues stashed away in his closet because he didn't even have a distribution system. He used it, like he used the summer seminars, to make contacts, to gather articles from people he wanted to meet. It was primarily an enterprise designed to make Henry known to great people around the world."[27]

Professor Stephen Graubard, a friend of Kissinger's who became assistant editor of the magazine, disagrees. "It had a distribution system and real, although modest, sales," he said. In addition, the articles tended to be serious, worthy, even interesting. But Graubard concurs that *Confluence* was used by Kissinger to build a network of influential acquaintances. "Both the journal and the International Seminar gave him an entrée for getting to know important people," Graubard said. "These were people he would not have met had he been just an ordinary graduate student."[28]

The fine art of cultivating influential people, so vividly on display at *Confluence* and the International Seminar, would remain a Kissinger specialty. At the core of his personality was an eagerness to impress prominent people that was matched only by his ability to do so. It was not merely crass power-climbing: partly he sought out important people because he was interested in exploring their thoughts. "I guess they found me interesting and appreciated my intelligence," he said. "I had nothing else to offer—not money or status. So my ability to befriend must have been a reflection on my intellect."

But there was more to it than that. Kissinger (like many people) was incorrigibly attracted to powerful, charismatic, and wealthy people. There was a streak of the courtier in him. Among his colleagues at Harvard, who were busier trying to impress their academic superiors, Kissinger's worldly ambitions prompted a mix of ridicule and jealousy; but his success in nurturing a name for himself in the outside world made him less vulnerable to the ivy-cloaked daggers of academe.

CASTLEREAGH AND METTERNICH

Among the graduate students in Harvard's Government Department, one tenet was widely accepted: the atomic bomb had fundamentally changed the nature of international relations. Consequently, most doctoral candidates were working on dissertations that involved the postwar period. "As children of the atomic era we felt that it was only natural that we should immerse ourselves in these new challenges," noted John Stoessinger, a graduate student in the early 1950s. But there was, he recalled, "one anomaly in our midst."

Henry Kissinger was known to the other graduate students for his mammoth undergraduate thesis, for his summa, and for burrowing in the stacks of Widener Library rather than fraternizing. One day he joined a lunch table with Stoessinger and some other colleagues. Soon he was discoursing on his dissertation topic: how two nineteenth-century statesmen—Austria's Prince Klemens von Metternich and Britain's Viscount Castlereagh—had created a peaceful European balance after the defeat of Napoleon.

Someone at the table asked, hadn't he heard of the atom bomb? Another made the suggestion, intended to be snide, that perhaps he should transfer to the History Department. Kissinger rebutted coldly. Hiroshima had not created a new world; it merely showed that man had yet to learn history's lessons about shaping a stable balance of power. So it made sense to explore the Congress of Vienna, one of the few successful peace conferences of the modern era. "It seemed almost as if he were carrying on a dialogue with himself, rather than with his interlocutors," Stoessinger said. "There was something austere and remote about him. And one also sensed a fierce ambition."[29]

Kissinger's doctoral dissertation—"A World Restored: Metternich, Castlereagh and the Problems of Peace 1812–22"—was odd not only because it seemed outdated. Among most scholars at the time, Prince Metternich was dismissed as a reactionary blinded by his desire to impose a conservative order on Europe, and Viscount Castlereagh was thought of as a diplomat who could not even secure his power at home.

But the thesis that Kissinger produced was actually quite relevant to the atomic age. He had become concerned about the challenge of Soviet communism, so he explored the threats posed during the early nineteenth century by a "revolutionary" power, France, that defied the legitimate international system. The parallels between Napoleon's France and Stalin's Russia were unstated, but clear. Likewise, there were unstated parallels between Britain of 1815—an "island power" in Kissinger's parlance—and the United States of 1950.

Kissinger showed how conservative statesmen, who sought to preserve world order, learned to deal with a revolutionary nation through artfully tending to balances of power. In doing so, he laid the foundation for his philosophy of realpolitik and the conservative outlook that endured throughout his career.[30]

Kissinger's conservative realpolitik, as reflected in his dissertation, was based on the principle, taught by realists from Karl von Clausewitz to Hans Morgenthau, that diplomacy cannot be divorced from the realities of force and power. But diplomacy should be divorced, Kissinger argued, from a moralistic and meddlesome concern with the internal policies of other nations. Stability is the prime goal of diplomacy. It is served when nations accept the legitimacy of the existing world order and when they act based on their national interests; it is threatened when nations embark on ideological or moral crusades. "His was a quest for a realpolitik devoid of moral homilies," said his Harvard colleague Stanley Hoffmann.[31]

On the first page of his thesis, Kissinger set up a basic premise that was to define his realpolitik outlook throughout his career. "Whenever peace—conceived as the avoidance of war—has been the primary objective of a power or a group of powers, the international system has been at the mercy of the most ruthless member of the international community," he wrote. A more proper goal, he argued, was for "stability based on an equilibrium of forces."

It is the mark of a true European-style conservative that he seeks stability even when it protects a system that is oppressive. Kissinger fell into that category. One day, Stoessinger asked him how would he choose between a legitimate state that pursued unjust ends and a revolutionary one that had justice on its side? Kissinger replied with a paraphrased quotation from Goethe: "If I had to choose between justice and disorder, on the one hand, and injustice and order, on the other, I would always choose the latter."[32]

A "revolutionary" situation occurs when a leader such as Napoleon does not accept the legitimacy of the international order, Kissinger wrote. In such cases, he argued, negotiations are futile.[33]

Because of the problems inherent in negotiating with a "revolutionary" power, Kissinger felt that summit meetings with the Soviet Union served only to raise false hopes. In his first piece in the popular press, "The Limitations of Diplomacy" in *The New Republic* in 1955, he argued that the only valid reason to hold summits with the communists was to assuage allies and score points with neutral nations. Later, he would come to the view that the Soviets (and the Chinese) could be coaxed away from their "revolutionary" status by gaining a stake in the legitimacy of the international system.[34]

Kissinger's views on the futility of negotiating with revolutionary powers would also have relevance during the Vietnam War. The North Vietnamese and Viet Cong were revolutionary, and they had no desire for any compromise with the U.S. Yet Kissinger dismissed their revolutionary rhetoric and sought a diplomatic bargain—thus falling into the same trap he warned against in his doctoral dissertation. Later, he would concede that it was a mistake not to recognize the true nature of the North Vietnamese.[35]

Kissinger's dissertation was interesting not for its research content (it contained a surprising dearth of primary research for a doctoral paper, even one in the field of government), but for the insights it provided into who Kissinger was and what he believed. His descriptions of Metternich bore an uncanny resemblance to Kissinger's own self-perceptions, or to his critics' perceptions of him:

> Napoleon said of him that he confused policy with intrigue.
>
> He was a Rococo figure, complex, finely carved, all surface, like an intricately cut prism. His face was delicate but without depth, his conversation brilliant but without ultimate seriousness.
>
> Methods of almost nonchalant manipulation he had learned in his youth.

With his undeniable charm and grace, subtly and aloofly conducting his diplomacy with the circuitousness which is a symbol of certainty. . .

He excelled at manipulation, not construction. Trained in the school of eighteenth-century cabinet diplomacy, he preferred the subtle maneuver to the frontal attack, while his rationalism frequently made him mistake a well-phrased manifesto for an accomplished action.

[He was] devious, because the very certainty of his convictions made him extremely flexible in his choice of means.[36]

"Metternich is not my hero!" Kissinger would later insist. Nor was he Kissinger's historical doppelgänger. But for better or worse, each of these descriptions of Metternich could be used to describe some action or another in Kissinger's later career. Kissinger's lapidary precision at character description makes it clear that he understands Metternich's flaws. Nonetheless, the dissertation is, at its core, a tribute to Metternich's mastery of complex diplomacy and his ability to play a game of sophisticated linkage among different negotiations.

Kissinger planned for his analysis of Castlereagh and Metternich to be the prelude for his true topic: Prince Otto von Bismarck, who united Germany and became its first chancellor. His dissertation was supposed to conclude with a section on Bismarck. By January of 1954, however, his thesis was long enough and late enough that he reconsidered the Bismarck section. "The part on Metternich is completed," he wrote to his father. "I shall continue to work on Bismarck, but I doubt that I shall finish it before April. The part on Metternich will be sufficient for a degree, however."[37]

It was. Kissinger's thesis was well received, he earned his Ph.D. in May, and three years later Houghton Mifflin published *A World Restored.* He saved his assessment of Bismarck for later.

THE LIFE AND RIVALRIES OF
A GRADUATE STUDENT

John Conway's suite in Eliot House was the hangout for many of the Government Department's graduate students in the early 1950s. There Kissinger found the comfortable mix of intellectual bull sessions and social camaraderie that makes university life seductive. The gatherings were ostensibly regular meetings of the graduate students who helped teach Social Sciences 2, a course on "Western

Thought and Institutions" given by Sam Beer, one of the most beloved professors ever to walk Harvard Yard. The sessions in Conway's room tended to range over a wide variety of topics, depending on who had dropped by and what issues happened to be hot.

Courses at Harvard typically consisted of three large lectures a week accompanied by smaller group discussions, known as sections, run by graduate students. Conway was the head section man for Social Sciences 2. A gregarious graduate student who had lost an arm during the war, he was a natural catalyst for informal discussions. Kissinger, by virtue of his summa, easily landed a job as one of Beer's section men and joined the club of fellow doctoral candidates who hung around Conway's room.

Adam Ulam, a junior faculty member who taught a course with Professor Elliott on the British Commonwealth, was sometimes there, as was Klaus Epstein, a graduate student who became a close friend of Kissinger's. Occasionally they would be joined by McGeorge Bundy, the young superstar at Harvard who had been given tenure as a professor without ever getting a doctorate.*

Beer was an affable fellow who liked to talk and liked to listen— and had the rare attribute of being good at both. He possessed an agile mind, a wide array of interests, and a lusty commitment to the liberal wing of the Democratic Party. In Conway's room he would join the discussions more as a participant than as a professor. "It was a great interdisciplinary study group," Beer recalled. "Kissinger was a valuable part because he had an intuitive grasp of the importance of ideas in history."

A reverence for the role of ideas in world affairs was much in vogue at Harvard then. Beer's approach to Western thought was an effort to counter Marxist interpretations; he stressed the role of religion, probing such events as the Puritan revolution and Becket's martyrdom. "Kissinger never talked about his own religion," said Beer, "but he was eager to discuss the formative influence religion had in history."

Beer attributed Kissinger's outlook to his background. "German refugees had firsthand experience of the effect that ideas can have on the world, of the notion that 'isms' can have real consequences. They also understand what can make a big country like Germany go crazy."

---

* Ulam became a professor and an occasional academic antagonist of Kissinger's at Harvard. Epstein died young. Bundy was made dean of the faculty at the tender age of thirty-four and was considered a possible successor to James Conant as president. When he was passed over, classics professor John Finley commented, "Sic transit gloria Bundy," and he instead went on to become President Kennedy's national security adviser.

Kissinger's conservatism fascinated Beer. Conservatism barely existed as an intellectual movement in America at the time; even the word was new. Kissinger used it to refer to the European thinkers of the nineteenth century who opposed revolutionary upheavals.

One favorite topic for Kissinger and Conway was whether this European conservatism bore much relation to American conservatism —indeed, whether America in fact had any real conservative tradition at all. "It was something we talked about a lot, both in my rooms or when I'd go to his place in Newton for dinner," Conway said. "Ann would sit there and not say anything; she was a bit timid. We would discuss it for hours."

The last topic covered in Social Sciences 2 was the rise of the Nazis in Germany. Kissinger was, on most topics, quite emotional about his ideas. But when it came to the Nazis, he was cold and analytic, not letting his sentiments show. During the discussions in Conway's room to prepare for teaching the Nazi era, Kissinger argued that the Treaty of Versailles, ending World War I, was to blame. The participants at that peace conference did not understand the importance of symbols to a culture, he said. They rid Germany of its princes and grand dukes and other national symbols, leaving an emotional vacuum. The Germans were a proud and gifted people, but their spirit was as turbulent as Wagner's music. Kissinger never spoke a word about his own firsthand knowledge of the Nazi mind-set.

Even as Kissinger was establishing his reputation for brilliance, he was also becoming the butt of the mild ridicule tinged with jealousy that would dog him throughout his career. His tendency to play up to powerful people prompted fellow students to take his middle initial, A, and behind his back call him Henry Ass-Kissinger, recalled Herbert Spiro, later a foreign service officer. "One heard an enormous amount about him, what an extraordinarily arrogant and vain bastard he was," said Professor Stanley Hoffmann.

Part of it was due to Kissinger's ponderous way of comporting himself. He came across as a man who had never had a childhood, which was in a way true. Until the 1960s, when he adopted a self-deprecating and wry sense of humor, Kissinger was generally quite solemn. "I never remember him laughing or making other people laugh, at least intentionally," said Conway. "People reacted badly to him because he seemed so pompous."

In the billiard room of Lowell House, Kissinger's picture was on display. Unbeknownst to him, junior faculty members such as Adam Ulam had posted his photograph with a bull's-eye target drawn over it. "Adam and the others would joke about Kissinger a lot," recalled Professor Beer. "I think some of the people even used it for darts."

Ulam, a specialist in Russian history, learned to like Kissinger, eventually. But early on, he recalled, Kissinger's arrogance was hard to bear. "He had a manner of carrying himself as if he were a senior faculty member," Ulam recalls. "He would make appointments with you, very precise as if his schedule was extremely tight, instead of just dropping around, even when he was just a teaching fellow." Kissinger had developed the habit of being fifteen minutes late, which he would be throughout his life, and carrying himself as a man always pressed for time.[38]

But the hostility toward him was tempered by admiration. Just as Ulam came to respect Kissinger's mind, so too did Hoffmann develop a complex mixture of attitudes. "I made the mistake of reading Kissinger and liked enormously what I read," Hoffmann recalled. "I liked his ideas and the way he wrote, a combination of epigrams and sweeping statements. He had an unfailing grasp of the essentials when he analyzed things." As Conway put it: "He was, in fact, almost as brilliant as he thought he was, so that made up for it."

Among the most intense rivalries in the Harvard Government Department was that between Kissinger and Zbigniew Brzezinski, who ended up not getting tenure at Harvard. Brzezinski recalls that Kissinger felt competitive toward him, but Kissinger claims that it was the other way around. Both were probably right.

One day in the mid-1950s, Hoffmann and Brzezinski were sitting in Carl Friedrich's reception area, waiting to see the professor. Kissinger breezed through and right into Friedrich's office, pausing to turn to Brzezinski and needle him. Brzezinski, who later became President Carter's national security adviser, claimed the rivalry was exaggerated by those looking at it in retrospect. "Henry didn't really make all that much impression on me," he said.[39]

Soon after he became a graduate student, Kissinger began finding projects that would take him overseas. In 1951, the Operations Research Office of the Army sent him to Korea to study the impact of the U.S. military on civilian life there. His feel for foreign affairs was not yet finely honed: he got letters of introduction from some Japanese friends, a gesture not likely to please the Koreans. "I did it in the absurd belief that it would make sense to be introduced by fellow Asians," Kissinger recalled. "It was very silly. Syngman Rhee almost threw me out of the country."

The following summer he went to Germany. "Whatever you may think of Germany, their recovery has been fantastic," he wrote to his parents. "The Bavarians drink as in the days of old, while the Hessians are as disgusting as ever." In his capacity as director of the Harvard International Seminar, the second-year graduate student met with leading German industrialists in Düsseldorf and was feted at a dinner in his honor—held in the dining room of the Krupp munitions plant. "Who would have thought?" he joked to his parents.[40]

When he finished his dissertation, Kissinger, who had a high opinion of his value to Harvard, hoped to be selected to the Society of Fellows, a group of pampered and exalted scholars that had included such notables as Arthur Schlesinger, Jr., and McGeorge Bundy. When that did not materialize, he let it be known that he wanted to be put on a fast track to tenure; instead of waiting the usual seven or eight years, he told Bundy, who was then dean of the faculty, he felt entitled to skip a step or two. It was a cheeky request, and Bundy rebuffed it with a gentle but slightly condescending smile. So Kissinger became an "instructor," a nebulous, open-ended appointment that left the timing of tenure in abeyance, and began casting around for other opportunities.

FIVE

NEW YORK

In the Service of
the Establishment, 1954–1957

> *Foreign policy cannot be conducted without an awareness of power relationships.*—KISSINGER, NUCLEAR WEAPONS AND FOREIGN POLICY, *1957*

THE COUNCIL ON FOREIGN RELATIONS

As Kissinger was crossing Harvard Yard one day, he ran into Arthur Schlesinger, Jr., who asked him to look at a paper he had just written on nuclear weapons. In it, Schlesinger attacked the doctrine of "massive retaliation," the official U.S. strategy of threatening a no-holds-barred nuclear response to any Soviet attack, conventional or nuclear. Kissinger's comments, written over the weekend, impressed the history professor so much that he sent them on to *Foreign Affairs,* the prestigious quarterly of the Council on Foreign Relations in New York. As a result, Kissinger's first major article on national security policy was published in the April 1955 issue.[1]

In it, Kissinger argued that Eisenhower's doctrine of massive retaliation was dangerously outdated now that the Soviets had built their own bomb. The American threat to unleash an all-out war was no longer credible enough to deter the Soviets from expanding into the peripheral or "gray areas" of the world. "As Soviet nuclear strength increases, the number of areas that will seem worth the destruction of

New York, Detroit, or Chicago will steadily diminish," Kissinger wrote. "An all-or-nothing military policy therefore makes for a paralysis of diplomacy." Kissinger argued for an alternative to massive retaliation: the capacity to fight localized "little wars."[2]

The *Foreign Affairs* piece had two notable consequences. It laid the groundwork for Kissinger's theory that the U.S. should be prepared to fight "limited nuclear wars"—a doctrine that became the intellectual precursor to the Kennedy administration's "flexible response" strategy and NATO's decisions to deploy intermediate-range nuclear weapons in Europe. In addition, the article helped get Kissinger a job at the Council on Foreign Relations, a post that would catapult him from the obscurity of an untenured instructor to the celebrity of a best-selling nuclear strategist.

After sending Kissinger's article to *Foreign Affairs,* Schlesinger sent Kissinger in person. The editor, Hamilton Fish Armstrong, was looking for a deputy. Armstrong concluded that Kissinger's prose was not as lucid as his mind and did not offer him a job. But perhaps Kissinger would consider instead being the staff director of a new study group at the Council that was analyzing the impact of nuclear weapons on foreign policy? It would involve writing a book at the end.

Kissinger was eager. The study group offered a vehicle like the Harvard International Seminar writ large: he would be able to meet the best and tap the brightest of the New York foreign policy establishment, have at his beck the foremost experts in the emerging field of nuclear strategy, and then be paid to write a book about the subject. In applying for the job, Kissinger solicited and received hearty recommendations from (left to right) Schlesinger, Bundy, and Elliott.

In the meantime, he had offers from the University of Chicago (which he had tentatively accepted) and an even better one from the University of Pennsylvania. "An embarrassment of riches," he wrote to his mother in February 1955. "The U. of Pa. offers more money but little prestige. Harvard offers more prestige but little money. The Council on Foreign Relations offers me to write a book. *Foreign Affairs* offers me nothing."[3]

He decided to back out of his plan to go to Chicago, take a leave from Harvard, and accept the post at the Council. The rarefied world of academe was not as enticing as the power-charged precincts of Manhattan.

The realization that life as a professor would not sate his ambitions represented a major turning point in Kissinger's career. Once ensconced at the Council on Foreign Relations, he came to realize that Harvard, for all of its graces and pretentions, was a backwater from the true power centers of the world. His sojourn in Manhattan would reinforce his desire to make his name in the real world as well as give him the opportunity to do so. Unlike his father and grandfather, he would not spend his life as a teacher.

For a person with Kissinger's courtier instincts, being a retainer at the Council on Foreign Relations was akin to being an angler amid a spawning run. The organization was filled with powerful and successful leaders who were eager to adopt bright young men as part of their retinue.

Founded in 1921 by members of Manhattan's internationally minded business and legal elite, the Council is a private organization that serves as a discussion club for close to three thousand well-connected aficionados of foreign affairs. Beneath the chandeliers and stately portraits in its Park Avenue mansion, members attend lectures, dinners, and roundtable seminars featuring top officials and visiting world leaders.

The most exalted enterprises at the Council are the study groups, which consist of about a dozen distinguished members and wise men who meet regularly for a year or so to explore a particular subject in depth. Each has a study director, often a rising star in the academic world. The group that Kissinger was asked to direct had been formed in November 1954 to probe the topic of "nuclear weapons and foreign policy."

The group, which met about once a month from five P.M. until ten P.M., was chaired by Gordon Dean, former head of the Atomic Energy Commission. It included such foreign policy mandarins as Paul Nitze, a former director of policy planning at the State Department; Robert Bowie, the State Department's policy planning director, who would later become Kissinger's antagonist at Harvard; David Rockefeller, who was soon to become chairman of the Chase bank and of the Council; and Lieutenant General James Gavin, whose belief in the potential of nuclear technology to cure American military deficiencies proved infectious.

Nitze had been a harsh critic of the doctrine of massive retaliation ever since he heard John Foster Dulles enunciate it in a January 1954 dinner speech at the Council. At the first meeting of the new study group, months before Kissinger arrived on the scene, Nitze suggested that perhaps the U.S. needed to develop the capacity to fight in small, regional conflicts—known as limited wars—using small nuclear weapons. As Nitze explained at the first meeting, in addition to conventional wars and all-out nuclear wars, "there would seem to be another alternative, that of the use of tactical atomic devices in a limited war."[4]

This was the thesis of "limited nuclear wars" that Kissinger would later make famous.

Nitze expanded on the idea at a January 1955 meeting, making the same "credibility" argument that Kissinger would express in his *Foreign Affairs* article that April. As Moscow's nuclear capability increases, Nitze said, the American threat to use massive nuclear retaliation against Soviet aggression becomes less believable. A more realistic policy, Nitze went on, was a policy of "graduated deterrence."[5]

Before signing on as the director of the study group, Kissinger attended the February 1955 meeting as a guest. (The discussion that evening touched on the topic of whether it would make sense to use nuclear weapons in a land war in Indochina.) By April, Kissinger was taking charge, formulating a detailed list of questions he wanted the group to explore and making pronouncements on the debates under way.

At first Kissinger did not agree with Nitze's argument that nuclear weapons could be of use in a "limited" or regional war. It was, he said, "an assumption I do not particularly share." Nitze, fifty years old and with a decade of experience in government, insisted that it would be possible "to keep a limited nuclear war within bounds." Kissinger, who was thirty-one, retorted that "once a war becomes nuclear, it is much harder to set any effective limits."[6]

The Nitze-Kissinger dispute also had a personal component. The patrician and somewhat snobbish Nitze, whose prosperous grandfather had emigrated from Germany just after the American Civil War and whose wife's uncle had donated the Council's Park Avenue mansion, was a panjandrum of the foreign policy elite. He found the rough-edged Jewish refugee who had rather brusquely taken over the study group to be far too self-important for his liking. "Henry managed to convey that no one had thought intelligently about nuclear weapons and foreign policy until he came along to do it himself," Nitze later said.[7]

By the end of the summer, Kissinger had decided that the study group should not meet as a whole; instead, he divided it into subgroups that would, in effect, serve as panels of experts to advise him on specific questions. The final book, he made clear, would be his, not the study group's. For the only time in the Council's history, a study group was transformed (not without some grumbling by its members) from a deliberative body into a support staff designed to help the director write a book.

One of the most important things Kissinger learned from his study group members had nothing to do with nuclear weapons. These were all sophisticated men, polished by success in a way that Kissinger yearned to be. Some had been born rich and had nevertheless gone on to prove that they had talent; others were self-made. They were practiced in the arts of persuasion and discourse among people of power. Kissinger watched how they interacted. He learned what swayed them, what evidence and anecdotes and self-deprecating tales they used to make their points. He was not always deferential, but he flattered them with his attention to their ideas and honed his skills of courtship and cultivation.

Just as he had once offered powerful people a chance to write for *Confluence* or to address the Harvard International Seminar, now he invited them to address the Council study group. He produced a steady stream of letters to high government officials, praising them and seeking the chance to discuss their ideas about nuclear strategy.

Among his guests was his dean McGeorge Bundy, who came down in December to lead a discussion. There Bundy engaged in a fascinating colloquy with Kissinger and Nitze on NATO strategy. It was one of the first times that abstract theorizing about limited nuclear war was related to the defense doctrine that later became known as flexible response. When Nitze noted that the threat of massive nuclear retaliation might come to be viewed as "bluffing," Bundy replied: "Can we not develop a concept for the graduated application of power? It is essential that we find some flexible policy." As national security adviser six years later, Bundy would help institute this flexible-response strategy.

Kissinger, with some discomfort, had by then come around to Nitze's view that, for the foreseeable future, the U.S. would have to rely on nuclear weapons in fighting even a limited war. It would be "extremely dangerous," Kissinger argued, to become paralyzed by the belief that any use of nuclear weapons would automatically escalate to an all-out war. Like Nitze, he endorsed the concept of graduated deterrence, which meant being willing to fight limited wars with tactical nuclear weapons. "One of the crucial problems facing the U.S.," Kissinger told the study group in November, "was to develop a doctrine for the graduated employment of force."[8]

NUCLEAR WEAPONS AND FOREIGN POLICY

At the last study group session in early 1956, the members departed by wishing Kissinger good luck. His task was daunting: to take all the issues they discussed and turn them into a book. Holing up in his East Seventy-third Street Manhattan apartment, he spent the spring and summer trying to synthesize the rambling discussions. The task would take concentration, he rather brusquely told Ann. She was thus not to disturb him or talk to him unless necessary. Trying hard to remain unheard, she dutifully slid trays of snacks inside the door of his study as he wrote.[9]

With sentences that drift across ideas like a thick fog, Kissinger wrote a 450-page book, *Nuclear Weapons and Foreign Policy,* which argued the case for a doctrine of limited nuclear war. As in his doctoral dissertation, he began with the realist credo that the avoidance of war cannot be the primary objective of foreign policy because diplomacy is sterile unless accompanied by the threat of force. Eisenhower's declaration that "there is no alternative to peace" was dangerous, Kissinger wrote. "The enormity of modern weapons makes the thought of war repugnant, but the refusal to run any risks would amount to giving the Soviet rulers a blank check."[10]

The U.S. decision to limit its options either to a limited conventional war or to an all-out nuclear one, with nothing in between, "may lead to paralysis," Kissinger wrote, and "play into the hands of the Soviet strategy of ambiguity which seeks to upset the strategic balance by small degrees." The deterrent value of a doctrine of massive retaliation is undermined by a basic flaw: "The greater the horror of our destructive capabilities, the less certain has it become that they will be in fact used." In addition, American policy is founded on the mistaken assumption that a war is likely to begin with a surprise attack. "We have failed to see how vulnerable it has left us to the preferred form of Soviet aggression: internal subversion and limited war."

From these facts Kissinger concluded that the U.S. had to develop the capacity to use nuclear weapons when fighting limited wars.

The argument against such a strategy is that the taboo against using nuclear weapons serves as a clear firebreak to prevent a limited war from mushrooming out of control. There is a tacit understanding that if either side "goes nuclear" during a war, then mutual destruction will result. Blurring the lines between a conventional war and a nuclear one is dangerous: there would be no rules to prevent a rapid escalation.

Nevertheless, Kissinger concluded that "limited nuclear war represents our most effective strategy." By excluding the option to use nuclear weapons in a small or limited war, Kissinger argued, the U.S. would merely allow the Soviets the chance to determine when the first nuclear blow would be struck.

Within a few years, Kissinger would reconsider his embrace of a limited-nuclear-war doctrine—but mainly because of practical problems in figuring out how such a war could be contained, rather than because of strategic qualms. "I never met a military man who could describe how it would happen, how it would work," he recalled.

Kissinger's concepts were not original. Many were derived from the participants in the study group, notably Nitze and General Gavin. In addition, other members of the growing fraternity of defense intellectuals had been exploring the notion of limited war in the nuclear age, most notably Basil Liddell Hart and Bernard Brodie.

But Kissinger's book was the most forceful synthesis of ideas on the topic. It would also soon be the most famous. "Other people had made the same arguments," Brodie later said somewhat resentfully, "but his book hit the market at the right time."[11]

NUCLEAR CELEBRITY

Serious books by obscure professors on the nuances of defense policy rarely make the best-seller list. In a major surprise to his publishers and to himself, *Nuclear Weapons and Foreign Policy,* which came out in 1957, was on the list for fourteen weeks. Harper & Brothers printed seventy thousand hardcover copies, and Book-of-the-Month Club made it a selection. "I am sure that it is the most unread best-seller since Toynbee," Kissinger told one officer of the Council, displaying the self-deprecating humor he had begun to adopt as an antidote to the resentment his arrogance provoked.

In fact, judging from the impact it had and the storm it created, *Nuclear Weapons and Foreign Policy* was widely read. Richard Nixon was photographed carrying a copy, and he later wrote Kissinger a note discussing the thesis. Dulles, whose policies were being called into question, pronounced the critique valuable. Edward Teller, a father of the hydrogen bomb, lavished praise on Kissinger in the *New York Times Book Review,* declaring: "In a limited nuclear war, as in any limited war, it is possible to avoid the big-scale conflict if our aims remain moderate and our diplomacy skillful."[12]

Within weeks of its publication, Kissinger's book had stirred enough debate to become page-one news in the *New York Times.* "For the first time since President Eisenhower took office, officials at the highest Government levels are displaying interest in the theory of 'little' or 'limited' war," wrote Russell Baker, then a reporter in the paper's Washington bureau. "The lead in the debate has been taken not by anyone connected with the Government, but by a scholar of foreign affairs, Henry A. Kissinger, in his recently published book."

In a long paean, *Time* magazine wrote: "In the Pentagon, the State Department, the White House, top U.S. policymakers are earnestly debating a new book, a brilliant, independent analysis of the nation's postwar diplomatic and military struggle with Communism."[13]

One review, however, was decidedly uncharitable. Paul Nitze, writing in *The Reporter,* lambasted Kissinger for embarking on a flight of cosmic theory without understanding the military realities that underlay the argument. "There are several hundred passages in which either the facts or the logic seem doubtful, or at least unclear," Nitze wrote.

Some of Nitze's criticisms were oddly off base. He claimed that Kissinger advocated a doctrine that "would have called either for a preventive big war or a series of little offensive wars during the period of our atomic monopoly." That is a misreading of Kissinger's argument. Other points Nitze made were more technical, even pedantic. Kissinger miscalculated the blast effects of nuclear weapons, Nitze charged, by referring to the "cube root of their stepped-up explosive power," rather than the "square of the cube root," which Nitze points out is the correct ratio. Thus Kissinger mistakenly included in his proposed arsenal for a limited nuclear war certain weapons that were actually too destructive.

More significant, however, was Nitze's fundamental criticism that Kissinger had not been able to explain how a limited war, once under way, would stay limited. "If the limitations are really to stand up under the immense pressures of even a 'little' war," Nitze wrote, "it would seem something more is required than a Rube Goldberg chart of arbitrary limitations."

Throughout his life, Kissinger was wont to take his enemies seriously. In most cases, he would display an immigrantlike eagerness to curry favor with his critics, seek their approval, and try to turn them around. "There is in Kissinger," a friend once said, "a deeply consuming need to make everybody love him." This was the approach he took toward Max Ascoli, editor of *The Reporter;* Kissinger, who called to complain about the Nitze review, worked hard (and successfully) to become Ascoli's friend, and he was soon featured as a regular writer in the magazine.

With Nitze, Kissinger's relationship became more complex. He at first threatened to sue Nitze for libel, but then never did. When he ran into Nitze at a meeting of the Bilderberg Group near Rome a few months later, he sought to smooth the matter over. *The Reporter* had offered him the chance, Kissinger said, to write a rebuttal at any length he wanted. "I got to page 147 of that rebuttal," Nitze quotes Kissinger as conceding, "and decided that if the rebuttal took that many pages, there must be something wrong with my position." Nitze recalls that he resisted being seduced.

Kissinger's usual efforts to court and convert his critics had a flip side: he could nurture a simmering, sometimes paranoid, grudge. Such was the case with Nitze. For the next three decades their relationship would be chilly, and that would have important consequences. When Kissinger was in power, Nitze nominally worked under him as an arms control negotiator, but he soon quit and became critical of Kissinger's concessions. Later, when they took opposing sides in a dispute over the need to keep short-range missiles in West Germany, they engaged in a bitter televised debate on the "MacNeil/ Lehrer NewsHour," their animosity vividly on view.

Looking back on their dispute over limited nuclear wars, Kissinger said: "Nitze wanted to do some work on the topic and maybe write a book of his own. He thought I should help him. I didn't want to be a research assistant to Nitze. It got very personal. He should not have reviewed the book." [14]

NELSON ALDRICH ROCKEFELLER

At Camp Claiborne, it had been Fritz Kraemer. At Harvard, it was William Elliott. In 1955, Kissinger found a patron far more powerful and influential than either of them: Nelson Aldrich Rockefeller, the exuberant and driven son of Standard Oil scion John D. Rockefeller, Jr.

At the time, Rockefeller was an assistant to President Eisenhower for international affairs. Kissinger met him when Rockefeller assembled a group of academic experts at the Quantico Marine Base near Washington to discuss national security policy. "He entered the room slapping backs, calling each of us by the best approximation of our first name he could remember, at once outgoing and remote," Kissinger later recounted. The experts took turns giving Rockefeller political advice on how to accomplish certain foreign policy goals. Finally, the smile left Rockefeller's face. "What I want you to tell me," he said, "is not how to maneuver. I want you to tell me what's right." [15]

The Quantico meeting launched a lasting odd-couple relationship between Kissinger and Rockefeller. One of the admonitions favored by Rockefeller's mother was "Always associate with your superiors." Unlike Kissinger, Rockefeller was secure in his place in the world and thus comfortable with those who challenged him. Though driven by ambition and too often shielded by a politician's gregarious shell, he had been bred with a sense of the social obligations that come from being born to great privilege.

"He has a second-rate mind but a first-rate intuition about people," Kissinger once said of Rockefeller. "I have a first-rate mind but a third-rate intuition about people."

Kissinger was right on both counts. Rockefeller knew how to make people feel important, how to create an aura of fellowship, how to listen, and how to be frank and straightforward about his wishes in a way that put people at ease. Kissinger mastered none of these attributes, but respected them all.

The two men were fundamentally different in other ways. Rockefeller was an ebullient American optimist, Kissinger a brooding Middle European with a sense of the tragic. Rockefeller, with an affability that seemed to mask a lonely aloofness, was preternaturally energetic, impulsive, a man who worked a crowd like a candidate on a final swing even when he was in a room full of friends. Kissinger was intellectual, vulnerable, searching for approval and affection. Rockefeller could use his favorite phrase, "the brotherhood of man and the fatherhood of God," and actually mean it. For Kissinger, such pieties seemed meaningless. Yet he possessed in abundance, according to Rockefeller's speechwriter Joseph Persico, "the combination of brilliance and egotism that Nelson always found entrancing," and thus became his closest intellectual associate.[16]

The report from the Quantico meeting, which had been written mainly by Kissinger, contained a series of military proposals that would require, among other things, more spending. Eisenhower balked. Partly because of this, and partly because he wanted to lay the foundation for a run for governor, Rockefeller decided to resign and launch one of his typical high-minded enterprises: a Special Studies Project that would explore the "critical choices" facing the nation. With a quintessential Rockefeller grandness, a distinguished troupe of American chin-strokers was enlisted, among them: Chester Bowles, Arthur Burns, General Lucius Clay, John Cowles, John Gardner, Father Theodore Hesburgh, Henry Luce, Charles Percy, David Sarnoff, and Edward Teller.

In March 1956, with his Council book half-finished, Kissinger agreed to become director of the Rockefeller project, overseeing a staff of one hundred as well as various advisory panels. The first meeting was in Radio City Music Hall's dance practice studio, amid mirrors and stretching bars. Kissinger, who was still only thirty-two, began by making a presentation on conceptual thinking; it was important, he said, to see the grand sweep of an idea rather than bogging down in details.

Kissinger was something of a terror as director. He was constantly perceiving slights, such as when reports would come in addressed to one of his assistants rather than to him. "He suffered a great deal by taking things personally, simple things, like whether or not a car met him at the airport and whether it was a Cadillac or not," recalled Oscar Ruebhausen, long a close associate of the Rockefellers. "He would weep on one's shoulders at some slight . . . it was candor and Machiavellian scheming at the same time."[17]

Kissinger was notoriously short-tempered with subordinates. His impatience could be withering: he would throw around words like *idiots* and *morons,* and he had not yet perfected the trick of softening his tantrums with occasional grace notes of self-directed humor.

In addition to coordinating the whole enterprise—which resulted in a 468-page book—Kissinger personally wrote the report on the international security panel's deliberations. It proposed the development of tactical nuclear weapons and "a bomb shelter in every house" as preparation for a limited nuclear war. "The willingness to engage in nuclear war when necessary is part of the price of our freedom," Kissinger wrote.

Published as a separate paperback with an introduction by Henry Luce, Kissinger's international security report became known as "the answer to Sputnik." When Rockefeller went on the "Today" show to discuss it, Dave Garroway mentioned that those who wanted a copy should send in their names to NBC. "You'll have to give away a Ford V-8 with every copy," one NBC staffer commented snidely. Not so. Within two days, 250,000 requests had come in, and the offer had to be cut off.[18]

In a "Dear Henry" note, Rockefeller sent Kissinger back off to Harvard in the fall of 1957 with effusive praise for his contribution "to the future security of our country and the Free World." Attached, as a "token of my admiration," was a check for $500. "It's also to thank Ann for her unfailing support. Maybe while she is in New York, she could get something for the new house."

Until he joined Nixon's staff at the end of 1968, Kissinger remained a part-time consultant to Rockefeller. His compensation—which was paid by Rockefeller personally—was based on the amount of time he worked each year. In 1958, for example, he was paid a total of $3,000. By 1960, he was making $12,000 a year.* The most he made

---

* Kissinger's $12,000 payment in 1960 was equivalent to approximately $45,000 in 1990 dollars; likewise, adjusting for inflation, Kissinger's 1964 payment was worth about $66,000 in 1990 dollars.

was $18,000 in 1964 and $20,000 in 1968, both years in which Rocke-feller made a stab at running for President.

"It was not a significant sum," Kissinger later insisted. "It was calculated on the basis of the academic pay I had to forgo." Nor, however, was it an insignificant sum, especially when combined with the $50,000 Rockefeller would give him as a severance gift in 1969 when he left the payroll to enter government.[19]

SIX

HARVARD AGAIN

The Professor, 1957–1968

It was not that Bismarck lied—this is much too self-conscious an act—but that he was finely attuned to the subtlest currents of any environment and produced measures precisely adjusted to the need to prevail.—KISSINGER, "THE WHITE REVOLUTIONARY," 1968

THE CENTER FOR INTERNATIONAL AFFAIRS

April 25, 1957

Dear Bob:

I talked with Henry Kissinger earlier this week and suggested to him that he should get in touch with you. . . . I found him just a little uncertain as to whether he wanted to come back to a department which had not been unanimously friendly to him a year ago, but I tried to cheer him up on that point. It is clear that the Government Department as a whole is enthusiastic about his return (the vote was unanimous), and I hope that he will not be too much troubled by any past feelings. I have recently read his excellent leading article in *Foreign Affairs* for this year, and I am confident that he is the man we want. What I offered him was a three or four year appointment as Lecturer, with a starting salary of about $8,500.

Sincerely yours,
McGeorge Bundy

Bundy was then dean of Harvard's faculty. The Bob he was writing to was Robert Bowie, the chief policy planner in Dulles's State Department, who had been a professor at the Law School. He was planning to leave government to direct a new research institute at Harvard, to be known as the Center for International Affairs. Bundy wanted Kissinger to be the associate director, a prospect that aroused mixed emotions in the gentle and patrician law professor. But Bowie ended up offering Kissinger the job.[1]

Kissinger accepted it, along with a position as a "lecturer" at Harvard. That rank was somewhat ill-defined and did not carry tenure. But it was often used to circumvent the eight-year road of toiling as an assistant professor before being considered for promotion. Bundy himself had served as a lecturer in the Government Department for two years before being made a tenured professor, and Kissinger understood, correctly, that his own path would be similar.

With Bowie and Kissinger at the helm, the Center for International Affairs (at first called the CIA, and then, for understandable reasons, changed to the CFIA) was launched with high expectations that were never fully fulfilled. Though the Center attracted an impressive array of research associates, it never quite found a niche or made a name for itself. One reason was the deep, personal animosity that developed between Bowie and Kissinger.

Bowie had helped formulate Dulles's doctrine of "massive retaliation," which Kissinger had just become famous for attacking. He was also an advocate of what became known as the multilateral force (MLF), a proposal to create joint units made up of troops from different NATO allies that would be equipped with nuclear weapons. Kissinger trashed the idea with a vehemence that went beyond pure intellectual disagreement.

Indeed, the Kissinger-Bowie feud had little to do with intellectual disagreements. Instead, it was personal: they grew to dislike each other intensely. "There were periods when they were literally not speaking," said Professor Thomas Schelling. "They had neighboring offices with an anteroom containing their two secretaries. They would sometimes check with their secretaries before coming out to make sure the other was not there."

Kissinger seemed quite paranoid about the dispute. After attending a CFIA meeting to discuss who should get certain fellowships, he became agitated and pulled aside Morton Halperin, then an assistant professor. "Do you know what was happening in there?" Kissinger demanded. Halperin, who had been at the meeting with Kissinger, allowed that he assumed Bowie was offering suggestions for new fellows. No, Kissinger replied, Bowie was trying to embarrass him; the candidate that Bowie was pushing, Kissinger explained, had written a bad review of his nuclear weapons book. Halperin, who later served as a Kissinger aide in the White House and then became a critic, was unable to convince Kissinger otherwise. He thought it politic not to remark that eliminating every scholar who had criticized Kissinger's book would severely limit the pool of potential fellows.[2]

Bowie came to resent Kissinger's unhelpful attitude toward the CFIA. Harvard had freed both men from teaching duties during the academic year of 1957–58 so they could get the Center launched. Kissinger, however, spent most of his time in New York, working on his Rockefeller projects. Bowie grew irritated. Starting the Center was a lot of work, and he had hoped to have a partner, but Kissinger seemed to be exploiting his connection to the Center while engaging in self-promotion. Bowie also felt that Kissinger did not help raise money. In fact, he hurt. After Bowie approached the Carnegie Foundation, Kissinger succeeded in diverting some of the funds to a personal grant for himself, Bowie would later charge.

At one point, the CFIA decided to produce a book of essays on Germany and Western Europe. Since Kissinger was responsible for that region, he was supposed to edit it and write an introduction. The participants all wrote their chapters, but Kissinger never wrote his nor edited theirs. The Center finally had to pay people and send their pieces back. Kissinger later claimed that the papers were not good enough to publish.

Although Bowie cast himself as the aggrieved victim of Kissinger's behavior, colleagues who worked with both men found them equally turf-conscious and petty. The main difference was that Bowie lacked Kissinger's brilliance. Stanley Hoffmann and a couple of other professors once complained to Bowie that the CFIA was not paying enough attention to Europe. When Kissinger expressed sympathy for the complaints, Bowie became infuriated, calling him "untrustworthy." He would later claim that Kissinger tried to undercut him by proposing the formation of a separate European center. Hoffmann and Professor Laurence Wylie remember the tale differently. Bowie was very sensitive, they recalled, and became upset over a proposal to launch a European studies program. Only later did it become an autonomous center.

"I don't suppose either of us covered ourselves with glory," Kissinger said, looking back on his feud with Bowie. "I had problems with his belief that the CFIA was a military hierarchy, that I would be his assistant." Bundy agreed. "Kissinger could play junior to a Rocky or a Nixon," he later explained, "but he did not know how to play number two man to a colleague."[3]

In addition, with his work for Nelson Rockefeller, Kissinger found himself stretched too thin. In March 1958, he wrote to his mother apologizing for not visiting on her birthday. "I got into an insane rassle with the malicious maniac, Bowie, which took all my energies for a while," he explained. "Then the benevolent maniac, NAR, had to keep me occupied with his article which turned into more work than one of my own. . . . I spent three days in New York staying at Nelson's apartment. He and his wife were very sweet. But right now I wish he would just leave me alone for a while."[4]

THE TENURED PROFESSOR

Competition for that golden ring known as tenure—a permanent, lifetime professorship—has always been intense at Harvard, and no more so than in the Government Department during the late 1950s. Among those struggling for whatever chair might become available were Henry Kissinger, Zbigniew Brzezinski, Samuel Huntington, Stanley Hoffmann, and a brood of almost equal talents.

In this race, Kissinger was not handicapped by excess humility. He was on the road to fame and power, had returned to Harvard with the implied understanding that he would soon be tenured, and gave the sense that he felt Harvard would be lucky to have him as a permanent faculty member. Nevertheless, recalled Henry Rosovsky, "Henry did not have an easy time getting tenure."[5]

Kissinger's scholarly work, although fascinating, was considered to be derivative and not based on extensive primary research. For example, the basic material for his dissertation on Metternich and Castlereagh came from secondary sources in Widener Library rather than original documents buried in the archives of the British Museum. In addition, like his mentor Elliott, Kissinger was regarded as too entranced by Washington rather than the prospect of a cloistered life in academe. Finally, there was his personality: arrogant and abrasive even by Harvard standards.

The Government Department had twenty or so tenured chairs. When one fell vacant, a search committee would be appointed to canvass the world to see who could best fill it. Some preference was given to junior scholars at Harvard who were on the tenure track. The academic writings of the finalists would be copied and distributed to the department's professors. Over dinner in the library on the second floor of the Harvard faculty club, they would meet to debate the merits of each candidate.

"The Kissinger tenure battle was a wonderful fight," recalled Sam Beer, who was chairman of the department. "He called me up one day and said he was worried that we had become 'estranged.' He wanted to have lunch to 'clear it up.' I don't think he was trying to manipulate me, but I do think he had become concerned about his tenure prospects."

Adam Ulam, later a friend, admits to being a leader of the opposition to Kissinger. "I had my doubts about him. I was strongly opposed to giving people tenure for a quasi-political role. My idea was that people should be appointed on scholarly qualifications, not because they played a role in policy formulation." Ulam, like many others on the faculty, particularly objected to Kissinger's nuclear weapons book, calling it "not appropriate" as an academic credential. An intense yet unpretentious man, Ulam also rankled at Kissinger's "overbearing arrogance and heavy personality." Yet he eventually regretted opposing him. "In retrospect, I found him very scholarly. After he became a colleague and developed a sense of humor, I changed my mind about him."[6]

In the end, Kissinger won tenure in a roundabout way. Bundy, as dean of the faculty, had secured funding from the Ford Foundation for two new "half" chairs in the Government Department for professors who would spend half of their time on other duties. One of these was for a professor who would split his time between the CFIA and the Government Department; Bundy had tailored it for Kissinger. The other "half" chair was tailored for Stanley Hoffmann. Thus, thanks to Bundy's maneuverings, Kissinger and Hoffmann were both given tenure, and the rank of associate professor, in July 1959. Three years later, Kissinger was elevated to the rank of full professor.

Kissinger's main course was "Principles of International Relations," which usually drew more than two hundred undergraduates enticed by his newfound humor and charisma. He started with Napoleon, dwelled on Metternich and Bismarck, and concluded with an analysis of the current trends in arms control. The daunting sixteen-page reading list became a legend. His lectures blended brilliant analysis with rambling, name-dropping vignettes about the famous people he was getting to know. "Kissinger is quite a sight as he struts back and forth across the lecture platform alternately praising Metternich, castigating Kennedy, and tossing laurel wreaths to Kissinger for Kissinger's solutions to the evils that beset our mismanaged foreign policy," reported the 1963 edition of the *Confidential Guide,* a student publication that evaluated undergraduate courses.[7]

Each class began with a question period that often resembled a press conference on the events of the day. Arms control issues, summits, the U-2 incident, and the like would be tossed up to him by undergraduates eager to extract his ironic or sharp commentary. Though some found the performance pompous and a waste of time, most regarded it as an enlightening show.

One regular topic was the unilateral disarmament movement, which peaked at Harvard in the late 1950s. Kissinger, who was predictably opposed to it, enjoyed debating the topic and trying to win over his student adversaries. In doing so, he honed the mixture of charm, wit, and forensic skills later displayed in his dealings with the press as secretary of state.

Kissinger became a fellow of Quincy House, one of Harvard's residential halls. Once a week he would hold court at a lunch table in the dining room, often with a foreign guest or dignitary in tow. "Even when he was young, he was a commanding presence," recalled Professor David Riesman. "He would not spend his time chatting at the table. He presided. He and his guest would hold forth, then entertain discussion."[8]

In 1958, Kissinger won a minor power struggle to take over Harvard's Defense Studies Program, a graduate-level course and related independent-study projects that had some outside funding. As with the summer school's International Seminar, the Defense Studies Program became a way for Kissinger to invite a stream of potential patrons from Washington to be his guest lecturers. Almost every session of his defense policy class involved a talk by a famous visitor followed by polite questioning from Kissinger. He also had an eye for the not-yet famous: one of his early visiting lecturers was Michigan congressman Gerald Ford, then an obscure Republican on the Defense Appropriations Subcommittee, who enjoyed the experience so much that he came back a few years later.[9]

Kissinger used much the same method in a seminar on Western Europe that he helped to teach. Open to twenty or so graduate students, the seminar was also cotaught by two other giants of the Harvard faculty: Laurence Wylie and Stanley Hoffmann. From the Rockefeller Brothers Fund, Kissinger wheedled about $8,000 a year to pay for visiting speakers. "Kissinger created a network by inviting anyone in power or who soon might be in power in Europe," Wylie recalled. "There was always a feeling of jealousy that this Kissinger guy so young could have become so important in the world."

The jealousy did not go unnoticed by Kissinger, whose sensitivity to slights, both perceived and real, was hair-trigger set. In addition, he tended to be contemptuous of minds that he considered less brilliant than his own, a category that spared few. As a result, he swung from moods of arrogance to insecurity, sometimes displaying both at once.

With colleagues, Kissinger could be meanspirited. Leslie Gelb, who went on to a distinguished career in government and journalism, was an acolyte at Harvard. "He was my intellectual hero," Gelb recalled. As a doctoral student in the early 1960s, he did some research for a book that Kissinger was planning to write. When Gelb began work on his own proposal for a book, in which he planned to analyze different approaches to foreign policy, he discussed it with Kissinger, who was encouraging.

One day Gelb called with good news: Harper's had offered him a contract to publish the book. Kissinger seemed delighted and proud, Gelb recalled. A week later, however, Gelb got a copy of a letter that Kissinger had written to the editor in chief of Harper's, Cass Canfield. It accused Canfield of going to "one of my former assistants" to write the same book that he had once discussed with Harper's; he insisted that the publisher "correct" the situation.

When Gelb read the letter, he was so upset that he started shaking. Repeatedly he telephoned Kissinger, who refused to accept his calls. Finally he wrote Kissinger a note explaining that their two books were in no way competitive. "You encouraged me," Gelb reminded him. Kissinger wrote back saying, "I know you'll do the right thing."

Gelb, who was awed by Kissinger, decided to abandon his book; Kissinger, as it turned out, never got around to writing his. Although they later reestablished a rapport, Gelb would thenceforth consider Kissinger to be "the typical product of an authoritarian background— devious with his peers, domineering with his subordinates, obsequious to his superiors."[10]

Nevertheless, Kissinger was able to engender deep respect— sometimes grudging, but still sincere—among many who knew him. If he wanted to make a favorable impression on someone, he would exude charm and turn on his self-deprecating wit. While slathering on flattery, he would forge a conspiratorial bond based on privately shared put-downs about the minds and quirks of colleagues. But most importantly, as he discussed his ideas and argued his positions, Kissinger displayed the brilliance, creativity, and persuasiveness that was, after all, the coin of the realm in academe.

He also conveyed, in an oddly vulnerable way, a great need to be liked. He cared deeply about the intellectual respect of those he admired. Although he could be cruel and arrogant, he was solicitous toward people he considered worthy of friendship. In fact, the passion of his attempts to win over his intellectual adversaries indicated a genuine warmth as well as a gnawing insecurity.[11]

It was a mark of Kissinger's insecurity that he was more fascinated by his enemies than he was by his friends, at times becoming obsessed with them. When William Kaufmann, an arms control expert at the Rand Corporation, wrote a devastating review of *Nuclear Weapons and Foreign Policy,* Kissinger pleaded with Professor Tom Schelling to arrange a visit to Rand. "Henry was desperate to convert them," Schelling recalled.

At other times, he would become paranoid about his enemies. When he was part of an arms control group visiting Bonn a few years later, Kissinger felt that Schelling and the Rand people were snubbing him. "He wrote a bitter letter to me accusing me of joining with the Rand people and making fun of him behind his back," said Schelling. "It was a wild letter. I gave it back to him and told him to throw it away so he would not feel embarrassed about it later."[12]

Kissinger's ego, combined with the seriousness with which he took himself, enhanced his reputation for arrogance. He always seemed busy with something gravely important, impatient with such trivialities as making small talk in the halls or advising his students. Tutees would have to call weeks in advance for a fifteen-minute appointment, then spend up to an hour waiting outside his door, then be treated as if they were keeping him from more important matters.

"He had a fantastically strong ego," said Professor Wylie. "Exceptionally pompous," according to Schelling. "More arrogant and vain than any man I've ever met," was Hoffmann's first impression. Yet each developed complex, mixed feelings about him. He was, after all, a respected friend with a mind of undisputed brilliance. His personality, however annoying, was at least always worthy of fascination.[13]

ON THE HOME FRONT

Until he won tenure, Kissinger and his wife lived in a modest duplex on Frost Street in Cambridge, alongside their best friends, Klaus and Elizabeth Epstein. Klaus was also a political scientist, insightful and intense like Kissinger but not conventionally ambitious. "We would take day trips and have dinners together all the time, just the four of us, or five if you count the Kissingers' dog," recalled Elizabeth.[14]

Kissinger was surprised when the Epsteins began having children before they were financially secure. Only after he felt assured of winning tenure—and with his salary supplemented by about $8,000 a year from work for Rockefeller—did he and Ann have their first child, Elizabeth, who was born in March 1959. Her brother, David, arrived two years later.

Although Kissinger was no longer a practicing Jew, and Ann had become affiliated with the Ethical Culture Society in lieu of religion, David was circumcised at a Bris, the formal Jewish ceremony performed shortly after a boy's birth. In a letter to his parents that Yom Kippur, Kissinger reflected on the hard times they had been through. "At the Bris of David we could all meet in good health and look back with pride over many difficult years. I am well aware that I owe almost everything to the spirit of our family, which has kept us together in good days as in bad. I wish my two grandfathers could have been present on that occasion physically as they were in spirit."[15]

By then the Kissingers had moved into a three-bedroom, white colonial house in nearby Belmont Hill. Ann—who for a few years took to spelling her name "Anne," perhaps in the belief that it seemed more sophisticated—was a relentless housewife who cooked and cleaned with Germanic efficiency. It was necessary, she explained, given her husband's growing stature. Two or three times a week they would give dinner parties, usually small affairs with eight or ten guests. The mix would usually include some favored students, especially when the summer seminar was in session, along with a faculty colleague or two. Sometimes, however, dinner might involve a visiting foreign leader or someone as exalted as Nelson Rockefeller.

Ann tended to be overwhelmed by some of the guests and to seek refuge in the kitchen. A professor recalls seeing her standing by the dining room door listening, as if afraid to venture in. "Kissinger was a very German husband," according to Marian Schlesinger, the former wife of Arthur Schlesinger, Jr. "He tended to treat Ann as a hausfrau, and he never paid much heed to anything she might have to say at the table."

Nevertheless, Ann took great pride in her husband's career and kept neat scrapbooks of every clipping that mentioned him. She also amassed a Christmas-card list of four hundred names, most of them her husband's important acquaintances. Because she wanted to include a personal note on each, she would start writing them in October.

Almost inexorably, however, the Kissingers were drifting apart. He had a private study built above their garage to which he would retreat. When he took one friend on a tour, Ann ventured inside to join them for a drink; Kissinger brusquely told her to leave, that this was his room. Their friends saw the studio as a sign of his gradual abandonment of Ann, but he saw it as an attempt to keep the household together as his desire for privacy increased. In either case, they drifted farther apart, had less to talk about. Although he doted on his children, he seemed to have little time for his wife. "Henry and Ann were just two people who couldn't live in the same house," recalled a friend.

Ann was, in her unpretentious way, rather sophisticated. She liked music and art, and she could be an engaging conversationalist around people who made her feel comfortable. Nevertheless, Kissinger grew somewhat embarrassed by her as he began to move in more glamorous orbits. She did not have the style to fit in, he thought, with a Rockefeller or Kennedy crowd. "She was not perceived by her husband as a suitable consort," said a Boston psychiatrist who knew them both. "She was not scintillating enough." [16]

From Ann's perspective, Henry did not fit into the comforting and ordered home life to which she aspired. She wanted a husband, not a statesman.

By the end of 1962, after taking a trip to Europe and Asia together, the Kissingers decided to separate. He got an apartment on Beacon Hill for a while, then one in Cambridge. In August 1964, they were granted a divorce in Reno, Nevada.

The breakup was sad, for him as well as her, but not especially bitter. They stayed on good terms, talked often about the children, and Ann would even have Henry around for dinner on occasion. She rarely spoke ill of him, even to friends. When he became famous, she protected his reputation and even once arranged for him to speak to a group she belonged to. Later she married Saul Cohen, a distinguished and kindly chemistry professor at Brandeis.

Although the dissolution of his marriage was not caused by another woman, Kissinger began to adopt a more rakish style as he and Ann drifted apart. He bought a sunlamp and a Mercedes, lost weight, and sported better clothes. Schelling realized the change when he told a friend who was meeting Kissinger at the London airport how to recognize him. "He's fat, dumpyish, pale, and sickish," Schelling said. His friend did not spot him. Only then did Schelling realize that Kissinger had begun to spruce up his style. [17]

INVENTING ARMS CONTROL

For three decades, from the late 1950s until the late 1980s, the theory and pursuit of "arms control" dominated international relations. Arcane negotiations over thresholds and throw weights served as a barometer of East-West relations and the coin of the realm at summit meetings.

It was not always thus. After the failure of the quixotic efforts in 1946 to control the atom bomb through the United Nations, experts such as Bernard Brodie began to explore nuclear strategies. But it was not until the U.S. and U.S.S.R. were both producing a steady stream of nuclear missiles that the theology and technology of arms control gave birth to a new field of intellectual endeavor.

The ferment over arms control doctrines was centered in Cambridge, where political scientists met with atomic scientists to explore the nuances of the nuclear age. From these meetings grew an informal discussion circle that became known as the Harvard-MIT Arms Control Group. Its members would dominate arms control thinking through six presidential administrations: Jerome Weisner, George Kistiakowsky, Robert Bowie, Paul Doty, Tom Schelling, Sidney Drell, Albert Wohlsetter, Arthur Schlesinger, Jr., Marshall Shulman, and others. Even before Kissinger had gone to New York to write *Nuclear Weapons and Foreign Policy,* he had been invited to these discussions.

In 1989, when arguing at a private gathering that the time had finally come to deemphasize the role of arms control in Soviet-American relations, Kissinger tried to establish his credentials by claiming, "I was part of the intellectual community that originated the concept of arms control." The sweeping statement had some truth. The Harvard-MIT group, Kissinger later said, "created the basis for what became known as arms control thinking."[18]

The group would generally meet on Saturday mornings at the CFIA offices just north of Harvard Yard. It was not just chatter: participants were expected to work up specific proposals, present them as papers, and then defend them in discussion. The goal was to come up with a workable concept of stability and proper methods for assessing force balances.

The group had a "liberal" or "dovish" cast in that most members favored as much disarmament as possible, supported the idea of building missile-defense systems, endorsed a test ban treaty, and were against building strategic bombers. Kissinger, more conservative, was skeptical on all these counts.

Kissinger's fascination with arms control led him to put aside his more academic writing—including, for the moment, Bismarck—and churn out a series of policy critiques, mainly for *Foreign Affairs.* Most were mildly critical of the Eisenhower administration. For example, when the president suspended nuclear weapons tests and called on the Soviets to negotiate a test ban treaty, Kissinger argued that "we should agree to a complete ban only as part of a general disarmament agreement which includes conventional [i.e., non-nuclear] weapons."

A hot issue at the time was whether the NATO allies would allow the U.S. to deploy medium-range nuclear missiles in Western Europe. Such a move would be the logical outgrowth of Kissinger's belief that the U.S. needed to be prepared to use tactical nuclear weapons in a limited, regional war. In a 1958 *Foreign Affairs* piece titled "Missiles and the Western Alliance," Kissinger argued in favor of the European missile idea. "It represents," he wrote, "the only means by which Europe can gain a degree of influence over its future." As it turned out, such a deployment became part of NATO policy and remained that way until the late 1980s. (When Ronald Reagan and Mikhail Gorbachev worked out a deal in 1987 to remove these missiles from Europe, Kissinger was opposed.)[19]

As he was honing his foreign policy ideas, Kissinger was also building a public visibility unusual for a junior professor. His 1958 article on the Western Alliance led to a story with his picture in the *New York Times* headlined, "Refusal of Missile Bases Seen as Danger to Europe's Future." And *Time* magazine boxed out a half-page story on his test ban article, calling Kissinger "tough-minded" and heartily endorsing his message of "beware the ban."[20]

THE NECESSITY FOR CHOICE

Kissinger's articles on diplomacy and arms control formed the basis for a book that he published—not merely by coincidence—a few weeks after John Kennedy won the 1960 election. *The Necessity for Choice* was a wide-ranging manifesto, Kissinger's first full exposition of his philosophy. Though it restated arguments he had made in previous articles, it was packaged as a coherent approach to foreign policy—and as a job application in case the new president decided to seek some fresh thinking from Cambridge.[21]

Acknowledgments in a book are often insincere, but Kissinger carried that art to an extreme. He began by noting that the book was published "under the auspices" of the Center for International Affairs

and praising its director, Robert Bowie, for his "incisive comments."
In fact, the book caused the final blowup between the two bitter rivals
and served to sever Kissinger's role as associate director. Bowie had
insisted that the book be published by the CFIA. Kissinger refused;
his nuclear weapons book had been published by the Council on
Foreign Relations, which meant that he received no royalties when it
became a best-seller. So he had *Necessity* published by Harper's, with
just a meaningless line inside about its being under the "auspices" of
the CFIA. "They had a horrible fight over the issue," recalled Professor Schelling. "Each would come into my office, pace up and down,
and tell me how horrible the other one was." Kissinger also gave
thanks to a Council on Foreign Relations study group in 1958–59 that
he drew upon only scantily, and he ends with thanks to his wife, Ann,
who "was patient and cheerful."

The book itself read like a manifesto for the Democrats. "Our
margin of survival has narrowed dangerously," Kissinger said in criticism of the Eisenhower years. Like Kennedy, he warned of a missile
gap. Because foreign policy "has been far too bipartisan," there had
not been enough skepticism about Eisenhower's course. As if writing
a campaign speech, Kissinger declared that "if these trends continue,
the future of freedom will be dim indeed," then added: "We can still
reverse these trends if we move boldly and with conviction."[22]

In the book, Kissinger revisited the question of "limited" wars,
those regional conflicts that remain below the level of an all-out war.
Some of his premises remained the same as in his first book. "As the
consequences of all-out war grow more horrible, reliance on it also
becomes more absurd," he wrote. Thus, the U.S. needed to be able
to threaten a limited response when faced with a limited challenge,
such as a Soviet threat to Berlin. "A country not willing to risk limited
war because it fears that resistance to aggression on any scale may
lead to all-out war," he argued, "will have no choice in a showdown
but to surrender."

But buried in all of this analysis was a pirouette that would have
dazzled Diaghilev: a major reversal in Kissinger's position on whether
the strategy for fighting limited wars should include the option to use
nuclear weapons. He had become famous for saying yes, that the U.S.
did need a limited-nuclear-war capability. "Some years ago this author
advocated a nuclear strategy," Kissinger admitted. Abandoning self-
reference, he added: "Several developments have caused a shift in the
view."

His main reason for changing his mind was not because he
thought the idea of limited nuclear war was theoretically or morally
flawed, but because it had practical problems. "It would be next to

impossible to obtain a coherent description of what is understood by 'limited nuclear war' from our military establishment," he wrote. The distinction between conventional and nuclear forces, Kissinger argued in his revised theory, provided a clear firebreak in keeping a limited war from escalating. "The dividing line between conventional and nuclear weapons is more familiar and therefore easier to maintain."

Even while rejecting his previous position that small nuclear weapons could play a role in fighting limited wars, he argued that the U.S. should develop them in order to deter the Soviets from using them. In addition, he argued, the U.S. should refrain from pledging "no first use" of nuclear weapons during a limited war. "If the aggressor accepts a renunciation of nuclear weapons at face value as indicating a decision to accept defeat by conventional forces," Kissinger wrote, "aggression may actually be encouraged."[23]

All of this may seem like theological arcana with scant relevance to the real world. Not so. From the 1960s through most of the 1980s, NATO doctrine was based on precisely the policies that Kissinger—along with others—advocated. The capacity to use tactical nuclear weapons to deter a Soviet invasion was developed. Despite recurring pressures, NATO never adopted a policy of "no first use." Yet both in doctrine and in reality, limited wars—in Vietnam and in other global nooks and crannies—were kept at a non-nuclear level.

BISMARCK

Kissinger's doctoral dissertation on Metternich and Castlereagh was intended as a prelude to a study of Prince Otto von Bismarck, who took power as Prussia's chancellor in 1862 and proceeded to unite Germany. But it took Kissinger thirteen years to finish his Bismarck piece, which he published in 1968 in the academic journal *Daedalus*. Though one of his least-known writings, it may be the most enlightening, not for what it reveals about Bismarck, but for what it says about Kissinger and his concept of realism in world affairs.

Bismarck's genius, Kissinger writes with the authority of a disciple, was the ability to deal with contending forces "by manipulating their antagonisms." Because his goals for Germany were incompatible with the European order that existed, Bismarck was a revolutionary; but because he believed in an authoritarian, disciplined state, he was a conservative, a white rather than a red revolutionary.

Bismarck's drive for power was based more on ego than a desire to implement a philosophy. "Patriotism was probably the motive force of but a few of the famous statesmen," the Iron Chancellor once wrote to a friend. "Much more frequently, it was ambition, the desire to command, to be admired and to become famous." The same would later be said, not without some justification, of Kissinger.

Similarly, Bismarck had an attitude toward truth that critics said fit Kissinger as well. "The root fact of Bismarck's personality," Kissinger wrote, was his "incapacity to comprehend" any moral standard outside of his own will and ambition:

> For this reason, he could never accept the good faith of any opponent; it accounts, too, for his mastery in adapting to the requirements of the moment. It was not that Bismarck lied— this is much too self-conscious an act—but that he was finely attuned to the subtlest currents of any environment and produced measures precisely adjusted to the need to prevail.[24]

Kissinger would later argue that it was wrong to draw too many comparisons between himself and Bismarck, that he was a student of the Iron Chancellor and not a devotee. Nevertheless, Kissinger's later predilection for realpolitik and his feel for balance-of-power diplomacy show that his appreciation of Bismarck was not merely academic. "Bismarck urged that foreign policy had to be based not on sentiment but on an assessment of strength," Kissinger wrote. That would also become one of Kissinger's guiding principles.

SEVEN

THE FRINGES OF POWER

Kennedy, Johnson,
and Rockefeller, 1961–1968

> *Politics is the art of the possible, the science of the relative.*—OTTO
> VON BISMARCK, *September 29, 1851*

CAMELOT'S OUTER CIRCLE

Although he was a cold war conservative on retainer to Rockefeller, Kissinger was registered as a Democrat, and he voted that way in the 1960 election between John Kennedy and Richard Nixon. He had known Kennedy since 1958, when speechwriter Ted Sorensen asked him to join a panel of academic advisers to meet with the young senator now and then in Boston. In addition, Kennedy was on the "Visiting Committee" of Harvard's Government Department, a largely ceremonial function that brought him into contact with the tenured professors there. And socially, Kissinger was friendly with the Kennedys' favorite historian, Arthur Schlesinger, Jr.

These connections, along with his published articles criticizing Eisenhower's ineptitude, made Kissinger a prime candidate for a position in the new administration. But he was reluctant to leave Harvard full-time and sever his lucrative ties to Rockefeller unless an important position was offered.

None was. Dean Rusk sounded him out about an unspecified mid-level job at the State Department. More promisingly, Kennedy invited Kissinger to the White House in early February, praised his new book (Kissinger suspected Kennedy had read the review in the *New Yorker* rather than the whole tome), and invited him to join the White House staff under his former dean, McGeorge Bundy, the new national security assistant. Kissinger later noted, however, that Bundy did not appear to share "the President's sense of urgency to add to the White House staff another professor of comparable academic competence."[1]

Beginning at Harvard and extending through the Vietnam War, Bundy and Kissinger had an uneasy relationship. In *White House Years,* Kissinger's portrait of Bundy was sharp. "I admired his brilliance even when he put it, too frequently, at the service of ideas that were more fashionable than substantial." Their discomfort with each other was largely a matter of style and class. "He tended to treat me," Kissinger said, "with the combination of politeness and subconscious condescension that upper-class Bostonians reserve for people of, by New England standards, exotic backgrounds and excessively intense personal style." In later years, Kissinger claimed to have mellowed on Bundy, saying that "he really did not deserve the description I gave of him in *White House Years.*"[2]

Bundy ended up offering Kissinger a job as a part-time consultant. Though disappointed, he accepted. From 1961 until 1968, he would remain only on the fringes of power, like an outsider with his nose pressed to the glass. During those eight years, he would continue as a professor at Harvard, teaching his courses and running his summer seminar. But his heart was in Washington as he buzzed around the periphery as an adviser to Kennedy, Lyndon Johnson, and Nelson Rockefeller.

The problems inherent in a part-time consulting arrangement were evident in a "Dear Mac" letter in which Kissinger described what days he might be available. "In March, I could come to Washington on Monday and Tuesday morning, March 13 and 14th. Alternatively, if you want to have another go-round on the paper we discussed yesterday before then, I could come down on Friday and Saturday, March 10th and 11th, if you can let me know by the 8th. In April, I can give you most of the week of April 2nd." And so on.[3]

Kissinger's tendency to pour on flattery worked well with patrons such as Fritz Kraemer and William Yandell Elliott, whose flamboyant egos could cope with constant feeding. It would also work on Richard Nixon, whose dark insecurities were soothed by sycophancy. But it did not succeed with Bundy, a man of puritan reserve and Grotonian tact. Kissinger tried nonetheless. "I need hardly add," he scribbled on the bottom of a February letter, "that in addition to the importance of the assignment it would be a great personal pleasure to be associated with you again." In a note of encouragement after he learned that Bundy was considering resigning after the botched Bay of Pigs invasion in 1961, Kissinger wrote: "Great things must still be done. And your friends and admirers would rest easier if they knew that you will continue to play a major, indeed a leading, part in them."[4]

Less than a month after he was hired as a consultant, Kissinger wrote Bundy to ask if he should "see newspaper men who have been after me." Bundy, betraying a note of polite condescension, replied that he could "see no reason for you to see newspaper men." He also saw no reason for Kissinger to see much of the president. He knew that Kennedy, who considered Kissinger brilliant but tiresome, was driven to distraction by his ponderous insistence that all issues be put in a long-range strategic context.[5]

So Kissinger started asking Arthur Schlesinger to help him get into the Oval Office. "Bundy pretty much blocked his access," Schlesinger later said. "Whenever Henry had a pretty interesting idea, I'd help perform an end run on Bundy. I'd bring him in to see Kennedy." The president's tolerance was short-lived. He called Schlesinger in and told him, "You know, I do find some of what Henry says to be interesting, but I have to insist that he report through Bundy, otherwise things will get out of hand."[6]

By May, Bundy was fed up with Kissinger's habit of swooping into Washington for a day or two and critiquing projects that other aides had been wrestling with full-time. "Mac quickly came to feel," Schlesinger recalled, "that Henry's part-time kibitzing was more annoying than helpful," and he let Kissinger know it. Kissinger responded with a wounded, two-page letter saying that it had become clear "that I should not come to Washington for the summer."[7]

But just as Kissinger was preparing to spend the summer of 1961 sulking at his International Seminar, his expertise came into demand. The nagging problem of Berlin erupted again. Since 1958, the Soviets had been threatening to deprive the West of access to West Berlin. At Kennedy's request, former secretary of state Dean Acheson prepared a policy paper that cast the issue as a critical test of Western will. If Nikita Khrushchev moved to cut off West Berlin, Acheson argued, American military divisions should be sent rolling down the autobahn.

Despite Kissinger's hard-line views, he was discomforted by Acheson's dismissal of diplomatic alternatives. He found himself siding, both at meetings and in memos, with the soft-liners such as Carl Kaysen of the NSC staff, Abram Chayes of the State Department, and Arthur Schlesinger. It was one of the few times that he would find himself lining up with the doves on an East-West military issue.

One Friday in early July, Schlesinger became concerned that the president was heading off to Hyannis Port with Acheson's memo and nothing on the opposing side to balance it. He discussed the problem with Kissinger and Chayes over lunch in the White House mess, then called them an hour later to come by his office and compose a memo arguing the case against Acheson.

As Chayes and Kissinger paced up and down dictating, Schlesinger stuck a cigar in his mouth and typed up a five-point paper, which they raced to finish before Kennedy's helicopter left for Cape Cod. "It is essential to elaborate the cause for which we are prepared to go to nuclear war," they wrote in attacking Acheson's belligerency. A refusal to negotiate, Kissinger emphasized in a separate memo to Bundy, should not be mistaken for firmness.[8]

(Kissinger took care not to alienate Acheson. Around this time he wrote him a letter saying: "The discussion at dinner the other day showed such an appalling absence of subtlety and lack of understanding of intangibles on the part of almost everyone that only your presence prevented a real disaster." A few years later, the flattery was still flowing. "While in Paris a few weeks ago, I spoke to a man who had an appointment with de Gaulle right after you," Kissinger wrote. "He told me that de Gaulle said, 'Voilà un homme!' . . . It is, of course, no surprise to your admirers.")[9]

The Berlin crisis dramatized the dilemma that Kissinger had long been writing about: the U.S. did not have any alternatives between fighting a conventional war and an all-out nuclear war. Along with the Schlesinger-Kissinger-Chayes Berlin memo, Kennedy took to Hyannis Port a Kissinger paper explaining the need for medium-range missiles that could be used to fight a limited nuclear war.[10]

Kissinger's document was part of the reassessment that led to the decision to adopt a "flexible response" capability. "You may want to raise this question with [Defense Secretary] Bob McNamara in order to have a prompt review and new orders if necessary," Bundy wrote to Kennedy in a note attached to Kissinger's paper. "In essence, the current plan calls for shooting off everything we have in one shot, and it is so constructed as to make any more flexible course more difficult."

Kennedy agreed. In his speech about the Berlin crisis on July 25, the president noted the need to meet "all levels of aggressor pressure with whatever levels of force are required." He went on to say, "We intend to have a wider choice than humiliation or all-out nuclear action."[11]

Kissinger's approach to foreign policy was to address each problem by asking what the desired long-term outcome was. As he explained to Bundy in an August 11 memo on Berlin: "One way of arriving at this choice might be to consider explicitly just what we are after in Central Europe. What would we envisage Europe to be like in, say, 1965?"[12]

Presidents rarely have the luxury to engage in such long-range thinking. Three days after Kissinger wrote this memo, the Berlin Wall suddenly went up overnight, changing the nature of the crisis. Kissinger considered Kennedy's response too muted; he favored threatening a confrontation to test what risks the Soviets were willing to take and to reassure the Germans that the U.S. took their security seriously.

The Wall, it turned out, served to defuse the crisis over Berlin: the U.S. and other Western nations retained free access to the sectors they controlled, and the refugee flood from the East was stanched. As the crisis waned during the fall of 1961, so did the last vestiges of Kissinger's influence at the White House. In October he cleaned out his desk. Bundy sent him a letter of perfunctory thanks, which added that the White House had decided not to make a public announcement of his departure.[13]

Policy differences had contributed to Kissinger's problems: he considered Kennedy's "bear any burden" rhetoric to be dangerously naive about the limits of U.S. power. But the main reason that Kissinger did not last was that he simply did not fit in with Kennedy or his people. He was a character out of Wagner trying to play in Camelot. "Henry was not the president's style," recalled Carl Kaysen. "He was pompous and long-winded. You could be long-winded if the president liked you. But I never heard anyone say that Kissinger was likable."[14]

Kissinger found the experience frustrating. "He was on the outside looking in," Chayes later said, "and that upset him." He knew that Kennedy's closest aides—polished, glib, fast-talking—made fun of him behind his back; Bundy had begun to do passable imitations of Kissinger's ponderous Germanic discourses and of Kennedy rolling his eyes.

"I consumed my energies in offering unwanted advice and, in our infrequent contact, inflicting on President Kennedy learned disquisitions about which he could have done nothing in the unlikely event that they aroused his interest," Kissinger later noted. One lesson he learned was that a president does not need a lot of people who tell him what he cannot do; it is better to be one of those telling him what he can do, or at least offering preferable alternatives.[15]

Even though he was merely a junior professor with an undistinguished stint as a midlevel government consultant, Kissinger had developed the knack of being a notable presence wherever he went, of projecting himself as a man of importance. Thus he was able to stir controversy on a trip to Israel, India, and Pakistan that January, even though he was traveling only as a guest of the U.S. Information Agency rather than as a representative of the administration.

In Israel, Kissinger opined that Soviet arms shipments to Egypt were provocative, which prompted such headlines as "Nasser Seen as Causing Crisis." After visiting the Khyber Pass, he submitted to an impromptu press conference where he breezily (and incorrectly) noted that Pakistan "would never do anything so foolish" as join an alliance with China. The Pakistani ambassador to the U.S. officially protested. Finally, Bundy sent him a telegram saying, "If you don't keep your mouth shut, I'm going to hit the recall button." Bundy felt compelled to tell reporters that Kissinger was not working for the U.S. government, and an answer along the same lines was included in Kennedy's briefing book if the question arose at a press conference (it didn't).[16]

In a letter to his father from Bombay, Kissinger complained that "emotions run so high here that even the most innocent remark is likely to get played up in a sensational fashion." The letter also conveyed birthday wishes, which tended to bring out Kissinger's sentimental streak. "I have met many great men of this world, or those who would be great," he wrote after describing his trip. "Nothing has diminished—on the contrary it has enhanced—my appreciation of your qualities. I know what I owe to the tradition you exemplify."[17]

ON THE PROWL

In the summer of 1962, Kissinger returned to Harvard full-time. No longer restrained by a White House contract, he resumed writing conservative critiques of American policy for *Foreign Affairs, The Reporter,* and other publications, most of them conveying his concern that America and its allies remain steadfast in the face of the Soviet threat. "He had an enormous capacity for gloom about the future of the republic when he was not in charge," recalled Bundy.[18]

Once again he began to wrestle with the issue of whether the U.S. should be prepared to use nuclear weapons in fighting a limited war, which he had advocated in his first book and partly retracted in his second. In a July 1962 *Foreign Affairs* article titled "The Unsolved Problems of European Defense," he wrote that NATO could not be counted on to undertake the massive spending that would be needed to match Soviet conventional forces. Consequently, Kissinger argued, "its other option would be to rely more heavily on tactical nuclear weapons."

"Tactical" weapons referred to those with a short range that were suited for battlefield use, as contrasted with long-range "strategic" ones that can fly between continents. The distinction, Kissinger now felt, could help solve his old dilemma of how to devise a doctrine for fighting a limited nuclear war that would not immediately escalate into an unlimited one. In his 1962 piece, he came down in favor of relying on tactical nuclear weapons, which could be easily distinguished from the strategic weapons designed for all-out war. "The most effective method for employing nuclear weapons in a limited manner appears to be their tactical use to stop a battle," he wrote. "It is easy to jibe at the 'Marquis of Queensbury' rules which limited nuclear war is said to require. . . . However, those who ridicule the concept of tactical nuclear war should explain what alternative they propose."

Having finally arrived at this position, Kissinger stuck to it. Even in the late 1980s, he opposed the rush to eliminate tactical nuclear weapons from Europe and warned against "continuing to stigmatize those weapons the U.S. has come to rely upon to deter Soviet aggression." The weapons would remain in place until the Soviet threat to Europe collapsed and President Bush, in September 1991, announced plans to eliminate America's European-based missiles.[19]

Most of Kissinger's writings during the early 1960s analyzed the strains that existed within the Western alliance. He synthesized these articles into a lecture series at the Council on Foreign Relations in March 1964, which appeared the following year as a book, *The Troubled Partnership*. A central theme is an attack on Robert Bowie's idea of a Multilateral Force (MLF) jointly controlled by NATO members. Kissinger's animosity reflected his deep and lasting mistrust of the Europeans as reliable military allies, especially on nuclear issues. Throughout his career he was skeptical that most Western European governments had the backbone to sustain a tough anti-Soviet defense policy.[20]

During this period, Kissinger was refining the realpolitik philosophy that undergirded his approach to foreign policy. One of its central tenets was that a nation's influence depends on the perception the world holds of its power and of its willingness to use power. As he explained in an analysis of the Cuban missile crisis for *The Reporter* late in 1962: even if one believed that there was not much military danger in allowing the Soviets to keep their missiles in Cuba, America could not afford a weak response because that would "embolden" its adversaries, "dishearten" its allies, and diminish its "credibility." He would use this same line of reasoning during the Vietnam debate.[21]

Early in 1964, Kissinger moved to a bachelor apartment on Beacon Street in Boston. Although he was never much of a lothario, even when he cultivated a reputation for being one in the late 1960s, Kissinger began to flirt and joke about women more. When a friend proposed introducing him to a woman who was "very attractive but happens to be very tall," Kissinger replied: "My ego can handle that."

That year he also became involved in politics, especially the presidential campaign of his new patron Nelson Rockefeller, who unsuccessfully challenged Barry Goldwater for the Republican nomination. Kissinger spent much of his time on the periphery, sending speeches down by messenger from Boston and grumbling as they were rewritten by the candidate's staff. But Rockefeller, who collected good minds with the same avidity and taste with which he collected Picassos, grew fond of having Kissinger around and invited him to come along to San Francisco for the convention.

Part of Kissinger's task was to be one of Rockefeller's emissaries to the platform committee. Running the operation was a young but influential Wisconsin congressman named Melvin Laird. Although he found Kissinger's seriousness and self-importance amusing, Laird enlisted him to handle the delicate work of drafting a foreign policy plank that could "pass muster with Goldwater and Rockefeller as well as with the John Birch Society members on the committee." Kissinger succeeded.[22]

At the convention, Kissinger met a gangly, WASPy, thirty-year-old volunteer researcher for Rockefeller named Nancy Sharon Maginnes. He had dealt with her in passing at the Rockefeller offices in Manhattan, but it was only when he ran into her in a campaign staff room in San Francisco that he took note of her. They agreed to meet again at the convention hall that night. For the next ten years, she would be known to his friends, though not to the public, as his most regular date.

By now Kissinger considered himself a Republican, or at least a Rockefeller Republican. But the fire-eyed crowds that descended on San Francisco's Cow Palace in 1964 did not make him comfortable. When Rockefeller was booed by Goldwater's legions, the governor faced down the hecklers defiantly, at one point returning an obscene gesture with gusto. Kissinger, however, was appalled by his first glimpse of the hurly-burly of American populist passions. That November, he voted without hesitancy for Lyndon Johnson.

Having seen the passion of the Goldwaterites, Kissinger would later seek to please and appease, with a clumsiness that was unusual for him, the populist right wing of the Republican party. It never worked. Even as he became more hawkish, the conservative movement never felt comfortable with him. The crowds that booed Rockefeller in 1964 were driven not only by ideology but also by anti-elitist sentiments and resentments. Kissinger never fully grasped that it was not merely his policies that activist conservatives found anathema, but also his style and even his background. They could accept a Nixon, who shared their populist resentments, but never the European-oriented Harvard professor who had risen through Rockefeller's patronage.

FIRST STEP INTO THE QUAGMIRE

Kissinger paid scant attention to Vietnam in the early 1960s. To the extent that he did, he saw the conflict not as an indigenous civil war or an anticolonial struggle but as a military attempt by Soviet-backed North Vietnam to conquer the sovereign country of South Vietnam. "I shared the conventional wisdom," he later wrote.

Initially he was skeptical about American involvement. When President Kennedy sent 16,000 "advisers" to Vietnam, Kissinger asked Walt Rostow, then the chief planner at the State Department, what made the U.S. think it could succeed with that number when the French had failed with ten times more. "Rostow gave me the short shrift that harassed officials reserve for rank amateurs," Kissinger recalled. "The French," Rostow explained, "did not understand guerrilla warfare." When the *New York Times*'s James Reston wrote a column criticizing Kennedy's decision, Kissinger telephoned to express his agreement.[23]

But as usual, Kissinger's views were complex, and he sometimes shaded them—or emphasized different facets of them—to please those he was talking to at the moment. To his intellectual friends, he stressed his qualms about America's growing involvement in Vietnam. To those in the government, he claimed to be in favor of standing firm against communist aggression.

When President Lyndon Johnson made the decision to send in U.S. combat troops, Kissinger wrote two letters to McGeorge Bundy, in March and April of 1965, proclaiming his support. "I thought the President's program on Vietnam as outlined in his speech was just right: the proper mixture of firmness and flexibility," Kissinger wrote.

Replied Bundy: "It is good to know of your support on the current big issue—I fear you may be somewhat lonely among all our friends at Harvard."[24]

Kissinger began his own ten-year personal involvement with Vietnam in October 1965 when Ambassador Henry Cabot Lodge asked him to visit the country as a consultant. He spent two weeks meeting with Nguyen Van Thieu and other leaders, consulting with generals, talking to religious leaders and students, and roaming the countryside. "We are well guarded," he wrote his parents, "so please do not worry."

The trip disillusioned Kissinger about America's tactics but not about its aims in Vietnam. At his first military briefing, he asked his basic question: what was the eventual goal five or ten years down the road? He noted in his diary: "No one could really explain to me how even on the most favorable assumptions . . . the war was going to end."

The U.S., he realized, had become stuck supporting an inept and corrupt government. The communist sanctuaries in Cambodia and Laos prevented a complete military victory, and the bombing of North Vietnam was "enough to mobilize world opinion against us but too halfhearted and gradual to be decisive." Nevertheless, he felt that a withdrawal would harm American credibility.[25]

As his trip ended, Kissinger became involved in a controversy that revealed as much about his sensitivity as it did about his thinking on Vietnam. At the urging of the embassy's press officer, Barry Zorthian, he attended an off-the-record luncheon with eight journalists. But one reporter, Jack Foisie of the *Los Angeles Times,* arrived late, overlooked the ground rules, and filed a story that ran the next day on the front pages of his own paper and of the *Washington Post.* "Recent emissaries from the White House are reporting that there is almost total lack of political maturity or unselfish political motivation among the current leaders of the South Vietnam government," Foisie wrote. "These are known to be the findings of Prof. Henry Kissinger, the noted political scientist, and Clark Clifford, the Washington lawyer."

The president was furious. Clifford sent him a brief letter saying he had not been at the lunch; Press Secretary Bill Moyers put out a statement saying that Kissinger alone was the source and had no connection to the White House. It was now Kissinger's turn to become enraged. In a manner typical of the way he would handle damaging press stories in the future, he reacted vigorously.

Kissinger denied, with more vehemence than sincerity, that he had expressed the sentiments that Foisie cited. "I doubt that I spoke three sentences during that lunch," Kissinger wrote in a two-page scrawled letter to Bundy. The views ascribed to him "were not distortions but inventions." He expressed his "astonishment" at Moyers's statement, said it had undermined his credibility, and concluded that "simple fairness requires a correction." Still worked up a day later, he sent a telegram to the White House in which he proclaimed himself "aghast at the damage done to American policy." In a three-page letter to Clifford, he declared: "I am depressed and shaken that my effort to be helpful . . . has ended so ignominiously." And finally, he denied to the Associated Press that he had been the source of Foisie's story.

But according to Zorthian, Foisie had correctly reported Kissinger's remarks. "Henry did a lot of talking and expressed deep pessimism about the Saigon leadership, which he said did not have popular appeal and was corrupt," Zorthian recalled. "I must say, Foisie's story was accurate. So was Henry's pessimism."[26]

To Bundy, a man who prided himself on never letting his emotions overwhelm his intellect, Kissinger's agitation was worse than any comments he may have made. He asked his brother William Bundy, the assistant secretary of state for Far Eastern affairs, to calm Kissinger down. "I don't blame him for feeling agitated," McGeorge wrote, "but I think he should know that everyone else is pretty relaxed about this right now."

Despite his loud protests, Kissinger in fact held the pessimistic views ascribed to him, and he spelled them out in the same letter to Bundy in which he denied the accuracy of Foisie's report. "The situation in Vietnam is less encouraging than I had believed before I left," he wrote. Particularly worrisome was the "weakness of the Saigon government." Nevertheless, he offered his support for the war. "Even though the situation in Vietnam continues to be graver than our military reporting criteria indicate, I continue to believe that our policy is essentially correct."[27]

In December 1965, a few weeks after he returned home, Kissinger defended America's policy in Vietnam in a satellite debate on CBS against British Labour Party firebrand Michael Foot and two Oxford students. Helping Kissinger argue in favor of the war were two Harvard students who eventually became noted liberals: Robert Shrum, later a speechwriter for George McGovern, and Lawrence Tribe, later a law professor at Harvard. "We are involved in Vietnam," Kissinger declared, "because we want to give the people there the right to choose their own government." Also that month, he was one of 190 academics, including such Harvard colleagues as Morton Halperin and Sam Beer, to sign a petition supporting President Johnson's conduct of the war.[28]

On a second visit to Vietnam in July 1966, Kissinger returned to a province where he had been told a few months earlier that 80 percent of the population was "pacified" (brought under government control). The provincial chief spoke of the "enormous progress" in pacification since his last visit. Recalled Kissinger: "When I asked him how much of the province was now pacified, he proudly told me seventy percent!" On a third visit that October, he learned from talking to peasants in one South Vietnamese village that 80 percent paid taxes to the Viet Cong. How, Kissinger later asked a U.S. adviser, could he thus claim the village was largely pacified? "The VC wouldn't dare enter this village," replied the adviser. "The people pay their taxes by mail." Kissinger's skepticism was thus reinforced, though perhaps not enough.[29]

Kissinger remained dubious about American tactics. In a briefing for experts at the Rand Corporation in Santa Monica, he criticized the Johnson administration for tying its policy to the survival of President Nguyen Van Thieu's government, a mistake that Kissinger would later make himself. At the Harvard Business School, participating in a seminar with the quaint conceit of "Vietnam as a management problem," Kissinger was asked what he thought of the "enclave theory" that the U.S. should concentrate on establishing a few very secure strongholds throughout South Vietnam. "Ah, yes," Kissinger said sarcastically, "the theory that we should have three more Berlins and two more Guantánamos."[30]

In an August 1966 assessment of the war for *Look* magazine, Kissinger began by asserting two premises. "Withdrawal would be disastrous," he wrote, "and negotiations are inevitable." Unlike Secretary of State Dean Rusk, he did not believe that an outright military victory was possible. He nevertheless felt that the U.S. should continue the fight with the aim of securing enough territory to create a strong negotiating position.

In the world according to Kissinger, it was dangerous for America to abandon one of its commitments even if the nook of the globe at stake was not, in itself, a vital national security interest. If a "third-class Communist peasant state" could beat the U.S., he wrote in his *Look* article, it would "strengthen" the hand of America's adversaries everywhere, "demoralize" allies, "lessen the credibility" of the U.S. around the world, and cause other nations to consider shifting their allegiance to the Soviet Union. This emphasis on credibility would become the underpinning of his policies when his turn in power came.[31]

THE PENNSYLVANIA NEGOTIATIONS, 1967

At a conference in Paris in June 1967, Kissinger fell into a discussion about Vietnam with Herbert Marcovich, a French microbiologist. Marcovich mentioned that a friend of his named Raymond Aubrac had become close to Ho Chi Minh when the Vietnamese revolutionary was living in exile near Paris in 1946. Perhaps, suggested Marcovich, the U.S. could use Aubrac as a secret negotiating channel.

Thus began Kissinger's first experience with secret diplomacy and his baptism into the difficulties of dealing with the North Vietnamese. The Kissinger initiative, code-named Pennsylvania, also resulted in a significant change in the U.S. position on what conditions Hanoi had to meet to get a halt to the American bombing of North Vietnam.

Kissinger convinced Secretary of State Rusk that the two Frenchmen should be used as intermediaries. So Marcovich and Aubrac went off to Hanoi, where on July 24 they met with Ho Chi Minh and Prime Minister Pham Van Dong. The North Vietnamese repeated their long-standing position: if the U.S. stopped the bombing "unconditionally," negotiations could follow.

After Kissinger relayed this information to Washington, a carefully crafted message was prepared in President Johnson's name for Marcovich and Aubrac to convey to Hanoi. The U.S. would stop bombing, the message said, "if this will lead promptly to productive discussions" and if North Vietnam "would not take advantage" of the halt by increasing the flow of troops to the South. This was the first time the U.S. had offered to stop the bombing without insisting that negotiations be formally agreed to beforehand.

As Marcovich and Aubrac waited in Paris for a North Vietnamese response, Kissinger shuttled between Paris, Washington, and his teaching duties at Harvard. "I was on a quick trip to Europe for Governor Harriman," Kissinger wrote to his parents. "Since then I have been commuting to Washington often three times a week. In the meantime, Rockefeller has increased his requests and next week-end I shall go to Detroit to see Romney. [Governor George Romney was planning a run for the Republican presidential nomination.] The International Seminar is going very well; we have had Charles Percy and Henry Cabot Lodge."

Finally, on September 10, the North Vietnamese representative in Paris called Marcovich with the news that his government had rejected the offer; the American bombing had to be "ceased definitely and without conditions" before there could even be discussions of negotiations. Kissinger responded with a flurry of messages to the North Vietnamese representative in Paris insisting that the U.S. was not demanding specific conditions before it would halt the bombing, only an indication that "productive" talks would then be forthcoming. But he was unable to budge Hanoi.

By early October, the two sides seemed stuck on a semantic point: whether the U.S. "assumption" that talks would begin soon after a bombing halt constituted a "condition" for such a halt. Kissinger kept refining the wording of his notes, sent to Marcovich from Cambridge, in an effort to express this "assumption" in such a way that it did not sound like a precondition.[32]

Here was an example of what would become a pattern in Kissinger's diplomacy: his attempt to mediate a dispute by finding a semantic formulation to finesse differences. In this case it was devising a phrase that linked the bombing halt to the negotiations without sounding like a condition. Later, at the end of the war, he would search for ambiguous phrases about the demilitarized zone and South Vietnamese sovereignty that could be read differently in Hanoi and Saigon. Sometimes these word games paid off. But usually they opened Kissinger up to accusations that he had left important disagreements unresolved by talking out of both sides of his mouth.

One weekend in mid-October, Kissinger went up to the Vermont farmhouse of his Harvard colleague Paul Doty, where the White House switchboard tracked him down. It was Lyndon Johnson, and Kissinger signaled to Doty that he could listen in on an extension. The president grumbled that he had grave doubts about the Pennsylvania negotiations. Kissinger urged yet another reformulated version of the U.S. position. Johnson reluctantly agreed. "I'm going to give it one more try," he growled to Kissinger, "and if it doesn't work, I'm going to come up to Cambridge and cut off your balls." Kissinger found Johnson's gruff manner somewhat unnerving, but not nearly so much as his tendency to call him "Professor Schlesinger" now and then.[33]

Before returning to Paris with the new plan, Kissinger went down to the White House for a Wednesday-night meeting with President Johnson and Dean Rusk. Joining them for the rambling two-hour discussion were Walt Rostow, Robert McNamara, Nicholas Katzenbach, Abe Fortas, and Clark Clifford.

Rusk expressed skepticism; the North Vietnamese, he said, were showing no flexibility. But Kissinger argued that there were signs that they were "eager to keep this going." He suggested that, if Washington was willing to "have a bombing pause, it would be desirable to do this through this channel."

Johnson was not impressed. "I know if they were bombing Washington, hitting my bridges and railroads and highways, I would be delighted to try out discussions through an intermediary for a restriction on the bombing. It hasn't cost him [Ho Chi Minh] one bit. The net of it is that he has a sanctuary in Hanoi in return for having his consul talk with two scientists who talked with an American citizen."

Katzenbach disagreed and argued for a bombing pause to give the talks a chance. McNamara, by now turning dovish, was even more in favor of halting the bombing, which he considered ineffective anyway. "I believe I can show beyond a shadow of a doubt that bombing Hanoi and Haiphong will not affect resupply in the South one bit," the defense secretary said. "My evaluation is that if the bombing were to cease, talks would start quickly," Bundy agreed.

But Clark Clifford, who would soon become defense secretary, took a hawkish line: the Kissinger channel showed no progress, it should be closed down, and "a bombing pause makes the possibility of peace much more remote." It was nine-thirty P.M. when the president finally brought the meeting to a close by saying he was not ready to make a new gesture. "I see a failure on their part to indicate any desire to talk," Johnson concluded. Kissinger should convey this to Marcovich and Aubrac.[34]

Although the Pennsylvania channel collapsed, the new formula for a bombing halt became the official U.S. position. A few weeks later, the communists began their most spectacular offensive of the war, which culminated with the Tet holiday of early 1968. The Tet offensive would shock many Americans into opposing the war and precipitate Johnson's withdrawal from the presidential race. Not until the offensive was over would discussion of a bombing halt resume. Because he had earned the trust of the Johnson administration's top negotiators in Paris, Kissinger would be able to keep himself well informed on the progress of these talks—a situation that would prove helpful in establishing his relationship with Richard Nixon.

In June 1968, Kissinger participated in an academic panel on Vietnam with a dovish cast: Hans Morgenthau, Arthur Schlesinger, Stanley Hoffmann, and Daniel Ellsberg. In the wake of Tet, Kissinger was downbeat. He still saw the North Vietnamese as puppets of China, though they were in fact aligned with the Soviet Union. But his main point was that the territorial stakes were not all that high. "The acquisition of Vietnam by Peking would be infinitely less significant in terms of the balance of power than the acquisition of nuclear weapons by Peking," he said.

Kissinger had come to the conclusion that the best the U.S. could get was what became known as a "decent interval." Washington should seek to negotiate an honorable end to its military involvement in Vietnam, he told the panel, and hope that the political issue of who would rule South Vietnam could be deferred until later when America's credibility was no longer on the line.[35]

ROCKY IN '68

Having alienated the party's right wing by his 1964 challenge to Goldwater, Nelson Rockefeller decided to sit out the 1968 race and back George Romney over Richard Nixon for the Republican nomination. He even offered Kissinger's services to the Michigan governor. But the Romney campaign was a disaster, capped by the candidate's confession that he had been "brainwashed" about Vietnam, and he dropped out before the primaries began.

So in March, all eyes turned back to Rockefeller. After listening to Republican leaders around the nation urge him to run, and gathering their commitments to support him, Rockefeller called a major news conference in the grand ballroom of the New York Hilton and —surprising everyone—said he wanted to "reiterate unequivocally that I am not a candidate."

The next day he began to reconsider again.

That was the situation confronting the New York governor's dozen or so closest advisers as they gathered in April for a secret meeting in his Manhattan office on West Fifty-fifth Street. Joseph Persico, a speechwriter, remembered it as a typical gathering of egos, each attempting to assert dominance as they waited for Rockefeller to arrive.

Someone asked Kissinger how much time he would be able to provide if Rockefeller decided to jump into the race. "Not as much as Nelson will want," Kissinger replied.

If that was the case, Persico suggested, perhaps Zbigniew Brzezinski, then at Columbia, should be brought in as a consultant.

"Not at all the required depth," Kissinger shot back. Persico got the impression that Kissinger quickly decided he would be able to make more time available for the campaign.[36]

After the April meeting, Rockefeller finally decided to jump into the 1968 race. But his stutter-stepping during the previous months had made it virtually impossible for him to overtake Nixon.

As Rockefeller was making his decision, the *New York Times* ran an article describing his staff. It noted that Oscar Ruebhausen, a New

York lawyer who had been one of Rockefeller's college roommates, was to be director of research, with Kissinger and a domestic adviser both reporting to him. "I am sure you will understand, Oscar," Kissinger intoned on the phone, "that someone of my stature cannot report through a staffer. I will report directly to Nelson." Ruebhausen did not fight the issue, but he bridled as Kissinger refused to coordinate even his hiring decisions.

"Henry always had feuds with people who were his equals," remembers Ruebhausen. "He was always very deferential to those in power, but he viewed his equals as threats."

Kissinger developed a reputation for being both brilliant and difficult. Once, when he had sent down a foreign policy speech from Harvard and Rockefeller's writers began disentangling its Germanic phrasing, Kissinger got on the phone with Rocky's aide Hugh Morrow and grumbled: "When Nelson buys a Picasso, he doesn't hire four housepainters to improve it." From then on, the speechwriting staff called themselves the housepainters.[37]

One of the struggles in the campaign was between Kissinger and chief speechwriter Emmett John Hughes on Vietnam. Hughes was a dove, constantly tugging Rockefeller toward advocating withdrawal. Kissinger would rebut Hughes by insisting that the U.S. commitment could not be abandoned.

The Vietnam War had by then become so polarizing that politicians were pressed to come out either "for" it or "against" it. But Rockefeller's position remained fuzzy, as the press repeatedly pointed out. He kicked off his campaign on May 1 with an important speech on the subject before the Philadelphia World Affairs Council.

The voice was Rockefeller, but the ideas were those of Kissinger, who had been the principal author. There were "no military solutions" to the Vietnam War, the speech said. The U.S. effort had been based on the false premise that control of territory was the important factor. As a result the war had been "Americanized." The goal should be to create secure local governments and turn the war back to the South Vietnamese.

Another topic in the speech was just as important but was generally overlooked: a call for a new policy toward communist China. Richard Nixon would later claim credit, with some justification, for conceiving the China breakthrough. But Kissinger was also exploring the idea even before he joined Nixon's staff, and he was casting it as part of a new balance-of-power framework that Nixon was slower to grasp.

Nothing was to be gained by "aiding or encouraging the self-isolation of so great a people," Kissinger's speech for Rockefeller read.

"In a subtle triangle with communist China and the Soviet Union, we can ultimately improve our relations with each—as we test the will for peace of both." This was precisely the philosophy behind the triangular diplomacy that Kissinger would inaugurate three years later when he surprised the world by showing up in Beijing.[38]

After much debate between Hughes and Kissinger, Rockefeller laid out a new Vietnam position in a speech on July 13. The proposal was for a phased withdrawal designed to end the war within six months. Joseph Persico was given the task of turning Kissinger's draft into a speech. In doing so, he slipped in a few dovish lines of his own, such as: "I pledge that we will not again find ourselves with a commitment looking for a justification." As he was sitting at his desk, he suddenly heard a grumbling voice demand, "Who rewrote my speech?" Kissinger stared at Persico and then smiled. "Good job. I can't remember what you took out," he said, then strode away. "It was a Kissinger miniperformance," Persico later noted, "calculated for effect."[39]

Despite his privileged background, Nelson Rockefeller displayed an understanding and affection for the messy glories of American democracy. Not Kissinger. Throughout his career, he was wary of popular passions and contemptuous of political meddling in foreign policy. Although he reveled in the camaraderie of Rockefeller's lavishly catered campaign plane, he never quite learned to love the hurly-burly of politics.

By the time they got to the Miami Beach convention, Rockefeller's staffers were so sick of Kissinger that they put him—partly as a provocation—on a different floor of the Fontainebleau Hotel from Rockefeller and his top staff. Kissinger was furious. His dignity affronted, he insisted on being moved as close to the candidate as possible. (He finally was.) "Henry's at it again" became a standard half-joking lament of the Rockefeller entourage. "Nelson would just shrug his shoulders, sigh, and refused to be bothered" when such tantrums would occur, Ruebhausen recalled.

At the convention, the Rockefeller forces, with little to lose, sent Kissinger to talk to the Iowa delegation. "It was so novel to me," he told a reporter at the time. "I'd never met working politicians before. I didn't attempt to talk their language. I just talked what I knew." The Iowa delegation voted overwhelmingly for Nixon.

Kissinger's main work at the convention was fashioning a compromise plank in the party platform on Vietnam. The original one had been drafted by Senator Everett Dirksen, a hawk. Rockefeller had slowly shifted toward a more dovish stance. Though he did not have enough votes to win the nomination, he had the power to affect the platform.

Kissinger began drafting new language using Nixon's campaign rhetoric to make Rockefeller's points about the need for a negotiated settlement—thus assuring the approval of both camps. Some of Rockefeller's men were suspicious that Kissinger was, as Ruebhausen later put it, "trying to worm his way in" and ingratiate himself with the Nixon people.[40]

At one point he met Nixon's thirty-two-year-old foreign policy adviser, Richard Allen, in the hotel to exchange notes. After talking for a few moments in the lobby, Kissinger went upstairs to get some wording cleared by Rockefeller. While awaiting Kissinger's return, Allen saw the columnist Robert Novak across the lobby. When Kissinger got off the elevator, Allen made a grand charade of bellowing Kissinger's name as if he had stumbled across an old friend, then steered him out of the hotel and behind some trees before they exchanged papers. It was done to keep reporters from thinking that any deals were being concocted, but Allen's odd behavior baffled Kissinger. He began to regard the boyish, ebullient conservative as a bit of a kook.[41]

Kissinger had been one of the most fervent Rockefeller partisans on the staff, with none of the detachment that often distinguishes an academic. He would rail against Nixon's "shallowness," his "dangerous misunderstanding" of foreign policy. "No one shared my contempt for Richard Nixon more than Henry," Ruebhausen recalled. "He thought Nixon was a hollow man, and evil." Kissinger helped keep the "black book" of clippings on Nixon, which the campaign used to guide attacks. Among its chapter headings were "The Tricky Dick Syndrome" and "The Loser Image."

When Nixon finally won the nomination, Kissinger did not disguise his despair. Casper Citron, the New York radio host, conducted a long interview with him the day after the convention roll call. "I'm not a Republican," a clearly distressed Kissinger said. "I consider myself an independent. My view was very deeply that Rockefeller was the only candidate at this time who could unite the country." He added that he had "grave doubts" about Nixon.

Henry Brandon, a columnist with the London *Sunday Times,* telephoned that week to bemoan Nixon's shortcomings. "Kissinger not only confirmed all my fears and misgivings," Brandon recalled, "but reinforced them in no uncertain terms." Talking to Emmett Hughes, Kissinger said of Nixon: "The man is, of course, a disaster. Now the Republican Party is a disaster. Fortunately, he can't be elected—or the whole country would be a disaster." And he told many friends just after the convention, "That man is unfit to be president."

Yet something about a change of administrations seemed tantalizing. Kissinger had tentatively accepted a visiting position at All Souls College, Oxford; after keeping the option open as long as possible, he finally informed the college at the end of the summer that he would be staying in the U.S. instead. Depending on how things worked out, he added, he might be willing to come the following year.[42]

Louis Kissinger and Paula Stern, engagement photograph, 1922. He was a thirty-five-year-old schoolteacher, intellectual and shy; she was twenty-one, the spunky and quick-witted only child of a prosperous cattle dealer. "My father was lucky he had an earthy wife who made all the decisions," their son would later recall.

The Stern family's home in Leutershausen. Until the Nazis came to power, the Sterns considered themselves assimilated members of the German middle class. For Heinz, his grandparents' home was a magical place where he spent summers playing soccer and going on hikes with other children in the village.

TWO PHOTOS:
COURTESY OF PAULA KISSINGER

Heinz Kissinger, later known as Henry, with his father, Louis, 1923. He was a kind and very religious man, and his son grew to revere him. But he could also be emotionally distant. "He couldn't understand children having problems," Henry Kissinger would later say, "nor could he understand the type of problems a ten-year-old would have."

Paula Kissinger with Heinz (right) and his younger brother, Walter, Fürth, Germany, 1927. Hidden behind her smile and unaffected grace was a toughness when it came to protecting her family. She was the hero of their saga; without her strength and keen instincts, they might never have survived.

Heinz Kissinger, eight, in Fürth, 1931. A dutiful and bookish boy, he went to synagogue every morning to study the Torah. His passion was soccer; after Jews were banned from public matches, he would often sneak into the stadium and risk beatings from Nazi youth gangs.

Henry Kissinger, sixteen, at George Washington High School, New York City, 1939. He was the quickest of his immigrant friends to adapt to a new environment, explore Manhattan, and discover the magic of baseball. A small epiphany occurred when he realized he could walk the streets without scurrying away when approached by groups of non-Jewish kids.

Kissinger, Ann Fleischer, Walter Oppenheim, 1943. The two boys had been friends in Fürth and remained so after immigrating to New York. Both dated Ann, a refugee from Nuremberg. Walter was more social and handsome, but Henry won her heart. In 1949, they would marry in an Orthodox Jewish ceremony at his parents' apartment.

With Fritz Kraemer, Germany, 1945. A flamboyant Prussian immigrant, Kraemer plucked Private Kissinger from an infantry division, became his mentor, and made him a counter-intelligence officer. "My role was not discovering Kissinger!" Kraemer would later bellow. "My role was getting Kissinger to discover himself!"

Louis and Henry Kissinger, Harvard doctoral degree ceremony, 1954. Other students felt that nineteenth-century diplomacy had little relevance for the atomic age, but Kissinger immersed himself in the realpolitik of Metternich, Castlereagh, and Bismarck.

With Eleanor Roosevelt, circa 1959. As a graduate student and then junior professor at Harvard, Kissinger ran a summer program and edited a journal called *Confluence*. From the start, he was intent on meeting, knowing, and impressing the right people.

Kissinger with his children, David and Elizabeth, Cambridge, Massachusetts, 1965. His wife, Ann, did not share his social and intellectual ambitions, and they drifted apart. But even after their 1964 divorce, they remained friends, and Kissinger continued to dote on their children.

John Mitchell, Kissinger, Melvin Laird, Richard Nixon, and William Rogers aboard Air Force One, 1969. Kissinger became national security adviser after feeding information to Nixon's 1968 campaign. In the subsequent turf battles, he tangled with Defense Secretary Laird, who was a wily match, and Secretary of State Rogers, who proved a pushover.

With Alexander Haig and Lawrence Eagleburger, 1969. By enduring Kissinger's tantrums and overseeing secret projects such as the Cambodian bombings and the wiretaps, Colonel Haig became the top deputy and eventually earned four stars; but behind Kissinger's back, he forged his own ties to Nixon. Eagleburger suffered a breakdown and left the staff, but returned when Kissinger became secretary of state.

In the Executive Office Building hideaway, 1971. Nixon liked to ramble around a topic for hours, making contradictory decisions, engaging in Walter Mitty fantasies, and plotting conspiratorial intrigues. Kissinger would often humor him and cater to his prejudices. But sometimes their seminars led to brilliant and bold initiatives.

With William Rogers, John Ehrlichman, Charles Colson, and H. R. Haldeman, 1971. Haldeman and Ehrlichman served on an informal "Henry-Handling Committee" to deal with his fits of paranoia about Rogers. In response to Kissinger's rage about the leak of the Pentagon Papers, Colson formed the Plumber's Unit, which led the way to Watergate.

NATIONAL ARCHIVES, NIXON PROJECT

On the Great Wall of China, October 1971. Kissinger was there to prepare for the president's historic visit, and he had been ordered to avoid publicity so as not to steal Nixon's thunder. So when this picture appeared around the world, the president was furious. Equally so was United Nations Ambassador George Bush, who that week was fighting (unsuccessfully) to preserve Taiwan's seat.

TWO PHOTOS: AP/WIDE WORLD

Toasting Zhou Enlai at the February 1972 summit. "He was equally at home in philosophic sweeps, historical analysis, tactical probing, light repartee," Kissinger wrote of Zhou in his report to Nixon. Kissinger was mesmerized; these were qualities that he not only appreciated but shared.

In Mao Zedong's cozy and messy study. Kissinger excluded Secretary of State Rogers from the first meeting betwen Mao and Nixon, an action that Kissinger later conceded was "fundamentally unworthy."

With Robert Evans and Ali McGraw at the premiere of *The Godfather*, March 1972. Amid the crisis surrounding the mining of Haiphong harbor, the Paramount studio boss, who was Kissinger's most eager pal in Hollywood, insisted that he come to New York for the opening.

With Pat Nixon at the Moscow Summit, May 1972. She grew to distrust Kissinger for seeking acclaim at the expense of her husband. He liked to tell of her response when, early in the first term, he told her how brilliant her husband was. "You haven't seen through him yet?" she replied.

At his parents' fiftieth wedding anniversary, Switzerland, 1972. From left: Jeanne and Walter Kissinger and their daughter; Louis and Paula Kissinger; Henry; Erica and Arno Kissinger (Louis's brother). At least thirteen relatives had been killed in the holocaust.

With Jan Golding Cushing, Paris 1972. By that fall, his Vietnam peace talks were no longer secret, and he enjoyed playing games with the press and burnishing his image as a "swinger." After lunch with Cushing in a bistro, the maître d' offered to slip them out the back. But Kissinger went out the front and walked her up and down the block for the cameras.

With Le Duc Tho near Paris, 1972. Kissinger had an easier time negotiating a peace plan with the North Vietnamese than he did selling it to the South Vietnamese. Later their achievement would earn them the most controversial Nobel Peace Prize.

On the way to Paris to initial the Vietnam peace accords, with Winston Lord, John Negroponte, and Peter Rodman, January 1973. The agreement allowed North Vietnamese troops to remain in the South; just over two years later, they took over.

TWO PHOTOS: NATIONAL ARCHIVES, NIXON PROJECT

With translator Viktor Sukhodrev, Leonid Brezhnev, and a game warden, Zavidovo, May 1973. On the wildly mistaken notion that Kissinger would like to shoot wild boar, Brezhnev brought him to a hunting preserve near Moscow. When he and Kissinger were alone in a tower at the preserve, the Soviet leader tried to forge a tacit alliance with the United States against China.

Introducing Jill St. John to Brezhnev in San Clemente, as a naval aide looks on admiringly, June 1973. His father worried that St. John did not sound like a Jewish name. Kissinger assured him, correctly, that her real name was Jill Oppenheim. The relationship, largely conducted on the phone and at public functions, never became a romance.

TWO PHOTOS: AP/WIDE WORLD

Swearing in as secretary of state, with his mother and Chief Justice Warren Burger, September 1973. Nixon later admitted he did not want to appoint Kissinger, and he showed it at the ceremony; his remarks "ranged from the perfunctory to the bizarre," Kissinger recalled, and the president did not stay for the reception.

On his first visit with Anwar Sadat, November 1973. Kissinger had viewed the Egyptian president as a clown until that meeting, at which Sadat took the bold step of approving disengagement talks. Sadat loved to flatter people and had a limitless capacity to be flattered in return; so did Kissinger, which made them a happy match.

With Golda Meir, February 1974. Obstinately committed to the safety of her country, she spent much of their time together lecturing Kissinger, a habit that led him to refer to her as "that preposterous woman." Yet they understood each other as well as a Jewish mother and son, and their bond ran deeper than any of their disagreements.

On his honeymoon with Nancy Maginnes Kissinger, Acapulco, April 1974. She was from a Social Register family and had the cachet that came from being an aide to Nelson Rockefeller. The ceremony was performed by a surprised family court judge in suburban Virginia.

Traveling with his son, David. Even after he remarried, his children spent the summer with him, and he liked to take them on his trips to exotic capitals.

Briefing Gerald Ford on the train to Vladivostok, November 1974. The new president's strength lay in his simplicity, solidness, and feel for American values. He was a man at ease with himself and his fundamental faith in the democratic system—qualities that Nixon and Kissinger, for all of their intellectual brilliance, did not share.

Returning from spending New Year's in Puerto Rico with Rockefeller and their wives, January 1975. Rockefeller gave Kissinger a $50,000 gift when he joined Nixon's White House. "He has a second-rate mind but a first-rate intuition about people," Kissinger said immodestly of his patron. "I have a first-rate mind but a third-rate intuition about people."

With Defense Secretary James Schlesinger, May 1975. The Harvard classmates became intellectual rivals and opponents on arms control issues. Schlesinger's abrasive style and imperious attitude finally provoked Ford to fire him.

With Elizabeth Taylor at Malcolm Forbes's birthday party, Morocco, August 1989. He enjoyed a glittering twilight as the star of a jet-set social world that included Manhattan's high-fashion crowd, Hollywood celebrities, and top media luminaries.

With Maurice "Hank" Greenberg, chairman of the insurance underwriters American International Group. Greenberg was a typical client: he valued Kissinger's advice, liked to travel with him, and became a friend. They went to China after the 1989 Tiananmen Square massacre and dined with Deng Xiaoping in the Great Hall of the People.

With Mikhail Gorbachev and Bush, 1990. Kissinger proposed a plan, later derisively dubbed "Yalta II," to encourage Moscow to loosen its grip on Eastern Europe. Then and afterward, he underestimated the radical change that was occurring.

With Bush and Secretary of State James Baker. In the early 1970s, Kissinger alienated Bush when he was U.N. ambassador and envoy to Beijing, and he crossed swords with Baker when he was Ford's campaign manager. In the 1990s, he discovered that the resentments he created while in power could come back to haunt him.

EIGHT

THE CO-CONSPIRATORS

Kissinger and Nixon, 1968

> *The new order was tailored to a genius who proposed to restrain the contending forces, both domestic and foreign, by manipulating their antagonisms.* —KISSINGER *on Bismarck, "The White Revolutionary," 1968*

HEDGING HIS BETS

Shortly after the 1968 Republican convention, Richard Allen called Kissinger and invited him to serve on Nixon's foreign policy advisory board. Kissinger hesitated for a few days, then declined. He would prefer to provide advice privately, he confided, rather than publicly. "I can help you more if I work behind the scenes," he said.

Kissinger did help Nixon behind the scenes in his race against Hubert Humphrey, although the nature of that help would later become a matter of dispute. The Paris peace talks were entering a crucial phase, which reached a climax on October 31 when Lyndon Johnson announced a halt to the bombing of North Vietnam just six days before the election. Kissinger passed along warnings to the Nixon campaign about the possibility of such a bombing halt. He also implied that he was privy to inside information about the negotiations, which was in keeping with the conspiratorial streak in his character. The question is whether he actually had secret knowledge about the Paris talks that he improperly provided to the Nixon camp.

That charge is most forcefully made in Seymour Hersh's *The Price of Power,* which relies heavily on accusations made by Richard Allen. The story that Allen told Hersh, and later expanded on in interviews for this book, was that he was working in his office at Nixon's national headquarters in Manhattan one morning in early September when he got an unsolicited call from Kissinger. Would the campaign be interested, Kissinger allegedly asked, if he could supply inside information on the Paris peace talks? He had friends on the delegation, he explained, and would be traveling there in a few days.

Allen eagerly accepted and told John Mitchell and H. R. ("Bob") Haldeman—Nixon's campaign chairman and staff chief—about the apparent intelligence coup. "I became a handmaiden of Henry Kissinger's drive for power," Allen later lamented.

Allen claimed that he subsequently received at least four calls, initiated by Kissinger from pay telephones to preserve secrecy. During one conversation, they even lapsed into German for a few moments, adding to the conspiratorial air. Allen briefed Nixon personally, at his Fifth Avenue apartment, on the Kissinger contact and reported each call in writing to Nixon and John Mitchell. These memos, like others of a sensitive nature, were addressed not to Nixon but to "D.C." in order to preserve deniability. The initials stood for District of Columbia, but outsiders would likely think they referred to Nixon's appointments secretary, Dwight Chapin. Allen stressed to Mitchell the importance of keeping Kissinger's involvement absolutely confidential.[1]

Allen's version corresponds to what Nixon revealed in his own memoirs. In early September, he wrote, "a highly unusual channel" was opened when he got a report, relayed through Mitchell, that Kissinger had offered assistance. "I told Haldeman that Mitchell should continue as liaison with Kissinger and that we should honor his desire to keep his role completely confidential," Nixon wrote. Kissinger "was completely circumspect," Nixon said, and he did not reveal any classified details of the Paris talks. But he did provide warning when he thought movement was about to occur, and this prompted Nixon to moderate what he was saying about the war in his speeches.[2]

When the Hersh book came out, Kissinger denounced it as "slimy lies." But he did not deny that he provided advice to the Nixon campaign. In a minimal reference to the matter in his own memoirs, he wrote: "Several Nixon emissaries—some self-appointed—telephoned me for counsel. I took the position that I would answer specific questions on foreign policy, but that I would not offer general advice or volunteer suggestions. This was the same response I made to inquiries from the Humphrey staff."[3]

Where does the truth in fact lie?

As Allen has charged, the process began in early September when Kissinger called and offered to provide insights into the progress in Paris. A few days later, on September 17, he arrived in France aboard the *Île de France*. Among the other passengers was the mother of Daniel Davidson, a young lawyer on Averell Harriman's Paris negotiating team who had become friendly with Kissinger during his "Pennsylvania" negotiations of 1967. Davidson had sent word that when he came to Le Havre to pick up his mother, he would be happy to pick up Kissinger as well; but Kissinger used the ship-to-shore phone to say that he had enough experience with Jewish mothers to know that it would be better if he left the Davidsons to drive on their own and took the train.

At the time Davidson was an ardent admirer. "I was charmed and enchanted by Henry," he later recalled. "He had an intelligence, a sense of humor, and a conspiratorial manner that swept you into his camp." In Paris, the two of them had dinner at one of Davidson's favorite restaurants, La Coupole, where they discussed the progress being made at the talks. The proposals that would lead to the bombing halt had not yet been made, and Davidson had no inside information about possible negotiating breakthroughs. But he freely shared his insights about how things were going.

Davidson got the strong impression that Kissinger disdained Nixon. "Six days a week I'm for Hubert," he told Davidson, "but on the seventh day, I think they're both awful." But no matter which man was elected, Kissinger confided that he thought he would be offered a top job, most likely as head of policy planning at the State Department or international security affairs at the Pentagon. If so, he wanted Davidson to work with him. Davidson agreed.

During his two days in Paris, Kissinger also spent time with Richard Holbrooke, another young aide to Harriman. "Henry was the only person outside of the government we were authorized to discuss the negotiations with," Holbrooke recalled. "We trusted him. It is not stretching the truth to say that the Nixon campaign had a secret source within the U.S. negotiating team."

Harriman had just returned from Washington, where ways to break the impasse in Paris had been discussed. But in mid-September there were no negotiations yet about any specific elements of a bombing-halt deal, and thus no secrets for Kissinger to spill, according to William Bundy, who was then assistant secretary of state for Asia and has researched the issue for a book. All Kissinger took away from Paris was a general sense that the American side was eager to get a bombing halt before the November elections.[4]

When Kissinger returned from Paris, he called Mitchell to warn "that something big was afoot." As a result, Nixon decided to shift strategy and put the heat on Humphrey for "playing politics with the war." A few days later, Haldeman sent Nixon a memo with more information from Kissinger, as relayed through Mitchell. "Our source feels that there is better than even chance that Johnson will order a bombing halt at mid-October."

On October 9, a break occurred in Paris: for the first time, Hanoi showed a willingness to make concessions in order to get a bombing halt. The communists' new attitude was flashed to Washington, and two days later it became public that the talks had taken a turn for the better.

Kissinger was by then back in Cambridge, where he received an important phone call from Davidson. During the transatlantic conversation, Kissinger realized that a breakthrough was imminent. He talked to both Allen and Mitchell, who sent a memo to Nixon reporting Kissinger's assessment that there was "more to this than meets the eye." Just before Johnson announced the bombing halt, Kissinger called Allen with a few hours' worth of early warning. "I've got some important information," he told Allen. The American delegation in Paris had "broken open the champagne."

These were, to be sure, hardly explosive revelations. Nixon himself called Kissinger's reports "uncomfortably vague" and became suspicious of his intentions. But Nixon soon overcame his doubts about Kissinger's true disloyalties. "One factor that had most convinced me of Kissinger's credibility was the length to which he went to protect his secrecy," Nixon later wrote, showing his appreciation for the finer points of duplicity.

Nixon, it turned out, had even better sources for what was happening in the Vietnam negotiations, ones that Kissinger knew nothing about. Nixon's aide Bryce Harlow had a close friend in the White House who was passing along information. Nixon was also dealing with Saigon's ambassador Bui Diem and, through Anna Chenault, passing hints to President Nguyen Van Thieu not to rush into a deal.

What Kissinger provided was not serious spying; rather, it was a willingness to pass along tales and tidbits. In doing so, he revealed less about the negotiations than he did about his own personality, his propensity to curry favor by sharing secrets. Years later, in January of 1972 when they were preparing for another campaign, Nixon and Haldeman worried about whether Kissinger would divulge their important secrets if he quit the administration. According to Haldeman's notes, Nixon said: "Remember, he came to us in '68 with tales."[5]

Meanwhile, Kissinger was also giving Humphrey's people the

impression that he wanted to play on their side of the street. Back when Kissinger was working for Rockefeller, Ted Van Dyk, a Democratic political operative, visited. "They showed off their voluminous files on Nixon," he recalled. "I was impressed." The files in question included thousands of Nixon newspaper clippings and speech texts compiled and indexed with the care that only a Rockefeller research staff could afford.

Late that summer, Kissinger was spending a week with his children on Martha's Vineyard, where Professor Samuel Huntington, a Harvard colleague, also had a house. Sitting on the West Tisbury beach, Kissinger offered the Rockefeller camp's Nixon files to Huntington, who was a foreign policy adviser to Humphrey. "It was a wonderful offer," Professor Huntington later said, "because we had no resources to compare to that."

Van Dyk and Huntington both tried to get Kissinger to make good on the offer, and they enlisted Zbigniew Brzezinski in the effort. "Look, I've hated Nixon for years," Kissinger told Brzezinski. But he always found an excuse for why he could not get the files at that moment. The Humphrey camp eventually realized that he was not going to come through.

Van Dyk also claims that he saw a letter Kissinger sent to Humphrey during the last days of the campaign, when the race was tightening, professing admiration and offering to help if he was elected. Kissinger was most heated in denying this charge. "It is a goddamn lie," he said. In fact, no letter has ever turned up, and it is not in the Humphrey archives. Nor does anyone else remember seeing it.

In a subtle dig that only a few people caught, Brzezinski took a swipe at Kissinger when they were both at a Senate-caucus-room ceremony honoring Humphrey, then dying of cancer, in 1977. "The greatest opportunity in my life was to serve in your 1968 campaign," Brzezinski said to Humphrey. Then, indicating Kissinger in the audience, he added: "And I want to publicly thank Dr. Kissinger for the assistance he offered during that campaign."

Humphrey remained an admirer, and he later said that he would have made Kissinger national security adviser. "If I had been elected, I would have had Kissinger be my assistant," the senator said in 1973. "That fellow is indestructible—a professional, able, and rather unflappable. I like the fact that he has a little fun, too." The voluble senator may have been the only person ever to describe Kissinger as rather unflappable.[6]

Kissinger later admitted that he was ambivalent during the 1968 election and could have given both sides the impression he was with them. "I cannot deny that I said most of the bad things about Nixon attributed to me at the time of his nomination," he said. "But in the end I was reluctantly for Nixon, and I voted for him."[7]

Soon after Nixon won, Gloria Steinem wrote a piece for *New York* magazine warning that "the New Nixon is the same person as the old Nixon." Somewhat to her surprise, she got a phone call from Kissinger praising the article. They began discussing the people trooping to the Pierre Hotel to be considered for jobs in the new administration. Kissinger said that the only way he would go to Washington would be if Rockefeller got a top job and asked him along.

He told Steinem, however, that he was interested in the theoretical question of whether one should work for Nixon if asked. Was it better to try to make things less bad by working from the inside? Steinem convinced him to write a piece for *New York* magazine to be titled "The Collaboration Problem." He had addressed the dilemma in his doctoral dissertation. "To co-operate without losing one's soul, to assist without sacrificing one's identity," he wrote of Metternich's collaboration with Napoleon, "what harder test of moral toughness exists?"

Kissinger would eventually find out that the part about not sacrificing one's identity was a lot easier than the part about not losing one's soul. But he would not, as it turned out, end up exploring the question abstractly for *New York* magazine. A few days later, Steinem got another call from Kissinger. "Guess what?" he said.[8]

THE JOB OFFER

Throughout his dealings and double-dealings on behalf of Richard Nixon's 1968 campaign, Kissinger never spoke to him directly. In fact, by the time Nixon was elected, Kissinger had met him only once, in 1967 at a Christmas cocktail party given by Clare Boothe Luce in her Fifth Avenue apartment.

Recently widowed from Time-Life tycoon Henry Luce, she had been a playwright, Connecticut congresswoman, ambassador to Italy, and high-octane power broker. "I knew that if Henry spent an hour talking with Nixon," she recalled, "the two men would get along famously."

Kissinger arrived early, fidgeted about, and was preparing to leave when Nixon showed up. Luce promptly spirited them into her library. The meeting was stiff, the pleasantries strained. Kissinger had not yet overcome his awkwardness with small talk, and Nixon never would. Their five minutes together was mainly consumed by Nixon's praise for Kissinger's book *Nuclear Weapons and Foreign Policy;* Kissinger later said he found Nixon "more thoughtful" than he had expected.[9]

It was Kissinger's willingness to provide back-channel insights about the Paris peace talks that first caused Nixon to pay much heed to him. "During the last days of the campaign, when Kissinger was providing us with information about the bombing halt, I became more aware of his knowledge and his influence," Nixon noted.

On a campaign swing, Nixon confided to Joseph Kraft that he was considering making Kissinger his national security adviser. The columnist proceeded to pass this along to Kissinger, who "became a totally scared rabbit," Kraft recalled. "Please don't mention this to anybody else," he begged Kraft. Several times that day he called the columnist—from the airports in Washington, New York, and Boston, then from his house in Cambridge. "Please don't mention it," Kissinger begged repeatedly. "Keep it a secret."[10]

Among those pushing Kissinger's selection most strongly was Henry Cabot Lodge, who had been Nixon's running mate in 1960 and then served as ambassador to Saigon. Lodge had known Kissinger at Harvard and was impressed by his intellect and grasp of global strategy. Right after the election, Lodge met with Nixon to push Kissinger for the national security post. When he did, he found that Nixon was already thinking along these lines.

As fate would have it, Kissinger was having lunch with Nelson Rockefeller in his Manhattan hideaway apartment on West Fifty-fourth Street when the call came from Nixon's transition headquarters at the Pierre Hotel a few blocks up Fifth Avenue. It was Friday, November 22, and Rockefeller had gathered his closest advisers to discuss what cabinet job he might accept if offered. Beneath the Toulouse-Lautrec paintings that covered the curved, crimson walls, some of his advisers were urging that he remain as governor no matter what was offered; Kissinger, on the other hand, was eager to go to Washington as a Rockefeller assistant, and he was arguing that Rockefeller should take a cabinet post, preferably defense secretary.

But when Nixon's appointments secretary, Dwight Chapin, phoned from the Pierre, it was Kissinger who was summoned from the table and invited to come see the president-elect on Monday. The Rockefeller discussion then resumed "as if nothing had happened," Kissinger recalled. "No one at the lunch could conceive that the purpose of the call could be to offer me a major position in the new administration."[11]

At their meeting on the morning of November 25, Kissinger was struck by Nixon's nervousness, which was poorly concealed by his feigned jauntiness. "His movements were slightly vague, and unrelated to what he was saying, as if two different impulses were behind speech and gesture," Kissinger later wrote. The president-elect's words, however, were tinged with a dark conspiratorial tone and weighted, it would turn out, with enormous implications.

He was determined, Nixon said, to run foreign policy from the White House. The State Department would be shunted aside and its foreign service officers treated with contempt, the way they had treated him as vice president. President Eisenhower had only been given options that "they" had approved, and even under John Foster Dulles it had remained "their" State Department.

Later, when he would recount Nixon's diatribe about the need to usurp the power of the State Department bureaucracy, Kissinger would end the tale by smiling and saying, "I agreed." He told Nixon that he should set up a strong National Security Council staff in the White House that would take over from State the responsibility for developing policy options.

A bond was struck. For three hours the intellectual German refugee and the driven son of a small-town California grocer talked about power and the need to grab control of policy-making. But at the end of the conversation, Nixon's awkwardness in dealing with people on a personal basis—and his fear of being rebuffed—took over. He implied that he might want Kissinger in his administration, though he was not specific. Kissinger vaguely indicated interest, noting that perhaps he might come in as part of Rockefeller's staff.

As the meeting ended, Nixon buzzed for his assistant H. R. Haldeman and told him to have a direct phone line set up to Kissinger's office at Harvard. Haldeman jotted down this curious request on a yellow legal pad and then never did anything about it. Kissinger made it back to Cambridge in time to teach his four P.M. defense seminar. [12]

The next day Kissinger got two calls (on his conventional office telephone) in quick succession: the first from Rockefeller, saying that Nixon had told him he would rather have him remain governor of New York than join the cabinet, then from John Mitchell, inviting him to return to the Pierre the next day.

"What have you decided about the national security job?" said Mitchell, puffing on his pipe, when Kissinger arrived.

"I did not know I had been offered it," replied Kissinger.

"Oh, Jesus Christ, he has screwed it up again." Mitchell lumbered down the hall, consulted with his boss, then fetched Kissinger to come receive the official offer. Three other possible national security advisers had been briefly interviewed by Nixon—Robert Strausz-Hupe and William Kintner of the University of Pennsylvania, and Roy Ash, president of Litton Industries—but Kissinger was the only one seriously considered.

He wanted the job. But he was worried about what his associates —both from the Rockefeller campaign and Harvard—would think. He sought to defuse any resentment at his leap to the enemy by consulting them and inducing them to bestow their approval. He told Nixon he would be of no use unless he came with the moral support of his friends and Harvard colleagues—"a judgment," he would later note, "that proved to be false." Nixon, no doubt wary about Harvard faculty members serving as his character references, gave Kissinger the names of some professors who had known him at Duke.[13]

In consulting with his Cambridge colleagues, most of whom were inveterate Nixon-haters, Kissinger played to their prejudices. Nixon seemed like a void, he said in describing his meetings at the Pierre; he lacked a commanding presence, could not carry a conversation without disquieting pauses. One friend recalled that Kissinger "remarked over and over again how timid and unstatesmanlike he found Nixon's demeanor." If he accepted the job, Kissinger confided, a chief challenge would be to impart a sense of purpose and confidence to Nixon and to shore up his uncomfortable personality.

McGeorge Bundy, who had originally suggested to Kissinger that he seek the job of chief policy planner at the State Department, was surprised to hear that he had been offered Bundy's old job. He advised against taking it. "You can't do the job without fully trusting the president," he said. "I can't see how you can trust Nixon." Fritz Kraemer also told him to decline. "The Right will call you the Jew who lost Southeast Asia, and the Left will call you a traitor to the cause."

Otherwise, his friends and colleagues, despite ill-concealed envy, urged him to accept, advice that Kissinger realized was "tinged by the desire to know someone of influence in Washington." At a conference in Princeton hosted by Carl Kaysen, Kissinger pulled various friends and acquaintances aside, soliciting their opinions and getting their blessings. "He began cultivating us," Kaysen said. The process was mutual. As word spread that day, others sought him out to flatter him with the counsel that he must accept the job.

Among the Rockefeller staff, there was a sense of betrayal. Oscar Ruebhausen was with other advisers in the governor's office when word came that Kissinger had gotten the offer. "We were shocked," he recalls. "There was a sense that he was a whore." Or, a chameleon. Kissinger's fickleness led some Rockefeller staffers to parody a popular song: "I wonder who's Kissinger now?"

But the governor seemed pleased. His only dismay was at Kissinger for having the temerity to keep Nixon on hold. "You have to get right on the phone and accept that offer," Rockefeller said. "You have no right to treat a president that way."

Rather than displaying resentment, Rockefeller offered Kissinger a generous lump-sum severance gift, to be used to educate his children, which served to cushion the financial burden of going into government. In a "Dear Henry" note, he wrote: "As a token of my friendship and my appreciation for the work you have done in service to the people of this country, I am arranging to have a gift made to you in the amount of $50,000." (This amounted to approximately $170,000 in 1990 dollars.) After checking with Nixon and the White House counsel's office to make sure that it was legal, Kissinger accepted the gift, which helped to seal his professional and personal debt to Rockefeller.[14]

Late on the afternoon of Friday, November 29, Kissinger called Dwight Chapin to accept the job. The following Monday morning, the forty-five-year-old Harvard professor walked with the president-elect to the podium of the ballroom at the Pierre Hotel.

There, a significant new wrinkle was added to Nixon's plan to gut the power of State and other cabinet departments in favor of a strong White House staff: the shift would be done secretly, even deceitfully. "Dr. Kissinger is keenly aware of the necessity not to set himself up as a wall between the president and the secretary of state or the secretary of defense," Nixon told the press. Kissinger would deal with long-range planning rather than tactics or operations, Nixon pledged, adding: "I intend to have a strong secretary of state." None of those statements was true.

Nixon's willingness to say the opposite of what he believed was an early sign of his penchant for conspiratorial and covert ways of conducting policy. Kissinger's willingness to go along was, in turn, an early sign of precisely that: his willingness to go along. When he got to the podium, he claimed that what Nixon had said reflected his own thinking.

For the moment, the deception worked. Lavishing praise on Kissinger's appointment, a New York Times editorial lauded the fact that he "intends to leave operations to the departments . . . and is unlikely to arouse suspicion that he is arranging the flow of information to win the argument for his own view." At a December 12 meeting with the incoming cabinet, Nixon asked Kissinger to give his views on Vietnam. Kissinger demurred; he replied that he considered it his job to pass along options, not give advice. Citing the event with approval, columnists Rowland Evans and Robert Novak reported that Nixon planned "to use his own staff strictly as an information-gathering device and leave to his Cabinet all of the major policy advice."[15]

In the meantime, Kissinger's appointment met with broad approval. The *Washington Post* called it "welcome," and James Reston in the *New York Times* called it "reassuring," adding that it was encouraging that Kissinger had taken his doctorate "under McGeorge Bundy." (This mistaken assertion threw Kissinger into the first of what would be rather frequent private rages at the idiocy of American journalists.) Adam Yarmolinsky, a Harvard law professor who served in the Pentagon, declared: "We'll all sleep a little better each night knowing that Henry is down there." And William F. Buckley, Jr., whom Kissinger had been cultivating ever since he invited him to his Harvard seminar in 1954, wrote to him that "not since Florence Nightingale has any public figure received such universal acclaim."[16]

THE ODD COUPLE

Richard Nixon, who liked to portray his actions as bold and unexpected, often stressed how different he and Kissinger were. "The combination was unlikely," he would recall, "the grocer's son from Whittier and the refugee from Hitler's Germany, the politician and the academic."

But it was some inner similarities rather than their surface differences that helped forge the murky bond that was to unite them. As each of them acquired the power he had long sought, they retained the personal insecurities that they found reflected in each other.

Both were practitioners of realpolitik, that blend of cold realism and power-oriented statecraft that tended to be, to use Kissinger's description of Bismarck, "unencumbered by moral scruples." They believed, as Kissinger had once written of his nineteenth-century subjects, that "foreign policy had to be based not on sentiment but on an assessment of strength."

In a conversation with Golda Meir, Nixon once twisted the golden rule into a power game, telling her, "My rule in international affairs is, 'Do unto others as they would do unto you.' " At which Kissinger interjected: "Plus ten percent." On a more personal level, ethical concerns were not paramount for either Kissinger or Nixon when it came to plugging leaks or circumventing the State Department.

Kissinger also wrote of Bismarck that he "knew how to restrain the contending forces, both domestic and foreign, by manipulating their antagonisms." Likewise, Nixon and Kissinger shared a mastery of manipulating antagonisms. Both of them could be suspicious and secretive; they tended to think the worst of other people's motives, and they liked to pit their perceived enemies against one another. Inveterate backbiters, they forged alliances by invoking mutual enemies and brooding about shared antagonisms. Just as Kissinger said of Bismarck that "he could never accept the good faith of any opponent," so it was that Nixon and Kissinger invariably ascribed sinister motives to anyone who challenged them.[17]

"Kissinger and Nixon both had degrees of paranoia," said Lawrence Eagleburger, long one of Kissinger's closest aides and most astute observers. "It led them to worry about each other, but it also led them to make common cause on perceived mutual enemies. They developed a conspiratorial approach to foreign policy management."[18]

In addition, they were both loners—and liked to think of themselves as such. This bred a fondness for secrecy and furtiveness. Because they were unwilling to share either information or credit, they tended to be evasive when dealing with subordinates or colleagues.

Likewise, they both relished pulling off surprises designed to astonish their adversaries. Instead of being carefully coordinated with the State Department, the negotiations on Vietnam and arms control and China would be done covertly, then dramatically revealed.

Heightening these similarities was Kissinger's chameleon-like quality of taking on the coloration of those around him. By reinforcing each other's prejudices and spending far more time together than was healthy, Kissinger and Nixon soon bonded together as co-conspirators against the bureaucracy and a hostile world.[19]

What truly bound Kissinger and Nixon together, however, was an appetite and affection and feel for foreign policy. Most of their time together was spent as if in a two-person seminar, touring the horizon of world affairs and discussing avenues to be explored. With Kissinger paving the way, Nixon became the first American president to visit Moscow and Beijing, and he did it in the same year. To fathom foreign policy, Kissinger has said, a person must be constantly thinking of all the connections involved, even while shaving in the morning. Though he may not have done either perfectly, Nixon was one of the few men who would think about foreign policy while shaving.

Despite sharing all of these traits, Kissinger and Nixon had a major personality difference that made them fundamentally dissimilar: Kissinger was acutely aware of the world around him and self-aware of his role in it. Nixon was not.

This difference was manifest in many ways. Kissinger was painfully sensitive to every critic's opinion, whereas Nixon tended to withdraw into Walter Mitty–like fantasies and pretend to be impervious to what others thought. Kissinger struggled to co-opt his enemies and ingratiate himself with his critics; Nixon brooded about getting even. Kissinger relished personal interaction; Nixon dreaded it. When Kissinger got angry, he would rage at those involved; Nixon would shrink from confrontation, avoid dealing with people, and stew about getting revenge.

When challenges arose, Kissinger became intellectually engaged, almost obsessively so; Nixon became detached, almost eerily so. Kissinger's mind mastered details; Nixon remained aloof from even some of the major components of issues he faced. Kissinger's analytic lucidity took him straight to the core of any problem; Nixon's more intuitive approach led him to roll a problem around for hours on end as he brooded on various conflicting options.

One of the most perceptive comparisons of Kissinger and Nixon came in a 1973 speech by Thomas Hughes, a State Department veteran who had departed to become president of the Carnegie Endowment:

> Both were incurably covert, but Kissinger was charming about it. Both abhorred bureaucracy, but Nixon was reclusive about it. Both engaged in double-talk, but Kissinger was often convincing. Both were fiercely anti-ideological, but Nixon had recurrent relapses. Both jealously guarded against any diffusion of power, but Kissinger dispensed balm. Both were inveterate manipulators, but Nixon was more transparent. Both insisted on extremes of loyalty, but Kissinger endeared himself to his critics. Both had a penchant for secrecy, but neither uniformly practiced what he preached. Both were deeply suspicious, but Kissinger was irrepressibly gregarious. Neither was widely admired for truthfulness, but Kissinger excelled at articulation. Neither worshiped the First Amendment, but Kissinger mesmerized the press.[20]

Each February during his first term, Nixon would give an intimate birthday dinner upstairs in the White House for Alice Roosevelt Longworth, the daughter of President Theodore Roosevelt. The tart-tongued Washington insider, who had an embroidered pillow in her salon that read, "If you can't say anything nice come sit here beside me," was the doyenne of the two groups that Nixon most resented yet felt a curious compulsion to impress: Georgetown society and the Washington establishment. Usually there were only six people at the dinner: the Nixons, Mrs. Longworth, Kissinger, columnist Joseph Alsop, and his wife, Susan Mary. "Nixon would have Henry perform," said Mrs. Alsop, "and he would sit back and beam with pride, as if Henry were some sort of prized possession." Whenever an issue came up, Nixon would lean over to his dinner partner and say, "Mrs. Long-worth, I think you'll be interested in what Henry has to say about that."[21]

Such was Nixon's initial attitude toward Kissinger: pride, perhaps a bit of awe, all tinged with the sort of resentful delight that an unpopular kid might feel when he finds himself showing off a possession that makes other people respect him.

Heightening his pleasure at having Kissinger by his side was that he had once belonged to Rockefeller, whom Nixon envied. "If someone worked for Rockefeller," said Haldeman, "Nixon coveted him and assumed he was good because he belonged to someone who could buy whatever he wanted." Nixon never enjoyed the Kennedyesque aura that lured intellectuals naturally to his side, nor could he afford to buy the best and brightest minds, as Rockefeller could. But now that he was president, he could pry away one of Rockefeller's crown jewels. "He took a certain delight in that," speechwriter William Safire noted.[22]

In addition, Nixon admired Kissinger's detached kinship to the American establishment: he had been embraced by the East Coast foreign policy elite, yet by breeding and temperament he could never become a true insider, and he was contemptuous of the conventional wisdom that formed the establishment consensus. Unlike a McGeorge Bundy, for example, Kissinger was not born into the establishment, and unlike John McCloy or Dean Rusk, he would never be fully absorbed into it. Throughout his career he would be solicitous toward venerable establishment pillars, such as McCloy and David Bruce and later Cyrus Vance. But privately he tended to be condescending about their crowd.

To Nixon, who had always been snubbed by the foreign policy elite, even when he was an international lawyer in Manhattan in the 1960s, Kissinger's case seemed the ideal: to be courted but not seduced, to be an outsider who felt condescending toward the elite rather than the other way around. Among Nixon's little fantasies was that he was proud of not caring what people in those hallowed precincts thought of him. With Kissinger as his Tonto, that dream seemed more convincing.

Nixon nevertheless quickly became rather wary of Kissinger's quirky personality and ambition. "I don't trust Henry, but I can use him," he told one of Kissinger's rivals at the outset of the administration. To Elliot Richardson, who began as undersecretary of state, Nixon warned: "Watch Henry! Check on him!"

Nixon became particularly distressed by the conflicting extremes of Kissinger's personality: his insecurity and paranoia on the one hand, and his ego and megalomania on the other. Although Nixon loved fomenting rivalries, he hated to deal with them. As a result, the feud between Kissinger and Secretary of State William Rogers quickly got out of hand, and Nixon's perverse glee turned to despair.[23]

Kissinger's socializing with the Georgetown set and the media elite would also become a source of resentment. On some evenings, Nixon would call John Connally or Al Haig or Bob Haldeman to his hideaway and make fun of where Kissinger might be. "I guess Henry's out with his Georgetown friends," he'd say, then brood for a moment. "He would joke about it," Connally recalled, "but it bothered him badly." Nixon suspected (not without reason) that Kissinger was regaling dinner parties with tales of his own triumphs and how he was holding in check a mad president's dangerous instincts. Most of what Kissinger said on the social circuit echoed back, amplified, to stoke Nixon's suspicions even further.[24]

During his five and a half years in office, Nixon's admiration for Kissinger would gradually become more infected by jealousy and suspicions of disloyalty. With no personal affection to serve as a foundation for their relationship, what had been a love-hate alliance eventually tilted toward the latter. As the president's dependency on Kissinger grew, his resentment and bitterness increased.

So oddly matched in many ways, so oddly repelled by one another: Kissinger and Nixon formed a curious pair. Franklin Roosevelt and Harry Hopkins? Woodrow Wilson and Colonel Edward House? No, in each of those cases the assistant was more subservient to the president.

Perhaps the best comparison is the relationship Kissinger wrote about as a graduate student: Metternich and Emperor Francis I of Austria. When Metternich became foreign minister in 1809, Austria had been beaten down in spirit by the Napoleonic wars and was, in Kissinger's words, a "government which had lost its élan and its self-confidence, which knew its limits but hardly its goals." America was in much the same way at the end of 1968, having lost not only the will to prevail in Vietnam but also the confidence that it had a worthy role to play in the world.

Francis I was far more pedantic, thickheaded, resistant to new ideas, and meddlesome than Nixon. But, like Nixon, he used his police to spy on political enemies, and he read their reports with relish. A taste of Kissinger's later attitudes toward Nixon's grim determination can be found in his description of Francis I: "Dour and suspicious, unimaginative and pedantic, he had seen so many convulsions that he regarded mere persistence as an ethical value."

Francis I and Metternich believed they lacked the domestic consensus needed to conduct an open and forthright foreign policy, so they resorted to one based on deception, cunning, and maneuver. The emperor, through a succession of hard knocks, became cynical about the will and loyalties of his people; Metternich arrived at this disdain intellectually. The same could be said of Nixon and Kissinger. The way they perceived their predicament in 1969 was not all that different from Kissinger's description of the one perceived by their predecessors in 1809: "Since Austrian policy could not draw its strength from the inspiration of its people, it had to achieve its aims by the tenacity and subtlety of its diplomacy."[25]

One Saturday afternoon in the summer of 1970, Kissinger was in San Clemente with Nixon. The president suggested that the two of them, along with his chum Bebe Rebozo, drive up to find the small house in Yorba Linda where he was born. There, seized by an emotional nostalgia and anger at having his privacy invaded, he ordered the two cars of Secret Service agents and press to go away, leaving him alone with Kissinger, Rebozo, and a Secret Service driver. Nixon, more relaxed than Kissinger had ever seen him, pointed out the landmarks of his young life and discussed the random events that had led him to become a politician.

"The guiding theme of his discourse," Kissinger later recalled, "was how it had all been accidental." But Kissinger saw in it a different theme, that of an insecure man who lacked a strong sense of who he was and where he came from. "Nixon had set himself a goal beyond human capacity: to make himself over entirely," Kissinger later wrote. "But the gods exacted a fearful price for this presumption. Nixon paid, first, the price of congenital insecurity. And ultimately he learned what the Greeks had known: that the worst punishment can be having one's wishes filled too completely."[26]

Kissinger's previous patrons—Kraemer, Elliott, Rockefeller—had been grand personas, commanding in style, larger than life in presence. But as Kissinger discovered at their meeting at the Pierre, Nixon was unprepossessing, weak, lacking in presence. He struck Kissinger as a Walter Mitty type, a person who, like James Thurber's fictional character, spun out fantasies of being a brave hero and whose "romantic imaginings embellished the often self-inflicted daily disappointments."

Kissinger also came to see Nixon as a shy man, one who dreaded meeting new people or conveying a disappointing decision to someone's face. "The essence of this man is loneliness," Kissinger would tell friends. Nixon would hole up in his hideaway office, slump in a chair, and write notes on a yellow legal pad. For hours or even days, he would shield himself from outsiders, allowing only a small circle of aides to join him in his rambling ruminations. "He was a very odd man, an unpleasant man," Kissinger later let slip into an open microphone at a diplomatic dinner. "He didn't enjoy people. What I never understood is why he went into politics."[27]

Not surprisingly, Nixon instilled distrust among those around him. For Kissinger, who was prone to paranoia, the reaction was acute. Soon after he took office, Kissinger had aides or secretaries listen in on his phone conversations with the president (as well as other callers), using a "dead key" that would allow them to pick up the telephone undetected. The aides would prepare a memo of the conversation.

Whenever there would be a particularly strange or frightening phone call from the president, or when he seemed either drunk or out of control, Kissinger would emerge from his office and ask who had been taking notes. Then he would roll his eyes. Can you believe that? he would grumble. Did you hear what "that madman" said? When a presidential call became particularly rambling or woolly, Kissinger would signal wildly for an aide to pick up and share the horror.*

Kissinger's rants against Nixon became a carefully guarded secret. He referred to him as "our drunken friend" and "the meatball mind." "If the president had his way, there would be a nuclear war each week!" Kissinger would say to his aides in a conspiratorial growl. Daniel Patrick Moynihan, a colleague from both Harvard and the Nixon administration, once noted of Kissinger: "It was his obsession that no one ever should appear closer to the president than he, while neither should anyone be seen to hold this president in greater contempt."[28]

But even as he was denigrating Nixon, Kissinger would throw in a few words of tribute to his courage. "Genuinely heroic," was a phrase he would sometimes use. "Kissinger always paid tribute to Nixon's decisiveness when a crisis finally came, even to us staffers, even when he was complaining about Nixon's weird personality," recalled former aide Winston Lord. In times of crisis, Kissinger insisted, Nixon would steel himself against outside pressures and take bold, forceful

* See Chapter 10.

steps. It was a "joyless, desperate courage," according to Kissinger, one that seemed tinged by "his fatalistic instinct that nothing he touched would ever be crowned with success."

Kissinger's tributes to Nixon's decisiveness rang somewhat hollow. Nixon did make some tough decisions, but in most of the major crises during his tenure, he was far from heroic, as Kissinger well knew. During preparations for the Cambodian invasion, Nixon went to Camp David with his drinking buddy Bebe Rebozo; when he called Kissinger, he was slurring his words and shouting profanities. Over the next few days, he took a drunken trip up the Potomac on the *Sequoia,* paid a spooky visit to the Pentagon, and made a predawn appearance with his valet at the Lincoln Memorial. During Kissinger's secret trip to Moscow after the mining of Haiphong harbor in April 1972, Nixon went with Rebozo to Camp David and spent his time firing off posturing cables. And during both the 1972 Christmas bombing of Hanoi and the nuclear alert following the October 1973 Middle East war, Nixon was out of touch. *[29]

THE COURTIER'S INSTINCTS

As a refugee, with a full share of the insecurities and ambitions that come from being a smart outsider, Kissinger had learned how to cultivate the patronage of powerful people. He could maneuver, amuse, impress, and occasionally dazzle. But more important, at least in the strange case of Richard Nixon, Kissinger had learned how to flatter.

Even while he was denigrating Nixon behind his back, Kissinger was fawning to his face. During his trip to Europe a month after taking office, Nixon "desperately wanted to be told how well he had done," Kissinger recalled. He obliged. That same month, after his first meeting with Soviet ambassador Anatoli Dobrynin, Nixon called Kissinger to his office four times to hear him tell him how well he had done. Again, Kissinger obliged.

After a later meeting with Dobrynin, Kissinger gushed: "It was extraordinary! No president has ever laid it on the line to them like that." It was around then that Kissinger first met Pat Nixon at a reception. He told her how impressed he was by her husband, lavishing praise on his grasp of issues and his sense of command. She frowned. "Haven't you seen through him yet?" she asked.

* See Chapters 13, 19, 21, and 23.

Kissinger's flattery extended to writing Nixon mash notes. Before an April 1971 speech on Vietnam, for example, Kissinger sent him a handwritten missive: "No matter what the result, free people everywhere will be forever in your debt. Your serenity during crises, your steadfastness under pressure, have been all that have prevented the triumph of mass hysteria. It has been an inspiration to serve. As always, H." The words of this and other notes were so fulsome that one could almost forget that the descriptions of Nixon's "serenity" were not exactly sincere.[30]

Kissinger's entire demeanor would change whenever he was talking to the president. Peter Peterson, then Nixon's international-economics assistant, said that when Kissinger would visit his Georgetown home, he would belittle Nixon relentlessly. Then a call would come on the red line. "Oh, yes, Mr. President," Kissinger would say over and over again. Recalled Peterson: "The contrast was striking between how he talked about Nixon to his friends and how he acted in Nixon's presence." Henry Brandon also remembered Kissinger getting presidential calls at his house. "He was so deferential he seemed like a totally different person."[31]

As with many of Kissinger's character quirks, he was fully aware of his obsequiousness and could prick the balloon with his self-deprecating humor. He often told the tale of Nixon returning to his cabin at Camp David and announcing, "I scored 126." Replied Kissinger: "Your golf is improving, Mr. President." To which Nixon growled, "I was bowling." When Kissinger's direct line from the president rang while a reporter was there, Kissinger dryly noted: "I don't want you to get the wrong idea just because I was on my knees when I answered the phone."

After a visit to brief former president Johnson down on his ranch, Lady Bird drove Kissinger back to the air base and asked how he thought her husband's demeanor struck him. Kissinger, in telling the story on himself, recalled that he mumbled something about "serenity in retirement" and she almost drove off the road. "I suppose flattery has to be related to reality, however vaguely," he would say.[32]

Nixon's White House tapes, when they are finally released, will be particularly damaging to Kissinger because they will show him fawning over even Nixon's most hair-raising notions, according to those who were there. In 1982, Kissinger ran into John Ehrlichman at the Beverly Wilshire Hotel in Los Angeles. "Sooner or later those tapes are going to be released, and you and I are going to look like perfect fools," Kissinger told Nixon's domestic adviser. Speak for yourself, Ehrlichman thought. "He was obsequious naturally," said Ehrlichman. "He would lard things unbelievably. Nixon would make an outrageous statement, and instead of humming and staring at the ceiling like I would do, Kissinger would eagerly rumble in with, 'Yes, Mr. President, your analysis is absolutely correct and certainly very profound.' I would cringe."[33]

The most egregious cases came when Nixon seemed to bait Kissinger, saying things—especially about Jews—that cried out for Kissinger to challenge him. Kissinger never would. Once, Nixon phoned and started a rambling attack on Jews and blacks as Winston Lord listened in on a dead key. "Why didn't you say something?" Lord asked afterward. "I have enough trouble," Kissinger told his aide, "fighting with him on the things that really matter; his attitudes toward Jews and blacks are not my worry."

Nixon seemed to take a fiendish glee in launching into diatribes against Jews and watching as Kissinger shifted feet nervously, afraid to contradict him. "Nixon would talk about Jewish traitors," Ehrlichman recalled, "and he'd play off Kissinger, 'Isn't that right, Henry? Don't you agree?' And Henry would respond: 'Well, Mr. President, there are Jews and then there are Jews.' " Kissinger sometimes made his Jewish aides keep a low profile in order not to inflame Nixon's bias. "Nixon shared many of the prejudices of the uprooted, California lower-middle class from which he had come," Kissinger later said in explaining the president's anti-Semitism.[34]

Even his second wife, Nancy, as protective and devoted as any spouse could be, was bothered by Kissinger's willingness to play along with the president's prejudices. At one of her first meetings with Nixon, he began attacking Rockefeller. Kissinger did not protest, just mumbled, "Oh, yes," and nervously tried to change the subject. Nancy, who worked for Rockefeller and admired him deeply, was upset. "I was about to say something," she later recalled, "and Henry knew it and his eyebrow shot up to keep me quiet."

When asked about this incident, Nixon insisted that Kissinger had always remained loyal to Rockefeller. "He knew that Rockefeller and I had been rivals for years," Nixon said. "If he had wanted to pander to me, he could on occasion have said something critical of Rockefeller."[35]

Kissinger later defended his actions by saying that challenging Nixon was futile, "almost suicidal." "Nixon's favor depended on the readiness to fall in with the paranoid cult of the tough guy," he said. "The conspiracy of the press, the hostility of the Establishment, the flatulence of the Georgetown set, were permanent features of Nixon's conversation, which one challenged only at the cost of exclusion from the inner circle." Besides, Kissinger argued, it was easier to fall in with

Nixon's "most extravagant" musings than to challenge them because they rarely led to anything.

One reason that Nixon was such a complex man was because of the many contradictory aspects to his personality. H. R. Haldeman, for example, compared him to a quartz crystal: "Some facets bright and shining, others dark and mysterious. . . . Some smooth and polished, others crude, rough, and sharp." And each of them changed, he added, depending on what light was striking it.

William Safire, a Nixon speechwriter and author of the most colorful memoir of his first term, used a layer cake as an analogy. The icing was the public face, "stern, dignified, proper"; the first layer "a progressive politician"; just below that "an unnecessarily pugnacious man." Other layers included "the hater," "the realist," the courageous "risk-taker," and "the loner." [36]

Kissinger likewise came to see in Nixon an odd admixture of conflicting traits. "Several warring personalities struggled for preeminence in the same individual," he later noted. "One was idealistic, thoughtful, generous; another was vindictive, petty, emotional. There was a reflective, philosophical, stoical Nixon; and there was an impetuous, impulsive, and erratic one." Nixon's grim ambition was the result, Kissinger believed, of "the titanic struggle" among his various personalities. "Most men mature around a central core; Nixon had several. This is why he was never at peace with himself."

Because Nixon was a man of many facets—some enlightened, others murkier—Kissinger could later claim that the dark deeds of their tenure, such as the wiretapping and the humiliation of the State Department and the petty deceits, were done at Nixon's behest. At worst, this defense runs, Kissinger was merely a facilitator, a person who made it possible for Nixon to do what he wanted. But because Nixon was multifaceted, the opposite argument can also be made: Kissinger *could*, if he had chosen, have appealed to Nixon's better instincts, as some other aides in the White House tried to do. If Kissinger had done so, would the conduct of policy have been more open and honest? Did Kissinger reinforce Nixon's dark side by catering to it?

Perhaps to a small degree. But Nixon would have been Nixon, with or without Kissinger at his side. There were plenty of people around Nixon—including Secretary of State William Rogers—who practiced a more open and forthright style; but the president quickly shunted them aside in favor of those more comfortable with being devious.

To get anything done, Kissinger quickly learned, required catering to Nixon's prejudices. "If you bucked Nixon on his petty biases and idiosyncratic pronouncements," Ehrlichman said, "he'd cut you dead. He wouldn't see you or return your memos." People who fought Nixon's darker musings, such as advisers Herb Klein and Robert Finch, soon faded away. "It would have been crazy to challenge Nixon or take a heroic stand against his prejudices," recalled Diane Sawyer, who served as one of his press assistants. "He would just shut you off. If you were going to get something done, you had to keep elasticity in the relationship."[37]

So Kissinger became an enabler for the dark side of Nixon's personality, someone who joined in his backbiting, flattered his ideas, and never pushed him into a corner. Honorable men were often ridiculed by Nixon as prissy and weak. He preferred those who could be brutal, from Patton to Connally to Colson. A willingness to talk tough and applaud ruthlessness was the best way to become Nixon's co-conspirator against a hostile world.[38]

Did Nixon's dark side infect Kissinger? If the president had been an open, uncomplicated, and forthright gentleman, would Kissinger, with his chameleon-like traits, have become that way, too? "It would have been very different under Rockefeller," Kissinger would sigh over dinner at a French restaurant with some of his aides after their first year in office.

Perhaps to a small degree. But Kissinger's own dark streak—tinged with paranoia and insecurity and furtiveness—ran deep. He was conspiratorial when he had worked under Robert Bowie at Harvard. Even under the open and gregarious Rockefeller, Kissinger had waged petty turf battles with perceived rivals. And later, when Gerald Ford became one of America's least devious presidents, Kissinger still found himself embroiled in pointless bureaucratic struggles.

Nixon's thirst for flattery and Kissinger's penchant for providing it helped to seal a complex relationship, but it did not make Kissinger a social chum like Bebe Rebozo or Robert Abplanalp. Indeed, he and Nixon never developed a personal warmth toward one another. "Henry, of course, was not a personal friend," Nixon later told David Frost, flinging in the "of course" as a subtle Nixonian put-down. "We were associates, but not personal friends. Not enemies, but not personal friends."[39]

Even so, Kissinger quickly became Nixon's favorite person to talk to and have at his side. And with a man so complex and conflicted, proximity translated into power.

Within a year Kissinger and Nixon would be talking five or six times a day, in person or by phone, sometimes for hours on end. In the morning, after the regular briefing, Nixon would sometimes keep Kissinger in the Oval Office for two hours. In the afternoons, he would summon him to the hideaway in the Executive Office Building.

Nixon loved rambling discussions. He would poke at a situation from all sides, make pronouncements, circle back, make contradictory ones. The habit would hurt him during Watergate; the tapes show him suggesting certain courses of action—such as paying off the burglars —when in fact he was engaged in a Nixonian ramble. The habit also gave Kissinger extraordinary leeway to shape foreign policy tactics.

Instead of arguing against Nixon's most harebrained orders, Kissinger learned simply to ignore them, the way Haldeman had with Nixon's request to install a private phone line to Kissinger's office at Harvard. "It was part of the assistant's task—expected by Nixon—to winnow out those 'decisions' that he really did not mean to have implemented," Kissinger later said. "A good rule of thumb was that the president's seriousness was in inverse proportion to the frequency of his commands."[40]

THE QUIET COUP

In order to understand the audacious power grab that Kissinger engineered in December 1968—which his aide Roger Morris later dubbed the "coup d'état at the Hotel Pierre"—one must begin by noting that it was done at Nixon's behest. Although he had declared when announcing Kissinger's appointment that "I intend to have a strong secretary of state," in fact he intended the opposite. "From the outset of my administration," he later admitted with a bit more candor, "I planned to direct foreign policy from the White House."

To do so required a change in the policy-making structure that would sap the traditional powers of the State and Defense departments and centralize control in the West Wing, specifically in the hands of Nixon and Kissinger.

Because he regarded the government bureaucracy as his enemy, Nixon was determined to create a cadre of courtiers beholden only to him, a Byzantine system in which the palace guards maneuvered to undercut the nobles who ran the cabinet departments. He wanted to be "shielded from his cabinet and their bureaucracies," Haldeman recalled. The cabinet was studded with small-town Rotarian types, unassertive sorts. But Nixon staffed the White House with hard-edged ethnic academics (Kissinger, Daniel Patrick Moynihan, Arthur Burns) and loyal Prussian foot soldiers (Bob Haldeman, John Ehrlichman).

Lyndon Johnson—a man whose desire for feeling plugged in matched Nixon's for isolation—loved reaching deep into the bureaucracy for information. He had a bank of phones on his ranch-sized desk, each with rows of buttons. "If I needed to get hold of somebody, all I had to do was mash a button. And I mean anybody—even some little fellow tucked away in one of the agencies." He recalled this to aides after a visit to the Nixon Oval Office. The new president, he reported with disbelief, "had just one dinky phone" with three buttons on it. His voice rose. "That's all! Just three buttons! And they all go to Germans."

Nixon was also obsessed with getting credit, something he felt had been denied him for much of his life. The only way to assure this, he decided, was to have important policies handled within the White House.

All of this led Nixon, as he had confided to Kissinger at their first meeting at the Pierre, to want to enhance the role of the national security adviser and place him in charge of a more centralized policy-making structure.[41]

Kissinger was happy to oblige. His quest for control reflected the reach of his mind: he felt, correctly, that he was better equipped to handle foreign policy than the new secretary of state, William Rogers, and it was not in Kissinger's nature to be charitable toward those he did not respect. A related factor was Kissinger's vanity: he did not have the sort of ego that found gratification in deferring to colleagues or helping other people to shine.

In addition, as William Safire noted, "intrigue was second nature to him, an exercise he went through without thinking." In a Byzantine court, Kissinger flourished. "The reason his role became so great," Nixon later said, "was because he is a very good infighter. He liked power, which is a compliment, and he knew how to use it."[42]

But there was also, it must be noted, a legitimate reason to usurp the prerogatives of the bureaucracy: it was something that needed to be done. By 1969, America's national security bureaucracy had been sapped of its confidence and creativity. In Vietnam, it had committed one of the worst errors in American foreign policy history by misjudging the strengths of a nationalist revolution while misconceiving

America's national interest and its will. It had largely ignored the most important geopolitical event of the decade: the split between China and the Soviet Union. Even as the Soviets engaged in a massive nuclear buildup, the bureaucracy could not come up with a coherent strategy on arms control, only haphazard interagency scheming. And despite the Six-Day War, it had not conducted a fundamental reexamination of America's Middle East policies.

The problems were mainly due to an intellectual constipation caused by a system that encouraged caution rather than creativity. There was no reward for challenging prevailing orthodoxies. Clear thinking, even simple declarative sentences, were considered dangerous. Establishing a new policy on any issue required painstaking negotiations among the institutional interests of countless desk officers at the State Department, Pentagon, CIA, and a dozen other agencies. The result tended to be glacial changes, fuzzy conclusions swathed in murky language, and a resistance to reopening issues once a bureaucratic consensus had been reached.[43]

But Nixon, to his credit, wanted to reopen a host of issues. And like Kissinger, he felt it would be easier to circumvent rather than confront the inert bureaucracy.

The vehicle they chose was the staff apparatus attached to the National Security Council. The NSC had been created in 1947 during the Truman administration in response to Franklin Roosevelt's habit of leaving certain agencies in the dark when he made decisions. Its membership—known as the NSC "principals"—included the president, vice president, secretary of state, secretary of defense, and other top officials (such as the director of central intelligence) designated by the president.

In 1953, Robert Cutler, a Boston banker, advised President Eisenhower to designate a "special assistant for national security affairs" to oversee the NSC staff and manage the flow of options to the president. Eisenhower did, and Cutler got the job. In addition, General Andrew Goodpaster was made "staff secretary," which involved handling the daily operation of the NSC.

During the Kennedy and Johnson administrations, the staff secretary and special assistant roles were combined. McGeorge Bundy and then Walt Rostow became powerful advisers to the president as well as coordinators of the national security bureaucracy.

This led to an odd shift. The importance of the NSC itself waned; Kennedy formed ad hoc committees that met at the White House to deal with various issues, and Johnson relied on a Tuesday lunch that was a rather informal gathering of the NSC principals. But the importance of the NSC *staff* grew. Headed by a special assistant who eventually became known as the national security adviser,* the staff became a personal minibureaucracy that could analyze policy, devise tactics, and carry out operations for the president—often without the other principals of the NSC being informed.

That was precisely what Kissinger and Nixon wanted. As vice president, Nixon had been frustrated by Eisenhower's practice of encouraging a consensus among NSC principals before a matter reached him for decision. Instead, Nixon would use the NSC staff to make sure that conflicting options came directly to the White House. It was a worthy goal, but was destined to be overshadowed by the related demand that Nixon made: as much power as possible should be shifted from the State and Pentagon bureaucracies to the NSC staff.

As Kissinger was preparing to set up such an apparatus, he flew to Cambridge on December 16 for the last of his Monday-afternoon defense-policy seminars. By chance, his guest lecturer was Morton Halperin, a young protégé who in the early 1960s had been a junior professor at Harvard and one of Kissinger's teaching assistants. In 1966, when he realized he was not going to get tenure at Harvard, Halperin went to work in the Office of International Security Affairs, the Pentagon's foreign policy arm.

Halperin, then only twenty-nine, spoke to Kissinger's seminar on the optimistic topic of "Asian Security After Vietnam." (Unlike when Nixon addressed the same topic in *Foreign Affairs* the previous year, the possibility of a U.S. opening to China was not analyzed.) Kissinger wiped his glasses, chewed his nails, and lobbed in questions. When it was over, the students bade Kissinger farewell with a standing ovation. "This will do wonders for my megalomania," he said.

Afterward, he asked Halperin to write a memo on how systems analysis techniques could be applied to the NSC staff. Halperin came down to the Pierre, then suggested it would be more useful if he instead helped to devise a concrete decision-making system of the sort Kissinger clearly had in mind. Halperin, who had become frustrated by the constricted flow that surrounded Johnson's Tuesday lunch, liked the idea of forcing a variety of options out of the overly cautious bureaucracy.

Halperin proposed two subtle but significant changes in the NSC system. The first was to eliminate something called the Senior Interdepartmental Group, which was chaired by the undersecretary of state and was in charge of reviewing all options and proposals before they

---

* Kissinger had his title upgraded from "special assistant" to "deputy to the president for national security," and he was the first to regularly use the informal title "national security adviser."

reached a formal NSC meeting. In its place would be a Review Group —to be chaired by the national security adviser. That would give Kissinger the power to approve any papers submitted to the president by the State Department or other bureaucracies. It also gave him effective control of the agenda for NSC meetings.

Halperin's other proposal was to give the national security adviser the power to order what were dubbed National Security Study Memoranda (NSSMs, pronounced "NIZ-ums"). The NSSMs would determine the work that State, Defense, and the other departments did and when they did it. These directives became a key tool that Kissinger used to decide which policies should be reconsidered. It also allowed him to conduct negotiations secretly but with input from the State Department; he would simply issue a NSSM on a topic that he was privately negotiating. "It enabled me to use the bureaucracy without revealing our purposes," he later explained.

Kissinger gave Halperin's paper to one of his new aides, Lawrence Eagleburger, a career foreign service officer, and asked him to recast it into a memo from Kissinger to Nixon. But don't tell Halperin, he admonished in a conspiratorial way. What Kissinger had trouble learning was that information has a tendency to echo around. Eagleburger, baffled about the background of the paper he was supposed to rework, went right to Halperin. Explaining that he had his paper but was supposed to keep it secret, Eagleburger sought Halperin's help in turning it into a memo. Halperin was happy to oblige, and they laughed at Kissinger's secrecy games.[44]

In order to win approval for the plan, Kissinger enlisted a potent ally: General Andrew Goodpaster, Eisenhower's NSC staff secretary. Kissinger had courted him ever since they'd met at Rockefeller's Quantico study group in 1955, and Kissinger had once impressed the erect West Pointer by taking him to lunch at the 21 Club in Manhattan.

Goodpaster agreed that the national security adviser should run the key committees, a structure somewhat similar to the one Eisenhower had used. "Defense doesn't like taking orders from State," he rationalized. "It was my conviction—and Henry seemed to agree—that control of the agenda had to be with the White House man."

Nixon summoned his designated secretary of state, William Rogers, and of defense, Melvin Laird, to Key Biscayne to discuss the Kissinger plan on Saturday, December 28. In typical fashion, Nixon had approved it the day before, but not told them. After the discussion, he approved it again.

That evening, Kissinger conducted his first informal press briefing. Wearing a colorful sports shirt that clashed with his serious mien, he dined with a small group of reporters at the Jamaica Inn and spoke of his hope "to seize firm control of the decision-making process." The next day the *New York Times* reported that Nixon "clearly intends to elevate the prestige and enlarge the role of the NSC."

As with most Nixon decisions, it was hardly final. Rogers, all too often oblivious to bureaucratic maneuverings, had shown little concern about how the Kissinger plan would affect the power of the State Department. "What do all these committees mean anyway?" he asked.

But he soon found out from his excitable underlings. Leading the charge was Undersecretary of State U. Alexis Johnson, a proud defender of the prerogatives of the foreign service. "From the start," Johnson later said, "it was obvious that Kissinger was extremely insecure and had an obsession, which persisted throughout his White House years, that the State Department and Foreign Service were determined to undermine him." On January 6, more than a week after Nixon had approved the new structure, Johnson and Rogers came by Kissinger's office in the Pierre to discuss the matter.

The following day, Kissinger wrote Nixon a long memo casting the issue as a test of his leadership and pleading with him to resolve it once and for all. But Nixon was loathe to force a resolution that might demand a face-to-face confrontation. "Suddenly Nixon was unavailable for days on end," Kissinger recalled.

The issue was finally settled when Nixon secluded himself in Key Biscayne to work on his inaugural address. Word was sent through Haldeman: Nixon was signing an order implementing the Kissinger plan, and anyone who objected should resign.[45]

The result was a national security apparatus well crafted for a diplomacy based on bold new approaches, secrecy, surprise, and tactical maneuvering. On the other hand, it was not as well suited for building a bureaucratic and public consensus for major policies, nor for creating institutional checks on a defiant president who was prone to acting on impulse.

NINE

WELCOME TO VIETNAM

Secret Options, Secret Bombings

However fashionable it is to ridicule the terms "credibility" or "prestige," they are not empty phrases; other nations can gear their actions to ours only if they can count on our steadiness.
—KISSINGER *in* FOREIGN AFFAIRS, *January 1969*

A NEW DAY

When Richard Milhous Nixon appeared atop the Capitol steps on the blustery Inauguration Day of January 20, 1969, Kissinger noticed that the legs of his morning suit were, as with all of his trousers, a trifle short. "His jaw jutted defiantly," Kissinger later wrote, "and yet he seemed uncertain." Along Pennsylvania Avenue, bands of protesters chanted "Ho, Ho, Ho Chi Minh, the Viet Cong is going to win." And in offices around town, clerks acting at Kissinger's behest were placing on the desks of top officials the three decision memos—NSDM 1, NSDM 2, NSDM 3—that centralized power in the hands of the national security adviser.

That afternoon, while Nixon and Rogers watched the inaugural parade from heated bleachers in front of the White House, Kissinger drafted the first of the thousands of cables he would send to American ambassadors abroad. Eventually, he would establish his own back-channel method of secret communication. But for now, as he suddenly realized, he needed to use the State Department's channels. So he walked across the lawn to the reviewing stands, where Rogers, amiable as ever, smilingly signed his name for the serious, hardworking presidential aide.

Kissinger went back to his office to finish a series of private letters from Nixon to important heads of government, ranging from Leonid Brezhnev to Charles de Gaulle. "Nixon understood, correctly, that State would have taken four weeks to rewrite what he wanted to say and to make it mishmash," recalled Morton Halperin. So the State Department was not even informed about the letters. They were hand-delivered to the respective embassies in Washington, and thus became the first official secret that Nixon and Kissinger would share behind Rogers's back.[1]

Nixon inherited four major aberrations in American foreign policy:

- An ill-conceived war in Vietnam where victory was not feasible and withdrawal was difficult. More than 31,000 Americans had already died in a struggle as far away from Washington as the globe's geography permits. The U.S. had become involved because it viewed North Vietnam's actions as a manifestation of Chinese-Soviet expansionism. But by 1969, it was becoming clear that this was a misreading of the independent nationalism of the Vietnamese communists and of the relationship between China and the Soviet Union. In the U.S., the agony of the war was fomenting a new isolationism. A nation that began the decade with John Kennedy's pledge to bear any burden to assure the success of liberty around the world now had to adjust to an era of limits.
- The ostracism of China, home of one-fifth of the earth's people. America's notion of a monolithic communist threat had become outdated. Beginning in 1960, China had begun attacking Soviet "revisionism." The Soviets withdrew their advisers from China and stopped aid; old border disputes reignited. The U.S. faced the challenge, and opportunity, of playing a game of balance and maneuver. But entrenched attitudes about China made it difficult for Nixon's predecessors to see that its rift with the Soviet Union could be exploited.
- An escalating arms race between the U.S. and the Soviet Union that served the national interest of neither country. Throughout history, each addition to a nation's arsenal could readily be translated into increased global influence. But the 1960s brought the great irony of the nuclear age: the quantum leap in military force made incremental additions to each side's military power less meaningful. In addition, the rough parity between American and Soviet arsenals meant that the backbone of the containment policy—America's nuclear threat—was no longer believable. After

twenty years of the nuclear arms race, the time had come for a new era in which superpower relations would be defined by an arcane arms control process.

• A stalemate in the Middle East marked by American impotence. After the Six-Day War of 1967, Washington's influence with Arab countries had dissipated while Moscow's grew. Egypt and Syria, in particular, became virtual clients of the Soviet Union. The situation did not serve U.S. interests, nor ultimately those of Israel or the cause of peace in the region.[2]

Sometimes messily, sometimes brilliantly, Nixon and Kissinger would address all four of these aberrations. They would do so, however, in a manner that was relatively new in the conduct of American affairs: with a growing reliance on deception and secrecy and back channels to avoid having to deal with dissent in Congress, the public, or even within their own cabinet.

VIETNAM OPTIONS

When Nixon and Kissinger took office, the U.S. had 536,000 troops in Vietnam. Americans were being killed at a rate of about two hundred a week. The cost of the war to U.S. taxpayers was running about $30 billion a year ($100 billion in 1990 dollars). Nor was the proverbial light visible at the end of the tunnel. "There is no plan for any reduction in our troop level," outgoing Defense Secretary Clark Clifford declared early in December 1968. Later that month he added: "The level of combat is such that we are building up our troops, not cutting them down."

The Hanoi communists considered Vietnam to be one nation, as decreed in the 1954 Geneva accords, and its division into two administrative units to be merely a temporary aberration imposed by outsiders—first the French, then the Americans. Washington, on the other hand, viewed the war as the invasion of the sovereign nation of South Vietnam by its communist neighbor to the north. Casting the struggle in a cold war context, it sought to prevent a communist takeover and, in the words of the official study known as the Pentagon Papers, "to keep South Vietnam from Chinese hands."[3]

Though his later actions would seem to belie it, Nixon knew that an American military solution was not feasible. "There's no way to win this war," he told one of his speechwriters, Richard Whalen, in March of 1968. "But we can't say that, of course. In fact, we have to seem to say just the opposite, just to keep some degree of bargaining leverage."

After FBI director J. Edgar Hoover came up to the Pierre to brief him on the recording equipment Lyndon Johnson used in the Oval Office, Nixon told Haldeman: "I'm not going to end up like LBJ, Bob, holed up in the White House, afraid to show my face on the street. I'm going to stop that war. Fast." He ordered the recording equipment removed. He did not order his own bugging equipment installed until 1971, after the war had widened into Cambodia.[4]

Kissinger had spelled out his views on Vietnam in an article for *Foreign Affairs,* which was released with great fanfare shortly after his appointment was announced. A "remarkable analysis . . . free from the myths and prejudices of the past," the *Washington Post* called it. "A powerful mind, rising above knowledge of the details to identify the way out," wrote columnist Joseph Kraft.

The article began with a tough critique of U.S. strategy. "We lost sight of one of the cardinal maxims of guerrilla war: the guerrilla wins if he does not lose. The conventional army loses if it does not win." After the Tet offensive, it became clear the war was unwinnable, or to use Kissinger's more circumspect language, the U.S. "could no longer achieve its objectives within a period or with force levels politically acceptable to the American people."

Nevertheless, Kissinger contended, America could not simply cut its losses and withdraw. The reason, he said, was that the U.S. had to maintain its "credibility." This argument would be at the heart of his thinking on Vietnam and on every other global struggle for the rest of his career.

Even though the U.S. may not have been wise to get involved in Vietnam in the first place, Kissinger argued that it could not now withdraw without undermining its position throughout the world:

> The commitment of 500,000 Americans has settled the issue of the importance of Viet Nam. What is involved now is confidence in American promises. However fashionable it is to ridicule the terms "credibility" or "prestige," they are not empty phrases; other nations can gear their actions to ours only if they can count on our steadiness. . . . In many parts of the world—the Middle East, Europe, Latin America, even Japan—stability depends on confidence in American promises.[5]

Kissinger's emphasis on credibility was a constant in his personal brand of realpolitik. There was some merit to the notion. As the world groped its way into the nuclear age, the traditional methods of asserting national power—such as controlling more territory, forging new alliances, and adding to arsenals—were becoming less meaningful. The main way that a nuclear power could enhance its global clout was to increase the *credibility* of its commitments. Power thus depended more on perception—about a nation's will and the believability of its threats—than on military might.

In the case of Vietnam, Kissinger's "credibility" argument was based on the dubious premise that if the U.S. pulled out, people around the world would respect it less. But in fact, by pursuing a futile embroilment, the U.S. squandered the true sources of its influence—and of its credibility—in the world: its moral authority, its sense of worthy purpose, and its reputation as a reasonable and sensible player.

"Why not withdraw?" Charles de Gaulle asked Kissinger during a fleeting conversation when Nixon visited Paris a month after his inauguration.

"A sudden withdrawal might give us a credibility problem," Kissinger replied.

"Where?" asked de Gaulle.

Kissinger cited the Middle East. "How very odd," said de Gaulle, who had freed the French from the disastrous entanglement in Algeria. "It is precisely in the Middle East that I thought your enemies had a credibility problem."

An important corollary to Kissinger's credibility argument was left unstated. If preserving credibility was the main goal, then the U.S. did not have to save South Vietnam indefinitely. It merely had to achieve a "decent interval" between America's withdrawal and South Vietnam's collapse. Other justifications for the war, such as the domino theory favored by Lyndon Johnson, asserted that the U.S. had national security interests at stake in the wilds of Indochina that required the defeat of the communists. But Kissinger, according to both his friends and foes, felt otherwise. During 1968, he frequently said in private talks and seminars that the appropriate goal of U.S. policy was a "decent interval" of two or three years between the withdrawal of U.S. troops and a communist takeover in Vietnam.[6]

In order to get a negotiated settlement that would preserve American credibility, Kissinger suggested in his *Foreign Affairs* article that the military issues be separated from the political ones. Washington should deal directly with Hanoi on the military questions, such as the withdrawal of troops from South Vietnam and the return of prisoners. Saigon would deal directly with the National Liberation Front on political questions, such as the type of government that would emerge in South Vietnam and the possibility of a coalition. "If we involve ourselves deeply in the issue of South Vietnam's internal arrangements," he wrote, "we shall find ourselves in a morass of complexities."

The problem with this proposal was that the communists were not willing to stop the military struggle without having achieved their political aims. As Kissinger himself later noted, "They had not fought for forty years to achieve a compromise." They fought in order to overthrow the regime in Saigon; for the U.S. to propose that there should be a military settlement that was divorced from the question of who got to rule the South clearly missed the point of the whole exercise. As the Hanoi Communist Party newspaper put it: "The military and political aspects of the issue are inseparable because the underlying cause of the Vietnam War is the American imposition of a stooge administration on the South Vietnamese people."[7]

DANIEL ELLSBERG AND NSSM-1

Shortly after his appointment, Kissinger called his old colleague and occasional critic Henry Rowen, president of the Rand Corporation, a Santa Monica think tank that specialized in military studies for the government. Kissinger had attended many seminars about Vietnam at Rand, and he knew the people there to be tough-minded skeptics about U.S. policy. What, Kissinger would ask, were the alternatives? Now he wanted to hire a team of Rand analysts to explore these alternatives and analyze the range of options.

To lead the team, Rowen picked what would seem, at least in retrospect, an odd couple: Daniel Ellsberg, Rand's foremost Vietnam expert, who later leaked the Pentagon Papers and became a hero to the Left; and Fred Ikle, head of Rand's social science division, who later became an adviser to Ronald Reagan and a hero to the Right. Ellsberg had known Kissinger since the late 1950s, had lectured at his defense policy seminar, and had given him advice when he visited Vietnam in the mid-1960s. Ikle had been a research associate under Kissinger at Harvard in the early 1960s. On Christmas Day of 1968, they flew with Rowen to New York, where for four days they met with Kissinger at the Pierre Hotel to discuss their report.

Their paper, which has never been made public, laid out seven options. At one extreme was "military escalation aimed at negotiated victory." Among the military actions that this could entail: "air and ground operations in Cambodia," "unrestricted bombing of North

Vietnam including Hanoi," and the "mining of Haiphong." The goal, according to Option One, was "to destroy the will and capability of North Vietnam to support insurgency."

At the other extreme was "unilateral withdrawal of all U.S. forces." The discussion of this option began with an admission that it "has no advocates within the U.S. government." Indeed, it went further than the "peace plank" rejected at the Democratic convention as too dovish, and even Ellsberg was not in favor of it. Nevertheless, the arguments in its favor were explored, beginning with the premise that "the war is unwinnable" and that "we should therefore cut our losses." As for the credibility question, "other nations will accept our action because we have met our commitments by large investments of men and resources, and shown wisdom in accepting the situation."

On the first day of discussions, the unilateral withdrawal option was eliminated. "Henry said it was so far outside what was going to happen that it didn't help the options paper, and it would upset Nixon," Ikle later recalled.

As a result, the most dovish option was number six: "Substantial reduction in U.S. presence while seeking a compromise settlement." The idea involved obtaining Saigon's "approval" for regular withdrawals that would bring the U.S. troop level down to one hundred thousand by the end of 1971 while building up the South Vietnamese army to take over.

In between were other alternatives. But nowhere was there any suggestion—for the analysts that Christmas would surely have thought it absurd—that the U.S. could pursue a policy based on a mix of the two most extreme options, that is, military escalation as well as regular withdrawals. Both Ellsberg and Ikle later said that it would have seemed paradoxical to conceive of a policy based on trying to beat Hanoi into submission through unrestricted bombings and the invasion of Cambodia, on the one hand, while at the same time embarking on a policy of substantial unilateral troop withdrawals.[8]

One reason that American policy would eventually turn into a crazy quilt of threats, bombing spasms, and inexorable withdrawals was because of what Nixon once dubbed "the madman theory." During the 1968 campaign, he and Haldeman were walking along a foggy California beach when Nixon began to explain that the key to a Vietnam solution was to get Hanoi to fear American threats. "I call it the madman theory, Bob. I want the North Vietnamese to believe I've reached the point where I might do *anything* to stop the war. We'll just slip the word to them that, 'for God's sake, you know Nixon is

obsessed about Communism. We can't restrain him when he's angry
—and he has his hand on the nuclear button'—and Ho Chi Minh will
be in Paris in two days begging for peace."

"Henry bought into the madman theory," according to Haldeman. "He was eager to let the Soviets think that the president might
at any moment take tough steps." Nixon later explained that, in his
mind at least, it became a good-cop, bad-cop routine: Kissinger would
come across as reasonable, but he would let it be known that he was
having a difficult time controlling his president's warlike instincts.

Fundamental to Kissinger's philosophy—and to the realist political tradition—was that diplomacy must be backed by the threat of
force. "Kissinger has a very strong ideological belief in the efficacy and
legitimacy of the threat of violence as a tool of power," Daniel Ellsberg
told Jann Wenner of *Rolling Stone* magazine in a 1973 interview. For
example, during the war between the PLO and Jordan in 1970, Secretary of State Rogers would argue that, in order to facilitate diplomacy, the U.S. should pledge not to use force. On the contrary,
argued Kissinger, diplomacy could work only if the threat remained.[9]

The Rand paper noted that there were disagreements over basic
facts within the U.S. government. So Ellsberg suggested that Kissinger put a series of questions to the different agencies, make them
answer separately, and compare the discrepancies. Kissinger liked the
idea, in part because it would swamp the bureaucracy and give him
leeway to develop policy. Fritz Kraemer's son, Sven, who had become
an aide to Kissinger, objected to the tenor of Ellsberg's questions.
"Sven, you're completely right, but you don't understand what I'm
doing," Kissinger replied. "I'm tying up the bureaucracy for a year and
buying time for the new president."[10]

The six pages, containing twenty-eight major topics and fifty-six
questions, were issued as National Security Study Memorandum 1 on
Inauguration Day. Through February and March, as the answers
flowed in from the departments and agencies, Ellsberg worked secretly
as a consultant collating them for Kissinger.

NSSM-1 did not serve to answer any questions. But it did give
Kissinger an insight into the disagreements that were simmering
within the bureaucracy. Was the "domino theory" correct that the fall
of Vietnam might lead to a succession of neighboring revolutions?
The CIA downplayed that possibility. The defense secretary's office
did, too. But the intelligence units of the army, navy, and air force
supported the domino theory. Within the State Department, the Bureau of Intelligence thought the theory was overblown, but the East
Asian Bureau endorsed it.

Were B-52 strikes effective? The military thought so, the CIA and

State Department did not. The CIA even argued that there was "substantial evidence" that the bombing made it easier for Hanoi to "mobilize people behind the Communist war effort." And on the key question (especially for those who might be considering whether to bomb or invade Cambodia) of how important the enemy supply routes through Cambodia were, the responses revealed that the U.S. military and the embassy in Saigon considered them very important, "while CIA disagrees strongly."

In general, the military and the Saigon embassy took optimistic views on most questions, asserting that the war was going rather well. The CIA, the civilians at the Pentagon, and most bureaus in the State Department were more pessimistic.[11]

Kissinger believed that he would be able to reach a peace settlement quickly. "Give us six months," he told a group of protesting Quakers, "and if we haven't ended the war by then, you can come back and tear down the White House fence."

The young intellectuals on his staff believed him. "For the first time, I'm satisfied with the Vietnam policy of the U.S.," Morton Halperin told Daniel Ellsberg that spring. Looking back on that period, Anthony Lake, a young foreign service officer who would resign as Kissinger's assistant the next year after the invasion of Cambodia, recalled: "I believe that Henry was sincere in believing he could negotiate an end to the war, and do it sooner rather than later."[12]

But Kissinger was not sympathetic to the idea of a quick withdrawal. "We could not simply walk away from an enterprise involving two administrations, five allied countries, and 31,000 dead as if we were switching a television channel," he later wrote.[13]

So Kissinger embarked on what would be a four-year quest for a negotiated settlement. At the outset the U.S. had two major demands: North Vietnamese troops must be withdrawn from the South, and the government of Nguyen Van Thieu in Saigon must not be ousted other than by free elections. Hanoi demanded the opposite: that the U.S. must withdraw unilaterally, and the "American puppet" Thieu must be deposed. By the end of 1972, the U.S. would be ready to concede the first point, and Hanoi, at least for a decent interval of two years, would concede the second.

LINKAGE

Nixon believed, as he said in his 1968 campaign, that the Soviet Union "was the key" to getting a settlement in Vietnam.

Kissinger was more skeptical; he warned in his *Foreign Affairs* article against depending too much on the Kremlin; the proper incentives, he felt, were not yet in place in 1969 to make it worth Moscow's while to help the U.S. extricate itself. In addition, one of the few areas of agreement found in NSSM-1 was that Hanoi was becoming increasingly independent of Moscow and Beijing.

Kissinger, however, quickly adopted a variation of Nixon's line that the path to peace in Vietnam went through Moscow. This led to an approach that Kissinger called linkage: American policies toward the Soviet Union on various issues—trade, arms control, Vietnam, etc.—should be linked.

In the crudest sense, this meant using trade or arms agreements as bargaining levers to extract Soviet help on Vietnam. But in a subtler sense, linkage was a way to assure that policy reflected reality. For example, it would be unrealistic to expect great progress in arms control at the same time as there was increased Soviet-American tension over regional wars, such as Vietnam. By acknowledging these linkages, Washington could create a framework of incentives and penalties that would, in theory, make it in Moscow's interest to be helpful on Vietnam.

Linkage was a policy that played to Kissinger's intellectual strengths: it appealed to a person who could conjure up the connections and motivations that linked far-flung events. That type of thinking came naturally to someone who was both a brilliant conceptualizer and slightly conspiratorial in outlook, who could feel the connections the way a spider senses twitches in its web.

Nixon was receptive to the idea of linkage, which Kissinger spelled out to a meeting of the National Security Council on the day of the inauguration. The subject was the Soviet offer to begin Strategic Arms Limitation Talks (SALT) as quickly as possible. Nixon made it clear that he did not want to set a date for renewed arms control talks until the U.S. got a sense of how helpful the Soviets were going to be on Vietnam.

For most Americans, few of whom had heard of Metternich, linkage was an uncomfortable concept. The tendency of the U.S. bureaucracy is to compartmentalize: let one group handle trade, another the Middle East, another arms control or Southeast Asia. And as a nation of pragmatic problem-solvers, led by people with legal-trained minds, Americans like to tackle issues on a case-by-case basis, examining each on its merits rather than as an element of a larger framework.

Linkage was immediately criticized as an obstacle to arms control and an impediment to improved relations with Moscow. Despite the

Soviet invasion of Czechoslovakia a few months earlier, American opinion leaders were eager for an East-West thaw. A Council on Foreign Relations study group called an early arms agreement "imperative." Another blue-ribbon panel called improved trade "a matter of major priority." A *New York Times* editorial in February attacked linkage by name. "East-West political issues," it said, "will be difficult to settle, while strategic arms issues are ripe for resolution." The *Washington Post* chimed in: "Nixon has got to stop dawdling and move quickly on missile talks. . . . Arms control has a value and urgency entirely apart from the status of political issues."

Opposition to linkage also erupted within the State Department. Nixon was loath to confront Secretary of State Rogers, who was pushing for an early opening of SALT. So Kissinger drafted a letter emphasizing the principle of linkage, which Nixon signed and sent out to the administration's top officials. "The Soviet leaders should be brought to understand," it said, "that they cannot expect to reap the benefits of cooperation in one area while seeking to take advantage of tension or confrontation elsewhere." [14]

Against this backdrop, Kissinger came up with a plan to send Cyrus Vance, the soft-spoken Democratic statesman who had been one of Johnson's negotiators in Paris, on a secret mission to Moscow to propose a package deal on Vietnam and arms control. The State Department would not be informed. The idea served many purposes. On a petty level, it would wrest control of the negotiating process—both on Vietnam and arms control—from Rogers and the State Department. It would also cement linkage: Vance would be authorized to begin the arms control talks only if the Soviets agreed to expedite the Vietnamese peace talks.

Most importantly, the Vance mission was intended as a test of Kissinger's theory of how the war could best be ended: make a bottom-line offer backed up by a tough threat. The U.S. would propose the most generous peace plan it could accept: an immediate cease-fire, mutual withdrawal of all U.S. and North Vietnamese troops, and a political solution that included a role for the National Liberation Front in governing the South. This went far beyond the current U.S. position, which was opposed to a role for the NLF or to a cease-fire until North Vietnamese troops began withdrawing. The flip side was the threat: if Hanoi would not come to terms, tough military measures would follow, along with a cooling of Soviet-American relations.

The Vance mission went nowhere. Kissinger presented the plan to Soviet Ambassador Anatoli Dobrynin with great drama, even showing him copies of Nixon's own notes on the talking points. But Dobrynin never came back with a response.

Thus began the slow death of linkage, at least in its crudest, most explicit form. On at least ten occasions in 1969, Kissinger would ask Dobrynin for Moscow's cooperation on Vietnam. Each time, Dobrynin would be evasive. Years later, Soviet officials, including the American-affairs expert Georgi Arbatov, insisted that the U.S. had overestimated the clout that Moscow had with Hanoi.

By June, the U.S. would announce that it was ready to begin SALT negotiations, even though it had not even gotten the courtesy of an answer to its proposals about Vietnam and the Vance mission. Three years later, the SALT agreement would be signed amid joyous toasts in Moscow—even though North Vietnam had just launched its most brutal offensive since Tet. Indeed, by then a reverse form of linkage would emerge: Washington found itself fearing (rather than threatening) that the arms control summit would be jeopardized by increased fighting in Vietnam. The ultimate irony was that, by its persistent involvement in Vietnam, the U.S. ended up preserving the vestiges of international communist unity by making reluctant bedfellows out of Moscow, Beijing, and Hanoi.[15]

EUROPEAN INTERLUDE: FEBRUARY 1969

For Nixon, travel was one of the most enjoyable perquisites of the presidency. It offered him a respite from the unpleasant tasks of sorting out disputes and enforcing unpleasant decisions, and it provided the pomp and protocol that can reassure even the most insecure leader that he deserves the honors that bathe him. During his 2,026-day presidency, Nixon would rack up 147,686 miles of international travel, a pace easily surpassing any other president's, and probably any other leader's, in history.

Just a month after his inauguration, Nixon went to Western Europe. His public reason was to consult with allies before negotiating with the Soviets. In addition, he wanted to make it seem that he was not obsessed with Vietnam. For Kissinger, a return to the continent of his youth, whose faded grandeur testified to the fallibility of human foresight, added a note of poignancy to his new stature.[16]

The centerpiece of the trip was a pilgrimage to French President Charles de Gaulle, whose independent attitude toward the NATO alliance had infuriated the Kennedy and Johnson administrations. In *The Troubled Partnership,* which Nixon had leafed through on the flight over, Kissinger had come to de Gaulle's defense. When they landed at Orly airport, Nixon looked out of the window and saw the general's imposing figure at the end of the ramp, coatless against the freezing February night. Nixon took off his own overcoat before leaving the plane.

De Gaulle strongly pushed the idea of an opening to China. "I do not feel that we should leave them isolated in their rage," he said. Nixon hedged. An immediate opening would be unsettling to allies in Asia, but over the long term it made sense. "In ten years, when China has made significant nuclear progress, we will have no choice," said Nixon. De Gaulle replied: "It would be better for you to recognize China before you are obliged to do so." A seed was planted.

On Vietnam, de Gaulle spoke as a man whose nation had been through it before, twice: in Vietnam itself, and in Algeria. In addition to his casual cocktail chatter with Kissinger when he dismissed the notion of "credibility," he proposed to Nixon that the U.S. simply decide to withdraw and set a timetable. When he suggested direct negotiations with the North Vietnamese, perhaps secretly in Paris, Nixon expressed interest.

The topic that most interested de Gaulle was the Soviet Union. There was a great opportunity to be exploited: the Kremlin's growing paranoia about China. "They are thinking in terms of a possible clash with China," he said, "and they know they can't fight the West at the same time. Thus I believe they may end up opting for a policy of rapprochement." He then used a word that was later to become a trademark for the Nixon-Kissinger policy. "To work toward *détente* is a matter of good sense: if you are not ready to make war, make peace." [17]

For Kissinger, the significance of the European trip had less to do with its substance than the chance to define his own role. A month or so into the job, he had not yet formed a personal relationship with the president. They communicated mainly in memos and stilted meetings. With his desire to wrest control from the bureaucracy, Kissinger spent much of the trip trying to establish his authority.

He tried to have his NSC staff put in charge of preparing the briefing books, but his aide Morton Halperin convinced him that this would be too blatant an assault on the State Department's duties. The State Department's books were late, and where they were not filled with useless mush, they were wrong. The anti–de Gaulle bias of the previous administrations went unchallenged. "We had to throw them out and rush to complete new ones," Halperin recalled. Kissinger was not shy in pointing out all of this to the president.

There had been quite a bit of jockeying about who would be on Air Force One with the president and who would be relegated to the backup "zoo plane" carrying most of the press and lesser members of the entourage. Although Kissinger made the cut, Haldeman (who was in charge of such matters) got a perverse glee in needling him about the possibility of having to bump him. Kissinger was not amused.

On the way over, Kissinger discovered to his horror that the traveling party was supposed to disembark from the plane and proceed through receptions in order of protocol—meaning that he would not be by Nixon's side. Worse yet, although he was the same rank as Haldeman, he was behind him alphabetically. "He was mortified when I told him that I went first," Haldeman recalled. "He told me that it would have a terrible effect on his ability to deal with foreign officials." Haldeman smiled and let him go first.

Kissinger, in turn, took out his anxieties on his own alter ego, Helmut Sonnenfeldt, an old colleague from the army intelligence school in Oberammergau who had joined his staff as the European and Soviet expert. Sonnenfeldt was bumped by Kissinger from Air Force One with the explanation that "I don't think there should be too many Jews around."

Kissinger's condescending treatment of Sonnenfeldt was partly a result of their love-hate rivalry, but it also reflected Kissinger's desire to be the only foreign policy staffer to have direct contact with the president. At their stop in Bonn, Sonnenfeldt was sitting next to Kissinger at a meeting when German officials unexpectedly invited Nixon to talk to the Bundestag. "You better start writing some talking points for this madman, or there's no telling what he'll come up with," Kissinger whispered to Sonnenfeldt. So he scribbled three pages on a yellow legal pad, which Kissinger then passed to Nixon. Sonnenfeldt was brooding because, while in London, Nixon had mistaken him for a local official and asked him about the weather. So he made a point of going up to Nixon after the Bundestag speech and saying, "I hope you could read my handwriting on those talking points I wrote for you." Kissinger heard him and blew up. "God damn it, Hal, you're always trying to get to the president. Stay away!"[18]

At a stop in Belgium, officials had set up a meeting with only four chairs, assuming that the prime minister and foreign minister would be conferring with their counterparts, Nixon and Rogers. "Their protocol had no provision for presidential assistants," Kissinger recalled. Since Kissinger showed no sign of retiring to a different room, another chair was added—along with one for a Belgian staffer who was roped into the meeting to keep the proper balance.

The trip was an enormous boost for Kissinger. Late on the first night, the president phoned and asked him to come by his suite at Claridge's Hotel. For a rare moment, Nixon was filled with joy. He had tried to get to sleep, but couldn't. The wine, the excitement, the stress, and the late hour combined to cause him to slur his words. "Nixon desperately wanted to be told how well he had done," Kissinger recalled.

What happened that night at Claridge's would repeat itself often over the months ahead, and it would be a bonding for their odd relationship. "He asked me to recount his conspicuous role in the day's events over and over again," recalled Kissinger, who did so fulsomely. What began that night would help sustain their turbulent partnership for more than five years. And on the night before his decision to resign, Nixon would again call Kissinger to his room late at night and once again ask him to recount over and over again his conspicuous role in world affairs, and once again Kissinger would find it easy to reassure him, to help him go gentle into the night.[19]

THE SECRET BOMBING OF CAMBODIA, MARCH 1969

Cambodia, a country half the size of Vietnam and with 10 percent of the population, had for centuries been bedeviled by its expansionist neighbor. Since 1941, the nation had been ruled by a wily and petulant showman, Prince Norodom Sihanouk, a man of great ego, quick to boast of sexual conquests, proud of his amateurish conceits as a band leader and filmmaker. With a squeaky voice and shifty demeanor, he made an unlikely chief of state. But for twenty-nine years he was able to keep his country independent through adroit duplicity and a delicate balancing act.

Part of his balancing involved permitting the North Vietnamese to set up sanctuaries along Cambodia's border with South Vietnam, which were supplied through the Ho Chi Minh Trail running through Laos to the north and through the port of Sihanoukville to the south. Even while the U.S. was bombing North Vietnam and the supply routes in Laos, it left the communist bases in Cambodia pretty much alone.

Nixon began reconsidering that policy even before taking office. On January 8, while the transition team was working at the Pierre, he sent Kissinger a note: "I want a precise report on what the enemy has in Cambodia and what, if anything, we are doing to destroy the buildup there. I think a very definite change of policy toward Cambodia probably should be one of the first orders of business."

By February, U.S. officials were becoming alarmed at the rate of

North Vietnamese infiltration into the sanctuaries along the border, and Nixon began casting around for a response. There was a general consensus, however, against resuming the bombing of North Vietnam —or, for that matter, doing anything that might cause a public outcry. "None of us had the stomach for the domestic outburst we knew renewed bombing would provoke," Kissinger later said.[20]

General Earle Wheeler, the chairman of the Joint Chiefs of Staff, was among the most ardent advocates of bombing the Vietnamese communists' sanctuaries in Cambodia. On February 9, he received a secret cable from General Creighton Abrams, the U.S. commander in Vietnam, that bolstered his argument. It concerned the whereabouts of the communists' Central Office for South Vietnam— COSVN—the elusive jungle headquarters from which the North Vietnamese and Viet Cong were supposedly coordinating their war effort.

"Recent information developed from photo reconnaissance and a rallier [Viet Cong deserter] gives us hard intelligence on COSVN HQ facilities in Base Area 353," said the Abrams wire. That was one of the border sanctuary camps in an area of Cambodia known as the Fish Hook, about seventy-five miles northwest of Saigon. "All our information, generally confirmed by imagery interpretation, provides us with a firm basis for targeting COSVN HQ." He suggested sixty sorties by B-52 bombers compressed into a one-hour strike and noted that there would be little likelihood of killing Cambodian civilians "if the target boxes are placed carefully."[21]

Word was sent to Abrams that his request was being considered at "the highest authority." Secrecy was emphasized. "Highest authority desires that this matter be held as closely as possible." At that moment, it was Kissinger who was acting on behalf of "highest authority." He set up a breakfast briefing featuring two colonels whom Abrams had sent from Saigon. The session also included Laird, Wheeler, and other top military officials. Because of the setting, the contingency plans were given the code name Breakfast.

Kissinger and Laird both argued that bombing the sanctuaries in Cambodia was not politically wise unless there was some provocation. On February 22, the day before he left for Europe, Nixon agreed, relieved not to have to take a controversial military action that could spoil his trip.[22]

The provocations began that same day: the North Vietnamese launched an all-fronts offensive that, in its first week, more than doubled (to 453) the rate of American deaths. Kissinger was outraged. Hanoi had not even waited to see what the new administration would propose before unleashing an offensive.

Kissinger arranged a military briefing in the Oval Office for Nixon. The president was seething. "All his instincts were to respond violently to Hanoi's cynical maneuver," Kissinger recalled. Nixon, who tended to personalize these things, later called the offensive "a deliberate test, clearly designed to take the measure of me." For the moment, however, all he did was tell Kissinger to call Ambassador Dobrynin and rail at the Soviets, adding one more fruitless attempt to enlist Moscow's help in rescuing the U.S. from its dilemma.

On the flight to Brussels, Nixon was suddenly emboldened: he ordered that the Fish Hook sanctuary be bombed as soon as possible. Kissinger wired a flash message to Colonel Alexander Haig, his military assistant, to get to Brussels at once to work out the details. Haig summoned Colonel Ray Sitton, a Strategic Air Command officer serving as a planner at the Pentagon. Haig, not one to be shy of the perquisites of power, scrapped their initial plan to catch a commercial flight from New York and instead ordered up a military jet to carry the two of them to Brussels.

There they met with Kissinger on Air Force One, sitting at the Brussels airport. Hurriedly they developed military and diplomatic scenarios. The bombings would not be announced, they decided, but they would be acknowledged if Cambodia lodged a protest. Sitton remembers Kissinger's obsession with keeping the operation covert. The missions should be conducted, he told Sitton, without the Strategic Air Command's normal reporting system. He even suggested that the B-52 bomber crews not be told that their targets were in Cambodia. Sitton was able to convince Kissinger that was impractical, but he did agree to figure out a way to set up a major bombing operation that would not be reported through the normal chain of command.

Nixon did not join in the discussion because, Kissinger later said, he could not do so "without attracting attention." Thus the desire to keep a major military operation secret—mainly from the American people rather than from the enemy, who would know soon enough—had its first impact: the planning proceeded without full presidential participation. Nor did anyone tell Secretary of State Rogers, who was on the same plane. Nixon waited until he and his entourage had arrived in London to give Rogers "a cryptic account of his thinking but no details." Haig went back to Washington to brief Defense Secretary Laird.

Laird supported the plan but was baffled and bothered by the premium being placed on secrecy. He cabled back his objections, saying that it would be impossible to keep the bombings covert and that any attempt to do so would backfire. If it made sense to take out

COSVN and the sanctuaries, he argued, then it should be possible to justify it publicly.

There was never much debate about the morality of bombing the territory of a neutral nation. It was accepted that since the North Vietnamese had violated the border area of Cambodia, then the U.S. could do so as well. Nixon had already conveyed to his cabinet the sense that he had little patience for moral prissiness. American policy was edging toward what had heretofore been an unfamiliar realm: the use of military power not anchored by concerns about morality and international law.

At the last moment, Nixon became bothered by the awkwardness of launching a major bombing operation while he was wandering through Europe. So a delay was ordered, but with a strange twist: a cable was sent to Ambassador Ellsworth Bunker in Saigon through the State Department's leaky channel saying that all discussions of bombing Cambodia were being suspended. But using a secret military system, a back-channel message was sent to General Abrams telling him to ignore the message to Bunker. He should proceed with contingency planning.[23]

For the first two weeks of March, Nixon's advisers tugged him back and forth. Once again, after getting a recommendation from Kissinger, he issued an order to bomb the sanctuaries; once again, after listening to Rogers, he backed down. Then, on Saturday, March 15, the North Vietnamese shelled Saigon, something they had not done since the October 1968 bombing halt. Kissinger's phone line from the president rang just after three-thirty that afternoon. Nixon was adamant: he ordered that the communist sanctuaries in the Fish Hook region of Cambodia be bombed right away.

When Nixon was hyped up, he had a style of talking that was becoming familiar to Kissinger. His sentences would be abrupt, staccato, and peppered with warnings that he would fire anyone who dissented. He would bark his decision, hang up, then call back with a further command. "State is to be notified only after the point of no return," he said. Slam. Then, a few moments later: "The order is not appealable."[24]

A meeting was scheduled with Laird, Rogers, and Wheeler for the next afternoon in the Oval Office. As with the December Key Biscayne meeting involving the new NSC structure, the participants were not informed that the decision had already been made. It was "vintage Nixon," Kissinger later wrote. "He felt it necessary to pretend that the decision was still open. This led to hours of the very discussion that he found so distasteful and that reinforced his tendency to exclude the recalcitrants from further deliberations."

In the private memo that Kissinger wrote to Nixon urging the bombing, he noted that the greatest risks would be strong Cambodian and Soviet protests, a public outcry, and military retaliation by the North Vietnamese. But the Greek goddess Nemesis, as Kissinger once wrote, had a fiendish way of punishing her victims by granting their wishes. Kissinger did not analyze the possibility that the attack would remain secret and that the Cambodians and North Vietnamese would make no response at all.

The unintended consequences from such a scenario would have seemed absurd to contemplate had they not all come to pass: the lack of protests would mean that the bombings would continue secretly for more than a year; the fear of leaks would lead to extraordinary security measures and a program to wiretap White House aides; after a year the sanctuaries would still be operating, as would be the elusive COSVN headquarters; and later all of this would publicly explode.[25]

Nixon's decision to authorize the secret bombing of the Fish Hook sanctuary was conveyed in a cable from General Wheeler— "Execute Operation Breakfast," it read—that reached Anderson Air Force Base in Guam on the afternoon of March 17. That night, sixty B-52 bombers took off over the Russian "fishing" boats that always seemed to be lurking around and embarked on the five-hour journey to Vietnam. It was a clear night. As they entered Vietnamese airspace, American ground controllers took over the navigation. When the controllers finished their countdowns, a string of bombs fell from the planes and exploded to earth in a "box" that was two miles long and a half mile wide. Early on the morning of March 18, for the first time during the war, forty-eight of the B-52 bombing boxes were on Cambodian territory.

Kissinger was in his West Wing basement office talking to Morton Halperin when Alexander Haig came in with a piece of paper. Kissinger smiled and explained that American planes had just attacked a North Vietnamese base in Cambodia. At least seventy-three secondary explosions had been reported, some of them five times the intensity of a normal explosion, indicating that the bombs had struck pay dirt and hit fuel or ammunition storage areas. Halperin was sworn to secrecy.[26]

A few people got a far less optimistic assessment of the bombing. Since 1967, U.S. Green Berets had been running secret forays into Cambodia code-named Daniel Boone. The two-man teams were disguised in Viet Cong pajamas, carried no identification, and traveled with ten or so local mercenaries. On the morning of March 18, the commanding officer of Daniel Boone arrived from Saigon and ordered a unit sent to Base Area 353 in Cambodia, which he reported had just been bombed by American B-52s. Lieutenant Randolph Harrison, who was one of the unit commanders, later recalled that the men were told to go in and pick up communist survivors. "They will be so stunned," the commanding officer assured them, "that all you will have to do is walk over and lead them by the arm to the helicopter."

Two Americans and eleven locals were flown to a clearing near the target area. "They were cut down before they could even get to the trees," Harrison later recalled. "I believe two or three of them got out alive; the rest of them were not even recovered, their bodies." Despite the exaggerated reports of secondary explosions, the communists' "headquarters" had not been wiped out. "The visible effect on the North Vietnamese who were there was the same as taking a beehive the size of a basketball and poking it with a stick," Harrison later said. "They were mad." Asked about his opinion of the effectiveness of B-52s, he replied: "My original enthusiasm for them has been tempered somewhat." [27]

The enthusiasm of Nixon and Kissinger, however, was whetted. The original decision, made with great difficulty, was for one secret raid to wipe out the communist COSVN headquarters supposedly located in the Fish Hook region. But when the raid neither accomplished that mission nor raised a great outcry, Nixon authorized further attacks on other sanctuary areas in Cambodia—all to be kept secret. Operation Breakfast was followed by Lunch, Snack, Dinner, Dessert, and with the available meals running out, Supper. Kissinger later called the names "tasteless." The whole program was dubbed MENU.

Colonel Sitton had established, after talking to Kissinger and Haig, an elaborate system to keep the bombing secret. A set of false reports was sent through regular Pentagon channels, and a secret set of books were kept that contained the actual targets. "I asked why we had to fake the reports," Major Hal Knight of the Strategic Air Command in Vietnam told a 1973 Senate investigation, "and I was told it was necessary for political reasons."

The air force secretary and other top officials were not informed of the raids at all, and even the State Department was kept in the dark. A few selected congressmen were informed of the initial raid, but there was no effort to consult with Congress formally or to be frank about the extent of the operations—something that Kissinger later admitted he regretted. Even in 1971, a year after the secret bombing program had ended and well after Cambodia had been plunged into an open war, the Senate Armed Services Committee in a closed hearing on bombing targets was told by military officials that there "was no B-52 bombing in Cambodia of any kind during the entire year of 1969."[28]

The secret bombing continued for fourteen months, until May 1970, during which American B-52s flew 3,875 sorties and dropped 108,823 tons of bombs on the six border-area base camps. The duration of the program belied the original argument that a single strike could knock out communist headquarters. It also undercut the rationale that the bombing was in response to an unprovoked communist offensive; that offensive, like the ones every spring, had begun in February and ended with the monsoons of May. The MENU bombing would come to a close not because it was successful, but because it was unsuccessful: the sanctuaries and elusive COSVN headquarters remained such a threat that Nixon would decide to launch a full-fledged ground invasion of Cambodia.[29]

The military was nonetheless pleased with the operation. American deaths, which had doubled to 450 a week at the start of the communist offensive, dropped to 250 after the bombing, then to less than half that number. JCS chairman Earle Wheeler also noted, as if it were a benefit, that the bombings had caused "increased dispersal of personnel and supplies" by the Vietnamese communists in Cambodia.[30]

What seemed beneficial to General Wheeler, however, was not necessarily so for Cambodia's Prince Sihanouk. By walking a tightrope —and turning a blind eye to the North Vietnamese sanctuaries and the occasional U.S. raids—he had kept his country from being plunged into the wars that were tearing apart Vietnam and Laos. The local guerrilla movement, the Khmer Rouge, numbered only four or five thousand in 1969. Although the North Vietnamese had violated Cambodia's neutrality, their camps had not yet disrupted the lives of the Cambodian peasants and fishermen. But that delicate balance began to falter when the American bombing campaign caused the communist camps to disperse over a larger area. The bombing may not have been the main cause of Cambodia's plunge toward chaos a year later, but it did not make Sihanouk's balancing act any easier.[31]

Kissinger and other officials later defended the legality of the bombing by saying that Prince Sihanouk did not object, and that in his heart he welcomed it. Indeed, he restored diplomatic relations with the U.S. in July 1969, even as the bombs were falling. "If Sihanouk invited us to attack the North Vietnamese bases," argued Peter Rodman, a former aide to Kissinger, "then we were defending Cambodia's neutrality, not violating it."

Pinning down precisely what Sihanouk truly felt at any point is a task beyond most historians, and his words offer little help. He usually said what he felt best served his needs of the moment; even his own memoirs and interviews contradict one another. In 1968, he indicated to American diplomat Chester Bowles that he "would not object if the U.S. engaged in hot pursuit" of communist forces stationed in Cambodia, though he could not say so publicly. Sihanouk later told William Shawcross, a British journalist who wrote a critical account of U.S. policy toward Cambodia, "I had told Chester Bowles, in passing, that the U.S. could bomb Vietnamese sanctuaries," adding, however, that "the question of a big B-52 campaign was never raised."[32]

The historical debate over whether Sihanouk approved of the U.S. bombing mainly serves to highlight the delicacy of his balancing act. Only vagueness could preserve the precarious peace he guarded for his country. The fact remains that Sihanouk and his government never formally asked for U.S. help in eliminating the North Vietnamese bases. Short of such an official request, the vacillating private comments of a prickly prince do not serve as much of a legal justification for the bombing of a neutral nation, and for doing so without consulting Congress.

Kissinger later argued that it was necessary to keep the bombing secret to avoid putting Sihanouk on the spot, forcing him either to denounce—or perhaps approve—American actions against the North Vietnamese sanctuaries. "It was kept secret because a public announcement would be a gratuitous blow to the Cambodian government, which might have forced it to demand that we stop."

There is some merit to that. But in fact, Washington also had reason to fear the opposite, that Sihanouk would approve the raids. That would have put the administration in an even tougher spot: openly taking steps to widen the war into yet another Southeast Asian country. The result would have been the domestic uproar that Nixon and Kissinger wanted to avoid.

Despite all the talk about "Sihanouk's sensitivities," that justification for the secrecy cannot bear the weight that Kissinger ascribes to it. The administration became obsessed with keeping the Cambodian bombing secret largely because it was worried about American reaction, not just Sihanouk's. The double bookkeeping, wiretaps, falsified records, misleading congressional testimony, circumvention of Congress, and outright lies—it was not all necessary just for Sihanouk's sake.

In one of the most disingenuous sentences in his memoirs, Kissinger wrote that if the bombing program had been announced, "it would surely have been supported by the American public." Not so. Like the invasion of Cambodia a year later, an announcement of the bombing program would have set off violent protests. Seeking congressional and public support would have been in keeping with the American system—but it would not have been easy.

Nixon was more honest in his memoirs. After citing Sihanouk's delicate position, he adds: "Another reason for the secrecy was the problem of domestic antiwar protest." But in a democracy, the problem of domestic protest is not a valid reason for keeping a major military action secret. [33]

The decision to keep the bombings secret reflected the style of the people involved. Even Lawrence Eagleburger, long a close associate and defender of Kissinger, saw in his former boss the traits that led to the decision. "With the players involved—mainly Kissinger and Nixon and to some extent Haig—it was sure to be done in a secret way," he said. "With other players—Rockefeller, Ford—it would have been different." [34]

Defense Secretary Laird was a supporter of the bombing; he felt strongly that "we should hit the hell out of them." But he also felt that "it was goddamned stupid to try to keep it secret." Kissinger's dual reporting had to be ordered by Nixon over Laird's objections. "Despite what Henry told me," Laird later said, "I refused to authorize the phony reporting of the locations of the bombing runs. I refused to send the message. Nixon and Kissinger sent it to [Ambassador] Bunker for delivery to Abrams."

The secretiveness of Nixon and Kissinger allowed the wily Laird to earn a few chits from his friends on Capitol Hill. "Without the White House knowing it, I briefed some of my congressmen, such as Gerald Ford, George Mahon, Mendel Rivers, and Edward Hebert," he later said. "It made them trust me, because I kept them informed when Nixon and Kissinger were deceiving them." [35]

The odd thing is that the secrecy was not originally intended to be as obsessive as it became. From the very start, the plans contained provisions for handling press inquiries: "Spokesman will confirm that B-52s did strike on routine missions adjacent to the Cambodian border but state that he has no details and will look into it." If Cambodia officially protested: "After delivering a reply to any Cambodian protest, Washington will inform the press that we have apologized and offered compensation."

But as the program grew, and as the deceptions became more intricate, the secrecy gradually became more important than the bombing itself. Soon, Kissinger and Nixon were paying little attention to the results of the regular bombing runs. But they were becoming more and more obsessed with the need for secrecy. [36]

The Downing of the EC-121, April 1969

In accepting his 1968 nomination, Nixon had accused the Johnson administration of being feckless when the North Koreans seized the Navy spy ship *Pueblo* earlier that year. "When respect for the United States falls so low that a fourth-rate military power like Korea will seize an American naval vessel on the high seas, it's time for new leadership," he declared. Nixon's chance to show how he would act more decisively came on the night of Monday, April 14, when a North Korean jet shot down an unarmed American EC-121 spy plane, carrying thirty-one crewmen, that was well over international waters about ninety miles off Korea's coast.

The crisis would lead to the first clear split within the administration between the hawks, led by Nixon and Kissinger, and the doves, led by Rogers, Laird, and CIA director Richard Helms. It also became a test of the power-and-credibility philosophy that Kissinger and Nixon embraced.

From the outset, Kissinger favored retaliation, as did Morton Halperin and the other top NSC staffers. The State Department was opposed; it suggested that the U.S. make its displeasure known by not showing up at a meeting of the Armistice Commission later in the week. Laird and the Defense Department were against any military steps that might detract from the Vietnam effort; in the meantime, they canceled all U.S. spy flights in the region. [37]

The full NSC did not meet until Wednesday, almost two days after the incident. A consensus was forming around a proposal to seize a North Korean merchant ship at sea. But there was one hitch: North Korea had no ships at sea, and hadn't for almost a year. There were reports of a Korean-owned ship under Dutch registry floating around somewhere; Nixon kept asking about it, but no one could ever locate it.

Kissinger began pushing for what he called a "sterile" strike against the air base of the Korean fighter jet. Laird and his military advisers ridiculed the presumption, always more popular among theorists than military men, that an air strike could be surgical or sterile. They recommended against it. So did the State Department; Undersecretary Alexis Johnson kept asking how the North Koreans were supposed to know that this was just a retaliatory blow rather than the start of a full war. [38]

Kissinger even ran into opposition on the political side. After the NSC meeting, he met with Haldeman and Ehrlichman to ask what domestic reaction would be to a retaliation. "Like what?" asked Ehrlichman.

"Knocking out the base where the Korean planes came from," said Kissinger.

"Okay," answered Ehrlichman, "but what if they knock out something of ours?"

"Then it could escalate."

"How far?"

"Well," said Kissinger, "it could go nuclear."

It was not the sort of scenario to bandy about, especially in front of Ehrlichman, who already had his fears that Kissinger reminded him a little too much of Dr. Strangelove. The word soon floated around the White House that Kissinger was suggesting the possibility of a nuclear option.[39]

Frustrated by the bureaucracy's mushiness, Kissinger told Halperin that they had to prepare a memo to the president. "That's what we're doing," said Halperin. "No," replied Kissinger, "I mean a serious one. The one you're doing is for the files." Halperin ended up writing two memos, an official one and a private one. Eagleburger was also assigned to write a version, unbeknownst to Halperin.[40]

The next day Nixon decided against a military retaliation. Instead he selected two very mild options: sending out armed escorts along with spy plane flights, and dispatching two aircraft carriers to steam around the Sea of Japan. Only then did the White House discover that the Pentagon had already canceled all spy flights in the area. It would take a while to get them resumed, the Pentagon told Kissinger, especially if escorts were required.

Kissinger went to see Laird and "ricocheted all over the walls," according to one of the defense secretary's aides. He accused the Pentagon of having "usurped the president's authority." Kissinger spent four weeks firing off memos to Laird trying to get the spy flights under way again, but it was not until May 8 that they were resumed. His academic writings on how bureaucracies resist executive decisions were being played out before him.

The carriers grandly showing the flag in the Sea of Japan were followed by television crews and even a blimp. But because the administration had not announced (and in fact never decided) what it wanted from North Korea—an apology? compensation? admission of blame?—the processional served no discernible purpose.[41]

When he met with Nixon after the announcement of the mild responses, Kissinger again argued that a failure to retaliate would hurt America's credibility. A tough response, on the other hand, would reinforce Nixon's "madman theory" of how to intimidate the communist world. "If we strike back," Kissinger contended, "they will say, 'This guy is becoming irrational—we'd better settle with him.' "

But Rogers, Laird, and Helms continued to oppose a military retaliation, and Kissinger finally accepted the consensus. "We discovered that it would split the administration apart and might lead to the resignation of some of the cabinet," Nixon later recalled. "The traffic wouldn't bear it."

After the decision was made, Nixon railed to Kissinger about how spineless Laird and Rogers had been. He would get rid of them, he vowed, and he would never consult them again in a crisis. "The result," recalled Kissinger, "was to confirm Nixon in his isolated decision-making."

There was another result as well: with his disposition to please his patrons, Kissinger took Nixon's anger at his less militaristic advisers to heart. By talking tough, Kissinger realized, he had brought himself closer to the president.[42]

The NSC machinery had flunked its first test, badly. It had not produced usable options or established clear goals, and it had operated at a clumsy pace that missed any openings for decisive action. In fact, it never even determined whether the Korean attack was a deliberate provocation or an isolated wayward act; intelligence intercepts indicated the latter, but these were never fully discussed.

So Kissinger moved to tighten his grip on crisis management. He formed a new body called the Washington Special Action Group, which he would chair. Other members would include the number two officers at State, Defense, CIA, and other agencies. In future crises, it would develop strategies and impose a sense of direction—all under Kissinger's stewardship.

Kissinger's hard-line position was largely guided by his contention that America's credibility was at stake, that weakness would encourage future challenges. In discussing the EC-121 incident in his memoirs, he cited the lesson that "hesitation encourages the adversary to persevere, maybe even to raise the ante." The failure to respond, he asserted, emboldened America's adversaries.

Though this makes sense in theory, there is little evidence that it was true regarding the EC-121 shootdown. The U.S. did nothing; it made no retaliatory strike and barely rattled a saber. Nevertheless, North Korea did not raise the ante.

The only serious military response that Nixon made to the North Korean action was to order another bombing attack on North Vietnamese sanctuaries in Cambodia. This odd version of linkage seemed to assume that an attack on the Vietnamese communists, conducted in secret, would serve to punish and intimidate the North Koreans.[43]

TEN

KISSINGER'S EMPIRE

The Boss's Power
and How He Operated

> *One of the paradoxes of an increasingly specialized, bureaucratized society is that the qualities rewarded in the rise to eminence are less and less the qualities required once eminence is reached.*
> —KISSINGER, THE NECESSITY FOR CHOICE, *1960*

THE RACE FOR DEPUTY

The day after Kissinger was appointed, he had run into his old Harvard colleague Arthur Schlesinger, Jr. How in the world, Schlesinger asked, do you plan to cope with having Richard Allen as your deputy? "Arthur," Kissinger replied, "I plan to treat Dick Allen the way Mac Bundy treated me, and he will be gone within a year."

Allen was the cherubic-faced conservative who had helped bring Kissinger into the Nixon camp and served as a secret contact for inside information from the Vietnamese peace talks during the campaign. Nixon had appointed Allen deputy national security adviser, and initially Kissinger poured on the charm, such as by asking Allen to do him the honor of escorting his parents to the Pierre Hotel press conference where Kissinger's appointment was announced. Allen proudly did.[1]

But even before the new team took office, Kissinger was trying to ease Allen aside. Behind his back, he referred to Allen as a member of the "sandbox Right," a phrase that was picked up in a brutal column by Rowland Evans and Robert Novak that concluded: "It is inconceivable that Kissinger will make much use of Allen." After promising him an office next to his own in the White House West Wing, Kissinger convinced Allen that he would be better off in a bigger suite on the third floor of the Executive Office Building—across the street. Then he began deleting Allen's name from those invited to meetings with the president. "Where's Dick Allen?" Nixon would ask, and Kissinger would mumble something about his not being available. Soon the president stopped noticing.

In the meantime, Kissinger swamped Allen with mammoth make-work projects: rewriting the entire U.S. strategic targeting plan, reviewing the military's worldwide basing requirements. By August, Allen had resigned.[2]

Kissinger took pride in the freedom Nixon gave him to choose the best professional staff he could find, irrespective of their politics. "You've got to remember that I didn't support this man either," he said of Nixon as he enlisted Roger Morris, a foreign service officer who was on Johnson's NSC staff. Nixon's loyal retainers tried to interfere, but Kissinger was able to fend them off. "In at least two cases," Kissinger said, "Haldeman challenged my selections on grounds of security, which turned out to be more a matter of liberal convictions or a propensity to talk to journalists. In both cases I overruled Haldeman."[3]

The appointees in question were Morton Halperin and Helmut Sonnenfeldt—both ambitious intellectuals who emerged as the two candidates most likely to replace Allen as Kissinger's deputy.

Halperin would later become one of the administration's sharpest critics. But in early 1969, according to Roger Morris, he was "one of the more grasping, calculating bureaucrats circling the West Basement." He was also one of the smartest, with an eight-cylinder mind and darting eyes that were always working. His expertise was in bureaucratic structures: he had written about the subject as an academic, had put his theories into practice when he helped to draft the new NSC structure for Kissinger, and played the game daily as he shuttled between Kissinger's office in the White House basement and the NSC staff offices in the Executive Office Building.

Kissinger was, like Nixon, a man of multiple facets and tended to reflect whoever was around him. Halperin appealed to Kissinger's academic side. He was like a star graduate student who was nimble both as a thinker and as an aficionado of faculty politics.

Though no more ambitious than Sonnenfeldt, he was more open about it. "Mort put Kissinger under a lot of pressure to put him in a deputy's role, to have people report through him," said Laurence

Lynn, who was a systems analyst on the staff. "It caused some heart-ache."[4]

"Halperin was hoping to be deputy, so he was always waiting outside of Henry's door," recalled Helmut Sonnenfeldt. The same could be said, and often was, of Sonnenfeldt; Kissinger in particular used to joke that he couldn't step outside his office without stumbling over Sonnenfeldt.

If Halperin played the role of star graduate student, then Sonnenfeldt's part was that of fellow European intellectual who appealed to Kissinger's philosophic side. They were compatriots and companions who shared a common heritage, with all the rivalries and secret bondings and grudging respect that go with it. "Tension crackled in the air whenever they were together," said Larry Lynn. "Hal was too much like Henry to avoid rivalry: ambitious, vain, paranoid."

Sonnenfeldt would keep watch out of his Executive Office Building window onto the entrance of the White House West Wing. If he saw Soviet Ambassador Dobrynin or anyone else who fell within his area of responsibility, he would bound from his office to be there at any meeting Kissinger had. "It would drive Henry nuts," Eagleburger recalled. "There was a love-hate competition, especially on Hal's part."

The primary source of their rivalry was Sonnenfeldt's resentment at being treated like a Kissinger staffer rather than an official in his own right who deserved independent access to the president. "From the very first day Henry felt a sense of rivalry with me," Sonnenfeldt recalled, "especially in terms of dealing with Nixon." Unlike previous national security assistants, Kissinger made sure that his staff did not have independent access to the president, the press, or diplomats. "It was," said Sonnenfeldt, "a manifestation of his insecurity."

Once, when Kissinger's aides could not fit into his schedule a White House lunch that Nixon was hosting for the president of Notre Dame, they knew they could enlist Sonnenfeldt to fill in. Just beforehand, when Sonnenfeldt was in a meeting with Kissinger, Eagleburger —as a prank—marched in and handed Sonnenfeldt a memo saying, "Hal, this is about your luncheon with the president." Kissinger, as was his wont, looked over and read it. Unable to contain himself, he came out of the meeting and insisted that his schedule be revised; he went instead of Sonnenfeldt. At another point, his aides devised a plan to solve the problem of getting Kissinger to look at and approve his calendar of future appointments. They simply put his proposed schedules in a folder labeled "Sonnenfeldt" and left it lying where he would spot it; invariably he would pick it up and look inside.

Kissinger apparently took pleasure in inflicting small humiliations on Sonnenfeldt. "Not you, Hal, you're not important enough," he said at a White House ceremony as he excluded Sonnenfeldt from a group picture. "Petty instances of friction began to accumulate," Sonnenfeldt said. "Once I realized how sensitive he was, I started teasing him and pretending I was really challenging him for access to the president. It was in order to get a rise out of him." Then, almost sadly, Sonnenfeldt added: "The more loyal I was, the more he would sense a vulnerability, and the more devious he would be."

Yet for all of their personal friction, Kissinger had a great respect for Sonnenfeldt's analytic ability. Repeatedly, he would turn to him for assessments of Soviet intentions or sound him out about a variety of policies.

The odd thing about Sonnenfeldt was not that he failed to thrive under Kissinger, but that he survived. Years later, when Kissinger had moved to the State Department and brought Sonnenfeldt with him, Kissinger was with his spokesman Robert McCloskey at Andrews Air Force Base as West German Chancellor Willy Brandt's helicopter arrived. Out stepped the chancellor followed by a familiar face. "Why is Sonnenfeldt with Brandt?" McCloskey asked. Replied Kissinger: "Why does Sonnenfeldt exist?"[5]

As Halperin and Sonnenfeldt were self-destructing in the demolition derby to be Kissinger's deputy, left standing was an outside contender, one who could protect Kissinger on his vulnerable right flank: Colonel Alexander Haig, whose square-jawed fealty to Nixon's hardline policies increasingly became more important than intellect, creativity, or a knowledge of foreign policy nuances.

Under Haig's picture in the West Point yearbook for 1947, the year that he graduated 214th in a class of 310, are the words: "Strong convictions and even stronger ambitions mingled with a deep understanding of his fellow soldier should form a 'warrior's chariot' to carry Alex to the top." He had been born into a working-class Irish Catholic family in Philadelphia, lost his father to cancer, and been raised by a driven and savvy mother. As an infantry battalion commander in Vietnam in 1967, Haig helped oversee the destruction of Ben Suc, a once-peaceful South Vietnamese village near Saigon that was suspected of providing sanctuary to the Viet Cong. Later he was decorated for his heroism—and earned a battlefield promotion to colonel—by taking over command of a brigade in a fierce two-day battle close to the Cambodian border. But each of his subsequent promotions, up to four-star general, came for valor behind a desk at the White House.

When Kissinger was looking for a military assistant, Haig was recommended by Joseph Califano and Robert McNamara, who had known him from his days as a staff officer in the Pentagon. Kissinger's old mentor Fritz Kraemer also urged him to tap Haig, whom he later called "my other great discovery." Haig was then serving as deputy commandant of West Point, where he was earning a reputation (and many young enemies) for making his cadets march with their elbows locked and fingers cocked at the second knuckle.

Unlike the substantive aides on the NSC staff who were quartered in the Executive Office Building next door, Haig and Eagleburger began as Kissinger's two personal aides—military and civilian—with desks just outside his office in the basement of the White House West Wing. Haig soon began handling the most sensitive materials and secrets.

With his ability to curse like a sergeant and hold his gin like a general, Haig quickly became popular with much of Kissinger's staff. Unlike the ambitious Halperin and the antsy Sonnenfeldt, he was no intellectual threat and usually did not presume to second-guess their reports and recommendations. Yet he was able to make the office run smoothly despite the frenzy caused by Kissinger's volcanic disarray. "I liked Al," said Anthony Lake, who was not an ideological soul mate. "He was an organizer, enforcer, stroker, steadying force."

When Kissinger would erupt, Haig could take it; a valuable aspect of his military training was that he'd learned to absorb abuse from overbearing superiors while remaining erect and unruffled. Afterward, when Kissinger had stormed away, Haig would amuse the other staffers by mimicking the scene, first pretending to be Kissinger stomping around and hopping, then making fun of himself as a stiff and mindless robot willing to march around in circles. "Only someone schooled in taking shit could put up with it," said Coleman Hicks, who briefly held the thankless job of appointments secretary.

When others felt the brunt of Kissinger's wrath, Haig was there with a hand on the shoulder, "posing as their irreverent, sympathetic advocate," said Roger Morris. He would cast himself as the good cop while portraying the boss as wild and intractable. It was a tactic Kissinger knew well, since he cast himself in a similar role with Nixon. "In that sense Haig hoisted me by my own petard," Kissinger later said.

Haig's quest to become Kissinger's deputy was helped by his willingness to work long hours. Kissinger would generally depart around eight for a dinner party or other social obligation, leaving Haig alone in the basement with a pile of work. Afterward, Kissinger would swing back by the office to find the work done and the secrets all safe. Haig's duties were manifold. He served as the emissary to FBI Director J. Edgar Hoover and others who might suspect Kissinger of being soft. He taught Kissinger about the perks of power, such as arranging for military planes to take him to New York for weekends. He was even the one who rented the white tie and tails Kissinger needed for his first White House dinner and came to his apartment to help him put it on.

Among the tasks Haig soon came to handle for Kissinger was overseeing a secret FBI program to wiretap the home telephones of other members of the NSC staff (see Chapter 11). Halperin and Sonnenfeldt, on the other hand, would be the first two victims of that program. That, it turned out, would pretty much settle which of the three would emerge victorious in the race for deputy.

There was one other component in Haig's triumph: Kissinger was convinced that Haig could never become a threat to his own relationship with Nixon. He was an unreflective man, Kissinger felt, not a strategic thinker, and he believed in the chain of authority. Kissinger was right about Haig's mind. But he would soon discover that he had been deeply mistaken about both his ambitions and his loyalties.[6]

KISSINGER'S OPERATING STYLE

One day, a few months after taking office, Kissinger emerged from a meeting and, as was his wont, bellowed for his personal aide. Someone pointed to the couch in the reception area. There lay Lawrence Eagleburger, who had collapsed from nervous exhaustion and was being taken to the hospital. "But I need him," Kissinger shouted. Ignoring Eagleburger's plight, he stomped around barking orders and grumbling that work was not getting done. Haig, who was there, later retold the tale with relish for staffers who had missed the show.[7]

Eagleburger, a roly-poly foreign service officer with an irreverent sense of humor, had the toughest job on the staff: being Kissinger's personal aide, which meant tending to everything from his laundry to his paper flow. After recovering from his breakdown, he found calmer work as a diplomat assigned to NATO in Brussels; Tony Lake took over his duties, lasted less than a year, then was succeeded by Winston Lord.

The turnover on the rest of Kissinger's staff was almost as high. Of the twenty-eight assistants who joined the NSC at the beginning of 1969, ten would depart by September—including Eagleburger, Halperin, Daniel Davidson, Spurgeon Keeny, Richard Moose, and Richard Sneider. By the summer of 1971, only seven of the original twenty-eight would still be around.[8]

Part of the problem was that Kissinger treated his staffers as menials rather than foreign policy professionals. At their first meeting, on the afternoon of Inauguration Day, he had informed them that they would not have dining privileges at the White House mess, even though they would be working late hours. Only domestic staffers would be able to eat there. He blamed the decision on Haldeman; but Haldeman later said it was made by Kissinger, who did not want his people forming alliances with staffers from the White House's political side.

Kissinger concluded his lecture at the meeting by saying, "The most important thing is that all of you instantly are to sever your relations to the press." He added with preemptive candor: "If anybody leaks in this administration, I will be the one to leak."

Kissinger also stopped the practice of allowing top staffers to meet directly with the president to discuss their areas of expertise. In fact, he did not even allow them to accompany him to meetings with the president except in rare cases. "It reflected his tremendous mixture of ego and insecurity," said Winston Lord. Since the chance to meet with the president provides the sort of thrill that makes long hours and overbearing demands worthwhile, morale was undermined.

When Halperin gave CIA director Richard Helms a routine rundown of the agenda before the first NSC meeting, Kissinger found out. He had no objection to what Halperin had said, but he was upset that one of his underlings had presumed to talk to a cabinet official. Kissinger sent word through Haig: "No staffer is to talk to principals."

Because Kissinger, ever disorganized, refused to delegate authority or manage his schedule, his office became a bottleneck. "In the first year it was like a Moroccan whorehouse, with people queuing up outside his door for hours," said Sonnenfeldt. Kissinger was invariably ten minutes late wherever he was supposed to be, even White House staff meetings; top officials grumbled that they were being treated like college undergraduates waiting for a professor to show up for a seminar.

Some meetings, such as those with the U.S. arms negotiating team, were repeatedly canceled at the last moment. When Kissinger did arrive, he would often be interrupted by a secretary a few minutes into the meeting, depart abruptly to take a phone call, and then return after a half hour or so while the others fumed.

Kissinger's management style was conspiratorial rather than open, secretive rather than inclusive. "He didn't like large meetings because he didn't want people to form factions and confront him," said Sonnenfeldt. "He created a bond by sharing confidences and making snide comments about everyone else."

This approach was often not a considered strategy; instead, it was simply part of his personality, something that came naturally to him. "He was able to give a conspiratorial air to even the most minor of things," said Eagleburger. "It was rather adolescent at times."[9]

By dealing with aides and colleagues privately, Kissinger could create a sense of intimacy. He would lead people to believe that they were among the few people he could trust, among the few who would understand the sensitive information he was about to impart. "Henry used to tell me I was the only person at State with a capacity for conceptual thinking," said Elliot Richardson. "Henry would say that I was the only journalist he couldn't manipulate," said Henry Brandon.

It was all extremely charming. "I have never met a man with greater powers of seduction," recalled Admiral Elmo Zumwalt, a member of the Joint Chiefs of Staff. "He was not only charming and witty, but he made me feel I was a person whose advice and assistance he uniquely sought."

After one of their private meetings, where he enlisted Zumwalt's support to work around Laird's back, Kissinger told the admiral what a pleasure it was to deal with him. "You are the only intellectual among the chiefs, the only one to take a broad view." As soon as Zumwalt left, Kissinger turned to his staffers and muttered, "If there's one thing I can't stand, it's an intellectual admiral."

With so many insatiable egos in government, Kissinger's finesse at flattery found fertile territory. He used it on Ellsberg repeatedly. "I learned more about Vietnam from Daniel Ellsberg than any other person," Kissinger said just after the 1968 election when they were both at a Rand seminar. On Ellsberg's visit to see Kissinger at San Clemente two years later, he tried again: "I've learned more about bargaining from Daniel Ellsberg than any other person." At the other extreme, he would lay it on thick with his hawkish rival in the administration, John Connally. "He was always telling me how smart I was, how much the president relied on me," Connally later said. "He was damn good at it, and I know, because I had some experience in that field myself."[10]

But Kissinger's charm had a downside: in his efforts to co-opt and flatter a broad spectrum of people, he inevitably developed a reputation for being two-faced. By dealing privately and secretly with people, he was able to shade his responses to what each person wanted to hear. What he never fully realized was that, both among his staff and around town, comparing notes on what Kissinger had said was a lively preoccupation.

Both Arthur Schlesinger, Jr., the liberal historian, and William F. Buckley, Jr., the conservative journalist, used to go to Washington regularly to meet with Kissinger. "I'd come home and tell my wife I was encouraged, that Henry was the best thing in the Nixon administration," Schlesinger later said. "Then one day I heard that Buckley was following the exact same scenario—having lunch with Henry and telling *his* wife how great he was. I realized that something was wrong."

Buckley's friends in the conservative movement used to warn him that Kissinger was being duplicitous. "Kissinger can meet with six different people, smart as hell, learned, knowledgeable, experienced, of very different views, and persuade all six of them that the real Henry Kissinger is just where they are," recalled Frank Shakespeare, who headed the U.S. Information Agency. David Keene, who was then Agnew's chief of staff, said: "He had one line for liberals, one for conservatives, and all the time he'd swear you to secrecy—'what I'm about to tell you is the highest-classified information'—and he'd give you some bullshit, and he'd give somebody else the opposite." [11]

Kissinger's attempts to appeal to varying viewpoints was particularly evident on Vietnam, which infuriated Nixon and his loyalists. "We knew Henry as the 'hawk of hawks' in the Oval Office," Haldeman recalls. "But in the evenings, a magical transformation took place. Touching glasses at a party with his liberal friends, the belligerent Kissinger would suddenly become a dove—according to the reports that reached Nixon." [12]

Kissinger's style began to cause problems on Capitol Hill, where comparing notes and swapping information was part of the power game. "Kissinger would often have back-to-back meetings with Bill Fulbright then John Stennis and somehow tell each what they wanted to hear," according to John Lehman, who was Kissinger's congressional liaison and later served as navy secretary. "But people talk on the Hill, especially the staffers, and what he told Fulbright would get back to Stennis within the day. They began to use Henry as a pawn." By trying to stitch together a broad consensus for his policies, Kissinger was pursuing a legitimate goal; but he sought to span such a wide spectrum that his credibility suffered. "You can't for long convince both Fulbright and Stennis, Katharine Graham and Jesse Helms, that you're secretly their soul brother," said Lehman.

Swapping tales of Kissinger's deceits soon became a staple of Washington dinner parties. Lehman told of listening as Kissinger ordered arms negotiator Gerard Smith to proceed with an antiballistic missile (ABM) proposal for two American sites rather than four, hanging up the phone, then taking Defense Secretary Laird's call on another line and saying, "I agree with you on the need for four sites, but that goddamn Gerry is constantly making concessions." [13]

But Kissinger did not generally resort to outright lies in his dealings with different factions. That was too crude, too prone to backfire. When challenged, he could invariably point to careful distinctions he had made or ambiguous statements that others had mistaken for assent. "If you had a tape recorder," said Ray Price, a Nixon speechwriter who was not a Kissinger fan, "you would find that what Henry told a Fulbright was not really different from what he would tell a Stennis. But the packaging would be custom-made."[14]

Kissinger was able to take on the subtle colorations of whatever environment he was in, almost as if by instinct. With conservatives, he could appear resolute, even celebratory, as he described Nixon's motives. With liberals, he could wring his hands and look anguished as he said much the same. In either case, he would listen well and nod gravely. Then he would mutter about "those idiots" or "the maniacs" on the other side of the issue, ask sympathetic questions, and solicit sympathy in return. He understood their concerns, he would tell people repeatedly. And they tended to go away thinking that he shared them, an impression he did nothing to dispel. "Whether my interlocutors considered a dialogue a sign of agreement or whether I misled them by ambiguous statements is impossible to reconstruct at this remove," Kissinger later wrote. "There was probably a combination of both."

Kissinger's management style was also marked by an enormous temper. Some people have quick tempers that erupt as a vent for their frustrations; they throw tantrums, then get over it. Others have brooding, moody tempers that nurture resentments indefinitely. Kissinger had both. "Why have I been inflicted with such incompetents!" he would bellow, grabbing a staffer's memo, throwing it to the floor, and jumping up and down on it. "When he stamps a foot in anger, you're okay," one aide said. "It's when both feet leave the ground that you're in trouble."

Kissinger was more tolerant of honest mistakes than he was of sloppy thinking and intellectual laziness. When Winston Lord made an error in a report on Laos that caused a public uproar, Haig was so cold and contemptuous that Lord threw up. But Kissinger stuck by him "like the Rock of Gibraltar," Lord recalled, and defended him both privately and in public.

Kissinger also had a softer attitude toward women, which is why aides always enlisted the prettiest secretary to tell him when there was a scheduling problem. When Diane Sawyer was an assistant press secretary for Nixon, she was in charge of proofreading transcripts. At one background session, Kissinger said he had "wrapped up negotiations" on an arms control issue. The version Sawyer released quoted him as saying that he had "crapped up negotiations," a description that some at State no doubt agreed with. As Sawyer recalled it: "Kissinger came rumbling down the hall into the press office where he found me trembling. After glowering while I profusely took the blame, he ended up not blowing up at me." Of course, since he later dated Sawyer, it is not clear that a Sonnenfeldt or a Haig would have gotten such soft treatment.

Eventually his staff learned to take his tantrums in stride. On one occasion, when he was standing outside his office bellowing, nobody even bothered to look up. Finally, he shouted: "I am angry. I am very angry. Isn't anyone going to pay attention?" His longtime secretary Christine Vick turned to him and said, "We know you are angry. When you calm down and speak in a normal tone, then we'll pay attention to you." [15]

What took the edge off of Kissinger's temper—and helped to ameliorate his arrogance—was his sense of humor. A naturally serious man, he had learned that a talent for tactical self-deprecation was useful in defusing jealousy and softening his self-important demeanor. "You could watch the sense of humor build as if he were consciously acquiring it to protect against the resentments he engendered," said Henry Brandon, a journalist who had known Kissinger at Harvard. "He had the good sense to know he needed humor to deflate himself, and he developed it with an intelligence that was astounding."

Much of Kissinger's mock self-deprecation was aimed at his own arrogance. "I have been called indispensable and a miracle worker," he once said. "I know, because I remember every word I say." At the first meeting between Israel's and Egypt's diplomats in Washington, he began by saying, "I have not faced such a distinguished audience since dining alone in the Hall of Mirrors."

Every now and then, he would attempt to be self-deprecating and self-inflating at the same time. When he went to the bar mitzvah of Israeli ambassador Simcha Dinitz's son, after becoming secretary of state, someone asked whether it was much different from his own in Germany almost forty years earlier. "Ribbentrop did not come to my bar mitzvah," Kissinger replied.

He could also poke fun at his temper. At one point, having moved to a bigger office, he complained that, when angry, it took him so long to stomp across the room and fling open the door that he sometimes forgot what had enraged him. "Since English is my second language," he once said, "I didn't know that *maniac* and *fool* were not terms of endearment." Kissinger even made jokes about his turf rivalries. "Everyone in the State Department is trying to knife me in the back except for Bill Bundy," he grumbled early on. "He is still enough of a gentleman to knife me in the chest."

William Safire once arrived at Kissinger's office to work on a presidential speech and found the place being torn apart as everyone searched for a piece of paper summarizing a secret new arms control proposal. While Kissinger boomed apocalyptic warnings, secretaries rooted through wastebaskets and staffers led by Haig scurried about. "I cannot work with you now, or do anything else, until I find a piece of paper I had in my hand not five minutes ago," Kissinger grumbled to Safire. "If we do not find it now, my vaunted staff will put it into a mill that distributes it all over the goddamn bureaucracy."

"Relax, Henry," Safire said. "It'll turn up."

"I have just misplaced the most sensitive, the most top-secret piece of paper that exists in the entire government," said Kissinger, looking at Safire in wonderment. "Somehow I think a greater sense of urgency is required than to sprawl all over my sofa and say, 'It'll turn up.' "

But it did turn up, the turmoil subsided, and the staff "began moving about the bunker at a normally hectic pace." Kissinger's aides, Safire later noted in his memoirs, "humored Henry, tolerated his rages, put up with abuse, and worked grueling hours because they knew they could say 'no' on enterprises of great moment and Henry would stop and carefully consider their views."[16]

Indeed, the aides who survived his petulant tantrums and tyrannies discovered that Kissinger's was one of the few staffs in Washington where independent thinking was prized and sycophancy was not. Kissinger's insecurities were easily triggered, and his intellectual arrogance could be overbearing. Yet he liked to be challenged on substance, and he enjoyed a solid analytic argument. Which is why, when important decisions were being made, he did not seal himself off like Nixon, but instead sought out the most assertive minds on his staff and made them feel, at least for a moment, that working for him was worthwhile.

This sense of intellectual excitement and challenge, along with the charismatic power of Kissinger's brilliance, was what earned him the loyalty of those beleaguered staffers who could put up with his demanding personality. As a result, he was able to extract great work from some of Washington's best minds. On one occasion, Winston Lord was assigned to write a thirty-thousand-word report on the 1970 Cambodian invasion. A day before it was due to the president, Kissinger read it and hurled it to the floor, declaring it "completely worthless." Lord stayed up all night rewriting it; the next day Kissinger pronounced it "great." Lord later said that he had not made that many changes, but it was Kissinger's way of driving him to do the best job he could. Roger Morris recalled Kissinger calling him at midnight to say, "I've read your draft. B-plus. You're only one draft away from an A-minus."

One oft-told tale about Kissinger, which was similar to one told about his old professor William Yandell Elliott, involved a report that Winston Lord had worked on for days. After giving it to Kissinger, he got it back with the notation "Is this the best you can do?" Lord rewrote and polished and finally resubmitted it; back it came with the same curt question. After redrafting it one more time—and once again getting the same question from Kissinger—Lord snapped, "Damn it, yes, it's the best I can do." To which Kissinger replied: "Fine, then I guess I'll read it this time."[17]

For better or worse, there was no one else in the bureaucracy who would hold his staff, and himself, to such high standards or demand that such effort go into making each report so perfect.

WILLIAM PIERCE ROGERS

In other circumstances, Kissinger may have gotten along well with William Rogers, for he was generally solicitous toward WASPish gentlemen whom he considered to be distinguished but unthreatening. In dealing with the affable members of the Council on Foreign Relations, or with honorable old-school statesmen such as David K. E. Bruce or Ellsworth Bunker or Cyrus Vance, Kissinger could ooze charm. The exceptions were those who threatened his turf, such as Robert Bowie at Harvard. Or William Rogers at the State Department.

Rogers and Nixon were old friends, if not exactly dear ones. They had met in the late 1940s, when Nixon was hunting communists as a congressman and Rogers was serving as a counsel for a Senate investigation committee. When Nixon ran for vice president in 1952, he asked Rogers to ride along. He was by Nixon's side when the campaign-fund crisis broke, and he helped him conceive the Checkers speech that saved his career.

When Nixon, defeated in his bid for president and then for California governor, came to Manhattan as a lawyer, he was snubbed by the town's Republican elite, who did not invite him to their homes or to join their clubs. Rogers was one of the few who showed him some kindness. One night Rogers and his wife, Adele, took Nixon and Pat to the 21 Club. All of them got a bit drunk, but happily so. Pat was the cheeriest of all; she was glad to be out of politics and around real friends.

Yet even then there was a little distance between Nixon and Rogers. They were competing for the same international corporate clients, and there was even a rift between them for a few months when Nixon unsuccessfully tried to lure away the Dreyfus Fund. More significant was Rogers's amiable haughtiness. He condescended to Nixon. He seemed to think, and made Nixon feel it, that Nixon was not quite his social or professional peer.[18]

Nixon's first choice for secretary of state was Robert Murphy, a retired diplomat who was chairman of Corning Glass. Nixon talked to him, but was rebuffed. He also considered William Scranton, the former governor of Pennsylvania, who sent back word he was not interested. Finally, Nixon turned to Rogers, a man he felt would be loyal, comfortable, and a good lawyerly negotiator. His lack of foreign policy experience was not a drawback; in fact, it may have been an asset: Nixon wanted to run diplomacy from the White House.[19]

John Ehrlichman believed that Nixon's choice of Rogers filled a dark psychological need to subordinate him. They never had much of a friendship, Ehrlichman said, because "Nixon was too jealous and resentful of Rogers." Secure in his social status, at peace with the world, Rogers was good-looking, even dashing, and had an intelligent wife. "I always had the hunch that Nixon wanted him in the cabinet as an inferior, even perhaps so that he could humiliate him," said Ehrlichman. Kissinger came to feel that this theory had some merit. "He might have been appointed, at least in part, because his old friend wanted to reverse roles," he later noted.

The problem was that Rogers did not play along. "He looked down on Nixon and couldn't bear the idea of working for him, which played into Henry's hands," according to Elliot Richardson, who launched his Nixon-era résumé as Rogers's undersecretary.

In addition, Rogers insisted that he would carry out orders he disagreed with only if he could discuss them with Nixon personally. Letters signed by Nixon would not do: Rogers believed (rightly) that these were written by Kissinger and his staff.[20]

Since Nixon hated confrontations and issuing direct orders, he started looking for ways to circumvent Rogers, to carry out policy behind his back. Kissinger was only too willing to oblige.

Rogers failed to win control over foreign policy because he knew little about the subject and worked at it even less. "Kissinger triumphed because Rogers opted out of thinking about strategy," Richardson said. "He had the defect of a lawyer: he dealt in cases rather than grasping a way to look at a situation strategically."

It also quickly became clear that Rogers did not have the fire for a scrap with Kissinger. Although he had served as the New York lawyer for the *Washington Post,* Rogers never bothered to meet with the press or establish any relationships with the city's opinion-making elite. He genially assured his deputies that he had the friendship of the president, which was all that mattered, and thus fighting over matters like the new NSC apparatus was silly. "Bill was a laid-back guy enjoying life and not looking for ways to be aggressive," said John Connally.

Nor did Rogers's worldview, such as it was, mesh with that of Kissinger and Nixon. "I don't accept the chessboard theory that we lose countries or gain them," he said in one interview. "What I favor for the U.S. is a more natural role, befitting our character and capacities."[21]

Kissinger and Rogers initially attempted to hold regular meetings, but Rogers did not consider Kissinger an official equal, and Kissinger did not consider Rogers an intellectual equal. "Rogers was too proud, I intellectually too arrogant, and we were both too insecure to adopt a course which would have saved us much unneeded anguish," Kissinger later said.

Instead, Kissinger began having breakfast (eggs at the State Department) and lunch (chef's salad at the White House) regularly with Elliot Richardson, Rogers's deputy. It was a potent alliance of convenience. Both had their share of arrogance and ambition, but they wore it with one another the way two Harvard classmates could, sublimating it into a stream of acerbic and conspiratorial commentary on the menagerie of fools around them.[22]

Kissinger's contempt for Rogers was boiling out of control by their first summer in office. He engaged in a constant derogation of Rogers that seemed almost automatic. When Nixon's speechwriters or other aides visited Camp David while Kissinger was there, they would come away thinking he was a man obsessed, unable to stanch his steady stream of snide remarks about how lazy, inept, and incompetent Rogers was.

Nixon did not discourage Kissinger's venom. He liked a little competition and feuding, as long as he did not have to resolve it himself. In March 1969, he met with the NSC staff for the first (and last) time. How hard it must be for them, he commiserated, to deal with all those "impossible fags" in the State Department.

But Nixon would drive Kissinger to distraction by inviting Rogers for dinner upstairs in the White House, sometimes a cozy foursome with spouses, treating him as a social friend the way Nixon did not (and never would) treat Kissinger. On those nights Kissinger would stay late in his office, pacing around and muttering ominous thoughts about what "idiocies" Rogers might be cramming into Nixon's head. As the hours dragged by, Kissinger would keep checking with the Secret Service to see if Rogers was still there. "Henry would brood and fume when Rogers was having dinner at the mansion," recalled Haldeman. "He would seem paranoid, ranting that he couldn't understand why the president would want to talk to Rogers. He'd pace around telling me exactly what Rogers must be telling the president and how outrageous it was."

"I'm sorry about how Henry and Bill go at each other," Nixon told William Safire one day. "It's really rather deep-seated. Henry thinks Bill isn't very deep, and Bill thinks Henry is power crazy." Then the president smiled and put his finger on the problem. "And in a sense," he said, "they're both right."[23]

MELVIN LAIRD

Kissinger's rivalry with Defense Secretary Laird was a lot more fun, and certainly more evenly matched. With a bullet head that was a boon to cartoonists, Laird was publicly perceived, quite incorrectly, as the administration's hawk. In fact, he successfully led the fight for a steady withdrawal of troops from Vietnam and unsuccessfully against most of the bombing-mining-invasion proposals. In doing so, he joyously defended his prerogatives as secretary of defense, becoming a worthy opponent in a war of maneuver against Kissinger. "Henry was very Machiavellian," Laird says, "but I knew how to beat him at his own game."

Laird had the keen political antennae (and ambitions) that come from having spent six years in a state legislature and sixteen in Congress. His service as the ranking Republican on the Defense Appropriations Subcommittee meant that, unlike Rogers, he had a sure grasp of his field. He could be as devious as Kissinger, plus he had enough ties with his former colleagues in Congress to outflank his rival.

An example of his style came when the White House decided to transfer to the Park Service some seafront land that the army owned in Hawaii. Kissinger warned Ehrlichman that it would first be necessary to close off Laird's escape routes. A direct order would be suicidal, and an argument on the merits only marginally useful. Ehrlichman thought that ridiculous. So he sent Laird a letter signed by the president directing that the land be transferred. "Laird treated this clumsy procedure the way a matador handles the lunges of a bull," Kissinger recalled. He pretended to accept the order, proclaimed that he would comply as soon as Congress authorized the funds, and then worked with his old friend George Mahon, chairman of the House Appropriations Committee, to pass a law requiring that the land be used for army guest accommodations. "Once in a while you have to do something like that to show you're not a pushover," Laird later explained. [24]

Kissinger found himself amused by Laird's "rascally good humor" and impressed by his graciousness in both bureaucratic victory and defeat. As with any rival, Kissinger railed mercilessly about Laird behind his back, but it was clear that he found their frequent tangles to be more challenging than maddening. "While Laird's maneuvers were often as Byzantine as those of Nixon," he later wrote, "he accomplished with verve and surprising goodwill what Nixon performed with grim determination and inner resentment."

Laird's position was that the Constitution gave him the power to set defense policy, and he was not going to take orders from a presidential assistant. Rogers, of course, felt the same way about foreign policy, but Laird knew how to pull it off, and his popularity among his congressional cronies immunized him from reprisal. He would sometimes arrive at a White House meeting with the Joint Chiefs of Staff and eloquently support their views, then pull Kissinger aside to confide with a smile that he shared his reservations, then go off to see Congressmen Mahon and Edward Hebert and nail down his real position. "Mel was a match for Henry," said James Schlesinger, a successor at the Pentagon and as a Kissinger rival. "He was just as devious, but he also had a Midwestern pol's instinct for power maneuvers."

When Kissinger tried to use the NSC's Defense Program Review Committee to exert control over the Pentagon budget in 1971, Laird pretended to play along. He got a meeting that had been scheduled for March postponed until April. Then he submitted papers that were so intentionally confusing that Kissinger had to ask his staff to rewrite them. A meeting was planned for July to sort it all out, but Laird got it postponed at the last minute until August. In the meantime, he had sent out three different versions of his proposed budget: one to the NSC staff, one to the Joint Chiefs, and one to his buddies Mahon and Hebert in Congress. At that point Kissinger gave up. "There goes the most devious man in government," Nixon said with a wink as Laird left the NSC meeting where he finally got his way. According to CIA director Richard Helms, who was admiring the scene, "Kissinger seemed a bit jealous at a rival being bestowed with that accolade." [25]

During a visit to the Vatican, Kissinger tried to exclude Laird from the president's audience with the pope, a futile effort when faced with a pol of Laird's ingenuity. At the end of the visit, Nixon was supposed to fly in a U.S. military helicopter from St. Peter's Square to an aircraft carrier in the Mediterranean. So Laird personally brought the helicopter there an hour before Nixon arrived. The pope invited him to come inside. How did the Holy Father know of his presence? "I guess he knew I was there," Laird laughingly recalled, "because he couldn't help but noticing my helicopter landing outside his window."

When Kissinger arrived with the presidential party, he was startled and not particularly pleased to see Laird waiting inside, chomping on a cigar. Asked what he was doing there, Laird mumbled that he was looking for the helicopters. "It was not clear what he thought these might be doing *inside* the Vatican," Kissinger later said. Since Laird was obviously intent on proceeding into the papal audience with the president's party, Kissinger asked him at least to stash his cigar. In the middle of the pope's welcoming speech, wisps of smoke began issuing from Laird's pocket. Quietly at first, then with frantic slaps, Laird tried to extinguish his cigar and smoldering pocket. Some in the audience interpreted the defense secretary's attempt to avoid immolating himself as applause and warily joined in. Vatican officials and the Swiss Guard, reflecting their centuries of experience in dealing with odd pilgrims, ignored the commotion.[26]

Laird could also match Kissinger as the master of the inspired leak, often followed by a call to Kissinger in which he feigned outrage at the resulting story. If something was too sensitive to leak directly, Laird would tell it to the five or six congressional leaders he regularly briefed; eventually it would get out, usually in a matter of days.

After the 1970 Cambodian invasion, which he opposed, Laird let it leak to the *New York Times* that he had ordered the Joint Chiefs of Staff not to provide any more military options to Kissinger without getting approval from the defense secretary's office. He also leaked each decision to withdraw troops from Vietnam, partly to outmaneuver the White House for political credit and partly to make sure that the withdrawals continued apace. "I had to leak out the figures on withdrawals so that Henry could not torpedo them," he later explained.[27]

Although Kissinger grudgingly tolerated Laird's bureaucratic maneuvers, he was obsessed about leaks. So he tried to cut Laird off from information, just as he had done with Rogers. "Cutting out Mel Laird is what we did for a living," according to Kissinger's aide Laurence Lynn.[28]

But Kissinger, though he never knew it, failed miserably in this effort. Laird's bureaucratic prowess, it turned out, arose largely from his success at snooping on the White House—and Kissinger in particular. As Laird later admitted: "I had my sources, and very good ones at that, to keep me on top of who was doing what."

When Laird took the job, he extracted from Nixon a written letter that promised he could appoint his own people to key positions. But it was not such posts as assistant secretary that most concerned him. The first thing he did was put his "own man," Vice Admiral Noel Gayler, in charge of the National Security Agency, the supersecret spy outfit that electronically intercepts satellite and other communications from around the world. When he appointed Gayler, Laird told him that he had better be loyal to him; if so, he would get his fourth star.

Laird got what he wanted. "The NSA gave me my own copy of every back-channel message Henry sent, though I made sure he didn't know that," Laird said later. "Sometimes you have to do these things and play someone else's game against them."

Laird even kept up with the most secret Kissinger secret of all: the private peace talks with the North Vietnamese in Paris. "Hanoi's negotiators sent very good reports, full of Henry's sniveling, back from Paris every time Henry went over there," Laird said. These cables quickly made it to Laird's desk, even though Kissinger was going to great lengths to make sure that the Pentagon and the State Department did not even know that these negotiations were under way.

For those cases in which the CIA had more information on some subject than he did, Laird had access to all overseas CIA cable traffic. Unbeknownst to the spooks at Langley, their cousins at the National Security Agency were not fastidious about whom they would eavesdrop on.

In September 1972, a few months before Laird left office, Gayler was made a four-star admiral.

Laird was also able to stay informed because Kissinger, ironically, did not trust the CIA's back-channel facilities. So when he wanted to circumvent the State Department, he would use the military's cable network. To coordinate messages involving the secret opening to China, which was arranged by using Pakistan as an intermediary, a secure channel was set up through the U.S. Navy's attaché in Karachi. Likewise, when Kissinger was secretly engaged in back-channel negotiations over the future of Berlin, he used a complicated link involving the navy attaché in Frankfurt. In both cases, Laird and navy chief Admiral Elmo Zumwalt knew what was happening each step of the way, even if the CIA and State Department did not.

Nor were any of Kissinger's secret air travels—to Beijing or to bargaining sessions in Paris—a secret from Laird. "I ordered the Special Air Missions, which ran the White House planes, to keep me fully informed," Laird later said.

In addition, the U.S. Army Signal Corps was providing Laird with secret reports on most overseas White House conversations. The White House had two phone systems at the time: the White House Communications Agency, which was run by the Army Signal Corps; and the civilian-operated White House switchboard. The Army Signal Corps's was more sophisticated and supposedly more secure. It was used to connect Nixon and Kissinger to phones and facilities around the world, it handled the calls from Air Force One, and it established the communications setup whenever Nixon traveled. For example, in 1969 the Army Signal Corps spent $307,000 for communications equipment in Key Biscayne plus $161,000 more for a system on Grand Cay, the island owned by Nixon's friend Robert Abplanalp.[29]

Also unbeknownst to Kissinger, his practice of having his secretaries listen in and transcribe his telephone conversations became another method for the military to keep track of him. "A naval aide would back up Kissinger's staff in monitoring calls and preparing the transcripts," said former navy chief Zumwalt. "It meant I had my own spies. I could see who was saying what about whom. Haig and Kissinger especially—each would get to the president and put in a few digs when the other was traveling."[30]

At the end of 1971, a scandal would erupt involving a navy yeoman on Kissinger's staff who was spying for the Joint Chiefs.* But this military spy ring, outlandish as it was, paled in comparison to the information that Laird was able to get on his bureaucratic rivals. Laird's ability to thwart Nixon and Kissinger at their own game highlighted yet another drawback of their love of secrets: they could never be sure who also knew them.

KISSINGER'S POWER GROWS

For Nixon, meetings of the full National Security Council quickly became bothersome. Whenever a subject was discussed there, it meant he had to deal personally with the objections of Rogers and Laird as well as put up with the time-consuming and leaky process of having the matter considered within the bureaucracies of both their departments. One morning in early June 1969, at his daily private meeting with Haldeman, he decided to make official what had

* See Chapter 18.

been evolving for five months: Kissinger's role would be elevated at the expense of the secretaries of state and defense. Instead of considering most foreign policy matters at full NSC meetings, Kissinger and Nixon would decide things alone.

"Cut NSC to one every two weeks—or once a month," Haldeman's notes of the conversation read. "More brought privately to President for his discussion with Kissinger." Later in the conversation, Nixon returned to the subject even more worked up. From now on, he told Haldeman, Kissinger should come directly to the president on issues, rather than putting them on the agenda for a full NSC meeting. Then they could come to a decision without Rogers and Laird. "No appeal," Nixon added, as he often did, for emphasis.[31]

This suited Kissinger just fine. From the start, he had been seeking to make foreign policy in private with Nixon whenever possible. For the very first NSC meeting, which dealt with Vietnam options, he had Halperin do a two-page cover memo summarizing the plans put forth from State and other agencies. There were little boxes for Nixon to initial. Kissinger looked at it and told Halperin, "Fine, but now tell him what to do." Halperin was a little taken aback, having heard all of Kissinger's pronouncements about how the NSC staff would merely pass along options. The summary documents, with Kissinger's recommended course of action, were to become another of the secrets that Kissinger had to keep from the State Department and the rest of the government.[32]

The press, which was at first thrown off the scent by what Nixon had said about delegating power to his cabinet officers, quickly caught on to the power shift. After just three weeks in office, *Time* put Kissinger on its cover. "Kissinger is already widely suspected in Washington of being a would-be usurper of the powers traditionally delegated to the State and Defense departments," the magazine noted. "Humility is not his hallmark." The *New York Times* likewise reported that Kissinger "is taking over the responsibility for coordinating foreign policy in the Nixon Administration, a mandate formerly assigned to the Secretary of State."[33]

So NSC meetings became a formality. Nixon would open them with a statement of the topic and turn to Kissinger to present the issues. The position papers from the various agencies would be distributed to each NSC principal, but only Nixon and Kissinger had the summary and recommendation page. "It was a heady experience to be asked to draft presidential decisions before NSC meetings had even been held," staffer William Hyland recalled.

Nixon would also have "talking points" prepared by Kissinger's staff. These would even predict what Laird or Rogers was going to say and provide a scripted response for the president to deflect their objections. Nixon would follow it carefully, putting his initials in each box as he went along.[34]

Kissinger's main source of power over the bureaucracy was his chairmanship of the NSC's Senior Review Group, which determined what issues should reach the president and when. But he quickly set up a covey of other committees, all of which he chaired, to give him better control over specific topics. They included:

• The Washington Special Action Group, set up after North Korea's downing of the EC-121 plane, which handled breaking events and crises.

• The Verification Panel, formed in July 1969, which ostensibly analyzed whether compliance with different arms control proposals could be verified by U.S. intelligence, but which was soon in charge of managing all arms negotiations.

• The Defense Program Review Committee, which considered the funding requests for weapons and other military needs.

• The Vietnam Special Studies Group, set up in September 1969, which coordinated military and diplomatic policy regarding the war.

• The 40 Committee, a new name for an older panel, which was in charge of authorizing covert actions by the CIA and other agencies.

The enhanced role of the NSC staff was reflected in its funding. Walt Rostow in 1968 had a budget of $700,000. By 1971, Kissinger's budget was $2.2 million. The staff had almost doubled to 46 assistants and 105 administrative personnel.[35]

One source of power in Washington is having direct access to information, rather than having to go through channels. Kissinger never felt very comfortable with CIA director Richard Helms, a patrician who shunned bureaucratic conspiracies, so he ordered the CIA to send more raw data—rather than merely assessments and conclusions—to the NSC staff. "It skewed our way of writing estimates, especially about the Soviets," Helms said. "The estimates had to provide a vast amount of data so Kissinger could make up his own mind."

Kissinger also began to deal directly with the military. Early in 1969, he called Admiral Zumwalt, the chief of naval operations, regarding a matter involving Africa. Laird got upset. Dealings with the military should go through him, he insisted. Kissinger responded that as a representative of the president he had the right to deal directly with the military. A few weeks later, when Zumwalt and Kissinger met at a social event, the navy chief noted that he shared Laird's objections to dealing outside of the chain of command. But Kissinger was adamant. It was a matter of both power and principle, he felt, and he insisted that he had the right to deal with all members of the Joint Chiefs of Staff directly. "From then on," says Zumwalt, "every time we got together for business, he referred to it as a 'nonmeeting.'" Without Kissinger's knowledge, Zumwalt kept Laird fully informed.[36]

Kissinger's desire to control foreign policy, it should be noted, was not wholly unwarranted. By riding herd on the bureaucracy he was able to dispel some of the stale thinking that permeated the State and Defense departments.

For example, in the summer of 1969, he ordered a study on chemical and biological weapons. He was dubious about whether they had much use in a war-fighting strategy, and assumed correctly that little thought had been given to the issue. By asking for a range of feasible options, Kissinger guaranteed that the possibility of eliminating the program would be listed, if only as an extreme option to set off the policy the military preferred.

What came back was a mass of opaque prose that caused Kissinger to bellow, "I can't even read this paper." But he knew that an opportunity had been uncovered. He had his staff sharpen the wording so that the options became clearer. In making his decision to renounce first use of chemical weapons and to dismantle production of biological ones, Nixon stressed the novelty of the review process and how well it had worked.[37]

By the end of their first summer, Kissinger and Nixon were no longer communicating by memos; instead, they were spending hours in rambling conversations. Nixon would tour the world every morning, his remarks ranging from grand strategic concepts to petty biases about various leaders and peoples; along the way he would cast a few aspersions on the State Department or engage in some bureaucratic gossiping. Kissinger would guide him along like a deferential tutor, praising his observations, adding a few insights, and pointing out various perfidies and idiocies of the State Department. Haldeman began to resent the time Kissinger monopolized, but he knew that these were the type of discussions that their boss relished: private, conspiratorial, a curious blend of the high-minded and petty.

THE BACK CHANNEL

One of the basic rules of American diplomacy is that all official contacts with foreign governments are handled through State Department channels—even the negotiations done by special presidential envoys, such as those that Harry Hopkins conducted for

Franklin Roosevelt. The advantages to this procedure are the same as its disadvantages: all the relevant agencies get to weigh in with their expertise and objections, diplomatic initiatives are made to conform to established policy, and the information (even when given a high classification) goes into the bureaucratic mill to be distributed to scores of analysts, department heads, and diplomats who have successfully asserted their need to know such matters.

Not surprisingly, this process did not appeal to Nixon or Kissinger. The type of foreign policy they envisioned involved secret maneuvers, dramatic surprises, and a desire for the White House (meaning Nixon and Kissinger) rather than the State Department to get credit. Thus was born a complex system of "back channel" operations that Kissinger set up to bypass the State Department. The most central of these, involving a secret negotiating conduit to Moscow, was known simply as The Channel.

In describing how this process developed, Kissinger later wrote: "Nixon increasingly moved sensitive negotiations into the White House where he could supervise them directly, get the credit personally, and avoid the bureaucratic disputes or inertia that he found so distasteful." That sentence is true. But it would be just as true—in fact, as time went on, more true—if Kissinger's name was switched for Nixon's. Neither man could have back-channeled the State Department without the involvement and active encouragement of the other, but Kissinger was perhaps the more eager to do so. "I undoubtedly encouraged it," Kissinger would later concede. "Like the overwhelming majority of high officials, I had strong views and did not reject opportunities to have them prevail."

Even as an academic, Kissinger had been in favor of short-circuiting the usual policy-making channels. At a seminar in the spring of 1968 at the University of California, almost a year before he entered government, he discussed the need to keep the bureaucracy "working away in ignorance" while key decisions were made. He explained:

> One reason for keeping decisions to small groups is that when bureaucracies are so unwieldy and when their internal morale becomes a serious problem, an unpopular decision may be fought by brutal means, such as leaks to the press or to Congressional committees. Thus the only way secrecy can be kept is to exclude from the making of the decision all those who are theoretically charged with carrying it out.

The underlying assumption here is that decisions made without public scrutiny are better than those made after an open discussion.

But even if one accepts this premise, one can still be taken aback by the disdain for democracy implied by his assertion that there is something "brutal" about allowing a congressional committee or newspaper readers to know about the debate.[38]

Kissinger began setting up the back channel to the Soviet Union within weeks of coming into office. At a reception at the Soviet embassy, an official came up to him and said that Ambassador Dobrynin, who was nursing the flu in his upstairs apartment, would like Kissinger to come up and meet him. With the well-practiced heartiness that had made him a Washington social figure, Dobrynin greeted Kissinger and suggested that they address each other by their first names. After discussing the various "opportunities" for better relations that had been lost, Dobrynin requested a meeting with Nixon to deliver a letter from his leaders.

Kissinger later said that Nixon wanted Rogers excluded from the meeting; Nixon recalled that it was Kissinger who wanted it that way. No doubt they were both right. In any event, the thankless task of informing the secretary of state that Kissinger rather than he would attend the first meeting between the president and the Soviet ambassador—a breathtaking breach of diplomatic procedure—fell to Bob Haldeman. His notes show that Nixon blamed the decision on Kissinger; Haldeman did the same when he talked to Rogers.

At the meeting, Nixon told Dobrynin that he should discuss any sensitive issues privately with Kissinger rather than the State Department. "Kissinger had suggested that we develop a private channel between Dobrynin and him," Nixon recalled. "I agreed."

"The Channel was thus formally established," says Kissinger. Thereafter Dobrynin would visit as often as once a week, usually coming through a little-known door to the East Wing of the White House and meeting Kissinger in the Map Room where Franklin Roosevelt used to plot war strategy.

It took a while for professional diplomats to get the hang of the new way of operating. Jacob Beam, who was appointed ambassador to Moscow mainly because he was one of the only foreign service officers to treat the peripatetic Nixon decently while he was out of office, was asked by Nixon and Kissinger to draft a letter to Soviet Premier Aleksei Kosygin and to keep it very secret. Beam did, but he quite naturally sent a report to Secretary Rogers. It caused an uproar: Rogers was upset (understandably) at being excluded from a meeting involving a letter to a Soviet leader, and Kissinger was outraged that Beam had violated "a private talk."[39]

Each use of a back channel, on its own, could probably have been justified as necessary for creative diplomacy. But when the litany of double-dealings is examined—the dozens of major negotiations that were conducted by Kissinger secretly from the State Department—it becomes clear that less exalted motives were also at play.

One consequence was that there was no incentive for officials to be flexible, to reexamine established policy or to come up with compromises. Once they began to suspect that Kissinger was secretly doing things on his own, they could remain pristine and adhere to the line favored by their bureau or agency.

Kissinger would later be defensive about the extent to which he used back channels, and it would show in the shifting array of justifications that he offered. Primarily, he pinned it on Nixon. "These extraordinary procedures were essentially made necessary by a President who neither trusted his cabinet nor was willing to give them direct orders," he later wrote. Kissinger also blamed Rogers, and everyone else in the bureaucracy, who resisted many of the president's policies. If policy-making had been left to the proper channels, he argued (with some merit), creative approaches would have been stifled by the inertia of the system.

In the short run, the back channels worked. The approach "was weird and its human costs unattractive," Kissinger wrote, "yet history must also record the fundamental fact that major successes were achieved." Among the back-channel successes: a SALT agreement, an opening to China, a Berlin accord, a Moscow summit, and eventually a peace treaty for Vietnam. But handling the negotiations in secret from the State Department did not make the SALT outcome sturdier, the China opening smoother, or the Vietnam settlement any speedier.[40]

Whether or not the ends justified it, the back channel complicated American foreign policy. The Soviets became adroit at whipsawing the U.S. by playing off one channel against the other. Pakistan was treated with absurd tenderness during the Bangladesh fighting because it was serving as the back channel to China. North Vietnam triumphed in the war of public diplomacy because the U.S. became addicted to the secret channels.

In addition, reliance on secret channels wasted the time and creativity of Kissinger's staff. Winston Lord had to organize three versions of many briefing papers, for example. "If I wrote a memcon of a meeting and then had to do sanitized versions because other parts of the bureaucracy were not supposed to know something, it would take three times as long," he later said. "It was like juggling a double or triple bookkeeping system."

It also squandered the staff's sense of moral worthiness. "Some secrecy is necessary in government," said Tony Lake, "but Henry crossed the line from secrecy to deceit." During the secret Paris peace talks on Vietnam, Lake would have to write a memo for the president that fully—sometimes fulsomely—reported on what Kissinger did. Then there would be paragraphs deleted before it was given to David Bruce, and then an almost totally sanitized version for other officials. "The levels of knowledge and duplicity were like a Mozart opera in complexity," Lake said. "One reason I quit was because I kept finding myself writing misleading memos."[41]

Kissinger and Nixon relied on the channel more because it suited their personalities than because it suited the security interests of the nation. They both had a penchant for secrecy, a distaste for sharing credit with others, and a romantic view of themselves as loners. Neither had the ability to rejoice in someone else's success. Neither believed he had much to learn from professional diplomats or congressmen. Nor did either have any faith that public input and the messiness of democratic debate might lead to wiser decisions. "They developed a conspiratorial approach to foreign policy management," said Lawrence Eagleburger. "They tried not to let anyone else have a full picture, even if it meant deceiving them."

Nor can vanity be discounted. "The Channel was done largely to feed Kissinger's ego and grandeur, if I may be so blunt," said Georgi Arbatov, the veteran Soviet expert on the U.S. "And perhaps for Dobrynin's ego, too." Kissinger, in retrospect, admitted that it was hard for him to judge "to what extent less elevated motives of vanity and quest for power played a role." But, he was willing to admit, "it is unlikely that they were entirely absent."[42]

THE "HENRY-HANDLING COMMITTEE"

Kissinger's obsession with Rogers began to get on Nixon's nerves. On a trip to San Clemente their first summer in office, even as he was basking in frequent visits to Nixon's patio and afternoon swims together in the Pacific, Kissinger continued his tirades against Rogers to all who would listen. "The president got into a snit," Haldeman recalled, "and asked us to form a Henry-Handling Committee to deal with it."

Haldeman's notes from the meeting capture Nixon's mood: "Kissinger is on Rogers kick again. . . . Comes in 2–3 times a day. . . . Insists Rogers is trying to get him. . . . Just keep this off his [Nixon's] desk."

So Haldeman, Ehrlichman, and John Mitchell invited Kissinger over to Mitchell's rented bungalow for a talk. "Nixon hoped that the relaxed, informal atmosphere might help calm Henry," recalled Ehrlichman, "and perhaps he thought our little committee would become a permanent sounding board for Henry, thereby relieving Nixon of some of the wear and tear."

Kissinger arrived with a typewritten manifesto. Point one: Rogers should not be allowed to make speeches unless "the White House" (meaning Kissinger) had cleared them first. Point two: Kissinger should have the right to deal directly with Rogers's deputies and assistants without going through the secretary. And so it went. Once he had finished presenting the list, he rattled off examples of Rogers's alleged (and indeed often real) ineptitude. "The man is a positive danger to the peace of the free world," Kissinger told the group, gravely shaking his head.

Mitchell nodded, puffed on his pipe, and promised to talk to Rogers. But nothing much came of it. The Kissinger-Rogers feud continued to simmer.

It erupted again in January 1971. "I may return to Harvard at once," Kissinger announced as he arrived (late) for a morning meeting with Haldeman and Ehrlichman. The two staffers looked at him quizzically. "That Rogers has written a letter to the Egyptian foreign minister," Kissinger explained.

Since communicating with other foreign ministers could be construed as a reasonable activity for a secretary of state, and since the Middle East was one of the few areas of responsibility that Nixon had reserved for Rogers, the outrage seemed more in the mind of the beholder. But Haldeman told Kissinger to prepare a list of his grievances and they could talk them over in a few days.

Kissinger put Haig and a few of his underlings to work producing a massive document entitled "White House–State Department Relations." Among the items that particularly infuriated Kissinger was a report from a German official that a State Department emissary had told him: "Kissinger won't come over to Germany because he will not leave the president's side for one day for fear he will lose his influence." Kissinger pointed to it, shaking. "Can you believe that!"

Kissinger then brought the document and his rage into the Oval Office, much to Nixon's annoyance. The president told Haldeman to reconvene the Henry-Handling Committee. They met in Haldeman's office, where Kissinger confronted them with another typewritten ultimatum. Among the points: "Attacks on Kissinger—direct or indirect —must cease. . . . All cables with policy implications—including especially the Middle East—must be cleared [with Kissinger]. . . . All contacts with Dobrynin must be cleared." Once again, there were nods and murmurs of sympathy, but the committee knew there was little they could do other than protect the president from spending too much time hearing the complaints.[43]

The situation worsened when the *New York Times* ran a series of front-page special reports on consecutive days, the first headlined "Decision Power Ebbing at the State Department" and the next "Kissinger at the Hub." When Rogers asked the White House to come to his support, Haldeman put Safire to work on a statement denying the thrust of the stories.

"If Rogers doesn't knuckle under, I go!" was Kissinger's unsmiling greeting to Safire when he arrived to talk about the statement. Safire, who was generally amused by Kissinger's tantrums, tried to jolly him up. Kissinger began to simmer down, then decided against it. "You and Haldeman don't think I'm serious about this, but I mean it!" Haig stood in the corner, nodding. Pointing to a paragraph in the *Times* story about a dispute over West German policy, Kissinger launched again into his diatribe against the State Department emissary who had disparaged him to a German official.

"You feel better now?" Safire asked.

"No," Kissinger said, resuming his rant. Finally, he announced that he would quit if Safire wrote a statement pumping up the State Department. "If you do anything that supports State at my expense, I've had it." In the end, Haldeman decided that it would be safest all around if no statement was issued.

A few days later Safire came back to help draft the State of the World speech. Kissinger was still in an uproar. "You guys think I'm kidding when I say this, but I'll resign."

"If you quit, Henry," said Safire, "you'll never get a phone call from a beautiful woman again. The secret of your attraction is your proximity to power."

"You may be right about that, Safire," said Kissinger, who even amid a tantrum was usually willing to consider a humorous or intriguing proposition. Power, as he had often noted, was the ultimate aphrodisiac. "It would be a tremendous sacrifice."[44]

For the Henry-Handling Committee, the feud with Rogers would be a constant struggle. It would erupt a year later, and the year after that. "It's like the Arabs and the Israelis," Kissinger used to complain. "I'll win all the battles and he'll win the war. He only has to beat me once." In fact, as Nixon was finally to conclude in 1973, there was only one way that Kissinger could serve in a government and at the same time admire the secretary of state: if he *was* the secretary of state. So after winning all of the battles, Kissinger would eventually win the war.[45]

ELEVEN

THE WIRETAPS

Office Bugs, Dead Keys, and Other Devices

> *The deviousness of Metternich's diplomacy had been the reflection of a fundamental certainty: that liberty was inseparable from authority, that freedom was an attribute of order.*—KISSINGER, A WORLD RESTORED, *1957.*

THE NATIONAL SECURITY WIRETAPS, MAY 1969

When Nixon visited his friend Bebe Rebozo in Florida, his staff usually stayed a few blocks away in the villas of the Key Biscayne Hotel. On the morning of Friday, May 9—about four months after they had come into office—Kissinger and some other aides were sitting by the pool, having breakfast and reading the newspapers. Suddenly, Kissinger stood up and began shaking a copy of the *New York Times.* "Outrageous!" he shouted as he pointed to a story on the bottom right of the front page and waved it in Bob Haldeman's face. The president, Kissinger insisted, must be informed at once.

"That's how it began," Haldeman recalled. "With Henry's anger."[1]

"American B-52 bombers have raided several Viet Cong and North Vietnamese supply dumps in Cambodia," the story began. It was by William Beecher, the *Times*'s tenacious Pentagon correspondent. The article received surprisingly little attention. No other paper picked it up, no congressman protested, no one demonstrated; although the secret bombing would cause a major uproar four years later when the details and the extent of the deceit became fully exposed, few people got excited that Friday.

Except for two men in Key Biscayne. "Henry was livid," Richard Nixon recalled, "and I became that way as well." He was struck by how "very emotional" Kissinger was—pacing, stamping his feet, a little short of breath—when he stormed into the presidential bungalow that morning. "We must do something!" Kissinger said. "We must crush these people!"

Kissinger tried to blame the leak on the State or Defense departments and even placed a call to Melvin Laird, who was tracked down on the golf course of the Burning Tree Club. "You son of a bitch," Kissinger said, "I know you leaked that story, and you're going to have to explain it to the president." Laird hung up on Kissinger.

Nixon had a different idea of where the blame lay. He told Kissinger that he ought to "take a hard and objective look" at his own NSC staff.

The accusation stung Kissinger, and frightened him. Nothing could so quickly undercut his fledgling relationship with the president as the suspicion that his shop was the source of leaks. So he set out to prove to Nixon and his Prussian staffers that he was more fervent than anyone in enforcing the cult of secrecy.

Kissinger immediately called FBI Director J. Edgar Hoover in Washington. The Beecher story was "extraordinarily damaging," Kissinger said, according to Hoover's notes of the call, and the White House wanted "a major effort to find out where that came from." Just after eleven A.M., Kissinger called back to mention other recent Beecher stories that should be investigated: one on arms negotiations and two on the Korean EC-121 shootdown. Kissinger called again two hours later to ask that the probe be handled discreetly "so no stories will get out." Hoover promised he would; he said that he had decided (quite sensibly) not to have agents ask Beecher directly about his sources, and would try instead to find out by asking other reporters.[2]

As Kissinger knew, Hoover was already suspicious of Morton Halperin and had opposed his appointment. In one memo Hoover had gone so far as to label Halperin "a harvard type . . . of the opinion that the U.S. leadership erred in the Vietnam commitment." (Hoover made a habit of lower-casing *Harvard*.) Since that description also fit himself, Kissinger ignored it.

Nixon had given Kissinger a free hand to recruit for his staff the best brains without regard to their political loyalties, and Kissinger had done so. But goaded by Hoover's phone calls, Nixon grew uncomfortable about having people like Halperin around. "These guys are bad news," he told Kissinger.

"No, Mr. President, they are professionals," Kissinger replied. "They will be honorable."

In recounting this conversation many years later, Nixon would flash a quick, slightly bitter smile and shake his head. He became convinced, he said, that Kissinger's decision to staff the NSC with doves and Democrats was the cause of a lot of the problems he later faced. The wiretaps, the Plumbers Unit, the general air of paranoia— Nixon came to believe that he may have been spared these seeds of his downfall if Kissinger had hired a more loyally conservative staff.[3]

When Nixon and Hoover again raised questions about Halperin on the morning that the Beecher story appeared, Kissinger concluded that he could no longer afford to keep him on staff. There was no evidence that Halperin had leaked classified secrets or was guilty of anything more heinous than a lack of love for Richard Nixon. But given the climate of paranoia and toughness that he had begun adapting to in order to survive, Kissinger decided that Halperin had become an albatross.

Halperin, it so happened, was in Key Biscayne that Friday, there to help Kissinger prepare Nixon's first major speech on Vietnam. That afternoon, while they were in the swimming pool together, Kissinger turned to him and said, "Let's take a walk." As they wandered along the shoreline in their bathing suits, the two Harvard colleagues discussed the accusations against Halperin that Hoover and others were making. Halperin pointed out that he could not have been the source of the Beecher story since he had not known the details of the Cambodian bombing.

Kissinger said he believed him, but he made a proposal. How about if he cut off Halperin's access to classified material for a while? Then, the next time there was a leak, he could prove that it was not Halperin. Kissinger made the suggestion sound so plausible, and presented it so smoothly, that Halperin was unaware that he was being beheaded.

As they arrived back at the Key Biscayne Hotel, Haldeman and John Mitchell were conducting a staff meeting in one of the cabanas. Kissinger wandered in and introduced them to Halperin. It was the first time, Halperin later noted, that he met the attorney general.[4]

While Halperin was being walked down the beach, an FBI agent in Washington named James Gaffney was heading to the headquarters of the Chesapeake and Potomac Telephone Company. Written on an index card he carried was 469–7818, the telephone number for 8215 Stone Trail Drive in suburban Bethesda—the home of Morton and

Ina Halperin and their three sons. Gaffney did not need anything else —no court order, no letter from the attorney general. It was urgent, he told his contact at the phone company.

Agent Gaffney had been given the number by Ernest Belter, who for twenty years had been supervising national security wiretaps for the FBI. This one, he figured, must be special; it had been ordered directly by the White House, and security was so tight that normal reporting procedures were scrapped. Belter later told journalist David Wise that he figured "it was a big spy ring somewhere."

By late afternoon, a line from Halperin's phone had been patched into Ernest Belter's switchboard at the FBI's field office on Pennsylvania Avenue and Twelfth Street. Continuously manning the board was at least one FBI clerk with a set of earphones, a notebook, and a tape recorder.

When he got back from the beach, Kissinger placed another call to Hoover, who reported that his agents had discovered that Beecher "frequented" the Pentagon pressroom (hardly a surprise since he was, after all, the *Times*'s Pentagon correspondent). There was, Hoover added, "speculation all the way through tying it [the leak] into this man Halperin." In his notes, the savvy FBI director never makes explicit mention of wiretaps. He did, however, jot down that Kissinger pledged that he would "destroy whoever did this if we can find him, no matter where he is."

Kissinger was pandering to Hoover's prejudices, and he would be embarrassed when his tough words later became public. At a Senate hearing in 1974, Kissinger rather sheepishly tried to explain: "My impression was that Hoover was rather suspicious of me as well, therefore in my conversations I might have had a tendency to show him that I was alert to the danger of security."

Halperin also placed a call when he got back from the beach. At six-twenty P.M., his wife, Ina, answered. The new red light on Ernest Belter's board lit up for the first time, and the conversation between husband and wife was recorded by their government.[5]

Among the conversations that would eventually be caught by the Halperin wiretap was one that must have surprised Belter and his crew. In August, when Halperin told him that he was planning to resign, Kissinger was sincerely upset, so much so that he called him at home—either ignoring or forgetting that the phone was wiretapped —on a Saturday afternoon to beg him to stay. As the FBI summary of the wiretap reported: "It was strongly stated by Kissinger that Halperin had a 'damned frustrating position there and some of my operators have behaved poorly.' Kissinger wants Halperin to know that his work was 'certainly the most creative of anyone on the staff,' and he doesn't want to give up on that without a struggle." Halperin, unmoved, resigned that September; the wiretap on his home phone, however, remained in place for twenty-one months.[6]

In Kissinger's conversations with Hoover from Key Biscayne that Friday, three other potential sources of the leak were discussed: Helmut Sonnenfeldt and Daniel Davidson of Kissinger's staff, and Colonel Robert Pursley, the military assistant to Defense Secretary Laird. The next day, at Kissinger's behest, Haig arrived at the bureau to submit a formal request for taps on all three, plus for the tap on Halperin that was already in place.

Haig told Hoover's deputy, William C. Sullivan, that the taps "will only be necessary for a few days." No written record of them should ever be made, Haig added. Sullivan, highly skeptical, decided to wait until he could discuss the orders with Hoover the next day. When the director gave him the go-ahead, he created a new folder with the code word JUNE.

Sonnenfeldt was a wiretap target for many reasons. As a State Department official, he had previously been suspected of leaking, though it was never proven. His wife, Marjorie Hecht, the heir to a Washington department store fortune, was a leading socialite and Democratic activist whose lack of admiration for Nixon was no secret.

In addition, Kissinger's complex relationship with Sonnenfeldt, marked by an intellectual rivalry (and perhaps a tinge of jealousy of the social status he had achieved by marrying Marjorie), made the prospect of monitoring his private conversations enticing. And Haig saw Sonnenfeldt as a rival. In retrospect, Sonnenfeldt would say the biggest factor was the insecurity of the men he worked for. "The odd thing was," he commented, "Nixon and Kissinger were both extremely insecure."

Sonnenfeldt, like Kissinger, was from a prosperous Jewish family that was forced to flee the fascism of Germany. He had a deep fear of being wiretapped, and he would regularly wander into Haig's office and tell him he was sure his phone was bugged. Haig smiled but never told him the truth.[7]

The tap on Colonel Pursley was, on the surface, also quite plausible: his boss, Laird, was a master leaker who had, in fact, helped Beecher by confirming the Cambodian bombing story. But the Pursley tap also served a bureaucratic purpose. He and Laird talked every evening, sometimes two or three times, discussing strategy and exchanging gossip. The tap became a way for Kissinger to keep abreast of the only man in the administration who could outmaneuver him.

Laird had his own phones, both at home and the office, regularly checked for bugs. "But I made one big mistake," he later said. "I didn't have Pursley's home phone checked." When Laird finally found out about the tap in 1974, he confronted Kissinger. "Henry blamed it on Al Haig," Laird recalled. "Pursley was a brilliant person, much smarter than Haig, and I'm sure Haig felt resentment at that, but I don't think he came up with the wiretap himself."[8]

Dan Davidson was a Democrat, a young and bright Averell Harriman protégé who had briefed Kissinger when he visited the Paris peace talks during the 1968 campaign. Davidson, who soon left the NSC staff, would later express surprise that Kissinger considered it a plausible defense to say that he went along with the program because others in the administration felt it was warranted. "Can you imagine anyone going to Mac Bundy and saying, 'Let's wiretap some NSC staffers'? To any honorable person the suggestion would be considered inconceivable."[9]

In all there would be seventeen FBI wiretaps ordered by the White House under the justification of national security—thirteen of them on government employees, four on newsmen. The program would last for twenty-one months, until February of 1971; some of the victims would be tapped for only a month or two, others for more than a year. As the summaries came to Kissinger's office, Haig would read them, show his boss the interesting parts, and then store them in a safe in the Situation Room.

Other aides began to suspect something. Soon after the wiretaps had begun, Roger Morris went to the hospital to visit Lawrence Eagleburger, Kissinger's personal assistant who had collapsed from nervous exhaustion. Tears came to Eagleburger's eyes as he told his old friend from the foreign service about the tapping. "Don't say anything you don't want Haldeman or Henry to read over breakfast," Eagleburger warned. Anthony Lake, another idealistic staffer, stumbled across a wiretap summary involving one of their colleagues, and he told Morris about it. "Roger and I decided not to confront Kissinger," he recalls. "We were fighting on enough fronts. But every now and then, when we were talking on the phone, we'd wish J. Edgar Hoover a merry Christmas."[10]

The wiretap program had its roots in Nixon's resentments, which became even more inflamed when leaks were involved. As Nixon read the papers or his news summary each morning, an aide would sit in and take notes. "What is this cock-sucking story?" the notes quote Nixon as saying. "Find out who leaked it, and fire him!"[11]

Nixon first approved the concept of the national security wiretaps at a meeting in the Oval Office on April 25, two weeks before the

Beecher leak, according to a 169-page deposition he gave in a lawsuit filed by Halperin. He was complaining to Mitchell and Hoover about leaks, and Kissinger was summoned to join them. Hoover explained that wiretaps were common tools in such cases, their use going back to the days of Franklin Roosevelt. Nixon and Mitchell left by helicopter for Camp David at four P.M., according to Haldeman's notes. Hoover, who preferred to drive, met them there for a six-thirty dinner where the subject of leaks was further discussed. Kissinger was not invited.[12]

A memo written by Hoover's deputy Sullivan reports, with specific detail, that Kissinger personally came to the FBI building with Haig on May 20, two weeks after the program began, to read some of the raw transcripts. Although summaries of the wiretapped conversations were delivered each day to Kissinger's office, the verbatim transcripts—page after page typed on onion-skin paper—could make for more exciting reading.

"Dr. Kissinger and Colonel Haig came to my office this morning around 11:45," Sullivan wrote in the memo to Hoover. "Dr. Kissinger read all the logs. On doing this he said, 'It is clear that I don't have anybody in my office that I can trust except Colonel Haig here.'" Sullivan then added: "Kissinger said he wanted the coverage to continue for a while longer."

In retrospect, despite this memo, no one later seemed able to remember such a meeting, not even Sullivan. "I do not ever recall Dr. Kissinger coming to my office to read a log," he said in a 1974 letter to a Senate committee after being asked about his memo. "In fact, I do not remember him coming to my office for any reason." Kissinger likewise told the committee that he did not remember ever going to the FBI to read the transcripts. "If I would have wanted the logs, I could have had them sent over to my office." Haig, who regularly went to the FBI by himself to read the transcripts, carefully hedged his answer when asked if Kissinger had accompanied him on May 20. "I do not recall the meeting," he said, ". . . but it would not surprise me if there had been one."[13]

Whether or not he brought Kissinger along on May 20, Haig did bring the FBI two more requests for wiretaps: on Richard Moose and Richard Sneider, both NSC staff members. Moose was a former aide to Senator J. William Fulbright, the dovish Democrat who chaired the Foreign Relations Committee. Sneider, a career foreign service officer, was Kissinger's Asian expert. They became targets five and six.

The next name that Haig submitted, on May 28, was of a journalist: Henry Brandon, the wry and well-connected Washington correspondent of the *Sunday Times* of London, who had telephoned

Halperin the previous day with a routine question. A dapper Czech refugee who combined continental sophistication with English charm, Brandon was one of Kissinger's first friends in Washington and a fixture on the Georgetown social circuit. He was a master at access reporting: from John Kennedy to Ronald Reagan, he became friends with those in power, harvesting their insights while honoring their confidences. "Dr. Kissinger is aware of this request," a wary Sullivan wrote to Hoover.

Hoover was the driving force behind the tap on Brandon, about whom the FBI director had an odd obsession. He could be "someone else's colonel," Hoover had once told Nixon and Kissinger, implying that Brandon might work for British or Czech intelligence.

Kissinger later denied that the wiretap summaries contained anything gossipy or personal. But the Brandon summaries show otherwise. One summary reports on "a divorced woman in whom he had a romantic interest" and notes that he "made arrangements to meet her in another state." (The woman was his future wife, Muffie, whom he married in 1970.) The Brandon wiretap remained on for a year and nine months. Transcripts of Muffy's conversations with Joan Kennedy, one of her close friends, were reported in full—and not because they contained leaks of classified national security information.

When the wiretaps became public in 1973, Brandon demanded an appointment with Kissinger. "He looked glum, his jowls were drooping more than usual, and his body was hunched heavily in his chair," recalled Brandon, who demanded to know whether Kissinger had ordered the wiretap on him. He assured Brandon that he was not to blame, and he begged the reporter to believe him. Kissinger implied that the tap had been directed at him, not Brandon, since he so often talked to the reporter. Indeed, in his first year in Washington, Kissinger spent many of his Sundays at Brandon's home, using the pool and talking on the phone. Often the president would reach him there, no doubt surprising Ernest Belter's clerks who were listening in.[14]

By June 4, only one of the first seven wiretaps, that on Pursley, had been removed. That morning another leak was in the New York Times: Hedrick Smith reported on page one that Nixon was going to announce the first major U.S. troop reduction of the Vietnam War. By nine-thirty, Kissinger was at Hoover's office, where he personally requested that a tap be placed on Smith's home phone.

Haig had prepared a set of "talking points" for Kissinger to use in his meeting with Hoover that day. They indicated two things: that Haig was handling most of the details of the wiretap program, and that both men were solicitous of Hoover. "Express your appreciation to Mr. Hoover and Mr. Sullivan for the outstanding support in recent weeks in uncovering security problems within the NSC staff," Haig wrote. "Ask Mr. Hoover for his views on how we could proceed with Halperin, who has been involved in indiscretions and who obviously has a reputation for liberal views but has yet to be firmly linked with a security breach."

To his credit, Kissinger was by then having qualms about the open-ended wiretap program. Haig's talking points suggest that Kissinger inquire how long the program would last, "making it clear that the President wishes to terminate them as soon as possible." Kissinger later testified that "I did express to Hoover at a June 4 meeting the view that the taps in general should be stopped as soon as possible."

Kissinger's claim that he was growing uncomfortable with the wiretapping is confirmed by some handwritten notes buried in boxes of H. R. Haldeman's papers in the Nixon archives. Reporting on a June 4 meeting in the White House with the president, Haldeman's notes read: "Kissinger getting list of who talked to H. Smith. Kissinger is afraid we may be turning screws a notch too far. . . . Next turn there is danger of kickback."[15]

Nevertheless, the program continued for another year and a half.

The pretense that the taps were for national security purposes was virtually abandoned on August 4, when speechwriter William Safire was targeted. The FBI memo pinned the request on Haig, but it came at the bureau's suggestion. The FBI noted that "the rationale used by Colonel Haig was that the coverage on Brandon revealed that Brandon and Safire were friends and that Safire told Brandon what would be in a speech by the President." The speech, it turned out, was on welfare reform and, recalled Safire, "we were told to leak the hell out of it."

Kissinger later claimed that he was not directly involved in the Safire tap. On July 22, he had left with Nixon on a round-the-world trip that included Guam, the Philippines, Thailand, South Vietnam, India, Pakistan, Romania, and Britain. On the day of the request regarding Safire, Kissinger had quietly peeled off from the trip and was in Paris for his first secret meeting with North Vietnam's negotiators. Later he said he was "astonished" to hear of the tap.

When the program was revealed in 1973, Safire had just become a *New York Times* columnist. He called Haig and reached him in San Clemente, where he was having breakfast with Kissinger. "Did you know I was tapped?" Safire asked. Haig would not confirm or deny anything about the operation. "As we spoke," Safire later wrote, "a voice with a Senior Official's accent kept badgering him in the background. 'Tell him it wasn't me, make sure he knows it wasn't me.' "

Safire never believed Kissinger. "Al Haig wouldn't go to the bath-room without first raising his hand and asking Henry Kissinger's per-mission," he wrote. "The suggestion that Haig asked for this tap without the knowledge of Henry Kissinger is patently ridiculous." He later wrote that "Kissinger's reaction to the entire tapping episode is un-Kissinger-like. He gets visibly upset; he lies in an unstudied, ama-teurish way that can be found out; he is not himself."

The pain of having his privacy violated added a healthy dose of sensitivity toward civil liberties to Safire's conservatism—and it also left a sour taste about Kissinger. "I hope it is not personal pique that changed my view of his role in the Nixon years, but a certain under-standing that comes when one is lied to by men who are convinced that consistent lying can be the right thing for the country." [16]

In May of 1970, a year after the wiretapping began, the FBI was still churning out summaries, but interest in the program was waning. Kissinger and Haig had not added any names since Safire's the pre-vious summer. Then came the invasion of Cambodia; as with the secret bombing of that country a year earlier, the May 1970 invasion spawned a front-page Beecher story that infuriated Kissinger. It re-ported that the invasion was being accompanied by renewed heavy bombing of North Vietnam. Haig requested that Beecher, who had somehow escaped so far, be tapped. The national security justification was still thin: by reporting on the bombings, Beecher was hardly giving secret information to the enemy (for they knew full well that they were being hit), but instead was merely informing the American peo-ple.

Haig also requested that the tap on Pursley be reactivated and that one be put on Richard Pederson, the State Department counselor who was a confidant of Rogers. Rogers's top aide on Vietnam, Ambas-sador William H. Sullivan (not to be confused with William C. Sulli-van, the FBI official overseeing the program), was also tapped.

Once again, part of the motive was to spy on Kissinger's top two administration rivals through their aides. Neither Pursley, Pederson, nor Sullivan were security risks; they did not even hang around with reporters the way Kissinger and his top staffers did. Tapping them, however, enabled Kissinger to know in advance the positions that Rogers and Laird would be taking at meetings with the president. "This gave Henry a bureaucratic advantage to say the least," Safire later noted.

In addition, Kissinger had begun using the wiretap summaries in his battle to discredit the State and Defense departments in the eyes of the president. He would come storming into the Oval Office expressing his outrage at each reported slight against the president or himself.[17]

The Cambodian invasion upset Kissinger's brightest young staffers, including Tony Lake, who resigned, and Winston Lord, who almost did. Lake and Lord were two of the most honorable men ever to have worked in the White House, and certainly in the Nixon White House. On May 12, 1970, two weeks after Lake resigned, taps were placed on his home phone and that of Lord. Both taps remained in place for nine months, during a period in which Lake was working for Senator Edmund Muskie, a likely Democratic challenger to Nixon.

Except for a few snippets that were used in congressional testimony, the records of the wiretaps have never been released. But Lake was able to get access to the FBI transcripts of his own conversations and those of other aides who talked on his phone, and he agreed to allow them to be quoted here, along with the summaries (code-named JUNE and marked "TOP SECRET—DO NOT FILE") prepared by the FBI. Two things stand out: that most of the material was, in the words Nixon would later use when complaining about how Kissinger had wanted the wiretaps, just "gossip and bullshitting"; and that the administration was as interested in picking up political intelligence as in plugging security leaks.

In addition, the transcripts show that some of the FBI agents who prepared the reports were astonishingly out of touch. For example, in one of the first transcripts, made on May 15, 1970, Lake tells his wife "that Bill has decided he is going off." He was referring to fellow Kissinger aide Bill Watts. The FBI transcriber, however, has written *Secretary Rogers?* in parentheses next to *Bill.* From there on in the conversation, references to Bill Watts are recorded in the transcript as ROGERS, as if the secretary of state were thinking of quitting and going into a business venture with Tony Lake.

Another of the transcripts, from October 27, is of a conversation between Lake and Roger Morris, who had both left the NSC staff by then. It records that "Roger told Tony he was writing a short thing he hoped he could get Mondale to do. . . . He wants to mention all the money being spent for the war, but the needs at home are not being considered." Nothing resembling a classified secret is discussed, and Lake does not say anything substantive about Vietnam. Yet the FBI dutifully sent a summary of the conversation over to the White House by hand and helpfully added: " 'Mondale' is probably identical to U.S. Senator Walter F. Mondale (D-Farmer-Labor-Minnesota)." The memo also advised that at the end of the conversation, Lake told Morris he had bought a farm in West Virginia and that Morris had replied, "If that son of a bitch Nixon wins in '72, I will go out and farm it for you."

The FBI summaries highlight conversations that might help the White House keep track of Edmund Muskie's political plans. One in December even reports on a conversation that Lake's wife had with a friend, even though she was not a suspected national security risk and there was no authority whatever for disseminating her private conversations. In it, she revealed that Muskie was planning to leave December 27 on a trip to Jerusalem, Cairo, and Moscow in an effort to establish his foreign policy credentials.

When the wiretapping was exposed, Lake wrote to Kissinger asking him to say that there had never been any indiscretion on Lake's part and that the program was wrong. Kissinger balked. Reluctantly, Lake sued him for a token $1 in damages; it was a matter of principle. In 1989, he settled for a "Dear Tony" letter. In it, Kissinger did not quite apologize. "It was Attorney General Mitchell's view that such techniques were within the President's powers," he wrote. But later court rulings made it clear, Kissinger conceded, "that the wiretap of your home phone was indeed unconstitutional." Kissinger went on to note that "your extraordinary loyalty and integrity was obvious to all during our years working together." It was not the mea culpa that Lake had hoped for, but he had the letter framed nonetheless.[18]

Winston Lord, whose integrity was also beyond question, never got such a letter. The day before the wiretaps were exposed, Kissinger called him into his office. Without any apologies, he said that the wiretapping had been something Nixon and Mitchell wanted. Since he was worried about being an outsider in the new administration, he had not felt able to fight the program. Lord felt that was a rather lame excuse, since by the time the tap was put on his phone, Kissinger had been in office for more than a year. Nevertheless, Lord stayed on staff.

One oddity of the tap on Lord's phone, illustrating the absurdity of the whole program, involved his wife, Bette Bao Lord, who was born in China and later became a best-selling novelist. Every morning she would speak to her mother, often using phrases from her regional dialect. She was a gourmet cook, and they would swap intricate recipes. The FBI had to hire language specialists to decipher them and even called in code-breaking experts to see if there was some hidden meaning to all the ingredients. The tap stayed on for nine months, to the benefit of free-lance translators if not the taxpayer. Bette Lord later blamed Haig for the wiretap. "Haig resented Win, and it was his way of putting him down," she said.[19]

•

The day after the wiretaps were placed on Lake and Lord, Nixon abruptly removed Kissinger from overseeing the program. At a White House meeting with Haldeman and Hoover, the president said that, from then on, all summaries of the wiretaps should go to Haldeman only; Kissinger would no longer have the right to request new wiretaps without Haldeman's approval. That night, Kissinger was told of the decision.

There were a variety of reasons for the transfer. Hoover, who was convinced that leaks were coming from Kissinger and his men, was eager to get the program out of his hands. In addition, Haldeman and Hoover were worried that Lord, who had just been promoted to be Kissinger's special assistant, might see the summaries if they continued going to Kissinger.

But the main reason for the transfer was that, in the wake of the Cambodian invasion, Kissinger was having one of his periodic feuds with Nixon, who was at Camp David not returning his phone calls. Haldeman's notes show Nixon brooding about Kissinger's disloyalty and the fact that "he can't handle Rogers and Laird." It was a particularly emotional period for Kissinger, and behind his back Haig had gone to Nixon to feign concern for Kissinger's stability. "Haig came to see me," Nixon later recalled. "He expressed great concern about Dr. Kissinger's very emotional and very distraught reactions to the Cambodian actions."

It would be best, Nixon decided, to shift responsibility for the wiretap program to Haldeman. "Henry was spending a hell of a lot of time on these things," Nixon said in an interview for this book, "and I knew that Bob would not waste too much time before tossing the reports in the circular file." Haldeman was even more blunt in recalling the problem. "Nixon was sick of Kissinger bounding into his office with wild overreactions to each wiretap report," he said. "Henry would get outraged at every indication he saw or imagined of any disagreement, especially if it came from the State Department."[20]

Haldeman placed only one wiretap on his own initiative: on James McLane, a relatively obscure assistant on Ehrlichman's domestic policy staff. But under Haldeman, the political uses of the existing taps continued. The original tap on Halperin was still in operation, even though he had resigned in September 1969. It had already produced one juicy tidbit: Clark Clifford ("probably identical with the former Secretary of Defense," Hoover surmised in his memo) was planning to write an article for *Life* magazine attacking Nixon's handling of Vietnam. The political operatives sprang into action, enlisting Jeb Stuart Magruder to neutralize it by leaking anti-Clifford information to the press. Ehrlichman later sent a handwritten note to Haldeman saying, "This is the kind of early warning we need more of." Haldeman scribbled on the bottom, "I agree with John's point," and passed it along to Magruder. Magruder went on to become the Nixon campaign official who pushed the plan to bug the Watergate offices of the Democratic National Committee.[21]

The wiretapping program finally came to an end in February 1971. Nine people were still under surveillance: Mort Halperin (at twenty-one months, the longest, even though he had quit the NSC seventeen months earlier), Henry Brandon, William Beecher, Richard Pederson, Ambassador William Sullivan, Lake, Lord, and—on their second go-rounds—Robert Pursley and Helmut Sonnenfeldt. Like the bombing of Cambodia, it became yet another dark secret that Nixon and Kissinger shared.

The wiretap program was the first step down a slippery slope. Once a precedent had been set for eavesdropping on White House staffers and reporters, using an increasingly flimsy pretext of national security, it was just a short step to the formation of a secret White House unit to bug political opponents.[22]

When the wiretapping was exposed by the press in 1973, Nixon would take full blame for authorizing it. "I wish to affirm categorically," he wrote to a Senate committee, "that Secretary Kissinger and others involved in various aspects of this investigation were operating under my specific authority and were carrying out my express orders." Yet privately he often noted, with some justification, that Kissinger had spurred him to authorize the wiretapping by getting so inflamed by leaks. In a secretly taped conversation with John Dean in 1973, Nixon grumbled, "They never helped us. Just gobs and gobs of material. Gossip and bullshitting." Then, he added of Kissinger: "He asked that it be done."[23]

Kissinger's main role in launching the wiretap program was that he fed Nixon's natural frenzy about leaks. New to Washington, naturally secretive, and with a growing list of secrets to protect, Kissinger wildly overreacted to each leak. Even the Beecher story on the Cambodian bombing was hardly worth getting overwrought about; neither the rest of the press nor the Cambodians paid attention. The story that set Kissinger shaking at poolside in Key Biscayne was nowhere near as damaging as his reaction to that story.

Kissinger would later claim that, once the program was under way, his participation was passive. All he did, he said, was follow the president's instructions to give the FBI names of "officials who had access to the classified information that had been leaked." The FBI would then decide whether to wiretap them or not. Did you ever "initiate" a tap? he was repeatedly asked at a Senate hearing in 1974.

"Not in the sense that I said, 'Tap this individual,' " he testified. "I carried out the criteria of a previous decision." The most he would admit to was that, when he submitted a name, he knew that "wiretapping could be a part of this investigation and was the probable result."

Like most of Kissinger's fine distinctions, there is some truth to this. In a deposition after his resignation, Nixon said: "It was his responsibility not to control the program, but solely to furnish information to the FBI." The head of the FBI's intelligence division testified to the Senate that "we can find nothing here indicating that Dr. Kissinger played any part other than furnishing names of logical individuals to be wiretapped."[24]

But also like most of Kissinger's fine distinctions, it was not as clear-cut as he contends. His explanation belied how the wiretap program ended up working in reality: Kissinger or Haig would submit a name, the FBI would tap the person, and reports on his conversations would start flowing in to Kissinger's office. The FBI referred to the names submitted by Kissinger as "requests," and with rare exception it placed such taps immediately.

As often happened when he discussed an action he found difficult to defend, Kissinger created a rotating lineup of rationales. He told some of his aides that he was actually doing them a favor: the wiretaps were designed to prove their integrity by showing conclusively, when a leak occurred, that they could not be blamed. In reality, a wiretap could prove nothing of the sort; aides such as Lord and Lake, who considered their personal integrity at least equal to that of Kissinger and Haig, would be justified in considering such an explanation as offensive as the spinsters of Old Salem must have found it when the citizens told them they would be dunked in water to prove they were not witches.

On a loftier plane, Kissinger defended the wiretaps as necessary "to prevent the jeopardizing of American and South Vietnamese lives" by those who leaked military information. Certainly, leaks that endanger American soldiers are abhorrent; but neither the disclosures about the Cambodian bombings nor any of the others that so excited Kissinger and Nixon fell into that category. They usually involved information that the enemy already knew, but the American people were being denied. None of them came close to meeting the standard that Kissinger himself embraced years later when seeking confirmation as secretary of state: "If human liberty is to be ever infringed, the demonstration on the national security side must be overwhelming."[25]

To some friends, Kissinger deflected blame for the wiretaps by pinning the excesses on Haig. Much of what was "requested" in Kissinger's name, he insisted, was done on Haig's own initiative. There is some truth to the charge; Haig used the program to further his own interests and spy on his rivals. But it is also true that Kissinger decided that it was in his own interest—and served to enhance his credibility with Haldeman and Nixon and Hoover—to let Haig do so.

Kissinger also resorted to the others-did-it-too rationale. As far back as Franklin Roosevelt's presidency, J. Edgar Hoover had been providing the service of national security wiretaps when authorized by the attorney general. "I don't think there was any more or less wiretapping" in the Nixon years than in previous ones, said James Adams, head of the FBI's intelligence division. He added, however, that "what was unusual about this [was] that it involved wiretaps on the NSC staff, on individuals that were part of the White House family." In other words, previous wiretaps had been mainly on suspected spies, potentially subversive union leaders, and the like. A regular program of wiretapping one's own aides was, according to Thomas Smith, another top FBI official, "unprecedented."[26]

At the time they were placed, the wiretaps were considered legal. The 1968 Omnibus Crime bill required police to get a court warrant before placing a wiretap; but it contained a disclaimer saying that the act did not limit the president's power to protect national security. Attorney General Mitchell told Nixon that national security wiretaps thus did not require a court order. The Supreme Court later rejected that doctrine when applied to American citizens.

The wiretapping reflected the desire of Nixon and Kissinger to know what their aides were up to behind their backs—quite a natural temptation, especially for two people with a touch of paranoia. To eavesdrop on what others are saying—colleagues, subordinates, rivals, and enemies—gives a heady sense of power that has tempted people even more ethically fastidious than Kissinger and Nixon. Kissinger was, Safire later noted, "capable of getting a special thrill out of working most closely with those he spied on the most."

The program—which ultimately led to the plumbers, which led to Watergate—illustrated what can happen when a White House is intent on pursuing policies, such as the bombing of Cambodia, that it feels it cannot dare let the public discover. "It is the part of my public service about which I am most ambivalent," Kissinger later said. Which is about as close as he ever came to admitting that he was sorry he did something.[27]

OTHER WHITE HOUSE INTRIGUES

There was one secret about the wiretap program that Kissinger was never told: he was, in some cases, an indirect target. Nixon and Haldeman thought, correctly, that he was one of the worst leakers of all. "Get Kissinger away from the press," Haldeman's handwritten notes quote Nixon as saying just before he was relieved of responsibility for the wiretaps. "He talks too much."

Among those Kissinger talked to was CBS diplomatic correspondent Marvin Kalb, who with his brother Bernard was about to write a book about him. In September 1969, Attorney General Mitchell phoned the FBI and asked that a wiretap be put on Kalb's home phone. The reason, he said, was that "the president thought that Kalb might be receiving information."

Mitchell added an unusual request: all summaries and reports on the Kalb tap should go only to him and Ehrlichman, not to Kissinger's office. The tap stayed on for two months, without Kissinger's knowledge.

One odd aspect of the Kalb tap was the unfounded rumor that he was a spy for Romania, which Hoover spread, Nixon accepted, and Kissinger apparently decided to play along with. One day in late 1969, Nixon erupted about Kalb's "instant analysis" of the president's Vietnam speech the previous evening. According to Jeb Magruder, who was at the meeting, Kissinger broke in and said: "Well, Mr. President, that man is an agent of the Romanian government." "That's right," Nixon replied. "That guy is a Communist." Nixon clung to the assertion for years. One of his daily news summaries in 1971 noted that Kalb had done a story about Hanoi's thinking on the peace talks. In the margin, Nixon scribbled a note for Kissinger: "K—he ought to know!" The following year, even as Kissinger was giving the Kalb brothers extensive interviews for their book on him, Nixon wrote a note for Haldeman: "H—Kissinger must never do a Kalb interview." [28]

Another tap that was partly aimed at Kissinger was one placed on his friend Joseph Kraft, a syndicated *Washington Post* columnist, in May 1969. It was done on the direct order of the president, through Ehrlichman. The FBI was not initially involved, and it was not one of the seventeen that were part of the "national security" wiretap program directed by Kissinger and Haig.

On Ehrlichman's staff was John Caulfield, a former New York City police detective whose vague White House duties included political security arrangements. When Ehrlichman told him that Nixon wanted a wiretap on Kraft's phone, Caulfield protested: "For Christ sakes, John, that belongs with the Bureau." Ehrlichman replied that the FBI was a "sieve" and could not be trusted.

Caulfield turned to John Ragan, a former FBI agent who was director of security for the Republican National Committee. Climbing a telephone pole behind the Kraft house, he attached a battery-operated transmitter. Conversations could now be taped on a voice-activated tape recorder in the trunk of a nearby car. But the Krafts happened to be in Europe at the time, and the tape ended up with only the conversations of their Spanish maid. In the meantime, Ehrlichman had changed his mind and decided to work through the FBI instead.

Ehrlichman asked the FBI to arrange with their French counterparts to bug the hotel room where Kraft and his wife, Polly, were staying. FBI deputy director William Sullivan flew over to Paris personally to make the arrangements, and the French gallantly consented to place (and even pay for) the microphone in the Krafts' bedroom of the Hotel George V. Using the tapes provided by the French service, Sullivan and his assistants prepared a nineteen-page report.

The FBI report reveals less about Kraft's knowledge of secrets than it does about the FBI's lack of knowledge about public figures. It reports that Kraft made a call and "asked for John Monay," presumably referring to Jean Monnet, the man who helped to forge the European Economic Community. Another notation was that Kraft had contacted a "Kay Graham," whose identity was "not known." One would have expected that the FBI, ever on the alert for what it considered subversives, would have been able to identify the owner of the *Washington Post*.

Kraft's lawyer, Lloyd Cutler, who was eventually able to get the transcripts and a letter from the Justice Department exonerating his client, said that Kraft (who died in 1986) "came to believe the wiretap on him was aimed at Kissinger." According to Ehrlichman, Nixon was, even back in 1969, "getting very concerned about Henry, and he knew he was leaking to Kraft."

The irony was that, every few weeks, when Nixon had some line he wanted to push, he would send a memo to Kissinger telling him to leak it to Kraft. After a favorable Kraft column early in 1970, Nixon wrote a note to Kissinger in the margin of the news summary: "K— You get the credit?"[29]

THE DEAD KEY SCROLLS

Kissinger also found it useful to wiretap himself. As soon as he came into office, he began the practice of having a secretary listen in on his phone calls, take notes, and prepare a memo of conversation. Gradually the system improved. A series of "dead keys" on phone extensions around the office were added so that secretaries or aides could pick up and listen in without the caller's hearing anything. When Kissinger moved in 1970 from the West Wing basement to the ground floor near the Oval Office, the White House Communications Agency, at Haig's request, set up an IBM Dictabelt system to record calls in a console behind the desk of Kissinger's receptionist.

For the first year or so, the transcripts were rather rough; even important conversations with the president tended to be paraphrased. After the taping system was working well, Haig and Kissinger set up a battery of professional transcribers who would work overnight turning out high-quality, near-verbatim transcripts.

The "dead key" extensions were not a secret within the NSC staff inner circle. When Nixon would call in a rage or slurring his words, Kissinger would wave to get various aides on the extension phones to hear the show. The same would often happen when Kissinger talked with Laird or Rogers or any other bureaucratic rival; Kissinger liked to roll his eyes and make faces to amuse his aides as they listened in.

Kissinger often used the transcripts to make a point or prove his own loyalty. If Rogers or Laird said something that would upset the president, or if someone else made a comment that would support one of Kissinger's arguments, he might pass it along to Haldeman or show it directly to the president himself.

William Safire, who dubbed the transcripts the "Dead Key Scrolls," said he once saw Kissinger altering one to shore up a point he wanted to make to the president. He had been chewing out a reporter from the Christian Science Monitor for writing a story that was unfavorable to Nixon; in doing so, he also tossed in occasional complaints about the perfidy of Secretary Rogers. Since he was planning to send the transcript to the president, Safire said, he had taken a draft and edited it, "adding to the fierce loyalty of his own remarks."[30]

By authorizing Haig to listen in on his conversations, Kissinger gave him an enormous source of power. Soon he was privy to all of Kissinger's secrets, and sometimes it seemed to other staffers that he would listen in on a call more out of curiosity than necessity. Eventually, as he began tending to his own ambitions more than Kissinger's needs, Haig began to curry favor within the White House by showing some copies of the telephone transcripts to Haldeman and Ehrlichman.[31]

Kissinger would later claim that having calls monitored and transcribed was a standard practice in Washington. That was partly true. Some officials, including Dean Rusk, had done so for important calls. And there was some justification for the practice. It helped Kissinger, who tended to be quite harried and disorganized, assure that someone followed through on the requests and orders Nixon gave by phone. In addition, it provided a record of their decisions.

But as with many of Kissinger's actions, including his support for the secret Cambodian bombing and the wiretapping, the initial rationales he used had little relevance to what the program became. The practice soon grew so that every call to Kissinger, except the most personal ones, were transcribed. After some busy days, a relay of secretaries would work late into the night typing out the transcripts, mostly of conversations with people who had no idea that their words were not private.

Despite his halfhearted defense of the practice, Kissinger seemed to realize that taping and transcribing his callers without their permission was a questionable act: that is one reason why he went to extraordinary lengths—as he had with the national security wiretapping and the Cambodian bombing—to keep the practice secret. The existence —though not the full extent—of Kissinger's self-taping operation briefly surfaced in the press in early 1971, when the *Washington Post* learned about a few of the transcripts from some of Kissinger's aides. A reporter asked him if he planned to use them someday for his memoirs. "These notes are strictly for the President's files," Kissinger replied. "I have no intention of writing a book."

As it turned out, the transcripts were used extensively as background for the two books he wrote about the Nixon years. Nor did he leave the notes "for the President's files." In early 1973, when he was thinking of resigning, Kissinger secretly shipped thirty crates of documents, including the telephone transcripts, to the bomb shelter at Nelson Rockefeller's Pocantico Hills estate in Westchester County, New York.

Later that year, after he decided to stay in the administration, he needed them back, especially since storing government records in an unauthorized location was illegal. Haig ordered a White House military liaison named Bill Gulley to send an unmarked plane up to the Westchester Airport along with an army sergeant. He flew the papers back to Andrews Air Force base, put them in an unmarked truck, and drove them back to the White House, where the bulk of the transcripts were hidden in a bomb shelter under the East Wing.

Even then, Kissinger left the most sensitive telephone transcripts up at Pocantico. It was his contention that they were personal working papers, not government documents. When he became secretary of state, the phone transcripts (other than the ones at Pocantico) followed him to the State Department and were put under Lawrence Eagleburger's care.

As he was preparing to leave office in 1976, Kissinger decided that he would keep the transcripts. But after the threat of a lawsuit by a reporters' group, he included them among personal papers he donated to the Library of Congress. By the terms of the bequest, they will not be available until at least five years after his death. A suit challenging Kissinger's right to treat the papers this way went up to the Supreme Court, which decided in Kissinger's favor.* [32]

The wiretaps and recording of telephone calls were part of a pattern in the Nixon White House. Secret snoops were everywhere and bugs abounded. John Ehrlichman, for example, had a switch beneath his desk that allowed him to tape his conversations and phone calls. The president, as would later become well-known, had his own voice-activated secret taping system, which he ordered installed in 1971.

Kissinger was convinced, not unreasonably, that he was a target. "Henry, whose anger at leaks really started the 1969 FBI national security wiretapping, was constantly worried that his own telephone was tapped," recalled Haldeman. "Time and again he would pass me in the hall and say, 'What do your taps tell you about me today, Haldeman?' "

When Haig took over Haldeman's job in 1973, he left Nixon's secret White House taping system in operation, and he did not tell investigators about it when they began to probe the Watergate cover-up. He did, however, tell Kissinger, who was unnerved: he realized that the tapes could be devastating to him. They would show him catering to the president's odd whims and prejudices. He felt violated, and raged at the horror of the secret taping system, though there is no indication that he saw the irony, or that it made him more sensitive to the feelings of those whose conversations he had secretly either taped or had wiretapped. [33]

Haig also led Kissinger to believe that there was a dead key on Kissinger's phone line that he did not know about: one that allowed

---

* The ones that are quoted later in this book were provided unofficially by people who kept copies or who have access to some of the transcripts.

Haldeman or his assistant Lawrence Higby to listen in on Kissinger's conversations. "I always believed that Kissinger's phone was bugged," said Charles Colson, Nixon's hell-bent political operative.

Both Haldeman and Higby later convincingly denied that they could directly monitor Kissinger's conversations. "I had no dead key on Kissinger's phone and neither did Haldeman," said Higby, now a publishing executive at the *Los Angeles Times.* "I was in charge of setting those up. I would know. I could listen in on Haldeman's calls, but neither of us could listen in on Kissinger's."

Instead, when Nixon desired to know whom Kissinger was talking to, there were other options. Usually it was done through the White House switchboard, according to both Colson and Higby. The switchboard kept a handwritten log of all calls made or received, and these could be used to indicate that Kissinger had been the source of a press item.

In addition, Nixon's political aides had ways of getting hold of the transcripts of Kissinger's conversations. Sometimes Haig would show a particular one to make a point; at other times, more junior aides wanted—quite naturally—to show juicy tidbits to friends in the White House. Kissinger loved to share confidences and talk about people behind their backs; what he never fully realized was that almost everyone who worked for him liked doing the same, especially about him.[34]

TWELVE

NO EXIT

Vietnam Swallows
Another Administration

> *We lost sight of one of the cardinal maxims of guerrilla war: the guerrilla wins if he does not lose. The conventional army loses if it does not win.* —KISSINGER, FOREIGN AFFAIRS, *January 1969*

VIETNAMIZATION, JUNE 1969

The reason that the U.S. was mired in Vietnam was simple: the South Vietnamese army was not able to fend off the communists on its own. Until it could, there was no way to negotiate a withdrawal of American troops that would not lead to the overthrow of the Saigon government. For it is a reliable rule of diplomacy that you cannot win at the bargaining table something that you would be unable to win on the ground.

Spasms of bombings could, perhaps, delay the day of reckoning, but not change this reality. So unless the U.S. was willing to stay in Vietnam indefinitely, there could be no solution that assured Saigon's survival until the South Vietnamese army could take over the burden of fighting from the five hundred thousand U.S. troops there.

That was the military rationale behind Nixon's policy of beefing up the South Vietnamese army. "Although Kissinger didn't agree, it was clear to me that South Vietnam would not be able to survive a peace agreement unless it had the military forces to do so," said Nixon.[1]

Building up Saigon's forces would permit the U.S. to reduce its own. In pursuing the war, the new administration realized that it was important to stay just ahead of the growing antiwar outcry, to buy time by keeping the public mollified through periodic withdrawals of U.S. troops. Taken together, these rationales led to a program that was originally called de-Americanization and that Defense Secretary Laird dubbed "Vietnamization," a more elegant but eerily callous term. It was a policy that Laird pushed, Nixon accepted, and Kissinger disparaged.

The idea was raised by Nixon in his 1968 campaign. "We need a massive training program," Nixon said in an off-the-record talk to Southern convention delegates, "so that the South Vietnamese can be trained to take over the fighting, that they can be phased in as we phase out." On an October flight with the candidate from Bismarck to Boise, Laird told the press that up to ninety thousand U.S. troops could be pulled out in a year. (President Johnson's defense secretary Clark Clifford publicly rebutted Laird and pointed out that troop levels were still rising.)

Despite Laird's backing, the U.S. military was appalled by the notion of Vietnamization because they considered it tantamount to a slow surrender. On June 7, Nixon scheduled a showdown in Honolulu with General Creighton Abrams, the U.S. commander in Vietnam, to be followed the next day by a meeting on Midway Island with South Vietnam's President Thieu.

Abrams seethed with contempt as he listened to Nixon's plan. The tight-lipped general realized that—however it was sugarcoated—the withdrawal proposal amounted to the end of the possibility that the U.S. would prevail and the beginning of a sad rearguard action by the American military. Kissinger later called Abrams's discomfort "painful to see."[2]

The President's entourage—including Kissinger, Rogers, Laird, and five hundred other officials, reporters, and support staff—then descended on the two-square-mile American atoll of Midway, under the blank stares of the thousands of gooney birds that are its main inhabitants.

Nguyen Van Thieu, a proud military man who had risen from platoon commander to become Vietnam's president, was desperate to be treated as an equal, as the leader of an American ally rather than as a puppet or a subordinate. Kissinger had asked that Thieu arrive first, so that Nixon would not have to wait for him. But Thieu had insisted that the American president was the host and thus should be there first to greet him. Kissinger acquiesced, but Nixon's plane nevertheless ended up arriving fifteen minutes after Thieu's.

Thieu had also asked that he and Nixon meet alone; Nixon, through Kissinger, insisted that Kissinger be there. So Thieu brought along one of his assistants. When he arrived in the meeting room at the U.S. naval commander's house, he noticed that there was one big chair, apparently for Nixon, and three smaller chairs flanking it. Thieu turned around, walked silently into the dining room, found a chair the same size as Nixon's, carried it back, and placed it squarely facing Nixon's.[3]

Thieu knew the size of troop withdrawals being planned—twenty-five thousand—because it had been well leaked beforehand. Displaying the dignity of a people used to the perfidies of foreigners, Thieu suggested the withdrawal on his own, saying that it should be called a "redeployment." The two men then walked to a sheet-metal Quonset hut to announce that they had jointly agreed that twenty-five thousand American soldiers were going to be redeployed back home.

It was clear to both presidents, as Nixon later recounted, that the announcement that day "would begin an irreversible process." Thieu later recalled a queasy feeling on that hot afternoon as he thought of an old Vietnamese saying: *dau xuoi duoi lot*—"if the head slides through easily, the tail will follow."

The moment was a historic coup for Nixon, and a political one as well. For the first time since the U.S. Marines' Ninth Expeditionary Brigade landed on "Red Beach Two" just north of Da Nang on March 8, 1965, American troops were withdrawing from Vietnam. He was jubilant.

Yet Nixon again showed his strange inclination, when given the choice of explaining the truth or engaging in deception, reflexively to opt for the latter, even if it served no purpose. The withdrawal decision, he declared to the press, was based on "Thieu's recommendation and the assessment of our own commander in the field." In fact, as every listener knew, Thieu and Abrams were the two people most opposed to the decision. It was a little lie, one that Nixon later called "a diplomatic exaggeration," but it was another indication of a larger syndrome: that Nixon, and to some extent Kissinger, felt that it was easier to deceive the American people than to nurture public understanding and support by being open about what they were doing.[4]

In this case, however, Kissinger was more honest, perhaps because he was less pleased by the policy. In a background discussion with reporters on the way to Midway, Kissinger said that Vietnamization could help if it placed before Hanoi the specter of an opponent that would grow stronger. "If, however, we withdraw at a rate that gives Hanoi the feeling that we are really just looking for an excuse to get out, then it will thwart negotiations, because they will just sit there and wait." In that case, he added, Vietnamization would be no more than "an elegant bugout."

As it turned out, the withdrawals would continue at a painful rate: slow enough to drag out U.S. involvement for another three years amid growing domestic anger, but fast enough to encourage Hanoi to sit and wait. When Clark Clifford publicly suggested later that month that one hundred thousand troops could be pulled out in 1969, Nixon bridled at the hypocrisy. This was the man who just six months earlier, when he was defense secretary, had been talking about the need for more of a buildup. But to Kissinger's dismay, Nixon added, "I would hope that we could beat Mr. Clifford's timetable."[5]

For Kissinger, Vietnamization violated his cardinal rule of realism: military force and diplomacy must work together. In *Nuclear Weapons and Foreign Policy,* he had lambasted the U.S. decision to cease offensive operations in Korea while armistice talks were being held. His words in 1957 foreshadowed what he would face trying to negotiate a settlement in Vietnam: "By stopping military operations we removed the only Chinese incentive for a settlement; we produced the frustration of two years of inconclusive negotiations. In short, our insistence on divorcing force from diplomacy caused our power to lack purpose and our negotiations to lack force."

He later wrote strikingly similar words as he looked back on the policy of Vietnamization. It was unrealistic, he said, to have demanded a mutual withdrawal at the negotiating table while making unilateral withdrawals on the battlefield. "The more automatic our withdrawal, the less useful it was as a bargaining weapon; the demand for mutual withdrawal grew hollow as our unilateral withdrawal accelerated."[6]

Laird continued to be the strongest advocate of Vietnamization. "I knew that time was running out for us because the public wasn't going to support the war any longer," he later said. "Henry didn't understand this because he wasn't a politician. Instead, all he worried about was that Vietnamization would undercut his diplomacy."

Whenever a withdrawal was due to be announced, Laird would go into a briefing frenzy, calling in reporters and favorite congressmen. "I felt I had to keep pressure on Kissinger and prevent him from getting Nixon to back away." One of these sessions produced a report on CBS News that "Laird has long since made up his mind we should be getting out faster"; on his news summary, Nixon underlined the phrase and scribbled a note to Kissinger: "His clever game!"

Laird also outflanked Kissinger in a bureaucratic coup a few weeks after they returned from Midway. In order for Vietnamization to work, Laird felt that it was necessary to change the "mission statement" that guided how U.S. troops were used. Instead of deploying them to confront enemy forces, Laird's new mission statement said their role should be to assist South Vietnam's army and to stake out a defensive rather than offensive posture of their own.

Without waiting for an NSC meeting or presidential decision, Laird sent out this significant change. "I informed Kissinger and the president I had done it on the same day I issued the orders," he recalled. Kissinger tried to convince Nixon to reject the change. But since Laird had already sent it out, it stood. "Kissinger was upset and called me deceitful," says Laird, "but you have to be willing to play the other guy's game now and then."[7]

During Nixon's long vacation in San Clemente at the end of that August, Tony Lake was visiting Kissinger to discuss Vietnam. "I said that the problem with Vietnamization was that it was like salted peanuts: once the public got a taste for it, there was no stopping it." It was therefore important, Lake continued, to get the best possible deal right away while the U.S. position was strongest.

Kissinger asked him to turn his thoughts into a memo. Lake wrote three pages. Kissinger took the memo, praised the part about how Vietnamization weakened the U.S. bargaining position, but then eliminated the conclusion that it therefore made sense to go for a deal immediately. He included it in a longer, pessimistic memo of his own to Nixon. "The more troops are withdrawn," Kissinger wrote, "the more Hanoi will be encouraged."[8]

That week Kissinger won his first (and last) skirmish against Vietnamization. Nixon had decreed that each round of troop withdrawals would depend on three criteria: a reduction in enemy activity, progress at the negotiating table, and improvement in South Vietnam's capabilities. But in mid-August, after an eight-week lull in the fighting, communist forces launched surprise attacks on Cam Ranh Bay and more than a hundred other targets in South Vietnam. At Kissinger's urging, Nixon responded by postponing the next phase of U.S. troop withdrawals that had been scheduled by Laird for late August.

In a private background briefing for a few journalists in San Clemente, Kissinger explained that the delay proved that the U.S. was not a prisoner of the withdrawal bandwagon. "We have to impress Hanoi with our staying power or we won't have flexibility," he said. "It is important that Hanoi understands—and the American people understand—that the three criteria do apply and that we are not just engaged in a mechanical exercise."

Nevertheless, the three criteria were soon ignored and the withdrawals did in fact become mechanical. Just two weeks later, Nixon decided to proceed with another withdrawal of 40,500 troops. At a meeting in the Oval Office, as Ehrlichman scribbled notes (and doo-dled a remarkably good likeness of Nixon's nose), Kissinger suffered his final defeat. When Nixon commented that Vietnamization was going well, Kissinger asked, "But how are we going to turn it off if necessary later?" The real problem, Nixon replied, was that the with-drawals were "not fast enough." Never again would he delay a with-drawal announcement, no matter how bad the news from the battlefield or grim the tidings from the bargaining table.[9]

THE NIXON DOCTRINE, JULY 1969

For more than twenty years, ever since the onset of the cold war, American foreign policy had been marked by a willing-ness to bear any burden to assure the survival and the success of liberty. That era was now over, a casualty of the Vietnam War and of the self-doubt it engendered. Taking its place would be an era of limits, one marked by a gun-shy attitude toward overseas involvement and the realization that the U.S. could not be responsible for each and every resistance to Soviet expansionism.

The era of interventionism lasted just over twenty-two years. It can be dated from February 24, 1947, when President Harry Truman decided that the U.S. would take over from Britain the burden of defending Greece and Turkey from communism. It symbolically ended, and America's twenty-year era of limits began, on July 25, 1969, when troops of the First Brigade of the U.S. Army's Ninth Infantry Division returned home to the U.S. from Vietnam's Mekong Delta, their mission unaccomplished. On the day of this first official withdrawal of U.S. troops from Vietnam, President Nixon happened to be chatting with reporters at an officers' club on Guam during the first leg of a round-the-world tour.

The most difficult task facing Henry Kissinger during his tenure, besides ending the war in Vietnam, was creating a framework for dealing with the post-Vietnam era of limits. A nation that had histori-cally oscillated between excesses of involvement and excesses of iso-lationism—and which showed signs of reacting to Vietnam by again swinging toward the latter—would face the challenge of charting a middle course.

In order to accomplish this, Kissinger felt, the U.S. should shape an overall framework of global order by creating a triangular balance with the Soviet Union and China. The U.S. would then delegate to certain regional allies the manpower burden of defending their neighborhoods against communism. This is the notion that would soon be dubbed the "Nixon Doctrine."

Like most of America's great foreign policy doctrines, the Nixon Doctrine was partly a response to a packaging problem. Nixon did not want the American withdrawals from Vietnam to seem like merely a helpless reaction to a sorry situation. Instead, he wanted to take the idea of Vietnamization and wrap it in the guise of a coherent, purposeful philosophy.

In addition, there was the challenge of making sure that there were no more Vietnams. Before the next local war broke out, Nixon and Kissinger wanted to have a policy in place ensuring that the U.S. would not be burdened with responsibility for sending in soldiers.[10]

For years, in the dusty symposia and journals where such topics are pondered, Kissinger had been exploring the role America should play in a post-Vietnam era. In fact, his fascination with the "doctrine of limits" went back to his turgid reflections in "The Meaning of History" as an undergraduate. A sense of historic inevitability, he wrote in his analysis of Kant, involves "the recognition of limits . . . the knowledge that one must set boundaries to one's striving." Likewise, his writings on Metternich and Bismarck explore the cold calculus of opportunities and limits that are at the core of the realist tradition.

In an essay written in early 1968, while he was still working for Rockefeller, Kissinger first laid out what would later become the Nixon Doctrine:

> In the fifties and sixties, we offered remedies; in the late sixties and seventies, our role will be to contribute to a structure that will foster the initiative of others. . . . We must seek to encourage and not stifle a sense of local responsibility.[11]

Kissinger had discussed this theme often with Nixon in their rambling daily sessions leading up to Nixon's July 1969 trip to Guam, Asia, then around the world. In the future, they agreed, the U.S. should distinguish between three types of security threats that could face a small Asian ally: internal subversion, attack by a neighbor, or an attack from the Soviet Union or China. But their discussions had been casual: there had been no formal preparations for the proclamation of a new doctrine, none of the NSSMs or NSDMs or acronymic acrobatics that would normally precede a major policy pronouncement.

Instead, the Nixon Doctrine was inadvertently launched when Nixon ambled into some off-the-record ruminations with the traveling press corps in Guam. It was a low-keyed and restrained talk—perhaps because Nixon had for once sated his penchant for hyperbole when he watched the splashdown of the *Apollo XI* astronauts, who had gone to the moon, and declared it the "greatest week in the history of the world since the Creation." (Likely adding to Nixon's adrenaline was that Edward Kennedy had effectively eliminated himself as an opponent that week by driving off a Chappaquiddick bridge.)

In response to a question, Nixon spoke about other Asian allies who might find themselves in the same predicament as Vietnam. "As far as the problems of internal security are concerned," he said, "the U.S. is going to encourage and has a right to expect that this problem will be increasingly handled by . . . the Asian nations themselves." The U.S. would feel compelled to get involved directly only if an ally was attacked by the Soviets or Chinese. Later he explained that "if the U.S. just continued down the road of . . . assuming the primary responsibility for defending these countries when they have internal problems or external problems, they were never going to take care of themselves." [12]

The remarks quickly became a major story, and Nixon agreed they could be put on the record. He also delegated to Kissinger a critical assignment: to make sure that the press, which had immediately dubbed the new policy "the Guam Doctrine," came up with a more felicitous label, one that did honor to the author rather than the island.

Recalling his words years later, Nixon conceded they were not intended as a major new doctrine, but he says they reflected the thinking he and Kissinger had done about Vietnam. "I believed it was a mistake to furnish the arms, the economic aid, and the men," Nixon said. "Whichever country was involved should furnish the men. Vietnamization fit into that." [13]

The Nixon Doctrine was soon cast as a global rather than a primarily Asian strategy. Instead of the 1960s doctrine of undertaking far-flung defense commitments through NATO knockoffs such as CENTO and SEATO, the U.S. would build up regional powers that would bear the burden of on-the-scene defense. In the Persian Gulf area, for example, the shah of Iran would be anointed with that honor, with a supporting role to be played by the Saudis. [14]

This shift in American policy came from two men who were at their core internationalists, but who felt it necessary to scale back America's global responsibilities in order to head off the full-scale retreat brewing among the American public. Revulsion over the Vietnam War had created a virulent mood of neo-isolationism and anti-imperialism, which denounced as inherently evil any American military involvement, covert activity, or economic links abroad.

The Nixon-Kissinger response to this isolationist tide—captured in George McGovern's 1972 campaign slogan, "Come Home, America"—took two forms. The first was to circumvent it by deceiving the American people. Acts that would cause popular protest, such as the bombing of Cambodia, were conducted in secret. The second was much the opposite: it involved a rational attempt to scale back America's commitments so that they would be more in keeping with its resources and its will. The principles that guided foreign involvements were reexamined and spelled out in brilliant (though little-read) documents such as the annual "State of the World" reports.

If half the effort expended on the first approach had gone into the second, then the structure of peace that Kissinger tried to build would likely have had more public support. Kissinger's talent for conspiratorial maneuvering was fully exploited in the Nixon years; but his talent as a teacher who could provoke thought and open up people to new ideas could have used a little more exercise.

As a way to gussy up Vietnamization to look like more than an elegant bugout, the Nixon Doctrine was useful; it at least added a little to the elegance. But as a substantive global policy, the doctrine never amounted to much: about the only regional ally pumped up was Iran, which did not prove a wise investment strategy.

THE SECRET PEACE TALKS, AUGUST 1969

After leaving Guam, Nixon embarked on a round-the-world trip. Near the end, Kissinger slipped away with his aide Anthony Lake and boarded a small U.S. military jet for Paris. There they joined up with General Vernon Walters, an American military attaché with a facility for both languages and discretion, and headed for the rue de Rivoli apartment of Kissinger's old friend Jean Sainteny. In a few minutes, two North Vietnamese negotiators—Xuan Thuy and Mai Van Bo—arrived and, with embarrassed smiles, shook Kissinger's hand when he held it out to them.

Thus began a fitful three years of secret negotiations between Kissinger and the North Vietnamese. Until then, Kissinger had played two roles for Nixon: as a personal adviser and as master of the NSC machinery. Now he was taking on a third and more exciting role: for the first time, he was serving as a negotiator. No longer would he have to remain in the president's shadow. As a high-flying superdiplomat—first in Paris, then Beijing, Moscow, and the Middle East—he could display the flair for dramatic diplomacy and creative manipulation that would make him the most famous statesman of the modern era.

At the beginning of August 1969, Kissinger was working on various other subjects that he had begun to see as linked to the Vietnam situation. The previous week, China had released some wayward American yachters who had wandered into its waters, a gesture Kissinger was convinced was motivated by more than merely kindness. In Romania just before Kissinger peeled off for Paris, Nixon had asked President Nicolae Ceausescu to send word to the Chinese that the U.S. might be interested in opening a channel of communication. Ceausescu was sure to let the Soviets also know of the overture, but there was nothing wrong with making the Soviets a bit uncomfortable. Indeed, that was the whole point of the Romanian visit. Nixon also confided to Ceausescu that if there was no progress in Vietnam by November 1, then "drastic steps" might have to be taken—which was also intended to get back to Moscow.

Kissinger and Nixon had only recently officially abandoned Lyndon Johnson's "Manila Formula," which insisted that North Vietnamese withdrawals begin six months *before* American ones. In Paris, Kissinger sweetened the American position by saying that, if Hanoi would agree to a *mutual* withdrawal, the U.S. would agree not to leave a residual force in the South.[15]

To illustrate America's new position, Kissinger directed Tony Lake to draw up a proposed timetable for a complete, mutual withdrawal. It was pretty haphazard because Lake had to concoct it on his own. "Henry was so nervous about people finding out he was holding this meeting that he wouldn't even make use of the Vietnam experts on his own staff," Lake recalled. So the young assistant had to telephone the Defense Department and find out the exact number of U.S. troops in South Vietnam, then ask the CIA how many North Vietnamese troops were there. "Basically, I then divided the numbers by twelve and drew up a month-by-month chart of a one-year mutual withdrawal schedule," he recalled.

There was one problem: on the flight back, Lake discovered, to his horror, that he had divided wrong. The monthly figures for U.S. withdrawals did not add up to the total amount of troops there. "Math was never my strength," he later said. "I looked for a porthole on the plane large enough to jump out of. But when I told Kissinger, he laughed. He was good on stuff like that."

Lake had emerged as more than just Kissinger's special assistant; he was his fair-haired young intellectual, an idealistic foreign service officer with the brains and breeding that Kissinger admired. One grandfather was a professor of divinity at Harvard; his other was the prominent journalist William Hard, a writer at *The New Republic*. Lake had attended Middlesex, Harvard, and Cambridge before getting his doctorate at Princeton. Like young gentlemen of an earlier era, he looked upon diplomatic service as a noble and proper calling, and he developed a genteel sensitivity to foreign cultures.

He and his wife, Antonia—also called Toni—had gone to Vietnam together in 1963. But by the time he had begun working on Kissinger's staff, she was occasionally outside the gates marching with the antiwar protestors.

Lake's relationship with Kissinger was intense; he strove to impress his boss, but was often infuriated by him. One day Kissinger asked him to write for Nixon a letter explaining Vietnam policy to a student at Georgetown in what was to be a publicity gesture. Kissinger kept rejecting his drafts. Finally, he growled at Lake, "Make it more manly!" Lake was livid. Here was a pudgy professor who on his visits to Vietnam revealed himself to be petrified of flying in helicopters, and he was accusing Lake of not being manly enough. He stormed out, slammed the door, then smashed his fist into a Coke machine in the White House basement. Haig, sitting nearby, calmed him down. "My God," said Lake. "Here I am a junior foreign service officer and I've just been screaming at the president's national security adviser." He went back and rewrote the letter.[16]

Lake's miscalculation in the withdrawal timetable that he had prepared for the Paris meeting turned out not to be a problem: the North Vietnamese never noticed. Nor did they care. Xuan Thuy launched into a forty-five-minute monologue recounting the Vietnamese struggle against centuries of outside aggressors. Each had withdrawn. America would have to do the same, unconditionally and unilaterally.

There remained a fundamental gap in perception: Hanoi did not see itself as an "outside force" in South Vietnam. It would not even formally admit that its troops were in South Vietnam, nor discuss whether they had a right to be there. So the North Vietnamese had no interest in a "mutual" withdrawal, just an American one. They would never, it turned out, deviate from that position.

The most that Xuan Thuy offered was that Hanoi would consider holding more secret sessions with Kissinger. But it would not be until the following February that the process would resume.

Kissinger told Walters that he should inform absolutely no one about these talks, not even the American ambassador or his superiors in the Defense Department. Walters, a consummate professional, expressed misgivings. The president as commander in chief would confirm these instructions, Kissinger replied, adding that Nixon had the right to conduct foreign policy any way he wanted. Walters insisted on getting approval for these procedures from Nixon personally, which he did on a trip to Washington that was quickly arranged. A communications specialist was sent to Paris to give Walters special codes and equipment—and to teach him how to use the contraptions —so that he could communicate directly to Kissinger without going through the embassy channels.

It took some temerity for Kissinger, in his memoirs, to call the North Vietnamese "indirect and, by American standards, devious or baffling." For they must certainly have considered Kissinger's super-secret diplomacy and his murky offers to be indirect and, by Vietnamese standards, devious or baffling. What really infuriated Kissinger was not that the North Vietnamese were devious, but the opposite: that they said the same things in the private, secret talks that they were saying in public—indeed, they stubbornly seemed to mean what they said.[17]

There was little justification for the secrecy fetish about the Paris talks—other than to cut out the American public and the State Department bureaucracy. In fact, it served Hanoi's purposes to have the true American bargaining proposals remain secret for months while it drummed up public propaganda in favor of its own positions.

American interests would probably have been better served if Kissinger had made his trips to Paris publicly and if he had explained the strategy (if not the actual details) of his bargaining positions. As he later discovered when he used such an approach on his Middle East shuttles, the resulting drama and world attention can create a momentum and be conducive to a settlement, rather than an obstacle. In addition, a visible and well-explained effort by Kissinger to negotiate a Vietnam settlement might have calmed some of the anger of the antiwar movement.

DUCK HOOK, NOVEMBER 1969

At his August meeting with Xuan Thuy, Kissinger issued an unveiled warning: if there was no progress by November, then the U.S. would have to "consider steps of grave consequence." November 1 was the anniversary of the Johnson bombing halt, and Nixon had been dropping threats around the world—especially with Ceausescu in Romania—that it would also be the deadline for diplomacy to produce some payoffs. "It will be the policy of this Administration to warn only once," Nixon warned, more than once. In fact, he issued so many warnings about the November 1 deadline that it soon became necessary to contemplate what the U.S. might do to back them up.

The most explicit warnings were made to Dobrynin. At the end of September, Kissinger called in the Soviet ambassador to say that Moscow's lack of help on Vietnam made progress on arms control talks unlikely. As they were talking, Nixon telephoned, by prearrangement. "The president just told me in that call," Kissinger said to Dobrynin, "that as far as Vietnam is concerned, the train has just left the station."

"I hope it's an airplane," said Dobrynin, apparently not overawed, "because an airplane can still change its course in flight."

"The president chooses his words very carefully," said Kissinger. "He said 'train.' "[18]

As part of his philosophy that diplomacy and force could not be divorced, Kissinger favored having a military threat as part of a Vietnam strategy. Otherwise, he felt, negotiations could not succeed. Without a threat component, the U.S. policy of withdrawals would remove all incentive for Hanoi to compromise.

So Kissinger gathered a group of aides in September to determine whether there was a military option or threat that could be effective, something that could make Nixon's repeated warnings about a November deadline more than merely bluster. Among those involved were Alexander Haig, Helmut Sonnenfeldt, Winston Lord, Laurence Lynn, Anthony Lake, Roger Morris, and William Watts.

Their task, Kissinger said, was to come up with the option for a "savage, punishing blow." As he explained at the opening meeting: "I can't believe that a fourth-rate power like North Vietnam doesn't have a breaking point." Their project—figuring out just what that savage, backbreaking escalation might be—was given the code name Duck Hook.

The military ideas that the group devised, with the encouragement of the Joint Chiefs of Staff, included mining Haiphong and other North Vietnamese harbors and intensive bombing attacks on Hanoi and other industrial areas. A black loose-leaf book was prepared containing a detailed scenario for the operation. There was even a draft of a presidential speech by Lake and Morris. The beginning of their key sentence became a mordant catchphrase around the office: "Today, pursuant to my orders . . . "

It was an eerie period. October 15 was the day of a massive nationwide Vietnam moratorium, and 250,000 protestors marched in Washington. That night, Nixon sat writing notes about Vietnam on a yellow legal pad. "Don't get rattled—don't waver—don't react," he wrote to himself.

William Watts, on the other hand, was writing an impassioned memo warning that an escalation could lead to uncontrollable domestic violence. "The nation could be thrown into internal physical turmoil," he wrote. One night he took a break from his task and walked around the White House lawn; there, just outside the gates, were his wife and children, holding candles, marching with the protestors.

Lake and Morris also produced a memo that argued against any escalation of the war. As Lake had done earlier, their memo attacked Vietnamization as unworkable: the South Vietnamese were never going to hold their own, and steady withdrawals would make Hanoi less and less likely to concede anything. Any deal that could be achieved later would be no better than what could be gotten now. As if to prove the point to history, they proposed then what in fact was accepted three years later: a cease-fire in place, with the communists permitted to retain control over the territory they then held. To show that they could be as tough as any hawk, Lake and Morris stated that if the Saigon government tried to block the plan, the U.S. should overthrow Thieu just as it had done Diem six years earlier. "The stakes would seem to warrant steps we have not contemplated since 1963," they wrote. Kissinger sent the memo to Nixon with no comment except that it was for his information.

The most important memo opposing escalation was written by Lynn, the cold-eyed systems analyst. It was a critical, systematic look at the Duck Hook plan. "Nixon and Kissinger asked if there could be a quick, crushing blow, whether we could get in and out," Lynn later recalled. "But the JCS plan was lengthy, and the complexities of the operations were messy. It would not have been decisive." Lynn's detailed analysis showed just how much a blockade would leak, how long it would take before Hanoi felt the pinch, and how the B-52 raids would be more costly to the U.S. than to Vietnam.

Although Kissinger had ordered the Duck Hook study, his mind was open—and his feelings mixed—about what it would conclude. He encouraged Lynn to be as forceful as possible in exposing the plan's flaws. "I got the impression Kissinger was against Duck Hook and that his goal was to show Nixon it was unworkable," says Lynn. "He told me, 'We can save the president from the JCS if we write a good memo. Otherwise he's likely to go with it.' "

Tony Lake had the opposite impression; he sensed that Kissinger was in favor of a military blow and that he was disappointed Nixon was not as tough as Rockefeller would have been. "He kept muttering afterwards, 'Nelson would have cracked them,' " Lake later said. Nixon got the impression that Kissinger wanted to make good on the threats. "Henry was very hard-line at that point in time," Nixon later said. "He felt we had to show the communists we could not be pushed around."[19]

Nevertheless, Kissinger finally recommended against the plan in a memo on October 17. "I concluded that no quick and decisive military action seemed attainable," he recalled, "and that there was not enough unanimity in our administration to pursue so daring and risky a course."

Nixon agreed. Despite his show of writing "don't waver" as the demonstrators marched, he cited among his reasons for not carrying out his November 1 deadline threat that "the Moratorium had undercut the credibility of the ultimatum."

Looking back on the decision years later, Nixon called it one of his great mistakes. "In retrospect, I think we should have done it," he said. "I was worried how it would affect our chance of improving relations with the Russians and Chinese. And I didn't feel the traffic would bear it within the administration." Laird and Rogers would probably have resigned, he felt, and "I just wasn't ready for that."

Kissinger later had similar second thoughts. When asked by Bill Safire at the time of the January 1973 peace accords what he would have done differently, he responded: "We should have bombed the hell out of them the minute we took office." Even in reflective moods, Kissinger expressed regret about the failure to follow through on the Duck Hook threat. "We could have ended the war much sooner," he said, "if we had been willing to do in 1969 what we ended up doing in 1972."[20]

Astonishingly, right after accepting Kissinger's recommendation not to carry through on his ultimatums, Nixon had a meeting with Dobrynin in which he personally repeated all of his threats and tough talk. Unless something happened soon, the U.S. would have to "pursue our own methods for bringing the war to an end," the president warned as Kissinger looked on. "We will not hold still for being diddled to death in Vietnam."

Once again, Dobrynin called the bluff. He had just returned from Moscow, and his leaders had nothing to offer on Vietnam, he said. But they were ready to begin arms control talks as soon as possible, he noted. Despite Kissinger's strategy of linkage—which was based on withholding progress on arms control until the Soviets helped out on Vietnam—Nixon accepted.

When the meeting was over, Nixon later recalled, Kissinger was fawning in his praise. "I wager no one has ever talked to him that way in his entire career! It was extraordinary! No president ever laid it on the line to them like that." Yet Kissinger knew that the U.S. had been taken. "The Soviets, in short, applied reverse linkage to us," Kissinger later admitted. And Dobrynin, no doubt, learned not to take Nixon's threats seriously.[21]

Instead of announcing a military escalation, the president in his November 3 speech called on the "great silent majority" of Americans for support. It was an odd speech in that it sounded resolute but in fact represented a retreat from his military threats. That night Nixon was so keyed up he could hardly sleep. "The RN policy is to talk softly and carry a big stick," he wrote in his diary, ignoring the fact that he had just done the opposite.[22]

Still, the "Silent Majority" speech was successful, for it did indeed demonstrate that a majority of Americans were still willing to back him. The outpouring of support was massive. The speech was able to sell (for a while at least) Nixon's case for Vietnamization and his argument that an abrupt withdrawal would be a mistake. It gave a hint at what could be accomplished by leveling with the American people, rather than resorting to secrecy and deceit.

"You Americans missed many opportunities to settle the war in our favor, and that was one of them," South Vietnam's President Thieu later said as he reflected on the scuttling of the Duck Hook plan. No, not likely. The decision was probably wise. A single military spasm would neither have weakened the will of North Vietnam nor turned the course of the fighting. What was clearly unwise was issuing a slew of threats in the first place, since there was neither a plan nor the inclination to act on them. For an administration concerned about credibility, the month of bluff and bluster squandered that resource.[23]

YEAR OF THE SECRETS

As 1969 came to an end, Kissinger invited out to dinner two of the young aides he felt closest to personally, Tony Lake and Bill Watts. Their wives came along, too, for this was a social occasion, and Kissinger invited Nancy Maginnes down from New York. In a secluded back room of an elegant French restaurant, Kissinger displayed the exuberance he felt at having achieved such a powerful position. "It was the first time I heard him say that power is the ultimate aphrodisiac," Watts recalls. Yet his joy was tempered by the strange relationship he had developed with his new boss. "It would have been very different with Rockefeller," he said wistfully. "So much more normal."[24]

It had been an exciting year, but not a good one. Mainly, it had been a year of secrets: the ongoing bombings of Cambodia, the wiretaps, the back-channel talks with Ambassador Dobrynin, the private peace talks with North Vietnam. The decision to continue the war for another year had cost the lives of an additional 9,414 Americans—bringing the total killed to 40,122—but that was less than the 14,592 killed in 1968.

Kissinger had taken full control of foreign policy, except on the Middle East, from the secretary of state. The only struggle Rogers had won was to get the SALT arms control negotiations started despite the lack of Soviet help in Vietnam; but Kissinger had meanwhile taken over the responsibility for putting together an arms control position, and he had the bureaucracy working away providing him with "building block" proposals that he alone would decide how to piece together.

By the end of 1969, with SALT talks under way, Kissinger abandoned the last vestiges of his policy of linkage. When Ambassador Dobrynin came by just before Christmas for a year-end review, he proposed that they start discussing other issues in the channel rather than holding all negotiations up pending progress on Vietnam. Kissinger agreed. Soon he would be conducting talks directly with Dobrynin on issues ranging from SALT to the status of Berlin.[25]

Most importantly, Kissinger had begun developing what he saw as a post-Vietnam strategy for America, one designed to prevent the nation from a headlong retreat into isolationism. He spelled it out in the first "State of the World" report that he and his staff wrote for Nixon. Secluded in a villa in Key Biscayne with a group led by Tony Lake and Roger Morris, Kissinger worked for a full week on the report, playing familiar roles as both a demanding professor and quick-tempered taskmaster.

The saga of one sentence in the 43,000-word tome shows how careful, and painful, the process was. Lake and Morris had written, rather clunkily: "We shall isolate our problems, but we shall not isolate ourselves." With unusual directness, Kissinger replaced it with: "America cannot live in isolation." William Safire was called in and showed his flair for elegant pacing and clear concepts by adding the phrase "if it expects to live in peace."[26]

The document reflected Kissinger's roots in the "realist" tradition of political thought. American policy, the report said, should be "based on a realistic assessment of our and others' interests," rather than on emotional or moral ideals. "The source of America's historic greatness has been our ability to see what had to be done, and then do it."

But Kissinger and his report downplayed an even more important "source" of America's greatness: the tendency to act based on moral principles and ideals. One reason for American influence throughout the twentieth century has been that it does not slavishly pursue realism when higher principles are at stake; instead it fancies itself a beacon for freedom and individual rights.

This sense of righteousness can be a source of true danger—it is one of the main reasons the U.S. got involved in a decidedly unrealistic undertaking in Vietnam. But it has also been a source of credibility and power. Just as it is perilous to base a foreign policy on these ideals, any American policymaker who disdains them is likely to find that the structures he has built rest on shaky foundations.

PARIS IN THE SPRINGTIME WITH LE DUC THO, FEBRUARY TO APRIL 1970

As 1970 began, Kissinger felt that conditions were right for a new round of secret Vietnam peace talks. For the moment, the U.S. was in a strong position: Nixon's "Silent Majority" speech had temporarily rallied public support, and antiwar sentiment was receding in the U.S. as withdrawals continued. "In one astonishing year," *Newsweek* reported, "Richard Nixon has taken the war off the front pages and tucked it in the back of most American minds." Even more surprisingly, Vietnamization was working better than many had expected: South Vietnam's army had grown from 850,000 men to more than a million in one year, and it had doubled (to 55 percent) the amount of countryside that it fully controlled.

But all of this, Kissinger knew, was likely to change, which is why he wanted to resume secret talks with the North Vietnamese quickly. In addition, with his healthy dose of ego, Kissinger was eager to pursue the type of diplomatic coup that wins Nobel Peace Prizes.[27]

After much discussion, Kissinger was able to persuade Nixon, who had a lot less faith that Hanoi was ready to make concessions, to authorize another diplomatic round. When Vernon Walters made the request to Xuan Thuy, there was no immediate response. Then suddenly, on February 16, the North Vietnamese told Walters they would meet with Kissinger that Sunday, five days away. Kissinger, though he considered such behavior "insolent," immediately accepted.

One reason for his eagerness was that Hanoi was sending to Paris a top member of its politburo, Le Duc Tho. He would serve as a "special adviser" to Xuan Thuy, who clearly did not have any leeway to negotiate. Kissinger and his staff knew that it was useless to continue negotiations at Xuan Thuy's level; their disdain for his role led

Winston Lord, the most prolific punster on Kissinger's staff, to come up with one of his most egregious: "Xuan Thuy does not a forest make." [28]

Kissinger would end up holding three secret weekend sessions with Le Duc Tho before the series broke off in April.

In preparing for his February 21 meeting with Le Duc Tho, Kissinger paced up and down his small office practicing what he would say. "We are both scholars, men with an acute sense of history," Kissinger intoned. Tony Lake and Richard Smyser, another foreign service officer on the staff, listened to Kissinger's rehearsal sessions and helped turn them into talking points. [29]

General Walters handled the logistics for each of the trips, relishing the challenge of keeping it secret. "If there was anything he enjoyed more than imitating the men for whom he was interpreting," Kissinger said, "it was arranging clandestine meetings." A Boeing 707 from the White House fleet would touch down briefly at a French air base near Bourges, drop Kissinger off, then resume what seemed like a routine training flight to Frankfurt. Along with Lake and Smyser, Kissinger would stay at Walters's two-bedroom bachelor apartment in Neuilly, while the general slept on the couch. [30]

Le Duc Tho was a slight man with gray hair, invariably dressed in a somber Mao jacket. He had luminous eyes that seldom betrayed the fervor that had led him to become a communist guerrilla at age fifteen. During the struggle against the French, he had spent ten years in various prisons, and though he could speak eloquently of peace, it had for him remained only an abstraction. Kissinger occasionally used the word *insolent* to describe Le Duc Tho, an odd label, different from *arrogant* or *stubborn* in that it is usually applied to someone considered an inferior. No doubt Tho likewise saw Kissinger as insolent, being no more than the latest in a long line of foreigners who mistakenly thought they could meddle in Vietnam.

(After the peace accords had been signed, Le Duc Tho—whom Kissinger was by then calling Ducky behind his back—would take Kissinger through a museum of Vietnamese history. But instead of noting his nation's ancient culture, he recounted how he had survived various prisons and operated under different disguises. Kissinger called them "tips that will prove invaluable should I ever decide to lead a guerrilla struggle in Indochina.") [31]

Kissinger tried to strike a personal rapport at his first session with Le Duc Tho through his standard mix of jokes, flattery, self-deprecation, and historical allusions. Tho was polite. He laughed at Kissinger's jokes, sometimes heartily. But Kissinger professed not to have been fooled: "He had not suffered in prison for ten years and fought wars for twenty years to be seduced now by what a capitalist fancied to be charm."

Kissinger has often said that his negotiating strategy involves making bold steps rather than countless piecemeal concessions. "I always tried to determine the most reasonable outcome and then get there rapidly in one or two moves," he has written, referring specifically to Vietnam. "Shaving the salami encourages the other side to hold on to see what the next concession is likely to be." But in fact, Kissinger kept subtly sweetening the American position in small doses.

He had already conceded that withdrawals could begin simultaneously and that the U.S. would leave no residual forces. To Le Duc Tho he made a further tiny concession: the withdrawal of North Vietnamese troops from the South would not have to be placed on the same legal basis as that of the Americans, nor need it be formally announced.

Kissinger cast much of his argument not on principle but on what was politically possible for the U.S. In discussing the demand that Thieu be overthrown, for example, Kissinger replied that "the president couldn't do it for domestic reasons. . . . I'll be realistic about your imperatives, you must be realistic about mine."

In attempting to convince Le Duc Tho that forces were not in his favor, Kissinger hinted at his strategy of playing off China and the Soviet Union. "The international situation has complications," he said, that "may mean that Vietnam will not enjoy the undivided support of countries which now support it." He also pointed out that Nixon had shored up his domestic support. But when Le Duc Tho rebutted by citing Gallup polls and statements made at Senator Fulbright's televised hearings, Kissinger replied sharply that he would "listen to no further propositions from Hanoi regarding American public opinion."

Particularly distressing to Kissinger was that Le Duc Tho shared his belief that the Vietnamization withdrawals undercut the American bargaining position. If the U.S. could not prevail with a half million troops, Le Duc Tho asked, "how can you succeed when you let your puppet troops do the fighting?" It was a question, Kissinger later admitted, "that was also tormenting me." [32]

Kissinger's second session, on March 16, was more memorable for the travel than the talk. The Boeing 707 developed a hydraulic fluid problem and the pilot decided that it would be dangerous to try touching down in Bourges. After a series of increasingly agitated secret messages describing the situation, General Walters got a telephone call from Al Haig saying that the plane had decided to go directly to Frankfurt. Walters should "bail Kissinger out."

After pondering the predicament for a few minutes, General Walters decided that his best bet was to call on President Pompidou, who knew of Kissinger's clandestine meetings. So he walked to the Élysée Palace, presented himself to the "rather startled" gendarme, and was eventually ushered in to see Michel Jobert, who was Pompidou's Kissinger. After hearing him out, Jobert went in to see Pompidou, who then invited Walters in and offered him the use of his personal plane. The pilot of the French Mystère 20 jet was actually able to spot Kissinger's Boeing 707, land just behind it at Frankfurt, and taxi to a stop right beside it.

On the flight back to Paris, Pompidou's pilot asked Walters what he was supposed to tell the German controllers, who were mystified by the unscheduled landing of the Mystère jet and the disappearance of a passenger from the U.S. plane. "Tell them it involves a woman," said Walters after a few moments of thought.

"But what if Madame Pompidou finds out?" asked the pilot.

"If Madame Pompidou finds out," Walters replied, "I give you my word of honor as a U.S. Army officer that I will tell her the truth." Kissinger was rather impressed with Walters's whole rescue operation, though he later noted, "I have often wondered why he thought the ground personnel could have been fooled about the sex of the passenger."[33]

Once safely at the bargaining table, Kissinger provided a very precise timetable of how the U.S. troops would be withdrawn. But Le Duc Tho rejected any plan that would call for a mutual rather than unilateral withdrawal, and he did so again at the meeting on April 4, where he told Kissinger that there was no need for further meetings until the U.S. changed its position. Kissinger led Nixon to believe, falsely, that he had followed Nixon's instruction to demand that a time limit be adopted for reaching an agreement, and that when the North Vietnamese refused, Kissinger broke off the talks.

The secrecy surrounding the talks raised problems beyond those of wayward jets in the night. Kissinger later claimed, "I cabled full reports after every session by back channel to Ambassador Ellsworth Bunker in Saigon to brief Thieu." Yet others involved said that the version that went to South Vietnam's president was very sanitized, with Kissinger often personally going over the memo and excising paragraphs.

In fact, a private memo that Kissinger sent to Nixon shows a conscious decision not to coordinate fully with Saigon. He wrote: "The lack of an agreed position with the Government of [South] Vietnam will require you to make decisions on our position which could, if later revealed, embroil us in difficulties with Saigon. This is risky, but I see no other way to proceed if we are to maintain momentum and secrecy."

Smyser later defended this secrecy. "Kissinger believed as a matter of principle—and on this he's absolutely correct—that you cannot settle anything in public," he said. "Negotiations within negotiations are not just a Kissinger characteristic, they're a Vietnamese characteristic."

Yet domestically, Kissinger's secrecy had a price. At the time, some news stories and Senate testimony claimed that Hanoi was offering reasonable peace terms but that the Nixon administration was being intransigent. In opening his influential televised hearings on the war, Senator Fulbright said that "recent visitors to Hanoi report that . . . the North Vietnamese would be prepared to make significant concessions in return for our agreement to the gradual, phased, but complete withdrawal of American forces."

If Kissinger and Nixon had been more open about the Paris channel and revealed the general outline of what they were offering there, it would likely have angered the North Vietnamese. But it would have made it more difficult for critics of the war to allege that Washington was the only stubborn party.

Even after the talks broke down in April, Kissinger was eager to keep the channel alive, and to keep it secret. As a result, his reports to Nixon were far more optimistic than warranted. "Aware of Nixon's skepticism," he later wrote, "I fell into the trap of many negotiators of becoming an advocate of my own negotiation." But it would not be until September that the North Vietnamese would reactivate the channel. Before then, the war would widen significantly.[34]

THIRTEEN

THE INVASION
OF CAMBODIA

An Expanded War,
Resignations, and Rage

> *It is not often that nations learn from the past, even rarer that they draw the correct conclusions from it.*—KISSINGER, A WORLD RESTORED, *1957*

THE DECISION TO INVADE, APRIL 1970

In the history of civilization, few countries have ever endured a greater hell than the holocaust that engulfed Cambodia in the 1970s. The blame falls foremost on the genocidal Khmer Rouge communists, who took power in 1975. But the creation of the killing fields had many causes, and there was more than enough blood to stain many hands.

The American share of the blame, and Kissinger's, arises not from insidious intent, but from a moral callousness that placed America's perceived needs in Vietnam above what would be best for a vulnerable neighboring nation.

Direct U.S. action in Cambodia had begun with the single secret bombing run back in March 1969 designed to take out the "central office," known as COSVN, that served as the headquarters for communist operations in South Vietnam. It failed, but the secret strikes continued. After a year of regular bombardments, involving 1,045 sorties unloading 108,823 tons of bombs on the border areas of Cam-

256

bodia, the elusive COSVN had not been eliminated nor had the Vietnamese communist sanctuaries been diminished.

So a year later, in the spring of 1970, the U.S. military pushed another idea for eliminating COSVN: a ground invasion that would send American and South Vietnamese troops across the Cambodian border.

Just at that moment, Prince Norodom Sihanouk's breathtaking twenty-nine-year balancing act came to a close. The mercurial, erratic Cambodian premier had gone to a clinic on the French Riviera to take the cure, as he regularly did, for his panoply of minor ailments. On his way home, he planned to stop in Moscow and Beijing to seek help in persuading the North Vietnamese to reduce their sanctuaries in his border areas. He left in charge his prime minister, Lon Nol, a right-wing military man known in Washington for little other than being a palindrome.

While Sihanouk was away, large protests, encouraged by Lon Nol, erupted against the presence of the North Vietnamese border sanctuaries. At first many American officials thought the marches might be a typically elaborate ploy by Prince Sihanouk to strengthen his hand as he tried to negotiate the issue. But on March 18 the Cambodian legislature voted to strip him of power, a fact he learned in Moscow from Premier Aleksei Kosygin, who was taking him to the airport for his trip to Beijing.

It was an odd sort of coup since the government did not change, only its head. In Phnom Penh, where Cambodia's elite considered the squeaky-voiced prince an insufferable eccentric, the news was greeted with general relief. But in the countryside, Sihanouk was considered godlike. In the town of Kompong Cham, infuriated peasants found one of Lon Nol's brothers, killed him, ripped out his liver, and took the trophy to a restaurant where it was cooked, sliced, and eaten by the demonstrators.

There were immediate suspicions that the CIA had sponsored the coup. But there is no evidence of direct American involvement. The CIA, at the insistence of Senator Mike Mansfield, did not even have a station chief in Cambodia, and the coup caught it by surprise. "What the hell do those clowns do out there in Langley?" asked Nixon, angered that he had been given no warning. The last intelligence report that Nixon got was the day before the coup, when Kissinger sent him a memo about the demonstrations. "It is quite possible this is an elaborate maneuver to permit Sihanouk to call for Soviet and Chinese cooperation in urging the VC/NVA [Viet Cong and North Vietnamese Army] to leave," it guessed incorrectly.

The only indirect U.S. involvement in the coup was that some military officials based in Vietnam may have led Lon Nol to believe that he would get American backing if he ever took over. Among America's Special Forces commanders, there was not a high regard for Prince Sihanouk.[1]

When Le Duc Tho, at their secret Paris session on April 4, accused the U.S. of fomenting Sihanouk's overthrow, Kissinger could not help taking a little jab at the CIA: "I despair of convincing the Special Adviser that we had nothing to do with what happened in Phnom Penh, although I am flattered of the high opinion he has of our intelligence services. If they knew I was here, I would tell them of this high opinion."

But the critical issue was not whether the U.S. had sponsored the coup, but whether the other players thought so. By its actions in the weeks that followed, the U.S. made the mistake of causing both Sihanouk and the North Vietnamese to believe that it had.

Kissinger and Nixon both claim that the U.S. was initially stingy in its support for Lon Nol because it did not want to prejudge the situation or compromise Cambodia's neutrality. But there was really no question that Nixon would cast his lot with the new military ruler. On the day after Sihanouk's ouster, Nixon sent Kissinger a confidential note: "I want [CIA director] Helms to develop and implement a plan for maximum assistance to pro-U.S. elements in Cambodia."

As usual, Nixon wanted it secret. Even the interagency group in charge of reviewing covert activities, known as the 40 Committee, should not be informed, he ordered. "From day one," said Marshall Green, then the State Department's East Asia chief, "Nixon was insisting on building up Lon Nol."

Sihanouk, meanwhile, having lost his balance, decided it was safer to fall to the left rather than the right. He landed in Beijing, was embraced by Zhou Enlai, and soon thereafter vowed to join in "resisting American imperialism." The Soviets, who viewed him as kind of wacky, kept their distance and officially recognized the Lon Nol government; but the Chinese and North Vietnamese, as well as the fledgling Khmer Rouge, endorsed him.

With greater gumption than wisdom, Lon Nol ordered the North Vietnamese and Viet Cong to leave Cambodia immediately. Instead, the Vietnamese communists launched an assault on the Cambodian government, whose ill-equipped forces had been trained on a golf course near Phnom Penh and ridden off to battle in Pepsi-Cola trucks.[2]

Thus it was that in April 1970, the Cambodians began pleading for emergency support, America's commanders in Vietnam began advocating intervention, and Nixon was faced with the most fateful military decision of his presidency.

It did not come at a good time. That April was turning into the cruelest month of the Nixon presidency. Kissinger's secret negotiations with Le Duc Tho in Paris had broken off, and a settlement of the war suddenly seemed hopeless. Soviet military advisers were pouring into Egypt. Nixon directed Kissinger to see if he could arrange a summit in Moscow, but when Kissinger went to see Dobrynin, all that the Soviet ambassador offered was, Kissinger recalls, a screening of "some films about tiger hunting in Siberia that he erroneously believed would interest me." The Senate, after earlier rejecting Clement Haynsworth, did the same to Nixon's next Supreme Court nominee, Harrold Carswell. The *Apollo 13* moon flight developed a major malfunction, and the astronauts were in danger of perishing in their module. And the threat of protests caused Nixon to cancel plans to attend Julie's graduation from Smith College, forcing him to face a daughter's tears.

So Nixon, not always the calmest of men, was even less composed than usual that month. Kissinger in his memoirs rather diplomatically notes that "the accumulated nervous strain" had caused Nixon to become "somewhat overwrought" and "increasingly agitated." In private, he used more explicit phrases, such as "basket case" and "drunk."[3]

In addition, Nixon had developed a rather disconcerting desire to see repeated screenings of the movie *Patton,* about the swashbuckling Battle of the Bulge general who made defiance seem like heroism. In a breathtaking scene at the outset of the film, George C. Scott as Patton stands in front of a mammoth American flag addressing his troops. "Americans have never lost and will never lose a war," he declares, "because the very thought of losing is *hateful* to Americans."

When the *Apollo 13* astronauts did finally land safely, Nixon flew out to Hawaii to greet them. There, on April 18, he was briefed by the U.S. Pacific commander, Admiral John McCain, whose pugnacity and crusty manner reminded Kissinger of Popeye the Sailor. Admiral McCain's son (later a senator) was then a prisoner of war. As was the admiral's style, his briefing map had large red arrows and claws sweeping across it, in this case showing big blotches of Cambodia stained red and the claws grasping at Phnom Penh and beyond toward Thailand. Nixon was so impressed that he asked McCain to fly back with him to San Clemente where he could give his briefing to other officials.

While in San Clemente, Nixon made his decision on the next

round of troop withdrawals. The secret Paris negotiations had broken off, the North Vietnamese were mounting an offensive, and Saigon's army was still weak, which meant that not one of Nixon's three Vietnamization criteria were met. But nobody was taking them seriously anymore. Laird wrote a memo urging a fixed monthly rate of withdrawals. Like much of the nation, Rogers spoke of the need for "diplomatic rather than military measures," as if the two were incompatible.

Kissinger, on the other hand, felt that military pressure was not only compatible with diplomacy, it was necessary for it. Le Duc Tho apparently shared that belief, which is why he began each session with a lecture about America's weakness on the ground and the correlation of forces. "We had seen enough of Le Duc Tho to know that without a plausible military strategy we could have no effective diplomacy," Kissinger later noted.

Yet Kissinger knew it was futile to resist a new round of withdrawals. So he came up with a ploy: announce a very sizable withdrawal but stretch it out for a year. After consulting with the chairman of the Joint Chiefs of Staff (but admonishing him to keep the talk secret from Laird), Kissinger decided on 150,000 troops to be withdrawn over a year, with the bulk coming out after the beginning of 1971. Nixon approved, but, typically, he decided to mislead Laird and Rogers about the plan.

When Laird and Rogers, both back in Washington, called San Clemente to see what the decision was, Nixon refused to take the calls. Instead they had to talk to Kissinger, who told them, at the president's behest, that the plan was to announce a regular monthly withdrawal rate but no overall numbers—the exact opposite of the truth. These deceptions got Nixon and Kissinger what they wanted: a chance to surprise people momentarily with their dramatic announcement of a 150,000 withdrawal spread over a year.[4]

The deliberations that led to the 1970 Cambodian invasion began when Nixon, still in a barely controlled frenzy, arrived back in Washington. There was no more pretense of keeping a distance from Lon Nol's right-wing government that had toppled Sihanouk. On Wednesday, April 22, Nixon was awake at five A.M. and dictated a memo to Kissinger: "I think we need a bold move in Cambodia to show that we stand with Lon Nol." Regarding the North Vietnamese communists, he added: "They are romping in there, and the only government in Cambodia in the last 25 years that had the guts to take a pro-Western and pro-American stand is ready to fall."

Three more memos followed rapidly, one of them ordering Kissinger to warn the Soviets that Nixon had made a "command decision" to react if the communists attacked Phnom Penh. Later that morning he met with Kissinger and told him to have Lloyd ("Mike") Rives, the U.S. chargé d'affaires in Cambodia, fired. "As with many Nixon orders to fire people . . . it was not meant to be carried out," said Kissinger, who didn't.

The full National Security Council—including Nixon, Kissinger, Laird, Rogers, and Helms—gathered that afternoon in the Cabinet Room to discuss what to do about the communist advances into Cambodia. Three options were on the table: watching and waiting, which is what Rogers and Laird preferred; attacking the communist sanctuaries just inside Cambodia using South Vietnamese troops supported by U.S. air strikes, which was Kissinger's preferred option; or sending in American troops as well.

The main target being discussed was the Fish Hook region, the same border area where the first of the secret bombing strikes had been conducted more than a year earlier. Once again, the military promised that the elusive communist headquarters, COSVN, could be found there and crushed. The other potential target was called Parrot's Beak, an area further to the south and only thirty-three miles from Saigon.[5]

Nixon usually kept his own counsel at formal NSC meetings, but this time he announced his decision on the spot: he chose the second option, sending the South Vietnamese into Parrot's Beak alone, with the U.S. providing only small-scale air support.

Out of the blue, Vice President Agnew spoke up. It was all "pussyfooting," he said. If the sanctuaries needed to be cleaned out, then the U.S. should get on with the job. Both Fish Hook and Parrot's Beak should be attacked and done right. Nixon, who hated to seem less tough than his advisers, was taken aback. He was already smarting because of Agnew's advice that he "damn well ought to go to Smith" and see Julie graduate.[6]

The next evening, Kissinger was at the house of J. William Fulbright, the gentlemanly Arkansas dove, for an informal discussion of Vietnam with Senate Foreign Relations Committee members. Three times the White House switchboard tracked him down with calls from the president. He was in a "monumental rage," Kissinger recalled, because his three-week-old order to open a CIA station in Cambodia had still not been carried out. When Kissinger returned to his West Wing office, the calls continued. Nixon was staying up late in the Lincoln Sitting Room. Seven more times Kissinger picked up his special line to hear Nixon bark something, then slam down the phone.

By the final call, after midnight, it had become clear to Kissinger that Nixon—bothered by Agnew's charge of "pussyfooting"—wanted to use American troops in the Cambodian operation. He ordered Kissinger to set up a meeting at seven-fifteen the next morning with CIA Director Helms and Admiral Thomas Moorer, the acting chairman of the Joint Chiefs of Staff, both of whom favored an American invasion. Tracking down his aide William Watts, who was having a nightcap at the Jockey Club, Kissinger told him to hurry back to the White House and get papers prepared for a full day of meetings. "Our peerless leader," Kissinger said, "has flipped out."[7]

Friday, April 24, was one of those days that show how odd moods and personal agitations can affect a decision of historic moment. It began with Nixon issuing orders to the military behind the back of his secretary of defense and ended with him drunk at Camp David with his blustering pal, Bebe Rebozo.

At his seven-fifteen A.M. meeting, Nixon told Helms and Moorer that he wanted plans drawn up for a joint U.S.–South Vietnamese invasion of the Fish Hook area; this was to be in addition to the South Vietnamese solo operation into Parrot's Beak that he had approved at the previous day's NSC meeting.

Laird and Rogers, who had not been invited, were off in their offices working to make sure that American logistical support for the planned South Vietnamese invasion of Parrot's Beak was kept to a minimum. Feeling unusually squeamish about keeping the defense secretary in the dark, Kissinger called Laird and told him that an American invasion was now an option. Laird was not happy.[8]

Another National Security Council meeting had been scheduled so that Laird and Rogers could have their say. But Nixon abruptly postponed it until Sunday, heading instead for Camp David with his longtime chum Bebe Rebozo, a Miami businessman.

Among the many things Nixon and Rebozo shared, especially on that Friday evening, was a fondness for martinis. Together they watched *The Cincinnati Kid,* an improbable poker tale involving an aging champ who pulls a straight flush, and afterward Nixon called Kissinger at the White House. Watts picked up on a dead key to monitor the call. Nixon was slurring obscenities as he discussed sending in American troops.

"Wait a minute," Nixon suddenly said. "Bebe has something to say to you." A new voice came over the phone. "The president wants you to know, Henry, that if this doesn't work, it's your ass."

Nixon's drinking was a tricky issue. He did not drink during the day, but in the evening he indulged in the manner common to his generation of men, and sometimes a bit more. When he asked John Ehrlichman, who as a Christian Scientist never touched anything stronger than ginger ale, to work on the 1968 campaign, Ehrlichman insisted on assurances that he would curb his drinking. "I can promise you right now that will not be a problem," Nixon said, and for a while it wasn't. The only time he drank a lot, says Ehrlichman, was in the evening with friends, especially in Key Biscayne with Rebozo. "Bebe made strong drinks," says Ehrlichman, "and Nixon was less tolerant than normal people. It didn't take a whole lot of gin to get him sloshed."

That was the excuse that Kissinger often used when defending Nixon: when he was tired and under strain, Kissinger would say, Nixon would begin slurring his words after just one or two drinks, even if he wasn't really drunk. Still, Nixon's drinking had become unsettling to Kissinger, who barely drank at all. He would poke fun at "my drunken friend" the way people joke about things that truly scare them.

The drinking was also a festering issue among his staff, who often listened in on the slurred late-night conversations. Kissinger used this to his advantage; he needed their support, he would tell aides, because as they alone knew, he was the one man who kept "that drunken lunatic" from doing things that would "blow up the world." Said Morris: "It became a justification to Henry for his manipulations."[9]

As Nixon was letting off steam that Friday night with Bebe Rebozo at Camp David, Kissinger was meeting with the doves on his NSC staff. Intellectually secure, he liked having his ideas challenged; socially insecure, he sought to win the approval of all those around him. Both of those instincts were at work that Friday evening when he invited to his office Tony Lake, Roger Morris, Larry Lynn, and Winston Lord. "Ah, here are my bleeding hearts," he said as they filed in. Then noticing Bill Watts at his desk outside the door, Kissinger called out: "Are you a bleeding heart, too?" Watts nodded uncertainly. "Well, then, you might as well sit in." As Lake later said: "To Henry's credit, he was gathering the people who might argue him out of the Cambodian thing."

The meeting was surreal, recalled Watts, because "with Henry you always knew he was keeping someone in the dark." The only decision that had officially been made was to send in South Vietnamese ground troops, and Kissinger did not tell the meeting that U.S. troops might also be part of the invasion. Oddly, Kissinger had privately told each person in the room of the plans to use U.S. troops; but none was sure that the others knew, so everyone talked circumspectly about this key point. "I argued that U.S. troops would inevitably be dragged in because I wanted to raise that issue," recalled Lake, "but he said, 'No, we'll be able to stay in control.' "

Lake, Morris, and Lord argued that the goal should be a neutral Cambodia; Lon Nol should be encouraged to negotiate some "private understanding" with Hanoi that it could "use the border areas in the same fashion as earlier." Likewise, Cambodia should tacitly permit "cross-border skirmishes" and bombing—in short, the situation that had existed under Sihanouk.

Kissinger later said that permitting cross-border skirmishes but not a deep-penetration invasion was "a distinction whose moral significance continues to escape me." But the distinction the young trio made was logical: a tacit understanding that there might be skirmishes in the border area would not risk dragging Cambodia into the conflict; but a large invasion would mean the country would soon become engulfed by war.

The meeting became heated at times, but perhaps not as heated as some participants later liked to remember. "Not for the first or last time," admitted Morris, "a policy in Indochina that warranted screaming was too gently opposed."

At one point Lake warned that the U.S. would find itself "bogged down in a wider war." Kissinger responded, "Well, Tony, I knew what you were going to say." The mild-mannered Lake was incensed, but he kept it to himself; if he was so predictable, he thought, then he might as well just resign.

Lord focused on the domestic equation: not only would there be an uproar, but it would destroy the domestic support that was needed to keep the Vietnamization program properly paced. Watts's arguments were the most prescient. He agreed that an invasion would cause an explosion of domestic protest. But he added that invading Cambodia this year would lead to invading Laos next year and blockading Haiphong the year after.

As during the Duck Hook planning, Kissinger was most interested in Lynn's more systematic and less emotional analysis. He presented a cost-benefit argument against any invasion. "My job was to get the most bang for the buck," Lynn recalled, "and my case was that the same resources could be more effectively used in South Vietnam." But his analysis was not merely cold calculations. "Tony Lake was arguing that you don't invade a sovereign country, but for me it was that the costs on the ground—mainly human costs—were going to be devastating. I felt there was a lack of sensitivity about civilian population." [10]

But the more he heard the arguments against it, the more persuaded Kissinger became that a full-fledged invasion of the sanctuaries led by American forces was the answer. Those who opposed it could offer no explanation of how Vietnamization could proceed if Cambodia became a conduit for massive communist infiltration and resupply. A limited operation into one sanctuary using only Vietnamese troops, which he had originally recommended, now struck him as pointless. It would stir up domestic discord, have little effect on the North Vietnamese, and combine the worst elements of all alternatives.

That Saturday morning, Nixon called to invite Kissinger to Camp David. There the president paddled around the heated pool as Kissinger walked along the edge. No longer was there any question that Nixon wanted to send U.S. troops in. Now he was thinking of going even further. Why not, he asked, also now implement the Duck Hook plan? As long as the public was going to get hysterical, why not mine Haiphong and bomb Hanoi?

Kissinger could not figure out whether Nixon was serious or whether he was just indulging in some musings so that he could later convince himself that he was tougher than all of his advisers. Kissinger replied that they had "enough on their plates." [11]

Nixon and Kissinger and Rebozo helicoptered back to Washington that afternoon and headed to the presidential yacht *Sequoia* where, joined by John Mitchell, they embarked on a four-hour cruise on the Potomac. With the decision made and the consequences damned, there was a sense of jubilation, reinforced by ample alcohol. As they sailed past the flag over Mount Vernon, the president suggested they stand at attention; it was a feat, Kissinger recalled, that they did not all manage with equal success.

Back at the White House, Nixon invited everyone to yet another screening of *Patton,* the second time Kissinger had been presented with that pleasure. "Inspiring as the film no doubt was," he recalled, "I managed to escape for an hour in the middle of it to plan for the next day's NSC meeting."

The NSC meeting of Sunday, April 26, was held because Kissinger had convinced Nixon that he simply could not invade another country without at least consulting the secretaries of state and defense. They had not been heard from since Wednesday, when it had been decided that the only action would be a South Vietnamese strike against Parrot's Beak. On Sunday morning, Kissinger sent Nixon a memo (a reference to which he deleted from the galleys of his memoirs) reminding him that Laird did not realize that the use of American troops against Fish Hook was seriously being considered. The U.S. military command in Saigon had been preparing for such an invasion, Kissinger's memo said, "but up until now Secretary Laird has not been aware of the likelihood of its being approved and opposition can be expected from him as well as the Secretary of State."

Once again, Nixon and Kissinger went into an NSC meeting with a decision already made and tried to maneuver around those officials they had cut out. This time they did it by pretending the meeting was merely a military briefing on possible options (a strange way to spend a Sunday evening) rather than a time for decision. Laird and Rogers said little. (Though legally a member of the NSC, Agnew was not invited this time.) As soon as it was over, Nixon summoned Kissinger to the living quarters of the White House and put his initials on the military orders. As if to emphasize his determination, he then signed his full name right below. [12]

The Nixon-Kissinger policy of turning NSC meetings into a charade created a self-defeating cycle. Instead of thrashing out issues at them, Laird and Rogers learned to try to whittle away a decision after it was made. On Cambodia, this process began Monday morning. Rogers called Kissinger asking if the directive he had just received meant that the president wanted to use American troops against Fish Hook. Precisely, Kissinger replied. Rogers called Nixon and asked for a meeting. Laird had a host of objections, and he also called the president. Just before eleven, Haldeman phoned Kissinger to tell him that he had better hurry over to Nixon's Executive Office Building hideaway because Rogers and Laird were both on their way.

Kissinger's memoirs ridicule Rogers for being mainly concerned over what he would say at a Senate committee hearing scheduled for later in the day. But Haldeman's notes show that the secretary in fact had a substantive confrontation with Kissinger. He complained, with justification, that he had not even known that the decision about an invasion was on the agenda at the NSC meeting the previous evening.

There is a telling detail in Haldeman's notes: everyone was referring to the action as the "COSVN operation." In other words, just like the secret bombing program, the ground invasion had been sold as a way to eradicate the communist "central office" headquarters. Rogers pointed out that COSVN was not a permanent location. Once again, he warned, they would be embarrassed by never finding it. (He was right.)

Laird unleashed a scattershot volley that included the contention that General Creighton Abrams, the U.S. commander in Vietnam, was not really in favor of the operation. Kissinger refuted him, and Laird waffled on the point. Laird also insisted that it was wrong to call it a "COSVN operation." As he later recalled his argument: "For Christ sake, that damn thing moves all the time and it's really stupid to make that our objective because we'll never get it."

After Rogers and Laird left, Nixon let loose his frustrations on Kissinger. He said he was committed to using American troops in the

Cambodian invasion, but he would suspend his order for twenty-four hours. In the meantime, Kissinger should send a cable to Abrams in Saigon secretly—not through Pentagon channels—and see if Laird was right about his reservations. When Kissinger left, Nixon confided to Haldeman: "Rogers is playing against any move in reaction to the Senate, the establishment, the press, etc.; Laird is trying to figure the President's position and be with it without his prerogatives being cut; Kissinger is pushing too hard to control everything."[13]

Kissinger was careful to send the back-channel message to General Abrams in a way that would keep it completely secret from Laird. What he did not realize was that, as soon as Abrams received it, he picked up the phone and called Laird to read it to him. The defense secretary was upset at being back-channeled, but he was used to it; what got him angrier was the way the question was phrased. The issue was whether Abrams felt American troops should be used; the way Kissinger had framed the question was: "Can you assure success using only South Vietnamese troops?" Laird felt Kissinger was being deceitful. "He had worded the question so he would get the answer he wanted Nixon to hear," said Laird. But he decided there was no more he could do. Over the phone he told Abrams: "Abe, I know how you're going to answer, and don't worry, I'll understand."[14]

Finally, on Tuesday, April 28, Nixon made up his mind yet again to authorize a two-pronged invasion of Cambodia involving American troops. He called Laird and Rogers back in and told them directly. Kissinger was not there; instead, Attorney General John Mitchell sat in as a note-taker. The president was still worried that Kissinger was trying to control things, so he asked Kissinger to sneak out a side door just before the two cabinet officers arrived.

Mitchell's notes show Nixon taking responsibility for the action and declaring that the record would show he acted alone—against the advice of the secretaries of state and defense and that "Dr. Kissinger was leaning against." In fact Kissinger by then supported the idea of using U.S. troops, but Nixon apparently liked the idea that he was acting with Pattonesque disregard for the weak-kneed retainers arrayed around him. He was still portraying the mission as being the elimination of the elusive communist command center. "The President expressed the opinion that the COSVN operation was necessary in order to sustain the continuation of the Vietnamization program," Mitchell wrote.[15]

THE CAMBODIAN "INCURSION," MAY 1970

One of the most important aspects of any military operation is how it is perceived. Because Nixon as well as his critics portrayed the Cambodian invasion as a bold and brazen expansion of the American war effort, it became so. If Nixon had chosen to, the invasion could have been cast in a more muted light: instead of being launched with a fiery presidential address, it could have been announced by General Abrams's press office in Saigon as an expansion of the policy of cross-border operations designed to clear out sanctuaries that were threatening American troops. It would still have provoked protest, but not the explosion that Nixon detonated with his April 30 speech.

But Nixon had by then watched *Patton* once too often and was ready to proclaim his defiance for all to hear. Sitting in his darkened hideaway in the Executive Office Building, Tchaikovsky playing on his stereo, Nixon's resentments and pent-up tension spilled into a speech he wrote in longhand, with his most pugnacious in-house wordsmith, Patrick Buchanan, called in for the polishing.

Ignoring the pleas of Laird and Rogers, Nixon pointed to a map and said that the goal was to "attack the headquarters of the entire communist military operation in South Vietnam." Since it was unlikely that the troops would ever find this much-touted communist Pentagon, the claim would result in a further widening of his credibility gap. America, he declared, would not act like a "pitiful, helpless giant." As William Safire, the more moderate speechwriter who was not asked to help on this one, later said: "Nixon had done what only Nixon could do—made a courageous decision and wrapped it in a pious and divisive speech."

Going beyond hyperbole, Nixon launched into an outright lie: "For five years, neither the United States nor South Vietnam has moved against these enemy sanctuaries because we did not wish to violate the territory of a neutral nation." Actually, the secret MENU bombing of these sanctuaries was by then in its thirteenth month. Kissinger in his memoirs called the sentence "as irrelevant to his central thesis as it was untrue." But Kissinger had said the same thing in his background briefing for the press that evening.* [16]

* In an NBC interview years later, David Frost reminded Kissinger that, like Nixon, he had claimed at the time that the U.S. had not previously attacked the Cambodian sanctuaries. Kissinger got angry and said it was "because I suppose to us this bombing of the sanctuaries had become so much a part of the landscape that we did not focus on that." He later tried to get NBC, with

By the next morning—May 1, 1970—more than 31,000 American and 43,000 South Vietnamese troops were pouring over the border into Fish Hook and Parrot's Beak. With little sleep, Nixon paid an impromptu visit to the Pentagon with Kissinger in tow. His comments about "these bums blowing up campuses" made headlines, but his words inside were more hair-raising. As the generals pointed to their maps and pins, Nixon began asking about the other sanctuaries. "Could we take out all the sanctuaries?" he asked. There was a long silence. "I want to take out all of those sanctuaries," he said. "Knock them all out." He became more agitated, cutting off the briefers and launching into an obscenity-punctuated harangue. "You have to electrify people with bold decisions. Bold decisions make history, like Teddy Roosevelt charging up San Juan Hill, a small event but dramatic, and people took notice." Kissinger and Laird looked at each other in embarrassment. "Let's go blow the hell out of them," Nixon shouted.[18]

The domestic calm that had been purchased by troop withdrawals was quickly shattered—especially after the May 4 tragedy at Kent State University in Ohio, where youthful National Guardsmen aimed their rifles at an unarmed crowd of student demonstrators and squeezed off a volley that killed two girls and two boys. The picture of a young girl with her face in a silent scream as she knelt over a crumpled friend came to symbolize the nation's horror; the country was convulsed and its system of authority was brought to the brink of a nervous breakdown. Kissinger, unable to sleep in his apartment because of demonstrators, had to move to the White House basement.

Close to one hundred thousand marchers converged on the White House that Friday, May 8; police ringed the president's home with sixty buses and troops were stationed in the basement. Nixon called Kissinger just after nine-twenty P.M. for a rambling discussion of the war and the root causes of the protests. Unable to sleep, the president remained in the Lincoln Sitting Room, brooding and making telephone calls until dawn.

The telephone logs of that night show that he called Kissinger seven more times, sometimes talking for two minutes, other times for twenty. The last came just after three-thirty A.M. U. Alexis Johnson, the undersecretary of state, remembers being awakened with a call from Nixon complaining about fifty junior foreign service officers who had signed a letter opposing the Cambodian invasion. "This is the

whom he had a consulting contract, to delete the exchange from the show, which caused Frost to resign. Eventually, it was broadcast.[17]

president," Nixon barked at the groggy career diplomat. "I want all those sons of bitches fired in the morning!" Slam. The call lasted twelve seconds. A couple of minutes later, Nixon called Kissinger with the same order. "When he got excited, he would go into a feeding frenzy of phone calls," said Kissinger.

Among the others aroused by Nixon's late-night telephoning: Bob Haldeman (seven times), Norman Vincent Peale, Billy Graham, Rose Mary Woods (four times), Bebe Rebozo (twice), reporter Helen Thomas of UPI (at 1:22 A.M. and 3:50 A.M.), Nelson Rockefeller (at one A.M.), and Thomas Dewey (at one-thirty A.M.). Nixon's last call was to his valet, Manolo Sanchez, at 4:22 A.M. As a startled Secret Service agent scurried to accompany them, the two men went to the Lincoln Memorial, where Nixon engaged a handful of amazed protesters in an awkward discussion of their college football teams, the importance of traveling while they were young, and his goals in Vietnam.

Nixon's "madman" strategy was backfiring on him: he was coming across as unhinged in the eyes of much of his own nation. As a result, the Cambodian invasion would turn into the greatest victory for Hanoi since it lost the 1968 Tet offensive. Despite its defeat on the battlefields during Tet, the North Vietnamese won the living-room war for American hearts and minds. And despite the marginal military gains the U.S. made in Cambodia, the invasion so deepened America's domestic divisions that it destroyed the remaining prospects for a sustained policy in Southeast Asia.

Nixon was still backed by a slim majority in opinion polls, but he had lost the domestic consensus necessary to maintain a commitment to Vietnam. The Senate began considering a series of amendments— Cooper-Church, McGovern-Hatfield—that would impose deadlines on American involvement.[19]

Psychologically exhausted, unnerved yet defiant, Nixon retreated to Camp David. He was annoyed at everyone, Kissinger included, and for the first time Kissinger knew what it was like to be frozen out. The president would not accept his phone calls on most days. Kissinger tried to rally his spirits by organizing supporters—including William F. Buckley, Jr.—to telephone the president with encouragement.

But to Nixon, it was Kissinger who was crumbling under the pressure, showing his anguish, becoming unglued. That, he later said, was why he became so upset with Kissinger. At one point when Kissinger was expressing second thoughts about the invasion, Nixon told him: "Remember Lot's wife—don't look back." Nixon liked retelling that tale as a way to contrast his fortitude with Kissinger's fecklessness, and he would occasionally rub in the salt by adding: "I don't know whether Henry had read the Old Testament or not, but I had." (This produced one of Safire's puns: "Two years later, in Moscow, Kissinger did indeed turn into a pillar of SALT.")[20]

It was during this period that Nixon took away Kissinger's control of the wiretapping program and ordered Haldeman "to get Kissinger away from the press." Kissinger's relationship with Nixon's other advisers also became strained, and he stopped attending Haldeman's eight A.M. staff meetings. One morning Haldeman tried to assert his authority by calling him and ordering him in. They were discussing the Cambodian invasion, he was told when he arrived, and they wanted to know how to answer questions about why the much-touted communist headquarters, COSVN, had not been found. "Kissinger was terribly offended," Ehrlichman recalled, "and was able to grumble and sputter at the same time. 'I do not deal with PR problems,' he said, and got up and stormed out."

As an act of personal friendship, even as her newspaper was running shard-sharp denunciations of the invasion, *Washington Post* publisher Katharine Graham asked Kissinger if he wanted to go out for a quiet evening at the movies. She took him to see *Cabaret,* and in the middle she realized it was a horrible choice. The story involves the heady hedonism of Weimar Germany that led to the rise of the Nazis. "I was freaked out," Graham recalled. She turned to him and whispered, "Do you want to leave?" He didn't. Afterward, they had a drink and Graham asked how he could have endured watching the movie. He replied that he was used to seeing the breakdown of social order. "When I was growing up," he said, "I took it for granted that when you saw certain people coming down the street, you stepped aside."[21]

After a month, Nixon gave a speech in which, with typical hyperbole, he called the Cambodian invasion "the most successful operation of this long and difficult war." Not once did he mention COSVN, or the lack of it. That evening, unable to sleep, he summoned Kissinger to ask him how his "Georgetown friends" received the speech. It was almost midnight, but Kissinger called columnist Joe Alsop, who had been to a dinner party with Ted Kennedy, former British Ambassador Lord Harlech, and stalwarts of the liberal establishment. Susan Mary Alsop would not wake her husband, so Kissinger explained the situation and grilled her. "I know you were at that party," he said. "We're curious what the atmosphere was like?" She replied bluntly: "It was very bad. Everyone was in a rage." She went on to lecture Kissinger until he finally cut her off to report to the president. "She says it didn't go over very well," he told him.[22]

Neither Nixon nor Kissinger regretted the invasion, only that they did not go far enough. Nixon later said he wished he had pursued the idea he broached at Camp David about bombing and mining North Vietnam as well. "We took tremendous heat on Cambodia," he said. "We would not have taken any more if we had done the bombing and mining then." If he had acted more forcefully, he lamented, he could have "broken their backs" and been able to get then "the agreement we got later." Kissinger also regretted that he dismissed the notion of bombing and mining North Vietnam then. "In retrospect I believe we should have taken it more seriously," he said. "The bane of our military actions in Vietnam was their hesitancy."

Although the communists did in fact have a command center in the Fish Hook area, it was never located. "The troops failed to find the always elusive COSVN headquarters, which the President had unfortunately mentioned as an objective," General Westmoreland recalled. The press accounts were mocking, and the result, Kissinger said, "was one of the famous, self-inflicted credibility gaps."

Nevertheless, Kissinger concluded that—at least on a military level—the operation was a success. It captured up to 40 percent of the enemy weapons stockpiled in Cambodia. For almost two years, there was a decline in fighting in the areas of Vietnam that bordered the Cambodian sanctuaries. The number of Americans killed per week—which had hit three hundred during the spring of 1969—dropped below one hundred per week for the first time since 1966; by the following May, it was down to thirty-five a week.

These statistics, however, are somewhat misleading. A Pentagon study later that year estimated that "captured supplies can be reinstituted in about seventy-five days with the opening of additional supply routes." The decline in American casualties was in direct proportion to the withdrawal of U.S. combat troops. Within two years the communist forces were killing even more than before; the difference was that South Vietnamese troops, not American ones, were bearing the brunt.[23]

Whether or not the Cambodian invasion was of marginal help to the American war effort in Vietnam pales beside the question of what it did to Cambodia. That nation's descent into hell had begun. Every dire prediction of those opposed to the invasion came true, but in a manner more gruesome than even the pessimists had predicted. The war widened. Cambodia inextricably became ensnared in the Vietnam conflict it had avoided for so long. The initial wary American commitment turned into a massive and addictive patronage of a cloddish Cambodian army and a regime that grew ever more corrupt.

When the U.S. invasion began, North Vietnamese forces had spread over one-quarter of Cambodia's countryside; when it was over, they had dispersed to over half of the country. Hanoi's troops had also begun creating a monster: as its allies, at least for the moment, the North Vietnamese communists began building up the local Khmer Rouge. A ragtag group of five thousand hapless rebels at the time of the invasion, the Khmer Rouge grew in number, in tenacity, and in savagery. By 1973, they were refusing Hanoi's pressure to negotiate a peace. By 1975, they were a murderous force of seventy thousand intent on brutalizing their own people in order to create the purest nightmare of a communist society.

"There are only two men responsible for the tragedy in Cambodia today," Prince Sihanouk has said. "Mr. Nixon and Dr. Kissinger. Lon Nol was nothing without them, and the Khmer Rouge were nothing without Lon Nol. They demoralized America, they lost all of Indochina to the communists, and they created the Khmer Rouge."

On a trip to Beijing in 1979, when he was a private citizen, Kissinger met the prince, then in exile, for the first time. They had their similarities: both could be charming, duplicitous, and eager to win over adversaries. According to Sihanouk, Kissinger insisted that the U.S. had nothing to do with the coup. "But why, immediately after the coup, did you extend de jure recognition to Lon Nol?" Sihanouk asked him.

"Yes, but we wanted you to return to power very quickly," Kissinger answered.

"Why did you refrain from telling me about it? Not only that, but you wanted Lon Nol to resist to the end my return."

"No. No. No. You must believe that we were favorable to your returning to power and we did not like Lon Nol. We liked you."

"Thank you very much," said Sihanouk.

"I want you to believe it," said Kissinger.

"Excellency, let bygones be bygones."

"No. No. No. I want you to say that you believe me."

"I apologize," answered Sihanouk. "I cannot say I believe you."[24]

The thesis that Kissinger and Nixon are to blame for the rise of the Khmer Rouge rebels is most forcefully made by British journalist William Shawcross in his book *Sideshow*. America's five-year intervention, he wrote, "created the conditions, the only conditions, in which they could grow." It destroyed the balance that Sihanouk had created and pushed the Vietnamese communists westward out of their border sanctuaries. With backing from the Vietnamese communists, the Khmer Rouge fed off the discontent in the provinces. Eventually, as they were brutalized by American bombing, they became more brutal. Likewise, the fabric of Cambodian society was obliterated by years of relentless bombing and military struggle.

Kissinger later dismissed this argument as "bizarre" and said that "no one can accept this as an adequate explanation except apologists for the murderous Khmer Rouge." The group's ideology had been fanatical for years, as Sihanouk himself knew when he ousted them from Cambodia in 1967. The forced dispersals of urban populations and official terror were, Kissinger's aide Peter Rodman wrote in rebuttal to Shawcross, "all standard Khmer Rouge practice in all the areas they controlled in Cambodia from as early as 1971." Genocide was a long-standing component of their fanatic ideology. By the time they took over Phnom Penh, American bombing had been stopped for twenty months; yet they savagely depopulated the city.

There is some merit to Kissinger's defense. Even in this most genocidal of all centuries, the Khmer Rouge stand on a par with the Nazis as being the most murderous of all. When they took over Cambodia in 1975, its population (after five hundred thousand or so deaths in the war that began at the time of the 1970 invasions) stood at about 8 million. By the time they were ousted in 1979, more than 3 million had died, many of them brutally, in a land turned into killing fields. It should not be forgotten that they—and not the U.S., nor Henry Kissinger—bear the direct and overwhelming moral responsibility for the unspeakable horrors that occurred. Kissinger's intent in opposing the Khmer Rouge and their North Vietnamese patrons was to avert precisely the type of bloodbath that eventually came to pass.

Nevertheless, statesmen must be judged not only by their intentions, but by the outcomes of their policies. By invading Cambodia, the U.S. joined with North Vietnam in spreading the war to engulf a beautiful nation that had struggled to remain peaceful.

Kissinger argued that the U.S. should not be blamed for violating Cambodia's sovereignty because it had been "already violated" by the North Vietnamese, as if she could not be raped because she was no longer a virgin. But each successive intrusion—the North Vietnamese sanctuaries, the American secret bombings, the North Vietnamese westward thrusts, the American military backing for the anticommunist Lon Nol junta, the invasion by seventy thousand American and South Vietnamese forces—sucked Cambodia further into the maelstrom.

At the very least, the U.S. is to blame for treating Cambodia as a "sideshow," a country whose peace and stability was callously disregarded as America sought to salvage the remnants of its own murky aims in Vietnam. In testimony to Congress when communist forces were completing their takeover of Cambodia in 1975, Kissinger conceded as much: "Our guilt, responsibility, or whatever you may call it toward the Cambodians is that we conducted our operations in Cambodia primarily to serve our purposes related to Vietnam, and that they have now been left in a very difficult circumstance." Very difficult indeed.[25]

"Without our incursion," Kissinger later argued, using the odd term that the administration chose in order to avoid the word *invasion,* "the communists would have taken over Cambodia years earlier." Perhaps. But it is hard to justify five years of war and five hundred thousand deaths in Cambodia by saying it delayed for that period the communist takeover.

Kissinger goes on to argue that had the communists come to power earlier, it "is not very likely" that they would have been less murderous. On this point the evidence seems to be against him. In 1970, the Khmer Rouge was small and relatively powerless, so the communists that would have taken over then would have been puppets of the North Vietnamese, who were certainly a less murderous crowd.

What is indisputable is that the catastrophe that befell Cambodia could hardly have been any worse.[26]

STAFF SHAKEOUT:
WATTS, LAKE, MORRIS, AND LYNN

The "bleeding hearts" club that Kissinger had convened on Friday, April 24, a week before the Cambodian invasion, had not come away converted. The next evening Kissinger called Bill Watts at home and told him that the president had asked him to act as staff coordinator at the Sunday NSC meeting. Watts spent a turbulent night. Less than an hour before the meeting, he finally decided that he could take no part. He walked into Kissinger's office and, taking Kissinger by surprise, announced: "I'm against this, and I'm resigning."

The exchange became hostile. Kissinger began throwing books around the room, a sure sign that he was angry. "Your views represent the cowardice of the Eastern Establishment." Watts started to go after Kissinger physically, then thought better of punching the president's national security adviser. Instead he stormed out into the Situation Room.

"What the hell did you say to Henry?" Haig asked. "He's throwing things all over the place."

"I'm not handling the Cambodian thing," said Watts.

"You can't refuse. You've just had an order from your commander in chief."

"Fuck you, Al," Watts explained. "I can, and I just quit."

When he got home, his wife said she could tell he had decided to quit. How? asked Watts. "Because you're smiling for the first time in six months."[27]

Watts's resignation upset Kissinger because their association went back to the Rockefeller days; together they had been the two people openly crying in Rockefeller's suite in Miami the night that Nixon won the nomination. But Watts did not evoke the warm affection that Kissinger felt for Tony Lake and Roger Morris, nicknamed the Gold Dust Twins by the rest of the staff because they had become the boss's fair-haired favorites. He took them out to dinner, cared about their ideas, and showered them with fondness as well as his fabled temper. (It was only after he resigned that Lake would be wiretapped, and Morris never was.)

Which is why, when they, too, decided to quit, they were afraid to tell Kissinger. So just before the invasion, they wrote a joint resignation letter and gave it to Haig. "We believe the costs and consequences of such an action far exceed any gains one can reasonably expect," they wrote.

They considered holding a press conference to make public the reasons that lay behind their resignations: the duplicity about the Vietnam policy, Nixon's drinking, their suspicions about the wiretapping. Not doing so, Morris later said, was "one of the greatest mistakes of my life." He and Lake, he recalled, "didn't want to do anything to hurt Henry, who we still saw as a lonely figure of sanity in a dangerous administration."

Kissinger was particularly devastated by Lake's resignation, and he asked Haig to try to change his mind. It was an odd assignment: Haig was jealous of Lake's talents, intellect, and relationship with Kissinger. Over lunch, Haig launched into a litany of how horrible they both knew it was to work for Kissinger. "He was very subtly working on all the feelings I had about leaving, all the embers of my resentment," Lake later said. If Lake really wanted to leave, Haig added, he could arrange for him to have a nice sinecure at the Peace Corps. Instead, he went to work for Senator Edmund Muskie.[28]

After the invasion, Larry Lynn spent a week in shock. "I couldn't work, couldn't write a memo," he recalled. He was not a committed dove. But the Cambodian invasion seemed monstrous to him, and for a systems analyst something almost as bad: completely counterproductive. "We were watching Nixon's speech in the White House basement when it hit me in the gut. This was Nixon's dark side, not his statesmanlike side."

Kissinger mobilized a major effort to dissuade Lynn from resigning, this time enlisting Nixon personally. After being invited to come see Nixon in the Oval Office, Lynn first went to get a haircut. "How old are you?" Nixon asked. Lynn replied that he was thirty-three. Nixon talked for ten minutes or so about what he had been doing at that age. Suddenly, as if to end the meeting, he reached into a little desk drawer, pulled out a souvenir tie clip and golf ball, and thrust them into Lynn's hand.

With Haig, Lynn had an experience similar to Lake's. "In the course of carrying out his assignment of trying to get me to stay," Lynn recalled, "Al did the opposite, on purpose. He tried to make sure I left. He was so manipulative it was transparent." [29]

Most of the bright, young intellectuals—Halperin, Davidson, Watts, Lake, Morris, Lynn—had now left Kissinger's staff. Their idealism and brilliance had appealed to Kissinger, and he had allowed himself to grow fond of each of them, even as he and Haig placed wiretaps on some of their phones.

Now Kissinger was left with Haig, who was pragmatic rather than idealistic, dutiful rather than brilliant, and who shared Kissinger's conservatism, ambition, and willingness to cater to the president. Kissinger was never fond of Haig. At times he treated him brutally, as he did most every other subordinate, but he rarely made up for it with the intellectual respect and warmth that he now and then lavished on his favorites. When Haig became Kissinger's deputy, he had settled into a role of beleaguered aide-de-camp and occasional co-conspirator; but he never became an intellectual colleague.

Kissinger thus began depending increasingly on the sole member of the bleeding hearts club who had not quit, Winston Lord.

Lord had not been aligned with the Lake-Morris axis on the staff; he was dovish on Vietnam, but only moderately so, and his feelings were mixed. Nevertheless, he had pretty much concluded that he would resign with them at the time of the Cambodian invasion. He was talked out of it by his wife, Bette Bao Lord. Look at the big picture, she told him. You can do more to change the world by working on the inside with such a remarkable man. Lord, then thirty-two, became Kissinger's special assistant, inheriting the mantle of Tony Lake.

Lord, who later served as president of the Council on Foreign Relations and ambassador to China, was a graduate of Yale and of Tufts's Fletcher School of Diplomacy, where he met his wife. He had the endearing demeanor of seeming—and probably being—both earnest and bemused at the same time. His self-effacing sincerity was leavened by a dry wit and a weakness for bad puns ("Hafiz Assad is better than no Assad at all").

Like Bill Watts, Lord came from a high-WASP background and was aligned to the Rockefeller wing of the Republican Party. His mother was Mary Pillsbury Lord, a granddaughter of the flour magnate; she was a wealthy Republican Party patron and an American delegate at the United Nations. Kissinger tended to display deference toward people with such social standing. Though he did not spare them from the sight of his frequent tantrums, as Watts and Lord will readily attest, he generally refrained from making them a target of personal wrath. He seemed to sense that their patrician view of him would deem such behavior rather emotional and exotic. "Henry's fits were rarely aimed directly at Win because I think he knew Win wouldn't do such a thing or stand for such a thing," said Bette Lord. "It would be like cursing at a dinner where no one else was cursing."

Lord was a fast and precise wordsmith who was willing to put up with Kissinger's constant demands for rewrites, so one of his major duties was drafting speeches and documents. He also became Kissinger's globe-trotting sidekick, sitting in on all major meetings, taking notes, and then serving as a sounding board. While Haig served as Kissinger's ambassador to the hawks and hard-liners, Lord was the more dovish voice who tended to the secret negotiations and arranged meetings with antiwar activists. At Christmas in 1970, Kissinger gave him a book of Andrew Wyeth prints. In it was a note: "To Winston, who serves as my conscience."[30]

COURTING BRIAN AND OTHER PROTESTERS

In the aftermath of the Cambodian invasion, Kissinger began a program of small, unpublicized meetings with students, protesters, and prominent antiwar activists. In May alone, he held ten such meetings, most of them in the White House, some in private homes or restaurants. By early 1971, he had held nineteen meetings with student groups, twenty-nine with intellectuals and academics, and thirty others with prominent public figures.

It was, for the most part, a sincere effort: the lapsed professor believed that the administration had a duty, whether Nixon thought so or not, to reach out to its critics, especially students. He also harbored the conceit, not altogether unjustified, that if given the chance, he could convince, cajole, and charm most critics into seeing his side of an argument.

In addition, he actually liked being intellectually challenged. Although he excelled at flattery and sycophancy when it came to his patrons, he found it tiresome when it was directed at him, much preferring a good argument.

Kissinger once said of Israel's Moshe Dayan that he was "a brilliant manipulator of people and yet emotionally dependent on them." The same could be said of Kissinger. He was drawn to his detractors like a moth to a flame. He craved their approval and felt compelled to convert or charm them.

At a Miami Dolphins game Nixon's staffers attended one Sunday while they were staying in Key Biscayne, Kissinger was asked what he thought quarterback Bob Griese should do. Since he hadn't passed long on first down yet, that would cross up the defense, Kissinger replied. Griese did just that, and it was intercepted. When the others looked at him for a reaction, Kissinger said: "There's a wonderful lesson in this: you should never listen to the experts on the sidelines." But Kissinger never followed that advice. He listened to the experts and critics on the sidelines, sometimes obsessively. [31]

Kissinger's compulsion to court his critics was reflected in his foreign policy triumphs. He was far more successful at making deals with adversaries than allies. In the Middle East, he charmed Sadat and even softened up two notorious haters of Jews, Hafiz Assad and King Faisal—but he had horrible problems dealing with the Israelis. He turned his attentions on Brezhnev, Dobrynin, Mao, Zhou Enlai, and Le Duc Tho—but his attitude toward South Vietnam's President Thieu was contemptuous.

One reason Kissinger spent time meeting with antiwar activists was because he feared that radical protests would lead to a right-wing backlash, perhaps with anti-Semitic overtones. "Unlike my contemporaries," he later said, "I had experienced the fragility of the fabric of modern society." He would tell his young, dovish staffers, "We are saving you from the Right." When Kissinger tried that line on Tony Lake after the Cambodian invasion, Lake replied, "You *are* the Right."

But Kissinger's vision of how brutal a right-wing reaction could be was far more vivid than anything a Tony Lake from New Canaan, Connecticut, could conceive. "Henry feared the Weimar thing in which he and the Jews would be accused of a bugout in Southeast Asia," said Roger Morris. According to Sonnenfeldt, "He felt the scapegoat might be the Jewish refugees in the government."

Kissinger discussed his fear of a right-wing, anti-Semitic reaction during a courtship of the author Norman Mailer over lunch at Sans Souci. "It was like that in the Weimar Republic—just the kind of wholesale debunking that may yet lead to totalitarianism," Kissinger said. "I wonder if people recognize how much Nixon may be a bulwark against that totalitarianism." Mailer was a rather pugnacious intellectual of the left with a tendency, as indicated by the title of his 1972 election book, *St. George and the Godfather,* to canonize Democratic antiwar candidate George McGovern. But like most others subjected to a Kissinger charm offensive, Mailer was not immune to the conceit that, deep inside, Kissinger was actually a soul mate who shared his concerns about the war and the president. Mailer later wrote that his "work might have been simplified if he liked the Doctor less."[32]

The most painful of Kissinger's meetings with academic critics was the first one he held after the invasion. On Friday, May 8, 1970—as police buses were ringing the White House—thirteen senior faculty colleagues from Harvard came down for lunch with the man they took pride in long knowing as "Henry." There was Paul Doty, who had advised him on SALT; Adam Yarmolinsky, who had served under Kennedy and Johnson; George Kistiakowsky, the science adviser to Eisenhower; Thomas Schelling, who had been part of the arms-control-strategy discussion groups; social relations professor Seymour Martin Lipset; Michael Walzer, a popular government professor who taught a course on just and unjust wars; Richard Neustadt, who taught on the powers of the presidency; and Ernest May, a personable history professor who had the misfortune of being the dean of the college and the target of protesters taunting: "Ernie May, Ernie May, how many kids did you kill today?"

"You're tearing the country apart domestically," said Dean May. "This will have long-term consequences because tomorrow's foreign policy is based on today's domestic situation." Others took their turn. The climax was a slow, pause-punctuated lecture by Schelling, who had been closest to Kissinger of them all. "As we see it," the economics professor said, "there are two possibilities: either the president didn't understand when he went into Cambodia that he was invading a sovereign country, or he did understand. We just don't know which is scarier."

Schelling saw the invasion as a moral issue. Even if it accomplished some of America's objectives, it was wrong to inflict war on a sovereign and innocent bystander nation. "Whether or not it succeeds on its own terms," Schelling argued, "it shouldn't have been done." But for Kissinger, no moral issue was involved in the invasion; it was "an essentially tactical" question, with the main consideration being whether it helped the U.S. get its forces safely out of Vietnam. There was no way their two minds could meet in rational discourse.

Kissinger asked his former colleagues if he could answer them off the record. No, said Schelling, this was a confrontation and not a discussion. In that case, Kissinger said, he could not go into details of the administration strategy. All he would say was that "the president has not lost sight of his original objective or gone off his timetable for withdrawal."

These were his old friends, but they left embittered. "The meeting completed my transition from the academic world," said Kissinger. What bothered him was not their opposition, but their "lack of compassion, the overweening righteousness, the refusal to offer an alternative." The wounds of this meeting were not healed even by the end of the war.[33]

Kissinger had a far more satisfying dialogue with a shaggy-haired twenty-seven-year-old pacifist named Brian McDonnell. A social worker from a middle-class Irish American family, McDonnell lived in the Roxborough section of Philadelphia with his wife, Alice. When the U.S. invaded Cambodia, he began a thirty-seven-day hunger fast, which he dramatized by sitting in front of the White House each day. Kissinger never noticed him until one morning in early June when they were introduced by a rather unlikely mutual friend, the actress Shirley MacLaine.

Without informing the White House (or anyone else), Kissinger visited McDonnell, whose wide-set eyes and beatific smile exuded an aura of innocence, at the simple home in Washington where he was staying. His pacifist purity, boylike innocence, and all-American sweetness were somewhat alien to Kissinger, who nonetheless found them deeply appealing. Kissinger was able to talk him out of his fast by assuring him that the decision to leave Cambodia had been made.

On the day that McDonnell left the hospital after ending his fast, Kissinger invited him and Alice to dinner in the back room of a quiet French bistro called Chez Camille. Winston and Bette Lord also came. They talked about books and philosophy and the war and disarmament. "Brian, you are so innocent!" Kissinger exclaimed at one point, shaking his head. For his part, McDonnell would concede that Kissinger was sincere in wanting the U.S. out of Vietnam, but that they disagreed on how "honestly" and speedily. "I can't get Henry into the nonviolence bag," he later said with some precision.

Kissinger subsequently met with McDonnell regularly to debate the war and, on occasion, discuss the phenomenology of Hegel and Kant. Later that year, his wife, Alice, who was black, was the victim of a random murder in the Philadelphia ghetto; Kissinger privately attended the funeral. "Brian was a perfect example of how desperately interested Kissinger was in being understood by his critics," said Bette Lord. "He tried to win people over with an intensity that is amazing. I think it stems from being an immigrant and a refugee, always anxious to win people over."[34]

About a year after he met McDonnell, Kissinger was the alleged target of a kidnap plot. Among the thirteen people named in the indictments were the noted antiwar priests Philip Berrigan and Daniel Berrigan, four other Catholic priests, and four nuns. Kissinger jokingly referred to the plot as being the work of "sex-starved nuns" (and had to call New York's Terence Cardinal Cooke to apologize). But privately, without informing the Secret Service or the Justice Department, Kissinger allowed McDonnell to arrange a Saturday-morning meeting in the White House Situation Room with three of the alleged conspirators.

Sitting in front of a map of the world that covers one wall, Kissinger said that the U.S. planned to have most of its combat troops out of Vietnam by mid-1972. His guests urged that a deadline be publicly set; Kissinger responded that doing so would reduce Hanoi's incentive to negotiate. He also opposed a coalition government, he told them, because that would leave South Vietnam in the hands of the communists. Surprisingly, they found Kissinger's hard line surprising. "I always thought of Kissinger as a liberal," Tom Davidson, a twenty-five-year-old activist, said afterward, revealing a rather common misperception, "but here he was, all hung up over the communist threat."

Nevertheless, Kissinger was able to charm his visitors, and their parting was friendlier than that of the Harvard professors. Kissinger even accepted their gift of a handful of "Kidnap Kissinger?" buttons their defense fund had made, joking that he could sell them to other White House staffers. "The scary part of it is that he really is a nice man," said Davidson. "He's got this weird thing for us who operate out of the morality bag."[35]

While in San Clemente at the end of the summer of 1970, Kissinger renewed his relationship with a man who was soon to become one of the war's most famous opponents, Daniel Ellsberg, the Rand Corporation analyst who had helped with the initial NSSM-1 study of Vietnam options. Lloyd Shearer, the editor of *Parade* magazine, was scheduled to have lunch with Kissinger and asked if he could bring Ellsberg, who had become an increasingly strident critic of the war. "He's a madman," Kissinger protested, but then said it would be all right. During lunch, Kissinger shunted Ellsberg off to Al Haig so that he could talk to Shearer privately. But he invited Ellsberg to come back to San Clemente to argue about Vietnam.

Their lunch, which took place in early September, lasted less than half an hour. Kissinger became annoyed as Ellsberg laid out the administration's policy in stark terms: slow withdrawals, threats, mad bursts of force such as Cambodia, the likelihood of future invasions or escalations, and a deception of the public. "I don't want to discuss our policy," Kissinger replied.

Ellsberg would not be deflected. He mentioned the Pentagon Papers, the secret study of how America got involved in Vietnam, which he would leak to the press a year later. "Have you read it?"

"No," answered Kissinger, "should I?"

"It's twenty years of history, and there's a great deal to be learned from it."

"But," Kissinger responded, "we make decisions very differently now."

"Cambodia didn't seem all that different," countered Ellsberg.

"You must understand," said Kissinger. "Cambodia was undertaken for very complicated reasons."

"Henry, there hasn't been a rotten decision in this area for twenty years which was not undertaken for very complicated reasons." As he ushered Ellsberg to his car near the gates of the San Clemente compound, Kissinger said that he very much wanted to see him again in Washington and continue the conversation. Appointments were set up, postponed, rescheduled, and postponed once more. They never got together again.[36]

Kissinger also met with such leading Democratic critics as George McGovern and Eugene McCarthy. McGovern was one of the few immune to his charms. "I can't see that this meeting served much purpose," he told the press when it was over. Kissinger even went so far as to invite Jane Fonda to the White House, a meeting that would not have endeared him to Nixon and his coterie. The one condition he put on the invitation was that the visit not be publicized in any way. Fonda refused to give such an assurance, and it was never held.[37]

Kissinger's willingness to appear sympathetic to critics of all persuasions, along with his desire to charm and please, made it hard to tell whether, deep inside, he was really more of a dove who was struggling to rein in Nixon's mad instincts or a hawk who truly believed that a bugout would destroy America's credibility. At the time, most of the doves working with him thought that Kissinger was a closet dove; virtually all of the hawks considered him a hawk.

The hawks were closer to the truth. "The overall lay of his soul was conservative," said his old mentor Fritz Kraemer. "Henry Kissinger is about the most conservative man I have ever met," according to his protégé Lawrence Eagleburger. "The real Henry was the hawk," said his former legislative aide John Lehman. "He was torn between his true hawklike instincts and his desire to appease his liberal academic and Georgetown friends," says Haldeman.[38]

Kissinger had a firm belief in the need to defend national interests through unflinching assertions of power. He believed the best way to end the war was to be credible with the threat of force. Even though he sometimes backed off a militaristic stance for practical reasons, his gut instinct in almost every crisis was to react forcefully. He had favored the secret bombing of Cambodia and a strong response to the downing by North Korea of the American EC-121 spy plane. He had recommended a South Vietnamese invasion of Cambodia and quickly embraced the idea of using American troops as well. And that September, Kissinger's voice would be the most hard-line of all Nixon's top advisers when he perceived challenges from the Soviet Union in three separate but concurrent crises.

FOURTEEN

TWO WEEKS
IN SEPTEMBER

An Hour-by-Hour Look
at the Art of Crisis Juggling

> *To foreclose Soviet opportunities is thus the essence of the West's responsibilities.* —KISSINGER, WHITE HOUSE YEARS, *1979*

BLACK SEPTEMBER, *1970*

Historians naturally treat the world in an unnatural way, plucking a particular event or crisis out of context, analyzing it, then moving on to the next one, even if they were in reality all jumbled up. For example, in Kissinger's memoirs, the Syrian invasion of Jordan, the discovery that the Soviets were basing a nuclear-armed submarine in Cuba, the visit of Israeli prime minister Golda Meir to the White House, the decision to order the CIA to block Salvador Allende from taking office as president of Chile, and the tabling of a new peace plan by the Viet Cong are discussed in five different chapters as far as 350 pages apart—even though they all happened in the same week of September 1970.

This approach is particularly problematic when analyzing Kissinger, whose greatest strength and occasional weakness as a global strategist was his tendency to see or imagine linkages that connected far-flung events. In his mind, for example, the events of September 1970—Chile, Cuba, Jordan, Vietnam—were related to a pattern of Soviet conduct designed to test the resolve of the United States.

Thus, instead of examining any of these crises separately, it may give a better sense of how Kissinger operated to look in detail at the way he juggled events during a single two-week period, beginning on Monday, September 14, 1970, and ending on Sunday, September 27. The willingness of some of the participants, including Kissinger and CIA director Richard Helms, to supply their daily appointment schedules and desk diaries for this period, and of others to provide meeting notes, memos of conversation, and telephone transcripts makes a rather precise reconstruction possible.

The background to this fortnight was as follows:

- **CUBA.** By early September, U-2 spy flights had revealed the construction of new barracks and a wharf at the port of Cienfuegos, on Cuba's southern coast. At the same time, an unusual flotilla of Soviet ships, including a tender normally used to service nuclear submarines, headed toward the area, arriving on September 9. Kissinger decided to authorize daily U-2 flights for the week of September 14 to see what the Soviets might be doing.

- **CHILE.** Since 1962, the CIA had been funneling aid to the opponents of Salvador Allende, a perennial Marxist candidate for president of Chile. But in 1970 the program was muddled because of the State Department's reluctance to back the main conservative candidate. On September 4, Allende won a slim plurality (36.2 percent) in a three-way race. At that point the administration began to consider ways to prevent him from taking office—either by convincing (and bribing) the Chilean Congress, which had the final say because no candidate had an outright majority, or through darker methods.

- **THE MIDDLE EAST.** Nixon had decided to cut Kissinger out of Middle East policy-making, partly because he was Jewish, and let Rogers handle it instead. This led to more than a year of sniping from Kissinger, who relentlessly undercut Rogers's plan for an Egyptian-Israeli cease-fire and comprehensive peace process. By September, that cease-fire was as unstable as the Kissinger-Rogers relationship.

- **JORDAN AND THE PLO.** Throughout the summer, Jordan's King Hussein had been struggling with the Palestinian guerrillas camped in his country. At the beginning of what it would later dub "Black September," the Popular Front for the Liberation of Palestine, which was one of the most radical factions in the Palestine Liberation Organization, hijacked four Western planes and brought them to an airstrip near Amman, apparently hoping to provoke a showdown between Jordan and the Palestinians and to scuttle the fragile peace process. Kissinger favored letting Israel take military action on Jordan's behalf if Syria or Iraq invaded in support of the Palestinians.

• **VIETNAM.** Kissinger's secret talks in Paris, which had broken off in April, resumed on September 7. Neither side offered much new: the U.S. was still stuck in the silly position of demanding a mutual withdrawal while it continued to withdraw unilaterally, and of asking a doctrinaire revolutionary movement to give up decades of struggle in favor of a Western-style electoral process. But the meeting was friendly, and both sides agreed to hold another secret session later in the month.

During the week of September 14, 1970, Nixon's popularity dipped below 50 percent for the first time in his twenty months as president. But the nation was noticeably calmer. Students were returning to campus, and there were no signs of major protests. Romance and sex were on people's minds: the best-selling novel was Erich Segal's sappy *Love Story,* and *Everything You Always Wanted to Know About Sex* displaced *The Sensuous Woman* as the nonfiction best-seller. That week was the debut of "The Mary Tyler Moore Show," which *Time* magazine dubbed "a disaster," and the big new movie was *Tora! Tora! Tora!*—a $25-million epic flop about Pearl Harbor. "Marcus Welby, M.D." swept the Emmy Awards. Phyllis George was named Miss America. And Jimi Hendrix died of a drug overdose.

MONDAY, SEPTEMBER 14

Pursuant to Kissinger's orders, a U-2 reconnaissance flight skirted the southern coast of Cuba early Monday morning to photograph the naval facility in the Bay of Cienfuegos. But Soviet-built MiG fighter jets from the Cuban air force chased it away. Kissinger asked that flights be attempted again as soon as weather permitted.

He was facing a busy period: the president was leaving in two weeks on a hectic nine-day trip through Europe, and this time Kissinger had wrested from the State Department the responsibility for preparing all of the speeches, statements, and briefing books. "We can't have a crisis this week," he liked to joke. "My schedule is full."

That morning he met with the ambassador from Yugoslavia to go over Nixon's scheduled visit with Marshal Josip Tito in Belgrade. Nixon had so enjoyed his tumultuous welcome the year before in Romania, and the discomfort it caused Moscow, that he decided to visit its nonaligned communist neighbor. Kissinger also met that morning with the ambassador from Spain to discuss Nixon's visit to

General Francisco Franco. The symbolism of flying from the lair of an aged communist dictator directly to that of an even more aged fascist one slightly bothered Kissinger, but he decided it was not worth rearranging the schedule.

Kissinger's lunch that day was with Attorney General John Mitchell, who wanted to talk about Chile. As a lawyer, Mitchell had handled many clients with business interests there; as a conservative, he expressed horror at the prospect that Chile might become the first nation to choose democratically to become Marxist.

After a quick detour to Capitol Hill to brief leaders about the crisis in Jordan, Kissinger returned to the subject of Chile at a four-thirty session with the 40 Committee, the small group of top officials that oversaw covert activities. On the agenda was how best to prevent Allende from being inaugurated president. Kissinger had requested from the U.S. embassy in Santiago a "cold-blooded assessment" of the chances for a military coup. The American ambassador, Edward Korry, had cabled back: "Opportunities for further significant U.S. government action with the Chilean military are nonexistent." Chile's armed forces, he added, were "in their current and customary state of flabby irresolution."

Instead, at the urging of Kissinger and CIA Director Helms, the 40 Committee agreed that afternoon on a plan that was dubbed the "Rube Goldberg gambit." Chile's Congress was scheduled to ratify the election of a new president on October 24; historically, it had always picked the front-runner in the popular election, in this case Allende. The idea, however, was to persuade it to select Allende's conservative runner-up on the condition that he would resign and open the way for new elections. Then the current Christian Democrat president, Eduardo Frei, barred by the constitution from immediately succeeding himself, would be eligible to run again. The committee authorized Ambassador Korry to spend $250,000 for "covert support" of the gambit—in other words, buying votes in the Congress.

The scheme was not as outrageous as some of the subversions that the Soviets specialized in. But it was still rather sordid. One can only imagine how Americans would have felt if it were discovered that a foreign government (especially a communist one) had spent money trying to bribe members of the Electoral College or Congress to deny victory to a conservative U.S. candidate who had won by a slim plurality. (Nixon, it should be noted, had won only 42 percent of the vote in his 1968 election against Hubert Humphrey and George Wallace.)

The 40 Committee that day also decided to increase the covert propaganda effort to convince Chile's Congress that the economy would be ruined if Allende was elected. More than twenty CIA-sponsored journalists from around the world were flown to Chile to produce anti-Allende stories, which they did.

As soon as the 40 Committee meeting broke up, Kissinger met with Admiral Thomas Moorer, the new chairman of the Joint Chiefs of Staff, and told him to make sure that the Sixth Fleet was being deployed so that it could be ready for an operation in Jordan, where Palestinian guerrillas were still holding hostages from their four hijacked planes. Then Kissinger spent an hour with Nixon's scheduler, Dwight Chapin, going over plans for the European trip before dropping by the Oval Office at eight P.M. for a final session with the president.

The time that Kissinger spent with Nixon that day was typical: a half-hour private briefing in the morning, a half hour with Nixon and Haldeman at noon, an unscheduled fifteen-minute session just after lunch, four phone calls, and finally the informal evening session.

It was just after ten-thirty when Kissinger arrived at the dinner party that columnist Joseph Kraft and his wife, Polly, were giving that evening in their Georgetown home. Polly Kraft, a punctual person who liked to serve at eight, used to get annoyed at Kissinger's habitual tardiness. But the excitement attending his arrivals usually made up for it.[1]

TUESDAY, SEPTEMBER 15

Augustin Edwards, publisher of the most respected newspaper in Chile, was visiting Washington to spread the alarm about Allende. He stayed at the house of his friend Donald Kendall, the president of Pepsi-Cola, who had given Nixon his first international legal account in the early 1960s when the defeated California politician had moved to New York and joined John Mitchell's law firm. So a lot of old private ties were involved when Attorney General Mitchell arranged for Edwards and Kendall to have breakfast with Kissinger that morning. The meeting lasted for more than an hour. Afterward, Kissinger met privately with Mitchell and then David Rockefeller, chairman of the Chase Manhattan Bank, which had interests in Chile that were more extensive than even Pepsi-Cola's.

Kissinger was persuaded that the U.S. should do even more to prevent Allende from being inaugurated. He called CIA Director Helms and asked him to meet with Kendall and Edwards at the Washington Hilton, where the two men had rented a room for discreet meetings. "They wanted to find some way to make sure Allende never came to power," Helms recalled.

Even without three brewing crises, Kissinger's schedule was full. That Tuesday, he gave an hour-long briefing to the press on the foreign aid bill; met with the Yugoslav and Spanish ambassadors again; had a short chat with Professor Sam Huntington, one of the few Harvard colleagues who remained supportive; had lunch with Robert McNamara; and met twice with the president.

In addition, he gave a background briefing to William F. Buckley, Jr., and his top editor at the *National Review,* James Burnham. Kissinger had gotten to know Buckley by regularly inviting him to lecture at his Harvard International Seminar in the early 1950s, and Buckley had at least twenty private briefings while Kissinger was in office; after this one, he wrote a column stressing that Allende had gotten only 36 percent of the vote and thus should not be made president. Burnham, on the other hand, took a dislike to Kissinger that day—he found him manipulative and insincere—and never came back.[2]

At three P.M., Nixon met with Kissinger, Helms, and Mitchell in the Oval Office for what would be one of the most fateful meetings on Chile. It lasted only thirteen minutes. Nixon barked orders as he sat hunched over his desk. He wanted Allende prevented from coming to power. Helms took a single page of notes on what Nixon said, which are sketchy but vivid: "Not concerned risks involved. No involvement of embassy. $10,000,000 available, more if necessary. Full-time job—best men we have. . . . Make the economy scream. 48 hours for plan of action." As Helms would later say, "If I ever carried a marshal's baton in my knapsack out of the Oval Office, it was that day."

This was the beginning of what became known as Track II, a top-secret plan for CIA action that would be pursued at the same time as the officially approved Track I plan to overturn Allende's plurality in the Chilean Congress. Ambassador Korry, the State Department, and even the 40 Committee were never told about Track II.

Kissinger had few qualms about meddling in Chile's internal affairs. As he told a meeting of the 40 Committee, only half in jest, "I don't see why we have to let a country go Marxist just because its people are irresponsible." His realpolitik outlook treated America's national interests as paramount, and moral concerns about another nation's sovereignty were secondary. Kissinger viewed Chile as linked to a broad web of tests of America's geopolitical will: the Soviets were trying to take advantage of the situation in Jordan, Vietnam, and Cienfuegos. "The reaction must be seen in that context," he later emphasized.

Nevertheless, the thirteen-minute Oval Office outburst was the type of Nixonian posturing that Kissinger was inclined to ignore. He never set aside the $10 million that Nixon had said was available. "You should not have paid such close attention to Nixon," Kissinger later told Helms. "He sometimes doesn't mean to be taken seriously." But Helms was not used to Nixon's flights of fanciful fury. "I've never seen a president more serious than he was that day," he recalled.[3]

As soon as they left the Oval Office meeting, Kissinger and Helms had to do a head-snapping change of focus to a half world away. Kissinger had scheduled a four P.M. session of the NSC's Senior Review Group to discuss Vietnam. A major policy change was being considered: offering Hanoi some form of "standstill cease-fire" or "cease-fire in place."

In effect, a cease-fire in place would be a tacit concession that the North Vietnamese could keep their troops in the South. It was a big step toward what Hanoi would eventually accept: a unilateral withdrawal by the U.S., survival of the Saigon government, and each side retaining de facto control over whatever territory it held when the peace accord was signed. By September 1970, the idea of a cease-fire in place was gaining public support. At the Senior Review Group meeting, a decision was made: the president should make such an offer sometime in October.

Kissinger went to the Oval Office shortly after five P.M. to discuss this decision, as well as Chile and Jordan, privately with the president. Helms headed to Langley, where he met at five forty-five with Thomas Karamessines, head of his covert operations division, and William Broe of his Latin American division to set up a Chilean task force. It would be so secret that few others at Langley would know of its existence.[4]

That night there was a black-tie dinner at which Defense Secretary Laird was being given an award at Airlie House, a former private estate in Warrenton, Virginia. After changing into a tuxedo at his office, Kissinger met Helms and other top officials to fly down by helicopter from the Pentagon pad.

At that moment, a cable was on its way from the U.S. ambassador in Jordan. King Hussein had just decided to form a military government, mobilize his troops, and have a showdown with the Palestine Liberation Organization. The king had indicated that, if Iraq or Syria intervened on behalf of the PLO, he might ask for American support. Al Haig phoned Kissinger in the midst of dinner to read him the message.

Gathering up Helms, Admiral Moorer, and others, Kissinger choppered back for an impromptu meeting of the Washington Special Action Group (WSAG, pronounced "wah-sag"), the committee he had created to coordinate crises. Kissinger, who chaired WSAG meetings and tended to dominate them, convinced the group, still clad in dinner dress, that the best course might be to encourage Israel to come to the support of King Hussein. In the meantime, American military supplies should be sent to Hussein.

It was important to stick by those nations, such as Jordan, that had risked taking a moderate, pro-Western approach, Kissinger argued; otherwise, Soviet influence in the Middle East would continue to increase. This was yet another test of U.S. resolve; it had to be seen in the context of Cuba, Chile, and Vietnam. As always, he felt that America's credibility was at stake.

Well past midnight, more than sixteen hours after he had sat down for breakfast with Don Kendall, Kissinger left for home.[5]

WEDNESDAY, SEPTEMBER 16

It was a day that showed the importance that Kissinger placed on the press.

Nixon was scheduled to fly to Chicago to brief a large group of Midwestern newspaper editors, and Kissinger had decided to go along. But first he had breakfast in the White House with C. L. Sulzberger, the Paris-based foreign affairs columnist for the *New York Times.* Among the items Kissinger let drop was "Soviet horsing around in Cuba these days." He hinted about American concern that the Soviets might base a nuclear-armed submarine in the port of Cienfuegos there. Partly it was a calculated leak designed to pressure Moscow; partly it was the result of Kissinger's congenital compulsion to talk. In either case, Sulzberger was a judicious gentleman who operated at the stately pace befitting his station in life. He did not publish a column on Cienfuegos until nine days later, at which point it would break into front-page news.

Before they left on their trip, Nixon and Kissinger had a very brief meeting to go over the recommendations from the late-night WSAG meeting. The president was surprisingly hostile to the idea of coming to Jordan's aid against the PLO or, even worse, encouraging Israel to do so. He wanted to avoid a confrontation, according to an angry note that he scribbled on the margin of Kissinger's report. Unlike Kissinger, he did not want to encourage or even permit the Israelis to take action.

If a military move was unavoidable, it should be a unilateral American one.

On the way to Chicago, Nixon stopped for a rousing rally at Kansas State University, where longitude and attitude intersected to define Middle America. One particular passage in his speech had an unintended irony to it. "There are those who protest that if the verdict of democracy goes against them, democracy itself is at fault, who say that if they don't get their own way, the answer is to burn a bus or bomb a building." At precisely that moment, Helms was holding a meeting at CIA headquarters with Karamessines, his deputy Cord Meyer, and three other trusted officials for the first meeting of the secret Track II task force that was considering ways to promote a military coup in Chile.[6]

When his turn came to brief the editors assembled in Chicago, Kissinger touched on all three crises. Although the session was on background, the editors were free to write stories based on what they had learned about "administration thinking." The situation in Cienfuegos was not yet public, but Kissinger used the briefing to send a private signal to Moscow. "If the Russians start operating strategic forces out of Cuba, say, Polaris-type submarines, and they use that as a depot, that would be a matter we would study very carefully," he said.

He also used the briefing to challenge the complacent attitude the American press was taking toward the election results in Chile. Indulging his taste for double negatives as a way to make his rumblings seem more cerebral, Kissinger said: "I don't think we should delude ourselves that an Allende takeover in Chile would not present massive problems for us."

On the Middle East, Kissinger sought to blame the crisis on Soviet behavior. "The Egyptians and the Russians violated the cease-fire literally, practically from the first day onward," Kissinger told the editors. He linked all of these issues with the debate over the U.S. commitment to South Vietnam, concluding: "A great deal of the peace and stability of the world depends on the confidence other people have in America's credibility."

Finally, he dropped a hint that American attitudes toward China might be changing. "The deepest rivalry which may exist in the world today," Kissinger instructed the assembled editors, "is that between the Soviet Union and China."[7]

THURSDAY, SEPTEMBER 17

Overnight, Jordan's King Hussein had ordered his army to secure the capital and evict any rebellious Palestinian units. Large-scale fighting broke out in northern Jordan, near Syria. In response, Syria moved tanks to its border. When Kissinger convened a WSAG meeting at seven-thirty Thursday morning, a new question was suddenly on the agenda: what if Syrian tanks swept down into Jordan?

At the ninety-minute morning meeting, and another thirty-minute one in midafternoon, Kissinger asked for a major increase in America's forces in the region. Two aircraft carriers were already in the eastern Mediterranean. Now the *John F. Kennedy,* on exercise in the Caribbean, was ordered in.

When Kissinger called Nixon, who was still in Chicago, to inform him of all the activity, Nixon's adrenaline got flowing. "There's nothing better than a little confrontation now and then, a little excitement," he told a somewhat surprised Kissinger. He ordered that the military moves be announced immediately. Kissinger, who thought this unwise, ignored it.

Nixon, meanwhile, was making news of his own—and sending a message to Kissinger—through yet another press briefing, this one an off-the-record talk to the *Chicago Sun-Times.* If Syria's tanks rolled into Jordan, he said, only two nations could stop them—Israel or the U.S. Rejecting Kissinger's repeated recommendations, Nixon said he preferred that America do it alone. He did not mind getting the Soviets worried; indeed, it might be beneficial if the Soviets thought that Nixon was "capable of irrational or unpredictable action," he said, splaying out the old "madman theory" with a candor that managed to be both disarming and alarming. The *Sun-Times,* unable to sit on such a scoop despite the off-the-record rules, printed the story in its afternoon edition. Press Secretary Ron Ziegler objected, but the next day Nixon called the reporter, Peter Lisagor, to praise his handling of the story.[8]

Despite the outbreak of war that morning, Jordan was not the main item on Kissinger's agenda that Thursday. Most of his time was consumed with Vietnam. He had scheduled meetings with Herbert Marcovich and Raymond Aubrac, the two Frenchmen with connections to Hanoi who were part of his efforts in 1967 to act as a backstage negotiator for President Johnson. He met with them and Winston Lord throughout the afternoon, breaking only to give a briefing to

Walter Cronkite, have lunch with Art Buchwald, and chair the half-hour afternoon WSAG session.

Kissinger wanted to get the Frenchmen's reading on how Hanoi might react to a cease-fire proposal. But it so happened that they arrived on the same day that the Viet Cong, a few hours earlier in Paris, had announced a new eight-point peace proposal. Kissinger ridiculed the proposal as merely a formula for American surrender. It did, indeed, set forth yet another plan for overthrowing Thieu and installing a communist-dominated coalition government. But there was one new element in the plan that Kissinger did not pursue: if Washington agreed to a nine-month withdrawal schedule, the communists would agree to begin talks on freeing all American prisoners of war.

Kissinger often argued, especially later, that Hanoi showed no signs of accepting even a unilateral American withdrawal; unless Thieu was toppled, the POWs would remain. The "ten-point" plan announced in 1969 had made release of the POWs contingent on agreement on all political issues. But that morning's "eight-point" plan represented a clear change on this issue.

In his talks with Aubrac and Marcovich, Kissinger was more interested in exploring the possibility of a cease-fire in place. There was general agreement that Hanoi would not accept one. But that made Kissinger favor it nonetheless: since so many doves were clamoring for a cease-fire offer, making one would be a low-risk propaganda coup. In the late afternoon Kissinger stepped out for a reception at the National Gallery of Art, then returned to work on cease-fire options until ten P.M. with two Vietnam staffers, Winston Lord and Richard Smyser.[9]

FRIDAY, SEPTEMBER 18

The eight-thirty A.M. WSAG meeting was an update on the situation in Jordan, but Helms stayed behind to talk to Kissinger about another matter. The U-2 spy flights over Cuba had finally been able to get good photographs. The conclusions were clear: a fairly large facility, including a barracks and wharf, had sprung up at Cienfuegos. Among other things, it included a soccer field. A CIA analyst noted that Cubans played little soccer, so it was probably there to provide recreation for Soviet seamen.

The soccer insight was not totally true. Despite Kissinger's jocular claim in his memoirs that "as an old soccer fan I knew the Cubans played no soccer," Cubans did in fact play the game some and had even reached the World Cup finals in 1938. But in this case the insight had some merit, since the facility did indeed turn out to be a Soviet one. In any case, Kissinger appropriated the CIA analyst's insight and did a Paul Revere ride through the West Wing.

Haldeman recalls him charging in that morning and slamming a file on his desk. "Bob, look at this!" he exclaimed.

Haldeman, not an expert at deciphering reconnaissance photographs, expressed some puzzlement. "It's a Cuban seaport," Kissinger explained, "and these pictures show the Cubans are building soccer fields. I have to see the president now." Haldeman made a snide comment about Kissinger perhaps partying too much the night before. "Those soccer fields could mean war, Bob," Kissinger continued. "Cubans play baseball. Russians play soccer." Haldeman went into the Oval Office, kicked out Ehrlichman, and ushered Kissinger in.

What the Soviets were doing, with clever ambiguity, was testing the fuzzy margins that had been established after the 1962 Cuban missile crisis. The facility that Moscow was building at Cienfuegos was not exactly a full-fledged submarine base but rather a semi-permanent support facility designed for stopovers, refueling, and recreation. This would allow the Soviets to extend the range of their submarines and to deploy ones carrying nuclear missiles near Cuba.

Kissinger was not one to minimize the nature of the challenge. The memo he had hastily drafted and brought to the Oval Office that morning began: "Analysis of reconnaissance flight photography over Cuba has this morning confirmed the construction of a probable submarine deployment base." Nixon wrote some orders in the margin demanding a report on "what CIA can do to support any kind of action which will irritate Cuba" and "what actions we can take, covert or overt, to put missiles in Turkey or a sub base in the Black Sea."

Nixon did not want a new Cuban missile crisis, especially at that moment. It would force the cancellation of his eagerly anticipated trip to Europe and distract from the crisis in Jordan. Likewise, Secretary Rogers urged Kissinger by phone that day to avoid "high-level tension."

Kissinger disagreed. At an early-afternoon CIA briefing, he was informed that the "support facility" (as the analysis carefully called it) would increase by 33 percent the amount of time Soviet subs could be within range of the U.S. He decided to put Cuba on the WSAG agenda for the next morning and to schedule a full NSC meeting with the president for the next Wednesday. Once again, Kissinger found himself in a more hawkish position than not only Rogers but Nixon. The need to show military resolve, he felt, was critical.[10]

After Kissinger's briefing by the CIA's Cuba watchers, Director Helms and his covert operations chief came by to report on the Track II secret project to get rid of Allende in Chile. The report was pessimistic. Chile's military was still disorganized and unwilling to act, Karamessines said, even though word had been passed that the U.S. would support a coup. For a while, the CIA was even offering $50,000 to those who would kidnap General René Schneider, the armed forces chief who was opposing any military efforts to disrupt the election. But nothing was working. "We tried to make clear to Kissinger how small the possibility of success was," recalled Helms. Kissinger told them to carry on.[11]

Despite a rather hectic day, Kissinger was able to get out in the evening to attend a reception for Akio Morita, the founder of Sony, and then have a late dinner at the Jockey Club. Washington was buzzing about an interview with John Mitchell published in that morning's *Women's Wear Daily*. The attorney general had, among other things, called Kissinger "an egocentric maniac." Kissinger sought to make light of the comment. "At Harvard it took me ten years to achieve an environment of total hostility," he told friends. "Here I've done it in twenty months."

SATURDAY, SEPTEMBER 19

Though he usually arrived late on Saturdays, Kissinger was in his office before eight A.M. preparing for the WSAG meeting. The first item on the crisis group's agenda was Jordan. Reports were starting to come in that Syrian troops might be crossing the border. It was hard to tell. The U.S. had poor intelligence in the area and was dependent on the Israelis, who had their own interests. The tanks moving in from Syria carried the markings of the Palestine Liberation Army; apparently they had been hastily painted, however, and were actually Syrian.

Regarding Chile, Helms reported that it was likely that the third-place candidate would support Allende—belying Kissinger's belief that the vote split indicated that a vast majority was strongly opposed to Allende. No mention was made of the Track II assassination and coup schemes because the WSAG members were not supposed to know about them.

Cuba was a last-minute addition to the agenda, and the WSAG members (generally the number two person at each agency) were not yet prepared with their bureaucratic responses. "Opinions therefore gyrated randomly in a conversational style," Kissinger recalled. There was a discussion of whether the Soviet actions violated the 1962 understandings. That was irrelevant, argued Kissinger, who had little patience with the American penchant for taking a legalistic approach to situations. The 1962 missile crisis occurred not because the Soviets had done something illegal, he reminded them, but because they had done something that was contrary to U.S. national interests. The current case was similar.

The debate showed how hard it often is for American policymakers to deal with ambiguous, gray-area challenges. Instead, they prefer to wish them away. In this case that would have been easy, since the Soviet action was not all that threatening. But unless it was stopped resolutely, Kissinger felt, the incremental challenges would continue and become even harder to oppose.

That night Kissinger phoned Nixon at Camp David. On Cuba, the president urged him to play down the problem. He did not want some "clown senator" demanding a blockade. On Jordan, Kissinger expressed some unusual, and unwarranted, optimism: he said that messages from the Soviet Union indicated that the Palestinians had been defeated and the Syrians were ready to back down. Nixon was dubious. Whenever the Soviets volunteered reassurances, he told Kissinger, something sinister was afoot. He was right. As they spoke, it was early morning in the Middle East, and Syrian tanks were pouring across the Jordanian border.

Kissinger spent his Saturday evening back at Airlie House in Virginia answering questions about budgeting before a Defense Management Group. He returned to the office to clear up paperwork before going home at ten-thirty.

In Vietnam during the week ending Saturday at midnight, fifty-two Americans were killed. It was the lowest weekly number since December of 1966. Since 1961, 43,674 Americans had lost their lives in the war. That week, 3,200 American servicemen were withdrawn under the Vietnamization program, leaving 396,300 still in country.[12]

Also that week, a minor change happened on Kissinger's staff, one that he probably did not notice. The Pentagon sent over a Navy yeoman named Charles Radford, whose job was to help with stenography and paper flow. He also began work on another task, one that Kissinger would not discover for more than a year: copying papers and transmitting them secretly back to the Joint Chiefs of Staff.

SUNDAY, SEPTEMBER 20

Since it was Sunday, Kissinger took most of the day off. But because the rest of the world didn't, he was back at his office by seven P.M. The other WSAG members and assorted additional crisis managers had gathered around the rectangular table in the windowless basement Situation Room. Until almost two A.M., Kissinger would preside over a running WSAG meeting devoted to the Syrian invasion of Lebanon. His only interruptions were to meet with the president.

Kissinger felt deceived by the reassuring messages he had received from the Soviet Union the day before. The war had become, in his mind, a clear contest between the U.S. and the U.S.S.R. for influence in the Middle East. Thus it was all the more important to show resolve there—and in Cuba, and in Chile.

Nixon had remained adamant throughout the week that the U.S., rather than Israel, should act unilaterally in Jordan if outside help was needed. Kissinger remained convinced of the opposite; he had prepared papers summarizing the benefits of each course and sent them to Camp David for the president.

The WSAG meeting, under Kissinger's guidance, quickly decided to recommend Kissinger's course: encouraging Israel to take action. He considered that choice preferable because Israel could sustain actions better than the U.S. and was less likely to provoke the Soviets into becoming directly involved. Another obvious reason to let the Israelis have the honors appealed mightily to Rogers and Laird: it would mean that U.S. troops would not have to be involved.

King Hussein had been hoping for *American* military help, especially air support, which would have been far less demeaning than displaying dependence on his *Israeli* enemies. But by late Sunday night Washington time, the King's messages to the American embassy in Amman expressed his eagerness for help "from any quarter."

Now Kissinger faced two further hurdles: getting Nixon to agree and getting Israel to agree.

Nixon was easy. Shortly before eight, he returned from Camp David and called Kissinger to his office. Kissinger's arguments over the phone had persuaded him that it was better to let Israel do the job. The president then met with the rest of the WSAG principals and gave them a pep talk. But on Kissinger's advice, the president did not reveal he had agreed with the recommendation to defer to Israeli action. He wanted them to continue deliberating without being influenced by his own inclinations.

The final WSAG recommendation was completed by nine-thirty P.M. It concluded that the U.S. should encourage Israeli air strikes against Syrian tanks. In addition, the group recommended a lot of Kissinger-style symbolic signal-sending on the part of the U.S., such as increasing the alert status of a brigade in Germany, putting the 82nd Airborne Division on alert in a manner that was sure to leak, and sending a reconnaissance plane from an American carrier to Tel Aviv so that it would be picked up by Soviet radar.

Kissinger later portrayed the actions that night as showing that the U.S. would "escalate rapidly and brutally" when necessary. This is odd, considering that the major decision they made that night was to step aside and convince Israel to do the saber rattling. America's actions were, in fact, all mostly hollow gestures rather than the display of guts and gumption that they became in the retelling; it had no plans actually to use the brigade in Germany or the 82nd Airborne.

Kissinger took the State Department's representative on the WSAG committee, Assistant Secretary Joseph Sisco, along to present the plan. Nixon, however, had chosen that time to go bowling. With the help of a Secret Service agent, they tracked him to the alley hidden in a distant part of the Executive Office Building basement. "Nixon," Kissinger reports, "approved the recommendations while incongruously holding a bowling ball."

Now it was Israel's turn. Prime Minister Golda Meir had flown to New York and on that Sunday night was attending a huge United Jewish Appeal dinner at the Hilton. Shortly after ten, a waiter handed Israel's Ambassador Yitzak Rabin a note: "Call Kissinger at the White House urgently." Using a hotel phone in a small anteroom, Rabin did.

King Hussein had not explicitly asked for Israeli military assistance. According to Kissinger, it was Rabin who first broached the idea by suggesting that Israel could help out with air support. As Kissinger put it: "Rabin, who was nobody's fool, asked whether we would look favorably on an Israeli air strike if the intelligence indicated significant Syrian advances," Kissinger later wrote.

That is not the way Rabin remembered it. He recalled that in his first phone conversation that night, Kissinger told him that Jordan had *requested* Israeli air support. The conversation, according to the Israeli ambassador, went as follows:

Kissinger: "King Hussein has approached us, describing the situation of his forces, and asked us to transmit his request that your air force attack the Syrians in northern Jordan."

Rabin: "I am surprised to hear the U.S. passing on messages of this kind like some sort of mailman. I will not even submit the request to Mrs. Meir before I know what your government thinks."

An hour later, Rabin says, Kissinger called back with an answer. "The request is approved and supported by the U.S."

Rabin: "Do you advise Israel to do it?"

Kissinger: "Yes, subject to your own considerations."

In any event, both the Kissinger and Rabin versions conclude with Kissinger pledging that the U.S. would make up any Israeli losses in armaments and protect Israel from an intervention by the Soviets.

Shortly after midnight, Kissinger got together with the WSAG principals one more time to assign topics to be studied for the next day. The most important of these was making contingency plans against a Soviet intervention. At two A.M., he left for home and three hours of sleep.[13]

MONDAY, SEPTEMBER 21

Kissinger was awakened at five-fifteen A.M. by a message from Ambassador Rabin that the Israelis were now considering ground action against the Syrians in Lebanon as well as air strikes. Since they would be using American weapons and would be regarded by the rest of the world as American surrogates, they would carry through only if the U.S. gave permission. Kissinger promptly woke the president with a call.

Nixon, after first asking Kissinger to consult with Sisco (but not Rogers), called back an hour later with an order: "I have decided it. Don't ask anybody else. Tell him [Rabin] 'go.' " Only reluctantly did the president agree to let his top cabinet officers consider it with him at the NSC meeting scheduled for eight-thirty that morning.

As in other showdowns, Kissinger believed that a display of resolve might force an end to the confrontation without further fighting. He was thus quite eager for Israel to begin preparing for a ground attack, which would involve two days of mobilizing its troops for all to see. "Israeli mobilization, added to our deployments, could spook all our adversaries and yet provide time for a solution short of war," he said. Syria now had three hundred tanks in Jordan and had captured the town of Irbid about fifteen miles from the border.

Secretary Rogers, on the other hand, pointed to the inconvenient fact that Jordan had not actually requested any ground support, especially from Israel. It was, in fact, still formally in a state of war with Israel. Any escalation should be slow and careful so as to avoid a confrontation, he said.

Kissinger argued the opposite: the best way to avoid a real fight would be to escalate rapidly and even with apparent recklessness. "Nixon and I held that if we wished to avoid confrontation with the Soviets, we had to create rapidly a calculus of risks they would be unwilling to confront, rather than let them slide into the temptation to match our gradual moves," Kissinger recalled. He would later claim that the main lesson he learned from Nixon was that a leader "must be prepared to escalate rapidly and brutally to a point where the opponent can no longer afford to experiment." For Kissinger and Nixon, this was one of the lessons of America's failure in Vietnam.

After listening to the opinions of Rogers and others at the NSC meeting, Nixon announced the decision that he and Kissinger had already privately made: the U.S. would encourage Israel to prepare for an air and ground intervention and would commit to protect it from a retaliatory response by the Soviet Union, Egypt, or any other enemy.

But in making the decision, Nixon included an element that did not please Kissinger. The State Department, Nixon said, should officially ask whether Hussein wanted Israeli ground help—or for that matter, Israeli air help. On this the president overruled Kissinger, who believed that "we should not mortgage the king's already precarious position in the Arab world by asking him questions he could not afford to answer."

Meanwhile, the responses to Kissinger's request for recommendations about the new submarine base at Cienfuegos were coming in. The State Department produced an analysis saying there was no cause for panic; Moscow's move was mainly symbolic, and Rogers should take the matter up quietly with Gromyko when they met at the United Nations in a month. The Pentagon, on the other hand, was alarmed that a stopover facility in Cuba could give the Soviets greater capacity in the Gulf of Mexico. Its recommendations were as wild as State's were somnolent; among them was to call up American reserves.

Although he knew that Nixon still hoped to defer the Cuban crisis until after his European trip, Kissinger felt it would not wait. So he put it on the agenda for a National Security Council meeting with the president, scheduled for Wednesday morning.[14]

TUESDAY, SEPTEMBER 22

Israeli tanks rolled toward the Jordan River and massed on the Golan Heights, threatening the flank of the Syrian troops that were marching south into Jordan. Kissinger, ever keen on signals, sent another American plane from a carrier to Tel Aviv so that the Soviet spy ships would see it. Bomb bays of Israeli planes were loaded in broad daylight.

There was one problem. King Hussein had come back with his answer: he was ambivalent about Israeli air strikes, but he rejected outright any Israeli ground support. Contemporary accounts of the crisis written with Kissinger's cooperation, such as a 1974 book by Marvin and Bernard Kalb, report that all of Israel's actions were in response to a Jordanian request. Indeed, Kissinger led Israeli officials to believe they were acting at King Hussein's request. It was not so. But Hussein's reticence did not worry Kissinger. He knew that the Israelis were not quite ready to invade, and he hoped that all the military maneuverings would lead to a diplomatic solution rather quickly.

While at the White House for a crisis committee session on Jordan, Helms and Karamessines gave Kissinger the CIA's update on Chile. President Frei, the Christian Democratic incumbent who was supposed to be the beneficiary of the Rube Goldberg scheme to allow him to run for reelection, would have no part in it. In fact, the Christian Democrats were less afraid of Allende's victory than of schemes to tamper with the election process, so they made clear that they would endorse Allende in the congressional vote.

As for the Track II military coup hopes, the army commander in chief, General Schneider, remained an obstacle. An upstanding officer, he felt that the dictates of democracy demanded that the military refrain from meddling in politics. In a better world, he was the type of person whom the United States would seek to exalt. Instead, the CIA was hatching plans to supply money and machine guns to right-wing renegades who were plotting to kidnap and kill him. The issue of what to do next in Chile was scheduled for a 40 Committee meeting on Thursday.

In order to show that the U.S. was not anti-Arab, Kissinger attended a party at the Egyptian embassy that evening. There he encountered the Soviet envoy who was in charge during Ambassador Dobrynin's absence, Yuli Vorontsov. With reporters watching, Vorontsov grabbed Kissinger and repeated his country's assurances that it was trying to restrain Syria. "We believe there should be no outside intervention of any kind," he said. Vorontsov professed to be concerned for America's reputation. If the U.S. intervened, it would become the target of anger throughout the Arab world. "In that case," Kissinger parried, "you should relax because you win either way." [15]

WEDNESDAY, SEPTEMBER 23

According to reports that Kissinger received when he arrived at his office just before eight A.M., the Jordanian crisis seemed to be winding down. The Soviets were telling all who would listen that they were pressuring Syria to withdraw. But Kissinger felt that it was important to keep up the pressure. Four more destroyers were dispatched to the Mediterranean, and at the WSAG meeting that morning, planning continued on how to counter a potential Soviet attack on Israel.

Kissinger attended a morning meeting of the National Security Council and a half dozen impromptu sessions with Nixon. All the while, reports kept coming in that the Syrian tanks were indeed beginning to depart from Jordan. For Kissinger it was an exhilarating moment. A show of force, he felt, had finally paid off. He called and congratulated each of the members of the WSAG who had helped to coordinate the crisis in the Situation Room over the past week.

One of them in particular impressed him: Joe Sisco, the brash and quick-witted State Department assistant secretary for the Middle East. Kissinger liked the fact that the fast-speaking foreign service officer had managed the trick of standing up to Kissinger while at the same time catering to his instincts. Almost despite themselves, they began to enjoy each other's company and good-humored barbs. Until then, Sisco had been a bureaucratic adversary, the man in charge of Rogers's Middle East diplomacy. But from then on, he would be a backstage ally of Kissinger's.

Kissinger's relationship with Rogers, however, remained bad. When the NSC meeting turned to the Soviet facility in Cuba, the secretary of state fervently opposed stirring up another crisis. The situation should be kept completely quiet, he argued, until after the congressional elections in November. This battle he won. Nixon ordered everyone to say nothing about the matter for the time being. Kissinger recalled being "extremely uneasy" about the president's insistence that the issue did not need to be solved right away.

Late that afternoon, Kissinger took time to give a briefing to columnist Joseph Alsop, a fellow believer in the efficacy of military might. Alsop's readers were soon to learn, with no attribution, that Kissinger's idea of getting the Israelis to mobilize was the main reason that the Syrians had retreated from Jordan.[16]

THURSDAY, SEPTEMBER 24

The smiling face of his unlikely new friend, the antiwar activist Brian McDonnell, greeted Kissinger when he arrived at his office the next morning. Winston Lord, who organized their breakfast, says that it served as a welcome release for Kissinger, while so much was swirling around him, to be able to spend time with someone who was so free of guile as the idealistic young man who had fasted in front of the White House during the Cambodian invasion.

With the Jordan crisis receding and Cienfuegos on a presidentially ordered hold, the only crisis on the day's agenda was Chile. For more than two hours that afternoon, Kissinger chaired a 40 Committee session to discuss covert strategy. The official Track I approach and the supersecret Track II (which the 40 Committee did not know about) began to merge. But it was not because the Track II emphasis on a military coup was being abandoned, just the opposite: the Track I scheme for complicated electoral shenanigans was being abandoned in favor of encouraging a coup.

General Schneider, the army's commander, was not the only military officer opposing a coup. Others feared that it might result in a cutoff of American aid. The 40 Committee decided to instruct Ambassador Korry "to approach selected military leaders." According to Kissinger: "They would be given to understand that their involvement [in a coup] would not jeopardize American military assistance."

Kissinger also took care to make sure that the Jordan story was being treated properly by the press. Although his lunches usually lasted less than forty-five minutes, that day he had a two-hour session with Time-Life columnist Hugh Sidey and two other members of *Time*'s Washington bureau. They were scheduled to have a formal interview with Nixon the next day and wanted guidance. Ask about China, Kissinger advised.

It was an unusual topic to raise in the midst of the swirling crises that week, but it was on the president's mind. He would snap a few heads at the State Department and elsewhere by responding: "If there is anything I want to do before I die, it is to go to China."

Sidey's column that next week in *Life* was headlined "The Exhilaration of Crisis," and it reflected Kissinger's briefing on how well the Jordanian showdown had been handled. In *Time*, a "senior White House official" was quoted as saying that "the threat of intervention helped to stabilize the situation." But the magazine added its own note of skepticism: "It probably did, although there was considerable bluff in all of the saber rattling, and that game is risky. At best, it can rarely work more than once."

Early that evening, as Kissinger was giving a briefing to columnist Joseph Kraft, he was interrupted by a phone call from Soviet Ambassador Dobrynin, who had just arrived back in Washington. Exuding joviality, the Soviet asked Kissinger how he could have broken his promise not to have a crisis while Dobrynin was away in the Soviet Union. Kissinger was not amused. Dobrynin said he wanted an appointment with Nixon to deliver personally a message concerning a possible summit; Kissinger said that he would get back with an answer the next day.

Nixon had been craving a 1970 summit in Moscow, preferably in October, just before the midterm Congressional elections. Though Kissinger knew it would be a total abandonment of linkage to be eagerly angling for a summit invitation even as the Soviets provided no help in Vietnam, he had put in a request through Dobrynin in August. The Soviets, discovering they had been given a new bargaining chip, played coy.

When Kissinger phoned to report his conversation with Dobrynin, Nixon told him to come over to the Lincoln Sitting Room. It was nine P.M., and Nixon was in an expansive mood. They decided that Dobrynin should be told to deliver his message to Kissinger, not the president, partly as a punishment for taking six weeks to come back with a response to the summit suggestion.

In 1970, it was still a rare treat, and occasional trial, for Kissinger to be invited to the residential part of the White House in the evening. It was Nixon's way of conferring favor, just as being cut off from contact was a sure sign that he was seething. After disposing of Dobrynin's request, the president turned to the Jordanian crisis. He was eager to recount each step of the triumph in detail and to hear Kissinger analyze repeatedly the wisdom of each decision they had made. It was after eleven P.M. when Kissinger finally left for home.[17]

FRIDAY, SEPTEMBER 25

Nixon's hopes that the problem brewing in Cienfuegos could be kept under wraps for a while were dispelled when C. L. Sulzberger's column finally appeared in Friday morning's *New York Times*, nine days after he had been briefed by Kissinger, under the headline "Ugly Clouds in the South." Kissinger had sent contingency plans to the Pentagon, State Department, and White House press

offices in case the story began to leak. They involved a typically Kissingerian multilayered approach to who should say what. The Pentagon
briefer, who was either less willing or less able to handle such complex
levels of secrecy, simply told reporters what he knew. An urgent story
went out over the AP wire: "The Pentagon said today it has firm
indications the Soviet Union may be establishing a permanent submarine base in Cuba."

As the briefing was under way, Ambassador Dobrynin, oblivious
of the controversy that was about to erupt, was at the White House to
give Kissinger the Soviet response to Nixon's summit request. Dobrynin said that yes, the Soviets would be happy to have a summit—but
not until the following summer. Like a playful man dangling a bone
before a puppy, Dobrynin inquired as to whether Nixon was perhaps
hoping to hold it in Moscow. "I allowed for the umpteenth time,"
Kissinger later noted, "that this thought had indeed crossed the president's mind." Dobrynin was noncommittal. He was not yet ready to
give up that bone.

Neither man raised the issue of what the Soviets were doing in
Cienfuegos. Instead, Kissinger told Dobrynin that he would be calling
him later that day.

The Pentagon briefing had meanwhile caused an uproar. Upon
finishing with Dobrynin, Kissinger went to see the president and convinced him that the leak meant that they would have to take the
course that Kissinger had urged all along. "I told the president that we
had no choice now except to face the Soviets down," he recalled.
Engaging in their proclivity for sending signals through ship movements, they decided to deploy a destroyer off Cienfuegos.

In the meantime, it was necessary to clear up one loose end from
the Jordan crisis. Kissinger called Israeli Ambassador Rabin with a
formal notification that the commitments America had made to protect Israel from the Soviets were now outdated. "If a new situation
arises," he said, "there will have to be a fresh exchange." This made
little impression on Rabin, perhaps because he considered it obvious.
The part of the message he considered most important read: "The
U.S. is fortunate in having an ally like Israel in the Middle East. These
events will be taken into account in all future developments." Rabin
later called the message "probably the most far-reaching statement
ever made by a president of the U.S. on the mutuality of the alliance
between the two countries."

The American commitment to Israel had long been a *moral* one.
Now, under the Nixon Doctrine and Kissinger's realpolitik approach,
Israel was being cast as a military and strategic ally in the region. By
arming and aiding Israel, the United States could avoid putting its

own soldiers on the line when its interests in the region were threatened.

It was a dangerous game. America and Israel had different security interests, which would not always be compatible. Moreover, it meant that someday, if the Soviet threat in the region ever diminished (as by the 1990s it would), Israel would no longer be needed as a strategic asset. By casting the relationship in strategic rather than moral terms, it meant that in such a situation there would be less of a basis for American support.

Kissinger had scheduled a background briefing with the press that day to tout the administration's success in handling the Jordan-PLO war and to discuss the presidential trip to Europe. But he knew he would get a chance to send a warning on Cuba, and indeed the question quickly arose. "The Soviet Union can be under no doubt," he said, "that we would view the establishment of a strategic base in the Caribbean with the utmost seriousness." He avoided flatly declaring that the base was being built, thus giving the Soviets a way out.

Kissinger also made that point when he met Dobrynin for the second time that day. The U.S. considered the construction at Cienfuegos "unmistakably" a submarine base, Kissinger told him, but it wanted to give the Soviets "a graceful opportunity to withdraw without a public confrontation." Kissinger also threw in one of his favorite phrases for such situations: "utmost gravity." Dobrynin said he would report all this back to Moscow.

Their talk did not end until after seven P.M. But Kissinger had one final meeting that evening. Tom Karamessines, the CIA's covert operations chief, came by to report on the status of the anti-Allende campaign in Chile. Things were still not going well, and no one in the military seemed ready to make a move. Kissinger thanked him but did not call off the Track II coup effort. He was keeping remarkably close tabs on the situation. This was his fourth private meeting with Karamessines.

Shortly before nine-thirty P.M., Kissinger got home. But he did not go to bed. Instead, he got his suitcase and headed for Andrews Air Force Base. A Boeing 707 was there to take him to Paris for another secret session with the North Vietnamese, after which he would link up with the presidential party arriving in Italy on Sunday.[18]

SATURDAY, SEPTEMBER 26

Before he could meet with the North Vietnamese, Kissinger had to handle the South Vietnamese. Vice President Nguyen Cao Ky was in Paris and had upset officials in Washington by hinting that he might visit there before going home. One of the pitiful disjunctures of the Vietnam War was that dozens of Americans were still being killed each week, yet it was not politically possible to have a member of the government they were dying for set foot in the United States. President Thieu had been allowed only as far as the gooney-bird-infested island of Midway the year before, despite his desire to be invited at least to Hawaii. Kissinger's first task in Paris was to assuage Ky and make sure that he did not come to Washington.

SUNDAY, SEPTEMBER 27

Le Duc Tho was not in Paris, so Kissinger was stuck with Xuan Thuy, who offered little beyond what was in the new public Viet Cong proposal. Kissinger broached a few ideas—a multifaction "electoral commission," possible cease-fire arrangements—that did not seem to interest Xuan Thuy.

Kissinger complained to his aides that Xuan Thuy clearly had no power to negotiate. What infuriated him most of all was that the North Vietnamese clearly did not share his zeal for secrecy, back channels, and saying different things in private. "Hanoi's 'private' view was identical to its public one," he later wrote with disdain.[19]

Kissinger arrived in Rome in time to join the president at a reception in the Quirinale Palace. The next day would include an audience with the pope as well as dealing with the news of the sudden death of Egyptian president Gamal Abdel Nasser. But for the moment, things were quiet. The Italians, in the midst of yet another government crisis, had no real desire to discuss foreign policy issues, and for better or worse, all of Kissinger's current crises—Jordan, Chile, Cienfuegos, Vietnam—had subsided, at least for the moment.

AFTERMATHS

The issue of the Cienfuegos submarine base would be resolved rather quietly when Kissinger returned from Europe in early

October. Dobrynin supplied a statement that the Soviets were not building a base, and Kissinger responded with a presidential note describing how Washington defined a "base." Work on the new facility was halted, anti-aircraft guns were removed, and visits by Soviet flotillas were limited to recreational port calls rather than servicing operations. The soccer field, however, was never converted into a baseball diamond.

Even in diplomatic triumph, Kissinger sought to cut out the rest of the bureaucracy. His liaison to the Joint Chiefs of Staff, Admiral Rembrandt Robinson, helped draft the note clarifying the meaning of "a base," but he was not allowed to consult with the State Department. When Elmo Zumwalt, the chief of naval operations, asked why, Robinson replied that "Henry does not like to bring Secretary Rogers into foreign policy matters that are delicate." As a result, Zumwalt later said, the note was "careless and unfortunate" because experts were not given the chance to define precisely whether nonnuclear submarines capable of carrying nuclear weapons were included. When Zumwalt confronted Haig with the problem, it was too late to fix it. Rolling his eyes, Haig told Zumwalt, "This is the way Henry does business."

Kissinger's style even baffled the Byzantine Soviet foreign minister, Andrei Gromyko, who visited the White House that fall. He came prepared to swap statements with the president that reaffirmed all of the understandings made about Cuba going back to the 1962 missile crisis. But Nixon never raised the topic. "To the convoluted, ever-suspicious Soviet mind," the convoluted and ever-suspicious Kissinger later wrote, "the President's omission had profoundly sinister connotations." Kissinger had to explain that Nixon had avoided the issue because Secretary Rogers was present, and he had been cut out of the deliberations.

Still, the Cienfuegos situation turned out well. The Soviets would probably have continued to enhance their port facility if Kissinger had not forced the issue.[20]

Things did not work out so neatly in Chile. Active efforts to provoke a military coup—both in Track I and Track II—continued. Kissinger and Haig were briefed on October 15 about a plot proposed by General Roberto Viaux, leader of a right-wing military faction, who wanted to kidnap General Schneider. Because Kissinger felt it was likely to fail (rather than because of any moral qualms about its succeeding), he vetoed the idea. "I saw Karamessines today," he wrote in a memo to Nixon. "That looks hopeless. I turned it off. Nothing would be worse than an abortive coup."

Kissinger later testified that he considered this to be the end of Track II or of any coup planning. The CIA did not see it that way. The agency was dealing with other military factions at the time, and a cable went out from CIA headquarters the next day saying: "It is firm and continuing policy that Allende be overthrown by a coup." Although it abandoned the option of using General Viaux, the agency supplied three submachine guns to an even more slapdash group of plotters, who made two failed Keystone Kops kidnapping attempts on General Schneider. General Viaux's claque, acting without CIA support, then tried to carry through its own kidnapping plan, bungled it, and ended up killing General Schneider. Two days later, on October 24, Chile's Congress voted Allende into office.

Although the effort was amateurish and unsuccessful, Kissinger later said that the attempt to prevent Allende from taking office "seemed right to me then and seems right to me today." Because of "the perils to our interests and to the Western Hemisphere" of having a pro-Marxist government in Chile, Kissinger said, Washington sought "to promote a clear-cut popular choice between the democratic and totalitarian forces." The Soviets regularly practice subversion, he noted, using this as an argument that Washington must do so as well. "I cannot accept the proposition that the United States is debarred from acting in the gray area between diplomacy and military intervention."

Even after he became resigned to an Allende presidency, Kissinger advised Nixon to reject the advice of Ambassador Korry that the U.S. attempt to work with the new leader. "A U.S. policy of seeking accommodation with him," Kissinger wrote in a memo, "is unlikely to deter him from an anti-U.S. course." Nixon in November approved Kissinger's recommended decision memorandum, known as NSDM 93, which ordered a "cool and correct" posture to the new Chilean government. Economic screws were to be tightened, investment discouraged, and credit blocked. In addition, over the next two years, the CIA was authorized to spend $8 million keeping track of and encouraging anti-Allende activities.

Some of Washington's actions were rather petty. On a trip through Latin America that February, Admiral Elmo Zumwalt, the navy's chief, stopped in Chile to visit military leaders. To his surprise, he was invited by Allende to come for a "fifteen-minute courtesy call," a sign of conciliation. The meeting lasted more than an hour and ended with Allende suggesting that the nuclear aircraft carrier USS *Enterprise,* then sailing around South America, make a ceremonial stop at the Chilean port of Valparaíso. It was an amazing gesture.

Zumwalt's counterpart, Admiral Raul Montero, urged him to accept. It would strengthen the prestige of an independent, noncommunist military.

Defense Secretary Laird and the Joint Chiefs agreed, and Ambassador Korry began sending out invitations to pro-American elements in the Chilean cabinet and military to come to lunch on board the carrier. In a public speech, Allende took personal credit for the invitation and the improvement in relations it signaled, and said that he would personally visit the ship. Then Kissinger, in Zumwalt's words, flew into a "black rage." He and Nixon overturned the plan and ordered the ship not to visit Chile.

The hard-rudder turnabout not only scuttled an opportunity to improve relations, it immediately blew up publicly because of all the invitations that had been issued to Chilean dignitaries. "The invitations had to be withdrawn awkwardly," the New York Times reported on the front page, "when a diplomatic cable arrived from Washington saying that the Enterprise would not be stopping at Valparaíso because of operational problems."

It would be wrong, however, to blame Chile's problems solely on Washington's harassment. Allende was no democrat. He began building a Cuban-armed personal militia outside the military structure and financing left-wing guerrillas. He also helped destroy his country's economy with a large-scale nationalization of private industries. Washington played no direct role in planning the military coup in 1973 that toppled Allende and led to his death. By then it had no need to: Allende's policies combined with the economic pressures applied by the U.S. had created a climate that was ripe for an indigenous coup.[21]

The outcome of the Jordan crisis was a victory for Washington: Arab moderates were strengthened at the expense of their Soviet-backed radical neighbors, the PLO was thrown into disarray, the hostages were released, and American influence in the region was reinforced. But was it truly as much of a direct confrontation with the Soviet Union as Kissinger thought?

Probably not. Syria's decision to invade was not instigated by the Soviets, nor was its decision to withdraw due to American pressure on the Soviets. "Moscow's involvement in fomenting the crisis did not exist to the best of our knowledge," according to Talcott Steelye, a veteran American diplomat who was at the time the State Department's director of North Arabian affairs. "The White House contention that we stood the Soviets down is pure nonsense."

Nonetheless, it is safe to assume that Moscow was willing to take advantage of the situation in Jordan had there not been any American or Israeli resistance. A victory by Syria and the PLO would have enormously increased Soviet influence in the region. Even if they did not provoke the confrontation, the Soviets stood to gain from it.

For Kissinger, this possibility had to be seen in a global context. In his geostrategic view, virtually every crisis—Vietnam, Cambodia, the Korean downing of the EC-121, Chile, Cienfuegos, the Egyptian-Israeli cease-fire, Jordan and the PLO—was first and sometimes foremost an East-West struggle. His belief, which had some merit, that the Soviets were always probing for areas of easy advantage was one that the president shared. "I had feared that in our handling of the EC-121 incident in 1969, the communists may have thought they had encountered mush," Nixon later wrote. "While our effort to prevent Allende from coming to power had failed, at least in 1970 in Jordan and Cuba, their probing had encountered our unmistakable steel."[22]

The North Vietnamese were not impressed by the idea of a cease-fire in place. When Nixon made the offer public in a speech October 8, 1970, they promptly rejected it, as Kissinger suspected they would.

The most important ingredient in the proposal was that it represented America's first step away from its insistence on mutual withdrawal. If accepted, it would inevitably lead to a situation in which Hanoi's troops could stay where they were while the American troops withdrew. So in effect, offering a cease-fire in place was only a short step away from offering a unilateral withdrawal.

Kissinger was vague and a little misleading about this at a background briefing on the day of Nixon's speech. "Are we abandoning the previous requirement for mutual withdrawal?" a reporter asked.

"No," Kissinger answered. "Of course, a lot depends on how you define 'mutuality.' But we are not abandoning this general principle."

That, it turned out, would take a few more months.

Kissinger was laying the groundwork for a resolution of the war that would provide a "decent interval" between American withdrawal and Saigon's collapse. "After we have put the South Vietnamese into the best possible shape that we can," he told a small group of reporters in an off-the-record session, "and after we can tell ourselves in good conscience that we have done it in a way that is not a cop-out, if then, after five years, it turns out that they can't make it anyway, I think we are facing different consequences than that of simply packing up and pulling out."[23]

THE YEAR OF CRISES

The end of 1970 represented a high point in Kissinger's relationship with the president. He was not yet a celebrity, he did not threaten or challenge the president's authority, but he was clearly in charge of running foreign policy.

No longer banished to a cramped office in the White House basement, Kissinger had moved up to a corner suite on the ground floor of the West Wing, near the president and Haldeman. As Kissinger padded about the new quarters with his serious mien one day, Haldeman and his assistant Lawrence Higby pressed their noses on the bulletproof glass of the floor-to-ceiling French windows and started making faces. "I've got to get some curtains," Kissinger grumbled. His old friend from Harvard, Guido Goldman, came to inspect his new quarters and made one pronouncement: "You're important enough to deserve your own private bathroom." Bryce Harlow, who had a small lavatory adjoining his office, soon lost it; the carpenters were called in, and the doorways changed.

Kissinger was also given Secret Service protection that fall, partly in response to kidnapping threats. "If such an attempt should succeed," he wrote Nixon in a serious private note in December, "I would like to ask you to meet no demands of the kidnappers, however trivial."

Working in its own mysterious ways, the Secret Service assigned him the code name Woodcutter, not the most fitting moniker for the sedentary intellectual. Kissinger persisted in getting it confused and referring to himself as Woodchopper, or actually "Vudchopper." Safire began dubbing him Woodpecker. Ehrlichman settled on calling him Wiener schnitzel. When a motorcade was about to leave, Kissinger would turn to Ehrlichman, look plaintively at the Secret Service radio, and say, "Would you work that movie gobbledygook to let them know where I am?"

Once again, Kissinger spent the end of the year putting together the annual State of the World report. These had originally been intended as a forthright explanation of policy principles and as such were a welcome antidote to the secrecy used in carrying out these policies. But this year's effort showed signs of falling victim to the penchant for deception that would eventually undercut support for Nixon's foreign policy and, more significantly, poison his presidency. On Chile, for example, the report proclaimed the principle of not trying to influence the internal affairs of "other sovereign nations" and pledged that "we are prepared to have the kind of relationship with the Chilean government that it is prepared to have with us." Unbeknownst to Kissinger, the president cared little about the report. "Henry's State of the World, it has no grand strategy," he told Ehrlichman privately in January. "It's a laundry list, ho-hum but necessary."

Under the rules of Harvard's faculty, professors may generally take no more than two years' leave from their academic duties. The time had come for Kissinger to give up his tenured professorship or to return. The decision was not the toughest Kissinger had ever faced: his love of power was almost matched by his disdain for most of his academic colleagues. Nevertheless, cutting such an important tie was difficult; ever since he had returned from the war twenty-five years earlier, he had been associated with the university.

In late December, he went back for a dinner in honor of Professor Carl Friedrich and to discuss the tenure matter with those in the Government Department. Privately, he was told he did not need to come back right away or do anything; his chair would be kept open for him. That settled, he proceeded to make a grand display of resigning. As the president, with apparent amusement, said to Ehrlichman in one of their private sessions, "Henry wants to make his Harvard resignation an event—a buildup." When Kissinger made the decision and wrote Nixon to inform him, the president was gracious, though perhaps slightly ambiguous, in the letter he released in response. "Frankly," he wrote, "I cannot imagine what the government would be like without you."[24]

FIFTEEN

SALT

Arms Control
in the Back Channel

> *Our generation has succeeded in stealing the fire of the gods,*
> *and it is doomed to live with the horror of its achievement.*
> —KISSINGER, NUCLEAR WEAPONS AND FOREIGN POLICY, *1957*

A CASE OF MIRVS

To a layman, MIRVs (rhymes with "nerves") can seem like an eye-glazing acronym for an arcane concept: Multiple Independently-Targetable Reentry Vehicles. In fact, the concept is simple and the issue is critical, one of the most fateful in the history of arms control failures. A MIRVed missile is a hydra-headed beast that carries two or more nuclear warheads, each programmed to hit a different target. They are a cheap way to increase the firepower of a nuclear arsenal without building more rockets, which is why the U.S. began testing them in 1968.

During Nixon's first term, the U.S. (and the Soviets) missed the chance to ban MIRVs before they were ever deployed. The result was that the number of warheads in the world increased and America's arsenal became more vulnerable to Soviet attack. In addition, the "stability" of the nuclear balance was undermined because MIRVs give an advantage to whichever side attacks first. "Refusal to ban MIRVs was the key decision in the entire history of SALT," according to William Hyland, a longtime Kissinger aide. "It was a truly fateful decision that changed strategic relations, and changed them to the detriment of U.S. security."[1]

Throughout 1969, there had been an effort to convince the Nixon administration of the dangers of MIRVs. Forty senators sponsored an anti-MIRV resolution, and the House Foreign Affairs Committee issued a report calling for a negotiated freeze on the weapons.

Among those who sought to persuade Kissinger was the clique of nuclear strategists he had met with each week back when he lived in Cambridge. Kissinger invited them to come down to Washington for regular Saturday-morning breakfasts to discuss arms control issues. The leader of the group was his old friend from Harvard Paul Doty. Also involved were Carl Kaysen, formerly of McGeorge Bundy's NSC staff; Marshall Shulman of Harvard, Marvin Goldberger of Princeton, and Sidney Drell of Stanford.

As old academic colleagues, they were properly irreverent about Kissinger (Goldberger persisted in calling him Siegfried), but also flattered at being called to such high counsel. Papers were presented and intricacies of nuclear strategy debated as Kissinger impressed his peers with his willingness to listen. But after a while, as it became clear that he was rejecting their pleas to ban MIRVs, many in the group began to feel they were being used. "It was a case of Henry cultivating his academic friends, wanting to be loved," recalled Kaysen. "One evening my train from Princeton had an accident and I found myself stranded in Philadelphia at two A.M. I asked myself, 'What the hell am I doing this for?' I got a Hertz car and drove back home. Nothing like a Philadelphia railroad platform at two in the morning to clarify your mind."

Also opposing the MIRV program were the elders of the arms control establishment, led by John McCloy. The former high commissioner for Germany and Wall Street banker was chairman of the President's General Advisory Committee on Arms Control, a bipartisan commission established in 1961. Among its Republican members were William Scranton, Nixon's first choice as secretary of state, and William Casey, later Reagan's campaign manager and CIA director. Even the Democrats—Dean Rusk, Harold Brown, Cyrus Vance— were hardly softheaded disarmament buffs. After studying the issue for a year, they formally recommended that MIRV testing be halted.[2]

The MIRV opponents found an inside supporter in Nixon's chief SALT negotiator, Gerard Smith, a gentlemanly Georgetown lawyer and Republican fund-raiser. Smith considered MIRVs "the most significant weapons development since the ballistic missile," and in May 1969 he wrote a memo to the president urging that testing be halted before it was too late.

Opposing him were the Joint Chiefs of Staff, who saw MIRVs as a cost-effective way to increase America's targeting capability and who generally recoiled from sacrificing any technological advantage, and Defense Secretary Laird, who somewhat surprisingly never seemed to grasp what MIRV technology was all about.[3]

Kissinger well understood the destabilizing nature of MIRV technology and was uncomfortable with it. But he had decided that banning MIRVs would be politically difficult now that the program had been tested. He was in favor of negotiating a limit on another program —the antiballistic missile (ABM), which was a ground-based defensive system designed to shoot down incoming enemy missiles. To fight against both, in the face of Pentagon resistance, would be "more than the traffic would bear," he said at the time.

Nor were there any strong opponents of MIRV on his staff. Even Morton Halperin was ambivalent, fearing that the time had passed when a MIRV ban was feasible. Halperin had a personal interest in backing a workable arms control stance: as a Pentagon official in the Johnson administration, Halperin had become a bureaucratic star by almost single-handedly maneuvering a complicated arms control negotiating stance through the bureaucracy. That package had not included a MIRV ban.[4]

Nixon never became engaged in the issue. His eyes would glaze whenever he was subjected to a discussion of arms control. On the advice of Kissinger and the Pentagon, he decided in May 1969 to proceed with the MIRV program.

Later that month Halperin was talking on the phone to his friend Leslie Gelb, then a scholar at the Brookings Institution, as the FBI surreptitiously recorded the conversation. Like Kissinger (or most anyone else), Halperin could take on some of the coloration of whomever he was talking to, and he conveyed the sense that he was upset by the MIRV decision. "What's cooking with the arms talks?" asked Gelb.

"We're waiting for the propitious international climate," Halperin said, mimicking Kissinger.

"Is it ever propitious?" asked Gelb.

Halperin: "No. . . . I had a meeting with Hal [Sonnenfeldt] and Larry [Lynn] and those guys are convinced, and have convinced Henry, there is absolutely no strategic rationale for an arms control view."

Gelb: "That's fantastic."

Halperin: "And that we prefer a world in which both sides have MIRVs. . . . "

Gelb: "This is really nutty."[5]

THE FIRST SALT PROPOSAL, APRIL 1970

This is how matters stood by the spring of 1970, when it came time for the administration to offer a comprehensive proposal at the Strategic Arms Limitation Talks (SALT) in Vienna. The April 1970 session would be the last time that a MIRV ban was possible, and the debate was engaged again.

Kissinger, who had wrested from Gerard Smith control of the arms control process, had established a "building block" approach to constructing an American negotiating proposal. He ordered each agency to come up with various outcomes it could accept on each major issue, and then he proceeded to construct privately whatever combination he thought best. But by early 1970, the proliferation of options had gotten out of hand. So Kissinger asked the Arms Control and Disarmament Agency to synthesize the possibilities into four options. The task was undertaken by Raymond Garthoff, a deputy to Smith.

The April 8 meeting of the NSC was a fateful moment for MIRVs. Under Kissinger's tutelage, Nixon pretended to consider the four options. "His glazed expression," Kissinger later wrote, "showed that he considered most of the arguments esoteric rubbish." The choices were:

Option A: Each country could build twelve ABM missile-defense sites, there would be no limits on MIRVs, and a high ceiling on offensive missiles would require no U.S. cuts. (The Pentagon liked this one.)

Option B: The same, except each side could have only one ABM site, which would be limited to protecting its capital.

Option C: The same as B, except there would be restrictions on MIRVs.

Option D: Each side would be limited to one ABM site, there would be deep missile cuts, but no MIRV restrictions.[6]

Kissinger favored option B. But as he later explained, "all hell would have broken loose" if this option had been chosen because "it would have been claimed we had never even explored a ban on ABM and MIRV." So Kissinger had Nixon approve both options C and D. "If the Soviets rejected them, as I firmly expected, we could then put forward option B from a much stronger domestic and bureaucratic position," Kissinger later said.

Option C was intended as an offer to ban MIRVs, but Kissinger attached two conditions that assured it would be rejected by the Soviets. The first was a requirement that there be on-site inspections. In his memoirs, Kissinger says that this provision was part of the proposal when it was submitted to the NSC. But Garthoff's papers show that this is incorrect. The Pentagon favored on-site inspection and said so in a dissenting note, but all other agencies were opposed. Everyone knew that the Soviets would reject any plan that called for such intrusion.

When Ambassador Smith presented the American package at the SALT session in Vienna that month, Garthoff watched as his Soviet counterpart copiously took notes. But once Smith read the on-site inspection provision, the Soviet put down his pen. Later he told Garthoff: "We had been hoping you would make a serious MIRV proposal."[7]

The second killer provision was a loophole permitting the *production* of MIRVs. Unlike what Kissinger said in his memoirs, the American plan did not simply call for "a ban on MIRVs." There are three phases of a program that can be banned: the testing of a weapon, the production of it, and the deployment of it. The U.S. proposal was to ban the testing of MIRVs and the deployment of them. But it would permit continued production. The rationale was that the testing and deployment of weapons can be verified by satellites, but enforcing a ban on production is far more difficult.

What made the production loophole unacceptable to the Soviets was that it would give the U.S. a tidy advantage: it could continue to produce MIRVs for its stockpiles in case a crisis arose or the treaty was broken. Since the Soviets had not yet tested a MIRV, it could not benefit from the provision allowing production. So Moscow came up with a MIRV proposal that was similarly one-sided: testing would be allowed, but production and deployment would not be.

It was all a bit confusing. But Gerard Smith and his SALT delegation came up with the obvious way to cut through it all: offering a ban on everything, including the testing, production, deployment, and anything else one could do with a MIRVed missile. Kissinger rejected the idea.

As Kissinger predicted, the American SALT negotiators began to accept as a fallback option B: high ceilings on offensive weapons and a limit of at most one ABM site around each nation's capital. One ill-considered aspect of the plan was that it would limit the number of *missiles* rather than *warheads*. This had just the opposite effect of a MIRV ban: with missiles limited to a fixed number, each side would have the incentive to cap them with MIRVs so they could end up with more warheads.[8]

Like a chess player seizing an opponent's unprotected queen, the Soviets accepted ("with amazing and totally unprecedented speed," Kissinger recalled) the offer to limit ABM systems to one around each capital. It was, as Kissinger quickly realized, a bad blunder by the U.S. A year earlier, after heated debate, Congress had approved by a 51-to-50 vote (Vice President Agnew breaking the tie) a modest ABM program that would protect two Western missile sites from a Soviet preemptive strike. There was no way that the public was going to support a much costlier ABM program that protected only the politicians and bureaucrats of Washington, D.C.

Yet that was the ABM option that ended up in the American SALT proposal in April. "In retrospect," Kissinger later said, "I find it hard to explain how this option could ever be considered, much less adopted." In his memoirs he made a halfhearted effort to blame it on others in the bureaucracy. But Garthoff points out that the issue was not even debated at the April 8 NSC meeting, and Kissinger made the decision on his own. It was, Kissinger later conceded, "a first-class blunder." He would spend the next year trying to extricate the U.S. from this position.[9]

Kissinger made another mistake on ABM that he would also spend the next year trying to undo. In March 1970, during one of their regular back-channel sessions, Soviet Ambassador Dobrynin had asked whether the U.S. preferred a "limited" agreement or a "comprehensive" one. By that he meant an agreement that was limited to restrictions on ABM defense systems, or one that included a comprehensive package restricting offensive weapons as well. But Kissinger did not realize the distinction Dobrynin was making. And he did not ask. He simply said that either course was suitable.

The principal Soviet concern at the time was to rein in ABM systems. The American negotiators hoped to use an ABM agreement as an enticement to get a cap on offensive weapons. Yet when Dobrynin came back in June and privately proposed an ABM-only agreement, Kissinger said that he and Nixon would consider it.

Kissinger sent the idea to Vienna for Gerard Smith's opinion, ordering him not to tell anyone else in the delegation about it. Smith, appalled, sat down and wrote a reply in longhand, to be coded and sent back immediately. "Any constraint on U.S. ABMs," he pointed out, "should be accompanied by constraints on U.S.S.R. offensive weapons systems." The ABM was "our strongest bargaining counter."[10]

Kissinger realized that Smith was right. But the Soviets had already tried to pocket what must have seemed like two unexpected concessions: an agreement to limit each side to one ABM system around its capital, and an understanding that this did not have to be linked to an offensive weapons agreement. It would take Kissinger a year to undo this mess.

Even if the U.S. had pursued a MIRV ban sincerely in 1970, the Soviets may not have gone along. The blame for the subsequent fifteen years of instability falls on both capitals. "While there may have been an opportunity missed," said Ambassador Smith, "it was not a clear one." Years later, Dobrynin would attempt to be evenhanded in assessing blame: "Washington continued to bet on U.S. technology, and the Soviet Union failed to make its MIRV proposals sufficiently consistent."

Kissinger came to see the MIRV decision as a mistake, one for which he blamed himself. "I would say in retrospect that I wish I had thought through the implications of a MIRVed world more thoughtfully in 1969 and 1970 than I did," he conceded at a background briefing in 1974.[11]

The lapse would eventually mar one of his and Nixon's most monumental achievements: the SALT I agreements of May 1972. The accords would become the backbone of détente and the most important strategic arms agreement of the cold war. But because they lacked a limit on MIRVs—in fact, they served to encourage the deployment of these monsters—the world would be condemned to another destabilizing round of the arms race.

THE BACK-CHANNEL "BREAKTHROUGH," MAY 1971

The U.S. was in a muddle over arms control by early 1971. It had no new offensive programs under way, while the Soviets were churning out land- and submarine-based missiles. But Kissinger had hurt the chance for a freeze on offensive programs by indicating to Dobrynin that a "limited" deal on ABMs might be acceptable.

In addition, Washington's confusion over what type of ABM system it wanted—one protecting missile sites (as Congress had approved), one protecting the national capitals (as the administration had mistakenly proposed to the willing Soviets), or none at all—somehow got even worse. Nixon and Kissinger in March suddenly ordered, to the horror of Gerard Smith and his negotiating team, that the U.S. propose that it be allowed four ABM sites protecting missile sites.

The Soviets rejected this, with Dobrynin pointedly reminding Kissinger that they had already accepted the American offer to have one ABM each protecting the national capitals. "I acknowledged this slightly embarrassing truth," Kissinger recalled.

In order to unravel this mess, Kissinger proposed a deal to Dobrynin: the two of them would privately work out, in their back channel, an approach to SALT as well as to the problem of Berlin. The issue of Berlin, which the Soviets had been anxious to resolve since 1958, involved ways to guarantee Western access to that city while defining the relationship between West Germany and West Berlin in a manner that was acceptable to the East Germans.

Dobrynin reacted favorably.

The negotiations that ensued illustrated two key elements in Kissinger's style of operating.

First, they showed him constructing a complex set of linkages within linkages. In order to get the ABM treaty that they wanted, the Soviets would have to agree to negotiate the limits on offensive missiles that the U.S. wanted. This process was, in turn, linked to a parallel set of negotiations on the status of Berlin, which the Soviets wanted resolved. When connected to other potential agreements— such as a grain deal, increased trade, scientific exchanges—it all formed a web that, in theory, would serve to restrain Moscow's adventurism, induce it to be more helpful on Vietnam, and lead to a lasting détente. What Kissinger created in 1971 was a more subtle, and successful, version of the crude linkage between arms control and Vietnam that Nixon had sought in 1969.

In addition, Kissinger's arms control and Berlin negotiations illustrated the successes and excesses of the back channel. In order for all of these carefully calibrated linkages to be made (and for the White House to be assured of credit for the outcome), Kissinger ruthlessly cut out the State Department and its arms control negotiators.

To set up the Berlin back channel, Kissinger sent a courier to Bonn with letters for Ambassador Ken Rush, who was America's delegate at the formal four-power talks on Berlin, and for Egon Bahr, who was Chancellor Willy Brandt's national security assistant. Both were invited to come to the U.S. for secret meetings with Kissinger.

Kissinger knew that the State Department would erupt if it discovered that he was negotiating privately with Bahr, so he arranged for Bahr to be invited to Cape Canaveral for the launch of the *Apollo 14* moon shot. On a military Jet Star aircraft down and back, the two advisers got to talk privately. Kissinger also invited, as cover, Kirk Douglas to fly with them; the actor spent his time sleeping in the back of the plane.[12]

The plan Kissinger worked out was that Bahr and Rush would come up with ideas to solve the Berlin impasse, Kissinger would negotiate them with Dobrynin, and then Rush and Bahr would put whatever was worked out back into the formal machinery. Both Bahr and Rush agreed that they would keep all of this secret from the U.S. State Department and the German foreign ministry.

Kissinger explained this game to Dobrynin, but Secretary Rogers was never told. In order to make sure that the State Department never knew what was happening, Kissinger decided not to use the diplomatic communications channel to the Bonn embassy when sending messages to Ambassador Rush. In fact, he would not even use the CIA's private channel because the agency's station chief in Bonn was too friendly with the foreign service officers there and might leak. So Admiral Rembrandt Robinson of Kissinger's staff established a super-secret cable link to a naval officer in Frankfurt who would act as a courier.

What Kissinger did not realize was that Robinson was working with Yeoman Charles Radford to gather Kissinger's secrets for the Joint Chiefs of Staff. In addition, the National Security Agency's intercepts of the communications link were being sent to Defense Secretary Laird. Fortunately, none of them had much interest in disrupting the Berlin negotiations.[13]

By early May 1971, Kissinger and Dobrynin had come close to reaching a back-channel agreement that would relink the ABM talks with those involving offensive weapons. Then the Soviets tried to pull what, to Kissinger at least, appeared to be the ultimate duplicity: they raised in the proper channels an issue that was being discussed secretly in the back channel.

This perfidy occurred at Gerard Smith's fifty-seventh birthday party in Vienna. After dinner, his Soviet counterpart, Vladimir Semenov, presented what Smith called "a birthday present of considerable interest." He offered that the Soviets would temporarily halt their offensive missile program while the ABM was being discussed. Smith, after getting his translator to be sure it was right, gleefully cabled the offer to Washington.

In its details, the offer was not quite as good as what Kissinger was working on with Dobrynin. But Smith had no way of knowing that. One of the many drawbacks to the system Kissinger had established was that Semenov had an advantage over Smith: he knew what his man in Washington was doing, unlike his counterpart in the Byzantine American system.

Kissinger confronted Dobrynin in a rage. The Soviets might think, he said, they could play off America's two channels against each other. But he should not doubt that "sooner or later the president's tenacity and my control of the bureaucratic machinery" meant that the White House channel would eventually be dominant. When that happened, "the president's anger at what he could only construe as a deliberate maneuver to deprive him of credit would be massive."

Within days, Dobrynin came back with wording that was acceptable to Kissinger. Nixon and Brezhnev jointly announced the agreement on May 20. Although Kissinger trumpeted it as "a breakthrough," it did little more than restore matters to where they stood a year earlier. The two countries agreed, the statement said, to try to agree on an ABM treaty "together with" measures that would limit offensive weapons.

Nixon left it to Haldeman to lie to Rogers and say that the agreement had suddenly occurred because of a letter Brezhnev had sent to Nixon (a tricky cover story since there was no such letter to show Rogers, who as secretary of state might reasonably ask to see it). Just before the announcement was made, Kissinger broke the news to Gerard Smith, showing him the proposed wording and summaries of some of his conversations with Dobrynin.

Smith was professional, even gracious, but not complimentary. He said that the "agreement to agree" formulation sounded silly, and the wording seemed as if it had been poorly translated from Russian. Miffed at discovering that it had been handled behind his back, he complained that the deal could have been done better in the normal channels. Back in December, his Soviet counterpart had suggested that they might be willing to engage in parallel offensive-defensive talks, and Smith duly reported it to Washington. "Was it necessary to pursue such a duplicitous diplomacy?" he later wrote.

But Smith's main objection was that the negotiating record indicated that Kissinger had made another blunder: he had told Dobrynin that the U.S. would not insist that submarine-launched missiles be included in the deal. "There is no evidence to indicate that this major change in SALT policy was ever considered in advance by anyone except Kissinger—and perhaps not even by him," Smith said. "It may have been a random answer of a fatigued and overextended man who did not realize the immense significance of his words."

Kissinger was indeed overextended during May 1971. His meeting with Dobrynin occurred in the midst of South Vietnam's messy attack on communist supply routes in Laos, an invasion that ended ignobly with Saigon's panicked forces clinging to the skids of departing American helicopters as television cameras rolled. In addition, fighting had broken out between Pakistan and India, and Kissinger had to resist the pro-Indian sentiments of the State Department because he was secretly using Pakistan as a conduit to China. That China initiative was paying off, and at the precise moment of the Smith-Semenov exchange, Kissinger was "vacationing" in Palm Springs and quietly sorting out plans for a secret trip to China.*

An advantage to relying on a bureaucracy such as that of the State Department is that one group of people can be working full-time on SALT while other groups are dealing with Vietnam, Berlin, China, and Pakistan. That makes linkages more difficult, and dramatic diplomatic surprises impossible, but it alleviates distractions. Realizing this, Kissinger would often launch the bureaucracy on a study of a certain issue without revealing that it was a matter of active negotiation. In the case of the submarine-missile question, however, there was no such process.

Nevertheless, despite what Smith and other critics charged, Kissinger had actually considered the submarine issue and, for better or worse, decided to defer it. One reason, according to journalist John Newhouse, who wrote an authoritative book on SALT I, was that "he feared that making an issue of SLBMs [submarine-launched ballistic missiles] might produce another stalemate" because the Soviets were eager to catch up in that realm.

Another reason for Kissinger's vagueness on submarines was never publicized. At the time, the U.S. was considering speeding up its own languishing submarine program, and Kissinger was waiting for Melvin Laird to make up his mind. "The decision not to nail down, for the time being, the SLBM issue reflected not a weak negotiation on Kissinger's part," according to William Hyland, "but a strategic decision that had not yet been made: would the U.S. proceed with a buildup, basing the missiles on an adaptation of an older submarine? This decision was pending until late in 1971, when Secretary Laird informed the president that it was unlikely that the U.S. could get a new SLBM before 1977."

Soon after the May 20 arms control announcement, the Soviets got their Berlin agreement. Once again, however, there was the difficulty of springing a back-channel deal on an unsuspecting bureaucracy. The State Department began to tinker with the proposed treaty that Ambassador Rush produced, unaware that it had already been

* See Chapters 16 and 18.

secretly settled between Kissinger and Dobrynin. Haldeman and Mitchell had to be called on to intervene with Rogers.

As Kissinger would later admit, the decision to conduct the SALT and Berlin talks in the back channel exacted a large price. Over the long run, he was doing damage to a democratic system of policy-making, where messiness can be a virtue as well as a vice. "It was certainly disruptive of departmental morale," he later wrote. "To individuals like Smith, it was unfair and demeaning. It was also tough on the nerves of the NSC staff. . . . And a lot of energy was consumed in duplicative channels." But Nixon's suspicious nature and the bureaucracy's disdain for him made it inevitable, Kissinger contended.

Perhaps the most telling criticism of Kissinger's back-channel method comes in the praise accorded it by Georgi Arbatov, the Kremlin's top American expert at the time: "The Channel made it easier for Kissinger to manipulate events by excluding the pressures of Congress and public opinion." But such a concentration of power, though it makes maneuvering easier, is precisely what the system of shared authority in the U.S. Constitution is designed to prevent. "At least in the Soviet Union, the whole politburo was consulted," Gerard Smith said of the May 20 agreement. "The bulk of the American national security leadership was never consulted."

But for all of its drawbacks, the back-channel method was producing some notable successes. The Berlin and SALT agreements were not perfect, but they were accomplishments that the State Department had not been able to achieve. "It was demoralizing to the bureaucracy," Kissinger argued. "But it worked. . . . The results should be judged on their merits."

For Kissinger personally, the back channel allowed him to become not only the nation's top strategist, but also its chief diplomat. "For the first two years, White House control had been confined to the formulation of policy," he said. "Now it extended to its execution."[14]

THE PENTAGON PAPERS, JUNE 1971

Charles Colson raised his glass of Scotch and soda. "To Henry Kissinger," he said. The toast by the president's hard-bitten political operative was in honor of Kissinger's May 1971 SALT "breakthrough." Nixon held up his own Scotch, Haldeman and Ehrlichman their ginger ales; Kissinger smiled appreciatively. The five men were enjoying yet another evening ride down the Potomac on the yacht

Sequoia, and once again they stood at rigid attention as they passed the flag at Mount Vernon, the *Sequoia's* bell ringing in salute. "It was a moment to savor," Colson recalled.

When they went below deck for their dinner of strip steaks and corn on the cob, Nixon tucked his tie into his shirt and began a long discourse on deténte with the Soviets and the prospects for peace in Vietnam. It was Nixon at his best: savoring a fine Burgundy, holding forth with a thoughtful assessment of foreign affairs. Suddenly he turned to Colson. "Do you think, Chuck, you'll get me an SST to fly to China?"

Kissinger blanched. The China initiative was among the most closely guarded of all his secrets. "Relax, relax," Nixon said. "If those liberals on your staff, Henry, don't stop giving everything to the *New York Times,* I won't be going anywhere." There was a flicker of Nixon's famous nervous smile, then he began working himself up. The mellow strategist was metamorphosing into the dark politician. "The leaks, the leaks," he fulminated. "That's what we've got to stop at any cost. Do you hear me, Henry?"

The president circled his finger over the rim of his wineglass as he continued to rant about his enemies. "One day we will get them— we'll get them on the ground where we want them. And we'll stick our heels in, step on them hard, and twist. Right, Chuck, right?" His nervous eyes then darted from Colson to Kissinger. "Henry knows what I mean. Just like you do it in the negotiations, Henry. Get them on the floor and step on them, crush them, show them no mercy."

Kissinger nodded and forced a smile.[15]

Such was the attitude toward leakers and enemies that permeated the White House even at the best of times. And such was the atmosphere that existed when the biggest leak of all came: the forty-seven-volume Defense Department study of American involvement in Vietnam, known as the Pentagon Papers. The classified report had been given to Neil Sheehan of the *New York Times* by Daniel Ellsberg, who a year earlier had begged Kissinger to read it. The *Times* began publishing it on Sunday, June 13.

The disjointed but detailed study, which Kissinger had worked on briefly as a consultant, was mainly a compendium of classified cables from the Kennedy and Johnson years, and as such threatened no political harm—and perhaps could even be a benefit—to Nixon. Nevertheless, Kissinger saw the leak as devastating to America's efforts to conduct secret diplomacy. He flew into a rage that shocked even those used to his explosions. "Without Henry's stimulus," Ehrlichman said, "the president and the rest of us might have concluded that the papers were Lyndon Johnson's problem, not ours."

Those who witnessed Kissinger's fury at the Monday-morning staff meeting would long marvel at the scene, speaking of it like old salts recalling a historic hurricane. "This will totally destroy American credibility forever," he ranted as he paced around waving his arms and stamping his feet. "It will destroy our ability to conduct foreign policy in confidence." He pounded his palm against a Chippendale table. "No foreign government will ever trust us again," he shouted. "We might just as well turn it all over to the Soviets and get it over with."

Kissinger's concerns had some validity, but what added to his rage was that he immediately surmised that the leak had come from Ellsberg. That, Kissinger knew, would reflect badly on himself. He had hired Ellsberg as a consultant on the NSSM-1 study of Vietnam and had even brought him into the compound at San Clemente for lunch. Years later, Nixon would shake his head and say, with a bitter smile, "I'm not sure people realize how good of a friend Kissinger was with Dan Ellsberg."

Not quite. *Friendship* was hardly the word for their relationship. Their last meeting, earlier that year at a conference at MIT, had turned into a muted confrontation when Ellsberg rose from the audience to ask, "What is your best estimate of the number of Vietnamese who will be killed in the next twelve months as a consequence of your policy?" Kissinger had called the question "cleverly worded." Ellsberg interrupted to say it wasn't meant to be so, that it was a basic question. As he often did when so challenged, Kissinger asked what the other options were. "I know the options game, Dr. Kissinger," Ellsberg said. "Can't you give us an answer?" Kissinger sidestepped, and the session was called to a close.

But since Nixon associated Ellsberg with Kissinger and lumped him with Halperin and all the other liberal renegades from Kissinger's staff, Kissinger felt vulnerable, which was an emotion that he tended to translate into anger.

At a meeting in the Oval Office later that week, Kissinger fulminated about Ellsberg to the president, Haldeman, Ehrlichman, and Harlowe. "Kissinger was still livid," Ehrlichman recalled. "He said he knew for a fact that Ellsberg had slept with his wife and another woman at the same time." Kissinger went on to describe in detail other sexual practices that Ellsberg allegedly engaged in, according to Ehrlichman's notes, and he charged that Ellsberg was "known to be a drug user." Recalled Ehrlichman: "Nixon was fascinated." In addition, according to Haldeman, Kissinger accused Ellsberg of riding in helicopters and taking potshots at peasants when he was visiting Vietnam. (There is no evidence for most of these allegations.) [16]

The release of the Pentagon Papers, it turned out, was not nearly as harmful as the Nixonian reaction that followed. As Charles Colson told the special prosecutors looking into the Watergate scandal, Kissinger got President Nixon so "psyched up over the leak" that he was "near hysteria." Ehrlichman also recalled the frenzy. "The Pentagon Papers problem was no larger than a bread box on the horizon until Henry got to the president," Ehrlichman says. "Henry managed to raise the heat so high that Nixon was giving orders left and right that could only lead to trouble."

The result was that, within a month, a new White House unit was formed that became known as the Plumbers because of its assignment to plug leaks. "Without any question, Kissinger's great alarm over the Pentagon Papers was the primary motivating influence in the formation of the Plumbers," according to Colson. "I was in private meetings with Henry when he told the president that this must be stopped no matter what we had to do to stop it. It was over the next few weeks that the Plumbers were formed as a direct response."

Haldeman also put a large share of the blame on Kissinger: "Henry got Nixon cranked up, and then they started cranking each other up until they both were in a frenzy."

Ehrlichman assigned one of his assistants, Egil Krogh, to be in charge of the unit, and in a stroke of bureaucratic cleverness tapped a Kissinger aide to be the codirector. The Kissinger recruit was a thirty-four-year-old Oxford-educated lawyer named David Young. Young had worked with Kissinger on the Rockefeller campaign and then joined his NSC staff as a personal assistant handling everything from scheduling to laundry. But he soon ran afoul of Haig and was reassigned to handle mainly clerical work. So he paid a call on Ehrlichman, confided that he was restless, and subsequently found himself enlisted for new duties.

Ehrlichman told Kissinger about Young's reassignment in mid-July, during a helicopter ride from San Clemente to Los Angeles. Reflexively, Kissinger protested: no one should be stealing his staffers without talking to him first. But the protest was rather perfunctory. Kissinger was never specifically told what Young's new duties were, and he had no direct dealings with him again.

Among those recruited for the Plumbers unit were Howard Hunt, a tough-talking former CIA operative, and G. Gordon Liddy, a former FBI man. With Colson goading them on, they organized a break-in at the office of Ellsberg's psychiatrist. Haldeman later blamed the operation on "the desire to find evidence to support Kissinger's vivid statement about Ellsberg's weird habits."[17]

The finger-pointing by Colson, Haldeman, and Ehrlichman reflected an effort at self-justification by three men who were convicted of Watergate crimes. Although he may have been guilty of riling people up in a way that led to the creation of the Plumbers unit, Kissinger's actions fundamentally differed from those of Nixon and his top political aides: Kissinger did not give any orders for illegal break-ins, nor did he engineer a cover-up of these illegal acts after they had occurred.

What can be said, however, is that the connection between Kissinger's fury over the Pentagon Papers and the subsequent formation of the Plumbers unit showed once again—just as the wiretap abuses had—that an obsessive desire for secrecy can be costly, and that the fear of leaks can be more dangerous than the leaks themselves.

THE UNILATERAL-WITHDRAWAL OFFER

One reason that Kissinger had gotten so worked up about the Pentagon Papers was that he was afraid that their publication would derail his diplomatic overtures to China by destroying any faith that Beijing had in America's ability to conduct discreet diplomacy. It was a misguided concern. China showed little interest in the inscrutable occidental approach to secrecy.

In addition, Kissinger was on edge because the secret Vietnam negotiations were at what seemed to be a critical juncture. On May 31, at a meeting with Xuan Thuy in Paris, Kissinger had finally offered a unilateral American withdrawal from Vietnam.

"The proposal sought to get us off the treadmill of demanding mutual withdrawal while we in fact carried ours out unilaterally," Kissinger recalled. In return, the U.S. demanded that Hanoi agree to a cease-fire in all of Indochina and drop its insistence that President Thieu's government be replaced.

The American concession was significant, as even the administration's detractors admitted. But was it the right one? Would it have been wiser to have abandoned support for Thieu instead? By conceding the military question, but remaining firmly against replacing Thieu with a coalition government, the U.S. tied itself to a regime that was eventually doomed. The U.S. became, said veteran diplomat George Ball, "the prisoner of President Thieu, a repressive, small-time dictator we had created."

A more conservative criticism was that conceding the right of North Vietnam's troops to remain in the South doomed the nation to continued war. Richard Smyser, Kissinger's Vietnam expert, held this view, and he made a last-ditch effort on the way to Paris to talk Kissinger into scaling back the new American concession. "If the North Vietnamese don't withdraw, there will never be peace," Smyser told Kissinger on the plane. "What we're proposing is simply an American withdrawal in which the war will go on indefinitely." Kissinger, Smyser recalled, admitted that he was right, but insisted the concession was necessary. "We need a settlement," he said.

As was his style, Kissinger relied heavily on ambiguity to camouflage the concession and make it palatable to South Vietnam's supporters. Employed were such phrases as "all other outside forces would withdraw," which skirted the fact that Hanoi did not consider its troops to be an outside force anywhere in Vietnam. Kissinger made no clear public explanation at the time, even on background, that the demand for North Vietnam's withdrawal was being dropped.

As a result, when a tentative deal along these lines was finally achieved in October 1972, President Thieu would be able to claim that he was shocked and outraged at the absence of a mutual withdrawal of North Vietnamese forces. In fact, he knew full well that the May 1971 proposal, which he reluctantly approved, conceded this point. Yet he did not really believe that it would ever be part of a deal. "I was informed that these things were being discussed, but I thought we would be consulted more before there was movement toward an agreement," he said rather plaintively in a 1990 interview.

Did the North Vietnamese know the extent of the concession? Yes, instantly. "They understood in a split second that we were yielding on the military issues and asking them to yield on the political one," said Smyser. "If you were an opera fan, and you heard a tenor drop a note from a phrase you'd heard hundreds of times before, you'd notice immediately. They did." Xuan Thuy started taking notes furiously. At the time, there was a flurry of hope. Le Duc Tho left Hanoi and headed for Paris.

As it turned out, the North Vietnamese were not ready to accept the proposal. After almost two decades of fighting, they were not going to agree to a cease-fire without accomplishing their goal of taking over the South Vietnamese government. That concession would not come for at least another year.[18]

SIXTEEN

CHINA

Creating a Triangle

Since Austrian policy could not draw its strength from the inspiration of its people, it had to achieve its aims by the tenacity and subtlety of its diplomacy. —KISSINGER, A WORLD RESTORED, 1957

THE ROAD TO BEIJING

Kissinger did not share the president's penchant for hyperbole. Instead, he tended to favor wry understatement as a way to emphasize a point. But when he received, in June 1971, a long-sought secret message from China inviting him to come and pave the way for a presidential visit, he presented it to Nixon with a flourish. "This," he said, "is the most important communication that has come to an American president since the end of World War II."

Grandiloquent though that statement was, it contained a kernel of truth; the creation of a strategic tie to communist China was probably the most significant and prudent American foreign policy initiative since the launching of the Marshall Plan and the creation of NATO. For both Nixon and Kissinger, it was a bold and in many ways brilliant coup, a dramatic stroke that, in Kissinger's more considered later assessment, "transformed the structure of international politics." Even that subtlest of statesmen, Chinese Premier Zhou Enlai, proclaimed that the world had been shaken.

With startling suddenness, the bipolar balance of power between

East and West, which had defined the world order for twenty-five years, gave way to a triangular system ripe for creative diplomacy and delicate leverages. In addition, as if by magic, the American attitude toward a mysterious land containing one-quarter of humanity was turned around. For a generation, the U.S. public and its professional policy elite had viewed China as a fanatic, revolutionary realm, a terra incognita of the sort that ancient cartographers used to label "here be dragons." The expansionism of Red China, American policymakers wrongly believed, had led to the Vietnam War. Now Nixon and Kissinger were ready to exploit a more nuanced linkage: by opening to China, they would be able to make North Vietnam feel more isolated and vulnerable.

Kissinger's approach to the China opening—his secret dealings with Zhou Enlai and Mao Zedong, his ability to play Beijing off against Moscow—was a prime example of how his personal style related to his diplomacy. In dealing with other people, he would forge alliances and conspiratorial bonds by manipulating their antagonisms. Drawn to his adversaries with a compulsive attraction, he would seek their approval through flattery, cajolery, and playing them off against others. He was particularly comfortable dealing with powerful men whose minds he could engage. As a child of the holocaust and a scholar of Napoleonic-era statecraft, he sensed that great men as well as great forces were what shaped the world, and he knew that personality and policy could never be fully divorced. Secrecy came naturally to him as a tool of control. And he had an instinctive feel for power relationships and balances, both psychological and geostrategic.

Because the U.S. and China shared the same concern about the Soviet threat, it was likely that a strategic relationship would develop eventually. The challenge for each nation was to see the other in geopolitical rather than ideological terms, an outlook that Nixon and Kissinger had no trouble adopting. Despite being a charter member of the "Who Lost China?" club of anticommunists, Nixon was an unemotional realist, as was Kissinger. Not surprisingly (except to a few American policy mandarins), the doctrine of realism was likewise not alien to the leaders of China, the world's oldest political entity.[1]

Kissinger had been thinking along these lines since 1968, when he wrote a campaign speech that Nelson Rockefeller gave that May. "I would begin a dialogue with communist China," the speech declared. "In a subtle triangle with communist China and the Soviet Union, we can ultimately improve our relations with each—as we test the will for peace of both."[2]

Nixon was among those who originally believed the Vietnam War was a manifestation of Chinese expansionism. It was, he said in a 1965 speech, "a confrontation not fundamentally between Vietnam and the Viet Cong . . . but between the United States and communist China." But even back then, he was fascinated by the possibility of going to China and almost succeeded in doing so that year. A Canadian client organized a trade mission to China and invited Nixon along. But Lyndon Johnson's State Department refused to give Nixon a visa.

By 1967, Nixon showed signs of being interested in better relations with China. Most frequently cited in this regard, especially by himself, is his October 1967 *Foreign Affairs* article, "Asia After Viet Nam," written with William Safire's help. "Taking the long view, we simply cannot afford to leave China forever outside the family of nations," he said. But the article as a whole did not actually advocate any immediate moves toward China; instead, it argued that China should be pressured to abandon its aggressive policies. "The world cannot be safe until China changes," Nixon wrote. "For the short run, then, this means a policy of firm restraint, of no reward, of creative counterpressure." China was then in the throes of its Cultural Revolution, and in an aside to Safire while working on the article, Nixon declared: "The current nuttiness in Peking underlines the manipulative techniques of the Chinese and their dangerous delusions."* 3

Those who favored a rapprochement with China in the late 1960s came to that conclusion from three different angles. First there were the liberals, who saw good relations as a valuable end in itself; typical of this view were a group of professors, led by Jerome Cohen and Doak Barnett, who publicly urged Nixon just after his election to make concessions on Taiwan that would lessen hostility.

A second school, which Nixon enrolled in, felt that improved ties to China could be an instrument to pressure the Soviet Union. Shortly after his inauguration, he told Kissinger to quietly "plant that idea" of a possible China-policy change as a way to unnerve Moscow. Later in 1969, Soviet Foreign Minister Andrei Gromyko visited the United Nations. Nixon sent Kissinger a confidential memo suggesting how to gig him: "I think that while Gromyko is in the country would be a very good time to have another move to China made."

Kissinger shared this view, but he also approached the China issue from a third, more subtle angle. Instead of using improved rela-

* Until 1979, "Peking" was the standard transliteration of the Chinese capital of Beijing. Likewise, Zhou Enlai was spelled "Chou En-lai" and Mao Zedong was "Mao Tse-tung." I have used the current Pinyin spelling system except when quoting documents that use the older style.

tions with Beijing primarily as a bludgeon to threaten Moscow, he envisioned a triangular set of relations that could create a more stable world balance. "We moved toward China," he later wrote, "to shape a global equilibrium. It was not to collude against the Soviet Union but to give us a balancing position to use for constructive ends—to give each Communist power a stake in better relations with us."

Kissinger was at first skeptical about any quick opening to China, and it was Nixon's dogged vision that propelled the initiative. On one trip early in 1969, Haldeman talked to Nixon on the plane and then came to sit next to Kissinger. "You know," Haldeman said, "he actually seriously intends to visit China before the end of the second term." Kissinger took off his glasses, polished them slowly, smiled, and replied, "Fat chance."[4]

The rising hostility between China and the Soviet Union in the spring of 1969—when shooting broke out along their border—stimulated both Nixon and Kissinger to think about new opportunities. Soviet Ambassador Dobrynin gave Kissinger an unsolicited emotional account of the incident, stressing that China was a menace they must work together to contain. Later that evening, Kissinger described Dobrynin's agitation to the president, who was "intrigued." A few weeks later, *Life* magazine ran an editorial on the Sino-Soviet dispute that urged the administration "to reject the temptation to play the split completely Russia's way and instead try to find a better way to live with China." In the margin of his news summary, Nixon jotted a note to be conveyed to the editor: "I completely agree. I urged this position incidentally on all European leaders on my recent trip."

Even though the State Department professionals were rather wary of a sudden change in policy, Secretary Rogers supported Nixon's goals. "Communist China obviously has long been too isolated from world affairs," he said in an August 1969 speech. "This is one reason why we have been seeking to open up channels of communications." Nonetheless, Kissinger once again sought to cut Rogers out of the action.

At first it was difficult for Kissinger to wrest control from the State Department because official contacts between the U.S. and China were handled by meetings between the nations' ambassadors in Warsaw. Since 1954, there had been 134 such sessions, making them a contender for the longest series of diplomatic talks that had produced not a single notable accomplishment. Each meeting was little more than a repetition of the stale but safe statements of the last.

In late 1969, after the talks had been recessed for a year, the U.S. ambassador to Poland, Walter Stoessel, acting on Kissinger's instruction, chased down the Chinese envoy at a reception and suggested the talks be resumed. When the Chinese agreed, the State Department bureaucracy followed its standard procedure of churning out a report and disseminating it to various embassies, desk officers, and other corners of its vast machinery that could claim a need to know such information.

Kissinger was horrified at this unsecretive method and told the president so. Nixon agreed, worrying that "we'll kill this child before it is born."[5]

Another, more valid, reason for seizing control from the State Department was that it contained too many entrenched attitudes to permit flexibility. At the next Warsaw meeting, to be held in January 1970, Kissinger wanted to propose sending a special envoy to Beijing. The various State Department officers disagreed. Besides blanching at the notion of a special envoy (i.e., someone outside their control), they felt it was important to emphasize that progress would depend on resolving long-standing issues, such as getting China to join in arms control talks and to pledge not to use force over Taiwan.

The battle ended with a typical bureaucratic compromise: the department could reiterate all the old issues it wanted, but it would also add a sentence Kissinger wanted saying that the U.S. "would be prepared to consider sending a representative to Peking for direct discussions."

Through the convergence of historical forces, and probably a similar spilling of bureaucratic blood in Beijing, the Chinese envoy, Lei Yang, had a similar phrase in his statement. "These talks," he said, "may either continue to be conducted at the ambassadorial level or may be conducted at a higher level or through other channels."

The problem now, for Kissinger at least, was how to get the talks out of the State Department channels. The inadvertent solution was the invasion of Cambodia. The Chinese canceled the May 1970 session, and no new meetings were scheduled. Kissinger later called the breakdown "providential." It spelled the end of the Warsaw talks and of State Department involvement in the process. "When we reestablished contact later in the year, it was in a different channel with a sharper focus."

Kissinger proceeded to make various attempts to create a back channel to Beijing. Among them was an effort by General Vernon Walters to establish a contact in Paris, which would have allowed Kissinger one-stop secret parleying. "But our back-channel system, which had so intrigued the Soviets, held as yet no attraction for the Chinese," Kissinger recalls. "Perhaps they did not understand how a serious government could be run in that way; if so, they were not alone." Another possible explanation was that Kissinger had blundered by proposing the channel through the Chinese military attaché; he was most likely aligned with the hard-line anti-American faction of Defense Minister Lin Biao.

In the meantime, the flirtation continued by interview. In response to Nixon's September 1970 interview in *Time,* where he said he wanted to visit China someday, Mao gave one to Edgar Snow for *Life,* saying that he "would be happy to talk to him, either as a tourist or as president."

The channel that China finally chose, after months of overeager signal-sending by Washington, was through Pakistan. Nixon had established the link on his August 1969 trip around the world, personally asking President Yahya Khan to convey to Beijing that Washington was willing to start a new relationship. The president gave another push in October 1970, when Yahya Khan came to the Oval Office. From there he headed to Beijing, whence he brought back a note that he gave to a courier who brought it to Pakistan's ambassador in the U.S. On the evening of December 8, the ambassador came to the White House to read it aloud to Kissinger. In the age of modern communications, couriers had taken six weeks to convey handwritten notes back and forth across the globe and read them aloud.

The message was from Premier Zhou Enlai. "In order to discuss the subject of the vacation of Chinese territories called Taiwan, a special envoy of President Nixon's will be most welcome in Peking." The focus on the Taiwan issue, Kissinger believed, was merely for show, to give China's leadership a way out if the meetings backfired. The important thing was that, in principle, a special envoy would be welcome.

Kissinger drafted a response, which was typed on plain Xerox paper, with no government watermark and handed to the Pakistani ambassador. It said that an American envoy would be willing to come and talk "on the broad range of issues" facing the two countries. In the note, Kissinger came up with a formula to deal with Taiwan that ended up being the basis for the agreements that were sealed more than a year later: "With respect to the U.S. military presence on Taiwan . . . the policy of the United States government is to reduce its military presence in the region of East Asia and the Pacific as tensions in this region diminish." It was yet another subtle linkage: American forces in Taiwan could be drawn down quicker if the Vietnam War was settled.

Neither Secretary Rogers nor the State Department was informed of the message. A copy was sent, however, through the Romanian government, which Kissinger and Nixon had enlisted as another back channel to China. One Soviet official later said that Moscow learned of the message through Romania. This resulted in the odd situation in which the foreign ministries of China, Pakistan, Romania, and the Soviet Union all knew about the American initiative to China, but the U.S. State Department did not.

Through the spring of 1971, little was communicated through the clunky conduits. Then, Glenn Cowan, nineteen, a Ping-Pong player from Santa Monica with the American team at the World Table Tennis Championships in Japan, stumbled into the act. After a match, he approached the Chinese team's captain and hitched a ride on their bus to a sight-seeing event at a nearby pearl farm. Later he gave his new friend a T-shirt as a gift and got a scarf in return.

The Chinese probably assumed, incorrectly, that Glenn Cowan's affability was a carefully considered policy signal choreographed from Washington. As a result, the American team found itself with a surprise invitation to visit Beijing the following week, and the world was suddenly transfixed by the spectacle of Ping-Pong diplomacy. "You have opened a new chapter in the relations of the American and Chinese people," Zhou Enlai told the players at a reception he personally threw in the Great Hall of the People.

A week later, on April 21, a new message from Zhou came through the Pakistani channel: "The Chinese Government reaffirms its willingness to receive publicly in Peking a special envoy of the President of the U.S. (for instance, Mr. Kissinger) or the U.S. Secretary of State or even the President of the U.S. himself for a direct meeting."

A crucial moment had arrived: deciding whom to send.

Kissinger would later claim that "originally, there was no thought of sending me." But it would be fair to say that the thought had crossed his mind. Nixon was merciless in toying with him on the issue. For the first time, the president showed signs of feeling some competitive resentment, even jealousy, toward his assistant.

So Nixon began to play with the notion of going to China first himself, with no emissary preceding him. That was certainly possible. The logistics of the visit would have to be worked out, but that could be done by anonymous advance men after the announcement of an impending summit. Kissinger worked hard to dissuade Nixon from such a course, arguing that an "unprepared presidential trip to China was much too dangerous."

Nixon acquiesced, but then began musing about a long list of possible envoys who could make the trip. Kissinger had originally proposed David Bruce, perhaps because it was easy for him to shoot down the idea when the time came; as the chief U.S. negotiator on Vietnam, Bruce would seem like a heavy-handed ploy. Nixon put forth other names. Henry Cabot Lodge? There was a similar problem since he had been ambassador to South Vietnam. George Bush, a former Texas congressman who was about to be named U.N. ambassador? He was considered insufficiently familiar with the nuances of the new policy toward China. Nelson Rockefeller? That proposal must have tortured Kissinger until Nixon decided that he was too visible.

Kissinger later said that "Rogers's name did not come up." Nixon remembered otherwise. "Well," he recalled saying, "what about Bill, then?" If the secretary of state went, Nixon reasoned, then the Chinese "will sure as hell know we're serious." Nixon later recounted, with some amusement, that Kissinger rolled his eyes upward. "Henry wasn't too enthusiastic," said Nixon. "Let me put it that way." Another discussion with Kissinger of possible envoys was held in front of Haldeman. Finally, having frazzled Kissinger's nerves enough, Nixon announced: "Henry, I think you will have to do it."

Kissinger felt "an immense sense of relief," he said. He fervently wanted to be the one to bring the enterprise to fruition. In choosing him, Kissinger realized, Nixon was partly motivated by a desire to retain most of the credit for the initiative rather than risk having some of his thunder stolen by a high-profile envoy. Kissinger was still a little-known assistant who had never given an on-the-record press conference. "I had no means of publicizing my activities except through the White House press office," Kissinger later wrote, stretching the truth somewhat.

The use of Pakistani couriers was becoming too cumbersome for arranging the final details, so Kissinger had the navy set up a private cable channel through its attaché in Karachi; as with the Berlin negotiations, this allowed the Pentagon, unbeknownst to Kissinger, to become privy to the secret.

On May 9, Kissinger used the channel to say that he would personally serve as the special envoy and to propose that one purpose of his trip would be to set up a subsequent visit by the president. On June 2 the reply came back that Kissinger would describe as "the most important" since World War II: Zhou Enlai approved his trip and expressed Chairman Mao's "pleasure" at the prospect of receiving President Nixon sometime soon thereafter.

Nixon was hosting a state dinner for Nicaraguan president Anastasio Somoza when Zhou's message arrived. Kissinger sent word in to him, and they were soon secluded in the Lincoln Sitting Room celebrating their secret triumph. Nixon found a bottle of old Courvoisier that he had been given and took two snifters from the cupboard. "Let us drink to generations to come who may have a better chance to live in peace because of what we have done," he said.

Yet the president seemed oddly disquieted, as he often was in moments of triumph. He could never bring himself to believe that a victory would not somehow turn sour. Specifically, he had started to worry that Kissinger would overshadow him. A new phase in their relationship was beginning.[6]

Privately the president began urging Kissinger to find a venue other than Beijing for his meeting with Chinese officials. If he met with them somewhere else—at an airport in southern China or better yet in Pakistan—it would detract far less from the drama of Nixon's subsequent trip.

In his memoirs, Kissinger would claim that he "procrastinated" on Nixon's request to meet somewhere other than Beijing because "I did not know how to put this either to the Pakistanis or the Chinese." In fact, as the exchanges of May and early June show, the Chinese were perfectly willing to have the meeting outside of Beijing.

The original plan, as discussed in April when he was chosen for the assignment, had been for Kissinger to meet with Chinese leaders in southern China or Pakistan. Even in the May 9 message informing Beijing that he was to be the envoy, Kissinger proposed holding the meeting "on Chinese soil preferably at some location within flying distance from Pakistan." The June 2 message made clear that such a plan was suitable to the Chinese; Kissinger "may fly direct from Islamabad to a Chinese airport not open to the public," Zhou's message said.

It was after the brandy had been sipped and the private toasts exchanged that Kissinger sat down with Winston Lord to draft a reply to the June 2 message. No longer was there any vague talk about "some location within flying distance" or about an "airport not open to the public." Instead, Kissinger's reply proposed that he would arrive on July 9, "flying in a Pakistani Boeing aircraft from Islamabad to Peking." Nixon was thus destined to arrive in the Chinese capital only after the American public had heard Kissinger's colorful descriptions of his own visit there.

Nixon made one other effort to preserve for himself more of the glory: he ordered Kissinger not to put his own name on the announcement that would be released after his visit. Even while Kissinger was on his way, Nixon kept badgering him. "Repeatedly I received instructions," Kissinger recalled, "saying yet again what I had already been told innumerable times before leaving: no names in the communiqué." Kissinger considered this absurd. "He did not explain how one could announce the visit of an American emissary to Peking without revealing the emissary's name unless one wanted to get a reputation in China for complete inscrutability." When the time came, Kissinger would simply ignore the request.

The secrecy leading up to Kissinger's trip was partly to preserve the drama of the announcement, partly to circumvent the resistant bureaucracy of the State Department, and partly to avoid a paralyzing public and congressional debate.

Later, Nixon would claim that the secrecy was also done at China's insistence. But that was untrue. When Ambassador Walter Stoessel had been invited to the Chinese embassy in Warsaw the year before, he had offered to come in secretly through a back entrance. No, said the Chinese, he should come through the front door. The April 21 missive from the Chinese had clearly stated their willingness to receive an American envoy "publicly." It was Kissinger's May 9 reply that mentioned three times, and underlined each one, the need to keep the preparations for his visit "strictly secret." "We learned later that the Chinese were extremely suspicious of our desire for secrecy," Kissinger said. The Chinese were a proud people who still felt the sting of John Foster Dulles's refusal to shake Zhou Enlai's hand at the 1954 Geneva Conference.

As usual, a price was paid for the secrecy. Secretary Rogers, oblivious to what was happening, publicly said in London in late April that China's policies were "rather paranoic." Kissinger had to search for ways of conveying to the Chinese that the secretary of state was not to be heeded, no doubt enhancing the reputation of Occidentals for inscrutability.

Over Kissinger's objection, Nixon decided that he would have to tell Rogers about Kissinger's secret mission once it was under way. "But State leaks," Kissinger protested, according to Nixon's memory. "So does your staff," Nixon replied. Nevertheless, he held off informing Rogers until the last moment and made it seem that the trip was due to an unexpected invitation that had come out of the blue.

The trip was also supposed to be secret from Defense Secretary Laird, but it wasn't. He knew what was being transmitted over the naval back channel to the attaché in Karachi, and the NSA kept him abreast of other messages. He could not help playing a puckish trick: he informed the White House that he planned to take a tour of defense installations on Taiwan during the first week in July, just when Kissinger was planning to be in Beijing. Without explaining why, and without knowing that Laird knew why, Kissinger had to ask him to rearrange his schedule.

But the secrecy surrounding the China initiative was more justified than most other attempts by Nixon and Kissinger to keep their actions covert. So many vested positions existed within the State Department that paralyzing bureaucratic demands would have been made each step of the way. There would have been pressures to seek concessions on items that were extraneous to the larger geopolitical issue at stake. Other nations would have sought various reassurances, and the initiative would quickly have leaked. Then, as Nixon says, conservative opposition would mobilize and "scuttle the whole effort."

Most foreign policy decisions, despite what Kissinger and Nixon generally thought, benefit from public input and have a greater chance of lasting support if developed in the open. But the China opening probably would not have taken place at such a timely moment —just as negotiations with North Vietnam and the Soviet Union were heating up—if it had been handled in official channels with open debate. "Simply put," Nixon argued, "we never could have done it if we had not kept it secret."

On July 1, 1971, Kissinger set out on what was announced as a fact-finding tour through Asia. Because Nixon had taken Air Force One and a backup plane to San Clemente, and Agnew and Laird had commandeered the other two private jets in the presidential fleet, Kissinger and his small entourage had to make do with a windowless communications plane from the Tactical Air Command.

No reporters came along. And few people gave much thought to the wire service report that was buried in most Saturday papers on July 10. The *New York Times,* for example, relegated it to the second item in its "Notes on People" column. It read: "Fleeing the hot, humid air of the plains around Rawalpindi, Henry A. Kissinger, President Nixon's national security adviser, spent the day at Nathiagali in the cool hills of northern Pakistan. He was described as 'feeling slightly indisposed.' "[7]

KISSINGER IN CHINA, JULY 1971

Kissinger never went to Nathiagali. A decoy motorcade, with sirens wailing and American flag flying, snaked up the cool hills. But Kissinger had been spirited away to the military section of the Islamabad airport where a Pakistani Boeing 707 with Chinese navigators awaited him. Three aides went with him: Winston Lord, Richard Smyser, and John Holdridge.

Also along for the ride were two of Kissinger's Secret Service men, John Ready and Gary McLeod, dedicated and earnest agents who had been worrying about the fact that they had not done a security check on the Nathiagali guesthouse when, without warning, they found themselves whisked away in a foreign plane with an enemy navigator to a place where there might be as many as 800 million communist sympathizers, many of them armed.

At the airport was a Pakistani journalist named M. F. H. Beg, who served as a stringer for the London *Telegraph*. Was that Henry Kissinger who just arrived? Yes, answered an airport official not briefed on the need for secrecy. Where is he going? China, the official answered. Beg breathlessly phoned in what would have been the scoop of the year to his desk in London, where his editor, assuming that Beg was drunk, listened politely then spiked it.

On the flight over, one Chinese official asked why there was such a need for secrecy. Was Kissinger ashamed to be meeting with Chinese leaders? No, he answered, and tried to explain as best he could his belief in the need for secrecy. As the plane neared the Chinese border, Winston Lord walked up toward the cockpit. He wanted to become, he later joked, the first American official to enter Chinese airspace.

Shortly after noon on Friday, July 9, 1971, Kissinger and his party landed in Beijing. They were taken to a Victorian-style state guesthouse in a walled park with a serpentine lake and elegant bridges. There Kissinger was met by Premier Zhou Enlai, the gaunt and graceful veteran of Mao's Long March who had been a leader of the communist movement in China for fifty of his seventy-three years. Kissinger, remembering the tale of Dulles's snub, "ostentatiously" stuck out his hand. "It was the first step in putting the legacy of the past behind us," he recalled.[8]

In his report to Nixon afterward, Kissinger took care to paint a vivid portrait of Zhou. "He was equally at home in philosophic sweeps, historical analysis, tactical probing, light repartee," he wrote in a description that also fit himself. Zhou's ability to dominate a room came not from his physical presence but from "his air of controlled tension" that made him seem "as if he were a coiled spring." His expressive face was dominated by piercing eyes that conveyed a mixture of intensity, wariness, and self-confidence. He wore with grace and inner serenity, as well as with a disciplined fervor, the burden of his role as Mao's only premier in the twenty-two years since the communists had controlled China.

Over the course of two days, Kissinger would hold seventeen hours of talks with Zhou. Their sessions would last up to seven hours at a stretch. Yet Zhou had that peculiar grace of all truly masterful leaders—a quality that Kissinger conspicuously lacked—of never seeming harried, never being interrupted, never giving the impression of having something more pressing to tend to, and never needing to take a phone call, despite his duties of running the world's largest nation. "I do not know how he managed it," Kissinger later marveled.

Kissinger had only one practical piece of business to settle: agreeing on an invitation to Nixon for a summit in Beijing. Other than that, he and Zhou had the luxury of being unburdened by mundane matters and could spend their time enjoying conceptual discussions.

As his two Secret Service agents eyed Zhou warily, Kissinger sat before his bulging briefing book and expounded on the strategic interests the two nations shared. Zhou spoke with only a single piece of paper in front of him. The stylized yet easy banter, Kissinger noted, was like "a dialogue between two professors of political philosophy."

The mutual interests they discussed mainly involved their shared distrust of the Soviets. Kissinger took the extraordinary step of showing the Chinese supersecret intelligence he had brought along regarding Soviet military activities. He even gave Zhou communications intercepts and high-quality satellite pictures of Soviet facilities along the Chinese border.[9]

Between sessions, Kissinger fully indulged his love for Chinese food. The banquets were so lavish that he remarked that a state visitor must have starved to death three thousand years ago and the Chinese were ever since determined to make up for it. After the trip had been revealed, Time noted that "an alert observer might have noticed that the man who was supposedly suffering from a stomach ailment had put on five pounds." The American party even got in some sightseeing; the Forbidden City was once again forbidden to the Chinese masses for an afternoon while Kissinger and his aides got a private tour of the fifteenth-century imperial palace.

Zhou finally broached the subject of a Nixon summit in a disconcerting way. He launched into a forceful recitation of the Chinese liturgy, using such standard Maoist catchphrases as "there is much turmoil under the heavens." Given the vast gulf between China and America, he concluded, would there be much point to a Nixon visit?

Replying that it was up to the Chinese to decide whether to invite Nixon, Kissinger began a rather brusque rebuttal, which seemed not to engage Zhou. He cut Kissinger off after just one point to tell him that the duck would get cold if they did not take a break for lunch. Zhou was genial as the lunch ended and offered his guest an explanation of China's Cultural Revolution, the radical social upheaval ordered by Mao that seemed to be winding down. That was an internal Chinese affair, Kissinger demurred. No, said Zhou, if the U.S. was to understand China, it must understand its Cultural Revolution.

When Zhou finished his analysis, Kissinger resumed his rebuttal of the morning diatribe. But after a few minutes, Zhou cut him off again. Nixon was welcome to come for a summit early the following year. Huang Hua, a top Chinese diplomat, would come to Kissinger's quarters to negotiate the communiqué.

Kissinger was elated, but it was short-lived. The draft that Huang offered declared that Nixon had solicited the invitation and that the purpose of the summit would be to discuss Taiwan. Kissinger responded that this was unacceptable. Instead of then proceeding to negotiate each point, Huang suggested another approach: each side should tell the other what its fundamental needs were, and then a text accommodating them could be attempted.

It was a typical Chinese approach to a negotiation, the opposite of the salami tactics of small concessions that Kissinger was used to. The Chinese liked to begin by laying out basic matters of principle that each side felt it simply could not compromise. Then, they would make and seek major steps to get quickly to an agreeable goal that preserved the fundamental needs of both parties. Kissinger often said that he embraced this method himself, though most of his negotiations with the Soviets, Vietnamese, and Arabs show little evidence of that.

After considering the American desires and needs, the Chinese came back the next morning with a new version of the communiqué. With just one small word change, easily made, it was all that Kissinger could have wanted. It mentioned Taiwan not at all. "Knowing of President Nixon's expressed desire to visit the People's Republic of China," it read, he was being invited to a summit early in 1972. The purpose would be "to seek the normalization of relations" and "to exchange views on questions of concern to the two sides." Despite Nixon's repeated instructions that Kissinger should not have his name in the communiqué, the document began: "Premier Chou En-lai and Dr. Henry Kissinger . . ."

A prearranged code word was flashed back to the White House when Kissinger emerged from China summit in hand: "Eureka." Upon his arrival at San Clemente, after a stopover in Paris for a secret session with North Vietnam's Le Duc Tho, Kissinger presented the president a fuller explanation: a forty-page, single-spaced report on his forty-nine hours in China. "We have laid the groundwork," it concluded, "for you and Mao to turn a page in history."

Nixon's brief televised announcement on Thursday, July 15, made with no advance warning of its content, left at least one of the network television commentators speechless for close to ten seconds. In a single stroke, the president had confounded all of his enemies: the Soviets, the North Vietnamese, the press, and the liberal Democrats.

For a moment Nixon could bask in acclaim. Wrote columnist Max Lerner: "The politics of surprise leads through the Gates of Astonishment into the Kingdom of Hope." In Paris, *France-Soir* ran a banner head declaring "Le Coup de Nixon" and said that it "turns the international situation topsy-turvy." Senate Democratic leader Mike Mansfield declared, "I am astounded, delighted, and happy," and George McGovern said that "I applaud the president's imagination and judgment."[10]

That evening Nixon celebrated with the unusual gesture of socializing with his staff. Along with Kissinger, Ehrlichman, Haldeman, and Ron Ziegler, he flew by helicopter to Los Angeles for dinner at Perino's. In the days when Nixon was young, Perino's had been a fashionable haunt, but its glory was now gone. It had been sold to a chain and catered largely to busloads of tourists. With the president coming, old Mr. Perino was quickly recalled to duty.

Kissinger and Nixon weightily discussed what Bordeaux was worthy of the occasion. The wine steward offered to bring out something special, and soon a dust-encrusted magnum of 1961 Château Lafite-Rothschild appeared. "To my uncultivated palate it seemed a bit sharp," recalled Ehrlichman, "but our two 'experts,' Nixon and Kissinger, proclaimed it outstanding."

The dinner was joyous, but it also had its serious side. They toasted the fact that the initiative had been kept secret, and Nixon stressed the need to limit future chatter and publicity about the new relationship. "There must be no further discussion with the press about Henry's trip," he said. Kissinger picked up the cue. "You are so right, Mr. President," he said. "If we talk about it any further, the Chinese will not believe we are serious people." They all agreed that absolutely no one would give further briefings to reporters.

At the end of the meal, Nixon went through the restaurant and lingered in the foyer introducing Kissinger, to the bafflement of the tourists who had not spent the evening watching televised announcements, as the man who had just gone to Beijing. "In his hour of achievement Richard Nixon was oddly vulnerable, waiting expectantly for recognition without quite being able to bridge the gulf by which he had isolated himself from his fellow men," Kissinger later wrote. "In this sense the scene at Perino's symbolized the triumph and tragedy of Richard Nixon."

Ehrlichman had a less elevated view of the same scene. After dinner, while "the president and Henry jumped up and began moving about the large dining room shaking hands," the naval aide handling the logistics pulled Ehrlichman aside. "That old bandit," he said, pointing to Perino, "wants six hundred dollars for that bottle of wine."

Ehrlichman told him to offer $300 spot cash, take it or leave it. Perino accepted. Ziegler later told reporters that the wine had cost $40.[11]

There was one sour note to the celebrations. The administration had bungled the trickiest element of the China opening: dealing with Japan. Tokyo had been given solemn assurances that Washington would not make any initiatives toward Beijing without full consultations. With his passion for secrecy, his disdain for Japanese concerns, and his desire to make no use of the State Department, Kissinger caused the breaking of this pledge to be as devastating as possible. "Few thoughts aroused more trepidation in the Japanese government over the years than the possibility that the United States would suddenly reverse its policy toward Beijing," recalled U. Alexis Johnson, a former ambassador to Japan who was then undersecretary of state.

Even allowing for the primacy given to secrecy, there were certainly less shabby ways to treat such an important ally. In fact, the plan devised by Rogers had been to send Johnson to Tokyo the day before the announcement so that he could deliver the news personally in advance. Kissinger vetoed the idea, telling Johnson that the president was too worried about the possibility of a leak. It was a curious excuse, since at that point a leak would not have had grave diplomatic consequences. "No leak could have created anything like the breakage resulting from our lack of consultation," said veteran statesman George Ball.

Alternatively, Kissinger could have allowed Smyser or Holdridge to fly to Tokyo just after leaving China. Although the Japanese would still have been upset, at least they would not have been publicly humiliated. Kissinger saw the failure mainly as one of etiquette. "It would have been more courteous and thoughtful," he said, to have sent an aide from the Beijing trip to Tokyo to inform the Japanese prime minister personally. "This would have combined secrecy with a demonstration of special consideration for a good and decent friend. It was a serious error in manners."

There was one curious footnote. The Japanese did not remain totally uninformed. Defense Secretary Laird, having canceled his trip to Taiwan, was in Tokyo instead. Through his own sources—naval communications channels, Yeoman Radford's reports, National Security Agency communications intercepts, and the special mission plane that Kissinger used—he knew exactly what was happening. Realizing that sharing information is a way to enhance your own power, he privately told his Japanese counterpart about the Kissinger trip and the forthcoming summit six hours before it was announced.[12]

The Soviets, who had been procrastinating on Nixon's desire for a Moscow summit, were also rattled by the Beijing announcement.

The following Monday, Ambassador Dobrynin appeared at the White House, full of charm, to ask about the possibility of having a Soviet summit first. "To have the two communist powers competing for good relations with us could only benefit the cause of peace," Kissinger later noted. "It was the essence of triangular strategy."

Kissinger indicated that the summits would occur in the order they had been arranged. Soviet coyness had a price. The Moscow summit was scheduled for May 1972, three months after the one in Beijing.[13]

The July 15 announcement of Kissinger's secret trip to China transformed him into an international celebrity. He was on the cover of the newsmagazines, featured on the network news, and profiled on front pages across the nation. "The 48-year-old foreign policy expert manages the development of Presidential diplomacy while creating the illusion that he is a full-time permanent floating cocktail party guest of honor," said the *New York Times* in an article headlined "The Inscrutable Occidental." Wrote *Time:* "At the height of a brilliant career, he enjoys a global spotlight and an influence that most professors only read about in libraries."

Blighting Nixon's fondest dream was the specter of his worst nightmare: Henry Kissinger, darling of Georgetown and the establishment press, was garnering much of the credit for the boldest coup of his presidency. Nixon was beside himself, as Haldeman's private meeting notes reveal. "There are to be no backgrounders whatever," the president demanded. "He has to quit seeing anyone from the *Times* or the *Post,* including columnists—except Joe Alsop." (The Alsop exception was somewhat quaint: he was an amateur archaeologist and Kissinger wanted to give him the scoop on a major new Chinese discovery involving a second-century B.C. tomb of a royal couple buried in jade body stockings. The resulting column took due note of Kissinger's brilliance.) A few days later, Nixon was even more adamant. Kissinger must set up "an *absolute* wall around himself—he must *not see* on *any* basis the *New York Times,* the *Washington Post,* CBS, or NBC."

Kissinger nevertheless embarked on a briefing frenzy which assured that within a week few publications in the Western world did not have a wealth of colorful details describing how he had slipped out of Pakistan, how many hours he had met with Zhou, how gracious and brilliant the Chinese were, and how much he had eaten. "I talked in English with the verbs more carefully placed than usual," he said in a session with newsmagazine correspondents.[14]

In order to capture from Kissinger the role of briefing the press about foreign affairs, and thus reclaim control over the public glory,

Nixon had recently hired the diplomatic correspondent of ABC News, John Scali. His job was to work directly for Nixon, through Haldeman, as a consultant on foreign policy and public relations. That led, rather quickly, to a bitter relationship with Kissinger. As Scali once told a reporter: "I don't have to give a good goddamn about Henry."

A few weeks after Kissinger's trip, Nixon called Scali into the Oval Office. On his desk were four articles about Kissinger in China, and the president was fuming. "Have you seen these?" he asked.

"Yes," Scali replied, sensing what was up.

"Where do you think these stories are coming from?" the president said, knowing full well it was Kissinger.

"Well, sir, it has to be Henry."

"But didn't he promise," Nixon asked with what passed for innocence, "not to talk to reporters?" The president paused and tapped his foot. "Can you get evidence that Kissinger has been talking to these reporters?"

"I can try," Scali responded.

In those days, all reporters going into the office areas of the West Wing had to get appointment slips, and phone calls made through the switchboard were logged. Scali went to the Secret Service with a little ruse. The administration, he said, had been getting a lot of criticism for not being open enough to the press. In order to disprove that, he wanted the names of all reporters who had talked to White House aides in the past few weeks. In the report he wrote back to the president, Scali revealed that Kissinger had held twenty-four sessions with reporters in his office during that period. All except two had written about him in China.[15]

There was, however, a schizophrenic quality to Nixon's attitude. At the same time he was complaining about Kissinger's affair with the press, he was also sending reporters to see him. Buried in Haldeman's papers is a memo from July 19 from Nixon to Kissinger, at about the same time Nixon was ordering Kissinger to cut off all contacts. In it the president refers to himself by his own initials:

July 19, 1971
To: Henry Kissinger
From: The President
    One effective line you could use in your talks with the press is how RN is uniquely prepared for this meeting and how ironically in many ways he has similar character characteristics and background to Chou. I am just listing a few of the items that might be emphasized.
    1. Strong convictions.
    2. Came up through adversity.

3. At his best in a crisis. Cool. Unflappable.
4. A tough bold strong leader . . .
5. A man who takes the long view . . .
6. A man with a philosophical turn of mind.
7. A man who works without notes—in meetings with 73 heads of state RN has had hours of conversations without any notes . . .
8. A man who knows Asia . . .
9. A man who . . . is subtle and appears almost gentle. The tougher his position, usually, the lower his voice.

You could point out that most of these attributes are ones that you also saw in Chou En-Lai . . .

Although he apparently could not go so far as to push the "subtle and appears almost gentle" line, Kissinger followed the president's mandate in an interview with Hugh Sidey the next day. In an illustration of Kissinger's relationship with the president and with the press, Sidey's column in *Life* the following week concluded:

> Kissinger found many similarities between the Chinese premier and the President. Chou spoke softly, like Nixon. He did not nitpick, a diplomatic device that Nixon scorns too. Chou expounded his ideology with fervor, but it never overwhelmed realism. Nixon does the same. Chou did not have to use a note in 20 hours of conversation. That's the way Nixon talks.[16]

Kissinger would go back to China once more that year, in October, this time publicly. While there, he had the pleasure, he recalled, of seeing a revolutionary Chinese opera, "an art form of truly stupefying boredom in which villains were the incarnations of evil and wore black, good guys wore red, and as far as I could make out the girl fell in love with a tractor." The next day he was treated to a very public walk along the top of the Great Wall, pictures of which would appear on the front pages of almost every newspaper, sending Nixon into another frenzy of resentment.

The main work on this second trip was to draft—in secret from the State Department—the communiqué that Nixon and Zhou would "negotiate" at the February 1972 summit. Kissinger proposed a text that was suitably mushy, and he was stunned when Zhou responded with a diatribe about how it papered over significant differences. He bestowed upon the American draft the ultimate Chinese insult: it was, he said, the type of document that the Soviets might negotiate.

Zhou made a novel proposal: a communiqué that pointed to common interests—resisting Soviet hegemony foremost among them—

but that also had a section where both sides declared unilaterally their positions on issues where they disagreed. Kissinger was at first horrified at the notion of producing an agreement of disagreements. "But," he later wrote, "as I reflected further I began to see that the very novelty of the approach might resolve our perplexities." With some give-and-take about what would be too explosive for either side to say, a draft was settled.

The Chinese had suggested that this second visit come in mid-October, and Kissinger had agreed, without realizing that it would thus coincide with the annual vote on whether to seat China rather than Taiwan at the United Nations. The Chinese probably thought it was a subtle way for the U.S. to concede the issue. In fact, America's new representative at the U.N., George Bush, was told to try to hold the line to prevent Taiwan's expulsion. But with Kissinger so prominently paying court in Beijing, that proved impossible. Taiwan was expelled by a 76-to-35 vote.

Bush had very few sharp words for anyone in his 1987 campaign autobiography. But Kissinger, lacking the foresight to see how it might someday work to his disadvantage, offended him. "What was harder to understand was Henry's telling me that he was 'disappointed' by the final outcome on the Taiwan vote," Bush wrote. "So was I. But given the fact that we were saying one thing in New York and doing another in Washington, that outcome was inevitable."

In order to keep Kissinger out of sight while the final United Nations roll call was taken, he was ordered to lay over in Alaska for a day on his way home. In addition, Nixon was still, in Kissinger's understated phrase, "restive at the publicity I was receiving." The White House went to the trouble of arranging for his plane to taxi to a far corner of Washington's Andrews Air Force Base, out of range of press and cameras, before he could get off. "It was not," he would later say, "a heroic homecoming." [17]

A rapprochement between Beijing and Washington was likely, no matter who was president, sometime during the 1970s. China's rift with the Soviets had worsened, and the de-escalation of American involvement in Vietnam erased Beijing's fears that there might be a U.S. invasion of China. But Nixon and Kissinger deserve credit, along with Zhou, for bringing about the transformation so rapidly. Nixon's original vision and persistence forced the issue; Kissinger brought the initiative to fruition and fit it into a foreign policy framework based on a triangular global balance with America at the fulcrum.

Kissinger's depth of intellect and philosophic sophistication made him well suited (compared to, say, a William Rogers) to engage the mind and imagination of Zhou. "Just as the China opening could not have begun or continued without Nixon's vision," said Roger Morris, Kissinger's former aide and frequent critic, "it never would have been so skillfully executed without Kissinger."[18]

In the midst of the anger over Vietnam and the resultant rise in isolationism, Nixon and Kissinger were able to capture, at least for a moment, the imagination of the American people. The dramatic opening to a faraway land was enchanting, exciting, and invigorating, as well as sensible. The pessimism about America's ability to engage in creative diplomacy or be a positive force in the world was thus temporarily dispelled.

With the suddenness of ice breaking on a lake, the opening to China made the Vietnam War seem like an anachronism. For Beijing and Washington, and Moscow as well, the clash in the Southeast Asian jungle—both as an ideological struggle and as a strategic one— abruptly seemed a nettlesome historical holdover. Now that they considered the Soviets rather than the Americans to be their prime antagonists, the Chinese would no longer be as thrilled by the prospect of a triumph by North Vietnam, which was aligned to Moscow. Likewise, now that it found itself being played off against Beijing, Moscow became more interested in détente than in prolonging America's agony in Vietnam. And in the U.S., the need to stop the spread of the Chinese communist menace—which is one way the war had been justified—no longer seemed quite so pressing.[19]

Within days of Kissinger's departure, Zhou went to Hanoi to assure North Vietnam's leaders that China would not sell them out. However, he soon began to pressure Hanoi to accept a compromise that permitted the survival of the Thieu government. China even passed along an American peace proposal, thus tacitly endorsing it, and advised that "the overthrow of the Saigon puppet regime is a long-term issue," meaning that it need not be a current one. Hanoi published some of these communications when it turned against China in 1979, in order to show how it had been betrayed.[20]

On the other side of the DMZ, it should be noted, there was similar discomfort. President Thieu wondered whether Kissinger had decided that South Vietnam's survival was not important enough to interfere in the rapprochement with China. "America has been looking for a better mistress, and now Nixon has discovered China," Thieu told his aides at the time. "He does not want to have the old mistress hanging around. Vietnam has become old and ugly."[21]

Perhaps the most interesting consequence of the opening to China was that it changed the American public's conception of foreign policy. Until then, world events that required American participation had usually been portrayed as struggles between good and evil. The U.S. got involved, with the reluctance of a sheriff in a Western movie, when right needed might to protect it, or so most Americans liked to think.

Now, suddenly, foreign policy involved something quite different: not a cold war confrontation between good guys and bad guys, but an intricate web of morally ambiguous relationships that the U.S. would have to balance in order to preserve international stability. It was a role that was not as simple, not as clean, and for a nation historically uneasy about balance-of-power diplomacy, not as comfortable to sustain.

SEVENTEEN

CELEBRITY

The Secret Life
of the World's
Least Likely Sex Symbol

Power is the ultimate aphrodisiac.—KISSINGER

THE SECRET SWINGER

Barbara Howar's party for Gloria Steinem in October 1969 was, like most of those thrown by the gregarious television personality, an informal affair. But for Washington it represented the ultimate in social excitement: a gathering of the Georgetown media elite along with a sprinkling of New York glitterati, Hollywood celebrities, doyens of the Washington establishment, and a few government officials considered either hip or powerful enough. When Henry Kissinger arrived, he was carrying a brown envelope. Howar asked whether it was a secret document. "No," Kissinger replied, "it's my advance copy of *Playboy.*"

"Oh, so you're really a swinger underneath it all," said Sally Quinn, the *Washington Post* reporter who was both the chronicler and the rising star of that social set.

"Well, you couldn't call me a swinger because of my job," he said. "Why don't you just assume I'm a secret swinger?"

The "secret swinger" remark appeared a day later in Quinn's story, along with a picture of Kissinger chatting up Steinem. The

ponderous and pudgy professor was on his way to becoming an unlikely celebrity and even unlikelier sex symbol. In an indication of
which way the zeitgeist was trending, George McGovern, who had
been posing with them, was cropped out of the photograph.

Kissinger lapped up the attention. When Steinem later joked that
"I am not nor have I ever been a girlfriend of Henry Kissinger's," he
responded in a dinner speech to the White House Correspondents
Association. "I am not discouraged. After all, she did not say, 'If
elected, I will not serve.' " Later, he took William Safire aside and
asked about his blossoming social image. "Do you suppose people will
think the president's national security adviser is gaga?"[1]

During his first two years in office, Kissinger's renown was confined pretty much to a local stage. What turned him into a global
celebrity—"Super-K," as a *Newsweek* cover dubbed him—was the
July 1971 news of his covert mission to China and the revelation six
months later that he had been flying off to Paris for secret sessions
with the North Vietnamese. "Henry Kissinger is a pop figure who has
far outdistanced in public curiosity his closest rival in official Washington—Martha Mitchell," the magazine reported, referring to the
outspoken wife of the attorney general.

Kissinger, with his thick glasses and even thicker accent, hardly
had the look of a superstar. Indeed, it seemed more likely that he
would be mistaken for a prosperous deli owner from Brooklyn than an
international sex symbol. Though charming, he was not polished. His
weakness for junk food meant that he was often munching on potato
chips while he talked. His most strenuous exercise was getting a massage, and the masseur at San Clemente noted that "he did not have a
muscle in his body."

Yet he had the ingredients to be a political celebrity in the 1970s:
power, flair, a fingertip feel for publicity, and above all a sense of
presence. "He had the quality of being at the center of wherever he
stood," Kissinger once said of Mao. "It moved with him whenever he
moved." Aware of this aura in others—in addition to Mao, he saw it
in Charles de Gaulle, Lyndon Johnson, Anwar Sadat, John Kennedy,
and John Connally—Kissinger cultivated it in himself. Hugh Sidey
was once allowed to observe a Nixon cabinet session. Upon Kissinger's
arrival, Sidey wrote, all eyes were drawn to him, adding: "Kissinger
dominates the room without doing anything." This heightened presence and energy helped Kissinger seem larger than life, both as statesman and celebrity.

One of the great truths about America in the media age is that
celebrity translates into power. Being famous creates an aura that
enhances influence. The period has passed when a passion for ano-

nymity—in, say, a John McCloy or Robert Lovett—could be considered a sign of backstage clout. Kissinger knew that. "Henry marshals everything to his goals," said Bette Lord. "He realizes that fame can make him powerful as well as the other way around."

But his pursuit of celebrity was not merely a means to enhance his power. Devoid of any passion for anonymity, he enjoyed recognition. In 1969, when his son, David, came down from Cambridge for a visit, Kissinger took him to a neighborhood pizza parlor. The proprietor recognized the new national security adviser, hugged him, and gave him the pizza for free. David later recalled fondly how surprised and proud his father was, and how his personal confidence grew over the next few years as he blossomed into a celebrity.[2]

THE GEORGETOWN SOCIAL SCENE

In Washington, like other one-industry towns, social status tends to be a function of professional position rather than family heritage. The inhabitants will tolerate almost any social lapse except for a fall from power. A foreign policy expert, for example, even one with Roman numerals after his name, may have some personal friendships during the time he spends ensconced at the Brookings Institution, but only during those years when he is an assistant secretary or name-brand journalist will he have a true A-list social life.

Since social standing is so dependent on power, a backwash effect occurs: social visibility becomes a way to enhance the appearance of power. This is important, because power in Washington—who's up, who's down—is largely a game of perceptions. Consequently, the appearance of power is a large component of the reality of power.

At the pinnacle of the social pyramid during Kissinger's day were a handful of venerable columnists and editors, a few stentorian yet socially amusing senators, a rotating crew of White House aides, and some elegant and tart-tongued widows of fondly remembered eminences. The geographic center of this world was the thirty-square-block core of Georgetown, known for colonial brick townhouses and dinner parties that ended by ten P.M. Here in the evening, the machinery of governance was lubricated, alliances formed, potential adversaries co-opted, stories planted, deals intimated, pulses taken, power calibrated.

Georgetown's social scene had been stagnant since the Kennedy years, and with Nixon's election the village hostesses searched desperately for some interesting new characters. As the most colorful and socially eager of the new White House aides, the Bavarian among the Prussians, Kissinger was quickly adopted. He had a good mind, a lot of charm, a desire to please, and a talent for sharing confidences that was admired in such salons. "Henry was the only interesting one in the new White House," recalled Barbara Howar. "And he played it to a hilt. So this little, round, obscure professor who claims to be a secret swinger became the darling of the Georgetown set."

His social world was dominated by the media elite that Nixon so despised. There was columnist Joseph Alsop and his sharp, sophisticated wife, Susan Mary; when Nancy Maginnes was in town, which was more often than the gossip columnists suspected, she had tea with them each afternoon. On Sundays, the Alsops would usually have Kissinger over for dinner along with Tom Braden and his spunky wife, Joan. Joseph Kraft, when he was not feuding with Kissinger, and his wife, Polly, an accomplished artist, were also part of the crowd. So were David and Susan Brinkley, Rowland and Kay Evans, and as the honorary chairwoman, Katharine Graham, owner of the *Washington Post*. Among the few nonjournalists were labor leader Lane Kirkland and his wife, Irena. The only other White House official who dared dwell in such realms was economic adviser Peter Peterson.[3]

Kissinger never entertained at home. In fact, he never even cooked for himself. "He'd rather go hungry than have to cook," Nancy Maginnes told friends, "which is saying a lot." He lived in a cramped two-bedroom rental on Rock Creek Park, for which his secretary had bought all of the furniture at a discount store. There were no comfortable chairs and no conveniently located lamps, but otherwise it had the decor of an early Holiday Inn. The only decorative elements, other than books piled about, were pictures of Kissinger with a wide variety of foreign officials. Once a week a cleaning lady would come in the early morning; she usually left about an hour later.

Despite Kissinger's reputation, his bedroom was no romantic lair. The bare room had two twin beds, one of them used as a laundry dump. A woman who stole a glance later reported that socks and underwear were scattered about and the mess "had so repulsive an aspect that it was hard to imagine anyone living there."

His only personal indulgence was his cream-white Mercedes. Until he was assigned a Secret Service driver, thus protecting his safety as well as that of other local motorists, he used to career around wearing black leather driving gloves and a rather distracted air.[4]

When he wished to entertain, Kissinger would often take friends to The Empress, a favorite Chinese restaurant with a large private room. Bette Bao Lord would help manage the affairs and pick the menu. She and Winston were among the few social friends Kissinger had drawn from his staff. Sometimes the Sonnenfeldts would be included, and before their resignations, the Lakes and Morrises.

For more formal entertaining, Kissinger would borrow the Bradens' rambling home in Chevy Chase to throw a dinner party of his own. The party he gave there in 1970, for example, was a seated dinner for thirty-two and included the Haldemans and Ehrlichmans among others. He was never able to ignite, however, a mutual admiration between his White House colleagues and the Georgetown set.

But mainly he enjoyed going out and being seen in public. On one occasion, he was due to have dinner at Rive Gauche, a trendy Washington bistro, with Kirk and Ann Douglas and the columnist Tom Braden and his wife, Joan. Nancy Maginnes was down from New York. Kissinger arrived late, and Douglas had already chosen a table in a secluded alcove near the back. Kissinger objected and asked for a "better" table in the front. There they ate, in full view, with people coming up for autographs and handshakes. Douglas was annoyed: Kissinger was in his glory. More than even most movie stars, Kissinger enjoyed being recognized as a celebrity.

STARLET-EYED IN HOLLYWOOD

Before 1969, Kissinger had made a dozen visits to the Rand Corporation, a think tank in Santa Monica, but had never once visited nearby Hollywood. As his celebrity status grew, the world of starlets and Tinseltown glamour suddenly opened up to him.

Perhaps it was the adolescent instincts he had never been able to indulge while growing up. Or perhaps it was because he had always been fascinated with American popular culture. More likely, it was simply the chance to party with stars and go out with starlets. Whatever the reason, Kissinger threw himself into the Hollywood social scene with an enthusiasm he had previously shown only for back-channel negotiations.

So even as he remained essentially a private person, one who did not bare his soul to other people, Kissinger sought out the limelight and a high-visibility social life. Karen Lerner, one of his West Coast dates, recalled that he asked her out one night and suggested that they attend the opening of the musical *Gigi* in Los Angeles. That was absurd, she said, reminding him that she was divorced from the author, Alan Jay Lerner, and would certainly not want to seem to upstage him by arriving with Kissinger. Let's go somewhere else to dinner, she suggested. Instead, he broke the date and asked out the actress Jill St. John. They were pictured together at the opening on page one of *Women's Wear Daily.* "Henry and Jill played their loving couple role more convincingly than the cast," the paper reported.

Even in Hollywood, where friendships are formed with a magical immediacy that eludes people elsewhere, it is striking that Jill St. John as well as producer Robert Evans both claimed that Kissinger was their best friend. He first met Jill St. John in early 1970 when she was seated next to him at a dinner given by Kirk Douglas. He began to telephone her late in the evenings just to talk. "It was a great tension reliever for him just to talk," she recalled. "We'd talk often and long." It worked both ways. "Whenever I had problems or felt depressed, even if it was three in the morning, I could call him and he would be loyal and talk for hours."

Kissinger dated her more often than any other movie star, so much so that his father, sensing that St. John did not sound like a Jewish name, called him to ask about her religion. Fortunately for his father's sensibilities, he was able to assure him (truthfully) that her real name was Jill Oppenheim, and that she was Jewish. But there was, in fact, never a romance. "Just a great friendship," she said.

Mainly they would go out to Los Angeles restaurants where they would be sure to be seen, places like the Coconut Grove and The Bistro. He would talk about how his old friends from the academic world were disloyal, how they had broken their friendships with him simply because they had disagreed with his policies. Hollywood people, Miss St. John told him, were much more real and understanding. "Since we were used to playing roles, we knew how to separate a person from his public policies," she said. "In addition, we have all had flops and we know what it's like."

When he was in public with Jill St. John, there would be a lot of fondling and, whenever eyes or cameras turned to them, a boyishly happy leer on Kissinger's face. He liked running his fingers through her red curls in a display that other diners sometimes found unseemly. Though resistant to real emotional intimacy with his starlet dates, he enjoyed its outward forms. He told her that he felt more open and free around her and his other Hollywood friends because they were more honest about their feelings and more natural at displaying them. She was at first a little puzzled, friends say, when he would drop her off at the end of the evening and not come inside. But she came to the conclusion that he mainly liked her because he could talk to her.

Like many of Kissinger's social friends, Jill St. John was a strong opponent of the war. After going to Vietnam on a Bob Hope Christmas tour, she came back and worked for Eugene McCarthy's 1968 peace candidacy. Over dinner she liked to argue with Kissinger. "He could run rings around me and punch holes in my arguments," she recalled, "but he could never convince me."

Nevertheless, she was his best supporting actress in public. At a Hollywood party thrown for Nixon during the 1972 campaign, she told reporters, "Henry has been trying for three years and he's finally gotten me to support the president." To which Kissinger added, "And you guys thought I'd been wasting my time out here in Hollywood." The party, at Nixon's villa in San Clemente, featured a cast of vintage Hollywood characters: Charlton Heston, who was a leader of Democrats for Nixon; George Hamilton, the perpetually tan former suitor of Lynda Bird Johnson; Frank Sinatra, a nominal Democrat who arrived with Vice President Agnew; Jim Brown, the Cleveland Browns fullback turned actor; Jimmy Durante; and Jack Benny. But the *New York Times* reported in its somewhat dry style: "The center of attention, of course, was Henry A. Kissinger, the president's national security adviser, who was accompanied by Jill St. John, an actress."[5]

Among the other stars Kissinger dated were Samantha Eggar, Shirley MacLaine, Marlo Thomas, Candice Bergen, and Liv Ullmann. He was photographed with the likes of Raquel Welch, Elizabeth Taylor, and Liza Minnelli. But he also had a weakness for young, beautiful lesser-known types who offered, at least in the abstract, the aura of something more illicit.

Lada Edmund, for example, was a blond Hollywood stuntwoman in her twenties, known for her agility at falling off motorcycles and driving cars into brick walls, talents that were displayed in such films as *Revolt of the Female Chain Gang.* One afternoon, she was spending an afternoon with Jill St. John while Kissinger was around, and he surprised her by coming on to her. "I thought it was a little weird with Jill sitting there," she later said, "but he and Jill have a strange relationship. They seem to get off on each other's sexual achievements."

So at St. John's urging, she accepted Kissinger's invitation for a date the following evening. It was not exactly what she expected. They went to a star-encrusted benefit for Milton Berle, after which Kissinger and his Secret Service driver dropped her off at home. He told her that he could not come in for a visit because the Secret Service felt that the narrow road she lived on could be blocked too easily. "And that was the end of my Kissinger experience."

Judy Brown, star of the X-rated Danish work *Threesome,* had a longer and somewhat more tumultuous relationship. She visited him in Palm Beach, where they lay in the sun, he reading *The Godfather* and she *The New Centurions.* They also went swimming together in the ocean at San Clemente, trailed by Secret Service agents. The affair ended rather publicly at The Bistro in Beverly Hills when paparazzi, tipped off by her press agent, arrived in force. Although the restaurant was not the sort of place one goes for privacy, Kissinger was upset at the prospect of that sort of publicity. He made her sneak out with him through the kitchen. "If you're so worried about being recognized," she asked, "why don't you take out secretaries?"

"I don't like secretaries," he said, reflecting a feeling that was often mutual. "I like actresses."

"Well, you can't have your cake and eat it," she shot back in a somewhat unclear metaphor.

"Then I'll do without my cake," he responded.

Miss Brown ended up revealing all in a fan magazine. "I forget that they are actresses," Kissinger later said. "Is there no end to my naïveté?"

Studio executives, such as Robert Evans of Paramount, were all eager to supply him with names, make introductions and phone calls, because they knew that fixing him up with one of their hot starlets would be good for all involved. Many young actresses remember getting a call from a studio boss and being offered the chance for a date with Kissinger to a high-visibility event; few declined.[6]

Why did Kissinger like socializing with starlets? When asked that question by the gossip columnist Joyce Haber, he replied, "I go out with actresses because I'm not apt to marry one," a comment that can be read on many levels. A somewhat more exalted journalist, the Italian inquisitor Oriana Fallaci, asked a similar question in 1972, and Kissinger's answer was less charming: "I think that my playboy reputation has been and still is useful because it serves to reassure people, to show them I'm not a museum piece. . . . For me women are only a diversion, a hobby. Nobody devotes too much time with his hobbies."[7]

Among Kissinger's male friends in Hollywood were the actors Kirk Douglas and Gregory Peck, and the media moguls Herbert Schlosser of NBC and Taft Schreiber of MCA. But the one who put the most energy into a friendship was Robert Evans, the actor and producer who was then the production chief at Paramount Studios. Their friendship began when Evans gave David and Elizabeth Kissinger backstage tours of the Paramount studios. "We were just excuses," David recalled. "Dad wanted to go. When we met Lana Turner, I asked who she was. 'You have destroyed one of the great moments of my life,' he joked."

Evans began helping Kissinger meet whatever actresses struck his fancy. One year, Kissinger told him that he wanted to spend New Year's Eve with Candice Bergen, an understandable desire. Evans called her up and she agreed. Along with Evans and Ali McGraw, who was then his wife, and one other couple, they had dinner at Evans's house and watched Woody Allen's *Sleeper* in his screening room.

Kissinger returned the favor in March 1972. *The Godfather,* which Evans had produced, was opening in Manhattan, and at the last moment Marlon Brando backed out of attending. Evans, who can get quite distraught at such things, knew he needed a great celebrity to make the premiere a success. He called Kissinger. It was not a good time: the North Vietnamese offensive had just begun, the Paris peace talks had been broken off, Kissinger was about to leave on a secret mission to Moscow, and he was planning the mining of Haiphong. So he begged off. "But I need you here," Evans pressed. Reluctantly, Kissinger took a flight up that night. Among those at the opening were Ali McGraw, Raquel Welch, Jack Nicholson, and Polly Bergen. "But the superstar was Henry Kissinger," *Time*'s people page reported. "So many people wanted to be seen talking to the president's national security adviser that the curtain was delayed about 15 minutes."

Kissinger's Hollywood diversions were a way to escape the atmosphere in San Clemente, where Nixon spent weeks at a time. As an alternative, Kissinger would helicopter to Palm Springs to visit producer Hal Wallis or baking magnate Ted Cummings. "He liked to get away to where he could hang around rich and celebrity types," said Lloyd Shearer, an editor of *Parade* magazine and sometime Kissinger friend.

By 1972, Kissinger's celebrity as an unexpected sex symbol would become an international gag. The *Harvard Lampoon* published a parody of *Cosmopolitan* that year featuring a foldout of Kissinger reclining nude on a Chinese-panda rug over the caption, "Forbidden fruit of the executive branch." (It was actually the body of a Boston cabdriver, with Kissinger's head attached.) More than 1.1 million copies were sold. Saigon's largest daily newspaper carried a picture of the centerfold on the day that Kissinger arrived there with a peace plan worked out in Paris; Thieu assumed that Kissinger had posed for the picture and was flabbergasted. Georgi Arbatov bought a copy and brought it back to Brezhnev, who pinned it up in his office.[8]

Nixon and his men were at first amused by Kissinger's social dallying. Ehrlichman even had a scantily clad photograph of Jill St. John blown up as a poster for Air Force One. When Kissinger was invited to take a table and bring seven dates to the annual dinner of the National Women's Political Caucus, he somewhat disingenuously requested the opinion of Charles Colson, in his capacity as White House political director, whether it would be proper to attend. Colson replied:

This is like the Pope seeking religious guidance from the vicar of my local Protestant church. Who am I to tell you about women? The National Women's Political Caucus are the bomb throwers—the Gloria Steinems of the world and a lot of your *other* girlfriends. I wouldn't be caught dead in the place—but then, I am not the Administration's "swinger." Under the circumstances, I don't see how you can possibly avoid it. . . . You simply have to go and run the terrible risk that you will not be attacked physically."

Nixon knew that the "swinger" image served a purpose. "I think it was helpful," he later said. "There were not many smiles in those days." In addition, the shapeliness of various actresses was something that Nixon and his pal Bebe Rebozo could joke about with Kissinger, a rare source of locker-room camaraderie. "It was great fun," Nixon recalled, "because we could talk about all those beautiful broads." At the helicopter pad in San Clemente one afternoon when Kissinger was flying up to Hollywood for the evening, Nixon patted him on the back and said loudly enough for the press to hear, "Don't do anything I wouldn't do tonight, Henry."

But there was also in Nixon a little envy, which came through when he tried to sound condescending about Kissinger's social life. "He likes parties," Nixon once said. "I despise them because I've been to so many. I used to like them, but Henry will learn to despise them, too, after he's been through a few more."

Eventually, Nixon's envy and disdain won out. At one morning staff meeting in 1971, he began ranting at Haldeman about "Henry's insistence on flitting around with movie stars." Haldeman, who agreed, said that it was because Kissinger loved being lionized. "He's making a fool of himself," Nixon insisted. "Grown men know better. Henry has got to stop this. Do something. Do something."

There was little Haldeman could do other than jot down the orders on his yellow legal pad. The only concrete step he took involved state dinners. Kissinger had made a pact with White House social director Lucy Winchester to be seated next to the prettiest women at formal affairs. When she let him down, he would accost her the next day and complain, "Lucy! You sat me next to a ninety-eight-year-old crone!" In 1971, Haldeman sent out an "action memo" reflecting a conversation with Nixon:

> In seating at State Dinners, the President feels that Henry should not always be put next to the most glamorous woman present. He should be put by an intelligent and interesting dinner partner and we should shift from the practice

of putting him next to the best looking one. It's starting to cause unfavorable talk that serves no useful purpose.[9]

THE ULTIMATE APHRODISIAC

One evening at Trader Vic's in the Los Angeles Hilton, the dancer Ann Miller saw Kissinger openly flirting and holding hands with Jill St. John. The next evening, Miller was Kissinger's partner at a Hollywood dinner party. In a friendly way, she criticized him for making such a frivolous public display "while our boys in Vietnam are getting their heads shot off."

Kissinger suddenly darkened. "Miss Miller," he said, no longer calling her Ann, "you don't know anything about me. I was miserable in a marriage for most of my life. I never had any fun. Now is my chance to enjoy myself. When this administration goes out, I'm going back to being a professor. But while I'm in the position I'm in, I'm damn well going to make it count."

With the boyish glee of a senior on prom night and the twinkle of a middle-aged rake, Kissinger reveled in the attention of women. He enjoyed their company and enjoyed being seen enjoying their company. Even on a Saturday at lunchtime, he would sometimes come into the White House mess escorting a striking blonde, sit at a table with Peter Peterson, and then whisper to him, "Eat your heart out, Pete."

His soft spot for pretty women could even defuse his temper. Whenever his staffers had a scheduling snafu sure to throw him into a tantrum, they would delegate the best-looking young secretary they could find to break the news to him. Likewise, the White House press office tended to use Diane Sawyer, then an assistant there, to perform similar tasks. It almost always worked.

The reverse was also true: women tended to be attracted to him. A poll of Playboy Club bunnies in 1972 ranked him number one as "the man I would most like to go out on a date with." His explanation for the phenomenon was that women were turned on by his power. As he had said in one of his most famous lines: "Power is the ultimate aphrodisiac."

Kissinger's secret with women was not all that different from his one with men whom he wanted to charm: he flattered them, he listened to them, he nodded a lot, and he made eye contact. But unlike the way he was with most men, Kissinger was exceedingly patient with women who wanted to talk. "Very few men in the 1970s actually listened to women," according to Bette Lord. "Henry talked to you seriously and probed for what you knew or thought." He was someone who could, and would, make a Jill St. John feel intelligent or a Shirley MacLaine feel politically savvy. "Next to Ingmar Bergman, he is the most interesting man I have ever met," said Liv Ullmann. "He is surrounded by a fascinating aura, a strange field of light, and he catches you in some kind of invisible net."

Over long dinners at public places, he would listen with sympathy while women talked about themselves, their lives, their hopes, and even sometimes their slightly wacky New Age philosophies. He would call them on the telephone late at night and talk for an hour or more at a time. "He was a great friend, especially a telephone friend, always there when you needed him," said Jill St. John.

The dirty little secret about Kissinger's relationship with women was that there was no dirty little secret. He liked to go out with them, but not home with them. His fascination with affairs tended to be foreign rather than domestic. "Henry's idea of being romantic was to slow down his car when he dropped you off after a date," said Howar. He may have been, in fact, the most celibate lecher in Washington. "People say, yes, he doesn't do anything with these girls," his friend Peter Peterson once remarked. "But that's beside the point. Nobody cared whether Sherman Adams actually wore the vicuña coat." [10]

A typical relationship was the one he had with Jan Golding (now Jan Cushing Amory), a smart, attractive, and socially aggressive New Yorker he dated in 1970 and 1971. She was twenty-two at the time, single and living in Manhattan. Kirk Douglas had given Kissinger her name, and he called out of the blue one afternoon and invited her to come down for dinner.

When she flew down, one of Kissinger's junior military aides picked her up at the shuttle gate and drove her to meet Kissinger at the Jockey Club, a high-visibility haunt in the old Fairfax Hotel. In the middle of dinner, he was called to the phone and, much to Golding's annoyance, stayed away for forty minutes, mumbling some apologies upon his return about the secretary of state needing his advice. But when he was with her, he was very solicitous, asking what she planned to do with her life and what she thought of various issues. "It was heady," she recalled.

Golding and Kissinger dated for the next five months or so, but only in Washington, because he had made a promise to Nancy Maginnes that he would not go out with any other women when in New York. But though Kissinger and Golding were both single, and she was willing, nothing romantic ever developed. Only once did they go back to his apartment; and when they arrived, an aide was there fielding telephone calls. By Golding's count, the phone rang forty times. "You couldn't do anything romantic in that place even if you were dying to," she recalled.

There were some awkward efforts, Golding later said, at injecting something more into their relationship, partly out of a sense that the other person wanted it that way. "We both felt we should try to make it romantic, but it ended up just being a friendship," she said. "I just don't think Henry was interested in sex. When it came time to perform —well, I just think he was too preoccupied for it. He didn't have time for it. Power for him may have been the aphrodisiac, but it was also the climax."

The relationship continued by telephone until it finally concluded amicably. She wrote Kissinger a note saying that she was marrying Fred Cushing, an investment banker and Newport social fixture, and moving with him to Paris. He should give a call if he was ever there.

During the Paris peace talks in 1972, he did call, inviting her to lunch. Should she bring Freddy? No, said Kissinger, that would spoil the fun. She made a reservation at Chez Tante, near the embassy, a no-star but respectable bistro about to enjoy its moment of fame. Kissinger's talks in Paris were no longer secret by then, and hordes of journalists dogged his trail. At the end of the meal, the maître d' mentioned that the press had gathered out front, but he could easily slip them out the back. No, Kissinger said. They marched out the front door, and instead of heading right for the waiting car, he walked her down the block for a while until all the photographers had gotten their fill. The picture of him with "an unidentified young blonde"—or "The Mystery Woman" as the Daily News put it—was on front pages around the world.

Jan Cushing also gave, with her husband, a series of dinners in Kissinger's honor that fall in Paris. When she asked him who should be invited, he said he wanted to be with fun international socialites and jet-setters. The guest lists ranged from minor European royalty to tycoons such as Adnan Khashoggi (who hugged him and said, "We are all Semites," during one discussion of the Middle East). It was a crowd Kissinger was beginning to enjoy. They, in turn, were fascinated by the inside anecdotes and insights he would dispense, although Freddy Cushing liked to bring Kissinger down a notch every now and then by shifting the conversation from politics to topics that would have been considered more suitable for a table at Newport.[11]

Another testament to Kissinger's lascivious celibacy was Marsha Metrinko, who had competed in a variety of beauty contests and had been named "Miss Love Bundle" by a Washington trade group. Although they went out dozens of times in both Washington and California, "mostly we ate," she recalled. "I was always home by midnight. He usually had work to do later."

Even when they were out to dinner, Kissinger would continually be called from the table. "There always seemed to be a crisis," Metrinko said. Yet when they were together, he was very attentive. "He's a very physical person. He touches your hair and holds hands under the table. He notices your hair and your nail polish." Much of their relationship was on the telephone; as they talked, she made a needlepoint map of the world set in a pillow, which she sent to him for his birthday.[12]

One French would-be paramour of Kissinger's even went public with her lament of unrequited love. Danielle Hunebelle was a prominent free-lance Parisian journalist. In the course of doing a television piece on him, she became rather more interested in her subject than even the laxer press standards of the day condoned. Particularly perplexing to her was Kissinger's manner of flirting with her publicly, talking to her sweetly by phone, but keeping her at bay when she tried to get close. "Giving up on understanding him," she wrote in a heartbroken confessional paperback titled *Dear Henry,* "I began to love him."

Hunebelle had his home number, and she would sometimes call early in the morning. He would be kind, reassuring, full of promises about setting up a lunch sometime soon. Once, after she had left a note in the door of his apartment, he called her back at two in the morning using, she recalled, "that warm, slow, emotion-filled voice that troubles me sensually."

Yet on those rare occasions when a lunch or dinner was arranged, he would turn cooler. His first wife, he later told her, had subjected him to emotional "blackmail" for years. "I can't stand pressure," he said, "above all from another woman."

Even by Hunebelle's own account, Kissinger spent most of his time trying to brush her off. He never answered her passionate letters and usually had his assistant call to cancel dates with her. One of their last times together was in early September 1970, just at the start of his month dealing with crises in Jordan, Cuba, and Chile. Hunebelle had hoped to sell her black-and-white French TV documentary on him to CBS, but the network decided instead to make one of its own. As a consolation, he took her to lunch at Sans Souci. Joe Kraft and Art Buchwald were among the regulars there who were amused at the somewhat emotional scene.

Over duck à l'orange, she chided him for going out with so many starlets. "Those actresses?" he replied. "They're getting free publicity out of me. I don't attach any importance to them."

She became rather emotional and asked for the key to his apartment. If she had it, she said, she would fix it up and fill it with flowers and make it romantic. "What good would that do," he responded, "since I only go there to sleep?"

"Henry, sometimes you give me the impression that you're taking revenge on me for your wife."

"Danielle, it's tragic. I have a lot of affection for you. But in my situation you have to run away from any emotion. I won't let myself get tenderized."

"Do you lie sometimes?"

"Of course," he replied. "When I have to defend myself."

Thus Kissinger was able to extricate himself from a somewhat fanatical female admirer and return to dealing with the PLO hijackings that had just occurred and the escalating crisis in Jordan.

His lunch with Hunebelle was on the same day as his final interview with Mike Wallace and the CBS crew. When Hunebelle came by the White House, she was enraged to discover that the CBS show was being handled by Margaret Osmer, a producer who had once quizzed Hunebelle in Paris about Kissinger. Osmer, a highly professional journalist, occasionally dated Kissinger, but she was able to keep her relationship in perspective.

Osmer was well versed in two of Kissinger's fascinations: the media world and foreign policy. (She later became director of meetings at the Council on Foreign Relations.) Kissinger enjoyed her company. One well-publicized date they had was when he was being trailed by journalists in Paris in July 1971, on his way home from his secret trip to Beijing and after another secret meeting with Le Duc Tho. *Newsweek's* Mel Elfin would later say that Kissinger was the only person who used his personal life to conceal his professional activities.[13]

Though he would become famous for his flirtations with starlets, Kissinger tended to prefer dating media-savvy professionals such as Diane Sawyer, Margaret Osmer, and Barbara Howar. He met Howar in 1969 at a party given by Evangeline Bruce, wife of veteran diplomat David Bruce. "Let's sit on this couch where we can touch knees," Howar said in her rolling Carolina accent. He told her he and Nixon were going to Midway the next day to discuss troop withdrawals with President Thieu, but after that he would like to call her for dinner.

"If you bring about a withdrawal from Vietnam," she said, "you can call me and do whatever you want with me."

"Dinner will be sufficient," he said. They subsequently became friends.[14]

Howar knew, soon after they started going out, that Kissinger was serious about only one woman, Nancy Maginnes, the lanky and well-bred Rockefeller researcher he had first gotten to know at the 1964 Republican convention. "She was very cool," recalled Howar, "and really the only one for Henry." Unbeknownst to all except his close friends, Maginnes had been coming down almost every weekend, staying at the Hay-Adams or the Fairfax and avoiding the high-visibility social scene. She was even familiar with the inside of his apartment, although the thought of how slovenly it was could make her recoil years later. She once had a loose button and poked around for a pair of scissors, only to discover that there was none in the house.

Unlike the other women in his life, Nancy Maginnes had the aversion to publicity expected of a well-bred lady. She came with the seal of approval of Nelson Rockefeller, for whom she worked as a foreign policy researcher, and with the social cachet of membership in New York's Colony Club. Kissinger had even once proposed marriage to her, shortly after they had first met at the Republican convention of 1964, and would do so again.[15]

EIGHTEEN

WINTER OF THE LONG KNIVES

After a Mishandled War, Kissinger Hits a Low Point

> *In every negotiation Castlereagh had to fight a more desperate battle with his Cabinet than with his foreign colleagues.* —KISSINGER, A WORLD RESTORED, 1957

THE INDIA-PAKISTAN WAR, DECEMBER 1971

Avid colonialists though they were, the British never mastered the art of decolonization. After finally granting India its freedom, the British created Pakistan in 1947 by carving off the Moslem areas. Pakistan had two segments, separated by a thousand miles of Hindu-dominated India between them. West Pakistan, inhabited largely by Punjabis, politically dominated the poorer East Pakistan, inhabited mainly by Bengalis. The only bond that tied the two Pakistans was their shared Islamic faith, which could not fully subsume their economic and ethnic differences.

The separatist sentiment in East Pakistan, which had taken to calling itself Bangladesh, was aggravated by a devastating cyclone in November 1970 that killed two hundred thousand people. In national assembly elections the following month, the Awami League, which favored autonomy for East Pakistan, won 167 out of 169 seats there. In West Pakistan, Zulfikar Ali Bhutto, who opposed splitting the nation, emerged as the strongest force. The results thwarted President Yahya Khan's plan to turn over power to a new civilian government.

Yahya Kahn's solution—which even his defender Kissinger would later label "reckless"—was to order a brutal crackdown and have the leader of the Awami League, Sheik Mujibur Rahman (known as Mujib), arrested. Sweeping into the city of Dacca with American M-24 tanks, the Pakistani army in March 1971 began a systematic massacre of its own citizens in an effort to crush the movement for an independent Bangladesh.

Even in a century marked by genocidal madness, the crackdown was horrifying. The women's dorm at the university was set ablaze, then the students were machine-gunned to death as they ran out. Newspapers carried descriptions of soldiers gouging out the eyes or crudely amputating the arms of hundreds of living children, then killing their parents. Within three days, some ten thousand people were killed; by the end of the year, the death toll would be more than half a million.

In addition, *10 million* refugees began to flee over the border into India in what was probably the greatest exodus of its kind in modern history. The flood led India's prime minister, Indira Gandhi, to call for autonomy for East Pakistan. Thus the gruesome civil war in Pakistan set the stage for a showdown with its historic rival India.

With a unanimity seldom seen in the State Department, a cry went up to denounce Pakistan's brutality. "This is a time when principles make best policies," cabled Kenneth Keating, the ambassador to India. As the carnage continued and Washington remained silent, the American consul in East Pakistan, Archer Blood, sent a petition from nineteen American diplomats based there. The failure to denounce the suppression of democracy, it said, "serves neither our moral interests, broadly defined, nor our national interests, narrowly defined." An interdepartmental group—composed of officials from State, Defense, the CIA, and Kissinger's own staff—concluded that the Pakistani army's brutality made it in America's interest to move closer to India.[1]

But Kissinger had other considerations in early 1971. Pakistan and its president were providing the secret back channel to China. April 1971 began with the American Ping-Pong team going to Beijing and ended with the letter conveyed by Pakistan's ambassador inviting Nixon to send an envoy. Kissinger sent back word thanking Yahya Khan "for his delicacy and tact," an odd description for a ruler who at that moment was being portrayed in papers around the world as waging the bloodiest of political crackdowns.

Because he was anxious not to disrupt this crucial channel or seem ungrateful to President Yahya Khan, the distortion of American policy toward Pakistan became yet another hidden cost of Kissinger's fetish for secrecy. He also felt that larger strategic issues—most notably, how to create a triangular relationship with China—should outweigh moral sentiments. He saw the tensions between Pakistan and India not in local terms but as a proxy confrontation between the U.S. and the Soviet Union. The conflict thus illustrated two of the basic themes of his diplomacy: the primacy of realism over moral concerns, and the tendency to see disputes through the prism of the Soviet-American competition.

Reinforcing Kissinger's pro-Pakistan outlook was Nixon's personal bias against India's Indira Gandhi. In conversation, he referred to her as "the bitch," except when he was angry; then he called her worse. She exuded an air of moral superiority, and her condescending silences in conversation, Kissinger noted, "brought out all of Nixon's latent insecurities."

After returning from his secret trip to China in July 1971, Kissinger presented a geopolitical analysis to a meeting of the president and his top advisers in San Clemente. India was likely to use the Bangladesh crisis as a pretext to dismember its historic enemy Pakistan. The Soviet Union was encouraging India, acting like "a pyromaniac" in an incendiary situation. If India attacked, China might come to Pakistan's aid. The Soviets would then come in on India's side. America should stick by Pakistan in order to discourage an Indian attack and Soviet meddling.[2]

The analysis, while brilliant, had one flaw: it was incorrect. India would claim throughout the crisis that it had no designs on Pakistani territory, and it ended up acting accordingly. The Soviets would claim they were counseling restraint, and they acted accordingly. The Chinese never offered to come to Pakistan's aid. And it would be Pakistan, not India, that launched the first full-scale attack.

The State Department disagreed with Kissinger. Its assessment, backed by the CIA, was that India did not plan to attack West Pakistan nor did the Soviets want them to. In the event of a war, Washington should work with India and the Soviet Union to prevent the Chinese from getting involved. When the department made this argument at a Senior Review Group meeting at the end of July, Kissinger blew up. "The President always says to tilt toward Pakistan, but every proposal I get is in the opposite direction," he said. "Sometimes I think I'm in a nuthouse." It was his first recorded use of the word *tilt,* which was soon to become the watchword for the administration's policy.[3]

Kissinger was further infuriated in August when India and the Soviet Union announced a new friendship treaty. The State Department was sanguine: the pact did not include the strong mutual defense obligations Moscow had with its closer allies, and an intelligence report suggested that it could serve as a useful restraining influence on New Delhi. Kissinger, however, called the treaty a "bombshell" and the intelligence report "fatuous."

The Soviet-Indian pact was partly a fallout from Kissinger's Chinese trip. Though the treaty was two years in the making, India sent an emissary to Moscow to conclude it right after Kissinger returned from Beijing. New Delhi's leaders were offended when they discovered that Kissinger's visit to India was just part of an elaborate charade to cover his trip to China. His flurry of briefings extolling how he and Yahya Khan had handled all of the logistics did not help. By forging a new American tie to China, which was an ally of Pakistan's, Kissinger drove India closer to the Soviets.

This was the unhappy situation when Indira Gandhi came to Washington for a state visit in November 1971. Kissinger later called her sessions at the White House the "most unfortunate meetings Nixon had with any foreign leader."

Even when she praised Nixon for opening up to China, Gandhi's tone struck Kissinger as that of a professor complimenting a slightly backward student. She then proceeded to ignore Nixon's points about the need for restraint in dealing with Pakistan and instead launched into a history lesson on the dispute. Nixon retaliated by keeping her waiting for forty-five minutes when she arrived for their second meeting.

Gandhi was surprised at the dominant role that Kissinger played in the talks. "Mr. Nixon would talk for a few minutes and would then say, 'Isn't that right, Henry?' and from then on Henry would talk on for quite a while," she later recalled. "And then Nixon would say two words and then he would say, 'Wouldn't you say so, Henry?' I would talk with Henry rather than Nixon."

Kissinger came away from the meeting convinced that Gandhi's aim was to destroy Pakistan. This fixed idea colored not only his recommendations but his perception of the facts. Thus, on November 22, when India conducted a cross-border operation into East Pakistan in support of Bengali separatists, Kissinger was one of the few (then or in retrospect) who considered this incident the start of full-scale war. "I had no doubt that we were now witnessing the beginning of an India-Pakistan war and that India had started it," he later wrote. The State Department, on the other hand, downplayed the seriousness of these skirmishes; even Pakistan's President Yahya Khan cabled the next day to say he still hoped a war could be avoided.[4]

Most objective historians instead date the onset of the 1971 India-Pakistan war as December 3, when Pakistan committed an act that was as reckless as its crackdown the previous March: it launched a sneak attack on India from *West* Pakistan, where there had previously been no fighting. This allowed India to engage in an all-out retaliation while retaining its pretenses as a peace-loving victim.

At the WSAG (crisis committee) meeting that day, Kissinger demanded that the State Department accept Nixon's pro-Pakistan "tilt." "I am getting hell every half hour from the President that we are not being tough enough on India," Kissinger told the assistant secretaries gathered in the Situation Room. "He has just called me again. He does not believe we are carrying out his wishes. He wants to tilt in favor of Pakistan."

What was most notable about the meeting was the way Kissinger was indisputably in charge of the government. Most of the paragraphs in the minutes of the session begin "Dr. Kissinger ordered" or "Dr. Kissinger also directed" or "Dr. Kissinger asked." The verb used for the other players is "suggested." The absent president is invoked occasionally by Kissinger as if he were a distant specter.[5]

But Kissinger was no mere channeler for a reclusive Nixon. Instead, he egged Nixon on. "If we collapse now," he told the president on December 5, "the Soviets won't respect us for it; the Chinese will despise us." The result, especially when compounded by America's inexorable withdrawal from Vietnam, would be to encourage Soviet "adventures" elsewhere. In another conversation with Nixon, Kissinger put it more bluntly: "We can't let a friend of ours and China's get screwed in a conflict with a friend of Russia's."

An odd display of Nixonian reality came the next day when the president convened the National Security Council twice—once for a sham meeting performed for NBC News cameras, and then for a serious one that bore little resemblance to what viewers saw. "Get the facts out about what we've done for the refugees and so forth and so on," Nixon told his advisers for the benefit of the cameras. Then, in the real session, Kissinger and Rogers got into a brawl. Rogers accused Kissinger of taking the "Chinese position," and Kissinger later groused that "Rogers had no grasp of the geopolitical stakes." Nixon, as usual, refused to confront Rogers at the meeting, so the secretary came to believe that the "tilt" policy was merely a product of Kissinger's baleful influence.[6]

Because the pro-Pakistan tilt was not popular in Congress or among the public, Kissinger tried to keep it secret. He gave a not-for-attribution press briefing on December 7 in which he labeled as "totally inaccurate" the allegations that "the administration is anti-Indian." A new credibility gap was promptly created when Kissinger's briefing was made public by Senator Barry Goldwater, who was trying to be helpful, and the "tilt" comments were revealed by Jack

Anderson, who was trying to expose the hypocrisy. In addition, Ambassador Keating sent a cable, with a low-level classification that ensured it would leak (it did in a day), punching holes in Kissinger's briefing point by point.[7]

Feeding Kissinger's anti-Indian frenzy was a CIA report that arrived that day. It said that Gandhi had told her cabinet she would not accept a cease-fire until some Pakistani-controlled territory in a disputed part of Kashmir was captured for India and until "Pakistan's armor and air force capabilities" had been eliminated. In his memoirs, perhaps simply by mistake, Kissinger quotes the CIA report as saying that Gandhi wanted to eliminate Pakistan's "army" rather than merely its "armor," meaning its offensive tank forces. At the time, Kissinger's exaggeration of the report was even more pronounced: he gave it a far greater credence than most other officials (including CIA Director Helms) did, and he insisted that it meant Gandhi wanted to "dismember" and "destroy" West Pakistan.

Kissinger's other driving thesis was that India should be viewed as the Soviet Union's proxy in a big-power confrontation, a notion that would have surprised the world's most populous democracy. The result was that—as in Vietnam, Jordan, and elsewhere—Kissinger came to believe that a regional dispute could be solved by putting pressure on Moscow. "We decided that the best hope to keep India from smashing West Pakistan was to increase the risk for Moscow," Kissinger said.

The Soviet number two man in Washington, Yuli Vorontsov, who was filling in for the vacationing Dobrynin, was repeatedly summoned and read stern warnings, just as he had been during the Jordanian crisis. Since there was little he could do, Vorontsov did little, thus exposing the American bluster as impotent.

This led to perhaps the silliest scene of the crisis. The Soviet agricultural minister, a bubbly and beefy man named Vladimir Matskevich, happened to be in the U.S. on a goodwill tour. He was a Soviet version of Earl Butz: big, friendly, brimming with good cheer though not excessive subtlety. When he found himself, to his surprise, brought to the Oval Office for an unscheduled meeting with the president, he thought (mistakenly) that Nixon had remembered him from a lunch they had had together when he visited Moscow in 1959. Matskevich heartily conveyed best wishes from Brezhnev. Nixon then launched into an explanation of the crisis on the subcontinent. "The Soviet Union has a treaty with India," said Nixon. "We have one with Pakistan." If India invaded West Pakistan, the U.S. would not stand idly by. Matskevich replied, no doubt sincerely, that such matters were outside his area of expertise.[8]

As in other crises, Kissinger also became fond of sending signals.

Just as he had sent a task force to the eastern Mediterranean during the Jordan-PLO war, this time he ordered Admiral Zumwalt (without consulting Laird) to send the aircraft carrier *Enterprise* steaming from Vietnam to the Bay of Bengal. As orders were issued then revised by Kissinger, Zumwalt became frustrated at the notion of using military deployments for sending signals rather than carrying out specified missions, especially when Kissinger asked him to have the *Enterprise* sail through the Strait of Malacca during daylight hours. Zumwalt kept asking what the "mission" of the task force was. "I felt it was taking an unnecessary risk to put a task group without a stated mission in precisely the place where harm was most likely to befall it," he recalled.

The problem with Kissinger's signal was that, with all sorts of British and Soviet and Indian ships sailing around the Bay of Bengal, no one quite knew what if anything it was meant to convey. In 1989, Zumwalt visited India and met with its retired naval chief. During their discussion, Zumwalt apologized for what he called "Kissinger's irrational hostility toward India" and asked if the Indian navy had felt unduly threatened by the American task force in 1971. No, the Indian admiral replied. In fact he had sent out orders to his fleet: "If you encounter U.S. Navy ships, invite their captains aboard for a drink."

By Sunday, December 12, after more than a week of fighting, it was clear that India was winning. That day a message reached Kissinger and Nixon at the White House: the Chinese ambassador to the U.N. had an official note that he wanted to deliver.

This was the first time Beijing had ever taken such a step in a crisis. Kissinger recalls that he guessed that the note was to say that China was coming to Pakistan's assistance. Working on that assumption, he and Nixon came to a remarkable conclusion: instead of doing everything possible to dissuade China from turning a regional war into a big-power confrontation, they would reply that if China became involved, the U.S. would seek to prevent any Soviet retaliation—in other words, the U.S. would encourage China to widen the war.

This decision was made without the knowledge of the State and Defense departments, which would understandably have been opposed. "It was not an ideal way to manage a crisis," Kissinger later admitted. Haig was sent to New York to receive the Chinese message and to pass along the American assurances if it said what Kissinger assumed.

It turned out, however, that Kissinger was wrong in his "guess" that China was planning to intervene on Pakistan's behalf. The message from Beijing merely said that it would be willing to support any U.N. call for a cease-fire.[9]

Although the Soviets also supported a cease-fire, Kissinger felt that they were not yet doing enough to restrain India. So in a not-for-attribution press briefing, he threatened that if the Soviet approach did not change, the president might have to reconsider his trip to Moscow scheduled for the following May. The *Washington Post,* believing this was too explosive to run without attribution, broke the background guidelines and quoted Kissinger directly.*

Kissinger's remarks caused a crisis at the White House. Although Nixon had privately grumbled to Kissinger about possibly canceling the summit, he did not mean to be taken seriously, for he was deeply excited about making his historic visit to Moscow. Press Secretary Ron Ziegler was trotted out to say that Kissinger was wrong, the summit was not being reconsidered. Other aides avidly spread the word that Kissinger had exceeded his authority. The signal Kissinger was trying to send to Moscow became as unguided as the wandering naval task force.[10]

All worked out well enough, however, because on December 16, India offered a cease-fire that Pakistan quickly accepted. Gandhi made her peace without trying to dismember West Pakistan or even to snatch away any part of disputed Kashmir. "There is no doubt in my mind," Kissinger says, "that it was a reluctant decision resulting from Soviet pressure, which in turn grew out of American insistence, including the fleet movement and the willingness to risk the summit."

It is hard to disprove that assessment, but it is probably at least an overstatement. Even before the meandering American fleet and other warnings to Moscow, India and the Soviets had declared that all they sought was independence for Bangladesh and a return to the status quo with West Pakistan. And indeed that is all they did seek. "India and the Soviet Union undoubtedly would have accepted this outcome at *any* time in the crisis, without the acrobatics of triangular diplomacy waged by a master geopolitician," according to former State Department official Raymond Garthoff.

But Kissinger was correct in realizing that, despite State Department predictions, America's tilt toward Pakistan would not permanently drive India closer to the Soviet Union. Later, when joking about India's lack of loyalty to Moscow, Kissinger quoted to Ambassador Dobrynin a comment by the Austrian minister Felix Schwarzenberg after the Russians had helped him quell the Hungarian revolt of 1848: "Someday we will amaze the world by the depth of our ingratitude."

* See Chapter 25.

The same was also true of Pakistan. Although the nation, under the rule of Ali Bhutto, remained a strategic ally of the U.S., there were constant disputes over its nuclear weapons program. After his overthrow, and until the day of his execution, Bhutto blamed Kissinger personally for his fall, according to his daughter Benazir Bhutto. When she became Pakistan's prime minister, Benazir was moderately pro-American, but she retained her father's animosity toward Kissinger.[11]

This fallout indicated that it was overly simplistic to view the India-Pakistan dispute mainly in terms of the global struggle between the U.S. and the Soviet Union. In many other ways, Kissinger's approach to the dispute was costly:

• Washington supported the side that was morally wrong in a civil war: the regime in West Pakistan had brutally suppressed a democratic movement that had won free elections, and it had massacred hundreds of thousands of innocent people in the process.

• The U.S. then compounded its moral error with a pragmatic one by supporting the losing side in a regional war: Pakistan had foolishly attacked India and been badly beaten; the Soviets had supported the side that was now clearly the area's dominant power.

• The perception grew that Kissinger's foreign policy was insensitive to human rights. Downplaying morality may be sensible at times, but being brazen about it is, in America, politically untenable. A major factor in the 1976 challenges by both Ronald Reagan and Jimmy Carter was that the foreign policies of the Nixon-Ford years lacked a moral foundation.

• The credibility gap of the administration widened when its claims to be evenhanded were exposed to ridicule by the leaks of the WSAG minutes. Mocking headlines flashed "Tilt! Tilt! Tilt!" like an old-fashioned pinball machine.

The main lesson that Kissinger drew from the India-Pakistan war was that a tough display of force and resolve was needed to deter the Soviets from seeking advantages in regional wars. "This knowledge stood us in good stead when Vietnam exploded four months later," Kissinger later wrote.

In the long run, however, the belief that the Soviets could be restrained from meddling in regional crises by threats and bluster, or that America's regional enemies could be controlled by putting pressure on Moscow, would turn out to be largely an illusion. And when an illusion this strong does not live up to its billing, it can lead to a powerful sense of disillusion.[12]

YEOMAN RADFORD'S SPY RING, DECEMBER 1971

Tartar Sam. The words were meaningless to most people reading Jack Anderson's newspaper column on December 14, and apparently they were meaningless even to Anderson. But Admiral Robert Welander recalls that they "hit me right between the eyes" as he was finishing breakfast that Tuesday. For the second straight day, Anderson's column, which the *Washington Post* had moved to the front page, contained secret documents exposing America's "tilt" toward Pakistan in its war with India. This one listed the names of the ships accompanying the aircraft carrier *Enterprise* into the Bay of Bengal. It was accurate except for one thing: Tartar Sam, or more precisely Tartar SAM, was not a ship but a type of surface-to-air missile that was deployed on the destroyers.

Admiral Welander, who was Kissinger's liaison with the Joint Chiefs of Staff, had dictated a memo a few days earlier that listed the ships in the task force. After the names of destroyers, he had added "with Tartar SAM" because he realized that Kissinger might not know which missiles were aboard. The sloppy wording meant that an outsider could misconstrue "Tartar SAM" to be the name of another ship with the task force, the exact mistake that Jack Anderson's column made. Since no other memo had mentioned the missiles, it was clear that Welander's had leaked.

But his memo had gone to only two people. After dictating it, Welander had asked his secretary, Navy yeoman Charles Radford, to make two copies and walk them across the street for Kissinger and Haig. Assuming that Kissinger and Haig had not leaked it, Welander's suspicions turned to Radford, and he began to piece together what he knew about him: the young yeoman had previously been stationed at the New Delhi embassy, he had developed strong feelings about the need for Indian-American friendship, an Indian student had stayed with him and his wife that summer, and he had expressed his dismay the previous week about the task force being sent to the Bay of Bengal. He also had access to all the other documents that had leaked to Anderson. In addition, though Welander did not yet know it, Radford had been friends with Jack Anderson for more than a year, and four nights earlier he had gone to dinner (at Kissinger's favorite restaurant, The Empress) with the investigative columnist.

Welander did not worry, at least then, about the safety of another very sensitive secret that he and Radford shared. He gathered up the incriminating memos, walked them over to Haig's office, and laid them out. Haig sent him over to present his findings to David Young,

Kissinger's former aide who was now working under Ehrlichman plugging leaks as part of the secret "Plumbers Unit."

The next day, Young and investigators from the Pentagon grilled Yeoman Radford, often brutally. A bastard, they called him, a traitor, a man who had probably caused the deaths of his fellow military men in Vietnam. Radford repeatedly broke down and cried. But though he admitted his friendship with Jack Anderson, he denied being the source of the leaks.

A few hours into the grilling, however, Radford spilled a totally different revelation, one that snapped the heads of his interrogators. One questioner said he suddenly felt as if he were in the movie *Seven Days in May*. What the yeoman told them was that, with the encouragement of Admiral Welander, he had been part of a spy operation that stole and copied the most secret documents in Kissinger's office and passed them along to the chairman of the Joint Chiefs, Admiral Thomas Moorer.[13]

Radford had joined Kissinger's staff on September 18, 1970, one of the days in which the crises in Cuba, Jordan, and Chile were all climaxing. He became the secretary to Welander's predecessor as the NSC's liaison with the Joint Chiefs, Admiral Rembrandt Robinson. One of Radford's tasks was to carry sensitive documents back and forth from the Executive Office Building, where most of Kissinger's staff was quartered, to the White House, where Kissinger and Haig had their offices.

A polite and self-effacing young man, "Chuck" Radford had an air of naïveté that served him well. His snooping did not stem from any manipulative strain in his personality. Rather it arose from an eagerness to please. He once remarked that he "would go to extra lengths to get a pat on the head." Although as a Mormon he never touched coffee, he took charge of making and getting it for everyone else in the office. When there were secret papers to be copied, he was readily available. Other secretaries knew that when they went on a break, Radford would be glad to sit in for them.

Yeoman Radford was fond of Admiral "Rem" Robinson because he took time to explain exactly how his secretary should handle office protocol. The admiral gave Radford a list of names—including Hal Sonnenfeldt, John Negroponte, and Al Haig—and said that when they visited, he should not tell anyone. "He said that if the wrong person found out that another person had visited him," Radford recalls, "they might think that something was going on."

One day when they were waiting for a car outside their office, Admiral Robinson rather casually mentioned to Radford that he might run across papers that the Joint Chiefs had not seen. If so, he should make a copy if he could. If he kept his eyes opened, the admiral said, he would soon learn what they were interested in seeing. It was not a direct order, but for a yeoman who wanted to impress his admiral, and who hoped to win a commission as an officer, it was all that needed to be said.

Radford began going to the White House offices at night and checking out the burn bags, where he would find discarded drafts of the private memos that Kissinger sent to Nixon. During the day, when he was copying documents for other secretaries, he started making an extra. Admiral Robinson even offered a tip for sanitizing such documents: he should copy the pages that had distribution lists and other identification on it, cut out the incriminating information with a scissors, then copy the page again with blank paper behind it so that the cutouts did not show.

When Haig visited Vietnam in December 1970, Admiral Robinson got Radford assigned to the trip. Keep your eyes open for any information that the Joint Chiefs might find useful, Robinson told him. Among the topics Radford was to watch for: troop withdrawal discussions, information about Cambodia, or any "eyes only" messages that Haig received from Kissinger.

Robinson left the NSC in June 1971 (and was killed the following year in a helicopter crash over the Gulf of Tonkin). The new liaison was Admiral Welander, who continued the same procedures. At Haig's suggestion, Yeoman Radford was assigned to Kissinger's July 1971 round-the-world tour to Vietnam, Pakistan, India, and Paris with the secret stopover in China. "Be careful and don't get caught," Welander told him.

By the time their plane reached New Delhi, which was before the China detour, Radford had gathered so many documents that his suitcase could not hold them. A friend from his days at the U.S. embassy there agreed to send them back by diplomatic pouch in envelopes Radford had sealed and coded to prevent tampering. In Pakistan, Radford went into Kissinger's room and foraged through his briefcases. On the flight to Paris afterward, one of the secretaries asked him to get some of Kissinger's cases out of the storage area, and he again took the opportunity to look through them. There he found the notes of Kissinger's conversations with Zhou Enlai, but since there was only one copy, he left it behind. He did, however, collect the drafts of Kissinger's report about China that were in the burn bag as well as memos about Kissinger's secret meeting with Le Duc Tho in Paris.

Despite Welander's frequent compliments, Radford did not feel comfortable working for him. When angry, Welander tended to "come apart at the seams" and curse; profanity offended Radford's sense of propriety, which was more that of a Mormon than a navy yeoman. Nor did Radford like Kissinger, whose tantrums and mistreatment of his staff made him seem cruel. Radford was also repulsed by the anti-Indian bias he saw in the administration. A final disenchantment came in December: he was passed over for a commission as an officer.[14]

With all of this weighing on his mind, Radford accepted a dinner invitation from columnist Jack Anderson, a fellow Mormon who seemed sympathetic. While serving in New Delhi, Radford had met Anderson's parents when they came by the embassy with a visa problem and asked about finding a local Mormon worship group. Afterward, Radford kept in touch by mail. When they visited Washington in 1970 to stay with their famous son, Radford was invited around for the evening. Later, Radford's wife became friends with Jack Anderson's wife and they worked together studying genealogy.

A few days after his December 1971 dinner with Radford, Anderson's disclosures based on secret NSC documents began to appear. John Ehrlichman and the Pentagon investigators quickly became convinced that there was a link. But by then, Radford's revelations about the admirals' spy ring had overshadowed the leak investigation.

Admiral Welander, who had first told Ehrlichman about Yeoman Radford, was summoned back to the White House on December 22 for a less friendly session. When he arrived, Ehrlichman and his chief plumber, David Young, had a clunky reel-to-reel tape recorder set up and a typed confession ready for him to sign. Welander spurned the confession, which would have him admit to charges of political spying against the White House. Yet he willingly submitted to more than an hour of taped questioning, during which he confirmed that he had received purloined papers from Radford and passed them along to Joint Chiefs chairman Moorer. Welander's defense was that he was simply following procedures set up by his predecessor, Admiral Robinson.

When Ehrlichman told Nixon the next morning about Admiral Welander's taped admissions, the president was not particularly shocked that the military was spying on Kissinger. Instead, he was mainly concerned with avoiding yet another Kissinger temper tantrum. He also wanted to protect his new ally on the NSC staff, Alexander Haig. Ehrlichman's notes quote the president as saying: "Talk to HAK. Not to be brot up w/ P. . . . Don't let K blame Haig." The part about not letting Kissinger bring the matter up with the president was underlined.

Ehrlichman brought Haldeman along that afternoon to help him break the news of the spy ring to Kissinger. The prospect did not please Haldeman, who complained that Kissinger had been "a tremendous problem" all week. He was still fuming, Haldeman warned, that he had been undercut during the Pakistan crisis.

To their surprise, Kissinger seemed rather calm, almost sleepy, when Ehrlichman and Haldeman broke the news. Actually, he was simply being wary. His problems with the president had caused him to believe that Haldeman was out to get him, and somehow this all seemed part of the plot. But as the news sank in, Kissinger's wariness soon gave way to fury. "I was beside myself," Kissinger later said. "I was outraged." Ironically, this outrage about being spied upon came from a man who secretly tapped the telephones of his closest associates and allowed Haig and Haldeman to read the transcripts.

At ten that night, Ehrlichman was at home with friends having a Christmas carol party when the phone line from the White House rang. It was Kissinger, and he was throwing a tantrum. He had just fired Admiral Welander. He wanted Moorer fired. And he wanted to know what other evidence Ehrlichman had about the snooping. Ehrlichman told him to come by the next day and hear the tape of the admiral's quasi-confession.

For an hour the next morning, the day before Christmas, Kissinger paced up and down in Ehrlichman's office, listening to the Welander tape and ranting. "This time Henry wasn't so calm," Ehrlichman recalled. His anger was directed largely at Nixon, who had decided to cover up the whole affair and not force a showdown with the chairman of the Joint Chiefs. "He won't fire Moorer!" Kissinger shouted in dismay. "They can spy on him and spy on me and betray us, and he won't fire them!" Ehrlichman jotted down Kissinger's demand that Moorer "must go," but he indicated that Kissinger was probably right, the president would not do it.

After fretting for another hour or so in his office, Kissinger burst uninvited into Nixon's hideaway in the Executive Office Building. "In a low, somber voice, he spread gloom and doom," recalled Ehrlichman, who was there at the time. Nixon was "at his jocular worst." Kissinger's anger turned into a Christmas Eve melancholy, unrelieved by Nixon's stabs at encouragement. On his yellow legal pad, Ehrlichman stopped his nervous doodling to characterize the scene in two words: "mood indigo." [15]

Encouraged by Haig, Nixon decided to downplay the Radford controversy on the theory that the military was only doing what was natural, especially given Kissinger's secretiveness. "I did some checking," Nixon later said. "I found it had been traditional that the JCS spied on the White House. They wanted to know what was going on." So he ordered Haldeman to "sweep it under the rug."[16]

Nixon gave a variety of reasons for covering up the spy ring: an investigation would hurt the military, it would be distorted by the press, it would jeopardize the upcoming Beijing and Moscow summits. But Ehrlichman and others later said the main reason was that, as chairman of the Joint Chiefs, Admiral Moorer had been willing to take orders behind Defense Secretary Laird's back. Now that Nixon knew about his spy ring, Moorer would be even more compliant. So the president sent his crony John Mitchell personally to Moorer "to let him know that we had the goods," Ehrlichman said. "After this, the admiral was preshrunk."[17]

The spying by the Joint Chiefs was inexcusable and unjustified, but it could partly be explained as a reaction to Kissinger's obsession with secrecy. Admiral Elmo Zumwalt, who was a member of the Joint Chiefs, later said it was an example of "the way Henry's duplicity left booby traps everywhere." Radford, who was never court-martialed, similarly blamed the whole atmosphere within Kissinger's shop. "It was factions and splinter groups and egos and professional jealousies," he told Len Colodny and Robert Gettlin, authors of *Silent Coup,* a book connecting the affair to Watergate. "A sewer. How does a government operate like that?"[18]

In the past, a revelation like that of the military spy ring would have drawn Nixon and Kissinger closer by stoking their shared resentment toward common enemies. This time, however, Nixon would become more distant.

THE GENERAL IN HIS LABYRINTH

Alexander Haig's reaction was odd. Instead of getting upset that the top brass was spying on his boss Kissinger, he became protective and defensive about the military. When Kissinger ordered Admiral Welander fired, Haig called David Young, his old rival on the NSC staff, and reamed him out for his handling of the investigation. He accused Young of "jobbing a fine military officer."

Young had his suspicions about Haig's true loyalties, which he freely shared with Ehrlichman. It was Haig who had insisted that Radford be on the secret China trip, Young said accusingly, and he probably did so to help his military colleagues keep tabs on Kissinger. Haig had "constantly sold Henry out to the military," Young told Ehrlichman.

Welander seemed to confirm these suspicions, at least obliquely, in his taped confession with Ehrlichman and Young. He revealed that Moorer would sometimes return the more sensitive of Radford's purloined documents, including the report on the China trip, by sending them to Haig—which indicated that Haig probably knew that secret papers were flowing to the Pentagon.

Nevertheless, even though Haig likely knew that the military was doing some snooping on Kissinger's operations, there is no evidence that he realized there was a full-scale spy ring. "Haig was partly involved," Ehrlichman later said. "I think he knew the Chiefs had a way of getting documents, and he abetted it, though I doubt he knew that Radford was rifling briefcases."[19]

Nixon was tantalized by the rift he saw developing between Kissinger and Haig. No longer merely a tireless deputy to the volatile national security adviser, Haig had begun to pursue an independent relationship with the president. For his part, Nixon was happy to forge a bond with the tough-talking military man who catered to his belief that Kissinger was both emotionally unstable and soft on Vietnam. One of Nixon's Walter Mitty conceits was that he was a tough and cool leader surrounded by less stable advisers.

"The relationship between Al and Henry began to get testy at that point," Nixon later recalled with some satisfaction. "Kissinger felt we should fire Admiral Moorer. Haig was sensitive. Being a military man, he didn't want to see a military man fired. He felt we should not make a big issue out of the spying, and that made Henry upset."

The rift reflected more than merely a disagreement over how to handle the Radford spy ring. With a disloyalty that caught Kissinger by surprise, Haig had begun denigrating him to the military, to his subordinates on the NSC staff, to Haldeman, and even to the president. Haig's underhanded crusade was motivated by both clashing principles and personality, as well as a heavy dose of personal ambition.

By late 1971, Haig was on his way to becoming the embodiment of Kissinger's darkest nightmare: an NSC staffer with a link to the president behind Kissinger's back. Haig began telling the president how unstable Kissinger was, describing him as a temperamental genius whose moodiness made him unreliable. "Kissinger was very emotional," Nixon recalled. "I got a lot of reports on how he could be rough on his staff, and I heard a lot of things like that from Haig, who kept me informed."

Haig's expressions of concern about Kissinger's equanimity began to strike Haldeman as less than selfless. "At first I assumed honorable motivations on Haig's part, like he was seeking advice on a problem he wanted to handle properly," Haldeman later said. "Now I don't have the same convictions. I think Haig inflamed the problems, roiled rather than stilled the waters, both because of his own ambitions and his vindictiveness at Henry's slights."[20]

Haig's personal version of triangular diplomacy began in late 1969. When he got his first star as a brigadier general in October of that year, Nixon decided to bestow it himself. "I know what hours you put in there, Al, because I walk around at night," Nixon told the assembled staffers, including Kissinger. "I passed your place the other night and saw that your light was on and Henry's as usual was off. I guess he had gone off to another party in Georgetown." Kissinger's smile, recalled his former aide William Watts, was weak and wan, as if he were being disemboweled. Then Kissinger walked over to the taller Haig, made a show of polishing the star as Haig became rigid, and said, "Be a good boy, Al, and we'll get you another one of these." This time it was Haig's turn to put on a sickly smile.

The following month, Kissinger and Nixon were going over a speech with William Safire in the Oval Office and needed a statistic about Vietnam withdrawals. Haig was called and soon came marching in with the number neatly typed on a slip of paper. Kissinger dismissed him with a nod. Nixon, however, looked up and invited him to stay. "Thought and action," the president muttered. It was a reference to one of his favorite lines from Woodrow Wilson, and was meant as a salute to a man who could succeed in both realms.

The first time that the president called and asked for Haig rather than Kissinger, a pall fell over the office. Kissinger was talking to Julie Pineau, his chief secretary, when the light began blinking on the private line from Nixon. Kissinger automatically walked toward his office to take the call in private. "It's for you, General Haig," Pineau said. For a few moments, Kissinger stood outside Haig's door and waited. Then, he walked back into his office alone and shut the door. "There was more tension than I could ever recall in that office," one aide recalled. Haig was "drenched in sweat" by the time he got off the phone.[21]

"Nixon developed a direct relationship with Haig in order to undermine Henry's self-confidence," said James Schlesinger, who served as CIA director and defense secretary in Nixon's second term. Partly it was because Nixon was upset at the way fate and the perfidy of the press was allocating to Kissinger all the foreign policy glories he thought should be his own. "Nixon began playing games and used Haig to torment Henry," said Diane Sawyer, who worked in the press office. "But Haig was a co-conspirator who was perfectly happy to play along. He became one of the bluntest instruments in one of the most complex, intricate courts in history."

To Nixon, Haig seemed tough, self-assured, cool, and all the other attributes Nixon would like to fancy for himself. Haig's cocksure attitude on Vietnam won him a privileged status with a president beset by inner weaknesses. Talking to his political hit man Charles Colson in early 1972, Nixon praised John Connally and Haig as the only two advisers willing to advocate tough action in Vietnam. "You know, Chuck, those are the only two men around here qualified to fill this job when I step down," Nixon said.[22]

Nixon's admiration for Haig would remain strong, even after he helped ease the president out of office during Watergate. In December 1980, President-elect Ronald Reagan wrote to Nixon wondering about whether to appoint Haig as secretary of state. In reply, Nixon sent back a quote he found in Charles de Gaulle's *Edge of the Sword*: "It is the worst of policies to exclude men of strong character from office for no better reason than that they are difficult."

When pressed about Haig's character in an interview, Nixon conceded: "Al is a bureaucrat. He can be devious. But so can Henry. So can I."[23]

Haig also formed a not-so-holy alliance with Haldeman, to whom he would pass along tidbits of gossip about Kissinger's social life. He took special care to keep Haldeman informed about each of the Georgetown dinner parties filled with people of dubious loyalties that Kissinger attended.

Haig's most duplicitous action—and the one that enraged Kissinger the most—was informally showing Haldeman and others transcripts of some of Kissinger's telephone conversations, often to make a point about his divided loyalties. It was not an organized procedure. Rather, said Haldeman, "Al was willing to provide us with informal intelligence" about Kissinger's activities. "He would come to me and talk about problems Kissinger was having or problems Kissinger was causing. If a question arose where the president wanted back-channel information about what Kissinger was doing—especially if something had appeared in the press and he wanted to know how it happened— we would go to Haig and say, 'Did Henry do this?' "

"Haig did not provide telcon transcripts as a matter of course," said Lawrence Higby, who was Haldeman's deputy. "But he would go in and talk to Haldeman and show him some conversations when he thought Kissinger had gotten out of line." Even though it was not a regular occurrence, Kissinger later became convinced that Haig was guilty of massive disloyalty.[24]

Haig's derogations of Kissinger involved anti-Semitic slurs. "Haig had a strong streak of anti-Semitism, which came through in the denigrating comments he would make," said James Schlesinger. "It reflected a gut bias, a feeling, an army and West Point feeling." Zumwalt got the same impression. "Very early on, Haig was bad-mouthing Kissinger by telling me he was someone we would have to watch, not an American, a Jew." Haig's anti-Semitism seemed to subside after a few years. "Al got over it," recalled Schlesinger, "especially when he began to have political designs."

When talking to military leaders, Haig tended to blame Kissinger rather than Nixon for any softness in American policy on Vietnam and arms control. He confided to Bruce Palmer, the army's vice chief of staff, "that there were times when he wondered whether Kissinger had the inner toughness and tenacity to stay the course." It was his role, Haig liked to say, "to stiffen Kissinger's backbone." But Haig used the backbone metaphor about the president as well. "Al said that he had to exercise considerable dexterity to stiffen the president's backbone when the president was in a bugout mood," recalled Admiral Zumwalt, "and that he lived in dread that the president would be with Henry instead of him when the bugout mood came on."[25]

Haig also tried to curry favor with the rest of the NSC staff by running down their boss. When Kissinger would leave a room, Haig would perform a devastatingly accurate imitation of him, right down to the voice and facial expressions and stomping feet. He liked passing along gossip about Kissinger's silly actions or weak moments and his paranoid fits about Rogers and Laird. "It was his way of trying to show he was one of us," said Laurence Lynn, who came to despise Haig. "He was excessively ambitious, manipulative, ingratiating, crafty, not at all intelligent, a dissembler, and untrustworthy."

When Haig was with Kissinger, however, he was as deferential as Kissinger was in Nixon's presence. With the instincts of a chameleon, he could tailor his insults and mimicry to fit any environment. In front of Kissinger, Haig would ridicule Nixon as being weak and make a leering face as he imitated his limp wrist and speculated about his relationship with Bebe Rebozo.

All of this might sound familiar, for it was similar to the games Kissinger was playing. As the sorcerer's apprentice, Haig had learned to out-Kissinger Kissinger.

When Kissinger first began to suspect in late 1970 that Haig was lancing him in the back, his response was to try to divide the deputy's job and hire back Laurence Lynn, the systems analyst who could not stand Haig. Lynn, then teaching at Stanford, wrote a paper describing how the deputy's job should be split in two, one for operations and the other for substance. But he refused to come back, even though Kissinger tried to persuade him three times.[26]

In Haig's defense, it must be noted that he had the difficult job of coping with Kissinger's moods and anarchic administrative practices. His temper could be brutal, and Haig bore the brunt of it, which would engender resentments in any mortal. "When Henry would blow up," said his former aide Peter Rodman, "Al would come out flushed, with a wry or weary half-smile on his face. He would make a few phone calls, solve the problem, and smooth things over." Then he would sit at his desk chain-smoking, with jaw clenched. "You could see him disciplining himself, visibly controlling himself."

Whenever there was even the smallest problem, particularly something such as overscheduling, Kissinger would charge out of the office and proceed to berate Haig in front of whoever was around. Haig always stood at attention while Kissinger ranted. During the diatribe, his face would turn beet red, his fists would clench, and his upper lip would sweat. Then, after Kissinger left, he would pretend to be a mindless robot, amusing others on the staff as he marched around in circles and saluted.

Many of Haig's challenges to Kissinger stemmed from substantive disagreements rather than ambition or disloyalty. Especially on Vietnam, Haig was forthright in his opposition to Kissinger. "Haig was not being disloyal when he came to me about his Vietnam disputes with Henry," Nixon said. "Haig was the one who had traveled to Saigon and knew what the traffic would bear." Unlike Kissinger, Haig had strong ideological convictions. "Al would be manipulative, but in pursuit of what he believed," according to Roger Morris.

As with any rivals, Kissinger and Haig shared a battlefield camaraderie that prevented their relationship from fraying completely. At times, especially when it counted, Haig would stick up for Kissinger. Within Haig's complex relationship with his boss, there was even a protective streak. Every now and then, when Kissinger would behave in a way that inflamed members of his staff, Haig would calm them down. Sure Henry is crazy, he would say, but no more so than most of the geniuses of this world. Then he might tell about the time he was on General Douglas MacArthur's staff in Korea, when the commander sent him back through enemy fire to the house they had been using so that he could throw a grenade into the tile bathtub and make sure that "no stinking Chinese general would get a bath that night." These things happened when you worked with men who were great but temperamental, he would say.[27]

Haldeman, Ehrlichman, and the Holiday Blues

After Kissinger's eruption about the Radford spy ring in the president's hideaway on the afternoon of Christmas Eve, Nixon asked Ehrlichman to stay behind. For almost an hour, as Ehrlichman took notes, they talked about Kissinger's mood swings, his emotional reaction to the spy ring, and his never-ending battle with William Rogers. "Nixon wondered aloud," Ehrlichman recalled, "if Henry needed psychiatric care."

The suggestion struck Ehrlichman as sincere rather than mean-spirited. But there was a stiletto sharpness to the president's musings, and at one point he said that perhaps he would have to fire Kissinger if he did not agree to seek psychological help. "Talk to him, John," Nixon implored. "And talk to Al Haig. He will listen to Al."

So Ehrlichman wandered over to Haig's office and spelled out the president's concerns. Despite his growing willingness to undercut Kissinger, in this instance Haig defended him, arguing that it would be bad if Kissinger were forced to resign. "The president needs Henry," Haig said, pointing out that the Beijing and Moscow summits were coming up. "You've got to realize that the president isn't doing his homework these days. It's only Henry who pulls us through the summit conferences."

But Haig agreed that Kissinger needed psychiatric help, and he told Ehrlichman so. He had repeatedly made that point to Haldeman. "Al told me that Henry had gone to a psychiatrist before," Haldeman later recalled, "and that he really needed psychiatric help again. He talked about it a lot. Al would complain to me all the time about Henry's temper and paranoia. Or he would rant about Henry's personal peccadillos and the demands he made. In the process, he would always get into Henry's psychiatric troubles." (Kissinger has said that he never went to a psychiatrist.) [28]

Ehrlichman could never come up with a way to broach the subject of psychiatry to Kissinger, nor could anyone else. "No one would bell the cat and tell Henry he should see a psychiatrist," Ehrlichman recalled. But years later, he decided to tackle the scene in a semifictional way. In a piece he wrote for an obscure British collection of spy tales, he recounted a meeting with Nixon and Haldeman, not even bothering to change the names:

Nixon mused. He looked sharply at Haldeman. "Do you think Henry is nuts?" he asked. "He comes in here and whines about Bill Rogers and complains about Shultz and demands that I fire some ambassador I never heard of. I think he's psychotic, for God's sake. . . ."

Nixon smiled, an instantaneous grimace that was gone in a blink. "Let's talk about what needs to be done. Someone will have to talk to Henry about his problem. I think you should do that, Bob, don't you think so?"

"I can do that, but what if he denies it?"

"Of course he'll deny it. They all deny that they have mental problems. You need to say: 'The president knows about such things, Henry. He has some experience in these matters. He is worried. . . .' Either he gets some psychiatric treatment, so he calms down and gets over that awful paranoia—that's what it is, I think, a persecution complex—or he must resign. . . ."

Haldeman shook his head as he made notes on his pad. Note-taking reassured Nixon that his staff took his instructions seriously. "I'll see what I can do," Haldeman said, "but I'm not optimistic. Henry is going to be very upset."

"Just tell him, don't ask him. Tell him: he sees a psychiatrist or he is out. Period. No appeal." [29]

When asked about it later, Nixon denied that he ever said Kissinger should seek psychiatric help. Others brought up the idea, Nixon admitted, and it was discussed, but he insisted that he never had much use for psychiatrists. He tended to think that those who saw them came out worse rather than better. [30]

Though often lumped together, Haldeman and Ehrlichman were occasional rivals with very different personalities. Haldeman was often a mechanical martinet who had as his overriding goal the protection of the president. This meant spending hours each day taking notes of Nixon's ramblings while sorting out the orders that should be enforced from the dark musings that were best ignored. He did his job well, almost well enough to save Nixon from himself.

There was a simple, straightforward aspect to Haldeman's personality, partly because he was free from excessive ambition. He had achieved what he wanted in life and did not need to engage in bureaucratic backbiting or maneuvering. As an outsider of the sort who would stick by Nixon after his 1962 California defeat, Haldeman neither forged ties with Washington's permanent power structure nor surrounded himself with people of independent judgment. To him, Kissinger's courtship of the media elite and Senate chairmen was an oddity, one that was vaguely contemptible.

Likewise, Haldeman considered an excessive concern over the substance of policy to be emotionally quirky. He treated Kissinger's passion for policy with a bemused tolerance only because he knew the president considered foreign affairs enjoyable as well as important.

Haldeman was not normally a puckish character, but he liked poking fun at Kissinger. Every day, he would eat lunch in his office with his assistant Lawrence Higby. Kissinger would often drop in to touch base, and he would instinctively circle the room and glance at the important memos on Haldeman's desk and table. "We used to have fun with him," Haldeman recalled. "We'd deliberately place letters or documents that looked very interesting in an exposed area. Then, when Henry got there, Higby would take his lunch tray and set it on top of the paper, as if by accident. So Henry would move around, and we'd always stay one step ahead of him. And everyone kept a straight face."

Kissinger cultivated a nonaggression pact with Haldeman and would often drop in on him to try out an idea or seek advice on how to approach Nixon. Since Haldeman had no ideological or foreign policy agenda of his own, he could be counted on to assure that Kissinger's ideas got a fair hearing.

Yet deep inside, Kissinger felt that Haldeman was dangerous. "He was a conservative middle-class Californian, with all the sentiments, suspicions, and secret envy of that breed," Kissinger later noted, using a description that he also used for Nixon. When Nixon started wearing an American flag pin in his lapel, Haldeman suggested at a staff meeting that everyone do the same—to stick it to the liberals. Kissinger, imbued with the memory of state symbols used as totems of hatred, was repulsed. Despite his desire to fit into the Nixon circle, he refused. Near the end of his tenure in office, three years after Haldeman resigned, Kissinger was talking off the record to a handful of reporters on his plane. "Haldeman was the kind of guy who would send you to the showers," he said quietly. "He had the soul of a Nazi." [31]

In the same conversation, Kissinger referred to John Ehrlichman as "actually a good guy, at heart a decent guy." Interested in substance, mildly liberal, Ehrlichman's downfall came because he got caught up in the Nixonian cult of the tough guy that was the price of survival in the inner circle. When Nixon demanded that leaks be stopped, Ehrlichman formed a group of zealous plumbers; it was he who coined an immortal phrase of the era by saying of FBI Director Patrick Gray, "I think we should let him hang there, let him twist slowly, slowly in the wind."

Ehrlichman was more ambitious than Haldeman; he wanted to climb from being in charge of logistics to being a top domestic-policy assistant (which he became) and a cabinet officer (which he did not). But he cared deeply about the dissent that was tearing the nation apart, and he tried to reinforce the president's better instincts. Before the Cambodian invasion, Ehrlichman spent a long time in the Rose Garden warning the president of the outrage that would follow; when it did, he set up a meeting between Kent State students and Nixon in the Oval Office. Three of his teenaged children were caught up in the protests, and he was a true family man who cared deeply about their feelings.

At first, Ehrlichman's relationship with Kissinger was easy. They spent time together at Camp David, and during the summer they rented houses near one another in San Clemente. The Ehrlichmans had a pool, and most afternoons they would invite Kissinger and his children over to swim. Once when they were all seated around a picnic table, Ehrlichman's son asked about the ABM debate. Ehrlichman appreciated how Kissinger took the time to explain it in a non-condescending way. "Henry hadn't developed his grand stage aura yet," he said, "and without it he was actually rather pleasant."

After they had been working together for a year or so, Kissinger began to strike him as "very insecure," Ehrlichman said. "I'd never seen fingernails bitten so close to the quick." He had no sense of proportion or humor about what people wrote of him. "Henry had erected a protective facade that was part self-deprecating humor and part intellectual showboating, but behind it he was devastated by press attacks on his professional competence."

Because Ehrlichman had a sense of humor, he and Kissinger were able to develop a bantering relationship that smoothed over their antagonisms. But their notions of what was funny were sharply different: whereas Kissinger had an intellectually clever wit, Ehrlichman had a fraternity boy's jocularity and fondness for insults. At the West Wing elevator one day, Haldeman archly noted that he had read in the paper that Kissinger had been with some beautiful woman at a party the night before. Then Ehrlichman started ribbing him: "Of course you'd be happier if it was a boy. Were there any cute boys at the party, Henry?" Kissinger was not amused.[32]

With Nixon and his men arrayed against him at the end of 1971, Kissinger found himself suddenly cut off from the president. There were no morning meetings, his phone calls went unreturned. "Nixon could not resist the temptation of letting me twist slowly, slowly in the wind," he later noted, playing off Ehrlichman's famous phrase.

The president also decided, just after Christmas, to order a complete review of the security procedures within Kissinger's staff. It was

Nixon's way of letting Kissinger know that his shop was still being blamed for leaks, and it implied that he was somehow responsible for the Radford spy ring. Adding injury to insult, Nixon designated Ehrlichman to be in charge of the security review.

Kissinger became so dejected that Nancy Maginnes began asking friends to telephone him with encouragement. She called Henry Brandon in tears because Kissinger had gone so far as to decide on a date—January 27, 1972—for his resignation.

What he did not know was that Nixon was thinking of firing him. The group known as the Henry-Handling Committee*—Haldeman, Mitchell, and this time Ehrlichman—was scheduled to meet with Kissinger on January 14 to hear a new set of his complaints. The afternoon before, Nixon met with Haig and then a couple of times with Haldeman to discuss whether this was the right time to let Kissinger go.

Take a hard line with Kissinger, the president told Haig. To Haldeman, Nixon said, "It's better for it to blow up now than after Russia," referring to the Moscow summit scheduled for May. An election year was beginning, and Nixon brought up what he regarded as Kissinger's duplicity about the Vietnam peace talks during the 1968 campaign, according to Haldeman's notes. "If we don't face up now, he may go off cockeyed during the campaign," Nixon said. "Remember, he came to us in '68 with tales."

Later, Nixon returned to the subject. Haldeman's notes read: "K —get him out now? Bite bullet now. Problem is he'll be in the driver's seat during the campaign."

At the January 14 meeting of the Henry-Handling Committee, the grievances poured forth. CBS correspondent Marvin Kalb, Kissinger claimed, had told him that the attacks on his handling of the India-Pakistan situation "came from the highest level at the State Department." The administration's policy of cutting off aid to India during the war had been thwarted by the bureaucracy, Kissinger charged, and "State refused to take the president's direction." At one meeting he had asked what aid to India was in the pipeline. The State Department representative said he had been ordered by Secretary Rogers not to give out that information. "Rogers never said he disagreed with the policy," Kissinger added, not quite accurately, "but the sabotage went on underneath."

The attorney general finally got a chance to respond. "We have to have a modus vivendi so Rogers knows enough to satisfy him," Mitchell said. The problem, retorted Kissinger, was that Rogers would

* See Chapter 10.

blow his top every time he found out anything he did not like. "He puts the President through hell," he said, "so we have to wait until the last minute to tell him things." Once again, nothing was resolved.[33]

With historic summits scheduled in Beijing for February and Moscow for May, the likelihood of Kissinger's resigning in January— or of Nixon's asking him to—was small. Soon, everyone had calmed down.

AND A HAPPIER NEW YEAR

Instead, Kissinger's fortunes rebounded in January just as quickly as they had fallen in December. As Nixon's moodiness about the handling of the India-Pakistan war dissipated and his excitement about going to Beijing and Moscow became more palpable, he began talking to Kissinger again. He even decided that, at the outset of an election year, it would be useful to reveal that Kissinger had been conducting secret negotiations in Paris with North Vietnam's Le Duc Tho—even though that would have the side effect of making Kissinger even more of a media star.

William Safire was summoned back to write the speech. He was in New Orleans watching Dallas beat Miami in the 1972 Super Bowl when suddenly, as if he were an obstetrician, the public address system paged him to call his office. "This has to be absolutely top secret, but get back here fast," said Lawrence Higby when Safire called. If it was so secret, Safire asked in response, why had he been paged before eighty thousand fans? Worse than that, Higby conceded, the page had been picked up on television, so 60 million others had heard it. Safire later noted: "We agreed that nobody would suspect I was being called back for a secret assignment because not even the Presidential staff of a banana republic would bumble like that."

Although he was about to make Kissinger even more famous by revealing his secret peace talks, Nixon was still eager to keep him in his place. He told Safire that Rose Mary Woods, the president's personal secretary, would be typing drafts of the speech so it would not have to be channeled through Kissinger. In addition, wherever Safire had drafted the phrase *I asked Dr. Kissinger,* Nixon crossed it out and replaced it with *I directed Dr. Kissinger.*

Nixon seemed weary of all of the problems that Kissinger's ego had caused. Ego, he explained to Safire, "is really just a compensation for an inferiority complex." In order not to feed Kissinger's ego or fuel

Rogers's ire, Nixon cut out as many references to Kissinger as possible from the speech. "What the hell," he finally told Safire, "it's down to the minimum."[34]

Despite the minimum nature of the mentions, Kissinger rather than Nixon was featured in the headlines after the speech. *Time* and *Newsweek* featured him on their covers, both billing him as "Nixon's Secret Agent." He asked one colleague, half jokingly, whether he could survive being on both covers. "No, Henry," came the reply, "but what a way to go."

By revealing the talks, Nixon quelled domestic dissent for a while and undercut critics who were demanding that he offer proposals that had in fact already been made. Indeed, there was little reason for the excessive secrecy in the first place; the North Vietnamese had been willing to conduct the talks in the same fashion as the regular Paris negotiations, meaning behind closed doors but with no secrecy surrounding their existence. Now that they were made public, Hanoi was put on the defensive for a change.[35]

In the midst of all the fanfare over the news about his latest dramatic role, Kissinger was featured at the Washington Press Club's annual salute-to-Congress dinner, a black-tie gala that includes humorous speeches by a luminary from each party. Kissinger's dry wit was on full display. He poked fun at his counterpart, Senator Frank Church, who had cosponsored the famous Cooper-Church resolution restricting the president's war powers. The senator was his old friend, he said, and they were even on a first name basis. "He calls me Henry, I call him Cooper."

But then, for the traditional but-seriously-folks end to the speech, Kissinger quieted his audience with some reflections that betrayed the deep malaise he had been feeling. Later, his inbred pessimism would become a political issue. That night, it was enough to silence what had been a raucous dinner:

> We are clearly living through one of the most difficult periods of our history. Some say we are divided over Vietnam; others blame domestic discord. But I believe that the cause of our anguish is deeper. Throughout our history, we believed that effort was its own reward. Partly because so much has been achieved here in America, we tended to suppose that every problem must have a solution, and that good intentions should somehow guarantee good results. Utopia was seen not as a dream, but as our logical destination if we only traveled the right road. Our generation is the first to find that the road is endless, that in traveling it we will not find utopia but only

ourselves. The realization of our essential loneliness accounts for so much of the frustration and the rage of our time.[36]

His melancholia was heartfelt. But it was not fully warranted, for 1972 promised to be a good year. With the upcoming one-two punch of summits in two communist capitals that no U.S. president had ever visited, Kissinger was helping to create a sweeping transformation in American foreign policy.

In addition, the U.S. was steadily disengaging from the most misguided war in its history. Of the 540,000 American troops in Vietnam when Nixon took office, 410,000 had already been brought home, and the withdrawal of another 70,000 had just been announced. None of the remaining forces would be combat units. The number of U.S. battlefield deaths had dropped to 10 per week, down from an average of 280 per week in 1968. American society, it now seemed, would survive not only the war but the most threatening antigovernment uprisings in this century.

In the process Hanoi was being isolated internationally. Kissinger's back-channel diplomacy, as sloppy as it was, had arranged a new opening to China and a détente with the Soviet Union which assured that, even in the post-Vietnam era, the U.S. would play a major role in the world and have the potential to protect its interests through creative diplomacy.

NINETEEN

THE TRIANGLE

Summit Spring

in Moscow and Beijing

> *Henry Kissinger is the only person who has learned to eat caviar with chopsticks.* —SOVIET AMBASSADOR ANATOLI DOBRYNIN

WITH NIXON IN CHINA, FEBRUARY 1972

In order to heighten the drama of his first handshake with Zhou Enlai, Richard Nixon decided that he would descend the steps of Air Force One alone when it landed in Beijing on February 21, 1972. Only his wife, Pat, was to be in the picture, a few steps behind him. At least a dozen times on the flight, Kissinger was reminded not to emerge from the plane until the handshake was completed. When the moment came, Haldeman left nothing to chance: an aide blocked the aisle until the moment was captured by the cameras and beamed back live over a new satellite uplink the Chinese had installed for the occasion.

Planning of the trip had been relentlessly geared to television coverage, much to Kissinger's dismay. In January 1972, a month before Nixon was to arrive, a logistics team from the White House descended on China in force. "It became the advance party's task to bring home the wonders of American public relations to a Chinese officialdom that had just barely survived the Cultural Revolution,"

Kissinger noted. "Fortunately for us, the Chinese had time-honored ways of withstanding barbarian invaders."

The Chinese were, in fact, more sophisticated about the power of television than Kissinger. Matters such as fiddling over the final communiqué, they knew, were far less important to Sino-American relations than the impact of having their nation presented in all of its magical glory to the American people on prime-time television, with superstars such as Richard Nixon and Walter Cronkite serving as masters of ceremonies. With an understanding that sometimes eluded Kissinger, China's mandarins realized that reshaping foreign policy required reeducating the masses, rather than keeping them in the dark.

So the Chinese happily agreed to help produce the televised spectacle. The handshake, the sight of Nixon on the Great Wall, a Chinese military band playing "America the Beautiful" at a banquet in the Great Hall of the People—these video images instantly transformed China, in the minds of American viewers and voters, from a forbidding and foreboding land into an enchanting and inviting one, a feat that even the most elegant communiqué could never have accomplished. Later Kissinger would admit that "the advance men had, after all, made their own contribution to history in a way that I had not comprehended or appreciated beforehand."

On the flight over, Secretary of State Rogers had told Nixon that he was worried because no meeting with Mao had been firmly scheduled. The State Department even worked out a plan to minimize damage if the chairman decided not to grant an audience. In addition, Rogers was concerned that Kissinger's eagerness had made it seem that the Americans were yet another delegation of supplicants coming to pay court in the Middle Kingdom. It was important not to be maneuvered into a situation, Rogers said, where Mao seemed to be above Nixon, such as waiting for Nixon as he climbed up a sweep of stairs.

Rogers's fears were unnecessary. What he should have worried about instead was a slight so unthinkable that it probably did not occur to him: that Kissinger would arrange a presidential meeting with Mao and exclude the secretary of state.

In the days leading up to any big event, Nixon invariably gave excited and contradictory orders about cutting people out of the action. For example, Haldeman recalled, Nixon frequently ordered that Kissinger not be invited to ceremonial events, such as the splashdown of the astronauts who went to the moon, though invariably Kissinger and a host of others would end up there. In one such conversation the week before the summit, Nixon had told Kissinger that Secretary

Rogers should not be allowed into any meetings with Mao so that Nixon "could discuss sensitive matters."

This rationale was as spurious as the instinct was petty. Kissinger could have ignored the instruction, as he did many others, and arranged for the secretary of state to be included. It was not merely a matter of protocol and propriety; the decision to cut out the State Department meant that it would be more difficult to get the bureaucracy to accept the new direction in American policy. One of the primary duties of a national security adviser is to guide a president away from meanspirited considerations that lead to unwise decisions. Kissinger did not rise to the occasion. Later he admitted how "fundamentally unworthy" his conduct had been. "The Secretary of State should not have been excluded from this historic encounter," he noted.[1]

Mao received Nixon and Kissinger at his disarmingly modest house inside the red walls of Beijing's Imperial City. His study was lined with bookshelves, and volumes were piled on tables and the floor, making it seem to Kissinger "more the retreat of a scholar than the audience room of the all-powerful leader of the world's most populous nation." The easy chairs had brown slipcovers, as if they belonged to a frugal family eager to protect the upholstery. Next to Mao was a V-shaped table piled with books and containing his cup of jasmine tea. In front was a spittoon.

Mao's smile when he greeted them struck Kissinger as "both penetrating and slightly mocking," as if to convey that he had seen enough of mankind's foibles that there was no use trying to deceive him. Kissinger began by noting that he had assigned Mao's writings to his classes at Harvard.

"These writings of mine aren't anything," replied the peasant's son who thirty-eight years earlier had launched the Long March. "There is nothing instructive in what I wrote."

"The Chairman's writings moved a nation and changed the world," said Nixon.

"I've only been able to change a few places in the vicinity of Beijing," Mao replied.

Rather than discoursing on his worldview, Mao conveyed his thoughts through a bantering Socratic dialogue that guided his guests, with deceptive casualness, toward his conclusions. His elliptical comments seemed to Kissinger like the shadows on the wall of Plato's cave, in that they reflected reality but did not encompass it. For the rest of the week, Chinese officials would cite Mao's phrases from the hourlong meeting as being concrete guidance verging on gospel.

The most important matter of substance, or so almost everyone thought, was Taiwan. In his elliptical fashion, Mao opened the way to a resolution by noting a truth so obvious that others had ignored it: Taiwan was *not,* in fact, the most important matter of substance between the two nations. It was a relatively minor dispute, certainly not worth impinging on the truly momentous matters that faced America and China. There was no need for haste in resolving the Taiwan issue; the matter had been unresolved for twenty years and could wait another twenty, or another hundred.

And so the great breakthrough on Taiwan was that there did not need to be a great breakthrough on Taiwan. At the summit, the U.S. would make some concessions, such as stating its long-term intention to withdraw its forces; China would make some concessions of its own, such as allowing the U.S. to assert an "interest" in seeing that the situation was not resolved by force. Kissinger would spend an inordinate amount of late-night energy haggling over what clauses should be conditional and where the punctuation marks should be in the communiqué. But in the end, what really happened was that the issue was deferred. The Taiwanese system that had existed for twenty years would (as it turned out) still be in place twenty years later, despite all the hand-wringing about concessions and sellouts.

The symbolism of the summit was established at the state banquet given on the first night by Zhou. There in the Great Hall of the People occurred one of the historic incongruities of the twentieth century: the sight of inveterate red-baiter Richard Nixon, a card-carrying member of the Who Lost China? club, holding aloft a glass of mao-tai, a Chinese spirit roughly akin to lawn-mower fuel, and quoting Chairman Mao—"Seize the day! Seize the hour!"—as justification for a change in U.S. foreign policy, all of which was broadcast live to the morning shows in America on George Washington's birthday. A Chinese military band then broke into "Home on the Range." Back in America, a fascination bordering on infatuation with a former enemy was born.

In his formal sessions with Nixon and Kissinger (from which Rogers was also excluded), Zhou preferred to speak philosophically instead of about the details of negotiations. This suited Nixon, who was at his best when discussing global strategies rather than bargaining. The emphasis was on the requirements of the balance of power; ideology was downplayed.

Zhou followed Mao's approach to the Taiwan issue by diminishing its importance. Beijing and Washington had more crucial mutual interests to pursue that took precedence over worrying about Taiwan.

The most important of these mutual interests was the one that had brought the two nations together: resisting the spread of Soviet influence. That was Mao's main concern in his meeting with Nixon and Kissinger. He employed two euphemisms for the Soviet threat: "the international context" and "hegemony."* Zhou picked up the theme in his talks that week, emphasizing that the primary task facing the two nations was "joint opposition to hegemonic aspirations."

China's eagerness for an explicit partnership to oppose the Soviets presented the U.S. with a dilemma, albeit a happy one. Kissinger's goal was to create a triangular diplomacy rather than simply to enlist a new ally in the old bipolar game. "We had no vested interest in permanent hostility with Moscow," Kissinger later explained. Instead, he wanted to ease tensions with Moscow as well as Beijing. America's interests would be best served if China and the Soviet Union each sought to enlist the U.S. in a partnership directed against the other— which is precisely what happened in early 1972. "It was a three-dimensional game," Kissinger recalled, "but any simplification had the makings of catastrophe."

For the U.S., a primary concern was Vietnam. If he could play the two communist giants off against each other in a contest for American affection, Kissinger thought, both would be less steadfast in supporting North Vietnam. This is the policy Kissinger pursued, and in early 1972 it was paying off. In fact, North Vietnam's Prime Minister Pham Van Dong had visited Beijing to ask Mao not to receive Nixon and was rebuffed.

What Kissinger failed to appreciate fully, however, was that the growing rift between Beijing and Moscow made it far less important for the U.S. to continue its struggle in Vietnam. Indeed, if it had withdrawn from Vietnam in 1969, the U.S. could have eliminated one of the last issues that bound China and the Soviet Union together— thus hastening their rift, which was a more important strategic interest than saving the Saigon regime. In the process, the Chinese would have felt compelled to take over the task of saving Indochina from Soviet hegemony. (This eventually came to pass, but only years later after U.S. support for South Vietnam was ended over Kissinger's objections.)[2]

In his memoirs, Kissinger dismisses the talks that the State Department held in Beijing with the Chinese Foreign Ministry as busy-

---

* *Hegemony,* from a Greek word for "leader," came to mean a quest for international domination, particularly by the Soviets. One of Mao's sayings was, "Dig tunnels deep, store grain, and never seek hegemony." The first two clauses convey that a nation should strive for self-sufficiency; the last is a more direct injunction.

work dealing with the bureaucracy's "obsessions," such as trade and cultural exchanges. In the meantime, he was free to craft in secret what became known as the Shanghai Communiqué. Other officials seemed not to have considered the task of bickering over this communiqué quite as exalted as Kissinger did. His counterpart was Qiao Guanhua, who was a mere deputy foreign minister. Nixon paid little attention to the communiqué, and he never discussed it directly with Zhou. The Chinese premier dropped in only once on Kissinger's talks. In fact, Zhou spent more time with Rogers and his team of negotiators.

The communiqué that Kissinger negotiated followed the format that Zhou had suggested the previous year. Part of the document listed shared positions, while another part contained unilateral declarations of each side's divergent positions. Regarding the Soviet Union, the two sides jointly denounced "hegemony." But on Vietnam, there were unilateral declarations. China "expressed its firm support" for the revolutionary struggle, but it also noted that "all foreign troops should be withdrawn to their own countries," which presumably included the North Vietnamese in Laos and Cambodia.

The Taiwan issue remained sticky until the end, even though both sides planned to declare separate positions. The Chinese wanted two concessions in the American statement. The first involved Washington's declaration that it had an "interest" in a peaceful settlement of the dispute, which is a word used to designate a foreign policy goal that a nation might fight for. Beijing wanted that "interest" toned down to a "hope." Kissinger refused. China also wanted the U.S. to commit itself to withdrawing its troops from Taiwan. Kissinger eventually agreed to declare that a total U.S. withdrawal was "an ultimate objective." In the meantime, the U.S. would "progressively reduce" its forces "as the tension in the area diminishes." This had the neat side effect of linking the rate of withdrawal to a quieting of the Vietnam War.

No negotiation would be complete without an effort by Kissinger to cut out the State Department. This one was no exception. On the first day, Kissinger spent an hour with Zhou explaining which U.S. officials should be privy to which aspects of the talks. The Chinese, Kissinger recalled, "scheduled the meetings and kept the information compartmentalized as if they had dealt with our strange practices all their lives."

Kissinger excluded the State Department's experts from all of the sessions where he worked on the communiqué; he even relied on China's interpreters so that no one at State would have access to what was happening. The final draft of the communiqué was not shown to

State's experts until Nixon and Zhou and the Chinese politburo had already approved it and the presidential entourage was on its way to Shanghai.

Not surprisingly (for it is the most predictable result of cutting people out), the State Department began pointing out flaws in the document, both real and imagined. "It is the price that must be paid for excluding people from a negotiation," Kissinger later admitted. "They can indulge in setting up utopian goals . . . or they can nit-pick."

Kissinger's memoirs make State's objections seem like the latter, pure nitpicking. He does not mention that the primary objection was that the communiqué did not mention the U.S. defense treaty with Taiwan, even though it cited similar commitments to other nations in the region. Rogers finally got through to Nixon with this and a host of lesser criticisms.

Nixon was furious at what he considered petty meddling by the State Department, an emotion abetted by Kissinger. As Kissinger watched, the president stormed around his guesthouse in his under-wear, cursing and threatening to clean out the State Department. Later that night he phoned John Mitchell in Washington with the somewhat misdirected order that he fire Secretary Rogers. (Mitchell knew this was one to ignore.)

Kissinger attempted to solve the problem by being completely candid with Qiao Guanhua, a tactic he never tried on Rogers. He explained the State Department's objections and how they had sud-denly arisen and asked if some changes could be made. "My argu-ments did not exactly overwhelm Qiao," Kissinger recalled. The Chinese negotiator agreed to discuss a few stylistic modifications, but nothing in the Taiwan sections, which had been debated and ap-proved by the politburo.[3]

A result of this latest spat with the State Department was that Kissinger insisted that any follow-up communications with China be sent back channel to his office, with State cut out. This led to some absurd exchanges. For example, when the musk oxen that Nixon gave the Chinese as a gift developed mange, a flurry of secret cables cir-cumventing State Department channels went back and forth as Kis-singer's harried aides had to seek recipes for a pomade that would keep the oxen's hair from falling out. "It's bad enough when Henry sneaks behind my back for peace in Vietnam," Secretary Rogers told an aide, "but when he does it on behalf of mangy musk oxen, that's too much."[4]

Nixon had conceived of the opening to China and had pushed it despite a reluctant bureaucracy. Kissinger, who had at first been more cautious, had developed the "triangular" foreign policy framework that surrounded the policy and was responsible for the fitful but successful moves that brought it to fruition. The result was a cascade of acclaim for both men—which did not make Nixon happy. "He seemed obsessed by the fear that he was not receiving adequate credit," says Kissinger.

Back in the White House, a brooding president began pestering Haldeman for a public relations campaign to get him the credit he deserved. In one seventeen-paragraph memo to Haldeman, Nixon gave a detailed description of his own foreign policy strengths that he wanted Kissinger to begin selling to his friends in the press. To make matters trickier, he ordered Haldeman not to show the memo to Kissinger, but to pretend they were "simply your observations with regard to points you think he might well make." Kissinger should quit talking about the communiqué, Nixon said in the memo, because "the average person is probably tired of hearing about it." He then went on to list (referring to himself in the third person) points he wanted Kissinger to stress:

> RN goes into such meetings better prepared than anyone who has ever held this office. . . .
>
> He is able to handle any question that comes up on the spot. . . .
>
> He never gives an inch on principle. As a matter of fact, he is perhaps more rigid on principle than his advisers would want him to be. . . .
>
> He never quibbles. . . .
>
> He always keeps his eye on the main goal. . . .
>
> The qualities of subtlety, humor . . . of speaking more quietly when he is making the strongest points . . .
>
> He never takes a drink during the course of the meetings. . . .
>
> He even carries it to the extent of resisting the temptation which was so obviously presented to him, particularly with the Chinese, of eating nuts and other goodies put before him. . . .

This last sentence was a dig at Kissinger, who—as Nixon loved to point out—tended to gobble up mouthfuls of any snacks within reach while he was negotiating. In his rambling memo, Nixon went on to explain to Haldeman his "theory" that "eating tends to dull the reaction time," then he added, in a classic Nixonian way, that he "of course would not apply this same test to others." (In an interview eighteen years later, Nixon was still talking about how many peanuts and snacks Kissinger ate during negotiations.)

The good soldier Haldeman sent Kissinger a memo the next day making, as if they were his own, most of the points that Nixon had suggested. Kissinger later wrote of it: "Some of Haldeman's suggestions were on the mark; others were bizarre."

During Nixon's visit to the Ming Tombs, an American journalist had noted that the colorfully clad girls playing there seemed to be staged rather than spontaneous, and wrote that in his story. At a photo session before the Americans left Beijing, Zhou brought up the matter. "It was putting up a false appearance," the Chinese premier said with a candor hard to imagine from the American president at his side. "Your press correspondents have pointed this out to us, and we admit this was wrong. . . . We do not want to cover up the mistake on this."

Nixon did not take to heart Zhou's discourse about the dangers of cover-ups. Instead, when his turn came to reply, the president said that the pretty girls had been enjoyable, and he then criticized the press as unreliable. Back in Washington, Plumbers Unit veteran Howard Hunt, using the alias Ed Warren, was hiring college students to infiltrate Democratic campaigns. His partner, G. Gordon Liddy, met with John Mitchell and John Dean to discuss a $500,000 plan to spy on the Democrats. As a first target for wiretapping, they selected the party's headquarters in the Watergate Hotel.[5]

THE SECRET TRIP TO MOSCOW, APRIL 1972

Nixon's successful summit in Beijing, and the prospect of the upcoming May summit in Moscow, did not weaken North Vietnam's resolve to launch its annual spring offensive. The communist invasion across the demilitarized zone began on March 30, and it quickly became clear that, like the 1968 Tet offensive, which also coincided with an American election, the 1972 effort was going to be a major one.

Nixon's immediate reaction was to attempt once again a blunt form of direct linkage. He wanted to hold Moscow, and to a lesser extent Beijing, accountable for the actions of the North Vietnamese. Kissinger disagreed. "Whereas Nixon wanted to confront Hanoi and its patrons as a group, I preferred differentiating our pressures," he later explained.[6]

The Chinese were adroit at staying out of this line of fire: their ties to North Vietnam were not as strong as the Soviets', and Nixon and Kissinger were still too smitten by the new friendship to want to pick a fight.

The Soviets, who had supplied most of North Vietnam's weapons, were a different matter. At Nixon's behest, Kissinger met with Ambassador Dobrynin at the White House on April 3 and threatened to cancel the summit if Hanoi's offensive persisted. Later that week, Dobrynin was called in again and given a similarly stern warning.

All pretense of subtlety in triangular diplomacy was dispelled on April 9 when Kissinger invited Dobrynin to the White House to view movies of his visits to Beijing. Dobrynin continued to ignore Kissinger's bluster about Vietnam, but he did pass the word that the Soviets would allow Nixon to take one hundred reporters to Moscow. He knew full well where the administration's priorities lay.

Kissinger added another threat to the mix regarding his secret negotiations with Le Duc Tho in Paris, tentatively scheduled to resume on April 24. "Anatol," he said to the ambassador, "it must lead to concrete results, and if it does not, there will be incalculable consequences." Dobrynin assured him that the Soviets were hoping that the April 24 session would go well.

Ignoring all of Kissinger's threats to cancel the summit, Dobrynin invited him to Moscow to finalize plans for the May meeting, a trip that in the parity game would serve as a counterpart to his secret trip to Beijing. When the idea had been broached in February, Kissinger had made such a visit "conditional on some move by Moscow to end the war." Since then the communists had launched a major offensive and the Soviets had done nothing to stop them. Nevertheless, Kissinger decided to accept.

"The proposition," Kissinger dryly noted of his invitation to Moscow, "evoked the most diverse emotions in Nixon." A simpler description would be that Nixon hated the idea, was able to work himself up to saying so, but then shrank from a confrontation when Kissinger was persistent. In his own memoirs, Nixon cited a diary entry he made at the time: "I think perhaps I was too insistent and rough on Henry today. . . . Henry, with all of his many virtues, does seem too often to be concerned about preparing the way for negotiations with the Soviets. However, when he faces the facts, he realizes that no negotiation in Moscow is possible unless we come out all right on Vietnam."

Ego, as Kissinger later admitted, played a role in his desire to make the excursion to Moscow. Having secretly negotiated with the Chinese and North Vietnamese, he now had a chance to pull off a hat trick. "Vanity can never be completely dissociated in high office from the perception of the national interest," he later wrote. "My eagerness to go was no doubt affected by my sense of the dramatic."

Without question, if it were Rogers who had been proposed as the secret envoy to Moscow, Kissinger would have opposed such a mission with a vehemence intense enough to shake his whole body. As it was, the fact that the trip would allow him yet again to blindside Rogers, who had been engaged in a bitter struggle with him over who would handle the summit preparations, made the plan seem all the more savory.

Just after Kissinger persuaded a reluctant Nixon to authorize his secret trip, the North Vietnamese declared that they were canceling his April 24 session with Le Duc Tho—indicating that the Soviets had not overextended themselves to convince their ally to make that session successful. Kissinger sent what he called "a strong message" to the Soviets that day "questioning whether any progress could be made on Vietnam during my visit to Moscow if the Soviet Union could not bring about even one meeting." Kissinger's memoirs call the note "bold." Yet Kissinger's continued willingness to pay his secret call on Moscow seems an astonishingly flaccid reaction given the situation.

That is what Nixon thought. "I told Kissinger that I did not think he should take his secret trip to Moscow until we found out what kind of game they were playing," he later said. He broke the bad news to Kissinger as they walked from the White House across to Nixon's Executive Office Building hideaway. Because several groups of tourists were milling about and watching them, they stayed deep on the lawn. Looking back on it, Nixon stressed that his decision reflected his belief "that Henry was getting carried away with the idea of being a negotiator."

In his diary entry for April 15, Nixon seems coldly bemused by Kissinger's reaction: "Henry obviously considered this a crisis of the first magnitude. I laid down the law hard to him that under these circumstances he could not go to Moscow. . . . I can see that this shook him because he desperately wants to get to Moscow one way or another."

All was not lost. Later that afternoon, the two men had another talk. The Moscow summit would inevitably be canceled, Nixon gloomily predicted, and it would be necessary to go "hard right" on Vietnam, which might mean massive bombing of the North and blockading its harbors. Given the political uproar that would cause, Nixon said, he had an obligation to look for a successor. Perhaps Rockefeller or Reagan, he speculated, or maybe John Connally if he could be persuaded to switch parties.

Nixon's dark musings were clearly designed to elicit emotional support, and according to his diary, they did: "Henry threw up his hands and said none of them would do. . . . Henry then became very emotional about the point that I shouldn't be thinking this way or talking this way to anybody."

Well aware of Nixon's almost congenital inability to deny a request, Kissinger telephoned after dinner to persist in his pleadings: Dobrynin was still eager for him to come to Moscow for a presummit secret meeting. As an enticement to convince Nixon to let him go, Kissinger held out a possibility that, as he later made clear, he knew would never come to pass: perhaps while he was in Moscow the Soviets would persuade the North Vietnamese to send their foreign minister there for negotiations.

Nixon relented. "You've just got to go," he told Kissinger. But the president's heart was not in that decision, as those around him soon found out.[7]

On the evening of Wednesday, April 19, Kissinger stopped off at a Georgetown party. Around midnight, his black Cadillac limousine picked him up, but instead of going home, he headed for Andrews Air Force Base. At about the same time, a White House station wagon met Soviet ambassador Dobrynin on a nearby Georgetown corner. Kissinger had agreed to give him a lift to Moscow for the meeting. The CIA, unfortunately, had not been informed, and when their agents saw the Soviet ambassador snatched up from a street corner at midnight, it decided to follow the station wagon. Much to his lasting happiness, the White House driver was able to cut through parking lots, go down small alleys, and finally lose his tail. It took a day or so for the CIA and FBI to sort things out.

Before Kissinger left, Nixon told him that he was to "just pack up and come home" if Soviet general secretary Leonid Brezhnev did not offer something substantive on Vietnam. Nixon was worried that Kissinger would disobey this order out of eagerness for a summit. So he sent a cable to Kissinger's plane as it was flying toward Moscow insisting that he immediately raise the topic of Vietnam and not move on to anything else until Brezhnev had approved "some sort of understanding."[8]

Kissinger's four days of meetings began on Friday morning, April 21, and were scheduled to last until the following Monday afternoon. He and his aides—Hal Sonnenfeldt, Winston Lord, Peter Rodman, and John Negroponte—were quartered in the Lenin Hills guesthouses, a walled complex of dachas overlooking the Moscow River. There was a swimming pool for Negroponte, a tennis court for Lord and Sonnenfeldt, and a supply of movies, including an amusing one about a bumbling jewel thief. Never one to pass up the chance to send an obscure signal, Kissinger decided to play Ping-Pong with a Soviet security man.

Rogers was not informed of Kissinger's trip until it was under way. Dobrynin's counterpart, U.S. ambassador to Moscow Jacob Beam, was also not told that Kissinger was in town. Such humiliation undermines an ambassador's effectiveness because it makes clear to his host country that his superiors do not trust him, and in this case apparently trusted him less than they did Dobrynin. Beam earned the accolade that Kissinger accorded repeatedly in his memoirs to those whom he had slighted: "He deserved better." Because Beam had been cut out, Kissinger's cables to Washington could not be sent through the embassy's wire room and instead had to be handled by the temperamental radio on his plane.

Georgi Arbatov, the Kremlin's top scholar on America, recalled that Brezhnev was nervous. A gruff yet gregarious man, he had no feel for foreign policy. The week before Kissinger arrived, Brezhnev invited Arbatov to his fifth-floor office in the Central Committee building just outside the Kremlin. For two hours they talked about Kissinger. "He has a tremendous ability to charm people and to feel intuitively what arguments will work with a person," Arbatov told Brezhnev.

Arbatov's most important piece of advice was that the way to Kissinger's heart was through his ego. "He has a huge ego, and you can use it," Arbatov said. "Stroke him, treat him as a special person, deal with him as if he were an equal and not just a presidential assistant." For four days Brezhnev tried to do just that, although he was never able to dazzle and fascinate Kissinger the way that Zhou and Mao could. Instead, he struck Kissinger as rather cloddish and thick.[9]

Following Nixon's orders, Kissinger raised Vietnam first. Because of Hanoi's offensive, the U.S. might cancel the May summit, he warned; it was a threat the Soviets had learned to ignore. Brezhnev responded by reading a message from Hanoi refusing to send an envoy to meet with Kissinger in Moscow, and he proudly showed Kissinger the cable (in Russian) as if to display his sincerity.

Brezhnev then suggested a Soviet version of a cease-fire that would allow all troops to remain where they were. It was similar to what the U.S. had proposed earlier, but Kissinger rejected it because it would leave in the South all of the new North Vietnamese divisions that had poured over the demilitarized zone during the spring offensive.

Kissinger later defended his rejection of Brezhnev's plan by arguing that it was something best considered only if Hanoi proposed it at a bargaining session. That never happened. If Kissinger had accepted the idea when Brezhnev suggested it, the Soviets may have felt compelled to help achieve such a solution.[10]

In defiance of Nixon's orders, including another explicit cable that arrived on Friday night, Kissinger then moved on to arms control issues during the Saturday session, even though nothing had been resolved about Vietnam. On the matter of limiting antiballistic missile (ABM) defense systems, Brezhnev proposed ending the morass caused by conflicting American proposals by simply allowing each side to build two sites, one that would protect its capital and one that would protect an offensive missile installation. On the submarine issue, he suggested that the Soviets would accept a ceiling on their deployments, although it was a rather high number and involved a complex option to "trade in" older missiles for newer ones. In addition, the Soviets agreed to allow the whole package of limits on offensive weapons to run for five full years, which is what Washington wanted.

All told, these were rather significant concessions. For the next two days, Kissinger explored them further, mainly with Gromyko. In doing so, he opened himself up to a barrage of sniping from his home front, which further undermined his faith in the loyalty of the man he had entrusted to serve as his rear guard, Al Haig.

The situation was ripe for a confrontation. Behind the guarded walls of the Lenin Hills compound, Kissinger was in self-imposed isolation from the American embassy and reliant on the faulty radio facilities of his plane. Biting his nails and pacing up and down, he railed at Nixon's "idiocies," while Lord and Sonnenfeldt attempted to draft reassuring cables home. Because Kissinger realized, even in his excitable state, that it would be unwise to let Soviet bugging devices record his denunciations of his president, the ranting was done to the accompaniment of what was known as the babbler, a tape machine that emitted a cacophony of voices and gibberish at different frequencies, which possibly thwarted eavesdroppers and certainly drove its users to distraction.

Back at Camp David, Nixon was spending the weekend with Bebe Rebozo, who was probably no more conducive to calm reflection than an electronic babbler. On Friday, April 21, Al Haig and Bob Haldeman helicoptered up, creating a rough audience for Kissinger's diplomatic disobedience. Through Haig, Nixon sent word to Kissinger that he should return home by Sunday evening, rather than Monday as planned.

Kissinger replied to Haig personally, asking for his help in restraining Nixon. "Brezhnev wants a summit at almost any cost," Kissinger cabled. "He has told me in effect that he would not cancel it under any circumstances. He swears he knew nothing of [Hanoi's] offensive," a line that struck Nixon as naive. Kissinger added that it was "essential" that the president trust him "to play out the string and not be provocative." At the end he added a plea to Haig personally: "I am counting on you to help keep things in perspective."

Although Kissinger eventually got permission to stay through Monday, it was accompanied by Nixon's exhortations to do so only if there was "progress on the Vietnam question." In the meantime, said Haig, the president was considering immediate bombing runs near Hanoi and Haiphong. Explaining Nixon's "starchy mood," Haig informed Kissinger of some new findings by the White House's private pollster. "You should be aware that President has received results of Sindlinger Poll which indicates his popularity has risen sharply since escalation of fighting in Vietnam."

Kissinger sent back a blistering cable to Haig, which urged that there be no escalation of the bombing until he could determine whether he could get the North Vietnamese to schedule a new secret Paris session on May 2. In it he made little effort to control his frustrations:

> I am reading your messages with mounting astonishment. I cannot share the theory on which Washington operates. I do not believe that Moscow is in direct collusion with Hanoi. . . . Please keep everybody calm. We are approaching the successful culmination of our policies. Must we blow it in our eagerness to bomb targets which will not move and when the delay is only one week?

Kissinger was able to persuade Brezhnev to send an envoy to Hanoi carrying American proposals. That would have been a major diplomatic coup—and would probably have assuaged Nixon's anxieties—if it could have been announced publicly. An open declaration by Moscow that it was now helping the U.S. to try to settle the war would serve to isolate and unnerve Hanoi. In addition, it would rally domestic support in the U.S.

That is why Nixon's instructions had been explicit: when Kissinger left Moscow, the text of the statement announcing his trip should clearly indicate that Vietnam had been discussed. Since in Nixon's mind that was the sole purpose for allowing Kissinger to go on the trip, it was not unreasonable for him to expect this order to be heeded.

But Kissinger had not made this clear to the Soviets when accepting the invitation to Moscow. At the end, Foreign Minister Gromyko proposed a text that implied that Kissinger had asked for the meeting and that the purpose had been to prepare for the summit. The best Kissinger could do was reword the announcement so that it did not address the question of who had initiated the meeting and declared:

"The discussions dealt with important international problems, as well as with bilateral matters, preparatory to the talks between President Nixon and Soviet leaders in May."

Kissinger argued that "important international matters" was an "obvious" reference to Vietnam. But since the Middle East and Berlin were among the "international matters" discussed, this exceedingly ambiguous phrase did not in fact make the point Nixon wanted.

The president was furious. He cabled Kissinger that Kissinger had been "taken in" by the Soviets. In a long memo he dictated at Camp David, Nixon was brutal. "It seems to me that their primary purpose in getting you to Moscow to discuss the summit has now been served," he chided, "while our purpose of getting some progress on Vietnam has not been served."

Kissinger had earlier cabled Nixon about the progress on SALT and predicted to the president, "You will be able to sign the most important arms control agreement ever concluded." In his memo, Nixon put down that prospect as of concern only to "a few sophisticates." As a kicker, he added a line or so of clearly disingenuous praise and concluded with a sentence that did little to warm Kissinger's heart: "Rebozo joins us in sending our regards."

In his memoirs, Nixon described his disagreement with Kissinger in a muted fashion and noted only that he was "disappointed." However, when he looked back on the events in an interview, he became more critical. "There were sharply worded cables," he said. "I wanted Henry to know that it was vitally important to see our priorities taken up first. I wanted him to emphasize that Vietnam had to be front and center. It was my belief that it was vital to link progress on things the Soviets wanted, such as arms control, with progress on what we wanted." [11]

None of this diminished the new wave of public acclaim for Kissinger that accompanied the announcement of his trip. "I'd do anything for caviar," Kissinger said in response to why he went to Moscow, "and probably did." James Reston, whose *New York Times* column certified the conventional wisdom, gushed: "How he performs this delicate and dangerous role is a miracle." Hugh Sidey in *Life* listed the diverse attributes that contributed to Kissinger's success. "No one else has the combination of physical endurance, scholarship, aplomb and the knack of getting along with the wide variety of human types in positions of power," he wrote. "You can't help but admire the man." [12]

A month before Kissinger's Moscow trip, Al Haig had been given his second star. He was now a major general. More important, he had won the favor of Nixon and Haldeman with his advice on how to handle the temperamental Kissinger. Haig's behavior during his weekend at Camp David reaffirmed what both Nixon and Haldeman had been feeling: Kissinger could be emotional and uncontrollable, but Haig seemed stable and reliable; Kissinger put too much faith in negotiations, but Haig was made of sterner stuff; Kissinger was willing to make concessions that would appeal to the left, but Haig knew the importance of hanging tough.

Nixon's diaries in April and May contain phrases that would have confirmed Kissinger's worst fears. In discussing Vietnam, Haig privately disagreed with Kissinger's advice that the bombing of North Vietnam remain sporadic; instead, he recommended more concentrated assaults. He also told Nixon how important it was to make sure that he survived politically. "Haig emphasized that even more important than how Vietnam comes out is for us to handle these matters in a way that I can survive in office," Nixon wrote in his diary after one session in early May. In short, the modern major general knew exactly how to curry favor with the president and fell all over himself to do so in a manner that would have embarrassed even Kissinger.

It paid off. The good soldier who had acted as the point man on the wiretaps, who had handled the details of the covert program in Chile, and who had joined with Haldeman and Mitchell in "handling Henry" and feigning concern over his psychiatric health had now created the ultimate back channel: one that went behind the back of the master of that game.

MINING THE HARBOR OF HAIPHONG, MAY 1972

The administration's Vietnam policy was in a shambles. Hanoi's offensive was rolling southward, mowing down civilians as well as the disorganized defending forces. Vietnamization appeared to be a delusion, with no signs that Saigon's army could even mount an orderly retreat. All of the Nixon-Kissinger huffing and puffing about canceling the summit if the Soviets did not provide help on Vietnam turned out to be a bluff. Instead, linkage was becoming a looking-glass phenomenon: the American side was the one that seemed more eager for a summit, and Moscow even had the audacity to send a note warning Washington that restraint in the face of Hanoi's invasion would improve its prospects at the May summit.

Throughout April, Nixon had responded with a series of ineffective bombing runs on North Vietnam, including the first use of B-52s since Lyndon Johnson's 1968 bombing halt. Yet the pullout of American forces inexorably continued: Nixon authorized, on April 26, the withdrawal of another twenty thousand American troops over two months, despite the fact that North Vietnam had canceled the April 24 Paris secret negotiating session and had launched that very day an offensive in the Central Highlands. The announcement followed the seventy thousand ordered withdrawn in January, leaving only forty-five thousand U.S. troops in country, none of them in combat units. The pretense of basing the pullouts on Nixon's Vietnamization criteria—reduction of enemy activity, progress in negotiations, increases in South Vietnam's military capability—was now a complete sham. Enemy activity was at its highest level in four years, Hanoi had broken off negotiations, and South Vietnam's army was in disorderly retreat.

"I have decided," Nixon said in announcing the pullouts, "that Vietnamization has proved itself sufficiently that we can continue our program of withdrawing American forces." In fact, his motive was political, as shown by an "eyes only" memo he wrote to Kissinger disparaging hope for a negotiated settlement. "What is vital," Nixon wrote, "is that a final announcement of some kind must be made before the Democratic Convention in July. . . . Our announcement must be one which indicates that all American combat forces have left. . . . Before the Democratic Convention we must make a final announcement of some type or we will be in very serious trouble."[13]

On May 1, the city of Quangtri fell. "Thousands of panicking South Vietnamese soldiers fled in confusion from Quangtri Province today, streaming south down Route 1 like a rabble out of control," wrote Sydney Schanberg in the New York Times. The South Vietnamese soldiers hurled rocks at newsmen filming their flight, while the North Vietnamese fired on fleeing civilians. When Kissinger got the message from General Abrams in Saigon, he walked it into the Oval Office. "What else does he say?" Nixon asked.

Kissinger cleared his throat nervously and answered, "He feels that he has to report that it is quite possible that the South Vietnamese have lost their will to fight."

Kissinger was scheduled to leave for Paris late that night for his rescheduled secret session with Le Duc Tho. "They'll be riding high because of this," Nixon said of the North Vietnamese, "so you'll have to bring them down to the ground by your manner. No nonsense. No niceness. No accommodations. And we'll have to let our Soviet friends know that I'm willing to give up the summit if this is the price they have in mind to make us pay for it. Under no circumstances will I go to the summit if we're still in trouble over Vietnam."

Nixon's threat to cancel the summit was reiterated in a rambling memo he dictated for Kissinger to read on his flight to Paris. "I intend to cancel the summit unless the situation militarily or diplomatically substantially improves," he noted. The only exception would be if "we get a firm commitment from the Russians to announce a joint agreement at the summit to use our influence to end the war." None of these things would happen. As for the North Vietnamese, Nixon advised: "You have only one message to give them—Settle or else!"[14]

The meeting with Le Duc Tho was, as Kissinger later wrote, "brutal." As an aficionado of the relationship between force and diplomacy, Kissinger should not have been surprised that Hanoi was unwilling to discuss a compromise or cease-fire while its troops were rolling across South Vietnam. After a series of exchanges that came close to shouting matches, Kissinger broke off the talks. As he was preparing to leave, Le Duc Tho pulled him aside and, with the smirk of a co-conspirator, said that the prospects for the North Vietnamese were looking good.

When Kissinger arrived home that Tuesday evening, Haig met him at Andrews Air Force Base with a helicopter that would take them to join Nixon on the *Sequoia*. It was a confirmation of Haig's new status that he was invited as a full participant in the floating discussion, rather than just as Kissinger's loyal deputy.

Over the rumble of the old boat's engine, the three of them sat around the wardroom table and agreed that a major military response was necessary. The main question was what to do about the Moscow summit scheduled for later in the month: Nixon reluctantly said it was necessary to cancel.

The prospect of losing the summit horrified Kissinger. Although his fury at the North Vietnamese had heightened his conviction that a hard military blow was necessary, he had no stomach for a breakdown in negotiations and further domestic turmoil. Above all, he wanted to put into place the keystone of what he called his "structure of peace." The Soviet summit would complete the new foreign policy balance he had worked on for three years.

"Henry was wavering and playing both sides," Haldeman recalls. "But when he listed the cons of taking a strong action and canceling the summit, he expressed it in more cataclysmic terms than the pro side." What Kissinger and Nixon both wanted was a way to go to Moscow in the midst of a North Vietnamese offensive without seeming like pushovers.[15]

As they searched for a rationale to back off their threats and save the summit, a shift occurred in the way they cast the question. The original considerations in favor of canceling the summit were the impropriety of clinking glasses in the Kremlin while Soviet-supplied tanks were killing American soldiers, and the need to make good on months of threats that Soviet-American relations would suffer if the situation in Vietnam did not improve. Suddenly, these considerations were no longer raised and a new consideration emerged as the main reason for canceling: since Nixon had tentatively decided to take strong military measures against North Vietnam, it made sense to cancel the summit immediately in order to preempt the Soviets from canceling first.

The night after he returned empty-handed from Paris, Kissinger met with Nixon in the Lincoln Sitting Room to go over military options. Haldeman, who was there, could not understand why Kissinger was convinced that the Soviets would cancel the summit if the U.S. attacked North Vietnam. "Henry, you keep saying you know the Soviets will cancel," Haldeman recalls saying to him in front of Nixon. "But you don't *know* what the Soviets are going to do. Nobody can *know.*" Kissinger protested that this was a foreign policy question outside Haldeman's purview. Haldeman replied that it was merely a logical point: there was no reason to pretend to know what the Soviets would do.

In fact, Haldeman would be proved right. After all, the Soviets had always opposed linkage of an arms control summit to Vietnam. What Haldeman and the political experts sensed more keenly than Kissinger was that Brezhnev was basically a political hack, not a geostrategist, and as such he was less likely to let Vietnam tangle up plans for a summit.

Nixon sent Haldeman and Kissinger to consult with Treasury Secretary John Connally, whose rawhide toughness, swaggering self-assurance, and hardscrabble political instincts had made him Nixon's latest golden boy.

When Kissinger arrived at Connally's spacious corner office facing the White House, he began "fretting and wringing his hands," Connally recalled, about the plan to mine the harbors. "Maybe we ought not do this," Kissinger said, "because if we do, we'll have to cancel the summit."

Connally's tough-guy instincts came flooding out. "That makes no sense," he replied. "If we cancel, it would look like we had done something wrong." Nixon should bomb and mine and do whatever else he thought necessary to punish North Vietnam, Connally counseled. "And if the Russians want to cancel the summit, let them. But I sure don't think that they will."

With a modesty that was more becoming than convincing, Kissinger recalled that "as soon as Connally had spoken, I knew he was right." Conveniently, by admitting what they both call their "mistake,"

Nixon and Kissinger could do what they wanted to all along: go to Moscow for a summit even though all of their warnings about the adverse impact of a North Vietnamese invasion had been ignored.[16]

There was, of course, still the question of whether the Soviets would cancel the summit in response to the new military measures Nixon decided to take in Vietnam.

On the afternoon of Thursday, May 4, a few hours after Kissinger's discussion with Connally, the president went to his hideaway in the Executive Office Building to make his decision on what military steps to take in response to North Vietnam's unabated offensive. With him were Kissinger, Haldeman, and the new addition to the inner circle, Haig. As usual, Secretary of State Rogers and Defense Secretary Laird were cut out. Kissinger had ordered Admiral Moorer, chairman of the Joint Chiefs, to prepare contingency plans without Laird's knowledge.

Having passed through his Patton phase, this time Nixon played MacArthur; he paced up and down the long office, gesticulating with and occasionally puffing on a pipe, which no one had ever seen him smoke before. Based on Admiral Moorer's suggestions and on a dusted-off version of the Duck Hook options that had been discussed in 1969, Kissinger recommended mining Haiphong and the other major harbors of North Vietnam and increasing the B-52 bombings, especially around Hanoi.

Both the Defense Department and the CIA had concluded that mining the harbors would have little military significance. The communist offensive, which was already under way, would not be affected. Kissinger disagreed. Most of Hanoi's oil came by sea and would be difficult to move by rail. Even though the mining would do little to blunt the current offensive, it would sap the communist assurance that it could fight on indefinitely afterward.

Kissinger's staff met on Saturday afternoon to work out the plans in the absence of participation by State and Defense. Hal Sonnenfeldt predicted the Soviets would cancel the summit, John Holdridge predicted the Chinese would freeze relations, John Negroponte predicted the impact on South Vietnamese morale would be dramatic, and the CIA's George Carver said that land supply routes would soon substitute for sea ones. Each was wrong.[17]

Kissinger sent a secret, back-channel message to Ambassador Bunker in Saigon informing him of the decision. "To put it in the bluntest terms," Kissinger wrote, "we are not interested in half-measures; we want to demonstrate to Hanoi that we really mean business." He asked Bunker to come up with statistics, for Nixon to use in his announcement, showing the high number of civilian casualties that the communists had inflicted on civilians in the South. Truthfulness was not a high priority. "Do not hesitate to give us ballpark figures," Kissinger wrote in the secret cable, "and we will not object if they incline towards the high side." [18]

At Camp David that Sunday, Kissinger and Winston Lord met with Nixon and two of his speechwriters, Ray Price and John Andrews. The summit was a goner, Lord lamented, and he engaged in a grim banter with Kissinger as they went over the speech. Any language we don't use we can put into next year's State of the World report, Kissinger said.

"Yes, the title of that will probably be 'The Collapsed Structure of Peace,' " Lord replied.

"With this speech," added Kissinger, "we can take a grim satisfaction in the fact that we are wrecking in twenty minutes what it has taken three and a half years to build." [19]

On Monday morning, Nixon held a meeting of the National Security Council to formalize what he had already decided. According to U. Alexis Johnson, who was undersecretary of state for political affairs, Kissinger tried to pull a scam on William Rogers. Even though he knew the decision to mine Haiphong and bomb Hanoi had been made, Kissinger tried to get Rogers to oppose it.

The deceit, according to Johnson, began on Sunday morning when he was called by Kissinger and told of the bombing-and-mining decision. Mining the harbors, Johnson argued, would provoke outrage from countless nations whose ships were there. He also worried that the summit would be canceled. Johnson recalls Kissinger's response:

> Henry said he agreed with me. He felt the chances of losing the summit were 95 to 5, while the President only rated it at 50 to 50. He said he had been trying to persuade the President against the mining, which he claimed was the brainchild of John Connally and John Mitchell, but to no avail. He said that he would have to rely on Secretary Rogers to sway the President's mind at the NSC meeting scheduled for Monday morning.

Johnson relayed all of this to Rogers, who said he doubted that Kissinger was telling the truth. At the NSC meeting, the secretary ended up waffling. "Rogers's hunch that Henry was only pretending to oppose the plan turned out to be right," Johnson later noted. "Given his addiction to Machiavellian intrigue, perhaps he was trying to discredit Rogers further with the President by setting him up to attack a decision the President had already made." Kissinger later denied any duplicity; his intention, he said, was merely to allow Rogers to have his say.[20]

On Monday afternoon, Kissinger went to Nixon's hideaway office with the papers for him to sign ordering the mining and stepped-up bombings. There he also found Haldeman, who had been listening to Nixon fume at Kissinger for being two-faced. The president had gotten reports, Haldeman later explained, that Kissinger was telling people that he had opposed the decision. So they decided to test him. As Nixon nodded, Haldeman said that they were having second thoughts, that the operation would have dire effects on the president's popularity, and that it might cause his defeat in the election. Kissinger defended the decision to mine and bomb. When Nixon stepped out to the bathroom, Kissinger wheeled on Haldeman to castigate him for allowing last-minute doubts. Haldeman grinned sheepishly as if to say that he had been put up to the charade, not to worry. Later, when the taping system became known, Kissinger concluded that Nixon's purpose was to get him on record supporting the plan to guard against stories that he had privately opposed it.

Nixon announced the escalation in a televised speech, and the instant analysis of both pundits and politicians was that the mines being laid in Haiphong harbor would sink the summit. Kissinger, too, was pessimistic, and he gave the impression to friends that he doubted the wisdom of the president's course, just as Haldeman had feared. His former aide Roger Morris, writing on the op-ed page of the *New York Times*, referred to "the artless leaks trickling through Washington that this was the decision Henry finally opposed." *Life's* Hugh Sidey, who had talked with Kissinger, wrote: "Henry Kissinger's private convictions, to the extent that they could be determined, seemed less than granite."

Ambassador Dobrynin was also gloomy, for he, too, assumed that his masters in the Kremlin would now cancel the summit. But the day after the speech, when Kissinger called him, he had no word to report from Moscow. Kissinger added another link to linkage: the West German government, he told the Soviet ambassador, had secured enough votes to pass the treaty relating to Berlin that had been stalled in the Bundestag. That was important to the Soviets, and Kissinger sought to gain some credit even though the U.S. had not really played a role in forcing Bonn's decision. (American control over the Bundestag was probably about the same as Soviet control over Hanoi's politburo, but each side imagined the other with far more clout.)[21]

In Moscow, the decision was delayed because May 9 was the Soviet version of VE day, and everyone was out celebrating the last great triumph of Soviet-American cooperation. Georgi Arbatov and other veterans from his World War II artillery regiment were having a drunken reunion. When he finally got home from lunch at eleven P.M., there were messages that Brezhnev and KGB boss Yuri Andropov had called. The question of how to respond to the American actions would be taken up at a nine A.M. meeting at Central Committee headquarters the next morning, and Arbatov was told to be there.

Brezhnev seemed surprisingly relaxed when he walked into the conference room at the appointed hour, Arbatov later recalled. Present were about a dozen people, including Gromyko, Andropov, and representatives of the Defense Ministry. Andropov, who would later become the Soviet leader, opened the discussion, much as CIA director Richard Helms might have at an NSC meeting. When he called on Arbatov, the American-affairs academician recommended not canceling the summit. "It won't help Vietnam," he argued, "and our main concern should be Germany and relations with the U.S."

With the support of most of the politburo later in the day, Brezhnev tentatively decided not to call off the summit. His strongest opposition came from Pyotr Shelest, the party boss in the Ukraine. "I will not shake the hand that has been bloodied in Vietnam," he said of Nixon. Brezhnev then turned to the politburo's other Ukrainian member, Vladimir Shcherbitsky. Did he agree? No, he said. Brezhnev turned to Shelest. "You see, Comrade, you can speak for yourself, but you cannot speak for all Ukrainians."

But Brezhnev did not feel secure enough in his leadership to act without fuller support. He showed Arbatov several cables he had gotten from the regional party secretaries, most filled with anti-American rhetoric. "A lot of them want to call off the summit, defeat Nixon in the election, and show our principles," Brezhnev told his adviser. So he decided to call a rather unusual special session of the entire Central Committee on May 19, three days before the summit was set to begin, in order to ratify the decision. "I do not want to take all the blame," Brezhnev told Arbatov.

Brezhnev asked Arbatov to write his speech for the Central Committee. He was assisted by Arkady Shevchenko, then an aide to Foreign Minister Gromyko and later a high-profile defector to the U.S. By the time the Central Committee met in the Kremlin, Brezhnev had already lined up enough support. Shelest was removed as Ukrainian party boss and replaced by Shcherbitsky, who did shake Nixon's hand when he arrived in Kiev the next week.

"Kissinger thinks it was China that played the decisive role in getting us to feel the need to preserve our relationship with the U.S.A.," said Arbatov in an interview years later. "But Berlin actually played a much bigger role, almost a decisive one. Having the East German situation settled was most important to us, and we did not want to jeopardize that."

During the Central Committee meeting, there was a critical Bundestag vote on the treaty. "Brezhnev called a recess so that we could hear the results come in," Arbatov recalled. It passed by one vote. "If things had gone the other way in Bonn, Brezhnev and the Central Committee would have decided to cancel the summit, I am convinced. But we had assurances from Kissinger that it was going to come out right."[22]

Kissinger got his first indication that the Soviets were going to go through with the summit when Dobrynin paid a call on May 10. The note of protest he brought was mild, and he tried to entice Kissinger into a sealed-envelope guessing game about what the politburo would decide. Then he tipped his hand by asking whether the president had decided to receive Trade Minister Nikolai Patolichev, who was visiting America as the guest of Commerce Secretary Peter Peterson. Kissinger allowed as how it might be possible to fit it into Nixon's schedule. Press and photographers were usually present, he added. Would the Soviets mind? Dobrynin said they would not.

When Patolichev arrived at the Oval Office, he and the president discussed how to say the word *friendship* in different languages. An NBC correspondent shouted out a question about whether the summit was still on. Responded Patolichev: "We never had any doubts about it. I don't know why you asked this question. Have you any doubts?"[23]

President Thieu of South Vietnam was never consulted about the American mining-and-bombing plan, but he was elated by the news. In retrospect, his only complaint was that the escalation was short-lived. "You had the chance to win the war," he said, looking back after almost twenty years. "If you had kept bombing Hanoi, you would have seen from your planes a white flag rise up over Hanoi. But Kissinger was worried too much about Russia and China. So you were doing the war without conviction."[24]

Unlike the May 1970 invasion of Cambodia, the May 1972 escalation provoked little popular uproar. Vietnamization had served to tamp down domestic dissent. In addition, the Soviet decision to proceed with the summit undercut the vocal handful that did protest.

Vietnamization also proved hardy in another respect: the North Vietnamese advance soon began to slow. By the end of the summer, it had been relegated to the history books as just another spring offensive, and Le Duc Tho was back at the bargaining table. "The mining at least halted the headlong North Vietnamese advance, and in a sense purchased time," former aide Roger Morris, generally a critic, later wrote. "More restraining on Hanoi than the blockade, however, may have been the cautious indifference of its patrons in Peking and, of course, Moscow."

The decision to hold the summit undermined the principle of linkage. Kissinger had originally argued that linkage was not merely a policy but a reflection of reality: arms control and trade deals with the Soviets could naturally occur only if tensions were reduced around the world. That was wrong. Likewise, it was wrong to think that crude pressure would force the Soviets to do something concrete to end the Vietnam War. When they wouldn't, Kissinger and Nixon, after a lot of huffing, backed down from their insistence that summits and trade agreements would be held hostage to progress on Vietnam.

Kissinger cast the result as a triumph for his more subtle form of linkage: both China and the Soviet Union had been enticed into a web that made it in each of their interests to seek better relations with the U.S., even if it meant turning their backs on North Vietnam. America's mining of Vietnam's harbors was a major, provocative move, one that in a different environment could have provoked a military showdown with Moscow, especially since some of its ships were in Haiphong harbor and were hit by bombs. As it was, there would be only a few muted protests followed by champagne toasts in St. Vladimir's Hall.

"I always rejected the theory that we could force the Soviets to actively help us," Sonnenfeldt later said. "But I thought we could erect a structure in which it would be in their interest to see the war wind down and their solidarity with Hanoi downplayed. And we did."

Kissinger was exuberant. The first major test of détente had resulted in the Soviet Union's tacitly accepting an American military blow in Vietnam. "This has got to be one of the great diplomatic coups of all time!" he exulted to the president as they headed toward Moscow on the mission that would culminate their quest for a new international structure.

If Kissinger had any regrets, it was that the mining and bombing had not been attempted earlier. If the harbors had been mined and the bombing of the North resumed in 1969, as contemplated in the Duck Hook plan, the war would have been over by 1970, he would later say.[25]

THE MOSCOW SUMMIT, MAY 1972

Shortly before midnight on Friday, May 26, Richard Nixon and the leaders of the Soviet Union met in the green and gold hall of St. Vladimir in the Grand Kremlin Palace to sign agreements that marked the end of an era of unfettered arms competition and ushered in one that would be defined by the fits and starts of arms control negotiations. Out of his pocket, the president pulled a silver Parker fountain pen, used it on the most important of the strategic arms limitation agreements, and quietly slipped it back into his pocket. Later, privately, he would give it to Henry Kissinger. When the champagne arrived, the president toasted his hosts. Then, across the hall, he caught Kissinger's eye. Silently, he raised his glass in tribute. Smiling broadly, Kissinger returned the gesture.[26]

In addition to the arms control treaties, the week-long Moscow summit that began on May 22 would feature at least six other accords plus plans for improved trade relations and grain sales. At the outset, the New York Times's Max Frankel asked Kissinger at a background briefing whether he planned "to dribble out announcements through the week or is there going to be one big orgy of agreements?" Kissinger answered: "Our plan is to dribble out an orgy of announcements."

During the summit, Nixon, Kissinger, and their top aides were housed in the Czar's Apartments in the Kremlin, a sprawling Italianate fortress facing Red Square. Rogers and others from the State Department were isolated at the Rossiya Hotel about five minutes away, where they had corridors of office space, an entire hotel floor, a grand ballroom as a work space, and virtually nothing to do.

Kissinger and his crew—led by Sonnenfeldt, Hyland, and Lord—used a piano in a converted Kremlin bedroom as a filing area for SALT documents. The Vietnam papers were kept on a window ledge. This makeshift office was located next to the room of Pat Nixon's hairdresser, Rita de Santis, who could not figure out the electrical gadgetry and repeatedly asked Kissinger's aides to crawl around the floor wiring things for her. "Our demeanor in those moments," recalled Hyland, "confirmed Kissinger's view that we were not taking the summit seriously enough."[27]

On the first afternoon, Brezhnev invited Nixon over for an opening talk. But unlike when he met with Mao, Nixon headed off to it alone, without Kissinger. "Kissinger was beside himself," recalled Georgi Arbatov. He paced around and railed at Dobrynin that he had to be allowed in. "This could be the most important meeting of the summit," Kissinger fumed, "and there's no telling what he's saying in there." Particularly irksome was a practice that he often indulged in himself: Nixon was using only the Soviet interpreter, Viktor Sukhodrev. Thus, there would be no American notes for Kissinger to review.

Sukhodrev went to the Central Committee offices to write up a transcript for the Soviet records. Dobrynin came by with a plea from Kissinger: would Sukhodrev give him a copy? After checking to see that Brezhnev approved, Sukhodrev complied.

But the experience of being excluded did not cure Kissinger's penchant for secrecy. He asked Sukhodrev to provide the memo in English so that the State Department would not have to be brought in to do a translation. Sukhodrev arrived at the Kremlin at midnight and began dictating to Kissinger's secretary, Julie Pineau. Kissinger wandered in, shirt half unbuttoned, and with his usual charm toward subordinates growled to Pineau that he wanted it by seven A.M. Then he turned to Sukhodrev. "Viktor," he said, "can I trust you with this girl?"

"The task you gave us," Sukhodrev replied, "means there won't be time for anything else."[28]

Though not officially on the summit agenda, Vietnam was the dominant topic at a strange session conducted at Brezhnev's dacha, a stolid country home in the birch groves along the Moscow River a forty-minute drive from the Kremlin. After a minor signing ceremony one day, Brezhnev unexpectedly whisked Nixon away in a speeding Zil limousine, followed by a frantic Kissinger, baffled Secret Service agents, and eventually Lord and Negroponte. Upon their arrival at the dacha, Brezhnev treated Nixon to a frenetic hydrofoil ride.[29]

When everybody finally got to the oval table in the dacha's conference room, a desultory review of various issues ensued until Nixon turned the focus onto Vietnam. Suddenly, each of the three Soviet leaders—Brezhnev, Premier Aleksei Kosygin, and President Nikolai Podgorny—took turns launching into a diatribe.

Despite the vehemence, the whole scene seemed almost theatrical, as if the Soviets wanted to make a formal record that could be shown to hard-liners at home and fraternal allies in Hanoi. Hyland's Soviet counterpart later told him it had all been carefully planned, although Podgorny, who had not been properly briefed, got carried away a bit. Underneath all the fireworks was a rather mild reaction: none of the Soviet leaders mentioned that a plane had recently landed bearing the bodies of two Soviet seamen killed in the American bombing of Haiphong harbor. Once the show was over, Brezhnev invited everyone up to the second-floor dining room for a lavish and jovial meal.

The next day, Kissinger had a more substantive discussion about

Vietnam with Foreign Minister Gromyko where he broached a possible modification in the American position. Washington had previously offered that an "electoral commission" could be established to conduct new South Vietnamese elections. Kissinger now made the subtle concession that this commission could be a tripartite group with representatives of the Saigon regime, the communists, and neutralists. This made the electoral commission look like the "tripartite coalition government" that Hanoi wanted established. The concession was minor but significant because it paved the way for an eventual solution that would fudge the distinction between an electoral commission and an interim coalition government.[30]

One of Kissinger's focuses at the summit was a thousand-word declaration of "the Basic Principles" of Soviet-American relations, which was designed as a road map to détente. In it, both sides agreed to forswear "efforts to obtain unilateral advantage at the expense of the other," and they pledged not to exploit regional tensions or to claim spheres of influence in various areas of the world.

Soviet officials gave this "Basic Principles" document a high priority, emphasizing it in the Moscow press even more than the SALT accords. Kissinger also considered it a key achievement. But most American officials, especially the president and the State Department, tended to dismiss it as boilerplate.

With good reason: the document sought to enshrine a nebulous and unworkable code of conduct that in later years would lead to disenchantment because it would be invoked at every evidence of Soviet adventurism. It did not restrain the Soviets from exploiting tensions in Angola, nor the Americans from seeking unilateral advantages in the Middle East. Indeed the very notion of forswearing attempts to exploit tensions or obtain unilateral advantage was part of the fatuous overselling of détente. "Even lifelong drinkers occasionally try to stay on the wagon," Stanley Hoffmann later noted, "but great powers rarely give up playing international relations."

Kissinger nonetheless was able to turn this declaration, as he had the Shanghai Communiqué, into another of his intrigues to cut out Secretary Rogers. For no legitimate reason, Rogers had not been told that the document was in the works. Consequently, as happened with the invitation to the summit and with the Shanghai Communiqué, Kissinger had to enlist the other side in a ruse to spring it on Rogers. Brezhnev was asked to pretend that he had suddenly proposed the document to the U.S. The Soviet leader readily agreed. "This was a game Brezhnev could recognize," Kissinger later wrote.[31]

One of the key elements of linkage was the American enticement of better economic relations. Nothing concrete was settled at the summit, but arrangements were made for a July visit by Commerce Secretary Peter Peterson to discuss "most-favored-nation" trade status. Nixon had originally brought Peterson into the White House as a special assistant for international economics, telling him that it was a field Kissinger knew nothing about. "Peterson, that's just a minor economic consideration," Kissinger once said to him as they debated a policy. Replied Peterson: "Henry, for you that's a redundancy because you see every economic consideration as minor."

Over the next few months, Peterson would reach an agreement that would grant the Soviets most-favored-nation trade status and settle the Lend-Lease debts from World War II. At the same time, the North Vietnamese would suddenly become willing to negotiate an end to the war. (By 1975, the trade status deal would come unraveled. So, at that precise time, would the peace in Vietnam. The Soviets have a favorite phrase that goes, "It is no accident that . . .")

One of the economic arrangements to emerge was the infamous grain deal of 1972, known as the Great Grain Robbery. Handled mainly by the ebullient agricultural secretary, Earl Butz, it arranged for the Soviets to make major purchases of surplus American grain in return for credit and the right to buy at subsidized prices. It was seen, at first, as a political coup for the president. What happened, however, was that instead of the $150 million worth of grain that Kissinger thought would be involved, the Soviets went quietly into the marketplace to cut deals with different U.S. companies. Soon it was discovered that they had bought an amazing $1 billion worth at subsidized prices, which ended up inflating bread costs for Americans in an election year.

"It was painful to realize that we had been outmaneuvered," Kissinger said. He claimed not to have known that a disastrous harvest had put them in such a desperate situation. But a Joseph Alsop column written at the time of the summit, with Kissinger transparently as a source, mentions in passing the importance the Soviets were placing on trade agreements. "Because of the Soviet crop failure," Alsop wrote, "there will surely be a big, immediate grain deal."

Kissinger had been working to eliminate the requirement that half of all exports to the Soviets be carried on American-flagged vessels. Kissinger even tried, rather unsuccessfully, to persuade American union leaders to go along with such a change. After the dimensions of the "grain robbery" became apparent, Peterson argued him out of this course. The Soviets had pulled off a sweet deal, he said, but at least they could pay the U.S. some of the shipping costs.[32]

•

Serving as the centerpiece of the May 1972 summit were the Strategic Arms Limitation Talks (SALT I). There were two main components: a treaty limiting antiballistic missile (ABM) defense systems and an "Interim Agreement" freezing offensive missile construction for five years. After inadvertently leading the Soviets to believe that the U.S. might accept an ABM accord on its own, Kissinger in May 1971 had succeeded in relinking it to an offensive freeze. But that "breakthrough" left open a lot of questions: how many ABM sites could each side have? Would submarine-launched missiles (SLBMs) be included in the offensive-weapons freeze? How much modernization or upgrading of land-based missiles (ICBMs) would be permitted under the freeze?

On his secret trip to Moscow in April, Kissinger had pretty much resolved the ABM mess. He agreed that each side would be allowed two ABM sites, one protecting its national capital and another protecting a missile installation. This was to America's disadvantage because it had no plans, and never would, to build a defense around Washington. But in the overall scheme of things, it was not very important. The ABM treaty would be a major achievement because it would assure that any defensive system would be strategically insignificant. Neither nation could now upset the stability of deterrence by trying to protect itself from a counterattack. A potentially costly and complex area of arms competition was thus contained.

Also during his April trip, Kissinger had been able to get the Soviets to include submarines in the Interim Agreement's missile freeze, albeit by conceding a rather high ceiling. What remained to be settled at the summit were some arcane questions about how these SLBMs would be tallied and how ICBM modernization would be defined. Their complexity argued for involving America's negotiating experts, but Kissinger's impatience and vanity contributed to the decision to keep them in Helsinki where they had been holding their official talks.

As a result, the details of the final agreements would prove less important than the Lone Ranger style in which Kissinger concluded them. With an amazing display of diplomatic dissimulation, he was able to infuriate a spectrum of influential Americans including arms negotiators Gerard Smith and Paul Nitze, Admirals Thomas Moorer and Elmo Zumwalt, and Senators Henry Jackson and Barry Goldwater. This did not bode well for the future of the SALT process.

At the crux of the dispute over ICBM modernization was America's desire to prevent the Soviets from upgrading their "light" missiles into ones that were bigger. This involved getting limits on how much they could increase two things: the size of the missiles and the volume of the silos in which they were deployed. But there was an obstacle. The Soviets were already in the process of building two new "light" missiles with MIRVed warheads that would be bigger than the old ones. Thus, the Soviets resisted accepting tight limits on missile size or silo volume increases.

In Helsinki, the two delegations had agreed on a vague provision that "no significant increase" in silo volume would be permitted, without defining *significant*. Kissinger later claimed that American negotiator Gerry Smith and his delegation tried to pin this down to 15 percent or less, and that they proposed making this a "unilateral statement" by the Americans after the Soviets refused. Kissinger disparaged this: "To rest an agreement on a unilateral statement which the Soviets had rejected seemed too risky." But Raymond Garthoff, the negotiator who was handling this issue for Smith, said that Kissinger was wrong. The Americans in Helsinki never proposed a 15 percent definition or a unilateral statement. That statement, he says, had been prepared as a fallback on Kissinger's own orders—against the wishes of the delegation.

To Kissinger's amazement, Brezhnev suggested they could solve the issue by taking out the word *significant*. Kissinger sent Gerard Smith an urgent message in Helsinki saying that Brezhnev's offer apparently meant that the Soviets had no intention of increasing the "size" of their missiles. In fact, it meant nothing of the sort: the statement referred to the silo, not the missile.

More important, the Soviet proposal effectively applied only to the silo's diameter, because the Soviets had been insisting on inserting the phrase "observable with the aid of national technical means." Translated, this means that size limits would be subject to verification only by satellites, which can gauge the diameter but not the depth of silos. The new light missiles that the Soviets were building could squeeze into the old silos if they were deepened.

Though Kissinger was not an expert on these nuances, he continued to insist on negotiating such details without letting the SALT delegation come to Moscow. He faced not only Gromyko but a brilliant and bullet-headed arms specialist named L. V. Smirnov, who flew into a fury every time Kissinger attempted humorous banter. The Soviets backed away from what Brezhnev had seemed to offer and said that they would agree merely to a provision that there be "no *significant* changes" in silo dimensions, and they would say nothing about missile size. Kissinger responded by saying that "significant" had to be defined as 15 percent.

Finally, Gromyko accepted a 15 percent limit on increases in silo "dimensions." Kissinger was exultant, and years later he claimed it was much better than what the SALT delegation would have accepted. But Garthoff later pointed out that Kissinger, even when writing about his triumph later, never quite understood that the word *dimensions* had been substituted for *volume*. This meant that the Soviets could, if they chose, increase the diameter by 15 percent, which would increase the total volume of a silo by 32 percent.

In addition, the compromise Kissinger accepted did nothing to limit increases in missile (rather than silo) size. Instead, he authorized a "unilateral statement" of the American definition of a "light" missile. He then came close to outright deception in a congressional briefing the next month where he told Senator Henry Jackson that there was a "safeguard that no missile larger than the heaviest light missile that now exists can be substituted." There was no such safeguard, only the unilateral statement. Oddly, this was the type of unenforceable solution Kissinger denounced in his memoirs as "too risky" when discussing the silo issue. Even more oddly, in a footnote just a few pages later, he laments that "we overestimated the restraining effect of such a unilateral statement."

This disingenuous attitude hurt the SALT process. Kissinger knew full well that the Soviets were planning to build a larger "light" missile; he even had telephone intercepts of Soviet leaders discussing the proposed new missile. Once it became obvious that the U.S. could not convince the Soviets to sign an agreement that would halt this program, Kissinger had two choices: an agreement that accepted this fact of life, or one that tried to hide this fact with unenforceable unilateral statements that the Soviets had rejected. By choosing the latter course, Kissinger paved the way for an uproar among American hard-liners about Soviet "cheating" when Moscow went ahead and built its new missile.

The submarine-launched missile (SLBM) issue was, if possible, even more numbingly esoteric. Only after fathoming its intricacies is it apparent how shallow the dispute was. It arose because the Soviets were in the midst of a building program, which the U.S. was not. In order to get them to include submarines in the "freeze," Kissinger offered an idea first floated by Melvin Laird: they could continue to build their new Y-class submarines, but in order to preserve the concept of a freeze they would have to "trade in" older missiles by scrapping them.

That was the simple part. The hard part involved deciding how high the Soviets would eventually be allowed to go (Kissinger agreed to 950 SLBMs deployed on 62 subs), what baseline would be used for the current number of Soviet SLBMs deployed or under construction (it was a somewhat arbitrary number that depended on whose figures you believed and how you defined "under construction"), and whether Moscow's aging G-class diesel subs should count as part of the baseline, the total, or those eligible to use as trade-ins.

Suffice it to say that the solutions Kissinger came up with were considered far too generous by all of those he had cut out of the process, ranging from Gerard Smith to Admiral Elmo Zumwalt. Kissinger tried to make the 950 figure seem low by commissioning a study of what the Soviets might build without any constraints. The top projection, based on the assumption that the Soviets would speed up their construction programs as much as possible, led to a figure of about 1,150 SLBMs, which Kissinger henceforth cited in defense of what he had achieved. As it turned out, however, the Soviets never even got to the 950 figure during the original five-year life of the interim accord.

As one would expect, most of the American officials who had been cut out of Kissinger's negotiations cabled their opinions that the number should be lower. But in fairness to Kissinger, the deal was as good as could be expected. The U.S. did not have an active submarine-building program of its own, and consequently had little leverage. Kissinger essentially got the Soviets to agree to limit their submarine deployments at about the level they were planning to anyway, and the U.S. did not give up anything at all.

Once again, however, Kissinger undermined future support for SALT by his trickiness in dealing with some of the details. For example, the Soviet right to trade in old missiles for new submarine-launched ones applied to the Americans as well. This was a moot point since the U.S. had no new submarine in the works for at least five years. But the Soviets sought a written assurance that the U.S. would not exercise its trade-in rights, and Kissinger assented. Not only that, he insisted that the written assurance be kept secret.

Under questioning by Senator Jackson the next month, Kissinger insisted that "there are no secret understandings." Later, as if it were an afterthought, he was a bit more candid: "There are, of course, in the discussions, general statements of intentions. For example, we have conveyed to the Soviets what I have also said here publicly on the record: that the option of converting the Titans into submarines, given our present construction program, was not something we would necessarily carry out." In 1974, the secret written note was made public. It came in a period of revelations concerning the wiretaps, Watergate, and the Radford spy ring. Despite the fact that Kissinger had half-mentioned it in his testimony, the revelation of the note undermined his credibility and public support for détente.[33]

"In retrospect," said Kissinger, "it would have been better to have brought both delegations to Moscow and let them continue their work there" during the summit. Leaving out the American delegation—which included such experts as Gerard Smith, Paul Nitze, and Raymond Garthoff—meant that misunderstandings occurred and hours were wasted sending coded messages from Moscow to the White House Situation Room to Helsinki and back. "Frankly, we hadn't come prepared for a whole lot of detailed negotiations," said Hyland. "We didn't have all our info, and it was a real mess at times."

In addition, the people who might naturally have been the most enthusiastic supporters of the SALT accord, officials such as Smith and Garthoff and Nitze, who had dedicated years of their lives to reaching such an accomplishment, ended up feeling resentful and dispirited.

Kissinger blamed the decision not to bring Smith and his team to Moscow on Nixon's desire to get the White House credit for concluding the negotiation, though he admits that his own willingness to go along was "not uninfluenced by vanity and the desire to control the final negotiation." If the primary goal was to assure that Nixon got credit, there were safer and simpler ways to do this. Kissinger might merely have explained this to Smith and insisted that he be deferential about the president's role. Gerard Smith, a Georgetown gentleman lawyer and diplomat of the old school, was not a self-aggrandizing man. "If Henry had explained to me what Nixon wanted," he later said, "I would have been happy to have obliged."

All along, the plan had been to fly Smith in from Helsinki for the final signing ceremony on Friday night. With the talks deadlocked Thursday night, the signing was pushed back until Sunday, and Smith was told to stay away until then. At midday Friday, however, Gromyko came from a politburo meeting to say that the final American modifications had been accepted and the signing ceremony should be held as planned that evening. Even though the final SALT wording had not been drafted much less typed, Kissinger and Nixon agreed. As a result, there was an unseemly and unnecessary scramble to put together the final document based on cabled instructions to the delegations in Helsinki.

In addition, it meant that Smith, Nitze, and the other senior delegation members would have to scurry to make it to Moscow for the big event. That afternoon a half dozen Soviet and American negotiators climbed into an old propeller-driven American plane and celebrated with beers that, as the plane bounced, almost soaked the parchment documents they had prepared.

Smith's frayed nerves faced another indignity when he landed in

Moscow and found that no car or official was there to greet him. A Soviet car took him to the Kremlin, but all the Americans were at the dinner Nixon was throwing for Brezhnev at Spaso House, home of the American ambassador. Smith then went to the embassy office compound, where he was to join Kissinger in a briefing, and ended up pacing an alley waiting for everyone to arrive from the Nixon dinner. All he had consumed since waking up at three A.M. was the beer on the plane. "Here I was in the Soviet capital for the signing of SALT agreements on which I had worked so long," he recalled, "and I felt like an alley cat looking for a scrap to eat while the great men dined in state."

The bungling had been honest, but as Kissinger later noted, "the administrative practices of the Nixon Administration tended to inflict this sort of indignity on decent and able men." In his memoirs, Kissinger recycled a phrase he used to describe his treatment of Beam, Rogers, and others: "Smith deserved better."

The joint press briefing got off to a gloomy start. Smith was peppered with questions about the exact number of submarines the Soviets had and how many they could build under the agreement. Smith conceded that a rather large buildup could occur. Finally Kissinger broke in and gave a brief answer saying that the numbers were in dispute.

"What were you trying to do, cause a panic?" Kissinger berated Smith as they left the briefing for the signing ceremony at the Kremlin.

Because of the many unanswered questions about the SALT accord, Kissinger agreed to hold another press briefing after the signing ceremony. But he passed word to Smith that this one was to be a solo performance, Smith not invited.

So Smith went back to Ambassador Beam's residence, and the two gentleman diplomats stayed up late drinking, listening to music, and venting their spleen about Henry Kissinger. It was evenings like these that gave Kissinger such a long list of establishment enemies.

In the meantime, Kissinger headed for the Starry Sky nightclub in the Intourist Hotel off Red Square, where he took center stage clutching a microphone like a borscht-belt comic. In the wee hours of the morning of his forty-ninth birthday, he regaled the press with jokes, profundities, careful explanations, and a little dancing around what was in the SALT I accords. The point he emphasized was that the freeze placed some restraints on the Soviets but none whatsoever on the U.S., which had no programs that could be deployed during the five years in question.

When asked how the U.S. determined what Soviet submarines were "under construction," Kissinger quipped: "Well, some of the most profound minds in the bureaucracy [pause]—which is not saying a great deal [laughter]—have addressed that question." He also parried when a reporter asked how many American submarines were going to be upgraded with MIRV missiles. "I know the number," he said, "but I don't know whether it is classified or not."

"It is not," said another journalist.

"What is it then?" Kissinger asked him.

"You have deployed eight."

"But you don't know how many we are converting."

"You are converting thirty-one," the journalist said to great laughter.

"I thought all my former staff members joined candidates," said Kissinger, drawing an even bigger laugh.[34]

The most serious criticism of the SALT agreement was that it enshrined the "freeze" approach for dealing with offensive missile launchers. Instead of requiring equality, this allowed the Soviets to lock in the numerical advantages they had acquired since the 1962 Cuban missile crisis. (The Soviets were ahead of the U.S. in the number and size of nuclear missiles, though not in bombers and other areas.) The Joint Chiefs of Staff began weighing in with this objection in the middle of the summit. The numbers, said Admiral Zumwalt, were "appalling."

Alexander Haig, back in Washington, transmitted these concerns. He also made clear in his cable to Kissinger that he shared them. What he did not tell Kissinger was that he was relentlessly bad-mouthing the SALT accords in Washington. On the day of the signing, Haig said to James Schlesinger, who would soon become defense secretary and one of Kissinger's hard-line rivals: "This is a day of national shame."

But as Kissinger pointed out, some form of freeze was advantageous, or at least the best outcome available, because "no American programs existed that could possibly produce new missiles for at least five years." In the meantime, the Nixon administration pushed ahead with development on two major missile programs for the future: the submarine-launched Trident and the land-based Minuteman III.

When the objections from the Joint Chiefs and Haig came, Kissinger felt they needed to be raised with Nixon. He found the president stretched out naked on a massage table as his personal doctor gave him a back rub in an anteroom of the Czar's Apartments. "Lying naked on the rubbing table," Kissinger later noted, "Nixon made one

of the more courageous decisions of his presidency." The gist of it was
that Kissinger should not worry about the doubts in Washington, but
should instead proceed to seek an agreement.

Afterward, Kissinger sent a sharp cable back to Haig. His job was
to rally support, Kissinger told him, not merely transmit concerns.[35]

One criticism of Kissinger's approach, barely made at the time,
turned out to be valid. The agreements froze the number of missile
launchers but permitted "modernization" and "replacement." This
allowed—in fact, encouraged—the rapid deployment of multiple warheads (MIRVs) on each missile. The instability and "vulnerability"
problems that plagued the U.S. through the Reagan years were partially a result of the decision to encourage MIRVs rather than to ban
them.

"The MIRV explosion was especially devastating and discourag-
ing," said Hyland. The number of U.S. warheads increased from 1,700
at the time of the agreement to 10,000 by the 1980s, and the Soviets
reached the same point. "Thus," Hyland adds, "the first strategic arms
agreement actually produced a sizable buildup in strategic weaponry."

Still, the development of a working relationship with Moscow was
an achievement of enormous historic magnitude, made even more so
by the coup of accomplishing it at the same moment as a new tie was
forged with Beijing. In the grand scheme of things, disputes over the
counting rules for a handful of clunky G-class diesel submarines, the
bruised egos of a few admirals and arms control mandarins, and even
the fact that the SALT accord had little effect on the world's nuclear
arsenals should not obscure what was in fact achieved.

In Nixon's report to Congress, Kissinger and Winston Lord wrote
a sentence that captured Nixon's penchant for grandiloquence and
had the added virtue of being true: "Never before have two adversaries, so deeply divided by conflicting ideologies and political rivalries,
been able to agree to limit the armaments on which their survival
depends." Two enemies, whose nuclear competition had kept the
world on the brink for a generation, had decided to become partners
in a new relationship based on realism rather than emotion. However
meager the SALT agreement's impact might seem on paper, it represented the most important insight of the nuclear age: that an uncon-
strained arms race was futile, costly, and dangerous.

In addition, the whole spirit of the summit made the ideological
enmity that had fueled both Soviet and American foreign policy since
1945 seem less relevant. On television each night, after the reports on
the signing ceremonies and the toasts and the ballets and the banquets, the newscasts in America would sign off with a shot of a floodlit
American flag flying high over the ocher-and-red exterior of the Krem-

lin, signifying that, for the first time, a president of the United States had come to Moscow. An odd disjuncture it was, yet a thrilling sight, too, just three months after similar scenes had been beamed from Beijing.

Thus was launched what became known, briefly, as the "era of détente," during which Washington and Moscow sought to modulate their global competition by pursuing areas of mutual interest and indulging in occasional displays of friendship.

The word *détente,* which refers to the loosening of tension as in a taut string, is French; in Russian it translates as *razryadka,* a relaxation of tension. It had been used by John Kennedy in an October 1962 message to Khrushchev after the missile crisis—"We are prepared to discuss a détente affecting NATO and the Warsaw Pact"—and in a speech a year later at the University of Maine. Kissinger first publicly used it in a talk to a foreign service association the week after Nixon hired him in November 1968. "NATO is not equipped for détente policy," he said. When he used the word in his background briefings in Moscow, the press picked it up and popularized it.

After Moscow in May 1972, summits became a regular fixture in Soviet-American affairs, serving as a subtle restraint to keep relations from getting out of control. The SALT process played a central symbolic role: it became a barometer of how the relationship was faring.

Strategic weapons were not the cause of the rivalry between the U.S. and U.S.S.R., but unlike more fundamental issues—such as how a government treated its people, how much it meddled in regional crises, whether it tried to impose its will on other nations—nuclear warheads were tangible, countable, fungible assets that could be bargained away more easily than basic principles could be. Thus they provided a convenient (although sometimes complex) coin of the realm to facilitate endless negotiations.[36]

The successful spectacle in Moscow completed Kissinger's transition into a global superstar, the first and thus far only celebrity diplomat of the media age. The type of public adulation he was now receiving was reflected in a lead written by the *Chicago Sun-Times's* Peter Lisagor, a tough-minded Washington veteran who was not one of Kissinger's cronies, for a story just after the summit:

> Henry Alfred Kissinger has ceased being a phenomenon. He has become a legend, and the word is not lightly used. . . . He is the compleat cosmopolitan, urbane without swagger, self-centered without smugness. As a reputed ladies' man, he undoubtedly has given aid and comfort to every squat, owl-eyed, overweight and middle-aged bachelor in the land.

On the way home, Nixon and Kissinger stopped in Iran to shore up the shah as America's surrogate in the region. While there, Kissinger reveled in his new celebrity, visiting a nightclub that featured a belly dancer named Nadia, whom he allowed to be photographed in his lap. "She's a charming girl and very interested in foreign policy," he said when asked what they had discussed. "I spent some time explaining how you convert the SLBMs on a G-class submarine into Y-class subs. I want to make the world safe for Nadias."

The picture ran on the front page of the *Washington Post* and other papers, relegating those of Nixon being greeted in Warsaw by three hundred thousand cheering Poles to the inside pages. Haldeman was not amused. "Enough is enough," he raged on the flight home. "It's inexcusable to upstage the president."

Other colleagues on the trip were more exuberant. "Been one hell of a week, Henry," said Safire. "What does the president do for an encore?"

Kissinger did not hesitate a second. "Make peace in Vietnam," he said.[37]

TWENTY

PEACE AT HAND

The Paris Talks
Produce an Elusive Accord

We have fought for four years, have mortgaged our whole foreign policy to the defense of one country.—KISSINGER *to President Thieu, October 22, 1972*

A LIGHT AT THE END OF THE TUNNEL

Soon after the U.S. mined Haiphong harbor and intensified the bombing of Hanoi in May 1972, North Vietnam's military offensive sputtered to a halt. The stalemate left the balance of forces in the South about where they had been after the Tet offensive four years earlier.

More important, the triangular global balance that Kissinger had helped construct was paying off: due to America's success in forging realistic relationships with China and Russia, the North Vietnamese found themselves feeling isolated from their primary patrons. With a fervor that would make American pundits blush, Hanoi's Communist Party newspaper *Nhan Dan* denounced the Russians and Chinese for "throwing a life buoy to a drowning pirate" and being "mired on the dark and muddy road of unprincipled compromise." It added: "The revolution is a path strewn with fragrant flowers. Opportunism is a fetid quagmire."

With 140,000 or so North Vietnamese troops in the South supporting perhaps an equal number of Viet Cong guerrillas, Hanoi now saw no immediate chance of defeating Saigon's 1.2-million-man army supported by American air power. So the communist leaders began to look more favorably upon a cease-fire. In August 1972, after more than twelve years of fighting, the politburo in Hanoi voted to authorize a negotiated settlement.[1]

Within a few weeks, the communist negotiators in Paris began hinting that they would drop their demand that Thieu be immediately replaced by a "coalition" government. From that point on, a final treaty was only a matter of dealing with the devil in the details. The trade-off that lurked for four years was about to arrive: the U.S. had dropped its demand that North Vietnam withdraw its troops from South Vietnam, and North Vietnam was now dropping its demand that Thieu be toppled.

In one sense, the U.S. no longer had much to negotiate. Its unilateral withdrawal was almost complete, with 27,000 GIs remaining in Vietnam out of 543,000 there in early 1969. The release of America's POWs could probably have been secured, despite Kissinger's later claims to the contrary, by a simple deal to withdraw the remaining U.S. troops and stop supplying air support to Saigon as the war continued. But Kissinger wanted a solution that would give some meaning to the loss of more than fifty thousand American lives—and that meant seizing the chance to reach a negotiated cease-fire that would allow Thieu's government in Saigon to remain intact.

Kissinger hoped to pull off a cease-fire before America's November 7 presidential election. The Democrats had nominated George McGovern, a dovish South Dakota senator who made the war a major issue. Kissinger's critics, as well as some of his White House colleagues, assumed that his eagerness for a cease-fire came from a desire to get credit for helping Nixon crush McGovern.

In fact, Kissinger's main motivation was that he felt the U.S. was in a better bargaining position before rather than after the election. The communists were pushing for a fast-paced negotiating schedule, apparently because they were fearful of what Nixon might unleash on them once he was safely reelected. Kissinger believed, and he turned out to be right, that the desire to meet this schedule could be used to extract concessions from Le Duc Tho and his Hanoi politburo.

In addition, Kissinger realized that, even if Nixon won by a landslide, a Democratic-dominated Congress would return in January and restrict funds for the war. There was no way that the U.S. would be in a stronger military position in 1973 than it was in late 1972.[2]

Nixon, on the other hand, was not eager to pull off a peace settlement before the election, despite what critics would charge. This was not out of reverence for the integrity of the electoral process.

Instead, he was influenced by his political gunslinger Charles Colson, who had been meeting with pollsters Albert Sindlinger and Burns Roper. They had concluded, according to Colson, "that any agreement we reached before the election would appear to be a political ploy." Nixon's hawkish image was helpful, as shown by the wide support for the bombing-and-mining decisions. An end to the war, on the other hand, would allow many blue-collar Democrats then in Nixon's camp to return to their old party loyalties, according to Colson and the pollsters. Many of these working-class and hard-hat Democrats, flag-waving and assertively patriotic, supported Nixon's conduct of the war but might otherwise have voted along more traditional economic lines for their own party's nominee.

Nixon, Haldeman, Colson, and Haig often discussed the political risk in reaching a peace accord just before the election. "We saw the disadvantages of pushing an agreement," recalled Colson. "Henry, however, desperately wanted to be the man who brought the war to an end in time to assure Nixon's reelection. We could never convince him otherwise. This was at the root of a lot of tensions during that month."[3]

Nixon also suspected that Kissinger wanted to grab some credit for the impending landslide, and he was by now in no mood to share any more with his assistant. "You have got to get Henry to slow down," he told Colson. Haldeman passed the word that a settlement "could backfire" politically, but Kissinger brushed him off. "He was obsessed by having a peace accord by election day," recalled Haldeman.

Contrary to Kissinger's assessment, Nixon felt that he would be in a stronger negotiating position after his reelection. "I am inclined to think that the better bargaining time for us would be immediately after the election rather than before," he wrote in his diary, explaining that "the enemy then either has to settle or face the consequences of what we could do to them." Explaining his feelings years later, Nixon was more forceful. "After a tremendous mandate, after the antiwar crowd had been totally defeated, I thought that then we could get these people to, shall we say, cry uncle."[4]

More significantly, Nixon did not share Kissinger's faith in negotiations. Throughout 1972, when Kissinger would send back reports about the promising nuances of a new Hanoi offer or, even worse, give an optimistic analysis of the atmosphere at a meeting or the food served, Nixon would fill the margin with question marks and sarcastic comments. "Nixon never really agreed with Kissinger that a diplomatic solution was possible," Kissinger's aide Peter Rodman recalled. "He was skeptical and wary about diplomacy."

•

Nixon increasingly began to share with Alexander Haig his caustic comments about Kissinger and his negotiations. Haig did not discourage such sentiments. He felt, Nixon recalled, "that the North Vietnamese would be more likely to make concessions after the election when I would be armed with a landslide mandate."

Haig's rise in rank was unprecedented, especially for someone in a civilian desk job. Entering the White House as a colonel in 1969, he had received his second star as a major general in March 1972. By that summer, to the outrage of much of the army's high command, the rumor began circulating that he was soon to leapfrog over the rank of lieutenant general and become a full four-star general and army vice chief of staff. Kissinger, who by now knew that Haig was bad-mouthing him, fully supported this idea of promoting Haig back into the Pentagon.

That August, Haig went to lunch in Elmo Zumwalt's office to ask his advice. The chief of naval operations, a bluff and humorous man who would later admit that he was "not above needling someone occasionally," pretended not to know of the rumors that Haig was in line for army vice chief of staff and suggested that it was time for him to serve in a field command. The general who ran the Southern Command in Panama was retiring, he reminded Haig. Why not go there? Zumwalt recalled "having in my mind as I said it an entertaining, if totally untrue-to-life, picture of Al Haig, chin in hand, thoughtfully watching the Gatun Locks slowly open and then slowly close." Haig spent much of the lunch criticizing Kissinger, but when he got back to the White House, he said to Kissinger: "I just had lunch with Bud Zumwalt, the most hypocritical man in Washington."

Haig's appointment as a four-star general and army vice chief came through in September 1972, just six months after he had been given his second star. But Nixon added a caveat. He would have to stay as Kissinger's deputy until the Vietnam negotiations were completed. Kissinger needed him, Nixon said. More important, Nixon did not trust Kissinger—nor did Haig—to handle the negotiations without Haig there to stiffen his backbone.[5]

At a secret meeting in Paris on August 14, Kissinger began to see signs that Hanoi was edging away from its insistence that Thieu be ousted as a prerequisite for a cease-fire. "We have gotten closer to a negotiated settlement than ever before," he wrote in the report he sent back to the president.

Nixon, contemptuous, scribbled some marginal notes to Haig: "Al —It is obvious that no progress has been made and that none can be expected. Henry must be discouraged—as I have always been on this front until after the election."[6]

Another key figure who did not share Kissinger's enthusiasm for negotiations was President Nguyen Van Thieu of South Vietnam. The slender, erect, and proud soldier-president had sparkling eyes and a thin smile that gave little clue to what he was thinking. He could be a master of gentle indirection. But he had certain rather obvious imperatives:

- His pride and nationalism (and that of his people) made it crucial that he be fully involved in each stage of the negotiations rather than have a settlement imposed on him by Kissinger as a fait accompli.
- Likewise, he expected to be treated as an equal, a partner rather than a puppet.
- He needed to have enough time and advance warning to prepare the people of South Vietnam for any compromise peace accord.
- His basic national interest was diametrically opposed to that of Washington: he did not want to see U.S. troops withdraw. Nor did he want a cease-fire that would allow the North Vietnamese to stay in the South. Any solution that allowed a leopard-spot arrangement where the communists controlled certain territory undermined his government's sovereignty.

Kissinger was not sensitive to these needs. "The North Vietnamese had always accused us of being America's puppet," Thieu later said. "Now Kissinger was treating us like one. There was no effort to treat us as an equal, for he was too arrogant for that. We wanted to be part of the negotiations, but he was working behind our back and hardly keeping us informed."[7]

Kissinger flew to Saigon in mid-August, carrying a new biography of Metternich to read on the plane. His most important task was to make it clear to Thieu that the cease-fire being discussed would not require the North Vietnamese to pull their troops out of the South. Thieu had previously aquiesced in American proposals that implied such an outcome, but it was now important to be candid with him— a style that was not one of Kissinger's proven strengths.

Thieu placed the point squarely on the table. What happened, he asked, to a memo he had written in April in which he insisted that any withdrawal must be mutual?

"Mr. President," replied Kissinger, "I couldn't get the Russians to accept your position."

"We wanted it restated as our joint position," Thieu insisted.

"We'll try, but we don't know if they will accept it," Kissinger answered.

In short, the issue of insisting on a North Vietnamese withdrawal was left ambiguous: Kissinger was being disingenuous in his offer to "try" to win the point since he knew it had already been conceded, but he did give Thieu a pretty good indication of where the issue was heading. Likewise, Thieu gave a pretty good indication that he did not accept this direction. "We did not pursue the disagreement with Thieu," Kissinger later explained, "since it did not seem relevant to the deadlocked negotiations."[8]

But Kissinger knew that the deadlock in Paris was breaking—a fact that he did not make clear to Thieu. Consequently, Thieu later said, he did not think it necessary to challenge the U.S. proposals very forcefully.

Thieu did not help matters by his rudeness. Repeatedly he refused to receive the gentlemanly American ambassador, Ellsworth Bunker, and at times he treated both Haig and Kissinger as mere messenger boys. "Insolence is the armor of the weak," Kissinger later wrote of Thieu's attitude.

At least six times in his memoirs, Kissinger referred to Thieu and his aides as "insolent," just as he did to Le Duc Tho. The use of this word implies a perceived inferior, or an uppity puppet. Likewise, Kissinger's memoirs are enriched by his insights into the national character of various peoples, but his descriptions of the Vietnamese veer close to ethnic insults. In recounting his August meeting, he writes that Thieu "fought with characteristic Vietnamese opaqueness and with a cultural arrogance." Yet Kissinger was the one who was being rather opaque (in hiding the fact that a breakthrough seemed imminent) and culturally arrogant (in acting as if the U.S. could negotiate a settlement without Saigon's full participation).

Thieu was far from opaque about his objections to Kissinger's diplomatic efforts when Haig visited him in Saigon on October 4. In an emotional four-hour meeting, he denounced the notion of allowing North Vietnamese troops to remain in the South and Kissinger's scheme of creating a "Committee of National Reconciliation" as a way to pay lip service to the communist demand for an interim coalition government. Thieu also railed against Kissinger, saying that he did not "deign" to consider Saigon's views when conducting negotiations.

Haig passed along to Nixon this criticism of Kissinger. In his memoirs, Nixon later said that he "sympathized" with Thieu's position, an impression he gave Connally, Haig, and others. But to Kissinger, he criticized Haig for leaving Saigon too soon and not staying to "work over" Thieu.[9]

A clash between Washington and Saigon was clearly in the making, and Kissinger should have foreseen it. Four years earlier, in a footnote in his famous *Foreign Affairs* piece on Vietnam, he had discussed why the U.S. tends to get in disputes with its clients. The analysis was uncannily—almost eerily—close to what would occur in late 1972:

> Clashes with our allies in which both sides claim to have been deceived occur so frequently as to suggest structural causes. . . . When an issue is fairly abstract—before there is prospect for agreement —our diplomats tend to present our view in a bland, relaxed fashion to the ally whose interests are involved but who is not present at the negotiations. The ally responds equally vaguely for three reasons: (a) he may be misled into believing that no decision is imminent and therefore sees no purpose in making an issue; (b) he is afraid that if he forces the issue the decision will go against him; (c) he hopes the problem will go away because agreement will prove impossible. When agreement seems imminent, American diplomats suddenly go into high gear to gain the acquiescence of the ally. He in turn feels tricked by the very intensity and suddenness of the pressure while we are outraged to learn of objection heretofore not made explicit.[10]

On the merits, Kissinger was right to seek the settlement that was emerging in the autumn of 1972. Hanoi was finally ready to offer a cease-fire and to leave Thieu in control in Saigon. This ticket out was in America's interest, and it was the best deal that South Vietnam could get. Yet Kissinger made a tragic blunder in the way he pursued this solution. By forging ahead toward an October agreement despite clear signs that both President Thieu and President Nixon were not supportive, he raced into a collision that was both inevitable and foreseeable.

Kissinger's diplomatic strength was as a bargainer. He knew how to fudge and feint and find ways to concede points that didn't matter, while obscuring a few that did. His diplomatic weakness was that he sometimes did not serve as a true conciliator, one who would line up support for a position and assure that all sides felt they had a stake in its success. He would figure out in his own mind the best possible outcome of a situation, but he tended to be insensitive to the importance of making sure that all of the other players felt fully informed and that their concerns were taken into account.

"PEACE IS AT HAND," OCTOBER 1972

As his private talks in Paris with Le Duc Tho became more serious, Kissinger realized that his penchant for secrecy was serving little purpose except to satisfy his own flair for the dramatic and to give Hanoi a chance to whipsaw public opinion. So he decided that henceforth each meeting would be announced, though the details discussed would remain private. This more sensible approach, Kissinger later admitted, "blunted one of the psychological weapons in Hanoi's arsenal." By then even he realized that the secretiveness of the prior three years had been overdone.

Even so, Kissinger had trouble shaking his clandestine habits. For his September 15 meeting, he went through an elaborate ruse involving Do Not Disturb signs at Claridge's Hotel and leaving his jet parked conspicuously at Heathrow while he secretly took another plane from London to Paris. "It was a pointless—even juvenile—game not worth playing, since we would announce the meeting with Le Duc Tho later in the day," he conceded.

At that meeting, Kissinger took a fateful step: putting forth a proposal that had been specifically rejected in advance by President Thieu. It involved a modification of America's long-standing proposal that an "electoral commission" containing the communists and other parties could be set up after a cease-fire to supervise elections in South Vietnam. What Kissinger now proposed was to give this electoral commission a grander name, the Committee of National Reconciliation, and spell out that the communists would have equal representation on it with the Saigon regime. It seemed like no big deal to Kissinger because the committee would act only by consensus and thus Saigon would have a veto over its decisions.

Kissinger's purpose was to make the electoral commission look more like the "interim coalition government" that the communists were demanding. He hoped Hanoi would buy his idea as a face-saving compromise. Thieu was repelled by anything that even smelled like a coalition government. But mainly he feared that Kissinger's plan might be acceptable to Hanoi and thus pave the way for the cease-fire that Thieu feared. So two days before Kissinger's meeting in Paris, Thieu rejected the proposal.

Instead of accepting Thieu's decision or attempting to bring him around, Kissinger cabled Nixon recommending that the new plan be put forward anyway. "If the other side accepts our proposal, which we believe quite unlikely, then the fact that government of South Vietnam was not totally on board to the last detail will be obscured by myriad other complexities in what will essentially be a new ballgame," he said. The "quite unlikely" part was disingenuous: Kissinger was chomping to make the proposal precisely because he thought it might be accepted.

Nixon expressed his lack of enthusiasm to Haig, who relayed it to Kissinger in a cable. "The NSC does not seem to understand," Nixon said, referring to Kissinger and his colleagues, "that the American people are no longer interested in a solution based on compromise, [and instead] favor continued bombing and want to see the United States prevail after all these years." Nevertheless, Nixon finally agreed that Kissinger could submit his new proposal as long as his talk with Le Duc Tho "be a tough one which in a public sense would appeal to the hawk and not the dove."

The North Vietnamese negotiator came with a revised proposal of his own: a "Government of National Concord" that would be set up after a cease-fire but not replace the Thieu government. This new entity would handle more than just the supervision of free elections, and Kissinger rejected it, but the direction toward a compromise was clear. All that was necessary was fudging the distinctions between the Committee of National Reconciliation that Kissinger had proposed and the Government of National Concord that Le Duc Tho had proposed. And fudging distinctions was one of Kissinger's greatest talents as a bargainer.

Kissinger knew that the next Paris session, scheduled to begin October 8, was likely to produce the fateful breakthrough. He flew there with Haig in tow because, he claimed in his memoirs, the general had a "firsthand sense of what the traffic would bear in Saigon." Kissinger would later be more candid, admitting that "I had Haig in Paris because I didn't trust him behind my back anymore."

The meeting, on a sunny autumn Sunday, opened with some banter about a racetrack in Auteuil where for part of the race the horses are, in Kissinger's words, "behind the trees so you can't see them, and I'm told that's where the jockeys decide who will win."

"But we, are we making now a race to peace or to war?" Le Duc Tho asked.

"To peace, and we're behind the trees!" said Kissinger. It was a metaphor that applied as well to the way Kissinger's moves were being partly hidden from Thieu and Nixon.

Le Duc Tho then put forward a new plan that was clearly designed to produce a breakthrough. Almost every element represented a major leap toward the American position. After a few modifications but a lot of agonizing fits and starts, it would form the basis for the final peace accords. Its particulars included:

- An immediate cease-fire without waiting for all the political issues to be resolved—in other words, without requiring that Thieu be ousted first.
- A unilateral withdrawal of all American forces from South Vietnam, with the North Vietnamese troops implicitly allowed to stay.
- The return of all prisoners of war.
- An implied though murky commitment not to infiltrate more North Vietnamese troops into the South.
- The right of the U.S. to continue to aid the South Vietnamese army, and for Hanoi to do likewise for the Viet Cong.
- An "Administration of National Concord" that would have as its main function the "organizing" of elections, would make decisions only by consensus, and would not displace the authority of the Saigon government or the communist Provisional Revolutionary Government, each of which would run things in the areas it controlled.

"For nearly four years we had longed for this day," Kissinger later wrote, "yet when it arrived, it was less dramatic than we had ever imagined. Peace came in the guise of the droning voice of an elderly revolutionary wrapping the end of a decade of bloodshed into legalistic ambiguity." Despite the drone and the incongruous setting—an isolated stucco house filled with abstract art—Kissinger would later say that the moment was the most thrilling of his entire career.

Kissinger asked for a recess. When the Americans were alone, he and Lord pumped hands and exulted to each other, "We have done it." Haig declared with emotion, Kissinger recalled, that they had "saved the honor" of the soldiers who had served and died in Vietnam.

Only John Negroponte, the handsome, Yale-educated foreign service officer who spoke Vietnamese and had served in Saigon, seemed worried. Though the plan was pretty much what Washington had been seeking since it had implicitly dropped its demand for mutual withdrawal on Memorial Day of 1971, Negroponte suspected it would stir trouble in Saigon.

Despite Nixon's desire to stall until the election a month away, and despite Thieu's phobia about anything resembling a coalition government or a cease-fire not linked to North Vietnamese withdrawals, Kissinger decided to proceed along the lines suggested by Le Duc Tho. Delay seemed unjustified. Nor could he accept the notion in Nixon's telegram of mid-September that through "continued bombing" the U.S. should seek to "prevail," especially now that Hanoi seemed ready to accept America's basic terms.

So he asked Negroponte and Lord to revise Le Duc Tho's plan by watering down the duties of the Administration of National Concord, firming up the ban on further North Vietnamese infiltration, and adding a provision that Hanoi withdraw its troops from Cambodia and Laos. That evening he had dinner with a date at a Paris restaurant, then walked alone along the Left Bank of the Seine and past Nôtre Dame.

Negroponte and Lord finished their redraft at three A.M., left it for Kissinger, and went to bed. He awakened them at eight A.M., furious. The provisions pushed by Negroponte were too tough. "You don't understand," Kissinger explained loudly. "I want to meet their position." He gave his aides until noon to come up with a more accommodating counteroffer.

Kissinger's decision to pursue Le Duc Tho's offer was sensible. His mistake was to proceed hastily and on his own, without taking a break to consult with the two presidents for whom he was supposed to be negotiating.

Instead of filling Nixon in, Kissinger merely sent a cryptic message to Haldeman with no details. "Tell the President there has been some definite progress," it said. Nixon did not respond. Over the next two days, Kissinger's cables to Haldeman followed this pattern. "We know exactly what we are doing," read one, "and just as we have not let you down in the past, we will not do so now."

He did not send back details of what was being discussed, Kissinger later explained, because he knew Nixon was spending most of his time with political operatives who might exploit the talks. "If that person were Charles Colson—with whom he was spending an increasing amount of time—there was no telling what would happen," Kissinger said.

As for informing Thieu, Kissinger's short message, sent through Ambassador Bunker, was so cryptic as to be misleading. "The other side may surface a cease-fire proposal during these meetings," Kissinger said, not revealing that they already had and that Kissinger was hoping to accept it before leaving Paris. Thieu did not help matters by bristling at the cavalier way he was being treated. He refused to see Bunker; he had his obnoxious nephew and press secretary, Hoang Duc Nha, say that he had gone waterskiing and hurt his foot.[11]

In a marathon sixteen-hour session on October 11, the fourth straight day of meetings, an agreement acceptable to Kissinger and Le Duc Tho was reached. The basic provisions were along the lines offered by Hanoi on October 8: the Thieu government would not be replaced by a coalition government, but it would have to share autonomy in South Vietnam with the Viet Cong's Provisional Revolutionary Government, which would administer the areas controlled by communist forces. The war would end, the Americans would withdraw, and the POWs would be freed.

Although still unable to force any North Vietnamese troop withdrawals from the South, Kissinger secured an understanding that there would be no new infiltration. Both Hanoi and Washington, however, would have the right to resupply their allies. In addition, while avoiding the word *reparations,* Kissinger pledged the U.S. to provide aid to both Vietnams in order "to heal the wounds of war."

The cease-fire did not apply to Laos and Cambodia, despite Kissinger's efforts. Hanoi pledged to seek one in Laos within a month, but protested that its influence on the Cambodian Khmer Rouge was dwindling. (Though the U.S. did not understand the situation well enough to know it, Le Duc Tho was telling the truth; the communist governments of North Vietnam and Cambodia would be at war with one another in a few years.)

This was the accord Kissinger had been working for, and he accepted it subject only to the resolution of a few tiny details. Ever one for the dramatic, he even worked out a schedule that would have him travel secretly to Hanoi—the last major enemy capital he had yet to conquer—on October 24, emerge, and then grandly initial the accords.

Either out of arrogance or optimism, he did not make it clear to Le Duc Tho (and probably not to himself) that the whole package was contingent on President Thieu's approval. In fact, in the agreement accepted by Kissinger in Paris, both sides "agreed to be responsible for the concurrence of their respective allies."

The North Vietnamese certainly must have considered the agreement a done deal when Kissinger gave his farewell speech in the predawn euphoria at the end of a sixteen-hour session. "The real victory for both, of course, will now be the durable relations we can establish with each other," he proclaimed. "So when my colleagues and I come to Hanoi, we will come to pay our respects to the heroic people of North Vietnam and to begin a new era in our relationships."

Amazingly, Kissinger did not send a copy of the peace accord he had just drafted—a document that would determine the fate of South Vietnam and its leadership—to Saigon. He did not even inform President Thieu about the basic provisions of the deal, or even that a deal had been struck.

Worse yet, he sent Bunker a cable from Paris on October 12 containing information for Thieu that was deliberately misleading. "My judgment at this juncture would be that they appear ready to accept a cease-fire in place in the near future," Kissinger said, hiding the fact that Le Duc Tho had just accepted a cease-fire package. He told the ambassador to press upon Thieu the need "to regain as much territory as possible" right away, in anticipation of a cease-fire going into effect. He also told Bunker to stress to Thieu "the need for greater flexibility on the political side."

Kissinger himself later admitted that "the second point was substantially devious" because he thought Thieu would be happy with the political arrangements, which no longer included Hanoi's demand that he be replaced by a coalition government. Kissinger's strategy was to frighten Thieu with the prospect of an even worse agreement, then capitalize on his relief when he saw the deal was not quite so bad. In order to mislead Thieu even further, Kissinger sent along Le Duc Tho's proposals of October 9, which had subsequently been improved. "It was not a very elevated method," Kissinger later conceded, "nor did it work."

The reason Kissinger's deviousness did not work was because it animated Thieu's greatest nightmare: the U.S. cutting a deal behind his back and suddenly seeking to impose it on him. No matter what Kissinger would say in the future, no matter how strong his arguments might appear, Thieu would never again trust him.[12]

The rationales that Kissinger later gave for misleading Thieu were as numerous as they were unconvincing. Among his reasons for not sending Thieu the agreement or even word that a deal had been struck: "partly because of security," "because of our growing mistrust of his entourage," and because Kissinger thought "that further improvements were possible." But perhaps the most misguided justification was the one he placed most emphasis on: "above all because I supposed he would be pleased by the outcome and therefore there was no need to engage him in detail."

When they arrived home from Paris on the evening of October 12, Kissinger and Haig went to Nixon's hideaway office to report. Kissinger's recollection was that the president was "affecting nonchalance." The president, on the other hand, recalled that Kissinger "was smiling the broadest smile I had ever seen." Having established an opening to China and a détente with the Soviet Union, they now seemed on the verge of accomplishing their remaining goal of ending the Vietnam War. "Well, Mr. President, it looks like we've got three out of three," Kissinger said.

Nixon approved the agreement as Kissinger outlined it. Its major provisions, he later said, amounted to "a complete capitulation by the enemy." In order to celebrate, the president ordered three steaks sent over on trays from the White House mess and asked his valet, Manolo, to bring a bottle of Château Lafite-Rothschild.

If Saigon objected to the agreement, Nixon declared, Kissinger should back off and wait until after the election. That could present problems, Kissinger realized. The North Vietnamese were planning to host an initialing ceremony in less than two weeks: if the U.S. backed out, they might go public with the agreement that Kissinger had accepted. Congress would then surely demand that it be signed rather than prolonging the war. Yet even after Nixon's decision that Saigon should not be pressured, Kissinger did not warn Hanoi that the schedule could be delayed.

A week later, after tying up all except one or two of the final loose ends at another brief session in Paris, Kissinger finally flew to Saigon to present what he had done—just five days before he was supposed to initial the pact in Hanoi. On the way over, Negroponte expressed his misgivings. Thieu had been treated shabbily and would likely balk, even though the deal was the best he could expect. The decision to leave North Vietnamese troops in the South, after all, could sow the seeds for the destruction of his government. Kissinger exploded. He thought it was inconceivable that Thieu would object.

Nevertheless, Kissinger had still not seen fit to send Thieu the draft treaty or tell him what it contained. Nixon agreed that it would be best to surprise the South Vietnamese president with the provisions and then capitalize on the relief he would surely feel at being spared a coalition government. He even offered some advice on trickiness from a master. "The President suggested," Kissinger later wrote, "that I treat the forthcoming meetings with Thieu as a 'poker game' in which I should hold back the 'trump card' until the last trick." Besides muddling the rules of poker, it proved to be a complete misreading of Thieu.[13]

Unbeknownst to Kissinger (even years later), Thieu had received from his intelligence officers a ten-page document captured in the underground command post of a Viet Cong commissar in Quang Tin province. Rushed by helicopter and plane to Saigon, it was placed on the president's desk just after midnight on the day Kissinger was to arrive. Thieu read it immediately. Entitled "General Instructions for a Cease-Fire," it contained a draft of the treaty that Kissinger had secretly negotiated with Le Duc Tho.* What enraged Thieu even more than the provisions was the appalling betrayal involved: Kissinger had yet to tell him about the accord, yet in an isolated province near Da Nang, it was already being distributed to the communist cadres.

---

* Apparently it was valid; when CIA station chief Tom Polger later showed him a similar copy captured by the Americans, Kissinger commented, "It has the odious smell of truth."

"Suddenly I realized that things were being negotiated for us behind my back and without my approval," Thieu recalled. For months he had been asking Kissinger to allow Saigon to negotiate for itself with Hanoi, rather than be treated in a way that reinforced the impression that it was merely Washington's puppet. "We asked to be treated as partners. Instead, we had not even been consulted."

Kissinger, he realized, was coming to Saigon to demand his approval of a done deal, with only three days to give it. There would be no chance to prepare the nation for the wrenching change, nor any way to cast the package as something that Saigon had helped negotiate. He decided on his course. The next night, banners went up around town demanding no cease-fire without a North Vietnamese withdrawal.[14]

When Kissinger showed up at the Presidential Palace on the morning of October 19, he was kept waiting for fifteen minutes as press photographers recorded the insult. Only then did Thieu's nephew and aide Hoang Duc Nha usher him in to present the draft treaty at a formal meeting of the Saigon leadership. Kissinger later wrote that the meeting seemed to go modestly well. Thieu, he recalls, "raised a number of intelligent questions, none of them going to the heart of the agreement."

Little did he know what Thieu was actually thinking. "I wanted to punch Kissinger in the mouth," the former president recalled. Only after Kissinger's half-hour "seminar" did he deign to offer Thieu a copy of the treaty—in English. Thieu asked for one in Vietnamese. Kissinger replied that he did not have one. So Thieu signaled for Nha, who had a reputation for dating blond coeds at Oklahoma State University, and asked him to come read it. As Nha translated the provisions, Thieu smoked a thin Schimmelpennick cigar and watched Kissinger like a cat. "This is not what we expected," Nha whispered in Vietnamese.

Nha, who was thirty-one and full of fervor, led the opposition to the agreement and delighted in tormenting Kissinger. At one point, Kissinger tried to loosen him up by taking out his address book, opening to a page filled with Hollywood starlets, and joking that he would give it to Nha if he would be friendlier. Nha responded by pulling out his own list of women and offering an exchange. From then on, Kissinger described the decidedly abrasive Nha as "egregious."

When the meeting ended, Nha went to lunch with the foreign minister and other top South Vietnamese officials. "This is not so bad," one of them said. Nha shot back: "What do you mean, not so bad? Have you read it carefully?"[15]

As Kissinger awaited Saigon's response, he received word from

Hanoi that it had accepted the final two American details. This should have been cause for a celebration, but Haig captured the mood in a note he sent to Kissinger when he relayed Hanoi's cable. "I recognize," he said, "this message adds immeasurably to your burdens."

Kissinger sent a cable back to Hanoi, over the president's name, informing the communists that the agreement was now "complete." The message contained no indication that Saigon might not accept the accord. Nor did it leave any leeway for the possibility that Saigon might want to make some changes. Despite the simmering resistance he was encountering in Saigon, Kissinger did not yet consider that Thieu and his government might have to be allowed some say in the wording of the peace treaty.[16]

Kissinger had taken the rare step, as he completed his package in Paris, of fully briefing Secretary Rogers and asking for his department's assistance in finalizing the accord. In an indication of how much easier things may have been if Kissinger had done this more often, Rogers became a staunch supporter of the agreement and told Nixon it could not be improved. On the other hand, General William Westmoreland, the retiring army chief of staff, suddenly began criticizing the plan because it would not require a North Vietnamese withdrawal.

The result was that Nixon became more adamant than ever that Thieu should not be forced to swallow the accord—in particular, he should not be pressured in a way that might cause him to object publicly before the election. "The essential requirement is that Thieu's acceptance must be wholehearted so that the charge cannot be made that we forced him into a settlement," Nixon cabled Kissinger on October 20. Later in the message, he added: "It cannot be a shotgun marriage."

"I began to be nagged by the unworthy notion that I was being set up as the fall guy," Kissinger recalled. He sent a sharp message back to Haig. "I am grateful for the helpful comments that I have been receiving," it began, not without a note of sarcasm. Slowing down the push for an accord would be difficult, he added, because it would provoke a damaging explosion from Hanoi. But Kissinger said he would be willing to do so if the president would take clear responsibility for what would happen. "If I am being told to stop this process, then this should be made unambiguous."

Back at home, Haig was not being helpful. Behind Kissinger's back, he was warning Nixon that the peace plan could threaten Saigon's security. In his diary, Nixon noted that Haig warned that there could be "a murderous bloodbath, and it is something that we have to consider as we press Thieu to accept."

"The differences I had with Kissinger, and that Haig had, were because we remembered that the 1968 bombing agreement came apart because Saigon balked," Nixon said. (Kissinger, who was intricately involved at the time, presumably remembered this as well.) "I felt the October agreement was a good one. I do not think Saigon should have balked. But the fact was that they did, and I knew it meant we could not have an agreement right then, even if Kissinger didn't know that."[17]

The South Vietnamese had two substantive objections to Kissinger's agreement: it permitted the communists to keep control of the territory they held, and it created a strange political entity that was really a powerless electoral commission but that smelled like a coalition government. These were key provisions that could not be renegotiated, for they were at the heart of the deal.

However, upon studying the text, the South Vietnamese led by Nha found some smaller problems that undermined Kissinger's credibility. For example, the proposed pact referred to "three Indochinese states," meaning Cambodia, Laos, and Vietnam. This implied that Vietnam was one country, rather than South Vietnam and North Vietnam being sovereign nations. Unconvincingly, Kissinger called this a typographical error. In addition, the line separating the two Vietnams was defined in a nebulous way. That was an intentional Kissinger fudge; he had been unable to get Hanoi to refer to it as an international border.

In the midst of Kissinger's efforts to sell the pact in Saigon, North Vietnamese prime minister Pham Van Dong gave an interview to *Newsweek's* Arnaud de Borchgrave. "Thieu has been overtaken by events," the communist leader said rather recklessly. "The situation will be two armies and two administrations in the South, and given that new situation they will have to work out their own arrangements for a three-sided coalition."[18]

Kissinger's climactic meeting with Thieu had been scheduled for Saturday afternoon, but Nha had it postponed for a day. Thieu's brash aide made repeated abrupt calls—"he must have seen Humphrey Bogart do this in some movie," Kissinger later noted—to the American embassy to bark new instructions and then slam down the phone. In their book *The Palace File,* Nguyen Tien Hung and Jerrold Schecter gave Nha's account of one of the conversations:

Nha: "I'm sorry, the President cannot see you now. He will see you tomorrow."

Kissinger: "I am the Special Envoy of the President of the United States of America. You know I cannot be treated as an errand boy."

Nha: "We never considered you an errand boy, but if that's what you think you are, there's nothing I can do about it."

Kissinger: "I demand to see the President."

Nha: "May I remind you again what I just told you? I'm sorry."

In his seventy-eight years, Ambassador Bunker had rarely shown anger, but this time he did. Kissinger, who was not as slow to anger, was in a monumental fury. "We felt that impotent rage so cunningly seeded in foreigners by the Vietnamese."

Thieu's showdown with Kissinger finally took place on Sunday. "I do not object to peace," the South Vietnamese president began, "but I have not got any satisfactory answers from you, and I'm not going to sign."

In his memoirs Kissinger says little about the meeting and records that he replied calmly. Nha and Thieu would remember it differently. Kissinger became enraged, they recalled, and threatened: "If you do not sign, we're going to go out on our own." Directing a challenge at Nha, who was translating, Kissinger said: "Why does your President play the role of a martyr? He does not have the stuff of a martyr."

Thieu laughed. "I am not trying to be a martyr. I am a nationalist." He then turned his back on Kissinger to hide his tears.

"This is the greatest failure of my diplomatic career," Kissinger told him.

Thieu, more concerned with his country's future than with Kissinger's career, was unsympathetic. "Why," he asked, "are you rushing to get the Nobel Prize?"[19]

Ever since October 1970, when Nixon first offered a cease-fire in place, it was clear that the U.S. would be willing to accept a peace accord that did not require the North Vietnamese to withdraw from the South. Kissinger often left this concession murky: he frequently told Thieu, most recently in August, that he would "try" to get a provision for *mutual* withdrawal included in the plan. But the fact that the U.S. was willing to settle for a unilateral withdrawal should have come as no surprise to Thieu.

The real problem was that Thieu did not want an agreement of any sort. He was not ready for a cease-fire, especially now that Hanoi's offensive was being turned back. "The U.S. made a deal over my head," he recalled. "It was another Munich."

Kissinger would later concede that he "surely made a mistake not analyzing what Thieu's domestic needs were and how we could help him prepare for what was coming." But he called this "a trifling error in human calculation." He continued to feel that his secretiveness and haste in October 1972 were justified as a way to use Hanoi's self-imposed schedule to extract as many concessions as possible.[20]

After Thieu had finished his diatribe, Kissinger sent a cable to Haig in Washington. "Thieu has just rejected the entire plan or any modification of it and refuses to discuss any further negotiations on the basis of it. . . . I need not tell you the crisis with which this confronts us." A little while later, he sent a message to Nixon at Camp David. "It is hard to exaggerate the toughness of Thieu's position," he wrote. "His demands verge on insanity."

There were two options, Kissinger noted in his cables. He could proceed as planned to Hanoi and try to conduct a shuttle diplomacy, or he could return to Washington. In either event, he recommended that the bombing of North Vietnam be stopped because the breakdown was not its fault.

Nixon, encouraged by Haig, reacted vehemently against both the idea of a Hanoi trip and of a bombing halt. The flood of ensuing cables ordering Kissinger not to go to Hanoi continued even after he had sent word that, upon reflection, he too was against the idea. The unabated outpouring from Nixon convinced Kissinger, according to Winston Lord, that Haig was not showing all of his cables to the president and was instead stoking Nixon's resentment at older messages.

In his conversations with the staff of the NSC, Haig's challenge to Kissinger was more overt. Already nominated to become army vice chief of staff, he no longer had to make any pretense of being the loyal deputy. He met with a handful of younger staffers, including Fritz Kraemer's hard-line son, Sven. Kissinger was insisting on going to Hanoi, Haig claimed, and the president was upset. In essence, recalled one participant, Haig's message was, "This time Henry's gone too far." Sven wrote a critical paper on the proposed agreement, which argued that it was a complete capitulation to Hanoi's 1969 demands.

Haig also began meeting regularly with Fritz Kraemer, who had been his mentor at the Pentagon just as he had been Kissinger's during World War II. While Kissinger was away, Haig brought the elder Kraemer in to see Nixon. Wearing his monocle, Kraemer paced the room and tried to convince the president of the need to resume bombing. When Kissinger found out about Haig's meetings with the two Kraemers, he was incensed.

The dispute prompted a flurry of sharp cables between Haig and Kissinger. In one of them, Haig suggested that Kissinger could simply denounce the entire agreement. That was sure to inflame Kissinger, who responded that it was inconceivable to "poor-mouth an agreement that we will not be able to improve significantly" and that should instead be touted as "a tremendous success."

As he headed home, Kissinger sent Haig his sharpest and most personal cable of all, one that revealed the depth of the rupture between them:

> As for your characterization of the content of the agreement, I would like to recall your view that it was a good agreement when we concluded it. . . . Many wars have been lost by untoward timidity. But enormous tragedies have also been produced by the inability of military people to recognize when the time for a settlement has arrived.[21]

When Kissinger arrived in Washington, he found that Nixon had little interest in the details of the impasse. Instead, he was mainly concerned with keeping it quiet for another two weeks until his reelection.

To Nixon's dismay, however, Kissinger began leaking that he had achieved an agreement in principle with Hanoi. On October 25, he called Max Frankel, the bureau chief of the *New York Times,* and invited him to Sans Souci. Frankel's front-page story the next day quoted "American officials" as saying that a cease-fire could come very soon "barring a supreme act of folly in Saigon or Hanoi." It added a blunt warning that Thieu had "no logical alternative" except to go along. When Kissinger told Nixon that he had briefed Frankel, the president "was so mad his teeth clenched," according to Charles Colson. Later he told Colson: "I suppose now everybody's going to say that Kissinger won the election."[22]

That night, even as Frankel's story was being printed, Hanoi was going public by broadcasting over Radio Hanoi the details of the agreement that Kissinger had accepted and the tale of how Saigon had scuttled it. The broadcast quoted the cable Kissinger had sent in Nixon's name calling the accord "complete," and it demanded that the agreement be signed immediately.

Kissinger had a press briefing already scheduled for the next morning. He decided to turn it into a full-scale news conference and, with the president's permission, to allow television coverage.[23]

Later Kissinger would be charged with trying to help Nixon's reelection effort by proclaiming, falsely, that a peace accord was imminent. In fact, by then he realized that Nixon had no political desire for an immediate peace announcement. Instead, Kissinger's declarations at the press conference were aimed at the two Vietnamese capitals.

To Saigon, he wanted to convey that the U.S. was committed to the agreement he had drafted. To Hanoi, he wanted to send assurances that the problems in Saigon were but a glitch, that the basic outline of the peace plan still stood, and that it was not all a big scam orchestrated by Washington and Saigon.

In his attempt to reaffirm—both to Saigon and Hanoi—America's commitment to the framework reached in Paris, Kissinger uttered at the outset of his briefing a sound bite that was to haunt him for years. "We believe," he said, "that peace is at hand."

He went on to claim that he had warned Le Duc Tho that, before any agreement could be completed, Saigon would have to be consulted. With no trace of irony, Kissinger told the press: "Hanoi seemed to be of the view that we could simply impose any solution on Saigon and that their participation was not required"—this from the man who had arrived in Saigon and presented, with no advance warning, a complex peace treaty that he planned to initial in Hanoi five days later.

Otherwise, Kissinger's upbeat presentation, praise for Hanoi's "seriousness," and solicitous nods toward Saigon's concerns were convincing. That afternoon, the stock market soared. James Reston, in a column called "The End of the Tunnel," * wrote, "It has been a long time since Washington has heard such a candid and even brilliant explanation of an intricate political problem." *Newsweek* ran a cover of a GI with "Good-Bye Viet Nam" splashed across his helmet. In its sidebar on "How Kissinger Did It," which was based on a briefing Kissinger had given to its White House correspondent, the magazine reported: "He cajoled, wheedled, lectured, using all the arts of negotiation, including praise for the bravery of the North Vietnamese." George McGovern plaintively (and wrongly) charged that it was "a deliberate deception designed to fool the American people for the sake of Republican votes."[24]

A few weeks later, after the phrase *peace is at hand* had become a source of derision, speechwriter William Safire asked Kissinger why he had used it. "I had to say that," Kissinger replied, "because we had just backed away from initialing the document, and Hanoi needed to be reassured that we were ready to sign."

"At least you didn't do it to mislead the American electorate," said Safire, trying to be nice.

"So they'll say I was naive," said Kissinger.

---

* "The light at the end of the tunnel" was first used as a metaphor for impending success in Vietnam by French general Henri Navarre in May 1953, one year before his humiliation at Dien Bien Phu and twenty years before America withdrew the last Western combat troops.

"Better naive than devious."

"Not in this job." [25]

Nixon was enraged by Kissinger's pronouncement. "I knew immediately that our bargaining position with the North Vietnamese would be seriously eroded," he recalled. President Thieu was likewise unhappy. In an emotional talk to a packed rally in the Presidential Palace, he declared that "our minimum demands are that North Vietnamese Army troops should pull back to North Vietnam."

But for someone who had just intentionally misled an ally and unintentionally misled an adversary, Kissinger escaped with his reputation remarkably unscathed as he began trying to put back the pieces. To show new solidarity with Saigon, he attended a celebration of Vietnam's National Day at its Washington embassy on November 1. "I'm uniting Vietnam," he joked to the reporters who were there. "Both sides are screaming at me." [26]

TWENTY-ONE

THE CHRISTMAS BOMBING

Hanoi Is Hit in Order to Convince Saigon to Sign

> *It would be difficult to imagine two societies less meant to understand each other than the Vietnamese and the American.*
> —KISSINGER, in FOREIGN AFFAIRS, JANUARY 1969

THE BREAKDOWN, DECEMBER 1972

On the weekend before the 1972 election, Kissinger strolled the beach near San Clemente with journalist Theodore White, kicking the sand and watching kids collect kelp. At one point, he burst into an angry denunciation of President Thieu. But then his mood turned more philosophical. As he relaxed, he ruminated about how, in the aftermath of the Vietnam War, the U.S. would have to scale back the global role it had played since 1945.

"How do you withdraw?" Kissinger wondered aloud. "How do you get out of a situation where every single crisis around the globe gets dumped on us?" As they continued walking, Kissinger answered his own question. What the world needed, he said, was "a self-regulating mechanism." And that is what he and Nixon had created by adding China into the global balance. White, easily impressed, was. Not since he had talked to George Marshall and Dean Acheson, he recalled, "during the dynamic days of American hegemony, had I heard the use of American power so carefully explained."

At the end of the three-mile walk, Kissinger noticed that people were waving at him. A middle-aged man with fuzzy gray hair on his chest asked if he could shake Kissinger's hand. He simply wanted to say that he was grateful for peace. Kissinger suddenly seemed rather shy, not his usual carriage. "Where else could it happen but in a country like this?" he asked White. "To let a foreigner make peace for them, to accept a man like me—I even have a foreign accent."[1]

That Tuesday, Nixon won 47 million votes, more than 60 percent of those cast, the second-largest landslide in American history. Kissinger wrote a note that he had placed on the president's pillow: "To take a divided nation, mired in war, losing its confidence, wracked by intellectuals without conviction, and give it a new purpose and overcome its hesitations—will loom ever larger in the history books. It has been an inspiration to see your fortitude in adversity and your willingness to walk alone."

Amid all of this adulation, however, loomed one uncomfortable fact: peace in Vietnam was still not at hand.

Right after the election, acting on the theory that Thieu's resentment of Kissinger was to blame for his unwillingness to accept the agreement negotiated in Paris, Nixon sent Haig to Saigon to have a soldier-to-soldier talk with the proud, stubborn president. But Thieu stuck to his insistence that any agreement must require the North Vietnamese to withdraw from the South. "You are a general," he said to Haig. "I am a general. Would you as a general accept this agreement? If Russia invaded the U.S., would you accept an agreement where they got to stay and then say that it was a peace?" Haig was unable to reply. "He knew that I was right," Thieu later said.[2]

There were sixty-nine modifications in the October accord that South Vietnam felt were necessary, Thieu told Haig. When Kissinger returned to the Paris table to face Le Duc Tho on November 20, he presented them all, indicating that they were Saigon's demands and were being presented for the record. "The list was so preposterous," Kissinger recalled, "that it must have strengthened Hanoi's already strong temptation to dig in its heels."

Le Duc Tho, perhaps feeling duped, was more in a mood to lecture than to bargain. Colonial powers had deceived Vietnam over the centuries, he said, but never as badly as in this instance. Even Kissinger felt that the charges of perfidy were understandable.

During four days of talks, some minor issues were resolved. But Hanoi was unwilling to make any basic changes in the accord reached in October. When Kissinger realized that the only concessions he could get would be cosmetic, he cabled Nixon that there were two options: accept the treaty this way and cram it down Saigon's throat, or break off the talks and resume the bombing of the North.

Partly because he never focused on the details, and partly because he had secluded himself with Haldeman at Camp David in a postelection funk, Nixon's contribution was an array of conflicting and confused suggestions. In a cable on Wednesday, November 22, destined to confuse future historians who find it in the archives, Nixon pretended to be tough: "Unless the other side shows the same willingness to be reasonable that we are showing, I am directing you to discontinue the talks and we shall then have to resume military activity." Yet a cover note he sent with it made clear that the cable was intended as a ploy: "not a directive—for possible use with the North Vietnamese."

The next day the president seemed to flip the other way; he expressed his resentment at Kissinger's "peace is at hand" statement and said it had made it politically impossible to break off the talks. "Because of expectations that have been built up in this country," Nixon pointedly wired, "we must recognize the fundamental reality that we have no choice but to reach agreement along the lines of the October 8 principles." The next day he flopped back, saying that if the communists would not budge, then Kissinger should come home, after which the U.S. would launch a massive bombing strike.[3]

All the while, Haldeman and others (including Haig) began putting distance between the president and Kissinger by leaking word that he had exceeded his authority during the negotiations in October. "When he was in Saigon, twice he cabled the North Vietnamese in the president's name to accept their October proposal," Haldeman explained to Ehrlichman. "Henry did that over Al Haig's strong objection and beyond any presidential authority." Kissinger blamed these leaks on Nixon. Nixon in turn blamed them on the State Department and denied that they were true. "HAK never exceeded his authority," Ehrlichman's notes of one staff meeting record Nixon as saying. "State is leaking false stories."[4]

With his home front in disarray, Kissinger decided to ask for a ten-day recess of the Paris talks. When they resumed, Le Duc Tho was moderately forthcoming; he made clear that the North Vietnamese were still ready to sign the October accord, and he agreed to drop the phrase *administrative structure* from the description of the new National Council that was to be set up, thus eliminating a dispute over translation.

But Kissinger could not pin the North Vietnamese down on countless details necessary for a final agreement. He became frustrated, angry, and convinced that he was being stalled. Haig was again in Paris with him, contributing neither to his calmness nor to his sympathy for Hanoi's demands. Repeatedly Kissinger sent back word that it was time to break off the talks, resume the bombing, and damn the consequences.

Once again, Kissinger had become concerned about "credibility." It was necessary, he felt, to achieve some improvements in the October accord in order to justify Saigon's decision to reject it. If the U.S. proved unable to produce some tangible improvement, he reasoned, it would make both Washington and Saigon seem helpless. As he cabled Nixon: "It would deprive us of any ability to police the agreement, because if the communists know we are willing to swallow this backdown, they will also know that we will not have the capacity to react to violations." His conclusion this time was clear: "Therefore I believe we must be prepared to break off the negotiations."

On December 5 and 6, Kissinger produced a torrent of pessimistic cables. In one, he recommended that he put forth Thieu's demand for the withdrawal of North Vietnamese troops and use Hanoi's inevitable rejection as a pretext for breaking off the talks. In another, he suggested a new bombing campaign could last six months.

For once, Nixon was calmer and more ready to let diplomacy work than was Kissinger. "I had to back him off the position that we really had a viable option to break off the talks with the North and resume the bombing," Nixon wrote in his diary. "It simply isn't going to work." Later, in response to Kissinger's strongest cables, he began blaming the predicament on what he called "Henry's now-famous 'peace is at hand' statement." As he explained it in another diary entry: "Expectations were raised so high prior to the election . . . [that] to order resumption of the war with no end in sight and no hope is simply going to be a loser."

But it soon became clear that a breakdown—and a new bombing spree—was likely, which led to an even more contentious issue: who should break the bad news to the public?

With an adamancy that seemed motivated by more than humility, Kissinger insisted that Nixon was the right man for the job, the only one who could inspire the American people to support renewed bombing. "I believe that you can make a stirring and convincing case to rally them as you have so often in the past," Kissinger cabled from Paris.

This flattery left Nixon unmoved. He was still annoyed at how Kissinger, in his press conference and background leaks of October, had taken credit for peace being at hand. "Instead of a frantic and probably foredoomed attempt on my part to rally American public opinion behind a major escalation of the war, I preferred an unannounced stepping up of the bombing," Nixon later recalled. "This would be coupled with a press conference by Kissinger to explain where we stood."

In what he later admitted was a "suicidal" move, Kissinger repeated his recommendation that Nixon should have the honor of announcing any decision to renew the bombing, and then repeated it again. "We will need a personal address by you," Kissinger insisted. "I believe you could convey this message in clear and simple terms in a 10 to 15 minute speech."[5]

After absorbing the brunt of Nixon's outrage at Kissinger's gall, Haldeman was left to cable the national security adviser with the news that it was his responsibility to explain things if there was a breakdown. "You should conduct a low-key, nondramatic briefing," Haldeman advised. "I have talked to a very few of the hard-liners here in total confidence, and it is their strongly unanimous view that it would be totally wrong for the President to go on TV."

Kissinger recalled that he was not quite sure how it would be possible to make a "low-key, nondramatic" announcement that peace talks had collapsed and bombing had begun. The prospect of being the one who would have to stand up and say peace was not at hand caused him to butt his head against the wall yet again. "We had better face the facts of life," he replied to Haldeman, and then proceeded to spell them out. "If we are to attempt to rally the American people, only the President can do that eventually."[6]

All of this was happening while Nixon was ensconced with Ehrlichman and Haldeman at Camp David, where criticizing Kissinger seemed to be the theme of the party. The only thing working in his favor was that he had dragged Haig back to Paris with him, so his once-loyal assistant was not among those who got to bad-mouth him to the president. "I could picture Nixon, cut off from the most knowledgeable senior advisers," Kissinger later wrote. "He would ruminate, writing out the issues on his yellow pad, all the while showered with the advice of his public relations geniuses."

The notes and recollections of Ehrlichman and Haldeman, which Kissinger never had the pleasure of seeing, reveal a scene that was in fact worse than Kissinger's most frightful nightmare.

It was snowing and bitter cold when Ehrlichman arrived at Camp David's main house, Aspen Lodge, on the evening of December 6, but Nixon was paddling around in his superheated swimming pool.*

---

* That pool had cost an astonishing $550,000 to build, according to the head of Nixon's military office, Bill Gulley, because the site Nixon had picked required that an underground bomb shelter be relocated.

When Ehrlichman arrived, Haldeman showed him a sheaf of Kissinger's cables urging that the president—rather than Kissinger—announce the resumption of the bombing. Haldeman asked Ehrlichman what he thought. "The President should explain successes," Ehrlichman replied, shaking his head. "The staff explains failures."

"I don't know if you realize it," Haldeman went on, "but Henry was very down when he left for Paris. He's been under care. And he's been doing some strange things." It was Haig's contention, Haldeman reported, that Kissinger was out of line in accepting the October accord without consulting Nixon.

The president, swathed in towels and a terry-cloth robe, emerged from the pool and began drying his hair. Haldeman explained that Ehrlichman also opposed Kissinger's suggestion of a televised presidential address. "The South Vietnamese think Henry is weak now because of his press conference statements," Nixon grumbled. "That damn 'peace is at hand'! The North Vietnamese have sized him up; they know he has to either get a deal or lose face. That's why they've shifted to a harder position."

Nixon then dictated a five-page set of instructions telling Kissinger "to go down a list of questions" with Le Duc Tho to pin him down precisely on each American proposal. "The purpose here is to make the record clear once and for all." Then, if there is a breakdown, "we will embark on a very heavy bombing of the North." Once again, he rejected the suggestion that he personally announce all of this on television. Then he rather pointedly noted what was expected of Kissinger upon his return: "The thing to do here is to take the heat from the Washington establishment."

After a colonel from Kissinger's staff had been dispatched with these instructions, Nixon returned to the subject of a television broadcast. "We can't rally them to support us when it's nothing new," he told Ehrlichman and Haldeman as they stood before the fire in Aspen Lodge. "Henry doesn't seem to understand that. Or does he? Maybe he just wants people to associate me with the failure."

Ehrlichman nodded.

At another meeting, Nixon fulfilled Kissinger's dark suspicions about the public relations forces guiding decisions at Camp David. "We need a telephone poll," the president told Haldeman and Ehrlichman. "Thieu insists that all North Vietnamese troops be withdrawn. We should poll the question, should we continue operations until all are withdrawn?" Nixon also suggested other elements of a possible settlement that should be included in the poll: freedom for the POWs, a free election, and preventing a coalition government.

During those rather grim days at Camp David, Nixon came up

with other suggestions. "Tell Kissinger to examine the NSC staff," Ehrlichman's notes record from one Camp David session. How many of them were McGovern supporters? "The President made a private check for McGovern supporters—14 were." Haldeman got his own assignment that day: "Tell Haig that Kissinger shouldn't smile in the pictures with Tho." Kissinger would later recall being rather baffled when, twice in one week, he received cables from Haldeman making it clear that smiles were frowned upon at Camp David.[7]

Kissinger ignored Nixon's suggestion that he put a list of questions to Le Duc Tho. The talks broke down on December 13. Although Moscow passed the word that it could convince the North Vietnamese to go back to the October agreement—the one that Kissinger had accepted—Kissinger and Nixon had convinced themselves that this was no longer good enough.

With neither Air Force One nor its sister aircraft available, Kissinger and his team had to fly back to Washington that Wednesday night on a windowless military plane. In the gloomy cocoon, which for all of its gadgetry could not communicate securely with the White House, Kissinger felt isolated and devastated. When he arrived at Andrews Air Force Base, a reporter shouted out, "Dr. Kissinger, do you think peace is at hand?"

"That's a good phrase," he replied with a weak smile. "Wonder who used it?"

Also there to greet him that night was Al Haig, who had returned from Paris earlier. The only option now, the general said, was a large-scale B-52 bombing assault on Hanoi and the rest of North Vietnam.

"They're just a bunch of shits," Kissinger replied, referring to the North Vietnamese. At a meeting the next morning in the Oval Office, Kissinger seemed to take the collapse of the talks personally. "Tawdry, filthy shits. They make the Russians look good."[8]

It was at this meeting—with only Kissinger, Haig, and the president present—that the decision was made to launch a major new bombing assault on North Vietnam. The real issue was not whether to bomb; that was a given. It was a question of just how brutal the bombing should be. Would Nixon, for the first time in the war, order the use (over his cautious military commanders' objections) of the huge, lumbering B-52 strategic bomber to hit Hanoi, Haiphong, and other urban centers in the northern part of North Vietnam? Up until now, the B-52s had been used to bomb supply routes south of the twentieth parallel and on selected targets outside major cities. For targets in civilian areas, smaller and more precise fighter-bombers, such as the F-111 or the F-4, had been used.

Among the arguments in favor of a B-52 assault on Hanoi was

that a massive shock was needed to get the North Vietnamese back to the table before Congress could reconvene and stop the entire exercise. So far, bombing had not been able to bring Hanoi to its knees; the argument was that a more brutal assault might do the trick.

Among the arguments against the attack was that it would be unproductive and not worth the high cost in lives, military expense, America's reputation, and public support. Ever since the Strategic Bombing Survey after World War II, those who believe that bombing industrial areas can weaken enemy resolve have repeatedly had to learn that this is not as easy as it may seem in front of a map in the Situation Room. In addition, it was not Hanoi but Saigon that really needed to be pressured. It was unfair to brutalize the North Vietnamese for a breakdown that had primarily been caused by President Thieu.

Haig was in favor of the most forceful option available, that of using B-52s without restriction. The president, he told John Scali at the time, "is going to stand tall and resume the bombing and put those B-52 mothers in there and show 'em we mean business."

One of Nixon's maxims was that if you had to use force, you would get no points for showing restraint. Once a decision had been made to apply military muscle, it was best to go all out. And he did. Agreeing heartily with Haig, he ordered that every possible B-52 bomber available—129 in all—be sent to Vietnam for a relentless series of daily assaults, beginning on December 18, on targets in Hanoi, Haiphong, and elsewhere.

Kissinger was initially reluctant. He wanted to resume heavy bombing south of the twentieth parallel (meaning the supply routes near the demilitarized zone rather than farther north near Hanoi). If targets around Hanoi and Haiphong were to be struck, he favored using fighter jets, which would be effective yet cause less of a stir.

Even after the decision to use B-52s was made, and he had come around to supporting it, Kissinger's discomfort was visible to all around him—particularly to liberal reporters. Yet his qualms did not restrain him from lavishing praise on the president while in his presence. "Henry talked rather emotionally about the fact that this was a very courageous decision," Nixon wrote in his diary the night the bombing orders were issued.[9]

Nixon got his way, sort of, on who would make the announcement: he said nothing, but sent Kissinger to give a press conference on December 16, two days before the bombing was to begin. As was often the case, Nixon provided memos dictated late at night telling Kissinger how to describe the president: unflappable, cool in a crisis, and firm.

But Kissinger was not to be outmaneuvered. In his "peace is at hand" press conference, he had mentioned the president only thrice. This time around, he mentioned the president fourteen times, and it was not to pass along Nixon's self-descriptions of his great attributes. With subtle phrases, Kissinger placed responsibility for the impasse on the president. "We have not reached an agreement that the president considers just," he said, repeating this thought in various other formulations. He also did not mention the decision to launch a B-52 bombing assault on Hanoi; if the president was not going to take responsibility for announcing it, Kissinger decided, then the raids would simply begin without any official explanation.[10]

On the Monday morning of December 18, Colonel James McCarthy, commander of the 43rd Strategic Wing at Anderson Air Force Base on Guam, briefed his twenty-seven crews. Most of the men had hoped that the peace-is-at-hand announcement meant they would be home by Christmas. "Gentlemen," McCarthy began, "your target tonight is Hanoi." For the rest of the briefing, he recalled, you could hear a pin drop. The operation was code-named Linebacker II, a sequel to the bombing runs conducted the previous May. To the rest of the world, and to history, it would become known as "the Christmas bombing."

That night, Cliff Ashley was one of the first to reach Hanoi in his lumbering B-52 when his port wing was hit by a surface-to-air missile. He headed for the Thai border, the inside of his plane looking like "a red wall of flame." An escorting F-4 Phantom radioed him, "I don't think you're going to make it." His six crewmen and deputy commander bailed out, watching in the air as the huge eight-engine jet rolled over with fusilage aflame and plunged to the ground.

During the entire war up to that point, only one of these $8 million planes had been destroyed, but that night two others in addition to Ashley's went down, and the toll was fifteen by the time the bombing campaign ended twelve nights later. Fifteen smaller planes were also downed, and ninety-three American airmen lost.

There was only one break in the relentless bombing runs—for Christmas Day. In fact, Nixon would later rankle at the phrase *Christmas bombing* because, he pointed out, no bombs were dropped on Christmas Day.

By Hanoi's count, 1,318 civilians were killed in Hanoi and another 300 in Haiphong. The toll was moderated by the evacuation to the countryside of almost all of Hanoi's schoolchildren and half its population of 1 million.

Although critics charged that the American assault amounted to an indiscriminate carpet bombing of civilian areas, it was not. There was no massacre comparable to the blanket bombing of Dresden or the firebombing of Tokyo. In fact, considerable care was taken to hit only military targets, according to the *Baltimore Sun*'s former Saigon bureau chief, Arnold Isaacs, who studied the bombing as part of a generally critical analysis of American policy. Pilots were even ordered to fly straight for four minutes before dropping their bombs in order to hit their targets more accurately.[11]

But the problem with B-52s, which drop their bombs from seven miles high, is that the precision that seems possible to planners is seldom as clean on the ground. The famous Bach Mai hospital in the heart of Hanoi was hit by a string from a B-52 aiming for a target several thousand feet away. Two children, two doctors, and twenty-six others were killed. The Egyptian and Indian embassies were also hit, as was a Polish freighter in Haiphong harbor, killing three crewmen.

Nor is it necessary to allege that the Christmas bombing was indiscriminate in order to conclude that it was unjustified by any proper moral calculus or sense of proportion. The December 1972 decision to bomb targets in the urban areas of North Vietnam was an action that should and does haunt the United States, and Kissinger, to this day.

Hanoi was bombed in order to force changes in a treaty that the U.S. had already seen fit to accept. The modifications for which these lives were lost were so minor that neither Nixon nor Kissinger would adequately remember what they were. "In fact, I'm not sure that Nixon ever really understood what those changes were," Kissinger later said.

Although the North Vietnamese were certainly infuriating during December, and they were probably even guilty of overreaching, the main reason for pummeling Hanoi was Nixon's and Kissinger's belief that it was necessary to force cosmetic concessions to help Saigon save face. President Thieu was the one who had defied Kissinger and who had remained intransigent. The bombs that killed the children in Bach Mai hospital were not just aimed at targets a few thousand feet away; their real target in a sense was in Saigon. "If Kissinger had possessed the power to bomb the Independence Palace to force me to sign the agreement," Thieu later said with a caustic smile, "he would not hesitate to do so."

The damage to America's prestige and to Kissinger's reputation was devastating. On Christmas Day, millions of American television viewers saw incongruous shots of Kissinger smiling as he attended a Washington Redskins game juxtaposed with stories about the rain of bombs on Hanoi. Columnist Joseph Kraft wrote that Kissinger "had been compromised and everybody in town knows it" and asked, "Is he just a good German lending a cover of respectability to whatever monstrous policy President Nixon is pleased to pursue?" James Reston called the bombing "war by tantrum." Tom Wicker wrote, "There is no peace. There is shame on earth, an American shame, perhaps enduring, surely personal." And David Broder recounted a conversation over breakfast in 1969 when Kissinger had mused, "Vietnam may be one of those tragic issues that destroys everyone who touches it."

Pope Paul VI called the bombing "the object of daily grief." The London *Daily Mirror* said it "made the world recoil in revulsion." In Hamburg, where air raids had flattened the city and killed fifty thousand in a single week, an editorial in *Die Zeit* used a phrase familiar to Germans: "Even allies must call this a crime against humanity." When Swedish prime minister Olof Palme compared the action to Nazi atrocities and tossed around names such as that of the German death camp Treblinka, Kissinger was so upset that he publicly mentioned that Sweden had remained neutral during World War II.

The stain to Kissinger's reputation caused by his complicity in the Christmas bombing remained among the most indelible. Anthony Lewis also used the phrase "a crime against humanity." A year later, he wrote: "A public that forgets the Christmas bombing may too easily accept in the future the use of such mass weapons as B-52s against targets in urban areas." Two years later, he added: "There are some things that should not be forgotten. That is why the anniversary has been and will be noted in this space." And for years afterward, December after December, Lewis resurrected this ghost of Christmas past.[12]

Nixon finally halted the bombing on December 30 after Hanoi agreed to return to the bargaining table. In retrospect, he would concede that what he called "the December bombing" was not worth it. Given what happened, he "would have preferred to have taken the October 8 agreement."

Soon after the bombing ended, Kissinger was asked in an off-the-record conversation to speculate on North Vietnam's motives for coming back to the bargaining table. He declined to do so. "I have enough trouble," he replied, "analyzing our own motives." Publicly, he conceded that the bombing was caused by the intransigence of Saigon as well as Hanoi. "It was decided to try to bring home really to both Vietnamese parties that the continuation of the war had its price," he said in a televised interview with CBS's Marvin Kalb. He went on to explain that the way of "bringing it home" to North Vietnam was by bombing Hanoi and to South Vietnam was by "sending General Haig to Saigon," actions that even Kissinger could not have believed were comparably dire.

In the interview, Kissinger continued to distance himself from the bombing decision. Tellingly, he called it "certainly the most lonely decision that the president has had to make."

In fact, although he was conflicted, Kissinger supported the Christmas bombing at the time, intellectually if not emotionally. In retrospect, he even concluded that Nixon was right to use heavy B-52 bombers rather than smaller tactical ones.[13]

Yet by displaying his anguish for all of his friends in the press to see, and by continually casting it as "the president's" decision, Kissinger assured that the perception of pundits would be that he was not to blame for the Christmas bombing. When columns to that effect started appearing, the simmering tension between Kissinger and his patron began to boil over.

"Have you read Reston's column?" John Scali roared over the phone to Chuck Colson. "It's a disaster!"

Scali, the former ABC News correspondent who had been hired by Nixon to counter Kissinger's control of foreign policy publicity, knew that the column in the Sunday *New York Times* would deepen the president's eerily glum holiday mood. It was December 31, the day after the White House had quietly announced it was stopping the Christmas bombing and going back to the Paris bargaining table. Nixon's primary preoccupation had been to keep the announcement low-key and prevent Kissinger from interrupting his Palm Springs vacation to claim credit. James Reston's piece was just the sort that would send the president into a black fury.

In a column entitled "Nixon and Kissinger," Reston declared that the presidential assistant "undoubtedly opposes" the bombing strategy. Displaying the confidence that comes naturally to pundits whose phone calls never go unanswered, Reston informed his readers that "Kissinger has a strong sense of tragedy about Vietnam and wants to get it behind us." But for the moment, Reston continued, Kissinger "is avoiding a break with the President." Then came the capstone threat, which clearly sounded as if it had recently reached Reston's ears with a guttural Bavarian rumble: "If . . . there is an open split between the President and his principal foreign policy adviser and negotiator, Mr. Kissinger will be free to resign and write the whole story of the Paris talks and why they broke down, and this would probably be highly embarrassing to Mr. Nixon."

What a way to spoil a secluded Sunday at Camp David. Colson read the column over the phone to Nixon, who exploded and ordered him to call Kissinger immediately, even though it was only six-thirty A.M. in Palm Springs. "I will not tolerate insubordination," Nixon barked. "You tell Henry he's to talk to no one, period! And tell him not to call me. I will accept no calls from him." With that, he slammed down the phone. For the rest of the day, according to his valet, Manolo, Nixon remained so glum that he could not even enjoy the Washington Redskins game on television.

Colson, as ordered, telephoned Kissinger, who was spending a nervous New Year's Eve in the California desert as the houseguest of retired businessman Theodore Cummings. Then Kissinger, as phone records reveal, did just the opposite of what had been ordered. First he tried to get through to Nixon. True to his word, the president did not take the call. Then he phoned columnist Joseph Kraft, who did.

What Kissinger did not realize was that Colson had been authorized by the president to get a log of Kissinger's phone calls from the White House communications agency and the Secret Service. Minutes after Kissinger's conversation with Kraft, Colson was back on the phone to remind him that he was not supposed to talk to the columnist or anyone else in the press. "I wouldn't talk to that son of a bitch," Colson claimed that Kissinger responded, even though Colson knew that they had just finished speaking.

At Camp David, Nixon continued to stew, working himself into a frenzy so fierce that he decided to cut short his vacation and fly back to the White House early New Year's morning. "Find out what the hell Henry's doing," he told Haldeman. When Haldeman called, Kissinger denied that he had spoken to Reston. A few hours later, after Colson had gone through all of Kissinger's phone conversations for the week, Haldeman called back. "In fact you did talk to him," Haldeman charged, citing the specific time and date. Although it did not strike him as particularly funny at the time, Haldeman was later rather amused by Kissinger's response: "Yes, but that was only on the telephone."

Reston had known Kissinger since 1951, when the young graduate student had invited the distinguished journalist to address his Harvard summer seminar. As the gray eminence of America's newspaper of record, Reston defined what was to be the conventional wisdom: that the bombing had caused a rift between Kissinger and Nixon. *Time* and *Newsweek* took up the theme in their next issues, and within a week CBS White House correspondent Dan Rather had informed 20 million viewers that the schism had now moved "past the rumor stage to the fact stage."

In the meantime, Joe Kraft came out with a column based on his New Year's Eve phone call. "Dr. Kissinger remains perhaps the only instrument for effective foreign policy available to President Nixon," Kraft wrote. "Unless he gets a new mandate from the President—the

kind of mandate he can only get by being made Secretary of State—
he should probably resign in the next year."[14]

THE GHOSTS OF CHRISTMAS PRESENT

Ever since the November election, Nixon had been
obsessed with shaking up his team rather than basking in his landslide.
His torment in victory was first displayed on the day after the vote
when he gathered his aides and cabinet officers in the Roosevelt Room
and stunned them by saying he expected every one of them to offer
his resignation. It was, Kissinger later said, an "appalling performance."

For most of November and December, Nixon had spent his days
secluded at Camp David with Haldeman and Ehrlichman. He had
met with Kissinger only rarely, refused to take most of his phone calls,
and reduced him to communicating through Haldeman.

According to Ehrlichman's copious notes from the period, the
president was spending a lot of his time figuring out how to reshuffle
his administration. Kissinger, however, took his own lack of access as
a sign of instability, later writing: "Ensconced at Camp David, surrounded only by public relations experts, Nixon was still deep in the
bog of resentments that had produced the darkest and perhaps most
malevolent frame of mind of his Presidency."

Part of Nixon's agenda was replacing Bill Rogers as secretary of
state. He had initially considered John Connally for the job, knowing
full well that tapping such a headstrong personality would cause Kissinger to resign. In the end, he settled on Kenneth Rush, the former
ambassador to West Germany who had been part of the back-channel
Berlin negotiations in 1971.

Rush was a courtly industrialist and lawyer who, during a year
spent teaching corporate law at Duke, had come to admire the young
Richard Nixon. When Nixon asked whether he should become, as
Rush had been, a corporate lawyer in Manhattan, Rush replied that
he had too much talent; instead he should go back to California and
enter politics.

Kissinger realized that he had no hope of getting the cabinet post
for himself, at least at the moment; he was considering leaving the
government, and either way he deemed Rush the least offensive possible replacement for Rogers at State. Shortly after the election, Kissinger stormed into Haldeman's office and demanded to know when
the change would occur. Haldeman deflected the question, but a few

days later he was up at Camp David ready to inform Rogers that Nixon wanted him out.

But when Haldeman sat Rogers down in Laurel cabin and gave him the news, he refused to quit, and in fact he refused even to discuss the matter with Haldeman. He would take it up with his friend the president, he said. Then he walked over to Aspen Lodge to do that. Nixon displayed his distaste for direct confrontation. Rogers made the case that he should stay for another six months and that he did not want his departure to look like "a victory for Kissinger." The matter was thus temporarily settled.

"Telling Henry was like placing a flaring match inside a high-octane gasoline tank," Haldeman recalled. "The explosion was predictable, but nonetheless searing." Kissinger did not realize that the timing would turn out to be ideal for his own ambitions. "You promised me, Haldeman," he raged. "You gave me your word! And now he's hanging on just like I said he would." Then Kissinger slipped from anger to despair. "There is a price you must pay," he said in a low voice. "Mine is Rogers. He will be with me forever—because he has the president wrapped around his little finger."

What Kissinger did not know was that Nixon was again brooding about getting rid of him as well as Rogers. A few days after his failure to fire Rogers, Nixon was alone with Chuck Colson in Aspen Lodge and walked him into a hallway leading to the bedroom. (Colson later realized that it was because the room where they were sitting was bugged.) "He told me that soon Kissinger would go," Colson recalled, "that it would be better for Henry, that he'd been away from Harvard too long, that he really should be back in academia. He was through with Henry." (Colson shortly thereafter wrote an op-ed piece for the *New York Times*, which made up in fervor what it lacked in truthfulness, in which he called reports of a rift between Nixon and Kissinger "a full-blown myth born in the Washington Georgetown cocktail circuit.")

Nixon also expressed his desire to be rid of Kissinger during an informal talk with Elmo Zumwalt. "He's telling the press I'm impossible to deal with," Nixon told the admiral. "I'm going to fire the son of a bitch." The president then asked Haldeman to find a way to "physically remove all of the memoranda from and to the president, especially the handwritten stuff, originals, and so forth, from the Kissinger office files." [15]

One of the most outrageous, albeit amusing, of Kissinger's blunders in his relationship with Nixon was the interview he gave during this period to the sharpshooting Italian journalist Oriana Fallaci, known for her elicit-and-eviscerate encounters with world leaders. "I did so largely out of vanity," he later admitted. "Fame was sufficiently novel for me to be flattered by the company I would be keeping in her journalistic pantheon."

Coyly if not cleverly, Kissinger added a condition: he would see her twice, but at the first meeting he would ask the questions, and if he felt comfortable with the answers, only then would he allow her to turn the tables. When she was ushered into his office on November 2, shortly after "peace is at hand" and before the election, he lapsed into a rather typical act of distractedness—turning his back and reading a long typewritten report while she waited—which she took as a "stupid and ill-mannered" power ploy. "He is by no means carefree or sure of himself," she concluded. "Before facing someone, he needs to take time and protect himself by his authority."

Kissinger's questioning made Fallaci ill at ease, but she soon found common ground by denigrating President Thieu. "Thieu will never give in," she taunted. "He'll give in," Kissinger responded. "He has to." Every time she said something bad about Thieu, she recalled, "he nodded or smiled with complicity." He finally decided she had passed her examination, but expressed one more qualm. She was a woman, and the love-struck French journalist Danielle Hunebelle had just published an embarrassing account of their non-affair. If he liked, she retorted, she would wear a fake mustache and pretend to be a man. He laughed and told her to come by his office that Saturday morning, two days later.

As soon as they began, it was clear the interview was not going well. Every ten minutes, Nixon interrupted with a phone call. "Kissinger answered attentively, obsequiously," Fallaci noted. Although usually a master at exuding warmth toward women, toward journalists, and especially toward women journalists, Kissinger stuck Fallaci as "icy." Preoccupied with the Paris talks, he remained expressionless throughout and never altered the tone of his "sad, monotonous" voice. Just when she finally felt she was penetrating him, Nixon called again and Kissinger excused himself for a moment. Two hours later, while she was still waiting, an aide came in to explain that he had unexpectedly left with the president for San Clemente.

The interview—published by *L'Europeo* in late November and reprinted a few weeks later in *The New Republic*—proved to be explosive. Bristling like a pine forest of first-person pronouns, it quoted Kissinger taking credit for the entire foreign policy of the Nixon years. That was not destined to endear him to the president's men, but it was his foray into personal introspection that opened him up to the worst ridicule. With a beguiling tone of innocence, Fallaci laid her trap with a question that no clear-thinking presidential assistant would have touched. But Kissinger leaped at the bait.

Fallaci: "Dr. Kissinger, how do you explain the incredible movie-star status you enjoy? How do you explain the fact that you are almost more famous and popular than a president? Have you a theory on this matter?"

Kissinger: "Yes, but I won't tell you. . . . Why should I as long as I'm still in the middle of my work? Rather, you tell me yours. . . ."

Fallaci: "Like a chess player, you've made a few good moves. China, first of all . . ."

Kissinger (avoiding the temptation to give Nixon some credit for the China opening): "Yes, China has been a very important element in the mechanics of my success. And yet that's not the main point. The main point, well, yes, I'll tell you. What do I care? The main point arises from the fact that I've always acted alone. Americans like that immensely. Americans like the cowboy who leads the wagon train by riding ahead alone on his horse, the cowboy who rides all alone into the town with his horse and nothing else. Maybe even without a pistol, since he doesn't shoot. . . . This amazing, romantic character suits me precisely because to be alone has always been part of my style. . . . I'm not looking for popularity. On the contrary, if you really want to know, I care nothing about popularity. . . ."

Fallaci: "How do you reconcile the tremendous responsibilities that you've assumed with the frivolous reputation you enjoy?"

Kissinger: ". . . I think that my playboy reputation has been and still is useful because it served and still serves to reassure people. To show them that I'm not a museum piece. . . ."

Fallaci: "And to think I believed it an undeserved reputation, I mean play-acting instead of reality."

Kissinger: "Well, it's partly exaggerated, of course. But in part, let's face it, it's true. What counts is to what degree women are part of my life, a central preoccupation. Well, they aren't at all. For me, women are only a diversion, a hobby. Nobody spends too much time with his hobbies. . . ."

Fallaci: "Are you shy?"

Kissinger: "Fairly so. But as compensation I think I'm pretty well balanced. You see, there are those who depict me as a mysterious, tormented character, and those who depict me as an almost cheerful fellow who's always smiling, always laughing. Both those images are incorrect. I'm neither one nor the other. I'm . . . I won't tell you what I am. I'll never tell anyone."

The notion of Henry Kissinger as Clint Eastwood had a certain goofy charm. He had never been on a horse in his life, and he could be merciless in ridiculing Nixon's own Walter Mitty fantasies. Yet there is something rather endearing and boyish about the romantic image he paints of himself riding alone, unarmed, into Moscow or Beijing or Paris. Still, it was not a portrait destined to appeal to the other man in the White House who was proud of being a loner. "That was not exactly how Richard Nixon saw Henry," said Ehrlichman. "If there was a Lone Ranger handling foreign affairs, the President would have cast Henry, I suspect, as Tonto."

When the interview appeared in Italy, Kissinger heard about it and was mortified. He called John Scali and asked him to see what he could do to stop it. "How?" Scali asked.

"Deny it," Kissinger said.

"Did you see her?"

"Yes, but I didn't say those things." But when Kissinger conceded that Fallaci had used a tape recorder, Scali told him to forget trying to suppress it.

Going to Scali, it transpired, was not the best way to tamp down interest in Kissinger's delicious gaffe. Part of the former TV newsman's job was to cut Kissinger down to size. Scali tipped off his friend Peter Lisagor, by then with the *Chicago Daily News,* who broke the story on Sunday, November 19. His piece was syndicated in the *Washington Star* and other papers, and *The New Republic* then reprinted the entire interview.

Kissinger claimed that his words were manipulated and taken out of context. And it is probably true that he was the victim of some judicious editing. Despite initially offering to play her tape for American journalists, Fallaci never did. She later claimed to have played it for CBS's Mike Wallace, but Wallace denied that account. He said he heard a few moments of a scratchy tape with Kissinger saying something that was not as simple as Fallaci claimed. "The essence of some of what he said was there," said Wallace, "but I did not hear him say the stuff about being a lone cowboy."

There was also the problem of translation. The interview was conducted in English, then printed in Italian, then retranslated back into English; the version in *The New Republic* was notably different from the one in the English-language version of Fallaci's 1976 anthology. Nonetheless, whether or not Kissinger said everything precisely the way Fallaci quoted him, he probably came close, and his rivals in the White House, from Nixon on down, certainly believed that he did.

Sven Kraemer, already upset about what he saw as the sellout of South Vietnam, underlined the most egregious parts, wrote scathing comments in the margin, and sent copies to Kissinger's conservative critics. Among the recipients was Sven's father, Fritz Kraemer, then a strategist at the Pentagon. What set the elder Kraemer's teeth on edge was not his former protégé's pomposity but his insecurity. "People who think Kissinger haughty are totally mistaken," he later said. "The Fallaci interview reveals a desperate attempt to find approval, a self-defense mechanism that would never occur to the haughty."

But for most of Washington, Kissinger's hubris was amusing rather than upsetting. As the sharp-witted commentator Nicholas von Hoffman put it in his *Washington Post* column, Kissinger "emerged in print not as a skilled student of foreign affairs, but as a girl-crazed happy hamster."[16]

Kissinger had planned to spend Christmas in Key Biscayne with the president, and had flown down on December 20, just as the bombing was beginning. But two days later, to his staff's surprise, he was back in Washington, where he moped around rather glumly until heading off to spend New Year's at Ted Cummings's house with producer Robert Evans and a few Hollywood friends. Nixon remained in Key Biscayne for what he later told David Frost was "the loneliest and saddest Christmas I can ever remember."

As 1972 ended, one final irritant afflicted Nixon: he ended up having to share with Kissinger, rather than enjoy on his own, the designation as *Time*'s Man of the Year. The distinction was little more than a marketing gimmick begun by Henry Luce as a way to put Charles Lindbergh on the cover at the end of 1927 after having failed to do it when he made his transatlantic flight that May. Yet Nixon became oddly obsessed by it. In one of his daily news summaries in late October, he circled a quote from ABC's Howard K. Smith suggesting Kissinger as Man of the Year and wrote a note to Kissinger in the margin: "Good!" But he immediately got his aides to work on trying to burnish his own image in relationship to Kissinger's. Ehrlichman's notes of the president's orders for one session at Camp David in November read: "President's genius needs to be recognized, vis-a-vis HAK."

Kissinger, realizing that a problem was brewing, called *Time*'s Hugh Sidey and pleaded to be spared the honor. "This is going to complicate my life enormously," he said. He carried his case up to the editor in chief, Hedley Donovan, but, Kissinger recalled, "Donovan put an end to it by replying that if my importuning did not stop, I would be made Man of the Year in my own right."

When Nixon found out that he was sharing billing with his assistant, Haldeman recalled, he was "white-lipped with anger." He saw it, said Ehrlichman, as "another self-serving grab for publicity by

Henry." In fact, the article, although celebratory, sought to prick a few of Kissinger's pretensions. "For all his outer ego," it noted, "Kissinger has a servant's heart for Nixon."[17]

PEACE IN HAND, JANUARY 1973

Inside the villa near Paris, all of the North Vietnamese delegates stood waiting, as if in a receiving line, to greet their American counterparts. One of them, Nguyen Co Thach, later recalled how eager Kissinger was to create a friendly atmosphere. "It was not my responsibility," he told Le Duc Tho as he shook his hand. "It was not my fault about the bombing."

Although this did not deflect the North Vietnamese from delivering a stern lecture, they quickly showed they were willing to get down to the business of reaching a new settlement. By the end of the next day—Tuesday, January 9, 1973—the basics of an agreement were reached.

With a mixture of exuberance and flattery, Kissinger wired back to Nixon: "We celebrated the President's birthday today by making a major breakthrough in the negotiations. . . . What brought us to this point is the President's firmness and the North Vietnamese belief that he will not be affected by either Congressional or public pressure."

Nixon responded in kind. "What you have done today is the best birthday present I have had in sixty years."

The fragile bond between the two men seemed to be on the mend. After a festive farewell dinner with the North Vietnamese delegation on January 13, Kissinger flew to Key Biscayne, arriving at midnight. For two hours, he and Nixon discussed the agreement and shared a rare mood of affection. "I felt that night an odd tenderness toward him," Kissinger recalled, "even though we both sensed somehow that too much had happened between us to make the rest of the journey together."

For his part, Nixon wrote in his diary:

I walked out to the car with him and I told him that the country was indebted to him for what he had done. It is not really a comfortable feeling for me to praise people so openly. . . . On the other hand, Henry expects it, and it was good that I did so. He in turn responded that without my having the, as he put it, courage to make the difficult decision of December 18 [the Christmas bombing], we would not be where we are today.[18]

The January 1973 accord was fundamentally the same as the one that had been reached in October: the fighting would cease, the U.S. would withdraw, North Vietnam's troops would stay in the South, Thieu would stay in power in Saigon, and both sides would administer the territory that they militarily controlled. An awkwardly named National Council of National Reconciliation would be established with nebulous functions.

Kissinger claimed at the time that the January agreement contained a subtle but important concession involving the demilitarized zone (DMZ) that separated North from South: a vague phrase saying that the two sides would decide how to regulate "civilian passage." This implied, Kissinger unconvincingly claimed later, that *military* passage across the zone was forbidden. When combined with restrictions on the reinforcement of each side's troops in the South, Kissinger argued, this meant that the North Vietnamese forces would eventually wither away.

In fact, the major concession involving the DMZ was made by Kissinger: the area dividing North and South would continue to be considered a temporary demarcation line rather than an international boundary between sovereign states.

This issue went to the heart of what the war was all about, and Kissinger found that he could not finesse it with semantic sleights. President Thieu had tried to insist that South Vietnam be recognized in the cease-fire as a sovereign nation, one that had been invaded by outside forces from North Vietnam. But Hanoi insisted, successfully, that Vietnam be treated as one nation. Its argument had some merit: the Geneva accords of 1954 had proclaimed the unity of Vietnam even as it decreed that it would be split into two administrative units separated by a temporary military demarcation line.

"The military demarcation line between the two zones at the 17th parallel is only provisional and not a political or territorial boundary," the cease-fire agreement reached in October declared. And its first article pledged that the U.S. would "respect the . . . unity and territorial integrity of Vietnam." Although Kissinger dabbled, between October and January, with some meaningless obfuscations elsewhere in the accord, this clear and forthright acceptance of Hanoi's fundamental contention remained intact in the treaty's final version. The wording, in fact, was almost identical to the ten-point program that the communists tabled in May 1969.[19]

Where Kissinger's genius came into play, for better or worse, was in disguising some of the concessions, fudging controversial issues, and wrapping it all in creative ambiguity. Some might see the purpose of a peace accord as being to set forth in clear terms precisely what both sides have accepted. Kissinger approached it from a different perspective: on some fundamental disputes, he purposely devised language that could mean one thing to one side and something else to the other.

For example, even though he had agreed that Hanoi's troops could remain in the South, Kissinger wanted language that would allow Washington and Saigon to say that they had not fully conceded the principle. To that end, he wrote a letter for Nixon to send to Thieu on January 17 that stressed: "We do not recognize the right of foreign troops to remain on South Vietnamese soil." This obscured the fact that North Vietnam did not consider its troops to be "foreign" anywhere in either part of Vietnam.

At Thieu's insistence, the U.S. issued its interpretation about foreign troops as a "unilateral statement" accompanying the agreement. The same was done regarding the sole sovereignty of the Saigon government. But as happened with the SALT agreement, the unilateral statements tended to highlight what had *not* been agreed, rather than explain what had been agreed.

Another example of Kissinger's furtive tactics occurred on the issue of American aid to North Vietnam. Hanoi had demanded "reparations." Kissinger had offered instead a package of "reconstruction" assistance. This was duly included in the Paris agreement. But Kissinger kept secret an arrangement he had with Le Duc Tho that a letter would be sent over Nixon's signature spelling out the details of this aid. In order to make it seem separate from the Paris accord, the letter would be sent three days after the official signing.

Even more underhanded was the way of getting around Hanoi's demand that the letter not say that the aid was contingent on congressional approval. To solve that, Kissinger wrote another letter, sent separately over Nixon's signature, which noted that the aid package would "be implemented by each member in accordance with its own constitutional provisions." This allowed Kissinger and Nixon to tell a congressional briefing, held in between the signing of the accords and the sending of the private letters, that there "are no secret deals" involving foreign aid. It also allowed Kissinger later to argue that the aid package had always been conditional on congressional approval.

The complex fandango that was choreographed for the signing ceremony showed how basic differences had been papered over by ambiguous phrases. Even at the end, Thieu's government would not recognize the existence of the Viet Cong's Provisional Revolutionary Government or sign a document mentioning it by name. So two different versions of the cease-fire agreement were drawn up. One referred to the PRG and was signed by Washington and Hanoi only.

Another did not mention the PRG by name and was signed at a separate ceremony by Thieu's foreign minister; the foreign minister of the PRG also signed it, but on a different page.[20]

VIETNAM: A DAMAGE ASSESSMENT

Was any of this final fiddling worth the Christmas bombing? Were there improvements from the October agreement that justified three more months of war?

No, the changes made were minor and soon to prove meaningless. The dilution of the functions of the National Council turned out to mean little, since that contraption never came into existence. The fancy phrasing designed to shore up respect for the DMZ was also moot, since communist forces controlled both sides of that zone.

Kissinger later admitted that the main justification for the Christmas bombing was to get cosmetic changes that would make Saigon feel more comfortable with the agreement. "We could not in all conscience end a war on behalf of the independence of South Vietnam by imposing an unacceptable peace on our ally," he wrote. Yet that is what happened. It was not hard for the world to see that Thieu had been forced to accept an agreement that he feared and loathed.

Some on Kissinger's staff, notably Negroponte and Haig, felt that the bombing should have been used to get a fundamentally more favorable agreement, one that would expel North Vietnam's troops from the South. "We bombed the North Vietnamese into accepting our concessions," Negroponte said. Richard Holbrooke, the former Harriman aide who later became assistant secretary of state for Asia, likewise saw the final accord as a capitulation. "Allowing the North Vietnamese troops to stay in the South made it just a camouflaged bugout," he said. "We could have gotten essentially the same deal anytime after the 1968 bombing halt."

Such criticisms raise questions that are even more fundamental —and troubling—than those about the Christmas bombing. Was the agreement reached at the beginning of 1973 any better than that available at the beginning of 1969? If so, was it worth the cost?

The North Vietnamese claimed that the 1973 agreement was essentially an acceptance by the U.S. of the terms that Hanoi had been offering since its May 1969 ten-point program. Anthony Lake, one of Kissinger's fair-haired assistants who resigned over the Cambodian invasion, visited Hanoi in 1984 and asked a top minister whether the

U.S. could have ended the war on the same terms in 1969 as it did in 1973. "You never would have proposed it," the North Vietnamese official said.

"But suppose we had?"

"No, it was necessary that you be defeated militarily before you would have accepted our 1969 terms."[21]

A point-by-point comparison of Hanoi's "ten-point program" of 1969 with the 1973 agreement shows that they are largely identical, even in wording. But there is one significant difference. Missing in the 1973 accord is point five of Hanoi's 1969 program: the political provision that the Thieu government had to be replaced by a communist-approved coalition before there could be a cease-fire. Until October 1972, Hanoi insisted on this. In addition, the "Vietnamization" program meant that by 1973 Saigon's army was more able to defend itself than it was in 1969.

But was it worth four more years of war in order to get a cease-fire that allowed Thieu to retain authority in Saigon?

The deal would turn out to be costly: an additional 20,552 Americans dead, the near unraveling of America's social fabric, a breakdown in respect for government authority, the poisoning of America's reputation abroad (especially among an entire generation of youth), and the spread of the war to Cambodia and Laos. Given the fact that this deal held together for only two years, after which the communists took complete control and ousted Thieu, the continued effort was not justified, even if the motives for pursuing a negotiated settlement were honorable.

But what, as Kissinger repeatedly asked over the years, were the alternatives? In retrospect, a wiser alternative would have been simply to announce in 1969 that the U.S. felt it had honored its commitment, that it was now planning to withdraw by a fixed date, and that it would not try to negotiate on behalf of Saigon. The U.S. prisoners of war were few in number and not much of an issue in 1969; Washington could likely have sustained a demand, backed up by the threat of a blockade, that they be released as soon as the U.S. had withdrawn.

An American withdrawal, as Kissinger often argued, would have done some harm to its "credibility," the faith that other nations had that it would stand up to the Soviets and honor its treaty commitments. On the other hand, it would have recaptured the support of public opinion, at home and abroad. The resulting damage to the nation's ability to sustain a role in the world would have been far less than what actually occurred.

Kissinger argued that a withdrawal timetable would have undermined U.S. bargaining strength. "For better or worse," he said, "our judgment was that a public announcement would destroy the last incentives for Hanoi to negotiate." The judgment turned out to be wrong: Hanoi never negotiated seriously until after the bulk of U.S. troops had left in 1972.

But all of this is clearer in hindsight. At the time, Kissinger sincerely believed that a negotiated settlement could come quickly, and he agreed with Nixon that it should not involve abandoning the Thieu regime.

But even if one accepts this goal, there were better ways to pursue it. In consultation with Congress, Nixon and Kissinger could have drawn up a minimum American position, one generous enough to command domestic support. In the absence of a domestic consensus, a coherent policy was impossible.

By not enlisting support from Congress and the public for a clear plan, Nixon and Kissinger soon became trapped by a need for secrecy. Military threats and pressure had to be applied covertly. Plugging leaks became an obsession. Troop withdrawals were announced less for policy reasons than as sops to buy time with an impatient public. And the occasional spasms of bombings and invasions produced more domestic discord than sustained advantage on the battlefield. In short, the policy pursued by Nixon and Kissinger became one that depended on deception and secrecy rather than democratic support for its sustenance.

As it turned out, the main thing that Nixon and Kissinger accomplished was a "decent interval"—two years—between America's withdrawal and the defeat of the government it had committed itself to defend. That had the virtue of providing a little fig leaf to help preserve American credibility, but it hardly justified four more years of fighting and domestic discord.

Kissinger had used the phrase *decent interval* at symposiums he attended in 1967 and 1968, before taking office. By the fall of 1971, when the South Vietnamese elections turned out to be a sham, he had come to believe that it might be all that the U.S. could achieve. That September, he wrote a secret memo for Nixon advocating a negotiated settlement. In his memoirs, he summarized the still-classified document extensively, but he did not quote its key sentences:

> A peace settlement would end the war with an act of policy and leave the future of South Vietnam to the historic process. We could heal the wounds in this country as our men left peace behind on the battlefield and a *healthy interval* for South Vietnam's fate to unfold [emphasis added].[22]

As soon as he finished negotiating the January 1973 agreement, Kissinger gave some people the impression that it would probably achieve no more than a healthy or decent interval before a South Vietnamese defeat. "How long do you figure the South Vietnamese can survive under this agreement?" Ehrlichman asked him at the time. He expected some reassurances, but was surprised—and shaken —when Kissinger was blunt. "I think," Kissinger said, "that if they're lucky, they can hold out for a year and a half." [23]

But this remark probably reflected Kissinger's penchant for pessimistic pronouncements rather than what he actually believed. At the time of the accords, Saigon's forces controlled 75 percent of the territory of South Vietnam. Its army was far larger and stronger than Hanoi's. If it had the will, it had the means to retain power. In addition, Kissinger thought that détente would entice Soviet leaders to restrain Hanoi; until détente soured in 1975, that was the case.

Most important, Kissinger assumed that the U.S. would enforce the agreement by retaliating against blatant violations. Along these lines, he and Nixon made secret pledges to Thieu that would cause an uproar when they were revealed two years later, as Saigon was falling. "You have my absolute assurance that if Hanoi refuses to abide by the terms of this agreement it is my intention to take swift and retaliatory action," read a Kissinger-drafted letter from Nixon to Thieu on November 14. Another sent on January 5 pledged: "We will respond with full force should the settlement be violated by North Vietnam." [24]

"These commitments were what finally convinced me to sign," Thieu later said.

Kissinger would later claim that it seemed obvious that the U.S. would enforce the cease-fire, so he did not hesitate to make such a commitment to Thieu. "It never occurred to me that we could lose fifty thousand men and then not insist on enforcing what they had achieved," he said.

This borders on the disingenuous. Kissinger knew full well the mood of his war-weary nation, and he was under no illusion that Americans would permit a renewed set of military commitments. If he truly believed that the U.S. would agree to enforce the peace agreement, then he would not have gone to such lengths to avoid saying publicly what he had written in Nixon's secret letters to Thieu.

Instead, Kissinger handled these pledges in a typical—and inevitably destructive—fashion: secretly, without consulting Congress or informing the public. The reason for this approach is no mystery. Kissinger was aware that if he were to allow a public discussion about the pledges, they would have been scuttled by the Senate.

When the pledges were exposed two years later, Kissinger insisted that he had revealed them publicly when they were made. In fact, he had not. Asked at a news conference in early 1973 if the U.S. "would ever again send troops into Vietnam" if the accord was violated, he responded, "I don't want to comment on a hypothetical situation that we don't expect to arise." And when Marvin Kalb in a CBS interview repeatedly tried to pin him down on whether any pledges had been made, he replied: "Marvin, we did not end this war in order to look for an excuse to reenter it." In an unusually harsh article in *Foreign Affairs*, McGeorge Bundy analyzed Kissinger's statements and then blasted "the gravity of his distortions."

"Not even the Joint Chiefs of Staff were informed that written commitments were made to Thieu," said Admiral Elmo Zumwalt. "There are at least two words no one can use to characterize the outcome of this two-faced policy. One is 'peace.' The other is 'honor.' "

By making secret pledges, Nixon and Kissinger violated the role Congress is supposed to play in consenting to American military commitments. As with other secret Kissinger arrangements, it backfired when Congress finally found out two years later, enraging senators such as Henry Jackson and contributing to an atmosphere that led to a cutoff of all funds for Saigon.[25]

Kissinger would later argue that if he and Nixon had been given the authority to bomb and retaliate against Hanoi's transgressions, the fall of Saigon might have been delayed. Both Kissinger and Nixon blame the failure of resolve on Watergate. "But for the collapse of executive authority as a result of Watergate, I believe we would have succeeded," Kissinger said. "Had I survived," said Nixon, "I think that it would have been possible to have implemented the agreement. South Vietnam would still be a viable noncommunist enclave."

But this gate cannot hold much water. Once America had found a way to disengage from Vietnam, neither the Congress nor public would have permitted a reengagement, with or without Watergate. In the summer of 1973, Congress passed a law forbidding all air operations in Indochina, even though the war in Cambodia was continuing and the Vietnam cease-fire was being violated. When the final test in Vietnam occurred, it was during the honeymoon of a new and untainted president, Gerald Ford. He had been one of the congressional leaders who helped pass the bombing cutoff in 1973, and neither he nor his former Capitol Hill colleagues were willing to reintervene in Vietnam. Irrespective of Watergate, Americans wanted nothing more to do with Vietnam.[26]

•

In the end, it is hard to argue that the strategic interests at stake for the U.S. in pursuing the Vietnam War for another four years were worth the human, financial, moral, and spiritual costs. In all, 58,022 Americans lost their lives. Of these, 20,552 were now dead who had been alive when Nixon and Kissinger took office, including 4,278 who were killed in the last year of fighting. The direct cost of the war to the taxpayer was about $140 billion, or approximately $1,900 for each American household.

The moral principle of proportionality decrees that in fighting a war a nation should do no worse than the evil it seeks to prevent. The total amount of bombs the U.S. dropped on Indochina, at a cost of $6 billion, was 7,975,000 tons, about four times the tonnage used in all theaters during World War II. All told, 924,048 communist soldiers and 185,528 South Vietnamese soldiers were reported killed.

From the standpoint of American foreign policy, the war did more to deflect the nation from its important interests than it did to preserve its "credibility." When Kissinger had his bitter showdown with a recalcitrant Thieu in October 1972, he snapped that "for four years we have mortgaged our whole foreign policy to the defense of one country." To a realist such as Kissinger, such a distortion of national interest should have seemed idiotic. For he knew Bismarck's dictum: "Woe to the statesman whose reasons for entering a war do not appear so plausible at its end as at its beginning."

When America first entered the war, the reason was to counter the menace of a monolithic communism directed from Moscow and Beijing. By 1969, Kissinger and Nixon knew that this was not the situation. Another reason for entering the war was to contain China. Kissinger's 1971 trip to Beijing made this strategic interest less compelling.

Finally, the reason for American involvement came down to preventing a pro-communist nationalist revolution from imposing its system on a reluctant people. That was a moral, decent goal. But if the South Vietnamese people and its rickety regime could not protect themselves after eight years of massive U.S. support—if they could not fight off the threat without American boys dying for them indefinitely—then the U.S. involvement served only to postpone the inevitable. This was hardly a goal worthy of great sacrifice.

Nevertheless, the criticism must be put in perspective. By the beginning of 1973, Kissinger and Nixon had brought the nation's military misadventure in Vietnam to an end. Instead of slinking away as the Vietnamese factions continued the war, Kissinger had secured a cease-fire that, at least for the moment, curtailed the killing. In addition, America's ally had been given a decent chance to survive.

Officials in the previous two administrations, many of whom became preening doves as soon as their responsibility ended, had overseen a foolish deployment of close to 550,000 American troops over eight years. The Nixon administration immediately reversed the process and began withdrawing. It had all troops and POWs home in just over four years. It would have been wiser to do it more quickly and cleanly, but at least it was done. "We found more than half a million American troops in Vietnam when we came into office, and we got them home without destroying those who had relied on us," Kissinger said.[27]

The Paris agreement was the final element of a reshaped American foreign policy that—rather amazingly—provided the nation with the chance to play as influential a role in the world as it had before the paralyzing despair of its Vietnam involvement. By engineering the end of that war along with the opening to China and the détente with the Soviet Union, Kissinger had helped create a triangular structure for global stability that was beyond the imaginations of the Kennedy and Johnson administrations as well as the inert bureaucracy of the foreign policy establishment.

And so it was that Nixon's second term began with the possibilities for creative diplomacy expanding. From a platform on the Capitol steps, Kissinger watched the second inaugural ceremony with his eighty-six-year-old father, Louis, the former schoolmaster from Fürth, at his side. As senators and dignitaries came up to congratulate his son, Herr Kissinger beamed as if he could hardly believe what was happening. "In a strange way all the anguish of his life seemed vindicated," Kissinger noted.

Three days later, on January 23, Kissinger flew to Paris to initial the final "Agreement on Ending the War and Restoring the Peace in Vietnam." He arrived back that evening in time for the president's televised speech announcing the cease-fire.

After addressing the nation, Nixon went to the Lincoln Sitting Room, ate a light dinner, put on some Tchaikovsky records, and ordered that all calls be held. Around midnight he phoned Kissinger at home. Every success brings a terrific letdown, the president said. Don't let it get to you and don't be discouraged. There are many battles yet to fight.

Kissinger thought it rather odd, as if Nixon had really been talking to himself. "I was at peace with myself," Kissinger later noted, "neither elated nor sad."

In what he called "a sop to Rogers," Kissinger had agreed not to attend the formal Paris signing ceremonies by the foreign ministers on

January 27, staying instead in Washington. What would he be doing that Saturday? Safire asked him. "I will be at home," Kissinger replied. "I will raise a glass and say, with amazement in my voice, 'Peace *is* at hand!' " But when UPI correspondent Helen Thomas called to ask what he was doing while the agreement was being signed, Kissinger had crafted a somewhat catchier answer. "Making love not war," he replied.[28]

A short while later, near the town of An Loc, about fifty miles north of Saigon, Lieutenant Colonel William B. Nolde was struck by an artillery shell and blown apart just a few hours before the cease-fire went into effect. He was the last American combat soldier to die in battle in Vietnam.

TWENTY-TWO

SECRETARY
OF STATE

A Rise That Was Helped
Because Everyone Else Was Sinking

> *Men become myths not by what they know, nor even by what they achieve, but by the tasks they set for themselves.*—KISSINGER *on Metternich,* A WORLD RESTORED, *1957*

HAIG REPLACES HALDEMAN, MAY 1973

The month of September 1970—with the crises in Chile, Cuba, Jordan, and Vietnam—showed Kissinger in action. At the other extreme, the month of May 1973—with America out of Indochina and the rest of the world quiet—offered a glimpse of Kissinger in relative repose, dealing with the professional, bureaucratic, and personal matters that occupied him in between crises.

By then the Watergate scandal had started to consume the Nixon White House. What began as a bungled attempt to bug Democratic Party headquarters had turned into a deepening cover-up in which Nixon and his top domestic aides sought to prevent the disclosure of their well-funded illegal campaign activities. On the last night of April, in an emotional and awkward speech, Nixon told the nation that Haldeman and Ehrlichman were resigning because they had been involved in the cover-up. Kissinger telephoned both men, former sparring partners in the White House turf bouts, to offer his sympathy. "There but for the grace of God go I," he told Haldeman.

The roots of Watergate lay in a phenomenon that Kissinger knew

491

well. Nixon would sit brooding for hours while an aide, armed with the ubiquitous yellow legal pad, would duly note each of his commands as if its execution awaited only the opening of the Oval Office door. Sometimes the orders came like a barrage of buckshot, flying off in different directions. Some were made to be carried out, others for effect or as a way to think through a problem. The aide, who had earned this spot of honor not by having challenged Nixon's notions, would murmur assent. People such as Haldeman had distinguished themselves by knowing which orders could and should be ignored— or usually knowing. But occasionally, as Bryce Harlow had explained Watergate to Kissinger early on, "Some damn fool walked into the Oval Office and took literally what he heard there."

Now that Haldeman was gone, the sensitive job of chief of staff needed to be filled. Nixon could not operate without one. When Kissinger called after the president's speech to give him encouragement, his faithful secretary Rose Mary Woods had stepped into that role. Nixon, she told Kissinger, was too distraught to speak to him or anyone else.

At Nixon's invitation, Haldeman slipped into the White House on May 2, the day after he had officially departed, to help the president sort through his new staff problem. At the top of Haldeman's yellow legal pad was a note he had made in anticipation of the inevitable question: "General Haig." Nixon agreed. Haig, who had been army vice chief of staff for only four months, was the right choice to be the new chief of staff.

While at the Pentagon, Haig had kept in close contact with Nixon through a private line linked directly to the Oval Office, and he had already proved his loyalty to Nixon over Kissinger. "What he might have lacked in political experience and organizational finesse he made up for in sheer force of personality," Nixon later said. "Equally important to me, he understood Kissinger."

Unable to ask Haig on his own, Nixon prevailed upon Haldeman to make the offer, even though Haldeman had just been fired. He tracked Haig down at Fort Benning, Georgia, and the general accepted. But the hard part lay ahead: breaking the news to Kissinger. Haldeman declined that assignment, so it fell to Rose Mary Woods.

That evening, with Nixon slumped in a chair nearby, Woods phoned Kissinger. As if taking him into her confidence, she told him that Nixon wanted to bring in Haig as staff chief. It would only be for a week or two, until someone else could be found, she said. But the president was afraid of how you might react, she told Kissinger. She urged him not to object when Nixon told him the news the next morning. The president needed all the help he could get.

Nixon was right to worry about Kissinger's reaction to having his former deputy become, in effect, his boss. "Henry threatened to resign," Nixon recalled, "and he told Rose Mary Woods so." She responded rather bluntly. "For once, Henry, behave like a man," she scolded him over the phone.

Haig came to pay a courtesy call on Kissinger the next morning. He would not take the job, he said, unless he had Kissinger's blessing. This was, as Kissinger later called it, "nonsense," but it was properly mollifying. He urged Haig to accept. Still, he could not resist warning that it would probably spell the end of his beloved military career. Haig replied with a cold put-down of Kissinger: he had risked not only his career but his life when he was in Vietnam, and it would be wrong to put his career ahead of the needs of his commander in chief.

Only then did Nixon officially tell Kissinger of the appointment, and he did it by phone rather than in person. This had the effect of providing Kissinger and his staff with a recording of the conversation. In it the president came up with the oddest rationale yet for why Kissinger should be pleased with the appointment: it would prevent Vice President Spiro Agnew from trying to encroach on foreign policy. It was important to keep Agnew from "trying to step into things," Nixon explained. "Well, Agnew can't—we just can't allow that to happen."

Kissinger did not buy the argument. Haig, he protested, had not been loyal to him. Nixon asked who might be preferable. Kissinger suggested Brent Scowcroft, the air force lieutenant general who had become Kissinger's top deputy. Nixon rejected the idea.

An honorable and self-effacing career air force officer from Utah, Scowcroft was a West Point graduate with a doctorate in international relations from Columbia. While serving as a military aide in the White House, he had been soft-spoken but nevertheless able to go toe-to-toe with Haldeman. He had never become close to Haig and in fact did not seem to like the ambitious army general very much, which suited Kissinger just fine. "I'm a Mormon," he told Kissinger. "I'm known for loyalty."

When Scowcroft had replaced Haig as Kissinger's deputy, Nixon wanted to make sure he would supply information about Kissinger's activities, the way Haig had. Haldeman broached the subject, but Scowcroft was never open to the suggestion. "Haldeman talked in general language about how I worked for the president and not Kissinger," Scowcroft later recalled. "But it was an indirect conversation and it never went anywhere."[1]

As expected, initially there was a lot of tension between Kissinger and Haig—especially when the new White House staff chief did such things as put cover memos, with his own opinions, on some of Kissinger's reports to the president. "I won't put up with it," Kissinger raged to Admiral Zumwalt that summer, and he threatened to leave if he was not made secretary of state soon.

Yet an interesting dynamic occurred as Watergate began to threaten their ship: faced with a true national tragedy, Kissinger and Haig again began to work in harmony, dealing with one another as equals, protecting each other from the scandal. Having become an important source for Bob Woodward and other reporters covering Watergate, Haig could easily have pulled Kissinger down a peg, or even off his pedestal. But he did just the opposite. "For all of his ambivalence about Henry and the private bitterness that sometimes existed between them," Sven Kraemer later said, "Haig was strangely protective of Henry."[2]

Soon after he took over as White House chief of staff, Haig told Kissinger that Haldeman had a "dead key" telephone extension that allowed him or Higby to eavesdrop on Kissinger's conversations. Both Haldeman and Higby would later flatly deny this, but the allegation showed the levels of paranoia that existed at the time. Kissinger believed it was true, but he also came to suspect that Haig had known about it back in 1972, when it was purportedly being used.

Haig likewise told Kissinger about Nixon's secret White House taping system two months before it was publicly exposed. Kissinger, with a reverence for history's judgment and a self-awareness of how bad his groveling might sound when played publicly, was horrified. He knew that he had been caught on tape assenting to, even encouraging, Nixon's darker musings and paranoid prejudices. "Yes, Mr. President," he would say as Nixon attacked Harvard or Jews or the State Department, and then he would often throw in some fuel of his own to reinforce the prejudice. His comments to the president, he would later explain, were often based on "the needs of the moment" rather than "to stand the test of deferred scrutiny." What may someday be seen as obsequious excess, he insisted, should be viewed in the context of Nixon's situation: "He was so much in need of succor, so totally alone, our national security depended so much on his functioning."

Ironically, Kissinger may have been one of the causes of the taping system. Nixon said that he had installed it because Pepsi-Cola chairman Donald Kendall passed along a recommendation from Lyndon Johnson. But according to Haldeman, this story, though plausible, happens not to be true. The main reason they set up the system, he said, was to get a record of what Kissinger was advising, especially after the 1971 Cambodian invasion. "Nixon realized rather early in their relationship that he badly needed a complete record of all that they discussed," Haldeman recalled. "He knew that Henry's view on a particular subject was sometimes subject to change without notice." As Kissinger later noted: "It was a high price to pay for insurance."[3]

BOAR-HUNTING WITH BREZHNEV, MAY 1973

On the day after Haig took over, Kissinger left for a week-long trip to the Soviet Union, a grand visit that showed how he had begun to be treated around the world like a touring leader rather than as just an assistant to a president. His purpose was to prepare for a Brezhnev visit to Washington, Camp David, and San Clemente the next month. With little substantive business to discuss, the Soviet leader invited Kissinger and his party—including Hal Sonnenfeldt and Bill Hyland—to stay at his own version of Camp David, a hunting preserve ninety miles north of Moscow called Zavidovo. No Western official had ever been so honored.

Brezhnev showed off his villa with the pride of a self-made millionaire. It was an oversize Swiss-style chalet stuffed with the stolid, out-of-scale upholstered furniture that conveys status in the U.S.S.R. The ground floor included grand reception rooms, a movie theater, and a passage leading to an indoor Olympic-size swimming pool and gymnasium. Out front, among his other cars, was the Cadillac that Nixon had given him. A new souped-up hydrofoil was docked at the nearby lake.

How much, Brezhnev asked, would all this cost in America? At least $400,000, Kissinger answered. Brezhnev's face fell. Détente suddenly seemed imperiled. No, Sonnenfeldt corrected, at least $2 million, if not more. Brezhnev beamed. Peace was again at hand.

Kissinger later told a joke about Brezhnev's trying to convince his mother that he had become the Soviet leader. To overcome her skepticism, he took her on a tour of his realm at Zavidovo with the boats and cars and grand lodge and pool and theater. She was finally convinced. "This is wonderful, Leonid Ilyich," she said, "but what are you going to do when the Communists take over?"

The underlying truth to the joke, in Kissinger's mind, was that the Soviet Union should no longer be perceived as a revolutionary state. Unlike China, it did not continually stoke the flames of ideological zeal. Instead, it had become, at least during the 1970s, an empire dedicated to the self-preservation of a party bureaucracy. In his dissertation and early writings, Kissinger explained the difficulty in dealing with revolutionary states; but dealing with the Soviets, he felt, was now possible.

One afternoon, Kissinger and Sonnenfeldt returned to their villa to discover some olive drab hunting uniforms and high Prussian-style jackboots, attire that these two German-born Jewish refugees would not likely have selected on their own. Under the wildly mistaken notion that Kissinger would like to do some boar hunting, his hosts had arranged for Brezhnev to take him, and for Gromyko to take Sonnenfeldt, to the elevated shooting blinds deep in the forest.

As with the Soviets' old notion of alliance with Eastern Europe, their notion of hunting boars was rather one-sided. A game warden laid out a trail of corn leading to the towers, where the hunters could then blast the boars at point-blank range. Kissinger, whose soft spot for animals ran deeper than that for his subordinates and colleagues, was repelled by the idea of shooting for sport. But Brezhnev insisted. Some boars had been earmarked for him, he said. Kissinger replied that, given his marksmanship, the cause of death would have to be heart failure. He agreed to go along, but only as an observer.

Brezhnev killed one boar, wounded another, and then dispatched the game warden and other attendants to find the wounded boar. This was all part of a plan arranged by the Soviet leader to have some time alone with Kissinger, according to Viktor Sukhodrev, the Russian interpreter who was the only other person left in the tower. Once everyone else was gone, Brezhnev pointed to a picnic hamper and bellowed one of his favorite sayings, "Enjoy good things in life with impunity." Out came loaves of dark bread, sausages, hard-boiled eggs, a bag of salt, and a large bottle of vodka.

Brezhnev began to talk about his childhood, his rise through the Communist Party hierarchy, his experiences in the Great War. He stressed how important peace was to him, and to the Soviet people. But rather abruptly, he then lurched into a lecture on China that clearly had been carefully planned. "I knew that he would have this discussion then," recalled Sukhodrev. "I didn't take out my notebook to make notes because I didn't want to ruin the magic of the moment."

The Chinese were treacherous barbarians, Brezhnev said as they sat in the cozy hunting tower. Now they were building nuclear weapons, and something had to be done. It seemed to Kissinger that Brezhnev was seeking tacit American approval for a preemptive Soviet strike against China. Having watched Brezhnev's method of hunting, Kissinger steered clear of the bait. The situation with China, he replied carefully, "was one of those problems that underlined the importance of settling disputes peacefully."

A Soviet-American condominium to control China was never, of course, in the cards. But just the fact that the Soviets sought it showed how fundamentally the world had been changed by triangular diplomacy—and how it had given Washington an upper hand. Under past administrations, foreign policy had been based on the fear that the Soviets and Chinese were naturally colluding against the U.S. Now, each of the communist giants was trying to collude with the U.S. against the other.

Sonnenfeldt emerged from the woods with a black eye he had received from the kickback of his rifle, but with the dubious distinction of having bagged two boars. (The heads were stuffed and sent to him.) Gromyko would henceforth refer to him as the "master huntsman." Kissinger pretended to be skeptical. The Soviets had probably put blanks in Sonnenfeldt's rifle, he suggested, and then hidden a Red Army marksman near the blind to fell the boars.

When Kissinger described Soviet hospitality at a briefing upon his return, he provided an example of the patter that so often charmed the journalists who covered him:

Kissinger: "They took me on a new speedboat they have developed, which, with all respect to the general secretary, is a rather harrowing experience—Mr. Ziegler [press secretary Ron Ziegler] said particularly with my weight load, which comes with ill grace—and he also gave me my first opportunity to go hunting, unsolicited."

Question: "Did you get anything?"

Kissinger: "I acted as his special adviser."

Question: "Did you fire?"

Kissinger: "No. I advised him how to conduct the hunt."

Question: "Where to aim the rifle you mean?"

Kissinger: "In which direction. Ignorance of a subject has never kept a Harvard professor from offering theories."[4]

THE WIRETAPS BECOME PUBLIC, MAY 1973

Not all of the briefing involved tales about the Soviet Union. In the middle came a question about the secret "national security" wiretapping program of 1969–71.

Two months earlier in *Time* magazine, Sandy Smith and John Stacks had reported the existence of these wiretaps, but the White House had flatly denied the story. When John Dean came in to discuss the story, Nixon was recorded on the White House tapes saying that their reaction to the story should be "stonewalling."

But the story continued to trickle out, especially after acting FBI director William Ruckelshaus tracked down the wiretap records, which Ehrlichman had left in his office safe when he resigned. (On the morning of his resignation, Ehrlichman had asked Kissinger to take them, but he had declined.) Among the many things Ruckelshaus discovered was that Daniel Ellsberg—who was then on trial for leaking the Pentagon Papers—had been recorded by the tap on Morton Halperin's phone. So Ruckelshaus informed the judge presiding over the Ellsberg case, who promptly dismissed the charges.

By the time Kissinger returned from Russia, the press was eager to ask him what he knew about the program. Suddenly Kissinger was no longer pithy. In a rambling display of doublespeak that is impossible to decipher, he discoursed on the notion of "duly constituted processes." Once he had everyone confused, he concluded: "My office has not handled or been aware of any activities that were conducted by other processes."

No one tried to pin him down, but the dam was about to break.

The *Washington Post's* Bob Woodward, whose investigation of Watergate with Carl Bernstein was now producing one or two big disclosures a week, decided to call a top official at the FBI. Who, he asked, had authorized these wiretaps? On many of them, the FBI man replied, Kissinger himself had sent over the names.

Woodward was not one of the reporters on a "Henry" basis with Kissinger. He called through the White House switchboard, gave his name, and soon the familiar German accent was on the phone. According to Woodward, Kissinger at first played coy. "It could be Mr. Haldeman who authorized the taps," Kissinger said.

Woodward asked if it could have been Kissinger. "I don't believe it was true," replied Kissinger.

"Is that a denial?" asked Woodward.

Kissinger paused. "I frankly don't remember." But then he allowed that he may have supplied to the FBI the names of people who had access to documents that leaked. "It is quite possible that they construed this as an authorization."

It was, for Kissinger, a relatively candid admission, and he went on to talk about having to take responsibility. Then, rather abruptly, he challenged Woodward: "You aren't quoting me?"

Yes, Woodward said, he was.

But he had been speaking only for background, Kissinger insisted rather heatedly. "I've tried to be honest and now you're going to penalize me. In five years in Washington, I've never been trapped into talking like this."

Woodward wondered what kind of treatment Kissinger was accustomed to getting from the press. He consulted Murrey Marder, the kindly and soft-edged diplomatic reporter who covered Kissinger for the *Post*. Well, Marder admitted, "Henry" was regularly allowed to put statements on background after he made them.

A few minutes later, Kissinger was on the phone to Marder, fuming. Afterward, Marder and Woodward went to talk to managing editor Howard Simons. Their boss Ben Bradlee had gone home for the evening, but he soon gave them a call. Simons put him on the speakerphone. In a mock German accent, the irrepressible Bradlee reported that "I just got a call from Henry. He's mad." Simons decided to hold the story for a day or so.[5]

By then it was too late for the *Post*. The *New York Times*'s Seymour Hersh also had the information.

His source was William Sullivan, the FBI's number-three man. Eager to become FBI director, he had sent Kissinger a memo describing what he knew about the wiretapping—a heavy-handed attempt to enlist his support. It almost worked: Haig passed along to incoming attorney general Elliot Richardson the recommendation that he appoint Sullivan. But Richardson rejected the idea, and Sullivan gave Hersh copies of the wiretap authorizations with Kissinger's name on them.

Among those who tried to dissuade Hersh from publishing the story was Haig. Even though he had repeatedly bad-mouthed Kissinger while serving as his deputy, Haig respected Kissinger's genius as a steward of foreign policy; now that he was the White House staff chief attempting to maintain some stability amid the swirl of Watergate, Haig began calling journalists and describing Kissinger as "a national asset" who did not deserve to be tarnished by the wiretapping story. "Some reporters have a commitment to destroy," he complained to friendly journalists.

He warned Hersh that the story he was writing might cause Kissinger to resign. "You're Jewish, aren't you, Seymour?" Haig asked. Hersh said he was. "Let me ask you one question, then," Haig continued. "Do you honestly believe that Henry Kissinger, a Jewish refugee from Germany who lost thirteen members of his family to the Nazis, could engage in such police-state tactics as wiretapping his own aides? If there's any doubt, you owe it to yourself, your beliefs, and your nation to give us one day to prove that your story is wrong."

Hersh did not delay his story. "Kissinger Said to Have Asked for Taps," was the headline on the front page of the *New York Times* the next morning. On that day, May 17, Senator Sam Ervin gaveled to a start the televised hearings into Watergate, which in the public mind became intertwined with such matters as the wiretapping program.

At the *Washington Post*, Marder followed up with a story presenting the situation from Kissinger's perspective. "This is one of the most anguishing periods in his skyrocketing career," Marder wrote. "During the past week, Kissinger emotionally told old friends here and abroad that he has been considering resigning." The story also noted that Haig had been vigorously defending the wiretapping program and urging reporters not to pin it on Kissinger. Among others, Haig had called columnists Rowland Evans and Robert Novak, who wrote that Kissinger "is being smeared with the muck of Watergate, an affair with which he had no connection."[6]

The pressure on Kissinger receded the following week when Nixon released a statement on the wiretaps saying, "I authorized this entire program." The issue would bedevil Kissinger again during his confirmation hearings as secretary of state later in 1973, and also in June 1974 when a new spate of stories came out during the climactic weeks of Watergate. For the time being, however, his problem became merely a personal one. During May 1973, he spent a lot of his time trying to explain to stunned friends such as Hal Sonnenfeldt, Winston Lord, and Henry Brandon why he had participated in the tapping of their phones.

KISSINGER AT FIFTY, MAY 1973

Despite the wiretap flurry, Kissinger was reaching the peak of his popularity. In a Gallup poll in 1972, he had ranked fourth on the list of "most admired" Americans, after Nixon, Billy Graham, and Harry Truman; in 1973, he ranked first (Nixon had fallen to third after Graham, and Truman had died). He achieved an unprecedented nine-to-one ratio between those who viewed him "favorably" versus those saying "unfavorably."

Congressman Jonathan Bingham proposed a constitutional amendment to allow foreign-born citizens, such as Kissinger, to run for president. He became the most popular political figure at Madame Tussaud's wax museum in London, and the contestants in the Miss Universe pageant overwhelmingly voted him "the greatest person in the world today."

His fiftieth birthday that month became the occasion for effusive public tributes. ABC's Howard K. Smith called him "a genuine star that tourists gather to get a glimpse of as they would Elizabeth Taylor." Russell Baker of the *New York Times* dubbed him "public celebrity number one." His friend and critic Joseph Kraft, in a column entitled "The Virtuoso at 50," took measure of the new world balance he had created with the Soviet Union and China and declared: "It is a diplomatic accomplishment comparable in magnitude to the feats of Castlereagh and Bismarck."[7]

Kissinger's gala birthday party, held in Manhattan, was officially hosted by Guido Goldman, a Harvard lecturer who had been Kissinger's student and remained his close friend.* But the real organizer was Nancy Maginnes, who arranged to have it at the Colony Club, a genteel enclave on Park Avenue for well-bred women such as herself.

Kraft decided not to attend the party in protest over being wiretapped (even though his was one of the taps that did not involve Kissinger). A few others also stayed away because, as William Safire wrote in his "Henry at 50" column, "these days, even Frank Sinatra thinks twice about being seen in the company of Administration officials." In fact, Sinatra had been invited but could not attend, whereas Safire put aside his own anger at being wiretapped and did attend. Those who were there, he wrote, "wanted to salute an authentic American hero midpoint in his first century."

In addition to Safire, three other wiretap targets were willing to revel among the eighty guests: Winston Lord, Helmut Sonnenfeldt, and Henry Brandon, along with their wives. Bette Bao Lord, wearing an elaborate Chinese gown, was seated next to Kissinger. Media stars included Katharine Graham, Rowland Evans, Mike Wallace, Walter Cronkite, Joseph Alsop, David Frost, and Barbara Walters. Governor Nelson Rockefeller and his wife came with fifteen staff members. Robert Evans escorted a striking Swedish actress. Notably missing were members of the administration; Nixon was not invited, and Haig could not make it.

"There's always been the question of whether history makes the man or the man makes history," said Rockefeller in his toast. "Henry has settled the question. The man has made history." Barbara Walters toasted him "for having made careers for the countless women who have sat next to him at dinner." Alsop rose to make an impromptu toast to the private woman who could bring a would-be swinger down to earth. "She's a great girl," the columnist said, nodding toward Nancy Maginnes, "even if she is taller than God."

When it was over, Nancy Collins of *Women's Wear Daily*, who was part of the press horde waiting outside the Colony Club, asked Cronkite what the best gift had been. "They gave him a pardon," the

---

* His father, Nahum Goldmann, a noted Jewish leader and philanthropist, was close to the family when they first arrived from Germany and used to hire Kissinger's mother, Paula, to do his catering. Guido Goldman dropped the last letter of his family name.

CBS anchorman said. The press moved on to Maginnes's East Sixty-eighth Street apartment, where she and Kissinger had gone. "He's never stayed longer than twenty minutes," the doorman told the reporters. Sure enough, in twenty minutes Kissinger emerged. Spotting the huddle of journalists, he said, "Glad I didn't stay longer," and sped in his limousine to Guido Goldman's bachelor pad, which he often used while in New York.[8]

Kissinger's fiftieth birthday month was capped by a very quiet and unpublicized event near Cambridge to which he had not been invited. Ann Fleischer Kissinger married Brandeis University chemistry professor Saul Cohen, a low-key widower with a far greater passion for privacy than her first husband. This seemed to liberate Kissinger from the swinging bachelor image he had been cultivating. Shortly afterward, he and Nancy Maginnes decided to get married, though the actual ceremony would turn out to be at the mercy of more global events.

AMERICA'S FIFTY-FOURTH SECRETARY OF STATE, SEPTEMBER 1973

Many years later, Nixon would admit that "I did not really want to make Henry secretary of state." The reasons he cited were high-minded enough. "I felt what we needed at State was someone with economic expertise," he recalled. "I thought that Henry had absolutely no competitors when it came to geopolitics, but economics is not his area of expertise." In addition, he felt that Kissinger was better off focusing on the big issues rather than trying to run the Department of State, "where he would have to do things like read all the cables from Upper Volta." Although Nixon would never admit it on the record, it is also reasonable to assume that four years of accumulated resentment at Kissinger's popularity and tendency to usurp credit did not add to Nixon's desire to elevate him to the cabinet.

Nixon's first two preferences were Kenneth Rush, who had tentatively been offered the job the previous November before Rogers had balked at resigning right away, and John Connally, the bullheaded former treasury secretary. But Connally was becoming tainted by the scandals whirling around Watergate, and Rush did not have the public stature needed to stanch the hemorrhaging of power caused by the revelations that barraged the White House in the summer of 1973.

Then, too, there was the matter of Kissinger's desire. "Henry wanted State, felt he deserved it, and let me know that he would resign if he didn't get it," Nixon later recalled with a tight, quick smile. By the summer of 1973, the president was in so much trouble that he could not afford to lose Kissinger. "With the Watergate problem," he later said, "I didn't have any choices."[9]

Nevertheless, it took Nixon quite a while and no little agonizing to make that Hobson's choice. He would often sit in his hideaway office with John Connally, bitterly joking about how badly Kissinger wanted the job. Contemplating his promotion, Kissinger later said, "must have been torture for Nixon."

Surprisingly, given their past relationship, Haig was the one who pushed the appointment. He knew it was the only way to preserve the administration's authority in foreign affairs, and—despite their past struggles—the general felt that Kissinger was the best man for the job. In May, as the Watergate hearings began, he told Kissinger that he would raise the subject with Nixon, and he subsequently kept Kissinger informed of each step of Nixon's tortured thought process on the matter.

What it eventually came down to, Nixon later explained, was that the new secretary would have to match Kissinger's intelligence if he were to be able to hold his own. But, he added, "Henry does not tolerate competition." There was only one possible appointee whom Kissinger would consider an intellectual equal yet not a competitive threat. And so that person got the job.

When Nixon finally decided on Kissinger's appointment in August, he never discussed it with him. Instead he told only Haig, and he added a caveat: he would give Kissinger the job if Haig would bear the burden of informing William Rogers. So Kissinger's unlikely new patron set out where Haldeman had failed, and promptly failed himself. "Tell the president to go fuck himself," Rogers told Haig. If Nixon wanted him to resign, he said, then Nixon should ask personally.

When Nixon finally worked up the nerve to do so, in mid-August, Rogers made it easy. He arrived at Camp David with a gracious letter of resignation.

On August 21, Kissinger was in San Clemente with Nixon. A presidential press conference was scheduled for the next day, and Kissinger assumed it would include the announcement of his appointment. But he had heard no word from the president. That afternoon, Julie Nixon called to invite David and Elizabeth Kissinger over for a swim. David, who was then twelve, recalled how miserable the televised Watergate hearings were making the president's daughter. Not having fully perfected his father's talent for providing reassurance, David told her that he was "the only kid in Cambridge who will defend your father." When the president arrived back from a walk along the beach, Julie polished up the thought and told him, "David here is your biggest supporter in Cambridge." Not overly impressed with that accolade, Nixon grunted.

At her father's suggestion, Julie then called Kissinger and asked if he wanted to join them all in the pool. Kissinger sat on the steps while Nixon floated on his back and kicked around questions he might be asked at his news conference. Suddenly, without warmth or enthusiasm, the president said, "I shall open the press conference by announcing your appointment as secretary of state."

"I hope to be worthy of your trust," responded Kissinger.

Kissinger was not invited to the press conference the next day. He watched it on television from his cottage. Nixon's praise for William Rogers was so effusive that it stands as a testament to how little regard he had for the truth. He was accepting Rogers's resignation "with the greatest reluctance and regret." Rogers had "wanted to leave" at the end of the first term, but "he had been prevailed upon to remain in office" because there was unfinished business that needed his attention, including the conclusion of the Vietnam negotiations. The comments were so warm, generous, and personal—including the release of a letter saying that he and Pat hoped to see Bill and Adele often—that they almost seemed aimed at diminishing the man whose appointment was being announced.

Nixon was terse about Rogers's successor. "Dr. Kissinger's qualifications for this post, I think, are well known by all of you," he said. That was it; no further elaboration. At just that moment, Norwegian actress Liv Ullmann telephoned from Oslo to chat, unaware of the occasion. Kissinger explained he could not talk, but by the time he had hung up, he had missed the fleeting reference to himself.

After surviving persecution in his native land, a foreign-born refugee was about to become America's secretary of state, the fifty-fourth in a distinguished line that stretched back to Thomas Jefferson. But as he stared at the television that August afternoon, while reporters peppered Nixon with questions about Watergate, Kissinger's capacity for joy was drained. "I had achieved an office I never imagined within my reach," he later said, "yet I did not feel like celebrating."[10]

"Do you prefer to be called Mr. Secretary or Dr. Secretary?" he was asked by the press the next day.

"I do not stand on protocol," he said. "If you just call me Excellency, it will be okay."

Kissinger realized that his toughest problem at his confirmation hearings would be the wiretaps. For a full day, he huddled with Bryce Harlowe, Thomas Korologos, and John Lehman to rehearse. He even went to the trouble of softening up the chief staffer of the Senate Foreign Relations Committee, Carl Marcy; just before the hearings began, he suggested that Marcy might want to be ambassador to Sweden, where his family had come from. (Marcy never got the appointment.)[11]

As it turned out, the hearings were rather gentle. "I never recommended the practice of wiretapping," Kissinger testified in a closed-door session. "I was aware of it, and I went along with it to the extent of supplying the names of the people who had access to the sensitive documents in question." Senators John Sparkman and Clifford Case conducted a special inquiry into the FBI files and concluded that there was no evidence that would "constitute grounds to bar Dr. Kissinger's confirmation."

The Senate vote to confirm Kissinger, which came on September 21, was seventy-eight to seven. His opponents included the most conservative and the most liberal Republicans, Jesse Helms and Lowell Weicker, along with five Democrats, George McGovern, Harold Hughes, James Abourezk, Gaylord Nelson, and Floyd Haskel. "We know enough about Dr. Kissinger," said Abourezk, "to know that he is capable of deceiving Congress and the public."

But most of the senators were strongly supportive—even McGovern called to give a private endorsement—and the comments tended to be effusive. Senator Jacob Javits called the nomination "a miracle of American history," and Charles Mathias declared, "He has proved not only to America but the whole world that this is still an open society."[12]

The swearing-in was scheduled for the next day, a Saturday, which was discomforting to Paula and Louis Kissinger, who as Orthodox Jews were diligent about avoiding travel on the Sabbath. So they walked, rather than rode, from their hotel to the White House. One of their friends had located a copy of the Old Testament published in Fürth in 1801, but Kissinger decided to use Nixon's copy of a King James version instead. None of this, however, could dampen the joy of Paula as she held the Bible, or of Louis as he watched his son reach the pinnacle of success in their adopted country.

Close to one hundred fifty friends, relatives, and dignitaries crammed into the East Room for the ceremony. Fritz Kraemer and Nelson Rockefeller were there, of course, as were Kirk Douglas and Robert Evans. For most of them, inspired by the notion of a refugee from tyranny becoming the top minister in his adopted land, it was a moving moment, both as Americans and as friends. "Most of us had tears in our eyes," recalled Bette Lord.

One exception was Paula Kissinger, who beamed throughout.

When Bette Lord asked why she wasn't crying, she laughed and said, "Henry forbade me." She was, in fact, enjoying every moment. The triumph of human will that had, almost inconceivably, led to this ceremony had begun thirty-five years earlier when she had packed up her family and moved them to a new land she had never seen. Now she was living out the fantasy of every mother. Earlier in the week, at a beauty parlor in Washington Heights, a friend had begun to tell her about the success of her own son, a lawyer, when she caught herself and remarked how silly it was to brag about a son to the mother of Henry Kissinger. Replied Paula: "A son is a son."

The one jarring note was supplied by Nixon, who seemed to Kissinger to be "driven by his own demons." His remarks, Kissinger later noted, "ranged from the perfunctory to the bizarre." The president stressed, rather incorrectly, that Kissinger had overcome intense opposition in Congress to be confirmed. Then he wandered into a rambling discussion of how Kissinger was not only the first secretary of state to be a naturalized citizen but also the first since World War II not to part his hair. This led to a discourse on how to classify Dean Rusk, who was bald, but Nixon resolved this weighty question by quoting White House barber Milton Pitts—"a very wise man"—who had declared that what little hair Rusk had, he parted.

Kissinger, accustomed to more effusive introductions, was somewhat taken aback, but his reply was graceful:

> Mr. President, you referred to my background and it is true there is no country in the world where it is conceivable that a man of my origin could be standing here. . . . If my origin can contribute anything to the formulation of policy, it is that at an early age I have seen what can happen to a society that is based on hatred and strength and distrust.

Pat Nixon, a close friend of Bill and Adele Rogers's, refused to join the traditional receiving line after the ceremony. Both she and her husband left immediately afterward, skipping the reception held in the State Dining Room.[13]

Even though Kissinger retained his job as national security adviser, his elevation meant that Brent Scowcroft, his deputy, assumed more of the responsibility for managing the NSC machinery. Discreet yet forthright, unflappable and able to keep human foibles in perspective, with a balanced and wise mind rather than a brilliant conceptual one, the air force general was decidedly different from his boss, which made both of them comfortable.

Most of Kissinger's other top aides moved over to the State Department, forming the core of his seventh-floor coterie. Winston Lord, the ever-loyal assistant and nonnagging conscience, became director of policy planning. The acid-tongued Helmut Sonnenfeldt, after being blocked from becoming undersecretary of the treasury by right-wing senators who considered him a Kissinger clone, became State Department counselor and retained his role as an adviser on Soviet affairs. Sonnenfeldt's deputy, William Hyland, a wry and insightful former Soviet expert at the CIA, became director of the Bureau of Intelligence and Research.

Most important, Lawrence Eagleburger, who had collapsed of exhaustion in 1969, came back as Kissinger's executive assistant and then deputy undersecretary for management. More than anyone else, the gregarious foreign service officer—who was one of the few people who could say, "Henry, you're full of shit"—was in charge of handling both the State Department and its volatile secretary. "A lot of people couldn't survive working for Henry," said Eagleburger, who with Scowcroft later became an associate in Kissinger's consulting firm, "but those who did were the ones who answered back, who stood up to him."

To everyone's surprise, including probably his own, Kissinger decided to keep maverick diplomat Joseph Sisco as the department's top Middle East official—proof that engaging in shouting matches with Kissinger could be a way to earn his respect. Exuberant, frenetic, and loud, Sisco cultivated a pugnacious manner that set him apart from the pusillanimous style of the State Department. He was once derided as "Bill Rogers's boy" by Kissinger, who sniped at their 1970 Arab-Israeli peace plan. Even after Sisco's transformation into "Henry's boy," Kissinger joked about being afraid to leave him back in Washington for fear he would lead a coup. Kissinger once described Sisco as "supplying more answers than there were questions." But when Sisco announced his intention to resign to take over the presidency of Hamilton College, Kissinger persuaded him to change his mind by easing William Porter out of the number-three post of undersecretary for political affairs and offering the job to him.[14]

A month after Kissinger's elevation to secretary of state, he and Le Duc Tho were jointly awarded the Nobel Peace Prize for the Vietnam accords, even though the cease-fire was in shambles. Response to the choice was far from peaceful. Le Duc Tho rejected the prize and his share of the $130,000, saying that "peace has not yet been established in South Vietnam." Two of the five members of the Norwegian parliamentary committee that picked the winner resigned in protest.

A *New York Times* editorial dubbed it "the Nobel War Prize." Professor Edwin Reischauer of Harvard declared that "either the people of Norway have a poor understanding of what happened out there or a good sense of humor." Sixty other Harvard and MIT scholars signed a letter calling the award "more than a person with a normal sense of justice can take." One of David Kissinger's Cambridge school-mates told him that his friends were saying that his father did not deserve the prize. "What does it matter?" the younger Kissinger replied. "My mother said the same thing."

Even Kissinger seemed somewhat uncomfortable about the prize. Although flattered, he decided against going to accept it in person, sending the American ambassador to Norway instead. He quietly donated his share of the money to the New York Community Trust to set up scholarships for the children of servicemen killed in Vietnam. And when Saigon fell to the communists two years later, he wrote the Nobel committee offering to return his prize and the money. The offer was rejected.[15]

CAN A SHOWMAN BE TAMED?

At his first press conference after his appointment, Kissinger was asked about his penchant for secrecy, his "lone cowboy" style, and his flair for showmanship, drama, and solo performances. This approach, he replied, was required by the "revolutionary changes" that were being made during the first term. "But now we are in a different phase. The foundations that have been laid must now lead to the building of a more institutionalized structure."

Translated from the gobbledygook, Kissinger was promising that, as secretary of state, he would no longer seek to conduct a virtuoso one-man show—as he had with the opening to China, the SALT talks, the Moscow summit, and the Vietnam peace accord. Instead, he would try to "institutionalize" the process by involving the bureaucracy and the six thousand members of America's diplomatic corps. "A foreign policy achievement to be truly significant must at some point be institutionalized," he later explained. "No government should impose on itself the need to sustain a tour de force based on personalities."

Kissinger's academic writings were filled with injunctions against the theatrical, personalized policy-making he had been practicing.

"The statesman is suspicious of those who personalize foreign policy, for history teaches him the fragility of structures dependent upon individuals," he wrote in 1966. And he criticized Bismarck by saying: "Statesmen who build lastingly transform the personal act of creation into institutions that can be maintained by an average standard of performance. . . . Bismarck's tragedy was that he left a heritage of unassimilated greatness."[16]

Yet as a scholar, Kissinger showed little interest in studying institutions. His joy was in analyzing individuals, those grand and flawed statesmen—Metternich, Castlereagh, Talleyrand, Bismarck—whose triumphs came from being virtuoso performers pitted against the constraints of their bureaucracies.

Kissinger was correct to argue that the initiatives of Nixon's first term required a personalized style of diplomacy. Especially regarding China, old bureaucratic ways of thinking had to be skirted. The theatrical aspect of Kissinger's diplomacy during the first term—particularly the delight that he and Nixon shared at pulling off grand surprises —also served a purpose. It engaged the American public and made foreign policy fun rather than distasteful. "His theater was, in part, a way of bringing the public along by dramatizing and energizing foreign policy," said Robert Hormats, who served in the State Department under President Carter. "He was afraid that after Vietnam, the American people would otherwise turn inward."

But a policy based on maneuver and breakthrough and surprise (and, it must be noted, vanity) can only play a limited role, especially in a democracy. As former Under Secretary of State George Ball noted: "A policy of maneuver risks subverting our institutions, puts a premium on furtiveness in the highest places, creates an obsession with . . . 'national security,' and provides a factitious justification for such trespasses on individual freedom as wiretapping and even burglary."

In addition, a policy based on personalized diplomacy tends, by necessity, to be bilateral in its dealings. No matter how great he is as a gunslinger, the lone cowboy cannot handle a policy based on tending to various complex alliances unless he is willing to share information and authority with the bureaucracy.[17]

Kissinger's desire for drama launched an age of "bombshell diplomacy" in which future presidents would take delight in trying to dazzle the world with surprise announcements rather than engaging in the careful consultation that was once the norm. In the long run this trend will probably prove more exciting than wise.

After he became secretary of state, Kissinger tried to some extent to rely more on the bureaucracy. But mainly, instead of institutionalizing his approach, he became the institution. For better or worse, the ego, the excitement, the desire for personal control, and the taste for drama seemed ingrained in his personality.

So when war suddenly broke out in the Middle East two weeks after he was sworn in, Kissinger did not try to manage a coordinated American response from the unwieldy bureaucracy he now oversaw. Instead, he rode off on his imaginary horse to shuttle around the Middle East for months on end and achieve—in yet another virtuoso triumph—an Arab-Israeli disengagement.

TWENTY-THREE

THE
YOM KIPPUR WAR

A Mideast Initiation,

a Resupply Dispute,

and a Nuclear Alert

> Any negotiator who seduces himself into believing that his person-
> ality leads to automatic breakthroughs will soon find himself in the
> special purgatory that history reserves for those who measure them-
> selves by acclaim rather than by achievement." —KISSINGER, YEARS
> OF UPHEAVAL, 1982

During Nixon's first term, Kissinger had played little role in Middle East diplomacy. It was the one realm reserved for William Rogers, partly because Kissinger's Judaism, the president thought, might make him less credible. As Rogers put forth a succession of peace plans based on the principle of getting Israel to surrender lands it had captured in 1967 in exchange for peace, Kissinger had worked to delay any progress.

To some extent his motive was substantive: a prolonged stalemate, he argued, would convince the Arabs that relying on Soviet patronage would lead nowhere. In addition, his rivalry with Rogers meant that he was not rooting for a quick success; no doubt he would have seen less value in a stalemate if he had been given the portfolio for the Middle East.

When President Anwar Sadat surprised the world (and Kissinger) by expelling Soviet military personnel from Egypt in July 1972, Nixon finally authorized Kissinger to set up a back channel to Hafiz Ismail, Sadat's national security adviser, secret from the State Department. By early 1973, a classic Nixonian situation had arisen: Ismail arrived in February for talks at the State Department and then, secretly, with

Kissinger at Pepsi-Cola chairman Donald Kendall's house in suburban Connecticut. Since State had not given Kissinger a report of its discussions, only Ismail knew fully what the different factions in the American government were thinking. "It was not the best way to project unity of purpose," Kissinger admitted. "But it demonstrated to the Egyptians at least that we, too, could be Levantine without even half trying."

In a region where the information-trading bazaar is even more active than in Washington, the back channel inevitably backfired. The Egyptians told the Saudis about Ismail's secret session with Kissinger. Word soon got to British diplomats based in Cairo. Kissinger had briefed top British officials in London (though not his own secretary of state), but he had pledged them to secrecy. When the British diplomats in Cairo found out from the Egyptians, they informed their American counterparts. The American envoy in Cairo then got a full briefing on Kissinger's activities from the Saudis, which he merrily sent back to the State Department in an open cable that was widely distributed. Thus ended Kissinger's secret-track system in the Middle East.

The back channel would become pointless for two other reasons. When Kissinger became secretary of state in September, his temptation to cut out that cabinet officer lost its appeal. In addition, Anwar Sadat had privately decided to upset the stalemated chessboard. There was no real need for secret talks because by mid-1973 the Egyptian president had decided that, in conjunction with Syria, he would soon go to war.[1]

THE YOM KIPPUR WAR, OCTOBER 1973

Kissinger was sleeping in his thirty-fifth-floor suite in the Waldorf Towers when Joseph Sisco came barging in. They were in Manhattan for the largely ceremonial task of feting the foreign ministers attending the opening of the United Nations General Assembly, and the trip was supposed to be an enjoyable respite after the pressure leading up to Kissinger's ascension. But now, just before dawn on Saturday, October 6, Sisco was jolting Kissinger awake with the news that would not only disrupt his weekend plans but would dominate his next two years as secretary of state: Egypt and Syria, he told the startled secretary, were launching a surprise attack on Israel.

The ensuing sixteen days of fighting became known as the Yom Kippur War because the attack came on that holiest day of the Jewish year. Among Muslims it was referred to as the War of Ramadan, for it coincided with that holiday as well. And the Egyptian-Syrian command code-named it Operation Badr, for it fell on the 1,350th anniversary of that battle in which Muhammad gained entry into Mecca.

A few hours after the war broke out, Kissinger flew back to Washington to chair a meeting of the Washington Special Action Group (WSAG), the NSC's crisis committee. Israel had already made an emergency request for military supplies, even though it was widely expected that they would beat back the Arab attack within a day or two.

Deputy Secretary of State Kenneth Rush, representing the department while Kissinger wore his national security adviser's hat for that occasion, argued against sending supplies to Israel immediately. "They have no real shortage," he said. The Pentagon was even more strongly opposed. "Shipping any stuff into Israel blows any image we may have of an honest broker," said Defense Secretary James Schlesinger, whose incisive mind and prickly ego had made him Kissinger's new rival within the administration.

"Defense wants to turn against the Israelis," Kissinger reported by telephone that evening to White House chief of staff Haig, who was down in Key Biscayne with the president.

"Sounds like Clements," replied Haig, referring to Deputy Defense Secretary William Clements, a Texas oilman with pro-Arab sympathies.[2]

Thus began a critical dispute that would dominate Washington for a week: to what extent should the U.S. resupply Israel?

Even more controversial would be the ensuing historical dispute over the roles played by Kissinger, Schlesinger, and Clements in deciding the resupply issue. Dozens of books and articles have tackled the question. Those sympathetic to Kissinger portray him as staunchly willing to help Israel as soon as its desperate needs became known by midweek, and they describe his efforts to overcome resistance from the Pentagon. Some critical accounts, on the other hand, accuse Kissinger of playing a devious game; they charge that he held back supplies from Israel in order to create a climate ripe for diplomacy, unfairly blamed the Pentagon for the delays when talking to Jewish and Israeli leaders, took credit for the delays when talking to the Soviets and the Arabs, and finally grabbed credit for the airlift of supplies when it began after a week.[3]

Because many of the participants recorded or transcribed their telephone conversations and kept notes at meetings—and because in the underhanded atmosphere of the Nixon administration such material tended to be copied and kept and sometimes shared—this historical dispute can now be greatly elucidated. Based on these semiofficial or surreptitious records and on interviews with most of the participants, it is possible to report who said what to whom at each moment of the week-long debate.[4]

For the duration of the war, Nixon was preoccupied with Watergate. When it began, he was in Key Biscayne trying to decide how to deal with legal demands that he surrender his White House tapes. During the next two weeks, Vice President Spiro Agnew was forced to resign because of a financial scandal, Gerald Ford was selected to replace him, and Nixon fired Attorney General Elliot Richardson and Watergate special prosecutor Archibald Cox in what became known as the Saturday Night Massacre.

Thus Kissinger had a freer hand than in previous showdowns. In fact, in many of their conversations, Haig and Kissinger made critical decisions without even consulting the president.

This process began with Kissinger's first telephone calls to Haig that Saturday when the war broke out. "The Israelis say they need some ammunition," Kissinger said. Unless the Arabs pulled back, "we ought to give it to them."

"No question," Haig replied. And they proceeded on that basis without consulting the president.

In his conversations that Saturday from Key Biscayne, Haig emphasized to Kissinger that he should give the public the impression that Nixon was making the key decisions, even if he wasn't. "It's very important for a number of reasons, one being the situation with the Vice President, which I can't go into over the phone, that he be portrayed as intimately on top of this," Haig explained.

Kissinger agreed. "I think we can bring home to the people the importance of future leadership through this," he said.

But Kissinger did not want Nixon to fly back to Washington suddenly, fearing that it would look "like a hysterical move." Referring to Nixon's fantasies about taking command in times of crises, Kissinger told Haig, "I would urge you to keep any Walter Mitty tendencies under control."

Haig agreed to try to keep Nixon down in Key Biscayne longer. "I know what you're up against," Kissinger told his erstwhile rival. "It's not the first one we've been through together."

Kissinger assumed that Israel would win quickly, and he opposed giving it major support that could make its victory too one-sided. "The best result," Kissinger told Schlesinger the first weekend, "would be if Israel came out a little ahead but got bloodied in the process, and if the U.S. stayed clean."

"The strategy was to prevent Israel from humiliating Egypt again," Kissinger later explained. American restraint, he hoped, might lead to an opening to Egypt, preserve détente with the Soviets, and make Israel see the benefits of a negotiated settlement.

On the diplomatic front, Kissinger wanted to delay efforts at the U.N. to impose a cease-fire in place for a few days until Israel had pushed Egypt and Syria back to their original lines. Otherwise, such a cease-fire would allow the Arabs to keep hold of the land captured in their surprise attack.

Instead, Kissinger proposed a cease-fire status quo ante—in other words, a cease-fire that would require each side to return to where it was before the fighting began. Publicly, he argued that this was the only fair way to make sure that Egypt and Syria were not rewarded for starting a war.

Privately, his agenda was more complex. He realized that there was no way to get the Arabs to give up their own territory that they had finally retaken. His real goal was to get Israel to demand this outcome—so that if the battle turned and Israel captured new Arab territories, it would already be on record as favoring a return to the prewar lines. "There was no hope for a cease-fire status quo ante," Kissinger recalled, "but I wanted to get the Israelis to sign on to the principle so we could use it against them if they turned the war around."

On the second day of the war—Sunday, October 7—Kissinger and Schlesinger agreed that the Pentagon would provide Israel with Sidewinder missiles and new ammunition, but it would be required to send unmarked El Al planes to pick up these supplies secretly at a Virginia air base.

"Are you willing to use U.S. aircraft?" Schlesinger asked.

"No," Kissinger replied, "they are coming here."

Late that Sunday night, Israel's Ambassador Simcha Dinitz called to say that the Israeli planes had not been given permission by American military officials to land at the air base. "Oh, those goddamn idiots," Kissinger exclaimed, promising that he would try to clear the matter up.

Simcha Dinitz had that special Israeli characteristic of being gruff and ebullient at the same time. Portly, pugnacious, witty, wise, and, when necessary, defiant, he had risen from being Prime Minister Golda Meir's personal assistant to the post of ambassador to Washington, one of Israel's most important jobs and the de facto leader of Zionist Jewry in America. In his role, he reported directly to Meir, not to Foreign Minister Abba Eban. To his critics, his weakness was an attribute that other ambassadors might have considered a great strength: he had become, professionally and personally, very close to Henry Kissinger.

Kissinger, to whom linkage came naturally, immediately established some trade-offs with Dinitz and Soviet Ambassador Dobrynin. They centered on the most-favored-nation (MFN) trade status that Washington had promised the Soviets in 1972. Congress, with Senator Henry Jackson in the lead, was threatening to block this new trade relationship unless Moscow lifted restrictions on Jewish emigration. So Kissinger began to link the resupply of Israel and the Soviet trade bill.

He told Dobrynin on Sunday that he would continue to push for most-favored-nation status if the Soviets showed restraint in the Middle East crisis. The next evening, he was scheduled to give a major speech at a Washington conference. "Let me read you what I've written," he volunteered, proceeding to recite a passage advocating the most-favored-nation trade agreement. "Frankly," Kissinger warned, "I may have to drop that section from the speech depending on developments tomorrow."

Early the next morning, Dobrynin called with a message from Brezhnev. "We feel we should act in cooperation with you," the note said. In thanking him, Kissinger reiterated his linkage. "I will include," he promised, "some references to MFN in my speech tonight."

As for the Israeli side of the linkage equation, Kissinger told Dinitz that he expected Jewish leaders, in return for the U.S. efforts to resupply Israel, to withdraw their support for Senator Jackson's amendment to the Soviet trade bill. He spelled out the deal explicitly to officials from the Conference of Presidents of Major American Jewish Organizations; reluctantly, the group decided to go along.

Kissinger told Haig about this deal in a phone conversation on Sunday morning. Speaking about the resupply of Israel, he explained: "If we support them, they would be willing to help with MFN." The next day, as he prepared to give his speech with the section he had promised Dobrynin, he called Ambassador Dinitz and warned: "I'm going in this speech to mention our MFN position and I hope to God this is not a week whatever Jewish league will start attacking me on this."

To the extent that Nixon was involved at all that first weekend, it was to exhort Kissinger to be tough with Israel. On Sunday morning, he told Kissinger by phone, "One thing we have to keep in the back of our minds is we don't want to be so pro-Israel that the oil states—the Arabs that are not involved in the fighting—will break ranks" and join in the war. The following evening, in another phone conversation,

Nixon expressed confidence that the Israelis would win—"Thank God, they should"—but then lamented that they "will be even more impossible to deal with than before."

This led to a discussion of how the Soviets were being more cooperative than they had been during the 1967 Middle East war. The colloquy, with Kissinger playing solicitous tutor and Nixon enjoying little fantasies, is interesting for its tone as well as its substance:

Kissinger: "In 1967, they [the Soviets] were steaming their fleet around, they were threatening war, they were castigating us in the Security Council, breaking diplomatic relations with us, threatening our oil installations. And no one has made a peep against us yet."

Nixon: "That's great."

Kissinger: "And that's a major triumph for our policy, and we can use it in the MFN fight. . . . We can brief the hell out of this one."

Nixon: "Why?"

Kissinger: "Just compare it to '67."

Nixon: "Yeah. I guess so. Well, we thought we could brief the [expletive deleted] out of Jordan. It didn't help much."

Kissinger: "Jordan we never briefed much."

Nixon: "Never did, did we?"

Kissinger: "No."

Nixon: "That was really a good one, though."

Kissinger: "But there we couldn't tell the truth."

Nixon: "We really—with no cards at all—just like India-Pakistan —played a hell of a game."

Kissinger: "Exactly."

Nixon: "This time we don't have any cards either."

Kissinger: "We're playing a pretty good game."

Nixon: "That's right. OK, Henry, thank you."

All of these reveries were upset on Tuesday, October 9, the fourth day of fighting, when it became clear that Israel was in trouble. The Israeli cabinet had been meeting all night and had decided, among other things, to put its nuclear-armed Jericho missiles on alert. Israel's nuclear program was a closely guarded secret, but U.S. intelligence at the time estimated that it had manufactured as many as twenty nuclear warheads. Early that morning, as the cabinet meeting ended, Golda Meir called Ambassador Dinitz. Israel was being defeated, she said. He should call Kissinger immediately.

"I can't speak to anyone now, Golda, it's much too early," Dinitz replied, noting that it was only one A.M. in Washington.

"I don't care what time it is," she said. "Call Kissinger now."

He did. Twice during the predawn hours, the excitable ambassador called to ask about expediting the resupply of weapons. Kissinger agreed to meet with him at eight-thirty that morning in the Map Room of the White House.

Dinitz's meeting with Kissinger was a tense one, especially after the ambassador requested that their two assistants (Peter Rodman and General Mordechai Gur) leave the room. Dinitz confided that Meir was willing to make a secret trip to Washington for a one-hour private session with Nixon to plead for more supplies.

Kissinger dismissed that suggestion as unnecessary. Later, he would say that it smacked of "blackmail" because it was designed to put the administration on the spot.

According to both Dinitz and Kissinger, Dinitz did not mention —or threaten—that Israel was prepared to resort to nuclear weapons if its survival was at stake. But since the U.S. knew of Israel's capabilities, the threat was implicit. As William Quandt, a Middle East expert on Kissinger's staff, later noted: "Without being told in so many words, we knew that a desperate Israel might activate its nuclear option. This situation, by itself, created a kind of blackmail potential. . . . But no one had to say it, and I don't think anyone did." Kissinger later mentioned casually to Herman Eilts, who had been U.S. ambassador to Egypt at the time, that Israel had given "intimations that if they didn't get military equipment, and quickly, they might go nuclear."[5]

After talking to Dinitz for more than an hour, Kissinger promised the ambassador that he would have a reply by late afternoon. Then Kissinger called a WSAG crisis committee meeting to prepare options for the president.

At the WSAG meeting, Kissinger was once again isolated. Secretary Schlesinger, reflecting the attitude of the Defense Department, warned that a major rearming of Israel, especially if it helped turn the war around, would poison America's relations with the Arabs. There was a distinction, he argued, between defending Israel's survival and defending its right to keep control of the occupied territories it had taken during the Six Day War of 1967.

The WSAG came up with a range of five options. Kissinger then met with Nixon privately in his Executive Office Building hideaway, where they agreed on the one that Kissinger preferred: a quiet and low-key resupply of Israel with a modest amount of new planes and ammunition. In addition, Kissinger got Nixon to approve a crucial pledge: the U.S. would replace all of Israel's losses once the battle was over; thus the Israeli army would not have to hoard equipment. However, there would be no immediate American airlift. The resupply operation would be kept "quiet," and Israel would have to make arrangements for picking up its new supplies.

"With this kind of movement, we won't be able to keep it quiet," Schlesinger told Kissinger that evening. "With all the Israeli planes flying around, it will be impossible for the Arabs not to find out."

"It is extremely important," said Kissinger, "to keep it as low-key as we possibly can." He then added that it would be wonderful "if we can get through this crisis without antagonizing the Arabs."

Schlesinger's concerns were twofold. Kissinger's requirement that the operation be kept quiet and not involve American planes was, he complained, "like nailing the military's feet to the ground," and it was easier said than done. In addition, he shared Deputy Defense Secretary Clements's concerns that the pro-Israel tilt might not be in the national interest. As he put it in a phone call to Kissinger early Wednesday morning: "I think that we are going to get into a position in which all our interests in Saudi Arabia are at risk, and it might be desirable to examine the fundamentals of our position."

By then—Wednesday, October 10—the Soviets had begun their own resupply operation, of Syria. It was a modest airlift confined to ammunition and fuel (rather than tanks or planes), but it was still more overt than the U.S. effort. In addition, the Israelis were having problems collecting the U.S. equipment they needed using only their seven available transport planes.

Kissinger then made a decision that turned out to be one of the most bothersome mistakes of the resupply effort: instead of allowing American planes to transport the supplies, he decided that Israel should hire private charter companies to do it. This halfway solution, it turned out, neither helped the Israelis nor pleased the Arabs.

The president, preoccupied with Agnew's resignation that Wednesday, had not been very involved in the decision-making about the war. He had approved sending Israel five new F-4 Phantom fighter jets, but he had not paid much attention to Kissinger's maneuvers to achieve a military stalemate or to the Pentagon bureaucracy's reluctance to resupply Israel.

The Soviet airlift finally engaged Nixon's fighting instincts. He was shocked to find out that five Phantom jets he had ordered sent to Israel two days earlier had not yet gone. "It should have been done," Nixon snapped at Kissinger. "Do it now!"

"I thought it was done, and every day they find another excuse not to do it," Kissinger said, blaming the Pentagon.

"I'm pissed off about this business of not getting the planes through," Nixon continued. "Clements is a good man, but . . ."

"They think there is a special relationship with the Saudis," said Kissinger.

That evening, Kissinger got Scowcroft on the case. "Look, Brent, the Defense people are just going to have to stop dragging their feet," he said. "The Israelis are going wild." Scowcroft promised that at least two of the Phantom fighters would go out the next day. Kissinger then called Haig. "Could you stiffen Schlesinger's back?" he said. "The guy is totally panicked. Clements is beating after him. If the Egyptians win, we will lose our position."

Israeli ambassadors seldom sit quietly in situations such as this, and Simcha Dinitz was more energetic than most. And more resourceful. The newspapers on Thursday, October 11, contained stories—leaked by Dinitz—saying that Israel's survival was threatened because the U.S. was slow about furnishing promised supplies. Senator Henry Jackson, who had spoken to Dinitz twice the previous day, telephoned Kissinger to apply pressure. "The big obstacle," Kissinger told him, "has been that some of the Defense people did not want to move anything because of their obsession with Saudi Arabia."

"Someone should give orders in the name of the president," replied Jackson. "I just talked to Schlesinger, and he says he has no authority to requisition charters."

Kissinger immediately called his chief Mideast deputy, Joseph Sisco, to complain that the Israelis were raising hell about the difficulty of getting charter planes to pick up their supplies. The problem, Sisco explained, was that none of the charter companies was willing to come forward for such a dangerous and politically controversial job. And the Pentagon had not used its full authority or leverage to force them to help.

So Kissinger ordered the military to charter twenty transport planes on its own for the Israelis to use. He then phoned Dinitz and, early on Friday morning, the president, to say what he had done. Still, the charter scheme continued to have trouble getting off the ground.

Although Senator Jackson and others were blaming the Soviets for stirring up the crisis, Kissinger felt that their behavior had been restrained. The Soviets were being modest in the amount of supplies they were sending to Egypt and Syria, they were cooperating at the U.N., and they were pushing Egypt to accept a cease-fire. In order to tout this triumph of détente, Kissinger called a press conference for the morning of Friday, October 12.

His new State Department public affairs chief, Robert Mc-Closkey, was determined that the press conference would suit Kissinger's standards. "Do you have any feelings about the Great Seal?" he asked, saying that it was now mounted behind Kissinger's podium but could be moved.

"For all I care you could get a seal from the zoo and put a thing around its neck," Kissinger barked back. Then, noting that McCloskey seemed hurt, Kissinger added: "I don't care about the Seal as long as there are two heralds in front of me as I come in. An Irishman ought to be able to know where some heralds are."

At the press conference, Kissinger chose his words carefully. He said that he did "not consider the airlift of Soviet military equipment helpful," but he went on to label it "moderate." This was to be balanced against "the relative restraint that has been shown in the public media in the Soviet Union and in the conduct of their representatives at the Security Council." In short, he argued, détente was not dead.

In the meantime, the charter situation had still not been sorted out, and Israeli leaders were in an uproar. Dinitz showed up at Kissinger's White House office just before midnight that Friday night and explained that the situation was dire. Israel, he said, would run out of ammunition in three days.

At this point an interesting shift occurred. Schlesinger became convinced that, as long as the U.S. was going to resupply Israel, it should use its own military planes rather than continue to flop around trying to hire private charter planes. But Kissinger, who was hoping to begin a new diplomatic round, still wanted to avoid the use of U.S. military planes.

Shortly after midnight, as soon as Ambassador Dinitz left his office, Kissinger talked to Haig on the telephone. "Jim told me that it's suddenly critical," Haig said, referring to Schlesinger. "He's ready to move MAC [U.S. Military Assistance Command] aircraft in there immediately. I think that would be foolish."

"That would be disaster, Al," replied Kissinger. "How can he fuck everything up for a week—he can't now recoup it the day the diplomacy is supposed to start." He went on to express his disbelief at the Pentagon's claim that it could not hire any civilian charters. "You know goddamn well they didn't try."

"We do have the option of sending some American planes in there," Haig noted again. "I think that's a high risk for us."

"I think it's stupid," said Kissinger.

As soon as he hung up, Kissinger telephoned Schlesinger, who was at home asleep. In his memoirs, Kissinger noted that he and the defense secretary were pretty much in agreement. But Schlesinger's recollection of the call was that Kissinger flew off the handle. "As Israel began to fall apart," Schlesinger recalled, "Henry began to fall apart."

Kissinger began the conversation by saying that the lack of ammunition had caused the Israelis to stop pushing forward against Syria. This was "near disaster," he said, for America's diplomatic strategy, and it was all due to "massive sabotage" within the Pentagon. Yet when Schlesinger suggested abandoning the ill-fated private charter plan and using U.S. military transports instead, Kissinger remained adamantly opposed. "One thing we cannot have now, given our relations with the Soviets, is American planes flying in there," he said.

Schlesinger got out of bed, dressed, and had his driver take him to the Pentagon. There he reviewed the options. Sometime around three A.M., he came to a conclusion: the resupply could not be handled other than through an American military airlift all the way to Israel. The option that Kissinger was insisting on, the use of private charters, would not work. Schlesinger had available three C-5A transport planes, the largest behemoths in the American arsenal, each able to carry up to eighty tons directly to Israel. As soon as the sun rose, he called Haig to urge this course on Nixon.

Nixon agreed and gave Kissinger the word as he was preparing to chair another WSAG crisis committee meeting that Saturday morning. "Do it now!" Nixon told him. Kissinger did not object. In addition, he and Nixon decided that smaller transports would fly in other supplies, and fourteen new F-4 Phantom fighter jets would be sent to Israel immediately.

Thus, on Saturday, October 13, a week after the fighting began, a major American airlift finally got under way. As the droning American transport planes reached the skies over Tel Aviv, cars stopped in the streets, apartment windows opened, and people began to shout, "God bless America." Golda Meir cried for the first time since the war began. A thousand tons of equipment a day began flowing, with flights landing almost every hour. More arrived on the first day than the Soviets had delivered to Egypt, Syria, and Iraq combined in the previous four days. After a week spent dithering over whether it was possible to get five F-4 Phantoms to Israel, forty were delivered over the next ten days.

On Sunday morning, Nixon thought it worthwhile to remind Kissinger that, despite the airlift, he did not want Israel to get too cocky. "We have to squeeze the Israelis when this is over, and the Russians have got to know it," the president said. "We have to squeeze them goddamn hard." Nevertheless, that was no reason to hold back on the airlift now that it had begun. "It's got to be the works," he said. "What I mean is, we are going to get blamed just as much for three planes as for one hundred."

To Kissinger, it was another example of Nixon's notion that once a military decision is made, one should not try to dampen criticism by executing it hesitantly. "Mr. President," he replied, "I remember in 1970, when we went into Cambodia, you wanted to do Haiphong at the same time, and you were right."

"At least we did all the sanctuaries," Nixon said, recalling the opposition he had faced on that decision.

"No one wanted to do that," Kissinger agreed.

Although there were recriminations among American Jews against Kissinger for delaying the airlift, he had been properly balancing a concern for Israel's safety with the demands of America's own national interest. Israel had originally insisted, during the first few days of the war, only on a guarantee that its losses would be made up. There was no hurry for new supplies, since it was thought the war would be over in days. Once the supply issue became critical, three days were spent dithering over private charters. For that, Kissinger was partly responsible, because he did not want to associate the U.S. too closely with a major resupply effort that could permit Israel to humiliate the Arabs.

Ambassador Dinitz, accused at the time of being too trusting of Kissinger, later defended him. The central problem, he recalled, was that Schlesinger left the logistics to the Pentagon bureaucracy, run by William Clements. In the middle of the first week, Dinitz was unable to get an appointment with Schlesinger for two days. "His office told me he had gone bird-watching."

But Richard Perle, then an assistant to Senator Jackson, said that Kissinger was largely to blame because he kept insisting that charter planes rather than American military transports be used. "We kept telling Henry that the leased-charter arrangement was a loser," Perle said. "Schlesinger wanted to use the air force, but Kissinger wouldn't let him."

All of the delays at least produced a silver lining. The airlift was seen in Moscow and Cairo not as a major American provocation, but as a response to the one launched by the Soviets. Within a few days, it became clear that, if a cease-fire was timed right, the airlift would result in what Kissinger had hoped for at the start: a modest Israeli victory that encouraged Egyptian and Israeli flexibility while preserving the potential for American diplomacy.

Kissinger had abandoned his original call for a cease-fire status quo ante (one that would require a return to the prewar line) and had instead accepted in principle the Soviet plan for a cease-fire in place. His goal, however, was to stall until just the proper moment when Israel had regained enough territory without completely humiliating its Arab enemies.

By Friday, October 19, after two weeks of fighting, that time for peace seemed to be at hand. The Egyptian Third Army was still east of the Suez Canal, recapturing a strip of what had been Israeli-occupied Sinai. But to the north, an Israeli division had crossed over to the west of the canal into Egypt and threatened to cut off the Third Army. On that day a message arrived from Brezhnev inviting Kissinger personally—"in an urgent manner"—to come to Moscow to negotiate an immediate cease-fire.

The invitation played neatly into Kissinger's stall strategy: it would give Israel another two or three days to make military gains. In addition, it was, for Kissinger, an almost irresistible summons. Once again, he was being asked to ride off secretly in the dark of night to play the Lone Ranger in pursuit of peace, called upon to do in the Middle East what he had done in Vietnam and China: act as the free-wheeling superdiplomat who would reap accolades for saving the world. Late that night, after attending a gala public dinner in his honor thrown by the Chinese, Kissinger secretly flew off to the Kremlin with Dobrynin in tow.

THE NUCLEAR ALERT, OCTOBER 1973

As Kissinger was flying to Moscow, he received a message from the White House that would normally have furthered his strategy and stoked his ego. The president, Scowcroft informed him, was cabling a personal letter to Brezhnev in which he granted Kissinger "full authority" to make an agreement. Though not usually averse to sweeping grants of authority, Kissinger was annoyed: this time he wanted the option to refer any proposals back to the president, thus giving him the opportunity to stall a cease-fire for a few more hours as Israel's military position improved.

Later, after being criticized by Israel's supporters for agreeing to a cease-fire too quickly, Kissinger would argue that his entire strategy had been to delay for as long as possible. Actually, he was playing a trickier game: although he wanted Israel to improve its position, he realized that it was not in America's interest for Egypt to be humiliated. So he was trying to time the cease-fire so that it would create a battlefield stalemate that left room for negotiations.

An even more disconcerting message from Nixon reached him in Moscow. The president provided formal instructions for what he was to propose to the Soviet leader the next morning. Not only was he to seek an immediate cease-fire. In addition, he was to say that the U.S. and the Soviet Union, viewing the Middle East situation dispassionately, "must step in, determine the proper course of action for a just settlement, and then bring the necessary pressure on our respective friends."

Nixon was saying that Washington and Moscow should jointly work out a comprehensive peace plan and impose it on Israel and the Arabs. Kissinger's entire approach to the Middle East had been to cut the Soviets out of the diplomacy, not join in a partnership with them. In addition, the idea of seeking a comprehensive peace and imposing it on Israel was anathema to him. Instead, his goal was to have step-by-step negotiations between the Arabs and the Israelis, with the U.S. serving as the middleman while the Soviets were relegated to the sidelines.

So Kissinger fired off another strident cable to Scowcroft, and not being one to leave bad enough alone, he picked up the telephone and called Al Haig directly. On an open line, he expressed his dismay at the instructions he had received.

"Will you get off my back?" Haig said. "I have troubles of my own."

"What troubles can you possibly have in Washington on a Saturday night?" Kissinger shot back.

Haig replied rather wearily, "The president has just fired Cox. Richardson and Ruckelshaus have resigned and all hell has broken loose."

Thus he first learned of the firing of the Watergate special prosecutor and the resulting debacle that would be dubbed the Saturday Night Massacre.

Given the situation, Kissinger proceeded to ignore Nixon's instructions. All that he was prepared to discuss, he told Brezhnev the next day, was a simple cease-fire.

When the Soviets were motivated, by what they would call the correlation of forces, to reach a quick agreement, they were able to dispense rather suddenly with their plodding tactics and cut right to a deal. In this case their motivation was the rapidly worsening military situation of their Arab allies. It took Brezhnev and his colleagues only four hours on Sunday, October 21, to accept the three elements that Kissinger sought and Joe Sisco hastily drafted: a cease-fire resolution to be voted on that night at the U.N. and to take effect twelve hours later; a reference to Resolution 242 but no demand for specific Israeli withdrawals; and a call for negotiations "between the parties concerned," meaning that the Arabs for the first time would have to accept the principle of direct talks with Israel.

Things went so quickly that Kissinger grasped at any excuse for a delay. When Foreign Minister Gromyko asked if he had any ideas on the technical details of implementing the agreement, Kissinger replied that he did, but he had left the relevant papers at his Lenin Hills guesthouse and thus would not be able to submit them until later in the day. His assistant Peter Rodman interrupted to say that he had in fact brought the papers with him, not to worry. No, said Kissinger, they were back at the guesthouse. Rodman was not to be dissuaded; he triumphantly pulled them from his briefcase. Kissinger glared. Only then did Rodman realize it had been a stalling tactic. Kissinger's rage that evening was such that, from then on, whenever he asked Rodman or Lord for a paper during a negotiating session, they would hold back on it until he insisted.[6]

Kissinger was playing a precarious game. As he had with the South Vietnamese, he was now negotiating on Israel's behalf yet without regular consultations. The Israelis made matters worse by ignoring his repeated pleas to keep him informed of their military situation and desires about timing. When agreement on a joint cease-fire resolution was reached that Sunday, he did not tell the Soviets that it was contingent on Jerusalem's approval. He did, however, insist that the plan—which became known as Resolution 338—not be voted on by the Security Council for another twelve hours so that he would have time to consult with Israeli leaders.

Consequently, he was in a hurry to send Golda Meir his report, which explained in glowing terms his success in achieving a cease-fire that did not demand any Israeli withdrawals and that called for direct Arab-Israeli negotiations. That accomplished, he lay down for an hour's rest. When he got up, he discovered to his horror that a communications glitch, perhaps caused by Soviet jamming, meant that the messages had not yet been transmitted.

Kissinger was one of those people who had no comprehension of the workings of mechanical objects but who sensed that, like humans, they were likely to perform better when shouted at. Lawrence Eagleburger, who was struggling to get the cables moving, later wrote a report to Kissinger recalling the scene in the workspace at the Lenin Hills guesthouse:

> There were some twenty to thirty people in the room, all talking, with Joe Sisco (never a quiet fellow) taking the lead. . . . Unbeknownst to me, you walked in that moment and obviously heard what I was saying (I still haven't figured out how). There was a bellow along the lines of: "What, the cables aren't out yet!?!" I looked up to find you standing in the middle of the room with smoke issuing from nose, eyes, and ears, and no one else (with an exception I'll mention in a minute) in sight. All twenty or thirty people—no doubt led by Sisco—had exited with a speed and facility that would

have put Houdini to shame. The single exception was Winston Lord, who was sort of huddled in a corner, but—God bless him—prepared to hang around for the pyrotechnics and clean up the blood (mine) when it was all over.[7]

Eventually the cables were sent in time to be digested before Kissinger arrived in Israel. His well-choreographed triumph was met with mixed emotion there; many Israeli leaders had hoped that the cease-fire could have been delayed until Egypt's Third Army was destroyed. When Kissinger arrived to present the plan, crowds of jubilant citizens met him at the airport as a bearer of peace. But when Foreign Minister Abba Eban embraced him at the foot of the plane, Kissinger whispered to him about the prime minister, "I presume she is wild with anger at me." Eban allowed that she was.

As when he had negotiated on South Vietnam's behalf with little consultation, part of the problem was Kissinger's Lone Ranger pretensions. Why, Golda Meir wondered, had he not kept Israel better informed about what he was doing? Kissinger explained the communications glitches and protested that the Israelis had not sent along the military updates he had requested. His explanations were valid. Yet, once again, Kissinger's behavior contained traces of the arrogance that so often led him to forge ahead in negotiations without being solicitous about the sensitivities of those whose support he would later need.

The main problem was that many Israelis, especially in the military, were upset that the cease-fire came just when they were about to surround Egypt's twenty-five-thousand-man Third Army Corps. This represented a fundamental difference between Israeli and American interests. As Kissinger later put it, "We did not think that turning an Arab setback into a debacle represented a vital interest" of the U.S.

The Third Army Corps was the pride of the Egyptian forces. It had crossed the southern end of the Suez Canal and gained a foothold almost ten miles wide and thirty miles long in the Israeli-occupied Sinai peninsula, which Egypt had lost in 1967. But in a daring move, the Israeli army had crossed the canal into Egypt north of the Third Army, then moved southward to cut it off from the rest of the Egyptian forces. The Israelis were close to capturing the Third Army's last supply link—the Cairo-Suez road—when Kissinger's cease-fire went into effect.

With Israeli leaders chafing to complete the encirclement of the Third Army, Kissinger made a bad mistake: he indicated to the Israelis, as he later admitted, that there could be some "slippage" in the cease-fire deadline. According to one Israeli account, after being told how long it might take to complete the operation, he responded: "Two or three days? That's all? Well, in Vietnam the cease-fire didn't go into effect at the exact time it was agreed on."

Kissinger later claimed that he had in mind a few hours, not days. Either way, it was a dangerous game to be playing with the Soviets and Egyptians. Before his plane had landed in Washington, word of renewed Israeli fighting reached him.

He was furious, all the more so when Golda Meir made the dubious claim that Israel was only responding to Egyptian provocations. Even if some Egyptians on a suicidal impulse had violated the cease-fire, the Israelis were the ones clearly on the offensive and capturing new ground.

The Soviets and Egyptians protested vehemently to Kissinger personally and to the world at large. Yevgeni Primakov, Moscow's top Middle East expert, who went on to become one of President Gorbachev's closest advisers, recalled that the Soviets felt that Kissinger had intentionally deceived them by giving Israel permission to violate the cease-fire. Brezhnev sent a note directly to Kissinger, a highly unusual procedure that indicated his awareness that Kissinger, rather than Nixon, was now running the show.

Kissinger responded with a proposal for a new U.N. resolution that urged the Israelis and Arabs to stop shooting and return to where they were when the cease-fire went into effect the day before. The problem was to get Israel to agree. Again, Kissinger resorted to suggesting that he would tolerate a bit of subterfuge. There was no real reason the Israeli forces had to pull back to where they were at the moment of the cease-fire. "How can anyone ever know where a line is or was in the desert?"

Golda Meir seemed unimpressed. "They will know where our present line is, all right," she said. Kissinger understood. The Israelis had now completed the encirclement of Egypt's Third Army Corps. As Kissinger later recalled: "A crisis was upon us."

Throughout Wednesday, October 24, the Israelis' noose around the Third Army tightened. Egypt, which had broken diplomatic ties with the U.S. after the 1967 war, invited the Americans to send forces to the region to help enforce the cease-fire. Then, in a startling proposal to a nation that had just completed a massive military airlift to his enemy, Anwar Sadat requested that American troops be sent to the Egyptian side of the cease-fire line in order to help prevent Israeli attacks.

Golda Meir, on the other hand, sent a furious message to the U.S. accusing it of collusion with the Egyptians and the Soviets. "It is impossible for Israel to accept," she wrote, "that time and again it must face Russian and Egyptian ultimatums which will subsequently be assented to by the United States."

Therein lay an ominous sign for Kissinger's policy of détente: it would likely face its most fervent opposition not from old-line anti-communists, but from pro-Israeli neoconservatives who feared that Washington's new pragmatism toward Moscow might lead it to cut deals at Israel's expense. Already, Senators Henry Jackson and Jacob Javits—in addition to opposing most-favored-nation trade status for the Soviets until Jewish emigration was eased—were accusing Kissinger of being sluggish about an American airlift to Israel out of a desire to nurture détente with the Soviets.[8]

The limits of Soviet-American détente suddenly—although briefly—became vivid late that night. Unexpectedly, after two weeks of wary cooperation, a superpower showdown occurred that at first seemed as ominous as any since the Cuban Missile Crisis.[9]

The October 24 crisis was prompted by Sadat's understandable, albeit surprising, desire to have American troops come to his country in conjunction with Soviet ones to enforce a cease-fire. The Soviets, under the guise of trying to be cooperative, readily agreed to the proposal. Then, with somewhat less claim to a cooperative intent, they went a dangerous step further. They indicated they would send troops on their own if the U.S. did not want to be part of a joint venture.

One of Kissinger's primary goals in the Middle East had been to eliminate Moscow's military presence there. Sadat had unexpectedly done that in Egypt in 1972, and Kissinger was resolved to prevent the Soviets from getting back in. "We were determined," he recalled, "to resist by force if necessary the introduction of Soviet troops in the Middle East regardless of the pretext."

From the outset, the evening of October 24 had an unnerving quality to it. Dobrynin called just after seven P.M. to say that Moscow had decided to support a U.N. resolution calling for the introduction of Soviet and American troops to enforce the cease-fire. Kissinger felt that it was important to get the Israelis to obey the cease-fire, but he considered it even more important to keep Soviet forces out of the area. He immediately told Dobrynin that the U.S. would not agree to this.

Kissinger's decision was probably one that Nixon, had he been in a rational frame of mind, would have approved. In theory, however, it should have been his call. And there were indications that Nixon, who was highly agitated by both Watergate and Israeli defiance, may have been willing to work with the Soviets. In his conversations and notes during the previous week, he had repeatedly emphasized to Kissinger how tough the U.S. would need to be on the Israelis when the war ended, and he added that the Soviets should be told that the U.S. had this attitude.

Kissinger had a chance to discuss the issue with Nixon directly, but decided not to. In the midst of his tense session with Dobrynin, Kissinger was interrupted by a call from the president. But Nixon's mood, Kissinger quickly determined, made it unwise to present him with a serious foreign policy matter.

Nixon was distraught over the talk of impeachment that had been swelling since the Saturday Night Massacre and was as emotional as Kissinger had ever heard him. During their conversation, which was recorded by Kissinger's office, the president said that his critics were attacking him "because of their desire to kill the president. And they may succeed. I may physically die." Kissinger tried to soothe him by telling him how good he was in times of adversity, but his fine hand for flattery for once failed. Nixon was inconsolable. "What they care about is destruction," he said. "It brings me sometimes to feel like saying the hell with it."

When Nixon hung up, Kissinger returned to his conversation with Dobrynin. The U.S. would oppose any attempts by the Soviets to send troops to the region, he said. Dobrynin replied that he would pass this along to Moscow, but warned that minds there had probably been made up.

Dobrynin was back on the phone shortly after nine-thirty that night. Even though it was four-thirty A.M. in Moscow, a message from Brezhnev had just come in. "If you find it impossible to act jointly with us in this matter, we should be faced with the necessity urgently to consider the question of taking appropriate steps unilaterally." In addition, the CIA reported that some Soviet transport units were in a higher state of readiness. Kissinger immediately called Haig, who did not fully share his agitation but agreed it would be risky not to take Brezhnev's message seriously.

Kissinger: "I just had a letter from Brezhnev asking us to send forces in together or he will send them in alone."

Haig: "I was afraid of that."

Kissinger: "I think we have to go to the mat on this one. . . ."

Haig: "Where are the Israelis at this point?"

Kissinger: "They've got the Third Army surrounded."

Haig: "I think they [the Soviets] are playing chicken. They're not going to put forces in at the end of a war. I don't believe that."

Kissinger: "I don't know. What's going to stop them from flying paratroops in?"

Whether or not Kissinger was overreacting, one thing was now clear: if the U.S. wanted to demand that the Soviets not send in their troops, it would have to make at least an implied threat of war. Troops would have to be put on alert. Even with the enormous power that Kissinger now wielded, no secretary of state would want to embark on this course without the commander in chief. "Should I wake up the president?" Kissinger asked.

"No," replied Haig rather curtly. Kissinger understood. Nixon was "too distraught" to be involved, was the way Kissinger later politely put it, so he would have to run things himself. "It was a daunting responsibility to assume." [10]

He summoned the top cabinet officers—including Defense Secretary Schlesinger, CIA director William Colby, and Chairman of the Joint Chiefs Thomas Moorer—to the State Department for what was, in effect, a rump meeting of the National Security Council. In this case, however, the president would not be in the chair. Nor would the vice president, for the nation was without one. Gerald Ford had been named but not confirmed, and he was not invited to the meeting.

Shortly before the session was to begin at ten-thirty P.M., Kissinger talked to Haig again. The meeting should be held in the White House, Haig said, and Kissinger should chair it as the president's assistant rather than as secretary of state. Kissinger agreed. Although the distinction might seem semantic, it would preserve at least the fiction of presidential control. Kissinger again asked whether they should telephone the president. Haig ignored the question.

At the meeting, a consensus emerged that the Soviets might start airlifting troops into Egypt at any hour. The group decided to send a letter to Sadat asking him to withdraw his request for Soviet and American troops, and to send a reply to Brezhnev, over Nixon's name, that firmly rejected the introduction of Soviet or American troops into the region.

Shortly before midnight, the group Kissinger had gathered in the Situation Room came to a momentous decision: the U.S. should send a threatening military signal to Moscow. As an expert on the relation between force and diplomacy, Kissinger was an inveterate signal-sender who placed great stock in having aircraft carrier task forces steaming (as he had done during the India-Pakistan war) and putting troops on alert (as he had done during the 1970 Jordan crisis). This time, he and his colleagues decided to put American nuclear forces and troops worldwide on a higher state of nuclear alert.

"You will keep this secret," Kissinger growled at Admiral Moorer as he left the Situation Room to transmit the decision to the Pentagon. "Not a word of this is to leak." In true Kissinger fashion, he was trying to calibrate a signal that would be noticed by the Soviets but kept secret from the American public. "Of course, Henry," the Joint

Chiefs' chairman said, with no trace of irony. Defense Secretary Schlesinger, however, rolled his eyes.

A few hours later, Schlesinger was back at the Pentagon when Kissinger phoned. "I am listening to the radio and it is broadcasting news of the alert," he growled. "I thought you people were going to keep this one secret."

"Listen, Henry," Schlesinger replied, "there is no way you can put more than two million soldiers and reservists suddenly on alert and make sure nobody else finds out about it." Later, shaking his head, Schlesinger recalled the discussion and said, "It was typical of Henry to believe that you could keep it a secret from everyone except the Russians."

Despite the line later purveyed to the press, Nixon was not part of the decision-making process that night, nor was he briefed. Kissinger never even spoke to him that night, nor did Haig or anyone else. When Kissinger briefed the president at eight A.M., he gave him a rundown on all that had occurred; he was struck by the fact that Nixon seemed to be hearing it for the first time.

By then, Egypt had already sent word that, in response to the American rejection, it would withdraw its request for Soviet and American peacekeeping troops and instead ask for a U.N. "international" force, which by tradition does not include any of the permanent members of the Security Council.

Later that day, Brezhnev's reply arrived. It simply ignored all of the overnight hullabaloo and politely accepted an American suggestion that nonmilitary observers rather than soldiers should be sent in. The Soviets, Brezhnev added, were happy to do this in conjunction with the U.S. He ended by expressing hope that such cooperation would continue.

To Kissinger, it was a sign that the Soviets had been cowed by American resolve. "The Soviets had backed off," he later noted. To others, it was a sign that Kissinger had gotten a bit too excited about Brezhnev's rather ambiguous previous message the night before. "Far from representing a Soviet threat, it [Brezhnev's original Wednesday-night message] urged reinforcement of superpower collaboration as the preferred course of action," Raymond Garthoff, a former State Department Soviet expert and Kissinger critic, wrote. "The Soviets had no reason to expect the American response would be a global nuclear alert."

Since Kissinger and his colleagues could not possibly know what the Soviets were truly intending, they were probably prudent to treat the matter as deadly serious, even if in retrospect the nuclear alert seems excessive. "We may have read it wrong," Kissinger said in an off-the-record conversation with Joseph Kraft the next day, "but at midnight you can't take chances."

One unfair criticism leveled during the ensuing days was that the alert and crisis had been precipitated at Nixon's behest in order to distract attention from Watergate. Whether or not the participants in the rump session that Wednesday night were correct in their assessment of the Soviets, they were sincere in their motives.

"Do you think we overreacted on Wednesday to that letter?" Kissinger asked CIA Director Colby.

"I don't think you had any choice," Colby replied. "The Soviets may not have had the intention of going much further, but they sure sounded like it."

Those eager to torpedo détente saw the crisis as an opportunity to solidify their alliance with Israel's neoconservative supporters. The morning after the alert, Admiral Elmo Zumwalt, the chief of naval operations, leaked a copy of the original Brezhnev message to Senator Henry Jackson. With some exaggeration, the senator quickly leaked its gist to his friends in the press, calling the missive "brutal" and "threatening."

Intent on defending détente, Kissinger held a press conference that day. He refused to discuss the Brezhnev letter, even when pressed to justify the decision to go on nuclear alert. Instead, he went to extraordinary lengths to sound conciliatory. "We do not consider ourselves in a confrontation with the Soviet Union," he declared. Instead, he said, "Détente will have proved itself."

But the main line of questioning was whether the alert had been a ruse to deflect attention from Watergate. "It is a symptom of what is happening to our country that it could even be suggested that the U.S. would alert its forces for domestic reasons," Kissinger replied. When pressed, he challenged the reporters: "It is up to you ladies and gentlemen to determine whether this is the moment to try to create a crisis of confidence in the field of foreign policy as well."[11]

Like Nixon, Kissinger could crave a bit of flattery after a tough press conference, and like Kissinger, Al Haig knew how to provide it. "You did a hell of a job," Haig called to say right after the session.

"Was it all right?"

"Superb," Haig reassured.

"We've won," Kissinger exulted. "And you and I were the only ones for it."

"You're telling me," said Haig. "You really handled that thing magnificently."

"I think I did some good for the president."

"More than you know. [Senator Birch] Bayh called with tears in his eyes."

Nixon also expressed his elation when he telephoned to praise Kissinger for his press conference performance. This time, it was Kissinger who was doing the flattering. "Mr. President, you have won again," he said.

"You think so?"

"The Soviets have joined our resolution at the U.N. barring permanent members, after screaming like banshees," Kissinger replied. "The [expletive deleted] are saying we did all this for political purposes."

"I know," said Nixon, who was furious about it. "Like Kalb and who else?"

"Kalb, McCarthy. Reston called here with a similar question. . . ."

"I hope you told him strongly," said Nixon.

"I treated Kalb contemptuously at the press conference."

"What about Scotty [Reston]?"

"I gave him a few facts. I said, 'What would you do if seven of eight Soviet airborne divisions were put on alert?' I didn't tell him about the Brezhnev letter."

"Just as well I will not be doing the press conference," said Nixon, who had canceled plans for one that night. "I'm not in the mood."

"Do it tomorrow night," Kissinger suggested. "I would treat the bastards with contempt, Mr. President. They asked me about Watergate. I said you cannot play with the central authority of the country without paying a price."

"Good," said Nixon. "Al told me you slaughtered the bastards. Keep it up."

Less than a minute after they had finished, Nixon called again. He had a request that was eerily plaintive. "I was thinking of going up to Camp David," he said. Then he added hesitantly, "You don't think you could go up, too?" Back in the old days, Kissinger would have leaped at a chance to go to Camp David with the president. This time he just stammered a bit. "I understand," said Nixon.[12]

Later that evening, Nixon called from Camp David. He had come up with an idea. The next day Kissinger should invite the heads of all three networks and the *New York Times* to the White House and give them a briefing that stressed how indispensable Nixon had been (a rather odd request since he had slept through most of the crisis). "Their main concern is Israel," Nixon helpfully noted. "Who saved Israel? Would anybody else have saved it? You have to tell them that."

A few moments later, he called again. Kissinger should also gather Jewish leaders and do the same.

Kissinger murmured assent and let the subject drop. The briefings were never held. It was true, he later said, that Nixon had the determination to stick by Israel. But the pleas for such briefings, Kissinger felt, were "pathetic."[13]

In his own press conference the next day, Nixon showed none of Kissinger's restraint. Ignoring the fury it could cause in Moscow, he accused the Soviets of provoking "the most difficult crisis we have had since the Cuban confrontation of 1962." Indulging in his self-image of toughness, he said that Brezhnev had understood his resolve because he had bombed North Vietnam despite public pressure. "That is what made Mr. Brezhnev act as he did."[14]

Kissinger was aghast, and angrily said as much to Haig, whom he phoned as soon as Nixon finished speaking. When Haig tried to reassure Kissinger that they were getting some great public reaction, Kissinger snapped, "Don't tell him that or he'll do it again."

In an attempt to mitigate some of the damage, Haig took it upon himself to call Dobrynin. Speaking as a personal representative of the president, Haig told the Soviet ambassador: "I just came back from the president and told him that his remarks tonight were, I thought, very much overdrawn and would be interpreted improperly."

Dobrynin agreed.

"And I wanted you to know," Haig continued, "that he did not in any way have the intention of drawing the situation as sharply as he did. What he was trying to do—and I don't think it came across—he thought he was doing—was trying to emphasize his strong personal relationship with Mr. Brezhnev, and it did not come across that way to me at all."

"Yes," Dobrynin agreed, "it didn't come to me either."

For once, Kissinger had not called Nixon after a press conference to praise him. In fact, he was fuming at the president's heavy-handed performance. Then the phone rang from the Oval Office. It was Haig again. "I am with the president," he said, betraying no irony. "We noticed you are the only one who hasn't called."

"No, no," Kissinger protested, "we were trying to get through. I think it was very effective."

"Stu Alsop, who was at dinner in Georgetown, said that most of the guests were in a state of stunned admiration," Haig prompted.

"Yes, he called me, too," Kissinger said for Nixon's benefit. As he imagined the president sitting there brooding, Kissinger's anger began to ebb and a feeling of pity kicked in. He searched for something nice he could say to Nixon about the press conference. "It was quite a tour de force," he mumbled. Later, Kissinger would note that this remark was made "not without ambiguity."[15]

With the nuclear forces on both sides returned to regular status, attention turned back to the plight of Egypt's Third Army Corps, surrounded by Israel after the cease-fire and now in danger of being starved into surrender. As much as Kissinger tried, he was unable to persuade the Israelis to let convoys containing food, water, and medical supplies through.

Within the administration, and especially at the Pentagon, pressure was growing for the U.S. to resupply Egypt's beseiged corps. It was, on the surface, a rather strange notion: the U.S. would have thus conducted two resupply airlifts within the space of two weeks to the opposing sides in a bitter war.

Kissinger was against the idea. But he knew that he would have to find a way to force Israel to free the surrounded Egyptian forces. "My ultimate responsibility," he recalled, "was as secretary of state of the United States, not as a psychiatrist to the government of Israel."

At first he worked on his friend, Israel's irrepressible Ambassador Dinitz. It was folly, Kissinger argued, to persist in violating the cease-fire. What was to be gained? When persuasion did not work, Kissinger tried cold threats. He produced a set of tough demands of Israel that were made in Nixon's name. "We cannot permit the destruction of the Egyptian army under conditions achieved after a cease-fire was reached in part by negotiations in which we participated," Kissinger explained.

Golda Meir's response was defiant. The U.S. was joining with the Soviets, she charged, "in order that Egypt may announce a victory of her aggression." This was a rather theatrical overstatement, since the issue was merely whether non-military supplies should go to a starving army whose supply lines Israel had cut in violation of a cease-fire.

But before another crisis could occur, Anwar Sadat broke the impasse. He agreed to engage in direct Egyptian-Israeli talks at the military level in order to resolve the problem of access to his Third Army along the Cairo-Suez road. All the Egyptian president asked was that one convoy be allowed through in the meantime to keep his men alive. Israel agreed.

Shortly after midnight on the morning of Sunday, October 28, at a marker designating Kilometer 101 on the road between Cairo and Suez, Egypt's Lieutenant General Abdel Gamasy and Israel's Major General Aharon Yariv approached each other, offered awkward salutes, and then shook hands. Kilometer 101 was destined to become, so to speak, a milestone. The first direct peace talks between Israeli and Arab representatives in the quarter century since Israel had gained its independence had begun.

Henceforth, negotiations would replace armed conflict in the Arab-Israeli dispute. It was, for Kissinger, a major diplomatic success. His strategy, which had seemed foolhardy during the war, had produced just what he had desired: a military stalemate that would require intricate negotiations. The Soviets had lost their influence, and America's historic difficulty in forging ties with Arab nations had been overcome.

Although Israel had nominally won on the battlefield, it became clear that its military supremacy could no longer guarantee its safety. Nor would it ever again be America's sole or even primary client in the region.

Likewise, although Egypt and Syria had nominally lost militarily, they had won politically. They had held their own and avoided humiliation as they upset a status quo that they could not abide. The sense of Arab decline and impotence, which in some ways had been manifest for five centuries, began to lift. Negotiations for the return of at least some of the territories Israel had captured in 1967 were now inevitable.[16]

As for détente, the October 1973 war and nuclear alert illustrated both its limits and strengths. In a press conference a month later, Kissinger said that détente had "played a role in settling the crisis though it had not yet been firm enough to prevent the crisis." James Schlesinger, a skeptic about détente, publicly said much the same thing. "To work out in collaboration with the Soviets the arrangement for two cease-fires is, I think, a tribute to the success of détente," he told a press conference.

One component of détente, as defined in the principles signed at the 1972 Moscow summit, was that neither side would maneuver "to obtain unilateral advantage at the expense of the other." Nobody should have taken such a pledge very seriously, but to the extent that such maneuvering occurred during the October War, it was mainly by the Americans, and rather successfully. As Kissinger undiplomatically admitted in his memoirs: "There was a growing debate over détente, a mounting clamor that in some undefinable way we were being gulled by the Soviets. The opposite was true; our policy to reduce and where possible eliminate Soviet influence in the Middle East was in fact making progress under the cover of détente."[17]

The reason that Senator Jackson and other strong supporters of Israel were uncomfortable about détente was *not* that they believed that Soviet-American cooperation was illusory. Exactly the contrary:

they were worried that détente could become all too real, and that it would come at Israel's expense. The reduction of tensions between Moscow and Washington made it more likely that Israel would be pressured to make concessions.

For Kissinger, the triumph of October 1973 was that he was able to maintain good relations with the Soviets while simultaneously reducing their influence in the Middle East. The fact that he had made it through the war—and even the one-night nuclear alert—without doing lasting damage to détente exhilarated Kissinger, and rightly.

On the day when the Egyptian and Israeli generals were shaking hands for the first time, the Soviet ambassador to the U.N., Yakov Malik, worked himself into a dither about a minor glitch that had long been solved. By then, Kissinger was bubbling in triumph. "You tell Malik to hold his water or I will send him to Siberia," he said to John Scali, who had become the American ambassador at the U.N. "I know Brezhnev better than he does. Ask him if he's ever been kissed on the mouth by Brezhnev. I have."

THE ROAD TO GENEVA, DECEMBER 1973

In all of his years of world travel, Henry Kissinger had never set foot in an Arab nation. That changed with a four-day, five-nation swing in November 1973. After paying courtesy calls in Morocco and Tunisia, where he proved remarkably clumsy in his first attempts at reviewing honor guards, he headed to a meeting in Egypt with President Anwar Sadat that would determine the success of his Middle East strategy.

That strategy was a brilliant but risky one. If Kissinger could pull it off, it promised to transform alliances in the Middle East to America's advantage as profoundly as his China trip and the policy of détente had altered the strategic balance. If it failed, there could be recriminations in Israel, the radicalization of the Arab states, an increased chance of war, and the breakdown of cooperation with Moscow.

At the outset, the strategy had five major components:

• Instead of dickering over getting Israel back to the October 22 cease-fire line, he hoped to convince it and Egypt to move directly to a more ambitious "disengagement" agreement that would pull all Israeli troops back from the Suez Canal.

• To fulfill the cease-fire provision that called for talks among the parties "under Soviet and American auspices," and to keep Moscow at bay, he would convene a peace conference in Geneva in December. This would have the added advantage of establishing a precedent for direct political-level talks between Israel and the Arabs. But the conference would be just for show, and it would not be allowed to interfere with his personal designs as a peacemaker.

• He would establish the principle that only the U.S.—and not the Soviet Union or the spineless European allies—held the key to peace. Only by dealing through Washington could the Arabs get back any of their land. "Our strategy has to be that when the Soviet Union, the British, and the French press, we stall—so all of them know only we can deliver," he explained to Defense Secretary Schlesinger and other top officials at an informal lunch. "All the Arabs are coming to us."

• Instead of seeking a comprehensive solution to all aspects of the Arab-Israeli dispute, there would be a "step-by-step" process to negotiate small-scale Israeli withdrawal agreements on a bilateral basis, first with Egypt, then Syria, and then perhaps Jordan. Fundamental issues—such as the Palestinian problem, Israel's final borders, the status of Jerusalem—would be deferred in favor of manageable, concrete accords.

• The U.S. (i.e., Kissinger) would mediate these bilateral negotiations without Soviet involvement, thus further reducing Moscow's influence in the region.

Kissinger approached his meeting with President Sadat, whom he had never met and tended to view as a clown, with more than his usual trepidation and fingernail biting. He was even worried about his own safety. His parents had advised him against the trip, he confided to Egyptian foreign minister Ismail Fahmy. (When Fahmy assured him that he would be able to walk the streets of Cairo with no one noticing him, that prospect also seemed to disconcert him, Fahmy half-jokingly recalls.) In addition, he had never dealt with an Arab leader and had no feel for how to handle one.

It was, indeed, an incongruous pairing that occurred on the balcony of the Tahra Palace in suburban Cairo on November 7: representing America to the Arab world was a plump, German-born Jew wearing an ill-fitting, rumpled blue suit; greeting him as if a long-lost friend was a tall, erect, swarthy former terrorist, peasant-born but aristocratic in bearing, wearing a crisply pressed khaki tunic with a Saville Row cashmere coat draped over his shoulders. Each was quickly and lastingly charmed.

Kissinger discovered that flattery is a universal language. Tell me, he asked Sadat, how did you achieve "such stunning surprise" with your attack on Israel? Smiling and puffing on his pipe, growing more animated as he went along, Sadat recounted how he had pulled it off. When he finished, they talked about peace in conceptual terms, "as a psychological, not a diplomatic problem," Kissinger later recalled.

But such reveries could not continue forever. Finally, Sadat abruptly brought matters back to earth. "And what about my Third Army?" he asked. "What about the October 22 line?"

There were two options, Kissinger told him. Egypt and the U.S. could expend all their energies trying to force Israel to move back to the cease-fire line. Or, with the same amount of effort but a little bit more patience, they might be able to arrange a genuine disengagement of forces that would move Israel back from the Suez Canal. In the meantime, arrangements could be made to get a steady supply of non-military material to the Third Army. Sadat could choose, Kissinger said. He would do his best either way.

Sadat sat in his gilded armchair, brooding silently. He did not haggle or try to wheedle some concessions. Instead, after two or three minutes, he said that he would be willing to go for a full-fledged disengagement, as Kissinger preferred, rather than insisting on redressing the Israeli cease-fire violations that had ensnared his Third Army. In addition, he would begin the process of restoring full diplomatic relations with the U.S.

With this sweeping gesture, Sadat moved Egypt from a reliance on Moscow to a reliance on Washington, and he was in effect putting aside not only the Third Army issue but also Egypt's strategy of seeking a comprehensive peace. In doing so, he paved the way for Kissinger's step-by-step approach, which became the basis for his shuttle diplomacy.

It was typical of Sadat: from that morning when he launched a new era of Middle East diplomacy, to the day four years later when he brought that process to a climax by deciding to go to Jerusalem, he was a master at making bold strokes that could serve his national interest. "Wise statesmen know they will be measured by the historical process they set in motion, not by the debating points they score," Kissinger later wrote of him.

Kissinger was exultant. Joe Sisco and Hafiz Ismail, who had been sitting on the lawn, were summoned over. "We will call this the Sisco Plan," said Sadat.

"If it fails," replied Kissinger with a smile, "we will call it the Sisco Plan. If it succeeds, we will call it the Kissinger Plan."

When the journalists were allowed in, one asked the Egyptian president if this meant the United States would curtail its airlift to Israel. "You should ask this question of Dr. Kissinger," said Sadat.

"Luckily, I didn't hear it," said Kissinger.

"I'd be happy to rephrase the question," said the reporter.

"And I'd be happy," replied Kissinger, "to rephrase my answer."[18]

There was still one hitch: in what was becoming a pattern, Kissinger had given short shrift to the ally on whose behalf he was nominally negotiating. Instead of consulting with Israel, or going there personally to present the deal, he sent aides Sisco and Hal Saunders.

Golda Meir and her cabinet, however, were not ready to accept his plan for negotiations. Sadat might feel that the safety of his nation required bold strokes; but Israelis, understandably, felt that their nation's safety required constant, excruciating vigilance.

In what was also becoming a pattern, Kissinger's penchant for diplomatic ambiguity—creatively fudging issues, as he had done during the Vietnam negotiations—ran afoul of the Israeli desire to pin down each distinction with a hairsplitting rigor that would dazzle a Talmudic scholar. For example, Kissinger had arranged for there to be U.N. checkpoints along the road to the encircled Third Army; Israel wanted it to be clear that it still "controlled" the road. This and other matters were finally included by Sisco and Saunders in a private "Memorandum of Understanding" with the Israelis.

These private memoranda of understanding between the U.S. and Israel that accompanied any peace plan were to become standard, and sometimes they would end up being more important than the accords they accompanied. There was one problem with them: given the Casbah atmosphere of the Middle East, and the hothouse of Israeli politics, there was no chance of keeping them secret. So the side deals and "interpretations" that Kissinger and his men cut with the Israelis kept becoming public.

In the meantime, the direct talks at Kilometer 101 were going better than Kissinger had imagined, disquietingly better. The problem Kissinger faced, it turned out, was not from the danger of disagreements there, but from the danger of a serious agreement, one that he would not control or get credit for. Israeli general Yariv and Egyptian general Gamasy, sitting in that isolated tent in the desert, began to disprove the maxim that military men do not know how to make peace. Once they cleared up the rules of the road for the convoys to the Third Army, they turned to more ambitious proposals for a full-scale separation of forces.

For Israel, it was a welcome chance to prove what it could negotiate on its own, freed from American tutelage. For Egypt, it was an opportunity to speed up an accord that would free the Third Army. For the two generals, the quips they exchanged in the desert about their chances of winning the next Nobel Peace Prize were not totally in jest.

The official positions of each government were, literally, miles apart. But each general was given permission to put informal proposals on the table. Israel's Yariv suggested that his country's troops would leave the western side of the canal and pull back up to twelve kilometers if Egypt would agree to create a semi-demilitarized zone for thirty kilometers on both sides of the canal. Egypt's Gamasy countered with a plan that would make the Israelis pull back farther, reduce the size of the restricted zone, put a U.N. buffer between them, and set up a timetable for future Israeli withdrawals from the Sinai.

Although still far from an agreement, the two generals were marching toward the type of disengagement accord that Kissinger hoped to negotiate himself. Rather than cheering them on, however, he began maneuvering to make them stop.

As was often the case, his motives were a mix of valid policy concerns and personal vanity. If a disengagement framework was reached before the December 18 opening of the Geneva Conference, he feared, the negotiations there would have to begin with more contentious issues. In addition, the chance to serve as the indispensable mediator was America's ticket to increased influence in the region. On a more personal level, Kissinger quite simply liked to control important negotiations himself and, not incidentally, garner the glory and potential peace prizes that came with them.

"What is Yariv selling there?" Kissinger demanded of Ambassador Dinitz. "Tell him to stop. . . . Suppose Yariv comes out a great hero on disengagement. What do you discuss on December 18?"

At Kissinger's behest, both Sadat and Meir reined in their generals at the Kilometer 101 talks. The Israeli ambassador, although a Kissinger partisan, felt that it was largely a matter of ego. "Kissinger's view was that if any concessions were to be made, they should be made by him," Dinitz recalled. "He was very upset when he found that things were actually being settled by the generals at Kilometer 101. We had to make them stop. Ego was a weakness of his. But it was also the source of his greatness."[19]

Back in Washington, President Nixon was consumed by his own form of jealousy. Kissinger was darting around the world garnering headlines (with hardly a mention of the president's name in his pronouncements) and a Nobel Prize while Nixon was being hammered daily by Watergate. To prove he was in charge, and to pull Kissinger down a peg, Nixon abruptly summoned Soviet ambassador Dobrynin to the White House in early December, just after Kissinger had left for the Middle East on a trip designed to finalize plans for the Geneva Conference. Haig and Scowcroft tried to block the meeting, but Nixon was undeterred. He wanted to discuss the Middle East with Dobrynin, he told them. And he wanted it to be private. No one else would be there. The meeting lasted about half an hour.

Scowcroft knew that Kissinger would be beside himself when he found out that Nixon was meddling in Middle East diplomacy—and worse yet, doing so by bringing the Soviets into the act. "I will see if Haig can find out what was discussed and will, of course, pass it immediately to you," Scowcroft said in his cable to Kissinger in Egypt. "While I know this is an upsetting development, it could have been worse."

"That last sentence was a tribute to Scowcroft's subtlety and finesse," Kissinger later wrote. "I did not view the meeting so objectively." The cables from Kissinger conveying his rage spewed back to Washington, one following the other throughout a sleepless night. In reply, Scowcroft explained how it could in fact have been worse: Nixon had then tried to call in the Saudi ambassador, but Haig was able to head it off. "The sun dawned over Cairo before I subsided," Kissinger recalled.[20]

Kissinger's only failure in bringing the December Geneva Conference together was that he was unable to secure the participation of Syria. President Hafiz al-Assad, who had burned into his soul the historic injustices that centuries of foreigners had wrought on his land, was a suspicious man. When Kissinger came to Damascus, he found the Syrian president seated beneath a grand oil painting of Saladin crushing the last of the Christian Crusaders.

Kissinger tried both humor and flattery. Aware that Assad was trying to learn English, Kissinger offered to help, adding, "You'll be the first Arab leader to speak English with a German accent." Assuming that the Syrians would share the fascination that other Arabs showed about his success with women, Kissinger made a few lecherous jokes. He also poked fun at Sisco, saying that he had brought him along out of a fear he would lead a coup against him if left in Washington. That finally drew a laugh from Assad, who had assumed power in a coup after Syria's ill-fated war on behalf of the PLO in Jordan in 1970.

When Kissinger raised the Geneva Conference, Assad indicated that there should first be some progress in removing Israeli forces from his territory. "Before Geneva convenes there ought to be a disengagement agreement," he said.

"Look," Kissinger said, "it took me four years to settle the Vietnam War."

Instead of wrestling with such larger issues, Kissinger sought to engage Assad in the details of organizing the Geneva conference. How should the letter of invitation be worded? How quickly could it begin? How should the reference to the Palestinians be worded in the letter of invitation?

Suddenly Assad seemed more agreeable. If a delay of a few days was necessary, that was fine with him. Other problems with the invitation seemed minor, and he would be pleased to defer to Sadat. "What about the language regarding 'other participants'?" Kissinger asked, referring to the euphemism being used for the Palestinians.

"Anything in that letter that you and President Sadat agree upon is agreeable to me," Assad said.

Kissinger began to believe that Assad's reputation for intractability was overblown. Was there anything in the letter that he objected to?

Well, yes, one part of the letter "is not accurate," Assad replied.

What was that? Kissinger inquired.

"It says Syria has agreed to attend the conference," Assad dryly noted. "I have not agreed."[21]

At first, Kissinger was shocked. He suddenly realized that the reason Assad seemed so nonchalant about the wording of the invitation to Geneva was that he did not plan to accept it.

Yet Kissinger quickly concluded that Syria's refusal to attend the Geneva Conference was a blessing, for it reduced the chance of an immediate blowup. "Not to put too fine a point on it," Kissinger recalled, "we were better off without Syria."

His put-down in Damascus even gave him something to joke about with the Israelis when he returned there. He would mimic Assad and portray him as the great exemplar of flexibility until—like a rabbit punch—he mentioned his intention not to attend. He worked it up into quite a routine, almost as good as the parody of staying up until dawn haggling with Golda Meir—"Miss Israel," he called her—that he later performed for Sadat.

When the Geneva Conference convened on December 21, with one empty chair, Kissinger's words were worthy of the moment. "The fate of Arabs and Jews has been inextricably linked throughout their history, rising and falling together," he said. In recent centuries the Jews have been dispersed and the Arabs oppressed by colonizers. But for the last twenty-five years they have had the chance to determine their own fate. "Thus, in the land of Arabs and Jews, where the reality of mistrust and hate so tragically contradicts the spiritual message which originates there, it is essential for the voice of reconciliation to be heard."[22]

The conference was not important for what happened there; nothing did. What mattered was the process of getting it assembled so that it would put a grand imprimatur on the first face-to-face peace negotiations at the political level between the Arabs and Israel since 1948. After that, Kissinger's main challenge was to keep the conference quiescent so that he could proceed, without Soviet involvement, along his step-by-step course of bilateral talks. Within months, every state in the region would regard America as the paramount force there, and Kissinger would become the personification—and to a large degree the cause—of that heightened influence.

TWENTY-FOUR

THE SHUTTLE

Step by Step Through Israel, Egypt, and Syria

He preferred the subtle maneuver to the frontal attack, while his rationalism frequently made him mistake a well-phrased manifesto for an accomplished action.—KISSINGER *on Metternich,* A WORLD RESTORED, *1957*

THE FIRST ISRAELI-EGYPTIAN SHUTTLE: JANUARY 1974

Shuttle diplomacy was born unplanned. When Israeli defense minister Moshe Dayan arrived in Washington at the beginning of January 1974, a month after the Geneva Conference's symbolic opening session, he brought a new troop disengagement proposal. Appealing both to Kissinger's instincts and to his ego, Dayan suggested that the secretary should personally present the plan to Sadat.

So off Kissinger went to Aswan, Sadat's winter residence, where the Egyptian president offered a suggestion with similar appeal: instead of now referring the matter to the Geneva Conference working group, why not push for a quick agreement by staying in the Middle East and mediating the details himself? After a foray to Jerusalem and back, a new style of diplomacy was born. "Welcome aboard the Egyptian-Israeli shuttle!" shouted the effervescent Joseph Sisco as the next trip began.[1]

Over the next two years, Kissinger would make eleven visits to the Middle East for four major rounds of negotiations. The first round, in January 1974, would lead to a military disengagement on the Egyptian front involving a pullback of Israeli forces from the Suez Canal. Then came the Syrian disengagement accord of May 1974, involving a marathon thirty-four-day, 24,230-mile trip during which Kissinger visited Jerusalem sixteen times, Damascus fifteen times, and six other countries in between. The only failure came in March 1975 when the second Egyptian-Israeli talks broke down. But Kissinger was successful in salvaging them that August, when Israel agreed to further withdrawals in the Sinai Peninsula.

Kissinger's decision to conduct the first Sinai disengagement talks on his own, rather than let the matter be handled in Geneva, served to cut the Soviets out of the action. In addition, Kissinger admits that "no doubt there was a touch of vanity involved." His reluctance to give up control over a diplomatic initiative was generally twofold: his belief that someone else could not possibly do it just as well, and, almost as worrying, his fear that someone else might possibly do it just as well.

Thus, he was "horror-struck," as he put it, to discover in January 1974 that the ideas suggested to him privately by Dayan had also been floated by the Israeli delegate to the Geneva Convention. Just as he had stopped the two generals at Kilometer 101 from proceeding on their own toward a disengagement accord, Kissinger pressed Israel to withdraw its proposals made in the Geneva forum. Even though he was now secretary of state, and thus in charge of the front channel as well as the back one, Kissinger's aversion to the use of official channels remained strong.

The heart of the Dayan plan was that Israel would withdraw all of its troops to a line about twenty kilometers east of the Suez Canal. There would be a U.N. buffer zone of about ten kilometers, and there would be limits on the numbers of troops, tanks, and missiles in the area extending about forty kilometers behind each line. Other provisions included an end to belligerency and the reopening of the Suez Canal.

Sadat would never accept this outright because, among other reasons, the forty-kilometer restricted zone would extend well into the main (non-Sinai) part of Egypt. But it was a good basis for discussion. As Sadat realized (far better than his generals or the Israeli cabinet), the details were pretty much beside the point. If the agreement led to a continued peace process, the locations of the lines at this first stage would soon be minor footnotes; if not, then the ensuing hostilities would make the proposed map moot. The important thing was that, if accomplished, the disengagement accord would mark the first time since 1956 that Israel had withdrawn from significant territory it had captured.

Therefore Sadat, to Kissinger's surprise, readily accepted that the Israeli forward line could be where Dayan proposed. All he asked was that the limited-forces zone plan be simplified. Neither nation, he suggested, should deploy missiles or artillery that could hit the other side's main forces. Dayan's plan that only two Egyptian battalions could stay on the eastern side of the canal, Sadat claimed, was an insult to his military that had captured that territory. He wanted ten battalions and some tanks. But in a gesture of trust toward the emissary of a nation that until recently had been an enemy, Sadat told Kissinger to seek the best possible numbers he could. Egypt would accept whatever he could get out of Israel.

In Jerusalem, Kissinger found the negotiators ready to haggle over the number of divisions that Egypt could keep on the eastern side of the canal. "On the number of battalions," Yigal Allon told him, "we had an argument among ourselves because when we said two or three battalions, we meant it. If you can settle it on five or six, you will be awarded the Ben-Gurion prize." Remarkably, both Allon and Sadat were speaking to Kissinger as if he were working on behalf of their respective sides.

"Six is impossible," Kissinger answered.

"If they stick to ten, and we stick to six, maybe eight," said Allon.

Kissinger convinced him that it was foolish to press the lower number in anticipation of a later compromise. If the Israelis could accept eight, they should say so right away. "If it takes too long," Kissinger warned, "his [Sadat's] advisers will turn against it." Kissinger was given the authority to accept eight battalions if necessary when he returned to Cairo the next day.

Sadat accepted that number. He was reluctant, however, to sign an accord with Israel, a nation Egypt did not recognize, that contained pledges about where Egypt would deploy its troops and when it would reopen the Suez Canal. So Kissinger worked out an idea, which he credited to Sadat, for putting all such arrangements in side letters that Egypt and Israel would present to the U.S. The U.S. could then produce letters offering these assurances to the other side. Though complex, it worked smoothly.

By Wednesday, January 16, it was becoming clear from the celebratory stories being generated on his plane that Kissinger was nearing success. Back at the White House, Nixon, besieged by Watergate and craving some glory, was feeling as cut out of the action as Andrei Gromyko. So he had both Haig and Scowcroft separately send cables to Kissinger telling him to come home before any agreement was reached. This would allow Nixon to make a public display of giving him some presidential instructions before he concluded the accord and thus permit the president to take some of the credit.

Kissinger, as might be expected, would have none of this. After waiting a day, he sent back word that leaving the region might "unravel the whole delicate fabric."

Instead Kissinger defied Nixon's orders and brought the nearly final agreement back to Sadat, who spontaneously decided to dictate the first direct message ever from the head of modern-day Egypt to Israel. Its content was a rather extraordinary endorsement of Kissinger's personal role. "When I talk of peace now, I mean it," Sadat declared in his letter to Golda Meir. "We never have had contact before. We now have the services of Dr. Kissinger. Let us use him and talk to each other through him."

Golda Meir, suffering from severe shingles, had been homebound all week. When Kissinger arrived in Israel, there was a massive snowfall, the most in decades. With the help of Israeli army vehicles, he was able to make it to her house with the Sadat letter, which he read her aloud.

"It is a good thing," she said laconically. "Why is he doing this?" Later that day, she composed her own letter. "I am deeply conscious of the significance of a message received by the Prime Minister of Israel from the President of Egypt," she began. After professing her desire for peace, she also ended with an encomium to Kissinger. "It is indeed extremely fortunate that we have Dr. Kissinger who we both trust and who is prepared to give of his wisdom and talents in the cause of peace."

The final touches of the disengagement accord were quickly accepted, and it was signed by the military chiefs of Egypt and Israel at Kilometer 101. Kissinger was by then back at Sadat's summer home in Aswan, and Sadat had just finished reading Golda Meir's letter when an aide came in with the news that the signing had occurred. "I am taking off my military uniform," Sadat declared. "I never expect to wear it again except for ceremonial occasions. Tell her that is the answer to her letter."

Nixon announced the agreements that afternoon in the White House pressroom, providing him a joyous albeit brief respite from his domestic travails. Most of the glory, however, went to Kissinger: a Harris poll found that 85 percent of Americans felt he was doing a good job, the highest approval rating for anyone in government since the polls were begun. He was portrayed on the front page of two Israeli papers as an angel of peace, there were mass celebrations in Egypt, and in Syria the public resentment was transformed into a private desire to be next on Kissinger's agenda.

Only from Moscow did denunciations flow. The U.S., Brezhnev complained in a formal letter to Nixon, was ignoring previous understandings that it would work jointly with the Soviets in dealing with the Middle East. To Kissinger, that plaintive criticism was one of the best compliments he could have received. At the core of his foreign policy was the goal of reducing Soviet influence around the world, and now he was proving that he could do so with dogged diplomacy.[2]

KISSINGER'S NEGOTIATING STYLE: AN OVERVIEW

On all of his shuttle missions, Kissinger used the Boeing 707 that had served as Lyndon Johnson's vice-presidential plane. Its relics included a mammoth kidney-shaped conference table and chair that LBJ had installed in the middle compartment. Each was hydraulically movable into a variety of positions; Kissinger, who did not have a knack for things mechanical, occasionally found his ample girth endangered as he got the chair and table moving in opposite directions by mistake.

The plane also had a couch-and-shower area for Kissinger, a staff area where Joe Sisco held sway, and a rear seating compartment that usually carried fourteen journalists. One of the stewards could do an uncanny imitation of Kissinger, and he would sometimes sneak up behind Larry Eagleburger and rumble some absurd order that caused the rather unsprightly aide to leap in terror. Up to thirty-five Secret Service agents were also along, and two bulletproof limousines were leapfrogged in front of them at every stop by Military Air Command transports.

As on a campaign plane, a ship-of-fools camaraderie developed on Kissinger's jet, especially among the regular journalists. NBC's Richard Valeriani had buttons printed up proclaiming "Free the Kissinger 14," who generally included, besides himself, ABC's Ted Koppel, CBS's Bernard or Marvin Kalb, the *Washington Post's* Marilyn Berger, the *New York Times's* Bernard Gwertzman, *Time's* Jerrold Schecter, and *Newsweek's* Bruce van Voorst. On most legs, Kissinger invited the press to his conference room or wandered to expropriate some of the meat loaf being served in the rear compartments. There, thinly disguised as "a senior official," he would give background briefings on the course of the negotiations. The briefings, especially when read in retrospect, seem designed to dazzle with brilliant conceptualizing rather than to illuminate with useful facts.

Before he became involved in the bazaar of the Middle East, Kissinger's preferred bargaining philosophy had been to have a desired outcome in mind before he began groping for ways to get there. "In negotiations," he said at a background briefing in 1973, "if you put down specific proposals before you know where you're going, it's almost suicidal." He loved the way the Chinese negotiated: they first determined a reasonable solution that accommodated each side's basic principles, then they would get there in one jump. Concessions were made voluntarily, rather than in response to pressure, thus inviting reciprocity.

On the surface, Kissinger's step-by-step method during the Arab-Israeli shuttles seemed contrary to this philosophy. It often degenerated into a kilometer-by-kilometer method, with each side struggling over the most minor concessions rather than making a graceful leap to a reasonable solution.

But step-by-step was actually more than just a method: it was the foundation for the outcome Kissinger preferred. He saw no need, or opportunity, to reach a comprehensive Middle East agreement solving such fundamental issues as the Palestinian question; instead, he felt that the best solution was coaxing Israel to withdraw from captured lands while enticing the Arabs to accept Israel and its right to secure borders. The magic about the step-by-step approach was that this outcome was implicit from the very start.

By personalizing his diplomacy in the Middle East, Kissinger was able to make use of the intangible goodwill that comes from what passes for friendships among statesmen. "He created a kind of personal relationship," said former Israeli defense minister Yitzhak Rabin, "a kind of intensive relationship that forced people in a way to be committed to him."[3]

The role of such personal factors in foreign affairs—as opposed to colder calculations of national interests—is ignored by many historians, including by Kissinger during his academic years. Yet the pressures and inducements that are created by personal bonds of trust can become part of the atmosphere in a high-pressure negotiating frenzy such as a shuttle mission.

This is especially true in the Middle East. The mentality that governs bargaining in the Arab world involves more than just a haggle over price. At a certain point before a deal is struck, "there must develop as well a personal bond between buyer and seller—a covenant of confidence and trust that excites the sentiment of friendship," according to Edward Sheehan, a Middle East scholar. Kissinger loved to excite the sentiment of friendship, particularly when it was accompanied by bargaining. "He was, after all, a Semite," noted Sheehan.[4]

The most significant personal bond he forged was the least predictable: with Anwar Sadat of Egypt. Kissinger often referred to Sadat, in reverential tones, as "a prophet." No other statesman he dealt with, other than Zhou Enlai, is accorded anything near this respect in Kissinger's mind, and none elicited the same affection.

As Kissinger left Aswan at the outset of his first shuttle in January 1974, Sadat took Kissinger to a tropical garden by his villa and beneath a mango tree, kissed him. "You are not only my friend," he said. "You are my brother." (A rather startled Kissinger subsequently told his press corps that "the reason the Israelis don't get better treatment is because they don't kiss me.")

Kissinger's relationship with Golda Meir, on the other hand, was far more tormented, like that between a strong-willed Jewish mother and a successful but ungrateful grown son. "Does Golda hate me?" Kissinger would frequently ask Ambassador Dinitz and others. No, they would reassure him, but they agreed that the relationship was stormy.

Obstinate, explosive, and unwaveringly committed to the safety of her country, Meir spent much of their time together lecturing Kissinger, a habit he found less than endearing and that led him to refer to her as "that preposterous woman." When Meir flew to Washington after the October 1973 war, she at first refused to see Kissinger, then he refused to see her. Finally they met that night and stayed up past one A.M. talking.

Despite her ability to frustrate and madden him, Kissinger had a reserve of affection for Golda Meir because he understood the intensity of her feelings for the safety of every one of her citizens and because he shared her emotional dedication to the survival of Israel. "What do you expect from me?" she asked during one long conversation when he was pressuring her to be, in effect, more like Sadat. "I was born in the last century."

"The nineteenth century is my specialty," Kissinger replied.

Meir's last official act as prime minister in 1974 was to throw a reception for Kissinger. There, amid great laughter, he gave her a big kiss, bigger than he had ever given or gotten from Sadat. "I never knew," she said, "that you kissed women."

Kissinger had a closer, though likewise often strained, relationship with Yigal Allon, the deputy prime minister and chief Israeli negotiator. Allon had been in Kissinger's International Seminar at

Harvard, and although Kissinger found him somewhat unreflective, he developed a deep affection for him. In 1959, when Kissinger went to Israel to talk at a seminar, he stayed with Allon at his kibbutz on the Sea of Galilee. One evening, as they were watching the boats go out, Allon explained why the Israeli fishermen had to cast so close to the Syrian shore. "The fish congregate there," Allon said, "because that's where the Jordan River flows in. Unlike humans, fish like to swim against the stream."

"Thank God all humans are not alike," Kissinger responded. "You and I, Yigal, are destined to swim against the stream." Perhaps. At the very least, they were destined to deal with the area on the far side of that lake, which was known as the Golan Heights.

With Ismail Fahmy, the Egyptian foreign minister, Kissinger tried hard but failed to form the rapport he had with Sadat. "We have only met twice, but I already feel we have known each other for a long time," Kissinger told Fahmy the day after he arrived in Washington in the wake of the October 1973 war. "I have known Abba Eban for six years and I still call him Mr. Minister. In your case, I feel we can call each other by our first names. May I call you Ismail?"

Fahmy acquiesced, but he became neither a friend nor a fan. "Pretending to be the peacemaker and the go-between, he was in fact always acting on behalf of Israel," he later wrote of Kissinger. "That is not surprising considering that he is a Jew himself and that, as he personally told me, his parents were 'extremist, fanatic Jews.' "[5]

What provoked Fahmy's disdain was that he found Kissinger to be two-faced. "He always tried to hide his bias by cursing the Israelis and constantly making funny and unflattering remarks about the Israeli leaders to convince us that he was on our side," he says. "Unfortunately, his rather obvious ruses were fairly effective with Sadat."

This question of Kissinger's duplicity, a charge leveled by many who dealt with him, is a tricky one. Shadings of the truth, sometimes up to and crossing the line of deceit, are a fact of diplomatic life, and Kissinger was engaged in no crusade to upgrade the morality of foreign policy. The line between diplomacy and duplicity, like that between charm and hypocrisy, is a fine one.

Kissinger was a very clever man, sometimes to a fault. As such, he often cast his words, acts, jokes, and style to appeal to his interlocutors of the moment. As he described the landscape they faced, he would stress to one side the hills and to the other the valleys. In order to insinuate himself, he would regale each side with tales and horror stories about the other. In Syria, he sarcastically referred to Golda Meir as "Miss Israel." In Israel, he made crude jokes about Assad and mimicked King Faisal of Saudi Arabia giving his lecture about the connection between communism and Judaism.

Yet Kissinger's cleverness also meant that he was careful to avoid outright duplicity and double-dealing; a study of his words—even the transcripts of relatively unguarded conversations—shows him phrasing his remarks carefully so as not to contradict directly what he was telling someone else. He would withhold information and even allow a listener to be misled—which comes close to the definition of deceit. But he seldom resorted to unadorned lying in his negotiating efforts. "I may have kept things secret," he later said, "but that's not the same as being deceitful."

In discussing deviousness in foreign policy, Kissinger once wrote that "I tended to share Metternich's view that in a negotiation the perfectly straightforward person was the most difficult to deal with." Judging from Metternich's actions, it is not clear that he actually held this view. Nor is it clear that Kissinger did. "Kissinger had a Metternichian system of telling only half the truth," said Israel's Yitzhak Rabin. "He didn't lie. He would have lost credibility. He didn't tell the whole truth."

"If you didn't listen word by word, you could be carried away by what he said," according to Shimon Peres, who later became Israel's prime minister. "But if you listened word by word, he wasn't lying." This did not, however, make Kissinger honest in Peres's eyes. He once privately told Rabin, "With due respect to Kissinger, he is the most devious man I've ever met."

When Peres was defense minister in 1974, he regaled his colleagues with a scathing prediction about an upcoming trip that Yigal Allon was taking to Washington:

> I'll tell you how it will go. Yigal arrives in America; Kissinger comes and tells him, "We've got to work out a joint American-Israeli strategy for the next stage." Yigal is delighted. Fahmy arrives; Kissinger tells him the same thing about American-Egyptian strategy. Fahmy is pleased. Each of them thinks Kissinger is on his side. Afterward there is a leak in an Israeli newspaper harmful to Kissinger. He calls in Simcha Dinitz and says in an offended tone, "I am your best friend." Then we apologize.

The wary humor Israelis felt about Kissinger's style was reflected in an old matchmaking joke that was told about him at the time. Kissinger decides to play matchmaker and informs a poor peasant that he has found the perfect wife for his son. "But I never meddle in my son's affairs," says the peasant.

"Ah, but the girl is the daughter of Lord Rothschild," says Kissinger.

"Well, in that case . . ."

Then Kissinger goes to Lord Rothschild. "I have the perfect husband for your daughter," he says.

"But she's too young," Lord Rothschild protests.

"Ah, but the boy is a vice president of the World Bank."

"Well, in that case . . ."

Then Kissinger goes to the president of the World Bank, saying, "Have I got a vice president for you."

"But we don't need another one."

"Ah," says Kissinger, "but he is the son-in-law of Lord Rothschild."

At a seminar in Jerusalem in March 1974, Professor Hans Morgenthau, a leading exponent of the "realist" approach to foreign policy, discussed the drawbacks of what he charged was Kissinger's devious style. "Henry has a magnificent gift, which I didn't expect of him, having known him for twenty years, to transform himself in every capital into a friend and promoter of the particular country where he happens to be," he said. "There is a danger in such a diplomacy, which works in the beginning, but doesn't work where the governments have good relations and talk to one another."

James Schlesinger, Kissinger's sometimes antagonist during those years, was the most scathing when making such charges. He explained it in terms of Kissinger's background. "Henry's style of deception is less condemned in Europe than it is here," Schlesinger said. "Being excessively manipulative does not go over well in Anglo-Saxon countries.

"What Henry didn't realize is that Arab leaders compare tales," Schlesinger added. In fact, Kissinger did realize this, at least intellectually. In describing the downside of deviousness during one of his very first shuttle backgrounders, he told reporters: "Eventually the two sides will get together and compare notes. If they find out they've been told different things, you're dead."

Despite this understanding, Kissinger came across as a chameleon—emphasizing different shadings to different listeners and attempting to ingratiate himself to one person by disparaging another. It was more than a negotiating tactic; it was a character flaw. His style with the Arabs and Israelis was not all that different from his style within the White House or at Washington dinner parties. In order to create a sense of intimacy, to hornswoggle as well as to charm, he shared denigrating confidences about other people.

Intellectually he realized that people compared notes. But instinctively he never understood that swapping tales about encounters with Kissinger—and perhaps exaggerating the loose comments he made—was a prime amusement from Araby to Georgetown. In fact, rather than being a master manipulator, Kissinger seemed quite a maladroit one. If he had been better at it, fewer people would have accused him of it.[6]

Related to Kissinger's tendency to shade his emphasis for each audience was his use of what he called "constructive ambiguity." In the Vietnam negotiations, he had devised murky wording regarding the DMZ and South Vietnamese sovereignty so that both sides could claim what they wanted; in the SALT talks, he left vague the limits on silo size changes and later dropped the word *ballistic* from limits on air missiles so that the Americans and Soviets ended up interpreting the meaning differently. Likewise, on the Middle East, Kissinger tried to fudge many of the theological disputes that stood in the way of practical disengagement accords.

Commenting on Metternich's negotiating style, Talleyrand cited "his marvelous command of words that are vague and void of meaning." Kissinger shared that talent. "Sometimes, the art of diplomacy is to keep the obvious obscured," he once said. The Rogers Plan of 1969, for example, was straightforward and unambiguous; it did not get far.

When a reporter tried to make him clear up the different interpretations that Israel and Egypt had about the Geneva Conference, Kissinger exploded: "For Christ's sake, leave everyone their face-saving formula! If it pleases the Israelis to consider it 'direct' if they are in the same room with Egyptians, and Sadat prefers to call this 'indirect' if somebody else is there, what the hell difference does it make?"

Al-Ahram, an Egyptian newspaper allied with Sadat, objected to this tactic at the outset. "The solution," it wrote, "does not lie in clever diplomatic formulas couched in double meanings which each side can interpret in its own way to suit its purposes." Yet that, as Kissinger would show, was a pretty good description of where the solutions did indeed lie.

For example, a variety of euphemisms were coined for the status of the quasi-peace that Egypt and Israel were agreeing to at each stage. Egypt was not yet ready to declare a full state of "peace" with Israel. During the first disengagement talks, it did not even want to go as far as providing a pledge that a state of "non-belligerency" existed between the two countries. When Kissinger brought to Egypt an Israeli proposal that had five different expressions that implied an end to belligerency, Fahmy erupted. So Kissinger devised some new language that said much the same thing.[7]

•

Unlike previous secretaries of state, who traveled less and delegated more, Kissinger insisted that major department decisions be made by him on the plane. Thus, instead of being run by an undersecretary in Washington, the State Department in effect traveled wherever Kissinger went. On some days more than two hundred cables went back and forth to his plane. At each stop, eight large trunks filled with classified working papers would be moved from the plane to the hotel. The flying circus was dubbed in one *Washington Post* story "the biggest permanent floating foreign policy establishment in history."

Even back when he had worn only one hat as the president's national security adviser, Kissinger's briefcase was considered a black hole. His aides constantly looked for new ruses to get him to deal with the buildup of paper awaiting his approval. In addition to leaving his schedule out on a secretary's desk in a folder labeled "Sonnenfeldt"—which they could be sure he would grab and peruse—aides began putting important decision memos they wanted him to see in folders mislabeled with other titles sure to entice him, such as "Adulatory Cables" and "Scowcroft Conversations with the President."

By the time of the Middle East shuttles, Kissinger was spread even more thinly. He was attempting to be both national security adviser and secretary of state and was wearing what amounted to four hats: the president's personal adviser on foreign policy, the manager of the NSC machinery, the nation's chief globe-trotting negotiator, and the cabinet officer in charge of managing the State Department's sprawling bureaucracy.

Handling all of these responsibilities would have been a tall order even for a great manager, something that Kissinger was not. He hated to delegate, was indecisive and unclear in his orders, had trouble setting priorities for his time, could not keep to a schedule, took out his frustrations on subordinates, and made no effort to conceal his contempt for the bureaucracy. These management shortcomings were exacerbated when he began wandering on open-ended negotiating forays, taking along top officials such as Eagleburger and Lord while leaving behind at the helm such people as Deputy Secretary Kenneth Rush, whom he did not trust to make substantive decisions.

Consequently, although shuttle diplomacy would bring some dramatic successes, a price was paid. Other problems got little of his attention, including such critical matters as the resurgence of war in Vietnam, the swelling resentment of the NATO allies that made a shambles of what Kissinger had declared to be "the Year of Europe," and brewing regional crises such as in Cyprus.

For days at a time, Kissinger would become bogged down in the intricacies of cease-fire arrangements and the details of exactly which hills and passes were in dispute, an endeavor that could have been delegated to a high-profile special envoy with only the major issues left for Kissinger to resolve. But such a sharing of responsibility was alien to Kissinger's character.

Nevertheless, the shuttles were probably, on balance, a good use of Kissinger's talents. His weakness as a manager was matched by his indefatigable resourcefulness as a mediator and his understanding that in diplomacy, as in design, God is in the details.

With great conviction, he would portray to each side, in the most graphic terms, the dire consequences of failure. Each day they dithered, Kissinger would warn the Israelis, the more likely it would be that the PLO would get into the process, that the American public would get fed up, that a war would start that they would have to fight without an American airlift. On the other hand, he would tell Sadat that if war broke out, "the Pentagon will strike at you." The Syrians were given a similar picture of their lack of options other than a settlement; there was no other way to get the Israelis to withdraw. "What are your alternatives?" he would ask each side over and over again.

With the Israelis, whose concessions he needed most, Kissinger was particularly vivid in analyzing the situation in historic terms, conjuring up visions of apocalypse and global isolation if they remained recalcitrant. The negotiators in Jerusalem developed a mock lexicon of Kissinger's pessimism. When he called a course "suicidal," he meant that it was difficult. "Impossible" translated as "unlikely." "Difficult" meant "achievable." And when he said, "I'll see what I can do," it meant, "I've already gotten that concession from them but haven't told you yet."

To this mix he added some conventional forms of pressure and leverage. In the Arab world, he would promise American technological investment. As an implied reward for signing the first disengagement accord, Egypt was given an American nuclear power plant, which Nixon announced on his visit there in June 1974.

The following year, after the Sinai II talks had broken down because of what he saw as Israeli inflexibility, Kissinger told Defense Secretary Schlesinger to slow arms deliveries to Israel. Schlesinger, still fuming over the dispute about the Yom Kippur War, demanded the order in writing. Yigal Allon met with his former teacher at Camp David to complain about the new strictures, but Kissinger denied that any pressure was intended. There would never be, he promised, a connection between diplomatic disagreements and arms shipments.

Allon, who knew full well that this was being said for the record rather than as the truth, was astounded, and furious. But it worked. The next time around, Israel was more compliant.

Kissinger plunged into his sales pitches with the intensity of a veteran rug merchant. "I felt that if he wanted to sell us a car with a wheel missing," said Abba Eban, "he would achieve his purpose by an eloquent and cogent eulogy of the wheels that remained." He seemed to take rejection personally, and he was tireless in his wheedling. Sometimes he appeared to be deliberately using exhaustion as a weapon; with an energy fueled by junk food and a momentum built on the sheer thrill he got from pursuing an agreement, he would hammer away at each side hour after hour, night after night. "I sometimes felt that I had been driven to the point where I would sign anything just for the chance to get some sleep," one Israeli said.

The shuttle process itself became a way to maintain this constant pressure on both sides. The whirlwind of publicity and the jet-powered pace of Kissinger's missions swept up the negotiators on each side and created a momentum that made last-minute breakthroughs more likely. Heightening the intensity was Kissinger's personal reputation as a magician—or perhaps conjurer—in pulling off what were seen as negotiating miracles. This was a self-fulfilling perception. "I don't think anybody else could have done it," said Yitzhak Rabin, who replaced Meir as Israel's prime minister. "Only by using shuttle diplomacy could he get both sides to create the atmosphere that in itself made agreement possible."[8]

In addition, the personal mystique and theatrical show that Kissinger created through his shuttle diplomacy served a purpose at home. He made foreign policy seem exciting and engaging, especially in contrast to the sordidness of domestic politics. Also, in a period of post-Vietnam depression, his shuttle successes served as dramatic demonstrations that America's involvement in foreign affairs could be good for the world. Like the triangular relationship he created with the Soviets and China, this highly visible antidote to the nation's loss of worldly confidence fit in with a fundamental goal of Kissinger's grand design: avoiding the neo-isolationism that would otherwise have seized hold in America in the wake of the Vietnam War.

THE WANDERING JEW

At the end of his visit to Jerusalem in December 1973, Kissinger had broken away from his press corps for a private visit to

Yad Vashem, the memorial to the 6 million Jews who died in the Nazi holocaust. The trip was not at his initiative; Israeli officials ask every visiting statesman to stop there, the better to appreciate what Israel is all about, and he was no exception. Though Kissinger the refugee from Fürth did not need to be taught about the holocaust, some in Israel believed that Kissinger the secretary of state might. "What do Israelis think of me?" he asked Steve Strauss, his favorite masseur at Jerusalem's King David Hotel. "A lot of them," he replied, "think you have forgotten who you are and where you came from."

On the visit to Yad Vashem, Kissinger displayed his emotional ambivalences about his heritage. He went "only reluctantly," an Israeli newspaper reported, and once there walked quickly past the memorial pillars. "When are we getting out of here?" he whispered to American ambassador Kenneth Keating after twenty minutes, glancing at his watch. But his Israeli host, Gideon Hausner, was not eager to make the visit short or pleasant. He told Kissinger that his name figured prominently in Fürth, and he showed him books that listed the names of the thirteen members of his family who were killed.

Kissinger, wearing a yarmulke, began to breathe heavily. He had a cold, he was tired, but he was also, he said later, "heartbroken." As a chilly rain pounded the hillside memorial, a cantor sang the kaddish, the prayer for the dead. Kissinger bowed his head in silence and stayed in that position for a while. One official who accompanied him said he seemed "paralyzed." He was reflecting, Kissinger later recalled, "on my own past, the pitilessness of history, and the human stakes in the exertions of statesmen."[9]

As America's first Jewish secretary of state,* Kissinger was forced to face the role that his religious heritage played in his life. During the first term, he had been kept away from Middle East policy partly because, as Nixon said, "I felt that Kissinger's Jewish background would put him at a disadvantage." More painfully, Nixon's prejudices came out in dark jokes, such as when he had looked around his cabinet after Kissinger gave an opinion on the Middle East and asked, "Now, can we get an American point of view?" As Kissinger later noted, Nixon felt that "Jews formed a powerful cohesive group in American society . . . that they put the interests of Israel above everything else . . . that their control of the media made them dangerous adversaries."[10]

During one private meeting with Egyptian foreign minister

---

* Not counting Judah P. Benjamin, who served as a senator from Louisiana from 1852 to 1861 and then as the secretary of state of the Confederate States of America from 1862 to 1865.

Fahmy, Nixon referred to Kissinger as "my Jew boy." It was a phrase he used often; it even turned up on one of the White House tapes released during the Watergate investigation.

The subject of his religion made Kissinger uncomfortable; he liked to think it irrelevant. "I was born Jewish, but the truth is that has no significance for me," he told a Jewish friend in the early 1970s. "America has given me everything. A home, a chance to study and achieve a high position. I don't know what other Jews expect of me, but I consider myself an American first."

He had not practiced his religion since he returned from the army and entered Harvard. Yet he never rejected Judaism, unlike his former wife, who embraced the Ethical Culture Society, or James Schlesinger, whose family converted to Protestantism.

In fact, Kissinger insisted that his son have a bar mitzvah. David resisted mightily, but the ceremony was something that Kissinger had promised his father, Louis, and a legacy he felt he owed to his grandfather David. In August of 1974, following three days of talks in Washington with Jordan's King Hussein about the chances of forcing Israel to withdraw from the West Bank, Kissinger flew to Boston for the service, which was held in the Brandeis University chapel.[11]

As was often the case, Kissinger's attitude toward his Jewishness was reflected in his humor, much of it directed at the pressure on him from "my co-religionists" to forgive any Israeli sin. At the height of his fury at Jerusalem for violating the October 1973 cease-fire and surrounding Egypt's Third Army, Kissinger grumbled at one WSAG meeting, "If it were not for the accident of my birth, I would be anti-Semitic." In other moments of exasperation, he would note that "any people who have been persecuted for two thousand years must be doing something wrong."

Kissinger felt, with good cause, that his Jewishness was a vulnerability when dealing with Nixon. The president's attitude toward Jews was as conflicted as it was toward almost all other people. His top staff included such trusted Jews as Kissinger, Arthur Burns, William Safire, and Leonard Garment; yet he once asked his assistant Fred Malek to make a list of all the top Jews at the Labor Department after it came out with some unfavorable economic statistics. In the margins of his briefing papers, Nixon repeatedly wrote bitter little comments that stressed how impervious he was to pressure from "the Jews."

"For Kissinger, being Jewish was a vulnerability as he saw it, and he was not fond of being vulnerable," said John Ehrlichman. "But Nixon liked him to feel that way."

Kissinger accommodated Nixon's prejudices. At times he indicated to Sonnenfeldt or Halperin that he wanted to keep them out of a meeting for fear of showing up with "too many Jews." When he introduced his congressional liaison John Lehman to Nelson Rockefeller, he joked that he was "an Irishman with a Jewish name—if it were the other way around, I would really have something."

Despite his ambivalences, deep inside Kissinger had an emotional commitment to the survival of Israel that led him to be one of its staunchest defenders when its safety was truly at stake—as well as one of its most emotional critics when he felt it was embarked on a suicidal course. "How can I, as a Jew who lost thirteen relatives in the holocaust, do anything that would betray Israel?" he would tell Jewish leaders.[12]

OIL SHOCKS AND THE SHAH

In the midst of the October 1973 Yom Kippur War, the Arabs had followed through on years of warnings and unsheathed their oil weapon. The Organization of Petroleum Exporting Countries (OPEC), with its Arab members in the lead, raised the price of oil from $3.01 per barrel to $5.12 and cut back on production by 5 percent. On October 20, the day after Nixon had requested $2.2 billion from Congress to pay for the emergency Israeli airlift, the Saudis led a move to impose a complete embargo on Arab oil shipments to the United States.

The embargo was more of a symbolic insult, since world supplies of oil were fungible and the U.S. would have no trouble finding replacement sources. But the overall cutbacks and price rises presented a very real crisis for the entire oil-consuming world. At a December 23 OPEC meeting, the shah of Iran pressed for the most radical price rise ever. Over the reluctance of the Saudis, the price per barrel was raised to $11.65, close to a fourfold increase from early October. "This decision," Kissinger said, "was one of the pivotal events in the history of this century."

The total energy bill to the Western alliance and Japan immediately jumped by $40 billion a year, launching a period of stagnation and inflation that lasted almost a decade. For underdeveloped countries, the new cost was more than their foreign aid from all sources combined, thus wiping out the effects of such programs. Even the oil producers, as the hapless shah would fairly soon discover, were not immune from the seismic dislocations that would result.[13]

On their way back from Moscow at the end of May 1972, Nixon and Kissinger had stopped for a day in Teheran to see the shah.

Britain, which had been the colonial power there, had withdrawn from "east of Suez" and declared itself unable to remain the defender of Western interests in the Persian Gulf area. Kissinger and Nixon decided that Iran would help the U.S. assume that role in accordance with the Nixon Doctrine, the strategy announced on Guam in 1969 that sought to rely on lavishly armed local allies to help defend America's regional interests.

"Protect me," Nixon had said to the shah, whose rather obvious aspirations of grandeur made him only too eager to agree. The American part of this bargain was a willingness to sell oil-rich Iran unlimited amounts of virtually any weapon. The Pentagon had been warning that Iran was getting too many sophisticated weapons for its military to absorb. But it was overruled for what were clearly political reasons.

In a July 1972 memo that was among the fifty-eight volumes of documents released by Iranian radicals when they took over the U.S. embassy in 1979, Kissinger told the defense secretary: "Decisions on the acquisition of military equipment should be left primarily to the government of Iran." In a 1973 report reminding Nixon of the policy, Kissinger explained that "we adopted a policy which provides, in effect, that we will accede to any of the Shah's requests for arms purchases from us."[14]

Kissinger later denied that the policy amounted to a "blank check" for the shah to buy whatever he wanted, but both the shah and the Pentagon seemed to read it that way. The shah was so excited that he called Kissinger "probably the most intelligent American ever."[15]

Despite this affectionate relationship, the shah was a major instigator of the OPEC price hikes in 1973. Kissinger was consequently faced with charges that an implicit part of the arrangement he had made with the shah was a wink and nod that he could pay for his new arms by jacking up the price of oil. James Akins, the energy expert who served as Nixon's ambassador to Saudi Arabia, later claimed that the Saudis had tried to get Kissinger to put pressure on Iran to scale back its demands for an oil price increase, but Kissinger refused.

Kissinger called the charges "absurd" and a "canard." He later would admit that he had assumed that the shah might hike oil prices by a dollar or two a barrel to pay for his new weapons. But since Iran was not a major producer, Kissinger did not believe that it would have a big impact on OPEC prices. When he was proven wrong, and Iran led the way to the whopping December increase, Kissinger immediately sent a telegram to the shah in Nixon's name asking that the decision be reversed, warning that it could cause "catastrophic problems" and "a worldwide recession."

The shah paid no heed. The new prices remained, and the arms flow continued. As Robert Hormats, a former NSC staffer, put it: "The shah turned around and screwed us."

Even though there is no evidence to support the charge that Kissinger encouraged Iran to push for a price increase anywhere near the magnitude that occurred, he was not free of all blame: it was a logical consequence of the Nixon-Kissinger policy of encouraging unlimited arms sales. The Iranians spent more than $16 billion for U.S. arms from 1972 to 1977, increasing their military budget sevenfold. By the end, military purchases accounted for 40 percent of the nation's bloated budget.

Iran could finance such a spending spree in three ways: by greatly increasing oil production, which it was not capable of doing; by bartering for the guns in return for providing the U.S. with excess oil for storage in a strategic reserve, a course that Nixon unwisely rejected; or by forcing a major oil-price hike. That it did the latter should have been no surprise. The October and December price rises meant that Iran's oil revenues jumped from $4.4 billion in 1973 to $21.4 billion in 1974, handily covering the new weapons bills that were part of the Kissinger-Nixon policy.[16]

Another deal that had been cut at the May 1972 meeting in Tehran was that the U.S. would provide covert aid to the Kurdish rebels who were waging a struggle against Iran's enemy, Iraq. Over the opposition of the U.S. ambassador in Iran, and without the prior approval of the 40 Committee, which oversaw covert actions, Nixon and Kissinger embarked on a $16-million program to arm the Kurds. When the shah in 1975 reached an accommodation with Iraq, aid to the Kurds was suddenly cut off. "Our movement and people are being destroyed in an unbelievable way," the Kurdish leader Mustafa Barzani wrote in a sad plea to Kissinger, whom he had considered a hero. Kissinger did not reply.

In a leaked version of a congressional report on intelligence activities, known as the Pike Report, Kissinger is quoted in secret testimony giving a cold-blooded explanation of why the Kurds, who were about to be crushed, were being abandoned. "Covert action," he said, "should not be confused with missionary work." Later, he was more contrite. In a newspaper column on the Kurdish tragedy following the 1991 war in Iraq, Kissinger said that his 1975 decision had been "painful, even heartbreaking."[17]

Energy czar William Simon, who was soon to become treasury secretary, argued at the end of 1973 that the arms relationship with the shah should be used to force him to hold down oil prices. But even after the December OPEC shock, Kissinger was reluctant to use leverage and linkage—usually the paired arrows of his diplomatic quiver—to put pressure on the shah. If the U.S. restricted the flow of weaponry, Kissinger argued, nations such as France would eagerly step in to capture the lucrative market.

Simon, a free-market conservative with a sharp intellect, inevitably engaged in some turf rivalry with Kissinger, but their sparring was remarkably friendly, especially by Kissinger's standards. "I have a treaty of nonaggression with Secretary Simon," Kissinger would later joke. "If I will not speak about economic matters, he will take over foreign policy only slowly." Like Commerce Secretary Peter Peterson, but unlike Defense Secretary Schlesinger, Simon had a sense of humor and an engaging aura that caused Kissinger to forgive him his formidable intelligence. (Many years later, they would still be friends, and Simon would serve on the board of Kissinger's consulting firm.)

In 1974, they had a dispute over Persian Gulf policy. Simon, who was friendly with Saudi oil minister Sheikh Ahmed Yamani, favored a close partnership with Saudi Arabia rather than Iran. In February, he lapsed into public candor with his feelings, publicly proclaiming that the shah of Iran was "a nut." Kissinger unleashed an angry cable to Simon, who was flying off to Saudi Arabia at the time. "I am besieged by queries on you calling the Shah 'a nut.' How am I supposed to explain this?"

The quote, Simon said, had been "taken out of context."

Kissinger's reply betrayed a touch of humor as well as exasperation. "In what context," he cabled back, "*can* you call the head of state of an American ally 'a nut'?"[18]

The Kissinger-Nixon strategy of relying on the shah to protect American interests in the region made theoretical sense, but it turned out to be a disaster in practice, compounded because so much had been invested in it. The shah's megalomania was fed by the awesome arsenal he was sold. By the end of the decade he was toppled by a fundamentalist backlash against his Westernized outlook and the heathen modernization that was a by-product of his petrodollars. The anti-Americanism that resulted was to weaken Washington's role in the region for years.

Kissinger's main contribution toward easing the energy crisis was simply to ply his skills as a Middle East mediator. In February 1974, there was a mini-summit of Arab leaders in Algiers. In public they issued a statement reaffirming the oil embargo. In private, they made a secret decision to ask Kissinger to launch a second shuttle mission designed to get a disengagement on the Syrian-Israeli front.

Kissinger was more than happy to embark on a Syrian shuttle.

Nixon, however, was obsessed with ending the embargo, a coup he thought might bring some relief from Watergate. "You see, my only interest is the embargo," he told Kissinger. "That's the only thing the country is interested in. They don't give a damn what happens to Syria."

Fortunately, Egyptian foreign minister Ismail Fahmy and Saudi foreign minister Omar Saqqaf had been authorized by the Arab leaders to deal with both issues when they flew to Washington to convey the request for Kissinger's services.

The two Arab foreign ministers stayed at the Shoreham, a sprawling convention hotel, where their fraternal rivalries became almost comical. After talking to them both on the night of their arrival, Kissinger met privately with Fahmy, who insisted on walking him down to his limousine afterward as a way to assure that he did not then meet privately with Saqqaf. Kissinger ordered his driver to go to the hotel's other entrance, where he took the elevator back up to see Saqqaf. Each minister, Kissinger said, asked for a secret meeting with Nixon from which the other would be excluded.

Fahmy later insisted that it was the other way around: Saqqaf had ushered Kissinger to his car, and he had snuck back up to see Fahmy. Whichever way it was, Kissinger called the incident an illustration of the "deviousness" of the Arab mind. Fahmy, on the other hand, says, "It was far too obvious that Kissinger wanted to create tension between Saqqaf and me; it was a standard ploy of his." Perhaps the only conclusion that less Byzantine minds can draw is that the different versions of the story—as well as the fact that the story even had different versions—give an indication of how Kissinger's style and that of his counterparts were somehow suited to one another.[19]

In the end, the Arab visitors conveyed to Kissinger and Nixon that the embargo would be lifted by March, and—with the linkage implicit—Kissinger was expected to begin a Syrian-Israeli shuttle soon.

THE SYRIAN SHUTTLE: MAY 1974

It became clear that the Syrian-Israeli shuttle would be an endurance test when Kissinger arrived in Damascus for a preparatory visit. President Hafiz al-Assad kept Kissinger talking until three A.M. before agreeing to the concept of disengagement talks—and then he insisted on staying up to rehash the 1970 Jordanian crisis. Kissinger finally got to his bed in his sparse, thin-walled guesthouse only to be bolted awake at four-thirty by the amplified wails of the muezzin of a next-door mosque calling the faithful to morning prayers.

Kissinger knocked at the door of his aide Lawrence Eagleburger. "There stood this short, fat German pleading, 'Can't you get them to stop that?' " Eagleburger recalled. He proceeded to make, in Kissinger's words, "the officious moves of a foreign service officer confronted by a demented secretary of state." Fortunately, he did not attempt to carry out the heretical order.

The ingredients that had led to a deal between Egypt and Israel were missing on the Syrian front. Syria's army, unlike Egypt's, had not captured any new territory, and Assad was adamant about winning at a negotiating table what he had not won in battle. The situation at the Suez Canal had been untenable: Egypt's Third Army was on the east side, but cut off from their supplies, and Israeli troops were on the west side, also in a vulnerable position. But the situation on the Syrian front could fester indefinitely. In addition, Assad was not the visionary that Sadat was and certainly entertained no statesmanlike dreams of a lasting peace with Israel.

At the outset, Kissinger explained to both sides that the settlement he envisioned would involve Israel's giving back all of the land it had captured in the October 1973 war as well as a symbolic slim slice of the Golan Heights that had been captured in the Six Day War of 1967. The two sides started off nowhere near such a compromise. Israel's initial offer was that it might consider giving back one-third of what it had taken in 1973. President Assad's opening demand was that Syria get back all of the territory it had lost in the 1973 war plus one-half of the Golan Heights.

When he arrived in Jerusalem on May 2, Kissinger discovered how hard it would be to convince the Israeli cabinet that Syria, which had started a war and then lost territory, should be rewarded with a disengagement line that was farther toward Israel than it had been before the war. In addition, the Golan Heights, unlike the Sinai desert, was accorded a military significance that bordered on the religious. Eight hundred Israelis had been killed in the Golan Heights during the most recent war. "Two wars in seven years, with the price we paid for it," Golda Meir told Kissinger at their opening session. "Then Assad says he must get his territory back. I mean, that is chutzpah of the nth degree."

Even Steve Strauss, Kissinger's masseur at the King David Hotel, was no more accommodating. Pounding on him with apparent affection, he told Kissinger he was praying for his success. "We must have peace," he said. "I would give up ten years of my life for peace."

"How many kilometers would you give up in the Golan Heights for peace?" Kissinger inquired.

"Give up? Kilometers? On the Golan? You must be crazy! Nothing! Not a millimeter!"

"Then I should break off the talks?"

"Absolutely not," said the masseur, pummeling away even harder. "I would give up ten years of my life for peace."[20]

Kissinger's main weapon in Israel was what its ministers, once they had heard it a few dozen times, began referring to as "Henry's Doomsday Speech." Conceding territory in the Golan was bad, Kissinger admitted, but letting the negotiations fail would be worse. "I think it is essential that the gravity of a failure be understood," he said that first day. If that happened, the U.S. (and Kissinger) would no longer be willing to act as a mediator, he warned. The pro-Israel coalition in Washington, which was based on "an odd combination," would quickly fall apart. Israel would find itself alone, helpless.

The Doomsday Speech made up in passion what it lacked in brevity. Yet the Israeli cabinet was able to remain unmoved. It refused even to come up with any proposal that Kissinger felt was safe to bring to Assad as a starting point.

In Damascus, Assad was just as inflexible. He insisted that Israel withdraw from half of the Golan Heights. "If my line is unacceptable, we won't reach agreement," he said. "I am not going to accept one meter less."

Before the Syrian shuttle began, the press had asked the Egyptian president whether he had any advice for his ally Assad. "Trust my friend Henry," he had answered, "just trust my friend Henry." Now, after his futile opening moves, Kissinger traveled to Alexandria to seek Sadat's counsel.

The key to a settlement, Sadat told him, was the small, now deserted, town of Quneitra, nestled in the foothills of the Golan Heights. Once a dusty tangle of unpaved streets with a population of twenty thousand shopkeepers and peasants, it had served as the provincial capital of the Golan area until it was captured by Israel in 1967. If Israel would withdraw from its 1973 conquests and agree to budge back the 1967 line so that Quneitra could once again be controlled by Syria, said Sadat, a settlement was possible. "It must include Quneitra," Sadat said. "I can sell it to the whole Arab world and save face for Hafiz Assad."

Golda Meir and her defense minister, Moshe Dayan, were at that time privately discussing Quneitra, which they had decided Israel could safely offer as a concession. But they did not tell Kissinger.

Instead, they decided to stick for the moment with a preposterous plan that involved splitting control of the village.

When Israel formally offered the plan for dividing Quneitra, Kissinger knew it was unworkable. But he also realized that, like King Solomon's proposal for dividing the disputed baby, it was not designed to be accepted. The importance of the Quneitra offer, Kissinger saw, was that it edged the Israelis over a major psychological hurdle: they would, after all, be willing to pull back somewhat from the 1967 line. The principle was established. The rest was merely haggling over kilometers—though in negotiations between Syria and Israel, the word *merely* does not attach itself comfortably to the phrase *haggling over kilometers.*

Kissinger decided upon his return to Damascus to exaggerate slightly Israel's retreat on Quneitra, but to withhold a few small concessions it had made in other areas. Since the Israeli plan would put Quneitra in a demilitarized area, Kissinger emphasized that Israel was "giving up" the town. "They are not giving back Quneitra," shot back Assad, who knew better from his intelligence sources. "They have just split Quneitra."

As for the other concessions, Kissinger did not plan to mention them until after he had visited Egypt and Saudi Arabia, so that he could present the changes as coming in response to appeals from Sadat and King Faisal. But before he got back, Israel's full position had leaked to the newspapers there. "What are you doing to me?" he shouted at the Israeli negotiators. Why hadn't the government censored the revelations?

Military censorship was legal, one negotiator explained to him, but not censorship for political purposes. Kissinger was furious and continued to rant. Finally, his old Harvard student Yigal Allon broke in to give him a lecture about democracy. Public debate and sometimes even leaks were prices that had to be paid in a democracy, he explained to the American secretary of state. The Arab states, he added, would have to learn to live with the fact that Israel was a democracy. Kissinger, he did not add, would have to as well.[21]

After a week of negotiating, Kissinger took a side trip to Cyprus to meet with Andrei Gromyko—more as a way to keep the Soviet minister at bay than to include him in the discussions. Both Sadat and Assad were now conspiring with Kissinger to cut the Soviets out of the peace process—representing an astounding turnaround in superpower influence in the region. At the Cyprus meeting, Gromyko argued that Israel had to be pushed to retreat from the Golan Heights. If he wanted to fly to Jerusalem and persuade Golda Meir of that,

Kissinger told the Soviet minister, he was welcome to try. It was a not very subtle reminder that the Soviets had little role to play in the talks because they could not deliver much to the table.

A few days later, Kissinger was able to insist to Syria that Gromyko not be allowed to come there until he had left. Gromyko had the dismaying experience of being told by Moscow's putative client to delay his arrival for ten hours. He then was forced by Syrian officials to circle in his plane for forty-five more minutes because Kissinger had still not quite finished.

As Kissinger's Damascus-Jerusalem shuttle runs continued, the step-by-step process became a street-by-street haggling over Quneitra. Israel gradually conceded control over the town. But it insisted on a military line right at its limits.

At stake were three fields on the edge of town cultivated by Israeli settlers, whose produce in a year would not have paid for the jet fuel Kissinger's plane used in one day. Yet there was a principle and not just three hardscrabble patches of land at stake; Israel had never given up cultivated land or withdrawn from land it had already settled.

On May 14, as the second week of shuttling was ending, Kissinger decided to bring matters to a head by demanding Israel's best offer. Golda Meir became indignant. "He can't have what he wants," she stormed about Assad. "He is not entitled to everything he wants."

Kissinger was no less indignant. "We are talking about half a kilometer at a line a kilometer from the old dividing line." Had it not been for America's support, he lectured her, Israel would be facing pressure to return to its pre-1967 borders, giving up all of the Golan. "We broke the oil embargo, we made the Russians ridiculous in the Middle East. If you had to face all of this, under Russian pressure, with the oil embargo on, you wouldn't be talking about the Druze village in the northern sector. You would be talking about a hell of a lot worse things."

Even Kissinger, ever one to relish a role as a bargainer, was beginning to realize that the petty haggling was demeaning for a secretary of state. "I am wandering around here like a rug merchant in order to bargain over one hundred to two hundred meters!" he shouted at one point. "Like a peddler in the market! I am trying to save you, and you think you are doing me a favor when you are kind enough to give me a few extra meters. As if I were a citizen of Quneitra!"

The session got angrier. At one point Kissinger suggested a complex ploy: perhaps the Israelis could prepare a map showing the military line—which was farther back from Quneitra—and ignore for the moment the line of sovereignty, which Israel was insisting be right next to the town. That struck Moshe Dayan as devious and not, he said, grasping for the English word, "constitutional." Kissinger turned scathing. Dayan should go to Damascus and explain the Israeli constitution to Assad, he said. In the meantime, he would go back to Washington and report that the negotiations had broken down because Dayan wanted to build a barbed-wire fence on the edge of a town. How would that play in America?

Dayan just shook his head. He did not know how it would look, he replied. But he knew that Kissinger's ploy was not right.

Kissinger began shouting and waving his arms. What was he supposed to tell Assad? "That I do not support your position? Because, sir, I really don't support it! Absolutely not!" Then, still screaming as Dayan remained motionless, Kissinger threw the map across the table at him. "Maybe you would like to add something more to the map?" Kissinger yelled. "Write on the map whatever you want. I no longer care. . . . The best thing that could happen is that this negotiation fail. . . . So please write. Why don't you write?"

Dayan did not touch the map. With his one good eye, he stared coldly at Kissinger. Kissinger was breathing hard, trying to compose himself.

Just then, a Secret Service agent walked into the room with Kissinger's glasses, which, like his briefcases and raincoats, were always being left behind. The room was silent, Kissinger frozen. He did not take the glasses from the nervous agent. Finally, fixing him with a glare, he asked whether the agent knew of the proper protocol. Then Ambassador Kenneth Keating got up to get the glasses and handed them to Joe Sisco, who handed them to Kissinger.[22]

Nixon was by then reeling from what would be Watergate's final blows. While the Syrian shuttle mission was under way in May 1974, the House Judiciary Committee began its famous impeachment hearings. Within three months, the committee would vote in favor of impeachment and Nixon would resign.

Nixon's only diversion was following Kissinger's spectacle in the Middle East, and he began applying some unsolicited pressure of his own. After a series of threatening letters to the Israelis demanding that they accept Kissinger's suggestions, the president ordered Brent Scowcroft to cut off all aid to the country unless they immediately complied.

Nixon's meddling, combined with the horror of the massacre at Ma'alot of sixteen schoolchildren by Palestinian terrorists that week, caused Kissinger to mellow. He and the Israelis came to an agreement:

Kissinger would put forward an "American proposal" that would have Israel withdraw from the cultivated area abutting Quneitra but still allow it to keep military control of three surrounding hills.

Assad was at first unreceptive. Kissinger went so far as to work out with him the announcement of the breakdown of the talks. But just as the secretary was preparing to return empty-handed to Washington, the Syrian president asked him to renew his negotiating efforts. On Saturday, May 18, he finally won tentative acceptance of the disengagement line in both Damascus and Jerusalem.

That still left an array of details to be resolved involving the buffer zones, limited-weapons areas, U.N. forces, and whether Syria would be responsible for enforcing the cease-fire on Palestinian guerrillas living there. It would take another nine days of shuttling, and another brinksmanship moment threatening Assad with the breakdown of talks, before these were settled.

Not since Robert Lansing had wandered off for seven months to the Conference of Versailles in 1919 had a secretary of state been out of the country for so long. In thirty-four days, Kissinger had traveled 24,230 miles on forty-one flights—leading some to suggest that Kissinger was immersing himself in endless discussions of minor negotiating points partly to avoid the sordid Watergate morass at home. "One suspects he may even be prolonging his shuttle in order to avoid the even more complicated and poisonous controversies of Watergate," wrote *New York Times* columnist James Reston. CBS's Marvin Kalb and NBC's Richard Valeriani followed with similar stories.

The charge had an element of truth. But whatever his mix of motivations, his decision to be engaged personally in each step of the process turned out for the best. Only through his attention to detail was he able to wear down the two sides and reach an accord. In doing so, he established the U.S. as the dominant diplomatic force in the region.

Newsweek pictured him on its cover as "Super-K," and *Time* headlined its story, "The Miracle Worker Does It Again." Golda Meir gave him a reception just as she was retiring and turning over power to Yitzhak Rabin. "In a quiz," she said, "you would beat most of us on the details of the hills, the roads, the town, and even the houses of the Golan Heights." From Yigal Allon, Israel's incoming foreign minister, came the most effusive toast. "You are the foreign minister of the century," his former student declared.[23]

On the flight home, Kissinger sipped champagne and savored his triumph, but he was a bit less effusive in his proclamations. "The Syrians and the Israelis," he told a few journalists off the record, "are the only two peoples who deserve each other."

TWENTY-FIVE

THE PRESS

How to Be Captivating
on a Background Basis

> *I have not had unfortunate experiences with the press.*
> —Kissinger news conference, Salzburg, Austria, June 11, 1974.

Reporters, especially those in Washington, face an old journalistic dilemma: because their stature tends to rise and fall with that of the people they cover, they thus have a stake in the successes of their subject. This symbiotic relationship was particularly true with Kissinger's high-profile shuttling, which made stars out of those who covered him.

"Wherever the Kissinger plane has gone, the newsmen aboard have been the envy of their colleagues on the ground," wrote Bernard Gwertzman in the *New York Times*. Another reporter, with the humility for which the trade is known, declared, "We know more than most U.S. ambassadors in the places we visit." When Kissinger's plane would land, the local correspondents and even a few diplomats would surround his press entourage on the tarmac and interview its members.

The road show led to another journalistic dilemma: that of reporters becoming too dependent on one source and thus wary of doing anything that could antagonize him. For the "Kissinger 14," as the flying press circus was dubbed, the man who spoke thinly disguised as "a senior official" was the only real source. On each leg he would disarm them with his wit, intimidate them with his brilliance, flatter them with his confidences, and charm them with his attention. Their stories were in the news summary that reached his plane each morning, and he would often wander back to take issue, poke fun, appear hurt, or occasionally erupt in anger.

When Kissinger would send word that they could come up to his conference cabin for a briefing, there was invariably a melee as they sought the seats next to him. During one scramble, Jeremiah O'Leary, a crusty ex-Marine who worked for the *Washington Star,* knocked down his rival from the *Washington Post,* Marilyn Berger, who was not quite as crusty but no less determined. Kissinger, forsaking his usual diplomatic delicacy, shuffled back later that day and asked, "Where's O'Leary? I want to see him hit another woman." The *Boston Globe's* reporter finally solved the dispute by working out a seating rotation that was promptly dubbed the Berger-O'Leary Disengagement Accord.

Adding to the symbiosis was that the journalists, in their human capacity, had a desire to see Kissinger's shuttles succeed. This was not a political campaign, about which a reporter could be impartial; it was a quest to prevent another Middle East war. Kissinger knew the reporters were rooting for him. "Some of this may have sprung from a wish to give purpose to the physical discomfort of the shuttle, or from the reality that our success would give a reporter more exposure and prestige," he later wrote. "I also believe that among their reasons was a hope that in the midst of Watergate their country could accomplish something of which they could be proud."[1]

Successful reporters in Washington generally fall into one of two categories: those who have good access, and those who have aggressive investigative instincts. Access reporters tend to be assigned to the best beats, such as the White House or the State Department, and are most often the ones who evolve into columnists and pundits. Investigative reporters tend to win the Pulitzers and a greater degree of gritty professional respect. Both types can produce informative stories. Neither has a monopoly on morality. The problem comes when one aspect of reporting dominates to the exclusion of the other.

Investigative reporting—muckraking as it was called back then—was not as fashionable in those days before Redford and Hoffman played Woodward and Bernstein. Drew Pearson and his successor Jack Anderson had carved out a special niche, and the Vietnam War had produced a new breed of more skeptical reporters along the lines of David Halberstam, Neil Sheehan, and Seymour Hersh at the *New York Times.* But establishment insiders such as Joseph Alsop, Walter

Lippmann, and James Reston, who rubbed elbows with the mighty at the Metropolitan Club, remained the model of journalistic grandeur.

Access journalism had become more exalted during the 1960s as many prominent reporters shed their image as ink-stained hacks and became social friends of the Kennedy clan, sharing confidences with the president or frolicking around the pool of his brother Robert's home, Hickory Hill. Increasingly, reporters became socially acceptable members of the establishment. In Washington by the late 1960s, the Georgetown social set was dominated not only by grandees such as Alice Longworth and Evangeline Bruce, but also by the likes of Joseph and Susan Mary Alsop, Katharine Graham, Polly and Joseph Kraft, Rowland and Kay Evans, David Brinkley, Tom and Joan Braden, and, later, Ben Bradlee and Sally Quinn.

Kissinger was a master at dealing with the access journalists of Washington, mainly because he was willing to lavish on them what they wanted, access. He was less adroit at dealing with a dogged investigator, as revealed by his disastrous telephone interview with Woodward about the national security wiretaps.* Fortunately for Kissinger, diplomatic reportage tended to be dominated by access reporters. Few of those who covered foreign policy approached stories the way that *Washington Post* metro-desk reporters approached the Watergate break-in. Instead, they made their mark by being able to get and interpret the private thoughts of senior officials.

The odd thing about this reliance on access is that American foreign policy is so prone to leakage that it can be covered by a good reporter with little access at all. Some of the best scoops of the period —such as the stories about the Cambodian bombing, the covert action in Chile, the wiretaps, the tilt toward Pakistan, the My Lai massacre —came from reporters who never broke bread with Kissinger. "Washington is the only capital city in the world where information is so freely available that political and diplomatic reporting can be done without the gift of access," according to British journalist William Shawcross. "But paradoxically, Washington is also the city where access is both most easily obtained and most treasured."

One Rorschach test for classifying journalists of the period was how they treated Kissinger: those who called him Henry—or, when on television, "Doctor" Kissinger—tended to be establishment pundits and top management, or aspired to be; those who rolled their eyes at such coziness and deference tended to be hard-nosed investigative reporters.

Kissinger often complained that the journalists who covered him

* Described in Chapter 22.

bent over backward to seem tough. "The media yearn for access to senior officials and yet are afraid to be taken into camp by them," he said. "Hence they often err on the side of skepticism or the facile pursuit of credibility gaps."

The opposite was more often the case: because of a desire for intimate access to Kissinger, most reporters who covered him regularly tended to be deferential, especially the columnists whose color and insight depended upon his returned phone calls. "The routine resembled an implicit shakedown scheme," charged Seymour Hersh, an intense investigative reporter and Kissinger critic.[2]

What many reporters failed to realize was that writing negative stories about Kissinger generally did not result in being cut off. Quite the contrary. Kissinger's compulsion to convert his critics extended to the media. Pundits who attacked him (up to a point) were likely to be called, cajoled, stroked, and invited to breakfast. Kissinger had never paid any attention to the reporter on his plane from the *Chicago Tribune* until the paper berated him editorially for putting too much pressure on the regime in South Africa. On the next trip, Kissinger came by the seat where the reporter was typing and began to make conversation. "Writing another editorial?" he joked.

Another reporter who was getting the brush-off asked Brent Scowcroft how he could convince Kissinger to see him. "Just write something critical of him," Scowcroft replied. "He'll call." The reporter did, and Kissinger did. "There is the theory," Bernard Gwertzman of the *New York Times* once said, "that the more you criticize, the more information you get because he wants to convince you."

Kissinger's assiduous quest for favorable coverage was not merely a craving of his ego; it was also a way to further his foreign policy. "His diplomatic successes were possible partly because of the power of his presence, his larger-than-life image," said Diane Sawyer. "He used the press to magnify and intensify that."

Former CIA director Richard Helms recalled going with Kissinger to his office and watching him sort through phone message slips. "The ones from reporters would be put right on top, and sometimes he would call one of them back right away while I waited." John Andrews, a young conservative speechwriter who admired Kissinger, had the same experience when he would go to Kissinger's office to work on a speech. "A columnist like Kraft or Alsop would call, and he would interrupt me to take it and do an incredible snow job with me listening in. He'd pour syrup all over the guy." In San Clemente, Kissinger would meet with a steady stream of journalists on his office-area patio, where Ehrlichman could listen in from his own patio next door. "I could not help hearing Henry's blandishments and his self-congratulation," Ehrlichman recalled. "It surprised me that veteran journalists would let him get away with using them as he did."[3]

Kissinger's primary tactic with journalists, as with most everyone else he wished to befriend, was flattery. "I am calling you because I know you are the only one covering me who will understand this," he would purr. Like a sorcerer's incantation, the flattery worked. "You know you are being played like a violin," says Christopher Ogden, who covered Kissinger for *Time*, "but it's still extremely seductive." Clark Mollenhoff, a hard-bitten reporter with the *Des Moines Register*, once explained. "He tells you what he thinks you want to hear, then asks what you think. It's very flattering."

Another tactic was intimacy. With an air of slight indiscretion and personal trust, neither totally feigned, Kissinger would share confidences and inside information. "You always have the feeling that he's told you ten percent more than he has to," said Barbara Walters. In social settings, or in offhand comments that he implicitly understood would remain off the record, he would be surprisingly revealing, especially in his descriptions of personalities. Even for veteran pundits used to the proximity to power, the stroking was a heady experience.

On the other hand, Kissinger could use rage effectively, particularly since it came as naturally to him as charm. Notoriously thin-skinned, he would respond to certain critical stories with a hand-waving fury combined with a genuine sense of hurt. For reporters who experienced such displays, it was as painful as Kissinger's stroking could be pleasurable.

Nixon's oft-stated philosophy for dealing with the press was to "show cold contempt" and remain aloof no matter what was written. Kissinger had the opposite approach, and his was by far the more effective.

It would be a mistake, however, to believe that Kissinger had friends in the media simply by dint of a calculated courtship. Journalists naturally liked him, and enjoyed talking to him, for the same reasons that so many others found him fascinating. He was well-informed and liked to share information. His wit had a sharpness that journalists found bracing. At dinners he was charming, in interviews he was thoughtful, and as a storyteller he had an eye for color and detail that reporters could appreciate.

Similarly, Kissinger genuinely liked talking to journalists. To most people, foreign policy pundits may not seem as interesting as, say, Hollywood starlets when it comes to choosing dinner companions. And Kissinger may not have thought of them that way either. But for him, they were at least a close second. "Henry gets up early in the morning and he likes to talk," his wife, Nancy, would later say. "He goes to bed late at night, and he's still talking. And one of the things he most likes to talk about is foreign policy." Few people, other than diplomatic correspondents, fit into this category.

On the flight home after his Middle East mission at the end of 1973, after he'd visited thirteen countries in fifteen days, Kissinger's eyes were red, his nose runny, his voice hoarse. Aides tried to get him to sleep, but instead he invited the journalists aboard up to his cabin to talk and sip champagne. For more than an hour, he chatted, told anecdotes, analyzed what had happened, asked questions, and listened. It was not merely designed to shape coverage of a story that was already over; for Kissinger it was a form of pleasure.

Likewise, on his final shuttle mission in August 1975, after a day that had included meetings in Alexandria and Damascus, Kissinger hosted a midnight birthday party for the *Washington Post*'s Marilyn Berger in his suite at Jerusalem's King David Hotel. By one A.M. most of the correspondents had drifted off to bed. But Kissinger continued to hold court on the couch, reminiscing about Assad and Sadat and then Zhou and Brezhnev. "Kissinger doesn't play golf," James Anderson of the UPI once said. "His hobby is talking to us."[4]

Kissinger perfected the Washington practice of using background briefings to shape news coverage. He refined a set of ground rules that fell between on the record (in which the speaker can be quoted) and off the record (in which the information cannot be used at all). Usually he would speak on "background," which meant that he would be quoted merely as "a senior American official" or some such label. Occasionally, he would speak on "deep background," meaning that reporters could use the information, but not quote or attribute it in any manner.

Few people were fooled about who the "senior official" was. In fact, it became a bit of a joke. Humorist Art Buchwald, along for the ride on one trip, wrote a column referring to a "high U.S. official with wavy hair, horn-rimmed glasses and a German accent." Bob Schieffer of CBS did a report about a "senior American official" taking time off in Germany to attend a soccer match.

The *New York Times*'s Joseph Lelyveld, not a regular in Kissinger's contingent, exposed how Kissinger's skillful backgrounders helped create favorable coverage of a trip to Beijing. "In case there is any lingering doubt, only one 'senior American official' normally briefs newsmen on the progress of Secretary of State Kissinger's sundry negotiations," he began his story. After describing the views of this official, Lelyveld concluded: "Reports emerging from Mr. Kissinger's trip that the Chinese were essentially satisfied with the relationship with Washington as it now stands had no basis in official Chinese statements. Rather, the reports testify to Mr. Kissinger's virtuosity in dealing with the press. Switching back and forth between 'background' and 'deep background' and 'off the record' comments, the Secretary masterfully shapes the coverage he receives."

The only serious challenge to this system came early. In December 1971, Kissinger said on "deep background" that Soviet conduct during the India-Pakistan war could cause the U.S. to take "a new look" at whether to attend the May 1972 Moscow summit. The wire services immediately sent out bulletins to that effect, but they did not cite Kissinger as the source. *Washington Post* editor Ben Bradlee, whose reporter had not been part of the pool at the briefing, felt that the news was too important to print without saying where it came from. "We have engaged in this deception and done this disservice to the reader long enough," he said. *Post* reporter Stanley Karnow printed the quote about the summit and attributed it to Kissinger by name.

Few human rituals compare to the breast-beating of journalists collectively debating the morality of their rules. The *Post's* action caused a widespread realization that reliance on backgrounders had gone too far. "He was misusing the press as a government messenger boy," columnist Tom Wicker said of Kissinger. "The backgrounder can allow officials to be irresponsible and reporters lazy, almost unwittingly placing journalists in a too cozy relationship with news sources." Yet there was also a feeling that cutting off backgrounders completely could be a disaster. The White House Correspondents Association passed a resolution urging that reporters abide by Kissinger's background-briefing rules.

The real danger of the backgrounders was that they often replaced rather than supplemented real reporting. Kissinger's Middle East shuttles, for example, were largely reported by the press on his plane, which meant that he was the source for most of the information. Only a few of the more enterprising reporters consistently tried to supplement the background nuances gleaned on Kissinger's plane with hard reporting on the ground, including interviews with Israeli and Arab parties or pressure groups. The popularity of the backgrounder arose from two great journalistic sins, coziness and laziness.

Nevertheless, the background rules served a legitimate purpose. In the diplomatic world, an official pronouncement by a secretary of state or other top official can have major policy ramifications. The same statement that is not attributed, even if the source is only thinly disguised, need not affect policy nor require a response from other nations. None of Kissinger's insights into his negotiations or about the leaders he was dealing with could safely have been made on the record. But they could be useful to a reporter and to a reader, especially if the reporter put them in context. Even the *Washington Post* soon recovered from its fit of purity and pledged to play by the rules again.[5]

Kissinger's friendships with members of the media ran from the beat reporters to the owners. A sampling of his most important relationships shows some of the ways he dealt with the press.

The three primary television reporters on his plane—Marvin Kalb of CBS, Ted Koppel of ABC, and Richard Valeriani of NBC—received special attention. Although Kissinger played along at times with the absurd White House suspicion that Kalb was a Romanian agent, he was not responsible for the wiretap ordered by Attorney General Mitchell. The FBI was told, in fact, not even to send Kissinger copies of any material on Kalb. The likely reason was that Nixon suspected (rightly) that Kissinger was a good source for Kalb. On the margin of one of his 1972 news summaries, the president wrote a note to Haldeman: "H—K must never do a Kalb interview."

Nevertheless, Kissinger gave plenty of interviews to Kalb for the book that he and his brother Bernard wrote about him in 1974. A colorful account of Kissinger's tenure in the Nixon White House, *Kissinger* the book tended to reflect the views of Kissinger the source, especially on key events such as the struggle he had had with James Schlesinger over resupplying Israel during the Yom Kippur War. Kissinger considered Kalb to be "sensitive and scholarly," an opinion he did not change when the book appeared. (He attended the publication party for *Kissinger* and when asked whether he had read the book, replied, "No, but I like the title.")

During the Syrian disengagement shuttle, after the book had been finished, Kalb walked into Kissinger's private compartment in the front of the plane to give him encouragement when it looked as if talks were about to break down. "Hang in there, Mr. Secretary," he said. "We know you can make it." Recounting the incident later, Kissinger wrote, "Few events in those nerve-wracking weeks sustained me so much as that brief conversation."[6]

Valeriani also wrote a book, lighter in tone, called *Travels With Henry.* Although he took glee in pointing out Kissinger's personal foibles, both on television and in his book, Valeriani was a fan of his as a statesman. "Henry Kissinger was the smartest man I know," he wrote. Kissinger was amused by Valeriani, who was the ringmaster of the flying press circus. "We took it in stride when we were teased by colleagues, especially anti-Kissinger colleagues, for being too close, and we teased back," Valeriani said. "Some of their teasing derived simply from a kind of personal envy."[7]

Ted Koppel became a personal friend, a relationship that survived into the 1990s and made Kissinger's furrowed brow a regular feature on Koppel's "Nightline." Kissinger once offered Koppel a job as his chief spokesman, which he declined. In 1974, as Watergate was climaxing, he produced and reported an hour-long documentary on Kissinger. "By the fall of 1972 we were half-convinced that nothing was beyond the capacity of this remarkable man," Koppel said in that broadcast. "Kissinger already threatens to become a legend, the most admired man in America, the magician, the miracle worker." The documentary aired just weeks before Nixon resigned and while Kissinger was embroiled in a new controversy over the wiretaps. "Henry Kissinger may be the best thing we've got going for us," Koppel concluded.

But Koppel's coverage of Kissinger, although favorable, was not soft. More than any other reporter on the beat, he seemed to have a feel for the strengths and weaknesses of the pragmatic realpolitik approach that informed Kissinger's assessment of the national interest.[8]

At the *New York Times,* Kissinger had a cordial but strictly professional relationship with the Washington bureau chief, Max Frankel, an expert in foreign policy. Kissinger was able to get the paper to delay publication of a scoop by Tad Szulc about the impending invasion of Cambodia after talking to Frankel. But generally, Frankel and his bureau provided the toughest coverage of Kissinger, including investigative stories by Szulc and Seymour Hersh.

Leslie Gelb, the paper's national security correspondent, had been a doctoral student and then a teaching assistant under Kissinger at Harvard. But his accounts of Kissinger's major decisions, which included inside looks at crises such as the one in Cyprus, were shard-sharp and often critical. State Department correspondent Bernard Gwertzman also showed no signs that his access compromised his judgment. The paper's columnists included one of Kissinger's friendliest boosters, James Reston, and one of his fiercest detractors, Anthony Lewis.[9]

With *Time* magazine, Kissinger had a warm relationship that began early in 1969, less than a month after he took office, when the magazine ran a cover on the then-obscure presidential assistant. Kissinger had barred his staff from talking to the press, but he made an exception for the *Time* correspondents on the story. As is usually the case when a newsmagazine discovers a new figure, the cover story was admiring and portrayed him larger than life. Over the next two decades he would appear on twenty-one *Time* covers, more than any person in the magazine's history except for Presidents Nixon, Reagan, and Carter.

Kissinger and the magazine's editor at the time, Henry Grunwald, shared similar outlooks: childhood refugees from the Nazis, they both possessed agile yet rigorous minds, intellectual senses of humor, and a Middle European attitude about the type of power-oriented realism that made for an effective foreign policy.

Kissinger's closest working relationship at *Time* was with the Washington bureau chief, Hugh Sidey, who wrote columns for both *Time* and *Life*. Kissinger knew that Sidey's forte was providing his readers with intimate color and detail, and he would take care to supply the columnist with the small inside facts that he needed. Sidey's pieces were almost always adulatory. "There has never been anything quite like Kissinger in mythology or fact," he began a 1972 article in *Life* headlined, "The World Is the Woodcutter's Ball." Kissinger often fed him anecdotes that he or Nixon wanted to see in print. In one case, Sidey wrote that Kissinger was struck during his China trip by the similarities between Nixon and Zhou Enlai; some of the attributes he then mentioned were the same as those Nixon had listed in a rambling memo to Kissinger that asked him to get the press to write this.*

Yet Sidey, unlike many columnists, was able to keep clearly in mind that his relationship with Kissinger was a professional one, each of them doing his job, rather than a personal friendship. He got from Kissinger at least as much as Kissinger got from him. During Nixon's first trip to China, the presidential party was secluded in the Forbidden City, so the press corps all went off to eat dinner. Sidey, however, put in a phone message for Kissinger through the White House signal corps and then waited in his hotel room. Sure enough, Kissinger soon returned the call and filled Sidey in on the details of the meeting with Mao. It made for the perfect Sidey scoop when it ran the next Monday. "One thing about Henry," Sidey said, "he knew how the game was played."[10]

At the *Washington Post,* where Ben Bradlee set a tone of tough-guy professionalism in the newsroom, Kissinger mainly courted the Georgetown-based clique of columnists. His most significant and complex relationship was with owner Katharine Graham. She "adored" him and would do just about anything for him—except meddle in the editorial decisions of her paper. They used to go to the movies together, sometimes just the two of them (and Kissinger's bodyguards), to a suburban theater to watch *McCabe and Mrs. Miller* or *The French Connection* or *Cabaret*. "He's the most truly funny man I know," she said. She would also host dinners, during the fury over

---

* See Chapter 16.

Vietnam, with just him and Robert McNamara so that the two of them could commiserate about their war woes.

One of the few times that Mrs. Graham decided to intervene on Kissinger's behalf was a disaster. It concerned a story that gossip columnist Maxine Cheshire was planning to run about a date Kissinger had had in Hollywood. Actually, two young women were involved in the "date," both strippers: one had costarred in a movie named *Trio*, about a man, a woman, and an animal the species of which no one now seems to remember; the other woman was famous for balancing full glasses of champagne on her breasts. Even for a man who had told the paper's other Style section reporter, Sally Quinn, that he was a secret swinger, the impending Cheshire story went too far.

"I was worried," Mrs. Graham recalled. "Maxine was good, but not always accurate. So I got down on bended knee to Ben and begged him not to run the story." Two days passed and nothing appeared. She thought it had all blown over. But then the story appeared, featuring two rather full pictures of the young women in question. Worst of all, the story happened to be true. "Henry was so furious that when he called I had to hold the phone away from my ear," Mrs. Graham said. He followed up with an angry letter insisting there was no way he could have known about the backgrounds of the women. Was he supposed to run security checks, he asked, on everyone he dated?

Mrs. Graham, not exactly sympathetic to that line of argument, sent back a reply that noted, "There are no security checks for taste." It took Joe Alsop to bring them back together after a few months. "Maxine makes me want to commit murder," Kissinger told Mrs. Graham after he calmed down. "Sally makes me want to commit suicide." [11]

Among the many *Post* columnists Kissinger cultivated were the hawkish Joseph Alsop and the more liberal Joseph Kraft. Kissinger had known Alsop from Harvard, where the journalist was a member of the Board of Overseers. Though brusque in argument, Alsop was refined in his tastes, style, and entertaining. Invitations to the table hosted by his wife, Susan Mary, were among the most coveted in Georgetown, and they were among the few that Kissinger rarely declined. Once, however, he was detained at the White House and had his secretary call to say he would be late. Afterward, Alsop berated him. It was permissible to be late in order to attend to the president, but it was an unacceptable insult to his wife to have a secretary telephone rather than do it personally. Kissinger hung his head and said, "Thank you for teaching me manners."

Alsop's columns, which sometimes sounded as if they had been written in Latin and then lost a little zing in the translation, provided rocklike support for the Vietnam War and lavish praise for each of Kissinger's successes. When he returned with the Syrian-Israeli disengagement accord, to what most people would have considered hearty enough acclaim, Alsop declared: "It seems reasonable to suggest a bit more celebration of a pure diplomatic feat by an American Secretary of State that is without any obvious parallel since Talleyrand's triumphant prestidigitation at the Congress in Vienna."[12]

Kraft had fewer pretensions and was less easily awed. He quickly discovered that criticizing Kissinger would not result in a cutoff of access. After the 1970 Cambodian invasion he wrote a piece, titled "The Bottomless Pit," which charged that "the Nixon administration is a government of weak men unable to think deep or see far." Kissinger, livid, had his secretary try to reach Kraft at home that night. Not up for getting a lecture, the columnist told his wife, Polly, that he would not talk to him. A few minutes later, Kissinger himself was on the phone, beseeching Polly to put her husband on. Kraft, getting petulant, still refused. About a half hour later, the doorbell rang. It was Kissinger. Late into the night, with Kraft wearing pajamas, they argued about Cambodia.[13]

Amid the Watergate finale in mid-1974, it was probably inevitable that Kissinger would have a showdown of his own with the press. It came over the issue of the wiretaps. Even though the story had been splashed on the front pages when the taps were first exposed in May 1973 and again during his secretary of state confirmation hearings that September when he admitted that he had supplied names to the FBI, a new controversy arose in June 1974. It involved a rather semantic dispute over whether he had misled the Senate when he denied responsibility for "initiating" any of the taps.

The frenzy began when Kissinger returned from the Syrian shuttle, exhausted but ready to be revived by applause, only to be hit with questions about the wiretaps. At his first press conference, on June 6, none of the questions dealt with the Golan Heights, but a college newspaper reporter asked whether he had "retained counsel" for "a possible perjury indictment"? Kissinger began to sputter. His face turned red and he began to stamp his feet. "I am not conducting my office as if it were a conspiracy." When Clark Mollenhoff of the *Des Moines Register* began bellowing follow-up questions about the wiretaps in his foghorn voice, Kissinger stormed out.

Most of the questions, and almost all of the stories, came not from the friendly reporters who covered him, but from the White House correspondents and investigative reporters who did not. The morning of his press conference, Laurence Stern of the *Washington*

Post had a story about a Nixon comment on the White House tapes that seemed to say, in reference to the wiretaps, that Kissinger had "asked that it be done." Seymour Hersh revealed in the *New York Times* three days later that Kissinger's office "was directly responsible" for aspects of the program. Bob Woodward and Carl Bernstein followed up with a banner story filled with leaked memos from the FBI detailing Kissinger's phone calls and requests. "An Ugly Blot on Mister Clean," headlined an article in *Newsweek*.

Kissinger left Washington with Nixon on June 10 for a grand tour of the Middle East that was supposed to serve as a triumphal distraction from Watergate. On the way over, sitting in the cabin just behind the president's, Kissinger fumed to Scowcroft and Eagleburger that he would have to hold a press conference immediately to clear his name. Eagleburger agreed; Scowcroft did not. When Kissinger consulted Haig, who was sitting up with the president, the chief of staff was aghast. A Kissinger press conference would distract from Nixon's mission. But by the time the plane landed in Salzburg, Austria, for an overnight rest stop, Kissinger had decided to proceed.

He and his aides stayed up until dawn discussing how to address the allegations. As the sun rose, notices were being slipped under reporters' doors informing them that buses would be taking them to an unscheduled press conference in the drawing room of Kavalier Haus on the outskirts of town. When Kissinger appeared at the microphone in front of a tapestry of a medieval forest, it was clear this was not going to be another rollicking discussion of the Middle East.

For an hour and ten minutes, through an anguished monologue then somber answers to questions, Kissinger did not smile once. After an exhaustive explanation of his role in the wiretapping program, he turned almost maudlin about the diplomatic goals he had achieved. "I would rather like to think," he said, "that when the record is written, one may remember that perhaps some lives were saved and that perhaps some mothers can rest more at ease, but I leave that to history." Then he made his threat: "If it is not cleared up, I will resign."[14]

The Senate Foreign Relations Committee agreed to investigate the matter once again. It did so the following month, repeating the tepid exoneration it had issued after his confirmation hearings. But the real exoneration would be decided by public reaction, and more specifically by that of the opinion-makers of the Washington press corps. Faced with Kissinger's threatened resignation, the pundits rallied around him.

"Do we really want the responsibility of hounding from office the most admired public servant in the United States?" asked Joseph Alsop. (His answer was no, that this would be "a major catastrophe.")

William F. Buckley said of the press conference, "It was as if Sir Francis Drake, returning from sinking the Spanish Armada, had been asked at a press conference whether he had submitted the sails on his galleon to competitive bidding."

"The assumption of some reporters who direct their fire against Kissinger is that diplomacy should be treated like the police beat," the columnist Marquis Childs wrote. Even Joseph Kraft was willing to stand up for him, though in a manner designed to infuriate. "While he almost certainly lied, the untruths are matters of little consequence when weighed against his service to the state," he wrote. "For my own part, I think the resignation threat is a piece of spring silliness, born of exhaustion and self-intoxication, which should best be forgotten." Two days after the threat was made, the *New York Times* both reported opinion and shaped it with a page-one headline that read, "Capital Rallying Round Kissinger."

Deep into his Salzburg press conference, Kissinger had stopped for a moment wallowing in his woes and noted, "I have not had unfortunate experiences with the press." It was a classic Kissinger use of a double negative to make an understatement. Yet it was striking that, even amidst this travail, the most thin-skinned of postwar secretaries of state had to admit he had been treated kindly by the media.

A year earlier, at the height of a previous controversy about the revelations of the wiretaps, William Safire had remarked on how the coziness between Kissinger and his press corps had helped to protect him. "Years of accessibility to influential newsmen is like money in the bank," Safire wrote, "enabling the prudent depositor to obtain shelter, or at least a sympathetic hearing, on rainy days." Even during the final deluge of Watergate, for Kissinger that still held true.[15]

TWENTY-SIX

TRANSITIONS

The Final Days,
and a New Beginning

> *It was a Greek tragedy. Nixon was fulfilling his own nature. Once it started it could not end otherwise.—spoken by Kissinger to James St. Clair, August 8, 1974*

NANCY MAGINNES KISSINGER, MARCH 1974

"Remember," the secretary said as she stuck her head into Kissinger's office that Saturday, "you shouldn't be late for that meeting you have scheduled." Normally, Kissinger would have growled, or worse, at anyone who tried to make him obey his contemptible schedule. But this time he merely turned to Israeli Defense Minister Moshe Dayan and suggested that it was time for him to roll up his maps of the Golan Heights. Dayan never suspected that Kissinger had anything special planned, nor did the clutch of journalists who cornered him in the hallway for a quick briefing on the Middle East.

At four P.M. that day, March 30, 1974, in a very private four-minute ceremony in the office of family court judge Francis Thomas near Washington's National Airport, Henry Kissinger, fifty, and Nancy Maginnes, thirty-nine, were married. Judge Thomas later recalled that he usually charged $25 to perform a wedding—and had once been paid $100 by the only other celebrity he had married,

Lana Turner—but in his excitement he forgot to collect from the Kissingers.

Nancy Sharon Maginnes had been born on April 13, 1934, in Manhattan, and raised in the Westchester County suburb of White Plains. Her father, Albert Bristol Maginnes, a former semiprofessional football player, was a prosperous Park Avenue trusts-and-estates law-yer; her mother, the former Agnes McKinley, was active in charity work. Both were from Social Register families of good Episcopal stock with memberships in the right clubs.

Nancy grew up with her two brothers and a cadre of male cousins on the family's twenty-acre estate. Tall, lanky, and athletic, with a pony of her own, she developed the tomboy toughness and intellectual self-assurance that came from being considered one of the boys. "If I had been one of those adorable, cute little girls," she later joked, "maybe I would have been treated like one."

While a student at the Masters School, a girls' prep school in nearby Dobbs Ferry, she edited the student newspaper and was voted in the yearbook as "the most absentminded" in her class. There she grew to her six-foot height, but she remembers the school "as a very gentle place, where I had no great feeling I was growing tall because there was no competition for clothes or dates." She graduated from Mount Holyoke College in 1955, earned an M.A. in history at the University of Michigan, then returned to the Masters School to teach for two years.

Restless, unattached, and in search of intellectual stimulation, she quit teaching after two years and headed off to Berkeley to pursue a doctorate. Her dissertation topic was the role of the Catholic Church in Vichy France, which led her to take a semester in Paris doing research at the Sorbonne.

During her summer vacations in the early 1960s, Nancy had worked as a researcher for Nelson Rockefeller at his office on West Fifty-fifth Street in Manhattan. Kissinger was in charge of coordinat-ing foreign policy research, and he would read her briefing papers and memos, returning them with scrawled comments and requests that they be rewritten. But Nancy had not caught his eye until the 1964 Republican Convention in San Francisco. At the Rockefeller cam-paign's hotel, Kissinger recalls, he saw Nancy talking to the other staffers and asked if she was going to be at the Cow Palace for the opening of the convention that evening. She said yes. "You have no idea how difficult it is to find someone in a crowd at a convention," he recalled, "but I found her."

In the summer of 1964, Nancy was thirty, single, self-assured, serious, and striking. She had streaked blond hair and smoky green eyes, a large smile, and a long, angular face. Her expressively arched brows conveyed the impression of curiosity, but her hooded eyes added an aura of ironic detachment. Long-stemmed and languid, with an assertive bearing and tobacco-cured voice, she was neither intimidated nor awed by Kissinger.

Once he had returned East, Kissinger wrote her. She invited him to talk to one of her graduate-school classes at Berkeley the next time he came to San Francisco. Later that year, pretending that important business was taking him there (in fact, he only had to go to Los Angeles), he called to ask her to dinner. That is when he first proposed marriage. She demurred. "I thought he was totally insane," she recalls. He was an older, divorced, Jewish intellectual with hopes of going into government. But she did accept his recommendation to return to New York as a full-time researcher for Rockefeller, giving up the chance to complete her doctorate.

Schooled in the graces of society, though averse to publicity in the manner of most women of her breeding, Nancy was commanding in social situations. She was the type who could impress a Rockefeller or an Alsop with her style, and who would never seem an embarrassment to an immigrant professor trying to make it in a more rarefied crowd. "For a Jewish kid from Germany wanting acceptance, the Maginnes type would be his dream," said one woman on Rockefeller's staff. "The right schools, the right clubs, the right kind of people."

Once he had scaled the bastions of America's power elite, Kissinger seemed fascinated by gaining entrée into its social elite. In this pursuit he was not particularly discriminating: he was drawn both to the café-society crowd of international jet-setters whose pictures frequented the pages of *Women's Wear Daily* and also to the more subdued social world inhabited by old-line New York Social Register families. Nancy's position at the intersection of these two worlds was one of the things that attracted Kissinger to her. He would astonish friends by remarking: "Can you believe that she's a member of the Colony Club and wants to marry me?"

Neither Kissinger's Jewish parents nor Nancy's Episcopalian ones were particularly pleased by the match, but that is not why it took so long for the marriage to occur. "If either Henry or I were religious fanatics," Nancy later said, "it would have been different." What delayed wedding plans was Nancy's reluctance to be married to someone in government, especially a person as prominent as Kissinger. Among the many things she did not share with him was his taste for publicity. By early 1973, however, Kissinger had decided to leave the government, and Nancy had agreed to marry him.

When the Watergate crisis and Nixon's offer of the State Department combined to change Kissinger's mind about resigning, he and Nancy decided to go through with their plans nonetheless, and a date was set for October. That was scuttled by the Yom Kippur War. At least six times in the next five months, a new date was chosen and a State Department lawyer would call Judge Thomas in Arlington and schedule a marriage ceremony for "an important government official."

Even on the night before the March 30 wedding, it was still not clear that it would occur. Kissinger had just returned from a five-day trip to Moscow, on which he had taken his children, David and Elizabeth. But he had not mentioned the planned wedding to them, and that Friday morning they flew back to Boston to go home to their mother. Nancy had been more conscientious about informing her family, and her widowed mother arrived in Washington that evening for a small dinner party. But Moshe Dayan had also just arrived, so Nancy had to settle for Lawrence Eagleburger as her dinner partner.

When Kissinger got home that night, Nancy checked with him to make sure that he had informed his family. "He replied that he had, but it was a very dubious sort of yes. A few moments later he left the room to make some phone calls."

As Nancy had suspected, he had not yet gotten around to telling his mother and father. It was about ten on Friday night, and his parents, as strict Orthodox Jews, were forbidden to answer the phone on the Sabbath. He could not get through to them. Eventually, with the help of his brother, he was able to get word to them, but they did not fly to Washington. They had stretched their observance of the Sabbath to see him sworn in as secretary of state on a Saturday, but they would not travel or attend a wedding ceremony on one. Kissinger's children, having just arrived home, returned to the Boston airport a few hours later to fly back to Washington and attend the ceremony.

At the State Department that Saturday, after Dayan and the press had drifted away, there was a prewedding luncheon in Kissinger's private dining room. In addition to family members, the guests included Joseph and Susan Mary Alsop, Winston and Bette Lord, Lawrence Eagleburger, Brent Scowcroft, and Carlyle Maw, the distinguished New York lawyer and State Department legal adviser who had helped arrange the ceremony.

Only the immediate family members went on to Judge Thomas's law office. The Kissingers exchanged the traditional wedding vows, except that, at their request, Judge Thomas had not included the word *obey.*

Nixon called Nancy that day to wish her well. For some reason that she could never fathom, the president began to warn her in vivid terms about the dangers of the poisonous snakes to be found in Acapulco, where she and Kissinger were going on their honeymoon. "Just remember," Nixon said, "if you get the venom out quickly enough, you'll be okay."

The Kissingers flew to Mexico in Nelson Rockefeller's jet, and they spent their honeymoon in an estate lent to them by Eustaquio Escandon, a wealthy pharmaceutical importer, banker, and socialite. It was not an intimate interlude. In addition to the Kissingers, there were twelve Secret Service agents, twenty Mexican police, plus forty reporters camped outside the gate. Kissinger's aide Jerry Bremer was there to handle logistics and communications, photographer David Hume Kennerly came down to do a shoot, and the house contained a mad green parrot that shrieked every time Kissinger entered the foyer. As they sailed on a thirty-foot sloop around the bay, Kissinger's arm around his new wife, a motorboat laden with newsmen and photographers followed alongside.

Nancy proved her diplomatic panache when she accompanied her husband on the Syrian shuttle two months later, in June. Standing next to Arab leaders, she would cock one knee so as not to tower over them (or her husband). Every detail of her actions was highlighted in the newspapers, Israeli and Arab as well as American. They noted that she attended her husband's briefings on the plane in her stocking feet, and also that her toenails were painted to color-coordinate with each day's outfit. When she dove into the pool at the King David Hotel, she impressed everyone with her ability to swim each lap with only four graceful strokes; one of her edgy Secret Service guards jumped in wearing shorts and a polo shirt to swim at her side. "More people here," said Golda Meir in one of her toasts, "now talk about Nancy than Dr. Henry."

Her poise helped her to hide the anxieties that resulted in her being hospitalized for ulcers soon after her return. Fiercely protective of her husband, acidic about his enemies, she seemed to internalize the problems that beset him. Though she rarely exploded in temper the way he did, she chain-smoked Marlboros and had enough nervous energy to maintain a slim figure despite freely indulging in chocolates and junk food.

Politically, Nancy was more conservative than her husband; she had fewer qualms, for example, about the use of American force in Vietnam. At the time of the January 1973 peace agreement, she confided to friends that she feared the U.S. was not living up to its commitments. "I just have the instinctive, gut reaction that if you get into a war, it is much less complicated if you win it than if you lose it," she later said. "Vietnam was incredibly mismanaged."

During the three years she spent living in Washington, Nancy never learned to like the town, which she regarded as rather provincial and swamplike. She dutifully attended the embassy receptions and large parties, but her preferred form of entertainment was hosting dinner parties for eight or so friends. Her spirit was more attuned to the New York City scene, especially the haute-couture crowd.

Among Nancy's great strengths were her intellect, her deeply held views, and her sure grounding in the subject of foreign policy. Often she would read Kissinger's speeches, analyze them, and make suggestions. But after their marriage, when she was forced to give up her work coordinating foreign policy research for Rockefeller's Critical Choices program, she began to take herself less seriously and—or so it seemed to her friends—shed her intellectual image for one that was more socially frivolous. Clothes and interior decorators replaced world affairs and ideas as her favored topics of conversation.

Partly it was due to the exigencies of her role: the wife of a secretary of state can express her personal views only at her peril. After a lifetime avoiding publicity, she suddenly found herself surrounded by a world of journalists, forcing her to watch every word she said. In addition, she was married to a man whose outlook tended to be heavy to the point of ponderousness. By helping him to lighten up more often, she was doubtlessly doing him a greater favor than by critiquing his policy pronouncements.[1]

THE DECLINE AND FALL OF RICHARD NIXON, AUGUST 1974

As Watergate engulfed the Nixon administration, Kissinger emerged as the foremost figure not crippled by the scandal. He had been buffeted by revelations about the wiretaps, and also by Senate investigations that exposed the secrets of the Cambodian bombings and the Yeoman Radford spy ring. But he was never sucked into the maelstrom of the Watergate investigation, nor was there ever a serious threat that he would be forced to resign or face criminal charges.

Instead, the consensus among Washington's establishment was that he should be protected. "He is the one figure of stature remaining amid the ruins of Richard Nixon's stricken Administration," *Time* wrote at the end of 1973. Even some of the president's most fervent opponents were protective of Kissinger: they feared that if the scandal spread to Kissinger, Nixon's impeachment would be *less* rather than *more* likely. "There is a genuine worry in the Senate that everything could come apart overseas if the president is impeached," George McGovern, the Democrat Nixon defeated in the disputed campaign, told a reporter off the record in April 1974. "If Kissinger was implicated in something like the Plumbers' operation, impeachment would be regarded as a much greater risk."[2]

Kissinger had been lucky that his natural tendency to kibitz from the sidelines about White House activities was deflected by his immersion in overseas activity at key moments of the Watergate affair. When the burglars made their first failed attempt on May 27, 1972, Kissinger was in Moscow at the summit. During the successful break-in on June 16, he was flying to Beijing to meet with Zhou Enlai. During the tidal wave of leaks by Deep Throat and others during October 1972, Kissinger was shuttling between Paris and Saigon in the final Vietnam negotiating frenzy. When John Dean spelled out the extent of the cover-up to Nixon on March 21, 1973, Kissinger was on a week-long vacation in Acapulco. During the Saturday Night Massacre of October 20, 1973, Kissinger was in Moscow securing a cease-fire of the Yom Kippur War. And when Nixon released the White House tapes on April 24, 1974, Kissinger was in Geneva for meetings with Soviet Foreign Minister Gromyko.

The president did occasionally ask Kissinger's advice as the scandal began to unfold, though usually in an offhanded way. They were together in San Clemente in April 1973 when Senator Sam Ervin began hearings as chairman of a special House-Senate Watergate investigation committee. That week, the president called in Kissinger to ask if he felt Haldeman and Ehrlichman should testify. No, Kissinger replied, that would be an admission of their guilt.

Kissinger learned more about the scandal later that month when Leonard Garment, a former law partner of Nixon's and now an adviser, dropped by his corner office one Saturday morning. Casually slouching on Kissinger's couch, Garment described the web of illegal campaign activities that fell under the Watergate rubric. They agreed that only "radical surgery"—firing everyone involved and making a clean admission of what had happened—could solve things. The problem, Garment suggested, was that Nixon himself might be involved.

Kissinger was stunned. That evening, he was at the annual White House Correspondents dinner when he was called to the phone. It was Nixon, and he was agitated. "Do you agree," he said, barking an abrupt question as he often did in such moods, "that we should draw the wagons around the White House?"

From his conversation with Garment that morning, Kissinger

knew that such stonewalling would not work. He believed—as he told friends at the time and as he repeatedly claimed later—that the only solution was to dig out all of the facts quickly and make a clean breast of everything. But it was not exactly the ideal setting to tell this to the president. More to the point, it was not in Kissinger's nature to tell the president what he did not want to hear. Even after four years, he was still prone to catering to Nixon's tough-guy mentality and telling him to treat his critics and the press "with cold contempt." So, in a telephone call that was taped for posterity and will someday be released, Kissinger muttered his assent. "All right," said Nixon, "we will draw the wagons around the White House."[3]

John Andrews, a conservative and idealistic young speechwriter, was among those who felt most forcefully that Nixon could save himself only by uncovering and revealing all of the facts about Watergate. In August 1973, just after John Dean had finished testifying, Andrews took a walk at San Clemente with Kissinger. The president, Andrews said, had to be turned around so that he would begin acting like a prosecutor rather than a fugitive. "Why doesn't he run with the hounds instead of the foxes?" Andrews asked.

"Because," Kissinger responded, "he's one of the foxes. He is the fox."

Andrews was then working on a major Watergate speech that Nixon planned to give. The president had told him to consult with Kissinger and Ziegler about the tone it should take. "The president needs to show contrition, just as Kennedy did after the Bay of Pigs," Kissinger told him. "There is a huge reservoir of sympathy the president can tap if he's contrite."

Ziegler thought otherwise. "Contrition is bullshit," the press secretary said when informed of Kissinger's advice. "No apologies." Nixon apparently agreed. He rewrote Andrews's draft and denied all of John Dean's allegations. (Andrews, citing his disillusionment over the handling of Watergate, resigned a few months later.)[4]

Kissinger was in Moscow during the October 20, 1973, Saturday Night Massacre, in which Nixon ousted Special Prosecutor Archibald Cox and Attorney General Elliot Richardson. But before leaving, Kissinger had met privately and discussed the situation with Richardson, who had long been a friend and bureaucratic ally. To his horror, Kissinger was faced upon his return from Moscow with stories implying that he had urged Richardson to carry out Nixon's orders and not to resign.

At midday on October 24—the day that the Israeli-Egyptian cease-fire he had negotiated was completely unraveling in a way that would lead to a nuclear alert—Kissinger took time out from the crisis to telephone Richardson and make sure matters were straight. "I can't tell you how saddened I am," Kissinger said, referring to Richardson's resignation. "I consider you one of the guarantees of virtue in this administration." Richardson agreed that it was all very sad. Then Kissinger got to the point. "The thing that bothers me is that Murrey Marder and Scotty Reston both allege that I tried to dissuade you from your course," Kissinger said in a phone call that was recorded by his office. "Now, our meeting was at your initiative, and as far as our discussion of general principles, it would have led you in the opposite direction." Richardson assented.[5]

Later that week, as the uproar over the firing of Cox grew, Nixon permitted some of the White House tapes to be given to the federal court. Kissinger had been telling his friends that he favored a policy of quick and full disclosure; but in private, talking to Haig, he questioned the decision to release the tapes. "How are we going to risk giving up other documents now?" he asked Haig. The president's staff chief replied that "we will just have to take them case by case."[6]

Spiro Agnew's resignation—the result of an unrelated tax and bribery probe—late in October 1973 caused Kissinger to worry about who might replace him as vice president. (Kissinger, because he was foreign born, was barred by the Constitution from being selected.) His greatest fear was that Nixon would choose John Connally, whose headstrong foreign policy views made up in fervor what they lacked in subtlety. Kissinger made it clear to Haig that Connally was the one choice he would find unacceptable. His preference, he said, was Rockefeller. When Nixon ended up selecting Congressman Gerald Ford, the choice left Kissinger cold but not upset.

After becoming secretary of state, Kissinger's approach to Watergate was to stay as far away from it—and Washington—as possible. From October 1973 until Nixon's resignation in August 1974, Kissinger visited twenty-eight countries, including six trips to the Middle East, and traveled a total of 196,000 miles overseas, an average of 600 miles per day. To one foreign minister he met in his office he joked: "I am happy your stay in Washington coincided with one of my visits here."

By mid-July 1974, Kissinger was convinced that Nixon had to resign, and quickly. Had he been on the House Judiciary Committee, Kissinger later said, he would have voted in favor of impeachment. That month, he and Haig were in San Clemente with the president. "How long can this go on?" Kissinger asked his former deputy as they sat in a little office near the president's home. Haig said he was not sure, and he solicited Kissinger's advice. Nixon's resignation, Kissinger said, should come as soon as Haig could accomplish it. Haig said he agreed.

The strains between these two crafty and ambitious men had receded in the face of Watergate. Though they had bickered like schoolboys a few weeks earlier over who would get the suite next door to Nixon's in the Kremlin at the final summit there (Haig won), they had begun putting aside their rivalry as they sought to guide Nixon toward resignation. Each day, Haig would call Kissinger to report on the progress he was making and the meetings he was setting up. Kissinger would help by arranging for telephone calls that would edge Nixon in the desired direction. By the end of July, the House Judiciary Committee had voted in favor of three articles of impeachment, and the full House was expected to do the same, thus sending the matter to the Senate for a trial.

On Saturday, August 3, the Haigs and Kissingers did something that was unusual for them: they went out socially together. Using the president's box at the Kennedy Center, they went to a performance of *Desire Under the Elms*. Even had it been one of Eugene O'Neill's better plays, it could not have competed with the real-life drama going on around them. Throughout the performance, Kissinger and Haig kept going to the back of the box to discuss strategies for forcing Nixon to face reality.

Yet Kissinger did not bring himself to advise Nixon to resign until August 6, the day before the decision was made. It was shortly after noon, following a meandering and inconclusive cabinet meeting. Kissinger wandered into the Oval Office uninvited, though with Haig's approval. If Nixon continued to fight, Kissinger said, the ensuing impeachment trial would paralyze the nation and its foreign policy. Nixon was noncommittal. He said he would be in touch.

The president did call back later that evening, but not to discuss resignation. He had just gotten a request from Israel for military aid. Not only was he going to reject it, he had decided to cut off all military shipments to Israel immediately until they agreed to a comprehensive peace and withdrawal from occupied lands. He told Kissinger he regretted not doing it earlier. To Kissinger it seemed as if this was Nixon's odd way of "retaliation" for the advice he had given earlier in the day, as if cutting off Israel was a way to punish his Jewish secretary of state. (Kissinger never sent the relevant papers to Nixon; President Ford reversed the order four days later.)

Late the following afternoon—Wednesday, August 7—Haig called Kissinger at the State Department and asked him to come right over to the Oval Office. There he found Nixon alone, staring out of the bay windows into the Rose Garden. He had decided to resign, he said, and would announce it in a speech the following night. It would become effective Friday at noon. Kissinger, seeking to make the conversation businesslike, began describing how other governments should be informed. As he did, Nixon began ruminating about the reaction that various leaders—Mao, Brezhnev, Zhou—would have when they read their cables that night.

"History will treat you more kindly than your contemporaries," Kissinger told him.

"It depends on who writes the history," said Nixon.

Kissinger had never been personally close to Nixon and was invariably nervous in his presence. After more than five years, he still called him "Mr. President" at all times. But at that meeting Kissinger did something unusual: he touched Nixon. Then he put his arm around him and, as he recalls, embraced him.[7]

That evening, Kissinger was having dinner at home with Nancy and columnist Joseph Alsop. Also there were David and Elizabeth, visiting from Boston on their summer vacation. Around nine P.M., the telephone rang. It was Nixon. He was alone. Could Kissinger come by for a talk?

The scene that ensued has become famous, largely due to a vivid account by Bob Woodward and Carl Bernstein in *The Final Days.* Only two people were present, Nixon and Kissinger, and each later told a slightly different version. But there are other sources who can testify secondhand. Lawrence Eagleburger and Brent Scowcroft were both sitting in Kissinger's West Wing office at the time, and when he returned after his ninety minutes with Nixon, he gave them a complete description of what had happened. Based on interviews with Kissinger, Eagleburger, and Scowcroft, plus a conversation with Nixon on the subject, the following version of that strange night emerges.[8]

Nixon had spent the early part of the evening in a rather manic effort to pose his wife and two daughters for a series of final family portraits he wanted White House photographer Ollie Atkins to take. Then he wandered alone to the Lincoln Sitting Room, a small alcove on the second floor of the living quarters that was his private refuge. His favorite Tchaikovsky and Rachmaninoff albums were lined up on a shelf, and he would play them repeatedly as he sat brooding in his overstuffed armchair, feet propped up on an ottoman, a yellow legal pad on his lap.

That was how Kissinger found him that hot Wednesday night. Here was a man, Kissinger thought, who had created a political persona from an amorphous identity, who had impelled himself to reach the pinnacle through a feat of will that was so intense as to seem almost demented, and then, in a process he could not understand, had been plunged into an unfathomable hell by what he still considered just a third-rate burglary. It was, Kissinger later said, "a fate of biblical proportions."

Thus it was no surprise that Richard Nixon was, as Kissinger later put it, "almost a basket case" that evening. He sought reassurance, and Kissinger sought to provide it. Together they began recounting each of the foreign policy successes, both of them adding their recollections, embellishing the anecdotes. Kissinger was kind: he kept stressing how each triumph had only been possible because of an act of courage by Nixon at the right moment.

Without the Cambodian invasion and the mining of the Haiphong harbors, there could never have been peace with honor in Vietnam, Kissinger told the distraught president. The willingness to risk the Moscow summit, Kissinger reminded Nixon, had been his decision alone, and it had worked. Kissinger was even willing, that evening at least, to give Nixon full credit for designing the opening to China. Again they talked about history's verdict, and again Nixon made his dark joke about its depending on who wrote the histories.

At one point, as Nixon was recounting the night that Zhou Enlai's invitation to China had arrived, he remembered the bottle of Courvoisier brandy that he had opened then for their private toast. It was still in the pantry, he said. It had not been touched since. Nixon padded down the dark hall, suddenly intent on finding the bottle. He poured two glasses, and they drank another toast.

For much of the conversation, Nixon was able to stay composed. But when he raised the prospect of facing a criminal trial after his resignation, he became overwrought. A trial would kill him, he said. That was what his enemies wanted. "If they harass you," Kissinger pledged, "I am going to resign." He would quit and tell the world why. As Nixon recalled the scene, Kissinger's voice broke as he made the promise, and he began to cry.

That, Nixon later recalled, caused him to cry as well. "Henry, you're not going to resign," the president said. "Don't ever talk that way." The country would need him; there was no one who could shine his shoes, much less fill them.

Kissinger confirmed the exchange if not the emotionalism that Nixon ascribed to it. "You would think that the purpose of meeting had been to discuss my resignation rather than his," Kissinger later grumbled upon hearing a version of Nixon's account.

Swept up by the emotion and shaken by the sight of Nixon coming unglued, Kissinger began to perspire. He was ready to leave, but the president wanted to go over one more time some of the triumphs they had shared. Kissinger obliged. Finally, an hour and a half after he had arrived, Kissinger stood up, and Nixon began walking him down the wide hallway that bisects the family quarters toward a private elevator.

But the wrenching evening was not quite over. At the entrance to the Lincoln Bedroom, Nixon stopped. You and I, he said to Kissinger, probably have different religious beliefs "if we were to examine them in a strictly technical way." But he knew that Kissinger shared his "strong belief in a Supreme Being." In fact, he was sure Kissinger's belief in God was as strong as his own. Late at night, Nixon confided, after working in the Lincoln Sitting Room, he would often stop and follow his mother's Quaker custom by getting on his knees in prayer.

Nixon then asked his secretary of state to kneel and pray with him. It was, for Kissinger, an awkward request; even as a child, back when he was religiously inclined, prayers did not involve kneeling. Nevertheless, tentatively bending one knee, then the other, he knelt down and prayed with the president.

Years later, Kissinger still felt uncomfortable discussing the scene, as if it were one last little humiliation inflicted on him by the oddest man he had ever met. Officially, he would say that his memory was unclear about whether or not he knelt—a patently unconvincing assertion about a moment that was surely not possible to forget. But in private, he did not deny that he knelt down to pray with his president, nor was there any cause to be ashamed of such action. To have spurned Nixon's request would have been heartless. Given the surreal and tragic circumstances, prayer seemed to Kissinger to be as appropriate as anything. His only problem was that no prayers came into his head at that moment, only what he later described as "a deep sense of awe which seemed its own meaning."

The president began to cry. He was not hysterical, nor did he pound on the floor. But through his sobs he bemoaned his fate and railed against the agony that his enemies had dealt to him. History, Kissinger assured him one more time, would treat him more kindly.

When he got back to his office, where Eagleburger and Scowcroft had been growing rather anxious, Kissinger's shirt was drenched in sweat. "Nothing I have been through has ever been so traumatic," he said. Scowcroft mentioned that he should be flattered that, on his final night, the president had turned to him. Eagleburger said he was surprised to see Kissinger so moved, so emotional, so sympathetic. "At times I've thought you're not human," he said, "but I was wrong." Kissinger talked for a while more about how wrenching the evening had been, what a shock it was to see Nixon in that condition. "He is truly a tragic figure," Kissinger said, but his tone conveyed sympathy, even sorrow, rather than disdain.

Then, as the conversation continued, Nixon's private line to Kissinger rang. As Kissinger answered it, Eagleburger went across the room to pick up a dead-key extension and listen in. At first they had trouble understanding the president, who was speaking in a low monotone and slurring his words from the fatigue and brandy. Kissinger must not remember the encounter as a sign of weakness, Nixon implored. Instead, he should recall all the times Nixon had been courageous and bared his soul. Above all, the president begged, he must never tell anyone what had occurred or that he had watched the president cry.

Eagleburger quietly put down the extension. Kissinger made the president a promise: if he ever spoke of the evening, he would do it with respect.

The tape machine in the cabinets of Kissinger's outer office, which recorded all of his calls, had automatically gone to work. The next morning, as was standard procedure, a transcript was prepared. But shortly thereafter, with Kissinger's permission, Scowcroft personally destroyed both the transcript and the tape.

Later, Kissinger (as well as his aides) would talk on background to Woodward and Bernstein, who were able to recreate much of the scene. But Kissinger would insist that he never said anything that portrayed Richard Nixon in a disrespectful light. "He had conducted himself humanly and worthily," Kissinger later wrote.

Kissinger's connection to Watergate was indirect. He was not involved in the break-in or even the cover-up, but he had acquiesced in —even contributed to—the mind-set that had bred the scandal. It was his fury at the leaks about the Cambodian bombing that had led to the wiretaps, and about the Pentagon Papers that had led to the Plumbers' Unit.

There was an important distinction between the wiretaps and the effort to bug Democratic headquarters at the Watergate: the wiretaps were done through the FBI and were at least considered at the time to be legal, whereas Watergate was a patently illegal rogue operation funded by secret contributions. But the mind-set that had led to the wiretaps—listening in on the home phones of close aides and unwary reporters, some of whom were chosen for political reasons rather than valid security concerns—resembled the mind-set that had led to bugging the Democratic Party chairman.

Kissinger played along with Nixon's tough-guy talk and catered to his paranoia about "enemies" because he knew that this was the price one paid for admission to the president's inner circle. This devil's bargain did not cause Watergate. It was not an indictable offense. It could even be justified, if one tried hard enough, as a trade-off for the foreign policy triumphs that also occurred. However, it was the willingness of so many officials, Kissinger high among them, to make such compromises that allowed the Watergate mind-set to prevail.

KISSINGER AND FORD: BREAKING IN A NEW PRESIDENT

Gerald Ford was one of the many contacts Kissinger had made through his Harvard seminars. In the early 1960s, when the Michigan congressman was the ranking Republican on the Defense Appropriations subcommittee, he got a call from a professor he did not know asking him to be a guest lecturer at a defense policy seminar. So Ford, who was flattered, went up to spend two hours teaching Kissinger's students. "Henry made the visit a very pleasant experience for me," recalled Ford, who enjoyed it so much that he came back two years later. "I found him to be bright and hospitable and attentive."

Their paths continued to cross: Ford became a participant in Rockefeller's Critical Choices program, which Kissinger helped to run, then was a regular at the Republican leadership briefings held at the White House during Nixon's first term. To anyone who asked, the uncomplicated congressman would proclaim his awe at Kissinger's intellect. So it was no surprise that as early as March 1974, back when the vice president was avoiding any comment about a possible Nixon resignation, he told reporter John Osborne of *The New Republic* that if he ever became president, he would keep Kissinger.

During Nixon's final month, Kissinger personally took over from Scowcroft the job of conducting the vice president's foreign policy briefing. Ford remembers that the sessions, under Kissinger, became longer and more frequent.

Nixon had only one piece of personnel advice when he called Ford to the White House to say that he was resigning: keep Kissinger. But Nixon added a caveat. "Henry is a genius," he said, "but you don't have to accept everything he recommends. He can be invaluable, and he'll be very loyal, but you can't let him have a totally free hand." Nixon put it more bluntly when speaking to one of his staffers. "Ford has just got to realize there are times when Henry has to be kicked in the nuts," he said. "Because sometimes Henry starts to think he's president. But at other times you have to pet Henry and treat him like a child."

That afternoon Ford phoned Kissinger, later saying that he felt it important to give him some reassurance. "Henry," he said, "I need you. . . . I'll do everything I can to work with you."

"Sir, it will be my job to get along with you and not yours to get along with me," Kissinger replied.[9]

Gerald Ford of Omaha, Nebraska, and Grand Rapids, Michigan, was about as different from Henry Kissinger of Fürth, Germany, as the political system permits two bedfellows to be. Ford's strength lay in his simplicity, his solidness, and his fingertip feel for the values that down-home Americans hold dear. He was a man at ease with himself and with his fundamental faith in the American system—qualities that Nixon and Kissinger, for all of their brilliance, did not share.

Either by luck, happenstance, or divine grace, the nation's constitutional process had come forth with an unexpected president who was right for the moment. Ford was straightforward rather than deceitful, and his rise had come by virtue of good human instincts rather than brilliant designs. He had a rocklike common sense that was neither cluttered by excess cleverness nor unduly burdened by a reflective intelligence.

This decency of Gerald Ford was sometimes belittled, as if decency were a pleasant enough virtue but not one to base a presidency on. If part of the job of Nixon's aides had been to save him from his worst instincts, Ford's aides felt they had to save their president from his best instincts. But in tough times, decency is more than a virtue; it is a grace. It was the word that George Orwell used for what kept Britons sane when their intellectuals were embracing tyrannies of the Left and the Right. After an administration that had been felled by its addiction to secrecy and conspiracy, a dose of decency was a welcome antidote.

Soon after Ford took office, reporters snidely asked Kissinger why the president had been brought into a meeting with Soviet foreign minister Gromyko concerning the details of the SALT II talks. Kissinger paused, smiled mischievously, and (knowing his press corps would not betray him by quoting him) replied: "We felt the need to get some technical competence into the discussions."

But a few months later, when North Vietnam was poised to capture Saigon, Ford would show the value of his own foreign policy instincts. Kissinger was raging about the need for the U.S. to become reengaged in Vietnam, despite a vote in Congress to stop all aid. Ford, on the other hand, understood that the American people would not support continued involvement and that Kissinger's predictions of doom to U.S. credibility were overblown. As in many other cases where the brilliant men around him were not so smart, Ford turned out to be not so dumb.

"It was a strange friendship," Ford said of his relationship to Kissinger. "You'll find none with more wildly divergent backgrounds. I trusted him, and he was not used to that. And I think that helped him trust me." [10]

The secret to Ford's success with Kissinger was that he was a secure man, unthreatened by Kissinger's brilliance. "President Ford made it clear that he considered my father intellectually superior to him, but he was comfortable with that," said David Kissinger. [11]

Ford was even unthreatened by Kissinger's appetite for publicity, and he realized that satisfying Kissinger's craving for recognition—something that Nixon took bitter delight in thwarting—would make everyone better off. "You get Henry to do better when he's in his glory."

Robert Hartmann, a gruff former newsman who joined Ford's congressional staff in the 1960s and became a counselor in the White House, captures this aspect of the Ford-Kissinger relationship:

> Henry was and is a congenital celebrity. His compulsion to crow is as natural as a rooster's, his propensity to preen as normal as a peacock's. Ford was wiser than most about this. He knew it was hopeless to fool with Mother Nature. Henry's vanity was part of his total ability to perform well. If he needed more reassurance than the rest of us, Ford gladly gave it. [12]

Kissinger felt much more relaxed around Ford than Nixon. When Ford invited him one weekend to Camp David, Kissinger felt free to bring along not only his son, David, but also the new yellow Labrador retriever, named Tyler, which Nancy had just bought. Kissinger was incorrigible about spoiling dogs. At dinner, he kept feeding Tyler under the table while the president watched. Ford's own retriever, Liberty, sat politely at a distance like a properly bred dog. Then Tyler went off and ate Liberty's food. As Kissinger fussed over his puppy, Ford smiled affectionately. "My father never would have felt comfortable enough with Nixon," David said, "to bring his dog along to Camp David."

What made Ford so tolerant toward Kissinger was that he was truly fond of him. Years later, when presenting him with the 1991 Nelson Rockefeller award for public service, Ford said of Kissinger: "I not only admire Henry immensely, I also like him." [13]

With the transition from a manipulative president deeply interested in foreign policy to a forthright one with little such interest, a question arose as to whether Kissinger's own style would change. "Will he move to a more open style, taking the cue from his new president?" asked Richard Holbrooke in a *Boston Globe* magazine cover story. "Or will he remain the elusive, manipulative, brilliant diplomatist of recent years?"

The issue went to the heart of Kissinger's character. Was his secretive style mainly a function of his service to Nixon, or was it part of his personal baggage?

The record indicates that Kissinger's style was largely a reflection of his own nature, reinforced but not caused by his association with Nixon. It had been evident in the past when he worked in less sordid surroundings: at Harvard, where he clashed with the gentlemanly Robert Bowie, and on the Rockefeller staff, where he had run-ins with Emmett John Hughes and others. And these bureaucratic rivalries would be evident, although not quite as pronounced, in the administration of genial and forthright Gerald Ford.

"He's about as supersensitive to criticism as anyone I know," Ford said. Tending to Kissinger's vulnerable ego meant regularly dealing with his sensitivity to slights. As often as once a week, he would arrive in the Oval Office anguishing over some anonymous quote attacking him or some perceived raid on his turf by another staffer. "It was usually on a Monday," Ford recalled. "He would unburden himself: 'All this criticism is too much,' he would say, referring to some comment in the press or some leak. He always felt it was conspirators. 'I have to resign,' he would tell me."

Soothingly puffing his pipe, Ford would listen and stroke and restore Kissinger's calm. "I would take however long it required, which was sometimes minutes and often a whole hour, to reassure him and tell him how important he was to the country and ask him please to stay." The task was not one that Ford particularly enjoyed, but he realized that managing such problems was one of his talents, just as managing the world's problems was one of Kissinger's.

What vexed Kissinger more than most any world problem was having to cope with yet another new set of top White House aides determined (or at least he so suspected) to diminish his power. He had outlasted Haldeman and Ehrlichman, and now Haig was on his way out. ("I wanted someone I could totally work with and trust," Ford later said in explaining why he ousted Haig.) The thought of becoming embroiled in the internecine rivalries and power struggles of a new clique, Kissinger recalled, "filled me with a sense of dread." [14]

After some floundering, Ford selected as his chief of staff Donald

Rumsfeld, a former Eagle Scout and Republican congressman from an affluent Chicago suburb. Rumsfeld was bright, charming, and ambitious, the last of these traits causing an inevitable clash with Kissinger. Rumsfeld also felt it was crucial to portray Ford as more in command, more "presidential." He angrily told the new president that it had begun to appear that he was delegating most policy decisions and leaving himself with "such tasks as meeting with the Sunflower Queen and receiving the Thanksgiving turkey." Solving the problem, Rumsfeld felt, required making sure that it did not seem as if Ford were merely lip-synching Kissinger's foreign policy.

Together with Press Secretary Ron Nessen, Rumsfeld put out the word at one point that Ford was seeking foreign policy advice from a broader spectrum of people. It was an innocent enough assertion that had the added attribute of containing a trace of truth. When CBS newsman Bob Schieffer asked whether this meant that Ford was pulling away from Kissinger, Nessen nodded yes.

The resulting story sent the press pack baying. Kissinger fumed, railed at Nessen and Rumsfeld, then threatened to resign. Nessen scurried for cover by telling other reporters that the stories about Kissinger's decline were totally fabricated. Then he did something he later confessed to being ashamed of: he fired a low-level staffer for being the source of the leaks, even though Nessen knew he was not. The result was that Nessen's stature was diminished, as was Kissinger's, as was Rumsfeld's, as was Ford's.

The effort to shrink Kissinger continued at a NATO summit in May 1975. Rumsfeld decided, and Ford concurred, that the president rather than Kissinger would conduct the press briefings while in Brussels, and he would be pictured conferring with NATO leaders without Kissinger included in the shots. This was not merely some personal prejudice of an anti-Kissinger cabal; even Kissinger should have realized (but didn't) that the president's stature was diminished by the perception that Kissinger was running foreign policy.

Kissinger stormed into Nessen's curtained-off cubicle next to the pressroom in Brussels to raise hell. If his rivals on the staff thought that he was going to allow himself to be nibbled to death, Kissinger railed, they were crazy. When angered, Kissinger warned, he knew how to strike back. "It became a ritual on virtually every trip," Nessen recalled, "for Henry to blow up at least once about anti-Kissinger leaks, his tone bitter and arrogant, his voice high-pitched and quavery."

On the flight home, Kissinger leaned over to Ford's gruff speechwriter, Robert Hartmann, and apologized for suspecting him as a prime leaker. "Now it is perfectly clear who has been doing it," Kissinger said. "But we have ways of dealing with those clowns." With a cantankerous facade but a humorous heart, Hartmann tended to take Kissinger in stride, figuring that anyone who hated Rumsfeld couldn't be all bad. In addition, as Hartmann once said about Ford's coddling of Kissinger, "people who employ geniuses, as Michelangelo taught several Popes, have to pay a price."[15]

Outweighing all of these new rivalries, however, was the presence of the man for whom Kissinger felt the most trust and affection of anyone in public life: Nelson Rockefeller, who was selected by Ford to become the new vice president, partly at Kissinger's urging. The Kissingers and the Rockefellers spent New Year's together at the outset of 1975 at Dorado Beach in Puerto Rico. Relaxing in the sun with a Rockefeller and married to a socially impeccable former Rockefeller aide, Kissinger seemed more at peace with himself than he had been for a long time.

To friends, he said the transition from Nixon to Ford was as if a nervous knot had, after more than five years, suddenly disappeared from his stomach. "It's much easier, infinitely easier, on human grounds," Kissinger told his traveling press corps off the record. Over the next two years, Kissinger would make, almost despite himself, some disparaging comments about the thickness of Ford's skull, but there was an affection to the remarks rather than a bitterness. "It was touching to hear my father talk about Ford and to watch how comfortable he seemed to be in this new president's presence," recalled David Kissinger.[16]

Though it would not prevent the staff rivalries and the personal insecurities from swirling, this new mood would slowly manifest itself in a somewhat more open and straightforward conduct of foreign policy.

TWENTY-SEVEN

THE DEATH
OF DÉTENTE

An Odd Coalition
Takes a Hard Line

> *Conservatives who hated Communists and liberals who hated Nixon came together in a rare convergence, like an eclipse of the sun.* —KISSINGER, YEARS OF UPHEAVAL, *1982*

STRANGE BEDFELLOWS

The policy of détente—with its reduction in Soviet-American tensions—had wide appeal. Businessmen liked the notion of dealing with the Russians in a businesslike manner, especially when it came to trade. Farmers liked having a new market for their grain, editorialists lauded the arms control agreements, and even some mainstream conservatives felt that Nixon and Kissinger had pulled off a savvy balancing act at a time when America's willingness to assert itself in the world was going through a post-Vietnam depression.

Yet for reasons that were personal as well as ideological, an odd coalition began to grow in opposition to the policy. As Nixon's power waned and Gerald Ford came into office, Kissinger found himself fighting a rearguard defense of détente against a shifting array of domestic critics:

• The 1972 trade agreements were attacked by Democratic Senator Henry Jackson, Jewish leaders, and human rights advocates, who sought to link it to a requirement that Moscow remove restrictions on the emigration of Jews and other citizens.

• Labor union leaders, who had never been fans of either the Soviets or freer trade, also opposed the bill.

• At the same time, the SALT process was attacked, by Senator Jackson and Defense Secretary Schlesinger among others, for allowing the Soviets to maintain a numerical advantage in heavy missiles.

• Later, the entire goal of détente was assailed on moral grounds by righteous prophets ranging from Daniel Patrick Moynihan to Ronald Reagan to Alexander Solzhenitsyn, who criticized it as a realpolitik accommodation of Soviet power that gave short shrift to human values and American ideals.

The combination of anticommunist conservatives and anti-Nixon liberals who came together to oppose détente represented, as Kissinger later noted, "a rare convergence, like an eclipse of the sun."[1]

The conservatives' critique was most consistent. Long wary of the communist menace, they argued that détente—and especially the overselling of its glories—would lull Americans into complacency. In cases such as the October 1973 Middle East war, where the cup of benefits that came from détente could be viewed as half-empty or half-full, they were quick to pounce on the pessimistic interpretation, pointing out that détente had failed to prevent a crisis. They were also ever suspicious that negotiations over European security arrangements, leading up to a treaty that would be signed in Helsinki in 1975, were new Yalta-like sellouts of Eastern Europe and the Baltics. Ronald Reagan, then California governor, became the political and symbolic flag-bearer of this flank of attack.

Among the conservative dissenters were Kissinger's old patron Fritz Kraemer and his son, Sven, who worked on Kissinger's staff. Sven felt Kissinger's problem was that "he was not metaphysically anchored—no religion, no close friends, a pessimist." The young staffer, who shared his father's intensity of convictions, would write long memos about the danger of being soft on the Soviets, attach them to Kissinger speeches with offending passages underlined, and send them through the State Department's "dissent channel." Finally, Kissinger had Sonnenfeldt order him to desist.

More damaging than the conservative assault, which was to be expected, was the opposition to détente from former liberals, including those who had just recently been part of the peace movement. The neoconservatives, as these newcomers to the anticommunist crusade came to be called, were spearheaded by Jewish intellectuals and other strong supporters of Israel. They were partly motivated by the fear that America's weak-kneed anti-interventionist mood would combine with an eagerness to curry favor with Moscow and thus make the U.S. a less staunch defender of Israel. "There was a strong sense that Israel was doomed unless U.S. power in the world was maintained," said Richard Perle, one of the group's mandarins. "The Jewish-neoconservative connection sprang from that period of worries about détente and Israel."

These worries were heightened by the October 1973 war, during which Kissinger went to Moscow to arrange a cease-fire sooner than Israeli hard-liners wanted. Many viewed the heavy pressures he put on Israel, especially during the "reassessment" of American relations after the initial failure to reach a second Sinai accord in 1975, as part of his policy of détente. "Especially after the 1975 reassessment," Kissinger said, "assaults on détente stemmed from accusations that I was abandoning Israel." He also has a more personal explanation: "They could forgive me for being Jewish and secretary of state, but not for being Jewish, secretary of state, *and* marrying a tall, blond WASP."

Nixon, the staunch anticommunist, and Kissinger, the power-oriented defender of American credibility, found it astounding to be criticized as too soft on the Soviets by the likes of Norman Podhoretz and his contributors at *Commentary* magazine, many of whom had opposed the Vietnam war and major military programs. The intellectual stars of the neocons included Podhoretz; his wife, Midge Decter, who became director of the Committee for a Free World; Eugene Rostow, chairman of the Committee on the Present Danger; Irving Kristol, editor of *The Public Interest;* and Moynihan, who in 1975 became America's U.N. ambassador.[2]

One common theme expressed by conservatives, neoconservatives, and many liberals was that the Nixon-Ford-Kissinger approach to détente was too cold and calculating, too focused on a realpolitik concern with power balances, and thus gave short shrift to human rights and the fundamental ideals that should undergird American policy. Jimmy Carter embraced this human rights line of attack against détente, just as Reagan had latched onto the conservative line of criticism; the reaction against détente thus helped propel the careers of two future presidents.

Another part of the anti-détente conglomeration was organized labor, which possessed a proud anticommunist streak. The longshoremen's unions had regularly balked at loading grain destined for the U.S.S.R., and George Meany and other AFL-CIO leaders resisted new trade agreements. Thus they were natural supporters of Jackson's efforts to saddle the Soviet-American trade bill with emigration provisions. "Some American businessmen are developing a vested interest in downplaying the repressive and inhuman character of the Soviet regime," Meany testified at a 1974 Senate hearing on détente. "We don't want any part of it. We're not interested in seeing cheap goods made by Soviet slave labor pour into this country."[3]

Some of the liberal opposition to détente was partly motivated by a reflexive disdain for Nixon. The reviled red-baiter was pursuing arms control and increased trade as liberals had been demanding for a decade. "But the blood feud with Nixon ran too deep," Kissinger wrote. "If Nixon was for détente, perhaps the Cold War wasn't all bad!"

Although there may be some truth to that plaint, it does not explain why the opposition to détente swelled after Gerald Ford took office. In fact, if a personal factor was involved, it was that many of détente's critics had developed a disdain for Kissinger. The debate over détente, said Professor Stanley Hoffmann, "served as a peg on which the most diverse oppositions to or hatreds of Kissinger's person and policy could hang."

One example of the personal nature of the attack was Kissinger's longtime nemesis Paul Nitze, who quit his job on the U.S. SALT negotiating team in 1974 and became a critic of détente. At one point, he asked CIA counterintelligence chief James Jesus Angleton if Kissinger could conceivably be a Soviet mole, as some right-wing conspiracy theorists suspected. Nitze concluded that he was not. Still, when an acquaintance brought up Kissinger's name in late 1974, Nitze sputtered, "That man is a traitor to his country."[4]

Immanuel Kant, in his essay "Perpetual Peace," which Kissinger dissected as a Harvard undergraduate, wrote that to achieve perpetual peace requires perpetual work, for peace involves a constantly shifting construct, not a final product. To Kissinger, the critics of détente misunderstood what that policy was. "It is a continuing process, not a final condition," he said at a September 1974 Senate Foreign Relations Committee hearing. The idea was not to give up the rivalry with the Soviet Union; instead, it was to create a web of ties that would moderate the conflict that comes with such a rivalry. "By acquiring a stake in this network of relationships with the West," Kissinger told the Senate, "the Soviet Union may become more conscious of what it would lose by a return to confrontation."

Kissinger's structure of peace thus relied on linkages: Soviet behavior in one field might be rewarded by agreements in another. But in the world according to Kissinger and Nixon, linkage should not extend to internal matters such as domestic human rights policies. "What is important is not a nation's internal political philosophy,"

Nixon told Mao at their first meeting in 1972. "What is important is its policy toward the rest of the world and toward us."

Kissinger made this argument in his September 1974 Senate testimony when he rebuked those who criticized him for ignoring human rights issues:

> Where the age-old antagonism between freedom and tyranny is concerned, we are not neutral. But other imperatives impose limits on our ability to produce internal changes in foreign countries. Consciousness of our limits is a recognition of the necessity of peace—not moral callousness.

The "other imperatives" that Kissinger was referring to included the fact that the Soviets had the bomb. That limited how fervently America could crusade against the Soviet system. "In a world shadowed by the danger of nuclear holocaust," he said in a London speech, "there is no rational alternative to the pursuit of a relaxation of tensions."

Another reason that détente was necessary, Kissinger argued, was that Americans had grown weary of intervention after Vietnam. The isolationist mood would make it more difficult to enlist support for countering Soviet probes in the third world or for funding a continued defense buildup. Only by relaxing tensions and relying on a more creative diplomacy, he felt, could America's mood of retreat be countered.

The great difficulty with détente was trying to sell it politically. "The trouble—no, the tragedy—is that the dual concept of containment and coexistence," Kissinger wrote, "has no automatic consensus behind it." Americans had traditionally viewed the world in a Manichaean way: nations are at peace or at war, they are either good or evil, friend or foe. This led to a historic oscillation between isolationism and overcommitment. That was the nature of the challenge that Kissinger found himself facing as the domestic support for détente deteriorated.[5]

THE JACKSON-VANIK AMENDMENT

The criticisms of détente might have amounted to little more than random sniping had it not been for Senator Henry Jackson, a Washington State Democrat with moderately liberal domestic views and a hawkish attitude toward the Soviets. He was able to unite many of the disparate elements of the anti-détente coalition —conservatives, neocons, cold war liberals, labor union leaders, Jews, and human rights activists—behind himself personally and behind his amendment linking normal trade with the Soviets to their policies on Jewish emigration.

"Scoop" Jackson was a man of Norwegian ancestry and Lutheran beliefs, which produced a stubborn yet thoughtful warrior whose strength lay in his plodding persistence and the stolidness of his manner. He was a close friend and supporter of John Kennedy, yet he was once offered the job of defense secretary by Nixon; he was able to earn the trust of such different men not because his philosophy was variable (it wasn't), but because he tended to be so solid in his beliefs.

There was, however, a factor that clouded Jackson's thoughtfulness: his yearning for the presidency. This made him receptive to a cause that could rally Jews and labor to his banner; it also made him less than eager for a compromise solution once his crusade had been launched. "For a long time I didn't realize that Jackson could not be placated," said Kissinger, who embarked on a two-year effort to negotiate a settlement that would be acceptable to the Soviets and the senator.

Jackson was not the type of leader who needed an impassioned aide to tell him what to think, but he had one anyway: Richard Perle, an intense, razor-sharp scourge of the Soviets who, despite his cherubic smile, earned the sobriquet Prince of Darkness from the legions he had engaged in bureaucratic battle. Among the kinder things Kissinger called him at the time were "ruthless," "a little bastard," and "a son of Mensheviks who thinks all Bolsheviks are evil." Perle would have little argument with the last description, and perhaps not even the other two.

Perle was the leader of an informal group on Capitol Hill that was intensely supportive of Israel and had the unusual characteristic of including paid pro-Israeli lobbyists as well as congressional staffers. Among its other members were Morris Amitay, then of Senator Abraham Ribicoff's staff and later the head of the American Israel Public Affairs Committee (AIPAC), the Israeli lobby; Dorothy Fosdick, of Senator Jackson's staff; June Silver Rogul, who worked for the National Conference on Soviet Jewry; and I. L. Kenen, a longtime AIPAC lobbyist.[6]

What launched them and their patron Senator Jackson into battle against détente was an event at the height of Soviet-American goodwill in August 1972: the Kremlin levied a prohibitively high "education tax," to be paid as recompense for state-funded schooling, on all Soviet citizens who emigrated. In effect it was an exit tax aimed primarily at Jews.

Even before then, Jackson had been considering ways to scuttle Kissinger's effort to grant most-favored-nation—or MFN—trade status to the Soviets. (Despite its grand sound, "most favored nation" means no more than the normal trade relations enjoyed by more than 150 countries.) "Jackson thought the whole MFN and trade agreement was bullshit," said Perle. "You can't have a truly reciprocal trade agreement with a nonmarket economy." The imposition of the exit tax gave the senator a way to fight détente and trade while at the same time displaying support for Soviet Jewry: he would attach an amendment to the MFN trade legislation saying that it could not take effect until Soviet restrictions on Jewish emigration were lifted.*

Jackson introduced his amendment, which was sponsored in the House by Ohio Democrat Charles Vanik, in October 1972, just as Kissinger's own linkage—between improved trade and Soviet help in getting a Vietnam peace accord—was bearing fruit. Kissinger was not pleased, especially since he considered the trade pact with the Soviets a done deal.

Yet to Kissinger's surprise, the Jackson-Vanik proposal appeared to do some good. The Soviets promptly abandoned the education tax. Elated, Kissinger told Soviet ambassador Dobrynin that no other issues stood in the way of the MFN trade agreement. What he did not realize was that his problems would be with Senator Jackson and not with the Soviets.

When Kissinger and Nixon invited some senators to the White House to show them the Soviet note agreeing to eliminate the education tax, Jackson was not impressed. "Mr. President, if you believe that, you're being hoodwinked," he said. Not only would the Soviets have to revoke the education tax on emigrants, the senator demanded, they would have to guarantee a hefty increase in the number of exit visas granted each year.

The idea of making such a demand on another sovereign nation was beyond Kissinger's ken. It was an attempt to pursue a goal that, although it might be morally laudable, did not involve a vital national interest of the U.S. Indeed, Jackson seemed willing to sacrifice true American interests—such as more trade, the future of détente, the ability to use economic ties as leverage on issues such as arms control

---

* The amendment did not actually single out Jews specifically, but that was its effect. The Soviet Union generally did not allow any of its citizens to emigrate, but it made exceptions for Jews who wanted to go to Israel. After the 1967 Arab-Israeli war ended, the number of Russian Jews seeking exit visas jumped, and Soviet officials began limiting the number of visas granted.

or Vietnam—in order to further the moral sentiment of championing Soviet Jewry. No one knew better than Henry Kissinger the value of helping people to escape repression, and he had worked hard behind the scenes to increase Jewish emigration from the U.S.S.R. But it was not, in his view, a suitable subject for formal diplomatic demands.

Nor did he believe that diplomatic pressure should be used to influence the internal affairs of another nation. A peaceful world order depended upon the concept of "legitimacy," which Kissinger wrote about as a graduate student, and upon a respect for national sovereignty. This meant not meddling in another nation's internal matters, such as their emigration rules.

Kissinger also feared that détente would be threatened if the U.S. added a major new condition to a trade deal that had already been initialed. "The demand that Moscow modify its domestic policy as a precondition for MFN or détente was never made while we were negotiating," he said in his Pacem in Terris speech in October 1973. "Now it is inserted after both sides have carefully shaped an overall mosaic. Thus it raises questions about our entire bilateral relationship." A breakdown of détente would require the U.S. to spend more on weapons and be ready to confront the Soviets in far corners of the globe, policies previously opposed by some of those now cheering the loudest for Jackson-Vanik. "Are we ready to face the crises and increased defense budgets that a return to cold war conditions would spawn?" he asked.

Finally, Kissinger had a more substantive reason for being appalled by the Jackson-Vanik amendment: he felt that making a public issue out of Soviet emigration was bound to backfire. His own quiet diplomacy had proven effective. In 1968, only 400 Jews had been allowed to emigrate. That number increased to 13,000 in 1971 and then to 32,000 the following year, when the summit and trade agreements occurred. It also steadily rose in 1973, when it reached 35,000 despite a temporary dip caused by the Yom Kippur War. "Soviet policy on emigration would clearly depend on the overall state of U.S.-Soviet relations," Kissinger later wrote. "If Jackson succeeded in souring the relationship, he was almost certain to reduce rather than increase emigration."[7]

The October 1973 war had given Kissinger more leverage in dealing with Jewish leaders, and he used it to try to beat back the Jackson-Vanik amendment. On October 25, the day after the nuclear alert, a group of American Jewish leaders—led by Jacob Stein, Max Fisher, and Richard Maass—were invited by the White House to a briefing by Al Haig. Just as it was beginning, Kissinger himself arrived, remarked that it resembled a Sanhedrin (an ancient rabbinical court), and sent Haig away. Israel's survival was at stake, and it was "a very poor time to slap the Soviets in the face," one participant quoted Kissinger as saying.

Kissinger told Soviet ambassador Dobrynin about the meeting in a phone call later in the day. "I had a meeting with the Jewish community on the MFN issue," Kissinger said. "We are making progress."

"Were my friends there?" asked Dobrynin.

"Fisher, Stein, and Maass," confirmed Kissinger.

Kissinger also raised the issue with Golda Meir and her entourage when she visited Washington a week later. He proposed a simple deal: if Israel could persuade its friends in Congress to remove their support for the Jackson-Vanik amendment, the path would be cleared for a policy that would benefit Israel in the long run.

But Israel was not supporting the Jackson amendment, protested its ambassador to the U.S., Simcha Dinitz.

That was not enough, Kissinger replied. Israel should become active in opposing it.

As Kissinger requested, the American Jewish leaders went to Jackson and asked him to back down. He refused, adamantly. "The administration is always using you," he said, showing his anger. "The only way to get Soviet Jews out of the Soviet Union is to stand firm." For good measure, he called Kissinger a "liar" for claiming that he had forced the Pentagon into action on the resupply of Israel during the war. "Jackson was aghast and then infuriated that Kissinger had put them up to it," recalled Perle, who was there. "He gave them a tongue-lashing that turned into a pep talk."[8]

So Kissinger was forced into conducting a shuttle diplomacy between Jackson and the Soviets that lasted through the summer and fall of 1974. The goal was to extract from the Soviets enough concessions on Jewish emigration to satisfy Jackson. In return, the senator would be expected to support a provision that would waive the effect of his amendment for a year or so.

In order to support a waiver, Jackson wanted assurances that a specific number of Jews would be allowed to leave each year, and he wanted these assurances to be as explicit as possible. Moscow, on the other hand, was insulted at the very notion of guaranteeing that a large number of its citizens would emigrate, and it was willing at most to give only vague, implicit, private assurances. "It was the beginning of a dialogue that made me long for the relative tranquillity of the Middle East," Kissinger recalled.

Jackson and his two main supporters—Senators Abraham Ribicoff and Jacob Javits—were suggesting annual emigration quotas of around 100,000 Jews, as well as other provisions regarding harassment and geographic distribution. At meetings in Moscow and then in Geneva, Foreign Minister Gromyko grudgingly conceded that a figure of 45,000 could be used "approximately as a trend." But Kissinger did not convey this back to Jackson right away. Instead he embarked on his thirty-four-day Syrian shuttle, leaving Jackson to rally support for his cause and brood about Kissinger's silence.

In addition, Kissinger was being blindsided, despite repeated memos from midlevel staffers, by an attempt led by Jackson and Senator Adlai Stevenson III to put a $300 million ceiling on credits that the Export-Import bank could lend to the Soviets. Although Kissinger focused on Jackson-Vanik rather than on the Stevenson issue, the latter was to provoke at least as much fury in Moscow.

One problem Kissinger faced in dealing with Jackson and the Jewish leaders was his reputation for being duplicitous. For example, President Nixon in a speech at Annapolis just before he resigned denounced Jackson-Vanik and declared, "We cannot gear our foreign policy to the transformation of other societies." Kissinger's staff had written the speech, and he had urged that it take that hard line. Yet when a group of Jews came to see him the next day on their way to a meeting with Nixon, Kissinger told them: please don't raise the Annapolis speech with him. He went a bit too far, but let me take it up with him. They later said they were not fooled.[9]

When Ford took over in August, he quickly made it clear that he was a more direct player. In a meeting with Ambassador Dobrynin that Kissinger arranged, Ford said that it was inevitable that the trade bill would contain some form of the Jackson-Vanik measure. More to the point, Ford said he was personally sympathetic to Jackson's aims. Dobrynin conceded that the Soviets could give an implied, oral assurance that 55,000 or so Jews would be granted exit visas each year, a number that Ford agreed was suitable.

The president's breakfast the next day—August 15, 1974—with Kissinger, Jackson, and others was not as successful. Although Senators Ribicoff and Javits expressed pleasure with the compromise, Jackson insisted that Ford was being too soft on the Soviets. "Boy, was Scoop ever adamant," Ford later recalled. "It made no sense to me because it was sure to be counterproductive. But he would not bend, and the only explanation is politics."

Nevertheless, Kissinger was able to work out—or at least think that he had—a deal with Ambassador Dobrynin and Senator Jackson that tacitly implied that 60,000 or so Jews would be allowed to emigrate in the coming year. It would be set forth in an exchange of letters that did not involve the Soviets directly: Kissinger would write to Jackson saying that he had assurances that Moscow would permit freer emigration, then Jackson would reply by saying that he had confidence that this meant at least 60,000 people would be given visas each year, then Kissinger would write back indicating that he did not disagree with Jackson's assumption.

Kissinger agreed that there could be a "definitive leak" of the letters, but he insisted that they could not be officially released. It was a weird way to make foreign policy: settling a major issue through a semiprivate exchange of letters with a senator who was not even the chairman of the Foreign Relations or Finance Committee.

As Jackson left the Oval Office on September 20 after going over the details with Ford and Kissinger, he ran into Gromyko, who was waiting to go in and confirm his side of the bargain. Jackson put two fingers up behind his own ears and joked that he was the devil in this negotiation. A nervous interpreter tried hard to explain to the Soviet foreign minister what this odd senator was trying to say, but finally gave up.

Just as Jackson was showing small signs of flexibility and humor, the Soviet attitude was beginning to harden. General Secretary Brezhnev, it later became known, was just then being confronted by challenges from hard-liners such as President Nikolai Podgorny. Press reports of the Jackson deal—readily leaked by Jackson and his staff—made it appear that the Soviet "assurances" were far more explicit than the Kremlin had authorized.

So Kissinger began to backtrack. He had Brent Scowcroft call Jackson's office to say that there would not be a third letter in the exchange; Kissinger would state his general feeling about Soviet policy, Jackson would respond by describing what he understood it to mean in terms of numbers, but then there would be no response.

Jackson and Perle were furious, but by this point Jewish groups were eager to prevent the whole deal from unraveling. They felt that if it did, Jackson and Kissinger could spend all their time finger-pointing, but Soviet Jews would bear the brunt of the fallout. So they began to apply pressure to Jackson to go along. Finally he agreed.

The deal was vintage Kissinger: it relied on deliberate ambiguity, and rightfully so. The Soviets would be able to claim they had given no explicit assurances about what was to them an internal affair; Jackson and his colleagues would be able to claim that there were in fact assurances that a specific number of Jews would be allowed to emigrate. And Kissinger's trick was that he allowed each side to believe it got its way. But it would only work if—and this was a pretty big "if" given that Brezhnev and Jackson both had their own political needs—both kept rather quiet about their respective interpretations.[10]

They did not.

On October 18, 1974, Jackson, Vanik, and Javits arrived at the White House for the exchange of letters. Kissinger signed a rather diluted one saying that "we have been assured" that the Soviets would follow certain practices in granting visas. Then Jackson signed a response containing his "understandings" of what this meant specifically, including that Jewish emigration "may therefore exceed 60,000 per annum." Then Ron Nessen invited Jackson into the pressroom to give a briefing.

As Jackson talked, Perle and Amitay distributed copies of the letters—precisely the type of "official release" that the Soviets had rejected. Worse yet, Jackson's remarks were clearly the crowing and preening of a presidential prospect rather than the careful words of a person who wanted to prevent a Soviet reaction. "I think it is a monumental accomplishment considering the fact that so many said it could never be accomplished," he said rather immodestly.

Kissinger claimed that he was appalled that Jackson gave a public press conference and released the letters. But Perle said that Kissinger was being, to put it politely, disingenuous. "Kissinger saw the text of Scoop's remarks in advance," he claimed. "I had taken a draft of them the night before to the Jockey Club, where Sonnenfeldt was having a drink." The arrangement to release the letters was approved by Ford, at Senator Javits's request. "You would have to be living on another planet to think they wouldn't be released," said Perle.

When Kissinger arrived in Moscow later in the month to pave the way for President Ford's summit in Vladivostok, Gromyko handed him an explosive diplomatic message. The Jackson letters and the publicity surrounding them, he wrote, "create a distorted picture of our position as well as of what we told the American side on this matter." It was a blistering and personal attack on Kissinger's honesty. "What we said, and you, Mr. Secretary of State, know this well, concerned only the real situation concerning the given question. And when we did mention figures—to inform you of the real situation— the point was quite the opposite, namely about the present tendency toward a *decrease* in the number of persons wishing to leave the U.S.S.R." The message concluded with rejection of the tactic that Kissinger was using to hold the deal together. "No ambiguities should remain," Gromyko said.

But Kissinger decided to try to preserve the ambiguity. He did not inform Senator Jackson about the letter. He did not send it back to the State Department in Washington. He did not even tell President Ford about it. As his loyal Soviet expert Bill Hyland later put it: "Kissinger made a mistake."

Kissinger later conceded as much. "I was wrong not to show it to Jackson and others," he said. His excuse was that Gromyko gave him the letter while they were on the way to the airport. Kissinger was leaving for India, then going on to Pakistan and Iran. In the next three weeks, he would be traveling to Japan, Korea, China, and Vladivostok. Thus he was, by his own admission, stretched rather thin. "I was going to discuss Gromyko's letter with Jackson and others when I had time to sit down with them," he said.

Kissinger also thought, or at least hoped, that the Soviet letter was written mainly for the record—perhaps as a way for Brezhnev to protect his rear if the Central Committee rebelled at the alleged assurances. "It may have been intended for use only in an emergency by Gromyko, Dobrynin, Brezhnev and others closely associated with détente and the emigration deal," wrote Paula Stern, who published a comprehensive study of the Jackson-Vanik amendment. With a little luck, and the proper stroking in Vladivostok and Washington, the trade bill could be signed and the letter then buried in a classified file to baffle historians decades hence.

In the meantime, Kissinger had to testify on December 3 before the Senate Finance Committee, which was preparing to approve the final version of the trade bill, which would include most-favored-nation status for the Soviets, the Jackson-Vanik amendment, and a procedure for the president to waive the amendment based on the supposed "assurances" that Jackson had accepted. If Kissinger revealed Gromyko's letter, the entire construct might collapse. So he decided to keep it secret.

The trade bill and all of its accoutrements passed on Friday, December 13, with Jackson, Jewish leaders, and the White House all in support. (Only organized labor broke with Jackson and campaigned against the bill.) The following Wednesday, the politburo met in Moscow. To Kissinger's horror, that afternoon the Soviet news agency Tass released the Gromyko letter, the first time since the Cuban missile crisis that the Kremlin's diplomatic records were intentionally made public.

But a strange dynamic was now at work in Washington: it was in almost everyone's interest to downplay the significance of the letter and to dismiss it as simply showy rhetoric. That applied to Kissinger, of course, who stood exposed as having sat on the letter. But it also applied to Jackson, who having achieved a politically potent bargain and having won the devotion of Jewish leaders had no interest in seeing it turn into a fiasco for which he would be blamed. Likewise, the Jewish groups assumed (correctly) that a collapse of the deal would mean a clampdown on emigration. "We should keep our cool," Jackson said. There was a lot of mutual reassurance that the letter was merely for domestic consumption back in the U.S.S.R.

It wasn't. Truly angered at the way their implicit concessions had been exaggerated and publicized, and even more upset at the less-publicized slap of having their Export-Import bank credits limited to $300 million, the Soviets had decided to repudiate the entire package. In January 1975, less than a month after the trade bill and its barnacles passed, the Soviet Union officially informed the United States that it would not seek most-favored-nation status or comply with the provisions of the bill.

Less than three years after the grand Moscow summit, détente was collapsing. Instead of an improved trade relationship, there was a significant new irritant in Soviet-American relations: even though the Soviets had rejected MFN status, the Jackson-Vanik amendment was now part of American law. In addition, Moscow felt free of its obligation to pay the rest of its World War II lend-lease debts.

Far more significant was the damage to the nebulous linkage that existed in 1972 between American trade concessions and Soviet help in restraining North Vietnam. For two years, the cease-fire in Indochina had been repeatedly violated, but the basic battlefield alignment had not changed. Within weeks of the collapse of the 1972 trade agreement, however, the communists in both North Vietnam and Cambodia launched offensives that soon brought them total victory.[11]

There is no direct evidence that the Soviets encouraged these communist offensives in Indochina in response to the collapse of the linkage that was established in 1972. But to use a favorite phrase of the Russians, the fact that one followed the other was probably no accident. When asked about it later, Kissinger said he did not consider the connection at the time, but it may have existed. "The collapse of the MFN deal led to a break with the Soviets and removed a restraint on Hanoi," he said. "They promptly attacked a provincial capital, something they had never done before."[12]

Kissinger's original fears about Jackson's efforts to pressure the Soviets publicly came to pass: instead of leading to an increase in exit visas, it led to a decline. Jewish emigration, which had reached 35,000 in 1973, went back down to about 14,000 in 1975 and 1976.*

---

* For the next fifteen years, the number would fluctuate based on the warmth of Soviet-American relations. In 1979, after a new wheat deal and the negotiation of a SALT II treaty by President Carter, it jumped to 51,000. In 1980, when the Senate held up the arms treaty and the administration imposed a grain embargo after the invasion of Afghanistan, the number dropped again to 21,000. It was only during the Gorbachev Revolution of 1989 that emigration restrictions were suddenly lifted. In 1990, the number of Jews leaving the

Kissinger was proved right in his assessment of the Jackson-Vanik amendment. It was a bad gamble by a stubborn senator, and it backfired, to the detriment of both détente and Soviet Jewry.

Yet Kissinger cannot fully escape blame for the fiasco he predicted. When the Jackson-Vanik battle was being waged, the secretary was trying to play superdiplomat while running the State Department from a cabin of an airplane. He was in the country neither on the day the amendment was introduced nor on the day it passed the House.

Nor did Kissinger spend the time to build a coalition in Congress to block the measure. Instead, he annoyed the powerful opponents of the measure—most notably Foreign Relations Committee chairman William Fulbright—by dealing privately with Jackson and his self-appointed clique rather than with the responsible leaders of the Senate. As was his style, Kissinger kept important information secret, including the real nature of the Soviet assurances and the explosive letter from Gromyko. At the end, his own chief congressional liaison, Linwood Holton, quit, claiming that he had been "hamstrung by Kissinger's mania for secrecy." [13]

Above all, it was a painful illustration of the limits of diplomatic ambiguity. No amount of artful dodging could cover up the fact that Jackson and the Kremlin had two completely different interpretations of what assurances had been made about the future of Jewish emigration.

VLADIVOSTOK, NOVEMBER 1974

While Jackson was pursuing his assault on trade and Jewish emigration, he was also leading a fight against the way Kissinger was conducting the strategic arms limitation talks. Shortly after the SALT I treaty was signed at the 1972 Moscow summit, the senator introduced an amendment requiring that future agreements be based on numerical "equality." This was a direct repudiation of the SALT I approach, in which Kissinger had sought to freeze both sides' arsenals despite existing Soviet advantages (such as in heavy missiles) on the theory that these were offset by American advantages in other areas.

After a flurry of phone calls, Kissinger and Jackson agreed on a

---

country exploded to 150,000, and up to 400,000 citizens of all ethnic backgrounds left. At the 1991 Moscow summit, President George Bush finally announced America's intention to waive the Jackson-Vanik amendment.

version of the "equality" amendment that the White House could swallow. The final wording was worked out in a vacant Senate office by Richard Perle, Kissinger's legislative adviser John Lehman (later navy secretary), and George Will, then a young staffer working for Colorado senator Gordon Allott and soon thereafter a celebrated columnist. "We had threatened to hold funding for the Trident submarine hostage," recalled Perle. "A deal was finally struck on the exact wording of the amendment as well as the words the White House spokesman would use in not disavowing it."

Another demand Jackson made was for a purge of the SALT negotiating team and the Arms Control and Disarmament Agency. Gerard Smith was forced out as head of ACDA, and Fred Ikle, a hardline strategic analyst, was brought in as its head. Kissinger quietly collaborated with Jackson—or at least gave that impression—by calling Smith and his crew "arms control zealots." But to those more sympathetic to arms control, Kissinger took a different tone in bemoaning the purge that Jackson had forced. "When your arms control team is to the right of the Joint Chiefs of Staff," he complained, "you are deprived of bureaucratic maneuvering room."[14]

Jackson's most formidable ally in the fight against SALT was Defense Secretary James Schlesinger, who had set himself up as Kissinger's intellectual rival in the Ford administration. Kissinger liked to pay Schlesinger, a Harvard classmate, what passed for the highest of compliments: "Intellectually he is my equal." Although Schlesinger's intelligence was not as subtle as Kissinger's, it was just as intense. So was his ego.

Schlesinger had already done battle with Kissinger over who was to blame for the delays in resupplying Israel during the October 1973 war, a dispute that was reignited in the fall of 1974 when Bernard and Marvin Kalb published a book about Kissinger that advanced his version of the event. Further enraging Schlesinger was Kissinger's disingenuous denial that he "did not know where the Kalbs could have gotten their impressions." From that point on, the rivalry became personal. "Think of the ethics involved," Kissinger shouted during one phone call when Schlesinger suggested that more pressure be put on Israel. "Henry, you are in no position to instruct anybody about ethics," Schlesinger shot back, and slammed down the phone.

Kissinger and Schlesinger, had they found a way to work together, would have been able to dominate the Ford administration. In Hal Sonnenfeldt's words, "their views were not as far apart as their conflicting vanities would indicate." But working in tandem was not Kissinger's style, nor Schlesinger's. And it was not in Kissinger's nature to forge equal partnerships. Indeed, he never seemed to treat his colleagues as true peers: not Robert Bowie at Harvard, nor Emmett Hughes in the Rockefeller campaign, nor Mel Laird, William Rogers, Thomas Moorer, Haldeman, Ehrlichman, Haig, Schlesinger, or Donald Rumsfeld.

Schlesinger had similar problems treating colleagues as partners, and his case was compounded by a haughty manner that deprived him of Kissinger's personal charm. Schlesinger's demeanor, Bill Hyland recalled, "was such that he seemed in a perpetual state of condescension." This imperiousness did not endear him to Ford, who found him painfully grating. The mere mention of Schlesinger's name could get Ford's blood boiling, though it took him almost two years to fire him.

Later, after Schlesinger became more mellow, he could reflect more dispassionately about his personality. "I tended to be self-righteous, a quibbler," he recalled. "Stubborn, too. It took me a while to understand how hard I must have been to deal with."

Kissinger's problems were compounded by his ungracious bureaucratic methods. As the SALT II discussions began, he limited all strategy sessions to his personal staff, with representatives of the Defense Department and uniformed military excluded. "This was both tactless and unwise," Kissinger conceded. It meant that Pentagon officials had no stake in the success of Kissinger's SALT proposals.

Schlesinger's arms-control focus became "throw weight," the lift capacity of a missile that determines what weight and number of warheads it can throw at the enemy. Since the Soviets had emphasized big, powerful land missiles, rather than more versatile weapons systems, they had an advantage over the U.S. in throw weight. As director of the CIA and then defense secretary, Schlesinger came to meetings with impressive scale models illustrating the disparity. "The throw-weight issue began to drive Henry wild," Schlesinger recalled with a faint smile, "and so did I." [15]

Schlesinger was aided from within the military by Chief of Naval Operations Elmo Zumwalt, whose fierce suspicions of Kissinger led him to plant informants on the NSC staff. He set up his own special task force on SALT that would brief him every day, and by his own admission he regularly supplied information to Senator Jackson. "Kissinger's tactics," he said, "had impelled all of us to watch more closely."

As Zumwalt's backbiting became blatant, Kissinger felt the rage of betrayal. "He had been the most obsequious in the extreme of all of the Chiefs," he would later angrily recall. "He was also the most dovish." All the while, Kissinger thought Zumwalt was spying for him, not against him. "He would bootleg to me all of the briefings of the Joint Chiefs and their preparations for discussions with the president. He was desperate to curry favor with me."

After a flurry of memos that sniped at the SALT process, Zumwalt was relieved of his post in mid-1974. Kissinger told Schlesinger to stay away from Zumwalt's farewell ceremony at Annapolis and not to award him a medal. But though his name did not appear on the program, Schlesinger did attend, and he did give Zumwalt the medal.

Zumwalt had accepted an invitation to appear on NBC's "Meet the Press" the day after stepping down, and Kissinger tried to get Schlesinger to force the admiral to cancel. According to Zumwalt's diaries, the defense secretary used such words as "paranoid" and "sick" to describe Kissinger. Zumwalt refused to back off the show. "I told him that it stemmed from the principle involved: that Secretary Kissinger had deceived us, lied to us," Zumwalt wrote. But unfortunately for Lawrence Spivak and the others at NBC News, Zumwalt held his tongue when he appeared on the show and did not criticize either SALT or Kissinger. The closest he came was quoting Horace: " 'The man who is just and firm of purpose can be shaken from his stern resolve neither by the rage of the people. . .' " His voice trailed off, however, and he did not continue with the final part of the Roman poet's phrase: ". . . nor by the countenance of the threatening tyrant."[16]

As the number-crunching began on potential SALT II proposals, probably the best course for Kissinger would have been to cede control. As it was, he was not able to focus much attention on it in 1974 as he shuttled through the Middle East and juggled his other duties. He could have left it up to ACDA director Fred Ikle and the new chief negotiator Alexis Johnson to extract a workable proposal from the bureaucracy, if possible. Even if they failed, the butting of heads and the new sense of real responsibility may have made the players more flexible.

At the very least, Kissinger could have settled for a simple approach. As his aide Bill Hyland said in retrospect, "The political timing was wrong for the kind of complicated and nuanced agreement that would have, in fact, served American interests." But ceding responsibility was not in Kissinger's nature, nor was he the type to ignore complexities he thought important.

Officials at the Pentagon demanded that any SALT II treaty achieve equality—specifically what became known as equal aggregates, or each side's being allowed the same number of weapons in each category. On the surface that seemed fair. But it did not reflect reality. The two nations had, by choice, built different types of arsenals and emphasized different weapons. The Soviets relied most on big, heavy land-based missiles; the Americans more on bombers, submarines, and smaller, more accurate missiles topped with multiple warheads. Since no one on either side was proposing significant cuts in his own weapons, an "equal aggregates" approach inevitably meant a treaty that permitted each side to build up and match the strong points of its adversary.

But the Pentagon had no plans yet to build new land-based missiles to match the Soviet arsenal, so it wanted a deal that would force the Soviets to cut their numbers. In other words, Joint Chiefs wanted to achieve at the bargaining table the missile equality that they had no way of achieving on their own. "They had put forward no building program to reach numerical equivalence," Kissinger later said, "yet they were asking me to negotiate the result with the Soviet Union."

As if this were not hard enough, Schlesinger and Jackson began emphasizing the need to negotiate equal throw-weight levels. Since the Soviet missiles were bigger, they enjoyed a four-to-one advantage in the weight of payloads they could throw. The Pentagon came up with various ways to calculate and cap each side's throw weight— ingenious plans whose only drawbacks were their total unpalatability to the Soviets.

Although Kissinger would have been overjoyed if the Soviets, in a fit of unexpected generosity, agreed to cut their land-based missile numbers and throw weight, he assumed that the U.S. would have to offer something in return. In addition, he felt that the number of missiles and their throw weight was not as important as how many MIRVed warheads were deployed on them. If the Soviets decided to MIRV most of their big missiles, that would lead to a destabilizing situation in which each side would be vulnerable to a first strike.

He was right. It must be noted, however, that he was preaching with the wisdom of a sinner: back in 1970, when there was still a chance to cage the hydra-headed MIRV monster, Kissinger had not heeded the pleas of his fellow nuclear strategists to seek a ban. Now that the U.S. had MIRVed much of its arsenal, the only way to stop the Soviets from following suit was through a complicated deal involving other trade-offs.

That is what Kissinger sought rather than the Jackson "equal aggregates" approach. Basically, he wanted to extend the SALT I freeze on new missile launchers for a few years, which would allow the Soviets to keep their numerical advantage. In return, the Soviets would agree to allow the American side to have more of its missiles topped with MIRVs, thus giving it more warheads. This approach was dubbed "offsetting asymmetries"—which may have been one of the many reasons it had trouble achieving great political appeal.[17]

On a trip to Moscow in October 1974, Kissinger tried out both approaches. In each case, the Soviets would be allowed to keep 2,400 missiles and bombers. Under the "asymmetries" approach, the U.S. would be allowed only 2,200 or so missiles and bombers, but it could have about 200 more MIRVs. Under the "equality" approach, both sides would be allowed 2,400 missiles and bombers, and both sides would be allowed to put MIRVs on about 1,300 of these missiles.

Surprisingly, Brezhnev said that the Soviets were amenable to either plan. It would be up to President Ford to decide. He invited the new president to his first summit, to be held in Vladivostok the following month.

At this point Kissinger, with Ford's approval, retreated. Schlesinger and Jackson were both pushing for the "equality" approach, and they were criticizing Kissinger for his willingness to "concede" the Soviets an advantage. "It was a mistake to accept equal numbers," Kissinger said in retrospect. "But we accepted the Jackson amendment and the Vladivostok position because of domestic political pressure."[18]

Ford and Kissinger landed at the port city of Vladivostok on Russia's Pacific coast on November 23, 1974, and embarked on an hour-long ride through barren terrain to the Okeanskaya Sanatorium, a primitive resort for vacationing workers that looked to Ford like an abandoned YMCA camp. A babushka tended a potbellied stove in the classic, gilded railway car as Ford and Brezhnev talked sports and hit it off with a breezy informality. "Both were rugged outdoor men of action," noted Bill Hyland, who was part of the entourage. "They loved sports and good stories, and in other times or in other places might have become genuinely friendly."

"When I get nervous, I eat," Kissinger has said, and apparently the prospect of Ford negotiating an arms agreement with Brezhnev did not infuse him with calm. The Soviets kept piling pastries on the table, and Ford recalled that "Henry simply couldn't resist them." He would glance around to see if others were looking, then pluck one from the plate. Soon it became obvious that everyone was noticing it, and his nervous appetite became a joke. He finished off three plates of pastries before the train ride was over.

Kissinger was lucky: that evening's bargaining session lasted until well after midnight, and dinner was canceled. Everyone else went to bed famished.

The bargaining session had been successful, so much so that the most troubling aspect was that the Soviets had accepted the American "equality" proposal with alacrity. The U.S. team took a long walk around their dacha during a break, braving the bitter cold and snow for a place they could talk unbugged. "It is always a bit disconcerting," Hyland later noted, "when the Soviets accept your proposal." A whole lot of details were still to be worked out, as well as a bit of sparring, but both sides agreed to announce a "framework" for an agreement that would limit each side's missiles and bombers to 2,400, including no more than 1,320 MIRVed missiles. A final treaty, they hoped, could be negotiated within months and signed at a summit in the U.S.

Kissinger dominated the discussions. "Who is this new president?" one Soviet diplomat asked *Time*'s Hugh Sidey the next day. "Every time something comes up, he turns to Kissinger, and he lets Kissinger talk." Far more surprisingly, Brezhnev actually deferred to Kissinger as well. During one extremely complex point, Hyland recalled, "Brezhnev took instruction from Kissinger almost as a student, while impatiently waving away his own advisers."

In a casual chat with Press Secretary Ron Nessen after the bargaining session, Kissinger praised Ford's style. He was more comfortable than Nixon in genuine give-and-take, Kissinger said, and unlike his predecessor he knew how to look someone in the eye. Nessen happily passed this praise along, with his own embellishments, to a small group of reporters. Later, on the train ride back to the airport, Nessen enjoyed a few glasses of vodka and became even more lavish. "It was something Nixon couldn't do in five years," he said of the equality agreement, "but Ford did it in three months."

This, not surprisingly, caused quite an uproar when it appeared in print. Kissinger, who had stopped off in China on the way home from Vladivostok (not the most diplomatic of scheduling) sent an angry telegram telling Nessen to control himself. Stoking the flames, former Nixon speechwriter William Safire wrote an article in *Harper's* magazine blaming Kissinger for Nessen's anti-Nixon comparisons. Kissinger responded with a three-page letter denying it, then made a public visit to see Nixon in exile in San Clemente. Safire fired back with a column concluding: "It is when men in high places cover up mistakes with blustering deceit that they get into terrible trouble."

The "framework" adopted in Vladivostok was grudgingly endorsed by Secretary Schlesinger, which given that he was in Ford's cabinet should not have been as difficult a hurdle as it in fact was. In addition, both houses of Congress passed resolutions in support.

Senator Jackson, however, continued his barrage of criticism, even though the principle of equality he had demanded was being enshrined for the first time. His main objection was that the ceilings were far too high and did not limit throw weight, thus doing little to end Moscow's missile advantage. There was some truth to that critique, but there was no indication that the Soviets would unilaterally trim their missile advantage.

The more serious problems with the Vladivostok framework were the devils that resided in its unfinished details. The first of these was whether the aggregate total of 2,400 would include America's new Tomahawk air-launched cruise missiles. Cruise missiles are jet-propelled to their targets, unlike ballistic missiles, which are rocket-blasted in an arc through space before coming down.

The military had considered abandoning the cruise missile in 1973, but Kissinger insisted that it might be useful, at least as a bargaining chip, and forced it back into the budget. Now the Pentagon was adamant about not restricting this program in any way. "Those geniuses," Kissinger muttered about his adversaries in the military, "think the goddamn thing is a cure for cancer and the common cold." The Vladivostok record left the status of cruise missiles unclear, and in hammering out the diplomatic messages explaining the framework, Kissinger and Gromyko could not resolve it. The issue would remain unsettled for the rest of the administration's term.

The other issue was the new Soviet bomber known as the Backfire. The Soviets insisted it was not a "strategic" weapon, meaning a long-range weapon that could strike at the other superpower. It had only a medium range and was planned as a weapon for use in Asia and Europe. Thus, the Soviets argued, it should not be part of the strategic arms limits. Kissinger generally agreed and indicated so both to the Soviets and to reporters that he briefed. But for the Joint Chiefs and the Pentagon, it was a major dispute, and they resisted Kissinger's willingness to concede it.

Later information made it clear that the Backfire probably did not have the range of a strategic bomber (even though, like most warplanes, it could be refueled in flight). The Tomahawk cruise missile, however, turned out to be rather valuable, and a video-guided version became a great star in the war against Iraq in 1991. "As I look back on it," said John Lehman, who was part of Kissinger's hawkish opposition on both issues, "Henry was probably right about the Backfire and I was probably right on the Tomahawk cruise missile." [19]

The SALT II treaty was not destined to be completed while Kissinger was in office. In January 1976, he would make a last effort to restore the momentum on a trip to Moscow, but while he was there a minirevolt occurred. The new defense secretary, Donald Rumsfeld, who was even less interested in a SALT accord than was Schlesinger, expressed his dismay at what Kissinger was doing. A secret rump meeting of the NSC was held behind Kissinger's back. And Ford was persuaded that, as the election year got under way, the SALT process should be shelved.

Later, Ford speculated on what would have happened if he had decided otherwise. Perhaps, he reflected, a SALT agreement and Brezhnev visit in the early fall of 1976 might have been enough to turn around the close election he lost to Jimmy Carter. In any event, Ford regretted that arms control had gotten wrapped up in politics. "The criticism of détente, by both Jackson and Reagan, was done for political reasons," he said. "And that upsets me. It meant we couldn't do what we should have done on arms control." [20]

TWENTY-EIGHT

THE MAGIC IS GONE

Setbacks in the Sinai and Southeast Asia

The generation of Buchenwald and the Siberian labor camps can-not talk with the same optimism as its fathers. —KISSINGER, *"THE MEANING OF HISTORY," Harvard undergraduate dissertation, 1949*

SINAI II AND THE "REASSESSMENT," MARCH 1975

After the Egyptian-Israeli accord of January 1974 and the even more surprising success on the Syrian front in May, Kissinger made a mistake: he hesitated about seeking a Jordanian-Israeli nego-tiation. King Hussein, aware of the difficulties involved in recovering the Palestinian-populated West Bank region taken by Israel in 1967, had patiently waited for his turn on the shuttle schedule. But the new government in Israel, led by Golda Meir's successor Yitzhak Rabin, steadfastly resisted negotiations with Jordan, even though (or maybe because) the kingdom had not directly attacked Israel during the 1973 Yom Kippur War.

Kissinger later conceded that everyone "took the path of least resistance and brought about the worst possible outcome." Israel was the greatest obstacle. Rabin had pledged that before signing a Jorda-nian disengagement he would call new national elections so that the public could have its say. Now that he was tenuously clinging to power, the prime minister recoiled at the prospect. Near the end of a visit to Israel in October 1974, Kissinger returned to his King David Hotel room and exploded to Joseph Sisco: "We are racking our brains to find some formula, and there sits a prime minister shivering in fear every time I mention the word *Jordan*. It's a lost cause."

The option of a Jordanian shuttle was closed later that month when an Arab summit convened in Morocco and, to Kissinger's surprise, designated the PLO (rather than Jordan) to negotiate on behalf of the West Bank. Israel's reluctance to deal with moderate Jordan had paved the way for Yasir Arafat. "It was a bad miscalculation," lamented Ambassador Simcha Dinitz, "and it was our fault."[1]

That left three options: do nothing (Jerusalem's preferred course), refer the Middle East mess back to the Geneva conference (Moscow's preferred course), or go back for a second Sinai accord pulling Israel farther back from its Egyptian front in return for additional guarantees from Cairo about improving relations. That, finally, became Kissinger's preferred course.

He scheduled a new mission for March 1975 based on what he thought was a tacit assurance from Rabin's government that it would agree to pull back another ten or fifteen miles in the Sinai. The plan was that Israel would vacate two key mountain gaps—the Gidi and Mitla passes—which would represent a withdrawal from about one-sixth of the desert peninsula.

"We felt we had Rabin's agreement to move through the passes," Kissinger recalled. He paid a courtesy call at the outset on Golda Meir to show the retired prime minister the plan. When she told him it would never be approved by the Israeli cabinet, Kissinger said to his deputy Joseph Sisco that it only went to show how quickly a person loses touch after leaving office.[2]

When Kissinger conferred with the cabinet, he found that Meir was right: instead of withdrawing completely from the passes, the Israelis insisted on manning at least a warning station in their midst.

The climax came on Friday afternoon, March 21, when Kissinger arrived in Jerusalem after two weeks of shuttling. The Israeli cabinet had just received a cable signed by Ford. "I am disappointed to learn that Israel has not moved as far as it might," it noted, adding that a breakdown would cause the U.S. to "reassess" its policy in the Middle East, "including our policy towards Israel." It was about as brutal as such diplomatic letters get, and the Israeli cabinet was shell-shocked.

Rabin had been Kissinger's friend back when he served as Israel's ambassador to Washington. He was no longer. Israel would not accept ultimatums, the new prime minister said. Kissinger replied that he did not give orders to the president, and he was not responsible for Ford's cable. (In fact, he *was* responsible for it.)

"I do not believe you," said Rabin, lighting a cigarette and staring directly at Kissinger.

The eruption back at the King David Hotel that Sabbath evening revised the Richter scale of Kissinger tantrums. Never had he been talked to in that fashion, he said as he stormed around the room.[3]

Kissinger decided to take a sight-seeing tour the next morning. He chose as his destination some ancient ruins on a cliff overlooking the Dead Sea—the famous fortress of Masada. There, on the eve of Passover in A.D. 73, more than seven hundred Jewish warriors and their families jumped to their deaths in a mass suicide rather than surrender to fifteen thousand troops of the Roman Legion. Although he was not known to have a passionate interest in archaeology, Kissinger was famous as an inveterate signal-sender.

Israel has often been accused of having a Masada complex, of being willing to commit mass suicide rather than make the concessions necessary to achieve peace. But Masada is also a symbol for glory and bravery in Israel. Recruits entering the army's armored brigades are brought there to take their oath of allegiance. "Masada shall not fall again," they pledge. The professor who gave him the tour was unsure whether Kissinger was sending a metaphorical warning to the Israelis about the dangers of indulging a Masada complex, or whether he was fortifying his own Jewish conscience and displaying his awareness of his people's historic plight.

At one point, worried about tiring Kissinger, the professor said it would be difficult to see one of the terraces because it required walking down a flight of one hundred fifty steps. But Kissinger forged ahead. "We don't have to do it in one leap," he said so that the press could hear. "We can do it step by step."[4]

After the Israeli cabinet rejected the withdrawal plan, Kissinger met with Rabin and his top advisers on Saturday night until well past midnight. Once again he gave a version of his doomsday speech, this time with such feeling that it betrayed a real sincerity. By the end, there were tears in the eyes of the Israeli stenographer.

Kissinger: "Step-by-step has been throttled, first for Jordan, then for Egypt. We're losing control. We'll now see the Arabs working on a united front. There will be more emphasis on the Palestinians. . . . The Soviets will step back onstage. The U.S. is losing control over events, and we'd all better adjust to that reality. The Europeans will have to accelerate their relations with the Arabs. . . . Let's not kid ourselves. We've failed."

Foreign Minister Yigal Allon: "Why not start it up again in a few weeks?"

Kissinger: "Things aren't going to be the same again. The Arabs won't trust us as they have in the past. We look weak—in Vietnam, Turkey, Portugal, in a whole range of things. . . . One reason I and my colleagues are so exasperated is that we see a friend damaging himself for reasons that will seem trivial five years from now. . . . An agreement would have enabled the U.S. to remain in control of the diplomatic process. Compared to that, the location of the line eight kilometers one way or the other frankly does not seem very important. . . . I see pressure building up to force you back to the 1967 borders. . . . It's tragic to see people dooming themselves to a course of unbelievable peril."

Yitzhak Rabin: "This is the day you visited Masada."[5]

Kissinger promised that he would not publicly blame Israel for the collapse of the Sinai II shuttle. But his anger at what he bitterly called his "co-religionists" was hard to contain. On the flight home, speaking off the record, he called Rabin "a small man," claimed the entire cabinet was cowed by Defense Minister Shimon Peres, and lamented that there was no strong leader like Golda Meir to take charge.

March 1975 was, even without the Sinai II breakdown, a disastrous month for American foreign policy and for Kissinger. The final North Vietnamese offensive had begun, and the imperial city of Hue fell the day after Kissinger arrived home from Jerusalem. Likewise, the American-backed government in Cambodia was being assaulted by the Khmer Rouge. In Portugal, a coup against the left-leaning government had failed, increasing Kissinger's fears that the country would edge toward a pro-Soviet Marxist regime. In Angola, a civil war began, with the strongest rebel faction being backed by Cuban forces and Soviet aid. The Jackson-Vanik fiasco had jeopardized détente, and the SALT framework agreed to at Vladivostok had collapsed in disputes over its details.

Kissinger took his rejection by Israel personally, and for weeks he raged around Washington criticizing the "lunacy" of Rabin's cabinet. His actions ranged from the petty to the momentous. He ordered the removal of the direct private telephone line that ran from his office to that of Israeli ambassador Dinitz, a once and future friend. He also ordered, with Ford's approval, a very public "reassessment"—formalized in a National Security Study Memo—of America's Middle East policy and its relationship to Israel.

"With the end of the step-by-step approach, the U.S. faces a period of more complicated diplomacy," Kissinger said at a March 26 press conference. "Consequently, a reassessment of policy is necessary." In response to a question, he made one of those statements designed to convey one thing by saying precisely the opposite: "The assessment of our policy is not directed against Israel."

Although the much-heralded reassessment was largely for show, Kissinger took the exercise rather seriously. Three options emerged:

- A revived Geneva conference. This would be accompanied by an American declaration of what it considered to be a fair overall settlement: a return by Israel to its 1967 border with minor modifications along with strong guarantees of the nation's security.
- A full Israeli withdrawal from the Sinai and a separate peace with Egypt, as was finally wrought by President Carter at Camp David.
- A return to step-by-step disengagement shuttles.

Kissinger convened various groups to discuss these options. One gathering of the foreign policy establishment's wise men—including John McCloy, Averell Harriman, George Ball, Dean Rusk, McGeorge Bundy, and David Rockefeller—not unexpectedly came down in favor of the first course. So did most of those in a group of academics including such fans from his Harvard days as Stanley Hoffmann and Zbigniew Brzezinski, both of whom had just written pieces attacking shuttle diplomacy.

The notion of retreating to Geneva, and thus letting the Soviets become involved in the process, held no appeal for Kissinger. Despite his doomsday speeches, it soon became clear he would be back to his shuttling, zealously guarding America's dominant role as well as his own.

Also helping to shorten the reassessment was the high-octane involvement of the Israeli lobby, led by the American Israel Public Affairs Committee (AIPAC). No holds were barred. Kissinger was attacked with special vehemence. The campaign was capped by a public letter sent to the president and signed by seventy-six senators. It demanded massive military and economic aid for Israel, and it called on the president to make it clear that "the U.S. acting in its own national interest stands firmly with Israel."

Kissinger, enraged, summoned Dinitz (whom he now called "Mr. Ambassador" rather than "Simcha") and berated him. "You'll pay for this!" he shouted. "What do you think? That this is going to help you? You are crazy. This letter will kill you. It will increase anti-Semitism. It will cause people to charge that Jews control Congress."

Ford was also upset. He had been a stalwart supporter of Israel as a congressman, but the AIPAC letter, he recalled, "really bugged me." As he later wrote: "The Israeli lobby, made up of patriotic Americans, is strong, vocal, and wealthy, but many of its members have a single focus."

•

When Kissinger resumed his shuttle on August 21, 1975, he was hounded in Jerusalem by mobs of protesters outside his hotel shouting accusations of perfidy. "Jew boy! Jew boy! Jew boy go home!" they chanted, using a phrase Nixon had used on one of the Watergate tapes, which they knew would drive Kissinger mad. It did.

The breakthrough that would save the talks was visible before the new shuttle round began: American technicians would take charge of the warning stations in the middle of the disputed passes, and Israel would withdraw to the eastern end. It took twelve days, climaxing with an all-night session in Jerusalem, to tie up this agreement.

Key to the accord, and with more long-term significance, was the memorandum of understanding attached to it, which pledged that the U.S. would provide what turned out to be $2.6 billion in military aid to Israel, including advanced equipment such as the F-16 fighter jet. This mammoth payoff to Israel in return for its Sinai II signature would turn out to be controversial.

As Kissinger was flying home in triumph, he was asked about a statement President Ford had just released calling the secretary's success "one of the greatest diplomatic achievements of this century." Kissinger responded: "Why 'this century'?" But Richard Valeriani of NBC was among those more cynical. On the "Nightly News" that evening, he proclaimed that "it was the best agreement money could buy."[6]

THE FALL OF CAMBODIA, APRIL 1975

As soon as the Vietnam peace accords were signed in January 1973, the violations began. Hanoi flagrantly infiltrated troops and matériel into the South, and Saigon blocked the establishment of the "National Council" that it saw as the first step toward a coalition government. In Cambodia there was not even a fictitious peace: the Khmer Rouge never accepted a cease-fire, and its war with Lon Nol's government in Phnom Penh continued unabated.

Throughout the spring of 1973, Kissinger argued that the U.S. should step up its bombing in Cambodia and make strikes against the Vietnamese infiltration routes as a signal that it meant to enforce the peace. This reflected his faith in the value of isolated B-52 bombing, a tactic that tends to appeal to civilians in the Situation Room more than military commanders.

The bombing war in Cambodia did little more than further tarnish the administration's image at home and abroad. During the six months beginning in February 1973, 250,000 tons of bombs were dropped on the Khmer Rouge–controlled areas—more than fell on all of Japan during the entire Second World War. Yet no regions were recaptured by Cambodian government forces. By that summer, Congress would no longer stand for it: it banned all air strikes anywhere in Indochina beginning in August 1973.

Even after the bombing ended, the pro-American governments in Saigon and Phnom Penh remained in control. If the Paris peace accords had merely been a way for the U.S. to withdraw with the fig leaf of a "decent interval" before a communist victory, as some critics charged, at least the interval was turning out to be more decent than many (including Kissinger) had expected.

It soon became clear, however, that the communist forces in each country—the Khmer Rouge in Cambodia and the North Vietnamese army and its Viet Cong allies in South Vietnam—were building toward a "final" spring offensive, similar to the ones in 1968 and 1972. By the beginning of 1975, they were ready. Their munitions had been replenished. The credibility of American threats and the authority of its presidency had been, as Kissinger warned, reduced. And any restraining influence the Soviets had been exercising had dissipated with the decline of détente: the passage of Jackson-Vanik led the Soviets to feel that the U.S. had reneged on the trade benefits that had been the quid pro quo for Moscow's tacit help in the 1972 Vietnam negotiations.

Although the final offensives in Cambodia and Vietnam came at the same time, it was a mistake to assume, as Kissinger and most American officials did, that the two communist forces were working in tandem. Thomas Enders, who was then deputy chief of mission in Cambodia, later admitted that this misperception lingered through 1975.

In fact, deep rifts had already developed between the two communist forces by the end of 1972, when the Khmer Rouge accused the North Vietnamese of selling out by agreeing to a cease-fire. And within a few years, after each had finally won its own civil war, centuries of Vietnamese-Cambodian animosity resurfaced, and border clashes between the two communist countries began. A full war erupted by 1978 and was settled only when the North Vietnamese army conquered Cambodia in early 1979 and ousted the Khmer Rouge regime.

Because Kissinger mistakenly assumed that the Khmer Rouge and the Vietnamese communists were close allies, he tried an ill-conceived diplomatic ploy in 1973 that, even when he wrote about it years later, he did not realize was based on false premises. His first assumption—which was correct—was that there was tension between the Soviet-aligned Vietnamese communists and the Chinese (they, too, would battle each other in 1979). His second assumption—which was wrong—was that the Chinese would want to prevent a Khmer Rouge victory in Cambodia because that would represent (or so Kissinger mistakenly thought) an expansion of Hanoi's and Moscow's influence in Indochina. So in June 1973 he proposed to the Chinese a plan that would restore Sihanouk to power as part of a coalition government and thus head off a total Khmer Rouge takeover. Although the Chinese briefly showed some interest in the plan, they soon rejected it. The Chinese realized that the Khmer Rouge communists were rivals of the Vietnamese communists, not their puppets.

Even in 1982, when he first wrote about this initiative, Kissinger was still insisting that his plan might have worked except for the fact that Congress cut off the Cambodian bombing just when he was selling it to the Chinese. He even advances the rather wild and unsupported opinion that the bombing halt helped to topple Zhou Enlai, who Kissinger surmised had put his prestige behind the scheme only to be caught by surprise when the U.S. unilaterally stopped its military pressure.

This explanation has many holes. The talks with the Chinese did not even begin until the month after the House and Senate passed separate bills to cut off the bombing, and it was clear to even a casual newspaper reader that some version of the measure was bound to become law soon. In addition, the proposal had not been presented to any representative of any faction in Cambodia—not Sihanouk, not the Khmer Rouge, not Lon Nol, not any member of his government. It is possible that the bombing halt was a factor in making the Chinese less interested in a negotiated settlement, but the basic premise of Kissinger's Sihanouk scheme was flawed. Since the Chinese no longer viewed the Khmer Rouge as puppets of Soviet-backed North Vietnam, they were more likely to support the Khmer Rouge than to conspire with Kissinger to thwart them.[7]

The final offensive in Cambodia began early on New Year's Day of 1975. Refugees clutching their belongings began streaming into overcrowded Phnom Penh, the capital of a land once teeming with fish and rice and people who knew no hunger. Now the marketplaces were teeming with penniless peasants and starving children, some begging, others trying to sell a few vegetables or a small bundle of firewood that they had carried from the countryside.

Some American military men remained officially optimistic. Lieutenant General Howard Fish, director of the Defense Security Agency, declared in January: "Overall, the military prognosis for Cambodia is promising." But the Cambodian army was doing little more than squandering ammunition with futile spasms of firepower before retreating. After five years and $5 billion of American support, the government troops were no match for the fewer and less-equipped rebels.

At the end of the month, President Ford requested $222 million in supplemental military aid for Cambodia "to facilitate an early negotiated settlement." It was a pointless gesture: no negotiations were under way that could be helped by buying more time. So unconvincing was the case for more aid that even conservatives felt that the administration was making the request mainly to lay off on Congress the blame for the inevitable disaster.

Hawk and dove were both angered. "It saddens all responsible Americans to see Cambodia collapse," said conservative Democrat George Mahon of Texas, "but it is just impossible to convince rank-and-file Americans that there is any end to this." Dovish Republican Paul McCloskey said after visiting Cambodia that the U.S. had perpetrated a "greater evil than we have done to any country in the world." If he could find "the architect of this policy," he added, "my instinct would be to string him up." Senate Republican leader Hugh Scott said: "I have not supported a dollar of this war without feeling guilty."

As the Cambodian aid debate stretched into March, it was staged against the backdrop of news footage of South Vietnamese soldiers being routed in the neighboring war. The end of Cambodia's war thus mirrored its onset: a sideshow to Vietnam. "The value of Cambodia's survival derives from its importance to the survival of South Vietnam," Defense Secretary James Schlesinger told Congress. *Baltimore Sun* correspondent Arnold Isaacs later wrote: "It seemed that after all they had endured, the Cambodians were at least entitled to have their case judged on their own circumstances, without the burden of Vietnam's faults and failures added to their own. But even that was denied."[8]

Congress decided to delay the Cambodian aid decision until after its Easter recess. When they reconvened in April, President Ford realized that there was little hope. In a "State of the World" report to Congress, he included a plea from the Cambodian government, but then he conceded, "I regret to say that as of this evening, it may be too late."

That day, April 10, 1975, Kissinger made a last desperate peace effort. He told George Bush, then the American liaison in Beijing, to contact Sihanouk and invite him to return home and take charge. But the wily prince knew that the Khmer Rouge would not stand for it, and he told Bush that he "would never betray" the rebels that way.

April 11 was dawning in Cambodia. The final American evacuation—called Eagle Pull, a code name unlikely to fool many—was set to begin. Lon Nol had already fled, and his replacement as president, Sirik Matak, was offered escape by the American ambassador via one of the helicopters landing near the embassy. "I cannot, alas, leave in such a cowardly fashion," Sirik Matak replied in a note. "I have only committed this mistake of believing in you, the Americans." A few days later, he was beheaded by the Khmer Rouge.

Ambassador John Gunther Dean, like Kissinger a refugee of Nazi Germany as a child, boarded a helicopter with the embassy's American flag folded under his arm. As he left, Khmer Rouge mortars began hitting the field where young Cambodian onlookers had gathered to wave good-bye. A teenaged boy was killed, another wounded. One of the Marines who had been ringing the field with rifles ready to fend off a feared onslaught by panicked and angry Cambodians stopped to bandage the surviving youth before boarding the departing helicopter.

"Cambodians and foreigners alike," wrote the *New York Times's* Sydney Schanberg, the only American reporter to brave the capture of Phnom Penh, "looked ahead with hopeful relief to the collapse of the city, for they felt that when the Communists came and the war finally ended, at least the suffering would largely be over. All of us were wrong."

Schanberg and Jon Swain of the London *Sunday Times* were able to bear witness, not just for their readers but for history, to the horrors that were just beginning. "In five years of war this is the greatest caravan of human misery I have ever seen," Swain wrote as he described how the rebels forced everyone out of the city. The conquerors even emptied the hospitals and pushed limbless and crippled patients out of their beds, creating a forced march that would eventually turn the countryside into killing fields. Phnom Penh, a city then crammed with 3 million people, was cleared within a day, producing a crush on the roads so dense that the heaving mass could sometimes move only a few hundred feet each hour. Those who hesitated were shot. Those too weak, even be they children, were shot. Those who cried were shot.

Across the country, there were frenzied, cultlike efforts by ruthless young Khmer Rouge fanatics to purge every vestige of civil administration from the country. One man survived to describe a scene in the village of Mongkol Borei where ten civil servants and their families were brought out into a field. First the men were killed, stabbed to death in front of their wives and children. Then the women were killed. And last, the children were stabbed to death. When it was over, said the witness, blood ran "like water on the grass." It was a scene repeated not hundreds, not thousands, but hundreds of thousands of times.[9]

THE FALL OF VIETNAM, APRIL 1975

The final communist offensive in South Vietnam also began in January 1975, two years after the U.S. had withdrawn from the war. At a politburo meeting in Hanoi that concluded on January 8, a resolution was passed that declared: "Never have we had military and political conditions so perfect or a strategic advantage so great as we have now; complete the national democratic revolution in the South and move on to the peaceful reunification of our Fatherland."

By early April, the North Vietnamese and their Viet Cong allies were bearing down on Saigon. With the Mideast peace process in tatters, relations with the Soviets at a four-year low, Cambodia collapsing, and now South Vietnam besieged, President Ford left Washington for a golfing vacation in Palm Springs.

The evening news shows contained jarring juxtapositions of Indochina's death throes with Ford's golf swings. The worst scene came on the day when the networks broadcast the tale of South Vietnamese marines storming an American refugee ship and looting, raping, and killing some passengers. When reporters tried to question Ford at the Palm Springs airstrip, he began shouting, "Oh, ho, ho!" and jogging away from them, with Helen Thomas of UPI hustling to keep pace.

Kissinger and Ford had sent General Fredrick Weyand, the army chief of staff, to Vietnam to assess the situation. As he was returning, his plane was diverted to Palm Springs so that he could provide his report in person. His recommendation: renewed B-52 bombing runs by American pilots along with $722 million in additional immediate aid to be provided to the South Vietnamese army. The first of these would have been against the law. As for the aid, it was a staggering sum even to the dwindling few who felt that there was still hope that the South Vietnamese could hold on. The proposed package would include more than 440 tanks, 740 artillery pieces, 100,000 rifles, and 120,000 tons of munitions.

Nor did Weyand try to claim that even this could save an army that seemed fleeter in retreat than the nimble-footed Ford had been on the Palm Springs airstrip. The general's report justified the new aid in words designed to appeal to Kissinger's geopolitical outlook. "Continued U.S. credibility worldwide hinges on whether we make an effort, rather than on an actual success or failure," it said. "If we make no effort, our credibility as an ally is destroyed, perhaps for generations."

In other words, the recommendation was to prolong the end of the war for the same rationale that Kissinger had once used to justify prolonging America's ground combat role: to preserve credibility elsewhere. At a hearing a few days later, Mississippi congressman Jamie Whitten asked, "Is there any basis for your request except to maintain an appearance . . . when we know the end is inevitable?" General Weyand responded: "Well, sir, let me say this, that sometimes the style with which we do things, or the appearance as you say, is equally important as the substance."

Even Kissinger opposed Weyand's bombing recommendation. "If you do that," he said, "the American people will take to the streets again." The debate among the president's men in Palm Springs came over the aid package. Most of Ford's domestic advisers were against it, led by counselor Robert Hartmann and press secretary Ron Nessen, who had been wounded while in Vietnam as an NBC correspondent. Also opposed was the president's personal photographer, David Hume Kennerly, who had covered the war for *Life* and had persuaded Ford to let him go on the Weyand mission. Young, hip, and irreverent, Kennerly had become like a son to Ford, who often quoted his wisecracks. Any hope that South Vietnam could be saved, Kennerly said, was "bullshit."

Another opponent was James Schlesinger, but he had been cut out of the deliberations by Kissinger and left back in Washington. The defense secretary felt that the South Vietnamese army was now in a hopeless situation.

Kissinger, congenitally a pessimist, agreed that the situation was beyond salvage. Nonetheless, he felt that requesting the $722 million from Congress was the only honorable course. Ford agreed, albeit without enthusiasm. On the way to the pressroom to brief reporters about the decision, Kissinger turned to Nessen and said of the South Vietnamese, "Why don't these people die fast? The worst thing that could happen would be for them to linger on."

At the briefing, Kissinger's argument was geopolitical. He stressed how the decision on aid would be perceived around the world, what signal it would supposedly send to friend and foe elsewhere, what impact it would have on American credibility—rather than on what military effect it might have in the region around Saigon. "We are facing a great tragedy," he said, "in which there is involved something of American credibility, something of American honor, something of how we are perceived by other people in the world."

Even in this context, the decision was dubious, for it assumed that America's reputation would be enhanced rather than hurt if it dedicated itself to extending a hopeless war for a little longer. "What was imperiled by America's performance in South Vietnam," *Time* magazine wrote that week, "was not so much the nation's credibility as its aura of competence."[10]

On the evening that Kissinger and Ford made the case for new aid, American viewers were faced with horrifying television pictures of a tragedy that contributed to the sense that their nation was cursed in Vietnam. A C-5A Galaxy transport, the largest airplane in the world, lumbered off the runway at Saigon's Tan Son Nhut air base crammed with 243 orphans. Some had lost their parents to war, others were abandoned by starving mothers, others were the offspring of long-departed GIs. They were part of a well-publicized Operation Babylift, which was designed to alleviate in a small way Vietnam's pain and America's guilt.

A few minutes out of Saigon, the plane began to lose altitude. A rear door blew off, and the pilot, realizing that he would not make it back to the base, tried to land in a rice paddy; the plane skidded across the small dikes, tearing apart and spewing maimed bodies all around. The wings snapped off and a fire erupted, killing and disfiguring the boys and girls still inside. Close to 140 children and 50 adults died. Television showed the unbearable scenes of small bodies in the mud, of babies being brought to hospitals, of piles of burned clothing and little dolls—and of Vietnamese soldiers looting suitcases and taking jewelry off the dead. A basic American humanitarian gesture had ended in horror, a metaphor for the war itself: yet another failure of the good intentions and technology that, a decade earlier, had been billed by Washington's brightest and best as the keys to Vietnam's salvation.[11]

On April 10, Ford went to Capitol Hill to ask Congress formally for the $722 million. Kissinger had worked until well past midnight on a draft version of the speech that blamed Congress for the collapse of the Paris peace agreement. The "credibility" argument that he had used at the beginning of the Nixon administration was the one he stressed at the end. In the message to Congress that he wrote for Ford, this argument was put succinctly: "U.S. unwillingness to provide adequate assistance to our allies fighting for their lives would seriously affect our credibility throughout the world as an ally. And this credibility is essential to our security."

Ford retained the language about credibility, but he toned down

Kissinger's rhetoric and took out the attacks on Congress. "Henry had written a 'go down with the flags flying' speech for me to use," said Ford. "My instinct was that this was not the right approach." With Hartmann's help, the president softened the speech so that the request for funds was combined with a call for national reconciliation.

Even so, there was not one clap of applause—from either side of the aisle—when the president made his aid appeal, and two Democrats, Congressmen Toby Moffett and George Miller, stood up and walked out. Neither Congress nor the public was willing to support further fighting in Vietnam.

In later years, Kissinger would blame the collapse of the Paris peace accords on Watergate, saying that the breakdown in presidential authority meant that the U.S. could not or would not enforce the cease-fire. But it was the horror and futility of the Vietnam War, not Watergate, that produced the isolationist reflex of the 1970s and made the public recoil at the prospect of prolonging the wars of Indochina.

Admittedly, the cynicism about presidential authority caused by Watergate infected the Vietnam debate; likewise, the passions produced by Vietnam probably heightened the anti-Nixon fervor of the Watergate investigation. In any case, even with Gerald Ford in the White House and Watergate over, Congress was not about to authorize an infusion of new aid to prolong the quest for honor in Vietnam.[12]

Gerald Ford rarely went against Kissinger's advice in foreign policy. One little-known but historically significant case was his decision on April 24, 1975—even as his $722 million aid request was officially pending—to declare in a speech at Tulane University that, as far as the U.S. was concerned, the Vietnam War was over.

A few days earlier, Ford had outlined to his longtime aide Robert Hartmann the message he hoped to convey at Tulane. "What I want to get across is the idea of all the challenges awaiting college students today," the president explained. "Vietnam has been going on ever since any of them can remember. Well, the war is over."

"Why don't you just say that?" Hartmann asked.

"I'm not sure Henry would approve," Ford said, furrowing his brow. Yet it was clear that he liked the idea. After a little more discussion, he told Hartmann to start work on such a speech and "see what you can come up with." Even more significantly, he decided not to risk inciting Kissinger yet. "Don't pass it around until I decide," he told Hartmann.

Like any speech draft, an early version was sent to Kissinger's NSC office. But it did not contain any sentences on Vietnam. Those lines were inserted into the final version, which was completed and typed aboard Air Force One and never sent to Kissinger. Hartmann brought a copy up to the president's cabin, and there they carefully went over it and marked it up. Ford was pleased.

So, too, was Nessen, who realized as soon as he read the line how important it would be. His only worry was that Ford, who had been through a tiring day and "had sipped a cocktail," might mess up the dramatic moment. Deliver the speech slowly, the press secretary suggested. Photographer Kennerly cut in. "What he's trying to tell you is, 'Don't screw it up.' "

Ford didn't. In front of six thousand students packed into the noisy wooden bleachers of the Tulane basketball field house, he declared: "America can regain the sense of pride that existed before Vietnam. But it cannot be achieved by refighting a war that is finished as far as America is concerned."

As he intoned the sentence slowly, the crowd began whooping and cheering and stomping their feet. For several minutes the pandemonium continued as students began jumping up and down on the bleachers and hugging one another. The wire services, rather than merely writing stories on the speech, sent out bulletins.

Something in those simple words—"a war that is finished"— struck a national chord. They reflected the generous, decent instincts of an old American football player who knew how to behave graciously, even in defeat, when the whistle had blown and the game was over. Kissinger's complex geopolitical goals and desire to pin blame on Congress may have had some logic, but they were no longer appropriate. The healthiest thing for America to do, both for its own domestic psychology and even for its credibility abroad, was to put the Vietnam War behind.

"Mr. President," one of the reporters asked when Ford wandered back to the press section of Air Force One on his way home, "did Secretary Kissinger have anything to do with the preparation of your speech or approve it in advance?"

"No!" Ford shouted loudly enough to be heard above the jet noise. "Nothing at all."

Even Hartmann thought that was stirring up matters too much. "Mr. President," he interjected, "I think you should explain that a draft of this text went through the regular system, including the NSC office." Ford did not seem overly pleased by the clarification.

A reporter asked if he had intended for his words to mark the end of an era in American history. "Yes," said Ford. "After all, it's been a pretty long era. I had mixed emotions. It's not the way I wish it had ended, but you have to be realistic. We can't always achieve perfection in this world."

Early the next morning, the buzzer on Hartmann's direct phone from Ford's office "sounded off like a smoke alarm," he recalled. He hurried down the hall to the Oval Office to find the president puffing on his pipe and Kissinger pacing like an enraged lion. Even Ford was having a hard time calming him. "This we don't need," Kissinger said, gesturing and glaring at Hartmann. "How is it I knew nothing about this?"

Hartmann muttered something about how the final draft was finished late and how they were unaware that the line on Vietnam might cause such an explosion. He did not mention that Ford had wanted the line in from the start. "We were a little pressed for time," Ford agreed. Hartmann thought he caught a small wink in the president's eye as he turned to him and said, "Just be sure it doesn't happen again."

Years later, as he pleasantly recounted tales from his presidency, Ford was boundless in his praise for Kissinger. But there was a guile-free glint in his eye as he talked about the Tulane speech. "The line about the war being finished—Henry didn't like that sentence," Ford said. "I knew he wanted to keep fighting for more aid and that he blamed Congress. And I did, too. But having been up there on the Hill for twenty-five years, I just didn't think it would be all that productive to give them unshirted hell. That's where Henry and I disagreed. And I was right. I understood the system better." [13]

Yes, he did; despite all of Kissinger's *Fingerspitzengefühl* when it came to making foreign policy, he did not have Gerald Ford's fingertip feel for the way it is made in a democracy.

At the last moment, Kissinger tried to find a diplomatic solution by authorizing Ambassador Graham Martin to suggest to President Thieu that he step down. A day later, the ambassador got another cable telling him to hold off so that Kissinger could get credit for Thieu's resignation as a bargaining chip with the Soviets (who he once again futilely hoped would help save the Americans). Martin ignored the second message. "It just went from the incoming basket to the file with absolutely no action at all."

Thieu did agree to step aside, though he heaped scorn on the U.S. in his rambling resignation speech. Calling America's abandonment of his government "an inhumane act by an inhumane ally," he asked: "Are U.S. statements worthy? Are U.S. commitments still valid?"

Kissinger later tried to make up with Thieu. In 1980, he sent him a letter that put forth his if-not-for-Watergate argument. "I continue to believe that the balance of forces reflected in the Paris Agreement could have been maintained if Watergate had not destroyed our ability to obtain sufficient aid for South Vietnam from Congress in 1973 and 1974," he wrote. But then he added, in something of a contradiction: "Our tragic dilemma in 1972 was that we had reached the limit of our domestic possibilities. Had we attempted to continue the war, the Congress would have imposed in 1973 what was done later in 1975." Kissinger concluded by asking Thieu not to remain angry at him. "Ironically, I am under vicious attack these days [William Shawcross's book *Sideshow* had just been published] for my efforts to defend Cambodia in order to ensure the survival of your country."

Thieu chose not to answer the letter. But subsequently his anger abated, both at Kissinger and at his erstwhile American patrons. In 1990, he and his wife quietly moved to the Boston suburb of Newton near their grown children. "I do not blame Kissinger personally," he said. "He never saw the war in a Vietnamese context the way we had to." [14]

Thieu's resignation did not halt the communist advance. On the morning of April 29 (Asia time) Ambassador Martin was given the order to execute Operation Frequent Wind, the Saigon counterpart to Eagle Pull. Armed forces radio began playing "White Christmas" and the announcer said, "It's one hundred and five degrees in Saigon and rising"—the prearranged signal for Americans and their dependents to gather at evacuation points. Helicopters began swooping down on the embassy roof and other locations as U.S. Marines fended off Vietnamese civilians trying to cling to the skids in hope of escaping.

At Tan Son Nhut airbase, as Viet Cong rockets burst beside the runway, the first in a series of C-130 transports rumbled into the sky rescuing the refugees. Standing guard near the U.S. defense attaché's office there were two young Marine corporals, Darwin Judge of Marshalltown, Iowa, and Charles McMahon of Woburn, Massachusetts. A round of rocket fire hit, and they were dead.

Unlike in Cambodia, the evacuation of Vietnam would not go smoothly. For years, the scene of panic that occurred as the helicopters left the embassy roof would be seared into the American psyche, yet another lasting wound of the war, another symbolic image of a decade-long debacle.

There were also the smaller scenes, even more painful because they were personalized. One television broadcast showed a Vietnamese mother holding out her paralyzed baby to the cameraman and begging him to do something for the child, to take him from her, to take him to America, to save him. The child's legs flopped uncontrollably, helplessly. The camera backed away, leaving only an indelible image of the paralysis and despair.

Kissinger wandered into Donald Rumsfeld's office late that afternoon where the staff chief, Robert Hartmann, and others were holding a vigil. "I'm the only secretary of state," Kissinger said with gallows humor, "who has lost two countries in three weeks." David Kennerly was shooting pictures of the scene. "The good news is the war is over," he said. "The bad news is that we lost." A while later, Nancy Kissinger arrived dressed for the theater. She and her husband had tickets for *Present Laughter,* a Noel Coward comedy. Kissinger informed her they would have to cancel.[15]

"For the first time in the postwar period," Kissinger later wrote, "America abandoned to eventual Communist rule a friendly people who had relied on us." It had been ten years since the first American combat troops had waded ashore at Da Nang. It had been twenty years since the French had pulled out the last of their units. It had been thirty years since the French had gone in to regain control over their prewar colonies.

All that the U.S. had left to show for the 58,022 dead were the shreds of credibility that came from having achieved a peace agreement that lasted long enough to disguise the American pullout. Neither the peace nor the honor that Kissinger claimed in January 1973 turned out to be long lasting. But the Paris accords had at least served the purpose of making America's abandonment of its commitment to Saigon, and the resulting loss of credibility, rather ambiguous—another case in which ambiguity was the best Kissinger felt could be achieved.

This provided little solace for Kissinger, who felt then and continued to feel that the final loss in Vietnam in 1975 represented a blow to America's credibility that sapped the force of its threats and commitments around the world. "By our self-indulgence," he said, "we damaged the fabric of freedom everywhere." The surrender in Indochina, he said, "ushered in a period of American humiliation" that stretched from Angola to Ethiopia to Iran to Afghanistan.

But the "domino effect" that Kissinger and others predicted, and later claimed to see, was not so clear. Vietnam and Cambodia both became communist, but also bitter enemies. When Vietnamese communist forces in 1977 invaded the Parrot's Beak border area of communist Cambodia—the exact same area where American and South Vietnamese troops had launched their own 1970 "incursion"—the American public had a right to wonder whether its leaders had really understood enough about the nationalist complexities of Indochina to justify sacrificing so many lives. Instead of tumbling through to Thailand, the dominoes seemed to bounce back and forth in ways that policymakers never predicted.

Likewise, the credibility argument turned out to be more complex. There is no denying that a nation's credibility in keeping commitments and resisting adversaries has an effect on the global balance, as Kissinger argued. But many other factors strengthen America's influence in the world: the perception that it stands for certain moral values; the impressive nature of its economic prosperity; the model of individual freedom that it represents; the respect it shows for the sovereignty and nationalist yearnings of other nations; and the common sense and competence it displays in pursuing its global goals and keeping threats in perspective.

By pursuing the chimera of credibility while downplaying these other considerations, Kissinger helped to reinforce America's reputation for being a land of ham-handed imperialists. When the U.S. government finally abandoned its policy of force in Indochina, it was slowly able to rehabilitate its reputation at home and abroad, which probably was the best way to increase its global influence.

As the Indochinese wars ended, Kissinger seemed to be wrestling with these issues. Sitting in the Madison Room of the State Department, he gave a long interview to Barbara Walters that aired on NBC's "Today" show the first week of May. At first he appeared as if he were just going to repeat his vintage cold war philosophy. "There is in almost every major event a domino effect," he told her, adding that this is partly due to "the general psychological climate that is created in the world as to who is advancing and who is withdrawing."

But then Kissinger began discussing how "we probably made a mistake" by being too concerned about this when dealing with Vietnam. "We perhaps might have perceived the war more in Vietnamese terms rather than as the outward thrust of a global conspiracy," he said. Stephen Rosenfeld, a foreign policy analyst for the *Washington Post,* called this statement "a burst of historical revisionism fit to make his bitterest critics weep for joy."[16]

THE MAYAGUEZ, MAY 1975

In the wake of the failure of the Sinai II shuttle in March and the collapse of Cambodia and Vietnam in April, Kissinger's foreign policy (and Ford's poll ratings) was at a low point. He was eager to find a way to show, at least symbolically, that America still had the resolve to defend its interests around the world. That chance came on the afternoon of Monday, May 12, in the Gulf of Thailand, about seven miles south of the Cambodian island of Poulo Wai, when Charles Miller, the captain of a clunky American-owned cargo ship named the *Mayaguez,* picked up his intercom to be informed by his third mate, "There's a launch with a red flag coming at us, Captain."

Quickly the word spread through the ship and out over the radio in a series of Mayday messages: "We've been captured by Cambodians."

"Cambodians?" said chief engineer Cliff Harington as he emerged from the diesel room. "We aren't even at war with Cambodia."

American ships had been issued no warnings of trouble in the region, even though a Panamanian ship—originally referred to as the *Unid* during White House meetings until it was discovered that was simply an abbreviation for *unidentified*—had been seized the week before for wandering into waters newly claimed by Cambodia. Now, for four days, the *Mayaguez* and its thirty-nine crewmen would be the focus of a showdown freighted with symbolism.

It was still before dawn in Washington. An NSC meeting was called for noon, at which Kissinger led the discussion. More was at stake than the seizure of an old merchant vessel, he said, leaning over the Cabinet Room table and speaking with emotion. This was a test of U.S. resolve. Nations around the world would be watching, he claimed, to see if the failures in Cambodia and Vietnam signaled that America had lost its will to resist aggression. Unless there was a strong response, the nation's credibility would suffer yet another blow. "At some point," he stressed, "the U.S. must draw the line." The capture of the *Mayaguez,* he concluded in a somber clarion call, was a chance to show that there was a point beyond which the nation would not be pushed. "We must act upon it now, and act firmly."

Although Defense Secretary Schlesinger was skeptical, Ford and his political advisers tended to agree. They also had another goal for this crisis: showing that Ford could take charge of foreign policy rather than merely lip-synch the line provided by Kissinger. That afternoon Kissinger was scheduled to leave on a day-and-a-half speaking trip through Missouri, and he was quite prepared to postpone it for the crisis. But Ford asked him to go ahead with it.

At ten-thirty Tuesday night, Ford chaired another NSC meeting. Kissinger, who had just returned from Missouri, was still adamant about the stakes: America must respond decisively with enough force that North Korea as well as Cambodia and Vietnam would not mess around in the future. Schlesinger took issue with the notion that the crisis should be seen in global terms. He agreed that getting the *Ma-*

yaguez and its crew back quickly was important, but he was not eager to turn the incident into a display of force designed to impress Asia and the world. It was just a ship, perhaps taken by a low-ranking local commander; it should be retrieved but not turned into a symbol. "Henry was an incorrigible signal-sender, even when it might have been dangerous," Schlesinger recalled.

The debate was continued at an NSC meeting the next day with a more specific focus: whether B-52 bombers should attack the Cambodian mainland as part of a military rescue operation. Kissinger and Rockefeller led the argument for such an assault; Schlesinger opposed it saying that bombing was not necessary, militarily or symbolically. Ford chose a middle course. The B-52s reeked too much of Vietnam. The mainland should be attacked, but with tactical fighter-bombers from the aircraft carrier *Coral Sea*. These would be less destructive and more accurate than a major B-52 attack.

Diplomatic efforts had been unsuccessful: even sending a message to Cambodia, which no longer had any major Western embassies, was difficult. A note passed to the Chinese was returned undelivered; another sent to the door of the Cambodian embassy in Beijing was mailed back to the U.S. So on Wednesday night, Ford gave final authority for the military action to rescue the vessel and its crew.

Two minutes before a 175-man Marine contingent started landing on Koh Tang island, the radio in Phnom Penh began broadcasting word that Cambodia was ready to give back the ship. Kissinger had just taken a shower at the White House and was getting dressed for a state dinner when an aide rushed in with the message. The Cambodian concession was couched in a long diatribe, and it said nothing about the crew. Kissinger's instinct was not to call off the military operation.

Ford was at that moment sipping a martini on the rocks in the White House Red Room with his guest, Dutch premier Joop den Uyl, who was destined to have a rather disrupted state dinner. When Kissinger phoned with word of the Cambodian broadcast, Ford agreed that the operation should proceed. He said, however, that it was important to find some quick way to answer the Cambodians and tell them that the military operation would stop as soon as the ship and crew were released.

The fastest way to get the message to the Cambodians, Kissinger decided, was to announce it to the press and let it be disseminated over the wires and airwaves. With his tuxedo now pretty much on, Kissinger picked up the phone and called Press Secretary Ron Nessen. "Come down here right away!"

Kissinger's voice sounded "agitated," Nessen recalled, but he did not like being ordered around. So he continued to work on the problems he was wrestling with in his office a few doors away in the West Wing. A moment later, Scowcroft (also in black tie) burst into Nessen's office and pulled him physically to Kissinger's. Within a few minutes, a bulletin was being sent out by the media quoting a presidential statement to the Cambodians that military operations would cease as soon as the crew was released.

Throughout the state dinner, aides repeatedly pulled Ford and Kissinger away to report on the situation. As soon as the dessert plates had been cleared, Ford and Kissinger went to the Oval Office to monitor the operation. Secretary Schlesinger called a few minutes later with the good news: the crew had arrived safely in a fishing boat— they had actually been released before the American rescue got under way—and were all accounted for. A roar went up.

Kissinger, however, still felt it was important to carry through with a bombing attack on the mainland, both as punishment and as a way to assure the Cambodians did not cause some last-minute mischief. "Is there any reason for the Pentagon not to disengage?" Scowcroft asked in the excitement.

"No, but tell them to bomb the mainland," Kissinger answered, according to Nessen. "Let's look ferocious! Otherwise they will attack us as the ship leaves."

But the full-fledged final strike against the mainland, which Ford and Kissinger had approved, never occurred. Schlesinger and his generals, who had never been in favor of making a display of the bombing, did not get around to carrying out the full program. Ford tried to find out why his order was disobeyed, but he never got a satisfactory answer.

The victory had been costly: in order to save thirty-nine seamen, eighteen American military men were killed in action and another twenty-three had been killed when their helicopter crashed during preparations for the operation. Yet even with fifteen years of hindsight, Ford considered the action worthwhile. In fact, he named it as his most significant foreign policy decision. "*Mayaguez* provided us with a shot in the arm as a nation when we really needed it," he said. "It convinced some of our adversaries we were not a paper tiger."

Kissinger was a little more cautious in his press conference right after the rescue. He took care not to say outright what he had been advocating in private, that the military action was designed for its global symbolism. "I don't want to transform it into an apocalyptic event," he said. "The impact ought to be to make clear that there are limits beyond which the U.S. cannot be pushed and that the U.S. is prepared to defend its interests. But we are not going around looking for opportunities to prove our manhood."[17]

The rescue of the *Mayaguez* served as a much-needed punctuation mark ending a disastrous spring for American foreign policy. Although it could not exorcise the demons of Vietnam that haunted the nation's soul—that would take at least another decade—the small spasm of military assertiveness in the Gulf of Thailand did serve to perk up public opinion about the Ford administration's handling of foreign policy. Americans have a deeply ingrained tendency to rally around a president after a bold-seeming use of force. That tendency had been submerged during the last years of the Vietnam War. But the *Mayaguez* operation, sloppy though it was, showed that it had not disappeared.

TWENTY-NINE

MORALITY
IN FOREIGN POLICY

Kissinger's Realpolitik
and How It Was Challenged

> *If I had to choose between justice and disorder, on the one hand, and injustice and order, on the other, I would always choose the latter.* —KISSINGER, *paraphrasing Goethe*

THE ROOTS OF REALISM

When Henry Kissinger was asked, at a secret congressional hearing in 1975, why the U.S. had abruptly cut off aid to Kurdish rebels fighting for their freedom from Iraq, he replied that "covert action should not be confused with missionary work." The answer, though glib, reflected a basic tenet of his philosophy. Moral crusaders, he felt, made dangerous statesmen. In a nation whose instincts tend to be idealistic, even at times crusading, Kissinger was a rare and unabashed disciple of the school of political thought known as "realism."[1]

Based on a pessimistic view of human nature (which Kissinger came to naturally), the realist tradition—and its Prussian-accented cousin realpolitik—holds that power is paramount in international relations. Nations have their own interests, which are destined to clash now and then. A realist keeps his eye on these national interests, rather than on some idealistic vision of morality or justice, and understands that they can be protected only by military credibility. With a disdain for ideology, the realist tends to view the goal of statecraft as stability, best achieved through unsentimental alliances, a carefully tended balance of power, and competing spheres of influence.

A classic exposition of the realist outlook comes from Thucydides in his book, *The Peloponnesian War.* "What made war inevitable was the growth of Athenian power and the fear which this caused in Sparta," he writes. In his accounting, the city-states that relied on fairness and fidelity to agreements lost out to those that made an unvarnished appeal to power politics.

In its modern form, the realist tradition is best defined by the German sociologist Max Weber and two German American professors, Reinhold Niebuhr and Hans Morgenthau. All emphasized the primacy of power, the circumscribed role of morality in foreign affairs, and a Hobbesian pessimism about human nature. As Bismarck wrote in 1854: "For heaven's sake no sentimental alliances in which the consciousness of having performed a good deed furnishes the sole reward for our sacrifice." [2]

Like much in the American political character, the debate between idealism and realism in foreign policy can be traced back to Jefferson and Hamilton. Jefferson saw America's world role in idealistic terms: "I have sworn upon the altar of God eternal hostility against any form of tyranny over the mind of man." Hamilton had a feel for realpolitik: "Safety from external danger is the most powerful director of national conduct." Jefferson's idealism triumphed, supplemented by an isolationist resistance to ensnarement in overseas alliances, as expressed in George Washington's farewell address.

The modern exemplar of American idealism was Woodrow Wilson, a liberal internationalist who declared that the goal of World War I was to make the world "safe for democracy" and who believed that national interests could be transcended through the moralistic-legalistic mechanisms of the League of Nations. "Sometimes people call me an idealist," he said when the war was over. "Well, that is the only way I know I am an American. America is the only idealistic nation in the world." [3]

KISSINGER'S REALISM

Kissinger tended to be dismissive of this strand in American policy. He once told Syrian dictator Hafiz al-Assad that Franklin Roosevelt had not understood at the end of World War II the importance of gaining the best possible military position vis-à-vis Moscow's Red Army in Europe. Roosevelt's grasp of geopolitical realities, he said, was not as good as his feel for the idealistic values of America.

For Kissinger, the reverse was true. "Americans," he once wrote, "are comfortable with an idealistic tradition that espouses great causes, such as making the world safe for democracy, or human rights." But it was not in the country's nature, he often lamented, to sit still for the unedifying work of tending to imperfect alliances or the never-ending meddling necessary to maintain a balance of power. The U.S. has historically been, in Stanley Hoffmann's words, "tradition-ally hostile to balance of power diplomacy with its closets of partitions, compensations, secret treaties and gunboats."

To Kissinger, this excessive aversion to secret treaties and gun-boats, and to all the other trappings of realpolitik and balance-of-power diplomacy, stemmed from the simple, often simplistic, naïveté and decency of most Americans. With a jarring use of the first-person plural that belies the fact that the descriptions scarcely apply to him, Kissinger once wrote that "our native inclination for straightforward-ness, our instinct for open, noisy politics, our distrust of European manners and continental elites, all brought about an increasing im-patience with the stylized methods of European diplomacy and with its tendency toward ambiguous compromise."

This idealistic streak in the American character, this desire to seek moral perfection rather than messy accommodations, was what caused the nation to lurch over the years between isolationism and interventionism, to embark on crusades (World War I, Vietnam), and then to recoil into self-righteous withdrawal. "Emotional slogans, un-leavened by a concept of the national interest, had caused us to oscil-late between excesses of isolation and overextension," Kissinger wrote. The way to moderate these pendulum swings, he said, was "by making judgments according to some more permanent conception of national interest."[4]

One key component of Kissinger's brand of realism was his special emphasis on the role of military might. "Throughout history," he once wrote, "the influence of nations has been roughly correlative to their military power." This view led him to favor great displays and pre-tenses of power: bombings, incursions, aircraft carriers steaming to-ward trouble spots, nuclear alerts.

Even from a realist perspective, this emphasis on military power was subject to criticism. Other sophisticated realists, such as George Kennan and Hans Morgenthau, emphasized that economic vitality and political stability are equally important elements of national power. Kissinger's best diplomacy came in China, the Middle East, and later Africa, where the direct threat of American force played little role; his greatest failures came in Vietnam, Cambodia, and Pakistan, where displays of force abounded. There was also a political constraint: the brutal and cold application of force was incompatible with America's self-conception and what its citizenry in the 1970s was willing to countenance.

Another component of Kissinger's realism was the stress he put on the role that "credibility" played in determining a nation's influence and power. An emphasis on credibility is why realism in foreign policy is not always the same thing as pragmatism. In dealing with Vietnam, for example, a pragmatist would have come more quickly to the conclusion that the war was simply not worth the effort, that the costs were greater than any potential benefits. Realists such as Kissinger, however, emphasized that America could not abandon its commitments or else it would undermine its influence elsewhere in the world.

From his *Foreign Affairs* piece in 1968, to his analysis of Vietnam options in 1969, to his arguments in early 1975 as Saigon was falling, Kissinger put enormous weight on the credibility argument. The problem with an emphasis on credibility is that it can—and in the case of Vietnam did—result in an inability to discriminate between vital interests and ones that are merely peripheral.[5]

A third aspect of Kissinger's realism was his lack of concern about supporting democratic forces and human rights movements in authoritarian countries. He was more comfortable dealing with strong rulers—Brezhnev, Zhou Enlai, the shah of Iran, Assad, and Sadat—than with the messy democracies in Europe and Israel.

In office and after, he opposed the crusades of moral activists who wanted the U.S. to push for domestic reforms in the Soviet Union, China, Pakistan, and the shah's Iran. "Why is it our business how they govern themselves?" an annoyed Kissinger asked at a meeting in 1971 when State Department bureaucrats were recommending pressure on Pakistan. This attitude was later reflected when Kissinger refused to join in the criticism of China after the 1989 crackdown in Tiananmen Square.

Though complex, even ingenious, in its design, Kissinger's realism began with a simple premise: any event should be judged foremost by whether it represented a gain for the Soviets or for the West in the overall global balance. That was the basis of his credibility argument in Vietnam: the war would show the rest of the world whether Washington had the will to stand up to Soviet expansion elsewhere. He embarked on the Middle East peace process partly as a way to undermine Soviet influence there. In the India-Pakistan war, the U.S. became involved on the losing side partly because Kissinger insisted on viewing the regional war as a proxy struggle between a Soviet and an American client.

This tendency to see global disputes through an East-West prism provided his foreign policy with a coherent framework, but it could also be distorting, as he later admitted. "We must outgrow the notion that every setback is a Soviet gain or every problem is caused by Soviet action," he said in May 1975, after setbacks in Vietnam, Cambodia, Portugal, and the Middle East put him on the defensive about his policy of détente with the Soviets. Yet the "we" in his speech fit snugly, for he had spent six years pushing that notion.[6]

SOLZHENITSYN, HELSINKI, AND HUMAN RIGHTS, JULY 1975

By 1975, Kissinger's critics, both on the left and the right, had begun to attack his dismissive attitudes toward idealism and morality. The fact that he had developed a personal reputation for being Machiavellian and manipulative did not help: it served to make his approach to foreign policy seem that way as well.

Without appealing to idealism or ideology, it was difficult for Kissinger to build a constituency for an interventionist foreign policy. America had become involved in foreign alliances such as NATO and SEATO after World War II largely as a response to the threat of communism. By pursuing a policy of détente with Russia and China, Kissinger undermined the populist rationale for overseas involvement. He also unnerved conservatives who saw a moral crusade against communism as the foundation of foreign policy. Liberals, already alienated by Vietnam and by Kissinger's faith in military force, made common cause with conservatives by criticizing the disregard for moral issues that was inherent in his realpolitik.

These issues were crystallized in the summer of 1975 by an imbroglio over whether President Ford should meet with exiled Russian writer Alexander Solzhenitsyn, who came to Washington to address a gala dinner hosted by the AFL-CIO on June 30. His presence created a symbolic showdown between the supporters of détente and its foes. Kissinger passed the word that it would be inappropriate for executive branch officials to attend the dinner, especially since Solzhenitsyn's speech was likely to include an attack on the administration's policy of détente. This assured that Defense Secretary James Schlesinger would attend, as would Daniel Patrick Moynihan, who had just been sworn in that day as U.N. ambassador.

President Ford, on Kissinger's advice, stayed away, then turned down a public offer by conservative senators to bring Solzhenitsyn to the White House on July 4. Ford's decision was based on personality as well as policy: he considered the Russian to be "a goddamned horse's ass," which was a rather harsh literary judgment but did reflect the fact that, like most moral prophets, Solzhenitsyn lacked a certain personal charm.

The controversy that erupted was fueled by Ford's various explanations of why he could not meet with Solzhenitsyn. First he said he was "too busy," which was not widely regarded as credible. Then a spokesman said that he "did not like meetings that are symbolic and empty of substance." This, too, was a dubious excuse, especially since Solzhenitsyn certainly had more of substance to say than some of the champion athletes and beauty pageant winners who were regular features on Ford's schedule.

Finally, Ford relented and issued an open invitation for Solzhenitsyn to drop by whenever he wanted. By then the Russian was no longer interested. "Nobody needs symbolic meetings," he said, flinging Ford's words back at him.

Instead, on July 15 he delivered a lecture on an upcoming summit conference scheduled to be held in Helsinki, at which Ford planned to meet with European and Soviet leaders to discuss ways to guarantee security. Solzhenitsyn called the Helsinki conference "the betrayal of Eastern Europe." Stretching his talent for poetic imagery, he warned that "an amicable agreement of diplomatic shovels will bury and pack down corpses still breathing in a common grave."[7]

That same day, Kissinger gave one of the most important speeches of his career, in which he sought to explain why he felt that morality had only a limited role to play in foreign policy. The speech, given in Minneapolis, served as his answer to critics who were using the Solzhenitsyn snub and the upcoming Helsinki summit to criticize his power-oriented approach to world affairs.

Like his trip through Missouri on the first day of the *Mayaguez* crisis, Kissinger's visit to Minneapolis was part of a laudable effort to explain the philosophy behind his foreign policy and to listen to grassroots reactions. He spent a considerable amount of effort working on what he dubbed "the heartland speeches," which involved fourteen major domestic trips in 1975.

The heartland program illustrated an interesting dichotomy in

Kissinger's style: no American statesman has ever been more secretive and conspiratorial in managing foreign policy tactics, yet (especially after he became secretary of state) none tried harder to explain to the press and the public the conceptual goals he pursued. "The heartland program attempted to build a domestic consensus by educating people about America's role in the world," said Winston Lord, who oversaw it.

Unlike the usual mix of pabulum and clichés that fill most foreign policy speeches, Kissinger's did not attempt to talk down to his audience or dilute controversial ideas. Before each trip, he would outline his thoughts for a speech, and Mark Palmer of the Policy Planning staff would write a first draft with Peter Rodman. Lord would then bring it to Kissinger and brace for the inevitable explosion. "It's not what I wanted at all," Kissinger would invariably shout. "It's fuzzy. It's conventional thinking. It doesn't force any decisions. It has no bite. It's not conceptual." Sometimes he would throw it to the floor and stamp on it to make his feelings clear, though Lord had usually gotten his drift by that point. At the end of the process, Kissinger would usually rework parts of the speech himself. "He would will himself to work on the speeches between cables and emergencies, even when a war was breaking out," recalled Lord.

Not everyone in the White House was impressed. "His erudite writers did their best to make him sound like a combination of John the Baptist, John Birch, and John Doe," said Robert Hartmann, who oversaw Ford's speechwriting. Nevertheless, Kissinger's heartland speeches garnered adulatory press notices, and his popularity in polls remained abnormally high. "Kissinger proved to be an accomplished barnstormer who hugely enjoyed the attention he received in a Middle America that still sees him as Supersecretary," wrote *Time* after one of them.

On his way to Minneapolis, Kissinger stopped in Milwaukee to throw out the first ball of baseball's All-Star Game. There were a few glitches: the stadium announcer introduced him as Dr. Harry Kissinger, and a few boos mixed with the cheers as he delivered a rather weak toss from the stands. The next day, his speech in Minneapolis was repeatedly interrupted by a handful of hecklers, prompting Kissinger to say, "I think I have some of my old Harvard students here in the audience."

The speech, entitled "The Moral Foundations of Foreign Policy," did not try to blur his realpolitik outlook. He emphasized the importance of "furthering America's interests in a world where power remains the ultimate arbiter."

In defense of détente with the Soviets, he argued that nuclear weapons made it imperative to "seek a more productive and stable relationship despite the basic antagonism of our values." Although he included some sentences of pro forma praise for American ideals, he tended to follow them with sentences that began with a "But." For example: "This nation must be true to its own beliefs, or it will lose its bearings in the world. But at the same time it must survive in a world of sovereign nations and competing wills."

By the end of the speech, the *buts* had clearly won. Kissinger assailed the supporters of Solzhenitsyn and of Jackson-Vanik by pointing out that a majority of the world's nations may be repressive, but the U.S. must have relationships and even alliances with most of them. "We have used, and we will use, our influence against repressive practices," he said. "But truth compels a recognition of our limits. . . . To what extent are we able to affect the internal policies of other governments and to what extent is it desirable?"[8]

At the press conference after his speech, Kissinger found himself on the defensive about the upcoming Helsinki conference. The summit was planned as the culmination of a two-year-long series of meetings, officially known as the Conference on Security and Cooperation in Europe, which had been an obscure and inconsequential process until Senator Jackson, Solzhenitsyn, and others began to attack it. When Ford announced that he would attend the conference finale, the criticism grew that Kissinger had persuaded a gullible president to become entangled in a nefarious sellout.

The desire for a European security conference to ratify postwar borders had been a staple of Soviet diplomacy since the mid-1950s. Moscow hoped it would consolidate its grip on Eastern Europe and perhaps ease American troops off the continent. Although the U.S. had long resisted, its Western European allies began favoring the notion of a security conference in the early 1970s, especially after the Berlin treaties settled many of the German issues. Washington unenthusiastically went along after it was agreed that decisions would be made only by consensus and that the U.S. and Canada would be full participants.

The conference eventually produced three "baskets" of agreements, which became known as the Helsinki Final Act. The first basket, "Security in Europe," confirmed the postwar borders, tacitly accepted the incorporation of the Baltic states into the Soviet Union, and required "nonintervention in the internal affairs" of sovereign nations. The second basket dealt with science, technology, the environment, tourism, and trade. The final basket, which at first seemed mere rhetoric, was "Humanitarian and Other Fields." It endorsed the free movement of people and ideas as well as respect for individual rights. Once the conference completed this work, it scheduled a July 1975 summit of national leaders to ratify the handiwork.

Since all of this had been agreed to by thirty-four disparate nations plus the Vatican, it should not have been a major controversy. Nevertheless, as Ford was about to depart for Helsinki, the political storm in the U.S. intensified. The White House was deluged with mail —much of it from those of Estonian, Latvian, or Lithuanian descent —objecting to the alleged relegation of those Baltic states to the Soviet Union. "Jerry, Don't Go," headlined a *Wall Street Journal* editorial. "I'm against it," said California governor Ronald Reagan, who avoided the temptation to offer further explanation.

Helsinki had touched a nerve, the Yalta nerve. It reminded conservatives of the 1945 Yalta summit, where Roosevelt and Churchill had allegedly given Stalin the impression that the Soviets had permission to impose communist regimes on the European nations that the Red Army occupied. Ever since, many Americans have worried that Soviet-American "spheres of influence" diplomacy would result in "another Yalta," another sellout of Eastern Europe.

The day before he departed, Ford met with ethnic American leaders. In his remarks, which had been written by his staff and cleared with Scowcroft, the president proclaimed: "The United States has never recognized the Soviet incorporation of Lithuania, Latvia, and Estonia and is not going to do so in Helsinki." That was a standard reiteration of American policy, and everybody liked it—except Kissinger. He was outraged that the sentence seemed to be a slap at Moscow, and he blew up at Scowcroft and Hartmann in the hallway just outside the Oval Office as other aides watched startled. "You will pay for this! I tell you, heads will roll." He insisted that the sentence be removed from Ford's departure remarks at Andrews Air Force Base, and it was. But since it was in the prepared text given to the press, it only meant the sentence got more publicity, along with stories about how Kissinger was trying to muzzle his boss.[9]

Because the Helsinki conference, like many of the foreign policy controversies of the Ford administration, was more about rhetoric than reality, disputes over speech texts took on a particular importance. Indeed, even back in the Nixon years, one of the few periods when actions did tend to speak louder than words, Kissinger had realized that foreign policy largely consisted of words uttered by a president, and he spent much of his time making sure that he rather than Nixon's speechwriting team had final say over foreign policy speeches. Now this was harder because the White House writing staff was managed by Hartmann, a longtime aide to Ford.

As usual, the first draft of the speech that the president planned to give in Helsinki was prepared by Kissinger's staff, in this case Winston Lord. "His own stable of writers," Hartmann said of Kissinger, "tended to be Ivy League WASPs whose six-bit vocabularies drove the President right up the wall." Hartmann considered the draft to be too bland; it was "diplomatic gobbledygook" with no ringing defense of American principles. The only part of it he liked was what he referred to later as "an exceptionally felicitous final sentence." It read: "History will judge this conference not by what we say today, but what we do tomorrow; not by the promises we make but by the promises we keep."

Ford sat through all of the speeches by other leaders during the two-day summit as the alphabet slowly made its way to the United States. It would be rude, he said, not to be in his seat when someone else was talking. Finally, a frustrated Hartmann passed him a note. "When can I talk to you briefly, but privately, about Henry's latest draft of your speech?" He finally got time to talk to Ford while the president was getting dressed for the state dinner.

When Kissinger realized that Hartmann and company were doing a rewrite, he assigned his own staffer William Hyland to keep them in check—and to prevent anything truly critical of détente or of the Soviets from creeping into the speech. As one of those with a six-bit vocabulary, Hyland regarded the Hartmann stable of writers as "somewhat a strange breed." He discovered that they were "inordinately proud" of the final sentence, which everyone by then had apparently forgotten was part of the original draft from Kissinger's office. Hyland, rather puckish, asked why they were spending so much time on a speech that concluded by saying that we would not be judged by what we said.

In the end, the Kissinger and Hartmann camps agreed that the best course was to emphasize the human rights basket over the security basket. "To my country, they are not clichés or empty phrases," Ford said, looking directly at Brezhnev. "It is important that you recognize the deep devotion of the American people and their government to human rights and fundamental freedoms." During the enthusiastic standing ovation that followed, Kissinger came over to Hartmann and smiled. "Your words were better."

The Helsinki conference started a chain of political reactions against Ford's foreign policy that culminated a year later with his "gaffe" of liberating Poland during a debate with Jimmy Carter.* In fact, the Helsinki conference contributed significantly to Ford's defeat

---

* See Chapter 31.

in the 1976 election. But in retrospect, he and Kissinger were right, more right than even they imagined at the time: Helsinki would eventually turn out to be a step on the way toward the West's ultimate victory in Europe.

The security basket of the Helsinki accords would turn out to be, contrary to what both the Soviets and the American conservatives assumed, the least important part of the agreements. The "acceptance of final borders" mainly referred to the border between West and East Germany, which turned out not to be so final after all. And by 1991, the Soviet Union had disintegrated and the Baltic states had regained their independence.

In his briefing book for a post-Helsinki press conference, Kissinger had prepared an answer for a question that no one ended up asking: did he feel that the accords tacitly granted the Soviet Union dominance over Eastern Europe? Had the question been asked, he would have pointed out that the final agreement contained language requiring nations to "respect each other's right freely to choose and develop its political, social, economic and cultural systems." To Kissinger this was an outright repudiation of the Brezhnev Doctrine, in which the Soviets declared after the 1968 Czechoslovakia invasion that they had the right to prevent their allies from straying from the communist bloc.

As for the human rights requirements, Brezhnev seemed to reject them in his speech when he said, "It is only the people of each given state, and no one else, that has the sovereign right to resolve its internal affairs." But after the summit, dozens of "Helsinki groups" sprang up, led by dissidents and democrats, to demand that communist governments honor the phrases about freedom and human rights. Among them were such organizations as Charter 77, led by Vaclav Havel in Czechoslovakia, and Solidarity, led by Lech Walesa in Poland. And a formal network of "Helsinki Watch" organizations was formed in the West to encourage these developments. Less than fifteen years later, Havel and Walesa would become presidents of the nations that had only recently jailed them for their political activities.

"What started at Helsinki was to be startlingly different from what Brezhnev expected, the consolidation of the postwar order Moscow had so long desired," Hyland later noted. "Instead, the political status quo in Eastern Europe began to unravel." Years later, after the transformation was complete, Ford claimed a small bit of the credit. "Henry and I were accused of trying to freeze Yalta," he said. "But what Helsinki really brought about was pressure for human rights, and that has got to be one ingredient for what happened in 1989." [10]

Unfortunately for Ford and Kissinger, the historical vindication

of Helsinki was years away. Political vilification, however, was immediate. Aggravating the issue was a secret briefing on Helsinki given to
a meeting of American diplomats in London by Kissinger's aide Helmut Sonnenfeldt. The briefing was summarized in a State Department cable, which promptly leaked to columnists Rowland Evans and
Robert Novak.

Sonnenfeldt, known as Kissinger's Kissinger because of the complex and occasionally tricky nature of his strategic views, was reflecting
his boss's own realpolitik outlook about the Soviet sphere of influence
in Europe. What Sonnenfeldt said at the London meeting was rather
subtle and therefore open to oversimplification:

> The Soviets' inability to acquire loyalty in Eastern Eu-
> rope is an unfortunate historical failure, because Eastern Eu-
> rope is within their scope and area of natural interest. . . .
> So it must be our policy to strive for an evolution that makes
> the relationship between the Eastern Europeans and the So-
> viet Union an organic one. . . . This has worked in Poland.
> The Poles have been able to overcome their romantic politi-
> cal inclinations which led to their disasters in the past.

Sonnenfeldt's point was that an "organic" relationship was better
because it would not be based on force. Even so, what became known
as the Sonnenfeldt Doctrine was pretty close to the conservative's
worst nightmare of a secret Yalta-like sellout: an admission by the U.S.
that the "captive nations" of Eastern Europe were naturally part of
Moscow's sphere of influence.

"The Sonnenfeldt doctrine exposes the underpinnings of détente," Evans and Novak wrote. The rest of the press quickly got hold
of the cable summarizing Sonnenfeldt's briefing and treated it as an
exposé of Kissinger's secret worldview. "Whatever was actually meant
by Mr. Sonnenfeldt, the latest mini-Metternich of Foggy Bottom, the
idea sent shivers up the spine," C. L. Sulzberger wrote in the *New
York Times*. "It would seem to be an invitation to the Kremlin to
assert fuller control of Eastern Europe, perhaps even absorbing it into
the U.S.S.R." The *Washington Post* editorialized: "One hears rumors
of gloomy private ruminations by Secretary Kissinger on very much
the same theme."

Ronald Reagan blasted the Sonnenfeldt Doctrine for saying, in
effect, that "slaves should accept their fate," and he linked it to other
cases where the "Kissinger-Ford" team had abandoned human rights
concerns. "At Kissinger's insistence, Mr. Ford snubbed Alexander
Solzhenitsyn, one of the great moral heroes of our time," said the

California governor, who was preparing to challenge Ford for the Republican nomination. "At Kissinger's insistence, Mr. Ford flew halfway around the world to sign an agreement at Helsinki which placed the American seal of approval on the Soviet empire in Eastern Europe."

Kissinger was at first bemused, then baffled, then outraged by the furor, especially when he realized it was making him anathema to Republican conservatives. Although he agreed with the underlying theory of Sonnenfeldt's talk—which was, after all, a pretty clear statement of Kissinger's own belief in the importance of stable spheres of influence—he knew that trying to explain it would only make matters worse. Instead he tried to dismiss the entire flap as having nothing to do with American policy. Sonnenfeldt had wandered off the reservation, he told friends in the press. To those who knew of his long-standing love-hate rivalry with his fellow German refugee, Kissinger would grumble: "If it were truly a new doctrine of this administration, it would not be named after Hal Sonnenfeldt."[11]

DANIEL MOYNIHAN AND AMERICAN IDEALISM

Daniel Patrick Moynihan, the U.S. ambassador at the United Nations, was among those who felt that Sonnenfeldt, in his London briefing to ambassadors, had honestly reflected Kissinger's thinking. "This is what Kissinger knew, and Sonnenfeldt and men whose roots were still in Europe knew," Moynihan later wrote. "I knew little of this. On the other hand, I knew what Wilson was all about."

Moynihan had studied Woodrow Wilson with the same fascination that his old Harvard colleague had studied Metternich. On the fiftieth anniversary of President Wilson's death, in 1974, Moynihan had given a lecture that was reprinted in the neoconservative journal *Commentary*. Wilson's "singular contribution," Moynihan said, was defining America's "duty to defend and, where feasible, to advance democratic principles in the world at large." From this Moynihan adduced the nation's duties in the world today. "We must play the hand dealt us: we stand for liberty, for the expansion of liberty."

This Wilsonian idealism was the polar opposite of Kissinger's Metternichian realism. It aligned Moynihan with the moral critics of détente, ranging from Alexander Solzhenitsyn to Henry Jackson to Norman Podhoretz. Involved was more than an academic dispute between two Harvard professors: when Moynihan began to both practice and preach the politics of morality at the U.N., he became a rallying point for those who opposed Kissinger's lack of regard for human rights.

Moynihan had long harbored a collegial disdain for Henry Kissinger of the sort bred at faculty club dining tables. They had both joined Nixon's White House from Harvard in 1969 as presidential assistants, but after two years Moynihan went back to academia and then to India as ambassador. Personally, Moynihan enjoyed Kissinger's company and admired his energy. But he considered him dangerous. Moynihan liked to repeat a line said to him by Helmut Sonnenfeldt: "You do not understand. Henry does not lie because it is in his interest. He lies because it is in his nature." Later Moynihan would say that Kissinger's conspiratorial nature "helped bring on" Watergate.

Moynihan had a keen eye for how Kissinger's conspiratorial intimacy worked. Kissinger would immediately divine the case that any petitioner wanted to make, Moynihan explained, and then promptly "proclaim that object to be his very own." Exuding a commonality of purpose and great respect, he would say how profoundly grateful he was for the chance to combine forces with his visitor. Then, his charm would turn conspiratorial: they faced powerful opponents who must first be thrown off the scent; it was important to bear with him as he indirectly pursued their mutual goal. Accommodations would have to be made. It would be important not to criticize what might seem like concessions, Kissinger would tell his interlocutors. Thus, Moynihan recounted, did Kissinger pave the way for his promotion to secretary of state.

Moynihan had made himself a natural choice to replace John Scali as U.N. ambassador by writing an article for *Commentary* entitled "The United States in Opposition," which was released with much publicity in February 1975. "Speaking for political and civil liberty, and doing so in detail and in concrete particulars, is something that can surely be undertaken by Americans with enthusiasm and zeal," he wrote. "It is time that the American spokesman came to be feared in international forums for the truths he might tell."

Kissinger began reading the piece in his limousine and canceled an afternoon appointment so he could finish it. He was impressed but bothered: in the wake of the Jackson-Vanik debacle, he was more convinced than ever that moralistic crusading about human rights would undermine détente. Ford, on the other hand, had come to the conclusion that Moynihan would be useful at the U.N. to counter charges that the administration's foreign policy lacked moral fervor. When he broached the idea, Kissinger initially balked. "Henry was not in favor of sending Moynihan to the U.N. and warned that he might use it as a political stepping-stone," Ford recalled. [12]

None of these doubts did Kissinger convey when, at Ford's insistence, he called Moynihan to offer him the job. The *Commentary* article, Kissinger proclaimed, was "staggeringly good," so fine that it had made him proclaim, "Why didn't I write that!" It was the highest compliment one lapsed professor could pay to another, and Moynihan lapped it up. He agreed to come around one Wednesday afternoon in late March—just after the failed Sinai II shuttle mission—at which point he accepted the U.N. job.

For the rest of 1975, Moynihan raised hell at the U.N. by challenging the hypocrisy of the repressive nations who dared assail American imperialism. The culmination of his outspoken crusade came on November 10, when the General Assembly passed an anti-Israeli resolution declaring that "Zionism is a form of racism." Moynihan had fought the measure vociferously, dismaying some at the State Department who felt it would have been better simply to cast a quiet vote against it and treat it with the benign neglect reserved for much of the General Assembly's nonsense.

A couple of days after the vote, following a state dinner, Kissinger invited Moynihan to his White House office for a drink. (When Moynihan accepted, Kissinger, who stuck to diet soda, could find nothing but mao-tai for the less abstemious ambassador to drink.) The conversation, to Moynihan, seemed nothing more than pleasantries. But the following Monday, he read in *Newsweek* that a senior administration official revealed that "Kissinger raked Moynihan over the coals at the White House last week for his behavior at the U.N. and his independent efforts to stir up Congressional reaction to the Zionism resolution." Kissinger promptly assured Moynihan that he had no idea where *Newsweek* had gotten such a silly notion, but Moynihan knew full well. It was another example, he later said, of Kissinger's devious methods.

So, too, Moynihan thought, was an attack by the British ambassador to the U.N., Ivor Richard. In a speech, Richard said of the U.N., "Whatever else the place is, it is not the OK Corral." The gist of the speech was that Moynihan (though his name was never used) was courting danger by turning the place into "a confrontational arena." After Richard made a point of coming up at a dinner and saying the thoughts were not his own but a reflection of British policy, it dawned on Moynihan that they had probably been inspired by Kissinger, who had just met with Prime Minister James Callahan. Kissinger denied this with unusual vehemence, but the press began to push such speculation. "Ivor took advantage of the kick-me sign that Henry pinned on Pat," wrote William Safire.

Moynihan, feeling humiliated, flew down to Washington intent on resigning. Ford, however, had other ideas. Moynihan's feistiness was catching on with the public, certainly far more than Kissinger's defense of détente. "As a sort of ambassadorial fighting Irishman, Pat Moynihan has become an American pop hero," wrote *Time.* Sitting alone by a fire in the Oval Office, the president asked Moynihan to stay. It took less than thirty seconds, a shorter period than consumed by most Moynihan sentences, for him to agree. After another half hour of pleasant assurances of support, Ford called in Kissinger, who had been waiting outside. "His face," Moynihan recalls, "was terrible. He assured me of his complete support."

The truce lasted another two months, until the end of January 1976. Earlier that month, Moynihan had decided not to return to Harvard when his leave expired, thus abandoning his tenure there. But another series of articles questioning whether Kissinger still supported him—especially a harsh one by James Reston saying that the secretary did not—persuaded Moynihan that it was time to resign his U.N. job.

Kissinger was convinced that the real reason for Moynihan's resignation was that he wanted to run for the Senate from New York, which he had pledged not to do when he took the U.N. job. "He had to get out of his promise not to run for the Senate, so he picked a fight with me," Kissinger later said. Moynihan, on the other hand, recalled that Kissinger, as a "friend," had urged him to make the Senate race during a conversation in early January. In any event, soon after leaving the U.N., Moynihan entered the Democratic primary for Senate, which he won, and then went on to defeat incumbent James Buckley.

As soon as he bolted from the administration, Moynihan officially joined ranks with the critics of Kissinger's policy of détente. On March 1, his first day out of office, he flew to Boston to campaign on behalf of Senator Henry Jackson's presidential bid, and later he helped write an anti-détente plank into the Democratic platform.[13]

The Moynihan defection set the stage for the foreign policy issues of the 1976 presidential race. He was the last in-house advocate of an outspoken moral component to foreign policy. With him gone, Kissinger's policies became a clearer target. In both his race against Ronald Reagan for the Republican nomination and against Jimmy Carter for the presidency, Ford would find himself faced with charges that he was selling out Eastern Europe and muting America's moral voice in order to save the dying embers of détente.

THE HALLOWEEN MASSACRE, OCTOBER 1975

Moynihan's leave-taking had been preceded by that of the administration's other counterbalance to Kissinger, Defense Secretary James Schlesinger. His departure was not voluntary. Schlesinger was doomed not just because Kissinger kept taking potshots at him, but also because his caustic and condescending manner aggravated Ford. Schlesinger became the focus of a fumbled cabinet shake-up at the end of October 1975 that became known as the Halloween Massacre.

The process began when Ford's "kitchen cabinet" of old friends and outside advisers met with him to discuss his sinking popularity. Bryce Harlow took the lead. All of the feuding, he said, caused an appearance of "internal anarchy" at the White House. After ticking off the people taking shots at one another, especially Schlesinger and Kissinger, Harlow concluded "you have to fire them all" if that's what it would take to put a stop to it.

Ford needed no great encouragement to fire Schlesinger, and later said his only mistake had been not doing it sooner. "His aloof, frequently arrogant manner put me off," Ford later noted. "I could never be sure he was leveling with me." Hartmann recalled that the animosity was aroused even in trivial ways. "Ford didn't like the fact that a cabinet officer couldn't remember to button his shirt and cinch up his tie when he came to see the president," he said.

In addition, Ford and Kissinger both felt that it was time for CIA Director William Colby, who was just finishing spilling the beans at congressional hearings about the agency's historic misdeeds, to go. "Every time Bill Colby gets near Capitol Hill," Kissinger would growl, "the damn fool feels an irresistible urge to confess to some horrible crime."

Once he had decided to get rid of Schlesinger and Colby, Ford proceeded with almost no consultation to choreograph a game of musical chairs:

- His chief of staff, Don Rumsfeld, would replace Schlesinger at Defense.
- Deputy Chief of Staff Richard Cheney (who later would become George Bush's defense secretary) would be promoted to Rumsfeld's job.
- Commerce Secretary Rogers Morton, at his own initiative, would leave to head Ford's presidential campaign.
- Elliot Richardson, whose latest line on his long résumé was

ambassador to Britain, would be sounded out about the CIA job, spurn it, but then agree to come back as commerce secretary.

• George Bush, who had written the president of his desire to come home from China even though he had been there only a year, was at first going to be tapped for commerce secretary, but he then became Ford's choice for the CIA.

• Vice President Nelson Rockefeller, independent of the cabinet shuffle, would be induced to eliminate himself as Ford's running mate for 1976.

• Kissinger would remain as secretary of state, but give up his White House job as the president's national security adviser, to be replaced by his deputy Brent Scowcroft.

Ford called in Kissinger and Rumsfeld on October 25 to lay out the plan. Although Rumsfeld wanted a top-level cabinet post, he later claimed that he was surprised by the timing. "Hell, the cow is out of the barn," Rumsfeld told Ford at the meeting. "It's too late for something like this to help your image. Let's wait until after the election." Kissinger also argued against the changes, but Ford's mind was made up.

The hardest part was getting rid of Schlesinger. Ford called him into the Oval Office early on Sunday morning for a session that dragged on for almost an hour. Schlesinger's face got increasingly tense; Ford's anger grew. When Ford referred to the need for Schlesinger's resignation, the defense secretary snapped: "I haven't resigned. You're firing me."

Like most of those involved, Kissinger saw the shuffle as a power play by Rumsfeld. He was sure that the former congressman wanted to be Ford's vice presidential running mate and had thus edged Rockefeller out of the way. In addition, by bringing Bush back to run the CIA, Rumsfeld had eliminated another rival, because the president had to make a pledge that Bush would stay out of politics if confirmed.

Rumsfeld later denied that his ambition was to be vice president. The choice would not have made much sense: like Ford, he was a moderately conservative country-club WASP from the Midwest. "I know Bush felt competitive with me, but I told him it was not true, and so did Ford," said Rumsfeld. But as Bush's star rose, Rumsfeld's governmental career sputtered to an end.

Rumsfeld's relations with Kissinger and Scowcroft were further soured when they discovered that, in addition to being the principal force behind stripping Kissinger of his national security adviser's job, he had urged Ford to give the job to Arthur Hartman rather than Scowcroft. By trying and failing, Rumsfeld ensured that the NSC interagency bureaucracy would continue to tilt toward State rather than the Pentagon.

Some of Kissinger's critics blamed him, rather than Rumsfeld, for orchestrating the changes. Among them was Fritz Kraemer, Kissinger's army mentor. Kraemer, who stalked the Pentagon with his walking stick and monocle as a free-floating strategist, had recently latched onto Schlesinger, whose anti-détente outlook he passionately shared. Together they would lament Kissinger's "dishonorable" side, his "historic pessimism," his defeatism, his willingness to cut a deal with the Soviets.

Kraemer was so enraged by the firing of Schlesinger that he decided to cut Kissinger off and make a grand gesture of principle by refusing ever to talk to him again. "To eat with him would be a political lie," Kraemer later explained. "As a human being you have to stand for political values. People must know that I do not approve of him. This is a political-ethical stance." Things got so bad that Nancy Kissinger, carrying her dog Tyler, went to visit Kraemer's son, Sven, who was on the NSC staff, to try to mediate, but it was to no avail.

Schlesinger, on the other hand, realized that Kissinger was not really to blame. Kissinger, he knew, had not really wanted him fired. It was just in his nature, Schlesinger recalled, to bad-mouth rivals incessantly. "He spent a lot of his time poisoning the well about me, almost reflexively, but I don't think he really wanted me to go," Schlesinger said. "He was far better off with me than with Rumsfeld, as he realized the moment the changes were put to him."

The loss of his job as national security adviser sent Kissinger into a momentous depression, and he brooded for days to all around him about the need to resign. Advisers and wise men were summoned from afar to give counsel, and perhaps to Kissinger's dismay, many did not beseech him to stay. David Bruce, the distinguished statesman out of another era, came by Kissinger's house to advise that his farewell letter be formal and brief. Dean Rusk said much the same by phone from Georgia.

A core group of close friends met for four nights in a row at Kissinger's and Winston Lord's homes. Besides Winston and Bette Lord, it included William Simon, Lawrence Eagleburger, David Bruce, and others. Draft after draft of the resignation letter was written. At Winston Lord's suggestion, it mainly put forth what foreign policy goals Kissinger hoped would be achieved in the future. A full scenario was worked out for informing ambassadors and leaders abroad. In order to make sure that Ford realized it was not just another ploy, the president would be given only fifteen minutes' advance notice.

But before the plan went into effect, Kissinger decided to discuss it with Ford. Gently and calmly, as he puffed on his pipe, Ford asked him to stay. It took an hour or so this time, but he was able to convince Kissinger that the situation was not as dire as it seemed. Once again, he decided not to resign. At a congressional hearing the following week, he was asked a rather complex question, and after a pause he responded: "I've been so busy figuring out what jobs I have left that I haven't had a chance to study this." Then he smiled.[14]

THIRTY

AFRICA

Covert Involvement
Followed by Shuttle Diplomacy

> *We must outgrow the notion that every setback is a Soviet gain or every problem is caused by Soviet action.—KISSINGER, speech in St. Louis, Missouri, May 12, 1975*

ANGOLA THROUGH AN EAST-WEST PRISM, 1975

In the spring of 1974, there was a military coup in Portugal that was neither predicted nor understood by American intelligence officials. The right-wing authoritarian regime of Marcello Caetano was deposed by a junta of indeterminate ideology led by a cartoonish general with a monocle. By summer, however, it became clear that the real rulers were left-wing army officers. The government they formed included communists and others with pro-Soviet inclinations.

Kissinger, who was always pessimistic about the threat of Eurocommunism and the spineless attitude of NATO allies, was willing to believe the worst about Portugal. In October, Mario Soares, the socialist foreign minister, came to lunch at the State Department to convince a skeptical Kissinger that the communists would not be able to take full control. To Kissinger, he resembled the idealistic socialists with similar thoughts in Russia in 1917.

"You are a Kerensky," Kissinger told Soares. "I believe your sincerity, but you are naive."

"I certainly don't want to be a Kerensky," Soares shot back.

"Neither did Kerensky," Kissinger replied.

Kissinger's gloomy predictions that Portugal had begun a slippery slide into communism were disputed by Ambassador Stuart Nash Scott, who urged continued economic aid for Portugal's new government to bolster its connection to NATO. Kissinger's response was to sack Scott and heed instead the warnings of some retired American conservatives with vacation homes in Portugal, including Admiral George Anderson, a former chief of naval operations.

To replace Scott, Kissinger appointed Frank Carlucci, a foreign service officer then in the midst of a career rise that would eventually make him secretary of defense. Carlucci's conclusions were the same as Scott's: it was best to cooperate with the Lisbon government and not worry too much about the communists in the cabinet. "Whoever sold me Carlucci as a tough guy?" Kissinger bitterly remarked.

Nevertheless, Kissinger tentatively adopted Carlucci's advice and—perhaps because the spring of 1975 brought so many other worries—quit wringing his hands about the Portuguese. It helped that the Soviet Union refrained from exploiting the situation: it did not push as hard as it could to help the communists, and its ambassador to Lisbon repeatedly stressed to Carlucci that his nation would not try to pull Portugal into its orbit. Moscow was apparently willing to accord some of the respect for America's sphere of influence in Europe that it was seeking in Helsinki for its own sphere. By the end of 1975, the communists had been eased out of power by the pro-Western socialists, and the crisis in Portugal receded.[1]

But there was one lasting fallout to the Portuguese revolution: the nation's new leaders—communists and noncommunists alike—were eager to divest the nation of its African and Asian colonies. And they did so rather abruptly. As a result, the drama over Soviet influence in Portugal evolved into an even more complicated one involving its mineral-rich colony of Angola on the western coast of southern Africa.

When Portugal decided to grant Angola its independence, it invited the leaders of the three tribal-based rebel forces to meet in January 1975 to form a coalition government that would take over the following November. All groups readily agreed to work peacefully together. Then, aided by various foreign governments, they began fighting.

One confusing aspect of the Angolan civil war, at least for outsiders trying to figure out which side to support, was that the three factions were primarily based on tribal loyalties and did not readily fit ideological or East-West categories. That, however, did not stop Kissinger and other strategic gamesmen from trying. The three groups:

• The National Front for the Liberation of Angola (FNLA), based in the Kongo tribe of the north, was run by the slick, globe-trotting Holden Roberto, who had long received a retainer from the CIA. This was the horse the U.S. decided to back, even though it was not noticeably pro-Western or capitalist. The FNLA's other patrons at the time spanned an astonishing gamut: China, Romania, India, Algeria, Zaire, the AFL-CIO, and the Ford Foundation.

• The Popular Movement for the Liberation of Angola (MPLA), based in the Mbundu tribe around Luanda, was run by Agostinho Neto, a medical doctor and poet. Since it included some intellectuals from the capital, it was the only group that had a real ideology, which was generally European Marxist. The group had support from the Portuguese Communist Party and from some of Western Europe's socialist parties. But its main patron was Cuba and, with a little less constancy, the Soviet Union.

• The National Union for the Total Independence of Angola (UNITA), based among the Ovimbundu of the south, was run by Jonas Savimbi, a charismatic and flamboyant fighter who had originally been aligned with the FNLA. UNITA cast itself, at least at first, as the most radical leftists of the lot. Savimbi denounced "American interests" and "the notorious agents of imperialism," and his pilgrimages in search of aid took him to North Vietnam, China, and, most importantly, North Korea, which trained his fighters and supplied most of his original equipment. Oddly, UNITA would end the war allied with South Africa and, loosely, with the U.S. Even more oddly, as he continued his guerrilla struggle after the Cuban-backed MPLA won, Savimbi would hire right-wing influence-peddlers in Washington who would cast him as one of the Reagan Doctrine's deserving "freedom fighters" struggling to roll back communism.

The stage was thus set in 1975 for Angola to become a vivid example of Kissinger's tendency to see complex local struggles in an East-West context. "In all respect to Kissinger," wrote Jonathan Kwitny in his study of the Angolan war, "one really has to question the sanity of someone who looks at an ancient tribal dispute over control of distant coffee fields and sees in it a Soviet threat to the security of the United States."

More than that, Kissinger saw in Angola the first test of the new rules of détente, a way to feel out the limits on how far each superpower could go in seeking an advantage in the third world. With the credibility of American commitments called into question because of

Vietnam and Cambodia, Kissinger felt that it was important to seize an opportunity to show that the U.S. still had the will to counter Moscow's moves. Thus the rather lethargic Angolan conflict suddenly found itself exalted into more than just another muddled African civil war.[2]

One of the later disputes regarding Angola was a chicken-and-egg argument: did America respond to a Soviet intervention or the Soviets to an American one? In fact, it was an escalating cycle that also involved the Chinese, whose support of the FNLA in 1974 spurred the Soviets and Cubans to back the MPLA.

The first significant American involvement came in January 1975 —a week after the Portuguese accord with the three rebel groups— when the 40 Committee, the interagency group that oversaw covert actions, approved a $300,000 secret program for FNLA political activities. It was a modest sum, and it included no weapons. But it emboldened Roberto to begin a military campaign against the MPLA. By March he had moved a motorized column into Luanda and attacked MPLA headquarters.

That month the Soviets stepped up their support for the MPLA, sending supplies in by ship and airlift. Neto also turned to Havana, sending an emissary and asking for the most important resource of all: trained combat troops. Cuban mercenaries began arriving in May. Though they were serving as Soviet proxies, recent documents show that Cuba had its own motives for supporting a communist victory in Angola, and they were not restrained by the caution that prevailed in the Kremlin. Thus reinforced, the MPLA began a major counteroffensive in July and was able to push back both the FNLA in the north and UNITA in the south.[3]

The fail-safe point had been reached: Kissinger had to determine whether the U.S. should throw itself into the contest or quietly step back from the fray. He scheduled a meeting of the 40 Committee for July 14—the day before he was to fly to Minneapolis for his "Moral Foundations of Foreign Policy" speech and Solzhenitsyn would attack him for being too soft on the Soviets—to decide whether the U.S. should embark on a covert war in Angola.

The State Department bureaucracy, led by Kissinger's handpicked assistant secretary for African affairs, Nathaniel Davis, was resolutely opposed. As might be expected, a department task force worked for weeks and came up with one option: "an effort to achieve a peaceful solution through diplomatic-political measures." Although there was some merit to hopes that diplomatic pressure could have produced a peaceful stalemate, the report was the kind of typical State Department mushiness that drove Kissinger to distraction. He took the task force off the case and turned down Davis's request to be invited to the 40 Committee meeting.

Thus excluded from the 40 Committee meeting, Davis wrote a prescient memo to be considered at the session. "The worst possible outcome would be a test of will and strength which we lose," he wrote. Even the backers of covert U.S. involvement, he pointed out, were not saying that it would lead to a victory but at best a stalemate. "If we are to have a test of strength with the Soviets, we should find a more advantageous place." In addition, he pointed out that "the risks of discovery are so great as to make compromise virtually certain."

Not even the CIA was fully in favor of a covert program. Director William Colby, shell-shocked by Vietnam and buffeted by the congressional hearings into the agency's past misdeeds, was not looking for any more trouble. (After the plan was approved, he would insist on going to Congress to have funds officially appropriated, which would result in the leaks that would kill the program.) The midlevel agents developing the plan also had doubts. "Soviets enjoy greater freedom of action in the covert supply of arms, equipment and ammunition," the CIA paper stated, and "can escalate the level of their aid more readily than we." It also made clear that even in the best of circumstances, an outright "win" did not seem possible.

"We were confronting the Soviets over a country that was of little importance to either of us," John Stockwell, the CIA agent in charge of the Angola task force, wrote in a book critical of the agency. The plan being discussed was too small to win and too large to be kept secret, he warned at the time. Most of the midlevel CIA officers felt that it made more sense to establish ties with all three groups and to take the moral high ground by calling for a mediated settlement. That way, even if the MPLA won, as was likely, the U.S. would not lose all influence in Angola, and it would gain it elsewhere in Africa.[4]

Nevertheless, Kissinger recommended, and Ford approved, a covert program involving $32 million in funds and $16 million worth of military equipment to be funneled to the FNLA by way of Zaire. A more limited program of support was approved for Savimbi's UNITA forces in the south, now aligned with the FNLA. Nathaniel Davis submitted his resignation as assistant secretary; Kissinger talked him into staying in the department and made him ambassador to Switzerland, not the worst prize to befall a foreign service officer who made the mistake of being right.

By now, the tote card of who was backing which horse was something only a Kissinger could fathom. Besides the covert aid from the U.S., the FNLA got a major arms shipment from China, another from Romania, plus training from North Korean military instructors based in Zaire in the summer of 1975. UNITA, the radical left group that had heretofore been aligned with the SWAPO rebels seeking to free Namibia from South African control, was suddenly getting major support from the white-ruled regime in South Africa. Among other things, this in effect aligned the U.S. with South Africa, which was the worst possible way to pursue influence in black Africa.

As the November 11 Independence Day neared, South Africa sent in more than five thousand of its own troops to join with UNITA and a faction of the FNLA in a march toward Luanda. The Cubans responded with a large-scale infusion of troops, which were equipped with Soviet rocket launchers and flown in on Soviet planes. It was hard to tell which was worse for the U.S., its new allies or its new adversaries. The Chinese liked the looks of neither: seeing no strategic advantage in being on a side that was both a sure loser and tainted by South African support, it quietly and quickly folded its hand and withdrew.

With Soviet arms and Cuban support troops, the MPLA was securely ensconced in Luanda by the end of November, the de facto rulers of a newly independent Angola. Unable to leave bad enough alone, the 40 Committee asked the CIA for another options paper.

The recommendation that resulted had two components: an additional $28 million in aid for the FNLA to continue its fight, and the introduction of American advisers. Since there was no more money left in the CIA contingency fund—and since Colby was not averse to getting a clear statement of congressional approval for any further operations—the decision was made to submit the $28 million appropriation request to Congress in a secret but official hearing.

The proposal to introduce U.S. advisers was more controversial, and midlevel officials disagreed over how to proceed. Edward Mulcahy, the acting assistant secretary of state for African affairs, who participated in the CIA's interagency working group, was delegated to discuss the issue personally with Kissinger on December 2. It was important to get his decision then because he was leaving the next day on a dizzying two-week trip around the world. "We were already in a sensitive situation," Mulcahy recalled, "because the CIA was letting a few agents go in [to Angola] for a day or two at a time to do such things as set up radio facilities."

At two P.M., the working group gathered on the third floor of the CIA's Langley, Virginia, headquarters to find out Kissinger's decision. Eleven men and women sat in a crowded room in front of a four-by-five-foot map of Angola. When everyone was ready, Mulcahy was called upon to report what Kissinger had said. He tamped on his pipe and sucked it nervously for a moment. "He didn't actually say anything," Mulcahy finally said.

"Did he read the paper?" Mulcahy was asked.

"Oh, yes," he responded. "He read it. Then he grunted and walked out of his office."

"Grunted?"

"Yes, like, 'Unnph!' " Mulcahy explained, imitating the sound.

Everyone found this rather disconcerting, especially since Kissinger was heading off for Beijing. "Well," someone asked, "was it a positive grunt or a negative grunt?"

Mulcahy paused. "It was just a grunt," he explained. "Like, 'Unnph!' I mean it didn't go up or down."

Stockwell, the agent in charge, marveled as a group of somber officials supervising the nation's only extant war sat around a table trying to decipher a Kissinger grunt. Mulcahy provided his imitation of the grunt once again, emphasizing its flatness. Someone else at the other end of the table tried it. There were a few experiments contrasting positive grunts, with the voice rising, then a negative one, with the voice falling. Different people attempted it.

"Well," asked the CIA officer who was chairing the meeting, "do we proceed with the advisers?"

Mulcahy scowled and puffed on his pipe. "We'd better not," he finally said, trying to decipher his boss's mind. "Kissinger just decided not to send Americans into the Sinai. . . ."

There were a lot of nods. The request for advisers was shelved. "It was an amazing way to run a war," Mulcahy said years later as he recalled the incident.[5]

Inklings of America's covert aid program had made it into some newspapers, but it was not until the CIA made its supposedly secret request to Congress for $28 million in new funds that the facts began to leak. A page-one *New York Times* story on December 13 by Seymour Hersh detailed the full extent of the covert program and revealed that it had provoked Nathaniel Davis's resignation. Senator Dick Clark of Iowa, who had been fighting the funding in secret sessions, promptly introduced an amendment to cut off all covert aid.

All this was occurring while Kissinger was hopping around the world. In China with President Ford, he met with an aged Mao and listened as Deng Xiaoping gave a toast that typically seemed both appropriate and inscrutable: "There is great disorder under heaven, and the situation is excellent."

Kissinger and Ford also visited Indonesia; the day after they left, that country used its American-supplied weapons to invade the tiny neighboring nation of East Timor, another recently freed Portuguese colony that was being taken over by left-wing rebel forces. Kissinger and Ford knew from U.S. intelligence of Indonesia's planned action, which violated the laws governing its purchases of American arms, but Kissinger was quietly content to permit the Timor rebellion to be suppressed, so the administration did nothing to stop the invasion.

After other stops with Ford in Asia, Kissinger proceeded on his own to Europe for a NATO meeting in Brussels and a conclave of American ambassadors in London (the one at which Sonnenfeldt expounded on his soon-to-be-famous "doctrine"). The trip concluded with a sentimental return to Fürth with his parents, where Kissinger received the town's Gold Medal for Distinguished Native Citizens and then privately visited the grave of his mother's father, Falk Stern.[6]

While he was away, Kissinger was also being hit with cables describing Moynihan's exploits at the U.N. In addition, the House committee looking into CIA activities hit him with a contempt-of-Congress citation after the administration refused to turn over some classified State Department historical documents. (It was later dropped.)

Thus Kissinger was primed, as he put it, "to raise a little bit of hell" when he arrived home to confront the Angola and East Timor issues at a senior staff meeting on December 18. According to a secret ten-page memorandum of conversation, Kissinger's main concerns— now as in the past—were with lapses in secrecy rather than with substance.[7]

His first eruption at the meeting was about East Timor, where the Indonesian invasion to oust the fledgling left-wing regime was proving to be shockingly brutal. Kissinger was upset that the department's legal staff had officially raised the issue—and worse yet, put it on paper in a cable to him—of whether Indonesia's use of American arms violated U.S. law and thus required an embargo. Kissinger knew that if the issue was formally raised, the answer would have to be yes. But especially in light of the situation in Angola, Kissinger did not want to cut off supplies; instead, he hoped to get away with a quiet, temporary suspension.

Kissinger: "Take this cable on Timor. . . . The only consequence is to put yourself on record. It's a disgrace to treat the Secretary of State this way. . . . What possible explanation is there for it? I told you to stop it [arms sales to Indonesia] quietly. . . ."

Assistant Secretary Philip Habib: "We made it NODIS [no distribution] so it wouldn't leak. We have to look at the issue."

Kissinger: "I didn't say you can't make a recommendation orally."

Habib: "Our assessment was that if it was going to be trouble, it would come up before your return. . . ."

Kissinger: "Nonsense. I said do it [suspend arms sales] for a few weeks and then open up again."

Habib: "The cable will not leak."

Kissinger: "Yes, it will, and it will go to Congress, too, and then we'll have hearings on it."

Habib: "I was away. I was told by cable that it had come up."

Kissinger: "That means there are two cables! And that means twenty guys have seen it. . . ."

Under Secretary Sisco: "We were told you had decided we had to stop."

Kissinger: "Just a minute, just a minute. You all know my position on this. . . . It will have a devastating impact on Indonesia. There's this masochism in the extreme here. No one has complained that it was aggression."

Legal adviser Monroe Leigh: "The Indonesians were violating an agreement with us."

Kissinger: "The Israelis when they go into Lebanon—when was the last time we protested that?"

Leigh: "That's a different situation."

Under Secretary Carlyle Maw: "It is self-defense."

Kissinger: "And we can't construe a communist government in the middle of Indonesia as self-defense?"

Leigh: "Well . . ."

Kissinger [after a digression onto Angola]: "On the Timor thing, that will leak in three months and it will come out that Kissinger overruled his pristine bureaucrats and violated the law. . . . You have a responsibility to recognize that we are living in a revolutionary time. Everything on paper will be used against me."

The Indonesian invasion ended up causing more than one hundred thousand deaths in tiny East Timor, close to one-seventh of the population. Kissinger managed to keep military assistance flowing to Indonesia after only a brief interruption. Neither the cable nor the dispute leaked at the time.

Kissinger railed about a handful of other issues during the staff meeting, but the one that concerned him most was Angola. As he hopped from topic to topic (and, according to one participant, from side to side) he kept coming back to the civil war there.

His first concern was with the way that Moynihan was handling the Angola issue at the U.N. Like many neoconservatives, Moynihan opposed American intervention, but he felt that the Soviets should be denounced as loudly as possible for violating the spirit of détente. The U.S., he urged, should take the issue to the Security Council "and never let the argument fade until the last Cuban was out of Africa." Kissinger, from Asia, cabled back that going to the Security Council made no sense.

So Moynihan launched his own public crusade. He went on a Sunday talk show to proclaim that "the Russians had invaded southern Africa." In the annual General Assembly debate over South Africa, he mounted the podium to denounce the Soviets as the "new colonial, imperialist power" in Africa. In the meantime, he continued to pepper Kissinger with cables requesting the chance to take the crusade to the Security Council.

"Not a day goes by without a cable from Moynihan on Angola," Kissinger complained at the staff meeting. "Who the hell is Moynihan anyway to get into Angola? We can get a cease-fire anytime, but it's not worth anything if we don't put some forces in fast." To Kissinger, the neoconservatives and putative hawks—notably Moynihan and Schlesinger—liked to talk a tough game, but they were inexcusably wimpish when it came time to authorize the use of American force.

Moynihan, on the other hand, felt that Kissinger could not see that there were more effective ways to assert American interests than by using military force. "Unforgivably—for he was bound to fail—he had got himself involved in trying to channel CIA money through Zaire to the FNLA and UNITA," Moynihan later said. "It was the same old pattern: still bombing Cambodia, still planning a deal with Le Duc Tho." Public diplomacy, Moynihan felt, would have been more effective than covert force.

After complaining about Moynihan, Kissinger moved on to the leaks:

Kissinger: "Now look at this basic theme that is coming out on Angola. These SOBs are leaking all of this stuff to Les Gelb [then covering national security for the *New York Times*]."

Sisco: "I can tell you who."

Kissinger: "Who?"

Sisco: "Hyland spoke to him. . . . He said he briefed Gelb."

Kissinger: "I want these people to know that our concern in Angola is not the economic wealth or the naval base. It has to do with the U.S.S.R. operating 8,000 miles from home when all the surrounding states are asking for our help. . . ."

Habib: "I think leaks and dissent are the burden you have to bear. . . ."

Kissinger: ". . . The President says to the Chinese that we're going to stand firm in Angola and two weeks later we get out. I go to a NATO meeting and meanwhile the Department leaks that we're worried about a naval base and says it's an exaggeration or an aberration of Kissinger's. I don't care about the oil or the base, but I do care about the African reaction when they see the Soviets pull it off and we don't do anything. If the Europeans then say to themselves, 'If they can't hold Luanda, how can they defend Europe?' the Chinese will say we're a country that was run out of Indochina for 50,000 men and is now being run out of Angola for less than $50 million."[8]

The next day, the Senate passed, 54 to 22, the Clark amendment cutting off new funds for Angolan operations. The House followed suit in January by an even wider margin, 323 to 99. The FNLA melted away, and Holden Roberto moved to Europe. UNITA remained a low-level guerrilla movement in the south for the next fifteen years, notable mostly for Jonas Savimbi's charismatic travels around the world seeking support.

Kissinger privately blamed Ford for allowing Congress to run roughshod on foreign policy. The president, he felt, should have put up a fight and forced the necessary funding for Angola—or, perhaps, circumvented Congress altogether, as Nixon would have done. Shortly after the Clark amendment vote, Kissinger was in Boston to give an off-the-record briefing to the *Boston Globe*'s editorial board. He was furious at Ford for backing down on Angola, and he even attacked him by name, shaking his head as he described the president's fecklessness. The *Globe* editors left the meeting startled at the vehemence of Kissinger's attack on his own president, though none of it appeared in print since the meeting was private.[9]

Angola became, as Kissinger feared, a Soviet-style Marxist economy. Though the nation was rich in oil and minerals, its economy shriveled. One of the few Western journalists to visit Luanda, David Lamb of the *Los Angeles Times,* wrote, "A visitor is struck by the eerie notion that he has entered a ghost town." The Cubans did help to provide social services—rural health clinics, new schools, and the like —but with the education came indoctrination in communist dogma.

On the other hand, the American oil companies—run by the sort of capitalists who are far more pragmatic than statesmen in dealing with third world leftists—got along just fine with the MPLA and the new government it formed. Indeed, Gulf Oil even backed the MPLA rather than the FNLA during the early stages of the war, convinced that it would win. "Gulf has not been unduly hampered by the socialist aspirations of the MPLA," said Melvin Hill, president of the company's exploration subsidiary, at a 1980 congressional hearing. "There is an underlying mutual respect and trust which I believe is the key to understanding the productive relationship we have in Angola." Gene Bates of Texaco said much the same: "They are pragmatic people. Although they lean toward a Marxist-style government, their Marxist friends can't give them what they need, so they have turned to the West."[10]

Kissinger's rationale for American involvement in Angola was not to protect specific vital interests there; instead, as usual, he saw it as a matter of credibility, of showing that the U.S. was still willing to counter Soviet meddling in the third world. "The question is whether America still maintains the resolve to act responsibly as a great power," Kissinger told Congress in January 1976 as funds were being cut off. "If the U.S. is seen to emasculate itself in the face of massive, unprecedented Soviet and Cuban intervention, what will be the perception of leaders around the world as they make decisions regarding their future security?" In a background session on his plane that month, Kissinger argued that "if Moscow gets away with this one, it will try again soon in some other area."[11]

The credibility argument is sometimes debunked, especially since Kissinger gave it far more weight than it could bear when applied to Vietnam. But it is not always spurious. Throughout the 1970s, the Soviets were heeding Khrushchev's call to support liberation movements around the world in an effort to create "people's republics" aligned to Moscow. To contest each of these, especially when local conditions were not favorable, would have been foolhardy. But to withdraw from the contest entirely, as many Americans seemed willing to do after Vietnam, could also have been dangerous. The trick was choosing the right place, and the right method, to take a stand.

Washington did not have to make Angola a test of credibility. The U.S. had no vital interests there, nor any historic commitments to fulfill. It could have treated Angola as it did nearby Mozambique, another Portuguese colony that was taken over by a leftist liberation movement at the same time. Instead, Kissinger decided to make Angola a test of American credibility. It was as if the U.S. were in search of an enemy in order to prove its willingness to contest the Soviets for influence in the third world.

Choosing to turn that local struggle into a display of resolve—voluntarily putting America's credibility at stake—made sense only if Kissinger was confident that the U.S. was willing and able to prevail. As Nathaniel Davis had pointed out, the worst possible outcome was to pump up a third-rate, distant tribal struggle into a test of will with the Soviets and then lose it. As it turned out, Angola was a paradigm of an unnecessary, self-inflicted defeat.

Given the outcome—a total Soviet-Cuban victory, an unnecessary loss of American credibility, a political debacle at home, and a costly program that pointlessly fueled a distant war—almost any alternative would likely have been better. Arming proxy fighters and applying low-level force for long periods of time in far-flung corners of the globe—especially covertly—was something that the Soviets were adept at doing. America, a congenitally idealistic and disputatious democracy, was not, as Vietnam and Angola showed.[12]

If Kissinger had reconciled himself to this fact, he would have devised a different strategy for asserting America's influence and credibility in the world. A good model would have been his Middle East shuttling; there, he had successfully asserted America's influence at the expense of the Soviets (in a far more critical region) through creative diplomacy rather than through an attempt to use force.

After the Angolan fiasco, Kissinger came to this conclusion. Instead of seeking new situations where he could prove America's military resolve, he rather unexpectedly embarked on a concerted diplomatic effort, involving shuttles and a basic reexamination of U.S. policy, designed to bring about peaceful change in southern Africa and to increase America's influence among the black nations of the region.

RHODESIA: A TURNAROUND ON HUMAN RIGHTS, 1976

As his Angola policy was collapsing in January 1976, Kissinger complained to a Senate panel that "Congress has deprived the president of indispensable flexibility." Détente had been based on carrots and sticks. When the Soviets behaved well, as they had in 1972 on Vietnam, they were rewarded, such as with trade concessions. When they were meddlesome, they were resisted, by force if necessary. The Jackson-Vanik amendment had eliminated the most important carrot. Now, the Clark amendment had sheathed the stick.

Senator Dick Clark, who was chairing the hearings, disagreed. He suggested a new tack for policy toward black Africa: pursuing influence by appealing to the values of human rights and racial equality that America shared with the nations there. If the U.S. tried that approach, said Clark, "our cold war interests in Africa may very well take care of themselves."[13]

It was not an argument likely to appeal to Kissinger. He regarded most national liberation movements and rebels as handmaidens of Moscow. But he knew that he needed a new policy, especially for Africa, where black resentments in the remaining white-ruled nations seemed ready to erupt. The Soviets, given a chance, would surely exploit that tension, and Kissinger now had few tools to stop them. Thus it was that a realpolitik analysis led to the adoption of an idealistic new component to American foreign policy.

In addition, Ford played an important role in bringing about the shift in policy, mainly by replacing the cold, bigoted atmosphere of the Nixon administration with a presidency that prided itself on its decency. "The new African policy in 1976 reflected my own sympathies," Ford later said. "I looked at regimes that would not survive and felt we ought to move toward a more humane point of view." [14]

Perhaps another factor was that Kissinger was an adherent of Talleyrand's maxim: "The art of statesmanship is to foresee the inevitable and to expedite its occurrence."

So beginning in April 1976, when he took a tour of Africa, Kissinger helped to transform American policy. Thenceforth it would be based on forthright opposition to white minority regimes and on financial support for emerging black nations. His new willingness to use moralism as a foreign policy tool—an approach he had cautioned against in his Minneapolis address the previous July—even spread to areas outside Africa. He began speaking of alliances based on common values, and he told the U.N., in a speech widely labeled "Wilsonian," that the world should seek a "just" new order based "not on the strength of arms but on the strength of the human spirit."

In attempting to tap the power of American values, Kissinger was following the advice of liberals such as Clark as well as the conservatives who denounced the amorality of détente. What these critics were to discover was Kissinger's knack for co-opting ideas that he had seemed to reject. "He showed a remarkable talent for undercutting his adversaries by annexing their ideas," said his old Harvard colleague Stanley Hoffmann in analyzing Kissinger's African policy of 1976. "This chameleon-like ability to embrace views that first seemed alien to him testifies to his cleverness." [15]

Kissinger's previous approach toward southern Africa had been set in 1969 after a secret National Security Study Memorandum, called NSSM 39, prepared by Roger Morris. It laid out five options, ranging from closer association with the white regimes of Rhodesia and South Africa to a complete dissociation. Morris and Kissinger had recommended, and Nixon had approved, option two, dubbed "the Tar Baby option." Its premise was that "the whites are here to stay and the only way that constructive change can come about is through them."

Some liberal sensibilities were assuaged by the argument that American economic ties to Rhodesia and South Africa might improve the plight of black workers. But in practice, the decision permitted a hypocritical policy. "We would maintain," the document declared, "public opposition to racial repression but relax political isolation and economic restrictions on the white states."[16]

Kissinger first indicated that this approach was being revised on April 23, 1976, in the departure statement he made as he left for a thirteen-day tour of Kenya, Tanzania, Zambia, Zaire, Liberia, and Senegal. He spoke of the "commitment of the U.S. to majority rule in the black African countries" and of the "ties of values and aspirations" between "all Americans" and black Africans.

Kissinger was even more forceful in a major address he gave at a lunch in Lusaka hosted by Zambian president Kenneth Kaunda. The speech—which Kissinger had worked on for six weeks and seven drafts —provided details of a sweeping change in U.S. policy. He urged his listeners to put aside their feelings about America's past attitudes toward their goals. "It is time to find our common ground," he said. Then he addressed the "problem" posed by white rule:

> Of all the purposes we have in common, racial justice is one of the most basic. This is a dominant issue of our age. . . . Our support for this principle in southern Africa is not simply a matter of foreign policy but an imperative of our own moral heritage. . . . The Salisbury regime [of Ian Smith in Rhodesia] will face our unrelenting opposition until a negotiated settlement is achieved.

At one point in the speech, Kissinger pointedly referred to Rhodesia as Zimbabwe, the name it would get officially when blacks finally took power in 1980. Americans living there, he said, should leave. In order to help neighboring black-ruled nations hurt by the embargo against Rhodesia, Kissinger proposed a financial aid program; he even included $12.5 million for Mozambique, despite the fact that it had been taken over by leftists aligned with Angola's MPLA. As for South Africa, he said that Pretoria still had time to dismantle apartheid peacefully, but he warned, "There is a limit to that time—a limit of far shorter duration than was generally perceived even a few years ago."[17]

The Lusaka declaration was greeted enthusiastically. President Kaunda called it "an important turning point," and one Kissinger aide gushed: "It's the first time in a long time that we are doing the moral thing."

Kissinger appeared rejuvenated by the praise and, unlike on most trips, seemed to relish the ceremonial tasks of public sight-seeing—so much so that he abandoned his rule of travel, which was never to go see in a foreign country things you would decline to see in your own. He cruised down the Zambezi and Zaire rivers, walked under Victoria Falls, ate wild boar and manioc leaves, and showed no boredom as he watched native dancers in Kenya one day, in Zaire the next, and then in Liberia. With Senators Abraham Ribicoff and Jacob Javits in tow, he toured Kenya's Masai Mara game park in a Land Rover. And in Zambia, he walked out onto the railway bridge that spanned the border with Rhodesia, momentarily stepped across the white line, and joked, "At least now I know what the issues look like." One of the few somber notes came in Senegal, where he insisted on being taken on a forty-minute boat trip to the House of Slaves on the isle of Gorée, where human cargo had been warehoused while awaiting shipment to America. "It makes you ashamed to be a human being," he said.[18]

Back home, American conservatives were reacting with considerably less enthusiasm—so much so that it was a mark of Gerald Ford's bravery that, in the midst of a tough primary challenge from Ronald Reagan, he continued to encourage Kissinger's new line on Africa. Speaking to a high-noon campaign rally in front of the Alamo, Reagan charged that Kissinger's Lusaka speech could lead to "a massacre" in Rhodesia and had "undercut the possibility of a just and orderly settlement there." Kissinger became visibly agitated when he read a report of Reagan's speeches and told the traveling press, on the record, that the California governor was "totally irresponsible."

A few days later, Ford was crushed in the Texas primary, losing every county to Reagan—a landslide that was widely attributed to the unpopularity of Kissinger's African pronouncements. Patrick Buchanan, the former Nixon speechwriter who had become a newspaper columnist (and would later work for Reagan and run for President), wrote: "It is too early to determine if Secretary of State Henry Kissinger's safari through black Africa did greater damage to U.S. policy interests or to President Ford's hopes in the remaining primaries." Congressman Robert Michel, a House Republican leader, said the trip had had a "devastating effect" in the South and that Kissinger should be "muzzled." When the results reached Kissinger's plane as it was about to land in Dakar, Winston Lord and other staffers, with a grim determination to shrug off the news, serenaded the secretary with a chorus of "The Eyes of Texas Are Upon You."

Upon Kissinger's return, the battle was engaged when he testified before the Senate Foreign Relations Committee. Liberals such as Hubert Humphrey and Dick Clark asked if he would push for repeal of the Byrd Amendment, which allowed the U.S. to ignore sanctions against Rhodesia and buy chrome. Kissinger promised that he would. Then Senator Harry Byrd, author of that amendment, took on Kissinger from the right. He called him "hypocritical" and charged, "I know you put great trust in communist Russia." Kissinger's face turned red and he displayed the temper that he could usually keep in check in public. "Absolutely wrong," he sputtered. "Absolutely not." [19]

Kissinger knew that his rhetoric regarding Rhodesia would have only a minimal effect on winning influence and calming tensions in black Africa unless he was willing to back it up with some action. So he decided to embark on what he did best: a shuttle mission. It was a somewhat audacious infringement on British turf, since they still considered Rhodesia part of their dwindling sphere of influence. But Kissinger worried that the Soviets—after successes in Angola and Mozambique—were eyeing black Africa as a new sphere of influence of their own, especially as the war in Rhodesia escalated. In addition, there was a touch of vanity: here was a fertile new ground where he could display his shuttling skills.

But there was a fundamental difference from his previous shuttle efforts. In the Middle East, both sides had wanted diplomacy to succeed. In Africa, the blacks wanted a negotiated transition to majority rule, but the Rhodesian whites wanted no such settlement and would have been quite happy with no diplomacy at all. So Kissinger modified his Mideast tactics, which involved cajoling and cozying up to both sides as he slowly closed a gap. Instead, he lined up as much pressure as he could on Ian Smith's white regime in Rhodesia. Most important, he convinced South Africa—which served as landlocked Rhodesia's economic lifeline—to join in applying pressure. Unless they helped, Kissinger warned South Africa's leaders, they, too, would face early pressures to move toward majority rule.

Kissinger first made this argument to South African Prime Minister John Vorster during a private two-day rendezvous they had in June in the Bavarian resort town of Grafenau. If South Africa would be willing to separate its destiny from Rhodesia's, he promised, there would be a wider acceptance of the South African government and more patience about letting it solve its own race problems. In September, they met again in Zurich for two days of discussion at which Vorster agreed to cut off Rhodesia's rail lines if Ian Smith proved intransigent. He would urge Smith to accept a negotiated settlement at a meeting they planned to have the following week.

"I believe that the conditions for a negotiation exist," Kissinger told reporters on his plane. A week later—on Tuesday, September 14

—Kissinger embarked with little warning back to Africa to begin his shuttle diplomacy.

He first stopped in Tanzania to find out from President Julius Nyerere what the "frontline" black nations felt. A general outline emerged: there would have to be complete transition to black rule within two years; until then, there would have to be some form of interim government in which blacks and whites shared power. As soon as this was accepted, the black states would be willing to support an end to sanctions and try to tamp down the guerrilla violence. To this proposal, Kissinger and British officials added their own sweetener, a $2 billion "safety net" fund to protect whites from seizure of their property and to compensate them if they felt forced to leave their land.

When Kissinger arrived in Pretoria on Friday afternoon, he became the highest-ranking American official ever to visit South Africa. Ian Smith was due to arrive there from Rhodesia the next day, ostensibly to see a rugby match. Kissinger sent word that he would meet with Smith only if the Rhodesian leader indicated in advance that he was willing to discuss Kissinger's plan for a two-year transition to majority rule. Smith reluctantly agreed and passed the word through Vorster. So early Sunday morning, at the home of the American ambassador, Kissinger met for four hours with Smith.

The meeting was cold and blunt, not filled with the cajolery and stroking that Kissinger practiced in the Mideast. He showed Smith the CIA's estimate that the Rhodesian economy would be crippled within a year and secret military assessments that showed the rebels gaining in strength. Communism would take hold, Kissinger warned, if there were not immediate negotiations to permit moderate blacks to take over.

That night a larger Rhodesian delegation met with Kissinger's party at Vorster's home. Kissinger had the five-point plan typed up and ready. It included the two-year transition, the economic package, and a complex arrangement for a transitional government. That government would have a council of state with two whites and two blacks; below it would be a council of ministers that would run the government departments.

"You want me to sign my suicide note," Smith said as he looked across the table at Kissinger.

Kissinger said absolutely nothing. Later that week he called it one of the most "painful" moments of his life watching as Smith agreed to go back to Salisbury and recommend to his government that it surrender their country. Or so Kissinger thought.

As with many of his other negotiations—Vietnam, Vladivostok,

Jackson-Vanik, the Middle East—Kissinger was willing to use some ambiguity to cover up areas of disagreement. In this case, Smith wanted two concessions. During the two-year transition period, the chairman of the interim four-person council of state should be white, and the ministers in charge of the police and defense should be white. Kissinger agreed to present these points when he went back to Zambia and Tanzania. He would send word back in time for Smith's presentation to the Rhodesian cabinet.

The final decisions on these and other details were supposed to be formally reached at a Geneva conference in November, chaired by the British, at which the various Rhodesian parties and their neighbors would negotiate an official agreement. Kissinger's role was to get the salient points accepted in principle. After his discussions in Tanzania, Kissinger cabled back word to Smith that the black leaders would not be "unduly" upset if the initial announcement made by Smith referred to a white chairman of the council of state.

The issue of the police and defense ministers was not as easy. So Kissinger decided to leave it ambiguous by sending a murky response to Smith. "We also believe on the basis of our discussions in Lusaka and Dar es Salaam" that a sentence could be added saying that the police and defense interim ministers would be white. Although Smith did not notice, the carefully worded cable made no mention of whether the black leaders had accepted this.

When Smith made his announcement, these unsettled details drew little attention. Banner headlines blared Kissinger's amazing diplomatic triumph of getting Rhodesia to accept a two-year transition to black rule. Television and newspaper photos showed him announcing the agreement while holding a ceremonial tribal sword and shield presented to him by President Jomo Kenyatta in Kenya. He was again featured as a miracle worker on the covers of the newsmagazines, and *Time* proclaimed it "the spectacular climax of a carefully and astutely planned push for peace."

When Smith arrived in Geneva in November to sit in a room with Robert Mugabe, Joshua Nkomo, and the other black rebel leaders fighting his regime, it seemed that the main hurdles had been cleared. But as it turned out, the details of the interim government continued to cause problems. Through November and December, under the chairmanship of the British, the conference considered various alternative arrangements, including a temporary British commissioner, but none proved acceptable to all sides.

In the end, the conference would break down. But the outlines of the Kissinger agreement would serve as the basis when his successor, Cyrus Vance, took up the cause. The deal would finally be sealed three years later at another conference held in London's Lancaster House.[20]

Even though Kissinger's shuttle did not immediately produce the solution that was celebrated in September, it succeeded in its larger aims. The nations of black Africa, whose attitude toward the U.S. had ranged from wariness to hostility, began to trust Washington as a force for majority rule. The growing appeal of the Soviet Union was countered. Indeed, the Rhodesian shuttle showed that even quasi-successful diplomacy could do more to thwart Soviet influence than ham-fisted intervention such as in Angola.

THIRTY-ONE

EXIT

Not with a Bang
but a Whimper

> *The acid test of a policy is its ability to gain domestic support.*
> —KISSINGER, A WORLD RESTORED, 1957

THE ELECTION OF '76

One of the principal maxims of American politics is that presidential elections are settled by pocketbook issues rather than foreign policy. Like most American political maxims, it bears little relation to American politics. Kennedy used an alleged "missile gap" against Nixon in 1960; Johnson portrayed Goldwater as a person who just might cause a nuclear bomb to annihilate a small child; the Vietnam War forced Johnson to drop out in 1968 and Humphrey to stay on the defensive against Nixon, and was the major issue in the Nixon-McGovern contest of 1972.

In 1976, the two most important issues were Ford's pardon of Nixon for Watergate and the nation's stagnating, oil-depleted economy. But in what turned out to be a close election, foreign policy helped to tip the balance, both by fueling Ronald Reagan's Republican nomination challenge and by leading to a debate gaffe that undercut Ford's claim of being more competent than Jimmy Carter. The foreign policy issue had many components: détente, human rights, Solzhenitsyn, amorality, secretiveness, and a sense that the U.S. was negotiating its own tactical retreat. But these could all be summed up in one word: Kissinger.

A succession of Gerald Ford's political handlers that year treated Kissinger as a dark sheep to be hidden away. Campaign chairman Howard ("Bo") Callaway urged the president to put as much distance as possible between himself and Kissinger. This quickly made the rounds in gossipy Washington, and Kissinger demanded that Callaway come over to the State Department and explain. Callaway did not prevaricate. He explained that by distancing himself from Kissinger, Ford would come across as a stronger leader. Kissinger countered that presidents were not credited with leadership by sidling away from their secretary of state.

Then Rogers Morton became campaign chairman and began to say publicly what Callaway had whispered privately, most notably that Kissinger would probably not have a job if Ford were elected to a new term. "I would anticipate, and I'm sure I'm right about this, that he would not go on beyond this year," Morton said at a press briefing. James Baker, Ford's manager, also let it be known that he considered Kissinger a political liability.[1]

Although he occasionally brooded about emulating his old patron Rockefeller and stepping aside, Kissinger seemed eager to keep his job. Metternich, it must be remembered, served as Austria's foreign minister for thirty-nine years, a tenure that Kissinger considered about sufficient. Talking to friends on his Boeing 707, he noted, "What university would give me an airplane like this?" In addition, his backbone was stiffened when he heard that Ford's managers were spreading the rumor, as the Texas primary approached, that John Connally was likely to replace him as secretary of state, a prospect that Kissinger found unnerving.

After discussing the matter repeatedly with Kissinger, Ford went public with a vote of confidence. "I would like Kissinger to be secretary as long as I am president," he said. When the issue came up at a press conference, the president punched the air with his hand and tried to praise Kissinger without seeming beholden to him. "Kissinger, working with me and at my direction, has done some of the most outstanding diplomatic work on behalf of the U.S. and world peace, I think, of any secretary of state in the history of the U.S."[2]

But Kissinger seemed to realize that he served Ford best by staying out of the limelight—and even out of the country. During Ronald Reagan's 1976 primary challenge, Kissinger embarked on a travel binge that sometimes seemed to have little point other than to keep him away during the campaign. In January, he went to Copenhagen, Moscow, Brussels, and Madrid. In February, he went to Caracas,

Lima, Rio, Bogotá, San José, and Guatemala City. In April, he went on his prolonged African trip, as well as to London and Paris. In May, he went to Oslo, Bonn, Stockholm (where his father's brother Uncle Arno came to hear him speak), Luxembourg, and London. In June, he went to Santo Domingo, Santa Cruz, Santiago, Mexico City, and Cancún, and then to Paris, Grafenau, London, and San Juan. In August, just before the Republican Convention, he went on a peregrination that even he seemed to find pointless, visiting London, Tehran, Nowshera, Kabul, Lahore, Deauville, and The Hague.

The heart of Reagan's challenge to the Ford-Kissinger foreign policy was a broad attack on détente, which the California governor denounced as "a one-way street." He cited every overseas setback—Vietnam, Angola, Portugal—as evidence that détente had failed. At each stop he would assail the treatment of Solzhenitsyn—"a true moral hero snubbed by Kissinger and Ford"—and the so-called Sonnenfeldt Doctrine. The Helsinki conference, Reagan charged, was a sellout of the "captive nations" of Eastern Europe, which Ford and Kissinger felt should "give up any claim of national sovereignty and simply become part of the Soviet Union."[3]

Most conservative criticism of détente had an odd element: despite the vigor with which conservatives denounced the Soviets, Reagan and others were rather anti-interventionist when it came to committing American forces. Unless a situation warranted a full-scale, unilateral U.S. invasion, they tended to favor a pose of righteous indignation. Their anticommunist instincts were tempered by old-fashioned conservative isolationism. For example, instead of demanding that the U.S. be resolute in aiding its allies in Angola, Reagan and others on the right tended to demand that the U.S. retaliate by chilling its relationship with Moscow.

The attacks prompted Kissinger, acting on his own, to put out a ten-page rebuttal, which served little purpose other than to infuse the Reagan campaign with new life and press attention.

Ford, on the other hand, scurried away from defending détente like a startled rabbit. Instead of pointing out the reduction in world tension that détente had managed to achieve, Ford acted as if he were embarrassed by the word. In a speech in Peoria on March 5, in one of the year's silliest moves, he publicly banished it from his vocabulary. "We are going to forget the use of the word *détente*," he said. Henceforth, he said, it would be replaced by the phrase "peace through strength."[4]

Kissinger was appalled. But it should be noted that he had been doing his own redefining of *détente*. In September 1974, he called it "the search for a more productive relationship with the Soviet Union."

By July 1975 (after the fall of Vietnam), he was calling it "a means to regulate a competitive relationship." In February 1976, he said that détente was "designed to prevent Soviet expansion." And finally, a month after Ford forswore the word, he was asked at a press conference, "Would you comment on the charge made by Ronald Reagan that détente is a one-way street?" With a wry smile, Kissinger began his answer: "Let me describe what the policy that used to be called détente involves." It prompted the desired laughter, which allowed him to deflect the need to do any more redefining.

Reagan also used the negotiations over the Panama Canal to attack Kissinger for plunging ahead with a "giveaway." Panama's leader Omar Torrijos should be told, Reagan declared at most of his stump stops, "We built it, we paid for it, and we're going to keep it." Kissinger thought it not quite that simple, and he worried about the nationalist fervor that could be whipped up in Central America if Washington pursued such a course. The U.S., he realized, had little reason to retain sovereignty over the canal and had a lot to lose if it tried. But the merits mattered less than the symbolism, for the Panama Canal "giveaway" would come to stand for American wimpiness in the world.[5]

Underlying Reagan's criticism of Kissinger was a more personal attack on his alleged pessimism, his Spenglerian gloom over the long-term ability of an irresolute America to counter the relentless thrusts of the Soviet empire. This theme had been suggested to Reagan by two anti-détente refugees from the Ford administration, both nominal Democrats: ousted defense secretary James Schlesinger and retired chief of naval operations Elmo Zumwalt.

At the time, Zumwalt was running for a Senate seat in Virginia, and he was using Kissinger as a foil. In his speeches, as well as in his memoirs, which came out that year, the feisty admiral charged that Kissinger's pessimism made him too eager to strike deals with the Soviets. He recalled a diary entry he had made after a train ride with Kissinger to a West Point game in 1970: "Kissinger feels that U.S. has passed its historic high point like so many earlier civilizations. . . . He states that his job is to persuade the Russians to give us the best deal we can get, recognizing that the historical forces favor them. . . . [Americans] lack the stamina to stay the course against the Russians, who are 'Sparta to our Athens.' "

Kissinger, bristling at Zumwalt's distortion of his worldview, later called the West Point story "a fabrication." The way he recalled the tale, he was riding on the train to West Point with Nancy when Zumwalt sat down beside them and began coming across as "a dovish, doltish admiral." When Nancy got mad, Kissinger took on the admiral in argument, "and he misunderstood the points I was making."

But Zumwalt's accusations about Kissinger's pessimism had a kernel of truth. With good reason, Kissinger had come to the conclusion that the U.S. was not willing to commit itself, especially militarily, to the struggle against Soviet influence in the third world. Added to that was his innately gloomy nature. Like Spengler, Kissinger was pessimistic about the course of history. Like Metternich, he saw his role as propping up a fraying world power that could hold its own only by fancy diplomatic footwork.

This pessimism was reflected in his thesis on "The Meaning of History," written in 1950 as an undergraduate at Harvard: "Life is suffering. Birth involves death. Transitoriness is the fate of existence. No civilization has yet been permanent. . . . The generation of Buchenwald and the Siberian labor camps cannot talk with the same optimism as its fathers." In the end Kissinger rejected the full implications of Spengler's pessimism and adopted a quirky interpretation of Kant to conclude that "the experience of freedom enables us to rise beyond the suffering of the past and the frustrations of history." In other words, people—and especially great statesmen—have some freedom to shape events and avoid tragedy.

Almost twenty-five years later, these same ideas emerged in a reflective interview that Kissinger gave to James Reston. "As a historian," Kissinger said, "you have to be conscious of the fact that every civilization that has ever existed has ultimately collapsed. History is a tale of efforts that failed, of aspirations that weren't realized, of wishes that were fulfilled and then turned out to be different from what one expected." Kissinger did go on to say that the job of a statesman was to prevent such declines from occurring. But he retained his claim to pessimism by adding: "I think of myself as a historian more than a statesman."[6]

Whether or not Zumwalt understood Kissinger correctly, the perception of Kissinger's pessimism was prevalent enough to become a political issue. "One hears rumors of gloomy private ruminations by Secretary Kissinger," chided the Washington Post editorial page, which was presumably familiar with his off-the-record thoughts, "that the East-West rivalry rematches an effete Athens (the forces of freedom) and a vigorous and disciplined Sparta (the Soviet Union), with which the faltering Athenians must make the best deal they can." George Will wrote similarly: "He knows that, strategically, time is not on the side of the bourgeois societies of the West."

Reagan made Kissinger's pessimism a part of his stump speech.

"Dr. Kissinger is quoted as saying that he thinks of the United States as Athens and the Soviet Union as Sparta, and that the day of the United States is past," Reagan declared. This lapse of faith, Reagan charged, made Kissinger too eager to strike a deal with the Soviets. (In defense of Athens, it should be noted that, even though it lost the Peloponnesian War to Sparta, it ended up as the triumphant city-state, historically and culturally, and outlasted Sparta by centuries.)

Rather than explain his view of Kant and Spengler, Kissinger flew to Dallas for a press conference in late March in which he rebutted Admiral Zumwalt and Reagan in simpler terms. "I am going to nominate the good admiral for the Pulitzer Prize for fiction," he said. "I do not believe the United States will be defeated. I do not believe the United States is on the decline." This did little to clarify Kissinger's philosophy of history, but it did help put the pessimism issue to rest.[7]

At the Kansas City convention in August, Reagan did not quite have the delegates to win, and his strategist John Sears came up with two last-ditch ploys to recapture the momentum. The first was a rule that would force each candidate to reveal in advance who would be his running mate, something Reagan had already done (Senator Richard Schweiker of Pennsylvania). The Ford forces dubbed it the "misery-loves-company rule," and they were able to defeat it narrowly.

The second ploy was more difficult to defeat. It was an amendment to the party platform called the "Morality in Foreign Policy" plank. With the thinnest of veils, it was an attack on Kissinger: "We recognize and commend that great beacon of human courage and morality, Alexander Solzhenitsyn. . . . In pursuing détente we must not grant unilateral favors. . . . We are firmly committed to a foreign policy in which secret agreements, hidden from our people, will play no part."

Kissinger was being kept away from Kansas City until the last possible moment, and he heard about this proposed anti-détente plank when Hyland came by his State Department office for a drink one evening. They agreed it was a clear slap, and Kissinger told Hyland that he was disgusted and hurt that the Ford people were considering not opposing it.

At the convention, the Ford camp split on how to proceed. On one side were Rockefeller and Scowcroft arguing that the plank must be vigorously opposed. On the other were the political types, led by campaign manager James Baker (later secretary of state) and Ford's chief of staff, Dick Cheney (later secretary of defense). Ford should fight the plank on principle, said Scowcroft. "Principle doesn't do any good if you lose the nomination," replied Cheney.

When they showed Ford the plank for the first time, he read it and snapped, "I don't like it. I'll fight it." But his handlers convinced him to hold off saying anything right away. It was a Reagan trap, they said, and Ford should not be eager to take the bait.

After winning the vote on the running-mate rule, Ford had to make his final decision on the foreign policy plank. He was now leaning against making it into a fight, realizing that if he did not oppose it, Reagan would win nothing if it passed. Rockefeller talked to Kissinger by phone and marshaled one final effort to persuade Ford that it would be wrong not to stand up to such an outrageous insult. But it was getting late, and Jim Baker noted that there were a lot of empty seats in the hall. With Reagan's forces being the more passionate, they would likely stay and win if there was a fight. Finally Rockefeller relented, as did Ford. The plank was allowed to pass unopposed.

Later Jim Baker would say that the Reagan side's biggest miscalculation was that they wrote the plank in a way that it could, in a crunch, be accepted by the Ford side. A tougher plank, he said, would have put them in a bind. "I could see a two-word plank: 'Fire Kissinger,' and we would have had to fight it," he said. "And if we had been beaten, we could have lost the whole thing."[8]

JIMMY CARTER, FALL 1976

Ford left the convention with a thirty-point deficit in the polls against Democrat Jimmy Carter. For the entire general election campaign that fall, he was on the defensive, even during the last ten days when it looked as if he had just about caught up.

From the start, the former governor of Georgia took up the attacks on Kissinger. He spoke of the "Nixon-Kissinger-Ford" foreign policy as "covert, manipulative, and deceptive in style" in one speech in September. "It runs against the basic principles of this country, because Kissinger is obsessed with power blocs, with spheres of influence."

Adding injury to the insult was that Carter's words had come, almost verbatim, from Kissinger's old nemesis at Harvard, Zbigniew Brzezinski, now a professor at Columbia and a Carter campaign adviser. In 1975, writing in *Foreign Affairs,* Brzezinski had launched an attack on Kissinger's policies using the same words. "Covert, manipulative and deceptive in style, it seemed committed to a largely static view of the world, based on a traditional balance of power, seeking accommodation among the major powers on the basis of spheres of influence," Brzezinski wrote.

Hearing Brzezinski's snide words slung at him each day, not with a slightly embittered Polish accent but a smiling Georgia accent, drove Kissinger to near distraction. "Under the Nixon-Ford administration," Carter told one group in a speech written by Brzezinski, "there has evolved a kind of secretive, 'Lone Ranger' foreign policy, a one-man policy of international adventure." It was a foreign policy based on "secrecy . . . closely guarded and amoral." To these stiletto attacks, Carter added his own preachy refrain. "Our foreign policy should be as open and honest as the American people themselves," he repeatedly said.[9]

By the time Ford and Carter met for their second debate, on October 6 in San Francisco, Ford was gaining steadily, and it looked as though he might overtake his Democratic challenger in the final month. The subject of the debate was foreign policy, which should have been both Ford's strong suit and Carter's vulnerability.

Foreign policy can cut against a candidate if voters decide that he seems too untested or naive, if they somehow feel uncomfortable entrusting him with the fate of the world. That had been Carter's problem. The other way it can cut against a candidate is if voters get the impression that he is bumbling and blind about the dangers of Soviet communism. After an astonishingly inarticulate answer to a single question in San Francisco, that would end up being Ford's problem.

The question that tripped up Ford—and which arguably cost him the election—involved the accords that Kissinger had persuaded Ford to sign in Helsinki and the related "Sonnenfeldt Doctrine" that allegedly consigned Eastern Europe to the Soviets' sphere of influence.

Then and later, Ford's words on the subject were treated as a gaffe, a silly mistake that revealed his ignorance. In fact, a serious philosophical issue was involved. Kissinger (and Sonnenfeldt) did tend to see the world, despite their quasi-denials, as divided into spheres of influence. The respect that the Soviets and the Americans showed for each other's sphere helped to make the world stable. This, however, was not a politic thing to say. Thus, Ford was determined to deny vociferously that he was willing to concede to the Soviets any special rights or influence in Eastern Europe.

Kissinger's aide William Hyland was among those preparing Ford for the debate, and he was sure that one of the questions would involve the alleged "sellout" of Eastern Europe at Helsinki and in the Sonnenfeldt Doctrine. "We planned that Ford should immediately deny that there was any such doctrine and stress that indeed we had not abandoned Eastern Europe," Hyland recalled. During a practice session with Ford in the White House theater, Hyland played the part of a questioner. He bore down so hard on Eastern Europe that the president began to get angry. "I had to remind him that I was on his side," said Hyland.

Buried in the second volume of Ford's debate briefing book, now in the Gerald Ford library, is the suggested answer that Hyland and the NSC staff prepared for such a question about Soviet dominance over Eastern Europe. Ironically, it was not all that different from what Ford would get in trouble for saying. The NSC staff's proposed answer read:

> I am baffled by this talk about a Sonnenfeldt Doctrine in Eastern Europe. You can't have it both ways. I have visited Poland, Romania and Yugoslavia as President. Our relations with and support for the countries has never been stronger. I don't see how you can talk about conceding Soviet domination in light of this record.

This answer was the type that a foreign policy expert would write, not a political strategist. A better answer would have been for Ford to recall the fact that in 1956, during Hungary's revolution, he had flown to the Hungary-Austria border as a congressman to help welcome refugees from the Soviet army onslaught. He knew firsthand the fears and the aspirations of the people of Eastern Europe. That is why he would never sign anything that would concede that the Soviets had any special rights there, and he looked forward to the day when Soviet military domination would end. Unfortunately, Ford did not say this; neither Kissinger nor Hyland knew that he had made that trip in 1956.

In response to the opening question of the debate, or, more precisely, in skirting the actual question, Carter unleashed a personal attack on Ford. "As far as foreign policy goes," he said, "Mr. Kissinger has been the president of this country. Mr. Ford has shown an absence of leadership and an absence of a grasp of what this country is." One of the little-known secrets about Ford was that he had a bad temper. As Carter finished, the president started to simmer. For the rest of the debate, he seemed flustered.

Finally, about halfway through, the Eastern Europe question was asked by Max Frankel of the *New York Times*. Actually, it was a rather broad query about détente and the Soviets, but in asking it Frankel asserted that "we virtually signed, in Helsinki, an agreement that the Russians have dominance in Eastern Europe."

Ford began by pointing out that the Helsinki Final Act was signed by thirty-five leaders, including a representative of the pope. "It just isn't true," he said of charges that it tacitly gave the Soviets domination of Eastern Europe. He should have stopped there. Instead, he wandered into the thicket of trying to explain what the Helsinki accord actually said. And he ended with a resounding oversimplification of the suggested response that his briefers had written for him. "There is no Soviet domination of Eastern Europe," he declared, his right hand doing a karate chop, "and there never will be under a Ford administration."

Frankel gave Ford a chance to recoup, even waving a little warning flag for him in the process. "Did I understand you to say, sir, that the Russians are not using Eastern Europe as their own sphere of influence and occupying most of the countries there and making sure with their troops that it is a communist zone?" Ford responded somewhat along the lines of the paragraph in his briefing book:

> I don't believe that the Yugoslavians consider themselves dominated by the Soviet Union. I don't believe that the Romanians consider themselves dominated by the Soviet Union. I don't believe the Poles consider themselves dominated by the Soviet Union. . . . And the United States does not concede that these countries are under the domination of the Soviet Union. As a matter of fact, I visited Poland, Yugoslavia, and Romania to make certain that the people of those countries understand that the president of the U.S. and the people of the U.S. are dedicated to their independence, their autonomy, and their freedom.

Carter knew an opening when he saw it. "I would like to see Mr. Ford convince the Polish Americans and the Czech Americans and the Hungarian Americans in this country," he said, probably mentally tabulating the votes flowing in from Chicago's ethnic wards, "that those countries don't live under the domination and supervision of the Soviet Union."

Back in the White House, Hyland let out a moan. Brent Scowcroft, watching in a room just off the stage in San Francisco, went white. But Kissinger, ever solicitous, called from Washington an hour later to tell Ford what a wonderful job he had done. He never mentioned Eastern Europe, and it was not until he talked on the phone with Scowcroft that he realized the answer was causing big problems.

The press was not interested in exploring what Ford had really meant. Instead, the story was that Ford had made a huge mistake, as if he did not even know there were Soviet troops in Poland. Scowcroft and Cheney, thinking they could straighten matters out, gave a post-debate briefing that night, allowing Ford to go to bed. The first question was, "Are there any Soviet troops in Poland?"

After Scowcroft allowed that, yes, there were four divisions, he attempted to explain Ford's answer. "I think what the president was trying to say is that we do not recognize Soviet dominance of Europe," he said. Cheney insisted that the answer was clear enough in context. But by not getting Ford out right away to clear up the matter, the next day's papers and television shows made it seem that he just might somehow be unaware that the Soviets did indeed dominate Eastern Europe.

The issue lingered for days as Ford stubbornly refused to admit publicly that he had been inarticulate, the type of confession that is usually required to close off a media flurry. Finally, almost a week later, he admitted that "I did not express myself clearly," and the issue began to recede. Kissinger put it in perspective that week at a press conference. "Under the pressure of a debate, he did not make the point as felicitously as he might have," Kissinger said. "Nobody who knows his record could believe that on this particular issue he did not know exactly what the facts were."

Yet some critics of détente saw Ford's remarks as more than just a misunderstanding. They reflected the fact that Kissinger had gotten him tangled up in a hopeless policy of defending détente and Helsinki. "The verbal gaffe was the President's, but the basic political blunder of Helsinki was the Secretary of State's," wrote William Safire the next week. "Henry does not realize that to this day."

In any event, the political significance of Ford's remarks turned out to be devastating. George Gallup, the opinion pollster, called it the "most decisive moment in the campaign." As political reporter Jules Witcover wrote, "There was no doubt that the engines of the President's comeback drive had stalled." Ford never quite got his engines to kick in again; he lost the popular vote by just two percentage points.[10]

In December, Kissinger took his last trip in office, to Brussels for a NATO meeting with a stop in London to make a futile effort to reinvigorate the Rhodesian talks. It brought his total travel as secretary of state to 555,901 miles, in the course of which he visited fifty-seven countries. Did he think his successor, Cyrus Vance, would travel as much? one reporter on the plane asked. Kissinger paused, thought of Brzezinski's rumored selection to his old job, and said, chuckling, "It depends on who the national security adviser is."

The trip had the feel of a farewell tour. Many of the NATO ministers presented him with gifts, and Secretary-General Joseph

Luns gave what sounded like a eulogy. "You will stand in history as one of the most effective foreign ministers of our century," he said. "May I summarize our common feeling by quoting Shakespeare: 'He was a man, take him for all in all, I shall not look upon his like again.' "

With the traveling press corps, Kissinger kept up his usual banter and avoided becoming too reflective or maudlin. "Can you tell me," asked one reporter at a press conference in Brussels, "what you consider to be your greatest success and your greatest failure?" Kissinger replied, "I don't quite understand your second point." When the briefing ended, the foreign journalists gave him a standing ovation, and a few of the American correspondents joined in. On the flight home, some of them even asked for his autograph.

Not until his final week in office did he allow himself some personal reflections. "I leave to you, for a time, the great domain of public policy," he said at a farewell speech to the National Press Club, his voice starting to choke with emotion. "It would be hypocritical if I pretended that to part is easy. I envy you the excitement, the responsibility, the opportunities." This time, the entire audience joined in the standing ovation.

Later that week, he spoke at a Foreign Policy Association farewell dinner in New York City. As he finished his prepared text, he began to reminisce:

> When I came here in 1938, I was asked to write an essay at George Washington High School about what it meant to be an American. I wrote that, of course, it was hard being separated from the people with whom I had grown up and from the places that were familiar to me. But I thought that this was a country where one could walk across the street with one's head erect, and therefore it was all worthwhile. What America means to the rest of the world is the hope for people everywhere that they shall be able to walk with their heads erect. And our responsibility as Americans is always to make sure that our purposes transcend our differences.[11]

THIRTY-TWO

CITIZEN KISSINGER

The Jet-Set Life
of a Minister Without Portfolio

I'm a world figure. I can't just lead a normal professor's life.
*—*KISSINGER *to Harvard dean Henry Rosovsky, 1977*

BACK TO NEW YORK, JANUARY 1977

For the first time in eight years, Henry Kissinger arrived in New York City without the luxury of being borne by one of the air force jets of the presidential fleet. It was the week after Jimmy Carter's inauguration, and the cherished perks of power were starting to slip away. But unlike any other previous secretary of state—indeed, unlike even any past president—Kissinger would be able, by dint of his dedicated efforts and his larger-than-life personality, to retain the trappings of grandeur long after he had left office.

So even without an air force jet at his disposal, Kissinger was not to be found waiting for his luggage at the air shuttle terminal. For that trip to New York his first week out of office, he borrowed Nelson Rockefeller's private plane, though adequate scheduled service did exist. His belief that commercial airline travel was too much of a hassle and humiliation for a man of his stature would soon become a topic of amusement among his friends. He made sure that his consulting and speaking deals, whenever possible, included transportation on private planes.

Similarly, Kissinger was anxious to retain his entourage of Secret Service bodyguards. This was not wholly unreasonable for a controversial public figure planning to settle in Manhattan, where the chance that he would be accosted by nut cases was relatively high. Yet a trace of self-importance was involved as well; arriving at restaurants or business meetings accompanied by a phalanx of Secret Service agents assures a certain cachet even in Manhattan's most jaded precincts, and certainly lessens the chance of being asked to wait at the bar for a table.

For several months the new administration continued Kissinger's Secret Service protection at government expense. But this indulgence would not be granted indefinitely by Jimmy Carter, who made a point of carrying his own luggage, or by his national security adviser, Zbigniew Brzezinski, who for twenty years had harbored a smoldering resentment toward Kissinger. Brzezinski began ridiculing the protection as an expensive ego trip, and soon it was canceled, a decision that Kissinger denounced as vindictive. He ended up hiring the head of his Secret Service team, a personable agent named Walter Boethe, to lead a group of five private bodyguards to provide the same around-the-clock protection at a cost to Kissinger of just over $150,000 a year.

The private planes and bodyguards were trappings of a style that helped to guarantee that Kissinger would not recede into obscurity. Secretaries such as Dean Rusk and even Dean Acheson had been able to slip back into private life with the pretense of enjoying the unassuming style that is the luxury of people who have already achieved great stature. Not Kissinger. In one of the most amazing gravity-defying feats in the American media age, he was able to maintain his heightened aura long after even his successors could reenter restaurants unnoticed.

Two years into the Carter administration, *Washingtonian* magazine asked, "Who is the biggest star in Washington?" Ted Kennedy? Elizabeth Taylor? Jimmy Carter? It found the answer at a gala at the Kennedy Center: "The biggest star in the super-glittery assemblage, the star most oohed and aahed over, the star the TV cameras zeroed in on first when they panned the audience, was ex–Secretary of State Henry Kissinger." That was somewhat surprising. What was truly astonishing was that the same story done fifteen years later would likely have come to much the same conclusion.

Kissinger's continued celebrity came partly from the force of his personality and mind. Even out of power, he could be dazzling in public and charming in private: he dispensed weighty insights on television, shared confidences at dinner parties, and regaled lecture audiences with a brilliant mixture of maxims and anecdotes.

In addition, he cultivated the high-wattage aura of a person who —both by the natural force of his presence and by careful work— knows how to be the center of attention in any room he enters. Never reticent about projecting his personality, Kissinger realized that his image was his most marketable asset. If people were to pay $30,000 to have him speak or $250,000 to act as a consultant, it would not simply be for the substance of his thoughts. Part of his appeal would be the power of his mystique, which made it all the more worth tending.

This "reluctance to be reduced to the dimensions of a mere mortal," he readily admitted, was also driven by his own ego, the size of which amused even him. When he arrived in Rome to do a television special for NBC, he was told the pope was busy planning a beatification ceremony for two new saints. "Who is the other one?" he asked.

But he brooded over small perceived slights, such as when his friend and successor Cyrus Vance escorted him to the public elevator after a visit to the State Department rather than the private one Kissinger had had installed directly to the secretary's office.[1]

When they moved to Manhattan, the Kissingers bought a four-bedroom duplex apartment in River House, a fashionable twenty-six-story brick-and-sandstone building overlooking the East River at Fifty-second Street. Two of the bedrooms were furnished for David and Elizabeth, who continued to spend part of their summers and holidays with their father.

With the help of decorators Vincent Fourcade and Albert Hadley, Nancy furnished the apartment in a comfortable and rather warm style. The long living room, with its bay window overlooking the East River, was covered in padded green fabric, a Fourcade specialty. Its furnishings included a Spanish impressionist oil painting over the fireplace, a Chinese silk screen, and one of the many Oriental rugs that her husband liked to buy. The dining room, which could seat forty at four round tables, had dark blue lacquered walls with gold trim and subdued still-life paintings.

For their country residence, the Kissingers bought, for $470,000, a white colonial-era clapboard farmhouse on fifty acres near Kent in the northwest corner of Connecticut. This area, which was sprinkled with small dairy farms and New England crossroad villages, became in the 1970s a quiet alternative to the Hamptons as a refuge for wealthy and artistic New Yorkers. Kissinger's friends who had houses there ranged from fashion designer Oscar de la Renta to Senator Abraham Ribicoff and his wife, Casey, to violinist Isaac Stern.

The previous owner had covered part of the property with a blueberry plantation, and local residents were allowed to come pick their own during the late-summer harvest. They would then weigh their pails and pay about eighty cents a pound, part of which the owner donated to the local Congregational church. As quaint and beloved as the activity was, Kissinger had no desire to allow strangers to roam his property. In addition, though his house was nestled amid soothing woods, he wanted to clear wide swaths of land to provide better views of the lake and small hills he owned. So, much to his new neighbors' noisy consternation, the blueberry patches were uprooted. "There's a little bit of emotion up here," said Ed Rapp, editor of the weekly *Kent Good Times Dispatch*. "We figured the blueberries are worth more to us than Henry."[2]

The Kent house, part of which was built in 1770, had the rambling charm of many old New England farmhouses that have been expanded over the decades. When he decided to add another wing for a bedroom and study, Kissinger, who enjoyed the study of architectural proportions and spatial relationships, decided on the dimensions that would suitably balance the design. His concern for order, structure, frameworks, and balance was given tangible expression.

All of these needs and desires produced a high-maintenance lifestyle. The $150,000 out-of-pocket cost for bodyguards was matched by the expense of keeping three lawyers on retainer to fight suits (from Morton Halperin and Tony Lake, among others) involving his role in the wiretapping and access to his papers and telephone transcripts. Thus, it was never very likely that he would return to the life of a full-time professor.

Nevertheless, he had put his old colleagues from Harvard through the motions of making him an offer. His chair as professor of international relations in the Government Department had been kept vacant for eight years, an unusual act of deference, and the university offered it back to him. But the post came with no special embellishments; it would require carrying a full teaching load and making do with the normal office space and single secretary provided any other professor.

Kissinger made clear that he expected to be offered something more, although he gave no indication he would accept if he was. His stature, he felt, made him worthy of one of the five University Professorships or similarly exalted chairs that carry more perks and fewer duties. Henry Rosovsky, his old army friend, was then dean of the faculty, and he came to see Kissinger at the Ritz Hotel in Boston. "I'm a world figure," Kissinger told the dean. "I can't just lead a normal professor's life."

But Harvard's president, Derek Bok, who had a profound lack of sympathy for Kissinger, was unwilling to bestow a special chair on him. The danger with a person such as Henry, he told Rosovsky, is that he would use the university only as a base.[3]

Rosovsky came to suspect, correctly, that Kissinger would have spurned a University Professorship had it been offered. Instead, because it wasn't, he was able to savor the sweet bitterness of feeling slighted once again by his old colleagues.

He came far closer to accepting a distinguished professorship at Columbia, which would have allowed him to write his memoirs and pursue other ventures in New York. But he withdrew when students began protesting his role in the Vietnam War. "Hiring Kissinger would be like hiring Charles Manson to teach religion," one demonstrator was quoted as saying. (Kissinger also had a standing offer to become a fellow at All Souls College, Oxford, but joked, "Tyler would have to go into quarantine, and Nancy would move into the kennel.")

The only full-time job Kissinger considered was from John Whitehead, chairman of Goldman, Sachs & Co., who tried to recruit him to come to the investment bank. Instead, Kissinger ended up signing on as a consultant for about $150,000 a year, which made the firm the first client in what would eventually become his international consulting business.

He also signed a five-year, $200,000-a-year contract with NBC as a commentator and consultant, which rankled many of the correspondents there. According to those who helped handle his personal finances, Kissinger's other sources of income during his first year included a $10,000-a-year fee as counselor to the Chase Manhattan Bank's international advisory committee; a part-time professorship at Georgetown University in Washington paying $35,000 a year; a senior fellowship at the Aspen Institute paying $20,000 a year; and a dozen or so speeches, mainly to corporate audiences, at up to $15,000 each.

But Kissinger's main occupation for his first four years out of office was writing his memoirs. His agent, Marvin Josephson, was able to secure $5 million worldwide for the book, including close to $2 million from Little, Brown for the U.S. hardback rights.

Most of the writing was done in an office Kissinger rented in Washington. Sitting at a long rectangular table, he and a small group of paid researchers—including former NSC staffers Peter Rodman, Rosemary Niehuss, and William Hyland—would go over thousands of documents, telephone transcripts, and memos of conversation to lay the groundwork for each section. For up to ten hours a day, Kissinger would write and rewrite drafts on yellow legal pads, which were then given to a relay team of typists.

By the fall of 1978, he had produced more than a thousand pages

—and was just getting through Nixon's first term. His contract was renegotiated to allow for two volumes, the first of which was scheduled to be completed in mid-1979. As that deadline approached, Kissinger accepted help from the *Sunday Times* of London, which had bought British serial rights. Noting the density of the prose, the paper's editor, Harold Evans, offered to edit and enliven the manuscript; couriers were soon shuttling drafts across the Atlantic. Evans later insisted, however, that rumors that he virtually ghostwrote the book were nothing more than "flattering nonsense."

White House Years, covering 1969–72, is an exquisitely detailed work, often defensive (especially on Vietnam and Cambodia) but at times unflinchingly reflective. Unlike most memoirs, which tend to be rambling reminiscences filled with loosely connected anecdotes, it was handled with a historian's care for scholarship. Yet it also showed a novelist's eye for detail and lapidary descriptions of personalities. Even many of Kissinger's political and academic critics praised the book, and it became a number one best-seller during the 1979 Christmas season.

Publication was briefly delayed, much to the consternation of the Book-of-the-Month Club, when Kissinger insisted on revising his manuscript to rebut *Sideshow* by British journalist William Shawcross, a book sharply critical of the Nixon-Kissinger policies in Cambodia, which was published in May 1979. Shawcross, who coincidentally was a star on Harold Evans's *Sunday Times,* had used the Freedom of Information Act to unearth Pentagon documents, particularly those dealing with the bombing campaigns of 1969 and 1973. His basic thesis was that the U.S. was largely to blame for ensnaring Cambodia in the Vietnam maelstrom and dispatching it on its descent into hell. Kissinger became incensed by the accusations and brooded about the book during a trip he took to China with Polly and Joseph Kraft. It also came up in discussions Kissinger held with friends about the possibility of entering politics. Although he told interviewers that all he did was "add one or two footnotes" to his book in response to Shawcross, in fact he added at least a dozen passages to the final galleys.[4]

Kissinger's second volume, *Years of Upheaval,* took three more years to write, and it covered only the year and a half of Nixon's truncated second term. After it was published in the spring of 1982, Kissinger gave up being a memoirist. He never began his scheduled third volume about the Ford years, nor did he ever write of his life before or after entering government.

Kissinger channeled his writing in another direction. He signed a contract with the *Los Angeles Times* syndicate to do about a dozen newspaper columns a year, which were picked up in the *Washington Post,* the *New York Post,* and dozens of other papers. The columns tended to be long—about three times the length of a normal op-ed-page column—and intricately analytic, rather than based on sharp opinions or inside reporting. Often written by Kissinger in the back of his limousine on the way to his country home, they lacked the charm and irony of his memoirs, but generally were carefully reasoned expositions on a situation based on his balance-of-power principles. In addition, he began writing major pieces along the same lines four times a year for *Newsweek.*

Kissinger also increased his work as a television commentator, becoming the most ubiquitous opinionmeister of the 1980s. His relationship with NBC was not an easy one. His first special, on Eurocommunism, was the least watched of all sixty-five network shows the week it aired. When NBC decided to broadcast an hour-long interview with him, it felt the need to enlist an outside reporter and hired David Frost, the British journalist who had interviewed Nixon and other major leaders. Among those who helped Frost prepare was William Shawcross, and a tense exchange ensued between Kissinger and Frost over the Cambodian bombing. Kissinger called top network executives to insist that this portion either be deleted or refilmed, which led Frost to quit and release the original transcript. The show was finally broadcast as Frost wanted.

Thus it was not hard for ABC executives, led by Ted Koppel and Roone Arledge, to woo Kissinger away once his NBC contract expired. That gave ABC the first (but not exclusive) call on his services, and he became a regular on Koppel's "Nightline." Peter Jennings, on the other hand, was less of a fan of Kissinger's, and used him little on the evening newscast he anchored. The relationship with ABC lasted until 1989, when Kissinger resigned in order to join the board of CBS.

He had also been elected a trustee of the Metropolitan Museum of Art, perhaps the most socially prominent board in the city, and to the board of the Council on Foreign Relations. His faithful aide Winston Lord was selected to be the Council's president. But to the great embarrassment of both men, something unusual happened four years later: Kissinger was defeated for reelection.

It was a quirky situation. Nine candidates had been nominated for eight board positions, with members allowed to vote for their preferred eight. In effect this meant that each of the council's three thousand members decided which one of the nine they wanted to vote against; as the most controversial contender, Kissinger lost out. The story was cast as a rejection of Kissinger by the heart of the American establishment. He displayed some humor by saying that he would have demanded a formal recount except that it seemed pointless to have a recount of just one vote. Later he became active in council study groups, but he never stood for the board again.

In early 1982, Kissinger began suffering sharp pains in his right shoulder. At first he and his doctor thought it was the result of a fall from a platform after a speech to a bankers' convention. But tests at Massachusetts General Hospital in Boston revealed that it was because three of the arteries to his heart were clogged. He began negotiating with the doctors to see if he could find a time in his schedule for an operation, but concluded that he was booked solidly for the next three months. Only after he was shown details of the angiogram did he agree to submit to surgery that week.

"My physician says I need a triple bypass," Kissinger said at a press conference at the hospital the next day, "but I'm holding out for a quadruple—I want one more than Al Haig." At least, he added, "it proves that I *do* have a heart." Four presidents—Reagan, Nixon, Ford, and, to his surprise, Carter—called to wish him well. The operation went smoothly, and a few weeks later he was at the home of MCA president Lew Wasserman in Palm Springs recovering.

The doctors, however, told Kissinger that he would have to lose weight and change his frightful eating habits. When he went into government in 1969, he was almost slim—155 pounds—but by the time he left in 1977, he had ballooned to 215 pounds. His favorite foods were sausages, bratwurst, eggs, cream, fried onion rings, and meat loaf, a diet designed to dishearten the American Heart Association. Subsequently, he switched to cholesterol-free egg substitutes, and Nancy took strict control of his diet. But while out of her sight, he would ask their cooks, especially one from Estonia who worked at their country home, to prepare meat loaf or sausages or other forbidden dishes.

While on the way to Boston for the surgery, an incident had occurred that showed why Kissinger liked bodyguards and private planes. While walking with Nancy through Newark airport, Kissinger was approached by a member of Lyndon LaRouche's cult. "Why do you sleep with boys at the Carlyle Hotel?" the woman kept shouting. Nancy grabbed her by the neck and before pushing her away shouted, "Do you want to get slugged?" The woman pressed assault charges, and the Kissingers had to face a one-day trial in Newark the following June. The judge declared Nancy not guilty, adding that her actions seemed "spontaneous" and "human."

•

A few weeks after Kissinger's operation, his father, Louis, died in the modest Washington Heights apartment where he and Paula had lived since shortly after their arrival in 1938. He was ninety-five, and the horrors that had disrupted his life as a gentle teacher in Germany had been swept away by the immense pride he took in his son's successes.

Throughout his later life, Louis had kept scrapbooks of stories about his son, volume after volume filled with clippings sent by fellow refugees and even friends back in Germany. They were all carefully pasted and annotated, the banner headlines about Vietnam and China alongside the gossip items about Jill St. John and Samantha Eggar. One night in the early 1970s, Kissinger was at the Stanley Cup hockey playoffs when he got a message relayed through the White House switchboard to call his father at home immediately. Thinking that something had happened to his mother, he jumped up and hurried to a phone. "What's wrong?" he asked. His father replied: "You know, Henry, the German newspaper *Aufbau?*" Yes, Kissinger answered. "Well," his father continued, "they have a nasty editorial about you. Should I write them a letter?"

Kissinger's reputation took a more serious beating in 1983, when Seymour Hersh's scathing indictment of his first four years as national security adviser, *The Price of Power,* was published. A cascade of columns and news stories highlighted Hersh's charges, most notably that Kissinger had provided back-channel help to both Humphrey and Nixon in 1968. For months Kissinger raged against the "slimy lies" in the book; he had researchers hunt for inaccuracies, and he became furious at Stanley Hoffmann for giving it mildly respectable treatment in the *New York Times Book Review.*

One amusing note occurred when Kissinger and Nancy traveled to Turkey with Ahmet Ertegun, the head of Atlantic Records, and his wife, Mica, new friends in the jet-set social circuit. Ertegun asked his office to send a shipment of Kissinger books ahead so that they could give them as souvenirs. When the boxes arrived, Ertegun opened them to find, to his horror, that they had sent Hersh's book rather than Kissinger's memoirs.[5]

Some of their Washington friends tended to disparage the new, rather glitzy crowd that the Kissingers were by then socializing with. "Up in New York, Nancy seems to like to dine with her dressmakers," said Susan Mary Alsop, referring to people such as Oscar de la Renta. "I find them to be very nice people, but they really aren't my sort."

Most of the old friends blamed Nancy for choosing a social life that revolved around the sort of people pictured in *Women's Wear*

Daily. In fact, however, her husband was the one who most seemed to enjoy the comfort and fun that came from hanging around international jet-setters. Whether it was Hollywood or Manhattan or Paris, he enjoyed a certain frisson when among the rich and socially prominent. And in Manhattan in the 1970s and 1980s, the most glittery strata of nouvelle society included such new Kissinger friends as de la Renta, Annette Reed, and Ahmet and Mica Ertegun.

"I think he made up his mind that he had been involved with too much intellectual stuff," said Jan Cushing Amory, who had once been a girlfriend. "He wanted a group that would put him on a pedestal." Indeed, although the Kissingers remained casual friends with Arthur Schlesinger and a few other academics, he tended to avoid the New York intellectual scene, partly from a sense that they had written him off due to Vietnam and Cambodia.

Yet the crowd that the Kissingers gathered around themselves was more diverse and stimulating than the gossip columns of the early 1980s made it seem, and it showed once again his desire to reach out to convert old critics. At his sixtieth birthday party, for example, there were at least five people who had been wiretapped: William Safire, Winston Lord, Helmut Sonnenfeldt, Joseph Kraft, and Marvin Kalb.

The full range of Kissinger's new circle was most visibly on display at his birthday party two years later, which was hosted by Barbara Walters at Le Cirque, the most fashionable café on Manhattan's Upper East Side. From the entertainment business, there were 20th Century–Fox's Barry Diller, MCA's Lew Wasserman, and Ahmet Ertegun of Atlantic Records. Top media executives included CBS's William Paley, ABC's Roone Arledge, Katharine Graham of the *Washington Post,* and publisher Rupert Murdoch. Neoconservative gurus Norman Podhoretz and his wife, Midge Decter, frequent intellectual critics, were there, as were Robert McNamara and William Simon. Among the others were Happy Rockefeller, the deposed empress of Iran, Mike Wallace, William Safire, Ted Koppel (who did his Kissinger imitation in his toast), Winston and Bette Bao Lord, as well as the omnipresent Oscar de la Renta.[6]

It was not exactly a coterie of intimates and soul mates. But the crowd represented the blend of glamour and power and wealth that had long fascinated Kissinger. It was this world that had attracted him back to New York in the first place, and now he and his wife had become two of its most glittering stars.

MINISTER WITHOUT PORTFOLIO

For all of the pleasures of his new life in Manhattan, Kissinger retained his taste for public power. When he left Washington as a new Democratic president took office, he would have been dismayed to realize that two Republican administrations would follow and that neither would offer him a job. Throughout the 1980s and into the 1990s, he would remain on the sidelines, looming large but never summoned back onto the field.

During the Carter years, the long-standing mutual coolness between Kissinger and national security adviser Zbigniew Brzezinski was balanced by the warm relationship Kissinger had with Secretary of State Cyrus Vance. A mainstay of the Council on Foreign Relations and other precincts of gentrified foreign policy discourse, honorable and kind, Vance was the type of establishment figure Kissinger naturally courted.

Kissinger's greatest clash with the Carter administration came in 1979, when the shah of Iran was overthrown. "The biggest foreign policy debacle for the U.S. in a generation was the collapse of the shah of Iran without support or even understanding by the U.S. of what was involved," he publicly declared, downplaying a few other debacles.

Earlier that year, Kissinger had been asked by Vance's State Department to help find a home for the shah in the U.S. as a way to encourage him to abdicate gracefully. Kissinger doubted the wisdom of this policy, but he accepted the task, and with the help of David and Nelson Rockefeller, a place was found.

The Carter administration, however, decided after the shah left Iran that it did not want him to continue on to the U.S. Would Kissinger help dissuade him? He indignantly refused, and in fact he did the opposite: he made it clear to all concerned that he felt it was America's moral imperative to give an old ally asylum. Twice he visited Vance to urge that the shah be let in, and on at least three occasions he called other top officials, including Brzezinski. Brzezinski suggested he call President Carter, and in early April he did. When Carter said that he did not feel it was in America's interest to court a disaster, Kissinger decided to go public. It was morally wrong, he said in a speech later that month, to treat the shah as a "Flying Dutchman looking for a port of call."

Working closely with David Rockefeller and John McCloy, Kissinger took on the shah's cause. Rockefeller found a place for him to live temporarily in the Bahamas; Kissinger called the president of Mexico and arranged for asylum there; McCloy handled the visa problems for the shah's children, who were studying in the U.S. In late October, when Kissinger was traveling in Europe, the shah became seriously ill and asked to be allowed to visit New York for medical treatment; the Carter administration decided to let him in, and the resulting fury in Tehran led to the takeover of the American embassy and the capture of its personnel as hostages.

For Kissinger it was another case of America's credibility being at stake. "The issue of the shah's asylum goes not only to the moral stature of our nation but also to our ability to elicit trust and support among other nations," he argued.[7]

Kissinger had a strong case, but he was vulnerable on a deeper issue: the overthrow of the shah and the virulent anti-Americanism that ensued showed that the Nixon-Kissinger policy of giving enormous support to the shah and making him a pillar of the Nixon Doctrine was a policy built on dangerously shifting sands.

One path back to power that intrigued Kissinger as he settled into his New York exile was the possibility of running for the Senate. His friend Jacob Javits was up for election in 1980; he would be seventy-six at the time and was in poor health. Kissinger's name naturally came up as a replacement, raising the specter of New York's having the combustible combination of two lapsed Harvard professors, Kissinger and Moynihan—both towers of intellect and ego—as its Senate delegation.

The electricity that Kissinger generated as a potential candidate was on display at a party fund-raiser dinner in Manhattan in October 1978 featuring him and Gerald Ford. The former secretary of state overshadowed the former president. Fat-cat businessmen unabashedly asked Kissinger for his autograph, and wives were overheard asking their husbands to please find a way to introduce them. "Kissinger is catnip in New York politics these days," wrote David Broder in the next day's *Washington Post,* "and his prospective bid for the Empire State's Senate seat is . . . mesmerizing to the state's Republican politicians."

One person at the party told the tale of walking through Manhattan with Kissinger. "It was like being with Muhammad Ali," he said. "People in passing cabs rolled down their windows to shout hello. They were even leaning out of windows in the office buildings, pointing at him."

Yet Kissinger was not a natural pol. That night he left the fund-raiser early to have his own private dinner with West German Foreign Minister Hans-Dietrich Genscher. Publicly, he made it clear he would not run if Javits wanted to seek a fifth term. Privately, he worried about living on the $57,000 salary of a senator. And Nancy Kissinger indicated that her reaction to his entering politics would fall somewhere between becoming a Democrat and seeking a divorce.

Knowing that he would need bipartisan support, Kissinger asked financier Felix Rohatyn to put together a dinner of Democrats to discuss the possibility of the race. The guests ranged from labor leader Victor Gotbaum to author Peter Maas. Why, Kissinger was asked, given all you've done, would you want to be a senator? "I have ten years of capital left to my reputation," he replied. "Each year it will diminish. Soon I'll be forgotten unless I replenish it. I need a platform." Maas then brought up the Shawcross book on Cambodia, noting that it would bedevil him on the campaign trail. Kissinger erupted. "It's a tissue of lies," he said, hitting the table. The group concluded that his thin skin would be a hindrance in politics.[8]

In the end, Javits decided that he wanted to run, Kissinger decided that he did not, and Alfonse D'Amato became the next senator.

At the Republican Convention in Detroit in 1980, Kissinger was involved in an audacious set of political negotiations that almost resulted in a restructuring of the American presidency and—though this was one of the touchiest points of contention—his own return to power. Ronald Reagan was about to capture the nomination and, while casting around for a running mate, began toying with the notion of a dream ticket: former president Gerald Ford, defeated by Carter four years earlier, might be persuaded to accept the vice presidential slot. Ford had previously rejected the idea, but on the second day of the convention—Tuesday, July 15—he met for more than an hour with Reagan and agreed to reconsider. The one thing he wanted, said the man who had already been an unelected president and vice president, was a guarantee that his job would have meaningful responsibilities.

Kissinger was planning to go to dinner that Tuesday night with Nevada senator Paul Laxalt, who was one of Reagan's closest friends and a chieftain of the rugged brand of wild-West conservatism that had always considered Kissinger an alien. As he was ready to leave his suite in the steel-and-glass silo of the Detroit Plaza hotel, he received a phone call from William Casey inviting him up to his room. Casey, whom Kissinger had eased out of a job as undersecretary of state for economic affairs five years earlier, was now Reagan's campaign chairman.

When Kissinger arrived, he found Casey and Reagan's other top aides, Edwin Meese and Michael Deaver. Rather hurriedly, Meese explained that Reagan had decided he wanted Ford on the ticket and asked Kissinger to help persuade him. Perhaps, said Meese, he could go right away to see the former president on the floor just above. Kissinger was excited to find himself back in the thick of things, to be asked for help by his old conservative tormentors, and by the prospect of a Ford restoration that could call him back into power. He agreed to raise the issue later that night.

In the meantime, Kissinger had a chance to gain favor with the fervent Reaganites of the sort who had jeered him and his patron Rockefeller in 1976. That night he was scheduled to address the convention, and he had prepared an unusually bellicose stem-winder. He had even been able to wrangle a private meeting a week earlier with Reagan, who listened with a genial smile and glazed eyes as Kissinger went over the points he planned to make in his speech.

The speech went well. Though there were scattered hecklers as he came to the podium, he soon had the crowd aroused by his denunciations of the Democrats, whom he accused of "making the world safe for anti-American radicalism." There had been divisions within the Republican Party, he noted, "but the time has come to close ranks." His plea for unity was hardly necessary; his underlying text was that the time had come for the Reaganites to allow Kissinger to be part of those closed ranks.

Back in his hotel suite around midnight, Ford gathered with his wife, a couple of political aides, economist Alan Greenspan, and Kissinger. Also along for a ringside view of history was David Kissinger, then eighteen and about to enter Yale. Henry Kissinger expressed doubts whether a power-sharing plan between a president and vice president could work, but he appealed to Ford's patriotism and prevailed upon him to consider it. The nation, in fact the entire free world, was facing a dire situation, he said. If the Democrats were not defeated, disaster would ensue. He knew Ford would be sacrificing a lot, he said, but the country needed him.

After the meeting had been going on for an hour, Ford got up and asked Kissinger to come with him to a bedroom, where the two could talk privately. "But Henry, it won't work," he said. Kissinger replied again that the country needed him.

From the outset, the role that Kissinger would get to play in the new administration had emerged as a sticking point. Reagan simply did not trust him, did not like him, and thought he was too soft on the Soviets. The California ex-actor was a crusader and ideologue who saw simple truths where Kissinger saw nuances.

In addition, at Reagan's side as his chief foreign policy adviser and constant traveling companion was Richard Allen, the cherub-faced conservative whom Kissinger had brusquely shoved aside twelve years earlier after Nixon's first victory. Allen was personally repelled by Kissinger, whom he considered utterly lacking in principles. That Tuesday, he made it his mission to stay by Reagan's side to guard against whatever weird schemes Deaver and Meese might come up with, especially any involving the return of Kissinger.

Aware of the animosity he engendered, Kissinger told Ford on Tuesday night that no "personalities or names" should keep the deal from being done. He also called Deaver the next morning to say much the same thing. But Ford made it clear that he wanted Kissinger to become secretary of state again, and Kissinger did not remove himself from contention. "I decided," Ford recalled, "that if I was going to be on the ticket, I was going to insist pretty strongly that Henry be secretary of state. I told Henry that was one of the things we were going to negotiate."

On Wednesday, as rumors of the possible dream ticket began rippling across the convention floor, Ford authorized four advisers, including Kissinger and Greenspan, to meet with Reagan's top aides and see if a deal could be struck. Together they produced a two-page treaty that would, in essence, have made Ford the chief operating officer and staff chief in the White House, with supervisory authority over the National Security Council and its domestic-side counterparts. Reagan would remain as chairman and chief executive officer, with final decision-making authority. Kissinger pronounced the paper "not unreasonable."

Late that afternoon, Ford called and asked if he could come see Reagan. He had decided it was time to press the Kissinger issue. "Ron, I'm making a sacrifice here," he said when he arrived. "And now I'm asking you to make a sacrifice. I want you to appoint Henry Kissinger as secretary of state."

Reagan was blunt and, he later told aides, annoyed. This was going beyond the bounds of what he had expected. "Jerry, I know all of Kissinger's strong points," Reagan told Ford. "I would use him a lot, but not as secretary of state. I've been all over this country the last several years, and Kissinger carries a lot of baggage. I couldn't accept that. My own people, in fact, wouldn't accept it."

"I was pretty insistent," Ford recalled. "But Reagan wouldn't commit to it." After less than fifteen minutes of conversation with Reagan, Ford left to go back up to his room and mull the matter over a little more.

But the magic had gone from what was, as most participants admitted in retrospect, a rather wild notion. The Kissinger issue had pricked the balloon and spared the nation a rather unpromising effort to restructure the executive branch. That evening, Ford went on television to ruminate publicly about what Walter Cronkite called "a copresidency." Impatiently, Reagan called Ford and said he needed a decision that night. An hour or so later, Ford called back to say he had decided against joining the ticket.

Reagan wasted little time making his next phone call. George Bush, who had been the top prospect until the Ford flurry, was sitting in his hotel room a few blocks away, dejected, watching the drama unfold on television and drinking a Stroh's beer. When the phone rang, his campaign manager, James Baker, picked it up. "Who's calling?" he said. "Governor Reagan," was the answer. Bush braced for the bad news. Word had reached him that the Reagan-Ford deal was set. Then, suddenly, his tense face broke into a grin. Waving his arms at his wife, Barbara, and Baker, he flashed them a thumbs-up sign. "I'd be honored," he said into the phone. "Very honored."

One small legacy of the misbegotten Ford affair was that it would enter the back of Bush's mind—along with his treatment at the U.N. and as emissary to China—as another little reason to be cool toward Henry Kissinger. Though it had not been his scheme, Kissinger had seemed just a little too eager to get Ford rather than Bush on the 1980 Republican ticket.[9]

Reagan's appointment of Al Haig as secretary of state had the effect of keeping Kissinger at a distance. Although their relationship had been partly repaired during the climax of Watergate, they remained suspicious of each other, and Kissinger was contemptuous of his former aide's shallow mind. But soon enough, Haig rather ingloriously self-immolated and was forced out by Reagan after a brief and undistinguished tenure.

Replacing him was George Shultz, a man Kissinger genuinely liked and admired. In public Kissinger had said that Shultz was the type of person he would appoint president if given a chance. Yet in private, he could not refrain from denigrating him to friends, especially when his Middle East peace efforts bogged down. As usual, the information traveled. Kissinger's intimate insults were soon buzzing around the Washington circuit, and Shultz heard them. Coldly furious, he curtailed his courtesies of keeping Kissinger abreast of each new initiative. People who knew both men, such as Peter Peterson and James Schlesinger, marveled that Kissinger had still not learned that the way he bad-mouthed people behind their backs—it was like an addiction—inevitably got him in trouble.

Surprisingly, Kissinger found that most of his disagreements with Reagan's policies were from the Right. Reagan had entered office critical of the arms control process for merely *limiting* rather than *reducing* missiles. The Soviets, to the surprise of the administration hard-liners, decided to call what looked like a bluff and accept real reductions. The result was an agreement, known as the Zero Option, to remove all medium-range nuclear missiles from Europe.

Kissinger was dismayed, and said so forcefully in his columns; he had been an advocate of the Euromissiles ever since propounding his theories about "limited nuclear wars" in the 1950s. The missiles, which had been politically difficult to deploy, finally assured a NATO deterrence against a massive Soviet land assault.

Even more horrifying was Reagan's willingness, at the 1986 Reykjavik summit, to accept Gorbachev's vision of "eliminating all nuclear weapons from the face of the earth" and to embrace the Gorbomania that portrayed the new Soviet leader as representing the end of the cold war. As it turned out, Kissinger proved far too skeptical of Gorbachev's willingness to make sweeping changes in Soviet foreign policy, but he was right to be dismayed by Reagan's starry-eyed personal infatuation with the new Soviet leader.

Although Kissinger's objections to Reagan's policies were sincere, his increasingly conservative public posturing sprang from a mix of motivations. Among them was his desire—which seemed at times as desperate as it was doomed—to win the hearts and minds of the far Right. Even before they captured control of the Republican Party in 1980, their fervor gave them the power to stymie the careers of those they targeted, which is why politicians such as George Bush tried so hard to curry their approval.

Kissinger did the same. In addition to his natural yearning to win over all critics, he realized that it was the true believers on the Right rather than his old academic colleagues on the Left who had the power to prevent him from serving in another Republican administration. With an eagerness that struck his more moderate friends as unseemly, even craven, he courted the conservatives with all eight cylinders of charm.

It was a difficult task. The die-hard movement conservatives had been his foes since the early days of détente. But it was not just Kissinger's policy positions that they objected to. They were also put off by his style and even his background. At its core, the Reagan Revolution had a populist, often resentful tinge. Most of its activists espoused an America First blend of isolationism and unilateralism, and they mistrusted sophisticated internationalist gobbledygook about such things as the Atlantic Alliance. The revolution's bogeymen were members of the East Coast establishment, the Rockefellers, the media and banking elite—in other words, all of Kissinger's patrons.

At Reagan rallies, activists handed out leaflets that purported to expose the insidious reach of the Council on Foreign Relations and the Trilateral Commission, filled with exclamation points and arrows leading inexorably to boxes marked "Rockefeller" and "Kissinger." This was the Kissinger "baggage" that Reagan had mentioned to Ford. Even by sidling to the right, Kissinger could not eliminate the lingering distaste among the cadres of the movement.

The best he could hope to do was neutralize some conservative opposition. That effort was on display early in 1988 when he addressed a dinner of the Heritage Foundation, the intellectual incubator of the conservative movement. The U.S., he said, should focus more on political differences with the Soviet Union and less on arms control. Part of his speech was an intellectual argument about why the Russians would represent a threat even if they were led by czars rather than communists, but the applause came for the juicier red meat. "I am not swept away by the Gorbachev euphoria," he told them. Afterward, James Hackett, a national security specialist at the think tank, said: "It's amazing the way Kissinger has changed his views since leaving office."[10]

Kissinger kept up a strained but correct relationship with Richard Nixon. Never personal friends, always mixing wariness and codependency in their relationship with one another, their jealousies had become more bitter in 1977 when Nixon gave a series of interviews to David Frost. In them, he described Kissinger as secretive, conspiratorial, prone to making outrageous remarks in private, and power hungry. Kissinger had been timorous in resupplying Israel during the 1973 war, Nixon revealed, until Nixon ordered him "to send in everything that flies." He, not Kissinger, had plotted the diplomacy with China and the Soviet Union. With an acidic tone, Nixon spoke of Kissinger's fascination with the celebrity set and his emotional instability when hit by good and then bad news.

Kissinger, not knowing what to expect, had gone to Susan Mary Alsop's house to watch that Nixon interview. He began sputtering and storming around the room, not so much because of Nixon's descriptions of his personality, but because Nixon was downplaying his role in their foreign policy achievements. Mrs. Alsop became so upset that she wrote Nixon a letter. Nixon's response, written in a squiggly hand, was composed more with Kissinger's eyes in mind than hers:

> No one could be more distressed by the impression created by the foreign policy program with regard to my evaluation of Henry. I taped ten hours on foreign policy and only

80 minutes survived—over which I had no control. I pointed out over and over that without Henry's creative ideas and diplomatic skill we would never have succeeded with our China initiative, the Soviet SALT I agreement, the Vietnam Peace Agreement and the progress toward reducing tensions in the Middle East. My own evaluation is that he will be remembered as the greatest diplomat of our times. . . . P.S. If you see Henry on his birthday—Friday—give him a hug for me! —RN.[11]

In his memoirs, which came out the following spring, Nixon treated Kissinger kindly if a bit condescendingly. He portrayed himself as a resolute president handling a brilliant but temperamental foreign policy genius.

Once he finished writing his memoirs, Nixon moved back to the New York City area. He eventually bought a graceful ranch-style mansion in the woods near Saddle River, New Jersey, and commuted by limousine to a Manhattan office where he wrote books and worked on restoring his reputation. By the early 1980s, as Kissinger struggled with the animosity of conservative populists and liberal intellectuals, Nixon was enjoying another comeback. He retained his base among die-hard conservatives, while Reagan's saber rattling against the Soviets made the foreign policy elite yearn for Nixon's cold pragmatism.

The Kissingers did not include the Nixons in their social circle, nor did the Nixons show any inclination to go to dinner parties. (Pat Nixon, in fact, made no social appearances at all after a stroke in 1976.) Once, at Nixon's request, Kissinger held a stag dinner in Nixon's honor, and a couple of times a year he would invite his old mentor to lunch, usually at a highly visible restaurant. Nixon did not like to go out for lunch, and sometimes he would reply that he preferred simply to come by Kissinger's office for a Pepsi to talk about world affairs. Once when they did go out to Le Cirque together in 1984, William Safire wrote a column on "the curious transposition of reputations of the two men coming full circle at Le Cirque."

Publicly and privately, Nixon urged Reagan to make more use of Kissinger. In one television interview, he suggested him as a "heavy-weight negotiator" for the Middle East, though the recommendation was less robust than Kissinger may have liked. "Now, Henry is devious, Henry is difficult—some people think he's obnoxious—but he's a terrific negotiator," Nixon said on "Meet the Press."[12]

The Reagan team, however, kept Kissinger on the sidelines. His only assignment was the thankless task of heading the bipartisan commission on Central America that Reagan appointed in 1983—which

was little more than a cover to help the administration win approval
for its $110 million aid package for El Salvador and to bring some
coherence to the on-again, off-again policy of supporting contra rebels
fighting the Sandinista government in Nicaragua. Kissinger was not
thrilled. "They give me all the good ones," he said sarcastically to
friends. But at least the appointment provided, finally, official Reagan-
ite blessing. He accepted and, preening his new hawkish feathers,
threw himself into the task of providing bipartisan backing and intellectual underpinning for Reagan's policies.

Should we bemoan Kissinger's return? asked historian Ronald
Steel in the *Washington Post*. "Not, I think, if we want to restore a
needed measure of professionalism to our diplomacy. . . . Yes, if we
think our foreign policy should have some connection with the values
we profess." From the Left came the criticism that "the man who gave
us the bombing of Cambodia," as Congressman Norman Minetta put
it, was now giving the U.S. a rationale for involvement in Nicaragua
and El Salvador. From the Right came criticism that, as conservative
fund-raiser Richard Viguerie put it, "Kissinger's track record is one of
losing countries."

But the mainstream consensus was that recalling Kissinger to
duty was a good idea, and even Democrats working with him began
pouring forth praise. They noted that, unlike when he was in power,
Kissinger was willing to be conciliatory and build a consensus. "For a
man who has been secretary of state and had world fame, he has been
infinitely patient and fair," said Henry Cisneros, the liberal mayor of
San Antonio. "Dr. Kissinger is brilliant. It's marvelous to watch him
take an issue and frame it in another way so you can understand it."

In October, the members of the Kissinger Commission took a
televised six-day, six-nation tour of Central America that, against all
odds, actually ended up deepening their appreciation of the issues.
When they landed in El Salvador, where the U.S. was funneling
military aid, they were "aghast," as one member said, by all of the
evidence that the army was linked to right-wing death squads. Roberto d'Aubuisson, then the leader of the far Right (and later president), stunned the group, and especially AFL-CIO president Lane
Kirkland, by accusing moderate union leaders of being communist
sympathizers.

A consensus was formed in favor of tying future Salvadoran aid
to the end of death squad activity, and Kissinger issued a rare public
warning about human rights abuses as the group left the country. "My
proudest day as a member of the commission came in San Salvador,
watching some of my conservative colleagues become increasingly
outraged by the mounting evidence that right-wing death squads were

not a liberal fantasy," said Carlos Diaz-Alejandro, an economics professor at Columbia.

During their next stop, Nicaragua, the group was similarly antagonized from the left. Those on the panel who had believed that the nation's Sandinista regime might not be dominated by Moscow were disillusioned by a very undiplomatic harangue from President Daniel Ortega and other top leaders. They even used Soviet intelligence reports and maps to display their military superiority. This helped Kissinger in his effort to get the commission to endorse the basic premise that the region should be seen as a battlefield in the global East-West struggle.

The commission's whirlwind tour, recorded by hordes of reporters at each stop, displayed how, at age sixty, seven years after leaving office, Kissinger "retains the aura of a world leader," as the *Washington Post* reported. Indeed, the commission's work would have been conducted in relative obscurity had not Kissinger been at its head; instead, with his tarmac press conferences and top-level meetings, the trip took on the look of one of his shuttle missions while in power. When the group landed in Managua, Kissinger stepped off the plane and was mobbed by waiting reporters. The official greeting party from the foreign ministry stood slightly dazzled at the side while he completed his bantering and briefings.

The final product was a 132-page consensus report that generally endorsed Reagan's policy. While noting that "indigenous" roots existed for much of the unrest, it declared that the U.S. was facing a "Soviet-Cuban" challenge in the region. Kissinger's efforts to get everyone aboard meant that there was a lot in the report to please different sides: $400 million more in immediate military aid, as well as an $8 billion Marshall Plan–style program for economic and humanitarian needs in the long term. There was tacit endorsement of the contra resistance in Nicaragua, though two Democrats expressed their reservations in notes at the end.

The greatest compromise involved making the Salvadoran military aid strictly conditional on the end of death squad killings. There was a strong consensus in favor of that in the commission, even though Kissinger had some objection. In the end he agreed to include his reservations in a note—just as the Democrats had on the contras —and let the majority view prevail.

Reagan made a great show of praising the report, and he immediately submitted requests for both the military and humanitarian aid. The $8 billion package, however, was never taken seriously, either in Congress or the White House. More significantly, the White House shot down—even before the report was officially released—the idea of making Salvadoran aid contingent on the curbing of the death squads. When President Reagan sent his aid request to Congress, he insisted that he retain the final authority to decide whether continued right-wing killings should cause the flow of funds to be curtailed.

As a result, Democrats on the commission, led by Lane Kirkland and former party leader Robert Strauss, began denouncing the result. The main object of the commission—to drum up bipartisan support for the president's policies—was thus scuttled by the White House's unwillingness to go along with the report's key compromise. In the end, the Kissinger Commission report—although well written and well conceived compared to others in the genre—was consigned to the dusty shelf where bipartisan reports are destined to languish unread.[13]

The lure of elective office once again enticed Kissinger in 1986, when he sounded out state Republican leaders about the possibility of running against Mario Cuomo for governor. Kissinger as a senator would have made sense; but to most objective observers, the notion of him as a governor, milking cows at state fairs and wrestling with legislators over highway funds, was on the face of it ridiculous. Most state Republican leaders felt the same, but they were so eager to find someone to take on Cuomo that they gave him encouragement. "The Republican Party is scraping the top of the barrel," said political consultant David Garth. After a few weeks of consultations, Kissinger thought better of the idea.[14]

In the race for the 1988 Republican presidential nomination, there were two candidates who would likely have brought Kissinger back from the wilderness: Senator Robert Dole and Congressman Jack Kemp, both of whom were secure in their conservative credentials and in need of some foreign policy expertise. Unfortunately for Kissinger, the situation of the front-runner was the opposite: George Bush was secure in his foreign policy expertise but was not secure in his conservative credentials.

More significantly, he did not like Kissinger very much. Bush's aides recalled an incident when he was ambassador to the United Nations and Kissinger was withholding information from him at a meeting; Bush stalked out in anger, muttering, "I don't have to take this shit." In Bush's studiously polite campaign autobiography, Kissinger was the only person who got needled; Bush complained that both as envoy to Beijing and to the U.N., he was cut out of policy-making by Kissinger, and he described in a mildly mocking tone one of Kissinger's imperial visits to China.

So when Bush became president, Kissinger was faced with one of life's reminders that antagonisms made while on high can later come back to haunt you. Not only did Bush not offer Kissinger a job, he stole away his top two associates in his consulting firm, Lawrence Eagleburger and Brent Scowcroft. Actually, Kissinger was pleased by the Eagleburger and Scowcroft appointments, to deputy secretary of state and national security adviser respectively. He liked both men, and it gave him fine access to the heart of the new administration.

Both Bush and his secretary of state, James Baker, were Texas-style pragmatists with little feel for what Bush dismissively called "the vision thing." Kissinger, who had geostrategic visions galore, was not their sort.

Evidence of this came early, just after Bush's inauguration in 1989, when Baker subtly humiliated Kissinger over an idea he proposed that would become known derisively as "Yalta II." With the effortless air of a skeet shooter, Baker sent the idea floating into the sky, eyed it with bemused interest, and then casually blasted it away.

The notion behind Kissinger's Yalta II plan was similar to that behind the Code of Conduct signed at the 1972 Moscow summit and the Helsinki final act of 1975. Under Kissinger's new scheme, a quiet and tacit "framework of accommodation" would be hatched—preferably by a secret envoy such as himself—in which Moscow would agree to allow liberalization in Eastern Europe, and in return the U.S. would agree not to exploit these changes in a way that would threaten Soviet security (such as trying to lure Moscow's allies out of the Warsaw Pact).

It was the ultimate in Kissingerian diplomacy: a sweeping secret deal based on spheres of influence and balance-of-power considerations that would lead to unabashed détente between the Soviets and the Americans. There were enormous political risks. The scheme raised the specter of Yalta, the 1945 summit where, according to conservative demonology, Roosevelt sold out Eastern Europe to Stalin. It would also reopen the battle over the Sonnenfeldt Doctrine and the Helsinki summit, where Kissinger and Ford were accused of a similar sellout to Brezhnev. But Kissinger felt that, on the contrary, his plan would lead to "the reversal of Yalta, not the revival of Yalta."

Kissinger suggested this package plan to President-elect Bush, Scowcroft, and Baker at a private meeting in December 1988. Bush would be the first president, Kissinger stressed, with the opportunity to end the cold war. But it would require vision and caution. Bush seemed interested, and he authorized Kissinger to broach the idea with Soviet president Gorbachev.

When Kissinger explained the plan at a private meeting with Gorbachev on January 18, 1989, the Soviet leader leaned forward and inquired whether there was a hidden meaning. Was it a device to get the Soviets to reveal their ultimate intentions in Eastern Europe? Kissinger replied that there was no agenda other than the one he had just outlined. Gorbachev designated Kissinger's old back-channel partner, Ambassador Dobrynin, to serve as a conduit with Kissinger for future talks, if the Bush administration desired.

But Baker, despite being initially receptive, was not eager to encourage a grand diplomatic gambit that would be handled by Kissinger rather than himself. In addition, top-level officials at the State Department were leery of such a scheme, especially since events in Eastern Europe seemed to be moving in America's direction on their own. "Why buy what history is giving you for free?" one Soviet expert said. Others dubbed it with the poisonous moniker, Yalta II.

By February the plan began leaking from the State Department, with a spin. "Some specialists on European affairs have expressed dismay bordering on horror at Kissinger's concepts," reported the *Washington Post*. In an op-ed piece in the *New York Times,* Zbigniew Brzezinski was snide: "Others even advocate, in the tradition of real-politik, an American-Soviet deal regarding Eastern Europe, a kind of new Yalta."

James Baker was far more velvety and deft in skewering Kissinger's plan. On March 28, he gave an interview to the *New York Times*'s new diplomatic correspondent Thomas Friedman. "I think it's worthy of consideration because it's a novel approach," Baker said of the Kissinger plan, distorting it slightly. After some restrained words of praise, he proceeded to suggest a few problems with the idea, most notably that it was not necessary. Favorable trends were already under way in Eastern Europe, "so why not let the process move forward for the time being?"

Kissinger felt hurt, angry, and betrayed. At a Trilateral Commission meeting in Paris, he vented his fury at the secretary of state. "Baker has developed a new art form," he told some of the participants. "He defends a proposal I didn't make, then says he was interested in it in purely intellectual terms, then rejects it on the grounds that it will give away Eastern Europe to the Soviets."

Kissinger went so far as to write a defense of his proposal in a newspaper column that attacked Baker by name. He claimed that the secretary had seemed to endorse a "fragmentary summary of a private conversation" and had then proceeded anonymously to reject "a distorted version" of the idea. Baker's belief that there was no need to negotiate anything as long as things were moving along well in Eastern Europe was flawed, Kissinger said, because "once there is anarchy and the tanks roll, it is too late for diplomacy."

There were, however, plenty of flaws in Kissinger's scheme. It assumed that the Americans and Soviets still had the clout to negotiate matters affecting the fate of their allies. In addition, Baker turned out to be right: the Soviet satellites got their freedom without any security concessions by the West. If a grand new Yalta compromise had been reached, it may have preserved the Warsaw Pact's power, unlike what happened when history's forces were allowed to proceed naturally in 1989.[15]

From the Yalta II incident on, Kissinger's relations with Bush and Baker were chilly. Although they would occasionally meet and talk with him, they made no effort to involve Kissinger in the administration's momentous decisions as the Soviet hold on Eastern Europe crumbled.

Cut off from the main players, Kissinger eventually found himself in an odd-couple relationship with Vice President Dan Quayle, whom he had coached for his 1988 debate and courted thereafter. Quayle was not the sort Kissinger would have normally sought as a dining companion. This seemed apparent to many of the guests at a dinner Kissinger hosted in September 1990 at his River House apartment for the vice president. As usual, Kissinger invited a mix of his business and media friends. Laurence Tisch of CBS was there and Thomas Murphy of ABC; investor Warren Buffett and insurance magnate Maurice Greenberg; Jim Hoge of the *Daily News* and Lester Crystal of the "MacNeil/Lehrer NewsHour."

What struck many of the guests was how incongruous Kissinger and Quayle seemed together, how little they had in common. A question would be raised, Quayle would stumble around like a C student searching for a safe response, then Kissinger would give the correct answer. But the relationship was based on reciprocal needs. To Quayle, Kissinger could provide the heft and substance that seemed so missing in the vice president's vacant visage. And to Kissinger, Quayle offered a link to conservatives—and a chance, perhaps, to be influential someday in the future.

THIRTY-THREE

KISSINGER ASSOCIATES

How the World's
Most Famous Consultant
Struck It Rich

> *This guy is larger than life. It's like traveling with someone who is*
> *still a secretary of state. And there's a reason: he works at it.*
> —ROBERT DAY, *chairman, Trust Company of the West*

DIPLOMAT FOR HIRE

• Argentina's state-owned insurance company decided in the
early 1980s to get into the international reinsurance business. Among
the policies it bought up were some that had been issued by the American International Group, the largest commercial underwriter in the
U.S. But the insurance market went into a bad cycle, the Argentine
state company began losing money, and in 1987 it quit paying off on
claims, which left AIG holding the bag. Maurice Greenberg, the
chairman of AIG, turned to Henry Kissinger to bring about a resolution.

On a trip to Argentina, Kissinger met with the finance minister to
figure out what could be done. What impressed Greenberg was not
simply that Kissinger could open doors—though the ease with which
he got an appointment with the finance minister was impressive—but
also that he studied the details of the problem and worked on ways it
could be mediated. "He helped bring both parties off their fixed position," Greenberg says. While the matter was being discussed, Greenberg traveled to Argentina with Kissinger, where the former secretary

of state was an honored guest at the inauguration of President Carlos Menem.[1]

• Freeport-McMoRan, a Louisiana-based mining and exploration company, had an arrangement with Kissinger that was fairly typical: he was a member of the company's board of directors, and his firm, Kissinger Associates, was on retainer as an international consultant. When the company wanted to drill for oil and natural gas in Burma, Kissinger set up a meeting between top Freeport-McMoRan officials and another of his major clients, Daewoo, a huge Korean conglomerate. Together they worked out a $4 billion joint venture: Freeport-McMoRan would do the exploring and drilling, and Daewoo would build a plant to make liquefied natural gas and then ship it to Korea.

A hitch occurred in 1990 when Burma's military junta allowed an election, ended up losing, then refused to give up power. Amid the turmoil, the project was put on hold. Nevertheless, Kissinger Associates collected, in addition to its $200,000 annual retainer, close to $500,000 in monthly fees for working on the case—and that did not include the retainer and fees it got from its other client, Daewoo.[2]

• Trust Company of the West, an investment management firm, was a leader in raising investment capital for privatizing state-owned industries in Latin America, particularly in Mexico. Kissinger, who was on the TCW board and also served as a consultant on various projects, gave the company regular briefings on the political climate of Mexico along with colorful assessments of its leaders. But he also did something only he could do. In March 1990, while in Acapulco on vacation, he invited TCW's energetic chairman, Robert Day, to come for a visit. Then he arranged a day trip to Mexico City. They flew in Day's corporate jet, had a breakfast meeting with the finance minister, and in the course of the day met with every other major cabinet minister. That evening, Day went to a reception thrown for Kissinger by the American ambassador, John Negroponte, who had once been a member of Kissinger's White House staff. On hand were eighty of Mexico's top political and business leaders. At midnight, they flew back to Acapulco.[3]

The secretive world of Kissinger Associates involved a lucrative blend of strategic advice, foreign affairs insight, good connections, some door opening, and the cachet that came from one of the world's most marketable names. The consulting firm, which was founded soon after Kissinger left office, became an active business in July 1982, when he realized that he did not feel like writing a third volume of

memoirs and that Ronald Reagan was never going to make him secretary of state. With no legal training and little financial acumen, he
could not follow the usual revolving-door practice of returning to a
law firm or bank. So he set himself up as a statesman for hire, one
who would, for a hefty fee, purvey foreign policy expertise to private
corporations, undertake diplomatic assignments for them, and serve
as a personal national security adviser to their chairmen.

In the sleazy realm of Washington lobbying and influence ped-
dling, Kissinger's behavior was relatively benign. Unlike the scores of
top officials who leave government and immediately set up shop as
lawyers or lobbyists in order to sell their connections to major corporations, Kissinger decided that he would never lobby the U.S. government on behalf of any client. In addition, he waited five years,
more than a full presidential term, before actively pursuing business. Although he occasionally traveled with his clients and helped
them get in to see world leaders whom he knew, he was not primarily a door-opener living off his connections. Instead, the product that he sold was mainly his own insight and analysis of foreign
affairs.

Nevertheless, his phenomenal success provided an interesting
glimpse into the world of influence, where prestige and access come
with a big price tag.

With $350,000 lent to him by Goldman Sachs and a consortium
of three other banks, Kissinger opened an office on Park Avenue at
Fifty-first Street in Manhattan and another on Eighteenth and K
streets in Washington. The loans were for five years; by the end of the
second year, he repaid them in full. His annual revenues reached $5
million by 1987, and by the early 1990s were close to double that.

As the first associate in Kissinger Associates, he tapped his longtime deputy, former national security adviser Brent Scowcroft, who
was doing some private consulting work of his own in Washington.
Scowcroft signed on as a contract employee, manager of the firm's
Washington office, and vice chairman of the board. Although he kept
his own private clients in Washington, he would eventually make close
to $300,000 a year from Kissinger Associates.

The other principal was Lawrence Eagleburger, who was lured
aboard as president in June 1984 after serving as undersecretary of
state. Uncowed by Kissinger, jovial and likable, he helped build the
firm into a major enterprise. Having served as ambassador to Yugoslavia, he brought in clients from that country such as the makers of
the Yugo car and Enerjoprojeckt, a major construction firm. He also
joined the board of ITT, which became a client. In 1988, his final year
with the company before joining the Bush administration, he made

$674,000 in salary and more than $240,000 in severance and other payments.

In addition there was Alan Stoga, referred to by Kissinger and his clients simply as "the economist." He had worked in the Treasury Department during the Ford and Carter years, then had become the economist assigned to the Kissinger Commission on Central America. When the commission's work was done, Kissinger signed him up to be the economist at his firm. Low-key, unassuming, and good-natured, but also bright, he was a good complement to Kissinger.

After Eagleburger and Scowcroft left in 1989 to rejoin the government, Kissinger hired L. Paul "Jerry" Bremer, who had been his personal aide in the State Department then the chief antiterrorism official during the Carter administration. In addition, William D. Rogers, a lawyer and former undersecretary of state (not to be confused with former secretary William P. Rogers), began working in the Washington office on a part-time contract.

By the early 1990s, Kissinger Associates had more than two dozen corporations as clients, about three-quarters of them American. The list was a closely guarded secret, and the contract with Kissinger Associates barred either side from revealing the relationship. Yet from proxy statements, other financial forms, government disclosure requirements, interviews, and the tendency of businessmen to talk about their relationship with Kissinger, it is possible to come up with a list of the major clients that had contracts or project arrangements with his firm in the early 1990s:

- American Express and its subsidiary, Shearson Lehman Hutton
- American International Group, the insurance underwriter
- Anheuser-Busch, brewers of Budweiser and other beers
- ASEA Brown Boveri, a Swedish manufacturing firm
- Atlantic Richfield, the oil company
- Banca Nazionale del Lavoro (BNL), a Rome bank that made illegal loans to Iraq
- Bell Telephone Manufacturing of Belgium
- The Chase Manhattan Bank
- The Coca-Cola Company
- Continental Grain, a privately held grain company
- Daewoo, a Korean trading and construction conglomerate
- Ericsson, a Swedish telecommunications manufacturer
- Fiat, the Italian automobile company
- Fluor, a global engineering and construction company
- Freeport-McMoRan, an oil, gas, and mineral company
- GTE, the Connecticut-based telecommunications company

- H.J. Heinz, the food-product conglomerate
- Hollinger, Inc., a Toronto-based global newspaper company
- Hunt Oil Co., a Texas-based firm
- Merck and Co., the pharmaceutical giant
- Midland Bank, a British retail bank
- Revlon, the international cosmetics company
- Skandinaviska Enskilda Banken, a Stockholm-based bank
- Trust Company of the West, the investment management firm
- Union Carbide, the chemical and manufacturing conglomerate
- Volvo, the Swedish automobile company
- S.G. Warburg, the British investment bank

Kissinger Associates was not listed in the telephone book. Nor was its name on the directory of the steel-and-glass Park Avenue office tower that housed its headquarters. A visitor getting off the elevator at the correct floor would find a sparse waiting area with a receptionist behind a Plexiglas window. No name was on the door.

Inside, the undistinguished contemporary decor—white sofas, standard-issue desks—was that befitting a midsized insurance agency. Kissinger's L-shaped corner office was decorated with scores of signed photographs of world leaders smiling at him. Smaller offices along the hall included his security and logistics coordinator, his personal assistant, his scheduler, and his secretary. Stoga and Bremer had their offices on another corridor a safe distance away.

When Kissinger was in, the office buzzed with a mixture of low-level terror and excitement. He did not tend to sit quietly at his desk. Instead, he paced around, padded in and out of everyone's office, demanded clarifications of various decision memos in his folders, glanced warily at his future schedules, and then rejected them all as completely unacceptable. In between, he would proclaim certain things, some global and others trivial, to be total outrages. The staff he had been burdened with, he would growl, was surely some cruel punishment inflicted by vengeful gods. Then, just as suddenly, he would toss out an incisive suggestion about a project in the works, offer a compliment, or make a joke.

One such day was January 15, 1991, the deadline that Bush and the U.N. had set for Iraq's withdrawal from Kuwait. Kissinger was preparing to go to an all-day meeting of the Chase Manhattan Bank's International Advisory Board, which had been scheduled for six months. This did not make him happy; he wanted instead to be available for calls from worried clients and, just as important, for television networks that might want to broadcast his opinions. "This is never to happen again," Kissinger raged as he stomped around the corridors.

"Do you understand me?" Everyone nodded gravely, although they seemed unclear as to how they would henceforth convince the United Nations to plan its wars around Kissinger's corporate board meetings.

A surprisingly large portion of the work around the office involved revising Kissinger's schedules. He did not travel simply. He preferred private planes, required bodyguards, and expected to be met at each stop by cars and drivers. Although he hated being overscheduled, when he noted some looseness he tended to come up with an idea for another person he might see while he was in some far-flung locale. Then, after daily revisions and complaints that the schedule was too full, he was likely to cancel or postpone the trip at the last moment.

Yet the tantrums were leavened by an undercurrent of humor, a shared realization that it was partly an act. With a distracted air, Kissinger jumped from flashes of anger to compliments, from weary resignation to self-deprecating jokes. His staff learned to cope. When he was out of the office and telephoned in, his call was put through on a special extension, so everyone reacted as soon as they saw that light blinking. The office security system had a monitor with a camera on the elevator bank; the staffers watched it whenever he left, and they would let loose an audible all-clear sigh as soon as it showed the doors closing behind him. There was a sense of indulgence at times, as if they were dealing with an exceedingly gifted but temperamental child. There was also a deep sense of loyalty, which seemed to come more from respect, even affection, than from fear.

The typical annual retainer for Kissinger's services in the early 1990s was $200,000, with specific special projects costing an additional $100,000 or so per month—plus expenses. For that, corporate clients generally received a full briefing on world events two or three times a year. Usually conducted by Kissinger and either Stoga or Bremer, these were given orally to the firm's top handful of officers. Nothing was put on paper. Kissinger had no desire to see his insights photocopied, passed around, and referred to months later.

Each briefing was tailored to the client company's particular interests, but it did not involve specific investment advice. The view was usually medium range: what to expect in the European Community or Russia or Indonesia in the next five to ten years. Latin American debt and privatization were big issues, as were the trends in Eastern Europe.

In addition, Kissinger, Stoga, and Bremer were available for regular telephone consultations. As the war against Iraq erupted in 1991, five or six calls from major clients came in each day asking for insights. In such cases, the advice sought generally had little business connection. Corporate executives were not immune from the ego kick that comes from being able to say, "Well, I talked to Henry this morning and he feels . . ."

In fact, part of what Kissinger Associates had to sell was the famous name and rumbling accent. An executive who had to make a tough foreign investment decision could feel safer if, when presenting the plan to his board, he could talk about the breakfast he had with Kissinger on the subject and invoke his insights. "If something goes wrong in one of the countries where we've made an investment," explained one corporate executive, "I know that we will not look negligent if we'd discussed the situation with Henry beforehand."

More specific matters were handled on a project basis at an additional $100,000 per month. Typically this involved helping a company get some foreign venture approved and launched. Kissinger insisted that any project he took on be justifiable as being in the interest of the host government. This allowed him to do what he did best: act as a mediator, as he had in the Mideast, to help two sides get together on something that was in their mutual interests. During such negotiations, he liked to cast himself as the middleman trusted by both sides rather than as an agent serving only the interest of his client.

Kissinger recoiled at the notion that he sometimes served as a glorified fixer, but at least one-quarter of his project work was cutting through bureaucratic problems that clients faced in foreign countries. This often involved making a few well-placed phone calls to friends in top government positions.

Similarly, Kissinger used to deny rather heatedly that he served as a door-opener. "Everywhere I have traveled in the past year," he said in 1986, "the heads of government receive me. I do not ask them to do a favor for a client, and I do not bring the client in with me." He liked to tell of the time he refused an offer of $1 million simply to set up a meeting between a corporate executive and a foreign finance minister, something that could have been done with one phone call.

But as time went on, Kissinger became less fastidious about refusing to do any door-opening—partly because it is a natural business instinct to help provide introductions and to call on well-placed friends for help, and partly because the impropriety of doing so receded the longer he remained out of office. For example, H. J. Heinz chairman Anthony Reilly proudly describes how Kissinger helped him get in to see the presidents of Zimbabwe, Turkey, and the Ivory Coast. Just as Kissinger traveled to Mexico City with Trust Company of the West chairman Robert Day and introduced him around to top leaders, he did the same with James Robinson of American Express in Japan, with Maurice Greenberg of American International Group in China, and with James Moffett of Freeport-McMoRan in Indonesia.

Kissinger Associates was also active in many of the business groups that promoted trade and friendship with specific countries. These served as a way for corporate leaders to meet high officials of the country involved. A typical example was a group called the Malaysia-U.S. Private Sector Consultative Group, which had Kissinger and Greenberg as the American co-chairmen. Its nineteen members, some of whom were Kissinger clients, included Continental Grain chairman Michel Fribourg, ITT chairman John Hartley, Coca-Cola executive John Hunter, and Motorola chairman Robert Galvin.

One group that caused some unfair embarrassment was the U.S.-Iraq Business Forum, which existed before the two countries went to war in 1991. Although neither Kissinger nor his firm was a member, Alan Stoga, the economist, had been invited along as a guest on its 1989 trip to Baghdad, which later prompted a story in *The New Republic.* Later, "60 Minutes" aired a scathing segment that linked Kissinger's representation of the Italian bank BNL to imply that Kissinger was indirectly connected to illegal loans made to Iraq. The show contained no hard evidence for this allegation, and an outraged Kissinger later blamed the piece on executive producer Don Hewitt's pique at not being invited to a reception that Kissinger had organized after CBS chairman William Paley's funeral—an allegation for which there was also no real evidence.

Increasingly during the speculative boom years of the 1980s, Kissinger sought to branch into the field of putting together deals, such as the joint venture he tried to assemble in Burma involving Daewoo and Freeport-McMoRan. As he watched his investment-banker friends such as Peter Peterson, a neighbor in River House, rake in millions in percentage fees on big deals, Kissinger came to realize that this was how the real money was made. Kent Associates, a subsidiary of Kissinger Associates named after his country home, was formed partly for that purpose, and Alan Batkin, an investment banker with Shearson Lehman Hutton, was hired in 1990.

Commercial acumen, however, was not a prominent component of Kissinger's genius, and the business of deal-making, already in decline when he became involved, did not become a major part of his work. The distinction between Kent and Kissinger Associates withered away. "Just because he's a genius," said Maurice Greenberg, "doesn't mean he has a feel for commerce or the makings of an investment banker."

During the 1990s, one area of deal-making still offered promise: the privatization of government-owned enterprises—telephone systems, banks, heavy industries, transportation systems—as countries around the world moved more toward market-oriented economies.

Because American banks were nervous about making loans directly to third world governments, these countries increasingly had to rely on selling equity in state-owned businesses to foreign investors. "Privatization is the most important new trend," said Robert Day, the chairman of Trust Company of the West, "and Henry is perfectly poised to be at the fore. There is no one in the world today who has the personal contacts in so many governments and can help work out privatization deals."

Day was particularly interested in pursuing privatization deals in Latin America, and he worked on ventures in Mexico, Venezuela, and Chile. His company, a privately held asset-management fund group, handled $20 billion worth of investments for four hundred institutional and private clients in 1990. Kissinger, who sat on the board, did some work for TCW on a project basis. In addition, Day handled Kissinger's personal finances.

In 1990, TCW decided it wanted to put the money together to buy a major share in the Mexican national telephone system, Telemex. With Kissinger's help, TCW joined forces with GTE, which also happened to be a Kissinger client, and with Telefónica de España. It was while work on this venture was under way that Kissinger went with Day to Mexico City to meet with the members of the cabinet. He also advised James "Rocky" Johnson, the chairman of GTE, on the deal. Although the bid was not successful, TCW and GTE pursued other privatization deals in Latin America, and in December 1991 GTE paid close to $1 billion for a 20 percent stake in Venezuela's telephone company.

In addition to flying with Day to Mexico City, Kissinger traveled with him to Japan and China. "Wherever Henry goes, everyone wants to meet with him," said Day, a tan and fit Californian with an easygoing verve. "This guy is larger than life. It's like traveling with someone who is still a secretary of state. And there's a reason: he works at it."

A business relationship with Kissinger often brought with it a social component. When Day came to New York one week in early 1991, for example, Henry and Nancy Kissinger held a small dinner in his honor with a dozen or so of their most social friends. Among the guests were record magnate Ahmet Ertegun and his wife, Mica; Sid Bass, the oil heir, and his wife, Mercedes; Oscar de la Renta, the dress designer, and his wife, Annette Reed. All were names that regularly appeared in boldface in the gossip columns.

This type of spillover into the social realm was lagniappe, a nice little bonus that often comes with a business relationship. His dinner parties, especially those honoring visiting foreign leaders, were likely to include a sprinkling of client-friends such as Fiat's Giovanni Agnelli, AIG's Maurice Greenberg, and James Robinson of American Express.

AIG chairman Greenberg, known as Hank, was an example of someone who became both a client and a social friend in the early 1980s. A wiry and tightly wound man with a good sense of humor, twinkling eyes, and a secure smile, Greenberg had built American International Group into the leading U.S.-based international insurance company, with half of its revenues from foreign sources. In 1987, he made Kissinger the chairman of his International Advisory Group and began retaining him to handle three or four projects a year for the company, such as the one involving AIG's dispute with the Argentine state-owned insurance company. "Henry hasn't lost the spellbinding mystique he had when he was secretary of state," Greenberg said. "He gets immediate respect wherever he goes."

One of Kissinger's first assignments for AIG was to help it get a license to sell life insurance in South Korea, which it had been seeking unsuccessfully for fifteen years. Kissinger went to Seoul and spoke to members of the government, who blamed the problem on the lower levels of the bureaucracy. Greenberg was amazed at how thoroughly Kissinger mastered the substance of the licensing process; he did not simply raise the issue with the Koreans and let someone else deal with the details. "The fact that he took the time to understand the process so well," Greenberg said, "meant that he was able to clear away the bureaucratic underbrush that should not have been there in the first place." By 1989, AIG had opened a life insurance office in Korea.

Another project involved the government of Peru, where AIG had insured the facilities of an oil company named Belco. When the government of President Alan Garcia expropriated Belco's holdings, AIG faced a $200 million claim. During Garcia's term, negotiations with the Peruvian government for restitution went nowhere. But as his term neared an end in 1990, Kissinger got in touch with the Peruvian ambassador to the U.S., whom he knew, and suggested settlement talks. By 1991, negotiations were under way involving Kissinger, the ambassador, and top AIG executives.

In November 1989, Greenberg took a trip through Asia with Kissinger that showed the value of his relationships. Their first stop was in Singapore, where Kissinger's close friend Lee Kuan Yew, the prime minister since 1959, hosted a private lunch and then a large reception for him. At the latter, AIG's top local executives got to meet the prime minister in Kissinger's presence, a good way to establish a working relationship. Next, they went to Malaysia, whose prime minister, Mahathir Bin Mohamad, had been a student in Kissinger's international seminar at Harvard. During the visit, he asked Greenberg and Kissinger to set up the Malaysia-U.S. Private Sector Consultative Group. AIG is the largest insurance company in Malaysia. The trip ended with a three-day visit to Beijing, the first by Kissinger since the Tiananmen Square crackdown that June.

Kissinger and Greenberg went back to Indonesia and Malaysia in March 1991, but this time Kissinger flew with James Moffett, the chairman of Freeport-McMoRan. Moffett, who liked to be called Jim Bob, was an exuberant executive with the wildcat confidence of a man who has spent more than twenty years creating one of the world's most impressive phosphate, sulfur, gold, copper, oil, and gas exploration companies.

Bold, unvarnished, and optimistic, with few of the troubles that are spawned by excessive reflectiveness, Moffett was Kissinger's opposite. But he understood how much help Kissinger could be to a company with global aspirations. He consequently made Freeport-McMoRan one of Kissinger's most lucrative clients: in 1989, it paid his firm a $200,000 retainer and $600,000 in fees, plus it promised a commission of at least 2 percent on future capital investments made on the basis of its advice that year; in 1990, Kissinger's firm was paid a $200,000 retainer and $300,000 in fees. In addition, Kissinger made more than $30,000 annually in director's compensation for his service on the company's board.

Kissinger's name could lend credibility to a corporation such as Freeport-McMoRan, which was not well known in many countries. "We need stature and authentication when we're dealing with some foreign governments who don't know what we are," said chairman Moffett. "Having Kissinger behind us gives us credibility. We can get in to see people. They will take us seriously." When Kissinger came along on a trip, Moffett explained, he could be particularly helpful because of his personal relationships with many key leaders. "They will tell him things we might not be able to find out on our own."

On the eve of the company's January 1991 board meeting, Moffett took over Moran's Riverfront Restaurant on the edge of the New Orleans French Quarter and had a big square table placed in the middle. He was the type of executive who liked having Kissinger around simply for the joy of hearing him hold forth. So on this night the Freeport-McMoRan board and top executives were invited to eat oysters Rockefeller and shrimp remoulade while Kissinger expounded on the impending war with Iraq.

The situation in the Persian Gulf affected Freeport-McMoRan enormously. The company was about to make major new investments in the mining of gold, the price of which was bouncing around in response to war jitters. Likewise, its oil and gas operations were buffeted by each swing in the price of crude. Its largest new investment was in Indonesia, a secularized Moslem nation vulnerable to a rise in Islamic fundamentalism.

Kissinger did not try to give specific advice about the price of gold or the next OPEC pricing decision; his talk was more thematic, at times even abstract. Still, the board members and managers hung on his words as if they were received wisdom. Kissinger spoke of the coming upheavals in the Moslem world, the potential for isolating the Arab radicals and for forming a pro-West consensus in the Middle East.

No one came away from the session with a specific nugget of practical advice; in fact, most had trouble recalling anything concrete that Kissinger said. But even months later, many of them were still talking about how "brilliant" Kissinger's disquisition was. "It was fascinating," said Moffett. "He talked all about the long-range threat of a struggle between Muslims and the West."

Moffett also liked to use Kissinger for political and risk assessments, which were the core services that Kissinger Associates offered. For example, Freeport-McMoRan's biggest venture was a gold and copper mine in Indonesia. In early 1991, the company got a thirty-year permit to work the mine, which would require an investment of at least $550 million. Before completing the deal, Moffett asked Kissinger to provide an analysis of the political future in Indonesia for the next ten to twenty years.

Kissinger's associate William D. Rogers went to Indonesia to study the situation. In addition, Kissinger retained as a subconsultant his old NSC expert on Asia, John Holdridge, who had later served as ambassador to Indonesia. The results of their work were communicated by Kissinger to Moffett, after which the two men went on their March 1991 trip during which final details were worked out with the Indonesian government.

"When you're making a commitment of half a billion dollars," Moffett later explained, "a few hundred thou for a consultant who knows his way around the place is nothing." And if a revolution ever hit Indonesia and the mines were nationalized, Freeport-McMoRan's stockholders would have a hard time accusing their chairman of being negligent. (Nor, for that matter, could they hold Kissinger liable; under his contract, the company indemnifies him and holds him harmless for any bad advice he gives.)

In the late 1980s, Freeport-McMoRan wanted to set up a fertilizer deal involving Morocco. The company had the largest sulfur mine in the world, just off the Louisiana coast, and much of Morocco is built on phosphate rock. Both minerals are necessary for high-grade fertilizers, and Moffett wanted to work out a trade arrangement or joint venture. By 1991, although a deal had not been worked out, Kissinger had made three trips to the country during which he discussed possible projects. Particularly impressive, Moffett said, was that Kissinger even got to meet with King Hassan. "Henry is very close to the king," Moffett explained. "He not only gets involved in telling you the type of proposal that might appeal to the Moroccans, but he will also keep in touch with the people there, including those who know the king, and tell you which way things are going and what factors are important."

Another Freeport-McMoRan project involved Panama. The company had a gold mine there, which had to shut down when the U.S. slapped sanctions on that nation because of the actions of its strongman, Manuel Noriega. Hoping to sell its facilities, it needed to find someone in Panama who would help keep its leases active so that the mining rights would not be revoked. "Henry was able to find some rational people in the Panamanian government, even while Noriega was in power, who could help us out," Moffett recalled. "Henry can definitely cut the red tape for you in those countries where you've got some big bureaucracy who doesn't know who you are. He always has somebody he can call."

When Gerald Ford was retiring from the board of American Express in 1984, he recommended Kissinger as his replacement. "A lot of you fellows may not like Henry," Ford argued, "and he may be controversial in this country, but he is not controversial abroad. He knows people and can get doors open and can get things done." Another director demurred, noting that "a company as big and sophisticated as American Express doesn't need anyone to open doors for it." A few other board members argued that Kissinger might be too radioactive for a company such as American Express. But Kissinger was elected, and the firm's chairman, James Robinson, became one of his biggest fans.

The fee the company paid Kissinger Associates fluctuated, but for 1989, a typical year, it included a $100,000 retainer for advising Robinson on international affairs plus $200,000 as a consultant to Shearson Lehman Hutton, the company's investment-banking subsidiary. In addition, Kissinger personally received $120,000 for making speeches and appearances at company functions and $55,500 for his work as a member of the American Express board. At the start of most board meetings, Robinson would call on Kissinger to provide an assessment of the world situation.

"Henry has an incredible capacity to stay current," said Robinson. Before leaving on any major trip, Kissinger would usually call Robinson to see if there were any issues to be explored in the countries he planned to visit. Sometimes Robinson would cite a specific problem or two. For example, American Express was seeking a license for its banking subsidiary to do business in Hungary. When Kissinger traveled there, he raised the issue with the new government and stressed that the American Express bank should get priority because it would also serve to build the country's tourism industry.

Kissinger and Robinson traveled together frequently, especially to Japan. "He has introduced me to several high-level Japanese government officials," Robinson said. "I may have met them otherwise, but when you do it under Henry's auspices, it can be a more personal involvement." When Kissinger makes the introductions, it is as if he is saying, "I can vouch for these guys," according to Robinson.

One example was the deal by Nissei, Japan's Nippon Insurance Company, to buy a 13 percent stake in Shearson from American Express in 1987, a $530 million transaction. The Japanese government had reservations about the deal because it feared that it would increase anti-Japanese sentiment in Washington, so Nissei was holding off. But Kissinger traveled to Tokyo that March and met with his friend the Japanese finance minister. That was enough to settle the government's qualms, and the deal ended up going through. "He is able to handle shuttle diplomacy," Robinson said, "because both sides trust him."

In addition to his consulting business, Kissinger served on various corporate boards. In 1990, these included American Express, R. H. Macy, Hollinger, Union Pacific, Continental Grain, CBS, Revlon, Freeport-McMoRan, and Trust Company of the West, as well as the international advisory committees of Chase Manhattan Bank and AIG. The standard annual compensation for each of the boards was about $50,000, which amounted to approximately half a million dollars in additional personal income.

Added to that was his income from giving speeches. His average fee by 1990 was $30,000; leaving aside his contractual arrangement at American Express, he generally made more than one hundred speeches a year, about half for charity, the other half for a fee. In some years the income from his speaking business approached $2 million.

Kissinger's annual income thus was as high as $8 million. In 1988, Kissinger was ribbing Peter Peterson about how much money the investment banker must be making. Peterson replied with an I'll-show-you-mine wager: he would guess Kissinger's income, and if he was wrong by more than 20 percent, he would be willing to tell Kissinger his own. When Kissinger agreed to this rather odd game, Peterson made his guess about Kissinger's annual earnings: $7.5 million. Kissinger smiled, tacitly assenting that the guess was close to correct.[4]

CONFLICTS AND INTERESTS

Nothing that Kissinger did as a consultant was illegal, nor did he even skirt the edge of the law. In fact, his activities were generally more pristine than what was common practice in Washington. But like his foreign policy, Kissinger's world after he left office was filled with linkages. His attempt to juggle the roles of media commentator, business consultant, and unofficial government adviser provides an interesting case study of the standards of public, business, and journalistic conflicts of interest.

Kissinger was part of an old if not particularly venerable breed in Washington: top officials who leave government and then find themselves paid handsomely by clients who value not just their minds and talents, but also their connections, clout, and Rolodexes. Some make it seem more respectable by doing it under the thin guise of being lawyers. Others come right out and call themselves lobbyists and consultants. There is no clear line between what is acceptable and what is not. Rather, it is a matter of degree, discretion, and style.

Countless stabs at revising the Ethics in Government Act have produced a few principles for what is considered proper in this game: the longer you wait after leaving office, the less of an impropriety there tends to be, and it is best not to lobby those you once worked with. By these standards, Kissinger displayed a respectable propriety. Until he had been out of office for five years, he refused to join any corporate boards or pursue his own business actively. Unlike most eager-Deaver consultants, he provided his clients with substantive expertise rather than merely connections or introductions. In addition, he never did any domestic lobbying nor represented clients on White House, State Department, or congressional matters.

There was the possibility of a conflict between Kissinger's role as chairman of the bipartisan Central American commission and his private work as a highly paid consultant to banks and investment firms whose Latin American debt holdings led them to favor U.S. economic aid to the region. Such situations often arise when an outsider in private business agrees to serve on a public commission. The Kissinger case, for example, was more benign than, say, that of Brent Scowcroft, who headed a commission looking into strategic missile options while serving as a private consultant (in work outside of his duties at Kissinger Associates) to the Lockheed Corporation. In the end, unless the nation chooses to limit participation on boards and commissions to people who are uninvolved with the subject at stake, it must rely on the honesty of those who serve. "If you show me a situation with no conflicts," said American Express Chairman Robinson, "I'll show you a level of mediocrity and incompetence that means nothing will ever happen."

A clearer set of potentially conflicting interests arose out of Kissinger's work as a columnist and commentator. One of the basic rules of American journalism is that reporters and pundits should not have a financial stake in the issues they cover, especially if it is a secret. Kissinger, however, occasionally advocated positions, in his newspaper column and on television, that could benefit the interests of his clients.

Some perspective is warranted. People in journalism are more likely to recoil at this breach of the trade's ethics than would an average citizen. But Kissinger's readers would have been better served if, at the very least, he had disclosed any financial links his clients had in the issues he discussed.

In many cases this would not have been relevant. His analyses generally dealt with matters such as arms control, the future of NATO, and European security after the cold war, opinions that his clients may have found fascinating but that did not directly affect their business interests. Likewise, most of his comments on television dealt with breaking news events—the Iraq war, the Palestinian uprising, events in the Soviet Union and Eastern Europe—and his business relationships were not directly involved.

Every now and then, however, Kissinger tackled a topic in which his clients had a direct financial stake. In defending this practice, he argued that it was "absurd" to think that he would tailor his opinions to suit his clients' financial interests, and there is no evidence that he ever did. Yet it is reasonable to believe that his thoughts on some of these complex issues were influenced by listening to the strong opinions of people who were paying him quite well. In addition, consciously or subconsciously, his journalistic comments on foreign leaders could have been influenced by how friendly they had been in dealing with him and his desire to have a cordial relationship with them in the future.

Take, for example, Kissinger's columns on Mexico and its debt problem. The issue was of specific concern to companies that Kissinger advised, including American Express, Trust Company of the West, and the Chase Manhattan Bank.

In 1989, Chase added $1.15 billion to its reserve fund to cover its third world debt, which resulted in a major loss for the year; the bank's former chairman David Rockefeller and its current chairman, Willard Butcher, were active in urging Washington to help in paring Mexico's debt.

Similarly, the American Express Bank, the lending arm of that company, had more than $2 billion of Latin American debt in 1987, which it subsequently tried hard to reduce. Chairman James Robinson in 1988 publicly advocated the creation of an International Institute for Debt and Development, which would purchase third world loans at a discount and provide debt relief so that developing nations could trade and prosper. When Robinson announced this proposal, Kissinger read over the drafts of the speech and made numerous suggestions, most of which were adopted.

At Trust Company of the West, Chairman Robert Day was likewise interested in how the debt crisis was handled. In addition, he had a stake in specific ventures with the Mexicans, such as privatization, and he paid Kissinger to help him maintain good relations with whoever was in power there; he and Kissinger traveled to the country together three times.

Kissinger advocated Latin American debt relief in his role as a press pundit and as an informal adviser to top U.S. officials. In addition, his commentary about Mexico and its leaders was exceedingly sympathetic, which served to enhance the favored treatment he got when he traveled there with his clients.

For example, shortly after Carlos Salinas was elected president of Mexico in 1988, Kissinger wrote a long column for the *Los Angeles Times/Washington Post* syndicate praising him and warning of the internal communist threat to the country. He then went on to say that "the U.S. can play a major role in encouraging democracy and economic reform." How? By helping to ease the debt problem. "Salinas's liberal economic policy can be sustained only by growth. But the Mexican economy cannot grow so long as debt service consumes more than 6 percent of the Gross Domestic Product." The burden for this debt relief should not fall solely on the banks that made the loans. "Some of the burden of relief must be borne by creditor governments, including the United States," Kissinger wrote. He even proceeded to plug an "innovative proposal" along these lines by "James Robinson of American Express," without mentioning that he was a client and had formulated the proposal with Kissinger's help.

A year later, Kissinger wrote a column about the request made by major Latin American nations for a summit to discuss "their increasingly intractable debt problems." Kissinger argued: "It is an invitation the incoming Bush Administration should accept." It was "fortunate," he added, that Salinas had come to power at this time; Mexico deserved to be the first breakthrough on the debt problem. Again, Kissinger insisted that the burden should be on governments, not the banks. "Most of them have gone to the limit of what profit-making organizations can absorb," he wrote. "They have been generally innovative in designing financing schemes."

Kissinger's opinions were sincere; he held most of them even before his paying clients began pushing these causes. In addition, many of his suggestions ran counter to what his banking clients advocated. But his analysis was probably affected by the strong opinions of Rockefeller, Butcher, Robinson, and Day. "His views have influenced my thinking," said Robinson, who was paying Kissinger's firm close to half a million dollars a year, "and I like to think my views have had a modest impact on his."[5]

An even clearer and more controversial case of intertwined interests involved China.

On the day after the Tiananmen Square crackdown in June 1989, ABC News sent a Minicam to Kent to interview its paid consultant live on the evening news. "What should America do, Dr. Kissinger?" asked Peter Jennings. Emphasizing the importance of maintaining good relations with China, Kissinger advised, "I wouldn't do any sanctions." Throughout the summer, he continued to advocate these positions during appearances on ABC, with which he had a $100,000-per-year contract.

In his subsequent newspaper columns, Kissinger likewise argued strongly against economic sanctions against China. Although he wrote that he was "shocked by the brutality," he argued that this was an internal matter, that Deng should be praised as a real reformer, and that the stakes in maintaining good relations with China "could not be higher." After warning against being pushed into hasty reactions, Kissinger concluded that "the drama in Beijing is for Americans a test of our political maturity."

Later that summer he went further in a column that denounced Congress for voting sanctions on China "in reaction to events entirely within its domestic jurisdiction." Although he again expressed dismay at the brutality, he added: "No government in the world would have tolerated having the main square of its capital occupied for eight weeks by tens of thousands of demonstrators." Whatever Americans feel personally about what had happened, he said, "China remains too important for America's national security to risk the relationship on the emotions of the moment."

At the time, although the viewers of ABC or the readers of the *Los Angeles Times/Washington Post* syndicate did not know it, Kissinger's business involvement with the Deng regime in China was extensive. He had helped Atlantic Richfield negotiate a deal to market oil it had discovered in China. He had worked with ITT, which wanted to hold a board meeting in Beijing, and found an agency in China to act as the host. He provided advice and introductions for H. J. Heinz executives who were trying to set up a baby-food facility there. He was then negotiating with the Chinese government on behalf of Freeport-McMoRan, which was trying (unsuccessfully) to work out an arrangement for developing major coal and copper mines there. American International Group, whose international advisory board he chaired, was seeking licenses in Shanghai, where it was also building an office tower.

In addition, Kissinger's relationship with the Deng regime was such that he could bring clients and guests to China and be met by the top leadership, a highly marketable asset. He had gone there in late 1987 with Robert Day of Trust Company of the West. Early in 1988, he had set up an impressive itinerary for a meeting of the Chase's international advisory committee in Beijing, during which he and David Rockefeller met with Deng. One indication of his own blurred line between professional and friendly favors was that he asked a local Beijing business leader to host a dinner for the Chase group. Kissinger was infuriated when the businessman sent him a bill for performing the service.

Kissinger's most ambitious scheme for dealing with China was a limited investment partnership he established called China Ventures. Officially launched in December 1988, six months before the Tiananmen crackdown, its purpose was to allow a group of top American corporations to invest in new enterprises and joint ventures in China.

Kissinger was chairman, chief executive, and general partner of China Ventures. For that, he was to receive management fees that could total more than $1 million per year plus 20 percent of any profits that the partnership made after paying an 8 percent return on investors' capital.

The list of corporations making investments was secret, but most were Kissinger clients. Among the big investors: American Express, Freeport-McMoRan, American International Group, Trust Company of the West, H. J. Heinz, and Coca-Cola. Their chairmen were on the group's investment committee along with former treasury secretary William Simon, who was a member of the board of Kissinger Associates.

The total pool they created for investments was $75 million. American Express, for example, committed $10 million to the investment kitty and in 1989 paid $200,000 to Kissinger in management fees. Freeport-McMoRan, whose commitment was $3.3 million, paid $66,667 in management fees.

China Ventures never got off the ground. First of all, it suffered from Kissinger's limitations in the field of venture capitalism, according to his friend Maurice Greenberg. Most of the proposed projects did not make much economic sense. In the case of the mining venture, which Freeport-McMoRan was interested in, the Chinese wanted to retain control. A plan to manufacture textiles near Shanghai, said Greenberg, "was really too small to make much sense, a waste of everybody's time."

More significantly, the events in Tiananmen Square, and the ensuing outcry for sanctions, caused the partners to put the venture on hold. No investments were consummated, the committed capital was never called, and by the end of 1990 the partnership was formally dissolved. All of the investment money was returned to the corporations that had chipped in.

Kissinger insisted that it is wrong to charge that he had any business conflicts in publicly urging the U.S. to maintain good relations with China "because the fact is China Ventures never made any investments." However, if the American reaction to Tiananmen had been mild, as Kissinger urged, China Ventures would have proceeded, and Kissinger would have made a significant amount of money. In addition, Kissinger represented quite a few other business interests in China, and he was profiting from his good relationship with the Deng regime. Thus he in fact had a financial stake in Deng's survival. Indeed, the potential conflict was discussed within his firm, and there was great relief that China Ventures folded so that it would no longer be a public issue.

John Fialka of the *Wall Street Journal* revealed the existence of China Ventures in September 1989, and Kissinger was asked about it when he appeared as a commentator on the "MacNeil/Lehrer News-Hour." It was outrageous, he replied, to insinuate that personal financial considerations had prompted him to defend the Chinese regime. Congressman Stephen Solarz, a liberal Democrat, came to Kissinger's defense, sort of. I am sure finances played no part, the congressman said; Dr. Kissinger has always defended oppressive dictatorships whether or not he had a financial stake in them. Winston Lord, Kissinger's longtime aide who was ambassador to China at the time, split with Kissinger over his defense of Deng. But like Solarz he said of Kissinger, "If he didn't have a cent of commercial interest in China, he would have taken the same position."

The *Los Angeles Times* and the *Washington Post* subsequently printed an "editor's note" explaining, in light of his defense of Deng in his columns, that Kissinger had a latent business venture in China. It did not mention that he also had five or six clients for whom he had been handling other projects in China.

In November, Kissinger decided to take a highly visible trip to China to signify that, at least in his personal view, the time for ostracism was over. It was his fifteenth visit, and like his very first, it prompted an odd little tango with Richard Nixon. Just before that first trip, in 1971, Nixon had suggested that Kissinger could meet with Chinese leaders somewhere other than in Beijing so that Nixon would have the honor of being the first one into the capital. (Kissinger ignored the request.) Now, in November 1989, Nixon was planning to go to Beijing and sought the drama of being the first high official there since Tiananmen. Kissinger, who wanted to keep his trip as far apart from Nixon's as possible, repeatedly asked Nixon's office when the trip was planned, but he never got an answer. To Kissinger's annoyance, he read in the press that Nixon was arriving in Beijing just a few days ahead of him.

Joining Kissinger on his trip was Maurice Greenberg, the chairman of American International Group and one of the principals in the now-dormant China Ventures. Also along was Judith Hope, a prominent Washington lawyer, fellow board member of the Union Pacific, and member of the governing board of Harvard.

AIG was at the time in the midst of constructing a major office complex in Shanghai, where the company's founder had begun selling life insurance policies seventy years earlier. Although Kissinger did not work on the Shanghai project, just his presence helped AIG in its dealings with Chinese officials, according to Greenberg. "Henry's image and influence in China is such that just by the fact that you're with him there's a nice rub-off effect," Greenberg later said. "He is revered in that country, which is why it is so nice to travel there with him."

In his toast at the dinner given for them by the foreign minister, Kissinger noted that "some in America feel that China ought to make the first move in the present situation, while some in China feel the

U.S. should move first." Since both have an interest in maintaining the relationship, he concluded, "both countries should take steps together to put relations onto a smoother path."

At a small luncheon given for Kissinger and his guests by Deng Xiaoping in the Great Hall of the People, Tiananmen Square was raised. Kissinger explained that American policy had to reflect both values and interests, but that he hoped relations would soon improve. Deng talked about the Cultural Revolution, when he was purged and radicals threw his son out of a window and crippled him. The point of Deng's tale, Kissinger surmised, was that he felt he had faced another incipient revolution that past June, and that, like Kissinger, he had been taught by life to value order and authority.

Kissinger and Greenberg also met with other top Chinese leaders, including Premier Li Peng and party secretary Zhao Ziyang. Ambassador Winston Lord, Kissinger's former aide, threw a gala reception at the American embassy that featured the political, cultural, and financial mandarins of Beijing. Whatever was happening to Chinese-American relations, Kissinger's ties were still intact.

When he returned to the U.S., Kissinger was invited for dinner at the White House, where he briefed Bush, Baker, and Scowcroft. The U.S. would have to make a gesture, he said, if relations were ever to be restored. He explained how sensitive the Chinese were about outsiders who attempted to meddle in their domestic affairs. The Chinese had broken with the Soviets over the same sort of issue thirty years earlier.

What Bush decided to do made Kissinger seem even more influential than he was: he dispatched Scowcroft and Eagleburger, Kissinger's two former business associates and NSC staff colleagues, on a secret trip to China to toast Deng and repair the breach. Kissinger did not know of the plans beforehand and was flabbergasted when he found out. He realized that it would look as if he had been an unseen force behind the decision.

Kissinger's intertwined web of commentary, inside influence, and business connections remained in good shape. In February 1990, he gave a dinner in his River House apartment for the Chinese ambassador to the U.S. Some of his business clients were there, along with such media celebrities as Barbara Walters. In his toast, Kissinger noted that Americans do not fully understand China's proud tradition of resisting foreign meddling. As the party was ending, the ambassador huddled with Kissinger in the entry hall and expressed his worry about a resolution favoring sanctions that was being debated in Congress. As one of his business associates watched, Kissinger pulled out his black leather notepad and jotted down, "Call Brent." There is no evidence that he ever did. But it was the type of little gesture that could impress almost anyone, from a Chinese ambassador to a corporate chief executive.

"If I had known then what I know now, I wouldn't have wanted him on that broadcast, plain and simple," Peter Jennings later said about his interview with Kissinger on the day after Tiananmen. On the other hand, Kissinger's overlapping business, journalistic, and government interests made him more informed as an analyst.[6]

As with so many of his actions while in government, the problem with these overlapping interests was exacerbated by Kissinger's penchant for secrecy. Sunlight can be a good disinfectant; if he had disclosed his business and client interests in the issues he commented on, readers and viewers could have weighed that as they saw fit. Even if he did not wish to reveal the names of specific clients, he could have at least noted in general terms, when relevant, that he had given advice to clients who had a stake in the subject at hand. Being open about potential conflicts would not magically have made them go away, but it would have been the best policy for earning trust—which is what good journalism and business relationships, like good government, are based upon.

THE GLITTERING TWILIGHT

By the early 1990s, Kissinger's aura and energy were undiminished, but his hope of reentering high office was fading. As he neared his seventieth birthday, his life settled into a swirl of dinner parties and business trips and weekends in the country, a glittering twilight in the vortex of Manhattan's nouvelle society. His life remained tightly scheduled, minute by minute from dawn until midnight, months in advance. He still radiated nervous energy and an edge of impatience as he bustled about with retainers in his wake. Too driven and too overexposed to gain the mantle of a wise elder statesman, he appeared to have found just the right balance of business activity, media stardom, and jet-set socializing to keep his adrenaline at the hum he enjoyed.

During some particularly busy weeks, especially in the fall and spring, the Kissingers would host two dinners at their apartment and one on Saturday at their country home in Kent. Their parties tended to come in three styles: those centered around their social friends in Manhattan's high-fashion crowd, those that featured dynamos of the media and entertainment worlds, and those honoring statesmen and public officials.

A social-oriented dinner would typically include Brooke Astor, Happy Rockefeller, Isaac Stern, and Abraham and Casey Ribicoff, as well as the staples of the *Women's Wear Daily* party crowd such as Ahmet Ertegun, Oscar de la Renta, Sid Bass, Grace Dudley, and Jane Wrightsman.

Parties that featured a guest of honor from the media or entertainment world, such as the one for Swifty Lazar or for Barbara Walters's birthday, tended to be bigger, perhaps thirty to forty guests rather than a dozen. Generally they included one or two top media moguls—William Paley of CBS when he was alive, then Laurence Tisch; Thomas Murphy of ABC; Tom Johnson of the *Los Angeles Times* then CNN; Katharine Graham of the *Washington Post*. From the movie world would be friends such as Kirk and Ann Douglas, the Czech director Milos Forman and the British director Peter Glenville. In addition, there would be a sprinkling of celebrity journalists such as David and Susan Brinkley, Tom and Meredith Brokaw, Abe and Shirley Rosenthal, Henry and Louise Grunwald, and William and Pat Buckley, along with a couple of less celebrated editors from the newsmagazines or newspapers.

Dinners designed around a government official were particularly prevalent in the early fall when ministers descended on Manhattan for the opening of the United Nations. Among those feted in the early 1990s were the presidents of Brazil and Mexico; the Chinese foreign minister; the prime ministers of Singapore, Jamaica, Malaysia, and France; the South Korean trade minister; a former French president; and the American vice president. The guest lists usually contained a few journalists, a mix of top business leaders—most notably Kissinger's clients—as well as other power players ranging from AFL-CIO president Lane Kirkland and his wife, Irena, to former commerce secretary Pete Peterson and his wife, Joan Ganz Cooney.

Each February, the Kissingers spent a few weeks in Acapulco. Usually they stayed with Loel Guinness, the dashing scion of the banking branch of that famous British family, and his wife, Gloria, a beauteous Mexican-born adventuress who had once been married to an Egyptian prince. On a mountain high above the city, the Guinness compound included a mansion flanked by thatched-roof villas for guests. Until he died in 1989, Guinness was the social focal point of the American and European jet-setters who descended on the resort every winter.

A somewhat more gaudy social companion of the Kissingers during their visits to Acapulco was Baron Enrico "Ricky" di Portanova, an eccentric international gadabout whose money—an inheritance that provided more than $2 million a month—came from his maternal grandfather, Houston oil billionaire Hugh Roy Cullen. His title and theatricality came from his father, an occasional actor who was a minor member of the Italian aristocracy. In Acapulco, di Portanova and his wife, the Baroness Alessandra (formerly Sandy Hovas of Houston), built a Moorish fantasy palace, with thirty-two bedrooms, three swimming pools, two indoor waterfalls (one eighty feet high), and life-size plaster camels on the roof. At one of the many dinners in his honor there, Kissinger toasted "this amazing temple which centuries from now will have archaeologists in dispute over what strange religion was once practiced here."

At the other extreme in matters of style and taste was the British-born director Peter Glenville, who lived in Mexico and frequently came to visit the Kissingers in Acapulco. A man of refined sensibilities and dry British humor, Glenville was the director of such movies as *Becket* and *The Comedians* as well as dozens of plays in London and New York. Even when Kissinger was on vacation, Glenville recalled, "the huge Rolls-Royce engine that is incessantly humming along inside him is truly extraordinary. He will go to a party at the di Portanovas, come home at midnight, and start writing an article."

Every summer the Kissingers would spend all of August in Kent. Though not an adroit gardener, Kissinger took great interest in directing the landscaping. In particular, he continued to push back the forest and undergrowth to create open fields and vistas to the rock bluffs and lake on his property. (The de la Rentas and Erteguns gave Nancy a tractor one year as a birthday present.) With his Labrador retriever Amelia, bought by Nancy after Tyler died in 1989, he would take walks in the woods.

Most Christmas holidays were spent at a house party given by Annette and Oscar de la Renta at their three-acre beachfront estate in Santo Domingo, which included nine cottages as well as a rambling main house. Besides the Kissingers, the guests usually included Sid and Mercedes Bass, the Agnellis, Grace Dudley, Brooke Astor, Swifty and Mary Lazar, and John Richardson.

Kissinger remained close to his two children. Elizabeth went to medical school in Cambridge and became a doctor in the Boston area. David, who grew to look like his father, became a lawyer at a major Manhattan firm. But he then decided, to the partly feigned horror of his father, to abandon the bar and become a journalist. He became the top Los Angeles correspondent for *Variety*, the journal of the entertainment business, and later tried his hand as a television executive.

Kissinger's fanaticism for football, both American-style and soccer, grew over the years. Sitting with a few friends in front of the television each Sunday, he would dissect each team's strategies and predict the plays. In 1990, the boy who had once been barred from soccer matches in his hometown of Fürth was treated as a celebrity at the World Cup soccer games in Rome. "I have received more attention here at the World Cup games than in the non-soccer activity in which I've been engaged," he told a press conference. After helping to arrange for the U.S. to be selected as the host for the 1994 World Cup, he served as an honorary leader of the committee chosen to oversee those games. Bringing soccer to America, he said, was "sort of a missionary enterprise."[7]

Although not a clubby person, Kissinger liked to participate in a variety of groups that exuded power and prestige, the more exclusive and secret the better. On the scale of frivolous to ponderous, these ranged from the Bohemian Grove to the Bilderberg Group, and he had the unique distinction in May 1990 of being a featured speaker at the former's East Coast dinner and at the annual meeting of the latter the same week.

The Bohemian Grove is a secretive, all-male club whose main activity is an annual summer retreat in a rustic yet comfortable campground amid the redwoods north of San Francisco. There, major American tycoons and power brokers amuse themselves by singing silly songs, performing skits, listening to lectures, drinking, and relieving themselves on tree trunks. Among the members are four presidents: Bush, Reagan, Ford, and Nixon. Members and their guests bunk in a hundred or so camps, which are like clubs within the club. Kissinger belonged to Mandalay, which also boasted Ford, George Shultz, Nicholas Brady, Thomas Watson, Jr., and other titans of industry.

Kissinger was famous for performing in the skits. In 1988, he played the wolf in a Peter and the Wolf parody. The following year, a man appeared in the play known as the Low Jinks wearing a rubber Kissinger mask and speaking with an uncanny approximation of Kissinger's voice. Then he peeled off the mask, revealing himself to be, in fact, Kissinger. "I am here because I have always been convinced that the Low Jinks is the ultimate aphrodisiac," he rumbled. That year he was also remembered for the very un-Bohemian act of cutting in line at the telephones and for the ultra-Bohemian act of bringing the prime minister of France, Michel Rocard, as his guest.

The Bilderberg Group, almost as secretive, is as serious as the Bohemian Grove is sophomoric. With the goal of promoting better relations between European and American leaders, it was founded in the mid-1950s by Prince Bernhard of the Netherlands, the high-minded American statesman George Ball, a Polish resistance fighter named Joseph Retinger, and Burroughs Corporation president John Coleman. Its first session was held at the Hotel Bilderberg in Oosterbeek, Holland. Each year since, it has brought together eighty or so top leaders of Atlantic Alliance nations along with captains of industry for a well-guarded three-day conclave.

The May 1990 meeting, at an estate on Long Island, was one of the few to be held in the U.S. Kissinger was a featured speaker, and he helped arrange an invitation for Dan Quayle. The vice president, however, did not quite have a feel for what the group was all about, and organizers discovered to their chagrin that he was planning to swoop in for a brief appearance with a retinue of aides, advisers, and handlers. Kissinger, in consultation with David Rockefeller, was delegated to explain to Quayle that he should leave his entourage behind.[8]

When Kissinger sat down with Robert Day each year to budget his personal finances, they would make the assumption that the amount he would make from speaking fees would gradually decline. After all, now that he had been out of power for fifteen or so years, his fame and drawing power would surely diminish. But even into the 1990s, this never occurred. As if by magical suspension, his celebrity remained as high as ever, far above that of almost any other world figure. It is hard to hark back to a comparable case of a secretary of state's maintaining such an aura after leaving office—perhaps Dean Acheson, George Marshall, or Henry Stimson, though they maintained a more discreet style; maybe not since Martin Van Buren, the last secretary to become president.

How did Kissinger keep his celebrity so high for so long? Mainly by working at it. Like a trouper to the limelight, he was drawn to the television camera, and news producers found him an irresistible jewel for their shows. When Mikhail Gorbachev visited America at the end of 1988, Kissinger in a two-day period appeared on CNN twice, the "MacNeil/Lehrer NewsHour," ABC's "Good Morning America," the "CBS Evening News," the CBS late-news wrap-up, and the "CBS Morning News."

He even agreed to do the weather reports one day in 1991 for the CBS morning show, having confided to anchor Paula Zahn that prognosticating about meteorological rather than geopolitical trends was a secret ambition. "If you live anywhere between Egypt, Pennsylvania, and Lebanon, New Hampshire, I perceive peaceful weather for you," he intoned, and then went on to give the forecast for other American cities with foreign names while pointing in the wrong directions (the maps on weather shows appear on home screens through electronic wizardry but are not visible in the studio). The regular forecaster, Mark McEwan, interjected jokes about how he feared that Kissinger would take his job.

In working to maintain his image, Kissinger continued to be obsessed with converting his enemies, just as he had been ever since he met with antiwar protesters in the Nixon White House. He was drawn to his critics with a mixture of insecurity and arrogance that compelled him to explain himself and seek their approval. After Kissinger came out in favor of a campaign to block the construction of a large office complex on Manhattan's Coliseum Circle, he ran into the developer, Mortimer Zuckerman, and told him, "You know, I'm only doing this to appease my liberal friends."

Likewise, when journalist Ken Auletta wrote an unflattering account of Peter Peterson's role in the demise of Lehman Brothers, Kissinger commiserated with his old cabinet colleague about how unfair the attack was; Auletta got a letter from Kissinger praising his reporting. He also complimented editor Harold Evans on his book about his struggles with the newspaper magnate Rupert Murdoch, then later told Murdoch that he disagreed with the book's premise. Some of these stories may be exaggerated in the retelling, but there were so many of them precisely because Kissinger never realized how the retelling process worked.[9]

He even made a stab at winning over Garry Trudeau, the Doonesbury cartoonist who had lampooned Kissinger with lapidary precision over the years. When he read in a Liz Smith column that Trudeau and his wife, Jane Pauley, had considered but then rejected the name Tyler for their new son because it was also the name of Kissinger's dog, he wrote Pauley a letter signed by Tyler. "It is not that I fail to understand long-lived animosities," the letter said. "I still cannot pass the house of Sidney the poodle who bit me ten years ago without raising my hackles and peeing against his door. On the other hand, he had bitten me, and I do not recall ever having shown any hostility towards your husband."

Trudeau responded in a "Dear Mr. Kissinger" letter, referring to the missive purportedly written by Tyler the dog. "I was, in fact, delighted that Tyler was so named, as it undercut my wife's position that Tyler was a name 'not fit for a dog.' As it turned out, that position prevailed: our new son has the serviceable, if less elegant, name of

Thomas, in honor of a valued plumber we know who works on weekends. Tell your dog not to be so defensive."[10]

This unabated desire to court approval from a wide swath of
people, a common enough human trait but one that was particularly
pronounced in Kissinger, indicated to friends that the attainment of
great power and wealth had not dispelled the sense of vulnerability
that dwelled inside the refugee from Fürth. So, too, did his sensitivity
to attack, his obsession with his enemies, his paranoia about his
friends. For all of his sense of grandeur, there was still a trace of a
solicitous and even unassuming nature when he was around people
whose social respect he sought.

"He has always had a harder time feeling totally secure on a
human level than he has on an intellectual one," said Peter Glenville,
the British director who was Kissinger's occasional traveling companion. "The word *insecure* is usually a put-down, but I mean it as a
compliment when I say of Henry that deep down there are parts of
him that are still insecure after all of these years. There is a personal
vulnerability there, as well as a great strength of character."[11]

If there was anything missing from Kissinger's twilight in the early
1990s, it was that, both socially and professionally, his world was now
filled with more show than substance. Every now and then, in a humorous pang of self-reflection, he would refer to his new social circle
as "the bratty rich." With most of these friends, he lacked a soulful or
intellectual connection, and their frivolity remained somewhat alien.
Still, the parties were glamorous and the trips were grand and the
unchallenging camaraderie was comforting.

Likewise, his business success lacked some of the satisfaction to
be found in more substantive statecraft; making Indonesia safe for
Freeport-McMoRan was not quite as fulfilling as making the world
safe for China. Still, it allowed him to fly the globe in private planes
playing diplomat and foreign affairs adviser, the things he liked to do
best.

As a young man, Kissinger had conquered the world of academia.
Then came his triumphs in the world of Washington and foreign
affairs, then media stardom and celebrity, then big business and jet-
set society. In each of these fields—from the exalted realms of global
diplomacy to the petty precincts of the gossip columns—his mixture
of brilliance and abrasiveness, ego and insecurity, charm and furtiveness, humor and ambition had made him, for better and for worse,
one of the premier stars of his era.

•

In February 1991, Paula Kissinger—the cattle trader's daughter from Leutershausen who had married a schoolmaster, saved her family from the Nazis, and enjoyed from her apartment in Washington Heights every mother's dream of having a son become so famous that she no longer had to brag about him—turned ninety years old. As usual, she was spending the winter in Puerto Rico in a modest seaside apartment that she had first started renting with her husband years earlier.

She was as spry, witty, wise, unpretentious, and kind as ever. Also as healthy. Her apartment was on the tenth floor, and that month the elevator broke for a few days. She was offered a more convenient apartment, but did not want to move. Each day, she would walk up and down the ten flights of steps. Her only concession to age was to stop every three floors or so for a short rest; friends in the building would come out and give her a cup of tea when they saw her catching her breath.

The Saturday night of her birthday, one of Walter Kissinger's sons —a teacher, like so many of his forefathers had been—flew in from California to visit. He came to pick her up and brought her to the Caribe Hilton where he was staying. When she got to the room, there to her surprise were her sons, Henry and Walter, and the rest of her family.

At the dinner that night, Henry Kissinger spoke of his mother's strength. Because of her indomitable nature, he said, the family had escaped Nazi Germany. Because of it, they had been able to live comfortably after they arrived in America, and her sons were able to go to college. "In times of adversity," he said, "you were the one who held us together through your courage and spirit and devotion. Everything I have achieved, that our family has achieved, is due to you."

Paula Kissinger paused for a moment and took in the scene. Then she said, in her better-than-perfect English, "It was worth to have lived a life for." [12]

THIRTY-FOUR

LEGACY

Policy and Personality

The reaction against Metternich's smug self-satisfaction and rigid conservatism has tended . . . to take the form of denying the reality of his accomplishments.—KISSINGER, A WORLD RESTORED, 1957

Napoleon once said of Metternich that he confused policy with intrigue. Kissinger was a master at both, and as with Metternich, his policies reflected the complexities of his personality.

Kissinger's most salient trait, the one that underlay both his personality and his policies, was an intellectual brilliance that even his most ardent critics concede. In casual conversations or at formal meetings, he was able to weave together nuances and insights in a manner that brought discussions to a higher plane. As Zhou Enlai had said after exploring the world balance with him during their first meeting in Beijing in 1971, "You are a very brilliant man, Dr. Kissinger."

At the core of his brilliance was an ability to see the relationships between different events and to conceptualize patterns. Like a spider in its web, he sensed, sometimes too acutely, how an action in one corner of the world would reverberate in another, how the application of power in one place would ripple elsewhere.

In probing ideas, he was intellectually honest, surprisingly so to those who considered him otherwise deceitful. He surrounded himself with bright people of different philosophic hues, challenged them relentlessly, and was in turn willing to be challenged by them.

Critics contended that Kissinger's brilliance was mainly as a tactician rather than as a strategist. In other words, he was clever at plotting the steps necessary to accomplish a mission, but he did not have the vision to formulate grand goals. Rather than a Bismarck, Leslie Gelb wrote in 1976, he was a "Don Juan of international diplomacy, romancing and blundering his way through perilous affairs, to win out in the end."

In fact, Kissinger was both a strategist and a tactician. One of the strengths of his mind was its ability to engage on disparate levels, from the grand to the petty. In his writings, he mixed broad-brush maxims with detailed drypoints of small incidents. In his daily work, he would worry about sweeping historic forces at the same time as he fretted about the most trivial of bureaucratic slights. And he could envision overarching geostrategic frameworks—for the Middle East, for détente, for the Soviet-Chinese-American triangular relationship—while also tending to the countless tiny tactical bargaining levers he hoped to employ.[1]

Kissinger's European-style philosophy of international affairs—a power-oriented realism or realpolitik—was rooted in his background. Because he was a product of the Weimar Republic and a victim of the Nazis' ideological fervor, a yearning for stability and order was bred into his character. He grew up in an environment where trust was not readily instilled and where virtue was not its own reward, so he came naturally to the pessimistic view of human nature that underlies realpolitik. He had "the brooding melancholy of a man who has experienced tragedy as a child," said his old Harvard colleague Stanley Hoffmann. The ghost of Spengler walked at his side.

He became suspicious, prone to manipulating people's antagonisms more readily than appealing to their goodness. As he wrote in a 1945 letter describing concentration camp survivors: "They have seen men from the most evil side, who can blame them for being suspicious?" Power rather than righteousness, he came to believe, determined the world order. Nations that acted based on national interests were less dangerous than those that crusaded on the basis of ideology or their own perception of moral justice. Among the lessons he extracted from the holocaust was, as he wrote in a letter from Germany right after the war, that sometimes "one could only survive through lies" and that "weakness [was] synonymous with death."[2]

When Kissinger visited the Kremlin just before the 1972 summit there, Brezhnev showed him a row of urns in the Great Hall, all polished and carefully covered. The shrouds would be removed, Brezhnev said, just before Nixon's arrival, so the urns would be spotless. Kissinger later said that it was a sign of the deep insecurity that gnawed at the Russian soul. "But never forget," he added, "that feelings of insecurity can lead to bluster and arrogance."[3]

There was, as Kissinger would admit, an insecurity that gnawed at his own soul, and also a well-known streak of arrogance—the legacy, perhaps, of a childhood spent feeling both smarter and more beleaguered than those around him. Intellectually, he was self-assured: he enjoyed debating ideas and having his theories honestly challenged. But on a personal level, he brooded about adversaries real and imagined. His sensitivity to slights verged on paranoia, and his dealings with colleagues tended to be conspiratorial, attitudes reinforced by his odd alliance with Richard Nixon.

Kissinger's tendency to be secretive, even deceitful, was partly a reflection of this insecurity and nervousness. But it was also linked to the policies he pursued. Diplomacy based on moral idealism or international law is easy to wage openly; but a realist approach involving ambiguous compromises and power ploys lends itself to covert acts and deception, since it is likely to arouse popular disapproval if publicly articulated. Because Kissinger harbored the dark suspicion that many of his cold calculations of national security interests would not command popular or congressional support, he engaged in a foreign policy based on stealth and surprise. "If he were ten percent less brilliant and ten percent more honest, he would be a great man," Nahum Goldmann, an American Jewish leader and longtime friend of the Kissinger family, once said.

Kissinger's secretiveness, of course, was also largely due to Nixon's character and desires. Kissinger was reflecting—as well as reinforcing—the darker aspects of his patron the president. Both relished dramatic surprises, such as the announcement of the China opening; both were eager to control events and garner glory, rather than share responsibility; and both were basically distrustful, especially of the bureaucracy. So they preferred to plot moves in private and were inordinately fearful of leaks.

Kissinger's compulsion to cut his colleagues out of the action was motivated partly by vanity. But like much of his vanity, it had a basis in reality. Kissinger believed, with some justification, that in order to establish subtle linkages and calibrate delicate balances, he had to keep tight control over various strands of policy through back-channel machinations. In addition, he felt that he could better negotiate an opening to China if he kept the State Department in the dark, that he could more easily reach a settlement in Vietnam if he kept President

Thieu uninformed, and that he could piece together an arms control accord if he circumvented Gerard Smith and his SALT experts.

In these and countless other cases, Kissinger achieved some remarkable successes. But he also sowed the seeds of some destructive resentments. His furtive methods, though often dazzlingly successful in the short run, contributed to a Nixonian atmosphere of mistrust that undermined bureaucratic support and resulted in an unnecessary backlash against his policies.

Another reflection of Kissinger's combination of personal insecurity and intellectual ego was his compulsion to convert his critics and his conviction that he could do so. He became a masterly and rather indiscriminate charmer, one who knew how to appeal to people's vanity, stroke their egos, play them off against rivals, and share confidential put-downs of mutual friends.

Particularly striking was how wide he cast his net in his quest for approval: from Barry Goldwater to J. William Fulbright, Norman Mailer to William F. Buckley, H. R. Haldeman to Morton Halperin. "It takes an incredible combination of vanity and insecurity to cause someone to try to seduce everybody," said Polly Kraft, who had watched Kissinger work on her husband, Joseph, over the years.[4]

This trait reflected, in Arthur Schlesinger's words, "the soul of a refugee," and Diane Sawyer similarly called it "a typical immigrant's need to ingratiate himself." A simpler explanation is that Kissinger acted this way for the same reason that, to one degree or another, most people do: a desire to be liked and win approval. Naturally thin-skinned, he felt particularly vulnerable and besieged once he entered government. His look of worried sadness was animated by eyes that appeared to be eager for approval.

Kissinger's charm usually succeeded, for he was an engaging and intelligent and witty man. But it had a dark side: by trying to seduce a broad spectrum of people, he inevitably developed a reputation for duplicity. "Henry enjoys the complexity of deviousness," said James Schlesinger. "Other people when they lie look ashamed. Henry does it with style, as if it were an arabesque."

Kissinger once told Averell Harriman that, if Harriman refrained from attacking Nixon, he might be asked to play a role in the administration. Morton Halperin, who heard the conversation, asked if that was truly a possibility. "Henry replied that he hadn't really thought about it," Halperin recalled. "In deciding whether to say something, truth had little bearing."[5]

Kissinger's mixture of charm and seduction, flattery and duplicity, became part of his diplomacy. In the Middle East, for example, American policy was built around a process—step-by-step shuttle diplomacy—which in turn was built around Kissinger's personality. In Israel and Egypt, and even in Syria and Saudi Arabia, Kissinger was able to charm national leaders by flattering them, pretending to conspire with them, and making nasty comments about their adversaries.

At an emotional press conference in Salzburg in 1974, when he brooded about resigning because of stories about the wiretaps, Kissinger became unusually maudlin. He had been identified, he said, as someone who cared more about stabilizing the balance of power than about moral issues. "I would rather like to think," he added, "that when the record is written, one may remember that perhaps some lives were saved and perhaps some mothers can rest more at ease. But I leave that to history."

This historical judgment is unlikely ever to be a simple one. The structure of peace that Kissinger designed places him with Henry Stimson, George Marshall, and Dean Acheson atop the pantheon of modern American statesmen. In addition, he was the foremost American negotiator of this century and, along with George Kennan, the most influential foreign policy intellectual.

But Kissinger never had an instinctive feel for American values and mores, such as the emphasis that a Stimson would place on honor over intrigue or on idealism over national interests. Nor did he have an appreciation of the strengths to be derived from the healthy raucousness of American politics or from open decision-making in a democratic society. "Henry is a balance-of-power thinker," said Lawrence Eagleburger, one of his closest colleagues. "He deeply believes in stability. These kind of objectives are antithetical to the American experience. Americans tend to want to pursue a set of moral principles. Henry does not have an intrinsic feel for the American political system, and he does not start with the same basic values and assumptions."[6]

Kissinger came to power at a perilous moment for the foreign policy of his adoptive nation. America's isolationist reflexes were twitching as a result of its ill-conceived involvement in Vietnam. Congress and the public were in no mood to pay for new weapons or to engage the Soviets in marginal confrontations in the third world.

By ushering in an era of détente, Kissinger helped to assure that the competition with the Soviets would be more manageable and the showdowns less dangerous. And by devising a web of linkages, he provided the U.S. with some diplomatic leverage to compensate for its loss of military resolve. Looking back twenty years later, he could claim with some justification that "we perhaps deserve some credit for holding together the sinews of America at a time of fundamental collapse."[7]

Some of the initiatives that he pursued along the way were enlightened and imaginative, others impulsively brutal and blunt. Some were clever, others too clever by half. As the only European-style realist ever to guide U.S. foreign policy, a power practitioner unencumbered by the sentimental idealism that suffuses American history, he seemed painfully amoral at times. But he was able to take a clear-eyed approach to the creation of a new global balance, one that helped to preserve American influence in the post-Vietnam era and eventually contributed to the end of the cold war.

Although he was too likely to see a Moscow-inspired threat in every regional crisis, Kissinger was correct in resisting the dovish and isolationist forces of the period that sought to abandon the competition with the Soviets. And he was equally correct in resisting the hawkish and neoconservative pressure to abandon cooperation with the Soviets. As Kennan had pointed out in the late 1940s—and Kissinger had reiterated in the early 1970s—the rulers in the Kremlin could prop up their system only by expanding their empire or by invoking foreign threats. If denied these opportunities, the Soviet system would eventually disintegrate, as it did.

In addition, Kissinger and Nixon turned the world's bipolar tug-of-war into a three-dimensional chess game that provided the U.S. with more opportunities for creative diplomacy. The new relationship with China, which previous presidents had barely contemplated, gave both of the world's communist giants an incentive to maintain better relations with the U.S. than they had with one another.

It added up to a fundamental change in America's postwar foreign policy: for the first time since the Potsdam Conference of 1945, cooperation as well as competition with both Moscow and Beijing could be part of a great-power strategy of balance. That alone was a triumph of hard-edged realism worthy of a Metternich.

This new framework incorporated a recognition of America's limits with a belief that the nation still had a major role to play in resisting the spread of Soviet influence. Less ardently anti-Soviet than his conservative critics desired, and more interventionist than most liberals could abide, Kissinger was able to create an American role that kept the pendulum from careening too rapidly in one direction or the other after Vietnam.

The main lines of this policy were followed for the next two decades: a blend of containment and cooperation with Moscow that allowed the internal contradictions of the Soviet system to play out; a step-by-step process in the Middle East that kept the U.S. the dominant player in the region; and a realistic attitude toward China that created a global balance that was more stable and gave Washington more leverage. When the cold war ended, this dose of realism would help the U.S. operate in a new global environment based on multiple power centers and balances.[8]

But Kissinger's power-oriented realism and focus on national interests faltered because it was too dismissive of the role of morality. The secret bombing and then invasion of Cambodia, the Christmas bombing of Hanoi, the destabilization of Chile—these and other brutal actions betrayed a callous attitude toward what Americans like to believe is the historic foundation of their foreign policy: a respect for human rights, international law, democracy, and other idealistic values. The setbacks Kissinger encountered as a statesman, and the antagonism he engendered as a person, stemmed from the perceived amorality of his geopolitical calculations.

Kissinger's approach led to a backlash against détente; the national mood swung toward both the moralism of Jimmy Carter and the ideological fervor of Ronald Reagan. As a result, not unlike Metternich, Kissinger's legacy turned out to be one of brilliance more than solidity, of masterful structures built of bricks that were made without straw.

To Kissinger, an emphasis on realism and national interests—even though it might seem callous in its execution—was not a rejection of moral values. Rather, he saw it as the best way to pursue the stable world order that he believed was the ultimate moral imperative, especially in a nuclear age.

He tried to explain this relationship between realism and morality at a Paris gathering of Nobel Prize laureates in 1988. After being attacked in a closed-door session for his power-oriented and amoral approach—Argentine Adolfo Perez Esquivel, a former Peace Prize winner, accused him of "genocide and collective massacre"—Kissinger began to talk about his childhood. The room hushed.

More than a dozen of his relatives had been killed in the holocaust, he said, so he knew something of the nature of genocide. It was easy for human rights crusaders and peace activists to insist on perfection in this world. But the policymaker who has to deal with reality learns to seek the best that can be achieved rather than the best that can be imagined. It would be wonderful to banish the role of military power from world affairs, but the world is not perfect, as he had learned as a child. Those with true responsibility for peace, unlike those on the sidelines, cannot afford pure idealism. They must have the courage to deal with ambiguities and accommodations, to realize that great goals can be achieved only in imperfect steps. No side has a monopoly on morality.[9]

But Kissinger's realpolitik was ill-suited to an open and democratic society, where it is difficult to invoke distant ends to justify unpalatable means. A belief that America's actions are moral and noble is necessary to rally a naturally isolationist people. Whether marching off to war or rousing itself to counter the spread of communism, America draws its motivation from a desire to defend its values—rather than from a cold calculation of its geopolitical interests. Even when an American involvement is partly based on economic self-interest, such as the Persian Gulf War of 1991, the more high-minded goals are the ones that tend to be publicly emphasized.[10]

Kissinger considered this idealistic aspect of the American spirit a weakness in terms of sustaining policies in a messy world. To some extent he was right—but it was also a source of strength. The greatest triumph of political influence in the modern age was that of democratic capitalism over communism in the early 1990s. This occurred partly because Kissinger and others helped to create a new global balance during the 1970s, one that preserved American influence in the post-Vietnam era. But the main reason that the United States triumphed in the cold war was not because it won a competition for military power and influence. It was because the values offered by its system—among them a foreign policy that could draw its strength from the ideals of its people—eventually proved more attractive.

Acknowledgments

First, Strobe Talbott. He persuaded me to undertake this endeavor, infused it with his enthusiasm each step of the way, talked me through its themes, showered me with memos containing nuggets and insights, sharply edited my first draft, and—above all—provided in both his work and his life the model of honest inquiry that any journalist or historian should emulate.

The chance to work with Strobe was only one of the many joys of being at *Time* magazine, a stimulating, fun, and friendly place to share a curiosity about the world. Managing Editor Henry Muller was generous and understanding about this project as well as incisive in his suggestions. In addition, I'd like to thank those at the magazine who read parts of the manuscript, served as reliable sounding boards, or helped in other ways, among them: Richard Duncan, John Stacks, James Kelly, Margaret Carlson, Hugh Sidey, Michael Kramer, Richard Stengel, and Elliot Ravetz.

At Simon & Schuster, Alice Mayhew was, once again, a committed and intellectually demanding editor who was intensely involved in every aspect of this book, from concepts to commas. I am also grateful to her assistant, Ari Hoogenboom, for his sharp editorial eye and ability to keep matters organized, and to publisher Jack McKeown for his knowledgeable support of this project. From the inception of this book until its completion, Richard Snyder provided professional and personal guidance, sharply focused insights as well as great kindness. My agent, Amanda Urban, was always both enthusiastic and wise.

I am indebted to scores of people for providing insights, swapping Kissinger tales, and spending hours allowing me to sound out my ideas. But I particularly want to thank those who read parts of my early drafts, among them: Strobe Talbott, Richard Holbrooke, Richard Stengel, James Kelly, John Lewis Gaddis, Fareed Zakaria, Mortimer Zuckerman, Jonathan Alter, and Marilyn Berger.

My father and stepmother, Irwin and Julanne Isaacson, also read the entire manuscript and made copious comments and corrections. Their intelligence and love have always seemed boundless to me.

My most important reader, critic, and supporter was my wife, Cathy. Gently and lovingly, she was able to reinforce my judgments while reining in some of my excesses, encourage my convictions while attempting to prick any pretensions, and keep me honest to my beliefs. She was, and is, the truest touchstone of good sense and sensibility I can imagine; every day in every way, my debt to her is incalculable.

I would also like to thank my daughter for her, well . . . it would be stretching the truth to laud her patience, for she has all of the delightfully demanding nature that comes with being a two-year-old. In fact, to be honest, she was quite a distraction, whether she was seducing me from this desk or sitting on my lap pecking away at these keys. But as distractions go, she was the most magical one imaginable, and she made it all worthwhile. And so, to paraphrase P. G. Wodehouse, I would like to dedicate this book to Betsy Isaacson, without whose invaluable help it would have been finished in half the time.

Notes

Unless otherwise noted, all presidential statements are in the Public Papers of the President, and diplomatic statements are in the *Department of State Bulletin*. Telephone transcripts, memos of conversation, and other documents that are cited but not further sourced were provided to the author. Photocopies of all of the Kissinger letters cited are in the author's possession.

ABBREVIATIONS
LAT = *Los Angeles Times*
NPP = Nixon Presidential Papers, National Archives, Alexandria, Virginia
NYT = *New York Times*
WHSF = White House Special Files
WHY = *White House Years* by Henry Kissinger
WP = *Washington Post*
YOU = *Years of Upheaval* by Henry Kissinger

INTRODUCTION

1. Henry Kissinger, "Impressions of Germany," an unpublished story written as a letter to his parents in 1945, courtesy of Paula Kissinger.
2. Gallup poll, *WP*, Dec. 30, 1973; Valeriani, *Travels With Henry*, 33.
3. Robert Manning, Jan. 23, 1990.

ONE: FÜRTH

1. Paula Kissinger, May 8 and May 16, 1988; Kissinger family tree, an unpublished paper by Martin Kissinger; local birth records, vicar's office of the Rodelsee church.

2. *Encyclopedia Judaica,* passim; Martin Kissinger paper.

3. Henry Kissinger, Dec. 7, 1988; Lina Rau Schubach, Dec. 8, 1988.

4. Paula Kissinger, Dec. 17, 1988; Arno Kissinger (Louis's brother), Jan. 4, 1989.

5. Paula Kissinger, May 8, 1988; letter from Louis Kissinger to Lloyd Shearer, Sept. 22, 1971, courtesy of Shearer; Tzipora Jochsberger, Dec. 6, 1988; Mazlish, *Kissinger,* 21–22; Blumenfeld, *Henry Kissinger,* 18–33.

6. Letters of Louis Kissinger; Paula Kissinger, May 8, 1988; Jack Heiman, Dec. 5, 1988; Jerry Bechhofer, Dec. 2, 1988.

7. Paula Kissinger, May 8 and Dec. 17, 1988; Jack Heiman, Dec. 5, 1988; Henry Kissinger, Dec. 19, 1988; "From Fürth to the White House Basement," *Time,* Feb. 14, 1969; Mazlish, *Kissinger,* 26–27.

8. Paula Kissinger, Dec. 10 and Dec. 17, 1988. Some accounts say that his name was originally Alfred Heinz Kissinger. According to Kissinger, his mother, and his birth records, this is not correct.

9. Paula Kissinger, May 8, 1988; Walter Kissinger, Mar. 17, 1988; Henry Kissinger, Dec. 7, 1988; Harold Reissner, Nov. 30, 1988.

10. Blumenfeld, *Henry Kissinger,* 18–34; Paul Stiefel, Dec. 6, 1988; Henry Gitterman, Dec. 5, 1988; Jerry Bechhofer, Dec. 2, 1988.

11. Jack Heiman, Dec. 5, 1988; Paul Stiefel, Dec. 6, 1988; Henry Kissinger, Dec. 19, 1988.

12. Walter Kissinger, Mar. 17, 1988; Tziporah Jochsberger, Dec. 6, 1988; Paula Kissinger, May 8, 1988.

13. Walter Kissinger, Mar. 17, 1988; Paul Stiefel, Dec. 6, 1988; Jack Heiman, Dec. 5, 1988; Kalb and Kalb, *Kissinger,* 32.

14. Paula Kissinger, May 8, 1988; Henry Kissinger, Nov. 24, 1987. Other accounts say that Kissinger was expelled from the *Gymnasium* with Jews of his age; in fact, neither of the Kissinger boys was ever allowed to enroll in the *Gymnasium,* despite their parents' hopes.

15. Henry Kissinger, Dec. 19, 1988; Tzipora Jochsberger, Dec. 6, 1988.

16. "Kissinger's Boyhood Buddy," *Hadassah* magazine, Mar. 1974, 35; Menachem (Heinz) Lion, May 10, 1988; Heinz Lion changed his name to Menachem when he moved to Israel. His name is pronounced "Leon" and in some sources is incorrectly spelled that way. Kalb and Kalb, *Kissinger,* 34.

17. Jack Heiman, Dec. 5, 1988; Blumenfeld, *Henry Kissinger,* 18–33.

18. Lina Rau Schubach, Dec. 8, 1988; Tzipora Hilda Jochsberger, Dec. 6, 1988; Paula Kissinger, May 8, 1988; Henry Kissinger, Dec. 19, 1988.

19. Jack Heiman, Dec. 5, 1988; Menachem Lion, May 10, 1988; Jerry Bechhofer, Dec. 2, 1988; Lina Rau Schubach, Dec. 8, 1988; Walter Kissinger, May 8, 1988. Blumenfeld, *Henry Kissinger,* 18–33; Kalb and Kalb, *Kissinger,* 33.

20. Paula Kissinger, May 8, 1988; Henry Kissinger, Dec. 7, 1988.

21. Paula Kissinger, May 8, 1988.

22. "America's Clausewitz was banned from Fürth's city schools," *Fürther Nachrichten,* Oct. 15, 1958; Bernard Law Collier, "The Road to Peking," *NYT Magazine,* Nov. 14, 1971. As noted in *Kissinger* by Kalb and Kalb, p. 35: "Almost word for word, he has relayed the same disclaimers to other interviewers."

23. Lina Rau Schubach, Dec. 8, 1988; Paula Kissinger, May 8, 1988; Hunebelle, *Dear Henry,* 36–37.

24. Menachem Lion, May 10, 1988.

25. Blumenfeld, *Henry Kissinger,* 35–43.

26. Henry Kissinger, Dec. 7, 1988; Paula Kissinger, Dec. 17, 1988.

27. Interview with Menachem (Heinz) Lion, May 10, 1988; "Impressions of Germany," an unpublished letter home by Kissinger, 1945; Paula Kissinger, May 8, 1988.

28. *NYT,* Dec. 16, 1975; *WP,* Dec. 16, 1975; Paula Kissinger, May 8, 1988.

29. Paula Kissinger, May 8, 1988; Henry Kissinger, Dec. 7, 1988; Kissinger family tree, an unpublished paper by Martin Kissinger; Lina Rau Schubach, Dec. 8, 1988.

30. Henry Kissinger, Dec. 7, 1988; "Kissinger: Action Biography," reported by Howard K. Smith and Ted Koppel, ABC-TV, June 14, 1974.

31. Fritz Kraemer, May 14, 1988. Kraemer, who tends to repeat the same pronouncements almost verbatim years apart, gave a similar assessment to the *New York Post,* June 3, 1974.

32. Kissinger's childhood has produced a spate of clinical and psychoanalytic portraits—based on few biographical facts—that probe Kissinger's complexity by invoking Freudian concepts. Mazlish, *Kissinger;* and Dana Ward, "Kissinger: A Psychohistory," in *Henry Kissinger: His Personality and Policies* by Caldwell, ed.

33. Dickson, *Kissinger and the Meaning of History,* 43.

34. Arthur Schlesinger, Jr., Feb. 16, 1989.

35. Landau, *Kissinger,* 15; *WHY,* 229.

TWO: WASHINGTON HEIGHTS

1. Henry Kissinger, Nov. 24, 1987; Paula Kissinger, May 16, 1988; *WHY,* 229.

2. Paula Kissinger, May 8, 1988; Dorothy Zinberg, Aug. 28, 1988. In 1991, Paula Kissinger was still living in the same apartment she moved into the day they arrived more than fifty years earlier. Her cousin still lived across the hall, and they would meet their friends on a bench in nearby Fort Tryon Park and reminisce about the days in Fürth and the successes of all of their children, Henry among them.

3. Blumenfeld, *Henry Kissinger,* 34–44.

4. Henry Kissinger, Dec. 19, 1988; Kissinger's high school transcript, George Washington High School registrar's office; Blumenfeld, *Henry Kissinger,* 38–42.

5. Jerry Bechhofer, Dec. 2, 1988; Paula Kissinger, May 8, 1988; Erich Erlbach, Jan. 30, 1989.

6. Henry Gitterman, Dec. 5, 1988; Kurt Silbermann, Dec. 5, 1988.

7. Walter Oppenheim, Feb. 13, 1989.

8. Walter Kissinger, Mar. 17, 1988; Kurt Silbermann, Dec. 5, 1988; Blumenfeld, *Henry Kissinger,* 34–44. Paula Kissinger, May 7, 1988; Henry Kissinger, Dec. 19, 1988; Kurt Silbermann, Dec. 5, 1988; Henry Gitterman, Dec. 5, 1988; Walter Oppenheim, Feb. 7 and Feb. 13, 1989.

9. Henry Kissinger, Dec. 19, 1988; Blumenfeld, *Henry Kissinger,* 40–44; Alan Ascher, Jan. 30, 1989.

10. Henry Kissinger, Dec. 19, 1988.

11. Walter Oppenheim, Feb. 13, 1989.

THREE: THE ARMY

1. Letter from Henry Kissinger to Walter Kissinger, Aug. 13, 1943.

2. Henry Kissinger, Dec. 19, 1988; Blumenfeld, *Henry Kissinger,* 45–57.

3. Letter from Henry Kissinger to Walter Kissinger, Aug. 13, 1943.

4. Walter Oppenheim, Feb. 13, 1989; Charles J. Coyle, Feb. 8, 1989; transcript of academic record, Lafayette College.

5. Leonard Weiss, Dec. 10, 1988; Henry Kissinger, Dec. 19, 1988.

6. Paula Kissinger, May 8, 1988; Charles Coyle, Feb. 8, 1989.

7. This incident has been frequently recounted, often with minor variations. This version is from an interview with Fritz Kraemer, May 4, 1988, and with Henry Kissinger, Dec. 19, 1988. See also: Bernard Law Collier, "The Road to Peking," *NYT Magazine,* Nov. 14, 1971, 107; Mazlish, *Kissinger,* 49; Landau, *Kissinger,* 19.

8. Nick Thimmesch, "The Iron Mentor of the Pentagon," *WP Magazine,* Mar. 2, 1975; Fritz Kraemer, May 4 and May 14, 1988.

9. "Kissinger: Action Biography," reported by Ted Koppel and Howard K. Smith, ABC TV, June 14, 1974.

10. Fritz Kraemer, May 4 and May 14, 1988.

11. Blumenfeld, *Henry Kissinger,* 45–68; Henry Kissinger, Dec. 19, 1988; Fritz Kraemer, May 14, 1988.

12. Henry Kissinger, Dec. 19, 1988. For a similar version, see "Kissinger: Action Biography," reported by Koppel and Smith.

13. Kissinger's letter, written in 1945, is among the papers at his mother's apartment in Washington Heights.

14. Blumenfeld, *Henry Kissinger,* 4–5, 75; Harold (Helmut) Reissner, Nov. 30, 1988.

15. Letter from Kissinger to "My dear Mrs. Frank," Apr. 21, 1946, courtesy of Harold Reissner and Paula Kissinger.

16. "Memories of Mr. Henry," *Newsweek,* Oct. 8, 1973, 48.

17. Henry Kissinger, Dec. 19, 1988; Fritz Kraemer, May 14, 1988; Blumenfeld, *Henry Kissinger,* 68–80.

18. Harold Reissner, Nov. 30, 1988; Jerry Bechhofer, Dec. 2, 1988.

19. Paula Kissinger, May 8, 1988; Henry Kissinger, Dec. 19, 1988.

20. Henry Rosovsky, Feb. 24, 1989; Henry Rosovsky toast, Kissinger sixtieth birthday dinner, May 26, 1983; Donald Strong, Apr. 13, 1992; Blumenfeld, *Henry Kissinger,* 68–80; Fritz Kraemer, May 14, 1988.

21. Letter from Kissinger to parents, Dec. 22, 1946.

22. Joseph Kraft, "In Search of Kissinger," *Harper's,* Jan. 1971, 57; Henry Kissinger, Dec. 19, 1988.

23. Walter Kissinger, Mar. 17, 1988.

24. Letter from Kissinger to his parents, Aug. 12, 1947.

25. Paula Kissinger, May 8, 1988.

26. Fritz Kraemer, May 14, 1988; Henry Kissinger, Dec. 19, 1988.

27. Letter from Kissinger to Wesley Spence, Harvard counselor for veterans, May 10, 1947; application for admission to Harvard College, by Kissinger; veteran application for rooms, by Kissinger, Aug. 19, 1947; all in Kissinger's House file, Registrar's Office, Harvard.

FOUR: HARVARD

1. Smith, *The Harvard Century,* 168–178; McGeorge Bundy, Feb. 8, 1989. The college informed Kissinger that it did not give credit for night school, thus discarding his CCNY courses, but his record at Lafayette College and in the army qualified him to enter as a sophomore. When the Russian Research Center was founded, Harvard chose an anthropologist to run it, prompting Isaiah Berlin to remark that "the choice was based on the profound hypothesis that Russians are human beings."

2. Henry Rosovsky, Feb. 24, 1989; Sam Beer, Feb. 14, 1989; McGeorge Bundy, Feb. 8, 1989; David Reisman, Feb. 13, 1989; "Delmore Schwartz's Gift" in *Memories of the Moderns* by Harry Levin (Boston: Faber & Faber, 1981), 156; Henry Rosovsky,"From Periphery to Center," *Harvard Magazine,* Nov. 1979, 81; Nitza Rosovsky, *The Jewish Experience at Harvard and Radcliffe;* Marcia Synnott, *The Half-Open Door.*

3. Henry Kissinger, Mar. 8, 1989; Arthur Gilman, Feb. 14, 1989; Herbert Engelhardt, Feb. 27, 1989; Kissinger transcripts, House file, Harvard Registrar's Office.

4. Kissinger transcripts; Paul Doty, Feb. 13, 1989; Henry Kissinger, Mar. 8, 1989. Some accounts (such as Blumenfeld, Mazlish, and Graubard) report that Kissinger considered going into medicine. Kissinger says that, although he was interested in chemistry, he did not consider medicine as a profession. In December of his first term, his adviser noted in Kissinger's file that he "probably will go into social sciences or government."

5. Herbert Engelhardt, Feb. 27, 1989; Henry Kissinger, Mar. 8, 1989; Blumenfeld, *Henry Kissinger,* 86–87.

6. Henry Kissinger, Mar. 8, 1989; Stanley Hoffmann, Feb. 24, 1989; Sam Beer, Feb. 14, 1989; Arthur Schlesinger, Jr., Feb. 16, 1989; Sam Beer, Feb. 14, 1989; Landau, *Kissinger,* 42.

7. Kissinger tribute to William Elliott, Harvard Archives, Pusey Library; Kant, *Fundamental Principles of the Metaphysics of Morals,* 46.

8. Recommendation for Phi Beta Kappa, by Elliott, Kissinger House file.

9. Stoessinger, *Henry Kissinger,* 4. Elliott's book was *Western Political Heritage;* Friedrich's was *Inevitable Peace.*

10. Blumenfeld, *Henry Kissinger,* 87, 189.

11. Kissinger's transcripts; Henry Kissinger, Mar. 8, 1989.

12. Kissinger, "The Meaning of History" (the Descartes quote is on p. 4); Dickson, *Kissinger and the Meaning of History*. Kissinger's thesis has gone unread by most of those who have written about him, which is unfortunate. Dickson's book provides an excellent analysis.

13. Kissinger's two token British academic subjects, Arnold Toynbee and Viscount Castlereagh, serve as little more than sidebars to his main subjects.

14. Kissinger, "The Meaning of History," 1–17. Spengler also fascinated Paul Nitze, who in the late 1930s quit his Wall Street job to go to Harvard and study *The Decline of the West*.

15. Stanley Hoffmann, Feb. 24, 1989. Hoffmann, a Harvard colleague, is the foremost analyst of the relationship between Kissinger's intellectual ideas and his policies. Particularly valuable are *Dead Ends,* 17–66, and *Primacy or World Order,* 33–97.

16. Kissinger, "The Meaning of History," 133, 20, 234, 237, 238.

17. Friedrich, ed., *The Philosophy of Kant* (includes "Perpetual Peace"); Friedrich, *Inevitable Peace;* Kissinger, "The Meaning of History," 261, 280, 262, 324–28, 348; Dickson, *Kissinger and the Meaning of History,* 35, 47.

18. Blumenfeld, *Henry Kissinger,* 79, 89–90; Henry Kissinger, Dec. 19, 1988; Paula Kissinger, May 8, 1988; Harold Reissner, Nov. 30, 1988; Kurt Silbermann, Dec. 5, 1988; Arthur Gilman, Feb. 14, 1989.

19. Walter Kissinger, Mar. 17, 1988.

20. Scholarship application by Kissinger, Feb. 20, 1950, House files, Harvard Registrar's Office.

21. Kissinger's senior-year transcript and application to the Graduate School of Arts and Sciences, both in House files, Harvard.

22. Graubard, *Kissinger,* 55; Sam Beer, Feb. 8 and Feb. 14, 1989; John Conway, Feb. 13, 1989; Adam Ulam, Feb. 14, 1989.

23. Memo from special agent in charge, Boston, to the Central Research Division, FBI, July 15, 1953; see Sigmund Diamond, "Kissinger and the FBI," *The Nation,* Nov. 10, 1979.

24. Blumenfeld, *Henry Kissinger,* 95–97, 106; McGeorge Bundy, Feb. 8, 1989; Virginia Bohlin, "Summertime, Busiest Season of All," *Boston Traveler,* July 7, 1959; "Seminar Brings Together Future Foreign Leaders," *Harvard Crimson,* May 27, 1959; "Harvard Programs Received C.I.A. Help," *NYT,* Apr. 16, 1967.

25. Henry Kissinger, Mar. 8, 1989; Blumenfeld, *Henry Kissinger,* 107; *Confluence,* Mar. 1952. The final volume was Summer 1958.

26. Judis, *William F. Buckley, Jr.,* 300.

27. Thomas Schelling, Feb. 3, 1989.

28. Stephen Graubard, Apr. 23, 1989; Graubard, *Kissinger,* 59.

29. Kissinger, Apr. 25, 1989; Stoessinger, *Henry Kissinger,* 1–3.

30. Kissinger, *A World Restored;* Henry Kissinger, Mar. 8, 1989.

31. Hoffmann, *Primacy or World Order,* 36.

32. Stoessinger, *Henry Kissinger,* 14.

33. Kissinger, *A World Restored,* 1–2; for examples of these ideas applied to the twentieth century, see Kissinger, *Nuclear Weapons and Foreign Policy,* 4, 10, 203.

34. Kissinger, "The Limitations of Diplomacy," *New Republic,* May 9, 1955.

35. Henry Kissinger, Apr. 25, 1989.

36. Kissinger, *A World Restored,* 9–12.

37. Letter from Henry Kissinger to Louis Kissinger, Jan. 31, 1954.

38. Fritz Kraemer, May 14, 1988; Sam Beer, Feb. 14, 1989; Adam Ulam, Feb. 14, 1989; Herbert Spiro, June 9, 1989; John Conway, Feb. 13, 1989.

39. Stanley Hoffmann, May 11, 1989; Zbigniew Brzezinski, July 6, 1989.

40. Henry Kissinger, Mar. 8, 1989; letter from Kissinger to his parents, June 4, 1952.

FIVE: NEW YORK

1. Arthur Schlesinger, Jr., Feb. 16, 1989; Henry Kissinger, Mar. 8, 1989. "Massive retaliation" was spelled out in the NATO strategic concept MC 14/2, adopted by the North Atlantic Council in 1957. Epigraph is from *Nuclear Weapons and Foreign Policy* by Kissinger, 427.

2. Kissinger, "Military Policy and Defense of the Grey Areas," *Foreign Affairs,* Apr. 1955, 416–28.

3. Letter from Kissinger to Paula Kissinger, Feb. 23, 1955.

4. Council on Foreign Relations archives, nuclear weapons and foreign policy study group, minutes of the first meeting, Nov. 8, 1954, 11.

5. Ibid., minutes of the third meeting, Jan. 12, 1955, 3–4; Paul Nitze, "Atoms, Strategy, and Policy," *Foreign Affairs,* Jan. 1956; Nitze, *From Hiroshima to Glasnost,* 150.

6. Letter from Kissinger to George Franklin, Jr., Apr. 26, 1955, CFR archives; minutes of the sixth meeting, May 4, 1955, 2.

7. Talbott, *The Master of the Game,* 65.

8. Letter from George Franklin, Jr., to Carroll Wilson, Aug. 4, 1955, and from Wilson to Franklin, Aug. 12, 1955; from Kissinger to McGeorge Bundy, Sept. 22, 1955; from Kissinger to Maxwell Taylor, Oct. 24, 1955, and from Taylor to Kissinger, Oct. 29, 1955; subcommittee II minutes, Dec. 20, 1955, 7; letter from Kissinger to study group members, Sept. 23, 1955; minutes of Nov. 14, 1955, study group meeting; letter from Kissinger to Carroll Wilson, Dec. 9, 1955; all in CFR archives. Graubard, *Kissinger,* 104.

9. Kissinger, *Nuclear Weapons and Foreign Policy.* Ideas and excerpts from the book-in-progress were the basis for three articles by Kissinger: "Force and Diplomacy in the Nuclear Age," *Foreign Affairs,* Apr. 1956; "Reflections on American Diplomacy," *Foreign Affairs,* Oct. 1956; "Strategy and Organization," *Foreign Affairs,* Apr. 1957. Blumenfeld, *Henry Kissinger,* 119.

10. Kissinger, *Nuclear Weapons and Foreign Policy,* 4–7. Compare this idea and the invocation of the Greek goddess Nemesis to the virtually identical ideas on the first page of *A World Restored.*

11. Kissinger, *Nuclear Weapons and Foreign Policy,* 11, 12, 15, 132, 30, 199, 176, 180–81, 426–47; Henry Kissinger, Mar. 8, 1989; Freedman, *The Evolution of Nuclear Strategy;* Halperin, *Limited War in the Nuclear Age;* Bernard Brodie, "Nuclear Weapons: Strategic or Tactical?" *Foreign Affairs,* Jan. 1954; Bernard Brodie, "Strategy Hits a Dead End," *Harper's,* Oct. 1955; Blumenfeld, *Henry Kissinger,* 134.

12. Edward Teller, "A New Look at War-Making," *NYT Book Review,* July 7, 1957, 3; Kalb and Kalb, *Kissinger,* 54.

13. Russell Baker, "U.S. Reconsidering Small War Theory," *NYT,* Aug. 11, 1957, 1; "The Cold War and the Small War," *Time,* Aug. 26, 1957, 14.

14. Paul Nitze, "Limited Wars or Massive Retaliation," *The Reporter,* Sept. 5, 1957; Talbott, *The Master of the Game,* 65; Paul Nitze interview, U.S. Air Force Oral History Project, 468–72; Callahan, *Dangerous Capabilities,* 166; Mazlish, *Kissinger,* 109–10; unpublished paper on Paul Nitze by his nephew, Scott Thompson; Henry Kissinger, Mar. 8, 1989; "MacNeil/Lehrer NewsHour," May 5, 1989. The meeting near Rome is also recounted, with slightly different wording, in *From Hiroshima to Glasnost* by Nitze, 296.

15. Eulogy for Nelson Rockefeller by Kissinger, Feb. 2, 1979, Rockefeller family archives.

16. Despite some of Kissinger's and Rockefeller's published recollections (and such books as *Henry Kissinger* by Blumenfeld, 108–10), Kissinger was not at the first Quantico meeting of 1955 where the "open skies" plan was developed. The records of those meetings are now open and available from the Rockefeller family archives. Interviews with Hugh Morrow, July 12, 1989; Walt W. Rostow, July 18, 1989; Henry Kissinger, Apr. 6, 1989; Persico, *The Imperial Rockefeller,* 82.

17. Blumenfeld, *Henry Kissinger,* 117–18.

18. *Prospect for America: The Rockefeller Panel Report;* Philip Benjamin, "Arms Rise Urged Lest Reds Seize Lead in Two Years," *NYT,* Jan. 6, 1958; Kalb and Kalb, *Kissinger,* 56; "Rockefeller Report Seen Clue to 1960," *Christian Science Monitor,* Jan. 8, 1959.

19. Note from Nelson Rockefeller to Kissinger, undated, and Jan. 17, 1969, Rockefeller family papers; "Rates of Compensation Paid to Henry Kissinger by Nelson Rockefeller," documents and hearings of the Senate Rules Committee, Nov. 1974, 883; Henry Kissinger, Apr. 6, 1989.

SIX: HARVARD AGAIN

1. Letter from McGeorge Bundy to Robert Bowie, Apr. 25, 1957, records of the Harvard Center for International Affairs; McGeorge Bundy, Feb. 8, 1989. The epigraph is from Kissinger, "The White Revolutionary: Reflections on Bismarck," *Daedalus,* Summer 1968, 898.

2. Thomas Schelling, Feb. 3, 1989; Morton Halperin, Nov. 15, 1989.

3. Laurence Wylie, Apr. 22, 1989; Stanley Hoffmann, May 11, 1989; McGeorge Bundy, Feb. 8, 1989; Herbert Spiro, June 9, 1989; Henry Kissinger, Mar. 8, 1989.

4. Letter from Henry Kissinger to Paula Kissinger, Mar. 5, 1958.

5. Henry Rosovsky, Feb. 24, 1989.

6. Sam Beer, Feb. 14, 1989; Adam Ulam, Feb. 14, 1989; records of the Department of Government, Harvard University.

7. *Harvard Crimson Confidential Guide to Courses,* 1963.

8. David Riesman, Feb. 13, 1989.

9. Gerald Ford, July 24, 1990.

10. Graubard, *Kissinger,* 117–18; Thomas Schelling, Feb. 3, 1989; Paul

Doty, Feb. 13, 1989; Carl Kaysen, Feb. 12, 1989; Laurence Wylie, Apr. 22, 1989; Morton Halperin, May 24, 1988; Leslie Gelb, Jan. 9, 1990.

11. See also analysis in *Kissinger* by Landau, 83.

12. Tom Schelling, Feb. 3, 1989.

13. Laurence Wylie, Apr. 22, 1989; Tom Schelling, Feb. 3, 1989; Stanley Hoffmann, May 11, 1989.

14. Elizabeth Epstein Krumpe, May 5, 1989. (Klaus Epstein died in a car crash while a professor at Brown in 1967.)

15. Letter from Kissinger to "My Dear Parents," Sept. 8, 1961, courtesy of Paula Kissinger.

16. Virginia Bohlin, *"Traveler* Visits One of Nation's Outstanding Young Men," *Boston Traveler,* July 7, 1959; Arthur Schlesinger, Jr., Feb. 16, 1989; Leslie Gelb, Jan. 9, 1990; Blumenfeld, *Henry Kissinger,* 128–29, 144–47.

17. Tom Schelling, Feb. 3, 1989; Joan Dreyfus Wylie, Feb. 4, 1989; Blumenfeld, *Henry Kissinger,* 143.

18. Kissinger at the Council on Foreign Relations, June 9, 1989.

19. Kissinger, "Reflections on American Diplomacy," *Foreign Affairs,* Oct. 1956, 38–39. Kissinger discussed the implications of his ideas in two lectures to military conferences: "The Relation Between Force and Diplomacy," reprinted in *Armor Magazine,* July-Aug. 1957; "Strategy and Policy," reprinted in *Army Magazine,* Dec. 1957. Kissinger, "Missiles and the Western Alliance," *Foreign Affairs,* Apr. 1958, 389; Kissinger, "Nuclear Testing and the Problem of Peace," *Foreign Affairs,* Oct. 1958, 2; Kissinger, "The Search for Stability," *Foreign Affairs,* July 1959, 548; Kissinger, "Forget the Zero Option," *WP,* Apr. 5, 1987; Kissinger, "Arms Control Fever," *WP,* Jan. 19, 1988.

20. "Refusal of Missile Bases Seen as Danger to Europe's Future," *NYT,* Mar. 10, 1958; "Beware the Ban," *Time,* Oct. 6, 1958, 30. Also: interview with Kissinger, *Der Spiegel,* Feb. 9, 1959; "Professor Favors a Test on Berlin," *NYT,* Feb. 10, 1959; "NATO Cautioned on Atomic Shield," *NYT,* June 8, 1959. Kissinger, "As Urgent as the Moscow Threat," *NYT Magazine,* Mar. 8, 1959, 19; Kissinger, "The Khrushchev Visit—Dangers and Hopes," *NYT Magazine,* Sept. 6, 1959, 5.

21. The book appeared in stores and was reviewed during the second week of January 1961, a week before Kennedy was inaugurated. The book included two previously published articles by Kissinger: "Arms Control, Inspection and Surprise Attack," *Foreign Affairs,* July 1960, 557; "Limited War: Conventional or Nuclear?—A Reappraisal," *Daedalus,* Fall 1960, 800. The *Daedalus* issue is devoted entirely to arms control and contains important articles by Robert Bowie, Herman Kahn, Edward Teller, Jerome Weisner, and Thomas Schelling.

22. *Necessity for Choice,* ix–xi, 2–6; Tom Schelling, Feb. 3, 1989.

23. *Necessity for Choice,* 32–36, 57, 59, 81–83, 87, 89; Henry Kissinger, Mar. 8, 1989.

24. Kissinger, "The White Revolutionary: Reflections on Bismarck," *Daedalus,* Summer 1968, 888, 893, 898, 906, 910.

SEVEN: THE FRINGES OF POWER

1. Arthur Schlesinger, Jr., Feb. 16, 1989; McGeorge Bundy, Feb. 8, 1989; Abram Chayes, July 13, 1989; Ted Sorensen, Feb. 16, 1989; Henry Kissinger, Aug. 28, 1989; *WHY,* 9. Epigraph from Hugh Sidey, "An International Natural Resource," *Time,* Feb. 4, 1974.

2. *WHY,* 13–14; Henry Kissinger, Mar. 8, 1989.

3. Letter from Kissinger to Bundy, Mar. 1, 1961, national security files, Kissinger folder, Kennedy Library.

4. Letters from Kissinger to Bundy, Feb. 8 and May 5, 1961, ibid.

5. Letter from Kissinger to Bundy, Mar. 20, 1961, and Bundy to Kissinger, Mar. 22, 1961, ibid.

6. Arthur Schlesinger, Jr., Feb. 16, 1989; Kalb and Kalb, *Kissinger,* 63.

7. Letter from Kissinger to Bundy, June 5, 1961, national security files, Kissinger folder, Kennedy Library.

8. Schlesinger, *A Thousand Days,* pp. 386–88; Arthur Schlesinger, Jr., Feb. 16, 1989; Abram Chayes Oral History, 247–49, Kennedy Library; Abram Chayes, July 13, 1989. Schlesinger and Chayes disagree on whether they had lunch that day or merely met after lunch; I have used the Chayes account after discussing the discrepancies with him.

9. Letter from Kissinger to Acheson, July 18, 1961, and Dec. 14, 1966, Acheson papers, Kissinger folder, Yale University Library.

10. Kissinger memo to Bundy, July 15, 1961, national security files, Kissinger folder, Kennedy Library. Kissinger discusses the "missile gap" in *The Necessity for Choice,* 26–39. Bundy later criticized Kissinger's analysis in *Danger and Survival,* 346–48.

11. Bundy, "Covering note on Henry Kissinger's memo on Berlin," July 7, 1961, national security files 81, Kennedy Library; Kennedy's July 25 speech on Berlin, Public Papers of the President, 1961, 535; Bundy, *Danger and Survival,* 377. Bundy adds in his covering memo that he, Carl Kaysen, and other advisers "all agree [with Kissinger] that the current strategic war plan is dangerously rigid." For a fuller discussion of "flexible response" and "assured destruction," see Newhouse, *War and Peace in the Nuclear Age,* 162–64; Kaufmann, *The McNamara Strategy.*

12. Kissinger memo to Bundy, Aug. 11, 1961, national security files 81, Kennedy Library.

13. Henry Kissinger, Aug. 28, 1989; letter from Kissinger to Bundy, Oct. 19, 1961; from Bundy to Kissinger, Nov. 13, 1961, national security files, Kissinger folder, Kennedy Library.

14. Carl Kaysen, July 12, 1989.

15. Abram Chayes, July 13, 1989; Henry Kissinger, Mar. 8, 1989; Richard Holbrooke, Sept. 25, 1989; *WHY,* 9.

16. "Nasser Is Seen Causing Crisis," *WP,* Jan. 3, 1962; transcript of Kissinger remarks in Peshawar, Pakistan, Foreign Service Despatch, Feb. 13, 1962, Kissinger folder, national security files, staff memoranda, Kennedy Library; memo from L. D. Battle to McGeorge Bundy, Jan. 10, 1962, ibid.; Kennedy briefing papers, Jan. 15, 1962, ibid.; Kalb and Kalb, *Kissinger,* 63–64; *WHY,* 847.

17. Letter from Kissinger to Louis Kissinger, Jan. 25, 1962, courtesy of Paula Kissinger.

18. McGeorge Bundy, Feb. 8, 1989.

19. Kissinger, "The Unsolved Problems of European Defense," *Foreign Affairs,* July 1962, 525, 530, 531. Kissinger's 1989 comment is from the "MacNeil/Lehrer NewsHour," May 5, 1989.

20. Kissinger's writings included "Strains on the Alliance," *Foreign Affairs,* Jan. 1963; "The Skybolt Affair," *Reporter,* Jan. 17, 1963; "NATO's Nuclear Dilemma," *Reporter,* Mar. 28, 1963; "Coalition Diplomacy in the Nuclear Age," *Foreign Affairs,* July 1964; "The Illusionist: Why We Misunderstand De Gaulle," *Harper's,* Mar. 1965; "The Price of German Unity," *Reporter,* Apr. 22, 1965; "For a New Atlantic Alliance," *Reporter,* July 14, 1966.

21. "Reflections on Cuba," *The Reporter,* Nov. 22, 1962.

22. Melvin Laird, Dec. 18, 1989.

23. James Reston, Dec. 19, 1989; Walt Rostow, July 18, 1989; Reston, *Deadline,* 425; *WHY,* 230–31.

24. Letters from Kissinger to McGeorge Bundy, Mar. 30 and Apr. 13, 1965; Bundy to Kissinger, Apr. 12, 1965; national security files, Kissinger folder, Johnson Library.

25. Letter from Kissinger to his parents, Oct. 17, 1965, courtesy of Paula Kissinger; Hersh, *The Price of Power,* 46–48; *WHY,* 232–33; Landau, *Kissinger,* 157.

26. Jack Foisie, "Viet Regime Shaky, Johnson Envoys Find," *LAT,* Nov. 2, 1965 (also carried in *WP*); Barry Zorthian, Aug. 2, 1989. Letter from Kissinger to "Dear Mac" Bundy, Nov. 6, 1965; telegram from Kissinger to the White House, Nov. 7, 1965; letter from Kissinger to Clark Clifford, Nov. 10, 1965; all in national security files, Kissinger folder, Johnson Library. Clifford and Holbrooke, *Counsel to the President,* 429–32.

27. McGeorge Bundy memo to William Bundy, Nov. 10, 1965; Kissinger letter to "Dear Mac," Nov. 6, 1965; both in national security files, Kissinger folder, Johnson Library.

28. "Town Meeting of the World," hosted by Charles Collingwood, CBS News, Dec. 21, 1965; "Educators Back Vietnam Policy," *NYT,* Dec. 10, 1965.

29. *WHY,* 233; Kalb and Kalb, *Kissinger,* 69–70.

30. Kalb and Kalb, *Kissinger,* 67–68; Daniel Ellsberg, Aug. 8, 1989; Daniel Ellsberg interview, *Rolling Stone,* Nov. 8, 1973; Dan Davidson, July 31, 1989.

31. Kissinger, "What Should We Do Now," *Look,* Aug. 9, 1966.

32. The full documentation on the Pennsylvania initiative is contained in "The Pentagon Papers," volume VI.C.4, *Negotiations 1967–1968.* It is reprinted in *The Secret Diplomacy of the Vietnam War,* edited by Herring, 717–71. See also Kraslow and Loory, *The Secret Search for Peace in Vietnam;* Landau, *Kissinger,* 164–91. Kissinger's and Walt Rostow's notes are in the national security files, Vietnam, box 140, in the Johnson Library. Kissinger's letter to his parents is dated August 5, 1967, courtesy of Paula Kissinger.

33. Paul Doty, Feb. 13, 1989.

34. Transcript of the Oct. 18, 1967, meeting with President Lyndon Johnson, Henry Kissinger, Dean Rusk, and others, from the private papers of Clark Clifford; Clifford and Holbrooke, *Counsel to the President,* 457.

35. Transcript of the June 1968 seminar of the Adlai Stevenson Institute

of International Affairs; Pfeiffer, ed., *No More Vietnams,* 12–13. For more on Kissinger's belief in a "decent interval" solution, see Chapter 21.

36. Persico, *The Imperial Rockefeller,* 70.

37. Hugh Morrow, June 28, 1989.

38. Speech to the World Affairs Council of Philadelphia, May 1, 1968, the public papers of Nelson Rockefeller.

39. R. W. Apple, "Rockefeller Gives Four-Stage Plan to End the War," *NYT,* July 14, 1968; Persico, *The Imperial Rockefeller,* 73.

40. Oscar Ruebhausen, Aug. 3, 1989; Hugh Morrow, June 28, 1989; Henry Kissinger, Aug. 28, 1989; "Rockefeller Coup Gave Platform a Dovish Tone," *NYT,* Aug. 6, 1968.

41. Richard Allen, Aug. 7, 1989; Safire, *Before the Fall,* 52.

42. Oscar Ruebhausen, Aug. 3, 1989; Blumenfeld, *Henry Kissinger,* 167–70; Collier and Horowitz, *The Rockefellers,* 358; *WHY,* 7; "The Casper Citron Show," Aug. 8, 1968, transcript courtesy of Casper Citron; Brandon, *The Retreat of American Power,* 24; Henry Brandon, Nov. 15, 1989; Daniel Davidson, July 31, 1989.

EIGHT: THE CO-CONSPIRATORS

1. Hersh, *The Price of Power,* 12–13; Richard Allen, Aug. 7, 1989.

2. Nixon, *RN,* 323.

3. Henry Kissinger, Aug. 28, 1989; *WHY,* 10.

4. Daniel Davidson, July 31 and Aug. 3, 1989; Richard Holbrooke, Sept. 25, 1989; letter from William Bundy to the author, Feb. 24, 1991; William Bundy, Mar. 1 and 3, 1991; Clifford and Holbrooke, *Counsel to the President,* 691.

5. Henry Kissinger, Aug. 28, 1989; Richard Allen, Aug. 7, 1989; H. R. Haldeman, July 24, 1990; Hersh, *The Price of Power,* 13–18; Nixon, *RN,* 323–25; Haldeman meeting notes, Haldeman papers, box 45, WHSF, NPP; Bui Diem, *In the Jaws of History,* 235–42. (For Mitchell's denial of the quotes attributed to him by Hersh, see *National Review,* June 24, 1983.)

6. Ted Van Dyk, Aug. 3 and 7, 1989; Samuel Huntington, Aug. 6, 1991; Henry Kissinger, Aug. 28, 1989; *NYT,* Mar. 12, 1973.

7. Henry Kissinger, Aug. 28, 1989; Richard Holbrooke, Sept. 25, 1989.

8. Gloria Steinem, Nov. 29, 1987; Kissinger, *A World Restored,* 19.

9. Kalb and Kalb, *Kissinger,* 14–15; *WHY,* 9.

10. Nixon, *RN,* 340; Kraft's interview was filmed but not broadcast by WETA in Washington and is quoted in *The Price of Power* by Hersh, 19; Polly Kraft, Nov. 16, 1989; Sulzberger, *The World According to Richard Nixon,* 180.

11. *WHY,* 8; Henry Kissinger, April 25, 1989.

12. *WHY,* 10–12; Nixon, *RN,* 341; Morris, *Uncertain Greatness,* 63–64.

13. *WHY,* 14–15; *NYT,* Nov. 30, 1968.

14. Landau, *Kissinger,* 134; Henry Kissinger, Apr. 25, 1989; *WHY,* 15–16; McGeorge Bundy, Feb. 8, 1989; Bernard Law Collier, "The Road to Peking," *NYT Magazine,* Nov. 14, 1971; Fritz Kraemer, May 14, 1988; Carl Kaysen, July 18, 1989; Abe Chayes, July 13, 1989; Oscar Ruebhausen, Aug. 3, 1990;

H. R. Haldeman, Feb. 20, 1989; Kalb and Kalb, *Kissinger,* 26 (Kraemer is quoted as telling Kissinger he owed it to the country to take the job; Kraemer in 1989 did not remember it that way); note from Nelson Rockefeller to Kissinger, Jan. 17, 1969, Rockefeller family papers; *Rates of Compensation Paid to Henry Kissinger by Nelson Rockefeller,* documents and hearings of the Senate Rules Committee, Nov. 1974, 883; Henry Kissinger, Apr. 6, 1989.

15. *NYT,* Dec. 3, and editorial, Dec. 4, 1968; Evans and Novak column, Jan. 16, 1969; *WHY,* 16. (Based on interviews with H. R. Haldeman and other top Nixon aides, the *New York Times* on Nov. 14, 1968, produced a page-one assessment that would prove breathtakingly wrong: "Richard M. Nixon intends at this time not to allow his personal White House staff to dominate the functions or control the direction of the major agencies and bureaus of the Government. Sensitive to the possibility of empire building within his own small cadre of assistants, he plans instead to organize his White House staff in a way that will encourage and not inhibit direct communication between his Cabinet officers and the President. He is said to be firm in his view that his Cabinet officers should have the major responsibility for policymaking.")

16. *Time,* Dec. 13, 1968, and Feb. 14, 1969; *NYT,* Dec. 4, 1968.

17. Nixon, *RN,* 341; Kissinger, "The White Revolutionary," *Daedalus,* Summer 1968; *YOU,* 221; William Watts, Dec. 13, 1989.

18. Lawrence Eagleburger, June 25, 1990.

19. Similar analyses include: Ambrose, *Nixon,* vol. 2, 233, and Joan Hoff-Wilson quote, 490; Ball, *Diplomacy for a Crowded World,* 9; Brandon, *Retreat of American Power,* 34; Morris, *Uncertain Greatness,* 48.

20. Thomas Hughes, "Why Kissinger Must Choose Between Nixon and the Country," *NYT Magazine,* Dec. 30, 1973.

21. Susan Mary Alsop, Dec. 13, 1989.

22. H. R. Haldeman, Feb. 20, 1990; Kalb and Kalb, *Kissinger,* 29.

23. Richard Nixon, Oct. 11, 1990; Morris, *Uncertain Greatness,* 2; Brandon, *Special Relationships,* 292.

24. Richard Nixon, Oct. 11, 1990; letter from Nixon to the author, Oct. 12, 1990; David Frost interview with Nixon, broadcast May 12, 1977 (see *NYT,* May 13, 1977, for excerpts); John Connally, Apr. 16, 1990; H. R. Haldeman, Feb. 20, 1990.

25. Kissinger, *A World Restored,* 19, 83, 211, 322.

26. *YOU,* 74, 1183, 1185–86.

27. *WHY,* 11, 951, 1175, 1475; Henry Kissinger, Aug. 28, 1989; Nixon memo to Kissinger, July 19, 1971, H. R. Haldeman papers, box 140, NPP; Nixon memo to Haldeman, Mar. 13, 1972, H. R. Haldeman papers, box 162, NPP; Kissinger at dinner in Ottawa, in *Time,* Oct. 27, 1975; *YOU,* 95–96.

28. One of the first descriptions of Kissinger's taping system is in Woodward and Bernstein, *The Final Days,* 204. The descriptions I use are from some of the secretaries and aides involved and have been confirmed by Kissinger. Safire, *Before the Fall,* 169; Morris, *Uncertain Greatness,* 3, 147; Moynihan, *A Dangerous Place,* 8.

29. Winston Lord, Oct. 25, 1989; Henry Kissinger, Aug. 28, 1989; *WHY,* 163, 603.

30. Schulzinger, *Henry Kissinger,* 28; *WHY,* 93, 143; Nixon, *RN,* 369, 407, 715; Morris, *Uncertain Greatness,* 145; Kissinger letter to Nixon, Apr. 7,

1971, president's personal files, box 10, NPP; Hersh, *The Price of Power,* 40, 44.

31. Peter Peterson, Nov. 16, 1989; Henry Brandon, Nov. 15, 1989; Lawrence Higby, Jan. 29, 1990; Les Gelb, Jan. 9, 1990.

32. Safire, *Before the Fall,* 157–58; Hugh Sidey, "Shaking Down the Crisis," *Life,* May 22, 1970.

33. John Ehrlichman, Feb. 27, 1990; H. R. Haldeman, Feb. 20, 1990.

34. *YOU,* 202; Hersh, *The Price of Power,* 84–85; John Ehrlichman, Feb. 27, 1990; H. R. Haldeman, Feb. 20, 1990.

35. Nancy Kissinger, Jan. 25, 1990; Richard Nixon, Oct. 11, 1990; letter from Nixon to the author, Oct. 12, 1990.

36. Haldeman, *The Ends of Power,* 62; Safire, *Before the Fall,* 97–98.

37. *YOU,* 94, 112; John Ehrlichman, Feb. 27, 1990; Haldeman, *The Ends of Power,* 64; H. R. Haldeman, Feb. 20, 1990; Diane Sawyer, Sept. 7, 1990.

38. Morton Halperin, May 24, 1988; John Ehrlichman, Feb. 27, 1990. See also: Morris, *Uncertain Greatness,* 145; Kalb and Kalb, *Kissinger,* 92; Hersh, *The Price of Power,* 110.

39. David Frost interview with Nixon, syndicated broadcast May 12, 1977.

40. *WHY,* 305, 606, 696, 1168; Haldeman, *The Ends of Power,* 59; Henry Kissinger, Aug. 28, 1969; H. R. Haldeman, Feb. 20, 1990.

41. Nixon, *RN,* 340; *WHY,* 11; H. R. Haldeman, Feb. 20, 1990; George Ball, *Diplomacy for a Crowded World,* 10; Rather and Gates, *The Palace Guard,* 30.

42. Safire, *Before the Fall,* 437; Sulzberger, *The World and Richard Nixon,* 182.

43. Kissinger, *The Necessity for Choice,* 345–48; Morris, *Uncertain Greatness,* 24–36.

44. Morton Halperin, May 24, 1988; Kissinger memo to President-elect Nixon proposing a new NSC structure, Ehrlichman papers, box 19, NPP; Morris, *Uncertain Greatness,* 78–88; Sulzinger, *Henry Kissinger,* 24; *WHY,* 805; Kalb and Kalb, *Kissinger,* 90; Prados, *Keeper of the Keys,* 267; Shana Alexander column, *Newsweek,* Aug. 21, 1972; *YOU,* 414.

45. Morris, *Uncertain Greatness,* 83–85; Andrew Goodpaster, Feb. 7, 1990; *WHY,* 42–46; *NYT,* Dec. 29, 1968 and Jan. 24, 1973; Robert Semple, Sept. 28, 1990; Richard Moose, Feb. 1, 1990; U. Alexis Johnson, *The Right Hand of Power,* 514–16; Elliot Richardson, Dec. 13, 1989; Henry Kissinger, Aug. 28, 1989.

NINE: Welcome to Vietnam

1. *WHY,* 3; Szulc, *The Illusion of Peace,* 11–13; Morton Halperin, Nov. 15, 1989.

2. *WHY,* 56–57, 66; Brown, *The Crisis of Power,* 1–3, 142–43; *The President's First Annual Report on U.S. Foreign Policy* ("State of the World" report), Feb. 18, 1970, 1; Chang, *Friends and Enemies.*

3. *NYT,* Dec. 11 and 30, 1968; *The Pentagon Papers, NYT* edition, 496.

4. Whalen, *Catch the Falling Flag,* 137; Haldeman, *The Ends of Power,* 81.

5. *WP* editorial, Dec. 24, 1968; Joseph Kraft column, *WP,* Dec. 19, 1968; Kissinger, "The Viet Nam Negotiations," *Foreign Affairs,* Jan. 1969, 214, 216, 219. For a later version of the exact same type of credibility argument, see: Kissinger, "Decision Time in the Gulf," *LAT* syndicate, Sept. 25, 1990.

6. *WHY,* 110; Landau, *Kissinger,* 157–58, 249; Daniel Ellsberg, "What Nixon Is Up To," *New York Review of Books,* Mar. 11, 1971.

7. Kissinger, "The Viet Nam Negotiations," 231; *Time,* Feb. 5, 1969; *Nhan Dan* editorial, Aug. 31, 1972, cited in *Without Honor* by Isaacs, 33.

8. Fred Ikle, Oct. 2, 1990; Daniel Ellsberg, Aug. 8, 1989; Henry Kissinger, Oct. 2, 1990; Ikle and Ellsberg, "Vietnam Options Paper," Dec. 27, 1968, copy courtesy of Ellsberg; Jann Wenner interview with Ellsberg, *Rolling Stone,* Nov. 8, 1973; Hersh, *The Price of Power,* 48–49; Kalb and Kalb, *Kissinger,* 125; Nixon, *RN,* 347, 387.

9. Haldeman, *The Ends of Power,* 83; H. R. Haldeman, Feb. 20, 1990; Hersh, *The Price of Power,* 51; Eisenhower, *Mandate for Change,* 180; interview with Nixon, *Time,* Apr. 2, 1990; *WHY,* 195, 607; interview with Ellsberg, *Rolling Stone,* Nov. 8, 1973.

10. Sven Kraemer, Nov. 16, 1989.

11. Daniel Ellsberg, Aug. 8, 1989; interview with Ellsberg, *Rolling Stone,* Nov. 8, 1973; Hersh, *The Price of Power,* 50; *WHY,* 238; NSSM-1 (Jan. 20, 1969) and responses, inserted by Congressman Ron Dellums into the *Congressional Record,* May 10, 1972.

12. Kalb and Kalb, *Kissinger,* 120; Morton Halperin, Nov. 15, 1989; Tony Lake, Jan. 11, 1990.

13. *WHY,* 228, 261; Henry Kissinger, Oct. 2, 1990; Richard Nixon, *RN,* 348; Richard Nixon, Apr. 2, 1990.

14. *WHY,* 130–35; Kalb and Kalb, *Kissinger,* 103–5; Kissinger-Halperin memo quoted in *The Price of Power* by Hersh, 66; Garthoff, *Détente and Confrontation,* 129; Nixon's news conference, Jan. 27, 1969; Kissinger background briefing, Feb. 6, 1969; *NYT* editorial, Feb. 18, 1969; *WP* editorial, Apr. 5, 1969.

15. *WHY,* 265–68; Henry Kissinger, Oct. 2, 1990; Georgi Arbatov, Nov. 18, 1989.

16. Nixon, *RN,* 370; *WHY,* 105.

17. Nixon, *RN,* 371–74; *WHY,* 73, 95, 104–8, 170; Safire, *Before the Fall,* 123–26.

18. Morton Halperin, Nov. 15, 1989; H. R. Haldeman, Feb. 20, 1990; Helmut Sonnenfeldt, Nov. 16, 1989.

19. *WHY,* 79, 75, 93.

20. *WHY,* 239–41; Shawcross, *Sideshow,* 40–46.

21. Abrams to Wheeler, MAC 1782, Feb. 9, 1969. This was given to the House Judiciary Committee looking into impeachment charges against Nixon in 1974 but kept classified. It was obtained by William Shawcross under the Freedom of Information Act and is quoted in *Sideshow,* page 19. See also, *WHY,* 241; testimony by Gen. Earle Wheeler and Gen. Creighton Abrams, *Bombing in Cambodia,* hearings before the Senate Armed Services Committee, July and Aug. 1973, 131, 341.

22. McConnell to Abrams, JCS 01836, Feb. 11, 1969, and Wheeler to Abrams, JCS 03287, Mar. 1, 1969; Shawcross, *Sideshow,* 20–22; *WHY,* 242.

23. *WHY,* 243–44; Melvin Laird, Dec. 26, 1989; Henry Kissinger, Oct. 3, 1990; Hersh, *The Price of Power,* 60; Nixon, *RN,* 380.

24. Nixon press conferences, Mar. 4 and 14, 1969; Henry Kissinger, Oct. 3, 1990; Melvin Laird, Dec. 26, 1989; *WHY,* 245.

25. *WHY,* 246; Szulc, *The Illusion of Peace,* 53; Nixon, *RN,* 381.

26. Shawcross, *Sideshow,* 23–24 and 26; *WHY,* 257.

27. Testimony of Randolph Harrison, Special Forces unit commander, *Bombing in Cambodia,* hearings before the Senate Armed Services Committee, July and Aug. 1973, 232–45; Melvin Laird, Dec. 26, 1989; Shawcross, *Sideshow,* 25–26; Hersh, *The Price of Power,* 63–64.

28. Testimony by Maj. Hal Knight, Gen. Earle Wheeler, and Gen. Creighton Abrams, *Bombing in Cambodia,* hearings before the Senate Armed Services Committee, July and Aug. 1973, 5, 134, 484; Hersh, *The Price of Power,* 61–65; *WHY,* 250–53; *Department of Defense Report on Selected Air and Ground Operations in Cambodia and Laos,* submitted to the Senate Armed Services Committee, Sept. 10, 1973.

29. *WHY,* 247; *Department of Defense Report on Selected Air and Ground Operations in Cambodia and Laos,* submitted to the Senate Armed Services Committee, Sept. 10, 1973.

30. Gen. Earle Wheeler to the secretary of defense, Nov. 20, 1969, submitted to the Senate Armed Services Committee.

31. A fuller discussion of William Shawcross's thesis that the 1969 bombing and the 1970 invasion were responsible for the "destruction of Cambodia" is to be found after the section on the invasion. A good guide to the controversy is the 1987 Touchstone edition of Shawcross's *Sideshow,* which includes an analysis of how Kissinger's memoirs dealt with the allegations, an attack on Shawcross by Kissinger's aide Peter Rodman (from *The American Spectator,* March 1981), a response by Shawcross (from *The American Spectator,* Apr. 27, 1981), and a further response from Rodman (from *The American Spectator,* July 1981).

32. Shawcross, *Sideshow,* 417 (Rodman article reprint), 435; other quotes can be found in *WHY,* 251.

33. Morris, *Uncertain Greatness,* 154; *WHY,* 252, 245; Nixon, *RN,* 382.

34. Lawrence Eagleburger, June 25, 1990.

35. Melvin Laird, Dec. 26, 1989.

36. Impeachment of Richard M. Nixon, report of the House Judiciary Committee, dissenting views, 323; Shawcross, *Sideshow,* 22; *WHY,* 249; *NYT,* Apr. 27, 1969; *WP,* Apr. 27, 1969.

37. Richard Nixon, convention speech, Aug. 8, 1968; *WHY,* 351–53.

38. Melvin Laird, Dec. 26, 1989; Rogers speech, *NYT,* Apr. 17, 1969; Johnson, *The Right Hand of Power,* 524–25; Hersh, *The Price of Power,* 70–75.

39. H. R. Haldeman, Oct. 3, 1990.

40. Morton Halperin, May 24, 1988.

41. Richard Nixon, Oct. 11, 1990; Nixon, *RN,* 380–83; Hersh, *The Price of Power,* 70–75; Nixon press conference, Apr. 18, 1990; *WHY,* 320–21.

42. Nixon, *RN,* 384–85; Richard Nixon, Oct. 11, 1990; *WHY,* 319–20; Morris, *The General's Progress,* 107.

43. Garthoff, *Détente and Confrontation,* 75; *WHY,* 318.

TEN: KISSINGER'S EMPIRE

1. Richard Allen, Aug. 7, 1989; Arthur Schlesinger, Jr., Feb. 16, 1989.

2. Richard Allen, Aug. 7, 1989; Evans and Novak, "Nixon's Appointment of Assistant to Kissinger Raises Questions," *WP,* Dec. 26, 1968; Hersh, *The Price of Power,* 38; Lehman, *Command of the Seas,* 67; Evans and Novak, "Submerging Richard Allen," *WP,* Jan. 19, 1969.

3. Richard Nixon, Oct. 11, 1990; Hersh, *The Price of Power,* 37; *WHY,* 23.

4. Morris, *Haig,* 115; Lawrence Lynn, Jan. 12, 1990; Kissinger-Halperin phone call summary, Aug. 9, 1969, evidence in the case of *Halperin vs. Kissinger,* U.S. District Court, Washington; Szulc, *The Illusion of Peace,* 185; William Hyland, Oct. 22, 1990.

5. Helmut Sonnenfeldt, Sept. 12 and Nov. 16, 1989; Lawrence Lynn, Jan. 12, 1990; Valeriani, *Travels With Henry,* 57–58; Lawrence Eagleburger, June 25, 1990; Hersh, *The Price of Power,* 114–15; William Hyland, Dec. 11, 1989; Morris, *Haig,* 132; Woodward and Bernstein, *The Final Days,* 207; Robert McCloskey, Feb. 2, 1990.

6. Marjorie Hunter, "Four-Star Diplomat," *NYT,* May 5, 1973; West Point Yearbook, 1947; Morris, *Haig,* passim; Morris, *Uncertain Greatness,* 141–42; Schell, *The Village of Ben Suc;* Fritz Kraemer, May 14, 1988; *YOU,* 107; Tony Lake, Jan. 11, 1990; Bette Bao Lord, Aug. 15, 1990; Hersh, *The Price of Power,* 57–58; Winston Lord, Oct. 25, 1989. See also, Truscott, *Dress Gray.*

7. Lawrence Eagleburger, June 25, 1990; Tony Lake, Jan. 11, 1990; Morris, *Haig,* 115.

8. *NYT,* Sept. 12, 1969; I. M. Destler, "Can One Man Do?" *Foreign Policy,* Winter 1971–72; *NYT,* Jan. 19, 1971.

9. Lawrence Eagleburger, June 25, 1990; Szulc, *The Illusion of Peace,* 19; Helmut Sonnenfeldt, Sept. 12 and Nov. 16, 1989; Winston Lord, Oct. 25, 1989; Smith, *Doubletalk,* 109–11; Valeriani, *Travels With Henry,* 21.

10. Zumwalt, *On Watch,* 308, 397; Elmo Zumwalt, Aug. 9, 1990; Daniel Ellsberg, Aug. 8, 1989; John Connally, Apr. 16, 1990; Elliot Richardson, Dec. 13, 1989; Henry Brandon, Nov. 15, 1989.

11. *YOU,* 93; Blumenfeld, *Henry Kissinger,* 271; Arthur Schlesinger, Jr., Feb. 16, 1989; Judis, *William F. Buckley, Jr.,* 304.

12. Moynihan, *A Dangerous Place,* 50; Haldeman, *The Ends of Power,* 94; Nixon, *RN,* 734.

13. John Lehman, Jan. 11, 1990.

14. Ray Price, Jan. 23, 1990.

15. Peter Rodman, Nov. 16, 1989; William Hyland, Dec. 11 and 20, 1989; Lawrence Eagleburger, June 25, 1990; Nancy Kissinger, Jan. 25, 1990; interview with David Kissinger, Feb. 14, 1990; Valeriani, *Travels With Henry,* 24,

81; interview with Diane Sawyer, Sept. 7, 1990; Hyland, *Mortal Rivals,* 7; *Time,* Mar. 8, 1971.

16. Safire, *Before the Fall,* 389–90.

17. Winston Lord, Oct. 25 and Dec. 20, 1989.

18. Parmet, *Richard Nixon and His America,* 168, 243, 254; Safire, *Before the Fall,* 21–22; Ambrose, *Nixon,* vol. 2, 234; Klein, *Making It Perfectly Clear,* 308; Morris, *Uncertain Greatness,* 85.

19. Sulzberger, *The World and Richard Nixon,* 180; Evans and Novak, *Nixon in the White House,* 22; *WHY,* 26.

20. John Ehrlichman, Feb. 27, 1990; Henry Kissinger, Dec. 14, 1989; *WHY,* 28–29; Elliot Richardson, Dec. 13, 1989.

21. Elliot Richardson, Dec. 13, 1989; William Watts, Dec. 13, 1989; Hedrick Smith, "A Past Master of the Soft Sell," *NYT Magazine,* July 27, 1969; John Connally, Apr. 16, 1990; William S. White column, *WP,* Mar. 31, 1969; Milton Viorst, "William Rogers Thinks Like Richard Nixon," *NYT Magazine,* Feb. 27, 1972.

22. *WHY,* 31; Elliot Richardson, Dec. 13, 1989; Henry Kissinger, Dec. 14, 1989; Morris, *Uncertain Greatness,* 134.

23. Morris, *Uncertain Greatness,* 133, 156; John Connally, Apr. 16, 1990; Hersh, *The Price of Power,* 108, 113; John Andrews, Jan. 11, 1990; Joseph Sisco, Mar. 5, 1990; H. R. Haldeman, Feb. 20, 1990; Safire, *Before the Fall,* 406.

24. Melvin Laird, Dec. 18 and 26, 1989; *WHY,* 33.

25. Melvin Laird, Dec. 18 and 26, 1989; Evans and Novak, *Nixon in the White House,* 24. *WHY,* 32; Henry Kissinger, Dec. 14, 1989; James Schlesinger, Nov. 17, 1989; Zumwalt, *On Watch,* 335–36; Richard Helms, Nov. 15, 1989.

26. Melvin Laird, Dec. 26, 1989; *WHY,* 925. Laird insists Kissinger's version of smoke pouring out is exaggerated.

27. Melvin Laird, Dec. 18, 1989; *NYT,* June 11, 1970.

28. Klein, *Making It Perfectly Clear,* 311; H. R. Haldeman, Feb. 20, 1990; Morris, *Uncertain Greatness,* 136; Hersh, *The Price of Power,* 90, 112; Laurence Lynn, Jan. 12, 1990.

29. Some of this information was provided by former White House staffers who preferred not to be identified. It was corroborated through the following sources: H. R. Haldeman, Feb. 20 and Oct. 3, 1990; John Ehrlichman, Feb. 27 and Oct. 10, 1990; Melvin Laird, Dec. 18 and Dec. 26, 1989; memorandum for record, Maj. Frederick Swift, "Subject: Charlie Brown for John Ehrlichman," Feb. 6, 1990, White House Communications Agency files, NPP; Gulley, *Breaking Cover,* 158, 217, 219.

30. Elmo Zumwalt, Aug. 9, 1990.

31. Haldeman's handwritten meeting notes, June 4, 1969, Haldeman papers, box 40, WHSF, NPP.

32. Morton Halperin, Nov. 15, 1989; he tells a similar version of this story in Hersh, *The Price of Power,* 36.

33. *NYT,* Feb. 5, 1969; *Time,* Feb. 14, 1969.

34. Hyland, *Mortal Rivals,* 7; William Watts, Dec. 13, 1989.

35. *First Annual Report on U.S. Foreign Policy* ("State of the World"

report), Feb. 18, 1970, 124–25; John Leacacos, "The Nixon NSC," *Foreign Policy,* Winter 1971–72, 7; *NYT,* Jan. 19, 1971.

36. Richard Helms, Nov. 15, 1989; Elmo Zumwalt, Aug. 9, 1990; Zumwalt, *On Watch,* 310.

37. Morris, *Uncertain Greatness,* 96–103.

38. *WHY,* 29–30; Kissinger talk at the University of California, spring 1968, reprinted in *WP,* Sept. 17, 1973; see also Szulc, *The Illusion of Peace,* 14.

39. Haldeman's handwritten meeting notes, Feb. 15, 1969, Haldeman papers, box 40, WHSF, NPP; H. R. Haldeman, Feb. 20, 1990; Nixon, *RN,* 369; Hersh, *The Price of Power,* 40–41.

40. *WHY,* 728, 806, 822, 840–41, 887; Nixon, *RN,* 390.

41. Winston Lord, Oct. 25, 1989; Tony Lake, Jan. 11, 1990; *YOU,* 263.

42. Lawrence Eagleburger, June 25, 1990; Georgi Arbatov, Nov. 18, 1989.

43. H. R. Haldeman, Feb. 20, 1990; John Ehrlichman, Feb. 27, 1990; Ehrlichman, *Witness to Power,* 297–98; Haldeman's handwritten meeting notes, Aug. 27, 1969, Haldeman papers, box 40, WHSF, NPP.

44. *NYT,* Jan. 18 and Jan. 19, 1971; Safire, *Before the Fall,* 403–4, 391.

45. Haldeman's handwritten meeting notes, Jan. 14, 1972, Haldeman papers, box 45, WHSF, NPP; Safire, *Before the Fall,* 170.

ELEVEN: THE WIRETAPS

1. H. R. Haldeman, Oct. 3, 1990; Haldeman, *Ends of Power,* 100.

2. William Beecher, "Raids in Cambodia by U.S. Unprotested," *NYT,* May 9, 1969; Richard Nixon, Oct. 11, 1990; Nixon, *RN,* 388; Melvin Laird, Dec. 26, 1989; *Dr. Kissinger's Role in Wiretapping,* Senate Foreign Relations Committee, 1974, 23. Laird has said, and some books have reported, that Beecher based his story on a similar one that appeared in the London *Times* two days earlier. This is not true; no such story appeared. For a different version of Laird's conversation with Kissinger, see *Sideshow* by Shawcross, 105.

3. Richard Nixon, Oct. 11, 1990.

4. Wise, *The American Police State,* 31–33, 47; depositions in the case of *Halperin vs. Kissinger,* U.S. District Court, Washington, D.C., case 1187–73; Richard Nixon, Oct. 11, 1990; Morton Halperin, Nov. 15, 1989. Wise's excellent book, based on more than two hundred interviews, gives a colorful account of the wiretapping and was particularly helpful.

5. Wise, *The American Police State,* 33–38; depositions in the case of *Halperin vs. Kissinger,* op. cit.; *Dr. Kissinger's Role in Wiretapping,* op. cit., 23, 199; Gentry, *J. Edgar Hoover,* 632–36. In the documents released by the Senate, the names of the participants are all replaced by coded letters. Henry Brandon, for example, is referred to throughout as P, Helmut Sonnenfeldt as B. The code turns out to be simple: the people involved were listed in reverse alphabetical order and then assigned letters, starting with *A*.

6. Kissinger-Halperin phone call summary, Aug. 9, 1969, evidence in the case of *Halperin vs. Kissinger,* op. cit.

7. Helmut Sonnenfeldt, Nov. 16, 1989.

8. Melvin Laird, Dec. 26, 1989.

9. Daniel Davidson, July 31 and Aug. 3, 1989; Sullivan, *The Bureau.*

10. Tony Lake, Jan. 11, 1990; Roger Morris, Mar. 26, 1990; Morris, *Uncertain Greatness,* 159; Hersh, *The Price of Power,* 101.

11. Presidential news summaries and Butterfield memos, WHSF, NPP; John Ehrlichman, Apr. 2, 1990; Ehrlichman, *Witness to Power,* 175.

12. Nixon deposition, Jan. 15, 1976, and Kissinger deposition, Mar. 30, 1976, case of *Halperin vs. Kissinger,* op. cit.; Kissinger testimony, *Dr. Kissinger's Role in Wiretapping,* op. cit., 195; Haldeman's handwritten notes, Haldeman papers, box 40, WHSF, NPP.

13. Sullivan memo and written testimony, Kissinger and Haig testimony, in *Dr. Kissinger's Role in Wiretapping,* op. cit., 63, 64, 118, 124, 214, 259; Henry Kissinger, May 8, 1990. See also, Wise, *The American Police State,* 48; Szulc, *The Illusion of Peace,* 186.

14. Henry Brandon, Nov. 15, 1989; Richard Nixon, Oct. 11, 1990; Brandon, *Special Relationships,* 269–74; Wise, *The American Police State,* 49; Morris, *Haig,* 158.

15. *Dr. Kissinger's Role in Wiretapping,* op. cit., 104, 184–87; Morris, *Haig,* 159–60; notes for June 4, 1969, meeting, Haldeman papers, box 40, WHSF, NPP.

16. Safire, *Before the Fall,* 167–69; Safire, "Concerto in F," *NYT,* July 25, 1974; Haig testimony, *Dr. Kissinger's Role in Wiretapping,* op. cit., 254; Wise, *The American Police State,* 59.

17. Safire, *Before the Fall,* 167; Wise, *The American Police State,* 68; Shawcross, *Sideshow,* 155; Szulc, *The Illusion of Peace,* 286; H. R. Haldeman, Oct. 3, 1990.

18. Tony Lake, Jan. 11, 1990, Jan. 6, Jan. 8, Feb. 11, 1991; transcripts of wiretapped phone conversations, May to Dec. 1970, and related reports from the FBI to the White House, courtesy of Tony Lake; letter from Kissinger to Lake, Jan. 12, 1989; William Sullivan memo, May 13, 1970, in *Dr. Kissinger's Role in Wiretapping,* op. cit., 28.

19. Winston Lord, Oct. 25, 1989; Bette Bao Lord, Aug. 15, 1990.

20. Henry Kissinger, Oct. 9, 1989; meeting notes for May 11, 1970, and similar ones from May 10 and 12, Haldeman papers, box 41, WHSF, NPP; Nixon deposition, *Halperin vs. Kissinger,* op. cit.; Richard Nixon, Oct. 11, 1990; H. R. Haldeman, Feb. 20, 1990; memos to Sullivan on May 13 and 15, 1970, in *Dr. Kissinger's Role in Wiretapping,* op. cit., 28.

21. Helmut Sonnenfeldt, Nov. 16, 1989; William Sullivan memo of May 18, 1970, Hoover memo of Oct. 15, 1970, in *Dr. Kissinger's Role in Wiretapping,* op. cit., 28, 201–3, 277, 151 (includes reproductions of the Ehrlichman-Haldeman-Magruder correspondence); Hersh, *The Price of Power,* 322; Wise, *The American Police State,* 65–71.

22. Safire, *Before the Fall,* 169; Nixon conversation with John Dean, Feb. 28, 1973, the White House tapes, Nixon archives.

23. Nixon letter to Sen. J. William Fulbright, July 12, 1974, in *Dr. Kissinger's Role in Wiretapping,* op. cit., 111; see also, Nixon press conference of May 22, 1973; Nixon conversation with John Dean, Feb. 28, 1973, the White House tapes, Nixon archives.

24. Kissinger testimony, James Adams testimony, Elliot Richardson testimony, in *Dr. Kissinger's Role in Wiretapping,* op. cit., 99, 102, 186, 188; Nixon deposition, Jan. 15, 1976, case of *Halperin vs. Kissinger,* op. cit.; Henry Kissinger, Feb. 16, 1990. The three criteria for selecting wiretap victims are in *YOU,* 120; also, in Kissinger's testimony, nomination hearings, Senate Foreign Relations Committee, Sept. 7, 1973, 12. The criteria are so nebulous and convoluted that it is hard to believe that they were taken seriously at the time.

25. Kissinger testimony, nomination hearings, Senate Foreign Relations Committee, Sept. 7, 1973; see also, *YOU,* 429.

26. Adams testimony, Smith testimony, *Dr. Kissinger's Role in Wiretapping,* op. cit., 93, 94.

27. Safire, *Before the Fall,* 169; Szulc, *The Illusion of Peace,* 181; Richard Holbrooke, "The Price of Power," *WP* op-ed page, June 16, 1974; *YOU,* 121.

28. Meeting notes for May 11, 1970, Haldeman papers, box 41, WHSF, NPP; DeLoach FBI memo, Sept. 10, 1969, and Hoover memo, Nov. 4, in *Dr. Kissinger's Role in Wiretapping,* op. cit., 26; Nixon's handwritten notes, news summaries, Mar. 2, 1971, and Sept. 8, 1972, boxes 31, 32, WHSF, NPP, Wise, *The American Police State,* 62–64.

29. Wise, *The American Police State,* 3–30; Caulfield testimony to the Senate Select Committee on 1972 campaign activities (the Watergate committee), 1973; John Ehrlichman, Oct. 10, 1990; Polly Kraft, Nov. 16, 1989; Lloyd Cutler, Oct. 8, 1990; Nixon's handwritten notes, news summaries, Feb. 1970, box 31, WHSF, NPP. The Wise book is the source of the colorful details of the case.

30. Brent Scowcroft, July 16, 1990; Charles Colson, Sept. 10, 1990; Henry Kissinger, Oct. 9, 1989; Woodward and Bernstein, *The Final Days,* 203; Safire, "The Dead Key Scrolls," *NYT,* Jan. 16, 1976; Safire, *Before the Fall,* 169.

31. Lawrence Higby, Jan. 29, 1990; H. R. Haldeman, Oct. 3, 1990; John Ehrlichman, Oct. 10, 1990.

32. "Kissinger: No Book," *WP,* Feb. 22, 1971; Gulley, *Breaking Cover,* 208; *NYT,* Dec. 29 and 30, 1976. Interviews with Kissinger assistants. An excellent discussion of Kissinger's papers is to be found in "Who Owns History?" by Steve Weinberg, a paper for the Center for Public Integrity, Washington, D.C.

33. H. R. Haldeman, Feb. 20 and Oct. 3, 1990; John Ehrlichman, Feb. 27 and Oct. 10, 1990; Henry Kissinger, Feb. 16, 1990; Haldeman, *The Ends of Power,* 97.

34. Henry Kissinger, Feb. 16, 1990; Charles Colson, Sept. 10, 1990; H. R. Haldeman, Feb. 20 and Oct. 3, 1990; Lawrence Higby, Jan. 29, 1990; John Ehrlichman, Feb. 27 and Oct. 10, 1990; Lawrence Eagleburger, June 25, 1990; Roger Morris, March 26, 1990.

TWELVE: NO EXIT

1. Richard Nixon, Oct. 11, 1990.

2. Nixon talk to Southern delegates, Aug. 6, 1968, in Chester, Hodgson, and Page, *An American Melodrama,* 462; Evans and Novak, *Nixon in the White House,* 76, 82; *WHY,* 272.

3. Nguyen Van Thieu, Oct. 16, 1990; Schecter and Hung, *The Palace File,* 32–33.

4. *WHY,* 274; Nixon, *RN,* 392; Nixon press conference, June 8, 1969.

5. Kissinger background briefing, Laguna Beach, Calif., June 6, 1969; Clark Clifford, "A Vietnam Reappraisal," *Foreign Affairs,* July 1969; Nixon press conference, June 19, 1969; Ambrose, *Nixon,* vol. 2, 278.

6. Kissinger, *Nuclear Weapons and Foreign Policy,* 50; *WHY,* 275.

7. Melvin Laird, Dec. 26, 1989; Nixon note, news summary, Feb. 9, 1970, WHSF, NPP.

8. Tony Lake, Jan. 11, 1990; *WHY,* 284. Kissinger discusses the memo and reprints it in the notes of *WHY* (p. 1480), but does not describe its genesis or Lake's role.

9. Kissinger background briefing, Aug. 22, 1969; Ehrlichman notes, Oct. 6, 1969, Ehrlichman's meetings with the president, box 3, WHSF, NPP.

10. Inaugural address, John Kennedy, Jan. 20, 1961; *WHY,* 56–57; Richard Nixon, Oct. 11, 1990.

11. Kissinger, "The Meaning of History," unpublished undergraduate thesis, Harvard, 136; Kissinger, "Central Issues in American Foreign Policy," in *Agenda for the Nation* edited by Gordon, 612. See also, Brown, *The Crisis of Power,* 6–8.

12. *WHY,* 223; Nixon background briefing, July 25, 1969.

13. Richard Nixon, Oct. 11, 1990.

14. *U.S. Foreign Policy for the 1970s,* a report from the president to the Congress ("State of the World" reports), Feb. 18, 1970, 3, and Feb. 25, 1971, 11, 16.

15. Walters, *Silent Missions,* 508–12; Szulc, *The Illusion of Peace,* 138; *WHY,* 278.

16. Tony Lake, Jan. 11, 1990.

17. *WHY,* 259, 281, 448; Walters, *Silent Missions,* 511; Tony Lake, Jan. 11, 1990; Winston Lord, Oct. 25, 1989; Melvin Laird, Dec. 26, 1989.

18. Nixon, *RN,* 399; *WHY,* 280.

19. Tony Lake, Jan. 11, 1990; Winston Lord, Oct. 25, 1989; Laurence Lynn, Jan. 12, 1990; Peter Rodman, Sept. 12, 1989; Charles Colson, Sept. 10, 1990; H. R. Haldeman, Oct. 30, 1990; Richard Nixon, Oct. 11, 1990; Henry Kissinger, Mar. 26, 1990; "North Vietnam Contingency Plan," a memo from Kissinger to Laird, Oct. 24, 1969; Hammond, *Public Affairs,* 225; Morris, *Uncertain Greatness,* 164–67; Nixon, *RN,* 403; Hersh, *The Price of Power,* 125–33; Szulc, *The Illusion of Peace,* 150–56.

20. Henry Kissinger, Mar. 26, 1990; *WHY,* 285; Richard Nixon, Mar. 21 and Oct. 11, 1990; *Time* interview with Nixon, Apr. 2, 1990; Nixon, *RN,* 405.

21. Nixon, *RN,* 407; *WHY,* 305.

22. President Nixon's address to the nation, Nov. 3, 1969; Nixon, *RN,* 409–10; *WHY,* 306.

23. Nguyen Van Thieu, Oct. 15, 1990; Ambrose, *Nixon,* vol. 2, 311.

24. William Watts, Dec. 13, 1989.

25. U.S. Department of Defense casualty figures for the Vietnam conflict, revised as of 1985; *WHY,* 524.

26. *NYT,* Feb. 19, 1990; *U.S. Foreign Policy for the 1970s* ("State of the World" report), Feb. 18, 1970, 12, 17; Tony Lake, Jan. 11, 1990.

27. *Newsweek,* Feb. 10, 1970; *WHY,* 435; U.S. Department of Defense figures, submitted to the Senate Foreign Relations Committee, Feb. 20, 1970.

28. Winston Lord, Oct. 25, 1989; *WHY,* 438–40.

29. Morris, *Uncertain Greatness,* 172; Szulc, *The Illusion of Peace,* 226; Roger Morris, Mar. 26, 1990.

30. Walters, *Silent Missions,* 512–14; *WHY,* 439.

31. *WHY,* 441; Isaacs, *Without Honor,* 31.

32. Morris, *Uncertain Greatness,* 172; *WHY,* 442–44, 437; Szulc, *The Illusion of Peace,* 228; Winston Lord, Nov. 2, 1989; Anthony Lake, Jan. 11, 1990; Roger Morris, Mar. 6, 1990; Richard Smyser, Jan. 12, 1990.

33. Walters, *Secret Missions,* 578–80; *WHY,* 440.

34. Tony Lake, Jan. 11, 1990; Winston Lord, Nov. 2, 1989; Roger Morris, Mar. 26, 1990; Richard Smyser, Jan. 12, 1990; Henry Kissinger memo to Richard Nixon, Feb. 27, 1990, *WHY,* 447; Nixon, *RN,* 447; *Philadelphia Bulletin,* Feb. 22, 1970; *Vietnam Policy Proposals,* hearings before the Senate Foreign Relations Committee, Feb. 3, 1970, 4. One particularly good article about peace prospects was by Richard J. Barnet, who had recently visited Hanoi. He explained the Hanoi leadership's willingness to allow such prominent non-communists as Duong Van Minh, a once and future presidential candidate, to serve in a coalition. Richard J. Barnet, "How Hanoi Sees Nixon," *New York Review of Books,* Jan. 29, 1970.

THIRTEEN: THE INVASION OF CAMBODIA

1. Thomas Enders, Jan. 16, 1990; *WHY,* 457–69; Henry Kissinger, Dec. 21, 1990; Tony Lake, Jan. 11, 1990; Nixon, *RN,* 447; Shawcross, *Sideshow,* 112–27, 403; Richard Helms, Nov. 15, 1989; Hersh, *The Price of Power,* 176–83. Hersh argues that some U.S. military officials in Vietnam may have encouraged the overthrow of Sihanouk, but he does not pin such plots to Kissinger or Nixon. Roger Morris, in *Uncertain Greatness,* p. 173, says that the CIA had a station in Cambodia and gave advance warning of the coup, but based on interviews and papers I have seen, and the investigations of such Kissinger critics as Hersh and Shawcross, I think that this is incorrect. The day of the coup, a CIA report was circulated that quoted a businessman as saying the demonstrations in Phnom Penh might be a precursor to a coup (see *WHY,* 464).

2. Kissinger–Le Duc Tho memo of conversation, Apr. 4, 1970, and Nixon note to Kissinger on March 19 memo, in *WHY,* 468, 465; Shawcross, *Sideshow,* 124–25, 411; Sihanouk, *My War With the CIA,* 28; Nixon, *RN,* 447; Hersh, *The Price of Power,* 186–87; Thomas Enders, Jan. 16, 1990; Winston Lord, Nov. 2, 1989; Peter Rodman, Sept. 12, 1989.

3. *WHY,* 487, 489; Nixon, *RN,* 447; Roger Morris, Mar. 26, 1990; Tony Lake, Jan. 11, 1990; Winston Lord, Nov. 2, 1989; Kalb and Kalb, *Kissinger,* 154.

4. Shawcross, *Sideshow,* 136; *WHY,* 480, 482, 475–78; Szulc, *The Illusion of Peace,* 250.

5. Nixon, *RN,* 448; *WHY,* 489–92, 1484 (Nixon's version of the memo is slightly different from Kissinger's).

6. Shawcross, *Sideshow,* 410; Shawcross, "Through History With Henry Kissinger," *Harper's,* Nov. 1980, 90; *WHY,* 488–92; Thomas Enders, Jan. 16, 1990; Melvin Laird, Dec. 26, 1989.

7. J. William Fulbright, Jan. 30, 1989; Henry Kissinger, Mar. 26, 1990; William Watts, Dec. 13, 1989; White House logs of the president's telephone calls, Apr. 1970, WHSF, NPP; *Kissinger's Role in Wiretapping,* Senate Foreign Relations Committee, 358; *WHY,* 495; Safire, *Before the Fall,* 182; Kalb and Kalb, *Kissinger,* 157.

8. *WHY,* 495–96.

9. Henry Kissinger, Oct. 9, 1989; William Watts, Dec. 13, 1989; Roger Morris, Mar. 26, 1990; Winston Lord, Nov. 2, 1989; John Ehrlichman, Feb. 27, 1990; Wise, *The American Police State,* 92; Morris, *Haig,* 141; Morris, *Uncertain Greatness,* 95, 147.

10. Tony Lake, Jan. 11, 1990; Laurence Lynn, Jan. 12, 1990; Winston Lord, Oct. 25, 1989 and Apr. 24, 1990; William Watts, Dec. 13, 1989; Roger Morris, Mar. 26, 1990.

11. Richard Nixon, Oct. 11, 1990; *WHY,* 497–98.

12. *WHY,* 498–99; Diane Sawyer, Sept. 7, 1990; unpublished galley proof of *WHY;* William Shawcross, "Through History With Henry Kissinger," *Harper's,* Nov. 1980, 95; Kalb and Kalb, *Kissinger,* 160.

13. Haldeman notes, Apr. 27, 1970, Haldeman papers, box 41, WHSF, NPP; Melvin Laird, Dec. 26, 1989; Richard Nixon, Oct. 11, 1990; *WHY,* 499–501; Nixon, *RN,* 450.

14. Melvin Laird, Dec. 26, 1989.

15. Memorandum of meeting by John Mitchell, Apr. 28, 1970, country file: Cambodia, NPP; *WHY,* 502, 1485.

16. Nixon's address to the nation, Apr. 30, 1970; *WHY,* 503–5; Safire, *Before the Fall,* 183, 187–88; Kissinger background briefing, Apr. 30, 1970; William Shawcross, "Through History With Henry Kissinger," *Harper's,* Nov. 1980, 95; Shawcross, *Sideshow,* 407–8.

17. David Frost, Oct. 24, 1990.

18. Westmoreland, *A Soldier Reports,* 388–89; Shawcross, *Sideshow,* 152; Nixon, *RN,* 453–54; Melvin Laird, Dec. 26, 1989.

19. Egil Krogh memo, WHSF, and Nixon's telephone logs, May 8–9, 1970, NPP; Safire, *Before the Fall,* 202–4; Henry Kissinger, Oct. 9, 1989; Nixon, *RN,* 460; *WHY,* 512–14; Johnson, *The Right Hand of Power,* 530.

20. Henry Kissinger, Oct. 9, 1989; Richard Nixon, Mar. 13 and Oct. 11, 1990; David Frost, *I Gave Them a Sword,* 164; Safire, *Before the Fall,* 192.

21. Haldeman notes, May 11, 1970, Haldeman papers, box 41, WHSF, NPP; John Ehrlichman, Feb. 27, 1990; Katharine Graham, Dec. 14, 1989; Safire, *Before the Fall,* 192.

22. Winston Lord, Oct. 25 and Dec. 20, 1989; Nixon's address to the nation, June 3, 1970; Susan Mary Alsop, Dec. 13, 1989.

23. *WHY,* 508–9, 547, 693–96; Joseph Alsop, "Dobrynin on Mideast," *WP,* Sept. 9, 1970.

24. William Shawcross, "Through History With Henry Kissinger," *Harper's,* Nov. 1980.

25. Kissinger testimony, Apr. 18, 1975, *The Vietnam-Cambodia Emergency,* House International Relations Committee, Part 1, 152.

26. Morris, *Uncertain Greatness,* 175; Shawcross, *Sideshow,* 391–96, 414, and passim; *WHY,* 470, 497, 517, and passim; Henry Kissinger, May 10, 1990; Kissinger testimony, Apr. 18, 1975, *The Vietnam-Cambodia Emergency,* op. cit.; Szulc, *The Illusion of Peace,* 273; Kalb and Kalb, *Kissinger,* 171–72; Brown, *The Crisis of Power,* 57; Peter Rodman, "Sideswipe," *American Spectator,* Mar. 1981; William Shawcross, "Shawcross Swipes Again," *American Spectator,* Apr. 27, 1981; Rodman, "Rodman Responds," *American Spectator,* July 1981 (all reprinted in the Touchstone paperback of *Sideshow*); William Shawcross, "Through History With Henry Kissinger," *Harper's,* Nov. 1980.

27. William Watts, Dec. 13, 1989. See also, Woodward and Bernstein, *The Final Days,* 205; Hersh, *The Price of Power,* 191.

28. Roger Morris, Mar. 26, 1990; Anthony Lake, Jan. 11, 1990; Morris, *Haig,* 114; letter from Lake and Morris to Kissinger, Apr. 29, 1970, made available to the author.

29. Laurence Lynn, Jan. 12, 1990.

30. Winston Lord, Oct. 25, Nov. 2, and Dec. 20, 1989; Bette Bao Lord, Feb. 15 and Aug. 15, 1990.

31. Don Oberdorfer, "Kissinger's Open Line," *WP,* Mar. 25, 1971; *WHY,* 510; Brent Scowcroft, July 16, 1990; Joseph Kraft, "The Bottomless Pit," *WP,* May 3, 1970; Polly Kraft, Nov. 16, 1989; *YOU,* 102.

32. Mailer, *St. George and the Godfather,* 119; Kissinger background briefing, May 4, 1970; Roger Morris, Mar. 26, 1990; Helmut Sonnenfeldt, Nov. 16, 1989; Tony Lake, Jan. 11, 1990; Blumenfeld, *Henry Kissinger,* 186, 192.

33. Michael Kinsley, "I Think We Have a Very Unhappy Colleague-on-Leave," *Harvard Crimson,* May 16, 1970; Michael Kinsley, "Eating Lunch at Henry's," *Washington Monthly,* Sept. 1970; Thomas Schelling, Feb. 3, 1989; Paul Doty, Feb. 13, 1989; *WHY,* 514–15.

34. Brian McDonnell interview, Philadelphia *Bulletin,* Apr. 3, 1971; Bette Bao Lord, Aug. 15, 1990; *WHY,* 1015.

35. Mary McGrory, "Kissinger Meets Plotters," *Washington Star,* Mar. 12, 1971.

36. Daniel Ellsberg, Aug. 8, 1989; Lloyd Shearer, Apr. 18, 1990; Ellsberg interview with *Rolling Stone,* Nov. 8, 1973. Ellsberg also gave me his notes and some unpublished memoirs.

37. Joan Braden, Feb. 26, 1990; J. William Fulbright, Jan. 30, 1989; Barbara Howar, Dec. 8, 1989; *WP,* Mar. 21, 1971; Henry Kissinger, Jan. 21, 1990.

38. Fritz Kraemer, May 14, 1988; Lawrence Eagleburger, June 25, 1990; John Lehman, Jan. 12, 1990; H. R. Haldeman, Feb. 20, 1990.

FOURTEEN: TWO WEEKS IN SEPTEMBER

1. Henry Kissinger's appointment calendar, Sept. 14, 1970; Richard Helms's desk diary, Sept. 14, 1970; Richard Helms, Nov. 15, 1989; Haldeman papers, box 42, WHSF, NPP; Edward Korry cables, Sept. 12, 14, and 15, 1970, shown to the author; *Covert Action in Chile,* report of the Senate Intelligence Committee, Dec. 18, 1975; *Alleged Assassination Plots,* report of the Senate Intelligence Committee, 1975, 230 and passim; Edward Korry, "The Sellout of Chile," *Penthouse,* Mar. 1978; notes taken at the 40 Committee meeting,

Sept. 14, 1970, shown to the author; Hersh, *The Price of Power,* 270–73; *WHY,* 608, 637, 671–73, 929–30; Polly Kraft, Nov. 16, 1989.

2. Judis, *William F. Buckley, Jr.,* 302, 389.

3. Kissinger's appointment calendar, Sept. 15, 1970; Helms's desk diary, Sept. 15, 1970; Richard Helms, Nov. 15, 1989; Powers, *The Man Who Kept the Secrets,* 234–35; Helms's notes, Sept. 15, 1970; *Covert Action in Chile,* op. cit., 92; *Alleged Assassination Plots,* op. cit., 228; Ranelagh, *The Agency,* 516; Cord Meyer, *Facing Reality,* 186.

4. Kissinger's appointment calendar, Sept. 15, 1970; NSSM-99, shown to the author.

5. Kissinger's appointment calendar, Sept. 15, 1970; personal notes from WSAG meeting, provided by a participant to the author; *WHY,* 610–11; Joseph Sisco, Mar. 5, 1990; Quandt, *Decade of Decisions,* 112; Kalb and Kalb, *Kissinger,* 197; Nixon, *RN,* 483; Brandon, *The Retreat of American Power,* 133; C. L. Sulzberger column, *NYT,* Sept. 25, 1970; Sulzberger, *An Age of Mediocrity,* 655.

6. *Time,* Sept. 28, 1970; Kissinger's appointment calendar, Sept. 16, 1970; *WHY,* 612; Nixon speech at Kansas State University, Sept. 16, 1970; Helms's desk diary, Sept. 16, 1970.

7. Kissinger briefing, Chicago, Sept. 16, 1970.

8. Kissinger's appointment calendar, Sept. 17, 1970; *Chicago Sun-Times,* Sept. 17, 1970; Brandon, *The Retreat of American Power,* 134; *WHY,* 614–15; military deployment notes, from Adm. Elmo Zumwalt.

9. Kissinger's appointment calendar, Sept. 17, 1970; *WHY,* 978; Richard Smyser, Jan. 12, 1990; Winston Lord, Nov. 2, 1989.

10. Kissinger's appointment calendar, Sept. 18, 1970; Helms's desk diary, Sept. 18, 1970; Nixon's schedule, Sept. 18, 1970, president's personal files, NPP; Richard Helms, Nov. 15, 1989; H. R. Haldeman, Oct. 3, 1990; Garthoff, *Détente and Confrontation,* 77; "Soviet Naval Activities in Cuba," House Foreign Affairs Committee, 1971; Garthoff, "Handling the Cienfuegos Crisis," *International Security,* Summer 1983, 46; *WHY,* 638–42; Nixon, *RN,* 486.

11. Helms's desk diary, Sept. 18, 1970; Richard Helms, Nov. 15, 1989.

12. Kissinger's appointment calendar, Sept. 19, 1970; *WHY,* 617, 639–40; Helms's desk diary, Sept. 19, 1970; Richard Helms, Nov. 15, 1989 and Nov. 13, 1990; Ranelagh, *The Agency,* 516; weekly military report on Indochina, Department of Defense.

13. Kissinger's appointment calendar, Sept. 20, 1970; *WHY,* 620–23; Quandt, *Decade of Decisions,* 115; Kalb and Kalb, *Kissinger,* 201–3; Rabin, *The Rabin Memoirs,* 187–90; Nixon, *RN,* 485. Some critics (see Hersh, *The Price of Power,* 245–46) suggest that the invasion was really led by the Palestine Liberation Army based in Syria rather than by the Syrian army. The commander of the tank force was in fact a former Syrian prime minister, Yussef Zaylin. He was later arrested when his rivals within Syria, led by Hafiz Assad, came to power and denounced the folly of Syrian involvement in the war.

14. Kissinger's appointment calendar, Sept. 21, 1970; *WHY,* 622, 625–28, 640–41; Joseph Sisco, Mar. 26, 1990; handwritten notes of Sept. 21, 1970, NSC meeting, provided to the author.

15. Kissinger's appointment calendar, Sept. 22, 1970; Helms's desk diary,

Sept. 22, 1970; Richard Helms, Nov. 15, 1989, and Nov. 13, 1990; *WHY*, 628–29; *Time*, Oct. 5, 1970.

16. Kissinger's appointment calendar, Sept. 23, 1970; Richard Nixon, Oct. 11, 1990; Joseph Sisco, March 5 and 26, 1990; *WHY*, 630, 643; Quandt, *Decade of Decisions*, 119; Nixon, *RN*, 487; Hersh, *The Price of Power*, 253.

17. Kissinger's appointment calendar, Sept. 24, 1970; *WHY*, 675; *Covert Action in Chile*, op. cit., 26; Hugh Sidey, Oct. 16, 1989; *Life*, Oct. 2, 1970; *Time*, Oct. 5, 1970.

18. Kissinger's appointment calendar, Sept. 25, 1970; *WHY*, 631, 644–46; *NYT*, Sept. 25, 1970; Kalb and Kalb, *Kissinger*, 211–12; Brandon, *The Retreat of American Power*, 282; Hersh, *The Price of Power*, 255; Henry Kissinger, Mar. 31, 1990; Rabin, *The Rabin Memoirs*, 189; Quandt, *Decade of Decisions*, 123.

19. *WHY*, 979; Winston Lord, Nov. 2, 1989.

20. *WHY*, 649–50; Zumwalt, *On Watch*, 311–13; Elmo Zumwalt, Nov. 20, 1989; Garthoff, *Détente and Confrontation*, 79–81.

21. *WHY*, 676–83; *YOU*, 374–413; *Covert Action in Chile*, op. cit.; *Alleged Assassination Plots*, Nov. 1975 report, op. cit., 223–45; Phillips, *The Night Watch*, 220–23; Powers, *The Man Who Kept the Secrets*, 228; Hersh, *The Price of Power*, 283–90; Elmo Zumwalt, Nov. 20, 1989; Zumwalt, *On Watch*, 326–27; *NYT*, Mar. 7, 1971. My conclusions generally follow those of the Senate Intelligence Committee, known as the Church Committee after its chairman Frank Church. For further discussion of the extent to which the CIA and the Nixon administration's policies destabilized Chile after Allende's election, see: Sigmund, *The Overthrow of Allende and the Politics of Chile*, and Davis, *The Last Two Years of Salvador Allende*.

22. Neff, *Warriors Against Israel*, 41; Riad, *The Struggle for Peace in the Middle East*, 165; Quandt, *Decade of Decisions*, 124–27; Heikal, *The Road to Ramadan*, 98–100; Nixon, *RN*, 490. My conclusions generally follow those in Quandt.

23. Kissinger background briefing, Oct. 8, 1970; Kissinger background briefing, Aug. 14, 1970; Kalb and Kalb, *Kissinger*, 175; Richard Smyser, Jan. 12, 1990; Hugh Sidey, "The Story of a Peace Initiative," *Life*, Oct. 16, 1970.

24. Kissinger note to Nixon, Dec. 4, 1970, president's personal files, NPP; Ehrlichman notes of meeting with the president, Dec. 3, 1970, Ehrlichman papers, box 4, WHSF, NPP; Szulc, *The Illusion of Peace*, 376; *President's Report on Foreign Policy*, Feb. 25, 1971; Ehrlichman's notes of meeting with the president, Jan. 12, 1971, Ehrlichman papers, box 4, WHSF, NPP; Landau, *Kissinger*, 101; *Harvard Crimson*, Jan. 15, 1970; *Boston Globe*, Jan. 17, 1970; *NYT*, Jan. 17, 1970.

FIFTEEN: SALT

1. Hyland, *Mortal Rivals*, 43.

2. Carl Kaysen, July 18, 1989; *WHY*, 210–12, 540; Hersh, *The Price of Power*, 151–55, 164; *NYT*, June 20, 1969.

3. Gerard Smith, Aug. 1, 1990; Smith, *Doubletalk*, 158–61.

4. Richard Helms, Nov. 15, 1989; Powers, *The Man Who Kept the Se-*

crets, 211–12; *WHY,* 37; Garthoff, *Détente and Confrontation,* 135; New-house, *Cold Dawn,* 50; William Hyland, Oct. 22, 1990; Hersh, *The Price of Power,* 158; unpublished paper by Hyland analyzing Hersh's *The Price of Power,* used with Hyland's permission. Garthoff, who was on the SALT dele-gation and is often critical of Kissinger, has produced a useful documented survey of Soviet-American relations. Kissinger gave Newhouse access to the NSC staff and documents.

5. Halperin-Gelb conversation, May 27, 1969, part of the record of the case of *Halperin vs. Kissinger,* U.S. District Court, Washington, D.C., case 1187–73.

6. Smith, *Doubletalk,* 109; Morris, *Uncertain Greatness,* 210; *WHY,* 540–44; Garthoff, *Détente and Confrontation,* 138–39.

7. Garthoff, *Détente and Confrontation,* 138–39; *WHY,* 541–43; Smith, *Doubletalk,* 171–72; Gerard Smith, Aug. 1, 1990; Newhouse, *Cold Dawn,* 16.

8. *WHY,* 541; Kissinger press conference, June 15, 1972; Garthoff, *Détente and Confrontation,* 140. Kissinger, in 1972 testimony about why there had not been a MIRV ban, misstated the Soviet position by saying that they "refused a deployment ban as such. What they proposed was a production ban." In fact, they proposed banning both, just not testing.

9. *WHY,* 540–44; Garthoff, *Détente and Confrontation,* 142; Smith, *Doubletalk,* 152; Gerard Smith, Aug. 1, 1990.

10. *WHY,* 525, 534, 544–45; Smith, *Doubletalk,* 147; Gerard Smith, Aug. 1, 1990; Nitze, *From Hiroshima to Glasnost,* 309.

11. Smith, *Doubletalk,* 154; speech and arms control discussion by Do-brynin (attended by the author), Georgetown University, Nov. 17, 1989; Kis-singer background briefing, Dec. 3, 1974.

12. Egon Bahr, Mar. 19, 1991.

13. Melvin Laird, Dec. 26, 1989.

14. Gerard Smith, Aug. 1, 1990; Henry Kissinger, Mar. 31, 1990; William Hyland, Oct. 22, 1990; Winston Lord, Nov. 2, 1989; Georgi Arbatov, Nov. 18, 1989; talk by Anatoli Dobrynin, Georgetown University, Nov. 17, 1989; un-published paper by Hyland analyzing Hersh's *The Price of Power,* used with Hyland's permission; *WHY,* 805–30, 992; Garthoff, *Détente and Confronta-tion,* 148–60; Smith, *Doubletalk,* 195, 218–46; Newhouse, *Cold Dawn,* 222–29; Hersh, *The Price of Power,* 340–42.

15. Colson, *Born Again,* 43–45, 57–59; Charles Colson, Sept. 10, 1990.

16. H. R. Haldeman, Feb. 20, 1990; Daniel Ellsberg, Aug. 8, 1989; John Ehrlichman, Feb. 27, 1970; Ehrlichman, *Witness to Power,* 302; Hersh, *The Price of Power,* 384; Richard Nixon, Oct. 11, 1990. Ellsberg's name did not surface publicly until three days later, but Haig and Kissinger figured it was him the moment they heard the papers had been leaked. There is no indepen-dent evidence that these charges against Ellsberg are true and he has denied that he shot at peasants in Vietnam.

17. John Ehrlichman, Feb. 27, 1990; Ehrlichman meeting notes, June 17, 1970, Ehrlichman papers, box 5, WHSF, NPP; Ehrlichman affidavit, Apr. 30, 1974, U.S. District Court, Washington, Watergate special investigation; Haldeman, *The Ends of Power,* 110; Hersh, *The Price of Power,* 325, 330–31; 383–85; Charles Colson, Sept. 10, 1990; John Ehrlichman, Feb. 27, 1990; H. R. Haldeman, Feb. 20, 1990; Jack Anderson column, June 11, 1973, *WP;*

YOU, 118; Haldeman, *The Ends of Power*, 113–14; *Dr. Kissinger's Role in Wiretapping*, Senate Foreign Relations Committee, 174. The Ehrlichman notes of the June 17 meeting, along with the secret White House tape recording, were subpoenaed by the Watergate special prosecutor.

18. *WHY*, 1018, 1043, 1488, 1020; Ball, *Diplomacy for a Crowded World*, 77; Richard Smyser, Jan. 12, 1990; Henry Kissinger, Dec. 21, 1990; Nguyen Van Thieu, Oct. 15, 1990.

SIXTEEN: CHINA

1. Nixon, *RN*, 552; *WHY*, 163, 691. The belief that Chinese expansionism was behind the Vietnam War is reflected throughout the Pentagon Papers.

2. Speech to the World Affairs Council of Philadelphia, May 1, 1968, the public papers of Nelson Rockefeller (written by Henry Kissinger); Graubard, *Kissinger*, 250; *WHY*, 165, 169.

3. Speech to the Commonwealth Club of California by Richard Nixon, Apr. 2, 1965; Schecter and Hung, *The Palace File*, 9; Richard Nixon, "Asia After Viet Nam," *Foreign Affairs*, Oct. 1967, 121; Safire, *Before the Fall*, 366, 367.

4. Nixon memo to Kissinger, Feb. 1, 1969, and Nixon memo to Kissinger, Sept. 22, 1969, confidential files, box 6, China, NPP; Schulzinger, *Henry Kissinger*, 76; Haldeman, *The Ends of Power*, 91.

5. *WHY*, 172, 190; magazine news summary, Apr. 1969, president's office files, box 30, WHSF, NPP; address in Canberra, Australia, by William Rogers, Aug. 8, 1969.

6. Richard Nixon, Mar. 13 and Oct. 11, 1990; H. R. Haldeman, Oct. 3, 1990.

7. *WHY*, 686–732; Georgi Arbatov, Nov. 18, 1989; Nixon, *RN*, 550; Richard Nixon, Oct. 11, 1990; Garthoff, *Détente and Confrontation*, 227; Edgar Snow, "A Conversation with Mao," *Life*, Apr. 30, 1971; *NYT*, July 10, 1971.

8. *WHY*, 733–44; Kalb and Kalb, *Kissinger*, 245; Szulc, *The Illusion of Peace*, 406.

9. *WHY*, 743–46; Nixon, *RN*, 554; Winston Lord, Apr. 24, 1990; Garthoff, *Détente and Confrontation*, 233; Richard Helms, Nov. 15, 1989. Certain briefing papers and reports from the trip were shown to the author.

10. *Time*, July 26, 1971; Valeriani, *Travels with Henry*, 89; *WHY*, 749–55; Winston Lord, Apr. 24, 1990; Nixon, *RN*, 554–55; *NYT*, July 17, 1971.

11. Ehrlichman, *Witness to Power*, 293; John Ehrlichman, Apr. 2, 1990; *WHY*, 760; *Dr. Kissinger's Role in Wiretapping*, Senate Foreign Relations Committee, 1974, 174.

12. Morton Halperin, Nov. 15, 1989; Johnson, *The Right Hand of Power*, 553–55; *WHY*, 761–62; Ball, *Diplomacy for a Crowded World*, 22; Melvin Laird, Dec. 18, 1989.

13. *WHY*, 766, 836–37; Georgi Arbatov, Nov. 18, 1989.

14. *NYT*, July 17, 1971; "To Peking for Peace," *Time*, July 26, 1971; Haldeman meeting notes, July 13–16, 1971, Haldeman papers, box 44, WHSF, NPP; Joseph Alsop, "Jade Body Stockings," *WP*, July 21, 1971; "The Secret Voyage of Henry K," *Time*, July 26, 1971; "I Will Go to China," *Newsweek*,

July 26, 1971; "Blazing the Trail to Peking," *U.S. News and World Report,* Aug. 1, 1971; author's conversations with Hugh Sidey, Bruce Van Voorst, Jerrold Schecter.

15. John Scali, Nov. 15, 1990.

16. Nixon memo to Kissinger, July 19, 1971, Haldeman papers, box 140, WHSF, NPP; Hugh Sidey, "The Secret of Lincoln's Sitting Room," *Life,* July 30, 1971.

17. *WHY,* 779; Nixon, *RN,* 555; Bush, *Looking Forward,* 116.

18. Ball, *Diplomacy for a Crowded World,* 19; Morris, *Uncertain Greatness,* 205–7.

19. Isaacs, *Without Honor,* 27–29.

20. Richard Smyser, Jan. 12, 1990; Hersh, *The Price of Power,* 375.

21. Nguyen Van Thieu, Oct. 15, 1990; Schecter and Hung, *The Palace File,* 9–10.

SEVENTEEN: CELEBRITY

1. Barbara Howar, Dec. 8, 1989; *WP,* Oct. 10, 1969; Blumenfeld, *Henry Kissinger,* 211; Safire, *Before the Fall,* 159.

2. Valeriani, *Travels With Henry,* 2, 14, 98, 114; Hugh Sidey, "The Most Important Number Two Man in History," *Life,* Feb. 11, 1972; *Newsweek,* Feb. 7, 1972; Bette Lord, Aug. 15, 1990; David Kissinger, Feb. 14, 1990; Karen Lerner, Nov. 27, 1989; *Women's Wear Daily,* July 10, 1973; Jill St. John, Apr. 13, 1990; Robert Evans, Feb. 9, 1990; Joan Braden, Feb. 26, 1990; Lloyd Shearer, Apr. 18, 1990.

3. *WHY,* 20; Barbara Howar, Dec. 8, 1989; Nancy Kissinger, Jan. 25, 1990; Susan Mary Alsop, Dec. 13, 1989; Polly Kraft, Nov. 16, 1989; Joan Braden, Feb. 26, 1989; Katharine Graham, Dec. 14, 1989.

4. Barbara Howar, Dec. 8, 1989; Nancy Kissinger, Jan. 25, 1990; Hunebelle, *Dear Henry,* 102.

5. Jill St. John, Apr. 13, 1990; Blumenfeld, *Henry Kissinger,* 216; *Women's Wear Daily,* Sept. 8, 1971; *NYT,* Aug. 28, 1972.

6. Jill St. John, Apr. 13, 1990; Blumenfeld, *Henry Kissinger,* 216–22; Robert Evans, Feb. 9, 1990.

7. *Life,* Jan. 28, 1972; *Time,* Feb. 7, 1972; Fallaci, *Interview With History,* 42–43.

8. Robert Evans, Feb. 9 and Sept. 10, 1990; *Time,* Mar. 27, 1972; *Harvard Lampoon Cosmopolitan* parody, Oct. 1972; Georgi Arbatov, Nov. 18, 1989.

9. Lloyd Shearer, Apr. 18, 1990; memo from Charles Colson to Kissinger, Feb. 1, 1972, Colson papers, box 13, WHSF, NPP; David Kissinger, Feb. 14, 1990; H. R. Haldeman, Feb. 20, 1990; memo from Haldeman to Alexander Butterfield, Feb. 9, 1971, Haldeman papers, box 196, WHSF, NPP; Oudes, *From the President,* 215, 363; Richard Nixon, Oct. 11, 1990; Frost, *I Gave Them a Sword,* 72.

10. Blumenfeld, *Henry Kissinger,* 209–27; Bette Lord, Aug. 15, 1990; Jill St. John, Apr. 13, 1990; Diane Sawyer, Sept. 7, 1990.

11. Jan Golding Cushing Amory, Oct. 18 and Oct. 22, 1990.

12. Blumenfeld, *Henry Kissinger*, 211, 226.

13. Danielle Hunebelle, *Dear Henry*, 168–76 and passim; Kissinger appointment calendar, Sept. 9, 1970; Kalb and Kalb, *Kissinger*, 182.

14. Barbara Howar, Dec. 8, 1989; Nancy Kissinger, Jan. 25, 1990.

15. Nancy Kissinger, Mar. 6, 1991.

EIGHTEEN: WINTER OF THE LONG KNIVES

1. Christopher Van Hollen, "The Tilt Policy Revisited," *Asian Survey*, Apr. 1980, 342. At the time, Van Hollen was deputy assistant secretary of state for Near Eastern and South Asian affairs. His article strongly criticizes Kissinger's mishandling of the affair.

In addition, overall information on the India-Pakistan crisis comes from the following sources: Garthoff, *Détente and Confrontation*, 262–88; Jackson, *South Asian Crisis;* Blechman and Kaplan, *Force Without War*, 135–221; Nicholas and Oldenburg, *Bangladesh: The Birth of a Nation; WHY*, 842–918; Hersh, *The Price of Power*, 444–64; Morris, *Uncertain Greatness*, 214–27; Kalb and Kalb, *Kissinger*, 294–301; Anderson, *The Anderson Papers*, 205–69; as well as the interviews and documents cited below.

2. Nixon's annotated news summary, Feb. 10, 1970, box 31, president's office files, NPP; *WHY*, 848, 854, 864–65, 879, 915; Christopher Van Hollen, "The Tilt Policy Revisited," *Asian Survey*, Apr. 1980, 341, 347; Hersh, *The Price of Power*, 447.

3. State Department notes, Senior Review Group, July 23 and 31, 1971, Christopher Van Hollen, "The Tilt Policy Revisited," *Asian Survey*, Apr. 1980, 346–47; Kissinger memo to Nixon, July 27, 1971, *WHY*, 864–67, 876; Hersh, *The Price of Power*, 452; L. K. Jha, "Kissinger and I," *India Today* magazine, Nov. 1–15, 1979; Nixon, *RN*, 526.

4. *WHY*, 878–96; Nixon, *RN*, 531; *WP*, Dec. 30, 1979; Hersh, *The Price of Power*, 456; Christopher Van Hollen, "The Tilt Policy Revisited," *Asian Survey*, Apr. 1980, 350.

5. The full Dec. 3 WSAG minutes were published in the *NYT*, Jan. 6, 1972. Also, Jackson, *South Asian Crisis*, 213; Anthony Lewis, "Tilt," *NYT*, Jan. 10, 1972. The text, based on Defense Department copies, is slightly different from the brief quotes in *WHY*, 897.

6. *WHY*, 898, 887, 900; Nixon, *RN*, 527; Morris, *Uncertain Greatness*, 224.

7. Kissinger background briefing, Dec. 7, 1971, in *Congressional Record* (insert by Sen. Barry Goldwater), Dec. 9, 1971; "Regarding Government Duplicity," *Wall Street Journal* editorial, Jan. 14, 1972; Keating to State Department, Dec. 8, 1971, author's possession.

8. CIA report, Dec. 7, 1970, reported by Richard Helms at WSAG meeting, Dec. 8, 1971, minutes in *NYT*, Jan. 15, 1972; Joseph Sisco, Mar. 5, 1990; Christopher Van Hollen, "The Tilt Policy Revisited," *Asian Survey*, Apr. 1980, 351; Powers, *The Man Who Kept the Secrets*, 206; Garthoff, *Détente and Confrontation*, 268; Hersh, *The Price of Power*, 459–60; *WHY*, 901–4; L. K. Jha, "Kissinger and I," *India Today*, Nov. 1–15, 1979.

9. *WHY,* 767, 900–904, 909–13; Garthoff, *Détente and Confrontation,* 270, 276; Nixon, *RN,* 528; Elmo Zumwalt, Nov. 20, 1989; Zumwalt, *On Watch,* 368; Jackson, *South Asian Crisis,* 141.

10. *WP,* Dec. 15 and 16, 1971; *NYT,* Dec. 15 and 16, 1971; Tom Wicker, "Background Blues," *NYT,* Dec. 16, 1971; Kalb and Kalb, *Kissinger,* 261–62.

11. *WHY,* 913; Garthoff, *Détente and Confrontation,* 277, 284–88; Benazir Bhutto, June 9, 1989.

12. Christopher Van Hollen, "The Tilt Policy Revisited," *Asian Survey,* Apr. 1980, 358–59.

13. In addition to interviews, overall information about the Radford spy ring came from *Transmittal of Documents from the National Security Council to the Chairman of the Joint Chiefs of Staff,* the hearings of the Senate Armed Services Committee, Part I (Feb. 6, 1974), Part II (Feb. 20–21, 1974), Part III (Mar. 7, 1974), and *Final Report* (Dec. 19, 1974), referred to below as *Transmittal Hearings.*

Welander's testimony about suspecting Radford is in *Transmittal II,* 124–25 and 147–48; Radford's is in *Transmittal Hearings II,* 16–17.

David Young, "Special Report for the President," Young papers, boxes 23 & 24, NPP; interview of Radford by Ehrlichman, Dec. 23, 1971, Ehrlichman papers, special subject file, Young project, NPP. Most of these papers are still sealed, but participants with copies of them have made them available.

Silent Coup by Colodny and Gettlin provides a wealth of detail about the Radford spy ring. It argues that Haig was involved in the affair and was part of a military conspiracy to undermine Nixon. Haig's actions during Watergate, the authors say, were partly designed to force Nixon's resignation and to prevent Haig's involvement in the spy ring from coming to light. Although I am not persuaded of this thesis, the colorful book contains much useful reporting and information, including Admiral Welander's taped confession to John Ehrlichman.

14. *Transmittal Hearings II,* 9–16; Hersh, *The Price of Power,* 466–69.

15. John Ehrlichman, Mar. 27 and Apr. 2, 1990; Henry Kissinger, Feb. 16, 1990; H. R. Haldeman, Feb. 20, 1990; *Transmittal Hearings II,* 124–26, and *III,* 21; Ehrlichman notes of meetings, Dec. 13, 23, and 24, 1971, Ehrlichman papers, WHSF, NPP; Ehrlichman, *Witness to Power,* 304–8.

16. Richard Nixon, Oct. 11, 1990; H. R. Haldeman, Feb. 20, 1990.

17. John Ehrlichman, Feb. 27 and Apr. 4, 1990; Ehrlichman, *Witness to Power,* 305; Hersh, *The Price of Power,* 476.

18. Colodny and Gettlin, *Silent Coup,* 3–46. (See note 13 above.)

19. John Ehrlichman, Mar. 27 and Apr. 2, 1990; Henry Kissinger, Feb. 16, 1990; H. R. Haldeman, Feb. 20, 1990; Ehrlichman notes of meetings, Dec. 13, 23, and 24, 1971, Ehrlichman papers, WHSF, NPP; Ehrlichman, *Witness to Power,* 304–8.

20. H. R. Haldeman, Feb. 20, 1990; Nixon, *RN,* 600; Richard Nixon, Oct. 11, 1990; Charles Colson, Sept. 10, 1990.

21. William Watts, Dec. 13, 1989; Safire, *Before the Fall,* 165; Gulley, *Breaking Cover,* 143; Hersh, *The Price of Power,* 317.

22. James Schlesinger, Nov. 17, 1989; Diane Sawyer, Sept. 7, 1990; Morris, *Haig,* 199; Colson, *Born Again,* 67; Charles Colson, Sept. 10, 1990.

23. Nixon letter to Reagan, Dec. 1980, courtesy of Nixon; Nixon, Oct. 11, 1990.

24. H. R. Haldeman, May 7, 1990, also discussed Feb. 20, 1990; Lawrence Higby, Jan. 29, 1990; Brent Scowcroft, July 16, 1990.

25. James Schlesinger, Nov. 17, 1989; Elmo Zumwalt, Nov. 20, 1989; Palmer, *The 25-Year War,* 124; Zumwalt, *On Watch,* 399.

26. Laurence Lynn, Jan. 12, 1990; Roger Morris, Mar. 26, 1990; William Watts, Dec. 13, 1989; Morris, *Uncertain Greatness,* 143; Bette Bao Lord, Aug. 15, 1990; Winston Lord, Oct. 25, 1989; Woodward and Bernstein, *All the President's Men,* 211; John Ehrlichman, Feb. 27, 1990; *YOU,* 107; Hersh, *The Price of Power,* 318; Elmo Zumwalt, Nov. 20, 1989; Zumwalt, *On Watch,* 318–19; Kutler, *The Wars of Watergate,* 640; Ranelagh, *The Agency,* 507.

27. Peter Rodman, Nov. 16, 1989; Laurence Lynn, Jan. 12, 1990; Richard Nixon, Oct. 11, 1990; Roger Morris, Mar. 26, 1990; Charles Colson, Sept. 10, 1990; Morris, *Uncertain Greatness,* 142–44; Ehrlichman, *Witness to Power,* 308.

28. Ehrlichman, *Witness to Power,* 307–8; John Ehrlichman, Feb. 27, 1990; H. R. Haldeman, Feb. 20 and Oct. 3, 1990; Elmo Zumwalt, Nov. 20, 1989.

29. Tim Heald, ed., *The Rigby File,* 223–24. (Ehrlichman says this fictional account is based on the truth.)

30. Richard Nixon, Oct. 11, 1990.

31. Henry Kissinger, Feb. 16, 1990; H. R. Haldeman, Feb. 20 and Oct. 3, 1990; Lawrence Higby, Jan. 29, 1990; Charles Colson, Sept. 10, 1990; Colson, *Born Again,* 41; *WHY,* 648; *YOU,* 96–97; Robert Semple, Sept. 28, 1990; Christopher Ogden, Feb. 28, 1990; Haldeman, *The Ends of Power,* 95–98.

32. Henry Kissinger, Feb. 16, 1990; John Ehrlichman, Feb. 27, Apr. 2, and Oct. 10, 1990; Ehrlichman, *Witness to Power,* 288–314; *WHY,* 74; *YOU,* 94; Ehrlichman conversation with John Dean, Mar. 7, 1973; Christopher Ogden, Feb. 28, 1990.

33. Henry Kissinger, Feb. 16, 1990; Brandon, *Special Relationships,* 275; *WHY,* 918; Haldeman notes from meeting with Nixon, Jan. 13, 1972, and notes of meeting with Kissinger and others, Jan. 14, 1972, Haldeman papers, box 45, WHSF, NPP.

34. Safire, *Before the Fall,* 398–406.

35. *Time,* Feb. 7, 1972; *Newsweek,* Feb. 7, 1972; *WP,* Feb. 3, 1972; Hugh Sidey, "The Most Important Number Two in History," *Life,* Feb. 11, 1972; *WHY,* 1045.

36. Kissinger speech to the Washington Press Club, Jan. 27, 1972.

NINETEEN: THE TRIANGLE

1. *WHY,* 1050–67; Nixon, *RN,* 560; Ambrose, *Nixon,* vol. 2, 524; Winston Lord, Nov. 2 and Dec. 20, 1989; John Chancellor, "Who Produced the China Show," *Foreign Policy,* Summer 1972. (One unfair little rap Nixon has gotten: many commentators, including Kissinger in his memoirs, are rather snide in quoting him as saying, "This is a great wall," when he was shown the Great

Wall. They leave out the rest of his sentence, which was: "and it had to be built by a great people.")

2. *WHY,* 1057–79; Nixon, *RN,* 562–64; Winston Lord, Nov. 2 and Dec. 20, 1989; Hersh, *The Price of Power,* 442.

3. *WHY,* 1074–87; Hersh, *The Price of Power,* 497–500; Hugh Sidey, "Making History in Peking," *Life,* Feb. 25, 1972; Stanley Karnow, "Nixon Pledges Pullout of Forces in Taiwan," *WP,* Feb. 28, 1972; Kissinger press briefing, Feb. 27, 1972.

4. *WHY,* 1088–96; Henry Kissinger, Oct. 9, 1989; Winston Lord, Nov. 2, 1989.

5. Nixon memo to Haldeman, Mar. 13, 1972, Haldeman papers, box 162, WHSF, NPP; Nixon memo to Kissinger, Mar. 9, 1972; *WHY,* 1094–95, 1081.

6. H. R. Haldeman, Oct. 3, 1990; Richard Nixon, Oct. 11, 1990; William Hyland, Oct. 22, 1990; *WHY,* 1113.

7. *WHY,* 1104, 1114–22; Nixon, *RN,* 587–94; Richard Nixon, Oct. 11, 1990; Nixon's diaries are excerpted in his memoirs.

8. Hugh Sidey, "The Advance Man Strikes Again," *Life,* May 5, 1972; Gulley, *Breaking Cover,* 137; Nixon, *RN,* 592; *WHY,* 1136, 838; Kalb and Kalb, *Kissinger,* 295.

9. Viktor Sukhodrev, May 8, 1990; *WHY,* 1138–40, 1153; Georgi Arbatov, Nov. 18, 1989.

10. *WHY,* 1144–48; Morris, *Haig,* 198. John Negroponte, Kissinger's Vietnam expert who was on the trip, felt that the U.S. proposals in Moscow went further than previous ones. This analysis is reflected in Szulc, *The Illusion of Peace,* 545.

11. Winston Lord, Oct. 25, 1989; Helmut Sonnenfeldt, Sept. 12, 1989; *WHY,* 1148–54; Nixon, *RN,* 592; Richard Nixon, Oct. 11, 1990.

12. *Time,* May 8, 1972; *NYT,* Apr. 26, 1972; *Life,* May 5, 1972.

13. Nixon memo to Kissinger, Mar. 11, 1972, Haldeman papers, box 230, WHSF, NPP; Nixon address, Apr. 26, 1972.

14. *NYT,* May 2, 1972; Nixon, *RN,* 594–95; memo from Nixon to Kissinger, Apr. 30, 1972, the President's Office files, box 3, NPP (still classified); Hammond, *Public Affairs,* 870.

15. *WHY,* 1169–77; Nixon, *RN,* 602; Richard Nixon, Oct. 11, 1990; H. R. Haldeman, Feb. 20, 1990.

16. H. R. Haldeman, Feb. 20, 1990; John Connally, Apr. 16, 1990; Helmut Sonnenfeldt, Sept. 12, 1989; William Hyland, Oct. 22, 1990.

17. *WHY,* 1179–83; Kissinger back-channel message to Ambassador Ellsworth Bunker, May 4, 1972, NSC files, back channels, box 414, NPP (still classified); Hammond, *Public Affairs,* 878; Zumwalt, *On Watch,* 398; Szulc, *The Illusion of Peace,* 552; Winston Lord, Nov. 2, 1989.

18. Kissinger message to Bunker, May 6, 1972, NSC files, back channels, box 414, NPP (still classified); Hammond, *Public Affairs,* 881.

19. Personal memoir by John Andrews, June 25, 1972, courtesy of the author; John Andrews, Jan. 11, 1990.

20. Johnson, *The Right Hand of Power,* 534; Henry Kissinger, Dec. 21, 1990.

21. H. R. Haldeman, Feb. 20, 1990; *WHY,* 1186, 1188; Roger Morris,

"The Ultimate Betrayal," *NYT*, June 1, 1972; Hugh Sidey, "How the President Made Up His Mind," *Life*, May 19, 1972.

22. Georgi Arbatov, Nov. 18, 1989; Shevchenko, *Breaking With Moscow*, 211–12; Garthoff, *Détente and Confrontation*, 100.

23. Peter Peterson, Nov. 26, 1989; Sven Kraemer, Nov. 16, 1989; *NYT*, May 12, 1972; *Time*, May 22, 1972.

24. Nguyen Van Thieu, Oct. 15, 1990; Hung and Schecter, *The Palace File*, 60–61.

25. Morris, *Uncertain Greatness*, 186; Helmut Sonnenfeldt, Sept. 12, 1989; Henry Kissinger, Mar. 31, 1990; Nixon, *RN*, 609.

26. Morris, *Uncertain Greatness*, 1–2; Hugh Sidey, "Peaceful Victory in the Kremlin," *Life*, June 9, 1972.

27. Kissinger background briefing, Salzburg, May 21, 1972; Kalb and Kalb, *Kissinger*, 314; *WHY*, 1203; William Hyland, Dec. 11, 1989; Hyland, *Mortal Rivals*, 52.

28. Viktor Sukhodrev, May 8, 1990; Georgi Arbatov, Nov. 18, 1989; *WHY*, 1208.

29. Brezhnev gave Nixon a hydrofoil as a gift; Nixon responded with the gift of a Cadillac. In the Nixon archives a note from Haldeman to Dwight Chapin suggests he ask Ford Motors to donate a Lincoln, saying "it would be a pure business deal, since they are negotiating with the Russians for putting in a plant." As it turned out, Ford got to give a Lincoln when Brezhnev visited in 1973, but the Moscow summit was Cadillac's turn. Haldeman memo to Chapin, May 15, 1972, Haldeman papers, box 199, WHSF, NPP.

30. *WHY*, 1222–29; Hersh, *The Price of Power*, 527; Winston Lord, Nov. 2, 1989; William Hyland, Oct. 22, 1990.

31. "Basic Principles of Relations," May 29, 1972, *Department of State Bulletin*, vol. 66, 898; Hoffmann, *Primacy or World Order*, 64; *WHY*, 1205, 1209, 1213.

32. Peter Peterson, Nov. 26, 1989; Garthoff, *Détente and Confrontation*, 305–7; *WHY*, 1271; Trager, *The Great Grain Robbery*; Hersh, *The Price of Power*, 343–48, 531–34.

33. The description of the ICBM and SLBM dispute is largely based on *Détente and Confrontation* by Garthoff, 163–98. He was a negotiator of the agreement, and his resentment over Kissinger's intrusions are reflected in his criticisms. But his account is well documented. *Doubletalk* by Smith, 370–433, is likewise a SALT negotiator's perspective and is both more colorful and emotional. *Cold Dawn* by Newhouse, 246–55, is an early account by a journalist with good access to Kissinger's staff. *The Price of Power* by Hersh, 535–55, presents his far more critical account. William Hyland has written, and allowed me to use, an unpublished rebuttal to Hersh's account of the SALT talks. Kissinger's blow-by-blow recounting is in *White House Years*, 1216–41. See also, Zumwalt, *On Watch*, 400–404; Nitze, *From Hiroshima to Glasnost*, 318–28. Kissinger's comments to Senator Jackson were at a congressional briefing, June 15, 1972. I also relied on interviews with Winston Lord, William Hyland, Helmut Sonnenfeldt, and Gerard Smith.

34. William Hyland, Dec. 11, 1989; Gerard Smith, Aug. 1, 1990; *WHY*, 1230, 1243; Smith, *Doubletalk*, 433–41; press conference of Henry Kissinger

and Gerard Smith, Moscow, May 26, 1972; press conference of Henry Kissinger, Moscow, May 26–27, 1972; Kalb and Kalb, *Kissinger,* 329; Kenneth Rush, Jan. 9, 1991.

35. James Schlesinger, Nov. 17, 1989; *WHY,* 1233; Hyland, *Mortal Rivals,* 54; Ambrose, *Nixon,* vol. 2, 548; Garthoff, *Détente and Confrontation,* 311.

36. Henry Kissinger, Feb. 16, 1990; Safire, *Before the Fall,* 453; Garthoff, *Détente and Confrontation,* 191–93; Gaddis, *Strategies of Containment,* 287; Kissinger talk to foreign service officers, Nov. 30, 1968; Kissinger, *A World Restored,* 1–3; Nutter, *Kissinger's Grand Design,* 10–13; Brown, *The Crisis of Power,* 14–15; Kissinger speech to the Pilgrims of Great Britain, Dec. 12, 1973.

37. Peter Lisagor, "The Kissinger Legend," *Chicago Sun-Times,* June 18, 1972; Kalb and Kalb, *Kissinger,* 345; New York *Daily News,* May 31, 1990; John Andrews, Jan. 11, 1990; John Andrews, private memoir of the Moscow summit, June 1972; Safire, *Before the Fall,* 459.

TWENTY: PEACE AT HAND

1. Isaacs, *Without Honor,* 16–21; *WHY,* 1301.

2. Henry Kissinger, Oct. 9, 1989; *WHY,* 1308; Kissinger meeting with Hedley Donovan, Henry Grunwald, and others, Sept. 29, 1972, notes by Jerrold Schecter, cited in Hung and Schecter, *The Palace File,* 90–92.

3. Charles Colson, Sept. 10, 1990; John Connally, Apr. 16, 1990.

4. Richard Nixon, Oct. 11, 1990; conversation with Richard Nixon, Mar. 13, 1990; Nixon interview with *Time* magazine, Apr. 2, 1990; H. R. Haldeman, Feb. 20, 1990; Hersh, *The Price of Power,* 582; Sulzberger, *The World According to Richard Nixon,* 184.

5. Zumwalt, *On Watch,* 397–99; Elmo Zumwalt, Nov. 20, 1989.

6. Peter Rodman, Nov. 16, 1989; *WHY,* 1317–19; Nixon, *RN,* 701; Richard Nixon, Oct. 11, 1990.

7. Nguyen Van Thieu, Oct. 15, 1990.

8. Hung and Schecter, *The Palace File,* 66; *WHY,* 1315.

9. *WHY,* 1322–27, 1339; Nguyen Van Thieu, Oct. 15, 1990; Isaacs, *Without Honor,* 35, 41; Kalb and Kalb, *Kissinger,* 399; Nixon, *RN,* 690.

10. Kissinger, "The Viet Nam Negotiations," *Foreign Affairs,* Jan. 1969, 225.

11. *WHY,* 1313, 1330–32, 1341–53; Szulc, *The Illusion of Peace,* 626.

12. Nguyen Van Thieu, Oct. 15, 1990.

13. *WHY,* 1352–61; Isaacs, *Without Honor,* 37; Nixon, *RN,* 692–93; Richard Holbrooke, Sept. 25, 1989.

14. Nguyen Van Thieu, Oct. 15, 1990; Hoang Duc Nha, May 1, 1990; Hung and Schecter, *The Palace File,* 83; Isaacs, *Without Honor,* 38. *The Palace File* is by a former aide to Thieu and a former diplomatic correspondent for *Time.* It includes many documents from Thieu's files as well as information from him and Nha.

15. Hung and Schecter, *The Palace File,* 87–88; Snepp, *Decent Interval,* 27; Nguyen Van Thieu, Oct. 15, 1990.

16. Given the fact that it turned out to be a bad blunder, there is an odd

dispute between Kissinger's memoirs and Nixon's in which each man takes responsibility for sending this acceptance message to Hanoi. Nixon treats it by simply noting that "I sent a cable." Kissinger's version is: "I therefore sent a cable to Hanoi 'on behalf of the President.' " In fact, according to those who helped draft and send the cable, Kissinger's version is correct, and there is no indication that the president even read the cable at the time.

Two months later, when the agreement was breaking down, the president's men and Haig were more than happy to give Kissinger full credit for that cable. At Camp David that December, as Kissinger futilely tried to salvage a deal, Haldeman told Ehrlichman that Kissinger had been off the reservation in October. "When he was in Saigon, twice he cabled the North Vietnamese in the President's name to accept their October proposal," Haldeman said. "Henry did that over Al Haig's strong objection and beyond any Presidential authority." Kissinger does not recall any objections from Haig at the time; it is likely that they were made behind Kissinger's back.

WHY, 1361; Nixon, *RN,* 695; Henry Kissinger, Oct. 9, 1990; H. R. Haldeman, Feb. 20, 1990; Ehrlichman, *Witness to Power,* 314.

17. *WHY,* 1362, 1377–78; Nixon, *RN,* 697; Richard Nixon, Oct. 11, 1990.

18. Nguyen Van Thieu, Oct. 15, 1990; Hoang Duc Nha, May 1, 1990; Arnaud de Borchgrave, "Exclusive from Hanoi," *Newsweek,* Oct. 30, 1972.

19. Schecter and Hung, *The Palace File,* 100–105; *WHY,* 1385; Winston Lord, Oct. 25, 1989.

20. Nguyen Van Thieu, Oct. 15, 1990; Henry Kissinger, Oct. 9, 1989; *WHY,* 1391–93.

21. Nixon, *RN,* 699–702; *WHY,* 1388–94; Hersh, *The Price of Power,* 600; Winston Lord, Oct. 25, 1989; Sven Kraemer, Nov. 17, 1989; Fritz Kraemer, May 14, 1988.

22. Max Frankel, "Aides See a Truce in a Few Weeks," *NYT,* Oct. 26, 1972; Hersh, *The Price of Power,* 604.

23. Largely because of his Strangelovian accent, the White House had generally kept Kissinger off television. In his memoirs, he writes that "I appeared for the first time on national television" at the October 26 conference and jokes that the White House "finally took a chance on my pronunciation." In fact, his first televised news conference had been on June 24 of that year, at a White House press conference describing a follow-up trip he took to China. On that occasion, he joked that there would be "simultaneous translation" of his remarks. "Kissinger, Often Seen, Is Finally Heard on TV," *NYT,* June 25, 1972.

24. Kissinger news conference, Oct. 26, 1972; Safire, *Before the Fall,* 667; James Reston, "The End of the Tunnel," *NYT,* Oct. 27, 1972; *Newsweek,* Nov. 6, 1972; Max Frankel, "U.S. Threat to Saigon," *NYT,* Oct. 27, 1972.

25. Nixon, *RN,* 705–6; Hersh, *The Price of Power,* 606; Richard Nixon, Oct. 11, 1990; Charles Colson, Sept. 10, 1990; *NYT,* Oct. 28, 1972.

26. *NYT,* Nov. 3, 1972.

TWENTY-ONE: THE CHRISTMAS BOMBING

1. White, *The Making of the President 1972,* xi–xiii. White says that their

talk was on the weekend, but Kissinger's travel schedule indicates it was on Monday, Nov. 6.

2. Nixon, *RN,* 715; Nguyen Van Thieu, Oct. 15, 1990.

3. Haldeman (for Nixon) to Kissinger, Nov. 22, 1972, Haldeman papers, box 14, WHSF, NPP; *WHY,* 1419–21; Nixon, *RN,* 721–22.

4. H. R. Haldeman, Feb. 20, 1990; Ehrlichman, *Witness to Power,* 314; Ehrlichman meeting notes, Dec. 2, 1972, Ehrlichman papers, box 4, WHSF, NPP.

5. Kissinger cable to Nixon from Paris, Dec. 5, 1972, NSC files, box 1109, NPP (still classified); Nixon cable to Kissinger, Dec. 6, 1972, NSC files, Kissinger office files, box 27, NPP (still classified).

6. *WHY,* 1429–41; Nixon, *RN,* 723–28; Hersh, *The Price of Power,* 618.

7. Ehrlichman meeting notes, Dec. 6, Nov. 22, Dec. 2, 1972, Ehrlichman papers, box 7, WHSF, NPP; John Ehrlichman, Feb. 27, 1990; H. R. Haldeman, Feb. 20, 1990; Ehrlichman, *Witness to Power,* 313–16; Gulley, *Breaking Cover,* 149; Nixon, *RN,* 729–30; *WHY,* 1433. (Ehrlichman's account of Dec. 6 in his book is based on his meeting notes in the archives, which also contain some additional material.)

8. Winston Lord, Oct. 25, 1989; *WHY,* 1445–49; Kalb and Kalb, *Kissinger,* 412; Nixon, *RN,* 733.

9. Woodward and Bernstein, *The Final Days,* 212; Nixon, *RN,* 734; *WHY,* 1148–49.

10. Kalb and Kalb, *Kissinger,* 413; Kissinger press conference, Dec. 16, 1972; *WHY,* 1451.

11. Isaacs, *Without Honor,* 54–56; Richard Nixon, Mar. 13, 1990; McCarthy and Allison, *Linebacker II,* 30–50.

12. Hung and Schecter, *The Palace File,* 142–45; Henry Kissinger, Mar. 26, 1990; Ball, *The Past Has Another Pattern,* 420; Anthony Lewis, "Vietnam Delenda Est," *NYT,* Dec. 23, 1972; Anthony Lewis, "Ghosts," *NYT,* Dec. 24, 1973; Anthony Lewis, "Ghosts," *NYT,* Dec. 18, 1975; Tom Wicker, "Shame on Earth," *NYT,* Dec. 26, 1972; Joseph Kraft, "Twelve Days of Bombing," *WP,* Jan. 4, 1973; other reaction quotes from *Time,* Jan. 1, 1973, and *Facts on File,* Dec. 24–31, 1972.

13. Jerrold Schecter interview with Alexander Haig, Nov. 13, 1985; Hung and Schecter, *The Palace File,* 143; Richard Nixon, Mar. 21, 1990; Frost, *I Gave Them a Sword,* 138; Kissinger off-the-record briefing, Jan. 26, 1973; CBS interview with Henry Kissinger, Feb. 1, 1973.

14. Charles Colson, Sept. 10, 1990; James Reston, Dec. 19, 1989; H. R. Haldeman, Feb. 20, 1990; James Reston, "Kissinger and Nixon," *NYT,* Dec. 31, 1972; Reston, *Deadline,* 416; Colson, *Born Again,* 78–79; Charles Colson, "The Georgetown Blacking Factory," *NYT,* Jan. 30, 1973; Haldeman, *The Ends of Power,* 94–95; "CBS Evening News," Jan. 8, 1973; Joseph Kraft, "Twelve Days of Bombing," *WP,* Jan. 4, 1973; Hersh, *The Price of Power,* 630–31.

15. *WHY,* 1407–9, 1419; H. R. Haldeman, Feb. 20, 1990; John Ehrlichman, Feb. 27, 1990; Henry Kissinger, Oct. 9, 1989; Charles Colson, Sept. 10, 1990; Elmo Zumwalt, Nov. 20, 1989; Kenneth Rush, Jan. 9, 1991; Haldeman memo, Nov. 21, 1972, box 112, Haldeman papers, WHSF, NPP; news sum-

mary, Jan. 13, 1972, president's office files, NPP; Haldeman, *The Ends of Power,* 178–79; Charles Colson, "The Georgetown Blacking Factory," *NYT,* Jan. 30, 1973; Hersh, *The Price of Power,* 612; Klein, *Making It Perfectly Clear,* 309.

16. Fallaci, *Interview With History,* 17–44; Henry Kissinger, Oct. 9, 1989; Mike Wallace, Feb. 5, 1991; Ehrlichman, *Witness to Power,* 313; *The New Republic,* Dec. 16, 1972; *Time,* Jan. 1, 1973; *Time,* Nov. 19, 1979; Sven Kraemer, Nov. 16, 1989; Blumenfeld, *Henry Kissinger,* 231; Nicholas von Hoffman, "Slim Kissinger," *WP,* Dec. 22, 1972. The text in *The New Republic* is quite different from that in Fallaci's book, which is the source I used.

17. H. R. Haldeman, May 7, 1990; annotated news summary, Oct. 24, 1972, president's office files, NPP; meeting notes, Nov. 11, 1972, Ehrlichman papers, box 7, NPP; Hugh Sidey, *Life,* Oct. 16, 1989; Ehrlichman, *Witness to Power,* 316; Haldeman, *The Ends of Power,* 84; *WHY,* 1455; *Time,* Jan. 1, 1973.

18. Kissinger, *WHY,* 1463–64, 1468; Hersh, *The Price of Power,* 632; Nixon, *RN,* 747–48.

19. Draft peace agreement, Oct. 26, 1972 (reprinted in Porter, *Vietnam,* vol. 2, 575, and elsewhere); Hanoi's Ten-Point Peace Plan, May 9, 1969 (reprinted in Hung and Schecter, *The Palace File,* 446, and elsewhere); "Agreement on Ending the War and Restoring the Peace in Vietnam," Jan. 27, 1973; *WHY,* 1411–19; Isaacs, *Without Honor,* 52–53.

20. Nixon letter to Nguyen Van Thieu, Jan. 17, 1973, in Hung and Schecter, *The Palace File,* 394–95; Kissinger, "The Viet Nam Negotiations," *Foreign Affairs,* Jan. 1969, 217; *WHY,* 1464–72; *YOU,* 39–40; Nixon and Kissinger briefing to the joint leadership of Congress, Jan. 24, 1973, in Porter, *Vietnam,* vol. 2, 598.

21. *WHY,* 1466–67; Hung and Schecter, *The Palace File,* 112, 146, 356; Les Gelb, "The Kissinger Legacy," *NYT Magazine,* Oct. 31, 1976; Richard Holbrooke, Sept. 25, 1989; Anthony Lake, Jan. 11, 1990.

22. Memo from Kissinger to Nixon, Sept. 18, 1971, Nixon papers, National Security files, subject Vietnam, Alexander Haig special file (this memo is still classified); William Hammond, *Public Affairs,* 119; William Hammond, Aug. 13, 1991; *WHY,* 1038–39 (summarizes this memo, but leaves out the quote about "healthy interval").

23. Hung and Schecter, *The Palace File,* 446; Kissinger press conference, Oct. 26, 1972; annotated news summaries, box 45, president's office files, NPP; Ehrlichman, *Witness to Power,* 316.

24. The Nixon-Thieu letters were released by Nguyen Tien Hung, a South Vietnamese official, at a Washington press conference on Apr. 30, 1975, and are printed in the May 1, 1975, *NYT.* They are also reproduced and explained in Hung's book, *The Palace File,* by Hung and Schecter.

25. Nguyen Van Thieu, Oct. 15, 1990; Henry Kissinger, Mar. 14, 1988; Sylvan Fox, "Pledges to Thieu by U.S. Reported," *NYT,* Jan. 29, 1973; Kissinger news conference, Jan. 24, 1973; Marvin Kalb, "A Conversation with Kissinger," CBS News Special Report, Feb. 1, 1973; McGeorge Bundy, "Vietnam and Presidential Powers," *Foreign Affairs,* Winter 1979/80, 397–407; Zumwalt, *On Watch,* 413; *WHY,* 1373. See also *WHY,* footnote #2, p. 1495, where

Kissinger cites examples of public statements; none, however, is candid about the pledges made to Thieu. Kissinger's rebuttal of Bundy is in *YOU,* p. 304, and in a four-page footnote on pp. 1236–40.

26. *WHY,* 1470; *Time* interview with Nixon, Apr. 2, 1990; Ball, *The Past Has Another Pattern,* 420. For a similar analysis, see Hoffmann, *Dead Ends,* 43.

27. U.S. Department of Defense, report on the costs of the Vietnam War, Mar. 21, 1985; Bowman, ed., *The Vietnam War,* 358; *WHY,* 997, 1386; Henry Kissinger, Feb. 16, 1990.

28. *WHY,* 1469–76; Nixon, *RN,* 756; Nancy Kissinger, Feb. 23, 1991; Safire, *Before the Fall,* 670; Kalb and Kalb, *Kissinger,* 421.

TWENTY-TWO: SECRETARY OF STATE

1. H. R. Haldeman, Feb. 20, 1990; Richard Nixon, Oct. 11, 1990; Brent Scowcroft, July 16, 1990; Henry Kissinger, Oct. 9, 1989; Nixon, *RN,* 856; *YOU,* 108–9; Woodward and Bernstein, *The Final Days,* 17.

2. Brent Scowcroft, July 16, 1990; Elmo Zumwalt, Nov. 20, 1989; Zumwalt, *On Watch,* 420; Sven Kraemer, Nov. 16, 1989; Kalb and Kalb, *Kissinger,* 443; Hersh, *The Price of Power,* 90.

3. Henry Kissinger, Oct. 9, 1989; H. R. Haldeman, Oct. 3, 1990; Lawrence Higby, Jan. 29, 1990; *YOU,* 111–13; Richard Nixon, Oct. 11, 1990; Haldeman, *The Ends of Power,* 195. (In one interview with me, Nixon told with great gusto the story of how Don Kendall passed along Lyndon Johnson's recommendation for a White House taping system, and he added that I was the first reporter to be told this interesting historic footnote. In fact, Haldeman writes in his book that Nixon told him the same story several times. "It isn't true," Haldeman said, "and I have told Nixon that repeatedly to his great discomfort.")

4. Valeriani, *Travels With Henry,* 167–68; Viktor Sukhodrev, May 8, 1990; *YOU,* 228–35; Helmut Sonnenfeldt, Sept. 12, 1989; Kissinger briefing, May 12, 1973.

5. Kissinger briefing, May 12, 1973; Wise, *The American Police State,* 78–82; *Time,* Feb. 26, 1973; Woodward and Bernstein, *All the President's Men,* 344–47.

6. Seymour Hersh, "Kissinger Said to Have Asked for Taps," *NYT,* May 17, 1973; Hersh, *The Price of Power,* 400; Murrey Marder, "Kissinger Stung," *WP,* May 20, 1973; Rowland Evans and Robert Novak, "The Innocence of Dr. Kissinger," *WP,* May 24, 1973.

7. Gallup polls, *WP,* Apr. 22 and Dec. 30, 1973; Valeriani, *Travels With Henry,* 33; Joseph Kraft, "Henry Kissinger, the Virtuoso, at 50," *WP,* May 27, 1973.

8. Guido Goldman, Mar. 14, 1989; *NYT,* May 28, 1973; *Women's Wear Daily,* May 29, 1973; Nancy Kissinger, Mar. 6, 1991.

9. Richard Nixon, Oct. 11, 1990; John Connally, Apr. 16, 1990.

10. Henry Kissinger, Dec. 21, 1990; David Kissinger, Feb. 13, 1990; *YOU,* 3–4, 420–23; letters to and from Rogers and Nixon, Aug. 22, 1973; Nixon press conference, Aug. 22, 1973. (Some books refer to Kissinger as the fifty-

sixth secretary of state, but Daniel Webster and James G. Blaine served twice.)

11. Carl Marcy, Jan. 30, 1989.

12. Kenneth Rush, Jan. 9, 1991; *YOU,* 3–4, 420–23, 435–37; Osborne, *White House Watch,* 276; *NYT,* Sept. 21, 1973; *Confirmation Hearings of Henry Kissinger,* Senate Foreign Relations Committee, Sept. 7–17, 1973 (the Kissinger quote is on p. 293, from the Sept. 17 executive hearing, released in Oct. 1973).

13. Paula Kissinger, Dec. 17, 1988; Blumenfeld, *Henry Kissinger,* 231; *YOU,* 431–34; Bette Lord, Aug. 15, 1990; Marilyn Berger, Aug. 1, 1990.

14. Helmut Sonnenfeldt, Nov. 16, 1989; Lawrence Eagleburger, June 25, 1990; Winston Lord, Oct. 25, 1989; Kenneth Rush, Jan. 9, 1991; Joseph Sisco, Mar. 5, 1990; William Hyland, Oct. 22, 1990; Robert McCloskey, Feb. 2, 1990; Bernard Gwertzman, "Kissinger's Department," *NYT,* Apr. 26, 1974.

15. *NYT,* Oct. 17–23, 1973; *Christian Science Monitor,* Oct. 18, 1973; *WP,* Oct. 18, 1973.

16. Kissinger press conference, Aug. 23, 1973; *YOU,* 434; *Confirmation Hearings of Henry Kissinger,* Senate Foreign Relations Committee, Sept. 7–17, 1973, 46; Henry Kissinger, "Domestic Structure and Foreign Policy," *Daedalus,* Apr. 1966, 42; Henry Kissinger, "The White Revolutionary," *Daedalus,* Summer 1968, 890.

17. Ball, *Diplomacy for a Crowded World,* 14; Nutter, *Kissinger's Grand Design,* 17–18; Robert Hormats, May 9, 1990.

TWENTY-THREE: THE YOM KIPPUR WAR

1. Heikal, *The Road to Ramadan,* 200; *YOU,* 209, 224; Sadat, *In Search of Identity,* 241.

2. Kissinger-Haig telephone conversation, Oct. 6, 1973.

3. The divergent accounts of Kissinger's role in the Yom Kippur War include: Kalb and Kalb, *Kissinger,* 450–78 (reflecting Kissinger's cooperation); *YOU,* 450–544; Edward Luttwak and Walter Laquer, "Kissinger and the Yom Kippur War," *Commentary,* September 1974 (oriented toward Schlesinger's version); Szulc, *The Illusion of Peace,* 735–39; Edward R. F. Sheehan, "How Kissinger Did It," *Foreign Policy,* Spring 1976, 3–14; Sheehan, *The Arabs, Israelis and Kissinger,* 30–39; Golan, *The Secret Conversations of Henry Kissinger,* 33–62 (based on documents leaked by Kissinger's critics in Israel, which the government in Jerusalem then tried to suppress); Quandt, *Decade of Decisions,* 175–89 (a judicious but critical account that questions some of Kissinger's motives); Morris, *Uncertain Greatness,* 253–55; Nixon, *RN,* 927–30.

Sheehan's book was written with the cooperation of two of Kissinger's Middle East experts, Roy Atherton and Hal Saunders, who read him sections of memos of conversation. They acted with Kissinger's approval; but when Sheehan's work was published, Kissinger denied that the level of cooperation provided was authorized (just as he had done with John Newhouse's book, *Cold Dawn*), and he "reprimanded' Atherton and Saunders. See Sheehan's preface, pp. x–xi.

4. Various participants or aides allowed me to see telephone transcripts, memos of conversation, and meeting notes in their possession; in each case I was allowed to see the entire document and make use of all of the information it contained. In the text where I quote from one of these documents, I specify when the telephone conversation or meeting occurred and who was involved.

In addition, the narrative of the Yom Kippur War draws on the sources cited in the footnote above plus the following interviews: Henry Kissinger, Jan. 21 and May 8, 1990; James Schlesinger, Oct. 16 and Nov. 17, 1989; Simcha Dinitz, Mar. 16, 1990; Joseph Sisco, Mar. 5 and Mar. 26, 1990; Richard Nixon, Oct. 11, 1990; Seymour Weiss, Apr. 11, 1990; Richard Perle, Apr. 11, 1990; Robert McCloskey, Feb. 2, 1990; Kenneth Rush, Jan. 9, 1991; Arnaud de Borchgrave, Nov. 16, 1989; Elmo Zumwalt, Nov. 20, 1989.

5. Hersh, *The Samson Option*, 226–32 (Hersh argues that "obviously" Dinitz or some other Israeli explicitly made the nuclear threat); Simcha Dinitz, Mar. 6, 1990; Henry Kissinger, Nov. 20, 1991; William Quandt, "How Far Will Israel Go?" *WP Book World*, Nov. 24, 1991 (Quandt talked to Ambassador Eilts, who confirmed his quotes in the Hersh account); Jack Anderson, "Close Call," *WP*, Mar. 10, 1980 (like Hersh, Anderson suggests that the Israeli threat to resort to nuclear arms was explicit).

6. *YOU*, 544–52; Nixon, *RN*, 933 (Nixon's account ignores the ramifications of his letter to Brezhnev and merely notes that it was meant to sound tough); Garthoff, *Détente and Confrontation*, 371; Joseph Sisco, Mar. 5, 1990; Winston Lord, Dec. 20, 1989; Peter Rodman, Sept. 12, 1989.

7. Lawrence Eagleburger, June 25, 1990; *YOU*, 556–57.

8. Golan, *The Secret Conversations of Henry Kissinger*, 82–88; *YOU*, 568–74; Yevgeni Primakov, *The Anatomy of the Near East Conflict* (Moscow: Nauka, 1978), 173, quoted in Garthoff, *Détente and Confrontation*, 374.

9. As explained in source note 4, certain conversation transcripts and meeting notes were shown to me by various participants.

In addition, the following description of the alert is from *YOU*, 575–91; Garthoff, *Détente and Confrontation*, 375–83; Henry Kissinger, Jan. 21, 1990; James Schlesinger, Nov. 17, 1989; Brent Scowcroft, July 16, 1990; Lawrence Eagleburger, June 25, 1990; Simcha Dinitz, Mar. 16, 1990.

10. *YOU*, 585; Henry Kissinger, Jan. 21, 1990; Nixon-Kissinger conversation, Oct. 24, 1973; Haig-Kissinger conversation, Oct. 24, 1973.

11. Henry Kissinger news conference, Oct. 25, 1973.

12. Haig-Kissinger conversation, Nixon-Kissinger conversations, Oct. 25, 1973.

13. *YOU*, 597–99.

14. Richard Nixon news conference, Oct. 26, 1973.

15. Haig-Dobrynin conversation, Oct. 26, 1973; Haig-Kissinger conversations, Oct. 26, 1973; *YOU*, 606–7.

16. Quandt, *Decade of Decisions*, 203; Sheehan, *The Arabs, Israelis and Kissinger*, 12.

17. James Schlesinger news conference, Oct. 26, 1973; *YOU*, 594; Garthoff, *Détente and Confrontation*, 391–93; Kissinger news conference, Nov. 21, 1973.

18. *YOU*, 614–15, 636–45, 749–50; Ismail Fahmy, *Negotiating for Peace*

in the Middle East, 56; Sheehan, *The Arabs, Israelis and Kissinger,* 48–49; Valeriani, *Travels With Henry,* 252; Joseph Sisco, Mar. 26, 1990.

19. Simcha Dinitz, Mar. 16, 1990; Sheehan, *The Arabs, Israelis and Kissinger,* 79–91; Golan, *The Secret Conversations of Henry Kissinger,* 120–21; *YOU,* 651–53, 751–52.

20. *YOU,* 771–72.

21. Sheehan, *The Arabs, Israelis and Kissinger,* 95–101; *YOU,* 783; Joseph Sisco, Mar. 26, 1990.

22. Kissinger statement, Geneva, Dec. 20, 1973; *YOU,* 792–95.

TWENTY-FOUR: THE SHUTTLE

1. *YOU,* 818; Valeriani, *Travels With Henry,* 186. The first known use of *shuttle* in this context was in a *NYT* story, Jan. 11, 1974, by Bernard Gwertzman, which referred to Kissinger's "unorthodox bit of shuttle diplomacy."

2. *YOU,* 798–853; Sheehan, *The Arabs, Israelis and Kissinger,* 108–12; Golan, *The Secret Conversations of Henry Kissinger,* 144–78.

3. Valeriani, *Travels With Henry,* passim; Marilyn Berger, "If Today Is Tuesday, Kissinger Must Be In . . . " *WP,* Dec. 26, 1973; Bernard Gwertzman, "A Kissinger Seminar," *NYT,* Dec. 25, 1973; *YOU,* 747–52; Sheehan, *The Arabs, Israelis and Kissinger,* 115; James Schlesinger, Nov. 17, 1989; Joseph Sisco, Mar. 5 and 26, 1990; Ted Koppel, Nov. 16, 1989; Bruce van Voorst, Mar. 20, 1990. Rabin quote is on p. 193 of Valeriani.

4. Sheehan, *The Arabs, Israelis and Kissinger,* 120.

5. Ibid., 112, 128; Kalb and Kalb, *Kissinger,* 542; *YOU,* 646–51; Simcha Dinitz, Mar. 16, 1990; *Time,* Mar. 23, 1974; Fahmy, *Negotiating for Peace in the Middle East,* 31, 46.

6. Fahmy, *Negotiating for Peace in the Middle East,* 72–73; Henry Kissinger, Dec. 21, 1990; Simcha Dinitz, Mar. 16, 1990; lecture by Hans Morgenthau, the Institute for International Affairs, Jerusalem, Mar. 12, 1974; *WHY,* 411; *YOU,* 1055; Valeriani, *Travels With Henry,* 208–9; Golan, *The Road to Peace,* 127–28; James Schlesinger, Nov. 17, 1989; Bernard Gwertzman, "A Kissinger Seminar," *NYT,* Dec. 25, 1973; Sheehan, *The Arabs, Israelis and Kissinger,* 129, 135.

7. Nicolson, *The Congress of Vienna,* 187; Valeriani, *Travels With Henry,* 189–90; Quandt, *Decade of Decisions,* 90, 228, 275; Henry Kissinger, May 10, 1990; *YOU,* 767; Fahmy, *Negotiating for Peace in the Middle East,* 771–72; Rabin, *The Rabin Memoirs,* 259.

8. Valeriani, *Travels With Henry,* 20, 193, 210; Sadat, *In Search of Identity,* 268–69; Blumenfeld, *Henry Kissinger,* 208; Golan, *The Secret Conversations of Henry Kissinger,* 215, 221; *Women's Wear Daily,* Feb. 20, 1974.

9. Based partly on the account of Zvi Rimon, in *Yediot Aharonot,* Dec. 18, 1973. Also, *YOU,* 291; Blumenfeld, *Henry Kissinger,* 248; Valeriani, *Travels With Henry,* 242. One former American official discussed the visit with me on the condition that he not be quoted by name.

10. *WHY,* 559; *YOU,* 202–3; Nixon, *RN,* 477; John Ehrlichman, Feb. 27, 1990; H. R. Haldeman, Feb. 20, 1990; Hersh, *The Price of Power,* 84.

11. Simcha Dinitz, Mar. 16, 1990; Fahmy, *Negotiating for Peace in the*

Middle East, 78; Joseph Kraft, "Secretary Henry," *NYT Magazine,* Oct. 28, 1973; Blumenfeld, *Henry Kissinger,* 248–50; David Kissinger, Feb. 14, 1990.

12. Elmo Zumwalt, Nov. 20, 1989; Helmut Sonnenfeldt, Sept. 12, 1989; *WHY,* 559; *YOU,* 202; Safire, *Before the Fall,* 565; Hersh, *The Price of Power,* 85; John Ehrlichman, Feb. 27, 1990; Lehman, *Command of the Seas,* 77; introduction of Kissinger by Rabbi Alexander Schindler, Conference of Presidents banquet, Jan. 10, 1977.

13. *YOU,* 885.

14. Sick, *All Fall Down,* 14–15; Bill, *The Eagle and the Lion,* 201; Kissinger memo to the defense secretary, July 25, 1972, released by Iranian captors of the U.S. embassy, vol. 4; Senate Foreign Relations Committee, *U.S. Military Sales to Iran,* July 1976.

15. Ball, *The Past Has Another Pattern,* 453–58; Shawcross, *The Shah's Last Ride,* 167; Sick, *All Fall Down,* 15; Rubin, *Paved With Good Intentions,* 134; Taheri, *Nest of Spies,* 59.

16. "The Kissinger-Shah Connection," *60 Minutes,* CBS, May 4, 1980; Jack Anderson columns, *WP,* Dec. 5, 10, 26, 1973; William Shawcross, "Through History With Henry Kissinger," *Harper's,* Nov. 1980; *YOU,* 887–88; Rubin, *Paved With Good Intentions,* 130; Bill, *The Eagle and the Lion,* 202; Robert Hormats, May 9, 1990.

17. The Pike Report was leaked by former CBS correspondent Daniel Shorr to *The Village Voice,* which printed it on Feb. 16, 1976; see also *NYT,* Jan. 26, 1976; Daniel Schorr, "1975: Background to Betrayal," *WP,* Apr. 7, 1991; Bill, *The Eagle and the Lion,* 205–8; William Shawcross, "Through History With Henry Kissinger," *Harper's,* Nov. 1980; Henry Kissinger, "Hard Choices to Make in the Gulf," *WP* and *LAT,* May 5, 1991; William Safire, "Son of 'Secret Sellout,' " *NYT,* Feb. 12, 1976. In his column, Safire urged Ford to fire Kissinger as a way "to disavow this act of American dishonor."

18. William Simon, Mar. 4, 1990; Rubin, *Paved With Good Intentions,* 140, 155; Valeriani, *Travels With Henry,* 28.

19. Fahmy, *Negotiating for Peace in the Middle East,* 84–88; *YOU,* 894, 945–51.

20. Valeriani, *Travels With Henry,* 296; *YOU,* 958, 1054; Sheehan, *The Arabs, Israelis and Kissinger,* 125; Henry Kissinger, May 8, 1990.

21. Golan, *The Secret Conversations of Henry Kissinger,* 190–99; Simcha Dinitz, Mar. 16, 1990; *YOU,* 1056–71.

22. Golan, *The Secret Conversations of Henry Kissinger,* 195–201; Simcha Dinitz, Mar. 16, 1990; Joseph Sisco, Mar. 26, 1990; Peter Rodman, Sept. 12, 1989; *YOU,* 969, 971, 1034–36, 1050, 1059, 1063, 1096–99. Some transcripts were shown to me with the understanding that I would keep the sources confidential; the vigorous exchange on May 14 is in Golan's book.

23. Reston column, May 17, 1974; *YOU,* 1079–1110; Meir, *My Life,* 443–44; *Time,* June 10, 1974; *Newsweek,* June 10, 1974.

TWENTY-FIVE: THE PRESS

1. Murrey Marder, "Keeping Up With Henry Kissinger," *WP,* Dec. 8, 1973; Morris, *Uncertain Greatness,* 263; Valeriani, *Travels With Henry,* 366;

Marilyn Berger, July 21, 1990; *YOU,* 821, 1086; Bruce van Voorst, Mar. 20, 1990.

2. Shawcross, *Sideshow,* 96–98; *YOU,* 820; Hersh, *The Price of Power,* 204; Jonathan Alter, Aug. 19, 1991.

3. Brent Scowcroft, July 16, 1990; Diane Sawyer, Sept. 7, 1990; Valeriani, *Travels With Henry,* 341–42; Richard Helms, Nov. 15, 1989; John Andrews, Jan. 11, 1990; Ehrlichman, *Witness to Power,* 310.

4. Christopher Ogden, Mar. 5, 1990; Henry Brandon, Nov. 15, 1989; Morris, *Uncertain Greatness,* 195; *Time,* June 24, 1974; Nancy Kissinger, Mar. 7, 1991; Valeriani, *Travels With Henry,* 333; Bernard Gwertzman, "Mr. Kissinger Says a Lot," *NYT,* Mar. 14, 1976; Bernard Gwertzman, "A Kissinger Seminar," *NYT,* Dec. 25, 1973; Sheehan, *The Arabs, Israelis and Kissinger,* 8–10.

5. John Scali, Nov. 15, 1990; Valeriani, *Travels With Henry,* 352–55; Joseph Lelyveld, "Kissinger and Peking," *NYT,* Dec. 2, 1974; *Time,* Dec. 27, 1971; Kalb and Kalb, *Kissinger,* 261; *WHY,* 912; Tom Wicker, "Backgrounder Blues," *NYT,* Dec. 16, 1971; also, news stories in *NYT* and *WP,* Dec. 16 and 17, 1971, and Jan. 4, 1972.

6. Presidential news summary, Sept. 8, 1972, president's office files, NPP; Wise, *The American Police State,* 62–63; Kalb and Kalb, *Kissinger,* passim; *YOU,* 1086–87. Marvin Kalb later became director of the Joan Shorenstein Barone Center on the Press, Politics and Public Policy at Harvard; his brother later served as State Department spokesman.

7. Valeriani, *Travels With Henry,* 5, 368.

8. Ted Koppel, Nov. 16, 1989; "Kissinger: Action Biography," ABC Television, June 14, 1974; *Extra!* newsletter, Fairness and Accuracy In Reporting, Oct. 1989.

9. Leslie Gelb, Jan. 9, 1990; Robert Semple, Sept. 28, 1990; Morris, *Uncertain Greatness,* 197.

10. Hugh Sidey, Oct. 16, 1989; *Time,* Feb. 14, 1969; "The World Is the Woodcutter's Ball," *Life,* Sept. 22, 1972. I am on the staff of *Time* and have worked there since 1978.

11. Katharine Graham, Dec. 14, 1989.

12. Susan Mary Alsop, Dec. 13, 1989; Joseph Alsop, "Henry Kissinger's Success," *WP,* June 3, 1974.

13. Polly Kraft, Nov. 16, 1989; Joseph Kraft, "The Bottomless Pit," *WP,* May 3, 1970.

14. Kissinger press conference, June 6, 1974; Wise, *The American Police State,* 84–85; *YOU,* 1114; *Time,* June 24, 1974; Senate Foreign Relations Committee, *Dr. Kissinger's Role in the Wiretapping,* 1974, 30; *WP,* June 6, 1974; *NYT,* June 9, 1974; *WP,* June 13, 1974; *Newsweek,* June 17, 1974; Marilyn Berger, "Kissinger Sought Help Before Trip," *WP,* June 12, 1974; Woodward and Bernstein, *The Final Days,* 223–25; Nixon, *RN,* 1009; Kissinger press conference, Salzburg, June 11, 1974.

15. Joseph Alsop, "The Hounding of Henry Kissinger," *WP,* June 21, 1974; William F. Buckley, "Kissinger and the Miasma," *New York Post,* June 15, 1974; Marquis Childs, "The War Against Kissinger," *WP,* June 11, 1974; Joseph Kraft, "Kissinger's Threat," *WP,* June 12, 1974; *NYT,* June 13, 1974; William Safire, "Henry at 50," *NYT,* May 28, 1973.

TWENTY-SIX: TRANSITIONS

1. Nancy Kissinger, Jan. 21 and 25, Mar. 6 and 7, 1990; Henry Kissinger, Aug. 28, 1989, and Jan. 21, 1990; David Kissinger, Feb. 14, 1990; Irene Kirkland, Jan. 8, 1990; Susan Mary Alsop, Dec. 13, 1989; Blumenfeld, *Henry Kissinger,* 150, 162, 268; Meg Greenfield and Katharine Graham, "The New Mrs. Kissinger," *WP,* Apr. 21, 1974; *People,* Apr. 15 and June 20, 1974, and Oct. 6, 1975; *Time,* Apr. 8 and 15, 1975; *Women's Wear Daily,* June 24, 1974, and Oct. 15, 1975. Epigraph in *YOU,* 1212.

2. *Time,* Dec. 24, 1973; McGovern not-for-attribution interview, Apr. 8, 1974.

3. *YOU,* 75–79.

4. John Andrews, Jan. 11, 1990; Nixon televised address, Aug. 15, 1973.

5. Richardson-Kissinger conversation, Oct. 24, 1973.

6. Haig-Kissinger conversation, Oct. 27, 1973.

7. *YOU,* 1197–1205; *NYT,* Sept. 2, 1974; Henry Kissinger, Feb. 16, 1990; Nixon, *RN,* 1074; Richard Nixon, Oct. 11, 1990; Bette Lord, Aug. 15, 1990.

8. Henry Kissinger, Oct. 9, 1989; Lawrence Eagleburger, June 25 and 26, 1990; Brent Scowcroft, July 16, 1990; conversation with Richard Nixon, Oct. 11, 1990; Woodward and Bernstein, *The Final Days,* 469–72; *YOU,* 1207–10; Osborne, *White House Watch,* 312; Frost, *I Gave Them a Sword,* 98. Kissinger's memoirs say he was in with Nixon until midnight, but the president's telephone logs reveal that he left around ten-thirty P.M., after which Nixon called speechwriter Ray Price. Nixon's telephone logs, Aug. 7, 1974, Nixon papers; Ambrose, *Nixon,* vol. 3, 401; Price, *With Nixon,* 341. Kissinger was a source for some of Bob Woodward's revelations.

9. Gerald Ford, July 24, 1990; Osborne, *White House Watch,* 94; Morris, *Uncertain Greatness,* 2; Gulley, *Breaking Cover,* 133; Hartmann, *Palace Politics,* 116; Ford, *A Time to Heal,* 29–30; *NYT,* Aug. 9, 1974.

10. Gerald Ford, July 24, 1990.

11. David Kissinger, Feb. 14, 1990.

12. Hartmann, *Palace Politics,* 287, 363.

13. Gerald Ford, July 24, 1990; David Kissinger, Feb. 14, 1990.

14. Richard Holbrooke, "Henry Kissinger Is . . ." *WP,* Sept. 15, 1974 (reprinted from the *Boston Globe*); Gerald Ford, July 24, 1990; Henry Kissinger, Oct. 9, 1989.

15. Donald Rumsfeld, Apr. 16, 1990; Nessen, *It Sure Looks Different From the Inside,* 133–34; Hartmann, *Palace Politics,* 341–42, 347; Gerald Ford, July 24, 1990; Ford, *A Time to Heal,* 355; Osborne, *White House Watch,* 110.

16. Henry Kissinger, Apr. 25, 1989; *Women's Wear Daily,* June 24, 1974; *People,* Jan. 13, 1975; Nancy Kissinger, Feb. 23, 1991; David Kissinger, Feb. 14, 1990.

TWENTY-SEVEN: The Death of Détente
1. Garthoff, *Détente and Confrontation*, 24; *YOU*, 240, 983; Brent Scowcroft, July 16, 1990; Sven Kraemer, Nov. 16, 1989; Helmut Sonnenfeldt, Nov. 16, 1989.
2. Richard Perle, Apr. 11, 1990; Henry Kissinger, Jan. 21 and Sept. 29, 1990; Norman Podhoretz, "The Present Danger," *Commentary*, Mar. 1980; Garthoff, *Détente and Confrontation*, 405–7; *YOU*, 236.
3. George Meany testimony, Oct. 1, 1974, in Senate Foreign Relations Committee, *Détente*, 1974, 380–81.
4. *YOU*, 983; Hoffmann, *Primacy or World Order*, 71; private diaries of Paul Nitze's nephew Scott Thompson and a paper on Paul Nitze by Thompson, provided to me; Callahan, *Dangerous Capabilities*, 357–59; Johnson, *The Right Hand of Power*, 623; Zumwalt, *On Watch*, 489–90; Talbott, *Master of the Game*, 141.
5. Friedrich, ed., *The Philosophy of Kant* (includes "Perpetual Peace"); Kissinger, "The Meaning of History," 261–70; Hyland, *Mortal Rivals*, 201; Kissinger testimony, Sept. 19, 1974, in Senate Foreign Relations Committee, *Détente*, 1974, 238–60; Nixon, *RN*, 565; Kissinger speech, the Society of Pilgrims, London, Dec. 12, 1973; *YOU*, 240, 980–81.
6. *YOU*, 250–54, 984–85; Henry Kissinger, Jan. 21, 1990; Richard Perle, Apr. 11, 1990.
7. Stern, *Water's Edge*, passim (this thoroughly documented book is a basic source for the narrative about the Jackson-Vanik amendment); Joseph Albright, "The Pact of Two Henrys," *NYT Magazine*, Jan. 5, 1975; Lawrence Stern, "Two Henrys Descending," *Foreign Policy*, Spring 1975; Richard Perle, Apr. 11, 1990; Hoffmann, *Primacy or World Order*, 39; Kissinger speech, Pacem in Terris Conference, Washington, Oct. 8, 1973; *YOU*, 252–55, 987.
8. Stern, *Water's Edge*, 95–99; Joseph Albright, "The Pact of Two Henrys," *NYT Magazine*, Jan. 5, 1975; memcon of Kissinger conversation with Dobrynin, Oct. 25, 1973, provided to the author; Golan, *The Secret Conversations of Henry Kissinger*, 172; Richard Perle, Apr. 11, 1990.
9. Stern, *Water's Edge*, 111–23; Marilyn Berger, "Soviet Emigration Assurances, Trade Bill Linked," *WP*, Mar. 19, 1974; *YOU*, 991–99; Nixon speech, U.S. Naval Academy, Annapolis, June 5, 1974; *Time*, June 17, 1974.
10. Gerald Ford, July 24, 1990; Ford, *A Time to Heal*, 139; Jerry ter Horst, "Trade Bill Compromise," *Washington Star*, Oct. 23, 1974; Stern, *Water's Edge*, 146–62; Joseph Albright, "The Pact of Two Henrys," *NYT Magazine*, Jan. 5, 1975; *WP*, Sept. 21, 1974.
11. Stern, *Water's Edge*, 162–90; Henry Kissinger, Sept. 29, 1990; Richard Perle, Apr. 11, 1990; Gromyko letter to Kissinger, Oct. 26, 1974; Hyland, *Mortal Rivals*, 107; *Newsweek*, Dec. 30, 1974; Kissinger testimony, Dec. 3, 1974, in Senate Finance Committee, *Emigration Amendment*, 1974; "Remember the Refuseniks?" *NYT* editorial, Dec. 14, 1990. The Kissinger, Jackson, and Gromyko letters are all reprinted, along with a comprehensive story by Bernard Gwertzman, in *NYT*, Dec. 19, 1974.
12. Henry Kissinger, May 10, 1990.
13. Stern, *Water's Edge*, 208–9; *WP*, Dec. 28, 1974.

14. Richard Perle, Apr. 11, 1990; John Lehman, Jan. 11, 1990; Lehman, *Command of the Seas,* 88; Talbott, *Master of the Game,* 136; Henry Kissinger, Jan. 21, 1990.

15. James Schlesinger, Nov. 17, 1989; Hyland, *Mortal Rivals,* 152; Helmut Sonnenfeldt, Nov. 16, 1989; Les Gelb, "Schlesinger for Defense," *NYT Magazine,* Aug. 4, 1974.

16. Elmo Zumwalt, Nov. 20, 1989; Henry Kissinger, Dec. 21, 1990; Zumwalt, *On Watch,* 427–34, 507–10; "Meet the Press," NBC News, June 30, 1974.

17. Henry Kissinger, Jan. 21, 1990; James Schlesinger, Nov. 17, 1989; *YOU,* 263, 1011–29; Hyland, *Mortal Rivals,* 79.

18. Garthoff, *Détente and Confrontation,* 444–45; Ford, *A Time to Heal,* 215; Henry Kissinger, Jan. 21, 1990.

19. Hyland, *Mortal Rivals,* 76–97; Ford, *A Time to Heal,* 214–19; Leslie Gelb, "Vladivostok Pact: How It Was Reached," *NYT,* Dec. 3, 1974; Hugh Sidey, Oct. 16, 1989; Nessen, *It Sure Looks Different From the Inside,* 45–51; Garthoff, *Détente and Confrontation,* 444–50; William Safire, "Secretary Kissinger's Malicious Canard Roti," *NYT,* Feb. 17, 1975; Johnson, *The Right Hand of Power,* 605–16; Talbott, *Endgame,* 35; John Lehman, Jan. 11, 1990.

20. Gerald Ford, July 24, 1990.

TWENTY-EIGHT: THE MAGIC IS GONE

1. Henry Kissinger, Jan. 21, 1990; Simcha Dinitz, Mar. 16, 1990; Joseph Sisco, Mar. 25, 1990; *YOU,* 1135–41; Richard Ullman, "After Rabat," *Foreign Affairs,* Jan. 1975; Golan, *The Secret Conversations of Henry Kissinger,* 226–27.

2. Henry Kissinger, Jan. 21, 1990; Joseph Sisco, Mar. 26, 1990; Golan, *The Secret Conversations of Henry Kissinger,* 232–36; ABC News, Feb. 7, 1975 (in *NYT,* Feb. 8, 1975).

3. Henry Kissinger, Jan. 21, 1990; Joseph Sisco, Mar. 26, 1990; Golan, *The Secret Conversations of Henry Kissinger,* 236–37; Sheehan, *The Arabs, Israelis and Kissinger,* 159–62; Bernard Gwertzman, "Failure of Kissinger's Mideast Mission Traced to Major Miscalculations," *NYT,* Apr. 7, 1975.

4. Valeriani, *Travels With Henry,* 228–30.

5. Sheehan, *The Arabs, Israelis and Kissinger,* 161–62.

6. Ibid., 164–78; Kissinger press conference, Mar. 26, 1975; "What Now for Henry?" *Time,* Apr. 7, 1975; Simcha Dinitz, Mar. 16, 1990; Valeriani, *Travels With Henry,* 241.

7. Isaacs, *Without Honor,* 188–292 (Arnold Isaacs was a *Baltimore Sun* reporter in Cambodia and Vietnam; his book is a superb account of the end of the war in both countries. The following Cambodia narrative generally follows his reporting); *YOU,* 366–68.

8. Isaacs, *Without Honor,* 270–71.

9. Ibid., 283–87; articles on the fall of Phnom Penh by Sydney Schanberg, *NYT,* May 9, 1975, and Jon Swain, *Sunday Times* (London), May 11, 1975; Shawcross, *Sideshow,* 200–395; *YOU,* 335–55; exchanges between Peter Rodman and Shawcross in the *American Spectator,* Mar. 1981, Apr. 27, 1981, and July 1981, reprinted as an appendix to the Touchstone paperback edition

of *Sideshow;* memorandum for the historian of the State Department by Emory Swank and Thomas Enders, Oct. 1979, reprinted as an appendix to *YOU.* Kissinger's synopsis of the Shawcross thesis about the effects of the American bombing, which appears on pp. 336 and 348 of *YOU,* is oversimplified. The argument is an interesting one and is fully explored in the Rodman-Shawcross exchanges. For other aspects of the Shawcross criticism, see the earlier discussion of Cambodia in Chapters 9 and 13.

10. Dung, *Our Great Spring Victory,* 2; Porter, *Vietnam,* vol. 2, 658; Nessen, *It Sure Looks Different From the Inside,* 97–98; *Time,* Apr. 14, 1975; Snepp, *Decent Interval,* 235–37, 280, 306–8; Gen. Frederick Weyand testimony, House Appropriations Committee, *Emergency Supplemental Appropriations,* Apr. 21, 1975; Isaacs, *Without Honor,* 406–11; Schecter and Hung, *The Palace File,* 302–5; Kissinger briefing, Palm Springs, Apr. 4, 1975.

11. *Time,* Apr. 14, 1975; Isaacs, *Without Honor,* 396; Snepp, *Decent Interval,* 304.

12. Gerald Ford, July 24, 1990; Ford, *A Time to Heal,* 253–54; Isaacs, *Without Honor,* 408; Henry Kissinger, May 10, 1990; *WHY,* 1470.

13. Gerald Ford, July 24, 1990; Hartmann, *Palace Politics,* 321–23; Nessen, *It Sure Looks Different From the Inside,* 108; Casserly, *The Ford White House,* 80.

14. Nguyen Van Thieu, Oct. 15, 1990; Schecter and Hung, *The Palace File,* 328–31, 363; Snepp, *Decent Interval,* 392–94.

15. Isaacs, *Without Honor,* 448; Nessen, *It Sure Looks Different From the Inside,* 95, 109–11; Snepp, *Decent Interval,* 486. (Snepp, a CIA analyst who fought a court battle with the agency to allow his book to be published, provides a vivid insider's account of the fall of Saigon.)

16. *YOU,* 88, 369; Gelb and Betts, *The Irony of Vietnam,* 347; "Message to Congress Requesting Supplemental Assistance for Vietnam and Cambodia," Jan. 28, 1975; Kissinger interview by Barbara Walters, "Today" show, May 5–8, 1975; Stephen Rosenfeld, "Kissinger's Postwar Confusion," *WP,* May 9, 1975.

17. Rowan, *The Four Days of the* Mayaguez,passim (an excellent and colorful narrative that gives a good feel for the details of the crisis); "Seizure of the *Mayaguez,"* report of the comptroller general to the House Committee on International Relations, Oct. 4, 1976; Gerald Ford, July 24, 1990; James Schlesinger, Oct. 16, 1989; Henry Kissinger, Mar. 31, 1990; Ford, *A Time to Heal,* 276–83; Nessen, *It Sure Looks Different From the Inside,* 118–28; Henry Kissinger press conference, May 16, 1975.

TWENTY-NINE: MORALITY IN FOREIGN POLICY

1. Kissinger's statement was included in the Pike Report, which was leaked by CBS correspondent Daniel Shorr to *The Village Voice,* Feb. 16, 1976; see also, *NYT,* Jan. 26, 1976. Epigraph from *Henry Kissinger* by Stoessinger, 14.

2. Smith, *Realist Thought from Weber to Kissinger,* 1–16. This is an excellent analysis of the history of realism culminating with Kissinger. Henry

Kissinger, "Reflections on Bismarck," *Daedalus,* Summer 1968, 906; Fareed Zakariah, Aug. 17, 1991.

3. Woodrow Wilson speech asking for a declaration of war, Apr. 2, 1917; Wilson speech in Sioux Falls, Iowa, Sept. 8, 1919.

4. *YOU,* 50, 971; *WHY,* 59, 915, 1088; Henry Kissinger, "False Dreams of a New World Order," *WP,* Feb. 26, 1991; Hoffmann, *Dead Ends,* 35–37.

5. Stanley Hoffmann, "The Task of Henry Kissinger," *WP,* Apr. 27, 1969; Henry Kissinger, "The White Revolutionary," *Daedalus,* Summer 1968; Kissinger, *A World Restored,* 1; *WHY,* 195.

6. *WHY,* 594; Hans Morgenthau, "The Three Paradoxes," *The New Republic,* Oct. 11, 1975.

7. James Schlesinger, Oct. 16, 1989; Daniel Patrick Moynihan, Mar. 14, 1990; Gerald Ford, July 24, 1990; Henry Kissinger, Jan. 21, 1990; Hartmann, *Palace Politics,* 337; Ford, *A Time to Heal,* 298; Nessen, *It Sure Looks Different From the Inside,* 345; *NYT,* July 22, 1975; *Time,* July 28, 1975.

8. Winston Lord, Dec. 20, 1989; Peter Rodman, Sept. 12, 1989; Hartmann, *Palace Politics,* 363; "The Moral Foundations of Foreign Policy," a speech by Henry Kissinger, Minneapolis, July 15, 1975; Henry Kissinger press conference, Minneapolis, July 15, 1975; *Time,* July 28, 1975. The most important of Kissinger's heartland speeches, including the one in Minneapolis, are collected in the third edition of *American Foreign Policy* by Kissinger.

9. Hyland, *Mortal Rivals,* 115–20; Garthoff, *Détente and Confrontation,* 473; Hartmann, *Palace Politics,* 339–42; Ford, *A Time to Heal,* 301–2.

10. Hartmann, *Palace Politics,* 342–44; Hyland, *Mortal Rivals,* 118–22; Ford, *A Time to Heal,* 305–6; Hyland, *The Cold War Is Over,* 160; Gerald Ford, July 24, 1990.

11. Helmut Sonnenfeldt, Nov. 16, 1989; Sonnenfeldt briefing cable, reprinted in the *NYT,* Apr. 6, 1976; House International Relations Committee, *Hearings of the Subcommittee on International Security,* Apr. 12, 1976; Rowland Evans and Robert Novak, "A Soviet–East Europe 'Organic Union,' " *WP,* Mar. 12, 1976; Dusko Doder, "Sonnenfeldt Report a Shock to East Europe," *WP,* Mar. 26, 1976; C. L. Sulzberger, "Mini-Metternich in a Fog," *NYT,* Mar. 27, 1976; Stephen Rosenfeld, "The Sonnenfeldt Doctrine," *WP,* Apr. 2, 1976; Bernard Gwertzman, "Eastern Europe a Delicate Issue," *NYT,* Apr. 7, 1976; Schulzinger, *Henry Kissinger,* 228; Henry Kissinger, Feb. 16, 1990.

12. Gerald Ford, July 24, 1990.

13. Daniel Moynihan, Mar. 14, 1990; Henry Kissinger, Jan. 21, 1990; Moynihan, *A Dangerous Place,* passim; Moynihan, "Was Woodrow Wilson Right?" *Commentary,* May 1974; Moynihan, "The United States in Opposition," *Commentary,* Mar. 1975; Gerald Ford, July 24, 1990; Moynihan, "The Politics of Human Rights," *Commentary,* Aug. 1974; *Time,* Dec. 8, 1975; William Safire, "Henry & Pat & Ivor," *NYT,* Nov. 24, 1975; Leslie Gelb, "Moynihan Says State Department Fails to Back Policy," *NYT,* Jan. 28, 1976; Moynihan cable to Kissinger, Jan. 23, 1976, reprinted in *NYT,* Jan. 28, 1976; James Naughton, "Moynihan Resigns Post at U.N., Cites Harvard Job," *NYT,* Feb. 3, 1976.

14. Donald Rumsfeld, Apr. 16, 1990; Henry Kissinger, Sept. 29, 1990; James Schlesinger, Nov. 17, 1989; Bette Bao Lord, Aug. 15, 1990; Brent Scow-

croft, July 16, 1990; Sven Kraemer, Nov. 16, 1989; Hartmann, *Palace Politics,* 360–70; Ford, *A Time to Heal,* 319–30; Osborne, *White House Watch,* xxii–xxxii; "Ford's Costly Purge," *Time,* Nov. 17, 1975; "Reagan: 'I Am Not Appeased,' " *Time,* Nov. 17, 1975; "My Own Team," *Newsweek,* Nov. 17, 1975.

THIRTY: AFRICA

1. William Hyland, Oct. 22, 1990; Tad Szulc, "Behind Portugal's Revolution," *Foreign Policy,* Winter 1975–76; Hyland, *Mortal Rivals,* 131–35; Jack Anderson, "Lisbon Envoys, Kissinger Disagree," *WP,* Apr. 18, 1975; Miguel Acoca, "Envoy Reported in Disfavor," *WP,* Apr. 10, 1975; Garthoff, *Détente and Confrontation,* 485–87.

2. Kwitny, *Endless Enemies,* 133–36, 148; Garthoff, *Détente and Confrontation,* 503–5; Edward Mulcahy, Feb. 11, 1991.

3. Stockwell, *In Search of Enemies,* 67–68; Hyland, *Mortal Rivals,* 137–38; Garthoff, *Détente and Confrontation,* 506–7; Marcum, *The Angolan Revolution,* vol. 2, 257–59; Klinghoffer, *The Angolan War,* 17; see also, hearings before the Subcommittee on African Affairs, Senate Foreign Relations Committee, *Angola,* Jan.–Feb. 1976, particularly Kissinger's testimony, p. 50. John Stockwell was the CIA's Angola task force chief; he became disillusioned and wrote *In Search of Enemies,* a colorful and critical account of an agent's-eye view of the controversy.

4. Nathaniel Davis, "The Angola Decision of 1975," *Foreign Affairs,* Fall 1978, 113–15; Stockwell, *In Search of Enemies,* 68.

5. Edward Mulcahy, Feb. 11, 1991; Stockwell, *In Search of Enemies,* 21–23; Garthoff, *Détente and Confrontation,* 512–15; Klinghoffer, *The Angolan War,* 110–35.

6. Seymour Hersh, "Angolan Aid Issue Opening Rifts in State Department," *NYT,* Dec. 14, 1975; also, *NYT,* Nov. 7, 1975, and *WP,* Nov. 8, 1975; Nathaniel Davis, "The Angolan Decision of 1975," *Foreign Affairs,* Fall 1978, 119; *Time,* Dec. 15, 1975; Craig Whitney, "Kissinger Visits Home Town," *NYT,* Dec. 16, 1975.

7. Memorandum of conversation, "Department Policy," prepared by notetaker L. Paul Bremer, Dec. 18, 1975. It was excerpted in the *Nation,* with an introduction by Mark Hertsgaard, Oct. 29, 1990; I later obtained a full copy of the document.

8. See previous footnote; also, Moynihan, *A Dangerous Place,* 250–51. For a good analysis of the East Timor situation fifteen years later, see: Steven Erlanger, "East Timor, Reopened by Indonesians, Remains a Sad and Terrifying Place," *NYT,* Oct. 21, 1990; and "East Timor: The Shame Endures," *NYT* editorial, Dec. 8, 1990.

9. Robert Healey, Apr. 7, 1991.

10. Kwitny, *Endless Enemies,* 149–50.

11. Henry Kissinger press conference, Pittsburgh, Nov. 11, 1975; Garthoff, *Détente and Confrontation,* 520–21; Henry Kissinger testimony, Subcommittee on African Affairs, Senate Foreign Relations Committee, Jan. 29, 1976; Kissinger background session, Lusaka, Jan. 20, 1976.

12. Kwitny, *Endless Enemies,* 132; Anthony Lewis, "The Winds of Change II," *NYT,* Apr. 26, 1976.

13. Henry Kissinger testimony, Jan. 29, 1976, and Dick Clark statement, Feb. 6, 1976, in hearings before the African Affairs Subcommittee, Senate Foreign Relations Committee, *Angola,* 1976.

14. Gerald Ford, July 24, 1990.

15. Tony Lake, Feb. 8, 1991; Brown, *The Crisis of Power,* 135–37; Hoffmann, *Primacy or World Order,* 34; Kissinger speech to the U.N., Oct. 1, 1976.

16. Tony Lake, Feb. 8 and 11, 1991; Roger Morris, Mar. 26, 1990; NSC Interdepartmental Group for Africa, "Study in Response to NSSM 39: Southern Africa," Aug. 15, 1969; El-Khawas, *The Kissinger Study of Southern Africa,* passim; Lake, *The Tar Baby Option,* 123–57.

17. Kissinger speech in Lusaka, Zambia, Apr. 27, 1976.

18. Edward Mulcahy, Feb. 11, 1991; "Doctor K's African Safari," *Time,* May 10, 1976; Michael Kaufman, "Africa Tour Resembles Stampede," *NYT,* May 5, 1991.

19. Winston Lord, Dec. 20, 1989; Hyland, *Mortal Rivals,* 167; Jon Nordheimer, "Reagan Attacks Kissinger for His Stand on Rhodesia," *NYT,* May 1, 1976; "Kissinger Attacks Reagan," UPI wire story, May 1, 1976; Osborne, *White House Watch,* 326; Bernard Gwertzman, "Kissinger Vows Effort to Change Rule in Rhodesia," *NYT,* May 14, 1976.

20. Bernard Gwertzman, "Progress Cited in Kissinger Talk on African Issues," *NYT,* Sept. 6, 1976; John Darnton, "Challenge to the Shuttle," *NYT,* Sept. 16, 1976; Bernard Gwertzman, "Kissinger Expects Smith to Approve Black Power Plan," *NYT,* Sept. 19, 1976; Michael Kaufman, "Smith Accepts Plan for Rhodesia," *NYT,* Sept. 25, 1976; Robert Keatley, "Kissinger's African Policy," *Wall Street Journal,* Sept. 9, 1976; Bernard Gwertzman, "Rhodesian Response to Kissinger Hinged on Ambiguity," *NYT,* Nov. 16, 1976; "A Dr. K Offer They Couldn't Refuse," *Time,* Oct. 4, 1976; "Poised Between Peace and War," *Time,* Oct. 11, 1976; Bernard Gwertzman, "Kissinger and Briton Seek a Plan to End Rhodesian Deadlock," *NYT,* Dec. 12, 1976.

THIRTY-ONE: Exit

1. Hugh Sidey, "Kissinger's Personal Plan," *Time,* Mar. 15, 1976; John Osborne, "Kissinger's Troubles," *The New Republic,* Feb. 7, 1976, and "Pressure on Henry," May 22, 1976 (both in *White House Watch,* 268, 325); Philip Shabecoff, "White House Denies Aim of Pushing Kissinger Out," *NYT,* Apr. 6, 1976; Bernard Gwertzman, "G.O.P. Leaders Tell Ford He's Harmed as Criticism of Kissinger's Moves Rise," *NYT,* May 7, 1976.

2. Christopher Ogden, Mar. 5, 1990; Kissinger interview by Barbara Walters, "Today" show, May 17, 1976; Robert Keatley, "How Much Longer for Kissinger?" *Wall Street Journal,* May 24, 1976; James Naughton, "Ford Sees Wisconsin Vote as Kissinger Endorsement," *NYT,* Apr. 8, 1976.

3. Ronald Reagan speech, Rollins College, Winter Park, Fla., Mar. 4, 1976; Ronald Reagan television address, NBC network, Mar. 31, 1976; Wit-

cover, *Marathon,* 401; Schulzinger, *Henry Kissinger,* 225–31; "Kissinger, in Rebutting Reagan, Calls Charges 'False Inventions,' " *NYT,* Apr. 2, 1975.

4. Gerald Ford speech, Peoria, Ill., Mar. 5, 1976; Garthoff, *Détente and Confrontation,* 548.

5. Statement by Henry Kissinger, Sept. 19, 1974; "The Moral Foundations of Foreign Policy," a speech by Henry Kissinger, Minneapolis, July 15, 1975; "The Permanent Challenge of Peace," a speech by Henry Kissinger, Feb. 3, 1976; press conference by Henry Kissinger, Apr. 8, 1976; Ronald Reagan television address, NBC network, Mar. 31, 1976.

6. Elmo Zumwalt, Nov. 20, 1989; Zumwalt, *On Watch,* 319; Henry Kissinger, Jan. 21, 1990; Nancy Kissinger, Jan. 21, 1990; John Lehman, Jan. 11, 1990; "The Meaning of History," undergraduate thesis by Henry Kissinger; Kissinger interview with James Reston, *NYT,* Oct. 13, 1974.

7. "The Sonnenfeldt Doctrine," *WP* editorial, Mar. 28, 1976; George Will, "Is It Kissinger's Fault?" *WP,* Apr. 18, 1975; Bernard Gwertzman, "The Gloomy Side of the Historian Henry A. Kissinger," *NYT,* Apr. 5, 1978; Henry Kissinger press conference, Dallas, Mar. 23, 1976.

8. Nessen, *It Sure Looks Different From the Inside,* 229–30; Hyland, *Mortal Rivals,* 168; Witcover, *Marathon,* 500.

9. Schulzinger, *Henry Kissinger,* 231; Hyland, *Mortal Rivals,* 174; Zbigniew Brzezinski, "America in a Hostile World," *Foreign Affairs,* Spring 1975; Jimmy Carter speech, the Foreign Policy Association, Oct. 3, 1976.

10. William Hyland, Oct. 22, 1990; Hyland, *Mortal Rivals,* 176–78; Schulzinger, *Henry Kissinger,* 233; NSC debate briefing book, WHSF, box 2, Gerald Ford Library; Ford, *A Time to Heal,* 420–22; Witcover, *Marathon,* 598–608; Nessen, *It Sure Looks Different From the Inside,* 270–74; Kissinger, press conference, Oct. 15, 1974; William Safire, "Henry's Private Scorn," *NYT,* Oct. 18, 1976.

Richard Holbrooke, who coordinated Carter's debate preparations, says that the Democrat planned to attack Ford personally in response to the first question, whatever it was, in order to throw him off guard; interview, Oct. 12, 1991.

11. Valeriani, *Travels With Henry,* 392–99; *Time,* Dec. 20, 1976; Bernard Gwertzman, "Now, Kissinger Woos His Critics," *NYT,* Jan. 19, 1977.

THIRTY-TWO: CITIZEN KISSINGER

1. Marvin Kalb, "What Will Henry Do for an Encore," *NYT Magazine,* Apr. 16, 1978; "Who Is the Biggest Star in Washington?" *Washingtonian,* Mar. 1978; John Corry, "The Kissingers Find a Nice Place to Visit," *NYT,* Jan. 27, 1977; Judith Miller, "Kissinger Co.," *NYT,* May 27, 1979; Leslie Bennetts, "Kissinger Ponders What Challenge to Take On," *NYT,* Dec. 29, 1978.

2. Susan Mulcahy, "Kissinger Versus the Blueberry Patch," *New York Post,* Aug. 22, 1983.

3. Henry Rosovsky, Feb. 24, 1989; Curtis Wilkie, "Kissinger to Return to Hub Academics," *Boston Globe,* June 2, 1977.

4. Harold Evans, Apr. 8, 1991; "700,000 Words in Longhand," *People,*

July 2, 1979; Wolfgang Saxon, "Kissinger Revised His Book More Than He Reported," *NYT*, Oct. 31, 1979; Shawcross, "Kissinger and *Sideshow,*" appendix to the Touchstone edition, 403; author's conversations with William Shawcross.

5. Don Oberdorfer, "Kissinger Said to Have Courted Both Sides in '68," *WP*, June 2, 1983; "Kissinger Says Assertions of Double-Dealing Are Slimy Lies," *NYT*, June 3, 1983; Sydney Schanberg, "The Kissinger Debate," *NYT*, June 14, 1983; William Safire, "Henry and Sy," *NYT*, June 9, 1983; Stanley Hoffmann, "The Kissinger Anti-Memoirs," *NYT Book Review*, July 3, 1983; Charlotte Curtis, "The Kissinger Aura," *NYT*, Aug. 3, 1983; James Silberman, Oct. 24, 1991.

6. Nancy Kissinger, Mar. 5, 6, and 13, 1991; Susan Mary Alsop, Dec. 13, 1989; Jan Cushing Amory, Oct. 22, 1990; Liz Smith, "Stars Crowd the Big Night for Henry," New York *Daily News*, June 9, 1985.

7. Interview with John McCloy, conducted in 1985 for *The Wise Men* by Isaacson and Thomas, 733; Terence Smith, "Why Carter Admitted the Shah," *NYT Magazine*, May 17, 1981; Shawcross, *The Shah's Last Ride*, 151–55; Henry Kissinger, "The Controversy Over the Shah," *WP*, Nov. 29, 1979; Amir Taheri, *Nest of Spies*, 116–17.

8. David Broder, "Kissinger the Pol," *WP*, Oct. 4, 1978; Peter Maas, Aug. 3, 1990.

9. Gerald Ford, July 24, 1990; David Kissinger, Feb. 14, 1990; Richard Allen, Jan. 16, 1991; "Inside the Jerry Ford Drama," *Time*, July 28, 1980.

In 1980, I covered the Republican Convention as a *Time* correspondent assigned to the Reagan campaign; this section is partly based on notes of my background interviews with Edwin Meese, Michael Deaver, William Casey, Alan Greenspan, James Baker, and others at the time.

10. George Gedda, "Kissinger: Détente With the Right?" Associated Press, Jan. 16, 1988; Garry Wills, "The Unsinkable Kissinger Bobs Back," *NYT*, Jan. 17, 1989.

11. Susan Mary Alsop, Dec. 13, 1989; Nixon letter to Mrs. Alsop, May 24, 1977, courtesy of Mrs. Alsop; James Naughton, "Nixon Rates Kissinger Plus and Minus," *NYT*, May 13, 1990; Frost, *I Gave Them a Sword*, 89.

12. William Safire, "The Second Comeback," *NYT*, Apr. 16, 1984; "Meet the Press," NBC News, Apr. 10, 1988.

13. *Report of the National Bipartisan Commission on Central America*, Jan. 1984, and hearings before the Senate Foreign Relations Committee, Feb. 1984; Walter Isaacson, "Rolling Out the Big Guns," *Time*, Aug. 1, 1983; Ronald Steel, "Our Dark Ambitions for Henry Kissinger," *WP*, July 24, 1983; Edward Cody, "Kissinger: Same Act on Smaller Stage," *WP*, Oct. 17, 1983; Carlos Diaz-Alejandro, "Kissinger Report: An Insider's View," *NYT*, Jan. 18, 1984; Robert Greenberger, "Managua Visit Pushed Kissinger Commission Toward Harder Line," Jan. 12, 1984.

14. Jeffrey Schmalz, "Kissinger Is Called Able as Cuomo Challenger," *NYT*, Feb. 1, 1986; David Broder, "Kissinger Won't Run for N.Y. Governor," *WP*, Feb. 4, 1986.

15. I am grateful to Strobe Talbott, who with Michael Beschloss is writing a book on Bush and the Soviets, for his reporting and insights into Yalta II. Also, Don Oberdorfer, "A Kissinger Plan for Central Europe," *WP*, Feb. 12,

1989; Brzezinski column, *NYT,* Mar. 13, 1989; Thomas Friedman, "Baker, Outlining World View, Assesses Plan for Soviet Bloc," *NYT,* Mar. 28, 1989; Strobe Talbott, "What's Wrong With Yalta II," *Time,* Apr. 24, 1989; Henry Kissinger, "Reversing Yalta," *LAT* and *WP,* Apr. 16, 1989; Michael Gordon, "U.S. Isn't Planning East Europe Talks," *NYT,* May 7, 1989.

THIRTY-THREE: KISSINGER ASSOCIATES

1. Maurice Greenberg, Feb. 12 and Aug. 9, 1991; Alan Stoga, Jan. 15, 1991; L. Paul ("Jerry") Bremer, Mar. 4, 1991; AIG 1990 annual report and proxy.

2. James Moffett, Feb. 7, 1991; 1990 proxy statements, annual report, and 10-K forms for Freeport-McMoRan and Daewoo; Jerry Bremer, Mar. 4, 1991.

3. Robert Day, Jan. 24 and Mar. 12, 1991; 1990 information packet of Trust Company of the West.

4. James Moffett, Feb. 7, 1991; James Robinson, Mar. 4, 1991; Maurice Greenberg, Feb. 12 and Aug. 1, 1991; Alan Stoga, Jan. 15, 1991; Jerry Bremer, Mar. 4, 1991; Peter Peterson, May 4, 1991; Henry Kissinger, Sept. 29, 1990, Apr. 25, 1991; conversations with other business associates of Kissinger; confirmation hearings and related documents of Lawrence Eagleburger for deputy secretary of state, Senate Foreign Relations Committee, Mar. 1989; disclosure forms and related documents of Brent Scowcroft for national security adviser, Feb. 1989; 1990 proxy statements and annual reports of American Express, Freeport-McMoRan, Union Pacific, Chase Manhattan, American International Group, CBS, Daewoo; 1990 10-K forms of Freeport-McMoRan, R. H. Macy; 1990 information packet of Trust Company of the West; Martin Schram, "Geopolitics 'R' Us," *Washingtonian,* Feb. 1989; Jeff Gerth with Sarah Bartlett, "Kissinger and Friends and Revolving Doors," *NYT,* Apr. 30, 1989; Bonnie Angelo, "Fingerspitzengefühl," *Time,* Feb. 17, 1986; Margaret Garrard Warner, "The Kissinger Clique," *Newsweek,* Mar. 27, 1989; Walter Pincus, "Eagleburger to Limit Role in Dozen Countries," *WP,* Feb. 16, 1989; Leslie Gelb, "Kissinger Means Business," *NYT Magazine,* Apr. 20, 1986; Joe Conason, "The Iraq Lobby," *New Republic,* Oct. 1, 1990; Kissinger letter, *New Republic,* Oct. 15, 1990.

I also was helped by Charles Thompson, Ariadne Allan, and Mike Wallace, who reported a piece on Kissinger Associates for CBS's "60 Minutes" in 1992.

For a full description of the Iraq connection, see speeches of Cong. Henry Gonzales in the *Congressional Record,* Apr. 25 and May 2, 1991.

5. Henry Kissinger, "The Rise of Mexico," *WP,* Aug. 17, 1988; Henry Kissinger, "First, a Breakthrough With Mexico," *WP,* Nov. 11, 1989; Alan Stoga, Jan. 15, 1991; James Robinson, Mar. 4, 1991. See previous section for details of Kissinger's help for TCW in Mexico.

6. Henry Kissinger, "The Drama in Beijing," *WP,* June 11, 1989; Henry Kissinger, "The Caricature of Deng as a Tyrant Is Unfair," *WP,* Aug. 1, 1989; Richard Cohen, "Kissinger: Pragmatism or Profit," *WP,* Aug. 29, 1989; Ste-

phen Solarz, "Kissinger's Kowtow," *WP,* Aug. 6, 1989; John Fialka, "Mr. Kissinger Has Opinions on China—And Business Ties," *Wall Street Journal,* Sept. 15, 1989; 1990 proxy statements, Freeport-McMoRan and American Express; James Moffett, Feb. 7, 1991; Maurice Greenberg, Nov. 11, 1991; Henry Kissinger, Sept. 29, 1990; "MacNeil/Lehrer NewsHour," Sept. 19, 1989; "For the Record," *WP,* Oct. 11, 1989; Walter Pincus, "Kissinger Says He Had No Role in China Mission," *WP,* Dec. 14, 1989; Richard Holbrooke, Mar. 30 and Aug. 1, 1990.

7. Nancy Kissinger, Feb. 23, Mar. 6, 7, and 13, 1991; Peter Glenville, July 3, 1991; Robert Day, Mar. 12, 1991; interviews with various social friends of the Kissingers'.

8. Philip Weiss, "Inside Bohemian Grove," *Spy,* Nov. 1989; Ball, *The Past Has Another Pattern,* 104–6.

9. Robert Day, Mar. 12, 1991; "CBS This Morning," May 21, 1991; conversations with Mortimer Zuckerman, Ken Auletta, Garry Trudeau, Strobe Talbott.

10. Kissinger letter to Trudeau, Aug. 4, 1986; Trudeau letter to Kissinger, Sept. 16, 1986.

11. Peter Glenville, July 3, 1991.

12. Nancy Kissinger, Feb. 23 and Mar. 13, 1991; Paula Kissinger, Mar. 4, 1991; Walter Kissinger, Mar. 10, 1991.

THIRTY-FOUR: LEGACY

1. William Hyland, Dec. 11, 1989; Leslie Gelb, Jan. 9, 1990; Valeriani, *Travels With Henry,* 9; Leslie Gelb, "The Kissinger Legacy," *NYT,* Oct. 31, 1976; Safire, *Before the Fall,* 169.

2. Stanley Hoffmann, Feb. 24, 1989; Kissinger letter to Mrs. Frank, Apr. 21, 1946, courtesy Helmut Reissner.

3. *WHY,* 1138; Safire, *Before the Fall,* 439.

4. Polly Kraft, Nov. 16, 1989.

5. Arthur Schlesinger, Feb. 16, 1989; Diane Sawyer, Sept. 7, 1990; James Schlesinger, Nov. 17, 1989; Morton Halperin, May 24, 1988; Elmo Zumwalt, Nov. 20, 1989; Sven Kraemer, Nov. 16, 1989.

6. Lawrence Eagleburger, June 25, 1990.

7. Henry Kissinger, Jan. 21, 1990.

8. Henry Kissinger, Dec. 2, 1991; George Kennan (anonymously, as "X"), "The Sources of Soviet Conduct," *Foreign Affairs,* July 1947.

9. Kissinger off-the-record talk to Nobel laureates, Paris, Jan. 18, 1988, tape courtesy of the Elie Wiesel Foundation; *Washington Times,* Jan. 22, 1988.

10. The best example of Kissinger's emphasis on national interests and realism rather than idealism and morality in the aftermath of the cold war is his newspaper column "Redefining National Security," *LAT/WP,* Dec. 3, 1991.

Bibliography

A NOTE ON SOURCE MATERIALS

Kissinger's tenure in power coincided with two trends that seemed designed to flummox future historians: the rise of the Xerox machine and of the posterior-protecting memo. This meant that the documentary record became both voluminous and misleading. Future scholars, Kissinger himself noted, will have "no criteria for determining which documents were produced to provide an alibi and which genuinely guided decisions."

In addition, Kissinger rarely put anything on the record in normal diplomatic channels if he could devise a more secretive back channel instead. So when historians eventually get access to all of the archival material, they will have to determine not only what the documents reveal but also what they sought to conceal. "What is written in diplomatic documents never bears much relation to reality," Kissinger once told Daniel Davidson. "I could never have written my Metternich dissertation based on documents if I had known what I know now."

For example, early in his first year in office, Kissinger told Morton Halperin to prepare an action memo for the president regarding the downing of an American spy plane by the North Koreans. When Halperin said that he was already working on one, Kissinger answered: "No, I mean a serious one. The one you're doing is for the files." So Halperin wrote two versions. Likewise, during the Paris peace talks on Vietnam, both Anthony Lake and Winston Lord admit that, in preparing memos of conversations, they wrote three or more versions tailored for different audiences. As Kissinger was struggling to complete the Vietnam accord, Nixon sent him a tough cable threatening to resume the bombing—but the message was in fact just for use as a negotiating tool, as Nixon made clear in a separate note.

Since the archival record of the Nixon years can be very misleading, I have sought to combine a historian's respect for documents—many of which are available unofficially even though they will not be declassified and released for twenty years or so—with a journalist's eagerness to interview the various participants.

Since a book is partly shaped by the selection of sources, I decided to tote up whether there were more friends or foes among the 150 or so people interviewed. Some were easy to categorize, such as Gerald Ford (friend) and Daniel Ellsberg (foe). But despite the strong emotions Kissinger evokes, most of those I talked to had surprisingly mixed and complex sentiments about him.

Former South Vietnamese president Nguyen Van Thieu, for example, still felt a strong sense of betrayal, yet he managed to sound more understanding than spiteful as he spoke of Kissinger. H. R. Haldeman and John Ehrlichman, whom I had assumed would be rather favorable, turned out to be most revealing about the deceits that poisoned the atmosphere in Nixon's White House. Anthony Lake and Roger Morris, aides who resigned after the invasion of Cambodia, were thoughtful critics; yet both gave better insights than Kissinger's purer loyalists about his genius in reshaping the bureaucracy and transforming America's role in the world.

The person who was the most complex and ambivalent about Kissinger was Richard Nixon. His strange admixture of resentment and respect led him to sound denigrating and condescending even as he praised Kissinger's mind. A typical comment would begin: "Now, I'm not one of those ones who would say that Henry is paranoid, you know, but . . ."

I met with Nixon in his suburban New Jersey office for one formal and two informal sessions. He was typically awkward at times, such as when he said he wanted to record our interview. When the tape on his microcassette recorder ran out about a third of the way into the session, he fiddled a bit and gave up, announcing, "I was never very good at dealing with these tape machines." I looked carefully, but could not detect any sign of irony.

Nixon had worked hard to prepare for the interview; he had written out answers to a variety of questions I might ask, but he then made a point of telling me that he would not refer to these notes during our discussion. He seemed convinced that I was writing "a hatchet job" and that the only way to sell my book was "if you are hard on Henry." The day after our last meeting, Nixon sent me a long letter that began: "In reflecting on your question with regard to personal anecdotes, it occurred to me that while the major news interest will be what you are able to dig up on Henry's famous temper and other negative characteristics, your readers might like to see the warm-hearted, positive side of an authentic genius with an admittedly complex personality."

Nixon's letter went on to cite many examples of Kissinger's human side, which are, I hope, reflected in this book. Moreover, the letter's tone gives a feel for the complexities involved in Nixon's attitudes toward Kissinger. For example, after describing the time he met Kissinger's parents in the Oval Office, Nixon wrote: "I have often observed over the years that very successful individuals—and this is particularly true of those who consider themselves intellectuals—are somewhat embarrassed and even a bit ashamed of their parents. Henry, as we know, enjoys association with celebrities. But I sense that he considered his parents to be more important than any of these celebrities."

Kissinger's mother, Paula, a spry and unaffected and wryly honest woman, was an indispensable source as well as a delight to interview. While I was writing this book, she was still living in the modest apartment in upper Manhattan's Washington Heights where she and her family moved shortly after arriving from Germany in 1938. There, in her son's old bedroom, she kept boxes of his papers and childhood letters, including the short story about his relatives killed in the holocaust that he wrote at the end of the war when he returned to Fürth as an officer in the U.S. Army's counterintelligence corps. When I told him about the material she had given me, Kissinger said—jokingly, I assume—"You have co-opted my mother, and now even she is out to destroy me."

This book contains no allegations made solely by anonymous sources. This is not, I hasten to add, a high-minded statement of principle. I believe that reporters must be willing to talk to people on background, and I have. Yet most people, now that enough time has passed, never raised the issue of remaining anonymous. When sources who asked for anonymity made specific allegations—or for that matter compliments—I went back to them later to persuade them to go on the record, and they usually consented. Only five people insisted on remaining totally anonymous, and they are not listed below.

The primary source for documentary material is the Nixon Presidential Papers Project, located in a warehouse in Alexandria, Virginia. Due to post-Watergate laws and lawsuits, the papers are controlled not by the former president but by professionals at the National Archives, whose loyalty is to history and not to Nixon. Thus they willingly help with mandatory review requests to open material still sealed. The only significant time I was turned down involved some notes of a meeting where Kissinger's psychological stability was discussed (one of the participants later gave me a copy). Particularly useful are the handwritten meeting notes made each day by Haldeman and Ehrlichman, which are so fascinating that a researcher can spend weeks wallowing in them.

Starting soon after he took office, Kissinger had secretaries or aides listen in on his phone conversations on a "dead key" and take notes. This system evolved into a full-fledged taping system with a battery of secretaries who would transcribe the talks overnight. These are now under seal in the Library of Congress among Kissinger's personal papers, unavailable until at least five years after his death. Some people were willing to show me transcripts they had access to. When using these documents, I have cited the time and place of the conversation in the source notes.

This is also true for memos of conversation, known as memcons. Kissinger was a stickler for having a notetaker in all important meetings to provide a verbatim report. These, too, are still not public. Yet people who had access to them sometimes kept copies, and thus it was possible to turn up some of them while doing interviews.

INTERVIEWS

Richard Allen
Mort Allin
Susan Mary Alsop
Jan Golding Amory
John Andrews
Georgi Arbatov
Egon Bahr
Gerald Bechhofer
Samuel Beer
Benazir Bhutto
Arnaud de Borchgrave
Joan Braden
Henry Brandon
L. Paul (Jerry) Bremer
Zbigniew Brzezinski
McGeorge Bundy
William Bundy
Abram Chayes
Charles Colson
John Connally
John Conway
Charles Coyle
Lloyd Cutler
Daniel Davidson
Robert Day
Simcha Dinitz
Anatoli Dobrynin
Paul Doty
Lawrence Eagleburger
John Ehrlichman
Daniel Ellsberg
Thomas Enders
Herbert Engelhardt
Harold Evans
Robert Evans
Gerald Ford
J. William Fulbright
Leslie Gelb
Arthur Gilman
Henry Gitterman
Guido Goldman
Andrew Goodpaster

Katharine Graham
Stephen Graubard
Maurice Greenberg
H. R. Haldeman
Morton Halperin
Robert Healey
Jack Heiman
Richard Helms
Eric Hendel
Lawrence Higby
Stanley Hoffmann
Richard Holbrooke
Robert Hormats
Barbara Howar
Nguyen Tien Hung
Samuel Huntington
Fred Ikle
Tziporah Jochsberger
Carl Kaysen
Irena Kirkland
David Kissinger
Henry Kissinger
Nancy Maginnes
   Kissinger
Paula Kissinger
Walter Kissinger
Ted Koppel
Fritz Kraemer
Sven Kraemer
Polly Kraft
Elizabeth Epstein
   Krumpe
Melvin Laird
W. Anthony Lake
John Lehman
Menachem (Heinz)
   Lion
Bette Bao Lord
Winston Lord
Laurence Lynn
Karl Marcy
Robert McCloskey

James Moffett
Richard Moose
Roger Morris
Hugh Morrow
Daniel Moynihan
Edward Mulcahy
Richard Nixon
Christopher Ogden
Walter Oppenheim
Richard Perle
Peter Peterson
Ray Price
Harold (Helmut)
   Reissner
Stanley Resor
James Reston
Mahmoud Riad
Elliot Richardson
David Riesman
James Robinson
Peter Rodman
Henry Rosovsky
Walt Rostow
Oscar Ruebhausen
Donald Rumsfeld
Kenneth Rush
John Sachs
Jill St. John
Diane Sawyer
John Scali
Thomas Schelling
Arthur Schlesinger, Jr.
James Schlesinger
Lina Rau Schubach
Brent Scowcroft
Robert Semple
Lloyd Shearer
Marshall Shulman
Hugh Sidey
Kurt Silbermann
William Simon
Joseph Sisco

Gerard Smith
Richard Smyser
Helmut Sonnenfeldt
Herbert Spiro
Gloria Steinem
Paul Stiefel
Alan Stoga
Donald Strong

Viktor Sukhodrev
Strobe Talbott
Nguyen Van Thieu
Garry Trudeau
Adam Ulam
Ted Van Dyk
Christine Vick
Mike Wallace

William Watts
Leonard Weiss
Seymour Weiss
Laurence Wylie
Barry Zorthian
Elmo Zumwalt

BOOKS BY HENRY KISSINGER *(listed chronologically)*

A World Restored: Metternich, Castlereagh, and the Problems of Peace, 1812–22. Boston: Houghton Mifflin, 1957.

Nuclear Weapons and Foreign Policy. New York: Harper & Brothers, 1957.

Foreign Economic Policy for the Twentieth Century (ed.), Rockefeller Brothers' Fund Special Study Project. New York: Doubleday, 1958.

The Necessity for Choice. New York: Harper & Brothers, 1961.

The Troubled Partnership: A Reappraisal of the Atlantic Alliance. New York: McGraw Hill, 1965.

Problems of National Strategy (ed.). New York: Praeger, 1965.

American Foreign Policy (essays). New York: Norton, 1969, revised 1974, 1977.

White House Years. Boston: Little, Brown, 1979.

For the Record. Boston: Little, Brown, 1981.

Years of Upheaval. Boston: Little, Brown, 1982.

Observations. Boston: Little, Brown, 1985.

ACADEMIC ARTICLES BY KISSINGER *(listed chronologically)*

"The Meaning of History: Reflections on Spengler, Toynbee and Kant." Undergraduate thesis, unpublished, Widener Library, Harvard, 1951.

"Reflections on the Political Thought of Metternich." *American Political Science Review,* Dec. 1954.

"American Policy and Preventive War." *Yale Review,* Apr. 1955.

"Military Policy and the Defense of the Grey Areas." *Foreign Affairs,* Apr. 1955.

"Limitations of Diplomacy." *The New Republic,* May 6, 1955.

"Congress of Vienna." *World Politics,* Jan. 1956.

"Force and Diplomacy in the Nuclear Age." *Foreign Affairs,* Apr. 1956.

"Reflections on American Diplomacy." *Foreign Affairs,* Oct. 1956.

"Strategy and Organization." *Foreign Affairs,* Apr. 1957.

"Controls, Inspection and Limited War." *The Reporter,* June 13, 1957.

"U.S. Foreign Policy and Higher Education." *Current Issues in Higher Education,* Mar. 1958.

"Missiles and the Western Alliance." *Foreign Affairs,* Apr. 1958.

"Nuclear Testing and the Problems of the Peace." *Foreign Affairs,* Oct. 1958.

"The Policymaker and the Intellectual." *The Reporter*, Mar. 5, 1959.

"As Urgent as the Moscow Threat." *New York Times Magazine*, Mar. 11, 1959.

"The Search for Stability." *Foreign Affairs*, July 1959.

"The Khrushchev Visit." *New York Times Magazine*, Sept. 6, 1959.

"Arms Control, Inspection and Surprise Attack." *Foreign Affairs*, July 1960.

"Limited War: Nuclear or Conventional? A Reappraisal." *Daedalus*, Fall 1960.

"The New Cult of Neutralism." *The Reporter*, Nov. 24, 1960.

"The Next Summit Meeting." *Harper's*, Dec. 1960.

"For an Atlantic Confederacy." *The Reporter*, Feb. 2, 1961.

"L'Évolution de la Doctrine Stratégique aux États-Unis." *Politique Étranger* 2, 1962.

"The Unsolved Problems of European Defense." *Foreign Affairs*, July 1962.

"Reflections on Cuba." *The Reporter*, Nov. 22, 1962.

"Strains on the Alliance." *Foreign Affairs*, Jan. 1963.

"The Skybolt Affair." *The Reporter*, Jan. 17, 1963.

"NATO's Nuclear Dilemma." *The Reporter*, Mar. 28, 1963.

"Reflections on Power and Diplomacy," in E. A. J. Johnson (ed.), *Dimensions in Diplomacy*. Baltimore: Johns Hopkins Press, 1964.

"Les États-Unis et l'Europe," *Res Publica* 6 (Belgian Institute of Political Science), 1964.

"Classical Diplomacy," in John Stoessinger and Alan Westin (eds.), *Power & Order: Six Cases in World Politics*. New York: Harcourt, Brace, 1964.

"Coalition Diplomacy in the Nuclear Age." *Foreign Affairs*, July 1964.

"Goldwater and the Bomb." *The Reporter*, Nov. 5, 1964.

"The Illusionist: Why We Misread de Gaulle." *Harper's*, Mar. 1965.

"Kann Man Den Soviets Trauen?" *Die Welt*, Apr. 3, 1965.

"The Price of German Unity." *The Reporter*, Apr. 22, 1965.

"Domestic Structure and Foreign Policy." *Daedalus*, Apr. 1966.

"For a New Atlantic Alliance." *The Reporter*, July 14, 1966.

"What Should We Do Now?" *Look*, Aug. 9, 1966.

"NATO: Evolution or Decline?" *Texas Quarterly*, Autumn 1966.

"Fuller Explanation," a review of Raymond Aron's *A Theory of International Relations*. *New York Times Book Review*, Feb. 12, 1967.

"The White Revolutionary: Reflections on Bismarck." *Daedalus*, Summer 1968.

"Bureaucracy and Policymaking," Security Studies Paper #17. University of California–Los Angeles, 1968.

"Central Issues of American Foreign Policy," *Agenda for the Nation*. Washington: Brookings, 1968.

"The Vietnam Negotiation." *Foreign Affairs*, Jan. 1969.

OTHER BOOKS

Alroy, Gil. *The Kissinger Experience: American Foreign Policy in the Middle East*. New York: Horizon, 1975.

Ambrose, Stephen. *Nixon: Ruin and Recovery, 1973–1990.* New York: Simon & Schuster, 1991.

———. *Nixon: The Triumph of a Politician, 1962–1972.* New York: Simon & Schuster, 1989.

———. *Rise to Globalism.* New York: Penguin, 1985.

Anson, Robert Sam. *Exile: The Unquiet Oblivion of Richard M. Nixon.* New York: Simon & Schuster, 1984.

Aron, Raymond. *Peace and War.* New York: Doubleday, 1966.

Atwood, William. *The Twilight Struggle.* New York: Harper & Row, 1987.

Badri, Hassan, et al. *The Ramadan War.* New York: Hippocrene, 1978.

Baedeker, Karl. *Southern Germany,* 13th ed. Leipzig: Baedeker, 1929.

Ball, George. *Diplomacy for a Crowded World.* Boston: Little, Brown, 1976.

———. *The Past Has Another Pattern.* New York: Norton, 1982.

Bell, Coral. *The Diplomacy of Détente.* New York: St. Martin's, 1977.

Bellow, Saul. *To Jerusalem and Back.* New York: Viking, 1976.

Berman, Larry. *Planning a Tragedy.* New York: Norton, 1982.

Bill, James. *The Eagle and the Lion.* New Haven: Yale, 1988.

Blumenfeld, Ralph, and reporters of the *New York Post. Henry Kissinger.* New York: New American Library, 1974.

Brandon, Henry. *The Retreat of American Power.* New York: Doubleday, 1973.

———. *Special Relationships.* New York: Atheneum, 1988.

Brodine, Virginia, and Mark Selden. *Open Secret: The Kissinger-Nixon Doctrine in Asia.* New York: Harper & Row, 1972.

Brown, Seyom. *The Crisis of Power.* New York: Columbia, 1979.

Bundy, McGeorge. *Danger and Survival.* New York: Random House, 1988.

Bush, George, with Victor Gold. *Looking Forward.* New York: Doubleday, 1987.

Caldwell, Dan, ed. *Henry Kissinger: His Personality and Policies.* Durham, N.C.: Duke, 1983.

Callahan, David. *Dangerous Capabilities.* New York: HarperCollins, 1990.

Casserly, John. *The Ford White House.* Boulder: Colorado University, 1977.

Chester, Lewis, Godfrey Hodgson, and Bruce Page. *An American Melodrama.* New York: Viking, 1969.

Clifford, Clark, with Richard Holbrooke. *Counsel to the President.* New York: Random House, 1991.

Colby, William, and Peter Forbath. *Honorable Men: My Life in the CIA.* New York: Simon & Schuster, 1978.

Collier, Peter, and David Horowitz. *The Rockefellers.* New York: Holt, Rinehart and Winston, 1976.

Colodny, Len, and Robert Gettlin. *Silent Coup.* New York: St. Martin's, 1991.

Colson, Charles. *Born Again.* Lincoln, Va.: Chosen Books, 1976.

Dallek, Robert. *The American Style of Foreign Policy.* New York: Knopf, 1983.

Dayan, Moshe. *Story of My Life.* New York: Morrow, 1976.

Destler, I. M., Leslie Gelb, and Anthony Lake. *Our Own Worst Enemy.* New York: Simon & Schuster, 1984.

Dickson, Peter. *Kissinger and the Meaning of History.* New York: Cambridge, 1979.

Diem, Bui, with David Charnoff. *The Jaws of History.* Boston: Houghton Mifflin, 1987.

Dowty, Alan. *Middle East Crisis.* Berkeley: University of California, 1984.

Drew, Elizabeth. *Washington Journal: 1973–74.* New York: Random House, 1975.

Eban, Abba. *An Autobiography.* New York: Random House, 1977.

Ehrlichman, John. *Witness to Power.* New York: Simon & Schuster, 1982.

El-Khawas, Mohamed, and Barry Cohen. *The Kissinger Study of Southern Africa.* Westport: Lawrence Hill, 1976.

Elliott, William. *Western Political Heritage.* New York: Prentice-Hall, 1949.

Evans, Rowland, and Robert Novak. *Nixon in the White House.* New York: Random House, 1971.

Eveland, Wilbur. *Ropes of Sand.* New York: Norton, 1980.

Fahmy, Ismail. *Negotiating for Peace in the Middle East.* Baltimore: Johns Hopkins, 1983.

Fallaci, Oriana. *Interview With History.* New York: Liverwright, 1976.

Ford, Gerald. *A Time to Heal.* New York: Harper & Row, 1979.

Freedman, Lawrence. *The Evolution of Nuclear Strategy.* New York: St. Martin's, 1981.

Friedrich, Carl. *Inevitable Peace.* Cambridge: Harvard University Press, 1948.

———, ed. *The Philosophy of Kant* (includes "Perpetual Peace"). New York: Random House, 1949.

Frost, David. *I Gave Them a Sword.* New York: Morrow, 1978.

Frye, Alton. *A Responsible Congress: The Politics of National Security.* New York: McGraw-Hill, 1975.

Gaddis, John Lewis. *The Long Peace.* New York: Oxford, 1987.

———. *Strategies of Containment.* New York: Oxford, 1982.

Garthoff, Raymond. *Détente and Confrontation.* Washington: Brookings, 1985.

Gelb, Leslie, and Richard Betts. *The Irony of Vietnam: The System Worked.* Washington: Brookings, 1979.

Gentry, Curt. *J. Edgar Hoover.* New York: Norton, 1991.

Ghanayem, Ishaq, and Alden Voth. *The Kissinger Legacy: American Middle East Policy.* New York: Praeger, 1984.

Golan, Galia. *Yom Kippur and After.* New York: Cambridge, 1977.

Golan, Matti. *The Road to Peace: A Biography of Shimon Peres.* New York: Warner, 1989.

———. *The Secret Conversations of Henry Kissinger.* New York: Quadrangle, 1976.

Goodman, Allan. *The Lost Peace.* Stanford: Hoover, 1978.

Graubard, Stephen. *Kissinger: Portrait of a Mind.* New York: Norton, 1973.

Grose, Peter. *Israel in the Mind of America.* New York: Knopf, 1983.

Gulley, Bill, with Mary Ellen Reese. *Breaking Cover.* New York: Simon & Schuster, 1980.

Haig, Alexander. *Caveat.* New York: Macmillan, 1984.

Haldeman, H. R., and Joseph DiMona. *The Ends of Power.* New York: Times Books, 1978.

Halperin, Morton. *Bureaucratic Politics and Foreign Policy.* Washington: Brookings, 1974.

———. *Limited War in the Nuclear Age.* New York: John Wiley & Sons, 1963.

Hammond, William. *Public Affairs: The Military and The Media.* Department of the Army's Center for Military History, forthcoming.

Hartmann, Robert. *Palace Politics.* New York: McGraw-Hill, 1980.

Head, Richard, Frisco Short, and Robert McFarlane. *Crisis Resolution: Presidential Decisionmaking in the Mayaguez and Korean Confrontations.* Boulder: Westview, 1978.

Heald, Tim, et al. (including John Ehrlichman). *The Rigby File.* London: Hodder & Stoughton, 1989.

Heikal, Mohammed. *The Road to Ramadan.* New York: Times Books, 1975.

Herring, George. *America's Longest War.* New York: Knopf, 1985.

———, ed. *The Secret Diplomacy of the Vietnam War.* Austin: University of Texas, 1983.

Hersh, Seymour. *The Price of Power: Kissinger in the Nixon White House.* New York: Summit, 1983.

———. *The Samson Option.* New York: Random House, 1991.

Hodgson, Godfrey. *America in Our Time.* New York: Doubleday, 1976.

Hoffmann, Stanley. *Dead Ends.* Cambridge: Ballinger, 1983.

———. *Primacy or World Order.* New York: McGraw-Hill, 1978.

Hunebelle, Danielle. *Dear Henry.* New York: Berkley, 1972.

Hung, Nguyen Tien, and Jerrold Schecter. *The Palace File.* New York: Harper & Row, 1986.

Hyland, William. *The Cold War Is Over.* New York: Random House, 1990.

———. *Mortal Rivals.* New York: Random House, 1987.

Isaacs, Arnold. *Without Honor.* Baltimore: Johns Hopkins, 1983.

Johnson, U. Alexis, with Jef McAllister. *The Right Hand of Power.* Englewood Cliffs, N.J.: Prentice-Hall, 1984.

Joiner, Harry. *American Foreign Policy: The Kissinger Era.* Huntsville, Ala.: Strode, 1977.

Judis, John. *William F. Buckley, Jr.* New York: Simon & Schuster, 1988.

Kalb, Marvin, and Bernard Kalb. *Kissinger.* Boston: Little, Brown, 1974.

Kant, Immanuel. *Critique of Pure Reason.* New York: Doubleday, 1966.

———. *Fundamental Principles of the Metaphysics of Morals.* New York: Bobbs-Merrill, 1959.

Karnow, Stanley. *Vietnam: A History.* New York: Viking, 1983.

Kaufmann, William. *The McNamara Strategy.* New York: Harper & Row, 1964.

Klein, Herb. *Making It Perfectly Clear.* New York: Doubleday, 1980.

Klinghoffer, Arthur. *The Angolan War.* Boulder: Westview, 1980.

Kraslow, David, and Stuart Loory. *The Secret Search for Peace in Vietnam.* New York: Random House, 1968.

Kutler, Stanley. *The Wars of Watergate.* New York: Knopf, 1990.

Kwitny, Jonathan. *Endless Enemies.* New York: Congdon & Weed, 1984.

LaFeber, Walter. *The American Age.* New York: Norton, 1989.

Lake, Anthony. *The Tar Baby Option.* New York: Columbia, 1976.

————, ed. *The Vietnam Legacy.* New York: New York University, 1976.

Landow, David. *Kissinger: The Uses of Power.* Boston: Houghton Mifflin, 1972.

Lehman, John. *Command of the Seas.* New York: Scribner's, 1988.

Liska, George. *Beyond Kissinger: Ways of Conservative Statecraft.* Baltimore: Johns Hopkins, 1975.

Lukas, J. Anthony. *Nightmare: The Underside of the Nixon Years.* New York: Viking, 1976.

Mailer, Norman. *St. George and the Godfather.* New York: Arbor House, 1972.

Marchetti, Victor, and John Marks. *The CIA and the Cult of Intelligence.* New York: Knopf, 1974.

Marcum, John. *The Angolan Revolution.* Cambridge: MIT Press, 1980.

Mazlish, Bruce. *Kissinger: The European Mind in American Policy.* New York: Basic Books, 1976.

Meir, Golda. *My Life.* New York: Putnam's, 1975.

Morris, Roger. *Haig: The General's Progress.* New York: Playboy, 1982.

————. *Uncertain Greatness.* New York: Harper & Row, 1977.

Moynihan, Daniel. *A Dangerous Place.* Boston: Little, Brown, 1975.

Neff, Donald. *Warriors Against Israel.* Brattleboro, Vt.: Amana, 1988.

Nessen, Ron. *It Sure Looks Different From the Inside.* Chicago: Playboy, 1978.

Newhouse, John. *Cold Dawn.* New York: Holt, Rinehart & Winston, 1973.

————. *War and Peace in the Nuclear Age.* New York: Knopf, 1989.

Nicolson, Harold. *The Congress of Vienna.* New York: Harcourt Brace, 1946.

Nitze, Paul. *From Hiroshima to Glasnost.* New York: Grove Weidenfeld, 1989.

Nixon, Richard. *In the Arena.* New York: Simon & Schuster, 1990.

————. *Leaders.* New York: Warner, 1982.

————. *No More Vietnams.* New York: Arbor House, 1985.

————. *RN.* New York: Grossett & Dunlap, 1978.

Nutter, Warren. *Kissinger's Grand Design.* Washington: American Enterprise Institute, 1975.

Osborne, John. *White House Watch: The Ford Years.* Washington: New Republic Books, 1977.

Oudes, Bruce. *From the President: Richard Nixon's Secret Files.* New York: Harper & Row, 1989.

Palmer, Bruce. *The 25-Year War.* Lexington: University of Kentucky, 1984.

Parmet, Herbert. *Richard Nixon and His America.* Boston: Little, Brown, 1990.

Persico, Joseph. *The Imperial Rockefeller.* New York: Simon & Schuster, 1982.

Pfeiffer, Richard, ed. *No More Vietnams.* New York: Harper & Row, 1968.

Porter, Gareth. *Vietnam: The Definitive Documentation of Human Decisions.* Stanfordville, N.Y.: Earl Coleman, 1979.

Powers, Thomas. *The Man Who Kept the Secrets: Richard Helms and the CIA.* New York: Knopf, 1979.

————. *Vietnam: The War at Home.* Boston: G. K. Hall, 1984.

Prados, John. *Keepers of the Keys.* New York: Morrow, 1991.

Price, Raymond. *With Nixon.* New York: Viking, 1977.

Quandt, William. *Decade of Decisions.* Berkeley: University of California, 1977.

Rabin, Yitzhak. *The Rabin Memoirs.* Boston: Little, Brown, 1979.

Ranelagh, John. *The Agency.* New York: Simon & Schuster, 1986.

Rather, Dan, and Gary Paul Gates. *The Palace Guard.* New York: Harper & Row, 1974.

Reeves, Richard. *A Ford, Not a Lincoln.* New York: Harcourt Brace, 1975.

Reston, James. *Deadline.* New York: Random House, 1991.

Riad, Mahmoud. *The Struggle for Peace in the Middle East.* New York: Quartet, 1981.

Rosovsky, Nitza. *The Jewish Experience at Harvard and Radcliffe.* Cambridge: The Harvard Semitic Museum, 1986.

Rowan, Roy. *The Four Days of the Mayaguez.* New York: Norton, 1975.

Rubin, Barry. *Paved With Good Intentions.* New York: Oxford, 1980.

Sadat, Anwar. *In Search of Identity.* New York: Harper & Row, 1977.

Safire, William. *Before the Fall.* New York: Doubleday, 1975.

Saunders, Harold. *The Other Walls.* Washington: American Enterprise Institute, 1985.

Schell, Jonathan. *The Time of Illusion.* New York: Knopf, 1976.

————. *The Village of Ben Suc.* New York: Knopf, 1967.

Schlafly, Phyllis, and Ward Chester. *Kissinger on the Couch.* New York: Arlington House, 1974.

Schlesinger, Arthur, Jr. *A Thousand Days.* Boston: Houghton Mifflin, 1965.

Schulzinger, Robert. *Henry Kissinger: Doctor of Diplomacy.* New York: Columbia, 1989.

Shawcross, William. *The Quality of Mercy.* New York: Simon & Schuster, 1986.

————. *The Shah's Last Ride.* New York: Simon & Schuster, 1988.

————. *Sideshow.* New York: Simon & Schuster, 1979. (The Touchstone paperback, 1987, has added material and rebuttals by Peter Rodman.)

Sheehan, Edward. *The Arabs, Israelis and Kissinger.* New York: Reader's Digest Press, 1976.

Sheehan, Neil. *A Bright Shining Lie.* New York: Random House, 1988.

Sherrill, Robert. *The Oil Follies of 1970–1980.* New York: Doubleday, 1983.

Shipler, David. *Arab and Jew.* New York: Times Books, 1986.

Sick, Gary. *All Fall Down.* New York: Random House, 1985.

Sihanouk, Norodom, with William Burchett. *My War With the CIA.* New York: Monthly Review, 1973.

Smith, Gerard. *Doubletalk: The Story of SALT I.* New York: Doubleday, 1980.

Smith, Michael. *Realist Thought From Weber to Kissinger.* Baton Rouge: LSU Press, 1986.

Smith, Richard Norton. *The Harvard Century.* New York: Simon & Schuster, 1986.

Snepp, Frank. *Decent Interval.* New York: Random House, 1977.

Spengler, Oswald. *The Decline of the West.* New York: Knopf, 1928.

Stern, Paula. *Water's Edge.* Westport, Conn.: Greenwood Press, 1979.

Stockwell, John. *In Search of Enemies.* New York: Norton, 1978.

Stoessinger, John. *Henry Kissinger: The Anguish of Power.* New York: Norton, 1976.

Sullivan, William. *The Bureau.* New York: Norton, 1979.

Sulzberger, C. L. *The World and Richard Nixon.* New York: Prentice-Hall, 1987.

Synnott, Marcia. *The Half-Open Door.* Westport, Conn.: Greenwood Press, 1979.

Szulc, Tad. *The Illusion of Peace.* New York: Viking, 1978.

———. *Then and Now.* New York: Morrow, 1990.

Taheri, Amir. *Nest of Spies.* New York: Pantheon, 1988.

Talbott, Strobe. *Deadly Gambits.* New York: Knopf, 1984.

———. *Endgame.* New York: Harper & Row, 1979.

———. *The Master of the Game.* New York: Knopf, 1988.

Thornton, Richard. *The Nixon-Kissinger Years.* New York: Paragon, 1989.

Tivnan, Edward. *The Lobby.* New York: Simon & Schuster, 1987.

Toynbee, Arnold. *A Study of History.* Oxford: Oxford University Press, 1946 & 1957.

Trager, James. *The Great Grain Robbery.* New York: Ballantine, 1975.

Truscott, Lucian, IV. *Dress Gray.* New York: Doubleday, 1978.

Valeriani, Richard. *Travels With Henry.* Boston: Houghton Mifflin, 1979.

Viorst, Milton. *Sands of Sorrow.* New York: Harper & Row, 1987.

Walters, Vernon. *Silent Missions.* New York: Doubleday, 1978.

Westmoreland, William. *A Soldier Reports.* New York: Doubleday, 1976.

White, Theodore. *America in Search of Itself.* New York: Harper & Row, 1982.

———. *Breach of Faith.* New York: Atheneum, 1975.

———. *The Making of the President, 1972.* New York: Atheneum, 1973.

Wills, Garry. *Nixon Agonistes.* New York: Mentor Books, 1971.

Wise, David. *The American Police State.* New York: Random House, 1976.

Witcover, Jules. *Marathon.* New York: Viking, 1977.

Woodward, Bob, and Carl Bernstein. *All the President's Men.* New York: Simon & Schuster, 1974.

————. *The Final Days.* New York: Simon & Schuster, 1976.

Yergin, Daniel. *The Prize.* New York: Simon & Schuster, 1991.

Zumwalt, Elmo. *On Watch.* New York: Quadrangle, 1976.

U.S. GOVERNMENT REPORTS

Agreement on Limitations of Strategic Offensive Weapons. House Foreign Affairs Committee hearings, June–July, 1972.

Alleged Assassination Plots Involving Foreign Leaders. Senate Select Committee on Intelligence, 1975.

Background Information Relating to Southeast Asia and Vietnam. Senate Foreign Relations Committee, Dec. 1974.

Bombing as a Policy Tool in Vietnam. Senate Foreign Relations Committee, Oct. 12, 1972.

Bombing in Cambodia. Senate Armed Services Committee hearings, July–Aug. 1974.

Covert Action in Chile. Senate Select Committee on Intelligence, 1975.

Department of State Bulletin, 1969–77.

Détente. Senate Foreign Relations Committee hearings, Aug.–Oct. 1974.

Dr. Kissinger's Role in the Wiretapping. Senate Foreign Relations Committee hearings, July–Sept. 1974.

Impeachment of Richard M. Nixon. House Judiciary Committee hearings, Aug. 1974.

Intelligence Activities. Senate Government Operations Committee hearings, 1975.

Middle East Agreements. House International Relations Committee hearings, Sept.–Oct. 1975.

National Bipartisan Report on Central America. Senate Foreign Relations Committee hearings, Feb. 1984.

Nomination of Henry A. Kissinger. Senate Foreign Relations Committee hearings, Sept.–Oct. 1973.

Nomination of Nelson Rockefeller to be Vice President. House Judiciary Committee hearings, 1974.

Public Papers of the President. U.S. Government Printing Office.

Seizure of the Mayaguez. House International Relations Committee hearings, May 1975–Oct. 1976.

Situation in Indochina. House Foreign Affairs Committee hearings, Feb.–Mar. 1973.

Transmittal of Documents from the NSC to the Joint Chiefs of Staff. Senate Armed Services Committee hearings, Feb.–Mar. 1974.

U.S. Foreign Policy for the 1970s ("State of the World" reports), 1970, 1971, 1972, 1973. U.S. Government Printing Office.

U.S. National Security Policy vis-à-vis Eastern Europe ("The Sonnenfeldt Doctrine"). House International Relations Committee hearings, Apr. 1976.

U.S.–Soviet Union–China: The Great Power Triangle. House International Relations Committee, 1975–76.

The Vietnam-Cambodia Emergency 1975. House International Relations Committee hearings, Mar. 1975–May 1976.

Vietnam Policy Proposals. Senate Foreign Relations Committee, Feb.–Mar. 1970.

The War Powers Resolution. House International Relations Committee, 1976.

Index

in China summit (1972), 399, 400, 406–7
Christmas bombing and, 465, 466, 473
"dead key" used by, 232–33, 494
Ehrlichman's relationship with, 392
Haig's relationship with, 227, 231, 386–87, 388, 414–15
Haiphong harbor mining and, 417, 418, 419, 421
in Henry-Handling Committee, 209–11, 395–96, 415
JCS spying operation and, 384, 385
Kissinger as viewed by, 132, 191, 205, 330, 336, 392, 393, 438, 494–95
Kissinger-Rogers feud as viewed by, 198, 474–75, 503
Kissinger's China trip and, 347, 349, 350
Kissinger's relationship with, 170, 189, 227, 230, 271, 296, 314, 359, 364–65, 391–93, 604, 623, 763
Nixon as viewed by, 142, 479
Nixon's relationship with, 143, 391–92, 395
notes taken by, 136, 151, 202–3, 392
Paris peace negotiations as viewed by, 441, 449, 463, 465
Pentagon Papers and, 329, 330
resignation of, 393, 491, 492
Rogers's relationship with, 325, 327
Vietnam policy and, 163–64
in Watergate scandal, 330–31, 593
in wiretapping program, 212, 214, 217, 220, 224–25, 228, 498
Hallemann, Isaak, 28
Halloween Massacre, 669–72
Halperin, Ina, 215
Halperin, Morton:
arms control supported by, 318
as candidate for deputy national security adviser, 184–88
Kissinger's relationship with, 95–96, 119, 154, 155, 158, 165, 169, 175, 181, 214, 215, 329, 561, 763
resignation of, 215–16, 277
wiretapping of, 188, 213, 214–16, 218, 219, 224, 498, 708

Hamilton, Alexander, 654
Hamilton, George, 361
Hamilton College, 507
Handlin, Oscar, 73
Hard, William, 243
Harington, Cliff, 649
Harlow, Bryce, 132, 314, 329, 492, 504, 669
Harriman, Averell, 121, 131, 634, 763
Harris, Frank, 27
Harrison, Randolph, 176
Harris polls, 549
Hart, Basil Liddell, 88
Hartley, John, 737
Hartman, Arthur, 670
Hartmann, Robert, 603, 605–6, 641, 643, 644, 645, 647, 659, 661, 662, 669
Hartz, Louis, 60
Harvard Business School, 120
Harvard International Seminar, 69–72, 73, 74, 81, 83, 86, 99, 111, 121, 290, 552–53
Harvard Lampoon, 363
Harvard-MIT Arms Control Group, 104–5
Harvard University:
  Government Department of, 60, 67, 77–81, 94, 97–98, 109, 315, 708–9
  Jews at, 60
  Kissinger as professor at, 17, 43, 55, 81, 82, 83–84, 94–108, 114, 136, 154, 195, 206, 281, 297, 315, 475, 497, 604, 705, 708–9
  Kissinger as teaching assistant at, 68, 77–81
  Kissinger's application to, 57–58
  Kissinger's doctoral dissertation at, 31, 74–77, 87
  Kissinger's graduate career at, 69–81
  Kissinger's undergraduate career at, 45, 59–69
  Kissinger's undergraduate thesis at, 59, 64–67, 74, 240
  University Professorships of, 708–9
  veterans as students at, 57–58, 59
Haskel, Floyd, 505
Hassan II, King of Morocco, 742
Hausner, Gideon, 560
Havel, Vaclav, 663